THE PEOPLE'S ARTIST

THE PEOPLE'S ARTIST

PROKOFIEV'S SOVIET YEARS

Simon Morrison

OXFORD
UNIVERSITY PRESS

2009

OXFORD
UNIVERSITY PRESS

Oxford University Press, Inc., publishes works that further
Oxford University's objective of excellence
in research, scholarship, and education.

Oxford   New York

Auckland   Cape Town   Dar es Salaam   Hong Kong   Karachi
Kuala Lumpur   Madrid   Melbourne   Mexico City   Nairobi
New Delhi   Shanghai   Taipei   Toronto

With offices in

Argentina   Austria   Brazil   Chile   Czech Republic   France   Greece
Guatemala   Hungary   Italy   Japan   Poland   Portugal   Singapore
South Korea   Switzerland   Thailand   Turkey   Ukraine   Vietnam

Published by Oxford University Press, Inc.
198 Madison Avenue, New York, New York 10016

www.oup.com

Oxford is a registered trademark of Oxford University Press

Library of Congress Cataloging-in-Publication Data
Morrison, Simon Alexander, 1964–
The people's artist : Prokofiev's Soviet years / Simon Morrison.
      p.   cm.
Includes bibliographical references and index.
ISBN 978-0-19-518167-8
1. Prokofiev, Sergey, 1891–1953   2. Composers—Soviet Union—
Biography. I. Title.
ML410.P865M67 2008
786.2183092—dc22
[B]   2008018414

Publication of this book was supported by the Otto Kinkeldey Publication
Endowment Fund of the American Musicological Society.

1 3 5 7 9 8 6 4 2

Printed in the United States of America
on acid-free paper

For Galina Zlobina

Contents

Note on Transliteration

The transliteration system used in this book is the system devised by Gerald Abraham for the *New Grove Dictionary of Music and Musicians* (1980), with the modifications introduced by Richard Taruskin in *Musorgsky: Eight Essays and an Epilogue* (1993). The principal exceptions to the system concern commonly accepted spellings of names and places (Prokofiev rather than Prokof'yev) and suffixes (*-sky* rather than *-skiy*). In the bibliographic citations, however, the transliteration system is respected without exception (Prokof'yev rather than Prokofiev). Surname suffixes are presented intact, and hard and soft signs preserved.

THE PEOPLE'S ARTIST

Introduction:

Moscow's Celebrity Composer

According to those who knew him best, Sergey Prokofiev led an impulsive, impetuous life in the moment. He was smitten with the technological advances of the modern age and took full advantage of high-speed communication and intercontinental travel. In 1918, after completing the rigorous program of studies at St. Petersburg Conservatory, he departed revolutionary Russia for an extended tour in the United States and, after a two-year stay, settled in France, where, like other leading artists of the period, he made Paris his home. From the perspective of the Kremlin, Prokofiev was not an exile but an ambassador at large of Russian (Soviet) culture, a trustworthy fellow traveler. During these years he composed three ballets and three operas, fulfilled recording contracts, and played recitals of his own tempestuous piano music. Scores were packed in suitcases, scenarios and librettos hectically drafted on hotel letterhead. The transience tired him, but he prided himself on being an optimistic, progressive person of action—the embodiment of a new metaphysics.

For the ballet critic Vadim Gayevsky, the first half of Prokofiev's career suggests a story about a great escape artist: "When something threatened him, when there was a whiff of danger in the air, he would board a train, a steam liner, an airplane or, as [the writer Nina] Berberova narrates, get in a car and leave without explanation while he was still in one piece."[1] In 1936, Prokofiev left Paris, an often inhospitable place for foreigners, to take up permanent residence in the Soviet Union, specifically the Russian Soviet Federated Socialist Republic (RSFSR). He began visiting his transformed homeland in 1927, gradually building up his contacts and increasing his time there until the move became inevitable. Most writers on twentieth-century music argue that Prokofiev thereafter found himself trapped, unable after 1938 to travel abroad, and unable to compose in the manner he desired. "By the end of the 1930s, the leading composers were on the other side of the Atlantic, while Prokofiev was locked away in Russia," Francis Maes relates, in reference to Sergey Rachmaninoff and Igor Stravinsky.[2]

Prokofiev perplexed his anti-Soviet Parisian colleagues by migrating to a totalitarian state whose artists were obliged to curtail experiment in support of official doctrine. And indeed, though valued by the regime and supported by its institutions, he suffered correction and censorship, the eventual result being a gradual sapping of his creative energies. He sought to influence Soviet cultural policy, but instead it influenced him. Prokofiev revised and re-revised his late ballets and operas in an effort to see them staged, but, more often than not, his labors went to waste. Following his censure in a political and financial scandal in 1948, jittery concert and theater managers pulled his works from the repertoire. Moreover, physical illness, a series of strokes precipitated by chronic high blood pressure, cast a pall on Prokofiev's last years. Housebound, he turned inward, fulfilling modest commissions for works on the theme of youth. These technically unambitious scores could be interpreted as attempts at psychic healing or, less certainly, as evidence of atavistic withdrawal. Gayevsky here proposes that the composer's final escape took place "in creative, rather than geographical, space."[3]

But the question remains: what convinced Prokofiev to relocate to Moscow in early 1936? The period was marked by, among other things, the marshaling of cultural activities under the auspices of the All-Union Committee on Arts Affairs, the enforcement of official doctrine, and a broad-based attack against the leading Soviet composer, Dmitriy Shostakovich. Western historians have interpreted Prokofiev's move as a pragmatic business decision. Frustrated competing with Stravinsky, orphaned following the sudden demise of his ballet mentor Sergey Diaghilev in 1929, and dismayed by his failure to secure performances of his operas, he succumbed to the enticements of Moscow and Leningrad cultural and political operatives. Since the *glasnost'* period, Russian historians have looked at the matter from a conspiratorial perspective, asserting that the composer was deceived by colleagues who underreported the political situation in the nation. Then there is the position adopted by the composer Alfred Schnittke, who in a 1990 lecture argued that Prokofiev "saw the world differently, even heard it differently. No doubt nature had endowed him with fundamental gifts, means of perception, which were different from those of the vast majority of human beings." Even so, Schnittke adds, Prokofiev "knew the awful truth about the time in which he lived."[4]

The reasons for Prokofiev's decision continue to be debated, though the discussion is fueled less by ideological biases, which have dominated Shostakovich journalism, than by a lack of information stemming, in some cases, from restricted access to archival sources. The archival materials I have studied in Moscow and other cities furnish new details about Prokofiev's activities during this pivotal period in his career, as do the composer's vibrant, lavish diaries, which were published by the Prokofiev estate in 2002, and the memoirs and correspondence of his friends and contacts.[5] These materials trace a series of creative and personal upheavals that fascinate as much for their connection to the grave historical events that surround them as for their detachment from those events. For obvious reasons, Prokofiev does not reflect on the devastation and malevolence that defined Stalinism; the tone of his letters is controlled and businesslike, albeit enriched with dashes of acerbic humor and, in letters to friends, expressions of devotion. The reasons for his relocation are complicated and, in their own way, frightening. It emerges that the steel-willed composer never intended to remain in the Soviet Union. The regime needed celebrities, and he was lured into becoming one of them on the promise that nothing would change in his international career and that Moscow would simply replace Paris as the center of his operations.

This book is a detailed chronicle of Prokofiev's years in the Soviet Union, one that focuses on his tumultuous experiences, the genesis of his works (complete and incomplete, performed and unperformed), and his response to official doctrine. Chapters 3 and 5 concentrate respectively on the three scores that Prokofiev produced for the 1937 Pushkin centennial and three of his film scores; in the other chapters the discussion unfolds in loose chronological fashion, with considerable attention paid to his opera *War and Peace*, an ambiguous masterpiece that occupied him for a dozen years and exists in multiple versions. Biographical detail—again, most of it from archival sources—is provided where it pertains to Prokofiev's creative activities. I attempt, in essence, to document his artistic rather than his personal decision making, but I recognize that the two are often intertwined. For example, the shocking arrest and execution of Prokofiev's theatrical muse Vsevolod Meyerhold is described within the context of their collaboration on a Soviet-themed opera, *Semyon Kotko*, and on the scoring and choreographing of an outdoor athletics display; the details of his estrangement from his first wife, Lina (Carolina) Codina, are presented within a general account of his self-absorbed efforts to become the dominant Soviet composer. Prokofiev's health troubles and hospitalizations of necessity become relevant to the assessment of his late works.

Discussion of the composer's spiritual outlook is confined to discrete sections of the book, though it merits asserting, right at the start, that it governed his creative outlook. Beginning in 1924, long before his Soviet period, Prokofiev and his wife indoctrinated themselves in Christian Science, internalizing the foundational text of the faith, Mary Baker Eddy's *Science and Health with Key to the Scriptures* (1875), and consulting it for treatment of physical ailments. The composer subscribed to the principle that sickness was an illusion that stemmed from a loss of harmony with the godhead. Subsequent study convinced him that Christian Science and Kantian metaphysics had points in common, since "both reckon that the world surrounding us is only a representation."[6] A diary entry from February 6, 1926, finds him considering the difference between self-love and love for others. He also affirms the inevitable triumph of good, an "infinite" force, over evil, a "finite" one:

> Christian Science regards evil as unreal, for evil is a temporal entity; in eternity, where time does not exist, all that is temporal is unreal. The world instant is unrelated to eternity. Till when will evil last? Until individualities are strengthened to the extent that their mutual attractions no longer lead to fusion and annulment. Hence: a person's acceptance of good and rejection of evil is symptomatic of the maturation of his individuality.[7]

Prokofiev's emphasis on moral absolutes in his text-based works, and his preference for characters who believe in spiritual and nonspiritual causes over those who doubt, owes to his faith. In the 1930s and 1940s, he succeeded in tailoring his religious sentiments to a creative context that was relentlessly hostile to them.

It emerges from his diaries that Prokofiev defined his creative activities as embodiments of divine forces. His God-given talent came with great responsibilities: his life served his art, rather than the opposite, and this situation obliged him to take risks that defied external, nonartistic logic. In the mid-1930s, he composed a happy ending version of *Romeo and Juliet*. It irritated Soviet Shakespeare purists, who pressured him into reworking it. He also composed—after several years of contemplation—the *Cantata for the Twentieth Anniversary of October*, setting canonical Communist texts in such an unusual way as to ensure its official prohibition. The risks were artistic, the repercussions political and financial. Prokofiev disgruntled his ideological overseers, but he sincerely tried to win their approval. He was much less political than patriotic, but he solicited and absorbed the benefits of political patronage, and obligatorily adhered, in interviews and speeches, to the Party line. Unlike his lifelong Soviet colleagues, he received permission to travel abroad in the late 1930s, performing at Soviet diplomatic events in Western Europe and the United States in exchange for coveted exit permits. These trips are summarized in the first and second chapters; for a detailed account of Prokofiev's activities in the West before 1936, readers should consult the biography by David Nice, which is based on research conducted at the London Prokofiev Archive (Goldsmiths College), the principal holding of material about the composer's pre-Soviet career.[8]

In order to secure, or help to secure, commissions, performances, and publications, Prokofiev responded to official directives. However, despite heeding collegial and (more often) noncollegial requests for changes to his scores—simplifying complex harmonies, melodies, and rhythms—he did not, to his mind, forfeit his creative integrity. Prokofiev ascribed much more importance to the moment when musical material was conceived than to its subsequent, mandated reworking. His sketches are not sketches in the usual sense of the term. Invented in the abstract, they are preserved in elegant, legible notation. Prokofiev often jotted down his ideas in pencil and then traced over them in pen, thus preserving them in his notebooks in pristine form. Even when he assigned his melodies to odious political texts, even when he transferred them from one score to another, they retained, in his view, their divine essence. This notion altogether counters the principle, essential to Soviet aesthetics, that music could be tailored to support specific political agendas. The original, nonrepresentational status of the musical gesture seems to have mattered as much or more to Prokofiev than the context in which it was performed or published. To buttress this point, I give much attention in this book to his outlines, sketches, and unrealized compositions.

Invoking, as it does, binaries of matter and spirit, the finite and the infinite, his creative approach might seem ineluctably idealistic, but in one crucial sense it was not. Prokofiev subscribed much less to the problematic notion of musical transcendence than to its opposite: musical groundedness. The story of his Soviet years is one of an immensely gifted composer who, having rolled the dice on his career to become a public servant, sought to find public outlets and uses for his music. But State interests overshadowed personal ones in the Stalinist era: to solicit and accept commissions for official works, as Prokofiev did, meant setting vulgar verses that promoted falsehoods. For Prokofiev, as for Shostakovich, serving the State was an obligation. It was also, however, a stimulus for the creation of works that sought to elevate and ennoble the listener from a patriotic and spiritual standpoint. Such was the case with his Fifth and Sixth symphonies, the former a success, the latter the target of withering criticism.

In 1936, Prokofiev composed three major works (*Boris Godunov*, *Eugene Onegin*, and *The Queen of Spades*) for the 1937 Pushkin centennial. The first two works were conceived as incidental music for plays, the third for a film, but the cultural climate ensured that none of them ended up being used as intended. The waste of his labor was the first, and clearest, signal that his Soviet career would be fraught, subject to forces beyond his control. Prokofiev succumbed to subtle and not-so-subtle pressures to return to his homeland; the officials who choreographed the courtship, however, promised more than they delivered. In the rest of this introduction, I will discuss the terms of the Faustian bargain: in the eight chapters to follow, I will narrate its consequences.

The story begins on July 21, 1925, when the Central Committee of the Communist Party granted permission for Prokofiev, his rival Stravinsky, and the eminent concert pianist Aleksandr Borovsky to travel to the Soviet Union.[9] The impetus came from Anatoliy Lunacharsky, the People's Commissar for Enlightenment, who petitioned Iosif Stalin for permission to travel abroad for the purpose of cultivating cultural relationships with Western European nations, but also to engage with those Berlin- or Paris-based Russian artists, "for example the musicians Prokofiev and Stravinsky," who had achieved "world fame":

> These individuals are by no means hostile to us. I receive a lot of letters from them wishing to establish some sort of contact. Isolation from their homeland is obviously undesirable. Some of them might happily return to Russia for good. Others have too many ties abroad and consider themselves basically German, French, and so forth, rather than emigrants. But they would like to come to Russia more often to share the results of their work with us. I have neither the slightest

desire to repatriate emigrants in general nor to repatriate those outstanding individuals who, as emigrants, feel hostile to us. But it would of course be beneficial for those outstanding individuals who have kept themselves away out of misunderstanding or unspecified fear to renew contact with us.[10]

Such were the parameters of the task that Lunacharsky assigned himself, and that Stalin evidently approved: to reach out to those first-class talents who might consider relocating to the Soviet Union or, at a minimum, become regular visitors.

In August in Paris, Prokofiev, Stravinsky, and Borovsky received letters from Nadezhda Bryusova, a member of the Arts Department of the State Academic Council, on instruction of Lunacharsky, specifying the conditions under which they could travel to the RSFSR. Stravinsky and Borovsky ended up rejecting the overture; Prokofiev, in contrast, found it intriguing. Raised in a culture of musical support groups, he experienced feelings of estrangement abroad and sought to reestablish direct personal contact with colleagues in Moscow and Leningrad. Bryusova wrote the following to him:

> In response to your address to the Director of the Arts Department of the State Academic Council comrade [Pavel] Novitsky, the People's Commissar for Enlightenment Anatoliy Vasilyevich Lunacharsky instructs me to convey the following to you:
>
> > *The government agrees to your return to Russia. It agrees to grant you full amnesty for all prior offenses, if any such occurred. It stands to reason that the government cannot grant such amnesty for counter-revolutionary activities in the future. It likewise guarantees complete freedom of travel into and out of the RSFSR as you desire.*
>
> I am certain that the entire musical world of our Union will sincerely welcome your return.[11]

The final lines became, for Prokofiev, the ones that mattered, informing his decision, in May 1926, to accept in principle an invitation from a Moscow concert organizer for a homecoming tour.

Another, specifically musical consequence of Prokofiev's flirtation with the RSFSR was the Constructivist ballet *Le Pas d'Acier* (*The Dance of Steel*), which Prokofiev conceived with the Armenian artist Georgiy Yakulov as a celebration of the metamorphosis of Russian society after the Revolution. The political stakes were great, and Prokofiev fretted from the start that the ballet, which Diaghilev commissioned for the Paris-based Ballets Russes, might be taken for a lampoon by Soviet officials. For *Le Pas d'Acier* to succeed, it needed to be drained of ideology. Prokofiev soon realized, however, that such a nonpolitical work was "impossible, because present-day Russia is defined by the struggle of red against white, and thus a neutral stance won't characterize the moment."[12]

Yakulov convinced him otherwise by stressing that the ballet would unfold in a shape-shifting stage space representing the playground of the imagination. Although set in Russia and referring to developments since the Revolution, the drama would concern not politics but kinetics: the kinship between the workings of the human body and those of machines. The artist conceived *Le Pas d'Acier* as a fantastical construction with three overlapping spheres of action: a market on Sukharevskaya Square in Moscow, an NEP (New Economic Policy) enterprise, and either a factory or an agricultural exhibition—the latter denoting the remaking of Russia. Prokofiev found the conception too vague and prompted Yakulov to recast the ballet in two acts of eleven pantomimic scenes. Set in the years after the Revolution and the subsequent period of famine, the ballet featured stock types drawn from the upper and lower tiers of society who gather at a railway station platform, a symbol of transition. A sailor, the hero of the ballet, meets a coquettish worker girl, the heroine. There ensues an out-of-sync pas de deux, a parody inspired by Stravinsky's *Petrushka*, in which the male and female leads move around each other but do not touch. The stage clears; brigades of shock workers arrive to reconstruct the set, transforming the railway station into a factory. The second half of *Le Pas d'Acier* involved the performers in machine and hammer dances, which culminate in the reunion of the sailor and worker girl in proletarian guise. In a July 29, 1925, diary entry, Prokofiev described the apotheosis as follows:

> Suddenly the director of the factory appears and reports that, in view of a lack of money and material, the factory is shutting down. He presents the factory's books. The indignant workers drive out the director. But the facts cannot be

denied: the factory grinds to a halt. A sad meeting: what is to be done? At this time a children's procession announces itself with noise, *gambades*, and clattering percussion. (Yakulov says that this is very characteristic of contemporary Moscow.) The sailor and worker girl accompany the procession. The procession leaves, and the sailor urges the workers not to indulge their sadness, but to take up gymnastic exercises, since the health of the body is the most valuable thing of all. The ballet ends with cheerful gymnastic exercises.[13]

The ballet celebrates harmonious labor, with individual desire subordinated to the collective will; in the end, it proves to be neither about topicality nor ideology, but about dancing—about an idiosyncratic way of being in the modern world.

This, at any rate, was the plan. As Prokofiev sketched the music, which he conceived—at odds with the ballet's storyline—as an exercise in lyricism, Yakulov sketched the décor and choreography. The plans were then submitted to Diaghilev, who decided, after considerable vacillation, that the subject matter might not impress his audiences after all. He entrusted his newest protégé, the young Leonid Massine, with reworking the scenario and inventing the machine dances. The June 7, 1927, premiere performance disappointed Prokofiev.[14] Far from representing the enthusiastic transformation of the old world into the new, the ballet featured a parade of figures from Russian folklore. The new array of scenes devised by Massine—"Baba Yaga and Crocodile," "Street Bazaar and Countesses," "Sailor and Three Devils," "Tomcat and Feline," "Legend of a Drunkard," and "Sailor and Worker Girl"—baffled reviewers. During the industrial bacchanalia of the final scene, the dancers interacted with the décor in loose accord with the original scenario, but the overall effect was less of harmonious labor than of the subjugation, even enslavement of man to machine. In the words of one reviewer:

> Men and women in all stages of hurry and perturbation toiled and moiled, shifted heavy weights about, rained steamhammer blows on huge bars of imaginary steel, tried to look like pistons, connecting rods, cams and differentials, grew hot, and never, never smiled. It was all done in a way that only the mind of a Massine could imagine; and it came off hugely, grimly.[15]

Other writers described *Le Pas d'Acier* as a critique of Soviet plans for heavy industrialization, but could not decide if the critique was portentous or capricious. For Prokofiev, who was negotiating concert engagements with Soviet cultural officials, and for Yakulov, who had taken part in the design competition for the Lenin Mausoleum, the violation of their intentions was unsettling. The ballet was a success in Paris and London but, for political as well as aesthetic reasons, it did not receive a Moscow premiere.

Prokofiev's first visit to the Soviet Union, extending from January 19 to March 23, 1927, put to rest the question that had been dogging him since the time of his emigration: whether or not, because he had " 'fled from history,' " his "haggard" homeland would "embrace" him on his return.[16] The reception accorded his performances as a piano soloist with the Philharmonic in Leningrad and in Moscow with Persimfans—the Russian-language acronym for "First (Conductorless) Symphonic Ensemble"—far exceeded his expectations, although he admitted to losing his nerve before walking out onstage for the first event.[17] His other appearances included an orchestra and chamber concert mounted by the Association of Contemporary Music, a cash-strapped bastion of musical modernism, and six engagements in Ukraine. The indisputable highlight of the entire whirlwind affair was a Leningrad performance of his second completed opera, *The Love for Three Oranges*, under the direction of a longtime friend, Sergey Radlov. "I am astonished and delighted with the ingenuity and liveliness of [his] production," Prokofiev wrote in his diary on February 10.[18] By this time, he knew that plans were in the works for a Moscow staging of *The Love for Three Oranges*. Moreover, on February 16, Meyerhold, Radlov's mentor, approached him about directing his first completed opera, *The Gambler*. Prokofiev recalled the event with acerbic wit, noting in passing the service that Meyerhold had provided to Bolshevism:

> The honored Red Army soldier is such an important person
> I am surprised at how little fuss he made about coming to
> tell me he's agreed to direct *The Gambler*. But perhaps this
> is because in Paris I was the one who came to see him—to
> take him to Diaghilev's rehearsals. If the Mariinsky Theater
> is going to the trouble of getting a big fish like Meyerhold,
> then the production will go with a bang.[19]

Prokofiev found himself weighing proposals for different simultaneous stagings of his operas. It was a unique moment in his otherwise troubled operatic career, and one that he doubtless recalled in the interval between this and his second trip to the Soviet Union.

Upon returning to Paris, Prokofiev began to receive invitations for events at the Soviet Embassy (Plenipotentiary of the Diplomatic Mission), which, unlike the Comintern[20] organizations operating in the West, catered to non-Communist interests. He was contacted by Iosif (Ivan) Arens, a counselor with the embassy who had previously headed the press department of the Commissariat of Foreign Affairs and served as editor in chief of the French-language daily *Le Journal de Moscou*.[21] Arens prepared Prokofiev's Soviet travel papers and offered him financial and logistical advice, proposing that he use his earnings in Russian rubles to "build an apartment" for himself in Moscow and "hire Moscow engravers to engrave [his] compositions, if only for [distribution] abroad."[22] Prokofiev found the ideas compelling, but his international obligations prevented him from acting on them at the time. He wanted to remain cosmopolitan, fulfilling his contracts with European orchestras and retaining his contacts in the United States. The 1927 visit had been exciting and inspiring, but it also alerted him to the dark side of the workers' paradise. He had received a telephone call in his Moscow hotel room from an unnamed official with Comintern who asked him to participate in a concert celebrating the Communist takeover of Shanghai. Prokofiev managed to avoid the chore, but he found the overture unsettling, noting that "one has to be cautious if the Comintern is mentioned."[23] He knew about Soviet phones being tapped, random interrogations, and people being subject to all manner of bureaucratic humiliation. Through conversations and carefully worded letters, Prokofiev learned of the arrest and imprisonment of his cousin Katya (Yekaterina Rayevskaya), and her subsequent exile in the northwestern Russian town of Kadnikov.[24] Musicologist Nataliya Savkina adds here that "friends living in the USSR" asked him for medicine, but he was unable to send it. The terrible side was further revealed in "the vague recollections of acquaintances about people being taken away from work, committing suicide, and disappearing into thin air, no questions asked."[25] Another one of Prokofiev's cousins, Shurik (Aleksandr Rayevsky), was also arrested. Upon obtaining his release, he sent the composer a letter that ended with the words " 'don't write to me, it's not necessary.' "[26]

The disquieting news from his relatives doubtless reminded Prokofiev of the benefits of his unsettled Western existence. He was now a Soviet citizen with an external Soviet passport, but at the end of his 1927 visit to the Soviet Union, he renewed his French *certificat d'identité*.[27] His uncertain status irritated Soviet officials: in January 1930, for example, he received a stern letter from the Consul General of the USSR instructing him, "as a Soviet citizen," to refute an article in *L'Echo de Paris* that listed him among the Russian émigrés "living and working in Paris."[28] Prokofiev's commitment to Paris strengthened when his music unexpectedly came in for scathing ideological critique. Following a concert performance of six numbers from *Le Pas d'Acier* in Moscow in May 1928, hard-line critics and rivals declared that there was "nothing new" in the score, that "it had all been done before," that it was "too noisy," contained "too much of the 'white keys'" (C major), and that it was altogether "'too contrived.'"[29] There followed a harangue from the Russian Association of Proletarian Musicians (RAPM), an organization that attempted to be the Bolshevik Party's "mouthpiece for musical policy" while also aspiring "to define that policy."[30] In an essay in the RAPM journal, musicologist Yuriy Keldïsh complained at length about the discord and semantic sameness of the ballet's music. Keldïsh asserted that, even without the choreography, the score imposed bourgeois capitalist thought onto proletarian subject matter, and thus exhibited a hostile foreign attitude toward Soviet reality.[31]

The ballet did have some supporters in Moscow, chief among them the theater director Meyerhold and the State Academic Bolshoy Theater assistant director Boris Gusman, who both advocated staging *Le Pas d'Acier* with a new cast and choreography. Prokofiev learned of their plans during his second trip to the Soviet Union, from October 20 to November 18, 1929, and supported them in full. On the heels of a November 14 run-through of the score, Gusman proposed enlivening the scene at the bazaar with "giddily, enthusiastically rushing 'red sleighs.'" These sleighs would represent the "old Russian" forms of transport that had been supplanted by "new Russian" trains. Gusman also suggested replacing the three "commissars" with "bandits"—though he was cautioned that this change would contradict the music. For the factory scenes, lastly, Gusman wanted to include "cadres of Five-Year Plan workers."[32] Hoping to secure a Moscow staging of the ballet, Prokofiev engaged in repartee with skeptical RAPM representatives. In answer to the question "Why is the entire last part of the ballet shot through with machine-like, mechanical rhythms?" he dryly ad-libbed.

"Because a machine is more beautiful than a man." And when asked whether he believed that the factory scenes depicted "a capitalist factory, where the worker is slave, or a Soviet factory, where the worker is master," he quipped: "This concerns politics, not music, and so I won't respond."[33] His stubborn defense of the ballet (even of Massine's drastic changes) fell largely on deaf ears. *Le Pas d'Acier* did not reach the Soviet stage.

The hostile reaction dismayed and distressed Prokofiev. Beyond ending talk of a Moscow staging of his ballet, it thwarted his nascent campaign to have his beleaguered opera *The Fiery Angel* performed there under Meyerhold's direction.[34] Two of Prokofiev's conservatory classmates—the aesthetician, musicologist, and composer Boris Asafyev and the composer Nikolay Myaskovsky—would return to the subject of a Moscow staging of the opera in the mid-1930s, but the result would be the same. Prokofiev remained defiant, attributing the disappointment to the dilettantism of the RAPM rank and file and joking in his diary about the unsuccessful effort to "purge" his music from the Soviet repertoire.[35] He took comfort in the favorable reviews of the lavish Bolshoy Theater staging of *The Love for Three Oranges*, which he attended on November 13 and 16, and in the positive reaction to a November 17 concert of his Sinfonietta, First Violin Concerto, and *Overture on Hebrew Themes*. He managed to convince himself that the 1929 trip had been worthwhile: "It's a shame to part from the USSR," he noted in his diary on November 19. "The goal of the trip was obtained: I have certainly, definitely become stronger."[36]

On April 23, 1932, the Central Committee of the Communist Party mandated the liquidation of proletarian and non-proletarian arts organizations, thus resulting in the formation, first on a municipal and then on a national level, of Kremlin-controlled arts bureaucracies: the Union of Soviet Writers and the Union of Soviet Composers, among others, came into being.[37] During the grace period that preceded the establishment, in 1936, of the watchdog All-Union Committee on Arts Affairs (under the control of the Council of People's Commissars), the cultural climate appeared to moderate. Estranged and disgraced artists trusted that their reputations would be restored and the ideological constraints on their activities loosened. Prokofiev responded to the abolition of RAPM with distinct pleasure. Having endured the invective of uncouth opponents, he resolved to establish an authoritative presence in Soviet music. The evolution of his thinking can be gleaned from an October 5, 1932, letter to Myaskovsky—"It is time to come more often and to stay longer," he wrote[38]—and from a May 2–5, 1933, diary entry:

Lessons with students and several of their awkward attempts to compose something contemporary, and likewise the unsuccessful attempts of proletarian musicians (attempts at simplicity, which does not come easy without technique), and several hints that my music is too complicated for the masses—gave me the idea that what is needed now is to create for the masses in a manner that allows the music to remain good. My previous, melodic pieces and my search for a "new simplicity" have prepared me well for this task.[39]

By "new simplicity," Prokofiev was referring to the self-conscious shift in his musical approach that had begun in the mid-1920s. Stephen Press locates the beginning of the change in *Le Pas d'Acier*, specifically the Mozartian lyricism of the pas de deux.[40] From that point forward, Prokofiev's scores became more tuneful and their intended effect more uplifting. Perhaps unsurprisingly, the composer attributed this new disposition to his religious sentiments. In a December 3, 1932, conversation in Leningrad with the philologist Boris Demchinsky, an old friend, Prokofiev outlined the relationships among faith, music, and positive thinking:

Breakfast with Demchinsky. He tries to mount an attack on cheerfulness and joyfulness. When neither science nor public opinion provides solutions, music should express the general anxiety. I: the more the sea rages, the more precious a hard rock among the waves becomes. He: but no one will understand the meaning of this rock; besides, what is this feeling of calm based on—on health, self-assurance, individual personality? I: on the emphasis on God. He (immediately changing his tone): well, that's a different matter.[41]

Here is an aphoristic reworking of Prokofiev's definition of music as a manifestation of the divine. He would soon realize that the creation of art that dissolved ambiguities and contradictions, that invoked a realm beyond the intellect, was not only central to his personal beliefs but also to Soviet aesthetics. Stalinist-era composers proved adept at converting emblems of religious faith into emblems of political faith: "cheerfulness and joyfulness" are staples, however jejunely expressed, of their work.

Between his second and third trips to the Soviet Union while back in France, Prokofiev received insider accounts of cultural events there from visiting Soviet artists. Among them was the playwright Aleksandr Afinogenov, a former Russian Association of Proletarian Writers zealot who repented and became a founding member of the Union of Soviet Writers and—as one learns from the stenograph of his 1932 lecture "The Europe of Our Days"—a chronicler of Russian (Soviet) culture abroad.[42] (He had been granted an exit permit to conduct research on this topic for a new play.) Although he has not attracted the attention of Prokofiev biographers, Afinogenov exerted considerable influence on the composer during the period when he was assessing potential subjects for his first Soviet-themed opera. He, unlike the other Proletkult figures rumored to have been in contact with Prokofiev in Western Europe, actually befriended the composer.[43] Prokofiev regarded Afinogenov (and his American-born wife) as cosmopolitan and street-smart, and he was happy to listen to his advice. The two briefly considered collaborating on a stage work. In a June 16, 1932, diary entry, Prokofiev reports that Afinogenov "would like to write an opera with me. This suits my wishes: it's time to create a Soviet piece."[44] He informed the writer that he wanted the prospective work to have "a constructive rather than a destructive character." Perhaps recalling unhappy experiences, Prokofiev then changed his mind about writing an opera in the conventional sense of the term and suggested that he and Afinogenov collaborate on a hybrid work: "a play with rhythmic declamation" that would be less operatic and more realistic than even the prose-based operas conceived by Aleksandr Dargomïzhsky and Modest Musorgsky in the 1860s. Prokofiev added that he had conceived such a work eight years earlier, in 1924, but competing priorities had prevented it from being realized.

Also in 1932, Prokofiev briefly considered composing background music for Afinogenov's enormously successful 1931 drama *Fear (Strakh)*, which addressed the problems experienced by the pre-revolutionary Russian intelligentsia in adjusting to post-revolutionary Soviet life. For Prokofiev, the play doubtless had autobiographical resonances, since he was dealing at the time with his own adaptation to Soviet society. "It is a true-to-life play," he observed, "about the conflict between the old intelligentsia (those who are prepared to work with Soviet authorities) and the new administrative workers, who are less cultured but more energetic."[45] The precise reasons for the aborting of this project are unknown, but may relate to the Soviet cultural climate. In his notebook from this period, Afinogenov commented:

"Prokofiev plans to travel to the USSR in the fall; to go there now is not as unpleasant, RAPM is no longer, but I am all the same afraid of what will happen to [him], and what musicians' sentiments will be like, after the transition."[46]

When the time—and mood—was right, the task of convincing Prokofiev to relocate to Moscow fell to Levon Atovmyan, a music official, editor, and publisher who came to play an enormous role in the lives of Soviet composers following his appointment, in 1940, as Director and Deputy Chairman of Muzfond, the financial division of the Union of Soviet Composers.[47] Even by the chaotic norms of the Stalinist era, Atovmyan led a turbulent career. A native of Ashkhabad, Turkmenistan, he enlisted in the Red Army in 1919, working as a political instructor and the editor of a division newspaper. He contracted typhus in 1920 and received a permanent discharge; following his convalescence, he worked in the offices of the Bolshoy Theater for his benefactor Lunacharsky; there, among other tasks, he arranged concerts for workers at factory and institute social clubs. In 1925 he relocated to Tbilisi, Georgia, and resumed his interrupted musical education (he had studied cello and music theory in Moscow before enlisting) and worked in an experimental theater. In 1930 he was elected to the presidium of the All-Russia Society of Composers and Dramatists (then led by Afinogenov) and appointed executive secretary of the Composers' Division. In 1934 he became a theater administrator and briefly worked for Meyerhold. He thereafter returned to Ashkhabad, where he directed the local government cultural affairs department until his arrest in 1937 in a bureaucratic scandal. The reasons for his arrest remain obscure. His sentence was commuted in 1940 and his official status regained. Atovmyan returned to Moscow, working first for State Radio and then, most crucially, for Muzfond.

In his memoirs, which he completed in enfeebled retirement, Atovmyan recalls a 1932 summons to the NKID (Narodnïy Komissariat Inostrannïkh Del, the People's Commissariat for Foreign Affairs) to meet with the director of the Western European and North American Division:

> [The official] ordered coffee and pastries, invited me to the table and began to talk about our concerts in the Bolshoy Theater. In the discussion I was given to understand that it would be good to correspond with those musicians abroad, namely Prokofiev, Koussevitzky, Malko, and Pyatigorsky, who had taken part in these concerts and, if possible,

try to convince them of the merits of moving to the Soviet Union.[48]

Atovmyan sent letters to the first three people on the list; the cellist Gregor Pyatigorsky was excluded. Serge Koussevitzky, the conductor of the Boston Symphony Orchestra, did not reply, and Nikolay Malko, the conductor of the Danish State Radio Orchestra, agreed to visit for additional concerts, but insisted on returning abroad. Prokofiev, in contrast,

> answered very positively, but with the qualification that he was overloaded with concerts and would thus provide the actual date of his arrival a little later. They told me at *Narkomindel* not to answer Malko but to continue writing to Prokofiev, adding that if he agreed to stay in Moscow he would be offered a private residence (later they showed me a two-story private residence on the Garden Ring Road). I received a second and a third letter from Prokofiev, in which he articulated his desires concerning the programs of the planned concerts and performances, and the orchestral parts he was sending by registered book post. In lieu of this the planned program of the next concert of Soviet music was redone and now looked as follows: the Classical Symphony, the Fifth Piano Concerto, and the "Four Portraits" Symphonic Suite from *The Gambler*.[49]

Atovmyan ended his recollection by noting that "the entire musical (and not only musical) community lived in expectation of this concert and meeting with Prokofiev."

This and other concerts took place in Moscow and Leningrad during Prokofiev's third visit to the Soviet Union in late November and early December of 1932. He was hailed by the conductors and musicians with whom he performed, solicited for interviews and, despite informing Atovmyan that he disliked formal occasions, feted at a banquet at the National Hotel in Moscow and at a Congress of Arts Workers (S'yezd rabotnikov iskusstv) in Leningrad. His recollection of this latter event, which occurred on November 30, finds him flattered—if somewhat mystified—by the attention:

I am greeted with applause; thank God, I might not have to give a speech. They photograph me and draw my picture. We go to the Mikhaylovsky Theater, where composers and musicians have organized a reception in the foyer. Atovmyan telegrammed from Moscow that "Prokofiev hates ceremonial gatherings." Some seventy people in all. A speech by Iokhelson who, I just then realized, is the former chairman of the Leningrad branch of proletarian musicians. He says approximately what I wanted to say at the Congress: about the thriving interest in music, about the appeal of having me working on Soviet themes and creating ties with the Western musical world. All of this in a terrible flattering form: Sergey Sergeyevich this and Sergey Sergeyevich that.[50]

In his response, Prokofiev simply echoed Vladimir Iokhelson's points. His concluding statement "to the effect that I am planning to spend as much time here as possible" was "greeted with protracted applause." There followed a question-and-answer session, which Prokofiev deemed "friendly and factual, not treacherous as in 1929."

Atovmyan recalls that, in between the concerts, he arranged to speak with the composer about

business affairs; I found out during the conversation that [Prokofiev] had been obliged over the course of the year to give about 100 concerts and to compose in snatches, primarily on the train. Because of this he had to get used to writing [instrumental works] as piano scores and marking the instrumentation on them. When I suggested settling in Moscow he replied: "You should understand that I feel constrained in one country: even if I have 4–5 concerts in Moscow, Leningrad, or supposedly Kiev, Baku, and Tbilisi—that's the maximum I can have. I'll die here of starvation." "You won't die," I replied, "We'll guarantee you commissions for creative work." He took an interest in these commissions and, hearing the details, said: "Yes, it's worth thinking about your offer."[51]

Atovmyan appends that Myaskovsky and the music critic (and future Prokofiev assistant) Vladimir Derzhanovsky both lent heft to the discussions about his prospective relocation. The forty-four letters and telegrams exchanged by Atovmyan and Prokofiev between 1932 and 1934 attest to the seriousness of the recruitment effort. A letter from May 4, 1933, finds Atovmyan meticulously tending to the logistics of Prokofiev's latest visit to the Soviet Union. Having "heard rumors" that the composer "needed money," Atovmyan promises to promptly arrange a bank transfer for him. He then invites Prokofiev to a May 6 concert at the Bolshoy Theater, provides him with the details of his May 8 departure from Moscow to Tiflis (Tbilisi), and reminds him that "today at 6 o'clock" he would be giving a speech at the Composers' Union. On May 7, Atovmyan adds, the Moscow Philharmonic would be repeating its April 27 concert of Prokofiev's music, albeit without additional rehearsals. "I hoped to see you yesterday at the theater," he concludes, "but you were so closely surrounded by women and photographers that I fled in fear."[52]

During this period, Prokofiev received the first of the "guaranteed" Soviet commissions. It came from Gusman, who had lost his post at the Bolshoy Theater but had found a new one at Belorussian State Cinema—Belgoskino—which operated in Leningrad between 1928 and 1939. Like Atovmyan, Gusman careened from job to job in the 1930s;[53] also like Atovmyan, he supported Prokofiev financially and creatively, commissioning several scores from him and forwarding him potential ballet and opera subjects.[54] On December 2, 1932, in Leningrad, he approached Prokofiev with an offer to write a film score. The composer showed interest—although according to one source the interest was lukewarm[55]—and the next day he, Gusman, the scenarist and literary theorist Yuriy Tïnyanov, and the director Aleksandr Fayntsimmer met for several hours to hammer out the details.[56]

Titled *Lieutenant Kizhe*, the film was based on a novella written by Tïnyanov in 1927, which was itself based on a well-known anecdote about Tsar Pavel I, the irascible and manic son of Catherine the Great, who reigned for just five years, 1796–1801, before being murdered.[57] The clique that killed him circulated the rumor that he was mentally unbalanced. The anecdote, which comes from a 1901 publication, concerns the creation at Pavel's court "of a nonexistent officer by a scribal error, and the demise of a living one 'for the same reason.'"[58] Tïnyanov transformed the anecdote into a Gogolian satire about the absurdities of late eighteenth-century bureaucracy, which necessitated the interpretation of the letter, rather than the spirit, of the law to black comic ends. The film shows, near the start, a flustered young scribe writing up a regimental order for the tsar. Interrupted by an impatient aide-de-camp—who raps ("k k k") on the window—the scribe erroneously writes "Poruchik Kizhe" (Lieutenant Kizhe) on the order instead of "Poruchiki zhe" (while the lieutenants). The mistake cannot be undone: the fictitious officer must be reckoned with, accounted for, bundled and trundled away—so he is assigned to a guard post, blamed for waking the napping tsar, flogged and sent by foot to Siberia, restored to honor on a technicality, summoned back to St. Petersburg, married to a lovely maid-in-waiting (she stands at the altar alone, with an adjutant holding the nuptial crown over the head of her unseen groom), and sires a son. At the end of his career, he earns promotions to the rank of colonel and general, falls gravely ill with fever, dies, and receives a burial with full honors.

Beyond being a sociopolitical satire, *Lieutenant Kizhe* reflects Tinyanov's fascination with phonetic mutations and the manner that cinema, like poetry, traffics in apparent rather than concrete meanings.[59] The film involves frequent changes in perspective, representations of empty spaces, and distorted reflections. Images of soldiers and sweepers are doubled and quadrupled. The soundtrack teems, like the mind of a schizophrenic, with disembodied voices, sentence fragments, and isolated phonemes. Kizhe becomes a mirror image of Pavel I, an absent leader inhabiting a power vacuum. Prokofiev captures this sentiment in his score by surrounding Pavel I and his courtiers with hollow fanfares and stylized songs. Their music is no more subjective than that of the eponymous hero, who does not exist as a subject. Just as the film comments on its own status as fiction through the marionette-like behavior of its actors, so too does the music, which accompanies the visual representation of late eighteenth-century St. Petersburg with an anachronistic blend of modal and diatonic melodies. Given that tales about St. Petersburg tend to highlight the city's theatrical, artificial look, the inauthenticities in the film could be interpreted as oddly authentic.

Prokofiev composed the score in piecemeal, protracted fashion. Between mid-December 1932 and mid-April 1933, he traveled to France for the premiere of his ballet *On the Dnieper* (*Sur le Borysthène*) and then to the United States for a series of concerts. He returned to the Soviet Union on April 14 for an eleven-week stay. Lina joined him on May 6. It was her first visit to the Soviet Union since 1927.

The trip would involve residencies in Moscow, Leningrad, and two weeks of engagements, arranged by the ever-attentive Atovmyan, in the Caucasus.

On April 22, Prokofiev visited the set of *Lieutenant Kizhe* for the first time, and his recollection of the experience suggests that it had been underwhelming. He found Belgoskino "curious," and assailed both the training of the actors and their "manner of speech," contending that American acting was "more natural." He appreciated the fact that a "party" was organized after the final "cut," but he resented having to sit at the piano and perform for a newsreel: "The light is blinding and the spotlights are hot. It drags on. I play parts of my Toccata badly, but there is no time to redo them. I go home and sleep."[60] The unhappiness of this experience reflected Prokofiev's dissatisfaction both with the method of acting used in *Lieutenant Kizhe* and the state of early sound recording technology—a dissatisfaction that would be echoed by the film's reviewers. It did not lessen his interest in collaborating with Tïnyanov and Fayntsimmer, although the collaboration would end up demanding much more of his time than he could give.

The score for *Lieutenant Kizhe* includes seventeen short numbers ranging from 15 to 105 seconds in length, excluding repeats. Encouraged by Fayntsimmer, Prokofiev first wrote two songs—"Pavel's Song" and "Gagarina's Song"—for the film. The former imitates a children's clapping song and the latter uses the words and parodies the style of an eighteenth-century romance by Fyodor Dubyansky.[61] No sooner had they been completed than Prokofiev learned that the actor chosen to play Pavel I, Mikhaïl Yanshin, was tone deaf.[62] His discordant singing ended up enhancing the imbecility of "Pavel's Song," but it posed a logistical problem for "Gagarina's Song," which Prokofiev conceived in part as a salon-style vocal duet with harp accompaniment. Prokofiev and Lina, a trained soprano, both agreed to have their voices recorded for the film—the actress playing Princess Anna Gagarina, Nina Shaternikova, also seems to have had trouble holding a tune—but, save for several ghostly echoes in the background scoring, the duet ended up on the cutting room floor.

Prokofiev composed the bulk of the score in Paris between July and September 1933, forwarding it in installments to Fayntsimmer with instructions as to how the numbers could be lengthened or shortened to facilitate the editing and sound recording processes.[63] He finished the orchestration at Belgoskino on October 21. By this time, to his disappointment, the film had been reworked, with certain scenes added and others removed. Some of the changes were decided upon by Fayntsimmer, whose conception of *Lieutenant Kizhe* differed from that of Tïnyanov.[64] Others were mandated by a government commission dedicated to the correction of ideological deficiencies in Soviet cinema.[65] Prokofiev summed up the state of affairs as follows:

> On returning to Moscow I eagerly set to work on the music for *Lieutenant Kizhe*. I somehow had no doubts whatever about the musical language for this film. I went to Leningrad for the recording of the score....Unfortunately the ending was altered so many times that the film became confused and heavy as a result. The following year I made a symphonic suite out of the music. This gave me much more trouble than the music for the film itself, since I had to find the proper form, re-orchestrate the whole thing, polish it up and even combine several of the themes.[66]

The changes to the film did not affect the music, which, with the exception of the two songs, Prokofiev essentially conceived as an asynchronic background to the visuals. For the symphonic suite, he rescored the two songs for full orchestra. (The choice of timbre is perhaps the most crucial element of the score: the flute, a conventional bearer of sincere feeling, can be interpreted as maintaining the fiction of Kizhe's existence while the mocking, disrupting alto saxophone, on which Prokofiev lavished great care, seeks to expose it.)

The now-obscure film was a modest success both in the Soviet Union and abroad, but its unevenness proved to be fodder for ideological critique. Fayntsimmer described the critical response positively in a February 17, 1934, letter to the composer, noting that the "closed showings" in Moscow provoked "laughter and applause; in Leningrad, as always, the reaction was rather more restrained, but a good impression overall."[67] Nikolay Otten set the tone for the reviews in a January 10, 1934, piece in the newspaper *Kino*—heaping praise on Tinyanov's novella while accusing Fayntsimmer of transforming a historical lampoon with phantasmagoric tendencies into an anachronistic vaudeville. Otten chided Yanshin for his maniacal impersonation of Pavel I, but lauded Erast Garin for his Buster Keaton–like realization of the adjutant. For Belgoskino, Otten added, the film represented a creative and thematic setback but a significant technological achievement.[68]

Almost the same points were made by A. Petrovich, a reviewer for the official Soviet government newspaper *Izvestiya*, who commented that "in certain episodes of the film...the director had recourse to the grotesque, to merciless satire. But this was only in certain episodes; overall, the film is less modeled on a historical lampoon than on an operatic spectacle, a costumed concert." Prokofiev's "satiric, piquant" music "further underscored the thematic incongruities of the cinematic realization."[69] In essence, and in the opinion of two other critics, *Lieutenant Kizhe* "is a curious picture, worthy of attention, however it lies outside the mainstream of Soviet cinematographic development."[70] In later years, Prokofiev would seek both to occupy this mainstream and to define it. His greatest initial Soviet success would come in the realm of cinema.

Beyond the *Lieutenant Kizhe* commission, 1933 brought Prokofiev renewed promises of operatic commissions and productions from his Soviet backers. His discordant *Scythian Suite* and Third Symphony received well-intentioned performances. Prokofiev relished the attention given to the nettlesome scores by the Leningrad Philharmonic but blanched at the result:

> General rehearsal. The 3rd Symphony is thoroughly bad.
> I grapple with the orchestra inspector:
>   It sounds like cows hauling a manure cart up a mountain.
> He: Our orchestra was the first in the USSR.
>   I: To be the first in the USSR doesn't give you the right to
> play worse than they do abroad.[71]

Further, modest evidence that Prokofiev's approach—old and new—to composition would be indulged, rather than challenged, in the post-RAPM era came from the Moscow Conservatory, whose faculty invited him to become a "consultant" professor, the expectation being that he would advise advanced students nearing the end of the program of study. He accepted the position on May 27, 1933, and held it until March 22, 1937. Though his schedule blocked him from holding regular office hours, he tracked the progress of gifted students and commented on their progress in a notebook.[72] There is reason to suspect that after his permanent move to Moscow he neglected his duties: his file at the Conservatory claims "dismissal on account of the absence of a pedagogical load."[73]

Prokofiev's trips to the Soviet Union in spring, summer, and fall of 1934 included discussions with the writer Maxim Gorky (pseudonym of Aleksey Peshkov). Gorky served as the first chairman of the Union of Soviet Writers, whose constitution required its members to convene every three years to formulate policy and elect a presidium and secretariat. The first congress in August 1934, which Prokofiev did not attend, introduced the tenets of the official artistic doctrine of Socialist Realism and buttressed the rhetorical foundations of Stalinist cultural discourse. Prokofiev and Gorky had encountered each other at least twice before (in 1917 in Petrograd on the eve of the February Revolution and in 1926 in Sorrento during the period of Gorky's Italian sojourn). The writer, an ardent backer of (and fund-raiser for) the Bolshevik cause, disputed Lenin's political thought and despotic methods, especially his repression of intellectuals. Despite being even more repressive, Stalin managed to persuade Gorky to return to Moscow in 1928 for a triumphant, government-sponsored sixtieth-birthday celebration that named him the Soviet Union's preeminent public intellectual. He returned to Italy after the celebration, but visited the Soviet Union again in 1929 and 1932. Following his permanent return in 1933, he was forbidden from traveling abroad (in this respect Gorky's biography parallels Prokofiev's). Owing to his outspokenness and frequent clashes with officials, the circumstances behind his death in 1936 from heart failure have long been a subject of debate.[74]

Prokofiev eulogized Gorky on a June 19, 1936, Moscow radio broadcast. His remarks were trifling, but he recalled asking the writer for his thoughts on the type of music he should compose "for the new stage of socialist construction." The melodic streamlining of his style in the 1920s had fostered the composition of "cheerful and energetic" music, but Gorky suggested that it also needed to be "heartfelt and tender."[75] In a notebook, Prokofiev recalled the discussion in a more nuanced light, commenting that when he asked Gorky's counsel, the grizzled writer was "momentarily taken aback" but then opined that the Soviet people valued "goodness and strength, and therefore understand lyricism and feeling."[76] Although it remains a matter of speculation, it would seem that Prokofiev perceived his role in Soviet musical life as paralleling Gorky's role in Soviet literary life: he would be the lodestar of musical progress, improving and upholding standards in a fertile musical culture.

Prokofiev offered his thoughts on what he regarded as the proper course of Soviet music to *Izvestiya*. The November 16, 1934, article in question, "The Paths of Soviet Music," combined Party-speak with cautious, quasi-Tolstoyan pronouncements about artistic value. Prokofiev begins by noting the need, in the Soviet sphere, for "*great* music" corresponding "both in form and in content to the grandeur of the epoch." This music, he continues, "would be a stimulus to our own musical development, and abroad too it would reveal our true selves." Then a gentle rebuke (intended, perhaps, for RAPM dead-enders): "The danger of becoming provincial is unfortunately a very real one for modern Soviet composers."

Having noted the value of his own dual (internal and external) perspective on Soviet music, Prokofiev establishes that serious art need not be complex art, and innovation need not result in alienation:

> I believe the type of music needed is what one might call "light-serious" or "serious-light" music. It is by no means easy to find the right idiom for such music. It should be primarily melodious, and the melody would be clear and simple without, however, becoming repetitive or trivial. Many composers find it difficult enough to compose any sort of melody, let alone a melody having some definite function to perform. The same applies to the technique, the form—it too must be clear and simple, but not stereotyped. It is not the old simplicity that is needed but a new kind of simplicity. And this can be achieved only after the composer has mastered the art of composing serious, significant music, thereby acquiring the technique of expressing himself in simple, yet original terms.[77]

Prokofiev here renounces *enfant terrible* brashness: harmonic substitutions and chromatic displacements would continue to define his style, but its traditional tonal foundations would become more explicit. Prokofiev suggests, in the mildest of terms, that composers seeking to expand and extend the diatonic system must at least familiarize themselves with its antitheses. His own dalliances with dodecaphony and octatonicism, and his much more sustained exploration of poly-modality, had enriched the emotional and spiritual content of his scores without reducing them to technical studies. Prokofiev was not a system-dependent composer (hence the challenge he poses to music theorists): the spontaneity of the harmonic, melodic, and rhythmic shifts in his scores suggests an artist seeking to capture the moment of creative inspiration and then transfer it unmediated to his listeners. The "path" he proposed for Soviet music might be roughly likened to the path Lev Tolstoy chose for all art in a 1898 manifesto (*What Is Art?*): "The art of our time, in order to be art, must bypass science and make its own path, or else take direction from the unacknowledged science that is rejected by scientific orthodoxy."[78]

"The Paths of Soviet Music" marked the beginning of Prokofiev's absorption into Soviet cultural and political affairs. He remained, however, more a spectator of than a participant in those affairs, reacting to what he saw on the streets and read in the newspapers of Moscow and Leningrad with tourist-like wonder, offering, for example, an entertaining account of the May Day parade he attended in the Soviet capital in 1933:

> Atovmyan took it upon himself to get a ticket for me for the reviewing stand on Red Square to see the parade, but he made a mess of things, failing to get the ticket and then disappearing for five days, which ended up being more embarrassing than if he had stayed around. I watched from the corner window of my room. Tanks arrived at 5 in the morning. At 9 I tried to enter the square, but it was cordoned off everywhere and difficult to move, so I ended up back in the hotel. I was astonished by the airplanes: on my count 250 of them flew past, but they said 600. The tanks also shook the glass, but they say that one of them broke down right in front of the reviewing stand, unable to move forward or back. The most interesting thing: the processions of demonstrators. Beneath my window two ribbons (one from Gorky Street, the other from the Bolshoy Theater) merged like pavement onto pavement at the lower end of Gorky Street. They also say that from 11:30 to 5:30 on Red Square, people marched in formation in rows of eighty. From above the bright red scarves and hats of the women looked very beautiful. These were exchanged now and then for white and colored ones. A sea of banners and placards, predominantly red. An endless number of bands, which played a march, then something cheerful, then [the popular song] "Marusya Took Poison."[79]

Prokofiev maintained his distance from Soviet exotica in the early 1930s, but it thereafter became clear to him that he could not continue to count on Soviet patronage while residing abroad. Just as the cultural exchanges that had followed the dissolution of the proletarian organizations would dwindle after 1934, so, too, would Prokofiev's ability to reside contentedly outside of his homeland. The open borders agreement came with an expiration date.

Ever cognizant of the "task" that the NKID had "assigned" to him, Atovmyan continued to encourage Prokofiev to move to Moscow, and Prokofiev continued to warm to the idea.[80] ("When you come to the USSR," the composer generalized, "the first impression is of uncouthness, but under this uncouthness you begin to discern interesting, inspiring people.")[81] Because his published diary ends in 1933, much remains unknown about his thinking as he contemplated the paths between Paris and Moscow. Chapter 1 of this book offers more details about his decision, confirming that he conceived it less as repatriation than relocation. He tried, as long as he could, to keep his options open. Committed to sustaining a positive outlook that denied any finality or legitimacy to evil, he could not have imagined that his future career would be immortalized—and trivialized—in history textbooks as a parable about the traumatic upheavals of twentieth-century life.

An anecdote about a Moscow concert on May 25, 1933, in one of Prokofiev's final published diary entries, reads like a premonition: "Near the end of the entr'acte, Ptashka glanced at the loge and met eyes with Stalin, who had just then entered. His gaze was so intense that she immediately turned away."[82] *Ptashka*, or "little bird," was Prokofiev's nickname for his wife. In the years ahead, the composer's inner confidence would be no match for the tragic confidence of that malevolent stare. At the time, though, the future looked bright; it was a wonderful time to be alive.

1

Plans Gone Awry,

1935–1938

Vladimir Potyomkin, a historian who joined the Bolshevik movement after the Revolution, served as Soviet ambassador to Paris from 1934 to 1937 and as Deputy People's Commissar for Foreign Affairs from 1937 to 1940. A leading figure in Soviet foreign policy during the 1930s, he brokered a mutual support pact between the Soviet Union and France, and participated in the deliberations that resulted in the signing of a nonaggression pact between the Soviet Union and Nazi Germany in 1939. He dedicated much of his time to convincing prominent Paris-based Russians—the former general Count Aleksandr Ignatyev, for example, and the writer Aleksandr Kuprin—to relocate to Moscow and Leningrad.[1] Potyomkin played a leading role in persuading Prokofiev, a frequent guest at his residence, to complete the same move. Lina recalled Potyomkin "ma[king] many promises" to the composer "about the privileges awaiting him in the Soviet Union."[2] These included housing, commissions, performances, and income that would relieve him of the need to tour. Potyomkin iterated what Atovmyan, working at the behest of the NKID, had offered to Prokofiev. The promises began to be fulfilled even before the composer relocated. The year 1935 was one of the most lucrative of his career, the bulk of his income coming from Soviet sources.

Prokofiev had been delaying the move for several years, and he might not have relocated at all had he not been pressured. From the perspective of the French authorities, Prokofiev was a Soviet citizen with an external Soviet passport, yet he maintained his *certificat d'identité*. He routinely renewed both documents—the passport and the *certificat*—through written requests to the appropriate government bodies: the Central Executive Committee of the USSR[3] and the Ministry of Foreign Affairs of France.[4] Evidence of his hesitation about wholly departing France comes from his confidant Gabriel Paitchadze, the manager of the Paris office of Édition Russe de Musique:

> S. S. vacillated for quite a long time about leaving Paris and settling in Soviet Russia. He often talked with me about this. He was drawn on the one hand to his native soil and to the Russian public, but on the other hand, it was difficult for him to come to terms with such a radical change in his life. He had become accustomed to European comforts and his wife L. I. was such a European woman that it was difficult to imagine her in a Soviet context. There was also the question of the upbringing of his sons, who had just begun their studies in Paris and would have to change schools.[5]

Then the essential point:

> The vacillation between the West and the East would have continued for even longer if he had not been given to understand within Soviet circles that he had to bring his dual existence to an end and relocate to Russia and become an official Soviet composer. In sum, he would no longer be permitted to take trips to Russia. When the situation became clear to him, S. S. finally resolved to relocate for good and, at the beginning of 1936, they [Prokofiev and Lina] liquidated their Paris apartment and settled in Moscow, bringing some of their furniture and their automobile along with them.[6]

To decline the invitation to return would have been to sacrifice the commissions for the ballet *Romeo and Juliet*, the *Cantata for the Twentieth Anniversary of October*, the score for a filmed version of *The Queen of Spades*, and incidental music for productions of *Boris Godunov* and *Eugene Onegin*. This Prokofiev could not do. To assure him that he would not have to forfeit his international career, Potyomkin, according to Paitchadze, told Prokofiev that "he would be allowed annual foreign concert tours, and likewise the right to earn foreign royalties and concert fees."[7]

The decision was finalized in the summer of 1935, when Prokofiev for the first time brought his entire family to the RSFSR. They stayed together in Polenovo, the summer retreat of the Bolshoy Theater collective, with Prokofiev working in solitude in a stand-alone cottage and the rest of the family, who arrived after him, residing in the main building. Recreation included swimming in the Oka River, playing tennis and volleyball, and fraternizing with celebrated dancers and singers.[8] It was here, in a very brief time span, that Prokofiev composed *Romeo and Juliet,* a ballet about clandestine love that bears, in and of itself, a clandestine history.[9] Its path to the stage was extremely difficult. Prokofiev ascribed its negative initial reception to archaic tastes in choreography (Soviet ballet clung to the kind of melodramatic pantomime that Diaghilev and the Ballets Russes had abandoned) and old-fashioned approaches to Shakespeare (remarkably, the first version of the ballet featured a happy rather than a tragic ending). The composer perhaps delighted in the challenge of upending common practice, but cultural and political forces thwarted his ambitions. It took several years and much difficult revision before *Romeo and Juliet* became the greatest success of his career.

The Happy Ending

The conception of this (now) celebrated but (then) controversial work dates to late November 1934, when Prokofiev traveled to Leningrad to discuss prospective performances of his operas *The Gambler* and *The Fiery Angel* at the State Academic Theater of Opera and Ballet.[10] He arrived from Moscow, where he had been attending rehearsals of *Egyptian Nights*—a hybridized staging, by Aleksandr Tairov (real surname Kornblit), of scenes from Bernard Shaw's *Caesar and Cleopatra,* Shakespeare's *Antony and Cleopatra,* and a Pushkin poem for which Prokofiev composed incidental music. According to a 1934 diary fragment, Prokofiev met with Asafyev and the dramatist and artistic director of the Lenfilm studios Adrian Piotrovsky to evaluate the prospects for *The Gambler* and *The Fiery Angel* in Leningrad.[11] They also assessed potential subjects for a new dramatic work. These included Pushkin's *The Blackamoor of Peter the Great,* an unfinished historical novel and proxy biography about the poet's great-grandfather. "If [it is to be] *Blackamoor,*" Prokofiev informed his colleagues, "then [it will be] a ballet." Piotrovsky liked the idea; Asafyev did not. The latter was basking in the glow of the positive reviews of his Orientalist ballet *The Fountain of Bakhchisaray,* and perhaps feared losing the spotlight to Prokofiev. Following a trip to Moscow for the opening of *Egyptian Nights*, Prokofiev returned to Leningrad for additional brainstorming. "A get-together at Asafyev's," he wrote in a notebook. "I critiqued *Blackamoor*—too little material. We searched for a lyrical subject. Piotrovsky threw out [the names of] several classics including *Romeo and Juliet*. I immediately blurted out: a better [subject] cannot be found."[12]

Further details of the discussions come from Prokofiev's annotated 1951–52 work list.[13] Before recommending *Romeo and Juliet*, Piotrovsky proposed two other love stories: Maurice Maeterlinck's Symbolist drama *Pelléas et Mélisande* and Gottfried von Strassburg's epic *Tristan und Isolde*. To work with either of these texts would have been to contend with the operatic specters of Debussy and Wagner. By settling on *Romeo and Juliet*, Prokofiev joined the more agreeable (for him) company of Bellini, Berlioz, Chaikovsky, and Gounod. Once the decision was reached, he began to discuss the scenario with the innovative and influential director Radlov, a longtime friend. In April 1934, Radlov had mounted a stripped-down, unsentimental version of *Romeo and Juliet* with young actors at his Studio Theater in Leningrad. Prokofiev saw the production on tour in Moscow and admired its contrapuntal juxtaposition of comic and tragic scenes.

The scenario for Prokofiev's treatment of the drama passed through different hands and different drafts. The first five-act draft, dated January 1935, survives in the London Prokofiev Archive; a second four-act draft, dated May 16, 1935, is preserved at the Russian State Archive of Literature and Art. Prokofiev appears to have written the first draft himself in Paris and then turned it over to Piotrovsky and Radlov in Leningrad for their input. Noëlle Mann, who translated and published this document, remarks that it is unclear whether Prokofiev used an English-language edition of Shakespeare's play, a Russian-language edition, "or both."[14] It is also unclear whether this first version was intended for a ballet: it reads like an opera script.

On May 17, 1935, the Leningrad Komsomol[15] newspaper *Smena* (Change of Work Shift) released a habitually terse statement from Prokofiev about his work on *Romeo and Juliet*.[16] He reveals that the State Academic Theater had encouraged the creation of the ballet, yet an agreement had not been finalized. He does not indicate the reason for the turnabout, but it was likely tied to the infighting at the State Academic Theater that followed Radlov's extremely bitter resignation as its artistic director on June 22, 1934.[17] Vladimir Mutnïkh, the new administrative director of the Bolshoy Theater in Moscow, acquired the ballet a year later with the understanding that

Piotrovsky would remain involved as scenarist, and Radlov as both scenarist and director.[18] Radlov offered his general thoughts on the chain of events in an August 8, 1935, letter to Prokofiev:

> As before, I think ahead with enormous interest and happiness to that time when it will be possible to begin staging your wonderful ballet. Please inform Vl. Iv. Mutnïkh, if he's still in Polenovo, that I haven't yet signed the contract for the libretto *only* because I must consult with Adr. Piotrovsky about it. Meanwhile I'm not sure when and where I'll see him. In essence, however, nothing has changed because of this. That is, in the area of ballet I feel not the slightest surge of Leningrad patriotism. To the contrary, I'm more than loyally disposed to the Bolshoy Theater.[19]

With Mutnïkh committed to *Romeo and Juliet*, Prokofiev moved ahead on the assumption that, following an official hearing, it would be produced by the Bolshoy Theater in the spring of 1936. He worked on the music through the idyllic summer of 1935, finishing the piano score on September 8 and the orchestral score on October 1. Alterations and refinements extended into the late fall, when he was on tour in Morocco and Algeria. Insight into the creative process comes from two letters, the first to Vera Alpers, a St. Petersburg Conservatory classmate and lifelong friend, and the second to Myaskovsky. To Alpers, Prokofiev reported that the score involved fifty-eight numbers, "a list painstakingly worked out and annotated during my stay in Leningrad, and nothing gives me greater pleasure than putting a cross beside a composed number (a black cross if the music is conceived in principle and a red cross if the number is composed and written out)."[20] To Myaskovsky, he bemoaned the time it took to work up the orchestration. "I am maintaining a pace of about 20 pages a day ... but it is hard and the main thing is to avoid succumbing to Asafyevism, that is to say, the path of least resistance."[21] Such was the path evidently taken by Asafyev in *The Fountain of Bakhchisaray*, which Prokofiev obviously disliked, but whose success he at least hoped to replicate in *Romeo and Juliet*—even to the extent of consulting the same choreographer: Radlov's pupil Rostislav Zakharov.[22]

Prokofiev's full-time work on the ballet, and his signing of a contract to compose the *Cantata for the Twentieth Anniversary of October*, provided him leverage to petition Mossovet (the Moscow Council of Worker, Peasant, and Red Army Deputies—essentially City Hall) for permanent housing. Atov-myan had, of course, offered a two-story private residence on the Garden Ring Road, but Prokofiev declared that he "could not afford it" (ne po moemu karmanu).[23] He briefly considered inhabiting an apartment in the composers' residence then being built, but progress was slow and the thought of living alongside his colleagues did not appeal to him. Tired of living out of suitcases, Prokofiev on November 11, 1935, wrote to the chairman of the Executive Committee of Mossovet, Nikolay Bulganin, requesting an alternate arrangement:

> I have been commissioned by the Bolshoy Theater for a four-act ballet on Shakespeare's *Romeo and Juliet*, and by the Radio Committee for a large-scale cantata to commem-orate the twentieth anniversary of the Soviet accession to power, about which V. I. Mutnïkh and P. M. Kerzhentsev have already written to you. There is no point in undertak-ing such commissions unless they can be fulfilled to the very highest standards. At present, I do not have suitable condi-tions for working in peace, because I do not have a flat in Moscow. When I was living abroad, everyone told me (and quite rightly) that I ought to work in the Soviet Union; but when I arrived in Moscow, the more or less general opinion seemed to be: Prokofieff's used to traveling, so let him live out of his suitcase while he's here....
>
> Please do not refuse this request made on behalf of myself and my family for a quiet flat in Moscow, where I can concentrate on the aforementioned pieces. The present situation has become bizarre; in fact, it is almost like some-thing out of a story when a Soviet composer is forced to live abroad to work on pieces commissioned by major Soviet institutions, because there is no room for him in welcoming Moscow![24]

Prokofiev was promised an apartment for the spring, but did not receive it until the summer. For the time being, he lived and worked in temporary lodging.

Forces had already begun to align themselves against *Romeo and Juliet*. The October 4, 1935, run-through of the piano score at the Bolshoy Theater did not impress the audience. The conductor Yuriy Fayer, who served as Prokofiev's page-turner, described the event in grim terms, noting that the hall emptied out as the performance wore on. "When Sergey Sergeyevich finished playing, it became clear that there would be no adjudication: there was simply nobody to do it. This was an unexpected and hard blow to the composer."[25] Fayer, an ill-tempered conductor with a tin ear, deemed the music convoluted.

The rhythmic writing occasioned general critique for its terseness, the harmonic and melodic writing for its anti-Romantic rationalism. The greatest point of contention, however, concerned the plot of act 4. The title characters live rather than die in accord with a daring reconception of Shakespeare's drama as

> a play about the struggle for love, about the struggle for the right to love by young, strong, and progressive people battling against feudal traditions and feudal outlooks on marriage and family. This makes the entire play live, breathing struggle and passion as one—makes it, perhaps, the most "Komsomol-like" of all of Shakespeare's plays.[26]

This statement comes from Radlov, who decided, in consultation with Piotrovsky and Prokofiev, to update Shakespeare's play along proletarian lines. The decision to add a happy ending was vetted by several people, including Sergey Dinamov, a critic, writer, and Central Committee advisor who sat on the repertoire board of the Bolshoy Theater and exercised political control.[27] In a May 2, 1935, letter to Prokofiev, Radlov reports discussing the scenario with Dinamov, who "in general approves of it, even with the happy ending, but he recommends being careful naming it—adding something like 'on motives of Shakespeare' or another cautious subtitle."[28]

The May 16, 1935, version of the scenario (which does not bear a subtitle) details the happy ending. Juliet lies in her bedchamber, having taken the sleeping potion prepared for her by Friar Laurence. "Romeo enters," "dispatches the servant," and "pulls back the cover," but he is unable, like Paris before him, to rouse Juliet; Romeo concludes that she has died and, grief-stricken, resolves to commit suicide. The arrival of Friar Laurence prevents him from pulling out his dagger, and the two engage in a brief struggle during a break in the music (No. 51). "Juliet begins to breathe" (No. 52). Friar Laurence "strikes a gong"; Romeo clutches Juliet and bears her from the room "into a grove" (No. 53). The people gather, and Friar Laurence directs their attention to the lovers (No. 54). "Juliet slowly comes to herself." She and Romeo express their feelings of relief and joy in a final dance (No. 55), which Prokofiev intended to be "bright" but not overblown. It would not, he writes, "attain a *forte*."[29] The final three minutes and twenty seconds of the score (No. 56) are unscripted: in the apotheosis, the music expresses what the visuals cannot.

The composer found merit in Radlov's reconception of Shakespeare's drama, but his colleagues did not. Afinogenov mocked it in his journal:

> The librettist (Radlov) resurrected Romeo, did not allow him to take poison—the end is thus happy and unnatural. Shakespeare, he says, would have written this ending himself if he were alive now....But if Shakespeare were alive he would have written about something else. The issue is not one of fidelity but of the spirit of the work: "For never was a story of more woe / Than this of Juliet and her Romeo."[30]

Myaskovsky, for his part, called the music of the ballet "wonderful" but "undanceable," with a "ridiculous ending involving Juliet's revival (Radlov)."[31] Prokofiev resisted the criticism but shared it with Radlov, suggesting that perhaps the scenario might need to be rethought. On December 6, 1935, he sent his collaborator a jocular postcard from Casablanca, where he was on tour, asking, "Do you still remember *Romeo*? Are you pressing on with it? Have you devised an ingenious ending?"[32]

There followed a run-through of *Romeo and Juliet* at the offices of the newspaper *Sovetskoye iskusstvo* (Soviet Art) on January 25, 1936, with both Mutnïkh and Dinamov in attendance. Prokofiev performed the first three acts to mixed results. Even in its absence, act 4 remained a subject of discussion, now both positive and negative. Some lauded the idea of basing proletarian art on the classics, others decried it. Dinamov continued to approve of the happy ending, while also stressing the collective nature of the ballet's conception: eight people, he claimed, had weighed in on the scenario. "Personally I'm for changing the finale," he told the gathering. "Ballet is ballet. People need to leave the theater afterward feeling joy....Hence I conclude that in Prokofiev's work the two main characters of Shakespeare's drama must not die." The dramatist Osaf Litovsky and journalist David Zaslavsky concurred, noting that Prokofiev's hero and heroine were entirely different characters than Shakespeare's. (Litovsky, significantly, was not just a dramatist: from 1930 to 1937 he served as director of the censorship board Glavrepertkom.) The music critic Aleksandr Ostretsov disagreed, declaring that "there's nothing to fear if the ballet ends with death. A somber ending does not necessarily lend a pessimist character to the whole of a ballet. The life-enhancing tone of Prokofiev's entire piece, clearly manifest in the culmination, will not be weakened if he follows in Shakespeare's footsteps in the ballet's denouement." Radlov, for his part, no longer had the wherewithal to defend his scenario, commenting that it was not worth his dying "so that Romeo and Juliet should live."[33]

Irrespective of the debate over the ballet's ending, the Bolshoy Theater kept *Romeo and Juliet* in the repertoire; the premiere, however, was pushed back from the 1935–36 season to the 1936–37 season. Its eventual cancellation stemmed from an overhaul of the administration of the theater and a personal review of its repertoire by the imperious, repressive chairman of the Committee on Arts Affairs, Platon Kerzhentsev. A June 3, 1936, memorandum from Kerzhentsev to Stalin and Vyacheslav Molotov, the chairman of Sovnarkom (Council of People's Commissars), resulted in the dismissal of the conductor Nikolay Golovanov as part of a "decisive change within the theater." This memorandum still listed *Romeo and Juliet* as a forthcoming Bolshoy Theater production. Preparations were suspended, however, pending an "assessment" of the repertoire "by the theater's new leadership."[34] The arrest of Mutnïkh followed on April 20, 1937, as part of a wave of repression within cultural circles; he was executed on November 11.[35] Given its association with a vanquished "enemy of the people," *Romeo and Juliet*, a ballet involving murder, poison, and class struggle, became taboo, unfit for performance during the Twentieth Anniversary of the Great October Socialist Revolution. It disappeared from the repertoire. Kerzhentsev, meantime, had determined that Prokofiev required ideological guidance.

In 1941, the composer discussed the entire affair in an autobiographical essay commissioned by the editor of *Sovetskaya muzïka*, the journal of the Union of Soviet Composers:

> There was quite a fuss at the time about our attempts to give *Romeo and Juliet* a happy ending—in the last act Romeo arrives a minute earlier, finds Juliet alive and everything ends well. The reasons for this bit of barbarism were purely choreographic: living people can dance, the dying

cannot. The justification was that Shakespeare himself was said to have been uncertain about the ends of his plays (*King Lear*) and parallel with *Romeo and Juliet* had written *Two Gentlemen of Verona* in which all ends well. Curiously enough whereas the report that Prokofiev was writing a ballet on the theme of *Romeo and Juliet* with a happy ending was received quite calmly in London, our own Shakespeare scholars proved more papal than the pope and rushed to the defense of Shakespeare. But what really caused me to change my mind was a remark someone made to me about the ballet: "Strictly speaking your music does not express any real joy at the end." That was quite true. After several conferences with the choreographers it was found that the tragic ending could be expressed in dance and in due course the music for that ending was written.[36]

The crucial words of this confession are "in due course." Two letters from Prokofiev to his assistant Pavel Lamm reveal that he did not begin the music for the tragic ending—Nos. 51 and 52 of the score—until the late summer of 1936, and did not finish until the late summer of 1938.[37] Prokofiev trimmed the ending but did not entirely rewrite it. Indeed, comparing the ballet's two endings reveals a striking overlap: the music associated with the reunion of the two lovers in the happy version (No. 55) became the music of Juliet's death in the tragic version (No. 52). The theme in question comes from an earlier passage in the ballet called "Juliet the Young Girl" (No. 10 at rehearsal number 55). Once associated with wistful reverie, it comes to stand, in both versions of the ballet, for mature passion. Prokofiev enhances the theme's emotional impact by transposing it into the highest register of the violins.

In the happy ending, Prokofiev aligns this theme with another from "Juliet the Young Girl" (rehearsal number 53). Both express longing, an emotion sated when the two lovers avoid death and reunite. The positive sentiments are enhanced in the concluding measures, which develop a theme first heard in the "Love Dance" (No. 21 at rehearsal number 143) from the balcony episode. In short, the apotheosis of this version of the ballet embellishes the music associated with the hero and heroine's first declarations of love.

The happy ending begins with an elaboration of the tranquil, thinly scored theme first heard in "Juliet at Friar Laurence's" (No. 29). The post-awakening episodes (Nos. 53 and 54) feature a jubilant new theme: a rising arpeggiated pattern accompanied by ticking eighth notes and (in No. 53) the chiming of a bell and striking of a gong (by Friar Laurence) on the stage. Prokofiev does not use this theme anywhere else in the ballet and discarded it when he reconceived the ending. He did, however, eventually find a home for it. The nineteen-measure passage between rehearsal numbers 360 and 362 recurs almost intact at the start of the second movement of his Fifth Symphony (1944).[38]

In Shakespeare's play, the death of Romeo and Juliet cannot be undone; Prokofiev and Radlov perhaps wanted to believe that the two lovers had merely gone to sleep, that the fantastic energies in their relationship remained unaffected by potions and daggers. This formulation elaborates a central precept of Christian Science, whose teachings Prokofiev esteemed: "No form or physical combination is adequate to represent infinite Love."[39] The ballet accepts the existence of earthly evil but also the preexistence of celestial harmony. Prokofiev represents the two lovers willing away their reality—the Verona square and the palace—and entering another, greater one. But at the same time, the happy ending, with its various symbolic breaches of the proscenium, affronts the religious sentiment that lies at the heart of the play. In act 4, scene 5, Friar Laurence declares: "She's not well married that lives married long, but she's best married that dies married young."[40] Prokofiev and Radlov overturn this idea. Romeo learns in the nick of time that the potion only makes Juliet appear dead. The noble bride shakes off its effects in his arms. The ballet suggests that genuine tragedy, in the Russian conception, cannot happen by accident—as in Shakespeare's text.

Both versions of the ballet foreground the strife between the Capulets and Montagues and the disparities between the inner world of the emotions and the outer world of social codes. The metric shifts in the score correspond to Shakespeare's shifts between blank verse, rhymed couplets, and sonnet forms. The elaborate interweaving of themes captures the subtleties of the couple's emotional and psychological states. The force of fate is denoted by the earsplitting dissonances of "The Duke's Command" (No. 7) and by the ponderous "Dance of the Knights" (No. 13), which derives from music conceived for a diabolical swordfight in the inchoate 1930 version of *The Fiery Angel*.[41] Prokofiev would be pressured terribly into rethinking and reworking the ballet in the years ahead, and both the ordering of the numbers and their contents would be adversely affected. For example, the "Dance of the Two Captains" would be relocated from the end of the third act

(No. 49) to the beginning of the second act (No. 25) and renamed "Dance with Mandolins."[42] The issue of the ending aside, the 1935 version of the ballet makes more dramatic sense than the 1940 revision, which sounds in places like an exploratory draft.

Muddle Instead of Music

The summer of 1935, arguably the most productive of Prokofiev's career, involved work not only on *Romeo and Juliet* but also a set of twelve children's pieces for piano,[43] the libretto of the Cantata, and a collection of six group ("mass") songs that Prokofiev submitted to a contest organized by the Union of Soviet Composers, the Union of Soviet Writers, and the editorial board of *Pravda*.[44] Upon completing the ballet's orchestration, he returned to Paris with the children, while Lina stayed behind to participate in a broadcast on State Radio.[45] Prokofiev performed in a Brussels concert series ("Les Maîtres Contemporains de la Musique") and a festival of his works with Concerts Pasdeloup in Paris. The reviews of these two events noted his international fame.

Before liquidating their Paris apartment, the couple took a final trip to Moscow, ringing in the start of 1936 at the Moscow Arts Theater. Four weeks later, after they had left the Soviet Union, the Soviet musical world was thrown into turmoil by the publication of an unsigned article in *Pravda*. The article, dated January 28, 1936, condemned Shostakovich's second and final completed opera *Lady Macbeth of the Mtsensk District* for subverting operatic convention with perverse discord and ultra-naturalistic depictions of rape and murder. Two days earlier, Stalin and his assistants had attended a performance of the work, but exited the theater before the final curtain without a word. The article, titled "Muddle Instead of Music," described the opera as "an intentionally discordant flood of sounds. Scraps of melody, embryos of musical phrases drown, tear away, and disappear anew in the din, grinding, and squealing."[46] Ten days later, another unsigned article appeared, this time damning Shostakovich's third and final ballet *The Limpid Stream* for its inauthentic musical representation of life on the collective farm.[47] The attacks, and the anti-modernist, anti-Western invective they spawned, alarmed and angered Shostakovich.[48]

The articles appeared while Prokofiev was traveling in Eastern Europe. (Before settling in Moscow, he went on two massive concert tours, playing in Switzerland, Spain, Portugal, Morocco, Algeria, and Tunisia, then in

France, Belgium, Czechoslovakia, Hungary, Bulgaria, and Poland.) He read the articles while in Prague. Lina forwarded them to him from Paris, together with clippings from *Izvestiya* and the Russian émigré newspaper *Posledniye novosti*. The denunciation of Shostakovich demonstrated that the dismantling of the Russian Association of Proletarian Musicians and the founding of the Union of Soviet Composers had not put an end to dilettantish censorship. The extent to which the scandal prompted Lina and Prokofiev to reconsider their decision to relocate is unclear, but they seem to have concluded that Prokofiev's reputation in Soviet music circles had not suffered. In fact, his reputation seemed to improve. In the months ahead, Prokofiev allowed himself to believe that, with Shostakovich under a cloud, he had automatically become the preeminent Soviet composer. Altogether dissatisfied at earning the bulk of his income on the road, he pushed forward with the move to Moscow, reassuring Lina that if the experience soured, they could always return to Paris.

The Paris-based publisher Pierre Souvtchinsky (Pyotr Suvchinsky) was a family friend who financed and co-edited a journal devoted to the Eurasianist movement. Hostile to all things Soviet, he advised Lina to rethink the decision; he also kept her apprised of the fallout from the denunciation of Shostakovich, and drew her attention to the ongoing campaign in the Soviet media to eradicate bourgeois modernist influences from Soviet music. Souvtchinsky advised Lina to read, for example, the article "At the Gathering of Moscow Composers" from the February 17, 1936, issue of *Pravda*. According to Lina, the passage from this jingoistic piece that most bewildered Souvtchinsky was the following:

> Composers, critics, and performers, the leading representatives of Soviet music, came together to repudiate hostile influences on Soviet art.
>
> Professor H[enrich] Neuhaus, a Conservatory instructor and talented pianist, delivered a concerned, heartfelt speech. He called the *Pravda* articles a joyful event. Soviet existence is so great, so wonderful, that the music which purports to represent it should be nobler and grander than all that has come before it in art. We are scaling the Himalaya in art, Prof. Neuhaus said. How petty and insignificant are the feelings and passions represented in music like *Lady Macbeth*! This music is coarse and cynical. Its eccentricities

astonish at first exposure, but then, very quickly, they become merely tedious. The articles in *Pravda*, where the need for clarity in musical language and realism in art is forcefully argued, ought to be hailed.

It is interesting to compare the speech of a Conservatory instructor with that of one of the students, the young, talented composer [Tikhon] Khrennikov. He spoke in plain terms about the path he has taken, one that is typical of young musicians caught up in the sweep, grandeur and passion of the Great Proletarian Revolution. As artists, they sense all the beauty that is arising in our life. They want to join with the masses. But the western European composers Hindemith, Schoenberg, and Berg are given to them as examples and authorities. They are told that being a revolutionary involves finding new, intentionally complex forms and seeking out harsh sounds that are "original," even if incomprehensible. Clarity and lucidity of form and sound have for some reason become shameful.[49]

Souvtchinsky chafed at the conflation of Hindemith, a neoclassical composer with leftist tendencies, with the arch-formalists Schoenberg and Berg. The article signaled, in Souvtchinsky's opinion, that the neoclassical Prokofiev might likewise become an unwelcome presence in the Soviet sphere. He cautioned Lina not to "rush off with the furniture." Lina summarized Souvtchinsky's thoughts on the article for her husband, then voiced her own: "The musical idiots and cretins have suddenly used the opportunity to put forth their unwanted opinions—just like the period [1929] of the disputes—and others are silent." She told her husband to "be a little more cautious there all the same" and asked him to relay his "impressions" of Moscow back to her.[50]

This letter, dated February 22, 1936, exudes a mixture of anticipation and trepidation about the move. Lina seems to be a willing partner in Prokofiev's plans, but also cognizant of the risks involved. Her postscript, written in English rather than Russian or French, gives pause: "Please acknowledge receipt of letter. Perhaps you better destroy this one."[51]

Two days later, Lina wrote to Prokofiev again, this time referring more directly to the Shostakovich affair. She first reports visiting with Lyubov Kozintseva, the wife of the prolific novelist and journalist Ilya Ehrenburg, who, like her husband, tracked political events in the RSFSR and the shake-ups within its cultural agencies. (Ehrenburg worked at the time as a French correspondent for *Izvestiya*.) Kozintseva, who received "all of the Moscow newspapers," informed Lina that though the "attack" on Soviet composers appeared to have ended, it had shifted to architecture and would doubt-less affect "all branches of art."[52] Lina's specific remarks about the devel-opments in Soviet music reported in the newspapers suggest disdain. She determines that the struggle among the bureaucrats "to be the one who is showing the new way" stems from their having "achieved" and "mastered" little in their own dismal careers. "It is one thing to criticize, another to show in deeds," but "what have all those little insects [*bukashki*] shown? What have they achieved? What have they mastered?"[53] These comments are preceded by an expression of bemusement at the bungled efforts of uneducated and untalented musicians to define the parameters for Soviet music.

Lina indicates that because Prokofiev had already adopted a more acces-sible style, he would succeed in post-RAPM Moscow. The melodiousness of his last two ballets and his interest in the phenomenon of mass music had set the stage for his return. Although Lina recognized that diplomacy was not one of her husband's strong suits, she supported, and perhaps even encouraged, his efforts to inform the debate about Shostakovich's affront to proletarian taste. "I'm about to send you another *Pravda* article," she wrote in reference to the report on the meeting of Moscow composers. "It seems to me that in all of this drama you can play a very important role, but only, of course, with great tact, and without creating any unnecessary enemies."[54]

How Pioneer Peter Caught the Wolf

Prokofiev relocated to Moscow in early March 1936. He arrived ahead of his family, and resided in the National Hotel across from Red Square while waiting for his permanent residence—the apartment allotted to him for his work on the ballet and the Cantata—to be readied. On May 15, near the end of the Paris school year, Lina arrived in Moscow with the children. Pro-kofiev met his family at Belorussia train station. They stayed periodically at the hotel for five weeks (until June 29) before moving into a four-room apartment in a neo-Constructivist building at 14 Zemlyanoy Val.[55] (In 1938, the street would be renamed Ulitsa Chkalova.)[56] Part of the building was assigned to artist workers, another to Sovnarkom. The family's belongings included eleven crates of furniture and domestic items as well as an upright piano sent to Prokofiev as a gift from a Czechoslovakian firm.

Since Prokofiev had been away on tour, it fell to Lina to attend to the logistics of the relocation. Committed to maintaining her international way of life, she planned not only for the move to the RSFSR but also for future trips to France and the United States. Worries about the darkening political and cultural climate in the Soviet sphere—and the darkening political and cultural climate throughout Europe—mixed with practical concerns: the number of dresses customs officers would allow her to bring across the border, and the layout of the future apartment. In a March 11 letter to her husband she sends greetings from "the Potyomkins," whom she had visited the day before, and then asks: "When will the artists' building finally be done—have you received the apartment?"[57]

Lina also asks her husband about his work, referring to the contract he had received to write incidental music for a production of *Eugene Onegin*. She inquires after the dramatist Litovsky, with whom Prokofiev had discussed his plans for *Eugene Onegin*, and after Radlov. Unaware of the crisis within the Bolshoy Theater, she asks: "How is *Romeo and Juliet* coming along? I read somewhere that it will be performed 'in the spring.' Are they rehearsing it?"[58] It was not, of course, in rehearsal. But if Prokofiev recognized that the ballet was falling victim to the same type of anti-formalist, anti-Western backlash affecting Shostakovich, he could partly console himself with the news that the Leningrad Choreographic Technical College was interested in staging the ballet in 1938 to celebrate the bicentennial of its founding.[59] Such a production bore an artistic risk—it would be student-driven—but it would accord with the work's focus on youth struggling against repressive forces.

As the proposal was being floated, Lina arrived in Moscow with the children. It is unknown what Prokofiev said to his wife—in person or by telephone—about the *Pravda* articles. He spoke about them with his Moscow colleagues, whom he told that he considered Shostakovich's opera an example of first-rate stagecraft.[60] The report on the discussion at the mid-February meeting of Moscow composers mistakenly signaled to him that he was insulated from what had befallen Shostakovich. "The attacks on formalism," he wrote in a notebook, "neither affected me nor Myaskovsky."[61] He appended that Lev Lebedinsky, chief ideologue of the Russian Association of Proletarian Musicians, apologized for treating him discourteously in 1929.

Prokofiev's arrival in Moscow was cause for jubilation. "Of course we were all in seventh heaven about this," Atovmyan recalled, adding that he and his colleagues "tried in every possible way to look after [Prokofiev's] charming wife, Lina Ivanovna. We arranged concerts for her with performances of *The Ugly Duckling* and did everything to prevent her from convincing Prokofiev to return to Paris, which had, it showed, very much spoiled her."[62]

Excluding complaints about problems finding time to pursue her singing career, Lina's initial reactions to Moscow are unclear; Prokofiev, for his part, tended to view life in the city sardonically. Strolling by an election notice, he said to his wife: "Just look, Ptashka, at how everything interests them: they all vote for the same person."[63] To those left behind in Paris, Prokofiev described the relocation in matter-of-fact terms. He assured his mother-in-law, for example, that the family had adjusted to the move from Paris to Moscow without particular difficulty and had enjoyed another tranquil summer in Polenovo:

> We went to Polenovo in July and August, and returned on September 1 to Moscow, since Svyatoslav had to start school. In Polenovo he took Russian lessons each day and has quite passably adjusted to it. But he didn't stay in Russian school for long; now we've taken him to an English one. The enrollment is less English and American children than the children of Soviets serving abroad. Our little one flouted himself during the summer. Obsessed with chess, he walked around with a little board and figures in his pocket, and if he saw someone who knew how to play, he brought out the chess and requested a game. The apartment we received isn't very big—smaller than the previous one in Paris—but in other respects it's completely presentable. They've even shown our building to English tourists, and we've taken them into our apartment. But it was a wonder to put in order, and the process continues: it's difficult to find fittings, fuses, and so forth. The cupboards are insufficient to accommodate the books, linens, dishes, and other detritus. In light of this we've temporarily left Oleg in Polenovo, where he's in safe hands and enjoying a magical childhood summer (in contrast to the dust from the construction in our neighborhood; our road is being doubled in width). I'm working hard:

I wrote music for the film of *The Queen of Spades* and for
the drama *Eugene Onegin*, which Tairov is staging. Besides
this I wrote a big overture for a new symphony orchestra
(of 130 members) that is being formed here. We've heard
no news of you, which is entirely disagreeable. Ptashka
and Svyatoslav will write to you in a few days. Ptashka is
very tired from frayed nerves; the summer did not put this
right....I'm planning to be in Paris in December.[64]

In the summer of 1936, as in the summer of 1935, Prokofiev composed at
a Mozartian clip, producing two of the three commissions he received for
the Pushkin centennial of 1937. Polenovo—and the move to the RSFSR in
general—inspired the best-known music of his career, as well as a cluster of
lesser-known works he would mine for material in the future.

The most popular score is, of course, *Peter and the Wolf*, which arose
out of discussions between Prokofiev and Nataliya Sats, the indefatigable,
well-respected director of the Moscow Children's Theater. The result was a
pedagogical work that introduced the instruments of the orchestra within
the context of a spoken-word narrative about a Soviet boy scout, the headstrong, goodhearted Pioneer Peter, who sets wrong to right by defying an
elder. As the Slavicist Catriona Kelly remarks, "Conflicts of this kind were
passim...in children's literature (and in journalism for children) throughout
the 1920s and early 1930s."[65] Sats enlisted the poet Nina Sakonskaya (Anto-
nina Sokolovskaya), a prolific author of tales-in-verse for young readers, to
write the text. Prokofiev, however, rejected Sakonskaya's draft, complaining that it was too poetic, too rhymed. "The relations between words and
music in a work like this are very delicately balanced," he hectored Sats.
"Words must know their place; otherwise they may lead the listener's attention astray, instead of helping his perception of the music."[66] In keeping
with the Pioneer spirit of self-reliance, Prokofiev chose to write the text on
his own in consultation with Sats. After completing a draft, which he titled
How Pioneer Peter Caught the Wolf, he wrote a detailed set of performance
instructions in Russian and English. The English-language instructions read
as follows:

Each character of this tale is represented by a corresponding instrument in the orchestra: the bird by a flute, the duck

by an oboe, the cat by a clarinet playing staccato in a low register, the grandfather by a bassoon, the wolf by three horns, Peter by the string quartet, the shooting of the hunters by the kettle drums and bass drum. Before an orchestral performance it is desirable to show these instruments to the children and to play on them the corresponding leitmotivs. Thereby, the children learn to distinguish the sonorities of the instruments during the performance of this tale.[67]

The plot recalls, among other works, the folktale *Ivan Tsarevich and the Gray Wolf* and the Disney animated shorts *The Three Bears* and *The Wise Little Hen*.[68] It also derives from parables about nature spirits, however, of which the most frightening is the wood-goblin, which can appear as large as a tree, steal newborns, abduct villagers, drive them insane, and send them back to their homes mute and covered with moss. The wood-goblin's favorite beast is the wolf, which, according to folklore, must be domesticated.[69] Peter plays the role of the tamer in Prokofiev's tale. His controlling, rationalizing impulse mimics, on a sociopolitical front, the Soviet obsession with mastering nature, one clear-cut example being the triumph of the Moscow Metro over Mother Earth.

On the surface, *Peter and the Wolf* centers on two events: Peter's rescue of a songbird from the claws of a tomcat, and Peter's capture, with the assistance of the indebted songbird, of a displaced, famished wolf. Before the trap is set, the wolf swallows an inattentive duck. Peter summons a group of hunters to his aid, convincing them to place the wolf on exhibit in the zoo, and is finally dragged home by his unamused grandfather. The tale ends, for the purposes of narrative symmetry, with the sound of the duck quacking from within the wolf's stomach.

Prokofiev drafted the piano score for *Peter and the Wolf* in less than a week, after which he played and talked it through for a group of schoolchildren. (The piano score was completed on April 15, the orchestration on April 24.) He devised Peter's theme in advance of the others, working out several different versions in a sketchbook that also includes themes destined for *Romeo and Juliet*, the Sixth and Seventh piano sonatas, and the Seventh Symphony.[70] To affirm Peter's richness of character, his "polyphonic" persona, Prokofiev scored the theme for string quartet. He also transformed the theme, filtering it through different tonalities and presenting it as a miniature pastorale (when Peter steps through the gate into the meadow behind his grandfather's house), a waltz (when Peter convinces the hunters not to kill the wolf), and a mock heroic march (when Peter leads the parade to the zoo). The narrator addresses the lad's self-reliance, his love of animals and nature, and his vigilance—the Pioneer codes of conduct. Peter's theme cedes at the start of the score to the songbird's theme, which alludes to the bluebird variation in Chaikovsky's *Sleeping Beauty*. The two themes thereafter combine, assisting each other, as it were, to fashion a small ternary form.

The remarkable pictorialism of this and the other orchestral interludes in *Peter and the Wolf* ensured that it would be a success with children. Following a lackluster premiere with the Moscow Philharmonic on May 2, the work was re-premiered at the newly created Central Children's Theater, where it delighted the audience.[71] In search of a similar success with adults, Prokofiev wrote a pictorial work of a very different sort: the little-known, underrated *Russian* Overture.[72] This thirteen-minute piece exists in two versions, the first (1936) with a heavier woodwind and brass complement than the second (1937). Prokofiev reduced the scoring on the advice of the Hungarian conductor Eugen Szenkár, who had encouraged the creation of the work and become its champion. Pleased by the success of the October 29, 1936, premiere, Szenkár took the Overture on tour, conducting the first version in Leningrad and the second version in Paris and Tel Aviv.

Somewhat like Stravinsky's *Petrushka*, Prokofiev's Overture includes motives derived from Russian folkdance, salon song, and liturgical chant, all packaged into a sonata-rondo form. The composer highlights the folkdance motive in the first, third, and fifth sections, the salon song motive in the second section, and the liturgical chant motive in the fourth section. Toward the raucous climax, the motives are broken down and reduced to single-measure ostinato patterns that form the backbone for a grotesque portrayal, in the brasses and woodwinds, of wheezing accordions and shouting carnival barkers. The Overture, which invoked the nonrealist aesthetics of Stravinsky and the Ballets Russes, did not please the conservative Myaskovsky, who branded it "scathing and affected" after hearing the dress rehearsal.[73] Prokofiev did not attend the premiere; his absence, Myaskovsky reports, "suddenly caused anxiety."[74] The Overture earned positive initial reviews, however, with the infernal elements of the conclusion attracting less attention than what a critic for Leningrad *Krasnaya gazeta* dubbed the "freshness" of the "song-like melodic material" and "orchestral color."[75]

Karamzin

In their time, *Peter and the Wolf* and the *Russian* Overture fared well. However, the magnum opus of the mid-1930s, the ballet *Romeo and Juliet*, did not, even though it was conceived with the aim of raising the profile of Soviet ballet at home and abroad. First the prospective Leningrad State Academic Theater production fell through, then the contracted Moscow Bolshoy Theater production, and finally the prospective student-driven production for the Leningrad Choreographic Technical College. It would take two long years for *Romeo and Juliet* to reach the stage; the premiere, moreover, would occur not in Moscow but in Brno, Czechoslovakia, and would be partial, involving only the highlights of the score.[76] Prokofiev's frustration prompted him to initiate a salvage operation: he extracted the first of eventually three orchestral suites from *Romeo and Juliet*.[77] Detached from the ballet's controversial scenario, the suites would demonstrate to Kerzhentsev that Prokofiev, "a former captive of formalism," was clearly trying "to overcome formalism and approach realism."[78] Kerzhentsev's tepid praise came late—the quotation is taken from a December 19, 1937, report to Stalin and Molotov about Soviet musical affairs—and did nothing to hasten the ballet's Soviet premiere.

The difficulties with the ballet spurred Prokofiev in the spring of 1936 to express his concerns about the state of Soviet music. Even in the wake of recent setbacks and in the midst of the darkening cultural climate, he expected his opinions to be heeded. The tone of his pronouncements ranges from cautious to strident. Below is an example of his cautious approach (a document quoted in chapter 2 finds him reacting more heatedly). In answer to an April 23 questionnaire from the editors of the wall-newspaper of the Union of Soviet Composers, Prokofiev offered his opinion on the dissolution of the Russian Association of Proletarian Musicians:

1) It is difficult for me to speak about the overall significance of the April 23, 1932 Resolution, since it took place during my extended time abroad. I am thus obliged to restrict myself to a subjective point of view: I sensed opposition to my compositions before this time, which to a large extent diminished afterwards.

2) In much present-day music making, there is a depressing separation between the old-fashioned musical language of our composers

and present-day reality. They speak in Karamzin's language about present-day issues. Our composers have not yet found a language that is both comprehensible and new.

3)   For the twentieth anniversary of October I am writing a large cantata, but in addition I hope to complete some other projects.

4)   The Union of Soviet Composers has not helped me in my creative work. On the domestic front it has performed many valuable services. 3–4 years ago, moreover, it facilitated the performance of my works in Moscow and Leningrad.[79]

The answer to question 2 is most significant, for here Prokofiev articulates his long-standing view that the composer must at once divert and edify the listener. By referring to Nikolay Karamzin, Prokofiev forges a parallel between Soviet music and old-fashioned, sentimentalist aesthetics. To shed its Karamzinian bonds while also avoiding modernist abstraction, Soviet music needed to privilege what Prokofiev, in his 1934 article "The Paths of Soviet Music," called a "light-serious" or "serious-light" style.

The Cultural Diplomat

During his penultimate tour in the West—a three-month excursion that took him to Belgium, France, and the United States—Prokofiev boasted about the benefits of being a Soviet composer. He also justified his efforts, which had hitherto partly been a flop, to create appealing and ennobling works for the masses. "The composer working in Moscow needs to do this," he informed a Brussels radio reporter. "Today we have large new masses of listeners. It is the composer's duty to hold their attention in the concert hall, to offer them serious yet simple music, so as not to fatigue but to engage this segment of the public."[80]

Prokofiev spoke to the station on December 2, 1936, as part of an elaborate broadcast featuring the Second Violin Concerto, the Overture in B-flat Major, the Symbolist-inspired score Seven They Are Seven, and the suite from the ballet The Tale of the Buffoon. The first and second works evince his self-described transparency of expression; the third and fourth, dating from his unbridled, iconoclastic youth, do not. Long before his move to the RSFSR, Prokofiev reduced and refined his musical language, but he justified the change as an on-the-spot reaction to the conditions in his homeland. Touring abroad, he masqueraded as a born-again composer, a proud new

Soviet citizen who had rejected discord for concord, chromatic harmonies for flowing diatonic melodies.

Following a December 14 broadcast in Paris, during which he spoke with pride about *Peter and the Wolf*, he conducted and performed in Lausanne and Prague. He returned to Paris for another event on December 19, thereafter grumbling to Myaskovsky that "some Parisians like the suite from *Romeo*; others heaved sighs of regret over the simplification of my style."[81] Lina joined him in Paris on December 24, distressed about being harassed by French customs officials. The couple spent the holidays together in a flat on the rue du Dr Roux. On January 6, Prokofiev left for the United States, leaving Lina behind to care for her mother.

The American tour swung through the Northeast (Boston, New York, and Washington) and Midwest (Chicago and St. Louis). In interviews en route, Prokofiev advertised his latest works while making the argument that concert-goers must be introduced to accessible music before confronting challenging repertoire, lest they flee to dance halls for pure entertainment. He elaborated for a reporter from the *Chicago Daily Tribune*, describing *Romeo and Juliet* as the test of a "new melodic line." The First Suite from the ballet, Prokofiev asserted, offers "almost immediate appeal" like "nothing" in his oeuvre "that has gone before."[82] The sales pitch worked. The critic Edward Barry praised him for having the courage to change his method: "Far from adopting one theory of music to the exclusion of all others and devoting his whole life in an attempt to stuff it down the world's throat, [Prokofiev] changes his mind frequently and keeps himself ever open to new ideas."[83]

The American tour was a success: audiences and critics responded to his appearances with enthusiasm. The lone voice of dissent was the music critic for the *Christian Science Monitor*, who wondered why his two concerts in Boston did not include his latest works, in particular the incidental music for *Eugene Onegin*. "Surely the work must be done," the critic groused. "Might we not have heard something of all this?"[84] It was a reasonable question—but one that Prokofiev could not honestly answer, since he had been instructed in a December 3 memorandum to discontinue work on *Eugene Onegin*. The Committee on Arts Affairs had prohibited the staging of the drama on political grounds. The director, Tairov, had fallen out of favor with the Committee over another project; access to Molotov allowed him to retain his position and his theater, but not before he vowed to mend his ways.

Prokofiev did not speak about the cancellation while abroad, stressing instead—and without the slightest trace of irony—the benefits of Soviet government involvement in the arts. He was obliged to fulfill his patriotic duties. Doing so ensured he could travel and that he could retain the persona of a free artist. There were other paradoxes, other signs of internal conflict. He apparently took pride in being awash in work even as he learned that the work, when finished, would not always be performed. He also, it seems, reassured himself that he was immune to censure because of—rather than in spite of—the fact that Meyerhold and Tairov had come under fire. In this regard he was altogether mistaken.

Such was the opinion of one of his closest friends in the United States, Vernon Duke (Vladimir Dukelsky), who caught up with Prokofiev in New York and quizzed him about the tumult in Moscow. Duke maintained a successful career as a Broadway composer, penning a number of jazz standards while also competing in the arena of traditional symphonic and choral music. Like Prokofiev, he had abandoned Russia during the Revolution, thereafter leading a courageous and adventurous career that included a stint as a café musician in Constantinople (Istanbul), a commission in Paris from the Ballets Russes, freelance work as a songwriter in London, and tutelage from George Gershwin in New York. Resolving to write intelligent music for the general public, he settled into show business. From their letters and memoirs, it emerges that Duke and Prokofiev quarreled affectionately about their opposite career choices while also helping each other to secure performances.

When they reunited in 1937, Prokofiev spoke in upbeat terms about life in the Soviet Union, while Duke, accustomed to a competitive capitalist environment, recognized that the description was too good to be true:

> I took Serge to see Mother, who worshipped him. "Sergey Sergeyevich, do you mean to tell me that the Communists let you out—just like that?" she asked incredulously. "Just like that, Anna Aleksevna," Prokofiev assured her, slapping his thighs—a favorite mannerism with him. "Here I am all in one piece, as you see." "And Lina Ivanovna?" Mother persisted. "She will come back to the States with me in October—I have enough engagements to warrant a speedy return." "What about your boys?" At this, Prokofiev changed the subject abruptly. I later learned that the Soviet authorities would not let them travel with their parents;

in other words, they were forcibly left behind in Russia, as hostages.

At dinner—Mother having discreetly refused to join us as we had "so much" to talk about—I asked Serge a difficult question, then uppermost in my mind. I wanted to know how he could live and work in the atmosphere of Soviet totalitarianism. Serge was silent for a moment, then said quietly and seriously: "Here is how I feel about it: I care nothing for politics—I'm a composer first and last. Any government that lets me write my music in peace, publishes everything I compose before the ink is dry, and performs every note that comes from my pen is all right with me. In Europe we all have to fish for performances, cajole conductors and theater directors; in Russia they come to me—I can hardly keep up with the demand. What's more, I have a comfortable flat in Moscow, a delightful dacha in the country and a brand-new car. My boys go to a fine English school in Moscow. It's true, Lina Ivanovna whimpers now and then—but you know her. Being a composer's wife isn't easy."[85]

Anecdotes, especially amusing anecdotes, tend to be inaccurate, and this one is no exception: Prokofiev had only just purchased his car, an ostentatious blue Ford, and did not yet own a dacha.[86] Duke's story nonetheless draws attention to the strain in Prokofiev and Lina's relationship that had developed after their move from Paris to Moscow—here characterized as a sensible career option.

The last concert on Prokofiev's schedule occurred on February 8 at the Soviet Embassy in Washington, where the ambassador, Aleksandr Troyanovsky, honored him with a resplendent reception. His recital—which included *Visions fugitives*, the Andante movement from the Fourth Piano Sonata, and a selection from *Romeo and Juliet*—was heard by members of Congress, heads of diplomatic missions, and other local luminaries. According to a story in the *Washington Post*, the composer seemed "glad to be the guest artist for so responsive an audience" and played "with effortless composure and a crisp, brilliant style."[87]

On this glamorous occasion, Prokofiev greatly enjoyed being the toast of Soviet music. The rest of the 1937 tour suggests that he also relished his cosmopolitanism, paying greater heed to European and American accounts of his activities than to Soviet ones. To retain his status as a cultural attaché— to flourish, as it were, as a Soviet composer outside the Soviet Union—he needed to improve his standing with cultural and political officials. After his return to Moscow in late February, he started work on a cluster of party-line scores. In the opinion of his supporters, these works pointed the way forward for Soviet music; to his detractors, however, they proved that Prokofiev remained unwilling to abandon his formalist tendencies and adapt to new conditions.

Miscalculation

The effort to improve his standing began with the massive *Cantata for the Twentieth Anniversary of October*, which involved double mixed chorus, orchestra, accordion band, military band, and *musique concrète* (a siren, an alarm bell, recorded speech, and marching feet). Prokofiev conceived the work as a tribute to Lenin, but it evolved into a ten-movement narrative about the Revolution, the civil war, Stalin's pledge to Lenin, and the writing of the Soviet Constitution. It was a transparent high-stakes attempt by the composer to appease; it was also a profound miscalculation.[88]

The Cantata casts a long shadow over Prokofiev's career, extending from four years before his move to the RSFSR to thirty years after. The story of its creation starts in the summer of 1932, when Prokofiev rented a picture-perfect villa for himself and his family in Sainte Maxime in the South of France. The property belonged to Jacques Sadoul, an influential French Communist who worked as a foreign correspondent for *Izvestiya*.[89] Prokofiev had met Sadoul three years before in Paris; the correspondent was presumably one of those who urged Prokofiev to become a Moscow resident.

Sadoul's library included a French-language edition of Lenin's writings. Encouraged by Souvtchinsky, who was also vacationing at the villa, Prokofiev began to conceive a large-scale vocal and orchestral piece based on Lenin's speeches of 1917 (before his arrival at Finland Station in Petrograd) and 1920. In a September 10, 1932, letter to Afinogenov in Moscow, Prokofiev described the experience of reading Lenin in French. The translation, he deduced, softened Lenin's coarse locution. "You might say that this is aestheticism," Prokofiev told Afinogenov, "but I once read Chekhov and Dostoevsky in German and, I can assure you, it turned out quite well." Prokofiev added that some of Lenin's expressions were incomprehensible, both in Russian and in French. "My French is quite fine," the composer boasted, but in one of Lenin's writings

> I came across a word I did not understand: "*boisseau.*" A letter from Engels to Bebel had been lying under this *boisseau* for fifteen years, and Lenin was up in arms about it. Then suddenly it dawned on me that this letter had evidently been "*pod spudom*"! Then I realized that I didn't even know what *spud* means in Russian. Do you?[90]

The word *boisseau* means "bushel." Prokofiev refers to a letter from the German political economist Friedrich Engels to the German political activist August Bebel that had been withheld from publication. The letter, Lenin groused, had been lying under a bushel ("hidden in a haystack") for fifteen years. This was how Lenin's jargon came out in French. Prokofiev determines that, in the original Russian, Lenin declared that the letter had been *pod spudom*, meaning it had been "kept under wraps"—in other words, suppressed. The composer had evidently been reading chapter 4 of Lenin's 1917 manifesto *The State and Revolution*, which concerns Engels and Bebel.

Prokofiev asked Atovmyan to send him the six-volume collection of Lenin's writings (in Russian) that had been published in 1930 (volumes 1–3) and 1931 (volumes 4–6). Atovmyan did not find the requested books, since they were no longer available, having disappeared from bookshelves in anticipation of the release of a larger Lenin edition from the Central Committee Institute of Marx, Engels, and Lenin. "So I might have to wait the whole summer [to receive the books]," Prokofiev lamented, noting the irony of being unable to find Lenin in—of all places—Moscow. The peculiar absence, he mused, would likely inspire a "new Soviet anecdote (of the indecent kind)."[91] He ended up working with the new 1933 edition; most of the texts in the *Cantata for the Twentieth Anniversary of October* are found in its pages.

During his brief visits to the RSFSR in 1933 and 1934 Prokofiev broached the subject of the Cantata to his backer Boris Gusman, then the director of the Radio Committee arts division. Gusman found potential in the project and arranged a generous honorarium of 25,000 rubles. According to the June 26, 1935, contract, the "Cantata for the Twentieth Anniversary of the Soviet State," as it was initially called, needed to be suitable for radio broadcast, politically correct (in the Marxist-Leninist sense), and attentive to official artistic policy. The agreement came with a concrete deadline:

the full score had to be submitted to the Radio Committee no later than October 15, 1936.[92]

In its general aesthetic, the Cantata recalls Sergey Eisenstein's *Battleship Potyomkin* (1925) and Shostakovich's Symphony no. 2 (1927), two products of a liberal decade. Taking his cue from Souvtchinsky, who wanted the Cantata to be historically accurate, Prokofiev depicts the Revolution as two separate events: the first in February 1917, the second in October 1917. The first Revolution swept away the autocracy of Tsar Nikolay II in favor of a provisional government; the second Revolution replaced the provisional government with the Soviets, controlled by Lenin's Bolshevik Party. Prokofiev dramatizes the moment of victory with orchestral fireworks but frames the festivities with quotes from military and political speeches. Lenin's and Stalin's dicta spread the flames of October.

The libretto of the Cantata begins with the opening sentence of Marx and Engels's 1848 *Communist Manifesto*: "A specter is stalking Europe, the specter of Communism." Prokofiev does not actually set these iconic words but represents them with "stalking" music: fortissimo timpani rolls, chromatic pentuplets in the brass, and arpeggiated diminished-seventh chords in the strings. There follows a quotation from Marx's 1845 "Theses on Feuerbach," first published in Engels's *Ludwig Feuerbach and the End of German Classical Philosophy* (1886). The text in question, "The philosophers have only explained the world, in various ways; the point is to change it," comes from the eleventh thesis. Prokofiev initially planned to begin and end the Cantata with these words, but then the muse arrived, and he decided to devote the entire second movement to them.

Following an instrumental interlude, problems arise: Prokofiev abbreviates Lenin, setting three lines from the last paragraph of part 1, section 1 of the 1902 essay "What Is to Be Done?" These are taken out of context, a distortion of what the guardians of Lenin's legacy considered to be holy writ. After another instrumental interlude, Prokofiev depicts the Revolution through a musical pastiche, with special effects including the real-or-imitated sound of the leader's voice and tread of soldiers' boots. The text gathers quotations from Lenin's portentous October 1917 pronouncements. Stitching the texts together made musical but not political sense. From the perspective of the censors, Prokofiev had irresponsibly damaged Lenin's image.

And Stalin's. Movement 8 of the Cantata sets part of Stalin's January 26, 1924, speech at the Second All-Union Congress of Soviets, in which the ruler pledges to uphold the departed Lenin's teachings. (The first order of business was eulogistic: the Congress adopted a proposal to rename Petro-grad Leningrad and authorized the construction of a mausoleum on Red Square.) Movement 10 of the Cantata jumps forward to December 6, 1936. Prokofiev sets a passage from Stalin's address to the Eighth All-Union Con-gress of Soviets introducing the Constitution of the Soviet Union, which assigned control of the Russian Federation and the Union Republics to the Council of People's Commissars.

The original scenario for the Cantata did not call for this bureaucratic conclusion; it was the final salvo in a creative process that found the com-poser seeking to eclipse the efforts of his lesser-skilled contemporaries like-wise busy writing pieces for the twentieth anniversary of the Revolution. Prokofiev's efforts reflected the generous terms of his contract; they also stemmed from his intention to transform the least poetic of verbal forms (the political speech) into the most poetic of verbal forms (the choral ode). Lenin and Stalin served as the basis for the propagandistic reconstitution of the dithyramb. It was an enormous challenge, but the Radio Committee had placed its trust in him. Such trust was in fact conditional, as evidenced by the various escape clauses in the contract.

Prokofiev completed the outline of the Cantata in Paris in the early sum-mer of 1935. For help, he turned to Souvtchinsky and Sadoul. In an unpub-lished letter to the Soviet musicologist (and Prokofiev acquaintance) Izraíl Nestyev, Souvtchinsky acknowledged that he had provided Prokofiev with a working title for the Cantata, *We're On the Move*, and furnished a plan for the first three movements. He advised Prokofiev to write part 1 of the Can-tata for "*tutti* chorus" using words by Marx. For part 2, he advised him to represent "the dispute between Lenin and the defeatists." For part 3, finally, he suggested that Prokofiev compose a march "in which the formulaic phrase 'We're on the move' is repeated" end to end.[93] In another unpublished let-ter to the musicologist Malcolm Brown, Souvtchinsky supplied additional details about the project:

> In effect, it was I who suggested to Serge Prokofieff, at his request, those texts that form the basis for the first ver-sion of the Cantata (introduction: "A specter is haunting Europe…"; "Philosophers explained…"; "We march…"). I also gave him the idea of dividing the choirs into two parts to explain the polemic between the Bolsheviks and the Mensheviks.

The Cantata, Souvtchinsky points out, thereafter became a collective enterprise. "The project was reviewed by Jacques Sadoul and by those people—
I am unaware of their names—with whom S. P. spoke in Moscow." He
appends that "in my project there was no question of Stalin."[94]

The original and revised versions of the Cantata libretto are undated,
but appear to have been written between 1935 and 1936. (Part of the text
is on letterhead from the European Hotel in Warsaw.)[95] Departing from
Souvtchinsky, Prokofiev expanded the score from three to six movements:
"1. Epigraph from K. Marx; 2. Formation of the Bolshevik Party (Lenin);
3. October Revolution (on excerpts from Lenin's speeches and letters from
this time); 4. Victory (Lenin); 5. Stalin's pledge; 6. Repetition of the epigraph with a supplement that summarized the Party's work."[96] In the margins and on the back side of this handwritten list of movements, Prokofiev
added some explanatory notes, pointing out that the "fragmentariness of the
phrases" he had selected from Lenin's talks "does not distort their meaning,"
since they came "from the same period" and reflected "the same aspiration."
By assigning Lenin's words to "different sections of the chorus," they will
"give an impression of swift movement," offering "glimpses of the Revolution from different angles." In the "Victory" movement "the noise of the
cannonade" and the sound of the orchestra "culminates." The celebration,
Prokofiev comments, "is subdued." "The music calms," and then Stalin's
pledge is heard, solemnly at first, and then "all the more clearly and broadly,
reaching an apogee at the end."[97] The Cantata would conclude with a repetition of Marx's complaint about chattering philosophers.

The revised libretto provides additional details about Prokofiev's verbal
and musical intentions. His remarks, which appear in between stanzas of
the libretto, seek to assuage the concerns that the Committee on Arts Affairs
might have about the level of dissonance in the score. Prokofiev assures the
censors that his music would honor Marx's (and Lenin's) call for world
transformation. "Against a solemnly majestic backdrop," he explains,

> the choir articulates the epigraph: "Philosophers have only
> explained the world, in various ways; the point is to change
> it." The orchestra holds back; one senses a hidden force
> that has yet to break through the surface: "We are march-
> ing in close rank..." One feels the stride of a march, but it
> is not a march. The music's mood now abruptly changes:
> the orchestra expresses unease—the October Revolution is

imminent. Against this background separate choral groups less sing than declaim: "The crisis has matured. The entire future of the Russian Revolution is at stake..." Now the music becomes stormy: the civil war begins. One hears conflict in the orchestra; an alarm bell bursts in—this is the enemies' commotion. The accordions ring out—separate victories are celebrated. Against this background separate choral groups rush in: "We should, without losing a minute, organize the rebel ranks ..." The victory is subdued. Calm follows the orchestral climax, in which one hears the following: "Comrades, we are approaching spring..." Here the music takes on a marchlike gait, against which: "You will grow large. They will give you arms. Take them and learn the art of war well, not in order to shoot your brothers, the workers of other countries, but in order to achieve the end of exploitation, poverty, and wars."[98] For purely musical reasons, this text is a somewhat abbreviated version of the original. I don't think that the cuts change the basic meaning, however. The march recedes, leading to the solemn, reverent music of the introduction. Chorus: "Philosophers have only explained the world, in various ways; the point is to change it, and WE WILL CHANGE IT." End.[99]

No mention is made here of the three instrumental movements in the Cantata. Much more noteworthy, Prokofiev excludes the two Stalin-based movements from his description, even though the first ("Pledge," movement 8) was central to his initial conception, while the second ("Constitution," movement 10) brought the Cantata up to date politically.

From the transcript of a May 8, 1937, meeting of composers and musical officials, it emerges that Prokofiev had long discussed his plans for the Cantata with the Committee, but that he spoke little about its actual contents, noting only that he would be working with "large forms" whose impact on the listener would be cumulative rather than immediate.[100] Other composers strove for comparable grandiosity, but the titles of their works, works that have all been forgotten, indicate that their intentions were much different. The list of finished and evaluated works included Yevgeniy Golubev's *Return of the Sun*, a celebration of the "peoples of the North" (Eskimos) that included an address to the "Leader of the Peoples—Stalin." Aleksandr

Gedike wrote the "celebratory" cantata *Motherland of Joy*, while Mikhaíl Yudin wrote the like-minded *Spring*, "a cantata on the theme of the joy of Soviet life." The list of unfinished and unevaluated works included Nikolay Vilinsky's cantata "dedicated to the construction of Soviet Moldavia" and Vladimir Enke's cantata *Motherland*.[101] Neither of these compositions uses the actual words of Lenin and Stalin; the librettos are folkloric fabrications.

This was the correct approach to celebrating the Revolution, the approach backed by the Committee on Arts Affairs. Prokofiev was not the only composer to buck the trend—another 1937 work by Yudin, the *Heroic Oratorio*, would be discredited for its mishandling of select lines by Lenin and Stalin[102]— but he was certainly the most prominent. His pride in his effort is evident in two articles that he wrote for the newspaper *Vechernyaya Moskva*. In the first, dated January 28, 1936, Prokofiev comments that, in his Cantata, "Lenin's words will serve for the first time as the basis for a large-scale musical composition."[103] (The date of this piece coincides precisely with that of the infamous *Pravda* editorial "Muddle Instead of Music," which, as discussed, condemned Shostakovich for his opera *Lady Macbeth of the Mtsensk District*.) In a June 22, 1936, article, Prokofiev went a step further by saluting Lenin's powers of oration: "Lenin wrote with such pictorial, clear-cut, and persuasive language that it seemed a shame to resort to a poetic summary of his ideas. I wanted to go right to the original source and use the leader's actual words."[104]

Leonid Maksimenkov, the author of a landmark study of Soviet culture of the 1930s, confirms that the libretto angered Kerzhentsev, the chairman of the Committee on Arts Affairs.[105] Upset that Prokofiev had taken liberties with Lenin's words in setting them to music, Kerzhentsev insisted that the composer rewrite the libretto using verse rather than prose. In a letter to his superior Molotov, Kerzhentsev reported that though he "by all means supported Prokofiev's wish to compose his cantata," he felt the need to "point out the unacceptability of basing the entire cantata on randomly collected and unrelated quotations from Lenin." This creative approach, he emphasized, was "neither politically nor artistically justifiable."[106] The letter dates from May 4, 1936, the climax of the anti-formalist, anti-modernist campaign in the arts.

It is a telling irony that Kerzhentsev was busy at the time writing a monograph about Lenin, one that interwove biographical details with select de-contextualized quotations from the leader.[107] Perhaps aware of the monograph, Prokofiev dismissed the suggestion that he omit Lenin's words from the libretto. Unconcerned about retribution, he also lodged a complaint about Kerzhenstev with Marshall Mikhaíl Tukhachevsky, a nonvoting member of the Central Committee. Tukhachevsky was engaged at the time in a losing battle for his own survival (Stalin ordered him arrested in 1937) and did not intervene on Prokofiev's behalf. He instead slid the matter over to Molotov, who responded to the complaint by instructing Kerzhentsev to "rescind" his objection to "Prokofiev's project and allow him to address the question of the Lenin cantata himself."[108]

Prokofiev's bureaucratic triumph over Kerzhentsev was Pyrrhic: the chairman would have his revenge, ensuring, in the months ahead, the removal of *Romeo and Juliet* from the Bolshoy Theater repertoire and further problems with the Cantata. At the time, however, Molotov's backing emboldened the composer to expand the Cantata from a six- into a ten-movement structure. The score evolved from a Leninist montage into a depiction of what Marina Nestyeva (the daughter of Izraíl Nestyev) calls the "gigantic 'locomotive of history,'" traveling with "irresistible force, sweeping aside everything in its path."[109] The locomotive had to come to a halt, however, lest the Cantata lose cohesion. To this end, Prokofiev turned to his Leningrad friend Boris Demchinsky for help with the libretto. Prokofiev trusted Demchinsky's opinion on literary matters (he had consulted with him while writing the libretto of his opera *The Fiery Angel*), but in this instance Demchinsky appeared hesitant to help.

He did, however, provide Prokofiev with an honest critique of the Cantata's failings.[110] Demchinsky begins his May 7, 1937, letter by apologizing for the delay in responding to Prokofiev, and then he reports that he had visited the public library in Leningrad to peruse Lenin's writings, but the library refused to allow him to take home the index he needed, and he was loathe to spend eight rubles on his own copy. Turing to specifics, Demchinsky voices concern about the emphasis in the Cantata on historical chronicle. The events of 1917, he felt, needed to be represented in a valedictory fashion. "A Cantata for the Twentieth should be closer to conclusions than first steps," he informs Prokofiev. And rather than trafficking in names and dates, the libretto needed to celebrate the "brotherhood and independence of the peoples: the joy of being ('living has become better, living has become happier'),[111] work as an easy duty, as an honor; the Constitution, as the culmination of a long road." Fearing that Prokofiev might toss his letter into the trash in a huff, Demchinsky offers the Cantata some praise, lauding both the "harmonic chaos" of the Revolution movement and the decision to include Stalin's funeral pledge to Lenin. But there was still too much detail: why, Demchinsky asks, does the listener need to hear about officer cadets? Why are there six pledges rather than just one?

The Cantata has a historical foundation, he notes, "but where are the columns, where is the cupola?"

There were also problems with the ending. It was insufficient to quote from Marx: the Cantata needed to feature a "third party," someone whose words could somehow "synthesize" the 1917 experience. Demchinsky's choice was both timely and unassailable: Pushkin, who had, in the run-up to the 1937 jubilee of his death, become a "political figure." To enhance the Cantata's apotheosis, Demchinsky advised Prokofiev to set Pushkin's poem "To Chaadayev" (K Chaadayevu). The 1818 poem, which is dedicated to the dissident Russian dandy and Francophile philosopher Pyotr Chaadayev, protests political and religious oppression. Demchinsky specifically wanted Prokofiev to set the words "Believe, comrade, and it will come to pass" (Tovarishch, ver': vzoydyot ona), which predicts Russia's rebirth after an epoch of tyranny. By quoting Pushkin in the libretto and the "Internationale" in the score, Prokofiev would, in Demchinsky's opinion, give the Cantata the symbolism it so desperately needed.

Demchinsky ended his critique of the text by vaguely promising to help Prokofiev with the revisions, but he did not follow through. Frustrated, the composer upbraided him, pointing out that "one's word is bond," and bewailing the difficulties that he had revising the text on his own. "It fell upon me to clean up the mess," he grumbled in a May 31, 1937, letter. "For better or worse, I completed the basic outline of the *Cantata* right up to the final curtain."[112] The draft piano-vocal score was concluded on June 5, 1937; work on the instrumentation extended to September 21.

Prokofiev's irritation with Demchinsky was short-lived. In the same letter, Prokofiev proposes that they collaborate on another topical cantata, this one commissioned by the Moscow Conservatory. It was intended to celebrate the Soviet conquest of the highest of geographic peaks, the North Pole, and the establishment of a research station on an ice sheet located at 89°25' northern latitude. (The station existed from May 1937 to February 1938, at which time the ice began to break up and the four-man crew had to be rescued by plane.) Prokofiev described the project as follows:

> While I do not like to write "for an occasion" here it must be
> said that the event is unique and lends itself readily to musi-
> cal expression. Moreover, since this second, "little" cantata
> is for Conservatory students, involving simple music and
> comparatively modest performing resources, it would not be

difficult for me to compose, and would involve an entirely different style and means of expression than the first cantata. For the central material, I want to use in particular newspaper clippings about the discovery of the Pole. The literary quality of the material is irrelevant; what matters is that it comes hot off the press. You know from my experience with *The Gambler* and my first cantata that I like to set prose. It will of course be necessary to frame this material with other material—for example, poetry about the North, valor, and so forth. Here I once again (o, imprudence!) turn to you.[113]

For unknown reasons, the "North Pole" Cantata was not composed; the "October" Cantata, in contrast, was composed, but Prokofiev's multi-year labor on the score went to waste. He would hear just one portion of the score performed live, but only after it had been recycled in another work: the *Ode to the End of the War*.[114]

The portion in question comes from movement 9 of the Cantata, one of three untitled instrumental interludes that create moods of anticipation and foreboding. The music of these interludes derives from the Cantata's introductory movement, which opens the Pandora's box of Russian history. Movement 1 denotes primal forces; movements 3 and 5 invoke the ghosts of the Decembrists and the participants of "Bloody Sunday," the event that set the failed 1905 Revolution in motion; movement 9, in contrast, expresses triumph over adversity, but it is unclear whether the triumph is military or economic. The chronological placement of the movement in the Cantata's overall scheme indicates that it concerns the fulfillment of Stalin's first Five-Year Plan. The scalar whirls in the accordions can be interpreted as the sound of contented workers at well-oiled machines.

Movement 2, "Philosophers," bears the meditative, reflective traits of a traditional liturgical cantata, albeit in nonliturgical guise. The highlight of the movement is the glorious alto and soprano melody that begins in measure 21 and ascends from the overlaid ostinato pattern set down by the basses and tenors in the preceding measures. The opening measures scorn those passive academics who, according to Marx, have tried but failed to "explain" the world in "various" ways. The buffa repetitions of the word "philosophers" suggest stasis and stubbornness, being stuck in one's ways.

Movement 4, "We are marching in close rank," includes striking text-painting devices. The melodic line rises and falls in a fashion reminiscent of the aria "Every Valley Shall Be Exalted" from Handel's *Messiah* oratorio. To represent the Bolsheviks trudging "along a steep and narrow path," Prokofiev creates a rough and crooked line that struggles to define B minor.

The special effects of "Revolution" (movement 6) include rat-a-tatting snare drums, out-of-breath singing, and Lenin's radio voice. There are several references to Prokofiev's earlier scores, most notably *The Fiery Angel*, which narrates an apocalyptic conflict between those who believe in the occult and those who do not. An allusion to the lamentations of possessed nuns in act 5 of this opera precedes a musical depiction of the storming of the Winter Palace; the wails of the violins in the act 2, scene 2, séance conclude it. The principal characters in the opera find themselves submitting to unseen forces; much the same occurs in the Cantata, whose instrumental interludes imply the force of destiny and the inability of humans to resist it.

"Victory" (movement 7) denotes paradise, with a brass chorale ceding to a halcyon passage for the strings. The female voices describe the post-revolutionary winter of "cold," "hunger," "typhus," and general "chaos"; the lullaby strains in the violins signal that death has led to transfiguration. The cadential gesture that ends the varied melody is expanded on its final iteration to decorate the words "we nevertheless triumphed." There follows, in the second half of the movement, a vocal simulacrum of the tintinnabulation of steeple chimes. "Ice," the singers proclaim, "has broken at all corners of the earth." Then, in one of the cleverest sequences in the Cantata, Prokofiev shifts to a waltz rhythm to underscore that "a ponderous object" (capitalist oppression) "has been dislodged from its place." But the dance of the liberated proletariat no sooner begins than it ends. Prokofiev brings the movement to a close with a reference to the "measured tread" of "iron battalions" and the sound of Red Army soldiers trudging off into the distance.

The words of the Cantata's finale come neither from Marx (as originally planned) nor Pushkin (as Demchinsky suggested), but from Stalin. Having quoted Stalin in movement 8, which concerns Lenin's death, Prokofiev turned to him again in movement 10, which concerns the fulfillment of Lenin's legacy in the Soviet Constitution. The ratification of this document in December 1936 was celebrated by a Bolshoy Theater performance of Beethoven's Ode "To Joy."[115] For Prokofiev to set Stalin was much different, of course, than for Beethoven to set Schiller. It was also much different from setting Lenin, for the simple reason that Stalin was very much alive in 1937 and, like the tsars who had preceded him, oversaw his own portrayal in the media and the arts.

The *Cantata for the Twentieth Anniversary of October* was, in Maksi-menkov's opinion, a "dangerous," "politically incorrect," and potentially "criminal" experiment.[116] And indeed the June 19, 1937, run-through of the draft piano-vocal score at the offices of the Committee on Arts Affairs was a fiasco.[117] One attendee, the musicologist Moisey Grinberg, pointed out that even if Stalin had been left out of the mix, the Cantata would still have been denounced. Eager to settle scores, Kerzhentsev tore into Prokofiev, ask-ing him, "Just what do you think you're doing, Sergey Sergeyevich, taking texts that belong to the people and setting them to such incomprehensible music?"[118]

The language of Prokofiev's libretto is worlds away from the banter of the bazaar; it belonged less to the people than to the bureaucrats. Kerzhen-tsev resisted banning the Cantata outright (there was no ruling for Molotov to overturn); he simply ensured that it went unperformed. The newly appointed State Orchestra conductor Aleksandr Gauk, who had attended the June 19 run-through, appears to have been quietly advised not to rehearse it.

Prokofiev responded to the criticism with annoyance, twice complain-ing to Alpers that the Cantata had irritated, even alarmed his overseers. On August 26 he grumbled about having to devote two months of the summer "scribbling a Cantata for the Twentieth Anniversary," which, he added, "has already elicited more indignation than enthusiasm." "What," he mused, "will happen when they actually perform it?"[119] Sadly, nothing happened; despite his colossal efforts to finish the score near the deadline, it was not performed, and he only received 25 percent of his commission (the remaining 75 percent being contingent upon official approval of the score).[120] Hopes for a premiere shifted from the Revolution's twentieth anni-versary to its twenty-first. On New Year's Day, 1938, Prokofiev informed Alpers that

> my Cantata has still not been rehearsed: it is fiendishly dif-ficult and everyone (up to Kerzhentsev) is afraid of it. In order to soften hard hearts I wrote a different, somewhat simpler piece—*Songs of Our Days*, which has already been performed in Moscow and will probably soon be performed in Leningrad.[121]

Despite his cynicism, Prokofiev hoped that the Cantata would soon head into rehearsals. In January he sent a telegram from Paris to Gusman and

Lazar Kaufman (the assistant director of the Radio Committee arts division) requesting notification of the start of orchestral rehearsals.[122] That he did not receive an answer must have puzzled him. Kerzhentsev, after all, had not prohibited the score; in fact, Prokofiev indicates that the chairman's underlings advised him to continue working on it. He thus devoted the summer of 1937 to its orchestration.[123] In an attempt to spur action, Prokofiev at one point proposed rehearsing the singers himself. "Owing to the difficulty of the choral parts," he told Gusman and Kaufman, "it would be good if the chorus began learning them as soon as possible, before it gets bogged down with the other works of the season."[124] The recommendation was not honored.

The setback flattened the composer, who had assumed that his vision of historical development, framed by positive depictions of human striving, would be lauded. The spine-tingling highpoint of the "Philosophers" movement signals that his effort was sincere, the first major attempt to adapt his creative energies to an explicitly Soviet political context. The work may not have been inspired by the dogma of the Revolution, but it upheld beliefs in transcendence and transformation, beliefs found in political as well as religious faiths.

When it came time to write another tribute to the Revolution a decade later, Prokofiev was still dismayed that his Cantata had not yet been performed, and that his multi-year labor had gone to waste. The work received a partial premiere on April 5, 1966, twenty-eight years after its completion, and thirteen years after Prokofiev's death. By that time Nikita Khrushchev had come and gone as the Soviet leader; in his third year in power, he had forcefully denounced the "cult of personality" surrounding Stalin. The two Stalin-based movements of the Cantata were thus excluded from the performance, which occurred at the Moscow Conservatory under the direction of Kirill Kondrashin. In place of these movements, Kondrashin reprised "Philosophers," bringing the Cantata to a rhapsodic climax.

Songs of Our Days

Having learned a painful lesson in 1937, Prokofiev made sure that his future political works—his 1939 salute to Stalin and his 1947 *Cantata for the Thirtieth Anniversary of October*—did not breach protocol. These works substitute references to the actual events of 1917 with slogans about the blossoming happiness that occasioned the rise of Soviet power. Just as Kerzhentsev had administered the denunciation of Shostakovich in the pages of *Pravda*, so he had attended to the ideological reeducation of Prokofiev at the headquarters of the Committee on Arts Affairs. Prokofiev adjusted his creative method, but he did so less out of fear than bewildered frustration. In a notebook, he lampooned the unsuccessful run-through of the *Cantata for the Twentieth Anniversary of October* as the "Battle at Kerzhentsev," an allusion to the "Battle at [the River] Kerzhenets" scene in Nikolay Rimsky-Korsakov's opera *The Legend of the Invisible City of Kitezh and the Maiden Fevroniya*.[125] In the scene, foreign invaders launch an attack on unsuspecting Russians.

Prokofiev channeled his disdain for Kerzhentsev into simplistically doctrinaire, rather than subversive, music. He responded to the forfeiture of the Cantata with *Songs of Our Days*, a vocal suite that self-consciously shuns dissonance, chromaticism, even the faintest deviation from the reigning tonalities of C and G major. The effort suggests a sop to the Committee on Arts Affairs, but Myaskovsky, who supplied the title, described it as an escapist diversion. "Prokofiev," he wrote in his diary, "has composed an amusing (and splendid) suite from his mass and stage songs for soloist, chorus and orchestra." In another entry, Myaskovsky called it "magical."[126] Arguably the most entertaining number is "The Twenty-Year-Old" (Dvadtsatiletniy), a through-composed treatment of a text by Samuil Marshak, a prolific writer of children's tales about nature, animals, and the trials of growing up. (Marshak lived in the same apartment building as Prokofiev.) The song, a Gilbert-and-Sullivanesque tongue-twister, depicts, in the male voice parts, a search for the rescuer of a child from a burning building and, in the female parts, the chatter on the street about his heroism. Likewise engaging is the tripartite cavalry song "Over the Little Bridge" (Cherez mostik), which sets a poem by Anton Prishelets. In this song, the composer represents the workings of memory with accelerating, syncopated hoof-beat sounds.

In a *Pravda* article titled "The Flowering of Art" Prokofiev claimed that he composed original melodies for *Songs of Our Days*, but in a style that approximated folk music.[127] The distinction between imitating and borrowing folk music was a point of pride, since he had argued, in an April 9, 1937, speech at the Composers' Union, that his junior colleagues lacked an original approach to the national musical tradition. Rather than drawing inspiration from the folk repertoire for their mass songs, they had simply plundered it. Prokofiev's comments stand out for their self-confidence and fearlessness: he expressed impatience with the campaign against formalism, the staleness of Soviet music, and the perception that he was a disconnected foreigner. "Yes, I've been in the West a lot, but this does not mean that I've become a Westerner," he declared. He compromised this position, however, by boasting about his imported automobile and that he was able to assess the merits of Soviet music from an outside perspective. "A lot has been said about internal instabilities in the Composers' Union," he remarked, "but little has been said about actual creative issues," including the "challenge" of composing for the masses. Embroiled as he was in a battle to rescue his Cantata from oblivion, he tore into the leadership of the Composers' Union for its "mistakes" and "inexperience." Why, Prokofiev asked his listeners, had Soviet music fallen behind while other areas of Soviet culture strove forward? Industrialization and collectivization ensured a bright future. Why then did Soviet composers subsist on the folkloric equivalent of stale bread? Changing tack, Prokofiev offered his thoughts on how to improve the situation. The "battle against formalism," he began, is neither "a battle against perfecting and improving technique" nor a "cure-all" for bad composition. "Musiquette" (muzïchka) cannot be abolished, but this does not mean it should be emulated. "Mass music should be written with the same effort as symphonic music," he adds. "It would be better to write something a little more challenging rather than a little less so."[128]

Songs of Our Days shows technical skill, but sacrifices invention for academicism, becoming the folksy Soviet equivalent of one of Hindemith's *Gebrauchsmusik* compositions. The "Lullaby" (Kolïbel'naya), for example, is a routine exercise in musical rhetoric, with inflected thirds and fifths clouding the soothing text. The words come from Vasiliy Lebedev-Kumach, a newspaperman-turned-poet who supplied song texts for film comedies. He worked after the Revolution for *Rabochaya gazeta* (Worker's Gazette), *Krest'yanskaya gazeta* (Peasant's Gazette), and agitprop journals. Lebedev-Kumach had all the credentials for a successful career as an official writer: military training, obedience to the Party, and affection for innocent humor. The text he provided for Prokofiev likewise evinces a profound devotion to the Stalin personality cult: "There's a man behind the Kremlin walls, / All the land knows and loves him / Your joy and happiness come from him / Stalin! That is his great name!"[129]

Three other texts from *Songs of Our Days* purport to be folkloric—"Be of Good Health!" (Bud'te zdorovï!), "Golden Ukraine" (Zolotaya Ukraina), and (loosely translated) "From Sea to Shining Sea" (Ot kraya do kraya)—but actually derive from known sources. The second was written by a Ukrainian collective farm laborer whose verbal praise of the homeland made it into the October 1, 1937, issue of *Pravda*. The first and third texts came from two established poets of optimism, Adam Rusak and Mikhaíl Inyushkin. The words may be rustic, but they are not folkloric, unless evaluated from the fantastic perspective of Stalinist propaganda. The peasant paeans to the Soviet ruler were concocted in Moscow offices. Prokofiev enhanced the illusion, informing his listeners that he had modeled the melodies of his official works on authentic Russian, Belorussian, and Ukrainian folksongs that did not in fact exist. The absence is marked in *Songs of Our Days*, whose unwavering diatonic consonance sounds nothing like Prokofiev, and nothing like folksong.

The illusion was exposed in 1962, when the publishing house Sovetskaya muzïka issued a censured version of the suite, one that names the authors of the texts while stripping away their references to Stalin. "From Sea to Shining Sea" received the biggest overhaul. It was renamed "October Banner" (Oktyabr'skoye znamya), and each line was rewritten, at times to the detriment of the metric scheme. In the first version, the second strophe loosely translates as "O for Stalin, our own wise and beloved Stalin / The people are crafting a wonderful song"; in the revision, it becomes "We serve the Motherland as a single force / To make the age-old dream come true."[130]

Prokofiev earned only modest praise for *Songs of Our Days*; pandering to populism had in this instance not served him well.[131] The suite was premiered on January 5, 1938, in Moscow and re-premiered on November 19, 1938, the penultimate day of the second *dekada*, a ten-day festival of Soviet music. The performances went unacknowledged in *Pravda* and *Izvestiya*, a marked contrast to the praise accorded Shostakovich's Fifth Symphony and Aram Khachaturyan's *Symphonic Poem about Stalin*.[132]

Prokofiev did not consider his well-being at risk at the time, but most of his colleagues, Shostakovich included, lived in a state of apprehension. The NKVD (Narodnïy Komissariat Vnutrennikh Del, the People's Commissariat for Internal Affairs) conducted regular nighttime searches of apartments; people inexplicably vanished, not to be heard from again for years, if at all. (The case of Sats, the longtime director of the Moscow Children's Theater and the driving force behind *Peter and the Wolf*, is characteristic. On August 21, 1937, she was arrested on spurious charges of treason and sentenced to a Siberian work camp for five years. Her two children became wards of the State, and her apartment was converted into communal housing for the families of NKVD officers.)[133] Through it all, Prokofiev maintained the air—the external semblance—of indifference; Lina did not. Her nerves frayed, and she suffered extended periods of insomnia. The anxieties fueled arguments;

afterward, Prokofiev either withdrew into his study or left the apartment altogether. Lina asked him to honor his pledge to her that if she did not want to stay in Moscow, they would both return to Paris. He commented: "What I promised then can't be done now."[134] Elsewhere, Lina described the anxious, strained atmosphere in their building: "One night I learned to my great distress that an acquaintance had been taken away. I said that I wanted to go back to my mother. Sergey answered: 'Wait, it's temporary, it will all pass.'"[135]

For Lina, the situation was dire but not yet hopeless, for Prokofiev managed to arrange one more trip abroad for the two of them. Their children would remain behind in the care of a nanny, transferring from the English-language school where they had begun their studies in Moscow to a Russian-language school. The former was shut down without notice, forcing the two boys to adjust to new lessons in a new language without their parents there to support them.[136]

The Cultural Diplomat (Continued)

In coordination with his representatives abroad, Prokofiev organized a series of official and unofficial performances for the start of 1938. The schedule included chamber and orchestral concerts, sometimes hastily arranged, in Prague, Paris, London, and the United States (Boston, Boulder, Colorado Springs, Denver, Detroit, Los Angeles, New York, and Washington). Permission for the excursion did not come easily, as evidenced by Prokofiev's self-effacing petition to his nemesis Kerzhentsev (soon to be terminated as chairman of the Committee on Arts Affairs), in which he describes the potential political benefits of the trip:

> Aware of the significance of the historic events that are taking place in the Union, I have attempted to respond to the Twentieth Anniversary of the October Revolution and the elections. Having completed the Cantata, which you know about, I have composed a great choral and orchestral suite, which is straightforward and melodic, to contemporary texts from *Pravda*, as well as marches for wind band and songs for massed voices. I took part in the *dekada* of Soviet Music and the pre-election concerts. It has been suggested that I conduct concerts of my own works in London, Paris,

and Prague, as well as performing in a series of concerts in the USA.

There follows the promise that "in the course of numerous talks and interviews I shall have the opportunity to make favorable reference to the success of Soviet music."[137]

The promise was sincere, but it did not expedite permission to travel. That permission came late, forcing Prokofiev to postpone his departure for Paris and limit his time there to just two days and one concert. His performances in the United States were jeopardized.[138] A January 17 letter preserved at the Russian Ministry of External Affairs hints at the difficulties he and Lina confronted in seeking to exchange their internal passports for external ones. It was written by an official with VOKS (the All-Union Society for Cultural Ties Abroad) to his counterpart in London:

> We telegraphed you to the effect that the composer S. Prokofiev left on January 12 for Paris and London. Unfortunately, Prokofiev's departure only became definitely clear in the very last days and he left without managing to reach an agreement with us about his appearances with London VOKS. We do not even know exactly how long he will spend in Paris.[139]

Prokofiev did, in the end, perform in London at a VOKS concert—an event, like all of the other events on his schedule, overseen by Soviet officials. Regular reports on his activities were submitted from the Soviet embassies in Paris, London, and Washington to Moscow.

The Soviet ambassador to the United Kingdom, Ivan Maysky, hosted a Prokofiev recital on January 27, 1938. Before leaving London for the United States, Prokofiev gave Maysky the manuscript of a mass song that he had composed in 1935 in honor of the People's Commissar for Defense, Marshall Kliment Voroshilov. On Prokofiev's request, Maysky forwarded the song to its dedicatee, Voroshilov, for his approval, requesting that it be performed during the twentieth anniversary celebrations of the establishment of the Red Army.[140] He also reported on the overall reception Prokofiev received in London to the new chairman of the Committee on Arts Affairs, Aleksey Nazarov: "I consider it necessary to report to you," Maysky began, "that in the last days of January our eminent composer S. S. Prokofiev came through London on the way to America." There ensues a positive overview of Prokofiev's three concerts in the city—at Queen's Hall, the Embassy, and a reception at the Earl of Listowel's House—and a brief description of his encounters with British government officials.[141]

In the United States, Prokofiev performed for several hundred guests at a Soviet Embassy function in Washington.[142] He was also the focal point of a reception and musicale a week later at the American-Russian Institute in New York. At the embassy concert he played his Second Piano Sonata and accompanied his wife—who, according to Duke, possessed an appealing but unfocused voice[143]—in a pre-approved program of folksong settings and ballads by Shalva Azmayparashvili, Konstantin Makarov-Rakitin, Lev Shvarts, Aleksandr Zatayevich, Khachaturyan, and Myaskovsky.[144] The first two composers on the list—contributing, respectively, the "Shepherd's Song of Georgia" and "I Drink to Mary's Health"—had studied with Prokofiev at the Moscow Conservatory. Intended to represent the friendships among the Soviet peoples, the Washington event convinced at least one reporter, Hope Ridings Miller, that "the Union of Soviet Socialist Republics can hold its own against any country in the field of music."[145]

The events in Paris (a concert with Pasdeloup), Prague (a reception at the Soviet Embassy), and London came near the start of Prokofiev and Lina's period abroad; those in New York and Washington were at the end. The couple crossed the Atlantic on the *Normandie* between January 29 and February 3; after arriving in the United States, they parted company, with Lina staying in the New York area while Prokofiev headed north and west. In Boston he conducted the American premiere of *Peter and the Wolf*, the suite from *The Tale of the Buffoon*, and the Second Suite from *Romeo and Juliet*, trusting that these works would succeed where others had fallen flat. Indeed, he admitted to Warren Storey Smith, critic for the *Boston Post*, that the performance of *Peter* was a "rebuke to Boston for having failed to appreciate certain of his more complicated works, in particular the Fourth Symphony."[146] Before his March 25 and 26 concerts, he had decided to settle a score with the "supercilious" critics who had panned the Fourth Symphony, which had been commissioned by Koussevitzky and had received its premiere in Boston in 1930. Yet it had been dismissed by local critics as being "written in too much of a hurry." Prokofiev informed a *Time* magazine reporter that because audiences in Boston could not grasp his "serious music," he was obliged to pander to them with "simple things."[147] He did not report that he found himself in a comparable predicament in Moscow and Leningrad, where official attitudes, rather than public responses, influenced his activities. The press kit that accompanied his American performances exaggerated his interest in writing accessible music: "Still another public interest of Prokofiev's," the kit reads, "is the musical advancement of the large masses of Russian people who are now flocking to the concert halls. In some instances not yet able to understand and appreciate complicated music, these concert audiences are being introduced to the larger standard repertoire by means of specially composed popular songs for chorus, marches for military band, etc. In this respect it is Prokofiev's aim to compose music that remains simple and melodious."[148]

When interviewed, Prokofiev spoke positively on behalf of Soviet culture, but his tone was less upbeat than a year before. Avoiding any mention of recent political setbacks, he talked in inflated terms about the comforts provided by his "4 incomes": royalties from an ever-increasing number of performances; royalties from the publications of his works; commissions from theaters, orchestras, and film studios; and "modest but adequate" stipends from the Union of Soviet Composers. Moscow musicians, Prokofiev alleged, lived better than Wall Street entrepreneurs. Indeed, the reporter who spoke to him on this subject described his "cool and pleasantly untemperamental manner of address," which "bespoke the industrial executive rather than the creator of music." Prokofiev appeared to represent "a new social attitude towards the arts."[149]

To those who hosted him in the United States, Prokofiev came across as introverted and intemperate. Such was the impression he made on Jean Cranmer, a philanthropist who "improvised" the Denver Symphony Orchestra into existence. Speaking to a *Denver Post* journalist in 1972, Cranmer recalled the discomfort of billeting Prokofiev for ten days: "He hardly spoke to anyone, even though he did know English. He'd sit through a meal just not saying a word. Nobody could get anything out of him." Before giving piano recitals in Boulder and Colorado Springs, he conducted his Classical Symphony and performed his First Piano Concerto in Denver with the orchestra. The score of the Concerto, Cranmer lamented, was printed on "terrible Russian paper" which "had been re-fingered and erased and re-fingered again."[150] Since the orchestra had not had adequate time to rehearse the February 18 event, it was something of a shambles, with the orchestra unable to "keep pace" and the conductor, Horace Tureman, "working like a Volga boatman in an effort to tug and draw violins, violas, woodwinds, brasses, timpani and percussion into some sort of unity."[151] Upset with how things had gone, Prokofiev rudely told Cranmer after the post-concert reception that he "didn't like anyone who was there." Despite—or perhaps because of—his bad temper, she decided to win him over, taking him to see *Snow White and the Seven Dwarfs* at a local movie hall.[152] He was smitten with the film, asking to see it again the next night, but less than smitten with Cranmer. He later wrote a scathing letter to her about the quality of the Denver Symphony Orchestra, its conductor, and its board of directors—all of which, he huffed, she defended out of "false pride."[153] He nonetheless thanked her for her hospitality.

From Denver, Prokofiev traveled to Los Angeles, arriving on February 26 for a three-week stay. He had not planned on going there: the tour of the United States was to have been limited to the East Coast and Midwest. The invitation came from Rudolph Polk, a onetime violinist, musical director, and artist's agent who sought to engage Prokofiev as a Hollywood film composer. In a January 4, 1941, letter to Koussevitzky, Polk reported that Prokofiev had detoured from Colorado to California in 1938 "at my request." "During the visit," Polk continues, "I took [Prokofiev] to see Walt Disney with the idea of selling *Peter and the Wolf* for one of his animated cartoons."[154] On February 28, Polk and Prokofiev met with Disney and the composer Leigh Harline, who had just been contracted to write the music for *Pinocchio*, at the Hyperion Studio. Prokofiev played through *Peter and the Wolf* and declared, in the flush of the moment, that he had composed it with Disney in mind. The famous director was greatly impressed.

On March 4, Prokofiev wrote to his mother-in-law with the news that he had also, as soon as he arrived in Los Angeles, received a proposal from Paramount "to do music for a film and offered a nice big sum." He could not accept it, he lamented, because it would entail remaining in Los Angeles for ten more weeks, long after he was expected back in Moscow. "Thus," he lamented, the proposal "had to be turned down, and now we're in negotiations about a future season."[155] Elizabeth Bergman, who has studied Prokofiev's last trips to the United States in detail, reveals that Prokofiev took a tour through the Paramount facilities in the second week of March, presumably still enchanted by the proposal. He was guided by Boris Morros, "a native of St. Petersburg, a cellist (who claimed to be Gregor Pyatigorsky's first teacher), Russian émigré, and music director at Paramount from 1936 to 1940." Morros was also, Bergman points out, a Soviet agent.[156]

On March 13, the Russian-born stage and film director of Armenian origin Rouben Mamoulian arranged a dinner in Prokofiev's honor at the Victor Hugo Inn at Laguna Beach, after which he and the other guests returned to Mamoulian's house for an impromptu recital. Lina, who arrived in Los Angeles after her husband, recalls mingling with the stars Mary Pickford, Marlene Dietrich, Gloria Swanson, Douglas Fairbanks Jr., and, on a less glamorous note, the composer Arnold Schoenberg.[157] She encountered some of these celebrities at the Mamoulian gathering, and the rest at the March 10 Academy Awards at the Biltmore Hotel.[158] On March 27, just three days before he left the United States for Paris and Moscow, Prokofiev sent a pair of letters to Polk authorizing him to negotiate a contract with Disney Motion Pictures for the rights to *Peter and the Wolf*. Negotiations began in his absence on May 20, 1940, and a contract was signed on February 4, 1941.[159] Narrated by Sterling Holloway, the animated version of the score reached theaters in 1946 as part of a compilation titled *Make Mine Music*.

Prokofiev enthused about his California adventure, telling his sons, for example, that "in Hollywood, they manufacture entire homes, castles, and even cities out of cardboard." Besides visiting a set, he had been "*chez le papa de Mickey Mouse*."[160] To Myaskovsky, he boasted that Hollywood "showed unexpected interest" in his music. He added that, in order to pursue this interest, and in order to fulfill his promises to conduct in Boston and perform "several concerts of a political character [the Soviet Embassy events]," he needed to extend his time abroad. The letter (written on letterhead of the Roosevelt Hotel on Hollywood Boulevard) then becomes fretful. Cognizant of the fragile duality of his existence, Prokofiev grumbles to Myaskovsky about the lack of a final verdict on his Cantata. Kaufman, to whom he had written a few days before, had "broken his promise" to arrange for a reading. He expected little more from other colleagues, including Grinberg: "I won't be surprised if Grinberg also fails to keep his word, that is, he doesn't engrave the promised scores, and that Gauk isn't learning the Cantata."[161] Myaskovsky was unable to put his friend's mind at ease. In his March 18 reply, he confirmed what Prokofiev had been suspecting all along: Gauk had not prepared the Cantata, since he was devoting all of his time to performances of Shostakovich's Fifth Symphony. "Try not to think about your Cantata," Myaskovsky drily appended.[162]

For Prokofiev, the negative news from Moscow, coupled with the positive news from Los Angeles, must have fueled the nagging sensation that the Soviet regime had altogether deceived him. Despite his declarations that the regime published and performed everything he wrote, his recent works had not received premieres. He did not articulate his thoughts about the difficulties to his European and American friends, but some of them noted

a change in his demeanor. His confidant Paitchadze recalls that during Prokofiev's last trip abroad "he was very reserved, and while he did not express
regrets about the change in his life, it seemed that even with me, someone
he had known intimately for many years, he feared being candid." Both he
and Lina pledged, however, "that they would travel abroad again next year."
They bade farewell to Paitchadze with the words "until we meet again."[163]

Prokofiev ended his time in the United States with appearances in Boston
and New York, where Duke greeted him with the exciting news that he just
received a telegram from a Hollywood agent offering Prokofiev the outlandish sum of "$2,500 a week" to compose for cinema. (Duke is either misre-
membering or exaggerating here: the sum was actually a onetime offer of
$1,500 for the rights to *Peter and the Wolf*.)[164] Duke further claims that he
showed Prokofiev

> the telegram exultantly; there was a flicker of interest for a
> mere instant, then, his face set, his oversize lips petulant, he
> said gruffly: "That's nice bait, but I won't swallow it. I've
> got to go back to Moscow, to my music and my children.
> And now that that's settled, will you come to Macy's with
> me? I've got to buy a whole roomful of things you can't get
> in Russia—just look at Lina's list." The list was imposing,
> and we went to Macy's department store, another sample
> of capitalistic bait designed by the lackeys of Wall Street to
> be swallowed by oppressed workers. Although he wouldn't
> admit it, Serge enjoyed himself hugely in the store—he
> loved gadgets and trinkets of every description. Suddenly
> he turned to me, his eyes peculiarly moist, his voice even
> gruffer than usual: "You know, Dima, it occurred to me that
> I may not be back for quite some time...I don't suppose it
> would be wise for you to come to Russia, would it?" "No,
> I don't suppose it would," I answered, smiling bravely, my
> happiness abruptly gone. I never saw Prokofiev again.[165]

The sadness of the good-bye is echoed in the memoir of Berthe Malko (the
wife of the conductor Nikolay Malko), with whom Prokofiev spent a carefree evening in Prague at the start of his 1938 trip: "When we parted and
shook hands, he said, 'So where will we see each other next time and go

to the cinema? Why don't we say New York?' I never saw him again; they [Soviet officials] stopped allowing him to travel abroad."[166]

Prokofiev and Lina boarded the *Normandie* and left a fogged-in New York on March 31, their marriage, according to Duke, showing severe strain.[167] Upon arriving in Paris on April 6, they checked into the Hotel Astor. That evening, Prokofiev attended a reception at the Soviet Embassy in Paris. Shortly thereafter, he boarded a train for the long ride back to Moscow, his children, and his apartment. Lina followed him on May 7, after spending time with her mother.[168]

2

Seeking the Formula,

1938–1939

Following their conversation at Macy's department store in 1938, Vernon Duke did not see Prokofiev again, and in the years ahead he received just two letters (one survives) and a telegram from him. On April 5, 1940, he received a jocular letter that described, in French, the Leningrad premiere of *Romeo and Juliet* as a triumph beyond the imagining of the hitherto restive dancers, who came to the conclusion, after "15 curtain calls," that the watered-down novelties of the ballet "might be acceptable after all." Continuing his habit of ribbing Duke for his commitment to popular song, Prokofiev asked him what he had been composing both "by way of music" and "by way of tra-la-la."[1] Prokofiev comments that the war in Europe prevented him from traveling to the United States, where, one imagines, he would have immersed himself in Broadway and Hollywood musicals—if for no other reason than to alleviate his Moscow anxieties.

During the war years, Duke sent Prokofiev regular updates on his musical activities (these included the oft-delayed New York premiere of the oratorio *The End of St. Petersburg*, and the completion of his first book show for Broadway, *Cabin in the Sky*), which Prokofiev did not acknowledge until March 15, 1946, when he dispatched a telegram reading: "Thanks for very interesting letters. Please send scores. Letter follows. Greetings." The "letter" that followed a few days later is presumed lost; its contents cannot be verified. Duke simply describes it as a "strange" document "written in three languages," with "French, English, and German words artfully mixed, so as to baffle the censor, most likely." Strange, too, is Duke's cloak-and-dagger assertion that no sooner had he showed the letter to his friends in New York than it "mysteriously vanished."[2]

Duke's loss of contact with Prokofiev attests to the radical changes in the latter's career. On April 16, 1938, Prokofiev returned to the Soviet Union from his three-month trip abroad and never left again. Having reestablished contact with colleagues in Moscow and Leningrad, he lost touch with those in Paris and New York. Despite the resistance he met in organizing his 1938 trip, Prokofiev did not foresee being deprived of the opportunity to travel: the available evidence indicates that he intended to go abroad at least once a year, and that he had no intention of passing up opportunities for performances and premieres in Western Europe and North America. Although he turned it down, the proposal he received from Paramount could not have been far from his mind as he composed mass songs—the socialist equivalent to capitalist "tra-la-la"—for official occasions.

Prokofiev, it bears noting, received his first offer to write "fully accessible music for the masses" from an American rather than a Soviet source.[3] In 1930, Gloria Swanson asked him to create the score for the romantic comedy *What a Widow!* Predating *Lieutenant Kizhe* by four years, this rare film concerns a well-to-do, newly single socialite who finds herself pursued by four bachelors: a lawyer, a violinist, a baritone, and a lounge lizard. Prokofiev and Swanson did not come to an agreement (the deadline was tight, and he asked for too high a fee), but the project got him thinking; he began to weigh the pros and cons of composing for commercial film.[4] His 1934–36 notebook includes a list of the American, French, and German films that he saw (primarily) in Paris, with remarks about their casts, plots, and scores.[5] Of the 1936 musical *Sing Me a Love Song*, for example, he wrote: "Singing all the time, owner poses as a clerk in her own store. Rescue from bankruptcy. Kleptomaniac is apprehended." His tastes were eclectic, veering toward musical comedies. He enjoyed *San Francisco* (1936), a rags-to-riches story about a singer who escapes the squalor of the cabaret scene to become an opera star. She lands the part of Marguerite in Charles Gounod's *Faust*, and her career ascends. The spate of vocal performances "culminates [with an] earthquake." Prokofiev also enjoyed *Du bist mein Glück*, a Beniamino Gigli musical with "fine" operatic inserts. Other 1936 favorites included *Theodora Goes Wild*, a lark about a "provincial town" (Lynnfield, Connecticut) whose church-going residents are scandalized by the publication of a salacious novel (*The Sinner*) by a local writer, and *A Woman Rebels*, a Katharine Hepburn "melodrama" about the "struggle against women's rights." The composer favored detective films (especially singing detective ones): his 1936 list includes three examples, the most original being *Great Guy*, which pits a detective at the New York Department of Weights and Measures against corrupt deli owners. With the exception of an odd French dub of *Tarzan Escapes* (*Tarzan s'évade*), Prokofiev's taste in the fantastic and the surreal seemed unbounded: he drew special attention to the 1935 film *Die Ewige Maske* (*The Eternal Mask*), about a schizophrenic who takes a journey through his own mind looking for a cure. In Prague in January 1938, he and Berthe Malko saw the 1935 René Clair film *The Ghost Goes West*, a trifling romantic fantasy about a haunted castle that is relocated, brick by brick, from Scotland to Florida.

Had Prokofiev not returned to the Soviet Union from the United States, he might have contributed to Hollywood's Golden Age. His wife seems to have contemplated, perhaps naively, leaving the Soviet Union to reside long term in Los Angeles. Lawrence Creath Ammons, a Christian Scientist practitioner with whom Lina consulted in Paris, commented on the prospect in a March 15, 1938, letter to her. It began with a jarringly benign comment about European military and political affairs:

> It was good to hear from you even if it did recount the exhaustion of New York life. Yes, doesn't it make all these European cities seem like small villages? But just at present they are active ones with Hitler taking possession of Europe. This week's lesson page 95 line 12 shows what it all is but we have to see that we are on the "side of Science and peace" and thus bring more of it into one personal experience.
>
> Hollywood sounds promising and if it opens as you both hope I trust that that heaven planned place may be your quiet abode with the children for a few years. It has so much of the real Science about it there even if there is another artificial side in the movie life. Ideal American atmosphere for raising children! Page 591 line 16 tells us what Mind is and that it is our one and only Mind which outlines our future and present and we have only to accept the divine outline every day here we are on earth.[6]

The Hollywood promise went unrealized, as did the prospect of living, as Ammons put it, on the "side of Science and peace." Returning to the

Soviet Union, an illusory reality of another sort, was a traumatic, wrenching experience for Lina, even if she, like her husband, fully expected to travel abroad again.

Prokofiev lost the chance to work in Hollywood, but he could by the end of 1938 take some comfort in the fact that the arch-patriotic Soviet film *Alexander Nevsky*, for which he provided remarkable music, was playing in the largest theaters in Moscow, Leningrad, Kiev, and Minsk. No fewer than eight hundred prints were shipped around the nation.[7] It is perhaps fitting that strains from the now-classic score tend to resurface, in paraphrased form, in Hollywood blockbusters.

Hamlet

Intense work on *Alexander Nevsky* (discussed in chapter 5) followed the premiere of Radlov's staging of Shakespeare's *Hamlet* at the Leningrad Academic Theater of Drama named after A. S. Pushkin (the former Imperial Aleksandrinsky Theater). Prokofiev received a commission to compose incidental music for the production in August 1937, during work on the orchestration of his ill-fated *Cantata for the Twentieth Anniversary of October*. The play had been staged in experimental fashion throughout the 1930s, but by the time Radlov directed it, the Committee on Arts Affairs had launched its campaign against experimentalism. Radlov's staging, though successful, marked a creative retreat. It served as a pointed rebuttal to the madcap version of the play mounted in 1932 by Nikolay Akimov. That version, featuring incidental music by Shostakovich, seemed to comment on the power struggles that engulfed the Kremlin in the years following Lenin's death. "Almost unavoidably," the Slavic scholar Zdeněk Stříbrný notes, "Akimov's grotesque production was attacked by Communist critics and soon removed from the repertoire despite the fact that crowds of Muscovites were spending hours in ticket lines to see it and one New York critic called it 'the best show in Europe.' "[8] By 1938, however, political commentary of this sort was impossible. Radlov was forced to stage *Hamlet* along party lines.

Radlov resolved to strip away the complexities of the play, to represent Hamlet not as a ruminating melancholic but as a person of action, a force for change. In a May 9, 1938, article for *Krasnaya gazeta*, the director defined Hamlet as a "new man," less a "pitiful pessimist" than a "warrior" whose "indecisiveness" stemmed from "the enormous difficulty of the task that lay on his shoulders, and the persistent voice of his vigilant conscience, which so distinguishes him from his colonizing and plundering contemporaries." Radlov added that his production would right the wrongs committed by Akimov in his misguided, "formalist" transposition of the play.[9] It would also atone for the anthroposophy-inspired interpretation staged in 1924 at the Second Moscow Arts Theater (MKhAT 2). The Hamlet of that staging, realized by Mikhaíl Chekhov, experienced something akin to a disintegration of consciousness—an anti-Soviet phenomenon.[10]

To fulfill his aims, Radlov gave Prokofiev specific instructions as to the nature of the music that he wanted for *Hamlet*. These instructions tend to be paradoxical. He called on Prokofiev to compose ghost music for the first scene but pointed out that the result could not be "mystical." Mysticism, Radlov recognized, was anathema to Stalinist-era aesthetics. He also requested that Prokofiev compose four songs for the scene of Ophelia's descent into madness, but he did not want these songs to be irrational—likewise anathema to Stalinist-era aesthetics. "These are genuine little folk songs," the director told the composer, "I do not think that Ophelia's madness ought to produce an inaccurate rendering of the melodies themselves."[11] While she could not sound mad, Radlov conceded that she would at least have to appear so. He asked Prokofiev to append a postlude to the second of the songs, during which Ophelia would begin to dance erratically.

Prokofiev worked on the score intermittently through the fall of 1937. He did not complete it, however, until February 1938, while sailing to the United States. The orchestration was a logistical headache. Following his arrival in New York, Prokofiev sent his assistant, Pavel Lamm, instructions for orchestrating the parts, twice urging him to finish a part of the task in haste.[12]

Despite the delay, Prokofiev exceeded Radlov's expectations. His music for *Hamlet* comprises ten numbers, the most important being the music for the appearance of the ghost of Hamlet's father, the murdered King of Denmark. "There is no mysticism here," Prokofiev wrote in his program notes for the production, "which was how Shakespeare himself conceived it."[13] There ensues a march and fanfares for Claudius, "splendid" music that symbolizes the "brilliance with which the usurper king seeks to surround himself." Prokofiev next supplied music for the play-within-the-play, "The Mousetrap." Hamlet instructs the players to enact the death of his father, the intent being to provoke Claudius into revealing his guilt. Prokofiev conceived a gavotte for this scene, with the first and last sections representing what he called "outer cheer," the middle section "hidden tragedy." For Ophelia,

Prokofiev composed four short songs in Elizabethan-era style.[14] Her suicide by drowning is marked by a sardonic gravedigger's chorus. For the arrival of the Norwegian Prince Fortinbras in the final scene, Prokofiev provided a sober, ponderous march, one that reverts back to the chromatic strains of the opening ghost music. The opening and closing numbers in the score, which resonate with each other, find Prokofiev focusing on the theme of death. Hamlet is tormented by his father's death, guilt-stricken by Ophelia's, and caught up with thoughts of his own mortality. In the final scene, Radlov shows him reconciling with the fundamental uncertainties of death: it is neither positive nor negative, neither ennobling nor debasing. These uncertainties are maintained in Prokofiev's score: the soaring violin melody of the concluding march, for example, is undercut by heartbeat-like thuds in the bass drum and corseted by discordant trumpets and cornets. The significance of the march lies in its essential militarism. Fortinbras, the spiritual heir to Hamlet's war-mongering father, has ascended to the throne. In Radlov's staging, the same actor played the ghost and Fortinbras, just to emphasize that order has been restored in Denmark. The discord that Prokofiev builds into the march comments on the terrible cost of this restoration.

For the very last measures of the march, however, Prokofiev, in consultation with Radlov, fashioned an uplifting apotheosis: "A triumphant march, or rather an adagio in march rhythm, provides the backdrop for the last words of the dying Hamlet. Scarcely audible at first, it gradually ascends to the triumphant C major on which the curtain falls."[15] In keeping with the precepts of his chosen faith—Christian Science—Prokofiev wittingly or unwittingly devised an apotheosis for the score that serves as a paean to the human spirit, the manifestation of the divine. The divine did not have a place in Soviet theater, of course, but the transcendent did. Prokofiev's ending pleased Radlov, for it allowed him to represent Hamlet as a positive hero whose decisions, however agonized, illustrated his adherence to a higher purpose—the betterment of humankind.[16] To accommodate Radlov, Prokofiev appears to have reimagined the pursuit of a spiritual ideal as the pursuit of a political ideal; the teachings of Christian Science metamorphosed into those of Marxist-Leninism. Radlov told Prokofiev that

> Fortinbras's final march represents Shakespeare's constant, calm, trusting optimism. Heroes and villains die, but at the very moment of death, "there will be young life" and Shakespeare loves and has confidence in life. The true, courageous

and optimistic ending of the play will depend of your music, dear Sergey Sergeyevich.[17]

The "young life" to which Radlov alludes is that of a new world built upon the ruins of the old one.[18] The triumphant conclusion helped to make Radlov's staging of *Hamlet* at the Leningrad Academic Theater of Drama a success.

Given that his music for *Boris Godunov* and *Eugene Onegin* had not been performed, Prokofiev was doubtless relieved to see *Hamlet* reach the stage, and even more so to read the flattering reviews.[19] He took active part in the rehearsals and attended several performances. (Radlov's *Hamlet* ran for several seasons; Dmitriy Dudnikov performed the lead role seventy times, after which Boris Smirnov took it over.)[20] Lina, however, did not see the staging, for reasons that neither she nor her husband anticipated. Although she planned to travel from Moscow to Leningrad for the May 15 premiere, she did not board the train, because her travel papers were not in order.

This incident was the first signal that Lina—and Prokofiev—had lost a crucial freedom. In 1932, the Soviet government decreed that the residents of large urban centers had to obtain an internal passport, the purpose being to control the movement of the population. The police (*militsiya*) thereafter relied on "passport sweeps in cities as a primary way to bring in tens of thousands of people who fit the profile of the socially harmful—criminals and associates of criminals, the unemployed, beggars, prostitutes, itinerants, and other socially marginal populations."[21] Entire categories of citizens were prohibited from living in major cities or even being within one hundred kilometers of them. For a passport to be valid, it needed to list the bearer's date and place of birth, ethnic origin, address, education, place and type of work, marital status, and (for men) military service experience and readiness, with each entry stamped at a police station at the place of permanent residence. To further complicate matters, passports needed to be renewed every three, five, or ten years depending on the bearer's status and age (citizens forty-five and older were granted nonexpiring passports). If the bearer needed to leave his or her city of residence for more than twenty-four hours, he or she needed to obtain a permit (*spravka*) and to report at the police station at the place of arrival. To change cities, he or she would have to de-register the old address and register the new one. Standing in line at the police station became something of an endurance test.

Upon returning to the Soviet Union from abroad in early 1938, Prokofiev exchanged his external passport for his internal one bearing a Moscow residency stamp. Following this transaction, his ability to travel abroad came to an abrupt halt: the NKID henceforth declined to give him back his external passport, with various reasons being invented to explain the official change in his status from *vïyezdnoy* (allowed to travel) to *nevïyezdnoy* (disallowed). Even having the external passport would not have enabled him to leave the country, since he would also have needed to obtain an exit permit (*razresheniye na vïyezd zagranitsu*) from the police, issued on behalf of the NKVD. The setback was not, of course, announced to him—information regarding an individual's travel status was classified—nor did it at first affect him, since he had planned to confine his travels to the RSFSR in 1938. Lina, however, had a much harder time. On May 14, she went to the NKID to exchange her external passport for her internal one, but was told that the latter had expired on May 5, and that she needed to obtain a new one at the passport desk of her local police station. There she was told that the passport would take several days to be issued and, adding insult to injury, that her passport photographs were the wrong size. She wrote, with sarcasm surely intended, that instead of traveling to Leningrad to see *Hamlet*, she spent the day "standing in line with the polite citizens" of Moscow.[22]

The incident was galling, and it increased Lina's sense of apartment-bound isolation. Once cosmopolitan, she was now treated as an average Muscovite and subject to bureaucratic harassment. Opportunities to perform declined. She desperately wanted to return to France, and asked her husband to ascertain the procedures for procuring an exit permit. It remains unclear if he sought to do so.

Socialist Realism

For Prokofiev, the bureaucratic malfeasance was attenuated by professional accomplishment. During the period in question, he donned the mantle of a people's artist. *Hamlet*, his second (and greatest) success in the domain of incidental music, marked the start of his attitudinal adjustment, and *Alexander Nevsky*, his second (and greatest) success in the domain of film music, marked the finish.

Like most of the text-based works composed by Prokofiev in the years ahead, the film reflected, to different degrees, the tenets of Socialist Realism, the official artistic doctrine of the Soviet system. The doctrine came into existence in 1932, when the Communist Party Central Committee dissolved the proletarian arts organizations. The subsequent regulation of creative activity necessitated the fashioning of a creative protocol, one that would inform—if not dictate—the form and content of Stalinist art. The most famous example of Socialist Realism, Gorky's novel *Mother* (1906), predates the propagandizing of the term by almost three decades. The novel came to be seen in the late 1930s, however, as an ideal embodiment of three socialist realist principles: *partiynost'* (Party-mindedness), *narodnost'* (people-mindedness), and *ideynost'* (ideological content). The doctrine initially included a fourth principle, *klassovost'*, or class-mindedness, but it was excluded after 1936, when the government began to promote the concept of a classless society. In a classic study, Katerina Clark argues that socialist realist literature declined in quality from innovation to formulaic repetition.[23] In a caustic polemic, the exiled writer Abram Tertz (Andrei Sinyavsky) contends that the doctrine placed a paradoxical burden on Soviet artists:

> A socialist, i.e., a purposeful, a religious art cannot be produced with the literary method of the nineteenth century called "realism." And a really faithful representation of life cannot be achieved in a language based on teleological concepts.[24]

The "reality" of Socialist Realism is not the flawed reality of the present, but the perfect reality of the future, the existence guaranteed by historical movement. The characters in socialist realist literature are typecast according to an aesthetic "pleasure principle"—namely, the ability to detect evil, most often within their own consciousnesses.[25] They live according to strict moral codes, all reflecting their steadfast faith in the righteousness of the revolutionary cause.

The doctrine found timorous expression in the 1937 novella *I Am a Son of the Working People* by Valentin Katayev, which Prokofiev chose as the subject for his first opera on a Soviet theme (*Semyon Kotko*). Prokofiev recalled that the novella was brought to his attention by Gusman, a trusted contact who had been involved in the commissioning of *Lieutenant Kizhe*, the *Cantata for the Twentieth Anniversary of October*, and several smaller works.[26] Katayev, however, recalled that the suggestion came from the writer Count Aleksey Tolstoy, a mutual acquaintance.[27] (Tolstoy, an opportunistic and duplicitous bureaucrat, renounced his noble lineage and his years of exile in Paris and Berlin to become a devoted servant of—and apologist for—the

Stalinist regime. In 1938, he managed to take on the theme of themes, Lenin and Stalin in their public and private lives, transform it into a potboiler about the post-revolutionary civil war, and convert the resulting mélange into a successful play.)[28] It may be, of course, that both Gusman and Tolstoy pitched Katayev's novella to Prokofiev. Prokofiev might have also first asked Tolstoy to be his collaborator, since the writer was, as he somewhat cynically observed in 1927, such a "good little Soviet citizen."[29] He was also an experienced librettist.[30] Rather than an opera, Prokofiev and Tolstoy decided, toward the end of 1938, to collaborate on a ballet—Prokofiev informed his Paris assistant Mikhaíl Astrov (Michel Astrot) that he had a commission for it—but nothing came of the initiative.[31]

I Am a Son of the Working People had a long shelf life in the Soviet Union. Editions were printed in 1937 and 1938, the latter with illustrations. Katayev turned the novella into a popular stage play for the Vakhtangov Theater in Moscow and the Pushkin Theater in Leningrad. It was even made into an action film called—after the opening sentence—*A Soldier Came from the Front*.[32] Prokofiev settled on the novella after a long search for a subject and a creative approach that would, as he put it in a 1932 newspaper article, address "the heroism of construction, the new [Soviet] man, struggle and the overcoming of obstacles."[33]

I Am a Son of the Working People narrates a conflict between Bolsheviks, anti-Bolsheviks, and invading Germans in the immediate post-revolutionary years. The hero, Semyon Kotko, is a World War I soldier who returns to his native Ukrainian village after four years at the Romanian Front; the villain, Tkachenko, is an embittered kulak who colludes with menacing German officers to reclaim his confiscated estate. Central to the plot is the long-standing romance between Semyon and Sofya, who just happens to be Tkachenko's teenage daughter, and the blossoming romance between Mikola, an army cadet, and Frosya, Semyon's mischievous little sister. A tragic subplot involves the valiant sailor Tsaryov and his kindhearted fiancée, Lyubka. The sailor is hanged by Tkachenko's allies for his pro-Bolshevist sympathies; Lyubka loses her mind with grief. The crime occurs at the end of chapter 23, in which the Germans loot and burn down the village. Once Semyon and his Red Army cohorts set their minds to it (that is to say, once they realize their calling), they quickly rout the Germans. The climax of the battle comes in chapter 28, when Semyon, acting on orders from the Red Army high command, lobs a grenade into a church and rescues Sofya from forced marriage to one of Tkachenko's thugs. The novella's epilogue transports the hero and heroine through time and space to Red Square for a military parade. Semyon (now a well-to-do director of an aluminum plant) and Sofya stand on tiptoe to watch their son march by. They also hear Stalin make a pledge of allegiance to Lenin. (Prokofiev omitted this scene from his operatic version of the novella.)

In devising the plot, Katayev relied on his personal memory of the civil war period (a native of Odessa, he had covered the conflict for a hometown newspaper). He also relied on a collection of documents about the Bolshevik "intervention" in Ukraine that had, he claimed, "fallen into his hands."[34] The papers came from the archive of *Pravda*, where Katayev worked as a journalist, and contained the orders of the commander of the German occupation in southern Ukraine in 1918.[35] It is doubtful that Katayev simply came across the documents by chance; rather, his remark intimates that the subject of the novella had been assigned to him. In the late 1930s, the Union of Soviet Writers, acting in coordination or consultation with the Committee on Arts Affairs, issued contracts for educational books on approved themes: this was one of them. Katayev, a gifted writer, completed his presumed assignment with flair. Drawing inspiration from his literary idols (Bunin and Gogol), he infused *I Am a Son of the Working People* with arcane jargon, lavish landscape images, rustic humor, an apocalyptic dream scene, and an episode of grief-based madness. His symbolism, like his use of allegory, is intentionally clichéd. In chapter 5, for example, Semyon lifts up a millstone by his mother's hut and peers at the insect life beneath it. "Although spring had arrived," Katayev narrates, "the millstone was still ice-bound in the earth. It became sad and mournful."[36] Any schoolchild of the period would have understood the symbolism: the Revolution lifted the rock off the backs of the people. Had the civil war not been won, the people would have been weighed down again.

To be successful in Moscow and Leningrad, Prokofiev's new opera, his colleagues advised him, would have to be more accessible than his old ones. Upon outlining his intended "plan" for the score to Afinogenov, the writer unhappily replied: "But that's exactly what's considered to be formalism."[37] Musically, *I Am a Son of the Working People* allowed Prokofiev to express what he called (in a short essay for the program booklet) the "love of the young people," the "hatred of the representatives of the old world," pro-Bolshevik pluckiness, and anti-Bolshevik cowardliness.[38] The contemporary subject matter presented logistical difficulties for the composer, whose operatic method had a nineteenth-century grand opera pedigree. "For example," he remarked, "an aria sung by the chairman of a village Soviet could, with the slightest awkwardness on the part of the composer, be extremely puzzling to the listener. The recitative of a commissar making a telephone call may also seem strange." Prokofiev asserted, however, that Katayev's writing style eased these problems. The characters spoke like "flesh-and-blood" people, and the novella's symmetrical dialogues facilitated a hybridization of strophic and through-composed vocal forms.[39] Prokofiev acknowledged that his music was eclectic, contrasting ritual choral singing with propulsive, ostinato-driven declamation.[40] He asked listeners to "exert a little effort" to grasp the opera, in which he had tried to capture the true-to-life personalities of Katayev's characters, who "rejoice," "grieve," and "laugh" just like all people do.

Ultimately, Prokofiev's attraction to *I Am a Son of the Working People* had less to do with the novella's fictional paeans to peace, land, and bread than with real-world politics. Prokofiev needed to demonstrate his commitment to Socialist Realism, as did the intended director of the opera, Meyerhold, who was in serious trouble. In 1937, the director became a victim of the anti-modernist, anti-formalist campaign mounted by the Committee on Arts Affairs. His theater was liquidated on January 8, 1938, an event Meyerhold attributed to Kerzhentsev's machinations against him.[41]

In 1938, the director girded himself for arrest, but he did not think that the order would come from the top. In the illogic of the times, this belief offered solace. As Ehrenburg recalled: "We thought (probably because we needed to think) that Stalin was unaware of the senseless reprisals against the Communists and the Soviet intelligentsia." Vsevolod Emilyevich [Meyerhold] said: "Things are being concealed from Stalin."[42] Moscow was a vortex of lethal intrigue, but Meyerhold knew that there was no alternative but to continue to work. Deeply worried about Meyerhold's situation, his former teacher Konstantin Stanislavsky offered him a position, inviting him to become the creative director of his Opera Studio (henceforth the Stanislavsky Theater).

Stanislavsky unexpectedly died on August 7. Meyerhold heard the news as he was leaving for Moscow from the North Caucasus resort of Kislovodsk, a summer retreat of the Soviet artistic elite, and his stay at the resort overlapped with that of Prokofiev. Upon taking charge of the Stanislavsky Theater, Meyerhold beseeched Prokofiev to allow him to stage *Semyon Kotko* (the eventual title of the operatic version of *I Am a Son of the Working People*). Its subject matter was unassailable, and Meyerhold hoped that it would offer political cover. Katayev recalled the director becoming ever more "alarmed and agitated" as time passed. He "rushed Prokofiev, and wanted to mount the opera quickly, to get things done, and reach some sort of firm commitment as soon as possible."[43]

Prokofiev doubtless absorbed Meyerhold's anxieties and must have ruminated on the loss of some of his own creative and personal freedoms. For a person who took pride in mental toughness, the prospect of losing self-confidence was no less alarming than a summons from the NKVD. Prokofiev, to quote a leading Slavicist, eventually found himself in the paradoxical position of trusting "neither the inner rules that governed [his] own creative imagination, nor the outer rules that governed the society of which [he was] a part"—a situation that posed the threat of creative paralysis.[44]

Semyon Kotko came in for orchestrated criticism following its June 23, 1940, premiere. Long before then, however, the composer realized that the opera would not be the triumph he had trusted it would be. Kerzhentsev had been replaced as chairman of the Committee on Arts Affairs by Aleksey Nazarov, who was in turn quickly replaced by Mikhaíl Khrapchenko.[45] Prokofiev and Meyerhold hoped that the tumult would result in a liberalization of artistic doctrine, but this hope was violently dashed.

Katayev

On Meyerhold's urging, Prokofiev awarded *Semyon Kotko* to the Stanislav-sky Theater without a written contract. Intense labor on the project began in the early spring of 1939. The director worked in close quarters with the composer, but also consulted with the Ukrainian-born set designer Aleksandr Tíshler. Tíshler, who created dozens of sketches for the opera, encouraged Meyerhold to make the hero look like Saint Sebastian, a Roman martyr known as the protector against plagues.[46] The director conceived the spectacle as a collection of "fragmentary" vignettes, but Tíshler demurred on the grounds that the plotline was "monumental and integrated."[47] The two of them agreed in the end on a more stylized, abstract approach.

Putting aside other projects, Prokofiev composed the first three acts of the opera in haste, completing the piano score at a Chaikovskian clip of fifty-three days. He introduced the music to his colleagues on a tentative, scene-by-scene basis. On April 8, 1939, he played through acts 1 and

2 at a small gathering that included Meyerhold, Myaskovsky, and some Stanislavsky Theater personnel. Prokofiev admitted that he was too nervous at the time to present it to a larger audience. He read through the libretto of act 3, the heart and soul of the drama, and talked about the contents of acts 4 and 5.[48] Myaskovsky voiced approval to Meyerhold but, in his diary, expressed a prescient concern: "The other day I heard two acts of Prokofiev's opera *Semyon Kotko*: it is vibrant, piquant, and evocative, but as always, there are no set pieces."[49] Myaskovsky would eventually, however, recommend the opera for a Stalin Prize. His nomination letter, dated September 27, 1940, stressed the "deeply realistic" content of the score and the prevalence "from start to finish" of the "intonations of Russian and Ukrainian folksong."[50]

The absence of set pieces became a source of tension between Katayev and Prokofiev, one that lasted through the official run-throughs of the first three acts on June 2 and July 8, 1939. Prokofiev refused to convert the source text into a song-and-dance-filled spectacle: the opera would not, after all, feature Gloria Swanson in a lead role. Like his earlier operas, *Semyon Kotko* was to be largely arioso- and recitative-based, with the vocal lines governed in part by the accent and stress patterns of the Russian language. The technique, which has Musorgskian and Dargomïzhskian precedents, inspired Prokofiev to come up with novel ways of structuring the opera.[51] The Soviet musicologist Marina Sabinina, who wrote an extremely positive book on *Semyon Kotko* (she was appalled by the negative reception accorded the opera at the time of its premiere), comments that the visual action is often structured by the repetition of a single word or phrase. In act 1, scene 2, for example, a brief motive taken from the word *vzaimno* (likewise) provides a scaffold for a dialogue between Semyon, his little sister Frosya, and a group of inquisitive villagers. Sabinina notes that the scene assumes a rondo-like form, with *vzaimno* punctuating three separate exchanges. She charts the scene roughly as follows:

A: "vzaimno" (three old women and a villager)
B: two old men
A: "vzaimno" (Semyon)
C: three old women, Frosya, the villager, Semyon, two old men
A: "vzaimno" (Semyon)
D: three old women (outer sections) and Semyon (inner sections)
A: "vzaimno" (Semyon)[52]

Given the emphasis on arioso, Prokofiev planned to include just a handful of songs and choruses in *Semyon Kotko*, and each of these would be performed self-consciously by the characters. The singing, in other words, would be "diegetic"[53]—or, to use Carolyn Abbate's well-known term, "phenomenal"—emanating from the visual story space.[54] The characters would hear the singing and perceive it as realistic, emblematic of their harmonious Ukrainian existence.

Katayev was unhappy with this approach. He wanted Prokofiev to create a Soviet version of *La Traviata*—or at least a spectacle that would attain the level of success accorded *The Quiet Don*, a naively tuneful 1935 opera by Ivan Dzerzhinsky that famously received (if one is to believe the TASS account) qualified praise from Stalin.[55] Prokofiev found himself in the peculiar position of having to encourage the writer to stay true to his own prose style when fashioning the libretto. Katayev wanted to convert his evocative paragraphs into verse; Prokofiev hoped he would leave them intact. The writer described the tug-of-war between them to his biographer as follows:

> I worked on the libretto at the dacha, on the Klyazma [River], at a stressful pace. Prokofiev was extremely pedantic when working. He continually rushed me. When an act or scene needed to be written, he would impatiently demand: "Come on, what's wrong with you? You'll be the death of me." He collected it, judged it adequate, and went back to Moscow.
>
> I wrote the libretto in prose, for he would not have it any other way. "No, I don't want any of this, no verses of any sort." He himself supplied the plan for several scenes in accord with their musical conception. The use of counterpoint was interesting. In one act [II] he had two scenes in tandem, one on the right, one on the left. "I'm doing this for purposes of thematic development," he explained.[56]

Katayev paints himself as the victim of the impatient composer, but he had certain ideas of his own about the opera and a strong sense of his value to the project. He esteemed Prokofiev's talent, listening to his music "indulgently and contentedly" and describing him to his colleague Margarita Aliger as "our composer—a successful acquisition."[57] At the same time, Katayev resisted Prokofiev's operatic aesthetic and the effect it had on the libretto, which he considered to be his own exclusive domain. The writer likewise felt that he should be given full credit, and full payment, for the libretto.[58] Prokofiev ceded to the second request, but not to the first. There were too many "propagandisms" (*agitki*) in the text, he acerbically remarked to his friend Alpers, and these "quickly go out of fashion."[59]

In the end, a truce of sorts was reached between the two artists. Katayev begrudgingly accepted Prokofiev's changes to the libretto, and Prokofiev begrudgingly agreed to include lyrical numbers in the score, thus launching a preemptive strike against his critics in the cultural agencies. In accordance with the socialist realist principle of *narodnost'*, Prokofiev likewise saturated the score with the intonations of Ukrainian folksong, though he avoided actual folksong quotation. (The score contains just one such quotation: in act 1, scene 2, Frosya sings a song about her desires for romance to the tune of "Oh, don't frighten my timid little heart" [Oy, ne pugay, pugachen'ku], a tune also used by Chaikovsky in an opera.[60] Beyond this, the only other identified borrowing comes in act 2, when Tkachenko mockingly sings a fragment of "God Save the Tsar" [Bozhe, tsarya khrani], the Russian national anthem before the abdication of Nikolay II in February 1917, in anticipation of marrying off his daughter to a German invader.)[61] Upon consulting a published collection of Ukrainian folksongs, Prokofiev created a cluster of folklike melodies.[62] In a manner partially inspired by his Ballets Russes antipode Stravinsky, Prokofiev abstracted and stylized authentic folksong, a practice that allowed him to elevate his opera from a provincial, realistic plane to a universal, spiritual plane. The story of a mud-stained soldier treading home from the front becomes an allegory for the entire Soviet experience. Thus, on one level, the folklike music represents plain-spoken Ukrainians who have their hearts and minds in the right place. On another level, it offers political tutelage. Within this beautiful, alluring score, the voice of ideology—the voice of Prokofiev's musical narrator—is ever-present.

The folklike melodies are subject to development and modulation, and thus propel the action forward in a manner that actual folksong quotations could not. Prokofiev also connects his folklike music to individual leitmotifs. The giddy strains of the act 2 matchmaker chorus, for example, infuse Sofya's and her mother Khivrya's vocal lines.[63] In the middle of the opera, the army cadet Mikola sings the invented folksong "At the crack of dawn" (Rano-ranen'ko) while strumming on a guitar. (The text of the folksong comes from Katayev's novella.) The melody has been heard before, in the orchestral introduction to the opera, where it functions as a symbol of the Ukrainian homeland. It also appears in the betrothal chorus of act 2 and in the nocturne of act 3. Prokofiev extends Mikola's variant of this invented folksong to accommodate the chromatic line associated with Tkachenko's evil sidekick Klembovsky. The musical message is simple: the anti-Soviet villains are about to shatter the pro-Soviet peace of the village. At this point, however, Mikola has no clue as to Klembovsky's nasty plans; the grim warning is intended for the audience alone. Here Prokofiev's alteration of the folksong operates as a kind of musical double exposure: on the one hand, Mikola is singing; on the other hand, an invisible narrator is communicating through his voice.

Such inserted musical comments remind the listener of the controlling force at the heart of the work. The characters are cardboard cutouts, with preassigned roles—teacher and student, aggressor and defender—that derive from a Marxist-Leninist template. Their personalities devolve rather than evolve; over the course of the opera, they shed their individualities to become part of a like-minded collective. During the act 4 "artillery lesson" episode, for example, a jocular tune sung by Semyon is constantly bounced back to him by his comrades.

In act 5, Prokofiev elected to enhance further the political message of the opera. He once again reprised the invented folksong "At the crack of dawn," this time assigning it to a chorus of villagers and infusing it with march-like strains. The chorus celebrates the ragtag partisans' triumph over the Germans, even though, according to the plot, that victory is still some time away. In historical terms, the opera ends too soon. But the ideological principles at its core suggest a transformation of time. The ending completes a progression from nature (as thesis) to the people (as antithesis) to the Soviet national ideal (as synthesis). The transpositions of "At the crack of dawn" trace this tripartite movement.

Because Marxist-Leninist dialectics predetermines who will win and who will lose, the opposition between hero and villain in the score is artificial, since the future triumph of the Soviet system is assured. Prokofiev assigns the "good" characters in *Semyon Kotko* more melodies than the "bad" ones. Recitative-like passages dominate the opera such that singing stands out to denote exclusive pureness of spirit. To signal that the victory of the Ukrainian villagers over their German, kulak, and counterrevolutionary foes is assured, he subjected the music of the positive characters to heroic development and the music of the negative ones to hapless caricature.

In the instrumental preludes and postludes, however, harmonic and melodic repetition substitutes for conflict. The score's semantic sameness puzzled Sabinina, who felt that the pro-Soviet and anti-Soviet characters sounded too much alike. For instance, just before the episode in which Tkachenko hears of his daughter's plans to wed Semyon and settle down on a farm, the orchestra intones Tkachenko's first theme. Instead of the dissonant march-like music assigned to the other villains, however, one hears a variation of the tune used to represent the title's character's homecoming. The open fifths, doubled octaves, and descending eighth-note pattern all recall Semyon's "theme of return." The similarity obliges Sabinina to describe Tkachenko's music as untypical of the conventions in Soviet opera for representing nega-tive characters. Tkachenko's second theme is also problematic, in her view, because it "even more clearly demonstrates a connection to song, specifically Ukrainian folksong. Curiously, it first appears just when he reveals himself to be a deceitful informer, treacherous and cruel."[64]

The soldier-farmer Semyon and the landowner Tkachenko fulfill the duties assigned to them by ideology: the former directs the "movement to the Purpose"; the latter seeks to "hinder" this movement.[65] Prokofiev may or may not have held Socialist Realism in contempt, but his opera adheres to its guidelines. Present-day listeners may find—or may wish to find—irony in the two-dimensionality of the dramatic situations. These do not, however, reflect a desire on the part of the composer to be subversive; rather, they attest to the earnestness of his intentions. Prokofiev hoped to create a Soviet operatic classic, one that would rescue Soviet music from its decline into RAPMist dilettantism. Meyerhold, for his part, aspired to engineer a successful pre-miere of this obedient work and thus extricate himself from peril.

Meyerhold's Arrest

Tragically, he did not get the chance. On June 20, 1939, Meyerhold was arrested and, after seven months of torture in prison, executed. The director was detained in Leningrad, where he had traveled with Tishler, his set designer, to finalize details for an agitprop athletic spectacle organized by the Kremlin.[66] This was one of many such spectacles held in Soviet cities that summer as part of a campaign to increase the physical stamina of the adolescent population, the future conscripts of the ever-expanding Red Army. Wearing identical uni-forms and moving in unison, male and female "physical culturists" performed paramilitary exercises and executed hypothetical battlefield maneuvers.

The Leningrad Institute of Physical Culture summoned Meyerhold to serve as the choreographer for a July 6 spectacle involving 30,000 athletes. These athletes were but one component of a massive "All-Union" spectacle planned for July 18 and 20 in Moscow. (The July 18 performance was scheduled for Red Square; the July 20 performance for the Dynamo soccer stadium.) Meyerhold approached this very public task with tremendous seriousness and, to enrich the content of the spectacle, requested that Prokofiev be commissioned to write music for it. The composer scrambled over the course of a week (May 23–29) to provide six numbers for the "Gymnastic Exercises," which constituted just one part of the day-long event but bore their own narrative structure: "Introduction," "Apparatuses," "Free Exercises," "Obstacle Course," "Battle," and "Concluding Appearance of all Participants." The six numbers contain various cues indicating the types of activities they would accompany: "Work in unison," "work in ensembles," "pole jump," "long-distance jump," "start of the battle," "hand-to-hand battle," and so forth. Prokofiev's handwritten notes on the scenario provide insight into his time-saving creative methods, while also suggesting that he made no essential distinction between composing for pole-vaulters and floor-mat wrestlers and composing for ballet dancers. Chaikovsky's *Sleeping Beauty* and his own *Romeo and Juliet* served as fodder for the score. In the margins of the scenario for the apparatuses, for example, one reads:

> Waltz. 1 measure per second. 3/4. With the composure of circus acrobats. Like Chaikovsky's *Sleeping Beauty*, but with champagne.[67]

In a separate, lengthier note, he clarified these points:

> The apparatuses are brought in to the preceding [musical material]. Three chords at the start; the melody begins from the fourth. *Sleeping Beauty* waltz but merrier (more like Strauss). 3 minutes with possible extension to 3 1/2. 20-second coda. They come down at the end. 16 measures 16–20 seconds.[68]

In the margins of the scenario for the obstacle course Prokofiev noted that "40 seconds" of music would recall the music for Romeo's confidant

"Mercutio, but a little slower and not too impetuous."[69] For this project, Prokofiev thought primarily in metric schemes.

The music for the gymnastic exercises is a comparatively insignificant part of Prokofiev's oeuvre, but it was intended for a high-profile event and came with a generous commission. For seven days of work, he received 10,000 rubles, an amount that rivals the sums he earned for his film scores. He did not have to worry about hiring Lamm to handle the orchestration, because the task has already been farmed out to Zinoviy Feldman. Feldman had worked for Prokofiev once before, orchestrating the pomp-filled march he had composed in 1935 for the national games of the Soviet Union. (These games, known as the Soviet Spartakiade, were held every four years as a surrogate of the Olympic Games, which the Soviet Union did not join until 1952.) Feldman trembled at the thought of orchestrating the gymnastic exercises, however, and connived to break his contract, at which point Prokofiev tore into him, accusing him of acting like a "little child" and reminding him, in a fashion that could only have added to Feldman's stress, that "the entire government" was awaiting the spectacle.[70] Under great pressure, the two of them worked out a deal whereby Feldman would orchestrate the bulk of the music, with another composer handling the rest.

The Stalinist regime organized physical culture spectacles for didactic purposes; in this respect the spectacles were no different from the constant, droning speeches that filled the airwaves. By 1939, the public was accustomed to attending such mass rites, which, according to the official press, were greeted with enthusiasm and excitement. The freckle-faced participants beamed with joy, the clouds parted as they went into their routines, and the people in the stands marveled at the agility and strength of Soviet youth. Even Prokofiev was (or pretended to be) entranced: at the 1935 Spartakiade, he became totally "immersed" and was "joyfully smiling and happy."[71] This description comes from the musicologist Grigoriy Shneyerson, who also claimed that Prokofiev's fascination with the games was such that he seemed unaware of the sound of his own music. Whatever the composer's interest in the 1935 Spartakiade, it must have been greater than his enthusiasm for the 1939 spectacle. No sooner had he drafted the music for the latter event than he turned his back on the score, trusting that Meyerhold would transform his labor into something impressive.

Meyerhold traveled to Leningrad in mid-June to coordinate the sounds and sights of the spectacle. And then he disappeared. Tïshler recalls taking a stroll with him in the Botanical Garden on June 19; they arranged to meet again the next morning, but by then the director was gone:

> I returned to Moscow alone. The wall-newspaper hanging in the hallway of the [Stanislavsky] theater had photographs of Prokofiev, the conductor Zhukov, and me. Meyerhold's photograph was no longer there; it had been cut out. *Semyon Kotko* was staged by another director and, of course, in a different way.[72]

The official NKVD records of Meyerhold's arrest, like those of other victims of the purges, are stored in Moscow at the central archive of the Federal Security Bureau. Eighteen documents from the director's file have been published to date, and they provide harrowing and heartbreaking insight into NKVD tactics.[73] Following his transfer to the Butïrskaya Prison in Moscow, the director was questioned eleven times under unimaginable physical duress. (The first interrogation came on July 8, the last on November 9.) Prior to his execution by firing squad on February 1, 1940, he was beaten into signing a confession for espionage. He was then found guilty of conspiring against the Stalinist regime by following the teachings of the outlaw revolutionary Leon Trotsky, an "enemy of the people" who had fled the Soviet Union for Mexico. He, too, would soon be murdered.

Excluding a couple of passing mentions, Prokofiev left no record of his reaction to Meyerhold's disappearance. In the wake of the event, he tightly clung to his habits, continuing to compose, continuing to perform, and continuing to express his disdain for bureaucrats like the recently deposed Kerzhentsev. The fiasco of the *Cantata for the Twentieth Anniversary of October* eighteen months before had convinced him that the chairman of the Committee on Arts Affairs exacted revenge on those who did not follow his orders; it did not convince him, however, that he was, like Meyerhold, in harm's way.[74]

His wife, in contrast, became ever more fearful. On July 16, 1939, Lina learned that Zinaida Raykh, Meyerhold's wife and lead actress, had been gruesomely murdered. Lina had gone to the Stanislavsky Theater to collect her husband's advance for *Semyon Kotko*. The director of the theater, Zinoviy Daltsev, broke the news to her. "It seems," she wrote to her husband, "that the day before yesterday thieves broke into Z. Raykh's flat, first bludgeoned her housekeeper and then stabbed her twelve times. She died in the hospital an hour and a half later—what a drama!" Lina's distress was palpable: "I still can't get my head around this," she ended.[75] Nor could Prokofiev: "What horror about Zinaida!" he exclaimed in his July 19 reply, "Poor V. E. [Meyerhold]!"[76]

Lina's letter reached Prokofiev in Kislovodsk. Earlier, Lina had asked Daltsev if he could arrange for her to stay with her husband at the resort, but the director did not come through for her. The government mandated that vacations be distributed to individuals, not to their families, based on rank and merit. The needs of families came second to the needs of the regime; as a consequence, families broke apart. Lina remained in Moscow while Prokofiev lived in one of the rooms allotted to the Stanislavsky Theater collective, immersed in acts 4 and 5 of *Semyon Kotko*. Once he had patched together the simple final chorus of the opera he began the orchestration of the whole, completing the scoring of acts 1 and 2 on July 26, acts 3 and 4 on August 29, and act 5 on September 10—by which time he had left Kislovodsk, which had had a damp, cold summer, for warmer Sochi.[77] He intermittently met about the opera with Serafima Birman, an actress-turned-director chosen by Daltsev as Meyerhold's substitute, largely because she and Prokofiev were living alongside each other in Kislovodsk.

Although Prokofiev desperately wanted *Semyon Kotko* to be performed, he did not want to collaborate with Birman. He hoped instead to enlist Eisenstein as the director, but the filmmaker was occupied at the time with a project about the construction of the Fergana Canal in Uzbekistan, which was intended to facilitate cotton farming. Thus, before Prokofiev could invite Eisenstein to take the reins of the tainted opera, Eisenstein contacted him with a proposal to write the music for the film. Prokofiev seemed content to decline the request, since it would have meant creating background scoring for the encroachment of "threatening" sands on "a city parched to death"; it would have also meant reworking authentic Uzbek dances, the purpose being to narrate the transformation of the canal's heroic builders from desert nomads into industrial designers. In his reply to Eisenstein, Prokofiev dispassionately and somewhat opportunistically touched on Meyerhold's arrest: "Incidentally, after the catastrophe with M[eyerhold], who was to have staged my opera, my first impulse was to throw myself at your feet and implore you to take on the staging." This "dream" was scuttled when he learned that Eisenstein had taken on the Fergana Canal project.[78]

Evidence indicates that Birman, an untested director, had trepidations about *Semyon Kotko*; perhaps Eisenstein did as well. No sooner had Birman promised to stage the opera than she reneged. Daltsev needed to pester her from far-distant Moscow to sign her contract and expressed "bewilderment" at her tardiness. "I am unwilling to entertain the thought that you might decline [the offer]," he admonished her on July 14. "I recall your categorical promise to take on the staging of S. S. Prokofiev's opera. Believe me, Serafima Germanovna, you are assuming a very rewarding and noble task."[79] Further pressure came from Viktor Gorodinsky, editor-in-chief of *Sovetskoye iskusstvo* and former music advisor for the Central Committee, who told Daltsev that he would do "whatever it takes" to convince Birman to sign the contract.[80]

Daltsev reminded Birman of the favorable run-through of sections of acts 1–3 of *Semyon Kotko* at the Stanislavsky Theater on July 8.[81] The event was a lovefest, with the invited audience—which included Gorodinsky, the composers Lev Knipper, Georgiy Kreytner, and Gavriil Popov, the editors of *Sovetskoye iskusstvo*, the conductor Mikhaíl Zhukov, and some of the singers and musicians in the theater's employ—heaping praise on every detail of the score. Popov enthused that "act III was so captivating, that I don't have the words to express my feelings of delight," and Kreytner effused that acts 1 and 2 "marked a step forward in the creation of a classic Soviet opera." The group from *Sovetskoye iskusstvo* noted with approval the relationship between Prokofiev's and Musorgsky's text-setting practices, though one member noted that the folksy libretto less recalled Gogol than "thieves' cant"—the implication being that, for all of the score's exalted lyricism, debased creatures like Sofya's mother, Khivrya, are kept down in the gutter. The audience at the run-through backed the choice of Birman as director. Despite the brevity of her résumé, she had apparently demonstrated "profound originality and talent" in her work.

Prokofiev did not see it that way. His meetings with Birman, like his meetings with Katayev, left him gnashing his teeth. Numerous arguments arose. In a brief reminiscence, Birman acknowledged that the collaboration was anguished, with the inscrutable composer demanding the realization of Meyerhold's opaque vision of the opera, which she wanted to cast as a satire of the kulak class, freighted with symbolism about liberation from oppression.[82] (She took as inspiration the acclaimed 1898 production of Anton Chekhov's *The Seagull* at the Moscow Arts Theater.) Tishler, meantime, grumbled to Prokofiev that Birman lacked an understanding of his art and that he could not accommodate her requests. The singers, moreover, soon "tired of Birman's long-winded discussions and explanations." It was

a miserable situation, with the three principals having different agendas and
yanked in different directions, like "the swan, the crab, and the pike" in Ivan
Krïlov's eponymous nineteenth-century fable.[83] Birman tried to put a brave
face on it, but she could not help but notice that Prokofiev disliked her:

> It's a great pity that I decided only in very rare instances
> to approach Prokofiev with a question about what he
> wanted the orchestra to express in this or that fragment of
> the opera.
>
> "Sergey Sergeyevich, what's going in the orchestra when
> the enemies ambush the village?" "Bones. Don't you under-
> stand? Bones, I'm saying. Skeletons..." He did not explain
> further: if you got it, good, if not, blame yourself.
>
> But he could be fearsome, even rude. Once we were
> rehearsing a very difficult scene whose contents I don't
> precisely recall. We had to repeat the very same passage
> over and over again. The actors got distracted; my energy
> waned. Suddenly Prokofiev's angry voice emanated from the
> darkness of the hall: "Cadence! Cadence! It's imprecise!"
> I burst out: "Sergey Sergeyevich! I can't go on tormenting
> the actors." "Your work is careless!"[84]

Their one cordial meeting was their first, but even it had a black comic
dimension. Birman recalls Prokofiev visiting her room at the Kislovodsk
resort to introduce her to the opera. He had just completed a tennis match
and felt energized. There was no piano in the room; undaunted, he pulled
a chair up beside the bed, laid his large hands on the duvet, and proceeded
to thump through the entire score, singing both the instrumental and vocal
parts in his untrained voice. An attendant rapped on the door to report complaints from the neighbors: "Put a stop, please, to this noise and refrain from
disturbing the peace."[85]

The disappearance of Meyerhold, the quarrels with Katayev, and the
difficulties with Birman cast a pall over the rehearsals. An unrelated event
that no one could have predicted then spoiled the premiere. On August 23,
1939, the Soviet premier and foreign minister Molotov and his German
counterpart Joachim von Ribbentrop signed a nonaggression pact and
an appended secret protocol that were supposed to define the Soviet and
German spheres of influence for the next ten years.[86] Poland, the three

Baltic States, and the enclave of Bessarabia were suddenly left open to the depredations of either or both powers. The pact permitted Hitler to attack Poland a week later without fear of reprisal from Stalin. It remained in effect until June 22, 1941, when Hitler launched a three-pronged attack on the Soviet Union.

In the two years of the pact's existence, the Committee on Arts Affairs curtailed the commissioning and distributing of anti-German art. *Semyon Kotko*, like *Alexander Nevsky*, suddenly became politically incorrect. "There was a pause," Katayev recalls, and then some "diplomatic nastiness."[87] Marina Nestyeva claims that "a representative from the People's Commissariat for Foreign Affairs demanded that appropriate changes be made to the opera's text: 'The accent must be placed solely on the intervention. Europe is looking at you and your words, Sergey Sergeyevich.'" The composer bristled: "'I won't change anything in the music. So let Europe look at the comrade from the NKID.'"[88] The anecdote dates from April 17, 1940, nine days before the scheduled premiere of *Semyon Kotko*. It suggests that Prokofiev resisted bureaucratic intimidation even in the wake of Meyerhold's disappearance; as such, it is likely embellished. The "comrade from the NKID" was Vladimir Dekanozov, Deputy Foreign Affairs Minister (People's Commissar), about to be named Soviet ambassador to Nazi Germany.

The controversy led to a rescheduling of the premiere of *Semyon Kotko* from April 26 to June 23, the end of the 1939–40 season.[89] On June 1, Prokofiev wrote to Molotov in an effort to prevent an indefinite postponement:

> Highly esteemed Vyacheslav Mikhaylovich: You have paid great attention to my opera *SK*, showing interest in its fate. The presence in it of several foreign elements has elicited various reactions: as far as I know, comrades Lozovsky and Shcheglov find nothing wrong with it; comrade Dekanozov, on the other hand, considers it undesirable.... I know, Vyacheslav Mikhaylovich, that you attend many opera productions. Might I request that you schedule a closed review and attend it so as to be certain for yourself that there is nothing in it that might shock our neighbors? Reports by your colleagues and a reading of the libretto cannot provide an accurate perception of my conception, and the work might perish owing to an unclear perception of it.[90]

Molotov referred the matter to Khrapchenko and Andrey Vïshinsky, the Deputy Premier and the prosecutor of the 1936–38 show trials, jotting "What will it be?" on the June 8 letter. Vïshinsky jotted below: "Review scheduled for 11/VI at 11 a.m."

Two days later, on June 13, Vïshinsky informed Molotov that he had attended the review of *Semyon Kotko* with a lower-level official from the NKID press office and Khrapchenko. "I consider it prudent to make changes to the libretto, eliminating the episodes with the Austrian-German occupants," he stated. "S. S. Prokofiev agrees with these suggestions. The issue can therefore be considered resolved."[91]

The music of the opera remained the same, but the music was not in dispute, and Prokofiev, indignation notwithstanding, knew it. Since the libretto included a few German-language expressions, he and Katayev had at first simply decided to transform the villains from Germans into Austrians. This change obviously did not placate Vïshinsky. So the Austrians were transformed into *haydamaks* (Ukrainian nationalists), with some louts from the old imperial army thrown into the mix. Even Prokofiev's sons took part in the bizarre sequence of events: Oleg recalled playing dress-up—first as Germans, then as haydamaks—in the family apartment.[92]

Semyon Kotko received its June 23 premiere and held a spot in the Stanislavsky Theater repertoire during the 1940–41 season. It closed on February 2, 1941, after fifteen performances, including a radio broadcast of a montage from the score on December 21, 1940. Another such broadcast was heard on American radio on November 3, 1940, with Prokofiev offering remarks in English. During the season, excerpts from the first and second acts were performed as part of concerts at Moscow academies, institutes, and factories.[93] The fraught politics of *Semyon Kotko* made it unpalatable for most reviewers, who compared it unfavorably to the aria-and-chorus-filled opera *Into the Storm*, which was premiered on October 10, 1939, at the Nemirovich-Danchenko Music Theater.[94] That opera was written by a greenhorn composer from the provinces named Tikhon Khrennikov, who would make the right political moves to assume the leadership of the Union of Soviet Composers in 1948. Much like *Semyon Kotko*, *Into the Storm* narrates a struggle between pro- and anti-revolutionaries for control of a remote village. Unlike *Semyon Kotko*, it introduced, for the first time in Soviet opera, the character of Lenin, who, as a mark of transcendent otherness, speaks rather than sings. The two operas were compared in successive issues of the journal *Sovetskaya muzïka* and at meetings of the Moscow branch of the Union of Soviet Composers on November 27 and 29, 1939. Khrennikov asserts that his opera received the most attention, but that its assessors fell into two irreconcilable camps:[95]

> The head of the first was the musicologist Semyon Shlif-shteyn, the head of the second was the musicologist Georgiy Khubov (and each had his own "train" of people with like-minded views). For Shlifshteyn's lecture, which included a furious attack on my opera, I naturally asked to sing and play all of the musical examples myself. The situation became amusing (though at the time it did not seem amusing at all). The lecturer tore into me. "Listen to the crudeness here," he said. "Tikhon Nikolayevich, please demonstrate." And I obediently played the requested episode, compiling my own "dossier" of compromising sounds.[96]

Unlike Khrennikov, Prokofiev could not be accused of crudeness. Detractors of *Semyon Kotko* instead charged him with arrogantly disgracing the memories of Ukrainian revolutionaries by presenting them in a comic guise in the act 4 artillery scene. As Khrennikov recalls one critic remarking, "The partisans in this scene emit 'inarticulate sounds' and recall the grotesque figure of the lackey Stepan in Musorgsky's *Marriage*."[97] And although Prokofiev strove for tunefulness throughout his opera, he had not, according to a second critic, sacrificed his commitment to continuous declamation, the result being an uneven score:

> A contradiction arises between the aspiration to saturate the opera with *melos* and the aspiration to avoid cutting the musical-dramatic fabric into parts. As a result, despite an abundance of vocal lines of high melodic quality, the opera conveys an episodic, no-more-than-a-sum-of-its-parts impression. The impression of melodiousness would have been greater had Prokofiev not followed the irritating (to the listener) practice of more often than not assigning the singer mere "extensions" of the orchestral melodies (or partial themes, conveyed intact only in the orchestra). Several melodic episodes are not perceived as such by the listener, since they are heard at the same time as a recitative

or even the rhythmicized conversation of the other characters. Finally, the general melodic plan of the opera creates a
negative effect. Nearly half of the melodic ideas in the opera
are concentrated in act 1; in the remaining acts new themes
are introduced all the more sparingly.[98]

This critique is heavy-handed, an effort to isolate musical faults in a score
that Khrennikov, among others, privately deemed "brilliant" and "perhaps
the best of those [operas] written by Soviet composers on a Soviet theme."[99]
Even as the opera was pulled from the repertoire, it continued to gain defend-
ers. In mid-January 1943, Prokofiev entertained an offer to revive *Semyon
Kotko*—once certain large-scale changes in the dramatic structure were
made—but the plan fell through.

The Ballet Revised

As *Semyon Kotko* was being conceived, composed, and produced, work
continued behind the scenes on the much-delayed Leningrad premiere of
Romeo and Juliet. The ballet had a successful Czechoslovakian premiere at
the end of 1938, but suffered considerable vandalizing before it reached the
Soviet stage. On August 28, 1938, just before the Brno Opera House started
to rehearse the ballet, Prokofiev received a telegram from the Kirov Theater expressing interest in adding it to the 1939–40 season. The Leningrad
production, choreographed by Leonid Lavrovsky and conducted by Isay
Sherman, involved changes to the scenario and then the music that Prokofiev largely resisted, but that he did not fully know about until the January
11, 1940, premiere. In effect, the conflict with Katayev and Birman about
the dramatic structure of *Semyon Kotko* was reprised in a balletic context.
Just as his operatic co-collaborators implored him to traditionalize the opera
with tuneful numbers for the hero (Semyon) and heroine (Sofya), his balletic
co-collaborators pressured him to traditionalize *Romeo and Juliet* by including bravura variations in the ballroom and balcony scenes.

Prokofiev refused to rework the ballet along these lines, claiming that he
and Radlov had worked out the timings of the numbers to the precise second
and that he had left the ballet behind him for other projects—but Sherman,
acting as Lavrovsky's liaison with the composer in the ten weeks preceding the
premiere, cajoled him into changing his mind: "Sergey Sergeyevich, you write
cadenzas in your piano concertos—ballet variations are cadenzas, too. Why

deprive the dancers of the opportunity to display their balletic technique?"[100] After mulling the matter over, Prokofiev complied, drafting the requested variations (Nos. 14 and 20 in the score), and submitting them to the Kirov Theater for approval.[101] His effort satisfied the choreographer and his dancers only in part. On Lavrovsky's insistence, Sherman asked the composer to make the ending of Romeo's variation more emphatic and to eliminate six measures from Juliet's variation. Once again Prokofiev complied, informing Sherman:

> I have shortened Juliet's Variation in the following way: bars
> 68–72 without alterations. Then: further on, bar 80, i.e. the
> one with the four natural signs in the key signature. So, six
> bars have been removed as [the ballerina Galina] Ulanova
> requested. As regards Romeo's variation, nothing can be
> done there. It was agreed with Lavrovsky that it would end,
> dying away. Furthermore: the variations lead into other
> music *without a pause* so that even Romeo won't be able to
> milk applause: a hard fate for an ambitious dancer![102]

Prokofiev's compromise on the variations did not mark the end of the saga. Lavrovsky convinced the composer to add two blocks of music to act 4 (No. 51) for "Romeo's exit after the funeral" and "Romeo's death," and to add, for purposes of character development, a double reprise of Paris's theme in act 3 (No. 46).[103] Prokofiev was then asked to reduce Mercutio's variation (No. 15) from a three-part (ABA) form to a two-part (AA) one. The composer hesitated, noting (as Rimsky-Korsakov had taught him) that some cuts "lengthen, rather than shorten" a work.[104] He agreed to make the reduction only after seeing the choreography. Lastly, Lavrovsky asked for a group dance to be added to the opening of act 1, which was otherwise dominated by pantomimic scenes. Feeling besieged, Prokofiev refused to do so, but the choreographer did not back down. They quarreled, with Lavrovsky threatening to import the scherzo from Prokofiev's Second Piano Sonata into the ballet, and Prokofiev angrily forced into cobbling together a new number, the "Morning Dance" (No. 4).[105]

Much of the dispute centered on Prokofiev's disregard of the precepts of grand classical ballet in favor of a Diaghilev-inspired conception of the genre as one in which music and dance are free to set their own narrative agendas, to step out, as it were, from each other's shadows. *Romeo and Juliet* has a traditional framework, but as Vadim Gayevsky argues, the composer avoided traditional expressive modes. Committed to sober-minded stylization, he drained emotion from the "ball" and "sleep" scenes and, in the climactic episodes, suppressed "metaphysics," "conventional motives," "feeries," and "nocturnal poetry":

> Prokofiev's ball is not Berlioz's ball, and Juliet's sleep is not Aurora's sleep. It is a real but terrible sleep: it is as lifeless as death. The muffled chords of Prokofiev's music portray in almost palpable fashion the leaden tread, fading pulse, and falling, numbed body. The episode in which Juliet takes poison in order to fall asleep for forty-two hours is, on the level of emotion and orchestration, the least colorful episode of the score. It is as dry as a transcript and as brief as a death notice.[106]

The revised (tragic ending) version of *Romeo and Juliet* depicts death, but it does not celebrate it. The death scene denies the potential of reincarnation, transcendence, and—for the living left behind—consolation. Lavrovsky seems to have wanted the ballet to build up through the three acts to a *Liebestod*, with playful numbers from the original 1935 version of the score either rescored or removed. (At some point, he excised the "Dance of the Three Moors" in an effort to make the scenario gloomier.[107]) Prokofiev, in contrast, sought to depict the triumph of the spirit in the act 1 scenes of carefree abandon and guileless resistance to familial constraints. Uplifting Apollonian passion is embodied in the melodies of the ballroom, balcony, and morning episodes; the powers of fate govern the phobic ostinato patterns. The clash between the capricious, "neoclassical" Mercutio and hotheaded, "Scythian" Tibald establishes the parameters of the tragic ending.[108]

For the dancers, the challenge of the ballet was less aesthetic than practical. The loudest complaint came from Ulanova, to whom Lavrovsky assigned the role of Juliet. She found Prokofiev's rhythmic sequences inscrutable and pestered him to recompose them. Later, she ascribed the trouble to her training. The dancers in the troupe had been schooled in simple counts, not conflicting meters:

> To tell the truth we were not accustomed to such music, in fact we were a little afraid of it. It seemed to us that in rehearsing the Adagio from Act I, for example, we were following some melodic pattern of our own, something nearer

to our own conception of how the love of Romeo and Juliet should be expressed than that contained in Prokofiev's "strange" music. For I must confess that we did not hear that love in his music then.[109]

While *Romeo and Juliet* was in rehearsal, Prokofiev traveled back and forth from Moscow to Leningrad. He listened to the complaints about the score, ignoring most of them at first, but then, for the sake of the production, responding to them, tweaking rhythmic sequences, cadences, even the instrumentation. Sherman recounts the unusual fashion in which one of these alterations was made:

> During a break in one of the rehearsals, after the run-through of the scene in which Juliet takes poison, Ulanova told me that she nearly died of fright during her dance. She related basically the following: "Can you imagine, while dancing I saw Prokofiev in the mirror; startled, I had the fleeting thought: might this be a hallucination?"
>
> It turned out that she had previously complained to Sergey Sergeyevich that she could not hear the orchestra during the mirror scene, when [Juliet] decides to take poison. Prokofiev decided to validate the ballerina's complaint. He went onstage and walked behind Ulanova during her entire dance. At the break he silently came down to the orchestra pit, added something to a few instrumental parts, then he silently took the score and added something to it, and only then did he say to me: "The acoustics in the pit are such that not everything can be heard on the stage. See what I have added, without violating my conception...to my credit." So what did he add? In one place he gave the bass clarinet a held note; he added the triangle somewhere, and in two places he added short notes for the flutes and piccolos on strong beats in the measure...and onstage the ballerina heard everything.[110]

Given this and other adjustments, it is fair to say that the First and Second Suites from *Romeo and Juliet*, which date from 1936, provide a better sense of Prokofiev's intended orchestration of the ballet than the actual score— even though they were assembled for nontheatrical concert performance.

In the run-up to the ballet's Leningrad premiere, Prokofiev discovered that Lavrovsky had altered the music in places without consulting him.[111] He protested the changes to Sherman, but the conductor—to whom credit goes for shepherding the ballet to the stage—could not convince Lavrovsky to undo them. Prokofiev's final letter to Sherman on the subject shows enormous frustration:

> On numerous occasions I have appealed to the Kirov Theater
> to insert a number of corrections relating to the lack of coordi-
> nation between the choreography and the music, superfluous
> repeats, insertions, and so on. For four months nothing has
> been done and I do not know the state in which the produc-
> tion will reach Moscow. On March 31 I sent a registered letter
> to the management with an official request for an enquiry into
> this matter. But the management has simply not answered.[112]

Eventually, Prokofiev forgave Sherman and learned to tolerate, if not respect, Lavrovsky. He found it necessary, given all that had happened, to credit the choreographer as co-author of the scenario. The original scenarist Radlov, sidelined during the tortured process of revision, disowned the ballet, purportedly forewarning acquaintances who attended a rehearsal to "bear in mind that I don't take any responsibility for this disgrace."[113] Despite the alteration of the scenario and score and the fact that it premiered in blackout conditions in Leningrad during the Finnish-Russian War, *Romeo and Juliet* became a success. A March 23, 1940, memorandum from the Committee on Arts Affairs to Sovnarkom finds Stalin approving a performance in Moscow.[114] Later productions, including that presented by Lavrovsky in Moscow in 1946, received international notice. The aristocratic décor risked undercutting socialist principles, but it represented something of a diplomatic breakthrough, helping to reestablish cultural relations between Eastern and Western Europe. By 1946, Prokofiev could no longer conceive of traveling abroad; the altered, Stalin-approved version of the ballet went in his stead. His Shakespearean tale of woe came with a bittersweet ending.

Dissent

Such, of course, could not be said of the tale of *Semyon Kotko*. Prokofiev might have been ignorant of the details of Meyerhold's arrest, but he could not have been ignorant of the bureaucratic machinations that attended the closing of Meyerhold's theater and the gradual curtailment of the director's creative activities. In the fall of 1939, Prokofiev abandoned his fading hopes for a moderation in Soviet cultural policy. Indirect evidence comes from a lecture that he began but did not finish writing, perhaps because it had no chance of being delivered. The outline, which bristles with dissent, dates from November 12:

1. Soviet art, despite its enormous breadth, is declining in quality.

2. Among the arts (in general, not specifically in the USSR), music is the youngest. The process of hearing is refined with each generation and attains the ability to grasp increasingly complicated relationships between pitches. The music of all of the classic composers was not understood on first contact. In contrast, music that is immediately understood does not outlast its generation. Assessments of complexity and falseness are finite, not absolute. Perspective is needed.

3. The masses are developing faster than many composers think. The creation of music for the masses should be like an arrow in flight: moving forward toward its goal.

4. The music of [Isaak] Dunayevsky [an operetta, popular song, and film score composer] and [Dmitriy] Pokrass is based not on true folk music or the classics, but on operetta and cabaret songs. It does not transport the masses, but pushes them backward, schooling them in vulgarity.

5. The music of Dzerzhinsky is illiterate. His development of folksongs represents a decline in comparison to that which occurred seventy years ago. Lesser composers regard Dzherzhinsky's absence of talent as a marker of success.

6. But even more significant composers are in decline. Slogans about innovation and achievement are unconvincing, since even the slightest achievement is hailed. The critics' dangerous point of view: "I didn't understand this the first time—this makes it Formalism."

7. The official directive concerning the struggle against Formalism has been carried out too zealously. The baby has been thrown out with the bathwater. Composers have abandoned the search for new material (because to search for such material is Formalism). Music comprising second-rate material cannot be first-rate.[115]

Beneath the invective, one notes that while Prokofiev was not averse to composing music for the masses, he was averse to the notion that music should be oriented toward accessibility. The target of his complaint was the troika of cultural policy—Party-mindedness, people-mindedness, and ideological content—which remained, in his opinion, condescending to its intended audience, antithetical to the actual labor of music making.

The candor and the mere fact of the survival of these comments suggest that they were intended for posterity. Henceforth, Prokofiev prudently censored himself; his writings become less individual and more doctrinaire, choked with officialese. He maintained his international reputation, but he abandoned his international perspective. The government hastened this adjustment by refusing his requests to tour abroad.

It took some time before Prokofiev realized that he would no longer benefit from creative dialogue with colleagues and audiences in the West. Throughout 1938, he maintained regular contact with his Paris secretary Astrov, and continued to discuss potential engagements in Europe and the United States with his agent (S. S. Horwitz) and the Haensel & Jones firm. In December 1938, he arranged and, at the last minute, annulled a trip to Paris: "The time is not right," he wrote to Astrov on the 15th, "we will return to this question in a month."[116]

After scheduling the Paris performances, Prokofiev and his agent planned an entire month of events in the United States, including a week in February conducting the New York Philharmonic. Prokofiev proposed introducing his *Alexander Nevsky* Cantata (a noncinematic arrangement of his film score) to New York audiences. Irrespective of the work's xenophobic patriotic nationalism, he believed that it would have as large a success abroad as it did at home. Plans for the tour grew over time, with events on the East Coast, West Coast (the fascination with Hollywood had not decreased), and Chicago planned for February and March. Besides the *Alexander Nevsky* Cantata (which calls for eighty to one hundred singers), Prokofiev planned to conduct the *Love for Three Oranges* Suite, *Peter and the Wolf*, and the Second Suite from *Romeo and Juliet*. As in 1938, he would also perform his First Piano Concerto. The proposed tour received advance coverage in the *New York Times*, *Chicago Daily Tribune*, and *Los Angeles Times*. This last newspaper even reported that Prokofiev had "taken a house for several weeks" in Los Angeles in the spring of 1939 for the purposes of composing a film score.[117]

On February 9, 1939, Prokofiev informed Koussevitzky's assistant Nicolas Slonimsky that he had "expected to come to the States around this time," but that his engagements had been "postponed until next season."[118] The postponement became permanent as creative, personal, and political pressures mounted. Prokofiev wrote again to Astrov in June in hopes of arranging another tour to Paris, this time in January 1940, but he cautioned that the trip might have to be rescheduled on account of *Semyon Kotko*. The Stanislavsky Theater was planning a December 1939 premiere of the opera, but as Prokofiev pointed out—this time to Horwitz—"all premieres are susceptible to delay."[119] The composer could not have anticipated that he, Katayev, and Tïshler would be forced to rework the opera, and that the delay would last for over half a year.

On September 1, 1939, Nazi Germany invaded Poland. Two days later Western Europe exploded into conflict, with Great Britain and France entering full-scale battle against Hitler. Prokofiev expressed his fears about the conflict to his Parisian colleagues, and fretted about the health of his mother-in-law, whom he supported with proceeds from royalties. By November 15, 1939, prospects for a trip abroad had begun to fade. Although he still "counted on going" to the United States, he made it clear that he might have to cancel. "If I don't go to America," he told Astrov, "perhaps some personal effects and toiletries might be sent to me."[120] His list included 24-stave manuscript paper, an overcoat he had left behind, letter-writing paper, and a fashion magazine "pour madame." Near the end of the letter, Prokofiev's last to Astrov, he thanks him for helping his mother-in-law and for sending postage stamps of Mickey Mouse to his children for their collection.

Prokofiev's travel problems were described in accurate, succinct form in the January 10, 1940, edition of the *New York Times*: "Serge Prokofieff, Russian composer, will be unable to come to America this season to fulfill his engagement as guest conductor of the Philharmonic-Symphony Orchestra, it was announced yesterday. Political conditions have made it impossible for him to obtain the necessary visas."[121] Stravinsky, the newspaper added, would substitute for the absent Prokofiev at the podium—a bitter irony, given that Stravinsky's dominance of the international music scene had spurred Prokofiev's decision to relocate to the Soviet Union in 1936.

Stalin's Image in Music

Near the end of the traumatic year of 1939, Prokofiev wrote a paean to Stalin. The work, which was commissioned by the Radio Committee in October, is a thirteen-minute cantata titled *Zdravitsa* (A Toast), part of an inundation of musical and verbal salutations to the Great Leader and Teacher on the occasion of his sixtieth birthday (December 21, 1939). In explicit contrast to the reality of mass incarceration, starvation, and execution, these works offer benign images of resplendent harvests and harmonious labor. Their creators—Prokofiev included—represented Soviet life in whitewashed, future-perfect guise.

Prokofiev worked quickly on his birthday present, taking pains to ensure that its harmonic language did not stray out of bounds, and that the melodic writing conveyed something of the fixed-smile cheer of the libretto. To avoid repeating the fundamental miscalculation of the *Cantata for the Twentieth Anniversary of October*, he based the libretto on poems about Stalin. These poems came from a massive (534-page) Pravda publishing house collection dedicated to the twentieth anniversary of the Revolution. It bears the title *Folk Arts of the USSR*; the recently deceased Gorky is credited as editor in chief. Among other poems, Prokofiev set the first three verses of "The Sun Shines Differently" (Po-inomu svetit solntse) for the beginning of *Zdravitsa*; the first, fourth, and fifth verses of "Lenin's Great Pupil" (Velikiy uchyonik Lenina) for the ending; and the first verse of "I Would Travel to Moscow" (Ya bï s'yezdila v Moskvu) for a section of the middle.[122] *Zdravitsa* also includes a fragment of a Russian heroic ballad, or *bïlina*, called "The Praise to Stalin Will Be Eternal" (Slava Stalinu budet vechnaya).[123] (The ballad is fancifully credited to a storyteller named Marfa Kryukova, a resident of the village of Nizhnyaya Zolotitsa, near Arkhangelsk.) In setting these texts to music, Prokofiev changed some of the words and reordered some of the lines. The available evidence indicates that he did not rummage through the Pravda collection for suitable verses himself. Rather, they were chosen for him by Dina Ermilova, an editor with the literature division of the Radio Committee, and Aleksandr Tishchenko, the director of its music division. "Esteemed Sergey Sergeyevich," Tishchenko wrote on November 16, 1939, "I am forwarding you a selection of materials which, from our viewpoint, might be of particular interest as source texts for songs dedicated to I. V. Stalin."[124] The Radio Committee ensured that the *Zdravitsa* libretto did not breach protocol by assigning Prokofiev approved published texts. Had they been newly written, they would have been automatically sent for review to the Special Division (Osobïy sektor) of the Central Committee, which included a department "exclusively occupied with the State formation of the Stalin cult," including "preparation of collected works for publication, approval of journal and newspaper articles with accounts of Stalin's life and work, literary Staliniana, and so forth."[125]

The frontispiece of the 1939 piano-vocal score indicates that the *Zdravitsa* libretto comes from Russian, Ukrainian, Belorussian, Kumïk, Kurd, Mari, and Mordovian sources. The *Pravda* collection claims to represent thirty-five different peoples, with the contents devoted to five topics: Lenin, Stalin, the civil war, the Red Army, and Soviet nationhood. These claims, ethnographically speaking, are exaggerations. The sources for the libretto are distillates: they allude to, rather than actually come from, the peoples of the far-flung republics. Like the verses chosen for *Songs of Our Days*, the verses selected for *Zdravitsa* are examples of invented folklore. The "anonymous" texts are by official writers.

The third edition of *Zdravitsa* (1946) includes an English-language translation that Prokofiev had a hand in commissioning. ("Since Muzgiz is planning to publish *Zdravitsa*," he wrote to Atovmyan on September 20, 1945, "it would be good to commission straightaway an English translation from Shneyerson, who in collaboration with an American successfully coped with *Alexander Nevsky*.")[126] Besides this bilingual edition, the Moscow Conservatory library houses no fewer than eleven editions of *Zdravitsa* published between 1941 and 1984. The two editions (1970 and 1984) that postdate the Stalinist period replace the toast to the ruler with a toast to the Party. The ritualistic de-Stalinization of the score was undertaken by the same individual—the poet and librettist Aleksey Mashistov—who had de-Stalinized *Songs of Our Days*.[127] Prokofiev's *Cantata for the Thirtieth Anniversary of October* would also be cleansed of Stalin references under Khrushchev.[128] In every edition, however, the mood of *Zdravitsa* remains the same. The singers declare that happiness blossoms in the Slavic lands, and that Soviet life, like Soviet farmland, overflows with abundance. In the first (unaltered) stanza, the singers declaim: "There has never been a field so green / The village is filled with unheard-of happiness / Our life has never been so happy / Our rye has hitherto never been so plentiful."[129]

The sketches for *Zdravitsa* find Prokofiev conceiving it as a seven-part rondo, with each section terminating with a variation of a C-major refrain in the brass and strings.[130] (In accord with the composer's expanded definition of tonality, the refrain alternates between C major, C minor, and A-flat major harmonies.) After sketching the refrain, Prokofiev verbally itemized its appearances throughout the cantata. He indicated that it would first sound at the end of the orchestral introduction to the work, and then recur in the section devoted to an "old woman" from Mari who imagines being a teenager again and journeying to Moscow to thank Stalin for her good life. The passage dedicated to the old woman would be followed by a Russian *chastushka* or limerick tune.[131] For the beginning of the next episode, Prokofiev resorted to recycling, importing the text and music of "Send-Off" (Provodï), one of a collection of folklore-inspired mass songs that he composed between 1937 and 1939.[132] The text comes from the same 1937 collection as the rest of the *Zdravitsa* libretto: it tells the tale of a villager named Aksinya who is sent to Moscow for a Kremlin meeting with Stalin—her symbolic husband—in honor of her work. (The text is fancifully credited to Danila Letashkov, a twenty-five-year-old member of the Kommunar collective farm in Belorussia.) Prokofiev modeled the music of this episode on the laments that are traditionally sung in village settings before the weddings of young brides. There follows a reprise of the ending of the *chastushka*, and then an extremely unusual passage—the first section of *Zdravitsa* drafted by Prokofiev—involving ascending and descending C-major scales over A-flat and G pedal points in the brass. The scalar runs, which underscore a description of the suffering of the Russian people under the tsars, cascade through the bass, tenor, alto, and soprano parts. The overall sensation is one of a gigantic historical shudder.

The December 21 premiere of *Zdravitsa*, conducted by Golovanov, received positive reviews, as did the subsequent performances in the various jubilee concerts held in Stalin's honor.[133] The work remained in the repertoire until Stalin's death, and received special attention in an essay in *Sovetskaya muzïka* titled "Stalin's Image in Music." (The two authors struggled to find allusions to folklore in the score—"in the first chorus...the festive stamp of glorious, epochal folksongs is audible"—but then retreated, concluding only that "numerous themes, and the vigor and cheer of the score," charmed the listener.)[134] In addition to overseeing the publication of the first edition in 1939, Prokofiev served as a "consultant" for a May 11, 1940, recording.[135] His younger son Oleg remembered hearing *Zdravitsa* broadcast through loudspeakers on the street during either the winter of 1939–40 or 1940–41:

> Incredibly lonely it seemed as it resounded throughout the deserted Chkalov Street, where we lived then...Winter, the wind whirls snowflakes over the dark, gloomy asphalt, and the national choir booms out these strange harmonies. I was used to them, though, and that calmed me down. I ran

home to tell the big news: "Daddy! They are playing you outside..." But he already knew; and, as usual, the matter was never discussed again.[136]

The contrast between the sunshine-drenched imagery of the *Zdravitsa* libretto and the circumstances in which it was performed is telling; so, too, is the muteness of Prokofiev's response to its success. The last lines, which describe Stalin as the "flame" of the people's "blood," attest to the high political stakes of the commission.

In a brief essay on Prokofiev's Soviet period, the musicologist Vladimir Zak argues that the red-ink markings (the "crimson zigzags") made by Golovanov on his copy of the *Zdravitsa* score inadvertently emblematize the macabre context of its creation.[137] Perhaps: but one must keep in mind that the score was conceived in honor of the individual responsible for this macabre context. There is no subversion in the work, no contestation of cults of personalities. It cannot be rescued from the dustbin of musical agitprop. Far from denoting what Zak calls the "art of the subtext," it shows Prokofiev seeking, and finding, the formula for official approval.[138]

3

The Pushkin Centennial

February 10, 1937, marked the centennial of Aleksandr Pushkin's death. The celebration was an exhausting, protracted event that witnessed a reconception of the great poet's life and works. From the aristocratic, serf-owning, enlightened conservative of historical reality, who fathered a son by one of his serfs and sold others to the army, Pushkin became a political emblem of the freedom-loving Russian people, a social emblem of rustic values, and a cultural emblem of directness and transparency of expression. The editors of *Pravda*, who hyperbolically ascribed Pushkin's death to "a foreign aristocratic scoundrel and tsarist hireling," declared that he was "entirely ours, entirely Soviet, insofar as it is Soviet power that has inherited all of the best in our people and that is, itself, the realization of the people's best hopes."[1] The centennial, observed nationwide and involving thousands of cultural workers, interpreted Pushkin, through selective slanting of the facts, as an anti-tsarist advocate and radical democrat.

To certify this official version of Pushkin, the government published critical editions of his works, organized conferences and discussions, and commissioned cinematic and theatrical treatments of his life. The overseers of the centennial preparations were themselves overseen in an effort to ensure the consistency of the ideological distortions. The planning, re-planning, realization and—more often than not—cancellation of events took place in an atmosphere of dread. As Stephanie Sandler, to whom the preceding points are indebted, comments: "Newspapers in January and February 1937 featured two stories that received equally intense coverage:

the trial, sentencing, and execution of Karl Radek, Yuriy Pyatakov, and fifteen others; and the Pushkin celebration."[2] Ecstatic press accounts to the contrary, the centennial was the locus of different types of crisis, the most obvious—and wretchedly most benign—being the consolidation of State control over the entire Russian cultural heritage.

Prokofiev contributed to the centennial by fulfilling commissions for three large-scale orchestral works: incidental music for a theatrical production, by Tairov, of Pushkin's novel in verse, *Eugene Onegin* (1831); a score for a filmed version, directed by Mikhaíl Romm, of Pushkin's short story *The Queen of Spades* (1833); and incidental music for a theatrical production, by Meyerhold, of Pushkin's historical drama *Boris Godunov* (1825). The composer had formally committed to the three collaborative projects just after relocating to Moscow in the spring of 1936. He also composed three Pushkin Romances for soprano voice and piano, a setting of the poems "Pine Trees" (Sosnï), "Crimson Dawn" (Rumyanoy zaryoyu), and "In Your Chamber" (V tvoyu svetlitsu); he and Lina premiered this work in an April 20, 1937, radio broadcast. In addition, Prokofiev considered but did not undertake a setting of *Mozart and Salieri* (1830) for the actor and director Yuriy Zavadsky. Upon listing these projects to Alpers in a July 25, 1936, letter, Prokofiev joked: "Is this not just like the raving of a lunatic? But such is how it is, and the Pushkin centennial is to blame."[3]

Neither the theatrical productions nor the film were realized, for reasons unrelated to the composer. Meyerhold—who held a post on the original Pushkin centennial committee, formed by decree on July 27, 1934,[4] and on the second committee that was organized in 1936 after the death of Gorky—was censured for creative and political transgressions, as were Tairov and Romm. The three projects unraveled in succession, leaving Prokofiev with almost nothing to show for his inspired labor and his collaborators fearing, at a minimum, the ruin of their careers. Prokofiev reused some of the music in later works; for several decades, the rest of it languished in manuscript form, unorchestrated and unperformed. Recent recordings by Michail Jurowski for the Capriccio label have begun to give it its due. This chapter takes up each score in turn, lingering, as testament to its conceptual richness, on *Boris Godunov*.

Eugene Onegin

Of his five centennial projects, Prokofiev claimed that *Eugene Onegin* "interested [him] the most," largely because it allowed him to respond creatively to Chaikovsky's operatic treatment of the same subject—albeit in the realm of incidental music.⁵ In a June 22, 1936, article written for *Vechernyaya Moskva*, he explained his approach to the project:

> The play *Eugene Onegin*, adapted for the stage by S[igizmund] D. Krzhizhanovsky, highlights those parts of Pushkin's novel that are not included in Chaikovsky's opera. I believe it will be interesting to see Lensky arguing with Onegin over a bottle of Aÿ, Tatyana visiting his empty house, or Onegin "on the banks of the Neva." It is a well-known fact that opinions about Chaikovsky's opera were divided. Some considered the composer's interpretation to be perfect; others, on the other hand, believed that it robbed the novel of the intrinsic humor peculiar to the poet and gave it the pessimistic touch characteristic of Chaikovsky. I personally shall endeavor to capture the true spirit of Pushkin.⁶

One problem with Chaikovsky's opera, according to Prokofiev, was the absence of rusticity in the first dance-based episode (act 2, scene 1), which takes place at the estate of Olga Larina, Lensky's fiancée. In conversation with the dramatist Osaf Litovsky, Prokofiev derided Chaikovsky's use of "'chic,' metropolitan music" to represent a "provincial landholder's evening," whereas in reality, the attendees would have "danced to a piano" that sounded "a bit broken-down and jangling" with a coarse "tram-blyam" polka being the evening's highlight.⁷ When Prokofiev quipped that "new, more faithful" operatic versions of *Eugene Onegin* and *The Queen of Spades* could perhaps be written, Litovsky, whose tastes were exceptionally conservative, called his bluff: "So why don't you write them?" The purported answer: "What—compete with Chaikovsky?!"⁸

Prokofiev's desire "to capture the true spirit of Pushkin" proved problematic for the simple reason that Tairov planned to stage not a dramatic reading of *Eugene Onegin* but a dramatic enactment of it. He assigned the onerous task of adapting Pushkin's text to the ingenious litterateur Krzhizhanovsky, a prominent, if little published, member of the Moscow arts scene who improvised a career as a fiction writer, dramatist, historian, and educator. During his lifetime, just eight of his stories and one of novels appeared in print. Tairov first met Krzhizhanovsky after becoming familiar with his unpublished *Tales for Wunderkinder* (*Skazki dlya vunderkindov*); he thereafter invited him to join his theater, first as an acting instructor

(Krzhizhanovsky devised a course on the "psychology of the stage") and then as a dramatist.[9]

For Tairov, the first phase in the adaptation of *Eugene Onegin* involved teasing out its latent political content. In an April 6, 1936, public forum, he emphasized the importance, when staging a classic, of becoming intimately familiar with its original historical context. Such knowledge, he argued, enabled the director to identify and highlight those features most relevant to the present day. In his staging of *Eugene Onegin*, Tairov resolved to highlight what he perceived to be the title character's socially predetermined path to ruin. He reimagined Onegin as an "absolutely destroyed person," the antithesis of a "Decembrist" (a reference to the group of military officers and liberal thinkers who agitated to prevent the accession of Nikolay I to the throne in 1825).[10] Onegin becomes a superfluous person: dissolute, exhausted, and smitten because he lacks intention, the impulse to fulfill a goal. Tatyana, in contrast, "bears those natural Russian female features that could have allowed her to become the wife of a Decembrist—though it does not happen within the confines of the novel—consciously and willingly following him into exile." Her virtue resides in her decision to suppress, rather than indulge, her feelings for Onegin. Tairov's staging would not, it appears, have featured either a "tragic" or a "happy" ending, as in *Romeo and Juliet*; instead, the plot was to pivot around Tatyana's purposeful control of natural impulses and Onegin's purposeless submission to them.

For Krzhizhanovsky, the first phase in the adaptation involved replacing Pushkin's garrulous, self-conscious narrator with characters who speak in the first person. The narrator does not disappear entirely; rather, he is replaced by an itinerant "poet" (or, as labeled in the manuscript of Prokofiev's piano score, "companion") who appears onstage in the final scene to quote from book 1, stanza 1: "Will the hour of my freedom come? 'Tis time, 'tis time! To it I call."[11] The "poet" facilitates the bittersweet last encounter between Tatyana, who undergoes a psychological metamorphosis in the adaptation, and Onegin, who does not.

In consultation with Tairov, Krzhizhanovsky reordered scenes, deleted verses, blended others, and removed some of the philosophical, literary, and botanical asides. Elizaveta Dattel, the first musicologist to work on Prokofiev's music for the stage, points out that the scenarist transplanted the discussion between Larina and her neighbors about Tatyana's reluctance to settle down from long after her first encounter with Onegin (book 7, stanzas 25–27) to just before that encounter. Krzhizhanovsky also scrubbed the passage in which Onegin sends a letter to Tatyana (book 8, stanza 32). In Dattel's opinion, this change "destroyed" the psychological and emotional symmetry of the novel in verse, whereby the two characters, in different ways, upbraid one another in prose.[12] And there were remarkable additions to the drama: Krzhizhanovsky's adaptation begins with Lensky kneeling glumly at the grave of his fiancée's father, Dmitriy Larin, where he recites Pushkin's 1821 poem "I have outlasted all desire" (Ya perezhil svoi zhelan'ya). This poem, and the action it allegorizes, cannot be found in *Eugene Onegin*. It is one of several other Pushkin texts that Krzhizhanovsky included in his adaptation to compensate for having eliminated the narrator. Given the familiarity of Pushkin's tightly knitted text to Russian readers, the alterations could hardly have avoided drawing attention.

There was logic to the adaptation, to which Prokofiev responded even as others objected. The text would pass through several revisions, based first on positive exchanges between Tairov and Krzhizhanovsky, then on negative exchanges between Krzhizhanovsky, a commission of Pushkin scholars,[13] and, ultimately, Glavrepertkom, which was headed by Litovsky.

Prokofiev composed his music based on either the first or second version of the adaptation, which he heard at a May 1936 read-through in Tairov's office. The extant records of the project include Krzhizhanovsky's undated eighty-four-page typescript of either the first or second version with Prokofiev's marginalia concerning its musical possibilities, along with a four-page directorial lighting and blocking guide called "The Calendar of *Onegin*."[14] The autograph piano score contains both finished and unfinished passages (the former in ink, the latter in pencil), orchestration indications, and directorial references.[15] Comparing the typescript and the piano score reveals both consistencies and discrepancies. These latter attest to the reactionary uproar surrounding Krzhizhanovsky's adaptation and the pressure he came under to atone for his unorthodox distillation of Pushkin.

The most significant of the divergences concerns the chorus of frolicking students that Krzhizhanovsky may have devised for the final scene at a packed soirée in St. Petersburg—though, to be sure, in an upper-class salon it would never have been appropriate. Like the opening grave scene, this text, which comes from Pushkin's 1814 poem "To the Students" (K studentam), is not found in *Eugene Onegin*. Prokofiev drafted the chorus but did not assign it a number in his piano score, suggesting that Krzhizhanovsky perhaps decided to cut the chorus from the staging, with Prokofiev following suit. (Both the 1973 published score and the 2005 Capriccio recording include it as an appendix.) Further evidence of the problems with Krzhizhanovsky's adaptation appears in the autograph piano score, on page 6 in the lower margin. "Based on the new plan," Prokofiev jotted down in pencil, "Onegin and Tatyana at this point leave, following Onegin's lecture in the garden."[16] "The new plan" refers to either the second or third version of Krzhizhanovsky's adaptation, which restored something of the ordering of Pushkin's original.

The exact nature and timing of the Pushkin commission and Glavrepertkom adjudications of the adaptation are unknown, but they obviously caused enormous stress for Tairov, as evidenced by his communications to Krzhizhanovsky in the summer of 1936 (the former was in Kislovodsk, the latter in Odessa). Tairov specifically mentions Litovsky and Glavrepertkom, and desperately stresses the need to hasten the reworking of the adaptation to reflect their criticisms.[17] Prokofiev was in Moscow and Polenovo during the ordeal; his involvement in the negotiations over Krzhizhanovsky's text was evidently minimal.

Against this backdrop, Tairov's public remarks about the *Eugene Onegin* project seem almost absurdly benign. In a pair of interviews with *Krasnaya gazeta* and *Vechernyaya Moskva*, Tairov assures the reader that his work with Krzhizhanovsky on the adaptation, which had commenced in the winter of 1935, would be as true to Pushkin as possible:

> I have been working with S. Krzhizhanovsky on an edition of the text for the play for about half a year now. We are approaching this task with all of the necessary faithfulness toward Pushkin and trying in the main to bring to light those dramatic situations that Pushkin himself incorporated into *Onegin*. The work is complicated and laborious, especially since we began by relinquishing the narrator's role.[18]

In the first, more detailed interview, Tairov problematically assures his readers that "to be sure we won't be adding a single alien word and almost nothing will be taken from other Pushkin works." The staging, he added, posed "enormous difficulties" for Prokofiev, owing to the inescapable association of the subject matter with Chaikovsky. The composer later tempered this point, acknowledging that "to write the music for *Eugene Onegin* is a tempting proposition, but at the same time perhaps a thankless task." Although he managed to find "true" musical images for the characters, he "had to rewrite the themes and make several sketches" before arriving at what he needed.[19]

What he sought was sound that humbly served the characters and their actions. Prokofiev downplayed the significance of his music for spoken-word theater, commenting in an August 1936 interview for *Teatr i dramaturgiya* (Theater and Dramaturgy) that its role needed to be "modest":

> The listener goes to an opera or a ballet or a symphony con-
> cert with a special desire to hear the music, but the viewer
> going to the theater is not interested in the accompaniment
> to the staging. Hence music for a play does not need to
> solve particular problems; it must accompany it and, above
> all else, be understandable to, and calculated for, the less-
> skilled listener. It is best when a composer restricts himself
> to a handful of melodies and repeats them frequently: by
> the end the viewer will be humming them. For a play it is
> better to compose several simple melodies than many com-
> plex or hard-to-grasp ones.[20]

He added that the creative process involved translating visual images into musical ones: "I allow myself five to ten days in order to 'see' the perfor-mance, that is to say, to take in the actors' features, the illustration of their emotions, and the illustration of the events."

Accordingly, Prokofiev created distinct musical portraits for each of the characters in *Eugene Onegin,* which he nuanced over the course of the drama through transposition, modulation, and changes of timbre. His approach is subtler than his own comments would suggest: in several instances, the melodic shadings provide psychological insight into the char-acters. It also creates a very Chaikovskian feeling of fateful predestination. This is most apparent in the handling of the opening and closing melody of the score, associated with the poet Lensky and specifically his recitation of "I have outlasted all desire." Initially cast in G minor, the meander-ing, disconsolate melody lurks behind crucial plot events and represents Lensky's sad destiny. Sung by an offstage chorus of female and male voices in the interlude (the ending of No. 4 in the autograph piano score), it prefaces both Larina's musings with her neighbors about Tatyana's future prospects (" 'What should one do? Tatyana is no infant,' / quoth the old lady with a groan") as well as Tatyana's first appearance.[21] The melody returns over tremolo strings in the passage (No. 32) that precedes Onegin and Lensky's duel.

Prokofiev also represented Lensky's solitude. Solitude is the natural condition of Pushkin's novel in verse, but the narrator fills in the silences, the blank spaces (marked by empty stanzas in the text) between the characters. Prokofiev, in contrast, allows these silences to resonate. Although Lensky is romantically involved with Olga, the composer neither depicts their interactions nor assigns Olga a melody of her own. The broad C-major theme labeled "Lensky thinks about Olga" (No. 3) is static, nondevelopmental, and pastoral, reminiscent in its intervallic contours and transparent scoring of the pristine Ukrainian landscape music in *Semyon Kotko*.

The isolated mysteries of Tatyana's personality are captured in a cluster of interrelated themes. Her first appearance (No. 5) introduces a binary-form melody in B-flat major (the relative major of Lensky's fate music) that stresses the submediant and involves extreme contrasts of register. The first half of the melody belongs to the flute and the second half to muted first violins; the first half is then repeated by the clarinet in the pensive low register. There follow three variations, which increase in length and differ in timbre, adding nuance to Tatyana's emotional and psychological portrayal. The first (No. 8) accompanies Tatyana's initial meeting with Onegin; it comprises a single phrase in A-flat major scored for bassoons, cellos, and basses. The second (also No. 8), scored for English horn and alto saxophone, connotes her thoughts in two phrases that cadence respectively in A-flat and D-flat major. And the third (No. 9) comprises three phrases in the upper and lower strings that modulate from D-flat major to B-flat minor (phrase 1), then to E major (phrase 2), and then to D-flat major (phrase 3). This longest and most involved variation matches her unbridled declaration of love.

Listening to the variations can be likened to watching a painter adding detail to a portrait. Tatyana's music does not describe or narrate events but denotes a subjective interior where recollections and impressions coalesce. In the letter scene, for example (Nos. 10–12), Prokofiev repeats the three versions of Tatyana's melody intact, allowing them to commingle in the mind of the listener. His approach to the scene counters that of Chaikovsky, who represents the writing of the letter word for word. He strings together four Romances that depict both the physical act of putting quill to paper and Tatyana's conflicted emotions—her excitement as well as trepidation about exposing her feelings to her beloved.[22] The Romances impose an unnatural structure on the scene (each stands for a separate portion of the letter), but the boundaries between them are obfuscated, and their melodic and harmonic contents subject to unconventional transformations. The difference between Chaikovsky's and Prokofiev's approaches to the letter scene rests on the distinction between teleological and nonteleological modes of representation. The first composer charts Tatyana's *Bildungsroman* maturation, the second one does not. Prokofiev, like Pushkin, allows Tatyana to remain an enigma.

For the drama's conclusion (No. 44), which portrays Tatyana's triumph over her own helpless need for Onegin, Prokofiev repeats the second variation, initially associated with her psychological state in the wake of her first meeting with Onegin. Thus he poses a riddle: does the repetition reveal that, beneath the glitter and glamour of Tatyana's aristocratic trappings, "the indifferent princess, / the inaccessible goddess" remains the "enamored, poor and simple" maiden that Onegin had once spurned?[23] Does it reveal that Onegin cannot comprehend her transformation, and that his memory of Tatyana is more real to him than her physical presence? Does it confirm that Tatyana has not matured, because maturation is impossible for the honestly divided self? Or is something even more complicated happening: an acknowledgment that, in Olga Peter Hasty's words, Tatyana's "experiences are not stretched out in a line, but form instead an interrelated organic complex"?[24] Prokofiev collapses the past, present, and future of Tatyana's relationship with Onegin, presenting the organically interrelated variations of her melody in and out of order.

Toward the end of his score, moreover, he varies the variations, partitioning Tatyana's music into discrete blocks that can be distributed throughout the drama "at the director's discretion." On page 14 (recto) of the manuscript, Prokofiev helpfully lists the manner in which the blocks can be separated and combined: "1) A, 2) B, 3) C, 4) A+B, 5) A+C, 6) A+B+C, 7) A+B+C+D+E." His approach to *Eugene Onegin*, as it was later to *Boris Godunov*, counters the aesthetics of the *Gesamtkunstwerk* by eschewing through-composition in favor of redeployable and recombinable cells. One senses that he wanted his music to remain elusively distant from its own subject matter. Like Pushkin's Tatyana, a fantasist who does not allow her inner world to be tamed by the outer world, Prokofiev's music is not contingent or dependent on the stage events with which it is aligned.

Especially in light of the controversy surrounding Krzhizhanovsky's adaptation, it requires noting that the published piano and orchestral score of Prokofiev's *Eugene Onegin* misrepresents Prokofiev's intentions. Dattel, the editor of the score and the first person to attempt to document its history, puzzled over the inconsistencies between the novel in verse, its adaptation, and the music for the adaptation.[25] Supporting the 1960s and 1970s consensus that Krzhizhanovsky was a maverick writer who fell into political disfavor by bowdlerizing Pushkin, Dattel proposes that Prokofiev at first "refused to write the music" for his script, "only changing wrath to mercy under pressure and persistent pleading from Tairov who pledged to 'rework' the script jointly with the author."[26] There is absolutely no proof for this claim. And even if it existed the basic fact remains that Prokofiev honorably fulfilled his commission to write music *for* the adaptation. Dattel adheres to the claim, however, to justify editing the music of *Eugene Onegin* in a manner that reconciles it with the novel in verse. She suppressed Krzhizhanovsky from her edition in an effort to make it faithful to Pushkin, the result being a restoration of something that never existed in the first place. Dattel altered the sequence of episodes in the score, changed some of the composer's stage instructions, deleted some of those instructions, moved lines from one character to another, and, most strikingly, restored the role of the narrator. Some examples:

1. The comment that follows the second fermata of No. 1 in the manuscript—"[Lensky] lowered himself to the edge of the grave. He thinks."—is missing from the edition.

2. Prokofiev indicates that the music for No. 2 comes "after the words 'will my end come' [pridyot li moy konets]" are read; in the edition, the music is heard at the same time as these words.

3. The instruction preceding the music of No. 3 ("after the cuckoo sounds the hour") is missing from the edition.

4. Larina's words ("What should one do? Tatyana is no infant"), which Prokofiev intended to be heard against the backdrop of an offstage chorus at the end of No. 4, are missing from the edition.

5. For No. 5, Prokofiev specified that the music "accompanies Tatyana's words (perhaps not completely)"; in the edition, Dattel suppresses these words, which were written by Krzhizhanovsky, in favor of a direct quotation from Pushkin's novel in verse. The narrator, rather than Tatyana, speaks over the music.[27]

The edition implies that Prokofiev conceived his music as an accompaniment to a dramatic reading of Pushkin's verses. Several episodes in his score, however, were conceived as interludes meant to be heard between, rather than beneath, the verses. Thus Prokofiev's music lends form to the text, not the other way around.

Arguably Dattel's most striking violation of the original score affects the dream scene, which occupies book 5, stanzas 11–21, of Pushkin's novel in verse. After mentioning Tatyana's interest in fortune-telling, the narrator describes a nightmare in which Tatyana finds herself menaced by an outsized, appalling bear in a snow-filled valley. The creature helps her to cross a rickety bridge over a turbulent stream, but then chases her deeper into the woods; Tatyana loses her earrings, a shoe, and a handkerchief. Her frenzied, erotically charged flight ends at a festive gathering of mutant fairy-tale creatures. Onegin presides authoritatively over the feast, which is interrupted by the arrival of Olga and Lensky. The two men argue, and Onegin stabs Lensky. This last event would seem to be an obvious portent of the duel in book 6, but Pushkin skews the analogy by rendering the dream version of the event more realistic than the real version. And in accordance with Russian folklore, the bear would seem to be a stand-in for Tatyana's unnamed future husband, except that he has not yet been introduced to the plot. This is a dream that predicts, rather than recollects, events.

When Krzhizhanovsky revamped *Eugene Onegin*, he transplanted the dream scene from before to after Onegin and Lensky have their dispute in the party scene (Tatyana's name day fête). The dream still precedes their actual duel, but the anxieties that it represents are now justified. Art (the dream) no longer creates life (the duel) but reflects it. Or, more accurately, it competes with it—this being a central conceit of Krzhizhanovsky's phantasmagoric fiction. (His short story "Side Branch," for example, centers on the activities of a dream factory whose managers seek to conquer reality.) In his notes to Krzhizhanovsky's script for the dream scene, Prokofiev reveals his intent to infuse "Tatyana's main theme" with "tragic elements."[28] The result, in the piano score, is an A-flat major version of the theme appended to the tremolo-laden variation aligned with Onegin. The last five measures of the passage (No. 27) introduce an A-flat minor chord in the low brasses, a scalar descent in A minor, and then a return to the A-flat minor chord. The core of the dream scene (No. 28), in which Tatyana is chased by the bear, features a semitonal ostinato pattern in the tuba (representing the bear) and a melodic figure that leaps up and down by fourths and fifths in the upper woodwinds (Tatyana's efforts to elude the bear). Both figures are syncopated, and both are interrupted by falling eighth-note figures in the oboes (signaling her stumbling in the deep snow). The power of the music resides in its off-kilter, overlapping repetitions, which suggest an endless chase, an infinite pattern of kinetic impulses. It is the least sectionalized number in a score that relies on sectionalizing, that consists of isolated musical snapshots denoting thoughts and emotions.

Krzhizhanovsky's contentious decision to relocate the dream scene sets Tatyana's party at the center of the drama. The party scene opens with the strains of a "tryam-blam" polka emanating from a distant hall. Aberrant dance music represents aberrant events: much like Onegin himself, the dance music offends sensibility. It sounds wrong; it is a breach. Prokofiev scores the dance (No. 20) for two provincial, out-of-tune harpsichords, the invisible performers carelessly barreling through the five-measure phrases at an insane tempo—a comical comment on the hullabaloo that greets the arrival at the party of a pompous regimental commander. There ensues an enigmatic waltz (No. 21), which Prokofiev scores first for string quintet and then, in a jarring contrast, for the two harpsichords. Onegin enters the room and encounters Tatyana for the first time since responding to her letter. They exchange words; he gazes at her attentively, briefly warming her heart. In the waltz's opening section, the music is seductively languorous, the first violin sliding down a chromatic scale over a G minor accompaniment. But in the middle section, the sound turns brittle, with the harpsichords introducing a jagged second theme in C minor, the emphasis placed on intervals of the fifth and octave. The concluding section is interrupted by a recurrence of the polka (No. 22), this time scored for wind band. In the ensuing minuet (No. 23), Onegin engages in a repartee with the landowner Zaretsky, who will serve as Lensky's second in the duel. There follows a lyrical mazurka (No. 24), during which Onegin catches Olga's eye and begins to flirt with her. The scene concludes with a repetition of the enigmatic waltz, this time with the harpsichords preceding rather than following the string quintet. Onegin dances with Olga and, to Lensky's dismay, gains her favor.

The waltz is not, of course, realistic music; the clash, or duel, between the string quintet and the harpsichords suggests the breakdown of decorum that underpins the entire scene. In the party scene, more than in any other, the distinctions between the competing binaries in the tale—desire and decorum, art and life, the aesthetic and the social—dissolve. The first incarnation of the waltz in the sultry strings might be interpreted as representing Tatyana's encounter with Onegin, and then, in the brittle harpsichords, the false hopes this encounter engenders. As Onegin dismisses Tatyana in favor of

Olga, Prokofiev dehumidifies the languorous air. When, at the other end of the scene, the waltz recurs with the instrumentation reversed, Lensky realizes that his friend Onegin has betrayed him. The monotonous plinking of the keyboards cedes to the evocative strains of the violins: Olga is seduced.

But the waltz permits another, less literal reading. By conflating the two groups of instruments, Prokofiev signals that they might in fact stand for the same thing: the emptiness of Onegin's persona. The waltz blends a hackneyed Romantic sound with a hackneyed Baroque sound, and thus captures a central theme in Pushkin's novel in verse: namely, that Onegin has no actual identity, existing merely as a projection of Tatyana's overcrowded literary imagination. In the middle of book 7, which describes her visit to Onegin's gloomy aban-doned estate, she peruses his two or three favorite novels, wondering

> Who's he then? Can it be—an imitation,
> An insignificant phantasm, or else
> A Muscovite in Harold's mantle,
> A glossary of other people's megrims,
> A complete lexicon of words in vogue?...
> Might he not be, in fact, a parody?[29]

Prokofiev answers the question in the affirmative, twice representing Onegin in the score with a mock French song to words by Jacques Malfilâtre—"Elle était fille, / Elle était amoureuse"—and then, in the party scene, representing him with mock waltz strains.[30]

Ultimately, the waltz could be interpreted on a meta-narrative level as conflating the original eighteenth-century conception of Onegin with the subsequent nineteenth-century reconception. Prokofiev juxtaposes, in short, the passionate stylizations of Chaikovsky's operatic version of the tale with the dispassionate stylizations of Pushkin's source text. In the party scene, the historical reception of *Eugene Onegin* is mapped onto *Eugene Onegin* itself. Reading Krzhizhanovsky's remarkable adaptation, one can only wonder if this was part of his, and Tairov's, plan for the staging.

◆

Work on the staging ended abruptly. On December 3, 1936, Prokofiev received a note from the deputy director (surname Isoldov) of the Chamber Theater, who reported that "the All-Union Committee on Arts Affairs has categorically decreed that the spectacle *Eugene Onegin* cannot be staged by the State Moscow Chamber Theater. In view of this, the theater asks you not to carry out any further work on the orchestration of the music (of the score) for this spectacle; the contract of May 25 of this year, which required the score to be delivered to the theater and consultation work to be carried out during the rehearsal period, is hereby annulled."[31] The letter arrived when Prokofiev was in Brussels; news of the cancellation of the production, and that Tairov had taken ill as a consequence, came to him late.

The cancellation stemmed from the fallout over Tairov's previous project: a staging, in the form of a play with incidental music, of Aleksandr Borodin's 1867 comic opera *The Heroic Warriors*. The staging relied on a script written by the poet Demyan Bednïy (Pridvorov), who earned esteem in the immediate post-revolutionary period but faced a crisis in 1930 when Stalin questioned the ideological orientation of his poems.[32] Although confused as to the precise nature of his errors, Bednïy apologized and managed to restore, even improve, his previous standing. *Pravda* lauded his two decades of patriotic service to Bolshevism in a May 20, 1931, article, and he received a coveted Order of Lenin on the occasion of his fiftieth birthday in 1933—a first for a poet.[33] In 1934, however, Bednïy inadvertently erred again by accepting Tairov's invitation to collaborate on *The Heroic Warriors*. The original Borodin opera, which survived just one performance, relies on a pastiche of quotations and stylistic allusions to lampoon Russian operatic realism, French operetta, and grand opera. The plot takes on the clichés of heroic ballads, often to hilarious effect. In his revision, Bednïy sought to enhance the farce while also paying homage to the national traditions from which the farce sprang—a difficult feat that met with extreme hostility. No sooner had the play opened than it was closed by decree. On November 14, 1936, the Committee on Arts Affairs, echoing a Politburo decision, announced that Bednïy and Tairov had subverted history by depicting the "brigands" of Kievan Rus as "positive revolutionary elements" and slandering the epic characters who epitomize "the Russian people's heroic qualities."[34] On November 15, an article by Kerzhentsev on the topic appeared in *Pravda*.

Bednïy's and Tairov's colleagues were solicited by NKVD agents for their thoughts on the decision to prohibit *The Heroic Warriors*. Once the "Secret Political Department" of the NKVD had gathered the data, a report was generated. It opens with Tairov's admission that he committed a colossal blunder with *The Heroic Warriors*, though he qualifies that the Committee on Arts Affairs had itself at one time backed the staging. His actress wife, Alisa Koonen, remarks that the scandal had caused Tairov heart troubles, but adds, in a bow to official pressure, that it was a useful lesson for him about depending too much on his own artistic instincts. A director at the theater (Meyer Gersht) summarized the prevailing mood with the comment, transcribed by the NKVD, that "the Resolution is at root correct. We are obliged to stage *Eugene Onegin*. I expect that the history of this spectacle will be identical to that of *The Heroic Warriors*."[35]

The history was not quite identical. The Committee on Arts Affairs, guardian of the official Pushkin legacy, relieved Tairov and his employees of the obligation to stage *Eugene Onegin*. The disappointment manifested itself in different ways: Tairov avoided all mention of the project in his future writings; Krzhizhanovsky continued his principled journey into obscurity, piecing together an existence by writing encyclopedia articles, consulting on screenplays, and delivering lectures. In 1939, he belatedly became a member of the Union of Soviet Writers. In honor of his fiftieth birthday, a collection of his short stories went to press, but wartime deprivations prevented its publication. Prokofiev reused much of the music of *Eugene Onegin* in the opera *The Duenna*, the second movement of the Eighth Piano Sonata, the ballet *Cinderella*, the Seventh Symphony, and the opera *War and Peace*. (For example, the waltz that accompanies Onegin's encounter with Tatyana in the dream scene recurs in scene 2 of the opera, where it once again denotes transient passions.)[36] Transcending setbacks, Prokofiev would likewise recycle some of the music from the ill-fated *Queen of Spades* and *Boris Godunov* projects. These scores express the same reverence for—and resistance to—a nineteenth-century operatic model.

The Queen of Spades

Pushkin's thirty-three-page short story *The Queen of Spades* has been the subject of numerous transpositions, the best known being Chaikovsky's proto-Symbolist opera of 1890. There exist two completed silent film versions, dating from 1910 and 1916, and seven completed sound film versions (five Soviet, one German, and one French), whose relationship to the opera ranges from independent to dependent.[37] Director Mikhaíl Romm's film, one of a handful of unrealized adaptations, sought to distance itself from the opera. The extant records indicate that the director intended to highlight those stylistic features of Pushkin's story that Chaikovsky's opera had ignored: its tense, rapid pacing, caustic insights, and detached, analytic mode of narration.

Romm was not alone in the effort (in 1935, for example, Meyerhold staged a re-Pushkinized version of Chaikovsky's opera at Malegot, the Leningrad Malïy Opera Theater), but he was unique in seeking to untangle the relationship between Pushkin and Chaikovsky. Anatoly Vishevsky notes in this regard that "the line" between the story and the opera "blurred" in the twentieth century "and at times has disappeared completely." Vishevsky adds that "a number of educated Russians would be surprised to learn that the Winter Canal...does not appear in Pushkin's story, [and] that the words 'three cards, three cards'...are also not to be found there."[38] In his film version of *The Queen of Spades*, Romm endeavored to sever the story from its operatic adaptations by enlisting Prokofiev to write largely unsentimental music for it.

It is no small irony that, in an effort to make his film version of *The Queen of Spades* faithful to Pushkin, Romm enlisted a composer who would make it faithful to Dostoevsky. Prokofiev had earlier based an opera on Dostoevsky's quasi-autobiographical casino drama *The Gambler*. The style of Dostoevsky's prose differs wholesale from Pushkin's, as does the style of Prokofiev's music from Chaikovsky's. Both the libretto and the music of *The Gambler* represent the casino as a prison whose inhabitants less sing than speak—habitually a sign, in the world of opera, of deformation. Continuous arioso lends unstoppable momentum to the drama. And unlike Chaikovsky's *The Queen of Spades*, which terminates with a decisive invocation of malevolent, apocalyptic fate, Prokofiev's *The Gambler* does not appear to end at all. The winner at the casino (Aleksey) emerges as the loser, consigned to eternity at the roulette wheel. Prokofiev does not quote from *The Gambler* in his score for *The Queen of Spades*, but in addition to the general topic of gaming, the two works share, in their rhythmic language, an obsession with obsessive behavior.

In his memoirs, which date from 1948–51 and 1968–69, Romm recalled that he intended his film to be "maximally realistic" and "psychologically justified," an approach that justified his own departures from the source text.[39] In Pushkin's story, the protagonist Hermann is rationally opposed to gambling: he wants perfect odds, a guarantee that he will win. In the film, however, he suffers bouts of irrationality. The gravity of his condition becomes clear halfway through the film, when what he thinks is a ghost appears in his quarters to provide a magical three-card formula for reaping unprecedented profits at the casino. Pushkin leaves it perfectly unclear as to whether or not the ghost is an external apparition. But Romm sought to ascribe the specter to the internal night terrors of a "schizophrenic."[40] The three-card formula (3, 7, ace) remains a crucial feature of the plot. Hermann wins at the casino with the first and second of these cards, but loses when the final card he bids, an ace—which he has seen and chosen consciously—turns into the queen of spades. The shock from this event hastens his descent into madness. The harbinger in the film for the tragedy is not the middle ghost scene but the early barracks scene, which shows Hermann passing time alone playing faro. He deals right and left and by chance lays out the 3, 7, and ace cards. Later, one of his companions, Count Tomsky, regales him with a fable about an octogenarian Countess who gambled herself into near-ruin during her wild Parisian youth. As he tells the tale, Tomsky pantomimes the action at a casino, placing, again by chance, the 3, 7, and ace cards face up on the table (the other cards remain face down). Recognizing the combination, Hermann becomes fixated on it. He tells himself that he will be able to "treble" and "septuple" (rather than "double" and "quadruple") his savings by betting 37,000 rubles on the cards. Romm points out that, in Chaikovsky's opera, Hermann bets the nonsymbolic amount of 40,000 rubles.[41]

Beyond mental illness, the film, had it been completed, would have explored the disparities in Russian aristocratic society. In the original, Hermann woos the ward of the Countess in hopes of learning the three-card formula. The ward, Liza, falls in love with him and grants him access to her room, which also allows him access to the Countess's bedchamber, where he lies in wait for the old woman's return from a ball. Upon her arrival, Hermann beseeches her for the formula, threatening her with an unloaded gun when she refuses to provide it. The Countess suffers a fatal heart attack. Merely a semblance of these events occurs in Romm's film, and they are filtered through what he called "social analysis."[42] Romm expressed fascination with the final lines of Pushkin's text, which recount that Liza survived her experience with Hermann—she did not commit suicide in sentimentalist, Karamzinian fashion, as Chaikovsky has her do—to wed the son of the Countess's steward. Pushkin refers to these figures in passing to round off his story; Romm created actual parts for them in the film. In contrast to the Countess, who stands for the "growing impoverishment" of the "patrimonial aristocracy," the steward and his son stand for the "rising and expanding petit bourgeois class."[43] Romm justifies his approach by misleadingly claiming that Pushkin, despite being of noble lineage, considered himself to be petit bourgeois.[44] The director represents Hermann as a socially marginalized figure and condemns him for indulging his obsession, for trusting in chance. Pushkin does just the opposite, reproving Hermann for seeking to fix the rules of the game.

Although Romm's approach to Pushkin's story might have a political subtext, it also attests to his abiding interest in the plight of the outcast. His films teem with hardened antiheros. His first film, *Dumpling* (*Pïshka*, 1934), a silent version of Guy de Maupassant's 1880 story "Boule de Suif," addresses the treatment of the downtrodden by supposed people of honor. It takes place during the Franco-Prussian War. The downtrodden figure in this instance is an overweight prostitute who, despite being shunned by the passengers sharing a stagecoach with her, twice protects them, first by providing them with food, then by performing the repulsive deed with a Prussian officer who allows the stagecoach to cross Prussian lines. A later film, *The Dream* (*Mechta*, 1941), depicts the insect-like existence of the residents and employees of an oppressive boarding house. The ideological dimension of this film emerges at the end, when the Polish town where events unfold is liberated by the Soviets. Both films, considered cinematic masterworks, share with the unrealized *The Queen of Spades* a focus on human psychology and destiny, explored within claustrophobic spaces.

The Queen of Spades was to have distinguished itself stylistically through an emphasis on pantomime. To preserve the precision and terseness of Pushkin's story while also enhancing its psychological dimension, Romm sought to exploit mutable light and shadow effects; he also planned to make the film, in whole or in part, in color. The details come from a February 11, 1937, interview between Romm and the editors of the newspaper *Kino*. "*The Queen of Spades*," the director declared, "will be shot using the tricolor method. This poses an even more serious challenge than usual—ensuring an authentic, realistic style for the sets and costumes." To avoid turning the film into the kind of "cheap print" produced by Western filmmakers (here Romm may be referring to the 1935 tricolor film *Becky Sharp*), "the entire figurative, visual component of [*The Queen of Spades*] needs to be made at the highest artistic level."[45] To reach this level, Romm scripted entire scenes in wordless pantomime—a favorite device.[46]

Romm enlisted Eduard Pentslin to co-write the scenario of *The Queen of Spades* in the fall of 1934 and Prokofiev to compose the music in the spring of 1936. The circumstances behind the commission are unclear. The composer mentions it in a March 7, 1936, article in *Gazeta Polska*;[47] the actual contract, however, dates from May 29.[48] Romm began work on *The Queen of Spades* simultaneously with *Anka*, another uncompleted film, but a creative dispute with the scenarist of the latter placed his position at Mosfilm in jeopardy. Boris Shumyatsky, the head of the State Cinema Directorate (Gosudarstvennoye upravleniye kinomatografii) recommended his reassignment from Moscow to the Tajikistan city of Stalinabad (now Dushanbe). Romm successfully petitioned the Central Committee to be allowed to remain in Moscow, after which he agreed to co-write the scenario for *The Commander (Komandir)*. Romm took pride in this project, which boasted "psychological" as well as "lyric-dramatic and even epic elements," but to his frustration, the deputy director (soon to be acting director) of Mosfilm, Yelena Sokolovskaya, rejected it.[49] The decision precipitated a disastrous falling out between the two. Romm thereafter accepted the commission to realize a Soviet version of the American film *The Lost Patrol*, a 1934 John Ford adventure about a British cavalry regiment stranded and surrounded by unseen enemies in the Mesopotamian desert. The scenario for the film, *The Thirteen (Trinadtsat')*, was approved in the spring of 1936, after which Romm traveled with crew and cast to the scorching sands of Turkmenistan to shoot it.

Following the release of the epic on May 8, 1937, Romm returned to the camera obscura world of *The Queen of Spades*. He chose Boris Poslavsky for the role of Hermann and his own wife and lead actress Yelena Kuzmina for the role of Liza. A June 4, 1937, notice in *Kino* states that the casting and sketches for the sets and costumes were scheduled for completion on September 1, 1937.[50] A June 28 follow-up notice carped that most of the films for the Pushkin centennial had been "made in haste, which excludes the possibility of serious work. *The Queen of Spades*, to the contrary, has been 'heading into production' at Mosfilm studios for three years now, without a single frame being shot."[51]

No sooner had work on the film finally resumed than Romm's dispute with Sokolovskaya flared anew, the result being his forced transfer from Moscow to Kiev. And no sooner had he relocated to Kiev than Shumyatsky summoned him back to Moscow to work on a project that none of the other directors in his employ wanted to take on: the first biographical film about Lenin. The deadline was firm and the pressure enormous: Romm was told that he needed to complete the film, titled *Lenin in October (Lenin v Oktyabre)*, in four months.[52] (Bureaucratic trepidation would reduce the shooting schedule to a frantic two months and twenty days.) According to his memoirs, Romm accepted the challenge with Herculean gusto and received the coveted Order of Lenin for completing it to the satisfaction of Stalin and his aides, who viewed it on November 6, a day before its official opening at a Bolshoy Theater gala.[53] Romm relished his triumph over Sokolovskaya, who was arrested in 1937 as part of a purge of the film industry. Shumyatsky disappeared a year later.

These events took place a year after Prokofiev had peacefully completed the music for *The Queen of Spades* in Polenovo. He finished the piano score on July 12, 1936, and then dispatched it to Lamm for copying and, because he was traveling, safekeeping. Lamm completed the copy (designated a *klavierusluga*, a "service piano score") sometime between July 16 and 26, 1936, and forwarded it, through Myaskovsky, to Mosfilm. The piano score contains twenty-four concise numbers, with Prokofiev indicating the shot sequences to which each pertains.[54] Here and there in the manuscript, he offers Romm advice about coordinating the music with the visuals in the film. In the margin above No. 18 in the score ("Hermann makes a note, conceals it, and comes to the casino"), which pertains to shot sequence 568–90, Prokofiev comments: "If the excerpt is too long, a cut can be made in the middle, at measures 17–24, for example." In the margin beside No. 20 in the score ("Hermann goes to the casino a second time"), which pertains to shot sequence 624–29, Prokofiev adds: "I think the music should end when Hermann takes the glass of lemonade [stakan limonada]—or earlier—so that there will be a sufficient break before his next appearance." (As in the source text, Hermann is a teetotaler.)

Prokofiev played through the score for Romm shortly after it was drafted. The director found the music neither "dramatic" nor "lyrical" but as obsessive as piano studies: "three and then seven pitches repeat endlessly," which gave the film the barrenness, the "aridity" it needed.[55] Prokofiev, who told Romm that he considered Chaikovsky's *The Queen of Spades* to be "in very bad taste," depicted Hermann's torments with music that neither recalls nor reflects on events, but simply pushes them forward.[56] Rather than working with the number format, Prokofiev worked with numbers. Myaskovsky played through the score himself before leaving it with the studio and, like the director, considered it "successful." But he wondered why "the opening chords of the overture" did not recur in the score. "Why the wasteful extravagance?" he ribbed Prokofiev.[57] There is, in fact, no such extravagance. Although the opening chords do not recur in their original guise, they serve as the basis of the agitated ostinato patterns that begin in the eighth measure of the overture and do not relent, with modest exception, until the penultimate scene, in which Hermann, glowing from his winnings on the first and second card, loses everything on the third.

The opening comprises seven chords organized in two groups of three; the seventh, which concludes the phrase, establishes the key of B-flat minor (associated with Hermann) and is held under a fermata. The first three chords are triads as are the fifth and final ones. The others are minor-seventh chords, with the first built on the dominant of B-flat minor, and the second built on the mediant. Following the fermata, the first in a series of ostinato patterns is unleashed. It begins in quarter notes and then moves into sixteenths, with the three constituent pitches repeated seven times each. In subsequent passages, Prokofiev generates ostinato patterns out of three- and seven-pitch groups that highlight the interval of the major and minor third. His relentless emphasis on harmonic, intervallic, and rhythmic patterns of three and seven indicates—in calculated, empirical form—the anxious thoughts and repetitive behaviors of what would now be called obsessive compulsive disorder. The ostinato also signals that the Countess's ghost is neither a supernatural apparition nor an intoxicated hallucination but something psychological. The music he creates for her "visit" (No. 17) builds upon a preexisting ostinato pattern that defines the interval of the minor tenth on its initial ascents and the interval of the minor third on its subsequent descents. The pattern grows in strength over the course of the episode to become a musical simulacrum of palpitations. The melody around which the accompaniment wraps outlines the interval of the seventh three times, first falling from D sharp to E, then from C to D flat, and then rising by minor and major third from G to F.

Liza's melody, first introduced in No. 4 ("Liza"), is noteworthy for its absence of rhythmic regularity and its reliance on the tritone as well as the characteristic Russian Romance (or salon song) interval of the sixth. Although cast in C major, the melody features destabilizing, disquieting F sharps. No. 7 ("Hermann sees Liza") includes a variation of the melody in the key of E major—this being a tritone removed from Hermann's B-flat minor. Another variation occurs in the music for the third and final casino scene. Prokofiev transforms the melody into a cadential gesture that falls in half and quarter notes from the dominant to the leading tone of C major. The cadence is thwarted by march-like iterations of a D-flat-major chord in the inner lines of the accompaniment: the outer pitches of the chord resolve downward by a half step, but the middle pitch, F, does not. The cadential gesture sounds a second and then a third time, but the feeling of grinding non-resolution persists, forming an ironic correlate to Pushkin's devastating words "the game took its course" (igra poshla svoim cheredom).[58] Hermann's collapse at the gaming table is marked not by the appearance of the mocking specter of the Countess, as in Chaikovsky's opera, but by a recollection of squandered love. It is not the three-card formula but Liza who obsesses him at the end.

Perhaps because Lamm was unavailable, Prokofiev enlisted Derzhanovsky to orchestrate the score. Derzhanovsky completed twenty of the twenty-four numbers. The handwriting on the undated, fifty-six-page manuscript is slip-shod, seemingly a product of haste.[59] It wittingly or unwittingly bears the traces of the abrupt manner in which work on the film was resumed, cur-tailed, resumed again, and then curtailed again between 1936 and 1938. In December 1937, having survived the upheavals at Mosfilm, Romm relocated to Leningrad to begin shooting *The Queen of Spades*. The part of Hermann was reassigned from Poslavsky to a local stage actor. The outdoor scenes were shot in January and February, leaving the spring (March through June) to shoot the indoor scenes. Sometime after March 23, 1938—the precise date is unknown—the chairman of the newly formed Committee on Cinema Affairs (Komitet po delam kinomatografii), Semyon Dukelsky, called Romm to his office to break the news that work on the film would be terminated: the Committee had opted to cancel films based on classical subjects in favor of more topical fare. According to a March 14 memorandum submitted by Dukelsky to Molotov at Sovnarkom, the films then in production failed to fulfill the "thematic plan" that the State Cinema Directorate had devised in advance for them. Historical, anti-fascistic, and children's films were being made at the expense of those concerning, among other things, the life of the peoples of the Union, the Red Army, and the struggle against religion.[60] Romm protested the cancellation to Dukelsky, but the chairman held firm: "I don't understand you!" he bellowed at the persistent director. "Why are you always grieving *The Queen of Spades*—and thinking about three cards, three cards, three cards! If I were in your shoes I'd be happy. What don't you have? Money? You have it! Fame? You have it! Your films are even shown abroad. You have an apartment! What else do you need?"[61]

Thus ended Romm's third try—his third bid—to realize *The Queen of Spades*. In despair, he destroyed the scenario, most of the historical materi-als that had been gathered for him by an assistant, the costume sketches, and the photographs. The fate of the unedited footage is unclear, though it is presumed lost. Romm lamented not only the forfeiture of his own labor, but also that of his actors. The Committee on Cinema Affairs, meanwhile, was left to account for the squandering of more than 750,000 rubles on an unmade film. No record of Prokofiev's response to the cancellation of

The Queen of Spades has emerged to date. He acknowledged reusing material from the Liza-related passages in the first movement of his Eighth Piano Sonata, but he also did so in the third movement of his Fifth Symphony.[62] As always, he transferred melodic and harmonic ideas from one score to another without lamenting their decontextualization. Their essence remained intact, he believed, withstanding the manipulation that produced only a derivation of the inviolate musical idea, considered to be constant, eternal. Even within the score of *The Queen of Spades* itself, melodic and harmonic ideas assume different guises. They are no less mutable than the three-card formula.

Boris Godunov

Of the aborted Pushkin projects, the most conceptually complicated was Meyerhold's staging of *Boris Godunov*. Set between 1598 and 1605, the drama concerns the crisis-ridden reign of a tsar who came to be considered illegitimate and the challenge mounted against him by a pretender to the throne. Meyerhold intended to premiere *Boris Godunov* at the very start of the Pushkin centennial celebration of 1937, but political problems both inside and outside his theater forced him to delay and eventually to cancel the staging.[63] His contribution to the centennial consisted instead of a concert performance, in February 1937, of the realist composer Dargomïzhsky's 1869 setting of Pushkin's *The Stone Guest* (1830).[64] Meyerhold returned to *Boris Godunov* in March and April but, after a few rehearsals, abandoned it for good. His provocative plans for the drama, which he had developed in consultation with Prokofiev, were consigned to oblivion.

Given the level of apprehension and claustrophobia in the Russian capital, staging a drama about a Russian leader haunted by questions of legitimacy and plagued by real-or-imagined threats was ill advised, to say the least. In April 1937, the drama was removed from the repertoire of the Moscow Arts Theater on Molotov's order.[65] This was the same month that Meyerhold abandoned work on it. Eight months later, he came under direct political attack in the pages of *Pravda*.[66] Kerzhentsev thereafter signed a decree ordering the closure of his theater.[67] As discussed in chapter 2, the director both anticipated this event and prepared himself psychologically for the worst. Perversely, Kerzhentsev's downfall did nothing to prevent his own.

Meyerhold's adopted daughter Tatyana Esenina argues that Meyerhold began work on *Boris Godunov* long before he knew he was in trouble. She also argues that his staging was intended as a critique of the Stalinist regime.

The director sought with the drama to defend his modernist directorial technique—which ran counter to official artistic doctrine—and to protest, through none-too-subtle allegory, the advent of malevolent totalitarian rule. To support her assertion, Esenina refers to the scene 9 monologue in *Boris Godunov* weighing the uses and abuses of absolute power. Pushkin assigned the monologue to his quasi-fictionalized distant relative Afanasiy Pushkin, a foe of Godunov and incidental character in the drama, but one to whom Meyerhold devoted extensive attention in the rehearsals.[68] Esenina recalls that the actors involved did not understand why the director considered this monologue so important. In later years, she set out to find the answer:

> What needs explaining here? It was 1936, the time of the infamous open trials. I was abroad; I knew what was being written over there. Even we were whispering. The means of fighting for power were monstrous, though Stalin himself did not slink out of his office and stoke the pyres with his poker. Afanasiy Pushkin's monologue hit the bull's-eye. Spoken from the stage, it would have been like Hamlet's "Mousetrap." Years later I read the brilliant pages written by [Meyerhold's colleague Aleksandr] Gladkov about the rehearsals of the scene [10] at Shuysky's house. This was when Meyerhold, demonstrating how Pushkin's monologue should be read, leapt onto a table, flying into a rage that became a total frenzy. When he finished the monologue, he did not stop; over one hundred and twenty more lines poured out from him. These were improvised.[69]

This statement is complicated, to be sure, with Esenina equating Pushkin-the-author with Shakespeare and Pushkin-the-character with Hamlet, moving on to discuss a tempestuous rehearsal. To shore up her point about the ominous political subtext of *Boris Godunov*, moreover, Esenina quotes from Pushkin's text. The phrase "Stalin himself did not slink out of his office and stoke the pyres with his poker" derives from the opening section of the scene 9 monologue:

> Such uproar, that Tsar Boris will hardly
> Retain the crown on his clever head.
> And it serves him right! He rules us

Like Tsar Ivan (may his name not be invoked at night).
What does it matter that public executions have ceased,
That we do not sing the canons to Jesus
On bloodstained stakes, for all to see,
That they do not burn us in the squares, and that the Tsar
himself
Does not *stoke the pyres with his poker?*[70]

According to Esenina, Meyerhold wanted to represent Boris—and by extension Stalin—as behind-the-scenes instigators of historical processes that spiral out of their control. Despite her close relationship to Meyerhold, however, her interpretation contradicts the information found in the rehearsal transcripts. From these and other documents, it emerges that the staging had much broader artistic, political, and psychological concerns than Esenina indicates. Rather than conflating the evils of the early seventeenth century with those of the mid-twentieth century, the available evidence suggests that Meyerhold and Prokofiev intended to depict Russian rulers as impotent and, more generally, human striving as purposeless. Theirs was to have been a drama of primal forces and melancholy wanderers, a rumination transcending time and place. The rehearsal transcripts reveal that the Russian people, rather than their overseers, were to have occupied the secret space behind the scenes.

Meyerhold became obsessed with *Boris Godunov* long before he met Prokofiev, and this obsession was both a source of pleasure and torment for him. Although he regarded Pushkin's account of the rise, suffering, and fall of the infamous tsar as an ideal vehicle for testing new directorial methods, his efforts to stage the drama essentially came to naught. Indeed, the story of Meyerhold's involvement with *Boris Godunov* is one of almost constant disappointment. Productions were rehearsed and then abandoned because of practical problems, Meyerhold's uncertainties as to interpretation, and creative disputes with members of his troupes.

Even his lone success with the drama was partial. In 1911, Meyerhold had participated in a production of Musorgsky's *Boris Godunov* opera at the Mariinsky Theater in St. Petersburg. The libretto brought together both Pushkin's interpretation of the run-up to the Time of Troubles and that of the late eighteenth- and early nineteenth-century historian Karamzin. However legendary the staging of this opera, it did not allow Meyerhold to bring his modernist technique directly to bear on Pushkin. In 1918, as St. Petersburg endured the Revolution, Meyerhold published a directorial plan for an experimental production of *Boris Godunov* that he had developed in collaboration with a group of his own theater students. During the civil war (when Meyerhold was briefly imprisoned by the Whites), he turned to the drama anew, developing an independent directorial plan that reconciled Pushkin's stylistic dialogue with his Western theatrical models. This plan guided the rehearsals that he started in 1924 for a staging of *Boris Godunov* at the Vakhtangov Studio Theater in Moscow. Casting difficulties forced the director to shelve the project, but in 1934, Meyerhold came back to it one last time. He was by now desperate to perform it and vowed to do so—with his own troupe and in his own theater—in the spring of 1937.[71] This never came to pass.

It is unclear how the drama would have looked on stage, unfortunately, and how Meyerhold would have used physical gesture to represent the historical highlights of Pushkin's drama: the ascent of Boris Godunov to the throne, the social crises that accompanied his reign, the persistent rumors that he had murdered the Ryurikovich heir (Ivan the Terrible's son, the Tsarevich Dmitriy), and the appearance of the alleged pretender to the throne (an obscure figure, Grigoriy Otrepiyev, masquerading as the reincarnation of the Tsarevich Dmitriy). The rehearsal transcripts reveal, however, that Meyerhold wanted the acting to be energetic, even muscular, with certain scenes overlapping and the décor in constant motion. The barriers between auditorium and stage were to be eliminated, making the audience feel a part of the action; the actors would move between platforms via ramps, faces would appear in holes punched out in the walls, and indecipherable chatter would be heard from the wings. The acting, like the music, was to possess an element of lightness—but of a dispiriting, disturbing sort. Meyerhold told his cast: "With *Boris* it is very easy to fall into iconicity and sweetness, but this drains the blood from the images and text. Lightness does not mean bloodlessness."[72]

The initial meetings with the actors centered on improving their knowledge of poetic meter. The poet Vladimir Pyast, an expert on declamation, prepared a rhythmic and stylistic analysis of Pushkin's lines that specified "pauses, caesuras, accents" and "rises and falls" in vocal intonation.[73] In November 1935, Pyast provided Meyerhold with an analysis of a scene that Pushkin had in fact excised from his published version, titled "At the Monastery Wall (The Evil Monk)." It provides an explanation for Grigoriy's decision to masquerade as the incarnation of the murdered tsarevich.

Far from deciding his destiny on his own, the restless, adventure-seeking Grigoriy heeds external advice. Apparently deciding that this episode was thematically out of sync with the rest of the drama, Pushkin excluded it from the 1831 edition.[74] Pyast, however, was smitten with it and urged Meyerhold to insert it into his performance. The unholy monk, Pyast proposed, could visit Grigoriy as he slept, haunt his dreams, and, through the power of suggestion, lead him down the path of temptation. To this description of events, Pyast added the following thoughts:

> I even propose staging the "excluded" scene with the "Evil Monk" either as the last or, at the very least, the penultimate one. Not in the form of a whole scene, but if it is the last one, as an epilogue on the proscenium and, if it is the penultimate one, then as an intermezzo. Not with full décor, and if possible in the form of voices that "accumulate" from somewhere behind the scenes, voices saturated with oppressively rhythmical music. In the form of the tortuous dream of [the False] Dmitriy, who lies somewhere on the proscenium—his nightmare when he was about to become, or had already become, the tsar, his nightmare about the evil monk, who perhaps never existed.[75]

Persuaded by Pyast's argument, Meyerhold decided, in accordance with the original 1825 version of Pushkin's drama, to stage the exchange between Grigoriy and the monk after the nighttime episode involving Grigoriy and the hermit Pimen (scene 5 in the 1831 version) and before the daytime episode in the Patriarch's quarters (scene 6). Pyast reasoned that staging the appearance of the "Evil Monk" as a dream would solve a technical problem: the scene has a different verse structure (trochaic octometer) than the rest of the drama (iambic pentameter).[76]

Upon rearranging the text, Meyerhold enlisted Prokofiev to write incidental music, stressing (perhaps with Prokofiev's demon-filled opera *The Fiery Angel* in mind) that the score should involve a generous dose of acoustic *diablerie*.[77] In November 1936, Prokofiev completed a score for the drama that contained a half-Eastern, half-Western military tattoo, drunken singing, ballroom dancing, a reverie, and an amoroso characteristic of Hollywood melodrama. He framed these passages with their emotional inversions: a widow's lament, a sing-along for blind beggars, three behind-the-scenes choruses, and four songs of loneliness. As in Musorgsky's *Boris Godunov*, Prokofiev's score includes a poignant song for a bedraggled Holy Fool, who in a state of near-narcosis sings of the moonlight and a kitten's cry. Prokofiev suspended work on the score after completing twenty-four numbers; it is clear from his correspondence with Meyerhold, however, that he had planned on penning two more items, one for the Pretender's restless dreams, and another for the fortune-tellers who encircle and besiege Boris in his quarters. (The second item could have been improvised, since it involved onstage noisemakers: drums, sticks, bongos, and rattles. Prokofiev did not actually believe that the scene in question needed music, but Meyerhold wanted it to exude what he called the "jazz" of the sixteenth century.)[78]

Much of the score attests to Meyerhold's interest in expressing the profound isolation of the political elite of Russian history, the disregard of the masses for their striving, and the indifference of the cosmos to their sorrows. In accord with a central conceit of Pushkin's text, solitude became the structural dominant of the rehearsals. As Caryl Emerson explains, Pushkin "advocated neither Individuals nor the People as 'subjects of history' or 'heroes of drama'; they were the subjects and heroes only of their own personal fates."[79] This sense of self-willed entrapment, of being boxed up in the dramatic equivalent of a peep show, became a point of focus in Meyerhold and Prokofiev's collaboration.

On November 16, 1936, Prokofiev played through the piano score of his incidental music for *Boris Godunov* before a gathering of the actors involved in the staging. By all accounts, his score was rapturously received, with Meyerhold hailing the terse directness of Prokofiev's music. In his opinion, it accorded with the sentiments of Pushkin's text and filtered out its Musorgskian associations. Together, the director and composer sought to "return Pushkin to Pushkin," restoring the "sense of immediacy, intimacy, and risk that had been lost through the poet's canonization and the monumentalization of Musorgsky's opera."[80] The anxiety of Musorgskian influence lies not in the content of the incidental music to the drama but in what the incidental music leaves out. There are no discordant chimes, prolonged arioso death scenes, or text-based choruses in Prokofiev's score.

The director and the composer also endeavored to exaggerate the fragmentariness of *Boris Godunov*. Pushkin's characters are out of sync with one another: they speak in different rhythms and occupy different points on the time and space continua. This is clearest—and most comic—in the battle scene (scene 17), which Meyerhold strenuously praised. The battle is a polyglot jamboree in which the Tsar's "Asiatic" troops (represented by an octatonic pitch array), Grigoriy's "Western" troops, and some German mercenaries who side with the Tsar are in combat. Hilariously cast by Pushkin in French, German, and Russian, the three ensembles clash rhythmically and syntactically. Meyerhold noted that, in Prokofiev's conception, the identities of the Russian and non-Russian forces become pointedly confused. Boris's identity crises—the concerns about his authenticity and background—have been internationalized. "You just heard today the success Prokofiev had with the battle scene. Why do you think he succeeded?" Meyerhold asked after the November audition of the music. "Because he approached that scene with Pushkin's naiveté. Here you have a group of Western warriors imported by Grigoriy, a group of Asiatic warriors imported by Boris Godunov, and some Germans. He portrays this battle naively."[81]

The battle scene in *Boris Godunov* bears little resemblance to those in other Prokofiev scores, where sleigh bells and major-key fanfares confirm that victory for the Russians is assured, that the fight is over before it even begins.[82] Such is their nature in *Alexander Nevsky*, a film that served to mobilize the Soviet people for military conflict with the Nazis. *Boris Godunov*, however, does not rewrite history for propagandistic purposes. Instead, it mocks history. Prokofiev lampoons the three groups in their squabble over Eastern European territory by bringing them down to the same base level, by depicting them not as flesh-and-blood people but mere silhouettes.

Beyond the battle scene, the most striking music of the score comes in the middle dance scenes, whose polonaise and mazurka bear the influence of Chaikovsky. (Prokofiev, as noted, criticized portions of Chaikovsky's settings of *Eugene Onegin* and *The Queen of Spades*, but he nevertheless derived inspiration from them.) These dances, which served as preparatory studies for the ballroom numbers in Prokofiev's *War and Peace*, stand out for their sheer sonic exuberance. Owing to their agogic accents and suspensions across the bar line, they assume a slightly artificial, fantastic feel. Can one dance to such music? The sensation washes over the listener that the polonaise and mazurka are the products of delusion or dream, the acoustic tensions and releases intended for unnatural bodies. Indeed, the characters in *Boris Godunov* make no apparent effort to dance. In scene 12, which is set (like scene 13) at the Polish castle of the *voyevod* Mnishek, dance music is heard down a corridor lined with bright but unseen rooms, in and out of which couples stroll, rather than whirl.[83]

Prokofiev's *Boris Godunov* is an unusual score, going well beyond the composer's supposedly "modest" goals for his incidental music to offer much more than background atmosphere. The vocal music especially draws attention to itself, often telling a different story than the text. The composer conflates acoustic registers, bringing together, for example, duets and solo songs from the visible story space (the diegetic realm) and choruses from the invisible space beyond it (the nondiegetic realm). Yet the juxtaposition does not serve the purpose of dialogue; the onstage singing involves words (in the duets) and vocalized vowels (in the solo songs), but the offstage singing does not. During the monologues, Prokofiev works with two other types of sound. The first is imagined or, to use a term developed by the film scholar Claudia Gorbman, "meta-diegetic" sound: that which exists in the Tsar's and Pretender's multidimensional consciousnesses but which the audience is also permitted to hear.[84] The second type of sound is harder to define, since it is displaced in time, leaking into the present from the past or the future or both. The phenomenon might be likened to metempsychosis insofar as it concerns the transmigration of consciousness or, in the case of Kseniya's scene 10 lament, the transmigration of spirit.

Scene 10 opens with Kseniya grieving the death of her betrothed (an outpouring that worsens the Tsar's already terrible mood) and closes with the Tsar grieving the real-or-imagined enemies knocking (metaphorically speaking) at his door. The transcripts of Meyerhold's rehearsals from December 4 and 13, 1936, explain his intentions and shed light on the marriage of Pushkin's words to Prokofiev's background scoring. During the December 4 rehearsal, the director remarked that, despite the lack of "sentimentality" in scene 10, "a tone of sincerity must come from Kseniya." Since her bridegroom "did not die yesterday, but quite a long time ago, she will not weep now as she did on the day after his death. The expression of her sorrow must thus subside, though its ritual aspect must still be audible." By way of clarification, the director offered a personal anecdote, describing his experience at the funeral of the peasant poet Sergey Esenin. As Esenin's mother approached the coffin, he recalled, she began a ritual lament that exhibited vocal "technique," involving the hypnotic repetition of a familiar melody, one whose intonations offer her consolation. During the December 13 rehearsal, Meyerhold commented that the "egocentric" Tsar does not interpret his daughter's sorrow as an expression of personal loss; it is instead a generalized utterance, "the nation's lament."[85] The contemplative, introspective lament involves not one voice but many singing a single strain that repeats over and over again. The imaginative listener might interpret the sound—which is specifically associated with the Time of Troubles—as allegory for sorrowful recurrences in Russian history.

To convert a personal expression into a communal one, Prokofiev composed an eleven-measure piece that evokes the intonations of liturgical chant and thus refers to long-standing ritual. The ritual in question is a construct insofar as Prokofiev's music has no explicit connections to Russian chant of the sixteenth and seventeenth centuries, but takes as its point of reference later, post-Petrine concepts of liturgical modality and melody, such as that embodied in Rachmaninoff's *All-Night Vigil*. Kseniya sings amid a halo of strings. The first violins introduce a throbbing motive—a rising and falling minor third—which is adopted and embellished by the singer against a backdrop of rocking whole steps and semitones in the second violins. Gazing at an image of her lost betrothed, Kseniya grieves: "Why do your lips no longer speak, and your bright eyes no longer shine? Why are your lips sealed, your bright eyes set?" The peak of her melodic arch, on the word "bright," is marked by the insertion of F flat, D flat, and C flat in both the vocal and instrumental music—a literal flattening of the C-minor texture. By drawing upon the music of the background accompaniment, Kseniya imports nondiegetic sound into the diegetic realm, which from a narrative standpoint is the equivalent of transforming omniscient narration into direct speech. Kseniya quotes from a wordless chorus of string instruments; her lament is the lament of mourners before her, moving from the past through the present.

In 1944, Prokofiev included the music of Kseniya's lament in the score for *Ivan the Terrible* Part I. He used it in the scene in which Ivan's wife, Anastasiya, takes to her bed. She has fallen ill and will soon die, since her medicine has been poisoned by a treacherous courtier (Yefrosinya Staritskaya). In this context, Kseniya's lament serves the purpose of a nocturnal vigil. To enhance its emotion, Prokofiev added electronic feedback to the sound of the strings. In *Boris Godunov*, the acoustic extension is achieved not by electronics but by invisible human beings.

◆

Meyerhold defined *Boris Godunov* as "a struggle of passions against the backdrop of a seething sea,"[86] and throughout the rehearsal period, he equated the behavior of the masses with that of elemental nature. A letter he wrote to Prokofiev about the incidental music for the drama, and the detailed instructions that he inserted between the pages of Prokofiev's personal copy of the drama, describe the people as the embodiment of fierce meteorological events. In scene 22, Meyerhold sought to divide the sound of the people into two parts: in the first half of the scene, which features a speech about the demise of Boris and the triumphant arrival of the Pretender in Moscow, the people express a combination of "arousal, intensity, electricity"; in the second half, their utterances decay into white noise, the din of "rebellion, the roar of the sea, of a breached dam."[87] In his instructions for the final scene in the drama, Meyerhold extends his litany of metaphors. "The rumble of the crowd," he suggests to Prokofiev, should be

> dark, agitated, menacing, like the roar of the sea. One should feel their power growing, being restrained, an internal rage, a ferment that has yet to find an outlet. When their power has grown to the fullest, the people become organized, and nothing can stand against them.[88]

Here at the conclusion of Meyerhold's planned staging, the people (*narod*) are equated with a crowd or throng (*tolpa*)—an instruction that would have appealed to the neo-primitive or "Scythian" side of Prokofiev's musical persona.[89] It merits mention that in his letter to the composer that preceded these written instructions, Meyerhold commented that, in accordance with the 1831 ending of Pushkin's drama, the noise of the crowd would not be long-lasting and would calm down (*utikhayet*) with Mosalsky's words: "People! Mariya Godunova and her son Fyodor have poisoned themselves."[90] The omission of these remarks from his later written instructions to the composer suggests, perhaps, a mutation in his conception of the people from a passive into an aggressive force, from an embodiment of natural forces to the enactment of revolutionary power. He likewise came to argue for an alignment of man and nature, individual and mass, in the staging. Prokofiev, however, conceived not a violent deluge for the end of the drama but a block of sound that repeats insistently from end to end.

Meyerhold's instructions challenged Prokofiev to create a musical structure and language for the crowd scenes that would preserve the individual utterance within the collective or, more to the point, demonstrate that each form of expression enables the other. His response to the challenge was unique, insofar as it involved reducing the three choral episodes in the drama to the barest of harmonic, melodic, and rhythmic elements, and dispensing with words altogether. The three choruses in *Boris Godunov* feature, in the vocal lines, stammered eighth and quarter notes. These are accompanied by simple three- and four-note chords in the orchestra that repeat in rigid formations, give way to brief chromatic runs, and modulate up and down by whole steps. In terms of texture and dynamic, each of the choruses is cast in binary form, the first halves gradually increasing in density and volume, the second halves decreasing; each also alternates between homophonic and polyphonic passages. The music shuns development, depending instead on abstract patterns of cause and effect to generate meaning. Prokofiev omitted the music for the three choral scenes from the November run-through, but he talked about the general impact he wanted the wordless singing to achieve. "The noise of the crowd," he told the actors, "will be somewhere behind the scenes, the musical premise being as follows: there is a kind of musical foundation, which is accompanied by string bass, bassoon, bass drum, tam-tam, and kettledrums (these last are muted and emit only noise, not specific pitch). The chorus not only sings to this music, but also evokes the multi-voiced rumble of the crowd."[91]

These remarks pertain to the first and third choral scenes (Nos. 22 and 24 in the score), which convey a sense of temporal stasis, as though the people are locked in the historical moment, speaking neither to the past nor the future. In No. 24, the chorus that concludes the drama, the singing consists of bass and tenor voices that more often than not move in portentous lockstep. Measures 7 and 8 of the 16-measure repeating structure involve a chromatic run in the bass line that facilitates a modulation from C major to its relative minor, A. In the remaining measures (9–16), the bass line descends by half step from A to E flat; this last note drops to D with the return, following the double-bar sign, to measure 1. The repetition of notes within the formation as well as of the formation itself enhances the sense of stasis, the effect of building but bridled energy.

The first chorus (No. 22) achieves the effect through other means. Prokofiev drafted a series of rhythmic, harmonic, and melodic blocks, arranging them in palindromic fashion. The three measures of block "A" frame the chorus: the unit appears twice in the first ten measures and twice in the last ten measures of the episode. Block "B," which occupies two measures, serves as a second, internal frame, while blocks "C" (two measures) and "D" (three measures) define the center. The structure is not as rigid as a description makes it seem. For one thing, the four vocal-instrumental units are interrupted by passages that do not repeat; for another, the blocks are not always heard intact. The second repetition of block "A," for example, is missing one of its original measures, and the first repetition of block "D" is missing two. In other words, whereas the overall structure of the chorus is fixed, its internal elements are not: upon repetition, they tend to expand or contract in size. This elasticity, coupled with the changing rhythmic and harmonic relationships in each of the blocks, creates the overall impression of a marshaled cacophony. The chorus is a primal "ferment," to refer back to Meyerhold's instructions to Prokofiev, "that has yet to find an outlet."

For the middle chorus of the three, Prokofiev offered a musical self-analysis, noting that he devised the episode in an unusual fashion so that it could be fragmented and reconfigured to suit the needs of the director.[92] The chorus consists of a single eight-measure phrase that is transposed, upon repetition, from the tonalities of C to D, D to E, and E to F-sharp major and back down again. The seventh and eighth measures of the phrase facilitate these transpositions, which the composer defined as rises and falls in emotional intensity. To this chorus, Prokofiev added a chance element—a means for expressing primal spontaneity. In the bottom margin of the manuscript, he remarked that the four transpositions of the eight-measure phrase could be "combined as necessary" and performed at various tempos, though he cautioned that the melodic motives he inserted into the E-major transposition of the phrase should not be heard in succession.[93] Thus the actual published edition of the chorus, which includes seven repetitions of the phrase in four tonalities, does not reflect how the composer meant for it to be heard. The singing was to be partitioned into discrete blocks, with Meyerhold at liberty to rearrange and distribute them throughout the drama to capture the changing energies of the people. Here it should be noted that Pushkin scholars sometimes describe the narrative organization of *Boris Godunov* as a patchwork, a jumble of brief scenes providing different psychological angles on the same historical incidents. In her 1986 study of the drama, Emerson observes that "instead of a series of interlocking and exemplary life situations, we are given an assemblage of glimpses drawn from different points of view—what one critic [Mark Polyakov] has called 'poly-perspectival drama.' "[94]

Prokofiev's middle chorus is the invisible thread that binds the drama together. Akin to the chorus in a Greek tragedy, the singers inhabit a terrain inaccessible to the major players in Pushkin's text: Boris, Grigoriy, Fyodor, Kseniya, Pimen, and Shuysky. Unlike the commentators in a Greek tragedy, the singers react to the events onstage with wordless outbursts. They "speak" neither from the past nor the future; they do not remember what happened and cannot describe what will occur. Since history has not benefited the people, the people, it appears, have stepped outside of it.

◆

The lament and choruses constitute two of the three vocal layers of the incidental music for *Boris Godunov*. The third layer, a group of unaccompanied songs, is at once the simplest (in terms of syntax) and most complex (in terms of acoustic manipulation). The songs are heard both on- and offstage; they are sometimes remembered and sometimes imagined by the dramatis personae. Meyerhold proposed to distribute the songs "throughout the entire spectacle" and wanted "two or three" of them to exhibit an "Eastern character."[95] The first is performed by a melancholy wanderer, a figure who finds himself lost between borders. The "Song of the Lonely Traveler" occurs at the tail end of the scene on the Lithuanian border (No. 8), during which the Pretender Grigoriy takes flight from the Tsar's lansquenets. The listener, Meyerhold and Prokofiev believed, would equate Grigoriy with this song, even though it is sung (or at least appears to be sung) by someone else.

The "Lonely Traveler"—whose lack of identity reflects the devil-may-care Pretender's own lack of identity—brings to mind the shepherd from the devastating third act of Richard Wagner's 1859 *Tristan und Isolde*, which Meyerhold knew well.[96] Near the start of the act, Tristan awakes from a restless, feverish dream to ask a simple question: "Where am I?" He knows his nightmare is over but cannot bring himself out of it and does not know where he is. Recall that Meyerhold (at Pyast's urging) wanted his version of *Boris Godunov* to include a scene that Pushkin had omitted from the 1831 edition of his drama, one that involved Grigoriy, like Tristan, experiencing restless, feverish dreams. He declares, following a conversation with the "Evil Monk" who occupies the same room, that his future has been decided: "That's it! I am Dmitriy, the Tsarevich!"[97] Unlike Tristan, Grigoriy knows where he is and what he has become, but in Meyerhold's conception, he gains this knowledge with the assistance of a nocturnal interlocutor. Pushkin signals that Grigoriy is a habitual dreamer, and his egoistic vision in the presence of the monk marks his attempt to realize his most ambitious potential. The incident was to be staged as follows:

> The music begins, suggesting—like the delirium of someone in *War and Peace*—a state of pulsation, pulsing. And against the background of this pulsating music, somewhere

in the back behind translucent curtains it begins to get light, the decorations shake and throw light on *him*, next to the monk. He is in the monk's quarters. This is a sickly dream, like a delirium. He enters and speaks, but the actor who plays Dmitriy lies at the front of the stage.

I would entrust this scene not to actors, but to singers. This is not declamation in music, not recitation to music, which I don't like at all, but recitative. This should be done in the style of recitative, as in Mozart's *Don Giovanni*.[98]

In addition to recitative, Prokofiev offered to furnish Meyerhold with haunting, unsettled orchestral music for the scene: a throbbing backdrop consisting of leitmotifs from the reverie, polonaise, and mazurka that he composed for later pages in the drama.[99] The music for the dream scene, in short, would be a melodic congeries from the scene 13 gathering at the Polish castle and the scene 14 meeting between Grigoriy and Marina by the fountain. In a portentous inversion, Grigoriy would not be roused by the sounds of the past, the time and place of his authentic self, but by the sounds of the future, the time and place of his adopted selves. Time in the staging would run both forward and backward. In the "Evil Monk" scene, Meyerhold wanted the Pretender to hear the music of his fragmented destiny. Capable of multiply reinventing himself, he was to experience, in one jarring sequence, a compilation soundtrack of all his potential identities.

Rehearsals for *Boris Godunov* were suspended before the orchestral music for the dream scene came into being, leaving its relationship to the "Song of the Lonely Traveler" unclear. (Prokofiev kept the musical concept in mind, however, when he composed Prince Andrey's "piti-piti" hallucination for *War and Peace*; the episode involves the distant reprise of a waltz and a throbbing offstage chorus.) Perhaps the composer came to the same conclusion about *Boris Godunov* that Pushkin did: the drama needed to avoid the supernatural, since to invoke it would be to ascribe the decisions of the characters to events beyond their control.

In place of the dream music, Prokofiev composed three additional monophonic songs. Like the "Song of the Lonely Traveler," they are cast in the stripped-down style that Meyerhold regarded as the ideal counterpart to the disquieting directness of Pushkin's mode of expression.[100] The original manuscript of the songs reveals that Prokofiev conceived them as a group, with common phrases that could be shuffled around.[101] All intone the vowel "ah."

Songs one and two preserve the intervallic contours and cadential patterns associated with the Dorian (or natural minor) mode in both its liturgical and folkloric guises. Songs three and four, in contrast, bear a blank "Eastern" character, a reference, perhaps, to Karamzin's suggestion that Boris had Asiatic (Tatar-Mongol) ancestors.[102] The third song stresses the lowered second and lowered fifth scale degrees of the Locrian mode and a 9/8 rhythmic pattern that could conceivably have been inspired by the Turkish *Karsilama* and the motions of belly dancers: Prokofiev stacks one exotic cliché atop another. His fourth song involves—in an enharmonic respelling—the familiar "Eastern" interval of the augmented second. The melody ascends from E sharp to E natural, a span of a diminished octave, with the upper pitch repeated in a laconic diminuendo and diminution toward the end. The four songs represent no specific locale but remoteness as such. Prokofiev's score for *Boris Godunov* begins and ends in this ambiguous space.

The chance-based repetitiveness of the choral singing and the removal of context from the four songs evince calculated simplicity and intentional naiveté. Naiveté is the point at which comedy trips over into tragedy. In Prokofiev's score for *Boris Godunov* the boundaries of the two modes are probed—and found wanting—to eerie effect. The visible singers allow their unadorned cantilena to bridge the gaps between the scenes. The invisible singers, upon whom Meyerhold and Prokofiev lavished much care in their collaboration, issue their primal sounds from the hinterland, commenting on historic upheaval in a much different way than Pushkin's verses. Their distanced stammering opens a window into the minds of the Tsar and his rival, who are further and further detached from their handlers, the masses, and from their own previously constructed selves. Moving from the ending to the beginning of the music for *Boris Godunov* (and the ending to the beginning of Meyerhold and Prokofiev's interaction with Pushkin), one sees that the planned staging filled much greater psychological terrain than the seventeenth-century onset of the Time of Troubles or the twentieth-century onset of the Stalinist repressions.

The rehearsal transcripts for *Boris Godunov* imagine a terrain of unleashed primal forces that obliterate individuality and nationality. It is a much different place from the "alien theater" described by Kerzhentsev in a December 17, 1937, *Pravda* article of the same name.[103] That article, which accused Meyerhold of ignoring the "fundamental political and creative challenges" confronting the Soviet people in favor of abstraction and experiment, spelled the end of the director's career and, ultimately, his life. Had he staged *Boris Godunov*, his political opponents would doubtless have scorned its eccentric bleakness, with comparably dire consequences. Meyerhold was altogether fascinated by the figure of Pimen, whom he described as a very busy historian, someone who, despite a long-standing ban on the writing of chronicles,[104] "has always written," is "writing at the moment," and "still has a great deal to write."[105] This figure is Meyerhold himself, who still had a great deal to write in 1936, despite bans of a different sort and the shackling of his creative activities by Stalin's cultural servants. Pimen chronicled the erosion of the Russian State; Meyerhold imagined its end. Both feared the void that would be left behind.

4

War and Evacuation,

1940–1943

In 1938, Prokofiev's home life began to fall apart, the consequence of external pressures and internal disputes. In 1941, he abruptly abandoned Lina and their two sons to live in central Moscow with a twenty-six-year-old poet named Mira (Mariya) Abramovna Mendelson, a student in the Gorky Literary Institute. In the years ahead, Mira became Prokofiev's advisor, guardian of his time and health, and the co-author, with Prokofiev himself, of three opera librettos and several song texts. She took the lead role in preserving his legacy, and represented him in her writings in quasi-hagiographic terms. Her 1940–50 memoirs, a miscellany of personal observations, transcribed letters, and transcribed articles and reviews, contain select, decontextualized details about Prokofiev's day-to-day activities before, during, and after the Second World War. The summaries of their conversations tend to be banal, lacking substance, which suggests that she censored them in an effort to preserve the correct political picture of the relationship.

The two of them first met in August 1938, when Mira traveled with her parents to vacation at the resort in Kislovodsk where Prokofiev and Lina were also residing.[1] Mira pinpoints August 26 as the date of her first conversation with Prokofiev. They began to take walks, during which he spoke of his music and she of her attempts at verse. In an English-language interview, Lina recalls Prokofiev first describing Mira as "just some girl who wants to read me her bad poetry." Lina joked, "Well, take care of your little admirer."[2] Prokofiev defended his subsequent meetings with Mira on professional grounds: she "could help him find Soviet librettos." "Well, go ahead and see her," his wife answered, "I won't object; but that doesn't mean you have to live with her!"[3] He and Mira parted at the end of August— she returned to Moscow, he detoured to the Black Sea resort of Sochi—but they pledged to remain in contact. Mira was at this point entering the third year of her four-year program of studies, and living with her father, Abram Solomonovich Mendelson, and mother, Vera (Dora) Natanovna Mendelson, in two of the three rooms of a communal apartment across from the Moscow Arts Theater, in a building controlled by the State Planning Commission, the organization charged with drafting, implementing, and supervising the Five-Year Plans. The family had hard-won political credentials: Abram was an economist and statistician who worked in the 1930s for the State Planning Commission and the Central Administration for Economic Accounting, surviving the purges in those organizations and the Communist Party.[4] Vera, an active Party member, twice earned official recognition for her work.[5] Mira, for her part, studied in the Energy Sector of the Moscow Planning Institute before entering the Chernïshevsky Institute of History, Philosophy, and Literature and, after a year of study there, the Gorky Literary Institute. Her father appears to have steered her away from the type of career path, with its enormous Party obligations, he had taken. Through the four years of her advanced studies, Mira demonstrated a talent for translating prose and poetry from English into Russian but less skill as a creative writer.[6] The exact manner in which the young woman entered Prokofiev's life in 1938 remains unclear. Recalling the first months of her infatuation with him, Mira writes in clichés about riverside strolls, gift exchanges (in January 1939, Prokofiev gave her a photograph inscribed "to a blossoming poet from a modest admirer"), and dances at the Union of Soviet Writers club.[7] Rumors soon began to circulate about the nascent fall-spring romance.[8]

In the opening pages of her memoirs, Mira reports on Prokofiev's creative habits in 1938 and 1939, but provides nothing in the way of specific details. The account is at times naively self-serving: "During that winter, Sergey Sergeyevich was at work on the *Alexander Nevsky* Cantata. I often recall him telling me with a grin about all of the mistakes he had to scrape out of it, and how he thought of me at the time."[9] Her account of the ensuing months excludes mention of political events. Mira recalls Prokofiev asking her to meet with him again in the summer of 1939 in Kislovodsk, where he and the Stanislavsky Theater collective had relocated. In July, on the heels of the arrest of Meyerhold, he began his fraught collaboration with Birman on *Semyon Kotko*. He and Mira joked about his efforts to educate, or at least correct, the untested director: "How is the 'tuning up' [nastraivaniye] of Birman going?" Mira asked Prokofiev in a July 16, 1939, letter. "Thought of anything new?"[10] Ill-timed humor about the ill-timed opera notwithstanding, the romance provided a release of sorts from the extreme pressure under which Prokofiev was then working. Upon Mira's arrival in Kislovodsk in August, the two of them toured the Kislovodsk Castle of Wile and Love, and went on brief trips to three other North Caucasus resorts: Essentuki, Zheleznovodsk, and (together with one of the *Semyon Kotko* cast members) Adïl-Su.[11]

The real-world implications of their relationship began to become clear in the fall of 1939. At this time, Prokofiev became entangled in the disputes surrounding the Leningrad premiere of *Romeo and Juliet*, leaving Mira to prepare for her final-year exams. In a December 26 letter to her, he offers caustic insight into the discontent in the Kirov Theater. He claims that the challenge of coordinating the spectacle, the tense atmosphere, "stinging remarks," and "the hysterics of [Galina] Ulanova and the prophet Isaiah [Isay Sherman]" had led to the postponement of the premiere from December to January. "In the breaks between rehearsals, I am pasting in changes to the score, the primary purpose being to harden its edges, for the dancers cannot grasp anything even a little subtle and, having been taught to think with their feet, they get lost."[12]

Before his departure for Leningrad, Prokofiev told Lina about the affair. The stressful atmosphere in the apartment worsened to the extent that Prokofiev isolated himself in his study. It was there, during a period of anguished domestic conflict, that he composed his birthday present for Stalin. Mira recalls him musing about escaping to a distant corner of the planet with her. Life at home was "empty," since Lina "showed little interest" in him.[13] Here Prokofiev was being dishonest, since, as Mira herself comes close to declaring, Lina devoted herself entirely to him, supporting his decision to relocate to Moscow and placing her welfare in his hands upon joining him there.

Mira offers just one of three sides to the story that belongs to her, Prokofiev, and Lina alone. Certain other details, however, deserve brief mention, since they provide context for the composer's creative activities.

In the summer of 1939, before their separation, Prokofiev and Lina considered acquiring a summer house, or dacha, in Nikolina Gora, a cooperative of artists, composers, and writers established in the late 1920s on the western fringe of Moscow. (The area remains one of the wealthiest, and most exclusive, in all of Russia.) Lamm had a dacha there (with Myaskovsky as summer tenant), as did Lavrovsky. To finance the purchase, the couple decided to leave their Ulitsa Chkalova apartment—which had been allotted to them by the Committee on Arts Affairs—and move to a less expensive one. For a time, the family planned to move into a building at 40 Leningradskoye Shosse. It emerges from the letter in question (that in which Lina tells her husband about the murder of Zinaida Raykh) that she intended to vacation apart from Prokofiev in southern Ukraine, but that her travel permit, required for movement within the Soviet Union, had not appeared. Her plans were at a standstill, she lamented. "I sent two photographs and a telegram to Kiev with a request for a response of some sort but nothing has been heard—what happened there? It's now clear that I can't count on it—I absolutely don't know what I can do."[14] She traveled in the end to Gagra, a resort in the Abkhazian Autonomous Republic of Soviet Georgia, on the northeast coast of the Black Sea.[15] Later lines in Lina's letter attest to her troubles obtaining singing engagements. She had met that day with Georgiy Kreytner, a high-ranking member of the Committee on Arts Affairs, seeking a contract to perform repertoire in foreign languages for State Radio, but given the xenophobic cultural climate of the time, Kreytner could not or would not help her. "I am terribly distressed by current events," she comments with regard to her problems with State Radio.[16] The extent to which Prokofiev used his influence to support his wife's career remains unclear. In the fall of 1939, he started to untangle their lives, appearing less and less frequently with her in public. (Lina attended the premieres of *Romeo and Juliet* and *Semyon Kotko*; Mira was also in attendance at the latter, leading to an awkward, strained moment among the three of them.)[17] In the summer of 1940 he rented a dacha at Nikolina Gora—a purchase came later—and spent what turned out to be his last summer together with his family. He continued to see Mira, the justification being their collaboration on a libretto.

On June 1, 1940, Lina wrote her husband a trilingual letter that evinces profound despair, a letter that touches on their shared spiritual, creative, and personal outlook. References to Lev Tolstoy and Mary Baker Eddy, the founder of the Christian Science Church, collide on the pages. The following lines, written largely in Russian, illustrate her suspicions about Mira's background:

> Remember what you wrote after the first meeting. It was hardly you who chose them [Mira and her family], but they who "chose" you—where? At a health resort—you, not

some speck of sand, but S. S. P., the leading composer of the
nation, a famous person with a family-man aura, twice as
old. And it was not incognito. *Perhaps you will say "love at
first sight"—who will believe [that]?* There were sufficient
witnesses in Kislovodsk to the fact that she followed you
everywhere.[18]

For Lina, Mira's starstruck pursuit of Prokofiev seemed coarsely calculated
and transparent. In the months after her husband had decided to leave home,
she enjoined him to terminate what she considered to be a self-destructive
dalliance. Lina offers an insight—in English—taken directly from Christian
Science: "Turn to real identity and substance which will give you the real
support you are in need of now. No human theory, person or book, will give
it to you—real understanding is not intellectual, not the result of scholarly
attainments; it is the reality of things brought to life."[19] Prokofiev, in her
opinion, had been deceived in a fashion that would rob his life of spiritual
purpose. Here Lina invokes the Christian Science precept that earthly desires
impair the pursuit of the divine, exerting negative pressure on the immortal
mind. Lina ends her plea to her husband by once again paraphrasing Eddy:
"Mankind must learn that evil is not power. Its so-called despotism is but a
phase of nothingness."[20] This belief had enabled her and Prokofiev to cope
with the "terrible" present.

Prokofiev left Lina on March 15, 1941. Mira recalls that, late that night,
he unexpectedly called her from a Moscow train station to announce his
decision.[21] (Lina describes the departure as a panicked response to Mira's
"disgraceful" threats to take her own life if she could not be with him, but
also, more tellingly, as "a psychological escape from the terrible disappointment of reality.")[22] Prokofiev went to Leningrad to stay with Demchinsky;
Mira joined him there a few days later. The two of them were thereafter
inseparable, though the impulsiveness of their relationship obliged them
to live an itinerant, unsettled existence. Prior to the outbreak of the war
between the Soviet Union and Nazi Germany, they spent part of their time
in Moscow with Mira's parents, with whom Prokofiev developed an adequate relationship, and part of it in her family's dacha at Kratovo. Prokofiev
pledged to provide material support for his family, but ruled out the possibility of returning home. His relationship with Mira was much more than an
affair, but the beginning of a creative and personal partnership, despite the
difference in their ages and experiences.

Appassionata

Prokofiev's relationship with Mira inspired several realized and speculative operatic projects. The period was also marked by a tempestuous rededication to piano composition—one that invites all manner of allegorical interpretations. In the fall of 1939, according to Mira, Prokofiev conceived a trio of piano works (his Sixth, Seventh, and Eighth Sonatas), informing her that the first and second of them would be "restless and stormlike" and the third "tender and dreamlike."[23] He added that the first theme of the first movement of the Eighth Sonata—an *andante dolce* tune that floats in and out of B-flat major—came to him after one of his walks with her. Though his description of the character of these three major works recalls that of "Florestan" and "Eusebius" from Schumann's *Carnaval*—a favorite score— Prokofiev also appears to have drawn inspiration from Beethoven. In the summer of 1939, he read the original French-language edition of Romain Rolland's *Beethoven the Creator*, specifically those passages that addressed the "Appassionata" Sonata, a composition that, according to Rolland, comprised a "union of unrestrained passion and rigid logic."[24] Prokofiev's Sixth Sonata involves a comparable fusion between violent impulse and classical discipline; it operates, on syntactical and referential levels, from opposing standpoints of chaos and order. Myaskovsky deemed the work Janus-faced, a "mixture of the old and new Prokofiev."[25] The score suggested a dialogue between Neoprimitivism and Neoclassicism, which recalls the "Sturm und Drang" and "empfindsamer Stil" dialogue of another pianistic era.

The Sixth Sonata is cast in four expansive movements totaling, by Prokofiev's own calculation, twenty-five minutes in length. Traditional sonata form provides the framework for movement one, though the divisions between its thematic components are obfuscated and embellished and the harmonic polarities intensified.[26] The first theme—containing a nerve-jangling, compulsive motive that repeats in syncopated sixteenth and eighth notes—juxtaposes the tonic triads of A major and A minor. The teetering between C sharp and C natural, the mediants of the competing tonal domains, is one of several forces of destabilization in the movement. The development section involves contrapuntal imitation at the tritone rather than the fifth; the first and second themes are broken down into transposable units that become indistinguishable from one another. As testament to the movement's logical illogic, the bridge from the development into the recapitulation decreases, rather than increases, the energy level: the collision of semitonal forces reaches a stalemate with the deployment of interlocking whole tone scale fragments. The stalemate persists throughout the recapitulation: here, the thematic components of the exposition are concatenated. Prokofiev concludes the movement with a terse hammer stroke on the pitches B flat and A natural.

The drama of the movement resides in the foregrounding of dissonances over consonances, non-resolutions over resolutions, but also on something more visceral: the liquidation of pitch itself for sheer sonic effect. At the March 10, 1940, adjudication of the score in Prokofiev's presence at the Union of Soviet Composers, Klimentiy Korchmaryov asserted that the ostinato patterns and melodic and harmonic idiosyncrasies of the first movement bore much in common with Prokofiev's earlier sonatas and those of other, Prokofiev-inspired composers. Korchmaryov insisted that he "liked" the second and third movements of the work—the former a sped-up march, the latter a slowed-down waltz—much more than the first. (He essentially reserved judgment on the fourth movement, a sonata-rondo structure that features, in the development section and the coda, the recurrence, like a nervous tic, of the percussive first theme of the first movement.) Another adjudicator, Aleksandr Abramsky, countered that the first movement constituted a significant innovation owing to the "almost complete absence of figuration": there were no harmonies, he asserted, for the nonharmonic pitches to embellish. In place of figuration, Prokofiev stressed its opposite: four-note pitch groups played *col pugno*—with the fist. Abramsky also offered the thought that the Sixth Sonata evinced both "internal" and "external" simplicity, a reference to its symmetrical proportions and directness of expression.[27]

Two days before the adjudication, Prokofiev unveiled the Sixth Sonata at a gathering in Lamm's apartment. The audience included Svyatoslav Richter, who became Prokofiev's preferred pianist in the years ahead, after he recognized that his own technique had begun to wane owing to lack of time to practice and the effects of aging. On this occasion, however, Prokofiev evinced impertinent youthfulness, twice reading through the Sixth Sonata from the manuscript before abruptly departing. Richter turned the pages, deciding in the midst of the recital to learn the score.[28] Prokofiev premiered it on April 8, 1940; Richter performed it on November 26, his technique outshining that of the composer. In response, Prokofiev later fashioned for himself and for Richter one of the most challenging and mesmerizing movements in the piano repertoire, the finale of the Seventh Sonata, a *precipitato* toccata in 7/8 time. Befitting its impulsive character, the draft for this movement shows almost no signs of revision.[29]

Mira claimed that the Seventh Sonata was conceived alongside the Sixth and Eighth Sonatas, but the surviving source materials suggest another chronology. Melodic material for the three works dates as far back as 1935.[30] In the fall of 1939, Prokofiev produced two pages of sketches for the Sixth Sonata, but also penned, on the back of the second sheet, an outline of the entire Eighth Sonata.[31] The Seventh Sonata is the conception of a later time (1942) and place (Tbilisi), when Prokofiev felt less grounded but also less constrained. It is the most radical of the three works, which are as a group more radical than anything else in Prokofiev's mature oeuvre. They were also successful—more so than many of the works he calibrated for success. In the realm of Soviet piano music, accessibility was not a precondition for acceptability.

The three sonatas are united in the radiant discord of their melodic and harmonic language and the willfulness of their rhythmic writing. The music is abstract insofar as it avoids external references, but for the composer, abstraction bore programmatic, spiritualistic associations. One could fancifully argue that the three sonatas transcend their own structural and syntactical constraints, revealing those constraints to be the false postulates of false reasoning. This notion finds general support in the analytical literature: Deborah Anne Rifkin, for example, argues that the music of the second movement of the Seventh Sonata is both tonal and nontonal at the same time, owing to the substitution, right at the start, of implied chords for actual chords, motivic relationships for harmonic ones.[32] The erasure of tonal links suggests a process of dematerialization.

At the time of its dissemination, however, the Seventh Sonata was interpreted as an abstract embodiment of wartime struggle. Richter claimed that the first movement plunges the listener "into the anxiously threatening atmosphere of a world that has lost its balance.... In the tremendous struggle that this involves, we find the strength to affirm the irrepressible life-force."[33] His premiere of the work in Moscow on January 18, 1943, represented one of his greatest professional triumphs (he performed it twice), and ensured Prokofiev would receive a Stalin Prize (Second Class) for it. The announcement of the 50,000-ruble award was, according to Mira, a cause of "great celebration."[34] For the much more enigmatic Eighth Sonata, which Emil Gilels premiered in Moscow on December 30, 1944, the public and critical response proved more reserved. However, it earned a First Class Stalin Prize, testament to the bolstering of Prokofiev's reputation among his peers during the war years.

Leskov

Although the preceding comments might signal otherwise, the progress of Prokofiev's career between 1940 and 1943 affirms that he was first and foremost a theatrical composer, who relied, commissions permitting, on the great books for inspiration. The contradiction between his inclination toward abstraction and his reliance on literature is resolved by his text-setting method, which emphasizes the rhythm and cadence of language over its semantic content. Mira at first aided Prokofiev's constant search for operatic subjects by drawing his attention to writers who borrowed from folklore and street lingo to enrich the intonations of their syntax.

Following the belated Leningrad premiere of *Romeo and Juliet*, Prokofiev asked Mira to help him locate an opera subject. The text he eventually settled on, Richard Sheridan's 1775 comic drama *The Duenna*, or *The Double Elopement*, perhaps attests to his desire to depart a scarred present for a benign eighteenth-century fantasy. "Prokofiev," Richard Taruskin writes, "immediately sensed" the "possibilities" of Sheridan's text "for innocent musical 'champagne *à la* Mozart or Rossini.'"[35] Yet the path from the fraught ideological terrain of Prokofiev's first Soviet opera, *Semyon Kotko*, to the blatantly "anti-clerical and anti-mercantile" burlesque of *The Duenna* was hardly smooth.[36] Prokofiev explored several other subjects, and came close in 1940 to setting a drama by Nikolay Leskov, who was the author of the source text of Shostakovich's *Lady Macbeth of the Mtsensk District*.

After considering *The Dowerless Girl* (*Bespridannitsa*, 1878) and *The Thunderstorm* (*Groza*, 1859) by Aleksandr Ostrovsky, Prokofiev drafted an operatic synopsis for Leskov's melodrama *The Spendthrift* (*Rastochitel'*, 1867).[37] Like the Ostrovsky works, the drama concerns the exploitation of poor folk by mercantile ne'er-do-wells.[38] The improbable story line pits Firs Knyazev, a womanizing businessman with a cruel streak (tempered only by the onset of old age) against Ivan Molchanov, his dependent. It quickly emerges that Knyazev had murdered Molchanov's father in a business dispute, but had nonetheless become the boy's guardian. The tale traces Molchanov's maturation: his unhappy prearranged marriage, his studies abroad, and his rise in status. Eager to avenge the perverse injustice of his childhood, he turns to the courts to have his inheritance—which comes from Knyazev's unsavory business practices—assigned to a local orphanage. The old man foils the plan by accusing Molchanov of squandering the inheritance, and bribes the courts to rule in his favor. The upstanding Molchanov, unfairly branded a wastrel, winds up in an asylum. The story progresses to two outlandish climaxes: Molchanov escapes from the asylum and, in a strange purification ritual, sets the town on fire. He dies in the inferno, a tragedy that delights Knyazev until the courts, in an unexpected turnaround, send him to jail for corruption.

Even as melodrama, the story line is unconvincing, but Prokofiev, enamored of Leskov's use of dialect and colorful anecdotes, began to tinker with it. He conceived an operatic version of the tale in five acts, framing it with scenes in which Knyazev recounts his dreadful past in a delirium.[39] The voice of a hapless old merchant, whom the villain had once tried to drown, reverberates in his consciousness. "I am drowning...I am drowning..." Knyazev hears; "forget...forget..." he mutters to himself. To enhance the pathos of this scene, Prokofiev imagined a river coming into view upstage, and Knyazev slipping beneath the water's surface.

Prokofiev mapped out *The Spendthrift* along Chaikovskian lines, freighting the scenario with love duets and hypnotic orchestral interludes. He assigned the duets to Molchanov and his suicidal mistress, Marina. The romantic subplot dominates the middle scenes, which prevents them from getting bogged down in grimly satiric financial and judicial matters. The ending differs from that of the source text. There is no deus ex machina; the characters decide their own fates. In the last scene, Knyazev's factory is ordered burned to the ground, a much more substantial punishment for the villain than imprisonment. Molchanov and Marina are reunited and perform a "big love duet," but there is no relief in it, for she has taken poison. The defeated, enfeebled Knyazev makes a last-gasp attempt to stab his foe, but suffers pangs of conscience and another bout of delirium: "Save me...I am drowning..." The hero and heroine, conceived as positive characters in a negative world, submit to the approaching flames.

It is hard to imagine any operatic treatment of *The Spendthrift*, a tale of shattered spirits without a clear-cut moral, reaching the Soviet stage— especially after the setbacks suffered by Shostakovich for *Lady Macbeth of the Mtsensk District*. Before abandoning it for happier operatic terrain, Prokofiev wrote to his trusted friend Demchinsky. The February 11, 1940, letter bears more than a hint of special pleading:

> I really need your advice and input. I came across Leskov's drama *The Spendthrift*. On first glance, it is a dark, base thing. But what do you think? It might yield insight and enlightenment. I will have to take out the talk about money,

and enhance and expand the positive characters. But there will remain exquisite language, sharply drawn characters, and a series of dramatic situations that might bring to light something powerful.

Please read it. I am thinking of coming to Leningrad on February 18th or 19th. We could confer then—or earlier, if you are planning to be in Moscow beforehand. But don't be frightened by the first impression, and try to follow my train of thought. The greatness of the cockerel lies in his ability to find the pearl in the straw.[40]

The Aesop fable to which Prokofiev alludes in the last line—"The Cockerel and the Pearl"—concludes with the cockerel discarding the pearl for grain, the moral being that value lies in the eye of the beholder. Finding little of merit in the proposed opera scenario, Demchinsky told Prokofiev and his new co-librettist Mira to search the straw anew.

The Duenna

It was Mira who chose the subject.[41] She received a request from a former fellow student (Tatyana Ozerskaya) at the Gorky Literary Institute to assist with the translation of Sheridan's comedy *The Duenna*, a parody of parodies of English mores transplanted from the streets of London to eighteenth-century Seville. Sheridan enlisted his father- and brother-in-law (both named Thomas Linley) to provide music for the multilayered drama: the resulting work, a blend of original and borrowed songs, proved more popular during its opening run than the balladic farce that had inspired it: John Gay's *The Beggar's Opera*. Noting the success of the Moscow Arts Theater staging of Sheridan's *School for Scandal* at the time, Mira agreed to assist Ozerskaya with the translation. But her plans changed when she summarized the plot to Prokofiev, who found its variegated tomfoolery appealing. The two of them worked on the libretto in the spring of 1940 (the completed autograph dates from May 27), and then, according to Mira, shopped it around to Moscow theaters after it had been approved for development by Glavrepertkom. Prokofiev evidently conceived the work at this point as either a musical or a play with incidental songs. He completed the first draft of the actual opera between mid-July and September, traveling back and forth from Nikolina Gora (where he did not have the use of a piano) and Moscow (where he did) with draft material.

The project was undeniably escapist, as was the instantly appealing music that resulted. Prokofiev worked without an advance contract on *The Duenna* in uncomfortable domestic circumstances. On September 19, 1940, he played through the score for the artistic directors of the Stanislavsky Theater and representatives from the Radio Committee.[42] Both groups expressed interest, and both drew up contracts for the opera on the same day: October 28. (The thought seems to have been to have a simultaneous premiere in two venues, with Prokofiev hedging his bets that if Glavrepertkom did not approve the performance of the opera for the Stanislavsky Theater, it would at least be broadcast on State Radio, which was subject to less official control; this is exactly what came to pass.) The agreement with the Stanislavsky Theater specified an opera of nine scenes, with the piano score to be submitted on October 28 (the date of the agreement) and the orchestral score on January 1; Prokofiev would be paid 15,000 rubles in installments for the music and 7,500 rubles for the libretto, and the theater would set aside 3,500 rubles for assistance with the preparation of the orchestration.[43] The contract with the Radio Committee, involving the same fees, specified a lyric comedy of exactly two hours and twenty minutes, with the piano score to be submitted on November 1 and the orchestral score on January 15.[44] On October 16, 1940, Prokofiev gave an interview in the family apartment that summarized his progress and confirmed that the premiere would take the form of a broadcast: "Recently I finished the sketches of my new four-act opera. Its final title has still not been determined....I have now begun the opera's orchestration. All of these pages of manuscript paper, on which you see pencil annotations, have now been orchestrated. I hope that in the second half of the winter season the opera will be broadcast and perhaps staged."[45]

A broadcast of selections from the score occurred on June 7, 1941. By this time the opera was in preparation at the Stanislavsky Theater, but the troupe had begun to second-guess the score: the theater's "insufficient belief in the piece" and the beginning of war prevented the staging from being realized, Mira recalled.[46] In the absence of transcripts of the assessments it is impossible to pinpoint the exact nature of the concerns. The revisions that Prokofiev undertook in the spring of 1943 (after the Committee on Arts Affairs permitted the Bolshoy Theater to explore a staging) suggest that his dependence on declamation to motivate the drama—a dependence that stemmed from an aversion to dramatic stasis—had come back to haunt him. A list of alterations dated April 4, 1943, find him buttressing the lyrical content of the score at the expense of the declamation: melodies that had been the domain of the orchestra alone enter into the vocal parts.[47] Most of the changes bear the imprint of political doctrine; others, however, reveal an independent, nonpolitical impulse to compress the score and sharpen its dramatic contrasts: Prokofiev excised, for example, four measures from the overture to make the shift between two melodies more explicit. However, despite inspired work on both the first version and the revisions, the opera would not be premiered until November 3, 1946, in compromised form in Leningrad. (A more spirited staging would be organized in 1947 by VOKS for the Grand Opera of the Fifth of May in Prague.)

The plot celebrates the miscommunications, mistaken identities, and amorous caprice common to operatic wedding comedies. Don Jerome, a Seville merchant, betrothes his daughter Louisa to the rich but old Jewish fishmonger Isaac Mendoza. Louisa prefers the poor but young Don Antonio, and plots with her wealth-seeking governess, the duenna of the title, to engineer a solution to her dilemma. The two of them swap attire, the eventual result being Louisa's marriage to Antonio and the duenna's to Mendoza. Another story line involves Jerome's son Ferdinand, who enlists Louisa's help in his pursuit of Donna Clara, whose affluent father wants her to enter a convent. For this task, Louisa must disguise herself again and engage in another round of merry hoodwinking. The couples bribe the tippling prior of a local monastery to perform the three weddings, which Jerome, deceived into compliance, blesses. Prokofiev described the entire farrago with characteristic brevity: "The subject is old and banal, but developed by the English dramatist with great humor and brilliance."[48]

The libretto fuses rhymed and unrhymed passages in accord with Sheridan's original. Prokofiev took the lead in translating, abbreviating, and assembling the text: many of the draft pages are in his hand alone; those in Mira's hand show his corrections and suggestions for alternate wording.[49] They worked from a typescript of Sheridan's original, with Prokofiev writing translations of choice passages in the margins along with occasional musical comments. Of the twenty-seven songs and ensembles composed (or borrowed) for Sheridan by the Linley father-and-son team, Prokofiev and Mira kept those six that motivated the plot either by their content, something that happens within them, or by their affect, their ability to sharpen the distinctions between the comical (physical) and lyrical (emotional) characters in the plot.[50] He considered retaining two additional songs—Clara's "By him have we love offended," and Antonio's "How oft, Louisa, hast though told"—but discarded them in an effort to avoid redundancy. He altogether avoided those that smacked of anti-Semitism, such as "Give Isaac the nymph who no beauty can boast."

Prokofiev devised the first three scenes of tableau 1 independent of the source text.[51] These scenes establish right at the start a slapstick parallel between catching fish and reeling in spouses. Scene 2 enhances the depictions of Jerome and Mendoza while also mocking, on a meta-operatic level, the familiar operatic practice of assigning leitmotifs to the individual characters. Prokofiev first highlights the verbal tics of the two old men, and then introduces those background melodic figures that will stutter alongside them as the plot unfolds. Scene 3 moves the drama from the comic to the lyric plane. Prokofiev introduces Ferdinand and his servant Lopez. The former speaks of his love for Clara as he bumps into Antonio, who speaks in turn of his love for Louisa. Everything proceeds according to opera buffa conventions until scene 4—the first scene that Prokofiev calibrated according to Sheridan's text. Here the conventions begin to undercut themselves: the music, hitherto content to support the action and allow the characters to take themselves too seriously, begins to interrupt and interfere with them. Masked figures—participants in the carnival season festivities that frame the central amorous intrigue—enter the stage to report that Antonio, who plans to serenade Louisa beneath her window, will not elicit a response from her, since "the little beauty is sound asleep" (krasotka krepko spit). The serenade continues, and Louisa, contradicting the maskers, rouses herself to sing along with Antonio. The maskers return, this time urging Jerome to grab hold of the "mewing," moonstruck Antonio "by the tail" (lovi yego za khvost). In scene 6, the maskers stage an eerie, Orientalia-laden nocturnal dance that has the dual effect of overshadowing the drama and transforming it. The operatic characters are confronted by their balletic doubles: they appear quite literally besides themselves. In scene 7, the maskers perform a second such dance as a riposte, on the comic plane, to Jerome's imprecations. The opening woodwind melodies, snare drum accompaniment, and concluding brass cascades come straight from Maurice Ravel's *Boléro*. Henceforth in the opera the dance starts and stops in obsessive, impulsive fashion, symbolizing a kind of mechanistic anamnesis. The music, which is associated with adolescent celebration, allows the older characters in the opera to reexperience their forgotten youth.

Tableau 1 (there are nine in all) concludes with another sublime exchange, this time between sound and vision. From the very outset of his work on the opera, Prokofiev intended to conclude scene 7 of the tableau with an

avalanche of euphoric brass and percussion sounds, and scene 8 with a murmuring fade-out. "The maskers disperse," Prokofiev specifies in the score, "it
is quite dark. New maskers appear. They are visible only in silhouette and
dance without making a sound."[52] The music suggests a departing carnival,
but the visuals indicate the opposite—that the carnival has only just arrived.
From this point forward, the mysterious fancy of the two dances infiltrates
the sung and spoken dialogue of the principal characters.

The integration of song and dance, like the integration of the plot with
meta-operatic interpretation, further attests to Prokofiev's aversion to stasis irrespective of the dramatic situation. In tableau 6, for example, Jerome
casually gives his daughter his blessing to wed Antonio amid the discordant
strains of amateur music-making. Jerome blows a minuet tune of his own
composition through a clarinet while berating two other musicians—a trum-
peter and a drummer—to play in tune and in time with him. Distracted,
he gives Louisa away to the person he does not want her to wed. The half-
comic, half-tragic pathos of the scene resides in his failed attempt to surround himself with the aristocratic décor of neoclassical dance. In the final
wedding scene, he sheds the pretense. Echoed by the chorus, Jerome sings the
words "I've fixed up my son, fixed up my daughter and, by the way, untied
my hands" (ustroil sïna, doch' ustroil, kstati ruki razvyazal) while tinkling
glasses of champagne. Having given up his career as a court composer in
pressed linen and a powdered wig, he entertains the crowd in much more
modest fashion by playing spoons.

Prokofiev explained his general approach to *The Duenna* on several
occasions in the Soviet press. In *Vechernyaya Moskva* he emphasized his
juxtaposition of episodes of amorous euphoria with a lampoon of institu-
tionalized religion and Catholic confessionals:

> One of the most lyrical scenes in the opera takes place in the
> garden of the convent, where the heroine [Louisa] dreams
> about her beloved. This scene is contrasted with another,
> Bacchic one in the cellar of a monastery. The monks drink
> wine and after a series of comic peripeteia here they wed
> the lovers. Among the characters of this scene are Father
> Benedictine and Father Chartres.[53]

Prokofiev prefaces this general remark by noting his reliance in *The Duenna*
on arias, ariettas, and various types of ensembles. He endeavored to preserve

the mixed-world, *theatrum mundi* features of his previous comic opera, *The Love for Three Oranges*, while avoiding its coarse declamation-based grotesqueries. The result is a blend of allusions to Mozart (*Così fan tutte*), Gioachino Rossini (*Il barbiere di Siviglia*), Richard Strauss (*Der Rosenkavalier*), Carl Maria von Weber (*Der Freischütz*), and, as Shostakovich pointed out in a review of the Leningrad premiere, Giuseppe Verdi (*Falstaff*).[54] These references do not just showcase Prokofiev's encyclopedic knowledge of the repertoire; they enhance the philosophical weight of *The Duenna*, infusing it with a sense of cultural breadth, Orphic mystery, and Platonic introspection. Of course, Prokofiev also quotes himself, assigning, for example, the tune of "Elle était fille, / Elle était amoureuse" from *Eugene Onegin* to Carlos, Mendoza's impoverished, down-at-the-heels companion. This character sings the tune to Louisa in the exact middle of the opera, reminding her that even if time does not seem to move, even if "it seems suspended in the air" (kak budto ono povislo v vozdukhe), it does in fact move, irrevocably so. The paradox of the score, one embodied in other Russian operas, is that this motion tends to be circular, rounded.

No work in his oeuvre better attests to Prokofiev's melodic brilliance and to the inspiration provided by his relationship with Mira. Indeed, that ingenuity draws attention to itself in the score. Melodies that a less-gifted composer would covet are no sooner introduced than swept away in the carnival season gaiety. Since, however, the opera is a meditation on both forgotten and recovered youth, the melodies inevitably return in the vocal lines and orchestral background.

The Duenna took five years to receive a premiere, and then became a fixture in the Soviet repertoire after Prokofiev's death. Its history speaks volumes about the cultural and political constraints of the Stalinist era.

Tolstoy's Novels to Music

The problems that delayed the premiere of *The Duenna*, and the problems that would delay the time-obsessed ballet *Cinderella*, for which Prokofiev also signed a contract in late 1940, pale in comparison to those associated with *War and Peace*, his most significant Soviet achievement and the composition that arguably defines his legacy. From 1941 to 1952, this opera, a setting of disparate scenes from Tolstoy's eponymous, serialized novel of 1863–69, dominated his thoughts. It became for him what the grand opera *Les Troyens* was to Hector Berlioz: the governing obsession of his career.

The history of *The Duenna* dovetails with that of *War and Peace*, which shows the extent to which Prokofiev continued, even in the wake of *Semyon Kotko*, to aspire to create an iconic Soviet opera, whether in the comedic or patriotic mode. Although his greatest successes came in other domains, opera was the one he most cherished. Seemingly helpless in the face of his own creative drive, his life became, like his art, a manifestation of contrast-driven dramaturgy.

Prokofiev expressed an interest in setting *War and Peace* to music even before his permanent relocation to Moscow. In 1935, while touring in Chelyabinsk, he informed the singer Vera Dukhovskaya that he "long dreamt about writing an opera on this subject," but banished the thought owing to the monumental amount of labor the project would entail.[55] Given that projects on a grand scale defined the Stalinist era, his fascination with the operatic potential of the novel increased, rather than decreased, over time. On April 12, 1941, he drafted an outline for the opera in a notebook. It included eleven scenes, the first detailing the visit between the Rostovs and the elder Prince Bolkonsky, and the last describing the French retreat and the liberation of Pierre Bezukhov. (Prokofiev also jotted down a note about "Prince Andrey and the oak tree," the barrenness of the latter at first symbolizing for the prince the confutation—the falseness—of his life. Later, the tree denotes the potential of renewal.)[56] Four months later, Prokofiev returned to the outline and fleshed it out, adding a prefatory episode at the Rostov estate. This twelve-scene outline became the basis, with reconfiguring and compression in the second half, of the first version of the opera, which the composer produced in piano score between August 15, 1941, and April 13, 1942. His rapid pace astonished his colleagues.

In April, however, Prokofiev had not yet committed himself to *War and Peace*; instead he found himself attracted to another Tolstoy novel, one that related, at least obliquely, to his spiritual beliefs: *Resurrection*. His interest in this work was brief but intense, and it was brought about by another eminent composer: Shostakovich. On October 14, 1940, Shostakovich had signed a contract with the Kirov Theater to write the music for an operatic version of *Resurrection* called *Katyusha Maslova*, after the novel's heroine. The libretto was written over the course of ten months by the playwright Anatoliy Mariengof, a member of the composer's social circle. Mariengof drafted the first act of the four-act libretto in January 1941, after which he requested an extension of the deadline until April, since he had been unable to consult sufficiently with Shostakovich. He completed the draft in

March. Once the Kirov Theater had vetted it, the libretto was forwarded to Glavrepertkom.[57] By this time, Shostakovich had decided against composing the opera.

Knowing something of the negotiations between Shostakovich, Mariengof, and the Kirov Theater, Prokofiev wrote to his rival asking him to confirm whether he was planning to compose *Katyusha Maslova*.[58] Shostakovich gave Prokofiev permission to pursue the project in his place. His strange, rambling letter reads in part:

> I won't evidently be writing an opera on the subject of *Resurrection*. But for now, I request that you keep this circumstance between us. For an entire series of reasons, it is very hard for me now to decline the opera formally. With me it has come about that, as they say, "If a claw is caught, the whole bird is lost." My librettist and great friend, the writer A. B. Mariengof, will be very hurt and offended by my refusal to work with him and thus I need some time for a gradual modulation. I ask you not to be angry at me for adding my Katyusha Maslova to your life. But my personality is such that I am sometimes quite incapable of rashly and drastically causing people pain. In this instance I can't bring Mariengof grief, since in the first place we are friends, but most important because he (Mariengof) is having a very hard time of it: his seventeen-year-old son very recently hanged himself.[59]

In the next paragraph, Shostakovich abruptly changes the subject to Prokofiev's *Alexander Nevsky* Cantata, critiquing what he considered to be an overemphasis on musical illustration at the expense of thematic development in the score, but he also expressed the hope that Prokofiev would earn a Stalin Prize for it. He ends by praising Prokofiev's Sixth Piano Sonata. Nothing further is said about Mariengof, his son, or his libretto.

One can only speculate about Shostakovich's and Prokofiev's fleeting interests in *Resurrection*. The plot centers on the self-indulgent Prince Dmitriy Nekhlyudov, who is called to jury to decide the fate of a prostitute accused of murder. He recognizes the defendant, Katyusha Maslova, as a former ward of his aunt's whom he had seduced, gotten with child, and who, unbeknownst to him, had been cast out of the house when her dishonor was revealed. Although innocent of the crime for which she was charged, Maslova is sentenced by the bumbling, mumbling jury to four years of *katorga*—penal servitude. Racked by guilt for the injustices he has committed against Maslova, Nekhlyudov trails her to Siberia, where he arranges for a commutation of her sentence. She is unmoved by his intervention and disdainful of his effort to save himself by saving her. Nekhlyudov takes solace in the Gospels, having learned that time cannot be rewound to undo past wrongs. He deduces that, without the liberating possibility of atonement, he must either walk away from his past sins or suffer the torment of eternal remorse.

Resurrection concludes in the same bleak geographical place as Leskov's, though not Shostakovich's, *Lady Macbeth of the Mtsensk District*. In the former, *katorga* enables spiritual rebirth; in the latter it does not. Both plots involve seduction and violence, but *Resurrection* explores modes of redemption, a detail that doubtless interested Shostakovich, who had restored himself to official favor with his Fifth Symphony. Prokofiev may have been attracted to the plot for personal reasons, not least of all its meditations on self-affirmation and self-forgiveness. In his libretto, Mariengof added a scene in which Maslova is reading *Eugene Onegin* in bed while Nekhlyudov prowls around outside her window.[60] Had he ended up working with Mariengof and set this scene, Prokofiev would doubtless have assigned it some of the music he composed in 1936 for Tairov's unrealized staging of *Eugene Onegin*.

He did not have the chance. Mira's father strongly advised him against the project: "No, not *Resurrection*," he told his daughter over evening tea, "but if Sergey Sergeyevich wrote an opera on *War and Peace*!"[61] The suggestion took hold, and Prokofiev discarded the mental outline of *Resurrection* for the drafted outline of *War and Peace*. Even had he ignored Abram's advice, however, he would not have been able to compose *Resurrection*. On May 10, 1941, Glavrepertkom told the Kirov Theater that Mariengof's libretto had been banned. The scenes of unjust imprisonment and the commentaries on the power of evil to nurture evil provided sufficient cause for annulling the project. Subsequent historical events would offer additional cause.

Evacuation

On June 22, 1941, Prokofiev and Mira received word from the distraught wife of the watchman at Kratovo that Germany had attacked the Soviet Union, launching an aerial bombardment on several cities in the dead of night

(4 a.m.). Eisenstein, who also resided in Kratovo at the time, confirmed the State Radio report. That morning Molotov had been notified by the German ambassador, Friedrich Werner von der Schulenburg, that owing to numerous violations of the nonaggression pact, including the buildup of Soviet forces along its borders, his nation had declared war. The six-month German offensive, dubbed Operation Barbarossa, involved three armies, which advanced simultaneously on Leningrad, Moscow, and Kiev along the entire eastern edge of the Soviet Union, from the Barents Sea to the Black Sea. Within a month, German soldiers occupied a massive area of the Soviet Union (twice the size of France) and would, by September 10, 1941, overtake the city of Smolensk, located just 250 miles from Moscow. Though anticipated by the Soviet government, the attack nonetheless came as a shock; Stalin did not address the nation about the siege until July 3.

Atovmyan reports that, as soon as the conflict began, the membership of the Union of Soviet Composers rallied in support of the Red Army: "The decision was made to mobilize all composers for the creation of anti-fascist songs," he recounts, adding that Muzfond was directed to "expand" and "hasten" its activities in support of the troops.[62] These songs, written by poets and composers working both together and apart, were to be sent to the front as fast as the soldiers and tanks. Mira recalls, in the blandest of terms, that Prokofiev refocused his activities in the summer of 1941, first composing

> two songs—"Song of the Brave," text by [Aleksey] Surkov, and a song to words by [Vladimir] Mayakovsky—these being the fastest means to respond to current events. Soon he began to write the orchestral suite *The Year 1941*, in which he was able to represent these experiences more fully. We also at this time found ourselves urgently drawn to *War and Peace*: the events described within its pages had become close and made an especially acute impression. The Committee on Arts Affairs backed the idea of writing a *War and Peace* opera and advised us to present a plan for a libretto.[63]

At the start of August, Prokofiev returned to Moscow to sign the initial contract for the opera. The Committee on Arts Affairs informed him that he, Myaskovsky, and other major Soviet composers and actors were to be evacuated to Nalchik, the capital of the Kabardino-Balkarian Autonomous Republic in southeastern RSFSR (the north slope of the Caucasus).[64] Prokofiev vacated the dacha and stayed for two days with Mira in the apartment of his former student Makarov-Rakitin, who had been conscripted. Before leaving for Nalchik on August 8, Prokofiev asked Lina whether she also wanted to evacuate. She decided to remain in Moscow with her children, then aged seventeen and twelve. Lina recalls Prokofiev being "distraught" on the day of his departure.[65] He left her some money and later the authorization, through Atovmyan, to collect his income from the Copyright Agency (Upravleniye po okhrane avtorskikh prav) and the Stanislavsky Theater.[66]

The trip to Nalchik lasted four days (the artist-filled train was welcomed by a brass band). Prokofiev and Mira settled in the Hotel Nalchik, while most of the other composers who had traveled with them ended up in the city's outskirts in the Dolinsk district. Prokofiev swiftly settled into work on *War and Peace*, drafting the first six scenes between August 15 and November 12 to a libretto that he and Mira extracted section by section from the source novel. Both the April and July outlines called for separating the peace scenes altogether from the war scenes; in the former (scenes 1–6), Prokofiev strove for intimate character portraits and, in the latter (scenes 7–12), for historical panorama. (The opera in this regard juxtaposes two different conceptions of dramatic time and space.) On November 15, 1941, Prokofiev played through scenes 5 and 6 for the first time for Mira, who marveled at the composer's translation of Tolstoy's conceptions of Natasha and especially Pierre into music.[67] The heroic attributes of the latter character increased as the score evolved, but he nonetheless kept his original comedic features. The growing, unspoken love between Natasha and Pierre in the first half of the opera struck an obvious chord with both Mira and Prokofiev, and they agreed that it would be prudent to create a broader, nationalistic parallel for it in the second half. They thus decided to have Field Marshal Mikhaíl Kutuzov allegorically take the place of Pierre in the battlefield scenes, and to have Napoleon substitute for Natasha's malevolent bigamist suitor Anatol Kuragin, for whom she betrays Prince Andrey. This latter character would broadly embody the hopes and dreams of the Russian people, finding, through anguish, supreme clarity of purpose.

Other activities in Nalchik included fulfilling commissions that Khatu Temirkanov, the chairman of the Arts Affairs Administration (Upravleniya po delam iskusstv) in Nalchik, "courteously and efficiently" doled out to him and the other distinguished artists who had suddenly appeared in his midst.[68] Prokofiev composed additional songs to texts by Mira—the words came after, rather than before, the music—and the aforementioned three-movement orchestral suite *The Year 1941*.[69] He also began work on his String Quartet on Kabardino-Balkarian Themes, for which Temirkanov offered an 8,000-ruble contract and useful source material: the transcriptions of regional songs and dances that had been made by nineteenth- and twentieth-century composers, including Sergey Taneyev, a pupil of Chaikovsky.[70] Prokofiev described the conception of this work in a routine overview of his wartime activities for Sovinformbyuro, the propaganda agency responsible for military-related information broadcast on Soviet Radio, published in Soviet newspapers, and translated into foreign languages.[71] In an article dated May 24, 1944, Prokofiev commented that Temirkanov proposed merging "new and untouched Eastern folklore with the most classical of classical forms—the string quartet." The idea intrigued him, but he worried that Nalchik audiences would not "understand and appreciate" his music, since, "excluding its excellent folksongs, Kabardinian musical culture, from a European musical perspective, remains undeveloped." Temirkanov frowned on the stereotyping, instructing Prokofiev to "write what you feel: if we don't understand your quartet at first, we will appreciate it later."[72]

Composed between November 2 and December 3, 1941, the String Quartet has a choreographic impulse: Prokofiev based the first movement on a dance for old men, "Udzh starikov," and a four-part song, "Sosruko," named after a Prometheus-like character from Caucasian mythology. The movement also includes, beginning at rehearsal number 5, a dance taken from Taneyev's 1885 collection "On the Music of the Mountain Tatars."[73] The second movement of the String Quartet features a haunting, ethereal version of a familiar dance called "Izlamey." It is contrasted, at rehearsal number 22, with a second borrowing from Taneyev's collection, an animated shepherd's song.[74] The third and final movement, a sonata-rondo form, evokes a generic mountain dance.

Geographical precision was not Prokofiev's first concern: the borrowed melodies are trans-Caucasian. He mimed, moreover, the sound of both a Ukrainian *garmoshka* (a unisonoric folk accordion) and a Turkish *kemanche* (a spike fiddle) in the score. Prokofiev shared his borrowed materials with Myaskovsky, who used them in his Symphony no. 23 (1941). Myaskovsky stylized the material; Prokofiev did as well, while preserving and enhancing its perceived archaisms. Myaskovsky branded Prokofiev's score "wild-eyed and fantastical" in his diary, and "monstrously, even 'nightmarishly' interesting" in a letter.[75] In February 1942, Myaskovsky petitioned the Stalin Prize Committee to honor the String Quartet, but Khrapchenko dissented, claiming that the work did not make a particularly strong impression on him (he heard only a piano reduction). Even if, as Myaskovsky put it to him, Prokofiev had been "working insanely, composing an insane amount of music," it was insufficient reason to award him a Stalin Prize, since other composers worked just as slavishly. Khrapchenko's protracted opposition to Prokofiev gradually dissipated; in the years ahead, as Prokofiev's political fortunes improved, the chairman of the Committee on Arts Affairs would recommend (subject to Central Committee approval) both First and Second Class Stalin Prizes for him. The turnaround was occasioned in part by a pleasant business meeting between the two of them late in 1942, the principal topic of conversation being *War and Peace*.[76]

For Derzhanovsky, who attended the September 5, 1942, premiere performance of the String Quartet at the Moscow Conservatory, the open fifth and open fourth accompaniments, the parallel sevenths and seconds, and the (occasional) pitch clusters brought to mind, at least in the first movement, the primal energies of Prokofiev's 1915 *Scythian* Suite.[77] (The German air assault that delayed the performance doubtless increased the sense of implicit violence.) Stravinsky's 1913 neo-nationalist ballet *Le Sacre du Printemps* furnished another, much less convincing, point of comparison. Some proof that Prokofiev sought to embellish the exotic effects of the work along neo-nationalist lines emerges from a comparison of the draft and final versions of the score. The first movement of the latter (in Lamm's hand) shows a marked increase in tempo over the former, which lends the sound a sense of aggressive abandon.[78]

On November 20, 1941, Prokofiev and Mira received word that they would be relocated by overnight train from Nalchik, then under threat from the Wehrmacht, to Tbilisi, the secure capital of Georgia. They arrived in Tbilisi on November 24, settling in another, less agreeable hotel room in the Hotel Tbilisi. Both of them had become increasingly worried about the welfare of their families: Mira had altogether lost contact with her parents, and Prokofiev had received only brief secondhand reports—chiefly from Atovmyan, with whom he communicated by letter and telegram—about the well-being of Lina and his children. He began to hear directly from them in the summer of 1942, and the news, as he anticipated, was dire. There was little thought of his family leaving Moscow for a collective farm (an option offered to the hard-up families of leading musicians), since they feared losing their apartment. And there was obviously no chance of escaping the cold and grinding poverty of the capital for what Soviet propaganda termed "American darkness."

Lina, Svyatoslav, and Oleg received direct financial support from Prokofiev during the war. Atovmyan documents the amounts he transferred to them on a monthly basis from Prokofiev's publication and performance honoraria. At times, Prokofiev cut back on his own expenses in order to support his family. In Tbilisi, he and Mira briefly subsisted on just 13 rubles a day, a meager sum, until payment arrived for the String Quartet.[79] There was little available in the state-run stores and rampant inflation in the unofficial peasant markets. To persevere, Prokofiev took out a series of short-term loans from Muzfond, using the funds to help himself, his family, and those of his longtime friends who found themselves in extreme hardship.

In Tbilisi, as in Nalchik, Prokofiev devoted the bulk of his working time to *War and Peace*, but he now began to tinker with the outline, conflating two scenes (7 and 8) into one and composing the remaining ones out of order. The decision to do so, he noted, allowed him to avoid "stumbling blocks."[80] On January 15, 1942, he completed the renumbered scene 9, which depicts the torching of Moscow by its own citizens and the freeing of Pierre; on March 20, he finished scene 11, which concerns the chaotic French flight from Russia. Only then did he turn to the intimate episode of Natasha at the bedside of the delirious, wounded Prince Andrey. In her memoirs, Mira chronicled her and Prokofiev's methodical work on the opera in minute detail:

> November 17 (Nalchik): Seryozha has started the opera's seventh scene—before the Borodino battle. I rewrote the libretto of this scene for him. We selected an apt folk-song from the collection *The Expulsion of Napoleon from Moscow* [*Izgnaniye Napoleona iz Moskvï*, 1938]: "Hark, the foreign locusts have already swooped down upon us" [Chu, i k nam uzh naletela inozemna sarancha]. It seems this text will be good for the chorus.

◆

> November 27 (Tbilisi): He is mulling over the seventh scene. I copied out of the novel the characteristics of several fig-ures: Matveyev and the peasant Fyodor—whom we named ourselves—and Tikhon Shcherbatïy. Seryozha proposes a

baritone for Matveyev, a tenor for Fyodor, and a bass for Tikhon. Fyodor derived from the cheerful red-faced soldier whom Pierre meets on the Borodino battlefield; Matveyev, from the handsome fellow whom the French executed in Moscow.[81]

◆

November 30: I'm working on the opera's eleventh scene (the French retreat). The libretto is proving difficult, since it has to be borrowed and fashioned into a whole from different parts of the novel.

◆

December 16: Recently the Nechayevs, Gauks, Aleksandrovs, Massalitinova, and both N. Ya. and V. Ya. gathered at Lamm's.[82] Seryozha played the second act of *War and Peace*. It seems to have made a strong impression. But Nikolay Yakovlevich apparently did not like Pierre, who turned out, in his words, "to be a true operatic hero—a tenor."

◆

December 18: I worked entirely on the eighth scene (Napoleon at Shevardino Redoubt) and read the libretto to Seryozha. We decided to put the scene aside temporarily and to incorporate some changes further on.

◆

December 20: Seryozha played through the first act of *War and Peace*. Gauk noted: "It reminded me throughout of *Eugene Onegin*, with its enormous internal purity." I finished rewriting the libretto of the ninth scene (Moscow).

◆

December 23: I looked through Tolstoy's four Books [*War and Peace*] to make sure that I hadn't missed anything crucial for the opera. It seems the libretto now has a firm plan with the scenes following each other in logical order. The spectacle needs to be unified, even if at the painful expense of many wonderful pages. These had to be excluded owing to the impossibility of accommodating them in the opera, even though it would be performed over two evenings. Seryozha is writing Prince Andrey's arioso for the scene Before the Battle of Borodino.

◆

January 5: I am writing the song about Kutuzov for the scene Before the Battle of Borodino. Seryozha often asks for changes to the libretto of this scene.

◆

January 14: Today Seryozha finished the song that opens the Moscow scene. He used authentic French material in it. Now I am faced with writing the text. Today I was occupied with the Kazak song for the Borodino scene. The song is folkloric, but I had to redo the words, in part because Seryozha assigned it a fixed meter, for which, accordingly, verses needed to be written. He jokingly calls me "my Baron Rosen," a reference to Glinka's librettist, who often had to write to preassigned meters. Seryozha at first indicated the alternation of strong and weak syllables in his meters— "U"—for me, but later on this seemed too imprecise. Two additional signs were needed: a strong-weak "$\underline{U}$" for those syllables with a medium accent, and "=" for those strong syllables that mark the peak of the phrase. Seryozha placed some of the weak syllables in brackets, which meant that I could use them or not use them as I saw fit; put another way, Seryozha could either add a note in these places or, alternately, assign a single syllable to two slurred notes. If a certain place required an open sound, he added to the relevant measure the letter "a," which precluded the use of syllables with the letters "ï" and "u." When I wrote the song about the Kazaks we talked about the coarseness of the rhyme between "Kazaki" and "v drake" ["Kazaks" and "in a fight"], but since it exists in an 1812 folksong we decided to keep it.[83]

Beyond Mira's continuing education in the art of text setting, these select remarks attest to the surefootedness of Prokofiev's initial approach to *War and Peace*, despite occasional demurring from colleagues. They also reveal that, from the start, he intended the opera to be a two-evening production that captured at least something of the scope of Tolstoy's novel. The thematic parallels between the first and second half of the opera needed to be explicit, Prokofiev realized, in order for audiences to perceive them. Moreover, Mira's reference to *The Expulsion of Napoleon from Moscow*—and, elsewhere, Mikhaíl Bragin's 1941 *Field Marshal Kutuzov (Polkovodets Kutuzov)*—indicates that the decision to enhance the patriotic content of the opera stemmed as much from the composer and his co-librettist as it did from the bureaucrats who would, in the period ahead, adjudicate it.

Prokofiev kept Khrapchenko apprised of his progress with the score, alerting him, on December 1, 1941, that he had completed the first and second acts (scenes 1–6), and notifying him of the imminent completion of the third and fourth acts on March 29, 1942. In between the two updates came the first concrete news on the whereabouts of Mira's parents (they had evacuated to Samarkand, Uzbekistan) and on the well-being of Prokofiev's family. The composer learned that his cousin Katya urgently needed material support, and he immediately arranged to transfer 200 rubles a month to her. Progress on *War and Peace* continued despite a week-long excursion, at the beginning of February, to Baku, Azerbaijan, where Prokofiev performed for a packed audience of servicemen at an army cultural club, and for a smaller general audience at the Philharmonic.

Prokofiev hastily arranged these concerts following the outbreak of an epidemic in Tbilisi, forcing him and Mira to vacate their hotel, which, the management told them, required decontamination. The trip to Baku provided an unexpected benefit: the directors of the Azerbaijan State Opera and Ballet Theater (Azgosopera), having heard about *War and Peace*, arranged a hearing of select scenes for March 2. Their interest in the opera, expressed by letter and telegram, spurred Prokofiev to complete it quickly. For dramaturgical advice, he turned to the musicologist Semyon Shlifshteyn, who was then serving as the senior consultant for music on the Committee on Arts Affairs.[84] Shlifshteyn lauded the "coordination of the music of the waltzes [which were extracted, as Gauk picked up, from *Eugene Onegin*] with the dramatic action" in scene 3, but recommended a reconception of scene 10 to include a much more explicit musical depiction of the burning of Moscow. Prokofiev took the advice, but decided against symphonic portraiture in the scene in favor of additional choral writing. He assigned Mira the meter for a central Chorus of Muscovites, which she began with the words "Our white-walled mother city" (matushka nasha belokamennaya).

Near the end of the scene he added another chorus, "In the dark and moonless night" (V nochku tyomnuyu i nemesyachnu), whose text derived from various "folksongs composed in 1812." Shlifshteyn lauded these changes, but then recommended an aggrandizement of scene 7. Heeding the request, Prokofiev excised the original opening folksong ("Hark, the foreign locusts have already swooped down upon us") and replaced it with a "large choral and symphonic episode" that necessitated, to Mira's chagrin, a complete rewrite of the libretto.

Though the opera remained incomplete, Prokofiev returned with it to Baku for the prearranged March 2 run-through. A larger than expected audience attended his recital of the finished scenes and discussion of the unfinished ones. (Prokofiev was embarrassed by the turnout, since, owing to a "shortage of nightingales," he had to warble through all of the vocal parts on his own.) Mira described the "plan for the libretto" of scene 11. She completed this libretto in the days ahead with the assistance of passages extracted from the hedonistic, bravado-laden memoirs of Denis Davïdov, a writer-soldier during the 1812 Patriotic War (he led a hussar regiment and was later promoted to the rank of lieutenant general in the tsar's command). The writing process assumed circular contours, with Mira consulting a jingoistic source—Davïdov's *Diary of Partisans' Deeds in the Year 1812* (*Dnevnik partizanskikh deystviy 1812 goda*, 1838) that Tolstoy himself had used.

The event was a success, and the directors of the Opera and Ballet Theater appeared eager to stage the entire opera. (An official hearing would be arranged in Baku for June 1.) There followed two weeks of revisions, and a further two weeks of discussion between Prokofiev and his colleagues as to whether the score required abbreviation: Myaskovsky convinced Prokofiev not to make even the slightest of cuts. On March 18, Prokofiev capped the highly cinematic overture, which had, in his words, "fermented unconsciously" for the entire day. It featured at its core "the theme of the peasant militia and Kutuzov," against which sounded melodic fragments associated with "Pierre's anxious thoughts, the poetic hopes of Prince Andrey, and the tearful Natasha." *War and Peace* merited a grandiose unveiling, but neither Baku nor the other city involved in the discussions about the premiere (Yerevan, Armenia) could, Prokofiev suspected, be counted on to realize it. He placed his hopes for a premiere on the Soviet cultural capitals, but in the mid- and postwar periods those hopes would be repeatedly negated.

Cinematic and Theatrical Diversion

During the period of his evacuation, Prokofiev weighed proposals to compose music for several films, and, despite his immersion in *War and Peace*, fantasized about other operatic projects, the most provocative being a large-scale revision of Mozart's *Don Giovanni* with the dialogue scenes either trimmed (Prokofiev asked Mira to decide where cuts might be made) or replaced with musical numbers in the style of his own Classical Symphony.[85] Despite regular address changes, occasional shortages of food, perpetual and frustrating shortages of manuscript paper,[86] constant worry about the welfare of family and friends, and a worsening of the headaches that had plagued him throughout his adult years,[87] he managed to compose more music in less time than at any other point in his career. Personal contentment abetted his labors, as did liberation from bureaucratic chores: the more he traveled, the more he lived for himself. Eclipsing his prodigious prewar levels of productivity, he fulfilled simultaneous commissions for disparate cinematic and theatrical works.

As he steeled himself for the first adjudication, in Moscow, of the piano score of *War and Peace*, he received an invitation from Eisenstein to relocate to Alma-Ata, nicknamed "Hollywood on the border of China," to collaborate on a projected two-part film about Ivan the Terrible. (The letter was hand-delivered to him in Tbilisi on March 23, four months after Eisenstein wrote it.) Taking into account the growing success of *Alexander Nevsky*— just the day before, he and Mira had been writing an article to be published before the April 28 New York City screening—Prokofiev accepted Eisenstein's invitation with enthusiasm.[88] He and Mira left Tbilisi for Alma-Ata on May 29, arriving there, after an exhaustingly protracted trip involving many stops, on June 15.[89] The Ivan the Terrible project, which occupied Prokofiev on and off between 1942 and 1946, differed markedly from the other propagandistic films for which he provided music during the war: *Kotovsky*, *Partisans in the Ukrainian Steppe*, and *Tonya*. Prokofiev also worked on an oft-postponed pseudo-biographical film about the Romantic poet Mikhaíl Lermontov, who was killed in a duel at age twenty-seven, breathtakingly young given his artistic accomplishments.

Kotovsky involves simple people receiving an education in the Leninist concept of justified warfare. This principle is felt before it is thought of as part of an intuited communal consensus. The positive characters in the film—like the positive characters in *Partisans in the Ukrainian Steppe*—experience a political revelation, one that might be coarsely compared to the spiritual revelation experienced by Konstantin Levin, the central figure in Tolstoy's great novel *Anna Karenina*. Near the end of the novel, Levin finally discovers the "truth," the "certainty" that he has long "needed but could not find for himself—a collective certainty, a universal agreement, beyond reason."[90] The "certainty" in this instance is faith-based: fulfillment resides in service to the greater good, to the divine potential of human endeavor. Levin, however, is a pre-revolutionary private landowner, not the manager of a Soviet collective farm or a munitions plant. Although he speaks with ever-greater conviction about the divine and the cosmic, his philosophy has a private, intimate dimension. In *Kotovsky*, as in *Partisans in the Ukrainian Steppe,* the pursuit of the good is defined using abstract public slogans: the progressive building of socialism, the subsequent striving toward communism. The individual stages on the path to the ideal are marked by increasing political awareness and the overcoming of internal and external obstacles.

The central question raised by the two films concerns their status as art. Beauty in the metaphysical sense of the term is absent, but these films fulfill the duties that Stalinist critics assigned to artistic creation. The films are not intended to entertain but to inform, to instruct; they replace aesthetic experience with ideological enlightenment and learning through example. "Art" in this sense consists of communicating a proper model for consciousness, and of promoting party-line conceptions of the good, the moral, and the just. Under Stalin, art was wrested away from the guidance of a communal consensus and placed in the hands of particular individuals, the chairmen of the Committee on Arts Affairs, who wielded great power over the artists under their control. The definitions of the good, the moral, and the just had bureaucratic origins.

Kotovsky purports to represent separate episodes in the real life of Grigoriy Kotovsky, a rough-edged, Chapayev-like rebel fighter from an agricultural region of Moldova and Ukraine known as Bessarabia.[91] After leading a peasant revolt against Ukrainian landowners in 1905–6, Kotovsky joined the Bolshevik movement, eventually becoming the equivalent of a general in the Red Army (technically speaking, the rank of general was not introduced into the Red Army until 1940). For his harsh actions against White Russians in the post-revolutionary civil war, he earned pride of place in the annals of Soviet history.

Prokofiev received the commission for the film from the director Fayntsimmer, with whom he had collaborated on *Lieutenant Kizhe* in 1933 and 1934. *Kotovsky* was one of three patriotic films released by the Alma-Ata studios in recognition of the twenty-fifth anniversary of the Revolution.[92] It was scripted by the Stalin Prize–winning writer Aleksey Kapler and starred the Stalin Prize–winning actor Nikolay Mordvinov. The plotline highlights Kotovsky's recognition of the cause, his moment of sureness, which inspires him to take up arms. He avoids what seems to be certain execution, escapes from prison, and leads a peasant militia to victory after victory in his Bessarabian homeland.

Kotovsky's devotion to his place of origins attests in the film to his status as a paragon of simple values, natural essences. The structural dominant of the film's soundtrack is an artificial, rather than authentic, folk tune, which sounds whenever the hero appears on screen or whenever his homeland is invoked. As the musicologist E. A. Vishnevetskaya points out, the "Bessarabian Song," which Prokofiev set to a straightforward text by Mira, stereotypically stresses the sixth and seventh scale degrees of the natural minor scale and the intervals of the perfect fourth and fifth.[93] It is first sung by the chorus, after which the melody mutates to different orchestral instruments, each charged with illustrating a separate element of Kotovsky's psychology. The uniqueness of the music lies in the manner in which it was recorded: Prokofiev instructed that the first clarinet, the flute, and the first bassoon be placed directly in front of the microphone to emphasize what Vishnevetskaya calls their "pastoral" timbre. He—or perhaps Fayntsimmer—also wanted the music to be performed with microtonal inflections, although these do not appear in the actual score.[94]

In the battle scenes, Kotovsky is represented both by the "Bessarabian Song" and a solo trumpet fanfare. The latter is heard in the background during the scene in which Kotovsky and his ideological teacher—Kharitonov—are freed from prison. The soundtrack crackles with "hurrahs" and includes fragments of two revolutionary songs, the "Marseillaise" and "Varshavyanka."[95]

The hackneyed quotations attest to Prokofiev's dutiful, if uninspired, approach to this film, which appears to have occupied very little of his attention during his time in Alma-Ata. The film was shot in the summer of 1942, a period in which, as noted, the composer was involved in several unrelated projects. The multitasking resulted in some unusual cross-relations. For the card game scene in *Kotovsky*, for example, Prokofiev decided to include a waltz that he had actually conceived and earmarked for act 1 of *Cinderella*. Titled "Cinderella's Departure for the Ball," the waltz provides ambience for an episode in the film that begins frivolously but ends menacingly. The evil landowner Karakozin is confronted by Kotovsky, who demands the return of the money that has been stolen from the peasant workers—money that the landowner and his associates, including a local priest, have squandered playing cards. The episode ends in violent mayhem, with Kotovsky freeing imprisoned workers and setting the landowner's villa ablaze.

Prokofiev re-scored the waltz for chamber orchestra, providing the cinematic version with a more "salon-like" sound.[96] The inclusion of an aristocratic genre within the episode establishes a contrast between the debased, decadent world of the landowners and the progressive, promising world of the rebels. In the ballet, the waltz is associated with Cinderella's desire for an escape into romance, and her entry into a realm of beauty that has the potential to transform life. This latter notion, embodied in the music and dance of an escapist work, runs counter to the aims of propagandistic films like *Kotovsky*, which privilege the practical over the sublime.

On October 3, 1942, Prokofiev provided a summary of his activities to Myaskovsky, who had been relocated to the high-altitude city of Frunze (now Bishkek), the capital of Kyrgyzstan. Prokofiev commented specifically on his work for the Alma-Ata studios, rather crudely boasting that "film work is engaging, profitable, and does not require much creative exertion, and Alma-Ata is a pleasant city full of money. Besides films, I am writing a small dramatic cantata and received a commission from Moscow for a sonata for flute and piano."[97] Though he described his activities in carefree terms, the composer took on the bulk of his film work out of a practical need to support his wife and sons, who were living in dangerous and uncertain conditions in Moscow. Indeed, no sooner had he completed *Kotovsky* than he turned his attention to *Partisans in the Ukrainian Steppe* and *Tonya*. He also had to contend with *Lermontov: Pages from the Biography of the Great Russian Poet* (*Lermontov: Stranitsï biografii velikogo russkogo poeta*). This last film was conceived long before the onset of the war. Upon departing Moscow, Prokofiev had every reason to think that he had finished with it; *Lermontov* proved, however, to be the most nettlesome, least rewarding project of his evacuation.

Death and the Poet

For the centenary of Lermontov's death, as for the centenary of Pushkin's, Soviet cultural agencies planned lavish tributes, the ulterior motive being the poet's reconceptualization along proto-revolutionary lines. On May 15, 1941, in Moscow, Prokofiev accepted a proposal to write the music for a stylized cinematic treatment of Lermontov's life. The mastermind of the project was a dashing young director named Albert Gendelshteyn, who in 1935 had collaborated with Shostakovich on the civil war film *Love and Hatred* (*Lyubov' i nenavist'*) and who seemed assured of a distinguished career. The script of *Lermontov* was written by the dramatist Konstantin Paustovsky, who based it on one of his own plays.

For Prokofiev, work on the project proceeded swiftly, though the same could not be said for his collaborators. Within a month, he had completed a piano score for the film and had enlisted Lamm to realize the orchestration.[98] Gendelshteyn, however, lagged with the filming. By June, he had shot only the indoor scenes of *Lermontov*; he had not yet relocated, as the subject matter demanded, to the North Caucasus to shoot the outdoor scenes. His tardiness sparked a miniature scandal in Soviet cinema circles, with one critic making it his mission to track the amount of money that the project was overbudget and to document the perceived ineptitude of the crew.[99]

With the outbreak of war on June 22, 1941, activity in the cultural industries came to a temporary halt, and Gendelshteyn was forced to rethink *Lermontov* from start to finish. Paustovsky made use of the hiatus to draft a new version of the script, one that, in response to his own critics, placed increased stress on the poet's nationalism and excised emotion from his death scene.[100] The script received official approval in February 1942, at which point work on the film resumed. Prokofiev turned his attention back to the film in late May, while stationed in Tbilisi.

In the revised script, Lermontov is transformed from a dissolute fop into a heroic Russian patriot. He is represented as a key figure in the campaign to defend and expand the nation's southern borders. Having been dispatched by Tsar Nikolay I to serve in the Tenginsky infantry regiment, the poet defies his hesitant commander to lead a charge against fortified Circassian positions. Lermontov crosses a treacherous mountain pass on his trusty steed, all the while evading lethal volleys from above and to the side. Based on this and other battle scenes, one of the film's reviewers compared the poet's creative legacy to that of a brave Red Army soldier. "There exists in our army a fine and wise tradition (it began in the Tenginsky regiment, where Lermontov served as a lieutenant): if a soldier dies a hero, his name is heard along with the names of the living at morning and evening roll call." Just in case the point is missed, the author of the review repeats that, like a great soldier, a great poet "is immortalized in the memories of the living."[101]

Prokofiev's May 23, 1942, cue sheet contains twenty musical numbers, the most important from a narrative standpoint being the polonaise, quadrille, and three waltzes ("Youth," "Mephisto," and "High Society") of the two ballroom scenes.[102] He also composed a contradanse for the film, but it is not listed on the cue sheet, and evidently dates from a later phase in the writing process.[103] For the early scene depicting Pushkin's death, Prokofiev conceived a series of stark chords, each punctuated with a portentous pause. Later in the film, he planned to quote both from court music of the period and from an old soldier's song, "How delightful the Moscow road" (Moskovskaya slavna put'-dorozhen'ka).[104] The court music quotation would have prefaced the scene in which Lermontov, having fallen into disfavor with the son of the French ambassador Ernst de Barant, accepts a challenge to a duel, which ends in a feeble draw. The soldier's song quotation would have followed the scene in which the Tsar, having grown tired of the irreverent, recalcitrant poet, sends him to the Caucasus to serve in the Tenginsky regiment. Prokofiev sought to reprise the "Youth" Waltz in the scene set in the spa of Pyatigorsk, where Lermontov stops for rheumatism treatment en route to the regiment. The tragic climax of the film finds the poet involved in a dispute with Nikolay Martïnov, a retired officer. Less out of wounded pride than long-standing hatred for the poet, Martïnov challenges him to a duel with pistols, the result being Lermontov's ignoble death. For these scenes, Prokofiev conceived two passages of music, the first relating the poet's "spiritual state before the duel," which is "not tragic, but life-affirming." The second passage would have "derived from the music of Pushkin's death."[105] The fates of the two writers are immortalized as one.

The cue sheet also specifies a quotation from *La Muette de Portici* (*The Mute Girl of Portici*, 1828) by Daniel Auber. The curious decision to borrow from this opera came not from Prokofiev but Paustovsky, who set the third scene of the film (and the source play) at a St. Petersburg summer theater where *La Muette de Portici* is playing. Lingering at the entrance to the theater, Lermontov muses on the state of affairs in Russia with his friends. His elevated speech strikes the fancy of two aristocratic ladies:

> LERMONTOV: One recent night, I went on horseback to Tsarskoye. A thunderstorm was approaching. Before me in the darkness stood large, thick crops, thickets of century-old trees ascended, and it seemed to me that I was moving through a prosperous nation destined for happiness.

FIRST LADY: How poetic!

SECOND LADY: Extraordinary!

LERMONTOV (smirking): But the summer lightning flashed very brightly, and I saw each ear of wheat in the dusty fields. The ears of wheat were few and meager. Thus the illusion of a prosperous and happy nation vanished.[106]

Throughout the script, Paustovsky emphasizes Lermontov's disdain for the St. Petersburg elite. (In the scene quoted above, the banter, dress, and pretentious mannerisms of the theatergoers are subject to scrutiny.) Disregard for the theatrical artifice of aristocratic life is contrasted with positive portrayal of the natural world, which serves as a somewhat tired metaphor for harmonious social relationships and inner peace. In keeping with the standard readings of Lermontov's creativity, Paustovsky asserts that the poet found a balance and harmony in the natural world that he could not find in his interpersonal relationships. In the film, nature serves as the poet's muse and ally: his death, unmarked by his colleagues, provokes thunder and lightning.

The reference to Auber's *La Muette de Portici* in the film, moreover, places Lermontov's thinking in a proto-revolutionary context. The opera concerns an uprising against a corrupt aristocratic order, and portrays a mute peasant girl, someone who communicates through gesture alone, as the voice of progressive moral and social values. The libretto for *La Muette de Portici* was rejected by French censors, who insisted on changes to the plot and characters. This fact was not lost on Paustovsky, who represents, within his script, Lermontov's various feuds with the Russian imperial censors.

On May 25, 1942, Prokofiev wrote to Gendelshteyn expressing his happiness that work on *Lermontov* had resumed following the relocation of the assigned studio for the film (Soyuzdetfilm) to Stalinabad (Dushanbe), Tajikistan. Prokofiev lamented, however, that the news had reached him on the eve of his departure from Tbilisi to Alma-Ata. He assured the director that he would finish the music for the ball scenes, adding that the director could, if needed, increase the length of the dances by reprising their openings. The first sign of their eventual falling out comes when Prokofiev beseeches Gendelshteyn to restore the first scene of the film, which had been excised from the rewritten scenario, but which the composer found "very effective," since he had managed to use the melancholy melody he had quoted from *La Muette de Portici* in the leitmotif of Lermontov's immortal beloved (Varvara

Lopukhina).[107] Prokofiev ends the letter by reporting that a portion of the score had evidently become lost in transit from Tbilisi to Stalinabad. He asks that his assistant Lamm be paid an additional 200 rubles to reconstruct it.

Gendelshteyn's June 18 reply exasperated Prokofiev. The director reported that the theater scene could not be restored, and then asserted that, of the music Prokofiev had sent to him, only the "Mephisto" Waltz and the quadrille suited his needs. Gendelshteyn concluded that the polonaise lacked the imperial majesty merited by the St. Petersburg setting. The director also requested that the "Youth" Waltz, which Prokofiev had decided to remove from *Lermontov* and assign to *War and Peace*, be returned to it.[108] Prokofiev refused, and then inflamed the situation by offering a critique of Gendelshteyn's revised musical plan for the film, which included, in his words, "a heap of trifles" that no listener would be able to remember.[109] Prokofiev proposed that the film include only two waltzes and one polonaise to make the soundtrack more accessible and memorable. He pointed out that, in his experience, the varied repetition of a small cluster of themes over the course of a film enhanced its narrative flow.

There ensued a dispute over Gendelshteyn's decision to combine four numbers from the soundtrack into one. Prokofiev unnecessarily reminded the director that the film would be edited several times before its release, and thus the soundtrack should remain as adjustable, or "portable," as possible. "Your method would work if your montage was carved out of stone once and for all," he declared, "but this doesn't happen in the film business."[110] Then, in a July 11 letter, Prokofiev critiqued the visual content of the film. Upon reading the revised script, he griped that it was rife with historical inaccuracies, or "blunders," particularly when it came to the depiction of the habits and decorum of the Russian nobility. "Children," he remarked, "would not be allowed to play race-and-catch at a gathering where dignitaries like [Lermontov's benefactor Count] Benkendorf play cards."[111] Gendelshteyn pledged to correct the mistakes.

In their subsequent letters, Gendelshteyn continued to press Prokofiev about the "Youth" Waltz, but Prokofiev remained adamant about not restoring it to the film. "Alas," he told the director,

> that which has deceased cannot be resurrected, for it has crossed once and forever and conclusively into another world. Back in April, I presented the opera *War and Peace* (in which the waltz plays a very significant role) to the

Committee on Arts Affairs. It was first heard by [Khrap-
chenko's assistant Aleksandr] Solodovnikov, and then by
Khrapchenko and [the conductor Samuil] Samosud, and
then accepted and approved for staging. Now that a number
of theaters are heading into rehearsals, it is no longer possible to consider using the waltz material to other ends.[112]

In fact, Prokofiev was vastly overstating the rehearsal situation, and in
an effort to appease Gendelshteyn, the composer came up with a second
"Youth" Waltz for him, but Gendelshteyn considered it unsuitably repetitive. The relationship between them sank to name-calling:

I hope that the public, hearing the waltz in the film, will dis-
agree with the cantankerous director. Perhaps you haven't
learned, or more likely, that I haven't explained to you one
aspect of my conception, namely that, when in the further
development of the plot this waltz has to serve as a leitmotif, illustrating deeper moods, I will change it accordingly, in
the same fashion that I changed the theme that I sent to you
from [La Muette de Portici], whose original version sounds
relatively superficial.[113]

Upset that Gendelshteyn had twice criticized his music, Prokofiev was
all too happy to tell him on November 16, 1942, that he could not travel to
Stalinabad to complete the score, since he had undertaken another film project, *Partisans in the Ukrainian Steppe*, for the Ukrainian-born director Igor
Savchenko, which would require him to travel to Semipalatinsk, Kazakhstan.
Prokofiev suggested that Vasiliy Nechayev, a composer in desperate need of
work, be enlisted to complete *Lermontov*. Contact between Prokofiev and
Gendelshteyn ceased. The director did not in the end hire Nechayev, who
was living alongside Myaskovsky in distant Frunze, to finish what Prokofiev had begun. He instead entrusted the task to Venedikt Pushkov, a little-
known composer who had the advantage of already being in Stalinabad and
involved with the studio.

Mired in theater projects, and overwhelmed by the succession of acceptable and unacceptable commissions for propaganda films, Prokofiev opted—
as in the case of *Kotovsky*—to sacrifice creativity for expediency. In *Partisans
in the Ukrainian Steppe*, he recycled entire sections of his orchestral suite

The Year 1941, made elaborate use of a well-known Ukrainian folksong, and quoted the iconic melody of the "Internationale." He also included thematically related material from his opera *Semyon Kotko*, which bore the scars of a traumatic period in his career, but which, his colleagues constantly reminded him, merited revival. The opening cello melody of act 1, scene 1, which shows Semyon returning to his Ukrainian birthplace after four years at the Romanian front, became the music for the grave scene in *Partisans in the Ukrainian Steppe*. As Vishnevetskaya points out, Prokofiev first recycles the melody intact, and then transposes it up an octave, into the register of a lament. To further enhance its tragic pathos, he adds a tonic pedal point in the brass and a restless eighth-note pattern in the inner clarinet line.[114]

Partisans in the Ukrainian Steppe narrates a struggle between pro-Soviet Ukrainians and an invading German regiment for control of their land. The collective-farmer hero of the film bears much in common with the village-farmer hero of *Semyon Kotko*. Similar parallels can be found between the positive and negative figures in each work. The principal difference concerns the time of the action: the film is set at the beginning of a fictionalized World War II, whereas the opera unfolds at the end of a fictionalized World War I. Led by Salïvon Chasnïk, the director of a collective farm, the partisans first seek to thwart, and then to avenge, the ransacking of their village by the Germans. Salïvon loses his crops in the rampage, and takes out his ire on the self-serving speculator Dolgonosik, who has colluded with the Germans against the partisans. Salïvon confronts Dolgonosik, in the act of fleecing hapless peasants of their possessions, and forces him to hang himself, since he is not worth the cost of a single bullet made by an honest worker.

The film is cast in three episodes, each introduced by a Ukrainian peasant chorus, whose strains can be heard over the battle noises. The singing carries through the scene of the burning of the crops and, later, the scene in which the peasants, having been forced by the Germans to dig their own graves, are executed by a firing squad. Salïvon's wife, Pelageya, is among the victims.

The dismal struggle attains a climax in the middle episode. Singing a folksong at the top of his lungs, a grizzled, bearded partisan named Taras lures the gullible Germans, pied piper–like, into a minefield.[115] Following the slaughter, the exhausted, wounded old man returns to his hideout. Before falling asleep, he tucks his remaining grenades under his body, a final gesture of self-defense. He is discovered by a stone-faced German officer, who expresses disbelief that Taras has acted alone. The officer kicks him in disgust, and the grenades explode. The final scene of the film cuts from the charred Ukrainian steppe to the snow-covered Kremlin. It is the anniversary of the Revolution. Over the radio, Salïvon hears a morale-boosting speech by Stalin. The voice of the "father of the peoples" carries over hill and dale, and spurs Salïvon and his peasant brigade to keep up the fight.

The mind-numbing plot structure of the film is underscored by the varied repetitions of Taras's folksong, first on the diegetic level, as a symbol of the old man's cunning revolve, and then on the nondiegetic level, as a marker of the inbred heroism of the Soviet (Ukrainian) people. Prokofiev assigns two partial versions of the folksong melody to the violins.[116] The playful character of the second version—it unfolds in scherzando thirty-second notes—contradicts the sober events unfolding on the screen; one senses that the music, like Taras, is in a state of denial. Taras sings the folksong in a cheerful, energetic manner; his pluckiness illustrates that he is younger than the young, much in the same way that Lenin, according to a Soviet slogan, was "more alive than the living."[117] Having shared his political insights with Salïvon, the old man escorts the Germans to their death, fully aware that the deception will cost him his own life. The absorption of the folksong into the film's background scoring evinces that Taras's heroism will not be forgotten. It is the embodiment of *zeitgeist*, of the inexorable movement of history through the Revolution, the civil war, and World War II to Communist utopia.

Prokofiev, as noted, did not dwell on *Partisans in the Ukrainian Steppe*; his approach to the film was as schematic as the plotline—a point borne out by the autograph score of the grave scene, in which the composer dovetails a self-quotation from *Semyon Kotko* into one from *The Year 1941*.

Tonya

Excluding the Eisenstein projects, the most striking, if obscure, of Prokofiev's wartime films is *Tonya*, which stars the stage and screen actress Valentina Karavayeva, who earned instant celebrity (and a Stalin Prize) for her touching, magnetic performance in the contemporaneous *Little Masha* (*Mashenka*, 1942). The scenario of *Tonya* was written by Boris Brodsky for Prokofiev and the prolific director Abram Room. Although it was filmed and flown from Alma-Ata to Moscow for presentation to cultural officials, it was not released to the general public, for reasons that remain somewhat unclear.

Brodsky drafted the scenario in the spring of 1942, thereafter forwarding it for approval to the Committee on Cinema Affairs. After two readings the Committee told Brodsky that the scenario was "Good!" but needed to be "shorter and tenser," with "more meaningful short phrases."[118] Even before this verdict was reached, however, Brodsky had begun to rethink his text, excising one of the battle scenes and collating lines of dialogue, the result being a terse script for a thirty-two-minute film.

The scenario emphasizes person-to-person dialogue, a consequence of its original conception as a radio drama. Tonya works long, exhausting hours as a telephone operator, a position that requires fast fingers and multitasking, but no physical labor. We soon learn that she has a physical handicap, a stunted leg that has prevented her from enlisting in the Red Army. Tonya works with a girlfriend, Klava, who is as unmotivated as she is unappealing, and who ties up the phone lines flirting with male callers. There are two other characters of significance: Tonya's husband, Vasiliy Stepanovich, a newly recruited gunner for the Red Army, and Tikhon Petrovich, an old Bolshevik who oversees the operations of a train station.

The action takes place in an unnamed Soviet town, which has a telephone office, a train station, and a square lined with leafy trees. Tonya takes a break from work to stroll with her humorless, steel-willed husband, who announces his departure for the front, and enjoins Tonya to seek help with her day-to-day responsibilities from the station master. The next scene shows her going for another walk, this time with the stationmaster, who seeks to assure her of the value of her work to the Soviet cause. "If I was whole," Tonya comments in reference to her handicap, "you know I'd have gone to the front. But I'm only a telephone operator." The old Bolshevik fumes: "Banish those thoughts! They're good for nothing! Shameful, truly!"[119] Later, back at work, Tonya hears startling news: German soldiers have invaded the town, and the populace has begun to evacuate. Klava takes the first train out. The stationmaster takes the last train, but not before pleading with Tonya to leave with him. She tries three times to leave, but the switchboard continues to light up, and her dedication keeps her on the job.

The drama of the ruthless German takeover of the town is manifest in a series of chaotic telephone calls to a factory, a school, a hospital, even the NKVD. The commander of the local Red Army battalion phones in. Perplexed to learn that Tonya is alone, he asks her to serve as an advance post for the Soviet counterattack. "Describe everything you see from the window," he beseeches her, "but please don't be too afraid." "I'm not afraid,"

Tonya deadpans. "I'll look around once more, just don't leave the phone."[120] Peering through bullet holes, she pinpoints the locations of the German soldiers. The coordinates are relayed by the commander to his chief gunner, none other than Tonya's husband.

Soviet mortars explode with unexpected precision in the town square, destroying the German ordnance and filling the skies with debris and smoke. Tonya is thrown from wall to wall in the telephone office, but manages, despite near loss of consciousness, to retain contact with the regiment. Her husband grimaces as he orders the gunners to fire, for he recognizes that his wife's fate is in his hands. Despite the din of the battle—the sound of shattering glass and collapsing walls—Tonya's voice is overheard by a German soldier who has descended the damaged staircase behind her desk. Brandishing a rifle, the intruder orders her to shut down the switchboard. Tonya ignores the order, choosing instead to inform her husband, "I'm alive, Vasya, I'm all here. You haven't left? You're doing swell. Keep beating them, Vasik."[121] Tonya is shot at point-blank range; the sound of the rifle reverberates down the telephone line.

The film's denouement involves the Soviet retaking of the town and a closing episode at Tonya's gravesite. Ringed by an honor guard, the commander affixes one of his own medals, the Order of the Red Star, to the gravestone. Tonya's husband keeps shell-shocked vigil during the eulogies. One of the soldiers describes the martyred heroine "as tall and shapely, like a poplar tree, and beautiful."[122]

Even from this brief synopsis, it will be clear that Brodsky's scenario furnishes a convincing example of Socialist Realism, which became the official method for Soviet cinema in January 1935. It centers on a figure who, heeding the advice of a stern ideological tutor, overcomes her anatomical and psychological inhibitions to play a significant role in Soviet military history. Excluding the heroine, the characters in the film are stock types whose dependent thought processes reflect class consciousness. For the positive figures, there is no room for foreboding and second-guessing: Vasiliy pulls the trigger knowing that Tonya might be in the line of fire; the stationmaster keeps the trains running even as tanks shell them. The scenario involves simple metaphors: a change in the weather augurs the German invasion; the town's trees, under which Tonya first kissed her husband, are torched in the Soviet invasion. The socialist realist emphasis on comprehensibility (dostupnost' massam) is manifest in the direct visual contrast between the storm-cloud-covered German offensive and the sunshine-drenched Soviet counteroffensive. This counteroffensive unfolds with improbable ease, and then cuts to the extended epilogue at the graveside, where the political lessons of the film are stressed, and viewers are expected to reflect on the visual events for their own ideological betterment.

From this simple, even banal start, the scenario was subject to considerable manipulation, first by Room and then Prokofiev. The director and composer developed an audio-visual outline for the film that altered the sequence of events and the behavior of the characters. Klava was renamed Katya, and assigned a sidekick, Anya, who both bid a worried farewell to Tonya in the opening scenes. So as not to overstress the dullness of Tonya's telephone office duties, Room moved the narrative swiftly into the battle scenes through the use of inset titles. The second shot sequence, "The Russian People Abandon the Town" bleeds into the third, "The Dugout." The former shows the stationmaster gathering his belongings (the most valuable being a portrait of Gorky, credited with inventing Socialist Realism); the latter introduces us to the commander of the Red Army and Tonya's husband. Tonya appears as if in a dream in the action scenes, rising from a faint as the Germans begin their attack and whispering to her spouse in the shadows during the Soviet response. At the end of the film (during a long-distance, medium-range, and then close-up shot sequence titled "Tonya's Grave") the heroine's photograph comes to life and she is heard saluting her husband for his bravery.

However clichéd, the nonreality of this episode brings to mind one of Room's early experimental films, the little-known formalist masterpiece *A Strict Youth* (*Strogiy Yunosha*). Completed in 1936, at the onset of the Stalinist purges, this film was banned for ideological flaws, the most blatant being the representation of a future society whose citizens doubt, rather than uphold, totalitarian ideals. The film scholar Jerry Heil interprets it as an "undelimited dream-state...with a central 'dream-within-the-dream' of extreme artifice."[123] Heil notes that, following Room's denunciation, the director ended his flirtation with formalist methods: his subsequent films *Squadron No. 5* (*Eskadril'ya No. 5*, 1939) and *Wind from the East* (*Veter s Vostoka*, 1940) solidly promote wartime values. *Tonya* further attests to Room's change in direction.

It is nonetheless arguable that the ending of *Tonya* bears a trace of *A Strict Youth*. The "extreme artifice" of the grave scene betrays two other general features of Room's style: his reliance on words, rather than images, to ground his films in reality, and his stress on the texture of the voice to communicate psychological characteristics.[124] The central episodes of *Tonya*, moreover, are cyclical in nature, with the same telephone calls being made over and over again, taking on greater nuance and feeling.

Although Tonya symbolizes the bedraggled motherland and its bedraggled inhabitants, their presence is not actually felt in the film. The Soviet people—often depicted in artworks of the period as a suffering but resistant entity—do not play a role in *Tonya*: they are neither seen on-screen, in the diegetic realm, nor are they heard off-screen, in the nondiegetic realm. In accord with the pro-female orientation of Room's previous, full-length films, the nineteen-year-old heroine of *Tonya* is a physically weak but mentally robust figure.[125] She becomes an ideal, yet not abstract, emblem of the future perfect Soviet citizen, a model for 1942 filmgoers to adopt. She does not mimic the wartime struggle of the Soviet masses; rather, through the example of her heroism, she defines this struggle.

Like the *Tonya* cue sheet, which is included as Appendix B of this book, the score bears a September 1942 date. Prokofiev did not realize the orchestration himself, but as was his time-saving habit, enlisted Lamm for the task. His draft plan for the score (jotted down on an envelope glorifying Stalin), had ten parts:

1. Military march, then [the music of] the heroine, 50 seconds
2. [Tonya descends the] stairwell
3. Song, 160 seconds
4. Kat[ya] (from the overture), exit of the second girl (similar)
5. Military interlude, entrance of the Russians ("Tonya, it's you!")
6. Third military interlude
7. Train departure: the Russians abandon their hometown
8. The German pulls out his notebook
9. Tonya's death—5 convulsions
10. Graveside honor guard[126]

With the exception of the third item on the list, the song, this plan follows the plot of the film. The opening phrases of the song, which Prokofiev included in his *Seven Mass Songs* of 1942 under the title "A Warrior's Love" (Lyubov' voina), saturate the entire score.[127]

Upon conversing with Room, Prokofiev expanded and extended the score, adding an overture, a second farewell episode, and military action motives. The latter include a five-measure trumpet fanfare used for the scrolling text sequences, and ascending chromatic scale segments used for the stock footage of Soviet cannons being moved into position. The invading Germans, unsurprisingly, are represented by a repeating, one-measure motive built around the interval of the augmented second, a symbol, in nineteenth- and twentieth-century Russian music, of preternatural malevolence.

Prokofiev's emphasis, however, was clearly on the song, which he doubled in length while revising the draft score, and which he used in different textless variations in different scenes. When the film was edited, footage featuring the song was cut and the score lost cohesion. In an October 20, 1942, letter to Abram Mendelson, Prokofiev discussed the cut:

> The director Room finished his film *Tonya*, but the artistic council [*khudozhestvenniy sovet*] cut 200 meters, and the song to Mira's words suffered. But since the song itself was praised, it was relocated to the *konferans*. (Short films like *Tonya* are usually paired together and premised by so-called *konferansï*, i.e. slogans that move against a musical backdrop. In this case they move against the backdrop of two verses from the song.) Room has personally taken the completed film to Moscow to show to the administration [of the Committee on Cinema Affairs].[128]

Besides the opening title sequence, the song is heard (without words) in the episode showing Tonya working in the office and in the death scene. Its most prominent features are the descending interval of the minor third and its inverse mirror image: the ascending interval of the major sixth: chromatic inflections of the pitches that fill in these intervals suggest, in tandem with changes in timbre and rhythm, the heroine's fleeting feelings of despair, anxiety, and defiance.[129]

From their written remarks, it becomes clear that Prokofiev and Room intended the song to occupy an alternate time and space continuum than the rest of the soundtrack, which has an essentially illustrative character.[130] The number would fade in during a scene of humdrum activity, achieve full volume when the Germans are routed by the Red Army (in a fast-forward episode called "Vasya finishes off the enemy"), and fade out as the Soviet flag is slowly hoisted over the town. The text, written for Prokofiev by Mira, is found in the short score but not the orchestral score. The third strophe, from number 15 in the short score, captures the general sentiment:

At the hour of mortal battle the motherland summons
Her loyal son to provide a blood oath
To destroy the black regiments
And lead the Motherland like Suvorov!

◆

Klichet Rodina v chas smertnoy bitvï
Klyatvu krovnuyu ey vernïy sïn' dayot
Budut chornïye polki razbitï
Po Suvorovski za Rodinu vperyod![131]

This unambiguous exhortation is matched to a stripped-down accompaniment: sustained root position and first inversion D-major tonic chords passing to other chords built on the mediant, submediant, dominant, and subdominant. The texture expands through added thirds in the orchestral accompaniment and leaps of a fourth and sixth in the vocal line. Prokofiev assigns the third strophe a march-like tempo, with two cornets and a euphonium enhancing the armed services sound.

Overall, the song creates a peculiar impression. The music is unprepossessing, as though encoding within itself the comparative innocence of the newlywed nineteen-year-old heroine, but it is cast as a dirge with aspirations toward epic grandeur. Although linked with Tonya's sacrifice, the melody sounds outside the visual frame to take on a general meaning about masculine, rather than feminine, duty to the cause. The looped melody affronts the fast-pace visual action, suggesting the cessation of time associated with static camera shots. Reverberating throughout the soundtrack, the song takes on the guise of an air-raid siren, a repeated broadcast. Prokofiev wrote the music, of course, but it sounds like a poor copy of him. It suggests a composer seeking to limit his range of effects, to become, as it were, impersonal.

Why, then, was *Tonya* filmed but not released? There is no single explanation: ideological deficiencies, reduced distribution budgets and, as so often the case with Prokofiev, unhappy timing all contributed to the film not glowing on Soviet screens. In terms of its ideological deficiencies, one notes that the heroine dies at the hands of the bumbling, screwball Germans: hers is a passive end. Had the Red Army accidentally detonated Tonya, the film would have accorded with the definition of an "optimistic" tragedy, a prime tenet of Socialist Realism.

The music of *Tonya* was completed almost three months before the scenario was taken up by the Committee on Cinema Affairs. The bureaucratic delay irked Prokofiev: it was only after his intervention that the scenario was in fact adjudicated. On November 21 he petitioned Mikhaíl Tikhonov, the head of Mosfilm, for information about

> the fate of the picture *Tonya*, for which I have written the music. If deemed viable, then all for the better. If, however, it definitely won't see light of day, be kind enough to let me know, so that I can weigh my options.[132]

Prokofiev did not hear back from the studio about *Tonya* and did not refer to it again in his correspondence. By the end of November the film had for all intents and purposes been shelved; it remains unclear if Prokofiev received the 6,000-ruble payment stipulated in his contract for the score.[133] Although short wartime films, most often distributed in collections called "Battle Film Albums" (Boyevïye kinosborniki), served a useful purpose for the Stalinist regime, their production was curtailed in the fall of 1942, the low point of the Soviet war effort.[134] *Tonya* became the first half of an album titled *Our Girls* (*Nashi devushki*). The second half was the peculiar twenty-two-minute film *Once at Night* (*Odnazhdï noch'yu*), directed by Grigoriy Kozintsev. It concerns a female collective farmer who must decide which of the two Russian-speaking airmen who ask her for protection is a Nazi spy; her overriding concern, however, is her ailing sow Masha. This film, more so than *Tonya*, came in for criticism from the censors, who branded it "pathological"; Denise Youngblood, the source of this information, speculates that if *Tonya* had not been bundled together with *Once at Night*, it might well have been released.[135]

Antokolsky

The prohibition of *Tonya* was a comparatively minor disappointment for Prokofiev, whose wartime labors raised his stature within the Soviet musical world, allowing him to dictate both the volume and content of his commissions. His finances, if not his material circumstances, greatly improved in 1942, and he began to reach out in earnest to those of his friends who had suffered personal losses or found themselves without a source of income. Prokofiev showed, for example, extreme concern for the welfare of the widow of Demchinsky, who informed him, to his horror, that his close friend had died of hunger on February 16, 1942, the ghastly nadir of the Siege of Leningrad. On September 14, the grief-stricken, traumatized Varvara Demchinskaya wrote a tender letter to Prokofiev reminding him of the profound affection that Demchinsky had felt for him throughout his life. Her loss was his loss. "You were a part of Borik," the widow offered. "How he loved your family; with what love he spoke about your sons. Where are they now? If he knew my lot, even his philosophical peace of mind, which withstood an agonizing death, would be shaken. Don't ask me about his death. Sometime, if I see you, I'll tell you about it myself."[136] Prokofiev maintained an empathetic correspondence with the widow until 1947, much of it centering on her unsuccessful effort to turn the scenario of "The Craftsmen of Palekh" (Palekhovskiye kustari), one of Demchinsky's literary projects, into a film.

The composer likewise supported the widow of his longtime assistant Derzhanovsky, who died unexpectedly in Zagorsk on September 19, 1942. Myaskovsky broke the news to him. In a belated letter of condolence to Yekaterina Derzhanovskaya, Prokofiev deemed it "very shameful" that the Union of Soviet Composers "did not arrange an evening in V[ladimir] V[ladimirovich]'s memory, but don't grieve this... V. V. played a unique role in literary, musical, and concert life. But the perspective is still too close and people fail to see V. V.'s true significance. They will come back to his name, and this is much more important than any memorial concert."[137] As with Demchinskaya, Prokofiev kept in contact with Derzhanovskaya until 1947, often sending her money.

In this last letter, Prokofiev updates Derzhanovskaya on his musical activities, specifically mentioning his *Ballad of an Unknown Boy*, which he composed in piano score between August 12 and October 15, 1942, in Alma-Ata. Prokofiev prearranged the 12,000-ruble commission for this work—a cantata scored for soprano and tenor soloists, chorus, and orchestra—with the Committee on Arts Affairs.[138] Shlifshteyn, the work's dedicatee, facilitated the commission. Although Prokofiev did not finish the orchestration until the summer of 1943, *Ballad of an Unknown Boy* seems to have been conceived in honor of the twenty-fifth anniversary of the Revolution. In a March 8, 1942, letter sent from Tbilisi to Atovmyan in Moscow, Prokofiev addressed the circumstances of its conception while also prearranging an additional commission with Muzfond:

> Shlifshteyn said that the Committee on Arts Affairs will
> commission either a symphonic work or a cantata for the
> 25th anniversary of October. Independent of this I have
> begun several things—an 8th Sonata, a suite from *Semyon
> Kotko*, and a suite from *War and Peace*. I would be grateful
> if you gave me a commission for one or two of the afore-
> mentioned works.[139]

When he finished the piano score, he sent a letter to Shlifshteyn worriedly
seeking confirmation that the first installment of his honorarium for *Ballad of
an Unknown Boy*, 4,200 rubles, had been given to Lina. He expressed confidence that the cantata, a "very energetic and dramatic work," would "affect
the listener," but he nonetheless decided to postpone orchestrating it in favor
of more important tasks: writing the overture to *War and Peace* and orchestrating its last two scenes. "Let the cantata mature," he told Shlifshteyn,
"and it will be clearer to me how to orchestrate it."[140] The manuscript of the
piano score includes, on the back of the first page, a list of the percussion
instruments that he intended to use in the cantata; the actual orchestration
did not begin until June 25, 1943, in Novosibirsk. It was finished on July 28
in the Ural Mountains city of Molotov (henceforth Perm). Prokofiev turned
the cantata over to a short-term assistant, the Kirov Theater concertmaster
Mikhaíl Karpov, for copying, and then, on August 17, dispatched a letter to
Khrapchenko requesting a November or December premiere.[141]

Ballad of an Unknown Boy is based on an eponymous text by Pavel
Antokolsky, a prolific poet who joined the Communist Party on the eve of
the German invasion, and who, in the first year of the Soviet struggle, compiled a patriotic, mixed-genre collection entitled *Iron and Fire* (*Zhelezo i
ogon'*, 1942). The publication of "Ballad of an Unknown Boy" in the January 26, 1942, issue of *Literatura i iskusstvo* (Literature and Art) preceded the
death of Antokolsky's son, an anti-tank gunner, at the front after less than a
month of service.[142] Prokofiev read the poem in Tbilisi, thereafter describing
it to Sovinformbyuro as an

> anxious story about a boy whose mother and sister were
> killed by fascists, eradicating his happy childhood. The shock
> to his spirit matures him, and readiness for action ripens
> within him. During the German retreat from his hometown,
> the boy detonates a car containing fascist commanding

officers with a grenade. The boy's name and fate remain
unknown, but word of his brave deed spreads from the rear
to the front and beckons forward.[143]

Even in this official context, Prokofiev unmasks the ideological underpin-
nings of the poem: the boy does not have a father, thus his initiation into the
struggle occurs without a mentor. Nature offers the substitute, "just like in a
fairy tale," Antokolsky writes in the third stanza, "autumn walked alongside
him in order to cover his tracks." In the sixth stanza, the imagery is inverted:
the tale of the boy's deed spreads through the ranks, itself becoming a fairy
tale. Time, moreover, is made circular: the heroic legend that the boy creates
hastens him forward; he fashions and fulfills his own historic calling.

The cantata arguably captures this sentiment, but Prokofiev sensed that
it would be panned by the Committee on Arts Affairs, commenting, in the
aforementioned letter to Derzhanovskaya, that nobody "will make head or
tail out of it without my involvement; last January [1943], Shlifshteyn didn't
understand a thing and NYaM [Myaskovsky] only politely mumbled through
his moustache." These points pertain to the piano score only. The completed
work did not receive a premiere until February 21, 1944; Gauk conducted it
at the Moscow Conservatory, although Prokofiev's preferred choice had been
the more exciting and exacting conductor Yevgeniy Mravinsky. Myaskovsky,
who worried that the cantata "wouldn't take," owing to the "very idiosyncratic interpretation by the performers," called the premiere a "success, but
not a clear one."[144] He made his comments in private. In public, Shostakovich
called Prokofiev's creative method into question, deriding the emphasis in the
cantata on "accurate musical illustration of the text" at the expense of the
"integrity of the musical form." For Shostakovich, the cantata offered a cinematic impression: it comprised "a series of unrelated musical 'stills.' "[145]

The cantata's music is nondevelopmental, but it does cohere, and it
offers a powerful propagandistic statement about the surface anxieties of the
war and the higher truths that will vanquish them. The opening measures,
depicting the German invasion of the Soviet town of "B," are dominated—
both in the hobbled, labored accompaniment and the disjointed, discordant
vocal patterns—by the intervals of the minor second and major seventh. The
march is hazily cast in A minor, with the tonic pedal pitch briefly embellished
with a rising whole-tone scale in sixteenth notes—a glint of sorcery. With
the exception of two minuscule alterations, Prokofiev set Antokolsky's text
intact, generating awkward melodic lines from the awkward word choices:

"Mannequin behind mannequin," the Germans travel "bulkily along the dirt."[146] The introduction of the boy's theme, a simple cadential gesture sung by solo soprano, marks the beginning of extended crossover in the score from nonfunctional (A-minor) to functional (A-major) harmonic writing.

Prokofiev does not explicitly represent the positive hero: for obvious programmatic reasons, this character exists in the cantata more as an invisible concept than a tangible object. His part is not sung but embodied in the orchestra's primal forces. Rehearsal number 20 introduces a persistent three-pitch ostinato pattern that denotes the boy's pursuit of the Germans, and rehearsal number 29 inaugurates an exceedingly graphic orchestral representation of the horrors of the occupation of his hometown. The grenade throw is marked at rehearsal number 48 with a blast of white (key) light: a C-major chord, spread over six octaves. Prokofiev thereafter begins to smooth out the disjointed, discordant vocal patterns; he also harmonizes the hobbled, labored march of the opening measures, reprising it at rehearsal number 49 as part of a sensational cadential progression in C major, one that harmonizes the tonic (C) and subdominant (F) pitches along with their chromatic substitutes: C sharp and F sharp. The apotheosis, occupying rehearsal numbers 58–60, features a comparable progression that facilitates a modulation from C major to A major. Within Prokofiev's expanded conception of tonality, this progression is functional. Those nondiatonic pitches that customarily facilitate modulations—the lowered second scale degree, the raised fourth scale degree, and the lowered sixth scale degree—become part of the governing pitch collection. A major, in short, is enriched to include B flat, D sharp, and F natural.

Ballad of an Unknown Boy depicts a passage from darkness into radiance and chronological time into mythological time. Prokofiev does not purge the score of dissonance; rather, he renders the dissonance consonant. Evil becomes a fleeting, transient phenomenon. In the world of his music, as in the world of his faith, the higher, nobler instincts of humankind triumph over the lower, baser ones. The greater purpose cannot be dissipated.

Committee on Arts Affairs Evaluation

Ballad of an Unknown Boy was the last work completed in full by Prokofiev during his evacuation. Along with labor on this score and the cluster of film projects, Prokofiev began to revise *War and Peace* based on the evaluation of the piano score he received from the Committee on Arts Affairs. The detailed

May 10, 1942, assessment, compiled by Shlifshteyn and prefaced by a June 19 letter from Khrapchenko, reached him in Alma-Ata on July 6. Prokofiev finished the bulk of the requested revisions between August and October, updating Shlifshteyn of his progress each week by letter or telegraph.

Khrapchenko's letter, thin in concrete detail but thick in political import, established the groundwork for Shlifshteyn's recommendations for tilting the drama away from the quadrangular peacetime relationships between Natasha, Andrey, Anatol, and Pierre toward the broader wartime struggle between Russia (Kutuzov) and France (Napoleon). Khrapchenko argued that

> From our point of view (I'm speaking of my opinion and those of a group of my comrades, constituted from a joint hearing and assessment), you no doubt succeeded with the lyrical scenes of the opera. The story of the relationship between Andrey Bolkonsky and Natasha is expressed in music of profound artistic conviction. There are many wonderful passages, enthralling in their warmth and musical expressiveness. The lyrical pages of the opera offer rich material for performers, who will be able to "sing to their hearts' content."
>
> However, the second part of the opera, dedicated to the events of the Patriotic War of 1812, caused us serious doubts.
>
> The people's scenes in an opera about the Patriotic War cannot help but occupy a significant and, one could say, predominant place. It stands to reason that the issue is not one of quantitative correlation. The fundamental tone of the work is what matters. The people's scenes should be a distinct leitmotif, bringing all of the visual action to a climax. Unfortunately, this does not occur in the opera. The individual people's scenes in the opera are not, first and foremost, organically integrated with the overall progress of the action. They exist in and of themselves, in isolation.[147]

Shlifshteyn developed and embellished these brief points as follows:

> I will begin with the music, depicting the internal world of the characters. Everyone liked this part of the opera and it

can be said that it received unanimous approval. Your lyrical side has at last been recognized. For my part I will note
that you succeeded wonderfully with Natasha and Bolkonsky (Pierre to a significantly lesser extent). All of Natasha's
and Andrey's music in the 1st scene is true poetry. Natasha's
arioso in the 2nd scene is outstanding in its beauty and vocal
breadth; the entire 3rd scene (Bezukhov's ball) is exceptionally poetic; and Natasha's arietta is marvelously touching.
Then the following waltz and the episode of Anatol's declaration to Natasha—again, pure poetry, no matter what
kind. Everyone I showed it to was ecstatic. Whoever the
future soprano turns out to be, [Natalya] Shpiller or [Yelena]
Kruglikova, she will thank you for Natasha. And you don't
often hear that coming from vocalists. The 5th scene (the
"explanation" between Pierre and Natasha) leaves a very
good impression. The characters' personalities are represented expressively, particularly [the troika driver] Balaga
in the 4th scene.

   The essential inadequacy of this scene (also the 2nd
and 6th scenes) *is the abundance of conversation.* The episode about the defrocked priest [presumably the character
who will marry the bigamist Anatol and Natasha across the
border] held little musical interest for me and no dramatic
importance. The conversation beginning with the words
"Where's Khvostikov?" to the end of the scene seemed completely unnecessary.[148]

There follow some quibbles about specific lines of text, including the wrong-
headed assertion that the "cries of the delirious Andrey of 'piti, piti' and 'ti
ti'" in scene 9 would occasion laughter, and thus needed to be "replaced or
removed." Prokofiev left the episode intact, embellishing Andrey's extravagant recitation of the uninterruptible and uninterpretable "pi" and "ti" syllables with an offstage chorus of altos that expresses, on the one hand, his
disorientation and, on the other, his crossover into another world; the task of
the chanting, accordingly, is to articulate the transition from a physical to a
metaphysical condition, feverishness to pellucidness. The pseudo-conscious
admixture of musical and verbal utterances articulates something akin to the
experience of a severe migraine (such as the composer himself suffered) or, as

Taruskin proposes with reference to Tolstoy's novel, the hissing, ticking, and whining noises associated with tinnitus.[149] Gradually, Andrey experiences heightened consciousness, much as his nation does. Over time, Prokofiev would enhance the impact of the scene by adding five more measures for the offstage chorus and a reprise of the waltz that occasioned Andrey's amorous first meeting with Natasha.[150] Andrey recalls these and other sounds from his past life, but he cannot pull them into the present and define them. The scene becomes an echo chamber.

Shlifshteyn's remaining comments emphasize the need to enhance the patriotic and populist appeal of the opera. Scenes 7 and 10 seemed, in his opinion, most in need of enrichment along these lines:

> Now to the part of the opera that is inseparably tied to the subject of the Patriotic War of 1812, a subject that, *as Mikhaíl Borisovich Khrapchenko rightly indicates, should govern the performance*. There's a lot of good music in scene 7. The very beginning of the scene (B-flat minor), representing Borodino Field, creates a strong, impressive image. The entire episode of the approach of the Russian troops leaves a strong impression. The outstanding music for Kutuzov, the chorus of the popular guard, the Cossack song—all of this radiates power and authentic Russianness.
>
> *The inadequacy of the 7th scene is the presence* (chiefly in the first half) *of a large number of conversational episodes*. For me Pierre and Fyodor's conversation about death (the purpose and general dramatic conception of this episode is not clear), Andrey's question about the Masonic fraternity, and [Lieutenant] Dolokhov's dialogue with Kutuzov were uninteresting and unnecessary.
>
> *The nature of the representation of the common people raises serious objections (this again concerns the first half of the 7th scene)*. All of those "ish', tï," "ekh, vazhno," "dyaden'ka," "tyaten'ka," "mus'yev," "khfedor" and the like could possibly, albeit in a very small dose, serve as local color adornments of the musical depiction of the people, but by no means as its essential features. Moreover, in the entire first half of the 7th scene, with the exception of the B-flat minor chorus of the popular guard, the people appear

in the guise of some folkish "khfedor" [Fyodor], oh so kind and simple-hearted. *Where are the wonderful people Kutuzov speaks about* ("A wonderful people; the beast will be wounded by the whole mighty force of Russia"), and where is the power of the people in the music?...

The same thing in the 10th scene. Instead of the naive "wrap-up" (the entire episode with Pierre), *here it is desirable to have music of broad, mighty breadth, actual folk music* such as you have in your *Alexander Nevsky*. *The victorious people and their exultation need to be shown.* [The leader of the popular guard] Denisov, [the villager] Vasilisa, and Kutuzov must be presented to the listener in their full stature. Your Vasilisa is no more than a generic figure, but you *need to show this Russian woman's heroic character, so that associations arise within the listener between her and other revered, regular people, present-day avengers: Zoya Kosmodemyanskaya, Liza Chaykina, and others.* Likewise, the listener should discern in your Denisov the many heroes of the Patriotic War against Hitlerism, which will enter into the history of our people as their supreme patriotic and valiant struggle in their pursuit of happiness. The entire intimate world of this scene should cede to the expression of the people's essential nature.[151]

The key for Khrapchenko and Shlifshteyn was not to soften the image of the Russian people and to have their climactic choruses express partisan steadfastness, demonstrating that only a beast can wound a beast, only a thug can catch a thug. Prokofiev's real-life models were to be the young female guerrilla fighters Kosmodemyanskaya and Chaykina, hardened saboteurs who succeeded (before being captured and suffering hideous deaths) in destroying German weaponry and communications.

Mira fretted about the potentially debilitating workload occasioned by the requests for revisions, recalling Prokofiev mockingly muttering to himself at his desk: "Write, write, write write...write write write write."[152] On August 10, 1942, he hurriedly informed Khrapchenko that he had "finished the revision of the seventh scene; I'm now working on the scene of Moscow [aflame]."[153] On November 16, he submitted that he had completed the last item on his list of changes: establishing the importance of the Russian people to the action in a heroic choral epigraph.[154] Having consciously reconfigured *War and Peace* along Musorgskian lines (the rewritten "Moscow Aflame" scene absorbed features of the "Kromi Forest" episode in Musorgsky's *Boris Godunov*), Prokofiev arranged to leave for Moscow on December 15 to participate in its second adjudication, a prearranged, closed-door affair before what would prove to be a skeptical crowd.[155] Indeed, the best that Prokofiev would be able to claim for *War and Peace* by the end of the year was the forthcoming publication, on Atovmyan's initiative, of ten arias and choruses in collotype—hardly the resplendent unveiling the opera deserved.[156] To his dismay, he was asked to rename it *Natasha Rostova* in recognition of the fact that it lacked the scope of Tolstoy's novel. This he adamantly refused to do, since the bulk of his revisions had involved enhancing its historical grandeur.

Abbreviated Homecoming

In Moscow, Prokofiev stayed at the National Hotel; despite returning home, he remained an evacuee. The widow of Zinoviy Feldman (the composer who had scored Prokofiev's 1939 music for the physical culture spectacle) invited him to a subdued New Year's Eve gathering in her apartment. There he reunited with Atovmyan, who had spent part of 1942 shuttling between evacuation points as part of his duties for the Union of Soviet Composers, and with some of the artists (including Myaskovsky) with whom Prokofiev had stayed in Nalchik and Tbilisi. The actress Valeriya Massalitinova commented that Prokofiev looked thin but otherwise well.

Moscow existed in a state of siege, with returning citizens subject to interrogation at perimeter checkpoints and blackout regulations requiring the blanketing of windows at night. Amid extreme shortages of provisions and sporadic services, cultural life endured, becoming more rather than less relevant as the war raged. Prokofiev devoted the bulk of his time promoting *War and Peace* (on January 16, 1943, he performed excerpts from the score to those members of the Bolshoy Theater collective who had returned to the capital); he also advised Richter on the preparation of the Seventh Sonata for the January 18 premiere. (Richter recalled that the meeting was businesslike, save for the trifling fact that the two of them bumped heads while trying to repair a pedal on the piano; he also claimed, at odds with the chronology, that he learned the Seventh Sonata in a few days.)[157] Before Prokofiev's return to Alma-Ata, the musicologist David Rabinovich, who attended the Bolshoy Theater run-through of *War and Peace*, suggested that he undertake a revision of *Semyon Kotko*, which he felt had increased in topical relevance since the time of its removal from the Stanislavsky Theater repertoire. Rabinovich recommended "replacing the prologue and parts of the fourth and fifth acts," so that the opera ended "on a tragic plane, with the murder of Sofya, for example."[158] Absorbed elsewhere, Prokofiev dismissed the advice.

Prokofiev arranged to leave Moscow for Alma-Ata on January 23, but ending up delaying the departure until the start of February. Upon arriving in the Kazakh capital on February 13, he resumed work on the Ivan the Terrible project and *War and Peace*, taking into account both Eisenstein's recommendations for further thematic changes to the opera and those of the Bolshoy Theater conductor Samuil Samosud, who became a prominent, if inconsistent, advocate of the opera in the years ahead. During the spring, the editing of *Lermontov* at long last came to an end, the result being a beautiful cinematic patchwork. Prokofiev and Mira saw the film for the first time on July 28, the month of its general release. As testament to the vagaries of their existence, they saw it neither in Moscow nor in Alma-Ata but in Perm, where Prokofiev had been summoned to recommence work on an oft-postponed project: the ballet *Cinderella*.

He learned about the release of *Lermontov* from the local Perm newspapers, and he had no idea how the protracted dispute about the soundtrack had been resolved. Upon seeing the film, Prokofiev discovered that, of the pieces that he had provided for it, the polonaise, the contradanse, the "Mephisto" Waltz, and the second "Youth" Waltz had all survived the final edit.[159] Pushkov, the other composer participating in the project, supplied background music for the two duel scenes, a folksong for the central episode in the Caucasus, and an additional waltz. Prokofiev deemed the additions adequate, but blanched at the "mixture of his music with that of another composer."[160]

Released two years after the centenary of the title character's death, *Lermontov* received scant attention in the press, but great attention in official circles. The film was condemned, the result being Gendelshteyn's banishment from the elite studios; he spent the rest of his career making documentaries. A Sovnarkom document dated July 21, 1943, summarizes the reaction: "At the conference of film dramatists this film was harshly criticized, with the leading directors voicing regret that its creators 'rendered' the subject matter 'obscene.' It is no wonder that Soviet viewers have not accepted this film and have not gone to see it."[161] Of necessity, those who reviewed *Lermontov* in the press followed the official line. The most incisive of these reviews came from Viktor Shklovsky, who wrote at length on cinema in addition to his vaunted literary criticism. In a July 25, 1943, review in the newspaper *Trud* (Labor), Shklovsky labeled *Lermontov* "philosophically deficient" owing to its failure to provide the kind of "historically authentic" image of the poet that the Soviet populace "needed."[162]

Despite the prominence of the soundtrack, Shklovsky does not address it, though the cognitive dissonance that stems from the conflation of Prokofiev's neoclassical dances and Pushkov's neo-romantic dirges would seem to be prime interpretive fodder for a theorist of his stature. The score of *Lermontov* is nothing if not an example of unusual stylistic contrasts. On their own, Prokofiev's dances establish the film's central themes: Lermontov's extreme isolation from Russian aristocratic life and the aristocracy's coarse disregard for his talent. The polonaise, a musical emblem of triumphant tsarist militarism, opens and closes the scene in which Lermontov hears the awful news of Pushkin's death.[163] He alone is affected: the ladies and gentlemen of the court continue their indifferent whirl. The "Mephisto" Waltz dominates the second ball scene, in which Lermontov is pulled away from settling an argument with a diplomat, an unhappy portent. The scene is constructed in such a fashion as to signal Lermontov's forthcoming rendezvous with fate. Of the revelers, he is the only one without a mask; the poet is exposed, susceptible, it would appear, to the workings of Machiavellian—or "Mephistophelean"—forces. The frantic pace of the framing sections of the waltz and the chromatic descents assigned to the solo violin in the middle section enhance the tension of the scene.

But it is the indifferent whirl that beguiles. It suggests more about Prokofiev's creative approach and outlook than the astonishing propagandistic particulars of *Kotovsky*, *Partisans in the Ukrainian Steppe*, and *Tonya*. Prokofiev moved from place to place, project to project in 1942 and 1943, but rather than hampering his creativity, the disruptions appeared to drive it. In Atovmyan's words, "Prokofiev worked at the time with, I would say, rabid passion."[164] As part of his internal time-saving mechanism, he did not allow himself to dwell on the blind spots in his personal affairs. Work was his obligation, and he honored it with something akin to the Christian Science tenet that "constant toil, deprivations, exposures, and all untoward conditions, *if without sin*, can be experienced without suffering."[165] But suffering aside, Prokofiev was reaching the limit of his endurance.

Lina and Mira

Prokofiev lived in Perm from late June to early October, after which he returned to Moscow, in the same hyper-energetic frame of mind, to begin to reassemble his previous existence. Excluding his January visit, Prokofiev was one of the last of the evacuated composers to make it back to the capital.[166] Atovmyan, who seems to have expected Prokofiev to return much earlier, greeted him at the train station on October 5.[167] The government, which had itself relocated during the worst phase of the Great Patriotic War, advertised the cultural revival of Moscow to the world as a sign that the defeat of Hitler was imminent.[168] By the end of 1943, the upper hand in the conflict had moved for good to the side of the Soviets, with the Red Army repelling the Wehrmacht kilometer by kilometer along the entire stretch of the eastern front. The staggering failure to conquer Stalingrad (now Volgograd) and the horrendous human losses incurred in the effort to retain control of Kursk broke the back of the German campaign.

Prokofiev's return to Moscow was not self-willed: in Perm on October 2, 1943, he received a telegram from Vladimir Surin, deputy chairman of the Committee on Arts Affairs, summoning him to the capital to participate in the all-important competition for a new Soviet anthem, one that would replace the antiquated "Internationale," which had been in use since the Revolution.[169] (Surin, whose position on the Committee exceeded that of Shlifshteyn, signed off on the commission for *Ballad of an Unknown Boy*.) The authors of the text of the anthem, Sergey Mikhalkov and Gabriel El-Registan, believed that the task of writing the music should be assigned either to Shostakovich or Prokofiev, the best composers in the nation. To this end they wrote a letter to Marshall Kliment Voroshilov, the chairman of the Anthem Commission. Voroshilov dismissed the petition, resolving that, although "Shostakovich and Prokofiev are truly the most renowned composers of our day," the competition would involve "all of the composers of the USSR (perhaps even non-composers will participate), and the one who provides the best music for the anthem will be the author of this historic work."[170] In the end, some two hundred composers participated in the competition, and Prokofiev, like his colleagues, found his work intensely scrutinized. He introduced the first draft on October 10 to Shlifshteyn and Rabinovich, who "seemed to like it."[171] Khrapchenko, however, asked that the music be simplified and written with "greater sincerity." The next evening, Prokofiev wrote a new version, which both Surin and Khrapchenko approved. His entry did not, however, make it to the final and third round of the competition at the Bolshoy Theater (the entries were performed by the Red Army Chorus before Stalin), and he knew, by October 13, that the entries of Shostakovich and Yuriy Shaporin were considered more successful.[172] In the end, and after considerable infighting, the award went to Aleksandr Aleksandrov for his adaptation of a preexisting Bolshevik song to Mikhalkov and El-Registan's text. In 1945, Prokofiev would participate—as he had to—in a similar competition for an anthem for the RSFSR, though the outcome, despite two rewrites, would be the same.[173]

His involvement in the competition took a novel twist in December, when he enlisted the orchestrator Dmitriy Rogal-Levitsky to assist with the reconstitution of the orchestration of his ballet *The Tale of the Buffoon*, which the Kirov Theater had offered to produce before even becoming familiar with the music.[174] The offer, which Prokofiev received back in Perm, amounted to a bribe: hoping to steal the seemingly imminent premiere of *War and Peace* away from the Bolshoy Theater, the Kirov offered to resurrect a forgotten work from his Parisian youth. Prokofiev, however, did not have a copy of the then-unpublished orchestral score with him. "The sole orchestral manuscript, my original, was destroyed in Berlin during the bombings," he speculated. "On my instruction they searched for it there but did not find it. I assume, though I can't be sure, that it burned up."[175] Rogal-Levitsky hesitantly accepted the challenge of reconstituting the score based on the orchestral suite and the piano score, which Prokofiev managed to locate. The two of them met punctually—work time, Prokofiev insisted, must not be wasted—to discuss the project until March 16, 1944, at which point Rogal-Levitsky received notice that he had been appointed, by none other than Stalin, to undertake a new orchestration of Aleksandrov's prize-winning anthem since Stalin disliked the original one. Hearing the news, Prokofiev joked: "Now I have nothing to fear and can entirely relax about *The Buffoon*, since it is in sure hands, the hands of the 'State orchestrator.'"[176] Meantime, the Kirov Theater had quietly dropped its offer to perform the ballet. Rogal-Levitsky, who had been working on the orchestration without payment or even a contract, received Prokofiev's blessing to move on to other things.

Prokofiev did not have a permanent home in Moscow during this period, which forced him to reenact the hotel-based existence he had had in the Caucasus, Alma-Ata, and Perm. From October 1943 to January 1944, he and Mira lived in a single room with a piano in the Hotel Moscow (Moskva), an imposing concrete fortress located adjacent to Red Square (it was constructed in 1935, demolished in 2004, and recently reconstructed atop an underground parking garage). In February, according to Rogal-Levitsky, Prokofiev relocated to the Metropole Hotel and after that to the Savoy, his accommodations in this last hotel being much more modest than in the previous two.

Irrespective of events in his own unsettled life, Prokofiev remained extremely concerned about the well-being of his family, especially after he learned, on May 19, 1943, in Alma-Ata, that Oleg had contracted diphtheria.[177] In response, he immediately transferred the funds needed for his hospitalization to Lina. On June 5, she informed him by telegraph that Oleg's condition had improved, though he remained under observation for abnormal heart rhythms. July 24 brought the distressing news from Svyatoslav that Lina had contracted the same illness. On this occasion, Prokofiev asked Atovmyan to provide the needed funds for the treatment. Svyatoslav contracted tuberculosis in the autumn, and the family's health and general nutrition (their access to restricted meal halls) remained a pressing concern. He appealed to Khrapchenko, Sovnarkom, and the Union of Soviet Composers for assistance. On June 4, Khachaturyan, the deputy chairman of the Orgkomitet (Organizing Committee) of the Union and a Prokofiev ally, pledged to ensure that his family had adequate support.

According to a July 19, 1968, interview of Lina by Malcolm Brown, Prokofiev began to visit his wife and children following his return to Moscow in October 1943. "He was pleased," Lina commented, that "I had kept his suits and not exchanged them for sugar, lard, butter, or anything else." The conversation, she added, "tended to be strained and formal. He avoided mention of Mira."

5

The Eisenstein Films

rokofiev and the eminent director Sergey Eisenstein collaborated on three films: *Alexander Nevsky*, Eisenstein's first sound film, and on Parts I and II of *Ivan the Terrible*, two-thirds of a proposed trilogy about the first Russian Grand Prince to become tsar, and his transformation of the nation into an autocratic state. Filmed and edited on an extremely tight schedule, *Alexander Nevsky* went into general release on December 1, 1938. Part I of *Ivan the Terrible*, which was filmed in Alma-Ata and edited in Moscow, received its premiere at the Bolshoy Theater on December 30, 1944. It received official approval for general release twenty-four hours later, opening at the Udarnik, Khudozhestvennïy, and Rodina theaters in Moscow on January 18, and another nine theaters on January 19, 1945. Part II was banned from general release by a March 5, 1946, Central Committee decree. Fragments survive of Part III.

Politics and serious health problems put unforeseen constraints on the collaboration. Had Eisenstein and Prokofiev been allowed to work together after 1946, their innovations in sound cinema might have progressed to the point where Eisenstein's montage theories might have found equivalents in Prokofiev's scores. Instead, the collaboration finds the two of them seeking, with limited technical resources, to forge an effective sound-sight dialogue. In *Alexander Nevsky*, this dialogue expresses a clear-cut political message; in *Ivan the Terrible*, it assumes a mystical, spiritual dimension.

This chapter traces the evolution of these films while also challenging some assumptions about the Prokofiev-Eisenstein partnership.

Alexander Nevsky

Alexander Nevsky was a means for Eisenstein to salvage his distinguished international career following the prohibition of *Bezhin Meadow* (*Bezhin lug*, 1937) in mid-production. That film, on which some two million rubles had been spent, recounts in apocryphal form the martyrdom of the Pioneer Pavel Morozov, who defends the local collective farm from crop saboteurs, only to be murdered by his deranged kulak father. Following its prohibition, the film was destroyed—only stills remain. Eisenstein was accused of ideological transgressions—reverting to abstract biblical and mythological imagery, focusing on the domestic side of the tragedy over the uplifting social side, engaging in unspecified formalist experiments—by the head of the State Cinema Directorate, Boris Shumyatsky, with whom he had a history of such disputes.

The scandal posed a grave threat to Eisenstein, but Shumyatsky ended up taking the fall: having overplayed his hand in cultural affairs, he would be arrested on January 8, 1938, and executed on July 29.[1] Eisenstein survived, but his career was almost ruined. On April 16, 1937, eight months before Shumyatsky's arrest, he submitted a letter to the bureaucrat admitting grave errors of judgment in *Bezhin Meadow*. He begged for a chance to make a film showing "the country, the people, the Party, the work of Lenin, October."[2] He specifically asked to collaborate with the prose writer and dramatist Vsevolod Vishnevsky on *We, the Russian People* (*Mï—russkiy narod*). Shumyatsky reacted harshly to Eisenstein's request, forwarding it on April 19 to Stalin with a note recommending that Eisenstein remain permanently unemployed, irrespective of the fact that the director "in private conversations seeks to back his claims with threats of suicide."[3] To allow Eisenstein to rehabilitate himself, Shumyatsky contended, would be to undermine the March 5, 1937, Central Committee resolution prohibiting *Bezhin Meadow*. The Central Committee backed Shumyatsky, ruling on April 19 that Eisenstein could not return to work and ordering the newspapers to devote space to "the falsity of S. Eisenstein's creative method."[4]

On May 15, Aleksey Angarov, a leading official in the Central Committee's Cultural Enlightenment Division, overruled Shumyatsky in a report submitted to Stalin and Andrey Andreyev, a Politburo member and the Central Committee Secretary in charge of culture and ideology. "Shumyatsky has the wrong viewpoint," Angarov asserted, "because the director Eisenstein is for all of his formalist mistakes a talented artist and, if he is guided, can make a good Soviet film."[5] Angarov stressed that Eisenstein would follow Vishnevsky's advice if permitted to work with him. The director had earned a last-minute reprieve, and would henceforth appease. On May 9, 1937, the Central Committee instructed Shumyatsky to reenlist Eisenstein. He was to be given a proper subject on a preapproved scenario.[6]

In the end, Eisenstein did not film *We, the Russian People*, which concerned, in Vishnevsky's words, "Russia in 1916–17 and 1918, October, the creation of the Red Army, and battles with German interventionists."[7] The subject matter was passé; the celebration of the twentieth anniversary of the Revolution had all but exhausted the market for films about the Bolshevist triumph. *We, the Russian People* was assigned for revision to the director Efim Dzigan, with whom Vishnevsky had worked on the 1936 film *We Are from Kronstadt (Mï iz Kronshdadta)*. A creative dispute resulted in the project's annulment. Eisenstein, meanwhile, expressed an interest in filming the twelfth-century epic *The Lay of the Host of Igor (Slovo o polku Igoreve)*. The Mosfilm studios, heeding the thematic plan of the State Cinema Directorate, instead offered Eisenstein a choice of two newly completed scenarios. The first of these was Viktor Shklovsky's *Minin and Pozharsky (Minin i Pozharskiy)*, an allegorical tribute to the two figures credited with ending the Time of Troubles. According to historical legend, Kuzma Minin, a resident of Nizhniy Novgorod, and Dmitriy Pozharsky, a Rurikid prince, assembled the Russian army that expelled the Poles from the Moscow Kremlin. Eisenstein eventually adopted the second scenario, which concerned Alexander Nevsky, the Grand Prince of Novgorod and Vladimir who, for his defense of Russia, was sanctified by the Orthodox Church in 1547. This scenario was drafted by Pyotr Pavlenko, a prose writer, courtroom reporter, and wartime journalist who received four Stalin Prizes over the course of his prolific party-line career.

Originally titled *The Great Sovereign Novgorod (Gospodin Velikiy Novgorod)* and *Rus'*, the scenario served as a populist call to arms and national oneness in the face of impending Nazi aggression. Through allegorical extension, it also beatified Stalin.[8] The sparseness of the late thirteenth-century/early fourteenth-century chronicle of Nevsky's life provided Pavlenko and (later) Eisenstein with a comparatively free interpretive hand, the result being a film that, according to Russell Merritt, "mixes together different story formulae from different eras, much in the way Wagner fuses and alters elements from Teutonic and Old Norse mythology for his Ring Cycle." The film, Merritt proposes, interlaces the source chronicle with elements of medieval epic and chivalric romance, ultimately adapted to the political realities of the late 1930s.[9] A July 12, 1938, article in *Izvestiya* titled "Alexander Nevsky and the Rout of the Germans" shows the seriousness of Eisenstein's propagandistic intentions. The article avoids mentioning Nevsky's sainthood, depicting him instead as the thirteenth-century equivalent of a stalwart Bolshevik folk hero. Eisenstein draws attention to the "colorful figure of the governor of Pskov, Tverdil[o] Ivankovich, who betrayed Pskov to the Germans out of selfish personal interests."[10] This character occupies the twin socialist realist roles of military-industrial saboteur and counterrevolutionary. Having fallen under the sway of foreign forces, he must be liquidated. Eisenstein concludes the article by paralleling Russia's (reimagined) past and (hypothetical) future: "For, if the might of our national soul was able to punish the enemy in this way, when the country lay exhausted in the grip of the Tatar yoke, then nothing will be strong enough to destroy this country which has broken the last chains of its oppression; a country which has become a socialist motherland; a country which is being led to unprecedented victories by the greatest strategist in world history—Stalin."[11]

Pavlenko and Eisenstein published the scenario in the December 1937 issue of the journal *Znamya* (Banner) ahead of making the film. They received numerous solicited and unsolicited suggestions as to how the script might be brought (in the words of one critic) "closer to historical truth."[12] They prudently heeded the most trenchant, high-level criticisms, with Eisenstein reporting on April 26, 1938, that "after a lot of work, conducted in collaboration with historians, the scenario of *Rus'* has met its end. . . . Its successor is the *Alexander Nevsky* scenario."[13] Eisenstein navigated carefully. Vishnevsky noted in his diary that the director was "anxious and worried" about the film, darkly adding that "either [he] will again return to the fore, or . . ."[14]

Apart from the elimination of a scene featuring a quarrel between residents on opposite sides of Novgorod—a scene that Eisenstein conceived as the historical antecedent to the post-Revolution civil war in Russia—the last scene underwent the biggest change. The first draft depicted Nevsky's death following a diplomatic mission to the city of Sarai (assumed to have been situated on the lower Volga River) to meet with Sartaq Khan, the commander of the Golden Horde of the Mongol Empire. Knowing that he cannot dispatch the Mongols from Russia as easily as he had dispatched the Teutonic crusaders, Nevsky humbly submits to the Khan and pledges to help him defeat common enemies. The decadent, despotic Khan is served by a group of Russian traitors who, resenting and fearing Nevsky, poison him.

Nevsky tells the Khan that Russia's ancestral lands should be governed by Russians; the Khan replies that he alone will rule them. "I admire brave people," he ends the discussion, "return ye to your home!" Nevsky mounts his steed and heads northwest with his men through a ravaged landscape, pledging, as the toxin spreads through his blood, to defeat the Khan and restore his people's honor. He falls from his horse at Kulikovo Field (near the Don River), the future site of the defeat of the Mongols under the leadership of Prince Dmitriy Donskoy. Eisenstein intended to include an image of this victory in the film in the guise of a prophetic, end-of-life vision.[15]

In his memoirs, Eisenstein describes how the film's original ending was banned by one of his minders:

> On the way back from the Horde the poisoned Prince, looking before him at a distant field—Kulikovo Field—died. Pavlenko and I had our holy warrior take a small detour for this purpose from the historic path along which [he] actually traveled, and so he did not reach his own home.
>
> A hand other than mine drew a red line after the scene of the defeat of the German masses.
>
> "The scenario ends here," I was told. "Such a good prince must not die!"[16]

The identity of the censor remains unknown. Subsequently, on May 7, 1938, Stalin reviewed a typescript of the rewritten scenario and remarked "It seems it turned out not badly" on the first page.[17] The rewritten scenario culminates and concludes with the Battle on the Ice, a lament for the fallen Russian heroes, the ruthlessly efficient liquidation of woebegone, stupefied traitors, and a celebration, graced with touches of Gogolian folk humor, of the triumph in the central square of the newly liberated city of Pskov.

The conductor Frank Strobel, who reconstructed a hypothetical version of Prokofiev's *Alexander Nevsky* score for screenings involving live orchestra, believes that the loss of the original ending can be heard in the score. In a roundtable discussion following one of the screenings, Strobel remarked that the hymnlike music of the revised ending sounds hollow, owing to the silencing of the otherwise prominent chorus and the paucity of instruments playing in the middle register. "The film's finale lacks the sense of a powerful conclusion."[18] The point was challenged by the Eisenstein archivist Naum Kleyman, who claimed that the music enters a celestial plane at the end, with the thirteenth-century conflict between the Russians and Teutonic crusaders elevated, for powerful propagandistic purposes, into a conflict between the spiritual and the material. *Rus'* has the divine on its side:

> There is no sense of a joyful "Gloria," of a pompous musical eulogizing—those *tutti* trumpets and kettledrums that usually conclude this type of film. To be sure, the orchestra's final sound is not "empty": the celebration just isn't "materialized"; it remains light and "transparent," achieving, if you will, spiritual depth. It is like seeing the eternal, like floating in the cosmos, free from gravity's pull.[19]

Prokofiev did not work with the original ending of the scenario, and the extent to which Eisenstein discussed it with him remains unclear. If, as Kleyman suggests, the ending of the score has a spiritual component, it reflects Nevsky's penultimate declaration in the film—"Whoever comes to us with the sword shall perish by the sword"—a paraphrase from the New Testament Book of Matthew: "All who draw the sword will die by the sword" (26:52). The reference places Nevsky in the role of the Messiah.

Details about the actual filming of *Alexander Nevsky* in 1938 are scarce, owing to the loss of Mosfilm archival records during the war. The lucrative 25,000-ruble contract for the music provides something of a timeline: it specifies completion of the battle music by June 10, submission of the sketches for the Latin (Catholic) chant of the Teutonic crusaders by July 15, and completion of the entire score according to Eisenstein's instructions by November 1. Payment was made in four 6,250-ruble installments, the last one contingent on the film's approval for release.[20] Regular shooting began on June 5 on Lake Pleshcheyevo (Pereslavl-Zalesskiy), although as early as April test shots were taken of the actors and the artificial snow and ice that had been made in Potïlikha, the Moscow suburb that housed the Mosfilm studios, for the Battle on the Ice. An April 21 bulletin in *Pravda* describes "preparations" for filming; a July 8 follow-up mentions the "350 people" involved in the battle scene.[21] From mid-October to November 4, Eisenstein edited the footage. He had been given a firm deadline to complete the film by Semyon Dukelsky, the chairman of the Committee on Cinema Affairs. A first draft, including different versions of crucial scenes and the rough cut of the Battle on the Ice, was screened in the Kremlin in early October. Because Stalin approved it without demanding changes, Eisenstein lost the chance to trim the redundant Battle on the Ice footage—he had planned to remove 200 meters—and to improve the woeful sound quality.[22] For reasons that remain unclear, the "Fight on the Novgorod Bridge" (Draka na Novgorodskom moste) episode was cut from the film.[23]

During the frantic editing phase, Eisenstein studied the footage of each scene of *Alexander Nevsky* in his studio and manually edited it frame by frame, combining and contrasting shots for the purpose of boosting dramatic tension. His editing process, which emphasized axial cuts, bore musical logic—Eisenstein focused on dynamic and rhythmic contrasts—and it facilitated the assemblage of a soundtrack that bore visual logic. Eisenstein claimed that when Prokofiev watched the edited footage, he would impatiently and spasmodically tap his fingers

> as if receiving telegraph signals. Is Prokofiev beating time?
> No, he is "beating" something more complex. His moving
> fingers grasp the structural canons governing the lengths of
> time and tempo in the edited pieces, harmonizing these with
> the actions and intonations of the characters.[24]

Prokofiev, Eisenstein continued, timed the edited scenes with a stopwatch, and composed music for them in haste: "At night we look through a new sequence of the film. By morning a new sequence of music will be ready for it."[25] The cerebral concision of Prokofiev's style, Eisenstein appended, recalled the French realist writer Stendhal.

The nature of the collaboration merits closer assessment, since Eisenstein later theorized that *Alexander Nevsky* marries sight and sound in a special way: the emphasis in the film on the common internal elements of the two media, he suggested, allows the audience to *hear* the visuals and see the *music*. Prokofiev described the collaboration in characteristically matter-of-fact terms. In a September 20, 1938, article in *Literaturnaya gazeta*, he reported that Eisenstein "placed a series of serious demands" on him before, during, and after the filming. Following protracted discussions with the director at the start of the summer, he produced the sketches for the score. These guided Eisenstein in the shooting of certain unspecified scenes. But in September, after Prokofiev returned to Moscow from a two-month stay in the Caucasus (resorts in Teberda and Kislovodsk), the situation reversed itself: "I became familiar with the filmed scenes and wrote the music for them." The music, once the master of the visuals, became their servant.[26]

A letter to Alpers reveals that Prokofiev visited the Mosfilm studios on several occasions. "Leaving my Cello Concerto unfinished," he wrote on July 13,

> I threw myself into the composition of the music for *Alexander Nevsky*, which Eisenstein, doubtless our finest film director, is realizing with great pomp. Half of the film is taken up with the Battle on the Ice, which is being shot in the summer, the ice being made out of asphalt painted white, glass, and white sand (snow powder). I was at the filming several times; it's turning out great. Only the horses are behaving badly: the "ice" constantly needs to be cleaned.[27]

His visits to the studio marked, at best, the midpoint of his work on the score. In a follow-up letter to Alpers from Moscow dated October 26, he laments having to postpone traveling to Leningrad to conduct because he was "up to [his] ears" in the film.[28]

The memoirs of the innovative sound engineer Boris Volsky provide an entertaining anecdotal account of Prokofiev's adventures in the recording studio, including his experiments with microphone placement. The composer divided the unfinished orchestral score into equal halves, Russian and Teutonic, and worked with Volsky to ensure that the former sound sounded "pleasant" to the ear and the latter "unpleasant." The "grand" sound of the oboes eclipsed that of the "little" trumpets, and a Mosfilm office drawer augmented the percussion section.[29] The recording was made in three studios on just three microphones, and then transferred to film using the outmoded optical sound system invented in 1928 by Aleksandr Shorin and Pavel Tager. It is hiss-filled, distorted, and muffled (the orchestra, moreover, is out of tune). Although Eisenstein and Prokofiev doubtless intended to re-record it—even Lina complained about its woefulness—the rough cut, a product of on-the-spot contrivance and adjustment, went out as the final cut.[30]

The source materials for the project include an annotated eighty-four-page "director's scenario," dated March 1938, an eighteen-page bundle of sketches and drafts that seem to have been collected from different phases of the project and assembled in a convenient order, and forty-four-page orchestral score that finds Prokofiev tinkering with the instrumentation after hearing how it sounded when recorded. The director's scenario is the most revealing of the three documents, since it predates the start of the shooting of the film by up to three months, and shows the composer's intentions in embryonic form.[31] The text was written by Eisenstein's assistant director Dmitriy Vasilyev and the cinematographer Eduard Tissé based on the original "literary scenario." It comprises a precise description of each planned shot sequence, including camera positions, the amount of film stock to be used (1 meter = 2 seconds of viewing), and dialogue. In consultation with Eisenstein, Prokofiev jotted down his thoughts on the style and amount of music to be used in certain scenes, and indicated which passages he intended to compose before the shooting and after.

The foreword to the document contains a pair of quotations from Marx—the first from chapter 5 of *La Russie et l'Europe (Revelations on the Diplomatic History of the Eighteenth Century)*, the second from the "Chronological Tables" included in the second edition of the collected works of Marx and Engels—which further attest to the transformation of *Alexander Nevsky* from a historical chronicle into a military-political manifesto as it made its way through the approval process. "In the 13th century," Vasilyev and Tissé write,

> Russia was first subjected to aggression from Eastern and Western colonizers. German orders of Livonian and Teutonic knights intervened from the West. This was preceded by another intervention from the East—the Tatar invasion, which placed Russia under the yoke of the Golden Horde.
>
> "This yoke both oppressed and affronted the spirit of those people who became its victims. The Mongol Tatars established a regime of systematic terror; destruction and mass murder became its permanent institutions." K. Marx.
>
> "Despite this the Novgorod Prince Alexander Nevsky, having become the leader of a Russian popular defense, confronted the German knights, defeating them on the ice of Lake Peipus. The scoundrels were cast from Russia once and for all." K. Marx.
>
> With this Alexander prepared the ground for the liberation of Rus' from the Mongols—who were routed after his death by his great-grandson Dmitriy Donskoy—and forged the path to the future united Russian State.[32]

Taking this gloss on the facts as his prompt, Prokofiev confined his musical outline of *Alexander Nevsky* to seven, potentially eight, discrete sections:

"Rus' in Ruins," "Sunrise" (Prokofiev placed a question mark after this section), "Veche" (the medieval Russian term for a popular assembly, referring here to the Novgorod war council), "Mobilization," "Swine" (the Russian term for a "boar's head" cavalry wedge formation), "Russian *rozhki*," "*Sopeli*," and "*Kare*" (the Russian term for military camp, or "square," here referring to the gathering of Nevsky's forces at Lake Peipus).[33] The outline betrays an interest in historical precision that is absent from the finished score. Fixating on the references to period instruments in the scenario, Prokofiev planned on infusing his score with the sound of the thirteenth-century Novgorodian *rozhok*, a wooden pipe with a horn bellmouth, and *sopel*, a hybrid panpipe. Eisenstein shows these nasal-sounding instruments being blown upon in the film, but Prokofiev decided against including them in his score. He instead fantastically reimagined their sound on modern trumpets, trombones, flutes, oboes, bells, and tambourines. (On page 59 of the scenario, he indicates an intention to "test" the sound of these instruments at the microphone.)

For the "Rus' in ruins" section of the score, Prokofiev wanted the music to bear both a "Mongol nuance" and the echoes of ancient battles. The result was a three-note semitonal figure that sounds in the upper and lower registers of the string section three times, followed by a long-breathed oboe and clarinet melody accompanied by restless sixteenth- and thirty-second-note patterns. The music approximates the barrenness of Eisenstein's visuals, which suggest, on the one hand, the timeless grandeur of the Russian terrain and, on the other, the devastation that has been wrought upon it. For Prokofiev, this terrain obviously had points in common with another: the opening sonority of *Alexander Nevsky* is the same as the opening sonority of his music for Tairov's *Egyptian Nights*.

On pages 7–14 of Vasilyev and Tissé's scenario, Prokofiev offers some general remarks about the "pleasant" and "glorious" patriotic chorus "'Twas on the Neva River" (A i bïlo delo na Neve-reke), which he chose to write for the opening panorama of Novgorod. The words of the chorus detail Nevsky's past heroism—his victory on July 15, 1240, over Swedish warriors at one of the tributaries of the Neva—while also warning Russia's variable roster of enemies against crossing the border. Prokofiev brings the chorus to a close with a plagal cadence whose tonic chord lacks a stabilizing fifth. The sound is archaic and (taking into account the text) inconclusive. It suggests a grander future resolution after a grander future battle. Fittingly, in the final celebratory scene in the film the music of the chorus is repeated, this time with doubled rhythmic values, harmonization in tenths à la Mikhaíl Glinka, and an extended cadential progression to a thickly scored, fully voiced B-flat major chord. The singers fall silent at the end of the film, but in the *Alexander Nevsky* Cantata, they remain at full strength to toast the nation's subjugation of foreign thieves in a grand battle: "Celebrate, Rus', our motherland!" (Veselisya, Rus', rodnaya mat'!).[34] On pages 29–33 of the scenario, Prokofiev precisely outlines his plans for a second patriotic chorus, "Arise, Russian People" (Vstavayte, lyudi russkiye), which would become, after some simplifying and abbreviating, the most popular number in the score. The chorus, he writes, "sounds during the entire scene of [the Russians'] mobilization," but "in different guises" in "the orchestra" and "the voices." Prokofiev, in discussion with Eisenstein, decided to record the first two verses, which summon Novgorod's peasants to rally in defense of their land, in a mezzo piano to mezzo forte range, and to record the forward-looking final verse, which warns any and all "foes" that they "shall not occupy Rus'" (vragam na Rus' ne khazhivat') in the forte to fortissimo range. This chorus, like the last one, ends with a plagal cadence on an unstable chord.

While it was being recorded, Prokofiev told Volsky that the third vocal number in the score, the mezzo-soprano aria "Respond, Bright Falcons" (Otzovitesya, yasnï sokolï) of the post-battle (Field of the Dead) episode, sounded "strange" even to his own ears, like a conscious or unconscious adaptation from an epic Borodin or Rimsky-Korsakov opera.[35] (The mezzo-soprano aria most readily brings to mind the lament of the long-suffering Yaroslavna for her husband in act 4 of Borodin's *Prince Igor*; the falcon is a prominent metaphor in the lament and the opera as a whole.[36]) The feeling of de-familiarization perhaps related to the fact that Prokofiev at first intended to distribute the aria in different guises in different scenes in the film, rather than assigning it intact to a single scene. Its mournful strains would have lent gravitas to the battle preparations which, in the final cut, come across as uncomfortably lighthearted. Shot 356 (showing Nevsky and his longtime comrades Vasiliy Buslay and Gavrilo Oleksich assembled at the top of Raven Rock on the eastern shore of Lake Peipus) was to have involved at least part of the aria. Another part—the introduction—would have sounded in the orchestra at shot 303, a brief scene involving Nevsky's warriors skiing downhill. Had these fragments been preserved, they would have added emotional weight to a cinematic portrayal that could not, for artistic and nonartistic reasons, bear such weight. Whereas the patriotic choruses address the future, the aria is an interior monologue, addressing the past.

The verses for these numbers came from the well-known poet Vladimir Lugovskoy, who was brought into the *Alexander Nevsky* project by Pavlenko, a close friend of his at the time. Lugovskoy needed the work: he had come under attack for ideological deficiencies in *Literaturnaya gazeta* and *Pravda*.[37] The articles in question, centering in the first instance on a reprint edition of his poems from 1923–24 and in the second instance on his 1938 collection *October Verses* (*Oktyabrskiye stikhi*), sent his career into a tailspin. Together with the verses for *Alexander Nevsky*, which he wrote under a cloud, Lugovskoy also provided Prokofiev with folklore-derived and -inspired texts for *Ivan the Terrible* and, in January 1950, the text of a "Soldier's Marching Song," the latter a commission from Muzgiz arranged by Lugovskoy. In his annotated 1951–52 work list, Prokofiev reveals that he had "proposed writing an entire cycle of such songs, but in view of a lack of understanding of the first one the cycle was not continued."[38] Although the "Soldier's Marching Song" was "conditionally approved" by Muzgiz, it was not, in the end, sanctioned for publication.[39]

The Lugovskoy settings in *Alexander Nevsky* were, in marked contrast, successful. After 1948, when many of Prokofiev's works were barred from performance, "Arise, Russian People" continued to be heard on State Radio along with excerpts from *Romeo and Juliet*. "It's as though I haven't composed anything else!" Prokofiev complained to his older son.[40]

Alexander Nevsky also includes a non-Russian text—the Latin chant assigned to the Teutonic crusaders—but it was compiled by Prokofiev himself. The words are wittily nonsensical: "Peregrinus, expectavi, pedes meos, in cymbalis," which roughly translate as "A sojourner, I waited, my feet, with cymbals."[41] In a 1939 article, published in heavily edited form in the collection *Soviet Historical Film* (*Sovetskiy istoricheskiy fil'm*), Prokofiev explained that his original "inclination was to use authentic music of the thirteenth century" for the Teutonic crusaders, but that his "acquaintance with Catholic canticles of the thirteenth century was enough to show that this music had become so far removed from us during the past seven centuries, so emotionally alien, that it could no longer adequately stimulate the spectator's imagination. Therefore it seemed more 'advantageous' not to present it as it really sounded at the time of the Battle on the Ice, but in the style in which we now imagine it." The same precept, the composer continues, applied to the chorus "'Twas on the Neva River," which "needed to be given in a modern guise, leaving aside the question of how it might have been sung 700 years ago."[42]

The source from which Prokofiev borrowed the Latin words was exceptionally modern: Stravinsky's 1930 *Symphony of Psalms*.[43] The text of this three-movement score comes from David's Psalms in the Latin version of the Vulgate (as translated from the Greek rather than the Hebrew).[44] In the *Alexander Nevsky* Cantata, Prokofiev added the word *est* to his Latin script. It is not found in *Symphony of Psalms*, but it might be a footnote of sorts, since *es* and *t* add up to the first two letters of Stravinsky's surname in the Latin alphabet. Prokofiev enjoyed letter games of this sort, especially when they came at his Parisian rival's expense.[45]

In *Alexander Nevsky*, Prokofiev parodies Stravinsky's parodic approach to text setting, which privileged the sound of words, their phonic contour, over their semantic content, what they express. In *Symphony of Psalms*, phrases are often set with the accents in the wrong places and masked by the lower brass- and percussion-laden orchestration. Prokofiev acknowledged his Stravinsky borrowing, but explained that, in *Alexander Nevsky*, the borrowed words "have no literal meaning."[46]

The marginalia on the scenario and the sketches indicated that Prokofiev conceived the Latin (Catholic) chant and ostinato-driven attack music of the Teutonic crusaders, and much of the clamorous, percussion-filled music of the Battle on the Ice, in advance of the filming.[47] He expanded and enriched the contents of these sections of the score after seeing the raw footage. He composed most of the first part of the three-part battle, but paused when it came to the dramatic highlights of parts two and three: the death of the lad Savka (and the subsequent, grotesque use of his body to block spears), Vasiliy's exhortation to Gavrilo to show some courage; Nevsky's humiliating defeat of Graf German von Balk, the master of the Teutonic Order; and the climactic breakup of the ice. Prokofiev reminded himself, on the back of page 61 of the scenario, to write the music only after seeing "how [the footage] will be edited." On the back of page 63, he added: "Music to be put aside until I see it." His and Eisenstein's logic was simple: for the continuous through-composed action scenes in the film, they allowed the structure of the music to determine the structure of the visuals; for the discontinuous, fragmentary scenes, the opposite happens.

Prokofiev sought at times to translate sight into sound. By modulating from the minor to the major and stressing the upper registers of the orchestra, he ensured that the music for the climax of the battle "brightened, like a meteor" (page 64). Elsewhere (page 56), he decided to replicate the effect of close-up shots by placing instruments in front of the microphone and having them blow, sometimes overblow, "directly into the ear." (The effect is pronounced in the battle's denouement, where a four-measure Teutonic fanfare motive is subject to acoustic distortion and dissonant contrapuntal overlay. Once monumental, the motive becomes coarse and trivial.) Beyond finding these indirect correlations between the music and the visuals, Prokofiev was also confronted with the challenge of finding direct ones. Eisenstein asked him to imitate the sounds of thudding hooves, clanking swords, and buckling ice in the orchestra. The latter received the most elaborate treatment: Prokofiev composed five measures of music for crash cymbals, glockenspiel, snare drum, tambourine, tam-tam, timpani, and lower strings that could be repeated as often as needed to reinforce the sensation of the ice cracking, imploding, and engulfing the foreign profaners of Russian terra firma. The din of the pitched and unpitched instruments reflects the violent chaos of the visual events, while the lower strings, which descend in the last measure of the sequence from the dominant to the tonic of the key (F major), offer a long-postponed sense of resolution. The battle, a thirty-five-minute jamboree of thumping and whacking, has ended.

In an overview of the score, the semiotician Philip Roberts comments that "the visual irony of white swallowing up white, and, indeed (to a Western audience), of white being linked with evil and Roman Catholicism and black with good and Russian folk motives, is paralleled in Prokofiev's score by the 'medieval' organum-type harmonies of the Latin pilgrim's hymn which are linked with the antagonists, and the melodically rich but harmonically naïve songs which are linked with the Russian protagonists."[48] The details are inaccurate—Prokofiev neither uses "organum-type harmonies" nor, obviously, a "Latin pilgrim's hymn" to depict the Teutonic crusaders[49]— but Robert's basic point is generally well taken: the score privileges binary oppositions. It also, however, dominates the film like few other scores of the period, strengthening both the sentiments of the script and providing (in advance of the invention of the synthesizer and the development of multichannel recording equipment) special effects. The music, Roberts argues, is "not *able* to be conventional enough to escape being intrusive," by which he means that it avoids the kind of musical clichés that begin to inform Hollywood film in the 1930s.[50]

In *Alexander Nevsky*, the triumph of the Russians over their opponents becomes a triumph of musical perspective. The conclusion of the Battle on the Ice witnesses a metamorphosis of the Latin chant and the ostinato patterns that embellish it: the music is no longer heard through the ears of the enemies but through the ears of the heroes, in debased guise. In the Teutonic bivouac scene, Eisenstein depicts a hunched black monk playing the anachronistically harmonized strains of the chant on a portative organ, while two others tend to the bellows. The pitches are repeated in consonant fortissimo by an invisible chorus: the filmgoer hears the music both objectively and subjectively, both as it is (at the start of the scene) and as it is idealized by the crusaders. This same duality applies to the depiction of Nevsky's soldiers: in the Russian encampment scene, the visual image of Savka blowing a *rozhok* is reproduced by a multi-tiered fanfare. The sound is bigger than life, much like the nationalist cause it venerates.

On page 71 of their scenario for the Field of the Dead scene, Vasilyev and Tissé cryptically describe "a female figure [the Novgorod maiden Olga] moving against an illuminated backdrop. A lonely woman's song begins. She sings about brave men." In his music for the scene, Prokofiev at first planned to interweave verses of the song—the mezzo-soprano aria "Respond, Bright Falcons"—with the tolling of funeral bells. The bells are not heard in the finished film, however. The aria occupies the Field of the Dead scene alone, becoming the basis for a novel sound effect. Vasiliy, dazed but relieved to be alive, calls out to his comrade (and rival for Olga's affections) Gavrilo. Gavrilo certifies that he, too, is alive, and Vasiliy asks him if he can "hear the voice calling out to us" which could either be Olga's voice (she appears to be calling out their names as she ambles through the torch-lit plain) or the voice of the professional singer on the soundtrack. And then, as the valiant warrior asks his question, he looks straight into the camera, suggesting that he is not, in fact, speaking to Gavrilo, but to the viewers of the film in the theater—to the Soviet public.

◆

As this haunting highlight confirms, *Alexander Nevsky* blurs, for didactic purposes, the relationship between on- and off-screen, real and imagined sound. Eisenstein did not discuss the eerie effect of this infiltration in his description of the filmmaking process. He instead focused on a more abstract matter: his attempt to create sound-sight correspondences *without* recourse to didacticism.

The concept of the sound-sight correspondence is defined at length in the fourth chapter of his 1942 book *The Film Sense*, "Form and Content: Practice." Eisenstein claims that he avoided using Prokofiev's music simply to enhance the visceral impact in the film—although there are, of course, numerous passages in which consonance and high registers denote good and dissonance and low registers denote bad. He instead imagined the music articulating the inner logic of certain images: the shape of the lines etched by the landscape and the characters, the contrasts between light and dark, and the passage of the viewer's eye from left to right across the screen. His analysis is painterly because his film is painterly: the middle scenes involve long static shots that serve to stress the importance of a historical giant (Alexander Nevsky) and a monolithic event (the Battle on the Ice). Instead of coordinating the music and visuals along narrative lines, he sought to combine their common geometric shapes. The two processes sometimes yield the same results. Although Eisenstein disliked "platitudinous...visualizations" of music, he did not wholly avoid them.[51]

Prokofiev wrote the music for the film before and after it was shot. The music and visuals complement, rather than complete, each other, a situation that prompted the philosopher and film theorist Gilles Deleuze to ask: "Since the silent visual image already expressed a whole, how we can be sure that the sound and visual whole is not the same, or if it is the same, does not give rise to two redundant expressions?"[52] Each medium, Deleuze proposes, is on its own so powerful, so complete, as to render the other medium superfluous.

Although Eisenstein allowed for deviations, he believed that, by and large, audiences fixate on the same things: a jagged outline on the right side of the frame, for example, or a scalar descent on the last beat of a measure. He described music in terms of phrase lengths, meter changes, and harmonic contrasts, without acknowledging that the ear also perceives timbre, texture, and rhythm. His discussion of *Alexander Nevsky* focuses on the pre-battle dawn episode, in which Nevsky's all-volunteer force awaits battle atop Raven Rock. Melodic mutations increase the tension and govern the pacing of the scene. One such mutation, Eisenstein claims, marks the "farewell embrace" between Vasiliy and Gavrilo, which, like "the close-up shots of the German knights' helmets," could only have taken place when the music changes "its character from one that can be expressed in long shots and medium shots of the attack to one that demands rhythmic visual beats, close-ups of galloping and the like."[53] Here, evidently, the writing of the music occurred around the same time as the editing of the visuals, resulting in a compelling audio-visual montage.

Eisenstein formalized his theoretical principles after the fact, arguing for a degree of abstraction that neither his film's subject matter nor the circumstances of its commissioning could embrace. One senses that he did not respect himself improvising at his desk and felt that he had to leave posterity a tablet of rules. He excludes ideological matters from his musings, choosing instead to describe the film that would have been, that might have been, had he not been burdened with the task of creating a national myth.

The national myth proved to be a runaway hit. *Alexander Nevsky* was previewed at Mosfilm on November 6 and the House of Cinema (Dom kino) on November 23, 1938. The December 1 general release generated an avalanche of positive reviews, classroom discussions, pre- and post-screening lectures, and both literate and semiliterate letters of acclaim and critique to the director.[54] Eisenstein had honorably fulfilled his assigned task of "blurring together . . . the Russian and Soviet past" in anticipation of military conflict with the Third Reich.[55] However, the signing of the Molotov-Ribbentrop Nonaggression Pact abruptly terminated the festivities. Like *Semyon Kotko*, *Alexander Nevsky* was withdrawn from circulation; unlike *Semyon Kotko*, it was re-released, and reacclaimed, when the pact was annulled and the creation of anti-German art became the moral obligation of Soviet artists. Prokofiev's extravagant score for the film demonstrated that he was, as Stalin purportedly said to Eisenstein, "a good Bolshevik after all."[56]

The film score and the cantata derived from it merited a Stalin Prize, and Prokofiev's supporters advocated his belated awarding of one in 1941. Khrapchenko, however, remained unconvinced of Prokofiev's patriotism. In his January 6, 1941, report on the Stalin Prize Committee deliberations, he summed up the decision against him in a single blunt sentence: "For a long time S. S. Prokofiev resided abroad."[57] At the time, nothing could atone for his protracted exposure to Western values, not even jingoistic choruses like "Arise, Russian People."

Prokofiev's service to Soviet power during the Second World War erased the doubts about his ideological orientation. His second, much more intense collaboration with Eisenstein caused new concerns, but he, unlike the director, avoided direct critique.

Ivan the Terrible

The genesis of Eisenstein's two-part *Ivan the Terrible* film is well documented, although the structure and function of Prokofiev's music for it is not.[58] Eisenstein received the commission on January 11, 1941. He began the scenario following a period of assisted research and general background reading that included historical chronicles, legends, ballads, the Bible, and works by (among many others) Sigmund Freud, Johann von Goethe, Karamzin, and Shakespeare. He described the project in broad strokes in an article in *Izvestiya*: "We all met him in our childhood and youth," Eisenstein writes of his cinematic protagonist. "His strange, romantic figure haunted the imagination."[59] This rather mild comment is followed by a paraphrase of the official account of Ivan's life, which omits the multitudinous horrors of his reign in favor of "forgotten" details about his proto-Stalinist political and military achievements.[60]

Eisenstein first reminds his readers that Ivan became the Grand Prince of Moscow in 1533 at the astonishingly young age of three, and immediately and arrogantly foresaw great deeds for himself. Upon assuming the title of tsar (the first in Russian history) in an unprecedentedly elaborate coronation at age seventeen, he launched a campaign to improve trade routes and reclaim ancestral land occupied by the Mongol Tatars. (Although Ivan built a port on the river Narva in 1550, Russia lacked regular access to the Baltic Sea trade: foreign merchants preferred to deliver goods to the ports held by the Livonian Order.) He captured Kazan in 1552 and Astrakhan in 1556, liquidating their Tatar inhabitants and putting an end to a flourishing slave trade. Eisenstein highlights the effectiveness of Ivan's loyal guard—the *oprichniki*—against his enemies. He also touches on Ivan's decision to launch what became the disastrous bloodletting of a quarter-century war with Livonia and the defection of Ivan's longtime advisor, Andrey Kurbsky, to the enemy side. "By freeing [the Tsar's] history from lies and distortions, and basing it on those aspects of the epoch expressed by Marx, the image of the 16th-century Russian State looks entirely different," Eisenstein concludes. His future film would tackle the problem of depicting the sixteenth-century "poet of the idea of the State."[61] The twentieth-century "poet," he obligatorily implies, is Stalin.

These are the essential plot elements of *Ivan the Terrible*, but plot is of minor relevance to a film that consists of perplexing non-narrative fragments. The footage that survives Eisenstein's five-year struggle with himself, with Prokofiev, and with the Committee on Cinema Affairs is essentially a collection of drafts, unfinished and unfinishable, a jigsaw puzzle without a border. Eisenstein filled dozens of notebooks with plans and ideas; these are projections rather than formulations, conceived without interference, geared toward approximate or hypothetical realization. He perhaps shared his faith in drafts with Prokofiev: both artists recognized that caterpillars did not rely on butterflies to exist. Given the constraints imposed on him by the Committee on Cinema Affairs, Eisenstein seems to have determined that the most powerful ideas were the least incarnate ones. According to his colleague Mikhaíl Romm, who problematically defined *Ivan the Terrible* Part II as a "tragedy of tyranny," Eisenstein took the news that the film had been barred from release with "surprising calmness—he had a premonition, he knew this would happen."[62]

What exists of *Ivan the Terrible* is self-reflexive—the camera's eye constantly looks at itself—and deeply personal, an exploration of the relationship between the artist and his subject. Part I is considered to be much more conformist in its representation of Ivan than Part II, which shows him sliding into near-madness, sacrificing what German idealist philosophy—and Russian "mystic" Symbolism—would term the world of objects for the world of essences. Shadows, sleep, poison goblets, and near-death experiences loom large in the drama. Ivan forfeits reason in search of a utopian ideal, an "abstraction" known as the "Great Russian State."[63] For Eisenstein, this ideal became no less fictional than the cinematic depiction of its pursuit. The closing lines of his scenario for *Ivan the Terrible* Part III find Ivan alone on the eastern shore of the Baltic Sea, having finally carved a trading route for Russia through Livonia. He crosses a killing field to confront the waves, upon which he casts a calming spell.[64] There is nothing in front of him and nothing behind. This is the image of an individual who remains intact while everything else is shattered, but the preceding events in the scenario suggest the opposite, that *he* is the one who is shattered. In pursuit of a harsh nationalist ideal and in defiance of his own mortality, he has forfeited the higher integrated ideal of Christian faith. This concept is laid bare in the middle scene of Part II, as Ivan rejects the authority of the Church in order to impose his own will on man and nature.

The scenario passed through several revisions in 1941 and 1942.[65] The anti-German, anti-Polish sentiments of the text rose to the surface while the theme of Ivan's loneliness, a crucial element of the first draft, subsided. Eisenstein absorbed input from his assistant Lev Indenbom while also seeking advice from the eminent (official) historians Sergey Bogoyavlensky and Militsa Nechkina—who, like Eisenstein, had been evacuated to Alma-Ata during the war. He felt sufficiently confident about the scenario's initial prospects, however, to inform Prokofiev, in a December 23, 1941, letter from Alma-Ata to Tbilisi, that

> *Terrible* will be filmed. It appears I will begin at winter's end. Now I'm finishing the scenario and will send it with the next courier. At the beginning of next year it will be possible to form an agreement and meet, etc.

It came out in two parts, engaging to the highest
degree. Comrade composer is granted great freedom in all
directions.[66]

The courier (Nikolay Sliozberg) brought Prokofiev the scenario in March,
with Eisenstein encouraging Prokofiev "to begin the music whenever is convenient. I will begin filming at summer's end. You can begin in the spring, the
summer, the fall, even the winter—whenever is most opportune."[67]

Prokofiev took on the project, informing Eisenstein in a March 29, 1942,
letter that he was "writing up the last measures of *War and Peace*" but would
be able "to bend to [the director's] yoke in the near future."[68] He arrived in
Alma-Ata to begin work on the score on June 15—the meandering trip from
Tbilisi took seventeen days—settling with Mira in the modest Dom Sovetov
(House of Soviets) hotel, jampacked at the time with filmmakers, writers
(including Lugovskoy, Paustovsky, and Shklovsky), and composers. Since
neither the scenario nor the thematic plan for *Ivan the Terrible* had been
completed, Eisenstein was hardly in a position to provide what he called its
"specific features and themes" to Prokofiev, leaving him with some precious
time to work on the orchestration of *War and Peace*.[69] The *Ivan the Terrible* scenario received provisional approval from the Committee on Cinema
Affairs on September 5; the thematic plan was finished earlier, on August
14.[70] Both documents bear witness to Eisenstein's interest in fashioning the
cinematic equivalent of an operatic *Gesamtkunstwerk*, the principal point of
reference being Wagner's *Die Walküre*, which Eisenstein had directed at the
Bolshoy Theater in 1940.

While developing the scenario and thematic plan, the director relied
extensively on Lugovskoy's advice. The poet had met with Prokofiev in
Tashkent, Uzbekistan (while the composer was en route to Alma-Ata) to
discuss the types of songs to be used in the film. Lugovskoy's June 13, 1942,
letter to Eisenstein indicates that Prokofiev composed the songs to order:

I met with Prokofiev. He stayed overnight with me, and I had
the opportunity in the morning to read through most of the
songs with him (besides "The Beaver," the extra one, and
some trifles that I don't have with me).[71] He spoke highly
of them. The potential placement of the overture either
before or after the main titles elicited some puzzlement. He
also wondered if the canonicity of the furnace play would

be understood by the modern viewer, but he seemed quite interested in it. I told him that we'd planned out all the songs together and gave all kinds of passing explanations, which, of course, were only a weak approximation of your directorial concept.

Don't forget, dear patron, about the popularity of those songs that you selected for this purpose. Of course, the overture and the oath can be condensed and rearranged however preferable, depending on your and Prokofiev's decision. We'll work up the rest together.[72]

Hoping to preserve the formula that had worked so well in *Alexander Nevsky*, Lugovskoy insisted that the music of *Ivan the Terrible* be accessible, yet his actual poetic choices accorded with Eisenstein's darker cinematic conceits. The folkloric "Song of the Beaver" (Pesnya pro bobra), the one song he identifies by name, is performed by Ivan's boyarina aunt Yefrosiniya Staritskaya, who wants to see her dim-witted son Vladimir on the throne.[73] It occurs twice in Part II, first in the guise of a macabre lullaby, then as a macabre lament—two genres that are intertwined (many lullabies, after all, have a morbid lining, predicting the death of the child in sleep).

The disquieting effect of "The Song of the Beaver" resides in its mutation from a soothing strophic ballad into a violent through-composed tableau. Staritskaya loses herself in it, becoming spellbound by the words and the strident sounds she imagines underscoring them. The performance begins as a recitation of long-known verses and ends in near-demented improvisation. Prokofiev narrates her mental journey, transforming a rocking ostinato pattern in the strings (outlining the tonic and diatonic triads of B minor) into the strains of hunting horns and drums, and then into the strains of Ivan's coronation music. Through the transitions, Staritskaya mutters a portentous, nonpitched line of text, "The more [the beaver] bathed, the dirtier he became" (Ne vïkupalsya, ves' vïgryaznilsya), and then lodges herself in mantra-like repetitions of an A–E–A cadential gesture to the words "[He] dried himself down, he shook himself down, he looked around, he glanced around" (Bobyor nasushivalysa, otryakhivalsya, osmatrivalsya, oglyadïvalsya). Whole- and half-step modulations away from B minor betray Staritskaya's fragile hold on reality. Dissonant "stinger" harmonies mark her account of the panicked beaver being stalked, captured, and skinned. The gory scene mutates in Staritskaya's mind into a triumphant image of her son Vladimir, having wondrously supplanted Ivan as tsar, donning a cloak made out of the hide. Her final words, "to deck out Tsar Vladimir" (tsarya Volodimira obryaditi), are underscored by an orchestral simulacrum of a church chorus.

Lugovskoy's words and Prokofiev's music realize a prophecy that Eisenstein's visuals do not. Though Ivan is out of sight when "The Song of the Beaver" is performed, it nonetheless seems to affect him, becoming a subliminal prod, "the last decisive stimulus," in Tatiana Egorova's words, for the "annihilation of [Staritskaya's] family."[74]

Besides "The Song of the Beaver," Lugovskoy refers in his June 13 letter to Eisenstein to his text for the liturgical drama "The Fiery Furnace," which serves an allegorical purpose in the film. But his most impressive contribution goes altogether unmentioned: his text for the "Dances of the *Oprichniki*" (Plyaski oprichnikov) of Part II. As the Slavicist Avril Pyman observes, the "menacing one-stress refrain" of the dances almost exactly matches that of the 1906 quasi-folkloric poem "Merrymaking in Russia" (Vesel'ye na Rusi) by the Russian "mystic" Symbolist writer Aleksandr Blok. Lugovskoy's command "Da prikolachivay!"—which Pyman translates as "And nail it fast!"—mimes Blok's "Da pritopïvay!": "And tap out the rhythm with your foot!" The reference could only have been intentional, since, as Pyman concludes, Blok's text invokes the medieval allegorical image of "Death herself towering over Russia."[75] This is exactly the image that the *oprichniki* project in the frenzied, soul-less bacchanalia that concludes Part II, an episode that Eisenstein, making use of Agfa color film stock from Berlin (a spoil of the Red Army defeat of the Nazis), shot in crimson red.

Eisenstein's thematic plan indicates that Ivan's principal theme, nicknamed "A Storm Approaches," would be heard four times in Part I: in the overture, in the prologue showing Ivan as a boy, at the end of the scene showing the death of his wife, Anastasiya Romanovna (she is poisoned in her bedchamber by Staritskaya), and in the epilogue.[76] According to Leonid Kozlov, the nickname stems from the original scenario for the film, which fixates on the horridness of feudal Russia. The film represents Ivan's reign as the ear-splitting "thunder" that dissipated the "black clouds" of the feudal period.[77]

Although heard in its most explicit form only these four times, echoes, paraphrases, and transformations of the theme—a B-flat major march offset by ascending and descending sixteenth-note patterns in the violins—permeate the soundtrack. (The theme, for all its bellicosity, bears an archaic element: the substitution of the pitch E natural for E flat in the accompaniment suggests the Lydian mode.) The theme recurs in a quasi-liturgical guise at the end of Part I, which features one of the most famous images in the Eisenstein corpus: the colossal profile of the Tsar looming over the Russian people, who flow in single file over the horizon (from Moscow to Alexandrova Sloboda) to entreat him on hands and knees to resume his rule. Prokofiev here casts the Tsar as a demiurge, the literal creator of the world—albeit one who has willfully abandoned his creation. A subsequent metamorphosis of the theme, intended for the Part III scene of penitence, but also underscoring the Part I statement "I cannot rule the realm without the threat of force" (Ne mozhno tsaryu tsarstvo bez grozï derzhati), depicts him as Lucifer, a fallen but still light-bearing angel. The theme is introduced by a latticework of chromaticism in the strings; the opening intervals, accordingly, are compressed from whole to half steps. A fourth, "ironic" variant of the theme, running backward and forward in the woodwinds, underscores the shrewdness of Ivan's dealings with his enemies and of their dealings with him. It is heard throughout Part II.[78]

The thematic plan calls for the inclusion of a popular song (one that, in Eisenstein's prescription, "everyone" should be able to sing) titled "Ocean-Sea" (Okeyan-more). Prokofiev composed it to Lugovskoy's verses. This part of the film was to have comprised a concatenation of images from Ivan's unhappy childhood; the song was to have been sung by his nurse in the scenes framing the murder of his mother. But rather than a commentary on that tragic event, "Ocean-Sea" serves the broader purpose of instilling within Ivan a sense of future greatness, of the need to overcome obstacles preemptively, before they unite and overwhelm him. It furnishes psychological justification for his harsh, unsympathetic actions, actions that culminate in the expansion of Russia's boundaries to the Baltic Sea.

"Ocean-Sea" begins as a contralto solo but ends as a choral ode; Prokofiev elevates a meditative song to an epic plane. He and Eisenstein planned to include its opening strains, meta-diegetically, in four additional scenes in Parts I and II of the film: during Ivan's speech in the Uspensky Cathedral about the expansion and unification of Russia; following his unanticipated recuperation from near-fatal illness; in the "Dances of the *Oprichniki*"; and in the Livonian battle scenes. Despite the careful planning, the song never made it into the film, owing to the prohibition of the prologue by the Committee on Cinema Affairs.

Eisenstein and Prokofiev next map out their intentions in the thematic plan for the "Song of Kazan" (Kazanskaya pesnya) which, like "Ocean-Sea," was intended as a lyrical crowd-pleaser. It would have been deployed in much the same fashion as "Arise, Russian People" from *Alexander Nevsky*. This song was not written; the only vocal music heard in the battle scene is a brief (fourteen-measure) choral march titled "The Tatar Steppe" (Step' Tatarskaya) whose manuscript is presumed lost.

The thematic plan further describes the elaborate, beguiling music of "The Oath of the *Oprichniki*" (Klyatva oprichnikov), which Prokofiev cast in four different guises—chantlike recitative, song, dance, and unseen hummed chorus—but which was largely edited out. The loss of this particular music attests to the disorganization of his and Eisenstein's collaboration, and the impositions placed on them by the Committee on Cinema Affairs. The rest of the thematic plan for Part I centers on "The Fiery Furnace" and "The Song of the Beaver," which were both transferred to Part II. Eisenstein also planned at this stage to include a scene depicting the gruesome *oprichniki* campaign against the autonomous city of Novgorod. He first transferred the scene from Part I to Part II of the film, and then, in 1944, from Part II to the newly conceived Part III, which he did not complete. The requested background music for the scene went unwritten.

The plan for Part II is comparatively undeveloped, specifying music for the "galloping" *oprichniki*, liturgical music for Ivan's confession for the atrocities his henchmen have committed in the cities of Novgorod and Pskov, background music for the execution of the *oprichniki* leader Aleksey Basmanov (wrongly suspected by Ivan of treason) by his son Fyodor, and background music for the apocalyptic final battle that brings the aged Ivan to the Baltic Sea. These last three items were eventually relocated by Eisenstein from Part II to III of the film. So, too, was a number—for a boisterous scene featuring Queen Elizabeth I—called "The Ballad of the Red-Haired Bess" (Ballada o Rïzhey Bess). The scene was banned from the film, out of concern that it represented Ivan as an unapologetic Anglophile, too willing to align Russia diplomatically with England. The banning of the scene removed one of the few passages of real history from Part II. Unlike Part I, Part II is temporally and spatially hallucinatory, unhinged from actual events in Ivan's life.

◆

Political and logistical problems plagued the project from start to finish. Eisenstein had difficulties casting the parts and keeping up morale on the set, owing to shortages of electricity (provided to the studios only at night), food, fuel, and other material goods. He wanted to cast the well-known comic actress Faina Ranevskaya in the role of the treacherous Staritskaya, but the chairman of the Committee on Cinema Affairs, Ivan Bolshakov, overruled him, declaring her "Jewish features" unsuitable for the part of a Russian noblewoman.[79] Paradoxically, the role went to another Jewish actress, the ill-tempered Serafima Birman, with whom Prokofiev had an unpleasant relationship of long standing. Eisenstein had difficulties of another sort in casting the part of Ivan's wife, Anastasiya. He first offered it to the ballerina Galina Ulanova who, despite being flattered by the proposal, declined it—leaving him to scramble, late in 1943, to find a suitable substitute. He settled on Lyudmila Tselikovskaya, the wife of the celebrated actor Mikhaíl Zharov, to whom he had earlier allotted the role of Ivan's servant Skuratov. For the title role he was fortunate enough to again secure the services of the mime actor and committed Communist Nikolay Cherkasov, who had earlier played the part of Alexander Nevsky.[80] The filmmaking process was of proportions as epic as the film's subject matter.

Prokofiev worked with Eisenstein in the fall of 1942 and spring of 1943 in Alma-Ata, but the bulk of the music was written in 1944 and 1945 (in Moscow during the winters and outside of Ivanovo during the summers). Filming began on April 22, 1943; editing did not end (for Part II) until February 2, 1946. The dates of most of the twenty-nine items in Prokofiev's annotated piano score cannot be determined. The Sikorski (Urtext) Edition of the score assembled by the Glinka Museum researchers Marina Rakhmanova and Irina Medvedeva in 1997 further confuses this issue, since it includes hypothetical reconstructions of music that did not end up in the film while excluding music that did. The origins of the rest of the music in the film— the twelve liturgical items that, with one exception, were not arranged by Prokofiev—remain entirely unclear.[81] The question of origin is an extremely important one, because *Ivan the Terrible* was the first Soviet film to rely on liturgical music for positive and powerful rhetorical effect. (On September 5, 1943, Stalin announced a radical change in State and Party policy toward the Russian Orthodox Church, which explains the sudden lifting of the prohibition against religious music in concerts that year and, more pertinently, its inclusion in the score of *Ivan the Terrible*.)[82] The iterations of the hymn "My Soul" (Dusha moya) when Ivan expresses contrition for his actions, for example, underscore a central conceit of the film: the State cannot be put in order by rulers whose spirits are in disorder. Overall, the liturgical music attests to the iconicity of Eisenstein's cinematic conception, his half dreamscape, half Kabuki Theater meditation on the writing and rewriting of historical narratives.

The annotated piano score, written on fifty pages of manuscript paper of different types, contains twenty-nine dated and undated numbers.[83] A separate archival document, Lamm's realization of the orchestral score from Prokofiev's annotations, contains two other numbers.[84] The beguiling music for "The Oath of the *Oprichniki*" and "The *Oprichniki* and Vladimir" seems to have been the first that Prokofiev conceived for the film, and perhaps the only music, with the possible exception of the contralto song "Ocean-Sea," completed in Alma-Ata. "The Oath of the *Oprichniki*" did not make it into the film: in the opinion of Bolshakov and the Committee on Cinema Affairs, it depicted Ivan's loyal guard in a falsely negative light, whereas Stalinist revisionist historians described them in quasi-folkloric terms as a progressive force that vanquished the enemies of the State, hunting them down, tearing them up, and disposing of them (the *oprichniki* adopted as symbols a dog's head and a broom). Eisenstein managed to use part of the chromatic, murmured recitative that Prokofiev composed for "The Oath of the *Oprichniki*" in the balletic buildup to the climax of Part II, in which Ivan's black-robed legions escort Vladimir to his death. The discordant chanting, which is framed by shimmering strings, less suggests human beings than a force field, a vibrating power grid.

The "*Oprichniki* and Vladimir" scene, on which Eisenstein labored long and hard, did make it into the film. In a July 9, 1943, letter, he beseeched Prokofiev not to leave Alma-Ata for Perm (where he was expected to resume work on *Cinderella*) before the music was recorded:

> Without you the chorus and recording will doubtless be bungled (*if you know what I mean!*). They are obviously flogging themselves to no avail in the rehearsals, thus it would be very, very desirable to plan your departure not for Monday, but for the next possible departure time afterward.[85]

Eisenstein later requested that Prokofiev return from Perm to Alma-Ata at the end of October to complete the music for Part I of the film, but Prokofiev did not. He was again unable to make the trip, since he had been summoned back to Moscow to assist in the preparations for a prospective concert performance of *War and Peace* in December.

The performance never happened, even though Prokofiev, heeding previous advice from Shlifshteyn, had abandoned Eisenstein to attend to it.[86] "I'd like to hope that you aren't too upset with me for not coming to Alma-Ata," he wrote to Eisenstein on November 17, "I wasn't able to." Prokofiev adds that he had sent the music for "The Fiery Furnace," and asks Eisenstein to forward "detailed outlines of those pieces" that he could compose ahead of the director's return to Moscow.[87] The music for "The Fiery Furnace" is presumed lost: there survives, according to the Glinka Museum editors, merely a sketch of the central "Song of the Boys" (Peniye otrokov), which, for unknown reasons, was not included in the film.[88] Eisenstein appears to have patched together "The Fiery Furnace" using improvised choral singing. The Glinka Museum editors include a hypothetical reconstruction of "Song of the Boys"—based on the surviving sketch—in their score.[89]

The available evidence suggests that, for *Ivan the Terrible* Part I, Prokofiev composed most of his music to match Eisenstein's visuals. The difficult sound-recording process began in the late summer of 1944, after the belated return of the Mosfilm studios to Moscow, and after most of Parts I and II and a portion of Part III had been filmed. Eisenstein was now in a state of near-panic, having already been forced for logistical reasons to postpone the sound recording from March to July, and then, because he could not coordinate his work schedule with Prokofiev's, from July to August. Prokofiev was not in Moscow in July to greet Eisenstein; he had decided to spend the summer at the Union of Soviet Composers retreat outside of Ivanovo, an agricultural-industrial city 300 kilometers to the northeast of the capital. In a July 30 telegram, Eisenstein pleaded with Prokofiev to "come at once," to Moscow, because the delay was "threatening all of [his] plans for the release of both parts."[90] Prokofiev resisted, claiming, in a letter dated July 31, that he had been patiently waiting in Ivanovo to receive additional materials related to the film and, during that time, had become involved in a new project: his Fifth Symphony. His progress was such that he could "under no circumstances pause it and switch to *Ivan the Terrible*." Prokofiev pledged, however, to return to Moscow on August 15, after which he would "commit [himself] entirely" to the forsaken film, working "quickly and precisely."[91]

Mira described the sound-recording process as follows:

> Seryozha first looked at parts of the film in the studio. Then he wrote the music at home, and in doing so took into account the wishes that Sergey Mikhaylovich had voiced

while the film was being shown. Back in the studio: the music is recorded on tape with Seryozha at the piano; when singing is called for, he sings.[92] Immediately afterward they go through more materials. On the next occasion the tape recording accompanies the pictures, and when Eisenstein is satisfied, work on the instrumentation begins. The material that has been orchestrated is recorded in the studio on tape (immediately with choir and orchestra). Sometimes up to four hours are needed to record two minutes of music, since Eisenstein and Seryozha (who attended all the recording sessions) are extremely demanding.[93]

The work was not completed in August, as evidenced by a September 22 letter from Eisenstein (in Moscow) to Prokofiev (in Ivanovo). The letter included the revised scenario for the Kazan battle scene, along with "the seconds and markings so that you remember what is happening and what is desired in terms of character."[94] The revision was doubtless prompted by the August pre-screening of Part I at the Committee on Cinema Affairs, where it did not fare particularly well. Although the altered Part I eventually earned a First Class Stalin Prize, it elicited mixed reactions. The co-author (with Eisenstein) of the scenario for *Alexander Nevsky*, Pavlenko, wrote a negative review of *Ivan the Terrible* in advance of its general release. Since the film was on its way to the theaters, the review was withdrawn from publication; in its place, *Pravda* printed a positive review by Vishnevsky, who described the film as a "great triumph" for Soviet cinema. His lone comment on the music was that it sounded "confident and free."[95] Myaskovsky felt otherwise: "the music grunts somewhat, but in places it's interesting."[96]

The completion and recording of the music for Part II was delayed by Prokofiev's health problems. In a diary entry dated February 2, 1945, Myaskovsky reports that, about two weeks before, Prokofiev took a bad fall and suffered severe head trauma.[97] Although he never fully recovered from the accident, he managed during the summer (spent, once again, in Ivanovo) to resume full-time work. He informed Eisenstein, however, that he would not be able to return to *Ivan the Terrible* until at least October, which sent the director into despair: "This change puts my work in a catastrophic state," he wrote to Prokofiev on August 1, "based on your promise of music for the dance we built the corresponding décor for the filming and adjusted all of our plans and the schedules for the actors' arrival. Now everything will come

Prokofiev and Lina, 1933. [Russian State Archive of Documentary Film and Photography (Rossiyskiy gosudarstvennïy arkhiv kinofotodokumentov) (RGAKFD)]

The director Aleksandr Tairov, the singer Paul Robeson, the actress Alisa Koonen, Prokofiev, and the artist Pavel Kuznetsov at Tairov's Chamber Theater, Moscow, December 1934. [RGAKFD]

With Berthe Malko, Prague, January 1938. [Malcolm Brown (MB)]

Posing at the piano, Moscow, July 22, 1940. [RGAKFD]

With the cast of *Semyon Kotko*, Stanislavsky Theater, October 1, 1940. [RGAKFD]

The young Mira Mendelson, in a photograph inscribed "To my dear beloved daddy."
[Russian State Archive of Economics (RGAE)]

Abram Mendelson. [RGAE]

Receiving the Order of the Red Banner of Labor from Mikhail Kalinin, Moscow, 1943. [RGAKFD]

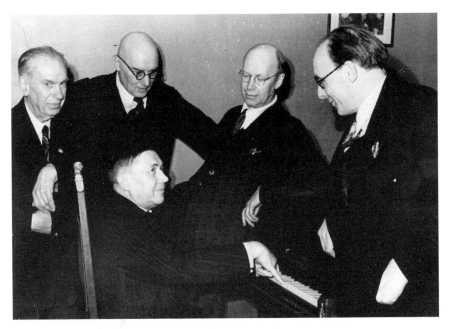

Sergey Vasilenko, Yuriy Shaporin, Nikolay Golovanov (at the piano), Prokofiev, and Mikhail Chulaki at a composers' gathering at the Central House of Art Workers, Moscow, 1943. [RGAKFD]

Metropole Hotel, Moscow, Fall 1943. [Russian State Archive of Literature and Art (RGALI)]

Metropole Hotel, Moscow, Fall 1943. [RGALI]

Prokofiev recalls his meetings with the English conductor Sir Henry Wood at a gathering at VOKS, Moscow, March 3, 1944. [RGALI]

Playing "Patience" at the Savoy Hotel, Moscow, April 1944. [RGALI]

Studio photograph, 1945. [RGAKFD]

Receiving the Medal for Valiant Labor in the Great Patriotic War from Aram Khachaturyan in his capacity as deputy chairman of the Orgkomitet of the Union of Soviet Composers, Moscow, 1945. [RGALI]

Prokofiev plays Levon Atovmyan's arrangement of six pieces for piano from *Cinderella*, Ivanovo, Summer 1945. [RGALI]

Prokofiev with Nikolay Chemberdzhi (in cap), Izraíl Nestyev (in front), and others, Ivanovo, Summer 1945. [RGALI]

Dmitriy Kabalevsky, Reinhold Glier, Prokofiev (seated), Vano Muradeli, the musicologist, and State Radio administrator Yakov Solodukho and M. Yu. Dvoyrin (standing), Ivanovo, Summer 1945. [RGALI]

With Mira and (a row behind) the musicologist Marina Sabinina at a rehearsal of *War and Peace*, Moscow, June 1945. [RGALI]

Lee Bland interviews Prokofiev at the dacha in Nikolina Gora, with Nikolay Myaskovsky listening, Summer 1946. [MB]

Lee Bland, Grigoriy Shneyerson, Pavel Lamm (in doorway), and Prokofiev at the dacha in Nikolina Gora, Summer 1946. [MB]

With Mira at the dacha in Nikolina Gora, Summer 1946. [RGALI]

With Mira on the balcony of the dacha in Nikolina Gora, Summer 1946. [RGALI]

The pianist and Leningrad Conservatory professor Nadezhda Golubovskaya, Prokofiev, Atovmyan, Shneyerson, and Mira at a rehearsal of the Sixth Symphony, Leningrad, October 9, 1947. [RGALI]

Nestyev, Atovmyan, Prokofiev, Shneyerson (partly obscured), and Mira at the premiere
of the Sixth Symphony, Leningrad, October 11, 1947. [RGALI]

Prokofiev and Yevgeniy Mravinsky following the premiere of the Sixth Symphony,
Leningrad, October 11, 1947. [RGALI]

Receiving applause following an encore performance of the *Ode to the End of the War*,
Chaikovsky Concert Hall, October 17, 1947. [RGAKFD]

The Moscow Philharmonic director Vladimir Vlasov, the conductor Konstantin Ivanov, and Prokofiev backstage at the
Chaikovsky Concert Hall, October 17, 1947. [RGAKFD]

Prokofiev and Tikhon Khrennikov at a plenary session of the Union of Soviet Composers, Moscow, December 27, 1948. [RGAKFD]

At Nikolina Gora, 1950, in a photograph taken by his son Svyatoslav. [Serge Prokofiev Jr. (SP)]

With Svyatoslav and Oleg, Nikolina Gora, 1950, in a photograph taken by Svyatoslav's wife, Nadezhda. [SP]

The French musicologist Rostislav-Michel Hoffman and Mira in Prokofiev's study, Moscow, November 1962. [RGAKFD]

apart at the seams and you won't be able to gather up the threads!"[98] Two days later, Mira informed Eisenstein that Prokofiev "can't possibly write the music for the second part."[99] In his place, Prokofiev suggested that Gavriil Popov, a composer whose talent he esteemed, be hired for the project. He wrote a letter to Popov to this effect and asked Eisenstein to deliver it to him, but the director refused, leaving the door open for Prokofiev to return to the project when his health had improved.[100]

In the fall, he managed to compose the two "Dances of the *Oprichniki*" for the concluding bacchanalia of Part II. Eisenstein shot the scene in a montage of crimson red (representing blood), gold (festive raiment), and black (death). Since Prokofiev could not spend extended periods of time in the studio, the director was obliged to tailor his visuals to match the timing of the precomposed music, which brought to an end the prospect of forging a fluid sight-sound dialogue. In a March 1947 lecture about the treatment of music and color in *Ivan the Terrible* Eisenstein confessed that adjusting "the pieces of filmed material" to "match exactly the beats in the music" ended up being an "awful job."[101] As his health improved, Prokofiev occasionally ventured to the studio, but he worked on the score for the most part at home, entrusting Eisenstein's sound engineer (Volsky) to fine-tune the orchestration in his absence. Volsky notes that, in the second half of 1945, he met Prokofiev in private to discuss the project. "He sat at the upright piano, familiarized me with all the details of the score, demonstrated possible variants with one instrument replacing another and suggested, in order to make the best choice, listening to them with live orchestra. He made 'crib notes' so that I'd remember all of his suggestions. Work on the selection of the dubs of the recorded material was wholly entrusted to me. Prokofiev worked only in the theater of the studio, watching the edited scenes for which he needed to write music."[102]

As noted, Part II was banned. On February 2, 1946, following the pre-screenings, Eisenstein submitted the film to the Committee on Cinema Affairs for assessment. That same night, at a gathering celebrating his receipt of a First Class Stalin Prize for Part I, he suffered a near-fatal heart attack.[103] The assessment went ahead on February 7, and both the film and its infirm director were denounced. (Prokofiev, its infirm composer, was spared the rod: the soundtrack was not a focal point of discussion.) A month later, on March 6, the Central Committee ruled that "the second part of the film *Ivan the Terrible* does not stand up to criticism in view of its anti-historical and anti-artistic qualities." The film was thus "prohibited from release."[104]

The months ahead would witness further denunciations and would compel Eisenstein to issue, according to Stalinist ritual, an abject letter of regret.

Eisenstein contemplated reworking Part II, but his frail health prevented him from returning to the studio. On February 25, 1947, he and Cherkasov attended a Kremlin meeting to discuss the perceived failings of the film. Upon agreeing to represent Ivan less like a Shakespearean antihero, to improve the image of the *oprichniki* (despite their black garb, they resembled the Ku Klux Klan), to remove the shadows, and to reintroduce the Moscow people, Eisenstein received approval to re-create Part II (now combined with Part III) with a wholly rewritten script. According to the transcript of the meeting, Cherkasov told Stalin "I am sure the reworking will be a success," to which Stalin jovially replied, "God willing, every day would be like Christmas."[105]

Part II was released finally in 1958. In 1962, the conductor Abram Stasevich, who recorded the soundtrack, transformed Prokofiev's score into a twenty-movement oratorio for soloists, chorus, and orchestra—with the task of linking the disparate movements together assigned to a narrator. Stasevich's oratorio is by no means an accurate representation of the soundtrack, nor, for that matter, are the six "songs and choruses" from *Ivan the Terrible* that were published as an appendix to the March 1958 issue of *Sovetskaya muzïka*.

Film historians usually contend that Part I glorifies Ivan and Part II eulogizes him, charting a mental and physical decline. The audio-visual content of the film traces a less straightforward path, however. In the coronation scene, Ivan is showered over and over again in gold coins. Time and space wrap around him. He exists outside of the phenomenal world, alternately projecting light and dark. The chief visual symbols are icons, nontemporal likenesses of divine figures; the chief musical symbols are chants bearing titles like "Eternal Remembrance" (Vechnaya pamyat') and "You Alone" (Sam yedin yesi). Over the course of the film, patterns of cause and effect, the logic of historical change as defined by Marx, are broken down to illustrate the cosmic forces to which humans can only helplessly submit. It is not surprising that Part II did not appeal to Stalin, who sought, through horrible means, to control time and space, to script existence in the manner of a film.[106]

6

The Forefront of Soviet Music,

1944–1947

Before returning to Moscow from evacuation in 1943, Prokofiev began to make inquiries about obtaining permanent housing there. On August 12, he wrote to Atovmyan from Perm, where he was involved in *Cinderella*, with the news that, in January, he had communicated with Khrapchenko, the chairman of the Committee on Arts Affairs, about "obtaining an apartment" in the capital. Khrapchenko was "sympathetic," and Prokofiev asked Atovmyan "to let me know the current possibilities on this front. I seek, of course, to obtain an apartment in the center of the city, though not in the composers' building."[1] The issue would not be settled until the end of 1944, and would involve much haggling with Mossovet, as signaled by Mira's January 4, 1945, comment: "Now we really do have apartment 210 on Mozhayskoye Shosse, building 11/13."[2] The large two-and-a-half-room apartment (substituting for the two-room apartment Mossovet had offered Prokofiev the previous summer) was located on the sixth floor of a building near the Kiev train station. It had a balcony, a telephone (Prokofiev's number was an extension of the number for the entire building; calls were monitored), and working gas. Tired of lugging suitcases between hotels and her parents' residence, Mira claimed to like the apartment, but the ringing of the telephone, the constant clatter of the elevator doors, the banter of the neighbors, and the blaring of their radios irritated Prokofiev beyond measure. He had resisted moving into it, arguing instead for housing closer to the center, but he was advised by Khrapchenko to make do. Prokofiev would live on Mozhayskoye Shosse for less than four months, thereafter relocating for health reasons to places outside of the city. One room of the apartment would remain in his possession until 1950. Atovmyan arranged to use it in Prokofiev's absence.[3]

In the summers of 1944 and 1945, Prokofiev and Mira were able to escape the constraints of wartime and post-wartime Moscow. For approximately three months each summer, they stayed at the Union of Soviet Composers retreat (a former imperial estate) outside of Ivanovo, which Prokofiev alternately nicknamed the "State Chicken Farm" and "State Pig Farm" in his letters to Atovmyan, owing to the presence of livestock on the grounds and the fact that some of the composers in residence worked in renovated farm buildings (Prokofiev composed in a glass-enclosed terrace overlooking a pond, Shostakovich in an erstwhile henhouse). "For wartime," Elizabeth Wilson writes, "the conditions were unique—composers enjoyed on the one hand the benefits of a kind of health farm, on the other an ideal haven to work in, plus the stimulus of the company of colleagues."[4] Volleyball was the recreation of choice for the energetic, including the sports-loving Shostakovich; Prokofiev defaulted to strolls in the woods and board games. On June 10, 1944, the day after his arrival at the retreat, Prokofiev sent a note to Mira's mother reporting that he was "totally delighted by the place," since "our room is big and quiet and they feed us wonderfully. Best of all is the forest with its fresh young leaves, profusion of flowers, and aroma of [pine] needles!"[5] The triteness of the note is tempered only by concerns about Mira's health: she had recently lost a lot of weight, and Prokofiev sought to assure her mother that he would see to her well-being. As a Stalin Prize laureate and recipient of the Order of the Red Banner of Labor (Orden Trudovogo Krasnogo Znameni), Prokofiev enjoyed greater benefits than most of his colleagues. Before leaving for Ivanovo, he arranged for Mira's parents to receive his allotment of Composers' Union food stamps.[6] Often, he used his status to obtain goods beyond the reach of the average citizen: coffee, dried fruit, white flour, and sweets.

He and Mira stayed at the retreat until August 27. That evening they took the overnight train back to Moscow, forfeiting sleep (their carriage was loud) in favor of conversation with Shostakovich and his wife, Nina, who were also returning to the capital. Upon arrival, Prokofiev and Mira checked into the same room at the Hotel Moscow that they had occupied between October 1943 and January 1944. Prokofiev had by this time received the two-and-a-half-room apartment on Mozhayskoye Shosse, and had even obtained stationery showing the apartment's address and telephone number, but he delayed moving into it for as long as he could.[7]

The summer in Ivanovo had animated and bolstered him, but the time there had passed too quickly, as his resistance to Eisenstein's urgent demands that he return to the capital to finish up *Ivan the Terrible* attests. The collaborative atmosphere had precipitated a rethinking of his compositional priorities, specifically a turn away from the aesthetic and practical demands of stage and screen toward instrumental music. At Ivanovo, Prokofiev finished his Eighth Piano Sonata and the piano score of his Fifth Symphony; the latter would emerge as his most successful, least procedurally problematic score of the 1940s.

The Dividing Line

The inspiration for the Fifth Symphony came in part from Shostakovich—it bears structural and stylistic elements in common with that composer's own Fifth Symphony, the archetype of successful Soviet symphonism—but its most enthusiastic proponent, and the person who witnessed its completion at Ivanovo, was Dmitriy Kabalevsky, a member from 1939 to 1948 of the Orgkomitet of the Union of Soviet Composers who was about to become, in April 1945, responsible for the solicitation and assessment of works for broadcast. This comment from Mira's memoirs, dated July 26, 1944, attests to Kabalevsky's involvement: "Seryozha had only just finished the Andante from the Fifth Symphony when he noticed Kabalevsky from the terrace. . . . Kabalevsky convinced Prokofiev to play the Andante for him. At dinner that evening he called it 'first of all humane, second of all symphonic, and third of all simple—though without a loss of character.' "[8] As his simultaneous work on the four movements progressed, Prokofiev repeatedly expressed his satisfaction with the symphony, the first that he had written in fourteen years. His confidence was bolstered by additional praise from Kabalevsky, Nina Makarova, Vano Muradeli, and Shostakovich when he unveiled the completed piano score to them on August 26. Myaskovsky extolled it in a pair of letters to Shlifshteyn, who had facilitated the 8,000-ruble commission.[9] Platitudes often masqueraded as accolades, Mira noted, but the overall reaction seemed genuine. To the delight of his supporters, Prokofiev produced an evocative score offsetting pastoral, ballroom, and military *topoi*, interpretable as a parable about the war—before, during, and after—and about civilization thwarting annihilation.

The Adagio, the third movement, opens with an elegiac waltz theme salvaged from the score for *The Queen of Spades*. The waltz cedes in the middle section to a languid lament, with the asymmetrical accompaniment (steady triplets in the upper strings combating syncopated quarter notes in the lower strings) ceding to a bombastic, brass-and-percussion-laden sequence of dotted eighths. In the massive, violent climax of the middle section, the lament cedes to a funeral march, after which the skewed dance pattern returns intact, bearing no traces of trauma.

The Scherzo, the second movement, revisits two sections (Nos. 53–54) of the original 1935 ending of *Romeo and Juliet*. The recycled music forms the toccata opening and closing sections of the movement. For the middle section, Prokofiev wrote another waltz, whose disorienting, Spanish-style percussion recalls Ravel; the eight-measure transition into and out of this waltz, moreover, involves a shrill theme (harmonized by alternating tonic major and augmented sixth chords) evocative of Ravel's disciple George Gershwin. Excluding a fanfare motive that punctuates repetitions of the toccata theme, the movement maintains the character of a capricious digression. Its wit resides in the stitching together of the pastoral Musette and the urban Bal-Musette, the former a product of the French Baroque, the latter a product of French café culture.

Thus two works from the mid-1930s, *The Queen of Spades* and *Romeo and Juliet*, came in service of an orchestral score of self-consciously epic proportions. The Andante and Scherzo are framed by a sonata-allegro movement with what Prokofiev called a "dithyrambic" character, and a ritornello movement expressing "folk festiveness."[10] Prokofiev emphasized the affirmative, victorious character of the Fifth Symphony in his public pronouncements, stating in one Soviet source that his "fundamental conception" was "the triumph of the human spirit," and in another that he sought to articulate "the greatness of the human spirit."[11] He waxed less poetic in the American media, informing an unnamed journalist for *Time* that the Fifth Symphony "is about the spirit of man, his soul or something like that."[12] The flip, one-size-fits-all nature of these remarks is only augmented by the fact that he used them again to describe his Sixth Symphony. Either he had become indifferent to the sameness of his own descriptive language or, much less cynically, he sought to stress the consistency of his creative outlook. If earlier in his career he had emphasized divine inspiration, now he stressed human potential. In his wartime and post-wartime statements, Prokofiev fashioned the discourse of Christian Science to accord with the discourse of Socialist Realism.

Prokofiev spoke in general terms about his approach to symphonic composition at the March 28 to April 7, 1944, plenary session of the Union of

Soviet Composers in Moscow. He comes across in the transcript as imper-tinently unimpressed by Shostakovich's wartime compositions. Training his sights on his rival's coolly received Eighth Symphony of 1943, Prokofiev lauds Shostakovich's "thinking, invention, and devising," but decries the "insufficient clarity of his melodic lines." Philosophical ideas are articulated at the expense of the actual sounding surface, he asserts, and calculation substitutes for inspiration. Prokofiev reminds his audience that "we often use the word 'compose,' but we don't always take into account what it means. To compose means to make up, to invent. My sense is that a mother who gathers her newborn into her arms and says 'And what are you getting up to now?' comes much closer to the meaning of this word than many composers when they write symphonies."[13]

The Fifth Symphony is a model of craftsmanship, with Prokofiev seek-ing, in the first and fourth movements, to integrate melodic material of alto-gether contrasting character. This material evolved over the course of some eleven years in his sketchbooks, but most of it dates from 1940 to 1944.[14] Although the two movements are cast in conventional forms (sonata alle-gro and ritornello), Prokofiev avoids traditional means of development. He subjects his themes to expansion, extension, and mutation within indi-vidual subsections of the forms; disruptions and dislocations, accordingly, substitute for transitions. The B-flat major opening theme of the first move-ment, a languid arioso in three phrases, is interrupted in measures 8–11 by an E-flat minor chord, a dotted rhythmic figure evocative of a distant fan-fare, and an ascending B-flat minor scale fragment. The asymmetric second theme bears points in common with the asymmetric first theme: they fill a similar range, and both involve a slippage between the dominant (F) and the augmented fourth (E natural) of the tonic B-flat major scale. As is typi-cal of Prokofiev, the slippage is mirrored in other parts of the exposition by the substitution of the flattened mediant for the mediant and the lead-ing tone for the tonic. In the Fifth Symphony, the destabilizing enrichment of the syntax has a dramatic purpose, lending the placid texture a strange feeling of disquiet.

The fourth movement offsets traces of the languid arioso of the first movement, an impish (giocoso) clarinet solo in B-flat major (enriched with raised tonic, supertonic, subdominant, and dominant pitches) and a soaring hymn in D-flat major in the strings and brasses. The composer conceived the discordant final measures as an enthusiastic and tempestuous evocation of Bacchic revelry, calibrated for twentieth-century ears. The symphony's forms are archaic but the syntax modern, with the tritone, rather than the fifth, providing structural coherence.[15]

The January 13, 1945, premiere, which Prokofiev conducted at the Great Hall of the Moscow Conservatory, glorified him in the eyes of the critics and the public. (The official assessment of the work by the Union of Soviet Composers came after the premiere.) The symphony immediately became a national success, and quickly, on the initiative of Koussevitzky and the Boston Symphony Orchestra, an international one.[16] Richter, who was in the audience for the premiere, absorbed the composer's glow: "The hall was probably lit as usual, but when Prokofiev stood up, it seemed as though the light poured down on him from on high. He stood there, like a monument on a pedestal."[17] As Prokofiev prepared to give the downbeat for the first movement, the concert's host entered the stage to update the audience on the progress of the Red Army on its final march to Berlin. The composer paused; guns blasted in celebration in the distance. "There was something deeply significant, deeply symbolic in this," Richter adds, "as if this moment marked a dividing line in the lives of everyone present, including Prokofiev himself." On or around January 20, just days later, Prokofiev tumbled from that allegorical summit, collapsing and suffering a concussion in the Mozhayskoye Shosse apartment.

The fall was the result of a blackout, brought on by chronic high blood pressure, for which Prokofiev had not been treated, despite a similar fall in 1943 in a market in Alma-Ata.[18] This time he almost died. Kabalevsky, just returned to Moscow from Helsinki, self-servingly recalls visiting Prokofiev in the apartment in February: "I'll never forget that sad visit. Prokofiev lay entirely motionless. At times he could not identify the people to whom he was talking and passed out. In a frail voice he asked a few questions about my encounter with Jean Sibelius and complained bitterly about the forced interruption of his work."[19] In the rough draft of an unpublished reminiscence, Mira's father supplies additional details about Prokofiev's precarious state:

> Mira telephoned: Sergey Sergeyevich has taken a bad fall, landing on his spine, hurting his head, and feels awful. During the next few days his condition worsened. The doctors confined him to bed. Toward the end of February his condition sharply deteriorated. Mira telephoned at 1 am in early March: "What can I do? He talks and talks; it's hard to make him out and I can't stop him." I had to get to him, but

I couldn't: my wife was ill and couldn't be left alone. Moreover, to reach Mozhayskoye Shosse from the center was
difficult: the Metro had already closed, taxis weren't yet
operating, and it would take too long to walk. I asked Mira
to report on Sergey's condition by telephone. She called a
little while later: he was calmer, drowsy.

   The next day I was at Sergey and Mira's. I sat on the
divan where Sergey lay with closed eyes. He had spoken
little the last few days. It was difficult for him to speak;
his condition was grave. His hands rested on the blanket,
his fingers in constant motion. His body was still, his eyes
closed, and his face pale—but his fingers kept moving....

   Mira sent for me the next day. Sergey was being treated
by Doctor Pokrovsky. The doctor was very worried; Sergey
needed immediate hospitalization. In an hour he was taken
by ambulance to the Kremlin hospital.[20]

Prokofiev entered this hospital, located at the time across from the Lenin
Library in central Moscow, on March 7. He received a course of treatment—
including the application of leeches—for what would eventually be diagnosed as ventricular hypertrophy. On March 15, Myaskovsky was able to
report in his diary that Prokofiev looked "relatively well, and feels better and
better."[21] From April 9 to May 28, Prokofiev convalesced, on Eisenstein's
instigation, at the exclusive Podlipki sanatorium in Barvikha, spending his
better mornings and afternoons reading, strolling, and receiving visitors. He
was not allowed to compose, but he apparently made a point of telling one of
his visitors, Vladimir Vlasov, that he was working on his *Ode to the End of
the War* "secretly...in my head."[22] Atovmyan tended to Prokofiev's requests
for warm clothing—spring had come late; his room was cold—newspapers,
and provisions. Mira, whose weight remained worryingly low, joined him at
the sanatorium at her father's insistence (her treatment consisted of warm
baths and exposure to ultraviolet light). "Seryozha feels quite well," she
wrote to her father on April 16, "but his blood pressure has increased somewhat."[23] Such would become the pattern for much of the rest of his life: his
health would gradually improve, allowing him to work full- or part-time,
but then suddenly deteriorate, leaving him bedridden with blinding headaches and nosebleeds. By the time he left Barvikha for Moscow, however, he
felt able-bodied, enthusing about an upcoming concert performance of *War*

and Peace at the Moscow Conservatory. Vlasov, the director of the Moscow Philharmonic, kept Prokofiev apprised of the progress of the rehearsals until he himself was able to hear them.

Yudina

This performance was prepared, on the instruction of the Committee on Arts Affairs, using singers and instrumentalists from the Bolshoy Theater, the Stanislavsky Theater, the State Symphony, the Chorus of the Republic (Respublikanskaya khorovaya kapella), and the Philharmonic. To be exact, it did not represent the premiere of the opera: that had taken place in Moscow on October 16, 1944, through the initiative of an ambitious young conductor named Konstantin Popov, who led the Ensemble of Soviet Opera of the All-Russia Theatrical Society (Ansambl' sovetskoy operï Vserossiyskogo Teatral'nogo Obshchestva).[24] Popov's performance, mounted in an inadequate space with piano accompaniment, featured seven of the eleven scenes from the opera, with a narrator reading from Tolstoy's novel as a means to bridge the missing scenes. Mira supplied the narrator with introductions to the two halves of the performance taken from Tolstoy's epilogue and the memoirs of the writer-soldier Davïdov.

Following this event, a modest success, the Committee on Arts Affairs granted approval for the large-scale concert performance of *War and Peace* at the Moscow Conservatory. Prompting came less from Popov and the Ensemble of Soviet Opera than from a foreign source: the Metropolitan Opera in New York City, whose director, Edward Johnson, had sought in 1943 to premiere *War and Peace*.[25] In response to Johnson's inquiries, Prokofiev wrote to Khrapchenko for permission to have the opera staged abroad, but was advised, as he expected he would be, that it first had to be staged in the Soviet Union, leaving him to express his frustration that "there were no signs of life on the part of the Bolshoy Theater."[26] The Metropolitan Opera continued to press for a staging, and VOKS also received an inquiry about it from the Royal Swedish Opera (Stockholm), but Khrapchenko's decision was, Prokofiev learned, "firm and final: *first in Moscow.*"[27] The growing foreign interest in *War and Peace* eventually motivated the Committee on Arts Affairs to approve, in lieu of a costly full-scale staging of the opera, the concert performance under Samosud's direction. Samosud had lost his post at the Bolshoy Theater in the summer of 1943, and sought with the performance to reestablish his credentials within the Soviet opera world.[28]

He conducted nine of the eleven scenes on June 7 and eight of them on June 9 and 11, 1945 (scene 6, "Pierre Bezukhov's Study," scene 8, "Shevardino Redoubt during the Battle of Borodino," and then scene 9, "A Street in French-Occupied Moscow," were excised). Once again, a narrator provided the details of the missing scenes. Prokofiev attended several rehearsals, and the first and the last of the performances—a headache kept him from the second one—publicly expressing delight that the opera had at last received a proper hearing.[29] Behind the scenes, however, his supporters chafed at the cuts. The eminent pianist, spiritualist, and nonconformist intellectual Mariya Yudina came forcefully to Prokofiev's defense in a letter of protest to Vlasov:

> The abridgement of Sergey Sergeyevich Prokofiev's *War and Peace* for the performances on the 9th and then the 11th of this month was, to numerous listeners, a grave error. The 9th scene is remarkable in its conception and realization, in its ingenious response to dramaturgical and compositional challenges, in the brilliance of its orchestration, in the profoundness of its individual episodes (Platon Karatayev, the appearance of Napoleon), in its musical ties with the past, in its maximal emotional impact, and in the richness of its patriotic grandeur. It can hardly be considered incidental to the work. How could one raise a hand against the "Burning of Moscow," which is close to everyone's heart, celebrated *at last* in all these great days of ours and in all the perfection of Prokofiev's craft? How could one be in favor of any sort of abridgement at the moment of the opera's realization, when it had *not previous been seen*, all the more so in the presence of the author, who owing to illness couldn't in any shape or form protest?
>
> I don't dare speak for Sergey Sergeyevich—it's possible that for some reason unbeknownst to me he didn't protest to you, either in general or in another context—but he didn't attend the performance on the 9th and on the 11th he was, as you know, sufficiently passive.[30]

Yudina additionally speculated that the opera had been shortened for pragmatic rather than aesthetic reasons, but noted that the performances occurred in the festive atmosphere of the postwar holidays, and that no one in the packed hall would be rushing home. "We all hope to hear the entire work as soon as possible," she concluded. "Being sometimes the first, at other times the only, performer of Prokofiev's works, I permit myself to consider my humble opinion important."[31]

The letter went unnoticed amid the avalanche of reviews that followed the June performances. Prokofiev and Mira gathered them all, taking special interest in a review and photo-spread published in *Vechernyaya Moskva*. The author, Georgiy Polyanovsky, lauded the balance in the score between romantic, epic, and patriotic themes: "The line of Natasha and Bolkonsky's love penetrates the entire fabric of the opera," he observed, "but without obscuring the lofty epic sound of the mass scenes, which bear the valor, faithfulness, and patriotism of the Russian people." Polyanovsky complained, however, that the thematic balance was upset by the presence of the narrator: "The idea of using an announcer to explain and connect the scenic action was a total failure. It was neither artistic nor essential; a large part of the text, moreover, could not be made out by the listener." Of the libretto, Polyanovsky quipped: "To leave Tolstoy's words, his aphoristic style, untouched—perhaps this was a tempting idea! But here the composer and the theater still have a lot of work to do."[32] In his view, the opera remained very much a work in progress.

Polyanovsky's observations would be echoed by later reviewers. In the August and September 1946 issues of *Sovetskaya muzïka*, for example, Anna Khokhlovkina-Zolotarevskaya compared and contrasted *War and Peace* favorably with the Russian operatic classics of the past: Musorgsky's *Boris Godunov*, Chaikovsky's *Eugene Onegin*, and Rimsky-Korsakov's *Legend of the Invisible City of Kitezh and the Maiden Fevroniya*.[33] Like Polyanovsky, Khokhlovkina-Zolotarevskaya praised the interpenetration of the public and private scenes in the opera. She took issue, however, with the wordiness of the libretto and the absence of folklore-derived material in the vocal lines. Prokofiev had anticipated this second concern, but his response to it had proved inadequate. In the run-up to the June 1945 performances, he had inserted a folksong-derived aria into the score titled "The iron breast does not fear severe weather" (Zheleznaya grud' ne boitsya surovosti pogod).[34] Sung by Field Marshal Kutuzov in scene 7, "Before the Battle of Borodino," the insertion marked the first phase in the metamorphosis of this character along nationalistic lines.

The response to the June performances was such that Samosud received tentative permission to stage the opera at the Leningrad Malïy Opera Theater (Malegot). He recognized the need for additional changes, but also the need to preserve Prokofiev's original conception of the opera as a two-evening production. His requests, however, threatened to expand *War and Peace* from two parts to three. Mira reports that, on March 3, 1946, she had a long conversation on the subject with Samosud:

> Several days ago he had advised Seryozha to include in the "Mïtishchi" scene [10] in *War and Peace* the waltz from the second scene, which he calls "magical." Yesterday he became enamored of a new idea: he wanted a new lyric scene written for the second part of the opera, namely the encounter between Natasha and Pierre at Princess Mariya's after the death of Prince Andrey. A lyrical element would thus be added to the second part; moreover, the Natasha-Pierre plotline would be brought to a close. After the conversation with Samosud I read the corresponding pages of the novel aloud to Seryozha. These pages are truly tremendous, but it seemed to me that the Natasha plotline should end with Andrey's death. Otherwise, for the new scene to have a place, a third part will have to be written.[35]

The opera would expand from eleven to thirteen scenes, but the idea of adding the scene for Natasha and Pierre would be dropped (it would have brought the opera perilously close to Tolstoy's anti-nationalistic epilogue). In the weeks ahead, Samosud further exhorted Prokofiev to drain *War and Peace* of declamation, the foundation of the 1942 draft, and to infuse it with transformative popular genres, the most spectacular of these being a suite of chimeric dances (a common-time polonaise, a mazurka, a waltz, and an écossaise) for a new scene involving a New Year's Eve ball.[36] With this new scene, the opera had twelve; one more would be added, detailing Kutuzov's startling decision to sacrifice Moscow in the struggle against Napoleon. This scene, "A Hut in Fili," would prove to be the most nettlesome of the entire opera; indeed, Prokofiev would still be working on it in the last year of his life. The difficulties stemmed from its allegorical significance and the political baggage it accrued over time. The representation of the Field Marshal's prosecution of the war against Napoleon gradually became a simulacrum of Stalin's prosecution of the war against Hitler.

On or around June 20, 1945, Prokofiev returned with Mira to Ivanovo. (The couple traveled there in Shostakovich's car and stayed temporarily in Shostakovich's cabin.)[37] There, after a five-month interruption, Prokofiev returned part-time to composition, beginning work in the mornings on the *War and Peace* revisions, another symphony (his Sixth), and several smaller projects, including a pair of Russian folksong arrangements for a competition organized by Kabalevsky.[38] His headaches and nosebleeds persisted; when bedridden, Mira read French and American literature to him (works by Émile Zola, Prosper Mérimée, and Theodore Dreiser). Toward the end of the summer he had rallied to the point where, as Mira explained to her father, "He seldom has headaches, even though he is working intensively. We have agreed that he will take Sundays off.... We have completed the libretto of the new scene for the opera and he has already prepared the waltz for Natasha and Andrey."[39]

The couple planned to remain in Ivanovo through the fall, but a telegram from the Bolshoy Theater abbreviated their plans. It brought the news that the ballet *Cinderella*, an oft-forsaken, oft-postponed work whose conception dates back to 1940, was in rehearsal for a November 1945 premiere. Prokofiev and Mira hurriedly returned to Moscow in October. The history of the ballet, a commission out of sync with the times, is complex, spanning the entire course of the war and bearing witness to the increasing ossification of the Soviet ballet school. That history must now be told in detail.

Cinderella

Following the successful Leningrad production of his ballet *Romeo and Juliet* in 1940, Prokofiev had entered into discussions with the Kirov Theater for a sequel, one that would equal the success of *Romeo and Juliet* while avoiding the political and logistical problems that had long delayed its premiere. The artistic director of the Kirov Theater, Ariy Pazovsky, had just passed on a scenario by Yuriy Slonimsky that was to have used the music of Chaikovsky, the safest of the Russian classics. Slonimsky, a major ballet critic and aesthetician, immediately turned to Prokofiev in the hope that he would write the music for his scenario, a paean to love and the onset of spring with more than a passing resemblance to the traditional Snow Maiden (Snegurochka) folktale. Ulanova, the Kirov Theater's prima ballerina, had also proposed this subject to Prokofiev, and had advised Slonimsky to meet with him.[40] No sooner had he read the scenario, however, than Prokofiev rejected it, admonishing Slonimsky for writing the kind of text that only an amateur composer would set. While dressing him down, Prokofiev offered an insight into the approach he intended to take in his new ballet:

> Balletomanes grumble that my *Romeo and Juliet* lacks dances. This is because they are used only to considering galops, polkas, waltzes, mazurkas, and variations as dances. I am not against traditional ballet forms. Don't you think that I know how to compose them? I can. I just don't want to. It's easy to compose in an old-fashioned way. But one has to move forward. And in Chaikovsky's ballets they don't always dance; sometimes they just walk about the stage. Why don't you complain about that? In my ballets, incidentally, everything has to be danced. It has to be and can be.
>
> It's a pity that there isn't a scenario that would allow me to illustrate how to compose waltzes, polkas, variations, and so on in a contemporary way. Your scenario doesn't allow this: it only requires imitating Chaikovsky![41]

These comments are instructive, illustrating a once-unthinkable fidelity to the forms of eighteenth- and nineteenth-century ballet but also an interest in updating their contents. Prokofiev readily composed in the number format, but sought to retain the unusual—for the time and place—rhythms and chromatic detours that defined his syntax. Both with and against his wishes, *Cinderella* became—in thick Soviet guise—the fourth Chaikovsky ballet.

Prokofiev signed a contract for the ballet with Yevgeniy Radin, the business director of the Kirov Theater, on November 23, 1940 (between the conclusion of work on *The Duenna* and the beginning of work on *War and Peace*). Owing to the "complexity" of the task and the various demands on Prokofiev's time, Radin offered him 20,000 rubles for its successful completion. The fee was approved by the Committee on Arts Affairs.[42] The first public notice of the ballet came on January, 17, 1941, in the final lines of an article in *Vechernyaya Moskva*. Prokofiev describes his conception of Cinderella as a "living Russian maiden with real, rather than fairy-tale experiences."[43] His choice of words suggests knowledge of the 1940 film *The Radiant Path* (*Svetliy put'*), whose title character (Tanya) evolves from an oppressed, illiterate housekeeper into a super-productive factory worker and recipient of the Order of Lenin; the original title of the film, directed by Viktor Ardov, was *Cinderella*.[44] Prokofiev further comments in the article that the ballet's scenario would be written by the dramatist Nikolay Volkhov—a rather predictable writer he had first met, through Meyerhold, in Kislovodsk.

In his memoirs, and in an article for the Kirov Theater newspaper *Za sovetskoye iskusstvo* (For Soviet Art), Volkhov offers a cheerful account of the ballet's creation, and supplies the striking image of Prokofiev solving technical problems in his head while playing the card game solitaire on the lid of his piano.[45] His "uncommonly amicable" collaboration with the composer resulted in a text that represented Cinderella as the "young romantic spirit," a "living presentiment" of true love. The Prince, in contrast, exudes "wind and flame"; rejecting courtly etiquette, "he leaps onto the throne like a horseman into the saddle." Comic interpolations included a lampoon of the stand-offish bourgeoisie and staid eighteenth-century court. The gentle fairy-tale world of the Fairy Godmother was filtered, according to Volkhov, through the imagination of a child, while the scenes in which the Prince searches for his beloved "from North to South, East to West" drew from adult adventure tales. The Ugly Stepsisters remain trapped, from the beginning to the end of the ballet, in the quotidian realm, tending to their wardrobe and coiffure in blissful ignorance of their failings.[46]

But the genesis of the scenario was more fraught than Volkhov relates. He and Prokofiev clashed over its contents almost from the outset. On December 24, 1940, Prokofiev told the theater that he imagined the ballet less in the French spirit of Charles Perrault than the Russian spirit of Aleksandr Afanasyev, whose version of the traditional Cinderella fairy tale has very dark hues. "I see *Cinderella* as an updated classical ballet with its particular forms, like the *pas d'action*, *grand pas*, and so forth," Prokofiev noted, adding that "insofar as Afanasyev's Cinderella tale relates to the eighteenth century," he would include other classical dances: a minuet, mazurka, and "no less than two or three full-scale waltzes." In a follow-up telegram to the theater dated January 6, 1941, he paradoxically emphasized the "need to create a Russian Cinderella of Elizabethan times."[47]

By the time *Cinderella* reached the stage, the story line had in places been altered beyond recognition. Prokofiev, the actor and director Zavadsky, and the choreographer Vakhtang Chabukiani all contributed to the revision, though Prokofiev seems to have had the final creative word. Volkhov's draft dates from May 15, 1941; Prokofiev's rewrite, which augments the buffoonery and suppresses the sentimentality of the draft, dates from much later—May 5, 1944—a month before Prokofiev's first summer in Ivanovo.

Comparison of the two versions finds Prokofiev deleting all but the most crucial narrative details. Where Volkhov created a traditional balletic storybook with elaborate descriptions of décor and dress, Prokofiev argued for concision, and for using the group dances, rather than stock-in-trade pantomime, to drive the action forward. There is, for example, a profound difference between the original and revised texts of act 1, scene 5, which depict the Fairy Godmother as a beggar-woman:

> VOLKHOV: The domestic situation threatens to become a tempest. But at this time—it is unknown how—a mysterious old woman appears in the room. Did she come through the door? Or straight through the wall? And her gait is such that she seems less to walk than to flow through the room. She appears to be a beggar. She leans on a crutch; a pouch hangs from her shoulder. And since nobody knows that the Fairy Godmother has arrived, they all take her for a beggar. The Fairy Godmother maintains this impression on purpose. With her hand outstretched, she first approaches the stepmother, then [the Ugly Stepsisters] Skinny [Khudïshka] and Dumpy [Kubïshka]. Nobody, however, gives her anything. Only Cinderella, in a fit of pity, wants to give the old woman something. Cinderella, however, owns nothing except her slippers. Gripped by a feeling of goodness, Cinderella quickly retrieves the cherished slippers from a small chest and offers them to the old woman. The Fairy tenderly looks at Cinderella and, concealing them in her pouch, disappears just as she had appeared.

> PROKOFIEV: In the room—it is unknown how—the Fairy Godmother appears in the guise of a beggar woman. She asks for a handout, but nobody gives her one. Cinderella, in a fit of goodness gives the old woman the cherished slippers. The Fairy disappears.[48]

Pantomimic detail was also excised from the ending of act 1, in the prophetic scene between Cinderella, her Fairy Godmother, and the Lilliputian timekeepers that control Cinderella's destiny:

VOLKHOV: The clock face lights up. The arms rise from 8 to 12. One after another, frightened dwarfs run out from the clock case. They don't understand what happened to the clock. But the old woman takes one of the dwarfs by the collar, shakes him and very strictly orders him to warn Cinderella about the arrival of midnight. At midnight the magic spell will disappear. And the princess will be in rags again.

PROKOFIEV: The clock face lights up. The arms move from 8 to 12. One after another, 12 dwarfs run out from the clock case. The old woman orders the dwarfs to warn Cinderella about the arrival of midnight. At midnight the magic spell will disappear.[49]

Although the scenario was drastically shortened between drafts, Prokofiev did permit a few scenes to be expanded. The depiction of each of the Four Seasons (the Spring, Summer, Autumn, and Winter Fairies), and the insertion of the "Dance of the Grasshoppers and Dragonflies" in act 1 evinces the influence, however remote, of the pantheism of the Snow Maiden folktale. Prokofiev had not altogether forgotten Slonimsky's proposal. Act 3, scene 1, moreover, includes three galops, which show the Prince traveling the globe in search of his beloved; along the way, he encounters temptresses from exotic nations. The Prince intently resists their advances.

On March 29, 1941, Prokofiev told a reporter for *Kurortnaya gazeta* (Resort Gazette) in Sochi that he had completed "half of the music for the ballet. Now I am working on the finale, after which the theater will begin to prepare the spectacle. *Cinderella* is scheduled as the first premiere of the season at the Leningrad Theater of Opera and Ballet."[50] Prokofiev added that the title role would be danced by Ulanova to choreography by Chabukiani. In 1941, Prokofiev met several times with Chabukiani, declaring in no uncertain terms that he would not permit alterations to his music to suit the choreography, as had been the disappointing case with *Romeo and Juliet*. On one occasion, Volkhov recounts, Prokofiev set a metronome on the lid of the piano and said to Chabukiani: " 'Now be good enough to dance through the entire second act. And remember one thing—since I've not yet written the music, you can change as many choreographic patterns as you like. But when I've written it, not a single note may be changed.' And Chabukiani began to dance and actually danced through the entire second act."[51] Following this silent demonstration, the composer drafted the music for act 2, taking care to establish melodic links between it and act 1. (In act 1, the love theme has the task of anticipating, through its harmonic digressions, new experiences; in act 2, the theme documents, through harmonic repetition, the moment of recognition.)

Prokofiev fell slightly behind schedule and requested an extension from the Kirov Theater from April 1 to June 15, 1941. (To show that progress had been made, he forwarded the piano score of act 2 and "1/3" of act 1 to the theater for perusal.)[52] The outbreak of war in the Soviet Union forced an unexpected, indefinite postponement of the premiere. Prokofiev and Chabukiani ended up together in Tbilisi, but they did not realize their work on the ballet. The music of *Cinderella* remained unfinished until July 1943, after Prokofiev had relocated to Perm. The Kirov troupe had also been evacuated to Perm, its administrators hoping to begin rehearsing the ballet in August, this time with choreography by Konstantin Sergeyev.[53] A production was planned for the cramped local theater in December. The conductor Sherman, who had also transferred to Perm, describes the state of affairs:

> As soon as he arrived in Perm Prokofiev worked on the ballet *Cinderella*. He composed in the morning, and then stopped by in the afternoon (we were all living in a hotel called "Semietazhka" [Seven Stories]; the sole upright piano in the hotel was in my room) to check what he had composed in the morning. At the piano Prokofiev checked only the complicated polyphonic passages. I was delighted to be the first to hear not only the music of Prokofiev's *Cinderella* but also that of his Flute Sonata. In 1943 in the hall of the Perm city library Sergey Sergeyevich played several excerpts from *Cinderella* at the piano. In that same concert the Kirov Theater Orchestra under my direction performed his Classical Symphony and his *Overture on Jewish Themes* (the orchestral version had been made by the author in 1936 at the request of the conductor Koussevitzky).[54]

Prokofiev completed the piano score in time for the rehearsals, but the premiere was once again postponed, this time owing to logistical problems. The theater in Perm had neither the means nor the clout to mount a large-scale ballet during the war.

The orchestration was begun in the spring of 1944. As is characteristic of Prokofiev's large scores, there are three systems of two-line notation on each page of the manuscript, with the selection of instruments indicated in shorthand in the margins. (As testament to wartime shortages, the 153-page manuscript of act 2 is written on poor-quality paper of different sizes.)[55] For acts 1 and 2, Prokofiev had Karpov, with whom he had worked on *Ballad of an Unknown Boy*, assist with the scoring; for act 3, he enlisted Lamm. On February 3, 1944, the Kirov troupe at last began rehearsals. These took place in a makeshift, leaky studio in the House of the Red Army in Perm. Half of the choreography would be set before the troupe returned to Leningrad, where its administrators confronted the daunting challenge of resurrecting its repertoire in deplorable conditions. The premiere of *Cinderella* would follow the return to the stage of an enduring favorite, Chaikovsky's *Swan Lake*, as a symbol of the survival of the city's people and culture through the blockade.[56]

In a March 26 broadcast Prokofiev described his conception of *Cinderella* and the premieres that had been promised (dates uncertain) for Moscow and Leningrad. "The fairy tale about Cinderella is encountered in many nations, many peoples," Prokofiev noted, adding that he and his scenarist "paid close attention to the dramatic side of the ballet." "It was our desire to make the characters real and living so that their sorrows and joys did not leave viewers indifferent." The music, Prokofiev conceded, reflected classical rather than modern ballet tradition. "It has several variations, a pas de deux, an Adagio, 3 waltzes, a gavotte, and a mazurka."[57] In a November comment, Prokofiev revealed that he had assigned three lyrical themes to the title character, the first designating Cinderella's suffering at the hands of her wicked stepsisters, the second her dreams of a better future, and the third her passion for the Prince.[58] Volkhov boasts of having given Prokofiev the idea of representing the hours of the clock and the chiming using tap-dancing dwarfs. He also took credit for the paraphrase, in act 2, of the March from Prokofiev's opera *The Love for Three Oranges* in the duet for the Ugly Stepsisters. (The decision to derive Cinderella's love theme from a portion of the incidental music to *Eugene Onegin* was Prokofiev's own.)[59] Finally, Volkhov seems to have advised Prokofiev to set the act 3, scene 1 episode between the Prince and the Cobblers, one of whom suffers from ill-temper brought on by a toothache.[60]

Prior to the ballet's Moscow premiere, several members of the Committee on Arts Affairs attended a rehearsal to vouchsafe its suitability for the stage. On November 16, 1945, the group met to discuss the ballet. For the most part, it was praised; the lone complaint concerned the orchestration, which had been changed on the insistence of the conductor, Yuriy Fayer, who decided that it was too light for the Bolshoy Theater. In the spring of 1945, he and the choreographer Rostislav Zakharov had sent Volkhov to the Podlipki sanatorium in Barvikha, where Prokofiev was recuperating from his January collapse, to discuss the orchestration. The composer unhappily agreed to the proposed changes, which were carried out by an in-house musician at the Bolshoy Theater, the percussionist Boris Pogrebov.[61] These did not sit well with the Committee on Arts Affairs. One of the appointed reviewers of the score, Khachaturyan, complained that "in some places the instrumentation is too heavy"; another, Shostakovich, observed that "nothing is said on the billboard about who took part in the orchestration or re-orchestration at the theater. It was well done; nothing shocked me about it. But I was nonetheless surprised that Prokofiev, who is such an outstanding orchestrator, had not completed the orchestration himself."[62]

In reality, the changes made a travesty of the ballet, since the composer had invested a great deal of energy in creating dreamlike timbres: the strings, for example, perform drawn-out phrases at the extreme limits of their registers. One potential explanation for the alterations to the score comes from Fayer's pupil Gennadiy Rozhdestvensky, who recalled that neither Fayer nor Zakharov felt comfortable reading scores. In the run-up to the premiere, the task of interpreting *Cinderella* fell to the rehearsal pianist, which resulted in a mismatch between the orchestral music and the dance. On one occasion, Rozhdestvensky notes, the choreographer heard the rehearsal pianist playing a forte section of the score and decided, in light of its robustness, to assign it to six men. At the first orchestral rehearsal, however, they found out that "these six men are dancing to a solo flute that just happens to be playing *forte*."[63] Sensing a fiasco in the offing, the dancers began protesting. At this point, Rozhdestvensky continues, Pogrebov was summoned to correct the orchestration. "In place of the unfortunate flute he inserted three trumpets in unison and added a large drum which beat the count of '1.' . . . Pogrebov reorchestrated *Cinderella* from A to Z."[64] (Rozhdestvensky, whose recollections evince a talent for exaggeration, if not an unbridled imagination, is overstating the extent of the alterations by a few letters.) Adding insult to an injury wrought by incompetence, the ballet's Moscow premiere included a scene that Prokofiev had deleted. It depicted the Prince searching for Cinderella after the ball in Africa. The music was adapted by the tunesmith Vladimir

Zakharov from the preexisting "Orientalia" of act 3 and orchestrated by Pogrebov.[65] In the original scenario, Volkhov scripted the scene as follows:

> The third galop brings the Prince to Africa. Some Negresses surround him. They have never before seen a slipper and attempt to wear it on their hands. The Prince unearths the jeweled shoe and returns to his native city.[66]

In the revised scenario, Prokofiev replaced this scene with a "series of brief meetings" between the Prince and potential Cinderellas.[67] The Bolshoy Theater disregarded his wishes.

Cinderella was first seen on November 21, 1945. The embellished orchestration gave the Moscow premiere a leaden grandeur that distracted from the dancing. Ulanova, for one, blanched at the louder and richer sound of the score; she also disliked the costume that Pyotr Vilyams created for her. (Inspired by a "French porcelain statuette of the eighteenth century," the outfit made Ulanova look like a cross between a shepherdess and a marquise.)[68] Prokofiev's doctors advised him against attending the premiere for fear that the excitement would precipitate a stroke. He defied them, seeing *Cinderella* three successive nights at the Bolshoy Theater, though he only managed to stay for one act each time.

The Leningrad premiere of *Cinderella* (April 8, 1946) brought back the original orchestration. Choreographed by Sergeyev, the production fared well with the critics: the writer for *Trud*, presumably heeding official instruction, applauded the Kirov Theater for respecting Prokofiev's intentions.[69] The conductor Boris Khaykin wrote to Prokofiev ahead of the premiere to assure him that the Kirov Theater had not tampered with the score. "I heard from Fayer that for some reason he didn't use your original score, and that the ballet is being done in Moscow in someone else's arrangement. I don't know Fayer's motives for doing this or what the arrangement contains; I can only say that we adhered strictly to the original score and the orchestra sounds simply marvelous."[70] The Leningrad staging, a modest, intimate counter to the excesses of the Moscow staging, came as a relief to the composer.

In the November 29, 1945, edition of *Pravda*, Shostakovich reviewed the Moscow premiere of *Cinderella*. His description is cluttered with vague adjectives and metaphors; it is a typical example of Communist official-speak. "In the production's visual-narrative development," Shostakovich comments, the music "creates a tremendous emotional-expressive buildup that achieves authentic tragedy." "The music," he emphasizes, "is symphonic: the composer develops the themes with authentic mastery that brings to light the dramatic force of the production."[71] To the extent that these remarks can be decoded, they contradict the broader Soviet and non-Soviet consensus about Prokofiev's score. In the words of the dance critic Arlene Croce, "Prokofiev's ballet…is not a conventional, sweet storybook romance; it is a brooding, disjointed affair."[72]

The central problem with the work is its defiance of fairy-tale logic. Cinderella's home life is less oppressive than her social life. The Ugly Stepsisters are buffoons, figures of fun who debase themselves alone, and Cinderella does not suffer their taunts. The music for the ball scenes is overscaled, characterized by dense chromaticism and heavy string and brass writing (especially in the Bolshoy Theater version): it does not allow Cinderella to forget her blue Mondays. Socialist aesthetics prohibited the composer from portraying the decadent, bourgeois court as a place of salvation. He avoided the issue by focusing on the clock tolling midnight, which marks the climax of an anxious ballroom sequence. For Cinderella and the Prince, the path to happiness is blocked not by social forces but by seconds and minutes. Having grown up in a debased world, both characters grasp at innocence and purity before mortality overtakes them. One senses here that, for Prokofiev, endlessly pressured by deadlines, paradise is a realm without clocks and chronologies. Croce approaches this point when she discusses the nature images in the scenario:

> Cinderella goes to the ball not as a social-climbing imposter but as Rousseau's naturally good human being in search of a non-brutalizing environment. She doesn't find it. (The Fairy Godmother should have known better, but she's naive.) Instead, Cinderella finds another child of nature, the Prince, who, even as she, has miraculously escaped environmental conditioning, and the two of them are united in the starry idealism of a world to come.[73]

The challenge the two characters face is one of dislocation: they need to find each other. In the absence of paradise, their reunion has to serve as its own reward in its own time. Such, at least, was the opinion of at least two reviewers of the Leningrad premiere of the ballet, who both felt that the staging lacked wonder until act 3.[74] (The music and décor bore the brunt of the blame for the preceding glumness.) In the final scene, Cinderella no longer behaves as if she is betrothed to a military man, but to a storybook hero.

The three waltzes embody the essence of the romance. The first two—the "Grand Waltz" and the "Waltz Coda"—dominate act 2. Both are foreshadowed in act 1, especially by the number "Cinderella's Departure for the Ball," which is suffused with a combination of hope and fear. The third "Slow Waltz" comes in act 3 before the concluding "Amoroso," which transports the heroine and hero into a magic garden, the sort of place that had vanished in twentieth-century ballet. In the scenario, Prokofiev noted that the "Amoroso" would begin with a "broad melody, calm at first," followed by "an exposition, then something of an abatement, and then the first melody once again, like a triumphant love song."[75] He might have added that the happy ending unfolds in a sound-scape reminiscent of *Swan Lake*.

The Grand Waltz is cast as an ABACA rondo, with the B and C sections subdividing into small ternary forms. These inner episodes offer a modest, intimate contrast to the violent outer episodes, which in turn suggest a contrast between the private and public, innocence and experience. The strings introduce grand melodies, but these are compromised, upon repetition, by oboes and muted trumpets, adding a grotesque, Gogolian lining to the waltz. Cinderella and the Prince appear to be caught in a realm that is out of sorts with itself: the downbeats are overstressed by the percussion and brass; intervals of the fourth and fifth are expanded and contracted by semitones; E and B tonic and dominant pitches are undercut by D-sharps and A-sharps. The E-flat major episode at rehearsal 217 alternates between semitonal turn figures and large intervallic leaps. The hairpin dynamics and the divided string chords at rehearsal number 220 and the twinkling arpeggios in the harp and piano at rehearsal 222 generate a phantasmal ambiance, but the interlude ends at rehearsal 225 with the oppressive incursion of the full orchestra and the opening melody: for Cinderella and the Prince the escape into the world of fantasy, the world of art, is short-lived: the waltz sighs to a close with a solo clarinet drifting down three octaves.

The Slow Waltz, a three-part structure depicting the reunion of Cinderella and the Prince, intimates that the two characters have gone to sleep. Prokofiev creates a sense of serene stasis in the opening and closing sections. The opening D-flat major theme unfolds at a leaden tempo (fifty-four beats per minute). Though it contains two-measure subdivisions, the contrapuntal interweaving of the inner lines renders them indistinct. Prokofiev holds pitches over bar-lines and, by postponing the cadential resolution, increases the theme's duration from eight to ten measures. The temporal distortions are exacerbated by changes in texture: the theme floats back and forth between muted strings and woodwinds. The middle (B) section shatters the calm mood, with the strings and brasses introducing machine-like ostinato patterns and hemiolas. It is not that dancers cannot perform this waltz, but that the waltz cannot perform itself—as witnessed by the insertion of a measure of 4/4 time between rehearsal numbers 376 and 377. Cinderella and the Prince have entered nirvana, but they still sense the regular world. According to the scenario, the middle section of the waltz expresses the reactions of the Ugly Stepsisters to Cinderella's newfound happiness. These reactions, however, are presented in fragments, the oneiric detritus of actual events. The closing section of the waltz reprises the opening theme, but Prokofiev pushes it toward abstraction by distributing it over several octaves.

The Waltz Coda, which occurs between the Grand and Slow Waltzes, is fretful rather than euphoric, with the languid first theme overpowered by the accompaniment and then transformed, upon its repetition, into a restless shadow of itself. The waltz moves from G minor to D major to G major, with the strident second theme, introduced by the glockenspiel and upper brass, sparring with the first theme. Toward the conclusion, the waltz takes a portentous turn, with the dancers overcome, as it were, by an extended orchestral crescendo. The tolling of midnight is nigh, and Cinderella and the Prince cannot avoid it. The ball becomes a modernist nightmare controlled by clockwork automata. Woodblock ticktocks are interpolated by orchestral references to the March of the grotesque gnome Chernomor in Glinka's 1842 opera *Ruslan and Lyudmila*—Prokofiev mimics the piercing piccolo notes of the March with a shrill flute line—and blends it with a chortling brass ostinato borrowed from the Constructivist ballet *Le Pas d'Acier*. High society imperils the heroine and hero, as does the inexorable progression of time. Act 3 finds the two characters stepping into a nostalgic cosmos where love stays pure, unsullied by experience. The tenuousness of this vision is denoted by its brevity: the concluding Amoroso, a digression in the narrative, lasts for just thirty-eight measures.

The more nuanced, less workaday reviews of the ballet focused on its wistfulness. Such is the case of the review in the illustrated journal *Ogonyok* (The Little Flame) by Yuriy Olesha, a gifted prose writer who had to ply his trade as a journalist because he had fallen out of favor with the regime. (Olesha is credited with penning the first proletarian fairy tale: *Three Fat*

Men [*Tri Tolstyaka*, 1924], which served as the basis of a ballet staged at the Bolshoy Theater in the infamous year of 1936.) "At times it seems that one is less listening to a ballet than a tender reminiscence of a ballet," Olesha wrote of *Cinderella*, "everything is graceful, nothing stressed." The music, he added, "does not seem to be the product of preparatory work; it comes into being in the moment, a narrative by the composer about how, in his opinion, a fairy tale should sound."[76]

Olesha seems to be conjuring up the intended rather than the realized ballet. Prokofiev wanted the music to sound increasingly spontaneous, but the alterations to the orchestration for the Bolshoy Theater premiere encumbered it, leaving Cinderella trapped in a doubly troubled world. To praise the ballet for its "realism," as a writer for *Sovetskaya muzïka* did, was actually to isolate its crucial defect.[77] In advance of the Kirov Theater premiere, Prokofiev responded to the problems with the orchestration by extracting three untampered orchestral suites from the ballet. He began planning the suites early in 1946 and continued working on them through the spring. None of them, however, would be published during his lifetime.[78]

Nikolina Gora

Also in early 1946, Prokofiev and Mira abandoned the apartment on Mozhayskoye Shosse for her parents' apartment (the third room of the three-room communal dwelling had evidently become available), which was a short walk from the major theaters and concert halls of the city.[79] March 8 witnessed the successful Moscow Conservatory premiere of the Third Suite from *Romeo and Juliet*, a reminder of that ballet's staying power in the repertoire. At the end of April Prokofiev and Mira relocated to Nikolina Gora, spending time with friends and acquaintances while also arranging the rental of a dacha from the physicist Mikhaíl Leontovich. Prokofiev's health made travel by public transit between Moscow and Nikolina Gora impractical, if not impossible. Mira's father used his privileges as director of the Institute of Economics to obtain a car, an Opel manufactured in Russian-occupied Leipzig, for Prokofiev's use.[80] An institute employee, Vladimir Tabernakulov, was tapped to serve as the composer's driver and courier.

On June 2, Prokofiev and Mira traveled to Leningrad with her parents for the staging of *War and Peace* Part I at Malegot. The four of them checked into adjacent rooms at the European Hotel, close to the theater. Prokofiev attended three dress rehearsals, after which he suffered a debilitating headache that necessitated his return to Moscow; the planned trip of eight days lasted just four.[81] What he heard of the opera satisfied him, even though in his absence Samosud and the singer Sergey Kazbanov had inserted, amid the waltz strains of scene 2, a conversation between Andrey and Natasha that Prokofiev had not actually composed. That addition, which Samosud claimed was inspired by the ballroom episodes in Chaikovsky's *Eugene Onegin* and Giuseppe Verdi's *La Traviata*, prompted yet another: a reprise, at the end of scene 2, of the portentous waltz music heard during the added conversation. The episode thus evolved, in the conductor's conception, from an unstructured divertissement into a fixed dramaturgical whole, the depiction of aristocratic decadence now wrapped around the foretelling of individual destinies. Although Prokofiev sanctioned the changes, he initially found them startling. Over the course of time, and sometimes without his knowledge, his opera had become a collective effort, subject to manipulation by other hands and further and further oriented toward nineteenth-century prototypes. During a rehearsal of scene 2, for example, he apparently "leapt from his chair as though stunned, grasped at the air, stood there dumbfounded, sank back down and . . . when the applause rang out, began clapping with everyone else."[82] His reaction was equivocal, but the reviews of the June 12 premiere were positive and the production destined for an unprecedented run of 105 performances during the 1946–47 season.[83] Prokofiev left Leningrad on June 6 with the expectation that *War and Peace* Part II would soon be staged, bringing his multi-year labor on the opera to a gratifying close.

As his political standing strengthened, so did his finances. On June 27, 1946, Prokofiev learned that he had been awarded a Stalin Prize (First Class) for *Cinderella*, which helped to ensure that the war-torn, mangled ballet remained in the repertoire for the rest of his life. The award came with a 100,000-ruble honorarium, money that greatly assisted with the purchase of a Nikolina Gora dacha, specifically the former residence of the Bolshoy Theater soprano Valeriya Barsova (Vladimirova), who moved for her retirement to Sochi. Prokofiev had long had his eye on the property, having rented a room from Barsova before the war, and quickly moved to purchase it. In a letter dated June 8, 1946, Prokofiev requested additional financing from the Presidium of the Orgkomitet of the Union of Soviet Composers, explaining that "owing to the poor state of my health and the doctors' insistence on the need for me to live permanently outside of the city, I have resolved to acquire Barsova's dacha in Nikolina Gora. The cost is 350,000 rubles, of which I will pay 200,000 rubles myself. I am requesting a loan of 150,000 rubles, which I will repay within two years."[84] The unquestioning nature of the letter betrays that the loan had been preapproved, worked out in advance between Prokofiev and Atovmyan. Mira almost confirms this point, noting that Prokofiev at first dismissed the idea of purchasing the dacha because they did not have "even a microscopic part of the sum in the bank." (Given the composer's pledge to cover two thirds of the dacha's purchase price himself, this claim would seem to be false.) To her "amazement," however, Prokofiev asked Atovmyan for a personal favor, an interest-free loan of 150,000 rubles. "Barsova's intentions came as no surprise to Atovmyan," she continues. "He already knew about them and said that, although Muzfond was arranging to acquire the dacha, if Seryozha needed it for health reasons he would try to help." Atovmyan and his assistant Boris Arkanov arranged the loan for Prokofiev through the Union of Soviet Composers and Muzfond; they also tended to the negotiations with Barsova's tightfisted husband.[85] By July 1, the papers were signed, a Steinway upright leased from Muzfond, a divan collected from the Mozhayskoye Shosse apartment, clothing gathered from Prokofiev and Mira's summer rental in Nikolina Gora, and the move completed. (Mira's father and ailing mother lived with them for the first several weeks.)

So settled in the countryside, Prokofiev resisted the tumult of Moscow, electing to commute to and from the capital rather than spending extended periods of time there. The house required serious attention—the interior and exterior had to be painted, the large porch enclosed in glass, and the neglected yard and garden cleared—but it was a place of comfort from the start, with an adopted cat (Mendoza) and rooster (Pyotr Ilyich) taking the place of the dog (Zmeyka) that had been his tagalong companion in Ivanovo. During the summer, leading artists populated the region, their abodes serving, like Prokofiev's, as focal points of creative exchange.

The social novelty of the summer was a July 14 interview, arranged through VOKS, between the renowned American radio broadcaster Norman Corwin and Prokofiev, Myaskovsky, and Lamm. Corwin had left the United States on June 15 to assemble a series of broadcasts on the state of the postwar world. (He received financial backing for the excursion from the Wendell Willkie Foundation, which gave him the inaugural One World Award in recognition of his wartime broadcasting.) Corwin had placed Prokofiev at the top of his list of people he hoped to interview, but no sooner had permission been granted for the meeting and the journey to Nikolina

Gora arranged than he came down with a bad case of strep throat.[86] His production engineer, Lee Bland, took his place, traveling to the dacha with a portable magnetic wire recorder for an English-language question-and-answer session on cultural and political matters. Since neither Myaskovsky nor Lamm spoke any English, Grigoriy Shneyerson, the VOKS official who oversaw the interview, acted as their interpreter. Lamm spoke to Bland about his work on Musorgsky's operas, and Myaskovsky offered his views on the American music scene. Prokofiev, according to Shneyerson, offered laconic responses to questions regarding "general political problems" and "contemporary art and literature."[87] Bland recalled the interview as follows:

> Prokofiev—very amiable and gracious, spoke excellent English. Checked gray tweed suit. Wonderful sense of humor. A regular guy, very relaxed. Hopeful for world peace. Believes cultural exchange of music and musicians important.
>
> Myaskovsky—graying beard, warm smile, twinkling eyes; black striped trousers, rather motley white jacket, wristwatch, cap. Shares Sergey's views on peace, exchange.
>
> Lamm—baldish, crew-cut style; snaggle-toothed, black high-necked shirt and belted velveteen jacket. Less outgoing, more introspective than others.
>
> My recollection of the dacha is that it was pleasant and comfortable, with plain and simple furnishings, badly in need of painting and had a tin roof. The house was nestled among tall pines and had a profusion of green shrubbery which lent privacy.
>
> Mrs. Prokofiev (his second wife, I presume) was dark, petite, attractive but shy, though she did pose with us afterward for outside pictures and provided a spread of cognac, wines, pork, candy and cakes before we parted.
>
> It was a fun visit with happy people, casual and spiced with good humor—a Sunday gathering of close friends who accepted me with warmth and cordiality and were seemingly unperturbed by my microphone or wire recorder.[88]

In fact, the photographs of the interview taken by the VOKS photographer Yevgeniy Umnov indicate that Bland's magnetic wire recorder surprised and delighted Prokofiev. Also contrary to Bland's recollections, Prokofiev's

English on the recording is less than excellent. He speaks for just two minutes during the interview broadcast on February 11, 1947, on CBS Radio, commenting that he neither composed moribund music ("I'm not doing myself reactionary art") nor had faced State censorship ("Nobody orders me anything, so I'm writing what I want"). Eisenstein and the *Pravda* editor David Zaslavsky are also featured in Corwin's broadcast, and provide similarly brief comments.[89]

Bland encountered a typical scene at Nikolina Gora: most days, Prokofiev, Lamm, and Myaskovsky met over tea, though by other accounts they did not discuss prospects for world peace. They coveted the relative isolation and sameness of their days, resisting, for example, having telephones installed in their dachas. Atovmyan, meanwhile, reliably tended to Prokofiev's Moscow affairs. Lavrovsky visited to discuss other potential ballets, and Kabalevsky proposed a reworking of *Semyon Kotko*, but for the most part, Prokofiev was able to devote the summer to "writing what I want." His unstable health constantly reminded him of his mortality, to which he responded by pursuing autobiographical writings.[90] He began to contemplate his legacy, bringing forsaken scores to efficient completion and putting the outlines and sketches associated with them in order. There was nothing morbid about the pursuit; it was a bid for posthumous longevity.

Puffing cigarettes at his desk—a habit that surely kept his blood pressure up—Prokofiev applied coats of polish to several chamber and orchestral scores, simultaneous commissions with private and public dimensions. His task list was such that he found himself obliged to abandon a large-scale project that, like *Cinderella*, languished for several years. The project in question, bearing the working title *Khan Buzay*, and the working subtitle "But the Shah has Horns!" (A u shakha yest' roga!), was a folktale-derived comic opera in the Eastern mode. Prokofiev had conceived it for the Alma-Ata Opera and Ballet Theater in 1942 and intended to base the brief score, in accord with the requirements of the commission, on regional folk music—forsaking, in effect, the type of *couleur locale* stylizations evident in *Semyon Kotko* in favor of direct quotation. Mira was commissioned to write the libretto, which, as she put it in a July 4, 1943, letter to a friend, obliged her to immerse herself in "Kazakh literature—fairy tales, legends, epics." Prokofiev, she added, had long been drawn to the "novelty and beauty" of Kazakh folk music.[91] The cause of the attraction dated back to an elaborate 1925 collection of Kirghiz and Kazakh melodies assembled by the composer and ethnographer Aleksandr Zatayevich, to whom Prokofiev was introduced in Leningrad on January 26,

1927, during his first visit to the Soviet Union. On that occasion, Zatayevich presented Prokofiev with an autographed copy of the collection; when it was reprinted in an expanded format in 1934, he gave the composer another signed copy. During preparatory work on *Khan Buzay*, Prokofiev systematically categorized the melodies in the collection according to their character and ritualistic use. He was aided by an essay published in the August–September 1939 issue of the journal *Literature and Art of Kazakhstan* (*Literatura i iskusstvo Kazakhstana*).[92] Ninety-nine of the melodies fell into the category of "calm lyricism" with a subgroup of twelve targeted for eventual inclusion in the opera. Other categories included "sad" and "anxious" melodies, "slow" and "fast" dances, "broad" melodies, laments, and marches. Some of the melodies lacked distinction: Prokofiev assigned this "objective" music to a category called "the main part," intending, perhaps, to include it in the background scoring rather than the vocal lines.[93]

The marvelously incongruous plot involves a superstitious Khan possessing a pair of horns that, as he despotically rhapsodizes to his captives, provide him with courage, wisdom, and control over the people. The people in question include the beguiling maiden Ayzhan and the gullible, Figaro-like barber, Dzhuman, to whom Ayzhan is betrothed. From time to time the Khan needs a haircut, but those who accept the honor of the task are invariably executed when they discover, beneath his turban, the grotesque horns. Dzhuman becomes the latest chosen victim (a jealous rival for Ayzhan's hand recommends him, through his treacherous father, to the Khan). Once the trimming and brushing is completed the Khan, true to form, sentences Dzhuman to death at the hands of his deaf-and-dumb henchman. Things begin to unravel for the Khan, however, when he discovers Ayzhan lurking in the corridors of the palace and, intoxicated by her looks, begins to flirt with her. Preternaturally fearful that Ayzhan might inform his wife of his indiscretion, he blanches when he hears from the now-captive Dzhuman that Ayzhan has arranged to meet with her for that very purpose. The second of three acts ends with the Khan granting Dzhuman a one-day stay of execution on the promise that he will prevent the meeting from occurring. The final act elevates the folklore-based slapstick into Orphic mystery. Dzhuman whispers the Khan's secret into a wishing well (he has vowed not to speak of it to anything that walks, crawls, or flies, but cannot resist uttering it into the enchanted waters); Ayzhan fashions a magical lute (as opposed to a magical flute or pipes) out of a reed taken from the well, and the lute, accordingly, begins to play the tune of a song with the words "but the Shah has horns!" Obsessed with Ayzhan, the Khan fantasizes about her replication into an entire harem of beauties. The plot reaches a climax with the arrival at the palace of the Khan's sensible wife: she, Ayzhan, and Dzhuman manage to convince the Khan that the Shaytan, the Devil of Muslim theology, has come to punish him for his misdeeds. He trembles in terror as Dzhuman, disguised as the Shaytan, cuts off his horns. "My friends," Dzhuman giddily announces to the gathered villagers, "the secret for which our barbers perished is no more. Khan Buzay grew horns, and he decided that they were a sign of his greatness, power, and gave him the right to oppress our people. He likened himself to Alexander Makedonski [Alexander the Great], and he compared himself with Eskender [Emperor of Ethiopia]—but what happened to him was just what happened to the sparrow."[94] Dzhuman thereafter recites the fable of the sparrow who thought he was an eagle, and ends up fatally snagged in the wool of a sheep he imagined he could whisk away, just like the eagle had before him. A mock sigh of pity for the Khan, and the commencement of Dzhuman and Ayzhan's wedding celebrations, bring down the curtain.

The surviving musical sketches (forty-nine two-sided pages) find Prokofiev enlivening the farce with musical double entendres; these reinforce the master-slave dialectic at the core of the plot.[95] In act 2, the triumphant march associated with Dzhuman's entrance into the palace becomes a despondent shuffle to the scaffold; the theme of his expected reward for serving the Khan becomes the dirge of his unexpected punishment. Here Prokofiev exploited the potential for European listeners to misperceive the major-mode affects of Kirghiz and Kazakh laments as jubilations. In acts 1 and 3, the minor-mode music associated with the Khan's supposed munificence blends with the music for his subjects' deprivations; the leitmotif of his secret becomes the leitmotif of its revelation. Falsetto and false chromatic relations would have underscored the Khan's self-delusions. The uniqueness of the planned score, however, resides as much in its structure as its syntax. As a consequence of his work with the filmmakers Eisenstein, Fayntsimmer, Romm, and Room, Prokofiev conceived *Khan Buzay* as a "cinematic" opera, the three acts partitioned into "shots" (*kadri*) of sometimes less than a minute in length, the static nature of their internal contents compensated for by their transience.[96] Before suspending work on the score, he had assigned twenty-two of these shots to act 1 and twenty-seven to act 2. Despite being conceived for a modest regional theater, *Khan Buzay* compelled Prokofiev to rethink his approach to opera on a grand scale. Whereas in *The Gambler*, *The Love for Three Oranges*, *The Fiery Angel*, and *Semyon Kotko* he had consciously replaced the number format with through-composition, here he replaced through-composition with cinematic vignettes. In *Khan Buzay*, dramaturgical thesis and antithesis reached a synthesis.

Most of the work on the libretto (Mira's task) and sketches took place in Perm in September 1943, the impossible aim (given Prokofiev's other projects) being to complete the piano score by September 15 and the orchestral score by November 1—the terms of the 28,000-ruble commission.[97] He set aside the opera upon traveling to Moscow to participate in the Soviet anthem competition, and did not return to it until the summer of 1946. Beyond, however, putting the sketches in order and having Mira type up the libretto, Prokofiev did little actual work on *Khan Buzay*; by August 23, he had permanently abandoned it. He waited until April 16, 1947, however, to file an official notice of the termination, informing the Committee on Arts Affairs on that day of his willingness to return the advance payment for the opera.[98]

Prokofiev shelved the opera in favor of his Violin Sonata in F Minor, which he had begun in 1938 but, as he confessed to Myaskovsky in a June 12, 1943, letter, he had found "difficult" to pursue.[99] The dark mood of the work cannot be explained by the sources, although the political climate of the 1930s could be one cause.

The first of its four movements features accented seventh chords in the piano and fleet, muted runs in the violin marked *freddo*, the latter likened by the composer to "autumn evening wind blowing across a neglected cemetery grave."[100] The spine-tingling return of that morbid breeze at the end of the fourth movement—indebted to the finale of Chopin's Piano Sonata no. 3 in B Minor—haunts the whole. Yet Prokofiev exerts strict control over the syntax and formal layout: at no point does the chilling sound threaten to destabilize or de-energize the score. For all its darkness, the Violin Sonata does not succumb to bleak midwinter.

Its completion was hastened by its dedicatee, the violinist David Oistrakh, for whom Prokofiev had earlier, in 1943 and 1944, transcribed his Flute Sonata. Prokofiev invited Oistrakh and his preferred accompanist, Lev Oborin, to the dacha to familiarize them with the rough draft of the Violin Sonata. Oistrakh recalls the composer describing the character and structure of each of the four movements before playing them without pause at the piano. His technique had slipped, but the effect produced by his hesitant, nervous performance was profound.[101]

Oistrakh and Oborin premiered the Violin Sonata on October 23, 1946, at the Moscow Conservatory, on the second half of a program that included

Shostakovich's Piano Trio in E Minor. Prokofiev heard the follow-up performance on October 25 before an audience that included members of the Stalin Prize Committee, who would, in the coming months, judge it an exceptional achievement, the "pride of Soviet music."[102] The composer's apprehension was nonetheless palpable, as was his relief that the performance succeeded. Upon congratulating the performers and engaging in amiable post-concert chatter with colleagues ("I don't like prescribing overdoses," Gavriil Popov enthused, "but the sonata is truly brilliant"), Prokofiev returned with Mira to Nikolina Gora.[103] The impressions of the evening kept him awake through the middle of the night.

His impressions were not, however, entirely positive. Irrespective of the official praise heaped on the Violin Sonata in *Pravda*—the reviewer was directed to interpret the score as a "meditation on the fortunes of the Motherland"—Oistrakh and Oborin's performance had disappointed him.[104] He griped that they had played the second and fourth movements dispassionately, "like two old professors," an approach he sought to correct by inviting them for a coaching session on November 18 at the Moscow apartment.[105] The score, which would not be published until 1951, remained a work in progress, with Prokofiev adding more accents and dynamic markings in an effort to prevent Oistrakh and Oborin's interpretation from becoming standardized. He even contemplated rewriting the second movement. In a sense, the Violin Sonata, an often desolate-sounding work, would not be realized until 1953, when Oistrakh played the first and third movements at the composer's funeral.

Cuts and Additions

Work on the Violin Sonata had taken a physical toll as the fall of 1946 approached. A spike in Prokofiev's blood pressure prevented him from traveling to Leningrad for the rehearsals, preview, and delayed world premiere of *The Duenna* at the Kirov Theater. The production was almost single-handedly mounted by the conductor Khaykin and director Ilya Shlepyanov under conditions that were, as Mira understated, "not entirely favorable."[106] *The Duenna* barely made it to the stage, owing to a harsh assessment from Glavrepertkom. "I won't describe in detail all of the upheavals to you," Khaykin meekly wrote to Prokofiev, "I'll just say that the Leningrad commission, having at first approved *The Duenna* and our performance, became scared and didn't know how to escape the predicament. In the end they simply decided to ban the performance."[107] The complaints ostensibly centered on the emphasis on declamation, the prominence of church figures, and the perceived emotional disconnect between the music and the text; behind the scenes, however, Glavrepertkom was reacting to a pair of Central Committee resolutions from August 14 and 26, 1946, the first concerned with the harmful, "anti-Soviet" content of the Leningrad literary journals *Zvezda* (Star) and *Leningrad*, and the second condemning the perceived overemphasis on foreign-authored plays on Leningrad stages.[108] *The Duenna*, a benignly foreign-themed opera, became a victim of an ideological cleanup operation. In despair, Khaykin appealed to the Committee on Arts Affairs for support; Khrapchenko decided to allow the opera to be shown to the public on November 3, 1946, but without advance notice in the press or even advertisements. The decision to permit subsequent performances stemmed from the positive reaction to the production by Yuriy Kalashnikov, the head of the theatrical division of Glavrepertkom. Posters and advertisements appeared thereafter, and the opera was re-premiered on November 9, with subsequent performances arranged for November 21 and 27.

Had he attended these performances, Prokofiev would doubtless have protested the cuts and modifications to his score. Khaykin blamed the changes on Glavrepertkom and the fallout from the October 26 dress rehearsal of the opera, but he simultaneously defended their merits. He was caught in a bind, neither wishing to offend Prokofiev nor, for obvious reasons, to risk the ire of the officials who oversaw his conduct. Khaykin assured Prokofiev that tableau 1 of *The Duenna* survived the adjudication relatively unharmed, save for the elimination of the eerie slow dance from scene 6 which, according to Khaykin, disrupted the flow of the action—even though this was its structural purpose. The duet between Louisa and the duenna at the start of tableau 2 merely lost a repeat, but the role of Clara's maid Rosina in tableau 3 disappeared altogether. Tableau 6, depicting Jerome's comically unsuccessful rehearsal of his amateur quartet, was shortened by four minutes—again to maintain a rapid dramatic pulse. These changes paled, however, when compared to the "two terrible blows" that befell the opera. Khaykin explained:

> First, the opera's seventh tableau (the convent) was entirely omitted. It was rehearsed until the last minute, and not badly. Part of it came out very well, and the music is simply magnificent. But it is too drawn out and the musical syntax departs, it seems to me, from the overall style of the opera.

> Most of our actors and musicians applauded the decision
> to remove this scene, saying that it helped the opera. I'm
> also confident it helps. The second blow is less important.
> In tableau 8, that is, the monastery, the carousing before
> the entrance of Mendoza and Antonio was significantly cut,
> almost in half. In general, the monks' revelry had to be sig-
> nificantly tempered, a great shame.[109]

Concluding his nightmarish summary, Khaykin mentions an unspecified "incidental" cut to the finale of tableau 9. There follows a feeble attempt to reassure Prokofiev about the success of certain scenes with the public (the maskers' dances, the monks' antics, and the finale, in which Jerome accompanies himself by tinkling perfectly pitched duralumin goblets). Banalities about audience laughter and applause could not, however, conceal that the production deviated from Prokofiev's half-operatic, half-balletic conception. Khaykin's explanation for this violation is equivocal: the slapdash changes, he coarsely suggests, improved the comedy—albeit at the unmentioned expense of the opera's dreamscapes.

The Duenna was at least staged; *War and Peace* Part II was not, and here Prokofiev confronted demands for changes of a different magnitude, demands that both frustrated and challenged him. Reviewing the score with the composer in the fall of 1946, Samosud complained that the battle scenes lacked an expository crux, an episode in which "the course of the war is settled." For over a year, he had been advocating the insertion of a new scene extracted from volume 1, part 3, chapter 12 of Tolstoy's sprawling novel, which concerns Russian battle planning. Prokofiev, ever-fearful of dramatic stasis, balked: "A council?...A war council?...In an opera?!" Such a scene, the composer recognized, could hardly be partitioned into fast-paced, cinematic vignettes. Beyond stasis, the greater problem concerned the depiction of Kutuzov. Tolstoy represents the Field Marshal as humble, devout, obese, and, in terms of wartime planning, rather limited; he is also down to earth with his soldiers and refreshingly foul-mouthed. He is a transcendentalist, committed, like Prince Andrey and Pierre, to something greater than himself, to an interconnected cosmos. In this regard he constitutes the antipode of the self-assured, vainglorious Napoleon. The Stalinist recoding of the novel required a different Kutuzov, a nineteenth-century simulacrum of Stalin himself, whose heroic persona (pipe in mouth and eyes twinkling at some distant horizon) would be projected in an epic aria, one that altogether lacked the concreteness and grotesqueness of the original character. Prokofiev conceded that, to win the war with Glavrepertkom, such an aria would need to be composed, however much it violated Tolstoy's conception of Kutuzov and, with it, his conception of historical movement. Prokofiev's discussions with Samosud about the style and shape of the aria became heated, however, with the impatient composer grousing "Just what do you want?" and "I can't write like that" to the patient conductor as one inadequate draft followed another. After eight attempts to compose something original, Prokofiev resorted to recycling, offering Samosud a number whose melody largely derived from the "Tatar Steppe" choral march of *Ivan the Terrible* Part I. The text for the aria was also recycled, but this time from within *War and Peace* itself. In the new scene 10, "A Hut in Fili," Kutuzov sings the words of the Chorus of Muscovites in the old scene 10, "A Street in French-Occupied Moscow."[110]

The already robust opera (or, as Prokofiev joked to Alpers, "operetta") had now expanded to thirteen scenes.[111] Prokofiev entertained the faint hope that Part II would be staged at Malegot in the spring of 1947 but, in the absence of an official assessment of the new scene, he recognized that the earliest possible staging would be the fall. The July 20, 1947, closed-door dress rehearsal of scenes 9 to 13 of Part II proved disastrous, however, leaving Samosud to break the news to Prokofiev, who was not in attendance, that the score, which had been well prepared for the hearing, needed additional work. Mira reports that, in August, Samosud and Vasiliy Kukharsky, the deputy director of the theater administration division of the Committee on Arts Affairs, traveled to Nikolina Gora to update Prokofiev on the difficulties with the rehearsals. Mira confines her recollections to the fact that Samosud and Kukharsky "requested small changes to the 'Fili' and 'Moscow' scenes" of the opera so as "to strengthen the theme of the Muscovite opposition" to Napoleon's forces. Prokofiev, she adds, agreed to make the changes.[112] These proved insufficient; when Part II was auditioned again three months later, Prokofiev's ideologically unmediated transposition of Tolstoy was condemned. Scenes 9 and 11 (representing Napoleon and Shevardino Redoubt and the burning of Moscow, respectively), were effectively banned, which ruled out a 1947 staging of Part II. Official attitudes toward opera, Prokofiev grimly realized, were hardening.

The impact on the composer of the truncated premiere production of *The Duenna* was minor; the problems with *War and Peace*, in contrast, would have a deleterious effect on his self-confidence. Despite his effort to monumentalize the opera, to bring its sound into accord with that of his orchestral works from the period, he had failed, according to his assessors, to represent the larger historical truths of the Russian historical progress toward Communism. Prokofiev worked at the problem but, owing to a downturn in political and cultural conditions, no solution could be found. At the end of 1947, pessimism breached optimism.

Public to Private

Yet 1947 had begun optimistically. In the first weeks, Prokofiev's health was stable, allowing him to attend several performances of *Cinderella* and the premiere of *Romeo and Juliet* at the Bolshoy Theater.[113] His business dealings with Atovmyan continued to benefit his career: in the realm of chamber and orchestral music, he usually chose what he wanted to compose, and Atovmyan obligingly prepared the contract in advance, sometimes exceeding Union of Soviet Composers rates for the genre of the work in question, a blatant conflict of interest. The negotiation for the Flute Sonata offers a typical example: the first draft of the contract, prepared by Orgkomitet employees in the early spring of 1943, specified a payment of 4,000 rubles. Upon reviewing the draft, Atovmyan informed Prokofiev that "no less than 6,000 rubles should be paid for a sonata at this time. I changed the amount to 8,000 rubles."[114] The capriciousness of his bookkeeping did not come under suspicion until the end of 1947, when he became the terrified focus of a series of State audits. In the meantime, Prokofiev remained the principal beneficiary of Atovmyan's largesse, securing in 1946 the funds for the purchase of the dacha, and increasing in 1947 the amount of support he provided to Lina and their two sons. The Committee on Arts Affairs was also generous to him, requesting eight large-scale works on patriotic subjects, all involving conventional forms and heavy orchestration. These commissions, facilitated by Shlifshteyn rather than Atovmyan (whose jurisdiction was the Union of Soviet Composers and Muzfond, not the Committee on Arts Affairs), contributed an additional 60,000 rubles to his income.

The period was also graced with a number of official tributes unexampled and unequaled in the annals of Soviet music. On June 7, 1947, Prokofiev learned that he had won a First Class Stalin Prize for his Violin Sonata. Other such awards were bestowed on the performers involved in the 1947 productions of *Romeo and Juliet* at the Bolshoy Theater and *War and Peace* Part I at Malegot. The 1946 Kirov Theater production of *Cinderella* had likewise received a First Class Stalin Prize. On November 5, 1947, Prokofiev would be elevated from the official status of Merited Activist of the Arts (Zasluzhennïy deyatel' iskusstv) of the RSFSR, a title given to him in 1944, to People's Artist (Narodnïy artist) of the RSFSR. These prestigious titles outshone the Order of the Red Banner of Labor that he had received from the Presidium of the Supreme Soviet in the summer of 1943,[115] and the two medals he had earned for his service "in defense of the Caucasus" (za oboronu Kavkaza) and "valiant labor in the Great Patriotic War" (za doblestnïy trud v Velikoy Otechestvennoy voyne). In 1947, he also earned a medal in connection with Moscow's 800th birthday celebrations, a widely distributed award that did not come with prize money.[116] The period of what the music critic Aleksey Ogolevets called the "inexplicable overlooking" of Prokofiev's "creative service" had clearly ended.[117]

According to a VOKS summary from the period, Prokofiev's foreign distinctions included a membership in the Boston Musical Academy, the honorary chairmanships of two Prokofiev societies in the United States, and a gold medal from the Royal Philharmonic Society in London.[118] A VOKS memorandum to the Central Committee Propaganda and Agitation Department (Upravleniye Propagandï i Agitatsii) dated July 27, 1947, similarly confirms Prokofiev's selection as an honorary member of the Royal Swedish Academy of Music; an inscription on the memorandum allows for notice of the selection to be printed in *Sovetskoye iskusstvo*.[119] In 1947, Prokofiev did not require Central Committee permission to accept the foreign award; the same could not be said for later years.

Prokofiev tended throughout his career to depend on mentors; he channeled his creative energy through the visions of others. Diaghilev, Meyerhold, and Eisenstein provided essential guidance in the prewar period. It could be argued that, in the immediate postwar period, official artistic doctrine itself became his muse. He accepted, for example, a commission from the Committee on Arts Affairs to write a pedagogical work for talented children, the most privileged of the sole privileged class of the Soviet Union, to perform in recitals and competitions. The result was a miniature three-movement Sonata for Solo Violin or Violins in Unison, accessible in both the practical and aesthetic senses of the term: a piece in the spirit of Fritz Kreisler's arrangements for budding violinists. The pedagogic intention is manifest in the etude-like progression from simple figurations in the sonata-allegro first movement to double stops in the mazurka-inspired third movement. The fascination of the score rests in its expressive dualities:

when performed by violins in unison, it assumes somber Baroque traits; when performed by a soloist it becomes starkly modern. For unknown reasons, neither Oistrakh nor any other professional played the Sonata for Solo Violin in public following its completion. The dual-purpose score actually went unperformed, by child or adult, until June 10, 1959, when the Italian-American virtuoso Ruggiero Ricci premiered it at the Moscow Conservatory.

Prokofiev embarked in June 1947 on a commissioned rescoring of his 1930 Fourth Symphony, itself related to the material of his 1929 ballet *L'Enfant Prodigue* (*The Prodigal Son*), the final work produced by Diaghilev's Ballets Russes. The stakes were high: Prokofiev resolved to redo a work from a different era, one that he had never been satisfied with, along the lines of his vaunted Fifth Symphony. It was a standard Soviet exercise in *pererabotka*: compliant adaptation to an approved template. The biblical subject matter of *L'Enfant Prodigue* and—by partial extension—the first version of the Fourth Symphony needed to be amended, the tale of an uncertain, questing liberal filtered through a heroic paradigm.[120] Having heard the criticism that the little-performed score affronted Soviet symphonic ideals (the performances that had occurred in Moscow on October 30, 1933, and November 20, 1937, had been equivalent flops), Prokofiev accepted a proposal to redo it.

He lengthened the Symphony by sixteen minutes, making the largest of the adjustments to the beginnings and endings of the first, third, and fourth movements, and subjecting most of the melodic material to internal expansion. Movement 1 was enriched by the addition of an invocational fourteen-measure introduction typified by flexible phrasing and, when reprised at the end of movement 4, excessive effects: fortissimo dynamics in the woodwinds and a brass choir evocative of clanging bells. Prokofiev reworked the transitions between theme groups and slackened the form, relying on recurrences of what Malcolm Brown calls "the toccata-like figuration" of the first theme of the exposition to lend unity to the whole.[121] Movement 1 was once a textbook sonata-allegro structure, but it became, as the revision progressed, increasingly disordered and inconsistent—less an accompaniment to a choreographic narrative than a narrative of its own. It adopted, in essence, some of the prolix, discursive traits of the Fifth Symphony: casual tempos, irregular groupings with the phrases, inconsistent assemblages of phrases within the period, thematic variation over repetition, and a misalignment of accents between the melodic and accompanimental lines. The melodic, harmonic, and rhythmic writing became the musical equivalent of verbal periphrasis. And, of course, the final stage in the conversion of movement 1 concerned the orchestration. Prokofiev thickened the sound, introducing accented staccato figures in the upper and lower registers and placing them in bold relief. *Divisi* became more prominent, as did combined pizzicato and non-pizzicato figures. The lower brasses and strings received greater emphasis in climatic passages, which Prokofiev transformed into emphatic declarations.

Mira's cheerful description of Prokofiev's revision of the Fourth Symphony makes the effort seem earnest, but in this context earnest might also have meant earnestly, sincerely acted: "Seryozha finds that there is a lot of good material in the Symphony [he had by this point launched into the first, second, and fourth movements], but the fact of writing the Fifth and Sixth Symphonies showed him that from the perspective of general construction the Fourth Symphony could be done more forcefully."[122] Prokofiev is either confessing that the framework of the symphony needed rebuilding, or pretending to confess to this effect, or allowing Mira to fictionalize this confession in her memoirs.

Subtle backing for this last assertion comes from what Mira excludes from her memoirs. Save for passing references to the dates and places of their premieres, she avoids discussing the chamber works that find the composer turning inward. Besides the Violin Sonata, the most beguiling of these scores is the Ninth Piano Sonata, which Prokofiev completed at Nikolina Gora on September 27, 1947 (thematic material dates from the mid-1940s). The inner movements of this modest masterpiece suggest a retreat into a world of nonvirtuosic, impenetrable rumination; the outer movements self-consciously revisit the basic (for him) elements of composition: sonata-allegro and sonata-rondo forms, C major, and the instinctive and intuitive movement of the hands at the keyboard. As Rita McAllister points out, Prokofiev's penchant for sudden contrasts between the "white" keys (C major, first and foremost, but also modally inflected D minor, E minor, and A minor) and the "black" keys (D-flat major and B-flat minor) can be partially ascribed to his working methods at the piano, where his imagination liaised closely with his fingers in the formation of melodic and harmonic material.[123] The Ninth Piano Sonata lays this method bare, although it is too deliberate, too preconceived to be called improvisation.

In a political climate based on absolutes, the vagaries of this music are striking. The opening melody of the third movement, in A-flat major, recurs with interpolations, coming to a decisive pause on a cadence in measure 8, a less decisive one in measure 26, and an even less decisive one in measure 72. The opaqueness of the line stems from an overlapping of opening and closing gestures; the eventual dissolution of the texture, moreover, reflects a methodical, step-by-step elimination of functional harmonies and the privileging of chromatic voice-leading patterns. The movement witnesses what Deborah Anne Rifkin, to whom these points are indebted, calls the "complete collapse of functional harmonic progression."[124]

The overall effect is one of deterioration, disintegration, as though the composer was attempting to find a dignified, non-clichéd way of fading out. But the music is not about silence, a marker of death. It is about the potential of sounding forever. Each of the four movements of the Sonata concludes with a quotation from the movement ahead, except, of course, the last movement, which concludes with a quotation from the first one. The tonalities of the quotations differ from the movements in which they appear, and from the movements to which they belong, making them apparitional. The music remembers the future; it is a circular set of reminiscences about that which has yet to occur.

But the Sonata also completes a trajectory of another sort: it evolves from fragments, coaxes those fragments into specific forms, and then returns to those fragments. It is not a cohesive work, but a set of sketches. The Sonata exposes the techniques of its own realization, a point borne out by the manner in which Prokofiev presented it to its dedicatee, Richter, a steadfast advocate of the composer's works:

> "I've something interesting to show you," he announced as soon as I arrived, whereupon he produced the sketches of his Ninth Sonata. "This will be your sonata. Don't think it's intended to create an effect. It's not the sort of work to raise the roof of the Grand Hall [of the Moscow Conservatory]."[125]

Disappointment with the Sonata's "domesticity" ceded to infatuation: "I love it very much," Richter declared in his memoirs.[126] Prokofiev anticipated that the Sonata would be premiered in early 1948, but politics got in the way. Richter did not unveil it until April 21, 1951, at a Composers' Union performance in early celebration of the composer's sixtieth birthday (April 23). Too ill to attend, Prokofiev listened to the performance on the telephone.

Chizhik-Pizhik

In the fall of 1947, the thirtieth anniversary of the Revolution obliged Prokofiev to emerge from introspection and compose tributes for official celebrations. During the summer, Myaskovsky had shared with Prokofiev his plans to construct a cantata for soprano *ad libitum*, chorus, and orchestra around select verses by the poet Sergey Vasilyev, the outcome being a "mystical nocturne" titled *Kremlin by Night*. Despite being dedicated "to the 30th anniversary of the October Revolution," Myaskovsky's score is equivocal, indicating an obsession with death and tragic silence: "Someone, somewhere, very muffled / Rang out in the night! It's Old Woman History / Fetching her keys" (Kto-to gde-to ochen' glukho / Prozvenel v nochi! To Istoriya-Starukha / Dostayet klyuchi).

Prokofiev, in striking contrast to Myaskovsky, quickly responded to the official summons with a pair of exceedingly tame compositions, the first being a thirteen-minute score alternately titled *Festive Poem* and *30 Years Overture* in the manuscript.[127] An arc-shaped work intended to express the mythic grandness of the Leninist-Stalinist timeline, but also including passages redolent of *Lieutenant Kizhe*, it no sooner received its Moscow premiere—on October 3, 1947, under the direction of Konstantin Ivanov—than it was dismissed as listless (in the opening and closing sections) and pallid (in the middle). Prokofiev had greater official success with his *Cantata for the Thirtieth Anniversary of October*, an economical setting of a Party-line poem by a Party-line poet (Yevgeniy Dolmatovsky) that bore the title—in the poet's final version of the text—"Praise to You, Motherland!" (Slav'sya Rodina!).[128] Once the text had been approved by the censorship board Glavlit, Prokofiev tweaked it for musical reasons, and assigned it a slightly catchier title: "Flourish, Mighty Land" (Rastsvetay, moguchiy kray). In 1962, when the Cantata was published with a de-Stalinized text, it took yet another title: "Praise to You, Our Mighty Land" (Slav'sya, nash moguchiy kray).

Prokofiev did not devote much of his limited time to these routine works. No sooner had he completed the orchestration of the *Festive Poem* on July 15, 1947, than he began writing "Flourish, Mighty Land." Four pages of sketches went into the first work, five into the second. Upon receipt of the commissions from the Committee on Arts Affairs, he bristled that his first and greatest paean to the Revolution—the 1937 *Cantata for the Twentieth Anniversary of October*—remained unperformed.

The November 12 premiere of "Flourish, Mighty Land" was conducted by Nikolay Anosov at the Moscow Conservatory following a visit to
Nikolina Gora earlier in the month to review the score with the composer.
The performance concluded a diverse concert that also featured selections
from *Cinderella* arranged for violin and orchestra. Mira indicates that both
Myaskovsky and Richter hailed "Flourish, Mighty Land," dubbing it one
of the best works written for the anniversary and an obvious improvement
over the *Festive Poem*. Others, however, found it trite, the melodic writing
reminiscent of nursery rhymes like "Chizhik-pïzhik."[129] Coarsely translated,
the rhyme begins "Chizhik-pïzhik where've you been? Drinking vodka on
the green!" (Chizhik-pïzhik, gde tï bïl? Na Fontanke vodku pil!) It was an
apt comparison—the Pioneer march in the opening and closing sections of
the Cantata recalls *Peter and the Wolf*—but Mira considered it demeaning.

"Flourish, Mighty Land" is at once the antithesis and *pererabotka* of
the *Cantata for the Twentieth Anniversary of October*. Gone are the historical references, the expressive grandeur, the *musique concrète*, and the
primary source texts. Dolmatovsky's poem and Prokofiev's music combine images of perky labor with paeans to the land. It consists of a single,
through-composed movement cast in the keys of A-flat major and D-flat
major, the scale collections enriched, as usual, with the second scale degree,
the flattened sixth degree, and the flattened seventh degree. In the opening instrumental passage, the trumpets and strings alternate marchlike and
hymnlike strains, after which a fanfare provides a bridge to the first and
second choral stanzas. These latter establish a mood of halcyon bliss. In the
middle section of the Cantata, the subject switches from the friendship of
the peoples—expressed using consonant harmonies—to the glorification of
Stalin, Lenin, and the Party.[130] The Cantata thereafter becomes animated,
introducing a pulsing accompaniment pattern similar to the opening march.
At the climax of this section, Prokofiev invokes a Russian operatic cliché:
he blends a chant of "Glory, glory, glory" (Slava, slava, slava) in the upper
voices with a stately recitative in the lower voices, the result being a simulacrum of jubilant chiming.

The Last Success

Besides the hypnotizing "slava" repetitions, the most distinctive feature of
the eight-minute Cantata is its emphasis on pastoral sounds—an emphasis
that is also found in the much more amorphous Sixth Symphony. Cued by

Prokofiev himself, critics of the period interpreted the work as a sequel to the Fifth Symphony, the somber, rustic persona of the latter complementing the strident, heroic persona of the former. (The same contrast, of course, marks Beethoven's middle symphonies.) Brown hears the Sixth Symphony as a quasi-theatrical amalgam of "orchestral recitatives," balladic passages redolent of folksong and, in the finale, an evocation of a dance-based "peasant celebration." The dramatic gestures, Brown qualifies, "are balanced by a loftier intellectualism."[131] In the compact developmental passages, the score signals a struggle between an external and internal, objective and subjective, representation of grand events. Overall, the ambiance is meditative. The bucolic murmurs of the woodwind-dominated exposition of the first movement might be likened to unseen life forces, which regulate both the body's agitations and the mind's calculations. The introversion of the Violin Sonata and Ninth Piano Sonata finds a large-scale orchestral equivalent.

Prokofiev intended to freight the score with this baggage, as gleaned from his remarks to Mira about the ending of the third movement, which recapitulates material from the first movement in portentous rhythmic expansion, the result being a fracturing of the form and deterioration of the mood. The climax comes between rehearsal numbers 116 and 117, with the staggering interpolation of chromatic sonorities—essentially vertical renditions of the descending motives assigned to the upper and lower brasses at the beginning of the first movement—whose aftershocks resonate through a pair of fermatas. At an October 9, 1947, rehearsal in Leningrad, Prokofiev told Mira that the interpolations represented "questions cast into eternity." One of the questions, he later disclosed, concerned the purpose of life.[132] This rare (even to Mira) explanation of programmatic intent permits a Mahlerian reading of the finale, one in which a celebration of life cedes to a premonition of death (musical, physical, and metaphysical). The concluding measures suggest less heroic affirmation than acceptance of the unknown.

The Sixth Symphony received its premiere on October 11, 1947, with the Leningrad Philharmonic Orchestra under the direction of Mravinsky, who had burnished his credentials in 1937 with a stunning premiere of Shostakovich's Fifth Symphony. Mravinsky, a staunch advocate of Prokofiev's music in the postwar period, became acquainted with the Sixth Symphony at Nikolina Gora. On March 21, 1947, he and Atovmyan traveled there to acquaint themselves with the score, which Prokofiev had composed intermittently in different locations, sketching it between June 23, 1945, and October 9, 1946, and orchestrating it between December 10, 1946, and February 18, 1947.[133] After hearing Prokofiev play through the Sixth Symphony, Mravinsky praised its grand sweep—the sound, he enthused to Mira, spanned "one horizon to the other"—and requested the privilege of conducting the premiere.[134]

On October 8, Prokofiev arrived at the European Hotel in Leningrad for a week-long stay. Beyond assisting Mravinsky in the rehearsals of the Sixth Symphony, he reunited, after long separations caused by the war, with two of his longtime friends: the pianist Vera Alpers and the philologist Varvara Demchinskaya, whom Prokofiev had been helping to make ends meet since the death of her husband in 1942. Business errands included meetings with Sherman and Nikolay Goryainov, the director of Malegot, regarding the stalled rehearsals of *War and Peace* Part II. Goryainov boarded Prokofiev's train just before he left Leningrad to discuss the "difficulties" of the situation. Before Part II could be staged, he grumbled, it needed further review by cultural policy-makers.[135]

The news depressed the composer, and cast a pall over his trip to Leningrad. Mravinsky's performance of the Sixth Symphony received strong initial notice in the press, however, and more than fulfilled his expectations. The most detailed review came from the musicologist Izraíl Nestyev, who traveled to Leningrad to report on the Symphony for *Sovetskoye iskusstvo*. Puzzled by the score, Nestyev had pestered Prokofiev for technical insights. He received the tersest of responses, and found himself having to concoct his own programmatic interpretation, one that assigned patriotic intent to the thematic structure. Nestyev proposes that, for narrative purposes, Prokofiev reversed the traditional roles of the exposition and development sections of the first and second movements. Melodic material is no sooner introduced than transformed in the opening sections; the middle sections, in contrast, involve a kaleidoscopic succession of images. The description of these images tends to be heavy-handed. Concerning the second movement, for example, Nestyev enthuses: "The new theme of the Largo is less a contrast than a continuation of the first—a beautiful instrumental arioso, suffused with reserved wisdom. Suddenly the lyric tone is superseded anew by the fantastic specters of war." The movement "culminates in a 'circular' reprise of the first two themes. 'I am young, I am strong, I defeated the powers of evil and I earned the right to happiness'—such can be divined from the assured major sounds of the Largo." Nestyev applies similar terms to the third movement. Here "a cheerful melody in the spirit of Mozart or Glinka" is intertwined with the strains of a rustic dance. But the life-affirming tableau is once more marred by the incursion of a "titan," a passage of "incessantly repeating fanfares" that revisits the traumas of the past.[136]

It remains unclear whether Prokofiev appreciated Nestyev's interpretation of the Symphony. (In later years, he and the musicologist would have a terrible falling out, owing to the latter's negative reevaluation of this score, along with Prokofiev's entire operatic output, for its supposedly modernist decadence.)[137] He probably preferred more abstract, poetic readings of the work, such as that offered by the musicologist Yulian Vaynkop. In a pre-premiere lecture, Vaynkop likened the opening trombone line in the Symphony to the "scrape" of a key in a "rusted lock."[138] The door holding that lock opened onto an elusive, eclectic creative domain. Extending the point, one could posit that, while the melodic and harmonic patterns have immanent narrative potential, the somewhat intangible character of their assemblage denies programmatic interpretation—and this may have been the composer's point. The Sixth Symphony embraces much of the surface rhetoric of a socialist realist narrative but little of its cohesiveness.

For the critics, there remained enough dialectical content in the Symphony to merit it a place in the repertoire. The same could not be said of Prokofiev's brief *Ode to the End of the War*, which received its premiere on November 12, 1945, under the direction of Samosud, but which, because of his health problems, Prokofiev did not in fact hear until October 17, 1947. Shortly after his return to Moscow from Leningrad, he attended a performance of the work at the Chaikovsky Concert Hall on a program that featured, as the main attraction, Shostakovich's Seventh Symphony. The audience included a group of Pioneers, to whom sweets were handed out as a special treat; Prokofiev, according to Mira, feigned snatching them away when he rose to take his bow. Despite receiving an encore and a cascade of bravos from the sated children, Prokofiev felt that the *Ode* was but a "modest success"; Mira, true to form, delighted in the "uniqueness" of the audience response.[139]

This score warrants comment less for its melodic and harmonic content than for its outlandish orchestration. In an October 12, 1945, article in *Sovetskoye iskusstvo*, Prokofiev reported that he intended the *Ode* to "glorify the arrival of peace" and to "reflect the joy of peaceful labor and the pathos of renewal."[140] These banal points fail, however, to capture the strangeness of the score, which translates Soviet architectural monumentalism into sound.

The *Ode* is the musical equivalent of an overdetermined Stalinist skyscraper. The instrumentation, which was partially inspired by the instrumentation of Stravinsky's rustic wedding ballet *Les Noces*, involves eight harps, four pianos, three tubas, three saxophones, and an expanded brass and wind section—the kind of expressive excess that totalitarian culture both fosters and demands.[141] To foreground the overlooked instruments of the orchestra, and to accentuate registral extremes, Prokofiev eliminated string instruments (violins, violas, and cellos) from the scoring. The *Ode* is cast from beginning to end in the major mode; the choice of gestures seems intended to overwhelm the listener. The music, a testament to State power, is awesome in both the positive and negative senses of the term.

Monumental music is not necessarily inspired music, however: Prokofiev conceived the *Ode* as a stack of building blocks of increasing heaviness, with drama ceding to surface display.[142] He outlined the score in a 1945 notebook as follows:

Part 1:   Slow
Part 2:   From the *Cantata for the Twentieth Anniversary of October*,
          fast, workman-like
Part 3:   Slow, but more ornate
Part 4:   Birth of joy
Part 5:   Russian, joyous (3rd theme)
Part 6:   Part 2, elaborated
Part 7:   Part 5
Part 1:   Part 1, against the background of parts 1 and 5
Coda: Solo, 4 timpani, F major, extract from part 2[143]

The manuscripts reveal that Prokofiev spent more time orchestrating the twelve-minute work than actually composing it. He began the scoring in Ivanovo on August 20, 1945, and finished it over five weeks later on September 29, whereas the composing took only half as long.[144]

The aspiration toward the monumental was not the only reason for the protracted creative process. In the summer of 1945 Prokofiev was still recuperating from his concussion. His health was so poor during the period that, as noted in the last chapter, he at first refused to work with Eisenstein on *Ivan the Terrible* Part II, suggesting that Popov be enlisted for the illustrious, high-stakes project in his place. His health improved, but he had frequent setbacks. Headaches and nosebleeds prevented him from attending most of the rehearsals and some of the performances of his new works. The October 18, 1947, performance of the *Ode* may have been a minor affair, but Prokofiev was grateful to be there.

He was also grateful to return to Leningrad in late November, where he managed to see both *The Duenna* (November 23) and *Cinderella* (November 24). The Kirov Theater production of the opera had substantially improved since its long-delayed premiere the previous fall—a premiere that Prokofiev, again owing to his health, had missed. By the time he saw *The Duenna*, it seemed of less personal importance: his central concern was the fate of *War and Peace* following the contentious July and October closed-door performances of select scenes from Part II. Nothing had happened with the opera since his last visit to Leningrad and his dispiriting conversation with Goryainov, and nothing was going to happen. In the absence of what Mira called a "resolution to the question of the staging" of Part II, Prokofiev was forced to bid a depressing farewell "to the dream of attending a rehearsal."[145] He was wholly unaware of the behind-the-scenes intrigue at Malegot, whose administration had decided, under extreme political pressure, to terminate work on *War and Peace* in favor of *The Great Friendship* by the second-tier composer Muradeli. This opera concerns the struggle between pro- and anti-Bolshevik forces during the civil war, and the struggle between Russians and the indigenous peoples of the North Caucasus. The pro-Bolshevik hero is based on a real-life figure, the "extraordinary Commissar" Sergo Ordzhonikidze.[146] Representing the heroism of a Stalin compatriot, *The Great Friendship* was staged by no fewer than thirteen Soviet theaters in celebration of the anniversary of the Revolution. Malegot was obliged to follow suit.[147]

In the absence of progress on *War and Peace*, Prokofiev, in a gesture of desperation and determination, signed a 10,000-ruble contract with the Kirov Theater for another, much shorter opera taken from the pages of recent Red Army history: *A Story of a Real Man*.[148] The choice of subject for the project (discussed in chapter 7) came from a Committee on Arts Affairs official (Kukharsky). Having settled on it, Prokofiev convinced himself that *A Story of a Real Man* would, upon completion, win favor—even if it included a grim episode in an operating room and, as Myaskovsky reminded him, lacked strong female roles.[149] Enslaved by his own theatrical imagination, Prokofiev continued, despite multiple frustrations, to define himself first and foremost as an opera composer. He trusted, as a matter of self-motivation, that his hospital opera would have greater fortune than the six operas—*The Gambler, The Love for Three Oranges, The Fiery Angel, Semyon Kotko, The Duenna,* and *War and Peace*—that had preceded it.

The end of 1947 marked the end of Prokofiev's tenure at the forefront of Soviet music, a position he had struggled to achieve for over a decade, at the expense of his marriage, his health, and elements of his technique. On December 25, Mravinsky conducted the Moscow premiere of the Sixth Symphony. The work remained in favor with the critics, who, writing in accord, continued to highlight its conception at the end of the Great Patriotic War and its depiction of triumph through sacrifice. According to the critical consensus, the traumatic harmonic and melodic deformations at the end of the third movement elevated the syntax to the level of the sublime.

The concert was Prokofiev's last unhampered, unmediated success.

7

1948

During the war, when Prokofiev devoted himself to the national struggle, his conviction that his music occupied a domain above and apart from the concerns of the real world did not waver and caused him no particular political problems.[1] Following the receipt of three First Class Stalin Prizes for the Fifth Symphony and the Eighth Piano Sonata, the Violin Sonata in F Minor, *Cinderella*, and another such award for his involvement with Eisenstein on *Ivan the Terrible* Part I, his official standing reached a zenith.[2] He earned generous advances and royalties from the Committee on Arts Affairs, Muzfond, the State theaters, and other parts of the disorganized State commission (Goszakaz) system. Prokofiev's greatest concern remained the absence of a complete premiere of *War and Peace* and the fact that many of his large-scale works remained unpublished. On January 6, 1948, he wrote to Molotov at the Kremlin requesting his assistance with the second of these concerns, remarking, as a transparent bargaining ploy, that foreign firms seemed more interested in publishing his works quickly than Muzgiz.[3] Prokofiev's complaint was rerouted from Molotov's to Khrapchenko's office, with a brief informative reply (a listing of Prokofiev's publications with Muzgiz) attached to it. It is less noteworthy that Prokofiev approached Molotov for assistance with a routine professional matter (Molotov had long served as a pastor to Soviet artists) than that the request went unheeded.

For elite artists living under Stalin, official approbation tended to alternate with official condemnation. The specific reasons for the changes in their fortunes are difficult to rationalize. Vacillations in cultural policies affected their careers, but so, too, did disputes within the cultural agencies, miscommunications between those agencies and other tiers of government, and personal rivalries. Prokofiev's standing declined radically in 1948, owing less to ideological considerations than the vagaries of policymakers, factionalism in the bureaucracy, and financial crises. The power of the regime was absolute in the sense that it followed no consistent rules.

On February 10, 1948, for example, Prokofiev attended a ceremony at the Kremlin elevating his official status from Merited Activist of the Arts of the RSFSR to People's Artist of the RSFSR—a title he received from the Presidium of the Supreme Soviet of the RSFSR on November 5, 1947.[4] (Prokofiev did not live long enough to receive the final award in the sequence: People's Artist of the USSR. His greatest honor, the Lenin Prize, was posthumously bestowed on him in 1957.) February 10, 1948, was also the day that finishing touches were put on a Central Committee Resolution that would, once it had been published, discussed, and enacted, abruptly curtail his creative plans. For unexplained, perhaps unexplainable reasons, the regime almost simultaneously lauded and condemned him, branding him and Shostakovich—who attended the same ceremony—both a People's Artist and anti-People Formalist.

The apparent target of the Resolution was *The Great Friendship*—which must have struck Prokofiev as bitterly ironic, given that this opera had supplanted his own *War and Peace* in the Malegot repertoire. The document dates from February 10 (it appeared on page 1 of *Pravda* the next day, page 1 of *Sovetskoye iskusstvo* on February 14, and page 1 of the January–February 1948 issue of *Sovetskaya muzïka*), but it articulated concerns about *The Great Friendship* and its composer (Muradeli) that had been festering since at least August 1, 1947, and that might easily have resulted in a cancellation of the premiere production. In a memorandum that day to the Central Committee Secretary and Politburo member Andrey Zhdanov titled "On the Prohibition of the Performance of V. I. Muradeli's Opera *The Great Friendship*," Georgiy Aleksandrov reported that the "propaganda directorate has familiarized itself with the content of this opera and considers it flawed, offering a distorted portrayal of the Bolshevik struggle in the North Caucasus in 1919–20 and the revolutionary activity of Com[rade] Ordzhonikidze during these years." Aleksandrov recommended "the withdrawal of published piano scores of the opera...and the issuing of an order to the Committee on Arts Affairs (C[omrade] Khrapchenko) to suspend work on the opera using the published piano score."[5]

Despite Aleksandrov's complaint, the Bolshoy Theater performed *The Great Friendship* in celebration of the thirtieth anniversary of the Revolution. The prohibition came only after hundreds of thousands of rubles had been spent on the opening run. Parroting points made by Aleksandrov, the February 10 Resolution attacked the opera for its misrepresentation of historical events (it failed, understandably enough, to portray the "friendship of the peoples" during the civil war), but also for its musical language, which excluded "the wealth of folk melodies, songs, refrains, formal- and folk-dance motives that so enrich the artistic creations of the peoples of the USSR, in particular the artistic creations of the peoples populating the North Caucasus, where the events represented in the opera unfold." Most of the score adhered in letter and spirit to the principles of *partiynost'*, *narodnost'*, and *ideynost'*, but it was nonetheless deemed a failure. The failure was not isolated; rather, it was symptomatic of the "unhappy state of contemporary Soviet music" and the pernicious influence of "composers of the formalist orientation."[6]

Here the real target of the Resolution comes into view: the Soviet musical elite, and the agencies that supported them. Shostakovich, Prokofiev, Khachaturyan, Vissarion Shebalin, Popov, and Myaskovsky are singled out for absorbing modernist creative techniques to the detriment of the listening public and for shunning the accessible Russian folk traditions in favor of inaccessible abstraction. Irrespective of the accolades heaped upon them by cultural agencies during World War II, their works were reinterpreted by Central Committee members as emblems of decadent distortion. They represented not Soviet culture, but "the contemporary modernist bourgeois [culture] of Europe and America," the "dementia" of this culture, its "complete negation of musical art," and its ultimate "dead end."[7] Despite its militant tone, the Resolution permitted a bureaucratic solution to the crisis: the dismissal of Khrapchenko from the Committee on Arts Affairs and of Khachaturyan and several others from the Orgkomitet of the Union of Soviet Composers.

Zhdanov oversaw the writing of the Resolution and took it upon himself to regulate the ideological content of the arts. (Also at the start of 1948, he devoted time to Communist Party activities in Eastern Europe, underproductive collective farms, and the Tito affair; he was an extremely busy individual.)[8] The history of the Resolution is complex, but thanks to recent archival work and the publication of memoirs by the people who attended to its recommendations, a picture is beginning to emerge of the interactions that resulted in the musical stars of the Soviet Union being undermined by lesser lights. Beyond the verbal and musical content of Muradeli's opera, the leadership questioned the staggering cost of the staging. On January 5, Stalin and his aides attended a performance of the opera at the Bolshoy Theater. The next day, Zhdanov and two other Central Committee employees, Dmitriy Shepilov and Polikarp (Aleksandr) Lebedev, met with the participants in the production and demanded an explanation for its political problems and financial excesses.[9] This meeting, which targeted Muradeli and Khrapchenko, began with Zhdanov damning the opera—in language reminiscent of "Muddle Instead of Music"—for its

> hysterical outbursts, exertions, and cacophonous jolts, which explode and literally frighten the listener.... The musical accompaniment does not accord with the moods and emotions of the dramatic personnel... and it is characterized by muddle and lapses—sometimes the chorus waits for the orchestra to end; sometimes the orchestra is silent while an artist sings.[10]

Fulfilling his obligatory role, Muradeli thanked Zhdanov for his "correct" observations and then, in an effort to deflect blame, expressed the hope that "all of our composers and musicologists hear this criticism" of the path taken by Soviet music in the postwar period. Shepilov stepped in to remind the gathering that the Central Committee Propaganda and Agitation Department had identified defects in the opera before its premiere.[11] He and Zhdanov then assailed Khrapchenko for not responding to Aleksandrov's memorandum.

This meeting was followed by a larger gathering at the Central Committee, a three-day event beginning on January 10 that involved artists of hard- and soft-line political mindsets. Zhdanov solicited opinions on *The Great Friendship* and Soviet music in general from former members of the Russian Association of Proletarian Musicians, career-minded faculty members at the Moscow Conservatory, and musical representatives from the Republics. Kiril Tomoff, the author of a history of the Union of Soviet Composers, contends that two "populists"—Vladimir Zakharov, an erstwhile RAPMist who contributed, against Prokofiev's wishes, to the score of *Cinderella*, and Aleksandr Goldenweizer, a Moscow Conservatory piano professor—inveighed against the "highbrow" composers Shostakovich and Knipper. Tomoff adds that, after the meeting, a Party official named N. S. Sherman submitted an unduly harsh report to Zhdanov that accused Myaskovsky of indoctrinating his Conservatory pupils in discredited techniques.[12]

Prokofiev at first declined to attend the gathering, but an official traveled to his dacha on the second day and convinced him otherwise.[13] Unhappy that his routine had been disrupted, he apparently fumed "Pust' Zhdanov 'podazhdanov'!"—a pun that translates as "Let Zhdanov wait!"[14] The cellist and conductor Mstislav Rostropovich recalls the following anecdote about the gathering:

> When Zhdanov launched into his angry speech against composers at the [Central Committee], Prokofiev was in the auditorium. A funereal silence reigned, but he was chatting with his neighbor, the future conductor of *War and Peace*. From two seats away a member of the Politburo turned to him: "Listen. This concerns you." "Who are you?" asked Prokofiev. "My name isn't relevant. But know this: when I tell you something you'd better pay heed." "I never pay attention to comments from people who haven't been introduced to me," Prokofiev threw back, unfazed.[15]

Khrennikov confirms the anecdote—it is potentially apocryphal—and identifies Prokofiev's addressee as Matvey Shkiryatov, the deputy director of a commission responsible for regulating the Communist Party ranks (and not a Politburo member, as Rostropovich claims). Shkiryatov participated in a massive purge of the Leningrad Communist Party in 1949–50, resulting in the arrest of some two thousand Party workers. Zhdanov took grim delight in Prokofiev's impetuous exchange with Shkiryatov: according to Khrennikov, he "broke off his speech and began to laugh" at the scene.[16]

The January meetings provided Zhdanov with the semblance of a mandate for restructuring the musical establishment. In accord with a January 26 Politburo memorandum, Lebedev replaced the discredited Khrapchenko as chairman of the Committee on Arts Affairs. Although battling a myriad of ailments precipitated by the Leningrad Blockade, Asafyev became titular head of the Orgkomitet of the Union of Soviet Composers. There were other changes: Khrennikov, a Zhdanov favorite, became General Secretary of the Orgkomitet of the Union. Two other contributors to the anti-formalist campaign, Zakharov and Marian Koval, served as his assistants.[17] Muradeli came in for severe censure, albeit less for his operatic misdemeanors than his administrative ones, especially his financial mismanagement. He lost his post as chairman of Muzfond.[18]

Atovmyan, Muradeli's shrewd deputy, was also sacked, an event that greatly affected Prokofiev, who had benefited from Atovmyan's creative, financial, and material support since even before his relocation to Moscow. In his memoirs, Atovmyan recalls facing extensive questioning about "Prokofiev's debt, in particular about the motives behind my granting of a 'fantastic' long-term loan to him for the purchase of a dacha in Nikolina Gora." "We invited Prokofiev to the USSR," Atovmyan commented, "promised him a two-story private residence and various forms of creative assistance. I was the initiator of this invitation and, recognizing the vital need for the loan, boldly took it upon myself to make the arrangements."[19] In an attempt to absolve himself of charges of corruption, Atovmyan asked Prokofiev, Myaskovsky, and Shostakovich to "declare in writing that their honoraria were received in the amounts certified by the Presidium of the Orgkomitet and that if the overseeing bodies considered the amounts incorrect, that they each bore responsibility for returning the 'excess' honoraria in their possession to Muzfond."[20]

Olga Lamm, the niece and adopted daughter of Pavel Lamm, relates that Zhdanov orchestrated the denunciation of the six composers named in the Resolution by pitting musical factions against each other. She further relates that Zhdanov solicited advice on the draft and final version of his Resolution from three members of the musical establishment: the ailing, fearful Asafyev, the old-fashioned conservatory pedagogue Goldenweizer (a devotee of Medtner, Rachmaninoff, and Scriabin who disdained Schoenbergian Modernism), and the mid-level composer Shaporin.[21] Olga Lamm's anecdotal recollection of the fallout from the Resolution includes paraphrases from conversations among the individuals it most affected. On the day of the Resolution's publication, she remembers, the composer Aleksandr Gedike informed her father

> I met Sasha [Goldenweizer] today, and he said to me: "Rejoice, true art has triumphed!" I replied: "How can you be happy when our wonderful musicians have been stigmatized. You must have lost your mind! This is a disgrace: each composer should be able to choose his own path in art. Come to your senses!"[22]

Most musicians reacted to the Resolution with silence, as though waiting for the other shoe to drop. Curious as to why Myaskovsky refused to comment on it, Olga confronted him:

> "Nikolay Yakovlevich, how can you be silent and not respond to the disgraceful and ridiculous accusations directed at composers?" Nikolay Yakovlevich looked at me very seriously and said only: "How can one communicate with people who speak in different languages? They don't even understand each other."[23]

Eisenstein's Death

Prokofiev did not immediately have time to contemplate the implications of the Resolution. On February 11, 1948—one day after the Resolution's release—his cinematic benefactor Eisenstein suffered a second heart attack and died, leaving his memoirs and two books unfinished, *Ivan the Terrible* Part II unrevised, and *Ivan the Terrible* Part III in fragments. He had jotted down his last thoughts on the trilogy in August and October 1947, in the rough draft of a comparative theoretical essay called "*The Idiot* and *Ivan the Terrible*" ("Idiot" i "Ivan Groznïy").[24] His last diary entries allude to Stalin's latest purge, the anti-cosmopolitan campaign; a last letter, to the director (and fellow montage pioneer) Lev Kuleshov, records the moment his scarred heart stopped working.[25]

From the start of 1946, Eisenstein believed that his end was imminent; he predicted that he would not live beyond 1948. In hospital after suffering his first heart attack, he informed Prokofiev: "Life is over—there remains only a postscript."[26] The director died nineteen days after his fiftieth birthday; the paperwork had just been prepared to award him an Order of Lenin, both in tribute to his birthday and his quarter century of "fruitful creativity in the realm of Soviet cinema."[27]

Prokofiev and Mira received the news indirectly from Eisenstein's longest-serving cinematographer, Eduard Tissé, and absorbed the blow in private. They reminisced about their long-term friendship with the director and, on the professional front, the essential help he provided in Alma-Ata with the original version of *War and Peace*. Mira also recalled Eisenstein teasing Prokofiev for "peddling old hoofs," that is to say, reusing tunes from previous works in his film scores. It remains unclear from her whitewashed account whether the recycling was a source of disagreement between the two of them. On February 13, 1948, the couple traveled to Moscow to pay their respects to the director at the House of Cinema: Prokofiev stood in the honor guard until 1 p.m. The funeral took place that afternoon at the riverside cemetery of Novodevichiy Convent.[28]

Over the next few days, Prokofiev consulted with his colleagues about the Resolution. According to Olga Lamm, Mira was "scared to death" by the document, and most likely convinced Prokofiev to write his humble response to it.[29] His reaction, like that of the other denounced composers, was monitored at the top, as evidenced by a memorandum submitted by Shepilov to Zhdanov on February 13, 1948:

> According to insufficiently trustworthy sources Prokofiev reacted to the resolution quite calmly; he's planning to send a letter to Zhdanov with a request for a meeting, specifically a consultation about a new opera on a Soviet theme, which Prokofiev has already begun composing (apparently based on the Polevoy novella *A Story of a Real Man*). Shostakovich is in a more anxious and nervous state, but he is similarly planning to compose the opera *The Young Guard* [*Molodaya gvardiya*]. Composer Shebalin officially welcomes the resolution; however, those close to him say that it is wrong for his name to be in the resolution, that it figures there as the result of someone's "machinations."[30]

A later portion of the memorandum involves the pianist Richter, who, in defiance of the Resolution, planned to keep performing Prokofiev's music:

> Certain artist workers are expressing their sympathies to the group of formalist composers. So at the adjudication of a concert program by the pianist Svyatoslav Richter, scheduled for February 17, Richter insisted on including works by Prokofiev. When employees of the Philharmonic advised him not to include one of the formalist sonatas of Prokofiev in the program, he declared, "Then I'll go to Prokofiev's home and play his sonata for him as a sign of respect."[31]

As these extracts from the rumor mill make clear, Shepilov and Zhdanov were interested in controlling but not silencing the composers named in the Resolution; they were to be redeemed once they made obeisance to the Central Committee apparatus.

Instead of submitting his letter of contrition to Zhdanov, as Shepilov predicted, Prokofiev sent it to Khrennikov and Lebedev, the new chairman of the Committee on Arts Affairs. Before receiving their approval, it was distributed to Stalin and other Politburo members, who offered it their tacit sanction. The letter was read in Prokofiev's absence at a General Assembly of Soviet Composers. Held February 17–26, the gathering sought to chart the future of music in the RSFSR and its satellites through the poison thicket of what the text of the Resolution called "formalist distortions and antidemocratic tendencies…foreign to the Soviet people and its artistic tastes."[32] Prokofiev excused himself from the gathering on account of health troubles. Myaskovsky, who was battling the flu, rejected the advice of his onetime student Kabalevsky and also declined to attend.[33] By telephone, Prokofiev informed Myaskovsky of his pragmatic decision to submit an apology. Dismayed by his friend's lack of resolve, Myaskovsky declared that he "found it impossible" to apologize for mistakes he had not made. Insincere expressions of atonement, he added, meant nothing in a society dictated by "ignorance and lack of good conscience."[34]

Prokofiev's February 16 apology has attained iconic status in music history, though not because it reflects the plight of nonconformist artists in totalitarian societies. Rather than responding to the Resolution with lip service alone, the prudent approach, Prokofiev sought to find an artistic escape route within it. He contends that he had already fulfilled official demands in his recent works, which shunned "formalist" esotericism in favor of tuneful "simplicity." He likewise justifies his reliance in his operas on continuous declamation by asserting the influence of Chaikovsky, whom Soviet cultural officials upheld as a positive example for socialist realist composers. Prokofiev pledges that his next opera would maintain a judicious balance between strophic and through-composed passages.

Perhaps the most striking feature of Prokofiev's letter is the reference to the 1936 denunciation of Shostakovich's *Lady Macbeth of the Mtsensk District*. Herewith, two separate paragraphs:

> Some elements of Formalism were characteristic of my music as early as fifteen to twenty years ago. I was probably

infected through my contact with a number of Western trends. After *Pravda* (under the direction of the Central Committee) had exposed the formalist errors in Shostakovich's opera, I pondered over the various creative devices in my own music and concluded that the path I had taken was wrong. In a number of the works that followed (*Alexander Nevsky*, *Zdravitsa*, *Romeo and Juliet*, the Fifth Symphony), I attempted to liberate myself from formalist elements, and I think I succeeded in this to some extent. The persistence of Formalism in some of my works can probably be explained by a degree of complacency on my part, and a failure to understand that our people have no need for such things. After the Resolution, which has had a rousing effect on the entire community of composers, it has become clear exactly what kind of music our people need; and now it is also clear how we can overcome the formalist disease.

In opera, I have often been reproached for allowing a preponderance of recitative over cantilena. I am very fond of the stage, and I think that all who come to the opera house have every right to expect stimulation not only for the ear, but also for the eye (otherwise they might as well have gone to a concert). But all kinds of stage action find a musical correlate in recitative, whereas cantilena brings the action more or less to a halt. I will recall, in some of Wagner's operas, what a torment it was for me to watch the stage over the course of an hour-long act when not a single character moved. It was this fear of stasis that prevented me from dwelling on cantilena for longer stretches. With the Resolution in mind, I have carefully reconsidered the issue and I have now come to the conclusion that in every opera libretto, some passages demand recitative, while others demand arioso, but over at least half of the opera, there are passages that the composer may present in either manner. Take, for example, Tatyana's letter scene in Chaikovsky's *Eugene Onegin*: it would have been a relatively simple matter to write most of this as recitative, but Chaikovsky decided to direct his music toward cantilena instead, transforming the entire letter into a huge aria; at the same time, the scene was able to benefit from some action on stage, thus providing food for the eye as well as the ear. That is the direction I want to take in my new opera, which is based on a contemporary Soviet plot, *A Story of a Real Man*, by Polevoy.[35]

Here one finds the composer backing away from his earlier operatic method, which stressed continuous declamation over melody, yet also implicitly damning the stand-and-sing style of Khrennikov's theater projects. There is little of Chaikovsky's *Eugene Onegin* in *A Story of a Real Man*, however. The Chaikovsky invoked by Prokofiev in his apology is not a post-Romantic composer, but a reimagined Soviet one.

Unlike Prokofiev, Shostakovich responded to the Resolution in journalistic point form, as though trying to dispense with an irritating formality as succinctly as possible. "In my *Poem of the Motherland*," he offered, "I attempted to create a symphonic work suffused with songfulness and melodiousness. It proved to be a failure." "But I will try again and again," he added, his language evocative of an ill-behaved schoolchild stuck in detention, writing the same line ad infinitum on a chalkboard.[36] Unlike Prokofiev, Shostakovich had been through the ritual of denunciation and rehabilitation once before, and had perfected the art of actively resenting, rather than actively resisting, a regime whose identity was wrapped up with his own.

Despite his fragile health, and despite the loss of his most important mentors—Diaghilev, Meyerhold, and Eisenstein—over the previous two decades, Prokofiev had maintained a mask of indifference to the setbacks in his professional life. In 1948, however, he became afraid. His past distinguished him from his "formalist" colleagues: he had departed Russia with Lunacharsky's blessing to spend his early career in France and the United States, repeatedly performed in the European capitals, visited Canada, Morocco, and Japan, and married a woman of Spanish descent in Ettal, Germany. In an effort to avoid self-incrimination, he disposed of the foreign books and journals in his possession and ensured that other compromising items, including letters to and from Russian émigrés, were cleared out of the dacha.[37] It was a common-sense course of action: the dacha was searched, and he risked detainment had such items been found. Prokofiev was Ukrainian-born and Russian-educated, but his peripatetic past marked him as an outsider. Lina, his estranged, foreign-born wife and the mother of his two sons, also bore this mark. She, however, lacked the protection of international fame.

Lina's Arrest

Throughout the war, Prokofiev had supported Lina and their two sons. Before his return to Moscow in October 1943 he routinely enlisted colleagues who were traveling on business to the capital to hand-deliver parcels to his family. Even after his return, however, he seldom crossed the doorstep of the Ulitsa Chkalova apartment and tended to communicate with his wife through intermediaries. Prokofiev asked Oleg to give a letter to Lina requesting a divorce. The request, dating from the summer of 1947, was not granted; indeed, the letter may not have been delivered. Oleg claimed that he did not have the heart to give it to his fragile mother, but Mira believed that he had.[38]

Lina still hoped to leave the Soviet Union. Following the example of her neighbor Annet Weinstein, she petitioned the authorities for an exit permit. Weinstein, a former French national married to an architect, received her visa; Lina did not.[39] Her desperate, depressed condition haunted Prokofiev, but it does not seem that he tried to help her to return to France. Even had he tried, he would not have succeeded.

There was no question of them reuniting. On November 22, 1947, Prokofiev filed a petition in a local court (in Moscow's Sverdlov district) to divorce Lina. His petition was rejected, albeit for reasons he could not have foreseen. On November 27, the court ruled that his October 1, 1923, marriage had no legal basis, since it had taken place in Germany rather than the Soviet Union and had not been registered with Soviet officials. The ruling stated that "marriages of Soviet citizens abroad have judicial standing only if they are registered by representatives of the RSFSR abroad with subsequent notification of the Central Department of ZAGS [Zapisi Aktov Granzhdanskogo Sostoyaniya]," the State Marriage Bureau.[40] Since this had not happened in Prokofiev and Lina's case, their marriage became null and void the moment they took up residence in the Soviet Union. Even by Soviet legal standards, the ruling was a farce: for one thing, it asserted that the marriage had taken place not in 1923 but in 1918, before Prokofiev had left Russia for the United States, and well before he even knew of Lina's existence. For another thing, the ruling asserted that the couple had been Soviet citizens at the time of their union, which, to be sure, they were not. The ruling did not address the status of their two sons.

Prokofiev came to terms with the strange decision after he verified it with a second judicial body.[41] Less than two months later, on January 13, 1948, he married Mira. They received a certificate bearing the signature of a ZAGS official and the seal of the Ministry of Internal Affairs (to which ZAGS belonged), and a new stamp in their internal passports.[42] By bureaucratic fiat, Mariya Ceciliya Abramovna Mendelson, born in 1915 in Kiev, Ukraine, replaced Carolina Llubera Codina as the legal partner of the composer Sergey Sergeyevich Prokofiev, born in 1891 in Sontsovka, Ukraine. Cutting his ties to Lina made Prokofiev less of an outsider in Soviet society, but it made her even more of one.

Lina was arrested on the evening of February 20, 1948—just four days after Prokofiev had submitted his statement of contrition for his musical misdeeds to the General Assembly of Soviet Composers. Desperate for contacts with the outside world, Lina had continued to attend diplomatic events—as "Madame Prokofieff"—and to interact with foreign embassy officials. Two of these officials, Anna Holdcroft and Frederick Reinhardt, offered Malcolm Brown brief accounts of their sightings of Lina, and of Lina's futile efforts to obtain permission to leave the Soviet Union. The most detailed of these accounts comes from Holdcroft, a British Foreign Office employee between 1944–48 and 1953–57. She and Lina met in 1945 at a diplomatic reception at the Metropole Hotel. "I visited her apartment very seldom," Holdcroft wrote to Brown,

> but I was there on the evening before she was taken away. I know I had been seen going there—but it was too late to retreat. I told her of this the moment I arrived; we agreed I should phone if I was seen going away. There was no need, for I saw no one "recognizable." We were to meet on neutral ground in two days time. On the next day I had a strange phone call telling me not to go to the place of the meeting. I feared the meaning of this—one acquires a sixth sense in the Union! My fears were confirmed later through mutual friends.[43]

Reinhardt, who was stationed at the American Embassy between 1941 and 1948, commented that "in the early postwar period," Lina brought herself "unfavorably to the attention of the authorities" by persisting in her effort to obtain an exit permit.[44]

Prokofiev learned about Lina's arrest on February 21. Svyatoslav and Oleg had taken the train from Moscow to the village of Perkhushkovo and then walked the remaining thirteen kilometers to Nikolina Gora. They told their father what had transpired as soon as he appeared at the door of the dacha:

> "Wait," he said, and left to get dressed. The three of us walked along the road. We told him about the arrest and search; he asked a few spare questions. The news we had brought obviously shocked him. He was dispirited and very reticent. He likely felt, of course, that some part of the blame lay on him: if they hadn't separated, perhaps this wouldn't have happened.[45]

In a published interview with Nataliya Savkina—from which the preceding information and quotation is taken—Svyatoslav recalls his mother receiving a telephone call on the evening of February 20 asking her to collect a parcel from some acquaintances. Lina left the apartment building and, according to neighbors, was muscled into a car parked by the front gate. There ensued a night-long search of the apartment by the police. Prokofiev's August Förster piano, a portrait of Lina by the eminent Silver Age painter Nataliya Goncharova, jewelry, record albums, photographs, documents, and other personal effects were all confiscated. In a muted aside, Svyatoslav, then twenty-four, describes the looters finding his postcard collection of Soviet leaders:

> The postcards had been with me a long time and in my thoughtlessness I did not recognize that it was necessary from time to time to remove the pictures of those leaders who had been repressed. During the search, one of the MGB [Ministry of State Security] officers came across a photograph of the latest enemy of the people. He laid it aside for the file. I attempted a protest: "I bought them all at once, just like they were sold at the store."[46]

Once inventoried, these and other incriminating items were either immediately bagged and hauled away or left behind in a sealed room in the apartment. The latter items were claimed by the police in the late summer and the apartment vacated.

Svyatoslav and Oleg approached Shostakovich for help, but in this sorrowful instance, the influential and concerned composer could do nothing for them. News of the incarceration reached Lina's mother in France, who sent an anxious telegram to the children. Soon after, they inquired at a police information outlet on Kuznetsky Most concerning their mother's whereabouts, and learned that she had been interned at the Lubyanka, the headquarters of the MGB and Ministry of Internal Affairs, the successors to the NKVD, before being transferred to Lefortovo prison, a solitary confinement facility in the northeast region of the city. Following a three-month investigation and six-month interrogation, Lina was court-martialed by the Military Collegium of the Supreme Court of the USSR (Voyennaya kollegiya Verkhovnogo suda SSSR). Svyatoslav reports that once the verdict had been rubber-stamped his mother

> was found guilty of espionage and betrayal of the homeland and assigned a sentence of twenty years in the harsh camps. Later, she never spoke about prison, about her questioning, but from separate, very brief recollections I know that she was confined to a cell, that there were nighttime interrogations with a bright light in the face, and much else. During the interrogations they called my father "that traitor," "that white émigré," and other similar things.[47]

The specific charges were enumerated by Lina in a 1954 petition for release addressed to the Soviet Attorney General: "attempting to defect"; "theft of a secret document from [Sov]informbyuro," the propaganda agency for which Lina had worked during the war as a part-time translator; facilitating the smuggling of a letter across the border from a certain "Engineer Shestopal" to his wife, Susanna Rotzenberg; and "criminal ties" to foreign embassy employees, including Holdcroft and Reinhardt. Lina concluded her exposure of the falseness of the charges with a simple question: "What am I guilty of?"[48] The question went unanswered.

Lina completed the first three years of her sentence in a large central camp at Inta, in the Komi Autonomous Republic (northeastern Russia). From there, she was moved to a facility at Abez, also in Komi, and then to a facility at Potma, in the Mordovian Autonomous Republic (southeastern Russia). The three camps were distinguished in the Gulag system by their large numbers of non-Russians. Inta and Abez included former peasant landowners from Western Ukraine and Belorussia (convicted for obstructing Soviet agricultural policy, specifically the program of forced collectivization) as well as citizens from the three annexed Baltic nations. Potma housed numerous Western Europeans. Details of Lina's time in the camps come from the memoirs of two other prisoners, the British Embassy staffer Inna Chernitskaya and the writer Yevgeniya Taratuta. Like Lina, they were incarcerated under the treason statute (58–1a) of the Soviet penal code. (Chernitskaya notes that she and Lina were both friends with the American reporter Edward Snow, and suggests that this friendship might have been another pretext for Lina's arrest.)[49] Life in the camps meant poor nutrition, a harsh climate, a brutal work regime, routine abuses, wretched housing, and inadequate clothing. Those who survived these conditions credit inner fortitude, spiritual faith, and the power of denial. Taratuta notes that Lina refused to "believe that what had happened to her was real, did not believe that the situation would persist, and did not believe at all in her twenty-year sentence."[50] She did not discuss the circumstances of her arrest with the other women in her barracks, except to say that the half-year interrogation was excruciating.

Men and women were kept apart in the Gulag system. At Inta, men toiled in coal mines outside the barracks; women cleared roads and plastered walls for new buildings. Chernitskaya mentions that Lina cleaned latrines, filthy labor that at least allowed her to converse with other educated women.[51] Letters from her sons lifted her spirits. She was rarely permitted to send letters, but she could receive as many as she liked, but not everything her sons wrote reached her. When packages arrived, she shared what the guards did not pilfer with the other women in her barracks. Lina took part in ideological reeducation programs, including a "cultural brigade" that performed in neighboring camps. At Abez, she sang in a choir whose repertoire came from film musicals, however by this time her voice had faded. Toward the end of her incarceration, she worked for a camp hospital.

Lina was released on June 30, 1956, three years after Prokofiev's death, which occurred, as is often noted, on the same day as Stalin's. Lina learned immediately about Stalin's death, but news about her husband took several months to reach the camp. Lina, Taratuta reveals, kept up with her husband's career as best as she could but knew little, if anything, about his last days. Returning to her barracks from a work shift, "someone came running from the bookroom and said: 'They just announced on the radio that, in Argentina, a concert was held in memory of the composer Prokofiev.' Lina Ivanovna began to weep and, without uttering a word, walked away."[52]

By the time she returned to Moscow after her liberation (she traveled using the prison camp release form as her sole means of identification), the family apartment on Ulitsa Chkalova had been confiscated by the government. It was reassigned to a popular graphic artist, Nikolay Sokolov, who received five Stalin Prizes, one for his grotesque caricatures of Hitler. Svyatoslav, his wife, and Oleg moved to a two-bedroom unit on Ulitsa Kupriyanova. Lina went with Svyatoslav to collect her certificate of rehabilitation from a bureaucrat who admitted that her case was a "fabrication."[53] In the months ahead, she sought to reassert her rights as Prokofiev's legal wife. On April 12, 1957, the oversight committee for the Moscow courts reversed the November 27, 1947, decision that nullified her marriage to the composer. The reversal, which restored Lina's claims to the Prokofiev estate, stemmed from a July 8, 1944, decree by the Supreme Soviet, the most powerful legislative body in the Soviet Union, to the effect that marriages conducted abroad remained legal at home. This reversal, however, was itself reversed. On March 12, 1958, the Russian Supreme Court renamed Mira as Prokofiev's legal wife. The issue at hand was not the fact of Lina's marriage to the composer but, once again, the fact that the marriage had not been registered with the Soviet government.[54] In the end, the composer's estate was divided between the two widows. Mira died on June 8, 1968, from a presumed heart attack.[55] Until Lina was finally allowed to emigrate in 1974, she lived in Moscow in a one-room apartment on Kutuzovsky Prospekt—a street named for the Russian Field Marshal who, as Prokofiev's *War and Peace* dramatizes, rebuffed Napoleon in 1812. After leaving Moscow, Lina resided in Paris and London and visited New York. She died in London on January 3, 1989, at the age of ninety-one. Her two sons had by this time also emigrated. Oleg, who became a noted visual artist, died at the age of fifty-nine in 1998. Svyatoslav lives in Paris with his son Serge Jr.

Deprivation

The events recounted in the preceding paragraphs concluded long after 1948, but they were all precipitated in that year. In the early spring, as Prokofiev absorbed the shock of Lina's arrest, he perhaps prepared himself for the same thing. He was not arrested, but as the repercussions of the February 10 Resolution intensified, his career went into freefall.

Between April 19 and 25, the First All-Union Congress of Soviet Composers took place in Moscow at the Hall of Columns, whose auditorium still bears the weight of the Stalinist show trials. Prokofiev and Mira attended for one day before fleeing back to the peace and quiet of the dacha. They heard

Asafyev's keynote address, which was read in his health-related absence by Vladimir Vlasov, and which marked the nadir of his career. Asafyev did not attack Prokofiev, whom he still considered a friend, in the text, but he tore into other eminent Russian composers. Asafyev began by comparing and contrasting Shostakovich's Eighth and Ninth symphonies (1943 and 1945). Unlike the Eighth Symphony, the Ninth had been denounced by reviewers, if not the actual public, as unpatriotic. "I once joked that this symphony went 'unheard' throughout musical society," Asafyev declared, "and not entirely because it was misunderstood. No, we understood it, correctly, and then we perceived this simple-minded, formalist composition as an insult, unworthy of our musical art."[56] He then turned to the expatriate composer Stravinsky, about whom he published an insightful book in 1929, but whom he now associated with "fascist 'aesthetics' and philosophy." "In my time," Asafyev commented, "I have written a lot about Stravinsky and must say that I, like many others, once misperceived the individualistic rebellion in [his] creativity as progressive. Stravinsky has come to the same end as many other petit-bourgeois 'rebels'—he has crossed over into the camp of darkest reaction."[57] This "darkest reaction," he continued, is most pronounced in Stravinsky's Norton Lectures at Harvard University, which were first published in English in 1942 under the title *Poetics of Music in the Form of Six Lessons* (the lectures were read in French). Asafyev quotes two lines from chapter 3 of the book, and conflates these with a paraphrase from chapter 4.[58] He refrains from taking up chapter 5, which includes a devastating indictment of Soviet music.

In his follow-up speech, Khrennikov offered an overview of Russian music since the Revolution, pointing out where composers had adhered to and deviated from the progressive enriching of the Glinka and Rimsky-Korsakov traditions. Dzerzhinsky's *The Quiet Don* was feted as the ideal, and Muradeli's *The Great Friendship* as its subversion. Most Soviet composers, Khrennikov conceded, had aspired to heed the dictates of the various "historic" *Pravda* articles about music making in Russia and the Republics. However, the move toward greater national content, ideological cohesion, future-perfect "Realism," and audience appeal held both potential and peril: Aleksandr Kasyanov's 1939 *Stepan Razin*, a folk drama about the rebellion of a seventeenth-century Cossack pretender to the tsarist throne, merited praise for its choral passages; Valeriy Zhelobinsky's 1938 *Mother*, a setting of Gorky's novel about the ideological awakening of the parent of a socialist agitator, merited critique for its primitive dramaturgy.[59] Khrennikov offered no specifics in his speech, opting instead to trudge through a long list of ideological successes and failures. He labeled Prokofiev (like Shostakovich) an out-of-touch radical, lumping together *The Duenna*, the Cello Concerto, and the Sixth Piano Sonata as examples of "extreme" formalism intended for a "narrow circle of aesthete-gourmands."[60] Without pausing to explain his culinary metaphor, Khrennikov proceeded to denounce Prokofiev's *The Year 1941* for failing to express the "sensation of historic events during the first phase of the Patriotic War."[61] Khrennikov also damned *War and Peace* for its "profound" dramaturgical "flaws." The composer's egregious departures from Tolstoy's novel attested to his "modernist" subjectivism.[62]

Asafyev's and Khrennikov's speeches bore the same workaday title "Thirty Years of Soviet Music and the Tasks for Soviet Composers." Khrennikov later claimed that they were penned by a team of ghostwriters, and their semantic similarity does indeed suggest a conspiratorial collusion.[63] Having heard the first of the speeches, Prokofiev decided not to remain for the second. Mira chatted in the foyer with some of the other escapees; Prokofiev wandered next door to look over the posted results of a chess tournament. Mira answered questions about the composer's health and well-being; one familiar figure, Kukharsky, lauded his "dignified behavior" in the face of hardship.[64] Mira did not at first know what he meant, but she later deduced that Kukharsky was referring to Prokofiev's pledge to engage the masses in his future work. Her confusion suggests that only a handful of people at the Congress actually paid attention to the proceedings. For most of the speakers and the audience, the event was a tedious ritual.

The Congress stenograph makes for depressing, redundant reading: speaker after speaker mounted the podium to salute Zhdanov, parrot rhetoric about consonance and folklorism, and point out the anti-democratic behavior of comrades Khachaturyan, Myaskovsky, Popov, Shebalin, Shostakovich, and Prokofiev. Day two of the Congress involved seven long reports by delegates from the Republics and newly annexed Baltic States; day three featured eight more. The next three days offered lectures from no fewer than forty-five composers, along with a dutiful reading of telegrammed greetings from the Committee on Arts Affairs, the Union of Soviet Writers, and a group of conductors and musicians from the Leningrad Military District. Of the censured composers, only Muradeli and Shostakovich chose to speak—the latter with apparent distress.[65] According to the stenograph, the gathering came to a close with pledges to continue the Russian classical tradition in opera, to create symphonies and tone poems evocative of the optimistic times, and to fuel the effort to build Communism with marches and choruses. The mandatory, groveling paeans to Stalin, the "inspiration" behind the Union's "creative victories" and "best friend of Soviet art," brought the crowd to its feet for "sustained and long-lasting applause."[66]

One item of business remained: the election of Union board members and administrators. The general discussion that preceded the secret voting was, according to Tomoff, fractious, with nasty notes passed from the floor to the podium, and petitions to add the names of "formalist" composers to the ballots ignored. "Of the fifty-one composers and musicologists elected to the governing board," Tomoff writes, "most of those who had been named to the Secretariat by the Central Committee resolution of 26 January finished far back in the pack. The new boss, Khrennikov, did the best, but he finished behind sixteen other candidates, most of whom were uncontroversial selections from the national republics or well-respected senior composers like [Mikhaíl] Gnesin, Dmitriy Arakishvili, and Sergey Vasilenko."[67]

For Prokofiev, the most obvious result from the Resolution and the follow-up meetings was financial hardship. Eight of his works were barred from performance—*The Year 1941*, *Ode to the End of the War*, *Festive Poem*, *Cantata for the Thirtieth Anniversary of October* "with Dolmatovsky's text," *Ballad of an Unknown Boy*, the 1934 piano cycle *Thoughts*, and the Sixth and Eighth Piano Sonatas.[68] In addition, the generous advances for new works, publications, and performances that enabled him to support himself, his family, and certain friends ceased. He found himself unable to keep up with the payments on the 150,000-ruble loan that Atovmyan had granted him for his dacha. Prokofiev's personal debt as of August 1948 was 180,000 rubles, which the Union of Soviet Composers—then under audit—demanded that he settle straightaway. He was forced to plead with the new chairman of Muzfond, the film composer Nikolay Kryukov, for a three-month grace period. As a gesture of good faith, he asked Kryukov to apply his anticipated honorarium from a *Cinderella* orchestral suite to the debt, though he acknowledged that it, like the 1,000 rubles he scraped together as a June payment, was "merely a drop in the sea."[69] Lamm decided to return the 6,000 rubles that Prokofiev had paid him for copy work, telling him to "pay it when you can."[70] Myaskovsky considered the degrading situation "dangerous" to Prokofiev's precarious health.[71]

Prokofiev's finances did not improve, as he hoped they would, in the three months ahead. In fact, it took over a year, and the lifting of the prohibition against performances of the aforementioned scores, before income began to trickle in again.[72] Rostropovich, who was presumably introduced to Prokofiev in the spring of 1947 and premiered his late works for cello, asserts that, in the immediate aftermath of the Resolution, the composer "did not even have money for food."[73] Although he lacked an extensive personal support network, Prokofiev relied for a time on help from others.

His financial troubles are sadly evident in a November 5, 1948, letter to the Moscow branch of the Union of Soviet Composers, in which he announces his intention "to compose 10 small pieces for children's repertoire, for violin and piano; I ask the [Union] to provide me with the necessary comradely support. The pieces could be unified by a common theme, based, for example, on the subject of a children's fairy tale."[74] Prokofiev proposes finishing the score by May 31, 1949; the commission was evidently not provided. Another glimpse into his situation comes from a September 2, 1949, letter from Mira to Myaskovsky, who was himself at pains to make ends meet following his post-Resolution dismissal from the Moscow Conservatory. Mira reports that after several trying months, the household finances had begun to improve. Prokofiev's 40 percent advance for the publication of the Third Suite from *Romeo and Juliet*, she reported, would see them through a few weeks. There was also hope that a new Cello Sonata, which Rostropovich was preparing for a run-through either at the Committee on Arts Affairs or the Union, would be approved for performance and publication. Although Prokofiev's doctors advised him against taking on any new projects, he decided that a vocal work on the theme of world peace might interest the Committee, but he did know who if anyone would endorse his petition to compose it. (It took over a year for the project, *On Guard for Peace*, to be completed.) Prokofiev added a tender postscript to the letter expressing gratitude to his old friend for the help: "Kolenka," he wrote, "you are an angel"—Myaskovsky had taken time away from his own work to correct the proofs for the Suite.[75]

A Story of a Real Man

In official circles, Prokofiev was viewed as a pariah for far longer than Shostakovich and the other composers targeted in the Resolution. The prolongation of his banishment stemmed from the fallout over a work that, incongruously, Prokofiev thought would return him to favor, and which he had touted in his February apology: *A Story of a Real Man*. Once the political and financial implications of the Resolution became clear to him, he resolved to complete the opera as quickly as possible. He began it on October 23, 1947, and handed the short score to Lamm for orchestration on May 11, 1948. Most of the work occurred between March and May. He toiled side by side with Mira on the opera, drafting the ten scenes in order once the libretto had been agreed upon, and taking pains to ensure that the score contained well-known folksongs and sing-along choruses. The choice of subject matter came, as noted in chapter 6, from Kukharsky, but in the aftermath of the Resolution the Committee on Arts Affairs official had second thoughts about his involvement with the chastened composer and decided to back away from the opera. He sheepishly told Mira that some of his colleagues "chided him for advising Seryozha to write *A Story of a Real Man*, fearing that he might take a fancy to the [source story's] morbid side." Mira sought to assure him that his worries were needless, since the score would focus on the "triumph over suffering, on courage, and on optimism."[76] Such, at least, is how Mira describes the incident in her memoirs, but even if—as her memoirs intimate—she adhered to Party teachings, it is unlikely that she would have communicated in such stilted, clichéd language.

In effect, Prokofiev decided that the ideological underpinning of his first Soviet opera, *Semyon Kotko*, would become the ideological underpinning of his newest one, with words and music once again blending to inform the listener that victory for the Soviet system is assured even before its enemies are engaged. The sole challenge confronting the battle-hardened heroes is the Christian Science–like mastering of mental inhibitions and physical weaknesses through acts of will.

A Story of a Real Man is based on an orthodox 1946 novella by Boris Polevoy (real surname Kampov), a World War II reporter for *Pravda* who turned his experiences at the front into propaganda tales for teens. Near the end of his career, he served as editor of the journal *Yunost'* (Youth). His novella, a recipient of a First Class Stalin Prize, gilds the real-life heroism of the pilot Aleksey Maresyev, whose plane was shot down behind Nazi lines in a dogfight and who, despite grave injuries to his legs and a weak constitution stemming from childhood malaria, survived for eighteen days in a snow-covered forest before being found by the children of displaced village farmers.[77] Commissioned to expand his original short-story version of the tale into a novella, Polevoy embellishes and exaggerates the central events. He relates in elaborate detail the wounded hero's struggle to keep himself from freezing to death, his pain-induced deliriums, his stand-off with a bear, and his poignant memories of his sweetheart, Olga. Aleksey's peasant rescuers ply him with soup and regale him with stories of their own suffering at the hands of the Nazis: their relatives were executed, their land torched, and their homes ransacked. His Red Army comrade Andrey arrives to transport him to a military hospital, where a well-known surgeon tells him that his gangrenous legs must be amputated below the knees. There ensue terrible nightmares in which Aleksey sees himself "crawling on stumps," with Olga "standing on the sandy riverside in a bright-colored frock blown about by the wind, light, radiant and beautiful, gazing at him intently and biting her lips." "That's how it will be!" he grieves upon waking. "And he broke into a fit of convulsive, silent weeping, burying his face in his pillow. Everybody in the ward was deeply affected."[78]

The co-occupants of the ward include a grizzled veteran of the civil war who, disdaining self-pity, challenges Aleksey to overcome his handicap in keeping with the spirit of the Revolution. In Prokofiev's operatic rendition of the tale Aleksey answers in woozy mixed metaphors: "A pilot without legs is like a bird without wings." "But you're a Soviet man," the veteran repeatedly assures him, each time pushing the phrase higher by half step in a halo of strings.[79] The final measures of the scene (rehearsal numbers 175 and 176) invoke a waltz rhythm, a marker in Prokofiev's operas for dream states, hallucination, and, in this instance, thought control. In the next scene, the veteran, having noted the splendors of springtime, passes away, a bittersweet event that highlights his role as magical helper in the tale. His is the spectral voice of socialist realist discourse, the instigator of the miraculous happy ending. (The veteran is a fictional character; he does not figure in Maresyev's actual biography. Polevoy inserted him into the narrative for didactic purposes.)

Aleksey's rehabilitation on double prostheses begins at an air force sanatorium in early spring. The sanatorium, once a tsarist palace, is depicted by Polevoy less as a scene of gritted-teeth resolve than ever-expanding optimism, with Aleksey's recovery aided by thoughts of returning to the skies, a letter from Olga, anecdotes with fellow flyer Andrey Degtyarenko, and soulful conversation with fellow patient Grigoriy Gvozdyov, a decorated tank commander fearful that his teenage pen pal Anyuta, who has stolen his heart, will reject him when she sees his facial scars. (The wounds are merely external: he suffers no internal damage; his organs, like his convictions, are intact.) The comradely repartee bolsters Aleksey's spirits, as does the arrival on the ward of a seductive physical therapist with flaming red hair, who offers, after much prodding on Aleksey's part, to teach him to dance on his artificial limbs:

> The terms on which she consented to teach him were severe: he must be obedient and diligent, try not to fall in love with her, since that interferes with the lessons, and chiefly—he must not be jealous when other partners invite her to dance, because if she were to dance only with one partner she would lose her skill, and besides, there was no fun sticking to only one partner.[80]

This incident became the pretext for Prokofiev's somewhat implausible insertion of a waltz, fox-trot, and even a rumba into the eighth scene, a sincere attempt to escape what Kukharsky deemed the "morbid" aspect of the drama, but one that completely backfired. His critics found the scene distasteful, and intimated that he had lost his judgment. The intent behind the drama, however, was rational: it endorsed the Stalinist-era endorsement of art about physical suffering. Caryl Emerson remarks here that, in socialist realist aesthetics, "to feel pain was by no means presented as a shameful thing. Pain was to be administered (in symbolic woundings, construction accidents, on battlefields), but it was to be transcended." This idea doubtless resonated with Prokofiev, who had been living with pain for years, and whose body, like Maresyev's, had become what Emerson calls "a 'classic' Stalinist-era text, wounded and hurting."[81]

The final chapters of the source novella for the opera find Aleksey committed to returning to combat, though the journey from hospital to hangar proves arduous, with the pilot confronting both physical and bureaucratic hurdles. In the penultimate scene, he finds himself cooped up in a communal apartment in Moscow, grumbling that the authorities have not allowed him back into combat. Katerina Clark notes that Polevoy "gives what was first done against the romantic backdrop of snow and dense forest a more prosaic rerun in the world of Soviet institutions." "Usually" in a socialist realist novel, "the situation is reversed," with "what was first treated at a prosaic level" transposed "to a more dramatic setting in the world of the elements."[82] In A Story of a Real Man, however, nature is embodied not in the forest but in the azure skies. Upon clearing the bureaucratic hurdles, Aleksey returns to flight, finishing the chore left undone when he crash-landed. He shoots down three enemy planes on low fuel during the Oryol-Kursk battle.

In the opera, the curtain falls as the hero reunites with his sweetheart and a journalist—Polevoy himself—appears with a request for an interview. The episode is altered in the truncated 1960 and 1963 performing editions of the score, with the chorus recapping a mass song about the regrowth of an oak tree felled by lightning. These editions likewise excise the role of Anyuta, the scene on the lake, and all mention of the place where Olga and Aleksey had first met: Stalingrad.[83]

The mass song is "The Song of the Motherland" (Pesnya o Rodine) that was recycled, in expanded form, by Prokofiev from his *Seven Songs for Voice and Piano* of 1939.[84] Evocative of prewar innocence, the tune does double duty as an emblem of the protagonist's heroism and, moving from the particular to the general, the Russian people's fortitude. It is first heard in scene 3 in the orchestra, as the peasant lad Seryonka, assigned a speaking part, recalls the Nazi assault on his village. It recurs in scene 6 as the veteran begins his hypnotic repetition of "But you're a Soviet man!" Aleksey falls under the spell, intoning the same words to the same tune with a faraway look in his eyes. The veteran's scene 5 ballad reprises the music of the first and second entr'actes, which narrate Aleksey's ordeal in the forest. Prokofiev here reveals that the old man, too, overcame physical and mental challenges in his service to the regime. When, in scene 5, Aleksey becomes anxious, the kindhearted head nurse Klavdiya sings "The Green Grove" (Zelyonaya roshchitsa), a lullaby Prokofiev previously arranged for a collection of twelve Russian folksongs for voice and piano.[85] His other self-references include "The Soldier's [Fighter's] Sweetheart" and "A Warrior's Love" from the *Seven Mass Songs* of 1942. The two melodies dovetail as Olga's theme, which first sounds in scene 2. A choral melody from the wedding in *Ivan the Terrible* Part I recurs in the scene 9 barcarolle performed by Aleksey, Andrey, and Anyuta on the lake by the sanatorium. (Olga is not actually present in the scene: her voice is heard from offstage, and Aleksey answers it.) The choral refrain in the film, an ode to Russian nature, is replaced in the opera with mention of a starlit journey to the front. The words bluntly affirm that Aleksey will succeed in his campaign to return to battle and, afterward, will settle down with his beloved—once she too enlists in the service. His semiconscious recitation in the forest scene of the self-deluding line "Everything will be fine" (Vsyo budet khorosho) literally works for him like a charm.

To further ensure that the audience would leave the theater humming, Prokofiev recycled four additional items in the opera: his 1944 March for concert band, the soldier's song "How delightful the Moscow road" from *Lermontov*, and the melismatic songs "What, Sashenka our joy, has made you so blue?" (Shto zhe tï, Sashen'ka-radost', priunïla?) and "My gentle dream, my happy dream" (Moy son milïy, son schastlivïy) from the Russian folksong collection. The first item provides material for the overture, the second for the final scene in the aerodrome, the third for the villager Varvara's dirge about her husband, from whom she has not received word since he went to the front, and the fourth for the tearful episode of the veteran's peaceful, wistful death. The profusion of self-borrowings finds Prokofiev virtually inventing a new genre: the catalog opera, consisting of tunes of his own that had succeeded in the past.

Excluding a scene 5 *chastushka* about Anyuta's seductive caprices, Prokofiev took pains in the framing and climactic scenes to forge motivic links between the solo numbers and mass choruses, or what official doctrine termed the inferior wishes of the individual and the supreme wishes of the collective. Despite the awkward backtracking from operatic realism to the number format, *A Story of a Real Man* demonstrates that the composer's talent for emotionally and psychologically reified text setting remained intact throughout his career.

The opera contains elements of oratorio while also, like the unrealized *Khan Buzay*, making extensive use of cinematic devices. One writer on the opera, L. Aleksandrovsky, argues that Prokofiev experimented in the first and second scenes with the operatic equivalent of fade-ins (the soothing voice of Olga's apparition), long shots (the thick forest, whose perils are implied by terse chromatic runs and the occasional augmented second), and close-ups (Aleksey's cries of distress).[86] The post-surgery delirium scene represents the macabre, recent past on one side of the stage and the halcyon, distant past on the other—the theatrical equivalent of a cinematic split-screen effect. Aleksey cannot help but listen to the amplified voices of the surgeons as they efficiently plan and perform the operation: like the villains of *Semyon Kotko*, they declaim rather than sing their lines. From childhood, Aleksey hears his mother advising him to wear warm socks in the damp cold; in semiconsciousness in the present, he sadly replies to her singsong patter: "Mama, what use are socks to me now?" (Mama, zachem teper' noski?) Olga emerges from a corner shadow to remind him that she expects him to return to her, whatever his condition. Her appearance is the emotional high point of the scene, and it comes with the quotation from the song "A Warrior's Love," which, as discussed in chapter 4, dominates the score of the unreleased film *Tonya*.

In scene 2 of the opera, moreover, Olga's photograph comes to life in much the same fashion as Tonya's does at the end of the film.

The verb "to wait" (*zhdat'*) links Olga's fade-out with the fade-in of Andrey, Aleksey's comrade, who reminds him that the air force, like his girl-friend, expects him to return to duty.[87] Individual and collective desire are subsequently synthesized in the protagonist's actions, resulting in his reunion with Olga and his fellow pilots on the airstrip.

Thus *A Story of a Real Man* combines the operatic, the nonoperatic, and even the anti-operatic. Its unevenness is less a reflection of hasty work than fundamental indecision. Prokofiev found himself struggling to preserve his artistic identity within un-artistic constraints. To accommodate official demands for melodiousness while also preserving some vestige of his text-setting technique, he relied extensively on borrowed vernacular melodies familiar to Soviet audiences. The jingles about chicken soup and farmers' daughters do not, however, mask the extreme anxieties behind the score. Future events would demonstrate that Prokofiev's effort to portray a "real" man like a "real" composer was all but futile, a waste of energy. Myas-kovsky felt from the start that the opera was in trouble, and that the months ahead would remain awful for his friend. "I looked over Prokofiev's [latest score]," he wrote in his diary. "As always it is extremely interesting, clear-cut, and expressive—but all the same it reflects notions of music drama that are now very 'passé.' I didn't like the libretto: grim emphases without coherent political direction. I fear it will be taken for a joke."[88] Myaskovsky articulates a hopeless double-bind: the more Prokofiev tried to make his music accessible, the more it lent itself to interpretation as sarcasm. Such was the power of the simple, rather than the complex, to convert and to subvert.

Alongside the lack of a strong female lead, the opera suffered from the fundamental implausibility of the opening scene, in which Aleksey performs an arioso while disentangling from airplane wreckage, and the "documentalism" of the surgery scene. Once the score was composed, Prokofiev refused—more from exhaustion than stubbornness—to alter either the text or the music. Myaskovsky's prediction came to pass, though instead of being perceived as a "joke" by the Committee on Arts Affairs, *A Story of a Real Man* was perceived as an insult. It is clear that even a revised version of the opera would have been panned. Prokofiev remained committed to a genre that other prominent composers abandoned, for they discerned, as he did not, that attempts to fulfill the guidelines of the

Resolution would not succeed in the near future, and perhaps not even in the long term. Soviet music was not thriving (as officialdom proclaimed), but withering.

For this reason, perhaps, Prokofiev both expressed high hopes for the success of *A Story of a Real Man* and prepared for its failure. Mere days after he announced that he had begun work on a topical opera about the "boundless courage" of "Soviet man," he began to scout for a backup project.[89] Recalling the grim lessons of *Semyon Kotko* and *The Duenna*, the latter a thematic riposte to the former, he decided to compose both a serious and comic score at the same time. The strategic retreat into humor, in short, would begin before the battle over his newest didactic opera was even waged.

Distant Seas

As discussed earlier, Prokofiev respectively conceived and evaluated two folklore-based projects in the immediate postwar period, drafting a libretto and sketches for *Khan Buzay*, and communicating with Demchinsky's impecunious widow about the scenario for a film about a Palekh craftsmen guild. The Muradeli affair, however, made him uneasy about the Eastern trope, even in its comic guise, and his interest in the film was half-hearted. Seeking benign fare, he thought about writing for the film *Spring* (*Vesna*), a trifling musical comedy about a female scientist, Irina, and her look-alike, the prima ballerina Vera. The plot is self-reflexive: a Moscow studio decides to make a biographical film about the scientist and hires the ballerina to play the lead role, the result being a series of mix-ups involving mistaken identities. Prokofiev was intrigued by the film-within-a-film structure of *Spring* but, after much pondering, decided against the project. The director, Grigoriy Aleksandrov (Mormonenko), instead enlisted a previous co-collaborator, the tunesmith Dunayevsky, for the task.

Prokofiev perhaps sensed that *Spring* would be panned, and indeed, when Mosfilm released it, critics charged that it was merely a pastiche of Aleksandrov and Dunayevsky's previous musical comedies, which included *The Carefree Lads* (*Vesyolïye rebyata*, 1934), *Circus* (*Tsirk*, 1936), and *Volga-Volga* (1938). "The copy appeared to be poorer than the original," Tatiana Egorova writes of *Spring* and *Volga-Volga*, "and less successful artistically."[90] Had Prokofiev taken on *Spring*, it might have fared better artistically, though it remains unclear whether his reduced political standing would have dampened its reception.

He next considered composing a comic opera on the subject of a play titled *Taymïr Calls You* (*Vas vïzïvayet Taymïr*, 1948), which was co-authored by Konstantin Isayev and Aleksandr Galich (Ginzburg). A situation comedy set in a Moscow hotel room, it concerns a geologist who is summoned from time to time by telephone for an excursion to Taymïr (a Russian territory situated above the Arctic Circle), the director of an orchestra, an apiarist, his granddaughter (an aspiring singer), and a lovestruck youth. Through a wittily irrational series of events, these characters end up assuming one another's identities. Prokofiev's interest in *Taymïr Calls You* did not last long: he abandoned it a few days after Mira drafted the outline of a libretto.[91]

Continuing to vacillate, Prokofiev next came up with the Brechtian idea of merging comic opera and vaudeville. For the source text of the experiment, he settled on the play *The Honeymoon* (*Svadebnoye puteshestviye*, 1942) by the satirist Vladimir Dïkhovichnïy.[92] The comedy also went by the name *Sladebnoye puteshestviye*, a one-letter misspelling that suggests a wedding (*svad'ba*) where the bride cannot manage her groom (*s nim sladu net*). The plot concerns amorous intrigue between graduate students of the marine sciences, and features episodes of drunkenness, mistaken identities, and bad cooking. Like other Soviet stage works about marriage, it takes the stance that happy couples pursue happy careers. To enhance this sentiment, which no doubt appealed to Prokofiev and Mira, they chose to expand and enrich the courtship scenes. They also decided to vary the time and place of the action. Dïkhovichnïy confined the seven scenes of his text to a dorm room and apartment in Leningrad. Prokofiev and Mira trimmed the number of scenes to six, setting the last three in a dacha, a train station, and an Eastern port.

Before starting the libretto, Prokofiev and Mira read up on the oceanic sciences, listing, for example, the types of research pursued by hydrologists and the prevailing conditions in the Sea of Okhotsk (located between the Kamchatka Peninsula and the Kurile Islands in the western Pacific Ocean). They noted that the "very dark" waters concealed oil reserves (especially off the northeastern coast of Sakhalin Island), and an abundance of salmon and herring. Prokofiev took note of the types of creatures that inhabit depths above and below 100 meters and wondered how benthic species survive under all the pressure.[93]

The plot addresses gender politics, with the female characters, true to Russian tradition, proving superior to the males in all matters of the heart and mind. Scene 1 introduces us to three graduate students: the biologist Kostik (tenor), the hydrologist Mark (bass), and the geologist Andrey (baritone), who together hope to join a research expedition in the Sea of Okhotsk. Mark and Andrey fret that Kostik is romantically involved with Zoya (soprano), the daughter of Professor Sinelnikov (bass), a distinguished oceanographer, and they determine that, for the sake of his career, they must alert him to the perils of marriage. They hatch a ludicrous plot: Andrey will pretend to court Zoya, wooing her with heartfelt poetry readings, and Mark will tearfully report that, during a recent trip abroad, he impulsively married a woman he had only just met. To complicate matters further, they take advantage of an invitation to the Professor's apartment to convince him that Kostik is unworthy of his daughter's hand: he drinks to excess, has to make alimony payments, and, worst of all, loses his temper during chess.

Nothing, of course, goes according to plan. Mark confesses that he married in error, but when the soprano actress (Nastenka) hired to play the part of his wife arrives at his door, she charms him with her domestic skills and fine manners, and he falls head over heels for her. Andrey feigns affection for Zoya, but he also falls in love. The Professor, meanwhile, receives an order to command the expedition to the Sea of Okhotsk, but refuses to add the lads to his crew, since they have behaved so foolishly in his presence. The three budding Jacques Cousteaus are crushed. The crisis is revolved through the intervention of the navigator, Olga Atamenko (mezzo-soprano), who, unbeknownst to Andrey and Mark, had eloped with Kostik a month before. She implores the Professor to take them all on his trip; against his better judgment, he agrees. The last scene, set on the deck of the research vessel *Ocean*, brings the three couples together. Each have a hand in preparing a meal, but they botch the recipe, and the Professor good-naturedly teases them for grossly oversalting his salad. The anchor is raised, and the Professor, looking to the horizon, declares: "Now, young men, to work: show me that you are true sons of the people."[94]

Though its subject is slight, recalling, at its headiest moments, the social and sexual mores (and partner swapping) of Nikolay Chernïshevsky's 1863 novel *What Is to Be Done?* and the ambiance of Jack London's Aleutian Island tales, Prokofiev needed official approval to move forward with it. To this end, he wrote to the Committee on Arts Affairs in hopes of securing a contract. His terse letter reveals just how far his musical standing and self-confidence had fallen in the wake of the anti-formalist campaign. The new score, Prokofiev assures Chairman Lebedev, would depict the hopes and dreams of Soviet youth in all their glory. He then lists the six "tasks" that he and Mira had assigned themselves in order to ensure the opera's public appeal and Party-mindedness:

1. Emphasize the ideological component [of the source text] and show the goal directedness and high-mindedness of our youth.
2. Strengthen the lyric line. We wish to call the opera a lyric comedy, not simply a comedy.
3. Replace the fragmented conversations with arias, songs, and ensembles.
4. Represent the characters' personalities as clearly as possible.
5. Change several places of action for more varied décor.
6. Reduce the number of scenes from seven to six or five and find another name for the opera.[95]

Prokofiev received an agreement-in-principle from the Committee for a production of the opera in 1952. In late July and August of 1948, he came up with six double-sided pages of sketches, drafted the first scene, and, with Mira, wrote and rewrote portions of the libretto. Fulfilling the requirements of point 6 in his letter to Lebedev, he christened the opera *Distant Seas*. On August 31, he halted work on the opera in order to attend to *A Story of a Real Man* and a new ballet, *The Tale of the Stone Flower*.

Owing to problems with these other two scores, Prokofiev would forget about *Distant Seas* until the start of 1952, at which point he looked over the drafts and, satisfied with them, decided to return to it. Since the deadline for the opera had passed, he was forced to petition the authorities for an extension. His request was bounced from the Theater Directorate (Glavnoye upravleniye muzïkal'nïkh teatrov) to the Union of Soviet Composers, whose secretary, Kabalevsky, advised him that, in order "to continue work on the opera," he needed the personal blessing of Nikolay Bespalov, who in late April 1951 had replaced the inefficient Lebedev as chairman of the Committee on Arts Affairs.[96]

Prokofiev heeded the advice. He sent a letter to Bespalov that detailed his health troubles, his reduced work schedule, and the pleasure he felt writing music on contemporary subjects. Turning to *Distant Seas*, he made the following plea for patience:

I am planning to renew work on the opera *Distant Seas*, which was curtailed owing to illness and the writing of two compositions on the pressing concerns of our present day. I implore you, highly esteemed Nikolay Nikolayevich, to assist me in this matter by giving me permission to prolong the agreement for writing the music and libretto of the opera *Distant Seas* until June or July 1953.[97]

Prokofiev defers to Bespalov like a courtier to a king. The language of the letter, however, does not reflect the full nature of the relationship between the composer and the bureaucrat. By 1952, Prokofiev had regained stature in official circles, as evidenced by Bespalov's effort, in the spring of that year, to secure Prokofiev a pension to supplement his reduced earnings from royalties. The pension—reduced after Central Committee review from 3,000 to 2,000 rubles a month—was awarded to him less on account of his health troubles than his celebrity status. Bespalov likewise granted an extension for *Distant Seas*, but the composer died before he could complete it.

What remains from the summer of 1948 is a pleasant first scene. It includes a flute solo derived from the opening of *Romeo and Juliet*, a sentimental arioso about lost youth, a vaudevillian "bit" about three drunkards, and a mock minuet.[98] The chordal writing involves quick-change effects. In the brief (thirty-eight-measure) instrumental prelude, a rising sequence of first-inversion major triads, each a half step apart, quickly bridges the tonic and dominant of E major. The verbal refrain of Kostik's arioso, "If only I were there!" (Tol'ko bï popast'!), conflates the pitches G-sharp and G-natural. The cross-relation is symbolic of Kostik's conflicted desires: will his career survive his marriage? Should he have heeded the advice of his buddies and remained a bachelor? The punch line of the drunkard anecdote, lastly, moves us from E-flat major to C minor through passing chords built on the pitches B-natural (the augmented fifth of E-flat major) and G-sharp (the augmented fifth of C minor).

Prokofiev planned to repeat the flute solo, which he associated with youthful reverie, in discrete variations throughout the opera, thus bringing together the sober and silly passages. Much as in Part I, scene 2 of *War and Peace*, he intended to organize Andrey and Zoya's love scene with waltz strains. These would have accompanied Andrey's recitation of "revolutionary" poems by Aleksandr Blok and Vladimir Mayakovsky, and would have continued through the next episode, in which Zoya implores her father to take the three lads on his expedition. For the scene at the Leningrad train station, Prokofiev planned to assign the first half of a duet to Nastenka and Zoya, and the second half to Andrey and Mark. To prevent the stage action from getting bogged down in the number format, the two couples would have alternated sitting on a bench in the waiting area, eavesdropping on each other from different hiding places. The two women feel free to express their emotions; the men do not. Embarrassed to admit to each other that they have fallen in love, they duck in turn behind a large potted plant to disclose their feelings directly to the audience.

Distant Seas finds Prokofiev backing into a world of libidinal adolescent caprice. Excluding the fact of its incompletion, nothing in the score speaks to the fraught circumstances of its conception. Vaudeville became for Prokofiev the ideal genre for authoritarian culture since within it the high and low could be crammed together without risk of censure. Forced in word and deed to tame his own creative instincts, he embraced a genre defined by pleasant banality. The three students are sentimental, the three drunkards besotted, and then vice versa. Had the work been finished, and had it survived into more rational times, the whole edifice might have been read as an exercise in high-seas escapism or, like *The Love for Three Oranges*, auto-parody. *Distant Seas* has no hidden meanings: its only subtext is the absence of a subtext.

The extant music is discussed in a short essay by L. V. Polyakova in the March 1963 issue of *Sovetskaya muzïka*. Even in the wake of the Khrushchev Thaw, ideological constraints prevented the author from making the basic point that Prokofiev took to vaudeville because of—rather than in spite of—its frivolity. Polyakova was also unable to address the anxiety and distress felt by Prokofiev in 1948. But she tried to: in the uncensored typescript of her essay, which is housed at the Russian State Archive of Literature and Art, she muses that Prokofiev would have finished *Distant Seas* "had it not been for the crushing blow brought on him by the tragic events of the last months of 1948." "One is hard pressed," she adds, "to find in the entire epoch of Stalin's 'cult of personality,' and the entire history of Soviet music, a more scandalous instance of reprisal against a composer!"[99] The editors of *Sovetskaya muzïka* deleted these lines, replacing them with the altogether false claim that "doubts about the suitability of the chosen text eventually convinced [the composer] not to write the opera."[100] For Prokofiev, the end of 1948 proved almost as traumatic as the beginning. He stopped work on *Distant Seas*, but he clearly sought to return to it.

Denunciation

Unsurprisingly, Prokofiev was further exhausted by the simultaneous labor in 1948 on a new opera and a new ballet (the aforementioned *Tale of a Stone Flower*), along with the preparations for the run-through of *A Story of a Real Man* and the relaunch of Part II of *War and Peace*, but he refused to curtail his activities. His work, ever his reason for being, now provided him shelter from the grimness of the outside world, even if, on a heightened allegorical level, it embodied this grimness. Ignoring his unstable health, he soldiered on, seeking both to honor his muse and appease cultural bureaucrats and ideologues. The pointlessness of the latter quest became obvious to him in December, when he once again came under attack. The attack stemmed from his supposed refusal to abide by the demands of the Resolution and the meetings that had followed from it, even though, by any rational standard of measurement, he had more than done so. The hostile denunciation of *A Story of a Real Man* left his creative life as debilitated as his personal one.

Mira reports that on May 25 the conductor Khaykin, the theater director Shlepyanov, and the violinist Dmitriy Tsïganov all gathered in Nikolina Gora to hear Prokofiev play and sing through *A Story of a Real Man*.[101] Trying to convince Khaykin of the sincerity of his intentions, Prokofiev looked at him in the eye and said: "I wrote this opera with my heart's blood."[102] Khaykin appeared to be delighted with the score, and offered to present it to the Committee on Arts Affairs, the hope being that the Committee would approve the minimal funding required for a staging at the Kirov Theater in Leningrad. Five days later, Khaykin relayed that the theater had received permission to begin work on the opera by the Committee chairman, Lebedev, with the question of payment for décor and costumes to be decided after a closed-door concert performance. Clinging to a modicum of optimism, Prokofiev asked Lamm to begin the orchestration. In September, however, the Union of Soviet Composers requested a copy of the libretto for internal review—a turn of events that galled the composer, since it signaled that the opera would be judged on its thematic content alone. Khrennikov could order changes before a single melody had been heard. The Union also requested that, following the review, the composer travel to Moscow to familiarize the membership with the music, a journey his doctors prohibited. Upon hearing the news, Khaykin pointed out that the Union's meddling was "senseless and illogical" and should be altogether ignored.[103] The libretto, he declared, would be assessed alongside the music by "responsible people" at the closed-door run-through in Leningrad. "If on this occasion the question of alterations arises, then we will be able to reach an agreement much more quickly. If we need to give not one but two closed performances, or need to repeat something, this will all be possible."

The run-through of *A Story of a Real Man* took place on the morning of December 3. Far from mollifying his critics with his topical subject matter, recycled folksongs, and hospital patient dances, Prokofiev endured a storm of derision, thus assuring that the opera would not be staged in his lifetime (the Moscow premiere took place in 1960 at the Bolshoy Theater, the Leningrad premiere in 1967 at the opera studio of the Conservatory). The rehearsals went very badly, since the singers had not learned their parts in advance and seemed distracted and unmotivated. The performance itself was by all accounts a fiasco; Prokofiev protested to Samosud that "I listened and didn't recognize my own music!...They didn't play my music!"[104] The available evidence indicates that the post-performance assessment of the score was scripted, planned in advance by the composer's opponents. Olga Lamm speculates that a "directive intentionally targeting Prokofiev came 'from above.'"[105] Mira writes that during the entr'acte Shlepyanov walked over to her seat and said, "Prepare yourself, there's going to be thunder."[106] The list of attendees included many of the surviving members of the artistic intelligentsia, thus ensuring that the criticism of the score would send a message across the disciplines. Mira recalls seeing the ballerina Nataliya Dudinskaya, the *Cinderella* choreographers Rostislav Zakharov and Konstantin Sergeyev, the conductor Mravinsky, and the composers Yuriy Kochurov, Vasiliy Solovyov-Sedoy, Oles (Aleksandr) Chishko, and Boris Arapov, who had, like Shostakovich, lost his post at the Leningrad Conservatory after the February 1948 scandal. The other locals and visitors at the event included the conformist writer Lev Nikulin and Maresyev, the real-life fighter ace whose near-fatal wounding, convalescence, and heroism Prokofiev's opera monumentalized. Looking around the audience, Mira wondered "Who's arranged all this, and why?"

Suffering a splitting headache, Prokofiev left the theater before the post-performance assessment. Mira remained with pencil and notepad, and recorded that all but one of the speakers who mounted the podium denounced the score. (The lone backer was Solovyov-Sedoy, a popular song composer who, in his speech, professed his lifelong love for Prokofiev's music.) Pavel Serebryakov, the director of the Leningrad Conservatory, set the ominous tone by branding the opera a "parody" lacking both "Russianness and feeling." The baritone Sergey Levik hastened to add that *A Story of a Real Man* and Prokofiev's comic opera *The Duenna* were "one and the same thing": a study in the "grotesque" tending "toward mockery." The score was characterized by "an absence of heroic images, an absence of characterization, and an ugly musical text." The musicologist Leonid Entelis branded the score a "defiled" and "wretched" contrivance expressing "neither truth nor heroism." The opera represented the "liquidation of music." "Prokofiev is no longer," Entelis added with seeming delight. "Prokofiev is finished!" The exceedingly ill-tempered composer Koval, an architect (with Khrennikov and Vladimir Zakharov) of the anti-formalist campaign, accused Prokofiev of a "deterioration of sonorousness" in his orchestration and "second-" perhaps even "third-rate" vocal writing. *A Story of a Real Man* attested to "the composer's unwillingness" to renounce his modernist tendencies and the Kirov Theater's "inadequate understanding of the [1948] Resolution."

There followed an act of personal betrayal. To Mira's dismay, Khaykin, who had advised and helped Prokofiev on the opera, revealed that, two days before the run-through, he had written to the Committee on Arts Affairs with a "forewarning" about the opera's various failings. Shocked that Khaykin had not voiced his concerns to Prokofiev and had disingenuously cast himself as the nervous composer's backer, Mira rose to speak. She described the pain she felt on Prokofiev's behalf and refuted the charge that he "had knowingly avoided writing what was required, that he did not want to reform" his style. The audience had no idea "how much effort Seryozha put into the opera, how he had tried to devise a new musical language that was accessible and close to the people." Unlike other composers hoping to return to official favor, Prokofiev did not "take the easy way out and write music for the cinema" but sought to respond to the "honorable and responsible challenge of writing an opera on a contemporary theme."

Mira held no sway. Following the orchestrated, fraudulent assessment of the performance, she returned to the Astoria Hotel and told Prokofiev what had happened. As he listened, he repeated "I just don't understand" over and over again. These words speak volumes about the earnestness of his aspiration to appease his antagonists. He had adhered to official doctrine in his topical opera, but had sought to elevate its crude precepts into art. This Pushkinian model of transcendence combined in his thinking with a model borrowed from Christian Science: the unreal circumstances in which he found himself could be transcended because they are unreal. On December 3, 1948, however, Prokofiev came to understand that he could not artistically overcome what could not be defined. The cultural climate was such that, no matter how earnest his attempt to honor Marxist-Leninist ideals, to represent them in the most glowing light, the attempt would always miss the target because the target did not exist. Socialist Realism, like formalism, had no concrete definition. It meant whatever officialdom wanted it to mean.

Kabalevsky telephoned Prokofiev after the run-through to offer his condolences, as did Mravinsky, who also commended Mira for defending A Story of a Real Man. Kukharsky, who had advised Prokofiev to compose the opera but then suffered cold feet about it, stopped by to inform him that the scandal was unwanted and criticized Khaykin for sending his letter to the Committee on Arts Affairs too late for the opera to be overhauled. Prokofiev accused Khaykin of inviting an antagonistic audience to the run-through; despite the conductor's claims to the contrary, Prokofiev held a grudge against him for the rest of his life.[107]

The composer was likewise betrayed by Kukharsky, who responded to the run-through by writing a harsh essay about Prokofiev's operatic methods. The essay, which appeared in the January 13, 1949, issue of Izvestiya, trotted out a familiar catalog of unspecific complaints about Prokofiev's supposed formalism, defined in this instance as "extremely pale, anti-melodic" syntax dependent on "unexpressive recitative" to amplify a "bad libretto."[108] Whereas "an authentic artist of our times would have found in B. Polevoy's story wonderful material for the creation of truthful and wonderful musical images of the remarkable Soviet people," Kukharsky expounded, "Prokofiev interpreted A Story of a Real Man from the discredited perspectives of Western Modernism." The result was an opera that replaced "real people" with "theatrical masks, spiritually vacuous personages with extremely primitive thoughts and feelings." The opera's weaknesses stemmed from the composer's "detachment from life" and his "armchair expert" approach to composition.

Since it would not have been helpful, from the perspective of political tutelage, to critique Prokofiev's opera without comparing it to other patriotic scores, Kukharsky in the final paragraphs of his essay trained his ideological lens on Dzerzhinsky's 1947 folk opera The Prince Lake, noting that its maker evinced only a "shallow knowledge" of his subject matter (this perhaps highlighting deficiencies in orchestration and voice-leading that had been ignored in the euphoric reviews of Dzerzhinsky's The Quiet Don). On the plus side,

Kukharsky drew attention to the young Armenian composer Aleksandr Harutyunyan's 1948 *Cantata About the Motherland*, a "talented, bright composition, suffused with the spirit of Soviet patriotism." The scenario featured "images of Soviet people raised in an atmosphere of inspiring creative labor, in the heroism and pathos of the struggle for Communism."

Like the affirmations of the Resolution published in *Kul'tura i zhizn'*, *Literaturnaya gazeta*, and *Sovetskoye iskusstvo* in early 1949, Kukharsky's *Izvestiya* article stemmed from a speech delivered at a special year-end meeting of the Union of Soviet Composers. During this event, held between December 21 and 29, 1948, Khrennikov, the newly minted General Secretary, cemented his authority. He arranged trial hearings of some 150 new works, and scheduled lectures by 27 composers and musicologists, who agonized in unison about the harm inflicted upon Soviet music by Western trends. Eminent artists—those who had benefited from Muzfond's munificence—were again petitioned to apologize, while an array of lesser talents from far-flung points in the empire basked in praise. The speeches bore the paradoxical distinction of being indistinct from each other: each touched on the inability of first-tier composers to rehabilitate themselves and the regrettable regression of second-tier composers from paragons of progress to recyclers. In the topsy-turvy post-Resolution period, sophisticated compositions were judged emotionally and psychologically primitive while unsophisticated ones were lauded as profound. Khrennikov closed the session with a prepared statement about the comradeship and conviviality shown in the talks.

Prokofiev was invited to the gathering, but remained too frail to attend, and thus managed to avoid another dressing down. He excused himself in a December 21 note to Khrennikov: "Dear Tikhon Nikolayevich: I came from the countryside to Moscow for the plenary but, not feeling well, I had to be confined to bed. I hope that I will soon recover and be able to participate in the work of the plenary."[109] On December 27, Prokofiev made a brief appearance at the gathering to have his photograph taken with Khrennikov; on December 28, he needed to stay home, but submitted a formal letter to the gathering that further outlined his views on the Resolution. As in his earlier apology, he invoked Chaikovsky, but this time with the aim of illustrating the differences, rather than the similarities, between their approaches to opera. The letter was read aloud in his absence:

> Comrade Zhdanov advised us to consult the Russian Classics. The guidance is important, offering a bearing for

a composer in his work. However, composing a Soviet opera presents us with a series of difficulties. Let us take for example one of the principal personages of the opera—the people. Chaikovsky and Rimsky-Korsakov concerned themselves with the people of the tsarist period. Our free Soviet people are a wholly different entity. In this respect it becomes obvious that the entire choral section of the opera must be composed in a totally different manner, one that still has to be found. I have often faced this problem. But I reasoned that the search is necessary, and if it is unsuccessful in the first opera, then it might turn out better in the next opera or the one after that.

In my opera I tried to be as melodic as I could, tried to make the melodies as comprehensible as possible. In representing my characters I was primarily concerned with disclosing Soviet man's internal world, his love for the Motherland, and Soviet patriotism. It was hard for me to hear the negative reactions of my comrades. I would nonetheless prefer, however, to write an opera on Soviet themes and even, in the event of failure, to listen to negative reactions—than not to write and not to listen.[110]

The letter is rhetorical rather than substantive, but it bears a hint of defiance: it is better to compose and be critiqued than not to compose at all. Prokofiev would not be silenced.

War and Peace (Part II)

There is no mention in Prokofiev's letter, and little mention at the plenary session, of the other opera auditioned in Leningrad during the month. On December 4, Part II of War and Peace, stripped of the elements that raised hackles in July and October 1947, received a rehearing at Malegot under the direction of Isay Sherman. (Prokofiev made the alterations following a resumption of negotiations about the score at the offices of the Committee on Arts Affairs.) In a peculiar reversal of fortunes, the unadorned concert performance, which occurred less than twenty-four hours after the catastrophe at the Kirov Theater with A Story of a Real Man, proved a modest success. Although the absence of decor and costumes "diminished the impression," the atmosphere in the hall was congenial. "Finally, after long months of anticipation," Mira wrote,

> I heard the following scenes: Napoleon at Shevardino Redoubt, Fili (with Kutuzov's new aria, so broadly Russian), Natasha's meeting with the wounded Andrey in Mïtishchi (during which I noticed tears in Seryozha's eyes), the Smolensk Road with a new ending that sounded much more impressive than the previous one. The Moscow scene [Moscow Aflame] wasn't done, since in the event of a staging they are planning to cut it.[111]

Mira does not specify who "they" were, but from the protocol of the discussion that followed the run-through, it emerges that the ideological sanitization of the opera stemmed as much from the Theater Directorate as the Committee on Arts Affairs. Mira reproduces the protocol in her memoirs, helpfully pointing out places where the record of the discussion deviates from her recollections.[112]

One such deviation is in the transcript of the musicologist Mikhaíl Glukh's reaction to Part II, in which he grumbles about the occasional blandness of the melodic writing for Kutuzov and Pierre, and the "impersonal construction" of Andrey's death scene. Like a latter-day Artusi inveighing against a Monteverdi, Glukh takes Prokofiev to task for his aberrant handling of dissonances (according to music theory textbooks); he also decries the coarseness of the jargon inserted into the scene 8 partisans' chorus—lines like "The black enemy will die...We'll leave neither hide nor hair; we'll rattle him like bones in a sack. We'll squash him like a flea; we'll crush him like a clove of garlic." Excluded from the transcript, according to Mira, is Glukh's praise of Prokofiev's lyrical writing. The transcript includes mention of a "series of positive lyrical passages," but omits Glukh's use of the adjective "ingenious" to describe them.

A second instance concerns the speech by Shaporin on the need to reconfigure the opera so that Part I, "Peace," and Part II, "War," could be performed in a single evening. Shaporin makes the reasonable point that, whereas Part I stands alone, Part II does not, especially when heard without the "Moscow Aflame" episode and the mass choruses, as was the case at Malegot. Shaporin advocates abbreviating the opera and revamping the vocal parts so that each scene evinces the beauty and pathos of the Part I ball scene, where Natasha and Andrey become smitten with each other, and the Part II death scene, which teems with hallucinatory waltz strains. He likewise calls for additional development of the "love angle" and greater elucidation of the characters' internal experiences. Mira comments here that the transcript excludes Shaporin's flattering comparison of *War and Peace* to Chaikovsky's *Queen of Spades*, which implied that, once banged into shape, Prokofiev's opera was destined for immortalization as a Russian—or Soviet—classic. Prokofiev concluded that this would happen only when each member of the Union had critiqued the score and it had been reworked to the point of non-recognition. In his "brief diary" (*kratkiy dnevnik*) of August 1952 to March 1953, he encapsulates the endless demands for changes in a single word: "disgusting."[113]

Given that Mira's memoirs fluctuate between hagiographic narration and dutifully researched chronicle, her corrections to the *War and Peace* protocol may or may not be accurate. One cannot help but note her careful adjustment of the opening of Kabalevsky's speech. In the transcript, he begins: "I didn't stay yesterday at the Kirov Theater for the assessment [of *A Story of a Real Man*] and did not speak out, since it was a day of great sorrow. I love S. S. Prokofiev very much and grieved this failure of his." Mira corrects the record to read: "I didn't stay for the assessment and did not appear yesterday because I was unable to speak positively about [*A Story of a Real Man*], and it is difficult for [me] to speak negatively, since [I] love Prokofiev very much and find personal delight in each of his successes and personal sorrow in each of his failures."[114] The transcript of the remainder of the speech, in which Kabalevsky echoes Shaporin's argument for reconfiguring *War and Peace* as a single-evening event, is, according to Mira, accurate.

Her appraisal of later events in the opera's sorrowful history finds support in the recollections of Valerian Bogdanov-Berezovsky, Samosud, and Prokofiev himself. Mira omits mention, however, of what occurred on December 5, two days after the abbreviated run-through of Part II. Dutifully heeding the counsel of the Committee on Arts Affairs, Prokofiev devised a new plan for the opera, one that excised not only "Moscow Aflame," but also "Napoleon at Shevardino Redoubt," the "Epigraph" of Part I, and scene 7, "Pierre Bezukhov's Study." Samosud comments that the plan also included provisions for trimming "the overture," "scenes four (at Hélène's) and five (at Dolokhov's), and even the tenth (Fili)"; he adds that Prokofiev's "desire to see *War and Peace* onstage" was "so persistent, so unshakable, that he was actually willing to cede to all manner of editorial modifications, abbreviations, and cuts if only it made it to theater."[115] The tinkering lasted much longer than either Prokofiev or Samosud could have reasonably anticipated.

Khrennikov

On December 30, the penultimate day of a nightmarish year, Prokofiev was once again summoned to the Union of Soviet Composers, this time for a face-to-face meeting with Khrennikov to discuss the defects in *A Story of a Real Man* and the fallout over the run-through.[116] Mira attended in his place, a now familiar ritual. During the meeting, she recalls, Khrennikov hailed Prokofiev as a "titan" and "colossus" among composers and dismissed Koval's invective about his "fall in mastery" as nonsense. Khrennikov's mood then soured, and he began to interrogate Mira about the choice of Polevoy's novel for an opera, rattling off a list of other topical novels and plays that might have been set. If Prokofiev hoped to write music about Soviet pilots, Khrennikov continued, he should have ventured out to an aerodrome to witness how the pilots worked and listened to their jargon. Mira countered that Prokofiev had tried his best with *A Story of a Real Man*, but that he was in no physical condition to conduct field research about aviation; his doctors forbade him to travel, even to make telephone calls.

At this point, Mira continues, Khrennikov abruptly changed the subject, asking her: "Why do you try to write librettos? You must know that you are very bad at it." Mira replied that she encouraged Prokofiev to collaborate with others on his librettos, but he always refused, preferring to write them with her at the same time as the music. She added in her own defense that, unlike the libretto for *A Story of a Real Man*, the libretto for *War and Peace* Part 2 had been well received. "Do you think so?" Khrennikov responded, "I don't find this to be the case."

Recalling how humiliated she felt, Mira did not suppress her disdain for the General Secretary. "Seryozha might be a 'titan' and 'colossus,'" she fumed,

> but Khrennikov will do all he can to ensure that his operas are not made available to the theaters and the people, and will defend Soviet music from Prokofiev, the "titan" and "colossus." He hated *Semyon Kotko*, and now he hates *War and Peace* and *A Story [of a Real Man]*. He will do all he can out of envy to guard the theaters and audiences from Prokofiev's harmful influence. And now he has the full

power to do this—his opinion is regarded by theaters, publishers, and music critics as directive.

Mira's candid remarks, a departure from the banal Soviet-speak of earlier
sections of the memoirs, end with a bitter insight: "Sincerity is a good thing."
Khrennikov's "sincerity," however, "bore a shade of malice."[117]

Khrennikov's "malice"—his purported ill-treatment of his colleagues—
and the entire series of events in 1948 traumatized the Soviet musical elite.
Olga Lamm believes that the Zhdanovshchina, the nickname given to these
events by musicologists, hastened the death not only of Prokofiev but also
of Asafyev (who died on January 27, 1949), Myaskovsky (August 8, 1950),
and Lamm (May 5, 1951). Shebalin, moreover, suffered a debilitating stroke
in 1949.[118] Of these figures, only Asafyev can be regarded as an agent in
his own demise, since he consciously cooperated with the regime. A fragile,
nervous person, Asafyev succumbed to pressure from above to abandon his
provocative journalism and academic writing for Party-line composition, the
result being a series of derivative scores on standard fare themes. His composer colleagues damned his efforts with faint praise, and even though he
heard his works performed, he wept over his loss of intellectual prestige.
Prokofiev scorned him, in public and private, for his 1932 French Revolution
ballet *The Flame of Paris*, since it absorbed, without the slightest alteration
or reworking, songs by French composers of the period that Prokofiev had
gathered for him in Paris. Lamm comments that on the night of the ballet's
premiere Prokofiev tore into Asafyev, telling him: "After such blatant pla-
giarism, they won't allow you into Paris."[119] Prokofiev provides a different
version of this episode in an autobiographical notation: "After *The Flame of
Paris*, I said to Asafyev that when he comes to Paris, the Société des Auteurs
will tell him to leave his suitcases at the station."[120] It testifies to Prokofiev's
uncommon ethics, which placed more value on creative integrity than personal integrity, that their friendship was spoiled more by Asafyev's artistic
betrayal than his political betrayal.

Upon learning in May 1948 that Asafyev had suffered a serious stroke,
Prokofiev nonetheless came to his side. During later visits, the two discussed
religion and reminisced about their comparatively paradisiacal conservatory days. According to a family intimate, Asafyev was guilt-stricken about
his creative and political hackwork and, "before his death, summoned a
priest."[121] He confessed his moral lapses to Prokofiev and Lamm, who both
forgave him. They perhaps did not know that, on December 16, he had

drafted a pathetic letter to Zhdanov in which he asserted, after describing his failing health, that the Resolution and its consequences were fair and just:

> I consider it my duty to convey to you in a proper man-
> ner several modest thoughts in connection with the news
> I received about the congress you led on the subject of our
> native music. Unfortunately, I was unable to appear in per-
> son. On May 14 last year I suffered a cruel misfortune: a
> brain seizure and loss of the use of my left arm and leg. This
> nagging condition was precipitated by high blood pressure,
> which dates from the days of the Leningrad Blockade, and
> of which I became acutely aware after January 1947. Yet
> I was compelled to complete my ballet on the theme of par-
> tisan Yugoslavians: *Malitsa*....
>
> Permit me to thank you for the powerful and intelligent
> words, in particular for your wonderful assessment of the
> value of the music of our Russian Classics, the music of our
> great people. I have come to believe that a new era will dawn
> in contemporary Russian music and that everything within
> it will be wholesome, expressed in a natural way, simple
> and beautiful. The tradition that extends from Glinka to
> the glorious masters of the Balakirev-Stasov circle (the new
> Russian school) and further to the great Chaikovsky (who
> used his talent and mastery of form to instill music in the
> hearts of the vast majority) will once again infuse our operas
> and symphonies with the strains of happy song.[122]

Owing, perhaps, to his failing health, Asafyev did not realize that he had written the letter in vain. Zhdanov had died four months earlier, on August 31, 1948.

Seeing the collapse of Asafyev's condition, Prokofiev and Lamm for-gave him for serving Zhdanov. Myaskovsky did not. After the release of the Resolution he refused on principle to speak to Asafyev and, owing to his own failing health (Myaskovsky was diagnosed with cancer in the spring of 1948), did not attend his funeral. He marked the event in his diary with cool dismissal: "Today B. V. Asafyev died. There was an entire epoch in his life. I hardly saw him these past two or three years."[123]

The mere fact that Prokofiev maintained his frenetic work schedule throughout 1948, embarking on a new fairy-tale ballet and persisting with *War and Peace*, attests to his steadfastness and irrepressible creative passion. His fervent desire to commit music to paper perhaps served as an anodyne. The Theater Directorate continued to funnel approved scenarios to him, and he continued to weigh new projects for stage and screen, despite the setbacks of the recent and distant past. He trusted that his health would not completely fail him while his musical imagination still sparked, and he invented musical worlds that he believed merited greater attention than the real world. Mira, herself a fabulist, shielded him as best as she could from external concerns, leaving him to negotiate increased work time with his doctors. Life, as Eisenstein had put it in 1946, was essentially over, but there still remained the postscript.

8

Affirmation,

1949–1953

rokofiev's final works composed after the storm of 1948 are characterized by a decline in melodic, harmonic, and rhythmic invention that reflects the parameters of his commissions and the difficulties he had concentrating as his health continued to deteriorate. The period also witnessed increased involvement (for good and for ill) in his creative activities by other musicians. In his final works, Prokofiev's authorial voice fades, and the voices of others, including Atovmyan, Samosud, and especially Rostropovich, threaten to crowd his out. He continued to construct his scores brick by brick from preexisting sketches but relied on interlocutors to provide the mortar. Once a meticulous proofreader, lambasting his hardworking assistants for not respecting his intentions when preparing his scores, he now ceded to their judgment, allowing them to realize his orchestrations based on their general understanding of his methods. He lacked the strength to prepare his manuscripts for completion on his own. Such meddling creates a paradox in his late works: while the syntax simplifies, hewing closer to standard diatonic collections, the scoring thickens to the point that each note becomes masked by several others.

After 1948, Prokofiev could no longer depend on the disgraced, deposed Atovmyan to attend to his business dealings; instead, Atovmyan depended on him, beseeching the composer to accept commission after commission for arrangements and transcriptions of preexisting works, which Atovmyan would then take the lead in bringing to order for performance and publication for a percentage of the fee. Proof comes from their 1949–52 correspondence, which finds Atovmyan encouraging Prokofiev to realize three (initially four)

orchestral suites from *The Tale of the Stone Flower* while also assembling
a pair of generic dance suites commissioned by the Radio Committee. The
commission for the dance suites dates from 1934 but went unfulfilled until
1950.[1] Evidently Atovmyan convinced the Radio Committee to revive a
defunct contract, and then took it upon himself to assemble the dance suites
without pausing for breath in his musical workshop. He kept Prokofiev
abreast of his progress, but one can only wonder whether the composer was
able to follow Atovmyan's tangled questions about arranging, formatting,
and transcribing the various interchangeable numbers. Atovmyan's letter of
July 11, 1950, with news of a successful premiere, may well have come as a
relief, even as it promised to keep the assembly line humming:

> Today the Dance Suite with the two new numbers (the Ser-
> enade and Minuet) was finally heard. I don't know why
> S[amuil] A[bramovich] Samosud was nervous about the
> instrumentation of the Serenade and Minuet. It all sounded
> wonderful. They performed six numbers: the Serenade,
> Minuet, Mazurka, Polonaise, and the 2 Pushkin Waltzes.
> I listened with immense pleasure. Did you hear it on the
> radio? What was your impression of the performance?
>   Now a new suite has to be done...We'll speak on this
> subject when we meet.[2]

The letter offers the unsettling impression of Prokofiev's music being plundered and patched together by an assistant who, out of his own need and
newly debased status, does with Prokofiev's dances what, back in 1936,
Meyerhold and Tairov were supposed to do with the composer's units of incidental music (assemble them, arrange them into effective dramatic wholes,
graft them, put them onto stage so that they sound wonderful), except that
here the whole process is driven by the need for income. Prokofiev did not
hear the Dance Suite, which was made up of spare parts from *The Duenna*
and the ill-fated Pushkin commissions, nor did he sanction the creation of a
sequel. Other projects and new compositions took precedence.

The Lower Depths

This is not to say that Prokofiev wanted to discontinue his relationship with
Atovmyan. Recognizing that his erstwhile benefactor had been reduced
to a hardscrabble existence, Prokofiev continued to involve Atovmyan

in his activities. (Atovmyan did not return to full-time work until 1953, when he became the administrator of the State Symphony Orchestra of Cinematography, holding the position for a decade.) The emotions and tensions in their long-term friendship are evident in their correspondence concerning Prokofiev's 1949 Cello Sonata, which Atovmyan rendered suitable for publication, though not without struggle.

The Cello Sonata was conceived for the twenty-year-old virtuoso Rostropovich, recent first-prize winner of an international festival for young performers in Prague, whom Prokofiev first heard play on December 21, 1947, in the Small Hall of the Moscow Conservatory.[3] On that Sunday evening, in a diverse concert dedicated to the Thirtieth Anniversary of the Great October Socialist Revolution, Rostropovich earned the composer's gratitude for performing his long-overlooked First Cello Concerto of 1938 (with a piano reduction of the orchestral score), which he had conceived in Paris for Gregor Pyatigorsky. Prokofiev thereafter pledged to compose something specific to Rostropovich's technique, the result being a productive friendship that extended through the remainder of the composer's life, with Rostropovich even periodically residing at Prokofiev's dacha, sleeping on the second floor. The contact between them must have been authorized, especially since Rostropovich, unlike Prokofiev, was sanctioned to travel abroad. They clearly knew each other before December 21, 1947. On June 8, Rostropovich sent a note to Prokofiev congratulating him on the Stalin Prize for his Violin Sonata while also wishing him "health, long years of life and many cello works."[4]

Prokofiev's initial inclination to rework the first Cello Concerto was set aside in favor of the Cello Sonata, a brand-new score commissioned by the Radio Committee. It was drafted in the spring of 1949 along the lines of Myaskovsky's Second Cello Sonata, which Rostropovich, being its dedicatee, obviously championed. Prokofiev sent the manuscript to Rostropovich in June with an invitation for him to travel with Atovmyan to Nikolina Gora to play it. The ambitious cellist was delighted to be at the service of the eminent composer; he became Prokofiev's advisor on revisions to the Cello Sonata, encouraging him to push its virtuosic side while ensuring its manageability. In an undated letter to Prokofiev, Rostropovich confirms: "I'm going to Ruza to prepare for my upcoming trip to Germany ('celebration of Bach's 200th'), but I'll be in touch with Moscow the entire time; so if I'm needed to change anything in the cello part I can always come to Moscow." He ends the letter with a plea for another project: "To avoid completely getting on your nerves, I won't ask anything about the Cello Concerto, but in my heart I'm hoping."[5]

Prior to its public unveiling, Rostropovich performed the Cello Sonata three times behind closed doors with Richter at the piano: the first run-through, on September 27, 1949, was for Union of Soviet Composers adjudication; the second, on December 6, highlighted a demonstration of Soviet music at the Union's 1949 plenary session; and the third, on January 12, 1950, was for Radio Committee adjudication. Mira reports that this last demonstration "was a success, but not the kind that the performers, expecting an ovation for Seryozha, had counted on. The mood in the hall was rather constrained."[6] The Cello Sonata was first performed for the public on March 1, 1950, in a well-received concert at the Moscow Conservatory. Serious illness—requiring hospitalization—prevented the composer from attending.

Prokofiev relies within the score on sonata, minuet and trio, and sonata-rondo forms, and highlights C and F major. But telltale signs of his idiosyncratic approach to harmony and tonality remain. In the opening movement, for example, the second theme group arrives on the dominant by way of a transition in F-sharp major, a tritone removed from C major. The recapitulation begins in the expected tonic but soon strays, and materials from the first and second theme groups are reordered and inverted—procedures that justify the absence of thematic development in the movement's core. The final movement, a quasi-symmetrical sonata-rondo, begins and ends in C major but wanders, as in the opening movement, through wide-ranging and unexpected tonalities. The middle episode offers an ethereal contrast to the upbeat refrain and first episode, which features several brisk themes tumbling one into the next (the order of the themes changes for the third episode). A coda supplants a final statement of the refrain. A version of the first theme of the opening movement returns—a gesture that recalls Prokofiev's Ninth Piano Sonata, whose ending also quotes from its beginning.

In addition to the Ninth Piano Sonata, there are other references in the Cello Sonata to Prokofiev's own works, some explicit, others surfacing like stylistic ciphers. Boris Schwarz notes the obvious similarity between the fourth melody introduced in the first movement (that is, the second melody of the second theme group) and the "Field of the Dead" mezzo-soprano aria in *Alexander Nevsky*, identifying it as an "almost literal quotation."[7] A more subtle example is the string of exposed rising triads in the center of the innocuous second movement, which recalls a similarly striking moment in the third movement of the 1943 Flute Sonata. The fourteen available pages of sketches for the Cello Sonata are essentially a gathering of melodic and harmonic material that had served Prokofiev well in the past.

Between the time of its first private adjudication and first public performance, Rostropovich entered several changes into the solo part. Atovmyan, having received the desperately needed commission to edit the manuscript and parts for publication with Muzgiz, found himself confronted with a mess. So, too, did Prokofiev, who complained about the state of the manuscript in a June 22, 1950, letter to Atovmyan:

> Rostropovich sent me his edit of the Sonata. I don't doubt that his remarks are reasonable, but the copy is blurred and stained. I don't think it's possible to send it to Muzgiz in this state. Besides, none of the changes made to the cello part has been entered into the score (everything has to be entered, except the fingerings). How does the Sonata end? You know, I wanted *two* variants, i.e. *ossia*. Now: if the 1st variant is completely unsuitable, then it's not worth publishing. Let Rostropovich + Richter decide this. I gave (and entrusted to) you an altogether clean and legible copy, and you're sending Muzgiz what? You can't, for example, send it to the engraver with an "8—" (for the cellos): the part has to be written out in the treble clef (or in the bass clef, if it's low).
>
> Unfortunately, I'm unable right now to deal with the corrections and tidying up, so I ask you, as a sufficiently experienced publisher, to put the Sonata into decent shape and send it to Muzgiz. What I hastily inscribed at the keyboard, working with Rostropovich, needs to look tidy.[8]

The criticism stung. "I don't understand why you attacked me," Atovmyan protested a week later.

> Instead of giving the Sonata to me (as I had asked him) Slava Rostropovich sent it to you in the state you found it in. But I wanted to put everything in order beforehand—then to send it to you in a final, ready-to-be-engraved state.
>
> Things turned out differently, but absolutely through no fault of my own. I'm working these days on the Sonata— I've entered all the corrections, including the bowings—and copied the coda once again, including as a second line the

second variant (*ossia*—the easier variant), and both the cello and piano parts. As proof I'm sending you the last 5 pages (so that you won't be in doubt). When I was preparing the Sonata for publication it seemed to me that the piano part was missing some phrase marks, but without your permission I didn't put them in. It can easily be done on the proofs.

The dedication wasn't clear to me. After it, was it necessary to include the Gorky quotation, the one that you have on the manuscript ("Man! The word has such a proud ring!")? To be on the safe side, I entered the quote. Today I submitted the manuscript in good condition to Muzgiz. It will go to the engraver at the beginning of July. When it's ready I'll send you the contract. In general, you scolded me for nothing.[9]

The correspondence finds Prokofiev including an optional ending to the Cello Sonata for less-virtuosic performers; it also finds him dedicating the score to Atovmyan, while also including, alongside the dedication, a quotation from Gorky's 1902 play *The Lower Depths* (*Na dne*), an almost grotesquely realistic, unsentimental depiction of destitute ne'er-do-wells in a flophouse in the town of Volga. The character Satin's famous declaration—"Man! The word has such a proud ring!"—underscores what is habitually considered to be the play's central concern with social justice, human equality. In an unfair world that privileges falsehoods over the truth, one can only preserve one's integrity. This, however, is the Stalinist cliché, the cynical rewriting of the play's message after Gorky's death. *The Lower Depths* is in fact highly nihilistic, with the characters slowly coming to terms with the idea that the universe is fundamentally indifferent to their plight. Prokofiev perhaps intended the quotation to comment on Atovmyan's humiliation, perhaps also on his own troubles. Muzgiz, he later learned, did not want to publish the dedication, which only confirmed to him Atovmyan's fall from grace within the cultural agencies. He intervened on his assistant's behalf, and the dedication was preserved—a triumph not for Stalinist bombast ("living has become better, living has become happier"), but for its Panglossian subtexts.

Over time, the affable, roguish Atovmyan rescued himself from the lower depths, improving his standing at Muzgiz and with it his personal finances. In the summer of 1952, he approached Prokofiev about the possibility of assembling a three-volume collected edition of his piano works, first making sure that the chief editor of Muzgiz, Aleksandr Zhivtsov, approved of the plan and would, if Prokofiev agreed, hire him as the compiler and arranger. On August 13, 1952, Atovmyan forwarded a provisional outline of the edition to Prokofiev; he planned to devote the first volume to sonatas, the second to shorter pieces, and the third to transcriptions and arrangements. Their ensuing exchange is notable for two reasons: first, Prokofiev, having responded with enthusiasm to the prospect of having his piano music gathered together by Muzgiz, found himself having to revise the Sixth Sonata, removing the dissonant *col pugno* pitch groups from the first movement. These, Atovmyan reminded him, would not be sanctioned for publication by Bespalov and the Committee on Arts Affairs. The Ninth Sonata was similarly excluded from the collection, since it had not yet been officially reviewed. "They aren't approving Sonata no. 9 for the three-volume edition of works for now," Atovmyan wrote, "next year I'll see about a separate edition."[10]

The second point of interest concerns Atovmyan's decision to publish, in the first volume, Prokofiev's E-minor and G-major sonatinas, which date from 1931 and 1932, respectively. The composer blanched, deeming the works too mild for placement alongside the heavier wartime sonatas. Atovmyan responded by relocating them to the second volume alongside the Fifth Piano Sonata, but this plan also bothered Prokofiev, who reported that "Atovmyan came by to show me his editorial changes to the first volume. Contra my expectations, it was well done. He said that the Fifth Sonata and perhaps the two Sonatinas, opus 54, will manage to be included in the second volume." Prokofiev looked over the three works and "took fright," concluding that the beautiful but impetuous sonatinas "had to be redone," and that the Fifth Sonata of 1923 (composed in Ettal, Germany, but showing the influence of the Parisian Francis Poulenc) needed substantial revision, "for example the final pages of the 1st and 3rd movements."[11] Thus began another exercise in commissioned *pererabotka*, but one that would remain mostly incomplete. Prokofiev finished the alteration of the Fifth Sonata in January 1953. Several of the changes soften the harmonic acerbities, but a few appear to be conditioned by voice-leading, specifically an interest in maintaining a flowing texture and a consistent mode of expression (excluding the coda of the third movement, where the aspiration toward homogeneity subsides: meandering, chromatic melodic writing cedes to percussive iterations of single chords). The new sections and substitutions, filling five pages of manuscript paper, range from two to ten measures in length, seemingly inadequate to merit assigning the work a new opus number, but that is what happened (opus 38 became opus 135). The pianist Anatoliy Vedernikov, who replaced Pavel Lamm as Prokofiev's assistant after Lamm's death in 1951, put the new version of the Fifth Sonata into shape.[12] Prokofiev at first refused to entrust Vedernikov with the realization of the score, but Mira, seeking to preserve his strength, convinced him otherwise. The job was finished in mid-February.

The sonatinas evolved in Prokofiev's imagination into the Tenth and Eleventh Piano Sonatas. Neither work was completed, however, and only the first even begun. The forty-four extant measures of the Tenth Sonata (composed on February 27, 1953) share the same tempo, meter, and tonality as the opening of the E-Minor Sonatina. Prokofiev eliminates the harsh edges in the original texture, delaying the introduction of modulatory pitches (the C-sharp in measure 6 of the Sonatina, precipitating the tonicization of B minor, appears in measure 10 of the Sonata) and filling in the sixteenth- and eighth-note rests that splinter the opening phrase. An impulse to traditionalize, to replace discordant musical fireworks with Mannheim rockets, governs the Tenth Sonata sketch, which was generated with ease, written in an even hand without alternates, cross-outs, or marginalia. It is nonetheless disquieting, showing the composer conventionalizing his own unconventional inspiration and suppressing, for the State Music Publisher, a transgressive past. After 1948 habitual recycling became habitual self-censorship.

Aside from these modest projects, Prokofiev focused on the ballet *The Tale of the Stone Flower*, *War and Peace*, *The Meeting of the Volga and the Don*, the Seventh Symphony, and additional realized and unrealized collaborations with Rostropovich. Between 1950 and 1952, doctors and nurses permitting, Prokofiev maintained the following routine: work in the mornings; light tasks in the afternoons; reading, listening to the radio, and strolling in the evenings. Given the circumstances, his perseverance with large-scale orchestral and theatrical works is impressive, although, as in the case of his chamber works, his achievement comes with reservations. At the end of his life, Prokofiev did not so much compose freely as respond to criticism, adapting his original thoughts to reflect the concerns of his helpers and minders who, with Mira's blessing, stopped by the dacha or apartment in the afternoons. He griped about the endless demands but accommodated them, even when it meant turning the clock back on his creativity to his Conservatory days, when he was obliged to compose fugues in the style of Bach and sonatas in the style of Haydn. To argue with his interlocutors was to forfeit income, a point proved by the fraught history of *The Tale of the Stone Flower*.

Bazhov

The ballet originated in the summer of 1948, in the wake of the fallout from the February Resolution. The endurance of *Cinderella* in the repertoire prompted him to entertain Lavrovsky's offer to collaborate on a lavish folklore-based spectacle. (Earlier, the composer had discussed writing a balletic version of the Eros and Psyche myth in collaboration with Volkhov, scenarist of *Cinderella*.)[13] Living near each other in Nikolina Gora, Prokofiev and Lavrovsky bounced ideas back and forth for several weeks, contemplating, for instance, a ballet based on Pushkin's imitation folktale *The Tale of the Dead Princess and the Seven Heroes* (*Skazka o myortvoy tsarevne i o semi bogatïryakh*, 1833), until they learned that another composer had already taken it up. Lavrovsky confessed an interest in the stories of Pavel Bazhov, a writer from the Siberian town of Sïsert who dedicated himself to animating the forgotten folklore of the Urals.[14] At this point Mira weighed in, proposing that Lavrovsky and Prokofiev base their ballet on one or more of the stories in Bazhov's 1939 collection *The Malachite Box* (*Malakhitovaya shkatulka*), which existed in several editions and had provided inspiration for a successful film, *The Stone Flower: A Legend from the Urals* (*Kamennïy tsvetok [Ural'skiy skaz]*, 1946).[15] Recognizing Lavrovsky's limited literary skills, Mira worked with him on the scenario. At the choreographer's insistence, the Bolshoy Theater offered Prokofiev a generous commission for the score: 40,000 rubles, to be paid in four installments. Bitter experience had taught him, however, to expect nothing more than the advance.

The cultural climate was such that Mira and Lavrovsky had no choice but to engage in ideological tutelage in the scenario. Here the film version of *The Stone Flower* furnished a useful model, filtering apolitical fantasy through political reality to honor socialist realist convention. Instead of never-never land, the story is set in late nineteenth-century Siberia, where magic events happen within the context of class struggle between masters and servants. The Mistress of Copper Mountain, a spiteful goddess with a surfeit of psychic energy, symbolizes the Motherland; Danila, an honest but obtuse stone carver, assumes the role of the artist-worker. Danila's obsession with creating a perfect stone flower out of malachite leads him to abandon his betrothed, Katerina, for admission into a fantastic mountain warehouse. Once there, he falls into the Mistress's clutches. Katerina meanwhile must fend for herself against the ogre Severyan. As in Ravel's *Daphnis et Chloé*, a work that Prokofiev once disdained, Eros intervenes to reunite the hero and heroine. Told on screen and stage, the story is self-reflexive—an artistic creation about artistic creation. Malachite, it bears noting, is sometimes believed to have magical healing powers, the ability to rejuvenate body and soul. For Prokofiev, the virtue of the story resided in its homage to craftsmanship and the search for perfection in one's work. In the last years of his life, the composer himself became a dutiful laborer, upholding the pre-Enlightenment notion of music making as a craft designed to please the patron and audience. Rather than subverting harmonic and structural conventions, he burnished his credentials as a retrospective composer.

Like all of Prokofiev's dramatic works, *The Tale of the Stone Flower* traveled a rough route to the stage. The initial outline of the four-act ballet, listing each number and each musical theme, is dated September 6, 1948. No fewer than seven versions of the scenario exist, the first dating from 1948 (four acts in eight scenes with a prologue and epilogue) and the last from 1954 (three acts in eight scenes with a prologue and epilogue). Before arriving at the final, simplified version, Mira and Lavrovsky filled 125 pages of paper with drafts. The third version includes a note in Prokofiev's hand: "8 copies right away, 3 on better quality paper."[16] The note is dated August 30, 1950, around the time of the first run-through of the piano score at the Union of Soviet Composers. (Multiple copies of scenarios were typically provided to opera and ballet adjudicators.) The fifth version includes another note in the composer's hand—"6 copies right away!"[17] This presumably refers to preparations for the second run-through. The final version of the scenario dates from after Prokofiev's death: he did not see the ballet on the stage, and did not finish all of the music himself: it was finished for him.

Herewith a summary of the contents of the first version of the scenario, which attests to Mira's, Lavrovsky's, and Prokofiev's efforts to create, according to an oxymoronic 1952 newspaper bulletin, "a realistic, authentically folkloric spectacle imbued with a strong socialist theme."[18] The prologue introduces the Mistress of Copper Mountain, who embodies the power and beauty of nature. She holds aloft her masterpiece—a stone flower—fused from the four elements of matter. Also introduced is Danila, who has taken on the task of carving a true-to-life image of a flower.

Act I, scene 1, comprises a solo dance in which Danila roams the Elysium fields seeking a flower to serve as a model for his carving. Finding none, he sinks into despair. Katerina consoles him as part of a lyric adagio. The crack of a whip is heard in the distance: Severyan, the foreman of a mine, is beating his workers for failing to meet their quota. Seeing the workers struggling to excavate the heavy lumps of malachite from the mine, Danila tries to intervene, but Katerina holds him back. An intermezzo reinforces the theme of the exploited worker: Severyan lashes an old man who has collapsed under his load. A broad-shouldered lad challenges the ogre, but Severyan threatens him with a pistol, at which point the would-be rescuer, having added the old man's load to his own, stumbles away. Fairy tales, of course, do not usually involve firearms.

The following scene combines diegetic dance with more pantomime. In anticipation of Danila and Katerina's wedding, the girls of the village perform a nuptial *khorovod*. The couple then bids farewell to the villagers in a pair of ensemble numbers. Severyan breaks up the nuptial celebrations, demanding to see the chalice and stone flower that Danila carved for the local baron. The ogre mocks the wedding and makes a crude pass at Katerina. After he departs, the focus of the action shifts to Danila's dissatisfaction with his art. His former teacher, the master carver Prokopich, tells the story of the Mistress of Copper Mountain: "In her garden grows a stone flower; those who experience it learn to create beauty. But not all are fit to meet the Mistress and enter her garden. She aids only the boldest, most decisive, and most freedom-loving people [the word *workers* is handwritten above *people* in the typescript]." As the old man tells his tale, Danila sees a dream image of the Mistress shimmering in a green copper dress and beckoning him with outstretched hands. He returns home to his hut obsessed, to Katerina's consternation, with visiting the sorceress's Ural mountain lair.

The two scenes of act 2 consist largely of group dances, with the intermezzo reprising the music of the act 1 intermezzo. Arriving in the Mistress's lair, Danila learns that he must pass through a series of trials before being allowed to see the coveted flower. He resists her amorous advances (trial one), which precipitates a lyrical adagio representing Katerina. The Mistress next promises Danila untold wealth, which he refuses on principle. "You won't take it?" the Mistress asks. "I won't think of it!" Danila answers (trial two). The third trial, which is partially deleted in the typescript, involves Danila justifying his quest for the stone flower. "He has come here," Mira and Lavrovsky write, "not for wealth, but to see the flower, to achieve great mastery and share it with the people." Danila mimes, "I can't live without the flower!" Having verified his socialist credentials, the Mistress admits

him into her garden, and there Danila disappears for several months. Fall
becomes winter; spring cedes to summer. During this period, the Mistress
appears before Severyan to explain that his capitalist exploitation of nature
will leave the foothills barren for the next generation. Katerina, left without
a source of income, enlists Prokopich to teach her carving.

Acts 3 and 4 involve significant repetition, and Mira and Lavrovsky
were obliged to delete events that provided symmetry but slowed the plotline. Act 3 opens in a peasant market, the pretext for the insertion of a folk
dance pageant. In the first scene, Katerina shows the fruits of her labors to
passers-by, only to be accosted by Severyan, who performs a drunken dance.
During the intermezzo, the Mistress reappears, heaping as much disdain on
Severyan as she had kindness on Danila. The ogre brandishes his pistol but
receives his comeuppance when the Mistress plants him in the earth, transforms him into a poppy, and finally erases him from view altogether. In act
4, Katerina resolves to find Danila. Aided by a magic helper—the sparkling
fire pixie Ognevushka-Poskakushka—she dances her way into the mountain warehouse, where she is reunited with her betrothed, who explains his
absence by unveiling the stone flower. Mira and Lavrovsky planned to preface this episode with a second *Magic Flute*–like trial scene, but for unknown
reasons changed their minds. The act ends with a group dance involving the
denizens of the mountain warehouse, the Mistress, and the happy couple.
A brief epilogue finds Danila sharing his creative talent with the liberated
workers of the village. The Mistress blesses them from afar.[19]

Once the scenario was drafted, Prokofiev, during periods of better
health, composed the music, beginning it on September 18, 1948, and finishing on March 24, 1949. Since the work needed to be freighted with discrete,
accessible numbers bearing no narrative content, Prokofiev opted to recycle
"Swan" from *Ivan the Terrible* Part I as the act 1, scene 2 *khorovod*. Other
self-borrowings—which Prokofiev identified in the original musical outline
for the ballet—include the number "Evening" (Vecher) from his 1935 *Music
for Children*, which serves as the hero and heroine's love theme, and the
songs "Dunyushka" and "The Monk" (Chernets) from his 1944 Russian
folksong settings.[20] Their melodies are heard in act 1, scene 2 and act 3. The
composer also recycled "To the Motherland" (K Rodine) from his 1939 song
collection to illustrate Katerina's domesticity.

In a fatuous account of their collaboration, Lavrovsky claimed that
Prokofiev began the score by "finding" the fanfare for the Mistress of Copper Mountain and devising a series of static recollection themes for the other

characters.[21] The choreographer acknowledges that he confounded the composer by insisting on the insertion of an ersatz gypsy dance in act 3 whose melody would recur in distorted guises to undercut Severyan's grotesque overtures to Katerina. Prokofiev told Lavrovsky that "yes, I understand that this scene is needed, but I must ask you, if possible, to lay out your wishes in more detail. I confess, I've never thought to write a gypsy piece, I don't know, I've never heard them." The claim was false: Prokofiev had had occasional exposure to gypsy music over the course of his career. Purporting to educate the composer, Lavrovsky brought Semyon Stuchevsky, the concert master of the Bolshoy Theater, to the dacha, and had him improvise some gypsy dances at the piano. Prokofiev was horrified: "Sorry, but I'm closing the window. I can't permit such sounds to come from [my] dacha." Upon working out his own version of a gypsy dance, he told the choreographer: "When friends hear what I'm composing and ask what I'm writing I say that Lavrovsky has bad taste and forces me to write these things."

The outline and sketches of the ballet reveal that Prokofiev struggled with the traditional ballet number format and with the need to feature folk dance.[22] The composer's greatest problems concerned the transitions between numbers, which had to advance the plot while also getting dancers positioned for their next routine. Ballet critics of the period advocated the integration of pantomime, solo variations, and ensemble dancing, but they also argued for greater diversity in the selection of numbers. In the opinion of one strident critic, Igor Moiseyev, a dancer and ballet master at the Bolshoy Theater, dance had become "the least interesting part of ballet," losing out to the expressive force of music. Moiseyev further argued that Soviet ballet suffered from a deficit, rather than a surplus, of abstraction. In his view, *Romeo and Juliet* and *Cinderella* overemphasized pantomime at the expense of audience-pleasing ensembles and variations; Prokofiev and Lavrovsky distrusted "the language of dance." To remedy the situation, Moiseyev advocated a partial reversion to classical norms. If, as he believed, nineteenth-century ballet had failed in its quest to incorporate sociopolitical content (or "rational concepts") into dance, then Soviet ballet had forsaken its commitment to the opposite: the incorporation of dance into sociopolitical content.[23]

Prokofiev, an erstwhile disciple of Diaghilev, found it difficult to revert to convention and wisecracked about the conservatism of his new ballet. His 1948–49 notebooks provide a characteristic example: "The 'Dance of the Little Swans' from *Swan Lake* was written by Chaikovsky under the strong influence of Prokofiev."[24] In his diary, he joked that

> I finished up the "Russian Dance" for *The Stone Flower*. Lavrovsky shifted one sixteen-measure passage [four phrases of four measures each]. The dance was played for members of the corps de ballet, who said that it was less like Prokofiev than Chaikovsky. Thankfully, it wasn't like Minkus.[25]

Although Lavrovsky encouraged Prokofiev to avoid asymmetry, the composer found it unpleasant to do so, pointing out that Stravinsky's *Petrushka*, which had been written forty years before, altogether lacked balanced four-measure phrases. Lampooning a nineteenth-century nationalist catchphrase about advancing "to new shores" (associated with Musorgsky and the arch-nationalist critic Vladimir Stasov), Prokofiev complained that the only way he could move "forward" was by going "backward to Chaikovsky."[26] Lavrovsky evidently convinced him, however, that the best way to represent the hero of the ballet, a traditional craftsman, was through a musical and choreographic translation of his tried-and-true stonecutting techniques. By composing perfectly balanced antecedent-consequent phrases, for example, Prokofiev would allow Lavrovsky's dancers to execute their *ronds de jambe en l'air* and *sissonnes en pointe* with chiseled precision. The reliance on rondo forms likewise allowed the ensembles to form concentric bands and other figurative shapes, imitating the look of polished malachite.

Confronted with the challenge of tacking stylistically back in time, Prokofiev transformed *The Tale of the Stone Flower* into a primer on nineteenth-century Russian music, filling the divertissements with *kuchkist*-era folksong abstractions. The roster of nationalist (exoticist) clichés includes the pentatonic scale, quartal-quintal cadences, and chordal progressions from the tonic major to the tonic augmented to the flattened submediant. Prokofiev uses folklike melodies as *canti firmi*, decorating them with orchestral figurations of increasing lavishness. He drew inspiration for his dances from recordings of folksongs from Sverdlovsk, which he obtained from the Moscow Conservatory library. In a traditional wedding celebration, ostinato-based dance tunes, or *naigrïshi*, would be repeated by either small ensemble or a balalaika or concertino player until fatigue overtook the dancers. Shunning verisimilitude, Prokofiev keeps his wedding dances implausibly brief. In the outline of the ballet, he separates act 1, scene 2, into ten numbers, permitting Katerina's girlfriends three minutes and twenty seconds for their group dance, and Danila's cronies (the picaresque bachelors of the village) one minute and forty-five seconds.[27] The preceding *khorovod* (No. 7) involves two melodies of similar intervallic content, which alternate in the first and third sections of the dance. In the second section, the two themes are fused. This clever example of self-conscious compositional craftsmanship recalls Glinka's *Kamarinskaya*, in which two melodies—one drawn from folk dance, the other from folksong—pass through each other. Prokofiev reprises his *khorovod* in No. 25, when Katerina laments the absent Danila, and in No. 28, when she rejoices his return to her.

Once one form of traditionalism was exhausted, others took its place. Arlene Croce notes that Lavrovsky's choreography for *The Tale of the Stone Flower* features "lyrical-adagio" numbers, "character-folk" numbers, and, "for the scenes in the glowing green underground kingdom of precious stones, a spiky type of *ballet moderne*" redolent of the machine dances of the 1920s.[28] Having determined the lengths of the numbers according to Lavrovsky's blueprint, Prokofiev assigned them emblematic Chaikovskian tonalities (D major defines the rustic world, A major the magic world, E major and E minor the powers of good and evil) and timbres (the oboe denotes Katerina, the French horn the Mistress, the E-flat clarinet Severyan). The interlacing of diatonic, modal, and chromatic gestures on the surface of the score resembles Glinka's *Ruslan and Lyudmila*.

The secondary characters, or *coryphées*, in *The Tale of the Stone Flower* all have direct antecedents in nineteenth-century Russian opera.[29] The rogue Severyan is an amalgam of the shameless seducer Vladimir Galitsky in Borodin's *Prince Igor* and the menacing blacksmith Yeryomka in Aleksandr Serov's *The Power of the Fiend*. The mournful variation "Where hast thou gone, Danilushko" (Gde tï, Danilushko) performed by Katerina in act 2 calls to mind Lyubava's lament in scene 3 of Rimsky-Korsakov's *Sadko*. The contrast between Katerina and the Mistress of Copper Mountain likewise parallels the contrast between Lyubava, a homemaker, and Volkhova, a sorceress, in that opera. Unlike Rimsky-Korsakov, Prokofiev elected to blur the border between reality and fantasy. Musically, the scenes in the village rhyme with the scenes in the Mistress's lair: Katerina's and Danila's diatonic leitmotifs inform the chromatic waltzes of the jewels and stones. The Mistress's leitmotif, moreover, leaks into the real-world dances at regular intervals. It is sometimes heard intact, other times in fragments, as though filtered through flawed human memory. The ballet's apotheosis likewise interweaves the magical and the real—a result that could be compared to the first and second acts of *The Nutcracker* being mapped on top of each other.

The score is unified on another level. Prokofiev reprises the melodies of the act 1 divertissement in the act 3 divertissement, forming a bridge between Danila and Katerina's wedding festivities and the folk dance pageant. By twinning the subjective (personal) and objective (national) in such a cheerful manner, the ballet affirms its fidelity to Soviet aesthetics. Thus the mood of *The Tale of the Stone Flower* differs from that of *Romeo and Juliet* and *Cinderella*, where the marriage of romance and politics is fraught. If, as Croce hypothesizes, Prokofiev's first and second Soviet ballets are "neurotic" and "brooding" affairs, his third ballet is perhaps best termed a surrender to popular demand, with the hero having "to choose between making art for the people and pursuing ivory- (or, in his case, malachite-) tower perfectionism."[30]

The references to the classics ensured *The Tale of the Stone Flower* a positive initial reception and prompted Lavrovsky to propose that he and Prokofiev work together on a ballet version of *Othello*, an idea that Prokofiev, disgruntled and exhausted, dismissed as a failure waiting to happen. Since he did not have the strength to introduce the piano score of *The Tale of the Stone Flower* to his overseers, he entrusted the task to Richter, explaining that he could not begin the orchestration until he knew what scenes would have to be recast, but that he nonetheless wanted to move forward with the task, since he needed the income from the ballet. Richter, however, left Moscow for a series of concert engagements on the eve of the June 24, 1949, run-through at the Bolshoy Theater, which forced Prokofiev to enlist a rehearsal pianist named Aleksey Zïbtsev and left him carping (in an unsent July 16, 1949, letter to Atovmyan) that "Richter is a swine."[31] Four days before the run-through, Myaskovsky jovially predicted to Prokofiev that Zïbtsev's performance would be uneven: "For the first act he'll earn a kiss, a smooch; for the second he'll be patted on the shoulder; for the third he'll have to be spanked."[32] The pianist rose to the occasion, however, providing an interpretation that garnered an enthusiastic response, with a member of the Committee on Arts Affairs declaring that the ballet was "a celebration, not only of [Prokofiev], but of all our art."[33] *Sadko* was a point of comparison in the assessment. (Perhaps for this reason, Prokofiev in 1950 recorded having a dream in which Rimsky-Korsakov played through a bowdlerized version of the opera for him. The title character, a fisherman blessed by a mermaid, had been transformed into a Red Army soldier.)[34]

The positive initial reception of *The Tale of the Stone Flower* delighted Prokofiev—he had been dreading a repeat of the *Story of a Real Man* debacle—but the strain occasioned by the run-through further compromised his health. On July 7, 1949, he suffered a stroke. Although he recovered, the headaches, fever, and nausea that had restricted his activities since 1945 significantly worsened. For a time, Mira and his children (who had begun to visit him more frequently) thought death was imminent. Olga Lamm saw Prokofiev that summer at Nikolina Gora and was struck by his red complexion, slurred speech, and problems concentrating. "Mira Aleksandrovna, holding his hand, tenderly and fearfully tried to calm him down and kept on repeating 'Seryozhenka, let's go home, let's go home now.' But Sergey Sergeyevich kept on turning to Nikolay Yakovlevich [Myaskovsky], evidently wanting to explain something to him."[35] Mira proposed transferring Prokofiev to a Moscow clinic, but the road from Nikolina Gora back to the city had become impassable owing to the rebuilding of a bridge. He was confined to the dacha until August, pining to travel to the south to rest by the sea.[36] Popov brought painkillers from the city; a hired nurse applied leeches (an efficacious but ghastly treatment for reducing swelling of blood vessels), and a therapist monitored his activities. " 'Could it be I'll never hear *War and Peace* or any of my other works again?' " he asked Mira. " 'Could it be that all of our works are unwanted, that they will all go to waste?' " he asked Myaskovsky.[37] Olga Lamm adds that one doctor, Rosa Ginsberg, humanely acquiesced to Prokofiev's pleas for more work time. "One cannot keep an artist from creating," Ginsberg mused, "the music will live in his soul, and the impossibility of writing it out will only worsen his moral and psychological state: 'Let him live a shorter life, but as he wishes.' "[38]

The Kremlin Hospital

Prokofiev recovered in the late fall, but his health declined again in the winter. On February 10, 1950, another caregiver, Nina Popova, and the physician-therapist E. I. Sokolov confined him—without pen and paper—to bed. Through the intervention of Shostakovich, who communicated urgently on Prokofiev's behalf to Molotov, Prokofiev was admitted into the Kremlin hospital, to which he no longer had privileged access, for treatment of hypertrophy. Shostakovich likewise used his political influence (he served at the time as a deputy on the Supreme Soviet of the RSFSR) to have Mira admitted to the hospital for a long-delayed operation to remove a cyst. "The professors who have been monitoring [S. S. Prokofiev's] health work in the *lechsanupr* of the Kremlin and can therefore monitor him if he and his wife are placed in the Kremlin hospital," Shostakovich redundantly beseeched Molotov. "S. S. Prokofiev is not registered in the *lechsanupr* of the Kremlin. If it can be done, he needs to be registered and, in any case now, perhaps by making an exception, admitted to the hospital."[39] Molotov signed off on the request on February 17. For three weeks, until March 15, Prokofiev and Mira wrote notes to each other from separate wards of the hospital. These furnish a humdrum chronology of doctors' and nurses' rounds, brief visits from select acquaintances—some, Rostropovich and Richter, more welcome than others, Kabalevsky and Lev Knipper—and laborious convalescences. For stimulus, Prokofiev read when he could, though one of his caregivers suggested that he spend less time with Chekhov and more with children's tales like *The Headless Horseman*.[40] Shlifshteyn dispatched a telegram congratulating him on his Cello Sonata, which Rostropovich and Richter premiered at the Moscow Conservatory on March 1. In a woeful recollection, Richter remarks that during the worst period of Prokofiev's illness, his doctors confiscated his manuscript paper, thus obliging the patient to jot down his ideas on napkins that he tucked under his pillow.[41] Later, when his doctors permitted him to work, he corrected the piano score of *The Tale of the Stone Flower*, which Pavel Lamm had helped assemble from the sketches.

Toward the end of his stay in the hospital (he was there two and a half weeks longer than Mira) and with his thoughts turning back to full-time work, Prokofiev received an invitation from the director Aleksandrov to write original music for a biographical film about Glinka. The film, Aleksandrov explained, would represent the cherished nineteenth-century composer as a strident defender of the peasant class and, by extension, an opponent of the Romanov family. As if to atone for its bowdlerization of history, the film would also include spectacular excerpts from Glinka's *Ruslan and Lyudmila* and *A Life for the Tsar*.

The project appealed to Prokofiev because it would allow him to merge his musical method—and his entire legacy—with that of his distinguished predecessor. He sought, in other words, to provide a context for his career that would have nothing to do with his catastrophic run-ins with the Committee on Arts Affairs and everything to do with the history of Russian culture. He even imagined writing an opera "based on the material of the film," though he quickly, and prudently, banished the thought. "Certain episodes" in Aleksandrov's screenplay "enthralled him," Mira recalled. "Others (the descriptions of Glinka's disappointments and the failure of *Ruslan and Lyudmila*) he found exceedingly painful."[42] Disheartened by the lack of performances of his own operas, Prokofiev decided against working on the film. The director instead enlisted Shebalin and Vladimir Shcherbachov, awarding Richter a cameo appearance as Liszt. Titled *Kompozitor Glinka* in Russian and *Glinka: Man of Music* in English, the film was released in 1952 to positive reviews.

On April 20, Prokofiev left the hospital and traveled with Mira to the Podlipki sanatorium in Barvikha, where he remained until the start of summer. The atmosphere at the facility ranged from restful to restive, with the composer receiving a steady stream of visitors and even attending the occasional concert. Kabalevsky, who both chided and appropriated Prokofiev's music during the period of their acquaintance, monitored his convalescence on behalf of the Union of Soviet Composers. The management of Prokofiev's return to political health—he remained, after all, a "fallen" artist—occurred at a higher level within the Party apparatus. During his stay at Barvikha, Prokofiev received a visit from the novelist Aleksandr Fadeyev, a depression-prone but committed servant of the regime elected to the Central Committee and Supreme Soviet. Fadeyev sanctioned Sergey Balasanyan, deputy director of the Radio Committee and the officer responsible for music programming, to commission an oratorio from Prokofiev.[43]

Fadeyev assigned the libretto to Marshak, with whom Prokofiev had worked in the fall of 1949 on a suite of children's pieces called *Winter Bonfire*. The suite, a Radio Committee commission broadcast in the last week of March 1950, features a chorus of Pioneer boys who sing in pairs and unison about their train ride from the city to the country to visit a collective farm.[44] Between the orchestral movements, a narrator describes the falling snow outside the train windows, the crackling of the winter bonfire, and the meeting of the Pioneers and the children on the farm. Prokofiev assigned the suite a symmetrical form, reprising the illustrative locomotive music of movement 1 in movement 8, balancing the whimsical snowfall movement (2) with a melancholic nocturne (6), and surrounding the Pioneer chorus with orchestral renditions of crackling flames. The rondo waltz (3) recalls Chaikovsky, which may explain why Prokofiev joked in his diary that he had helped Chaikovsky compose *Swan Lake*. In search of additional, neoclassical inspiration, Prokofiev seems to allude to the finale of Stravinsky's *Pulcinella* in movement 7 of the suite, but he made sure to avoid that score's capricious harmonic and rhythmic breakdowns. The suite adheres to C major, departing in the rustic bonfire scenes to a "pastoral" F major.

The success of *Winter Bonfire*, and the follow-up success of the oratorio *On Guard for Peace*, paved the way for the subsequent commissioning of *The Meeting of the Volga and the Don* and the Seventh Symphony.[45] All four works were composed for State Radio: the first, second, and fourth for the children's programming division, and the third for the adult programming division. Here it merits correcting the musicologist Stanley Krebs's intuition that the focus on children's issues in Prokofiev's late works has unsettling implications. "Adults deemed through boards or the court as chronically 'anti-social' are often sent to work with children in camps, orphanages and clubs."[46] Krebs adds that this practice was codified in the mid-1950s, after the Stalinist era. To be sure, artists, particularly writers, facing censorship routinely moved into children's literature, but they did so of their own volition, without instruction from "boards or the court." This practice dates primarily from the mid-1930s, before the worst phase of the purges, not after. In the late 1940s and early 1950s, Prokofiev was merely relying on the people and venues available to him for commissions: he had not been branded "anti-social" by the regime; rather, he remained a valued celebrity.

Marshak was Fadeyev's second choice as librettist of *On Guard for Peace*. His first, Nikolay Tikhonov, a Stalin Prize winner and chairman of a committee for the defense of peace, turned down the project, citing inexperience writing for children. Prokofiev had neither author in mind when he conceived the oratorio. He first discussed it with the music critic and dramatist Aleksandr Gayamov, one of his longtime acquaintances. Gayamov hoped to collaborate with Prokofiev on an opera and frequently encouraged the composer to set the first part of Aleksey Tolstoy's unfinished historical novel *Peter the First* (*Pyotr Pervïy*, 1929–45), an acclaimed work of the Soviet period. In consultation with Gayamov, Prokofiev worked up an outline for a five-part oratorio involving a "broad Russian theme," followed by an orchestral tableau representing the Great Patriotic War. There would ensue a recitative directed to "the peoples of the world" and a depiction of "the citizens of the future," who defend the "ideal" of peace. The oratorio would conclude with choral affirmations of this ideal.

Prokofiev thereafter discussed the oratorio with another associate, Ilya Ehrenburg, who offered to serve in Gayamov's stead as the librettist. Ehrenburg's conception of the work proved unacceptable, however, for it threatened to provoke an international incident, at least within cultural sectors. His twelve-part scenario details a U.S. nuclear attack on the Soviet Union.

1. The morning of May 10, 1945. Ruins. Part of a home with a gutted interior. Half of a bridge across a river: the bridge leads nowhere. Graves, graves, graves. The rockets' flames have expired; the ships' cannons have fallen silent. The soldiers return home in faded, tattered fatigues. They see ashes, children's hungry eyes, and grief in the home front.

How he desired Victory, how he dreamed of it. He came from the war; she went to meet him. But they no longer knew each other.

The exhausted solder, having returned home, seeks rest. But there is no rest: the ruins await builders. The people work in desperation, with all their strength, beyond their strength.

In America someone chuckles: "They won't rebuild the country." London's ruins. Rotterdam's ruins. Havre's ruins. Calm. Hammers ring out: the people rebuild Kiev, Voronezh, Stalingrad. A song, brought by a soldier from the war, carries into the timber felling.

2. Terrible drought; cloudless skies. The wheat withers. There's another struggle to endure. In America someone cheers: "They won't endure this."

3. A Stalingrad square. A Smolensk theater. An Oryol nursery. Warsaw rises from the ashes. Sofia's streets are rebuilt.

4. In America the enemies of peace conspire: "Release the atom bomb." They release it. Two bombs. Twenty bombs. Fish die in the sea. Grass withers. Life ends.

Business is good, very good. The stock market cheers. Shares of aircraft factories. Shares of Belgian uranium. Shares of war. Sell, buy. Release the bomb faster.

5. The French winemaker looks at the sky in horror. The Italian peasant girl covers her cradle. The old scientist gazes at his unfinished work.

The third world war. Atom bombs. Poison: one dose to end humankind. The stock market is satisfied. The Atlantic Pact. Let the French fight, we will reap the profits. The stock market celebrates.

6. A black cloud hangs over all of Europe's cities. Anxiety. The former soldier asks: "Could it be happening again?"

7. The Soviet people continue working. The old man plants a tree; it will grow after his death. He believes in peace. The people believe in peace.

8. The Soviet people continue to work: they know that Stalin means peace. But peace must be loved, peace must be defended...

9. The struggle for peace begins. Parisian workers march. Italian fishermen march. Czechs, Indians, Poles, and Hollanders march. China rises up, stands, and prevails in the war. Soviet song, like a spring breeze, embraces the world.

10. Grand meetings and street protests. Who is against peace? Only a small group of people: the stock market, the traders wearing suspenders, the traders of death. There are too few atom bombs. We need hydrogen bombs. The death of children, of the reefs, of everything is guaranteed.

11. But no. The people will not permit it. French maidens lie on the rails to delay the military echelons. Italian workers cast tanks into the sea. War will not be sanctioned. And everyone looks to Moscow. Moscow stands for peace.

12. Warning. Do not approach. Neither to the Soviet children nor to the Soviet flowers. This is the line that war does not cross.

    A gardener looks peacefully at a tree. A mother peacefully caresses her infant. Peace will defeat war.[47]

Fadeyev advised Prokofiev against setting this horrific text, and the enfeebled composer agreed. The nascent arms race between the United States and the Soviet Union—aggravated by the successful detonation of an atomic bomb in Kazakhstan on August 29, 1949, American advances in the development of a hydrogen bomb, and mutual espionage—mobilized the propaganda industries of both nations. Ehrenburg labored on the front lines of the anti-American campaign, receiving personal permission from Stalin to travel to Western Europe in January 1950 to research a book, *The Ninth Wave* (*Devyatïy val*, 1951), about the post–World War II peace movement.[48] His scenario for Prokofiev's oratorio derives from *The Ninth Wave* and reflects its tendentiousness.

On Fadeyev's counsel, Prokofiev agreed to work with Marshak, rather than Gayamov or Ehrenburg, on his oratorio. The bureaucrat monitored the creative process to ensure that the oratorio maintained a proper balance between pacifism and militarism. Fadeyev approved the inclusion of a chorus and solo parts for children but cautioned against making the work too saccharine. On July 11, 1950, Marshak reported to Prokofiev that Fadeyev was "very satisfied" with the draft plans for the oratorio and the fact that the "declarative" passages in the libretto had been rendered "more concrete" through the inclusion of a narrator. Marshak lamented, however, that Fadeyev vetoed a favorite feature of the score: the inclusion of real or represented cricket chirps in the "Lullaby" movement (7). These, apparently, would have made the sound too rustic.[49]

Fadeyev's influence on the project was such that Prokofiev needed his—rather than Marshak's—permission to adjust the libretto for musical reasons. The bureaucrat obliged him, enthusing, "In the first place, Marshak's verses are so fine that some of them can be assigned to the narrator: I think that these can be blended harmoniously with the music. In the second place, you should remove those verses that do not suit the music and that you find unnecessary."[50] Prokofiev thanked Fadeyev for his thoughts and filed a glowing progress report, affirming that the music was written, the piano score copied and in the hands of the conductor Samosud, and the contract signed. Balasanyan bore responsibility for scheduling the run-through. Prokofiev hinted that working on the score had sapped his strength, but he vowed to complete the orchestration by October.[51]

This exchange dates from September 22, 1950, two months after Prokofiev's return to Nikolina Gora from Barvikha, and just days after he had absorbed the news of Myaskovsky's death.[52] His friend of forty-four years had been battling cancer for nearly two, succumbing to it on August 8, 1950. Myaskovsky became aware of his condition in January 1949, when his doctor discovered and removed a small tumor. He recovered in time to hear Rostropovich premiere his folklore-inspired A-Minor Cello Sonata, a work that informed Prokofiev's C-Major Cello Sonata. The concert took place on March 5. The cancer continued to spread, but Myaskovsky insisted on working, hoping to conclude his prolific career with one last symphony (his twenty-seventh) and one last string quartet (his thirteenth). In May 1950, he underwent another, much more critical operation, with the doctors holding back the gravity of his condition from all but his intimates: his three sisters, Lamm, and Shebalin. Myaskovsky died at home on August 8. Mira broke the news to Prokofiev, whose doctors advised him against attending the public memorial service at the Moscow Conservatory, leaving him to grieve in private. He would later attend the mounting of a memorial plaque outside his friend's apartment.[53] Prokofiev himself was gravely ill. On August 28, a dizzy spell provoked a massive nosebleed and a precipitous drop in blood pressure. Following his tenuous recuperation, Mira vowed that the couple would spend less time at the dacha, which lacked a telephone, and more in the city, near emergency medical services.[54]

Collective Composition

Thus a troubled atmosphere surrounded the creation of *On Guard for Peace*, a work that aligns the quest for peace with the global spread of Communism. Prokofiev relies on declamation, martial strains, and open-ended structures for references to wartime deprivation; tripartite paraphrases of mass songs and unsullied harmonies greet the verbal paeans to Stalin. The oratorio collapses into cliché in movement 6, a strophic number about a dove's flight over the smokestacks of the Soviet capital. The high political stakes of this unambiguous, monological score can be gleaned not only from Fadeyev's interference in its composition, but also from Samosud's insistence that its sentimental content be made even more so to represent, as it were, the people's "helpless[ness] before the enchanting beauty of Communism."[55] The conductor proposed releasing doves during the performance, or surrounding the performers with images of doves, but the administration of the Hall of Columns rejected these ideas for logistical reasons.[56]

Samosud similarly beseeched Prokofiev and Marshak to include a crowd-pleasing number for boy soprano in the heart of the score. Marshak replied with two poems, "A Letter from an Italian Boy" (Pis'mo ital'yanskogo mal'chika) and "A Lesson in One's Native Language" (Urok rodnogo yazïka). The first poem, which Prokofiev did not set, involves a well-informed schoolboy who protests a shipment of rockets from the United States to Italy.[57] The second poem, which the composer did set, finds an entire classroom of Moscow schoolchildren repeatedly writing the slogan "Peace to all peoples of the world" (Mir vsem narodam na svete) on a blackboard. (Though it might appear paradoxical, the use of this optimistic slogan in a depressing after-class exercise suggests that a commitment to labor leads to the realization of dreams.) Prokofiev enhances the didactic tone by setting the choral refrain of the number, "We don't need war" (Nam ne nuzhna voyna), to a textbook example of a perfect authentic cadence.

The most striking passage in the score comes between the second and third movements, respectively titled "To the ten-year-old" (Komu sevodnya desyat' let) and "City of glory Stalingrad" (Gorod slavï—Stalingrad). The second movement opens with a chorus of boys recalling traumatic memories of the dark war years: the blacked-out windows, the blown-out street lights, the trains that pulled out of Moscow after midnight, and the frightful nights of the blitzkrieg. The rhythmic structure suggests a military march, but the melodic line lacks focus, wandering in chromatic darkness through A-flat major, D major, and F major. To heighten the sense of uncertainty, Prokofiev accompanies the first phrase of the vocal line with different versions of an A-flat triad: major, augmented, and minor. Each line of text is punctuated by a rising scalar pattern in the vocal lines, but Prokofiev varies their content, sometimes filling in an interval of a perfect fifth and other times the interval of a tritone. Apart from a representation in the orchestra of a train, Prokofiev refrains from word-painting. He ensures, however, that an emphatic cadence underscores the concluding words about the enemy's defeat.

The gloom clears in the transition between movements 2 and 3. At this point Prokofiev introduces one of four melodies associated in the oratorio with the pursuit of peace. Here it becomes obvious that the choristers have been groping toward this melody in the preceding measures. Its contours—a leap from the tonic to the submediant of G major, followed by a further ascent to the supertonic and a pair of affirmative cadences—have been anticipated in the preceding vocal lines. The melody and the optimism it signals become more prominent as the oratorio unfolds. In movements 3 and 4, the passage returns in the orchestra; in movements 8 and 10 Prokofiev places it in the chorus. The melody ascends from the "immaterial" orchestral realm into the "material" vocal realm, incarnating itself in the final rhapsodies about global peace and progress toward Communism.

Even with a boy soprano, children's choruses, and lyrical homage to peace, Prokofiev and his interlocutors worried that the oratorio might not be accessible enough for the authorities. Following a late September run-through of the score at the offices of the Radio Committee, Atovmyan, Balasanyan, Samosud, and the choral director Klavdiy Ptitsa enjoined the composer to rewrite the choral parts and the concluding movement to moderate the difficulties supposedly posed by the harmonic writing.[58] The changes were made well in advance of the December 19, 1950, premiere of the oratorio in the Hall of Columns. To explain the paleness of the score, Mira noted that Prokofiev began to compose it after a three-month break, that his doctors allowed him to work on it for no more than ninety minutes a day, and that his medication affected his concentration.[59] Mira does not, however, make the obvious point that the score suffered from external meddling; Prokofiev began the score, but it was finished by committee. Its paleness is the direct result of a bureaucratic compromise.

Excluding Prokofiev, Samosud played the most active part in the creative process. Mira's account of his concerns merits quoting at length, not least because her story changed over time. In the shorter, later version of her memoirs housed at the Glinka Museum, she is much less candid than in the longer, earlier version housed at the Russian State Archive of Literature and Art. Herewith, the Glinka Museum version:

> Samosud's hesitation was not groundless: he was troubled to know that some held a negative opinion of the oratorio, and he distrusted those who assured him that the performance would be "smooth" and immediately comprehensible. He was quite tense. But when I asked him for his own opinion of the oratorio and the impression the music made on him, I heard the highest praise. Trying to cheer Samosud up, I told him about the attention paid by A. A. Fadeyev to the oratorio and his keen interest in all of the work Seryozha and Marshak put into it.[60]

And the Russian State Archive of Literature and Art version:

> From this and subsequent [telephone] conversations with Samosud, it became clear that he was hesitant, worried, and tense. Though he greatly valued Seryozha's music, he voiced the fear that it would not be immediately comprehensible, that the performance might not be "smooth," since "they only want to hear simple music now." He evidently distrusted the assurances of those people on whom the oratorio's performance and right to exist depended, and trusted those with a completely different opinion. Samosud told me quite bluntly: "If I feel that things look bad for the oratorio I'll just say that I'm sick and can't conduct."

These words frightened me; I knew that it wasn't easy to say them, and that the oratorio's premiere might be canceled. I could imagine the difficulty of Samuil Abramovich's situation, but I was also acutely aware of the irreparable effect that the cancellation would have on the health of Seryozha, who had tried to finish the oratorio as quickly as possible and put so much effort into it. Trying to cheer Samosud up, I told him about the moral support given to Seryozha by A. A. Fadeyev. I also told him about the attention and keen interest paid by Aleksandr Aleksandrovich to each line of [Marshak's] text and Seryozha's musical plan.[61]

The premiere of the oratorio was preceded by a week of rehearsals, during which the conductor and performers pestered Prokofiev to thin the texture of the vocal lines, thus continuing the process of simplification that had begun after the critique of the oratorio by the Radio Committee. Prokofiev acquiesced, replacing octaves with unisons and removing large word-painting leaps in the vocal lines. (The 1973 edition of the score includes the altered passages in an appendix, enabling readers to compare "before" and "after" versions.) The premiere was a success, with sustained applause greeting the tuneful middle movements, though here, too, Mira's reaction differs in the first and second drafts of her memoirs. In the published Glinka Museum version, she opined that Prokofiev worried "in vain" about the oratorio; the premiere was a "triumph," testament to his timely dedication to "the struggle for peace." In the unpublished Russian State Archive of Literature and Art version, Mira focuses on the rehearsals rather than the premiere. Her reaction to the oratorio is cautious and qualified: "I of course understood that the oratorio's music wouldn't appeal to all composers and that it might provoke heated debates, but is this really sufficient cause for it not to be heard?"[62]

From this and other comparisons, it emerges that the later version of Mira's memoirs is much less reliable and forthright than the earlier version. She assembled the document piecemeal in the late 1940s and early 1950s, the worst of all times in terms of thought control, and her recollection of what happened to her and Prokofiev mutated into what might have or even should have happened. The premiere of the oratorio was noted in the national and international press coverage but it was neither a "triumph" nor impetus for heated debate. (The reception was positive enough, however, for the oratorio, together with *Winter Bonfire*, to earn a Second Class Stalin Prize.)[63] In the United States, a columnist for *Time* dismissed the oratorio as a jejune act of atonement for a composer seeking to "mend his ways." Here "Prokofiev's latter-day Peter comes across a new species of wolf: 'The sinister, evil voices of the warmongers and Wall Street merchants on their way to Korea, carrying hundreds of thousands of death-dealing bombs.' "[64] In its formulaic obeisance to the Party, *On Guard for Peace* bears more than just a musical likeness to Shostakovich's 1949 *Song of the Forests*. Following the Leningrad premiere of that work, Shostakovich reportedly "returned to his room at the Hotel Europe and began to sob, burying his head in a pillow. He sought consolation in vodka."[65] Priding himself on personal control, Prokofiev never sought solace in drink.

At the same time Prokofiev was revising the oratorio he completed the piano score and specified the orchestration of *The Tale of the Stone Flower* for his assistant Vedernikov. But the score hung in limbo. Despite having been well received at its first audition, the ballet faltered; rehearsals were delayed by officials at the Bolshoy Theater, who insisted that the composer remove some items from the score (the act 2 "Waltz of the Corals and Sapphires," for example), add others (the act 3 "Russian Dance"), and enrich the orchestration. Lavrovsky recalled that, during the run-throughs, "voices harshly critical of the music began to be heard. It was said that the music did not respect the artistic character of Bazhov's tales, that it was gloomy, difficult, and undanceable." The choreographer felt obliged "to hide a lot" of the "ill-considered, unforeseen, and sometimes even insensitive" comments directed at the composer out of concern for his health.[66]

Prokofiev balked at making the changes, at least until he received payment for the score in accord with his contract. On March 15, 1952, he dispatched a letter to Aleksandr Anisimov, the administrative director of the Bolshoy Theater, asking for the 10,000 rubles he was owed:

> The audition and assessment of the ballet took place in the summer of 1949 at the Bolshoy Theater. Representatives from the Committee on Arts Affairs, the administration of the theater, and members of the ballet troupe attended the audition. The piano score was approved, the ballet's music accepted, and it was agreed that I would proceed to the instrumentation.... I completed the ballet's instrumentation a long time ago. I spent more than a year on it. I implore

you, Aleksandr Ivanovich, to issue an order for payment of the funds owed to me for the score....Because of my illness, I am in great need of these funds.[67]

The response was disheartening:

The ballet is scheduled for production next season, but the Theater has the right to request that you make some changes and additions to the piano score and, by extension, the orchestral score. For this reason, it would be incorrect to consider the orchestration and likewise all of the work on the ballet finished. Nevertheless, I am confident that you will agree to go over the piano score and, by extension, the orchestral score to meet the needs of the Theater and its community. Hopefully, a consensus will be found that will allow me to pay you the portion of the honorarium in question.[68]

Artistic creation as Prokofiev understood it had been eradicated: rather than evolving from a private process into a public exchange, it began and ended in a bureaucratic tangle. While promoted as an antidote to the elitist inwardness of twelve-tone and serial composition in the West, the reigning Soviet aesthetic stupefied composers and audiences alike by emphasizing ideological obviousness. The impulse to demand one set of changes after another to *The Tale of the Stone Flower* debased what the bureaucrats claimed to honor.

Return to Renown

In the spring of 1952, the cultural establishment belatedly recognized that Prokofiev's health was in serious decline and that he required urgent financial support. The petition for this support came from Bespalov, the chairman of the Committee on Arts Affairs, who, on March 24, 1952, offered a candid assessment of Prokofiev's situation to Georgiy Malenkov, the Central Committee Secretary and the First Deputy Chairman of the USSR Council of Ministers. The letter and the response to it both merit quotation in full.

Sergey Sergeyevich Prokofiev, People's Artist of the RSFSR, is the preeminent Soviet composer. Prokofiev's name is known throughout the world, and each new work attracts enormous interest in musical society.

Prokofiev's creative path is complicated and replete with glaring contradictions. He promoted himself as one of the most blatant representatives of the formalist direction while also creating a large number of works of utmost significance to world musical culture. Such compositions as the Classical Symphony, the piano concertos and sonatas, the ballets *Romeo and Juliet* and *Cinderella*, the *Alexander Nevsky* Cantata, the oratorio *On Guard for Peace*, and many others have resolutely entered the musical repertoire, being performed everywhere with enormous success.

For his services in the work of developing Soviet musical art S. S. Prokofiev was awarded the Order of Lenin and medals of the Soviet Union. He has been bestowed the Stalin Prize six times.

Yet the sixty-year-old S. S. Prokofiev has been seriously ill for several years now. His illness—hypertrophy—progresses day by day. He is prohibited from undertaking any creative work. Consequently, S. S. Prokofiev, a famous composer, is extremely hard up at the present time, which only aggravates the poor state of his health.

At a time when he is deprived of the ability to provide a subsistence wage for himself with creative work, he should be offered immediate material assistance.

As such, the K[omitet po] D[elam] I[skusstv] petitions for

a)   establishment of a personal pension in the amount of 3,000 rubles a month for the composer S. S. Prokofiev;

b)   disbursement to him of a one-time-only benefit of 25,000 rubles;

c)   the costs of the pension and one-time-only assistance given to S. S. Prokofiev to come from the USSR Musical Foundation.

The draft of a Resolution for the USSR Council of Ministers is attached.[69]

For a composer of Prokofiev's stature to become impoverished was unacceptable to Bespalov, a lifelong civil servant whose tenure at the helm of the Committee on Arts Affairs lacked mean-spiritedness. To strengthen his argument, he exaggerated both the precariousness of Prokofiev's health—the composer was not entirely prohibited from working—and the quantity of his official honors, assigning him an award, the Order of Lenin, which he had not in fact received (Shostakovich had). The upper echelon was not impressed with the petition. On April 9, 1952, two cultural officials on the Central Committee, P. V. Lebedev (not to be confused with Polikarp Lebedev, former chairman of the Committee on Arts Affairs) and Boris Yarustovsky, dispassionately amended Bespalov's assessment of Prokofiev's needs.

> In accord with the instruction of the USSR Council of Ministers we are presenting our recommendation concerning the K[omitet po] D[elam] I[skusstv] petition for the establishment of a monthly pension and disbursement of a one-time-only benefit to the composer Prokofiev.
>
> Comrade Bespalov's report concerning the composer's "extreme hardship" does not correspond to the facts. This is clearly evident from the following tabulation of his honoraria in 1951:
>
> 1) Royalties: 87,833 rubles, 57,000 rubles after deductions;
> 2) Honoraria from the Radio Information Committee: 27,000 rubles;
> 3) Honoraria from the Committee on Arts Affairs: 20,000 rubles;
> 4) Total: 104,000 rubles.
>
> Thus it emerges that, on average, Prokofiev's monthly earnings were approximately 8,600 rubles, which cannot be considered an instance of "extreme hardship." It would be sensible, taking into consideration Prokofiev's importance, age, and poor health to arrange a monthly personal pension for him of 2,000 rubles, as supplemental material assistance.
>
> Disbursing a one-time-only benefit is not warranted.

Under the provisions of the government decision this
amount can be allotted from the resources of the USSR
Musical Foundation.[70]

For all their crankiness, Lebedev and Yarustovsky's recommendations and
their acknowledgment of Prokofiev's cultural impact marked the beginning
of his transformation into a Soviet Classic. Conscienceless officialdom had
begun to atone for the tribulations of 1948.

Two of Prokofiev's compositions were resurrected in 1952, the radical contrast between them attesting to the extremes of Prokofiev's Soviet career. On
September 12, *Zdravitsa*, Prokofiev's contribution to Stalin's sixtieth birthday,
was broadcast after years of neglect. "They played it well," Prokofiev noted,
"but with cuts, and not my own, but theirs (they excised the scalar runs in the
chorus, spoiling the form). Yet I'm so pleased they revived it that I've decided
to keep quiet for a while."[71] In the domain of hack work, Prokofiev relied on
inconstant musical structures to compensate for static verbal content. For this
reason, he opined that "Shostakovich's new cantata *Of the Party*" was "bland,
workmanlike, and too short."[72] *Zdravitsa* was re-broadcast on October 8, the
same day that the Bolshoy Theater performed *Romeo and Juliet*, with Ulanova
dancing the main role. Given the ballet's tortured genesis, its growing fame
surprised the composer: "This spectacle is so popular that, as they say, 'better
to refuse drink altogether than to drink just now and then.'"[73]

There followed more good news: the Bolshoy Theater had decided to
revive *Cinderella*, this time with the original rather than the altered orchestration. The theater retrieved the autograph manuscript from the Central
(Russian) State Archive of Literature and Art, where Prokofiev had deposited
it for safekeeping. Stuchevsky speculated that Fayer, director of the Bolshoy
Ballet, had become paranoid that he would be censured by cultural officials
for performing a corrupt version of the score, and so decided to restore it.
Prokofiev wanted no part in the drama. Yet in the end, and for reasons
that he could not discern, the Bolshoy Theater still used the corrupt version.
Prokofiev noted that the December 24 performance of *Cinderella* "was not
only a triumph but, they say, a 'wild triumph.' I wasn't there, but I will go
to one of the upcoming performances."[74] News of the success inspired him
to suppress his irritation with his assertive advisers and complete both *War
and Peace* and *The Tale of the Stone Flower* according to their suggestions.
He received assurances that the ballet, if not the opera, would be produced
at the Bolshoy Theater, rather than at one of its Moscow affiliates.

One last piece of good news concerned the Seventh Symphony, which Prokofiev composed from December 1951 to July 1952 (the draft piano score is dated March 20, 1952, the final orchestral score July 5), and which satisfied even his opponents. In keeping with the spirit of the commission, Prokofiev initially called it a "Children's Symphony"; he ended up changing the title, according to Rostropovich, on account of the Symphony's appeal to adults.[75] On August 26, Vedernikov played the piano score at the Union of Soviet Composers in Prokofiev's absence, and then traveled to the dacha to report that "even the negative people ([Viktor] Belïy, Koval, Goldenweizer)" found a way to praise it, the only quibbles concerning the proposed orchestration.[76] The Symphony also passed the test with the State Radio Orchestra—"Oh, wonder!" Prokofiev sarcastically noted.[77] (Still, the musicians exercised their collective right to adjust tempi.) The October 11 premiere had the feel of an old-guard reunion, with Prokofiev accepting congratulations from the veterans of the 1948 scandal. He mounted the stage and took the final bow of his career before an appreciative crowd. Goldenweizer, who had ridiculed A Story of a Real Man, began to cry, though Prokofiev could not quite believe it. "I didn't think that this dried-up old man could be moved to tears, but those in the hall corroborated that he cried into his sleeve."[78]

The positive reception signaled that the Symphony would receive an award, but Samosud, who conducted the premiere, warned him that the Stalin Prize Committee was not convinced that it merited the highest ranking, since the lugubrious conclusion did not accord with official taste. Samosud reported that "although seven members of the Stalin Prize Committee attended the Symphony and praised it," there was "a potential snag" in their deliberations: "The finale does not end in joy so, in order not to forfeit first prize for second prize, would it not be possible to create an alternate finale with a happy ending?"[79] Knowing that Prokofiev had little choice but to accommodate the Committee, Samosud returned the score to him for revision. Prokofiev at first blanched, calling the task "impossible," but then he rose to the occasion, writing a new, optimistic coda for the fourth movement, which Samosud premiered on November 6 and the composer pretended to like. To the melancholic recollection of the second and third themes from the first movement he added a jarring reprise of the glib opening tune of the fourth. For his efforts, he would posthumously earn a single-class Lenin Prize (the awarding of Stalin Prizes having been discontinued after the ruler's death).

In a bulletin written for the Telegraph Agency of the Soviet Union (TASS), Prokofiev defined the Symphony as a tribute to youth that sought to "reflect the spiritual beauty and strength of the young people of our country," the "joy of life," and the desire to move "forward to the future."[80] In a June 12, 1962, interview with Malcolm Brown, Mira clarified that the Symphony addressed "Soviet youth" as well as Prokofiev's "own youth."[81] Taking these remarks at face value, it would appear that he intended the work to be both forward- and backward-looking, both public and private. The music sounds sincere but fragile. After learning that the run-through of the Symphony at the Composers' Union had been a success, Prokofiev asked Kabalevsky whether it was "too simple."[82] He clung to the hope that one day, with one of his works, he would be asked to make the music more complex.

The Symphony clings to traditional forms and syntax, but the melodic writing meanders, with the abrupt tonal shifts serving less to dramatize the four movements than to slacken them. Prokofiev cast the first movement in a semblance of sonata form. There are three themes ranging in affect from nostalgic to inspired to withdrawn. The first is heard seven times intact: four times in the exposition, twice in the recapitulation, and once in the disquieting coda. Prokofiev harmonizes the theme with tonic and subdominant chords. The transition between the first and second presentations involves a running pattern that becomes the accompaniment of the third and fourth presentations. The modulation to the dominant for the repetition of the first theme, rather than the appearance of the second theme, recalls Haydn's monothematic sonata form expositions. Prokofiev introduces the second theme first in the horns and bassoons and then in the strings. The dynamic level dips to that of a lullaby, with the woodwinds and glockenspiel paired to present the closing theme.

There is little drama in the development section: the three themes are varied without contrapuntal overlay, this leading to a dominant pedal, the return of the home key, and the recapitulation of the first theme. Prokofiev here enlarges the tonal palette. The movement ends with the woodwinds and glockenspiel rousing the specter of the first theme.

The remainder of the Symphony is more spirited, with the composer manipulating waltz genres in the second movement and paying homage to a previous work, *Eugene Onegin*, in the third. (It reuses the theme and variations from *Eugene Onegin* that connote the heroine Tatyana and her feelings for Onegin.) The fourth and final movement combines a *valse à deux temps*, the historical precursor of the polka, with a giddy march. Brown notes that the composer's "favored effect of sudden tonal dislocation can be found throughout the symphony, both unexpected digressions within a phrase...as well as sudden displacements of the tonic between phrases and at cadences."[83] It is hard to avoid concluding that the Symphony was stitched together, with Prokofiev mixing and matching the elements of familiar forms. He perhaps amused himself by misaligning the harmonic and melodic writing, inserting cadences in the middle of phrases, and using leading tones—rather than the tonics and dominants—as pedal points. The distortions might be interpreted as programmatic representations of the fickleness of memory; they might also be interpreted as expressions of boredom. In the finale, the effortless handling of form at once transcends and mocks the trivial content. Brown defines the progression from "galop" to "march" as a "virtual thesaurus of familiar clichés from the conventional Soviet music of [the] day."[84]

In his post-1948 works Prokofiev muted his creative voice. Goldenweizer wept when he heard the Symphony—perhaps out of love for the music, perhaps also out of shame for the manner in which he had participated in the humiliation of a brilliant composer. So, too, did the Party-line Ukrainian musician Konstantin Dankevich, who had "insanely attacked" Prokofiev following the premiere of *Semyon Kotko*, but who himself came in for censure in 1951. Seeing the sadness and remorse on Dankevich's face, Prokofiev commented that "this was now a second evil-wisher (the first was Goldenweizer) who wept" upon hearing the Symphony.[85]

The Final Works

The other premieres of 1952 include the "festive poem" *The Meeting of the Volga and the Don* and its cerebral obverse: a taxing, large-scale composition for cello and orchestra that Prokofiev completed with the energetic assistance of Rostropovich. The first of these works, a throwaway composition representing inspired work brigades building a massive freight and passenger ship waterway between the Volga and Don Rivers, was broadcast on State Radio on February 22, 1952.[86] Prokofiev greeted Balasanyan, Rostropovich, and Samosud's proposal to compose the fifteen-minute score with skepticism, if not incredulity, but needing the income, accepted it. The composer developed the sketches piecemeal in August 1951 and worked out the orchestration from October 12 to November 18.[87] His knowledge of the gigantic engineering project to be celebrated by his score came from the numerous reports about it in *Pravda, Izvestiya,* and *Sovetskoye iskusstvo*—this last publication

celebrating the project as an architectural wonder. Rostropovich recalls Prokofiev summoning him into his study after receiving medical treatment and
playing "two themes from the future festive poem *The Meeting of the Volga
and the Don*, which he had written during the procedure in the margins
of a newspaper."[88] The upbeat press accounts of bulldozers and excavators
churning up the land between the rivers lent itself to the invention of an
awkwardly sectionalized score combining blustery fanfare motives—some
piercingly high in the trumpet—pioneer march strains, luxurious melodies
adapted from *Cinderella*, portentous lower brass harmonies, and a series of
false endings. In October 1951, Prokofiev robotically informed the readers
of the periodical *Novosti* that the subject matter of *The Meeting of the Volga
and the Don* had been "prompted by life."[89] A month later, he reported in a
column in *Sovetskoye iskusstvo* dedicated to the "upcoming 35th anniversary of October" that, while working on the score, he thought about "the
boundless width of our great rivers, the songs composed about them by the
people, and the verses dedicated to them by Russian classic and contemporary poets. I'm attempting to make the music... songlike, reflecting that
joy of labor that now grips all our people."[90] Prokofiev's score expresses
these panegyrics but also allows the listener to imagine hydroelectric station
turbines, the operation of the canal's thirteen locks, and the flowing waters
of the conjoined rivers, viewed from a distance. The false endings inadvertently predict the setbacks that delayed the canal's completion: it officially
opened on July 27, 1952, with the passenger ship *Iosif Stalin* making the
inaugural fifteen-hour journey, but the construction of dams at Kuybïshev
and Stalingrad extended into 1954.[91]

   The Meeting of the Volga and the Don was overshadowed in the press
by other works composed about the waterway; these were performed along
the banks by national and regional choruses and orchestras with the occasional participation of theater and circus brigades. The grandest work, the
choral-orchestral suite *Hail, Volga Don!*, involved three composers—Leonid
Bakalov, Konstantin Listov, and Sigizmund Katz—whose professional reputations resided solely in the mass song genre. The refrain of the opening
number of the suite, "Maritime Village" (Primorskaya stanitsa), typifies the
simplistic sentiment of the whole: "Tsimla, oh Tsimla, Tsimla Sea, Our deeds
are good, Our homeland flourishes" (Tsimla, oy Tsimla, Tsimlyanskoye
more, Khoroshi u nas dela, Kray tsvetet rodnoy). The verses address the
utopian transformation of the former Cossack village of Tsimla into a Soviet
canal-side resort. Not to be outdone by *Hail, Volga Don!*, the Voronezh

Russian Folk Ensemble mounted fourteen concerts in homogenized celebration of the "Stalinist builders of Communism" and, by extension, the economic and political might of the Soviet Union—which, according to banners and slogans of the period, disturbed and dismayed Wall Street bankers.[92] These and other Volga-Don festivities received exaggerated coverage in the six issues of *Sovetskoye iskusstvo* that preceded the canal's official opening.[93] Prokofiev's contribution to the festivities offers little of the mandated joyfulness of the others; he could not, or would not, compete with the displays being mounted at Tsimla.

Prokofiev's other new work of 1952, the Sinfonia Concertante (Symphony Concerto), gradually came into being over three years (up until the time of its premiere, it was titled the Second Cello Concerto; following its premiere, the composer expanded the orchestra's role, thereupon renaming it the Sinfonia Concertante). The 20,000-ruble commission came from Aleksandr Kholodilin, who led the music division of the Committee on Arts Affairs, and it specified a work of three movements for completion by November 1, 1951.[94] For source material, Prokofiev turned to his First Cello Concerto of 1938, which had not enjoyed success, generating the solo part in consultation with Rostropovich. The common assumption that the two of them worked side by side on the score stems from a single photograph and newspaper report.[95] It is undone by the primary source evidence, which finds Prokofiev composing the solo and accompanimental parts in relative solitude—and perhaps recalling the recommendations for corrections to the First Cello Concerto that he had received from Pyatigorsky back in 1940. Once the material was drafted, he gave the sketchbooks to Rostropovich for technical correction and refinement, who in turn forwarded them to Atovmyan for orchestration. On August 5, 1951, Atovmyan informed Prokofiev that "I'm sending you the realization of the first movement of the [Second Cello] Concerto with some questions of mine. M. Rostropovich is bringing around the 2nd movement tomorrow."[96] On August 25, he explained, "The delay in realizing the Cello Concerto wasn't my fault. Having begun the realization of the third sketchbook I ran across references to the first sketchbook, which Rostropovich sequestered.... When are you planning to give me the third movement of the Cello Concerto? I want to arrange my work schedule accordingly."[97] These letters elicited, on October 4, a wearied response from Prokofiev once again lamenting the sloppiness of Atovmyan's work. "There are many unclear notes, almost no dynamic markings, and so on. I'm unwell now, ordered to bed and forbidden to work." Prokofiev adds that he is short on income and asks how much he will earn for the "Gypsy Fantasy" suite from *The Tale of the Stone Flower*. He concludes, again with his finances in mind, that he had finished sketching *The Meeting of the Volga and the Don*.[98]

The Sinfonia Concertante does not require extended techniques, but it thoroughly tests the cellist's mental and physical stamina, emphasizing high-volume sound production, fingerboard precision (shifts and leaps, chromatic runs, and double stops), sustained phrasing, and rapidly shifting timbres. Muscular exertion is transformed into an expressive device. The antecedent of the opening phrase, for example, requires the soloist to bow exceedingly close to the bridge with the right hand while maintaining an intense vibrato with the left; the consequent of the phrase features large intervallic leaps along a single string of the fingerboard. The leaps demand seamless execution with a single bow stroke, while the ensuing double stops require subtle, rapid adjustments in the spacing between the first and third, and second and fourth fingers along the fingerboard. At times, the soloist must project two voices, transforming a typically monophonic instrument into a homophonic one.

The second movement is the longest, at seventeen minutes, and richest. It expands the technical challenges by obliging the soloist to navigate double-stop sequences as well as long-breathed melodies that incorporate double-stops mid-phrase. The swiftness of these passages makes generating the pitches as written exceedingly problematic; the sound of the soloist's physical exertion with the bow and fingerboard replaces the sound of the notated music. The finale, a variation movement in three parts, eases the strain. The opening theme offers a lyrical outtake from the technical obstacle course of the two preceding movements. The soloist first presents the melody as a single line and subsequently restates it in sixths, then subjects it to variation in a brush-stroke passage that metastasizes in the middle and closing sections of the movement. Pizzicato four-note harmonies and false harmonics characterize subsequent variations. Between measures 207 and 223, the soloist offers a repeat, in thick double stops, of the folklike tune that the orchestra had earlier introduced as a counterbalance to the main theme. The dash to the finish line, commencing at measure 368, involves a sequence of extremely fast, loud arpeggios that—optimally—find the performer overcoming technical limitations through sheer adrenalin.

The Sinfonia Concertante was premiered (as the Second Cello Concerto) on February 18, 1952, at the Moscow Conservatory, with the pianist Richter valiantly conducting the student orchestra while nursing an injury to his right hand. The soprano Vera Dukhovskaya, a champion of Prokofiev's Pushkin Romances who had been acquainted with the composer since 1927, wept bittersweet tears at the performance: the music, like its creator, seemed uncharacteristically morose to her.[99]

The performance received mixed reviews, but Rostropovich recalled it with great pride. He also provided some unverifiable details about his collaboration with Prokofiev, including being besieged "to compose some of the [solo] passages, but when I did so he always made some small but significant changes, leaving me wondering at how narrow, yet unbridgeable, is the gap between the mundane and the sublime." There follows an anecdote about the third movement:

> Prokofiev incorporated a theme [in the middle section] that was similar to a popular song by Vladimir Zakharov, an apparatchik who mercilessly vilified all "formalists." After the work was played at the Composers' Union, Zakharov stood up and said indignantly that he would write to the papers complaining that his own wonderful tune had been totally distorted. When I related this to Prokofiev he wrote a replacement tune (a waltz, which I never played), and said that once everything had settled down we could quietly revert to the original tune.[100]

If Rostropovich's interpretation of this event were accurate, if would have amounted to payback. Zakharov had in 1945 added music to *Cinderella* for the discarded scene of the Prince's wanderings through Africa without Prokofiev's authorization. But it is not accurate: Zakharov did produce a song with select points in common with Prokofiev's, but a much better rhythmic and melodic match comes from the Minsk arranger and composer Isaak Lyuban. Zakharov's common-time tune, titled "Be of Good Health" (Bud'te zdorovï), exists in print from 1939; Lyuban's triple-meter "Our Toast" (Nash tost) is dated 1948. Both songs became popular during the war, and both tended to be performed in concert in different variations, a practice good-humoredly reprised by Prokofiev in his score. Zakharov, a Stalin Prize winner, may have complained about the perceived mishandling of his—more likely Lyuban's—tune, but the allusion was not intended as a slight. Rather, it constituted a creative response to Zhdanov's 1948 instruction to Soviet composers to learn from popular music. The effort failed, and Prokofiev agreed to rewrite the offending passage.[101]

The date of the assessment of the Cello Concerto at the Union of Soviet Composers is unknown; it was reassessed by the Committee on Arts Affairs on August 30. This second review resulted in Rostropovich adding alternate, less demanding solo passages. The transformation of the Second Cello Concerto into the Sinfonia Concertante began on July 23, 1952, and essentially concluded, following a health-related interruption, on September 7, with the composer praising Rostropovich in his diary for his "very good advice concerning concerto performance and the general plan" of the work. Multitasking was now impossible for Prokofiev. Committed to the Sinfonia Concertante, he was forced to decline unceremoniously an offer to compose fifteen minutes of music for a cartoon titled *Flight to the Moon (Polyot na lunu)*.[102] At other times, such an offer would have fired his imagination; instead, so weakened, he told the filmmakers he was not interested.

Rostropovich returned to Prokofiev's dacha September 20–21 to discuss future projects, their relationship seemingly allowing the composer to relive the freer, itinerant years when he, like the cellist, performed for a living. Prokofiev could not wholly escape the present, however, noting that, "Yesterday [September 21], while strolling with Rostropovich in Nikolina Gora, we suddenly bumped into Khrennikov, his wife, and Yarustovsky. We conversed quite peacefully, even chatted—this appears (at least externally) to be a feature of our relationship."[103]

The other products of Prokofiev's interactions with Rostropovich went unfinished: these include a Sonata for Unaccompanied Cello in three movements, for which he completed fourteen pages of sketches between 1949 and (predominantly) 1952. The sketches for the second movement comprise a fugue, such as can be found in the Prelude of Bach's Fifth Suite for Unaccompanied Cello in C Minor, which Rostropovich played for Prokofiev at Nikolina Gora. For advice on constructing the fugue, Prokofiev turned to Shebalin, a former student of Myaskovsky and member of Lamm's musical circle who, after the 1948 Resolution, lost his teaching post at the Moscow Conservatory for three years. Shebalin was touted by his students as a master contrapuntalist (he composed several fugues for piano and wrote extensively for solo strings), but he was nonetheless "bewildered" that Prokofiev would turn to him for help. " 'I should be learning from you!' " he exclaimed.[104] The fugue had actually already been drafted, but when Prokofiev showed it to Rostropovich on September 28, 1952, the cellist recommended some fine-tuning. "Rostropovich is sure that after some small changes it will be a completely respectable fugue," Prokofiev noted, insecurely, in his diary.[105] Although he left the Sonata for Unaccompanied Cello incomplete, one of Shebalin's students, Vladimir Blok, managed to assemble a performing version of the C-major opening movement; it was premiered in 1972 in Moscow by Rostropovich's student Natalya Gutman.

Blok was also involved in the realization of Prokofiev's final work for cello, a "transparent" Concertino that the composer had conceived immediately following the completion of the Sinfonia Concertante.[106] Prokofiev intended to produce a finished manuscript in the spring of 1953; at the time of his death, he had completed the second movement in piano score but had only sketched the first and third movements. The cellist Steven Isserlis provides the details of its genesis:

> It was presumably intended as a vehicle for student cellists as much as for Rostropovich himself. It is not a "great" work—it is not trying to be one! It is what it is: tuneful, amusing, appealing. The first movement opens with a brooding melody exploring the darker regions of the cello; the second subject, in complete contrast, brings out the sun. The slow movement is relaxed, lyrical, with perhaps a touch of irony; as in the sonata for cello and piano, one can feel, in the aftermath of the 1948 [Resolution], Prokofiev's genuine desire to write accessible music mixed with a certain detachment, a musical raised eyebrow. The last movement opens with a gruffly humorous melody taken from the Symphony-Concerto (one of the few major themes from that work not derived from the [First Cello] Concerto, op. 58); the second subject, like that of the first movement, is charming, innocent.[107]

Rostropovich completed the first (sonata-allegro) and third (rondo) movements of the Concertino according to his understanding of Prokofiev's methods and premiered it, with piano accompaniment, on December 29, 1956. Kabalevsky, meanwhile, completed an orchestration that, despite referring to some of the annotations in Prokofiev's partial manuscript, was decidedly overblown, a violation of the composer's neoclassical intentions. In 1994, Isserlis approached Blok, who recognized that Kabalevsky's orchestration was "bad," about reducing and refining it for chamber ensemble. An eclectic new version of the Concertino, with Blok's orchestration, was premiered on April 11, 1997, with Isserlis as soloist.[108]

Another unfinished project was the Concerto for Two Pianos and Strings in C Major, whose 1951 inspiration, Prokofiev revealed, came from Bach's Concerto for Two Harpsichords and Strings in C Major (BWV 1061).[109] Prokofiev planned to dedicate the work to Vedernikov, who, like Rostropovich and Richter, participated in its formulation. The extant sketches are written both in Prokofiev's and Vedernikov's hands, which complicates the establishment of a chronology for the composition. There exist 65 measures of the opening C-major allegro movement, 101 measures of the middle G-minor andante (many of these just a single line), and 67 measures of the concluding allegretto. Around thirty measures of this last movement are in Vedernikov's hand, the rest in Prokofiev's. The change in the script is marked by a modulation from C major to E-flat major and by a deterioration in penmanship: compared to Vedernikov's script, Prokofiev's looks shaky. No orchestral indications are shown, except for one or two places indicating first violin.[110]

Prokofiev suspended work on the Concerto for Two Pianos in the fall of 1952 and directed his dwindling energies to another, greater project. The sketches for this and his other unfinished works are projections, pointing to a finished opus whose size and scope cannot be determined. (Prokofiev seldom outlined a piece on paper before beginning to compose.) The move back to Bach—to the enduring, unsullied musical landscape the eighteenth-century composer stereotypically emblematized—was to have been Prokofiev's concluding musical statement. The extant traces of that project are much less reminders of Bach, however, than of the openness, the imminent potential that Prokofiev saw in each of his sketches. He replaces the spiritual symbol of intricate counterpoint with another: the unrefined musical thoughts attributed to divine inspiration.

Noting how much Prokofiev seemed to be rushing to produce in his last days, Mira quoted him as saying, "But I could have written so much more."[111] The body, he knew, could no longer serve the spirit. The manuscripts of his finished and unfinished late works, particularly the manuscripts for *The Tale of the Stone Flower*, sometimes include in the margins Prokofiev's daily readings of his temperature and blood pressure—a painful detail that literally realizes the metaphor of work as lifeblood.

Kutuzov's Three Measures

The opera *War and Peace* had not been staged when the nation needed it. After 1945, it disintegrated into segments, which Prokofiev either removed, replaced, or rewrote to accord with ideological demands. His career-long effort to stage his dramatic works became a satire of itself as he was forced to haggle at smaller and smaller levels of detail over the representation of individual characters, the relationship between the war and peace scenes, the structure of the ballroom episode, the function of the chorus, and ultimately, the melodic writing in Kutuzov's climactic aria. The story of Prokofiev's Soviet years concludes, bathetically, with three measures of *War and Peace*, a snippet of a massive score that had dominated his thoughts for a dozen years, and that he still hoped to see staged in its entirety.

Based on the results of the December 4, 1948, assessment of Part II of the opera at Malegot, Prokofiev had begun a radical compression of the score from a two-evening (thirteen-scene) event into ten scenes performed in a single evening. A letter from May 28, 1949, to the Malegot conductor Eduard Grikurov illustrates both the coarseness of the changes and Prokofiev's willingness to accommodate the demands of his various interlocutors, even when those demands conflicted with each other. The letter finds him wishing entire sections of *War and Peace* out of existence:

> I agree with your proposal to exclude the scene at Dolokhov's. Samuil Abramovich [Samosud] is less in agreement with this, since he finds that the scene is needed in order to show the "golden" youth of that time and to justify the following scene at [Mariya] Akhrosimov's.
>
> I am not against the reductions to the Borodino and Shevardino Redoubt scenes. The Borodino scene leaves out the refugees and Pierre's part. In the concluding scene the episode between Pierre and Karatayev (from [394] to [398]) and the episode with the partisans (from [412] to [419]) are cut. I would prefer to eliminate all of Pierre's reflections on Hélène and the others, but then it seemed to me that they need to be preserved in order to determine the fate of the characters. However, if you find that this last scene is not abbreviated enough, then please express your views.

Prokofiev next remarks that, despite the elimination of scene 11 ("Moscow Aflame"), he valued the "patriotism and aspiration" of the concluding chorus and hoped to hear it somewhere in the Malegot staging. The changes to the entire opera would be shown in the new edition of the piano score that he was just completing, including "Natasha's new romance and Andrey's monologue, reworked as an aria."[112] Prokofiev appends that "this piano score can serve as the basis for the abbreviated version" of *War and Peace*, but that he would nonetheless "be very glad to hear further suggestions" from Grikurov.[113]

Grikurov did not move forward with the score, since neither the Composers' Union nor the Committee on Arts Affairs had vetted the changes. Prokofiev's last substantive talks with the two organizations about *War and Peace* came on February 10, 1950, and sent him into a fury. He was told that plans for the premiere of the truncated ten-scene version would be delayed until after the "staging of several operas on a contemporary subject." Prokofiev fired back in frustration: "What would you have me do, burn the opera?"[114] The bureaucrats mollified him with the platitudinous promise that Malegot would eventually stage the opera. The ensuing silence from the theater caused the composer terrible anxiety, as evidenced by his July 4, 1950, letter to Atovmyan, who helped assemble the new edition of both the piano and orchestral scores. Prokofiev twice requests assurance that *War and Peace* had, in fact, entered the Malegot repertoire plan:

> Will you be at the Malegot performances and meeting with Grikurov? It would be good to find out from him if *War and Peace* is part of the plan for the upcoming season (at the Arts Committee they said that it will be performed in the fall while other operas are running). If it won't be performed, try to find out the reasons. This issue worries me. Samosud related that Malegot sent a request to the Committee in the spring for permission to stage the opera. The Committee even said to me during the winter that it will be performed this fall, after several other operas are staged. If *War and Peace* is not included in the plan, I'd like to find out the reasons.[115]

Prokofiev never did find out, and hopes for a staging faded until the fall of 1952, at which time Samosud, perhaps nudged by Fadeyev, began the tedious process of arranging a performance for State Radio.[116] The administration of the Stanislavsky Theater also showed interest in producing the opera. On October 14, Prokofiev took a break from his Concerto for Two Pianos to orchestrate the three sections of *War and Peace* that existed only in piano score.[117] By this point, the Composers' Union had given its blessing to the two scenes ("New Year's Eve Ball" and "A Hut in Fili") that Prokofiev had added to the opera between 1945 and 1947, but the Committee on Arts Affairs—the greater obstacle to his plans—had not. Prokofiev believed that the Committee "stood in the way of *War and Peace*" out of a general "fear to permit anything" to be performed. He further grumbled that Kabalevsky, who had promised to speak on behalf of the opera to the Committee, had disappeared to China on a cultural exchange.[118]

Samosud nonetheless assured Prokofiev of his intentions to conduct the work for State Radio but annoyed him by advising that scene 10, "A Hut in Fili," needed to be reordered. Prokofiev reminded the conductor that *War and Peace* was an opera, not a film score: its parts could not be interchanged. But Samosud stood his ground, and Prokofiev gave way. "The most objectionable" part of the task involved sitting down "for the third time" with Kutuzov's aria to rewrite the trio middle section. He completed the task "with a feeling of loathing" and enlisted Vedernikov to attend to the rest of the changes in the scene.[119] This was by no means the end of the matter; the conductor also asked for Kutuzov's vocal lines to be transposed down a tone to accommodate the bass, Boris Dobrin, who was learning the part. Other irksome requests would follow.

Although he resented making the changes, Prokofiev conceded that they enhanced the dramatic potential of scene 10. By expanding Kutuzov's aria, he ensured that it stood above and apart from every other vocal number in the score. The aria completed the elevation of the character into the role of omniscient historical commentator, with Kutuzov absorbing something of the wisdom of Tolstoy's pedagogical epilogue to *War and Peace*. Tolstoy is not the sole source for the lyrics. During the process of revision, Prokofiev consulted an 1814 Kutuzov biography, which Mira procured from the Moscow branch of the Tolstoy Museum. He took part of the text of the aria—including Kutuzov's ominous prediction of the scattering of enemy bones throughout the Russian lands—directly from its pages.

Samosud conducted scene 10 for State Radio on February 4, 1953, the first phase of his effort to arrange a performance of the entire opera. Separate broadcasts of scene 1 (depicting Andrey at the Rostov estate in Otradnoye), scene 2 (the ball), and scene 12 (Andrey's death) took place over the course of the year.[120] The creative process came to an ignominious end. Samosud argued with Prokofiev over three measures in Kutuzov's aria, complaining they did not match the style of the whole.[121] The composer believed that they did. The dispute, emblematic of the tremendous effort that Prokofiev had to put into the slightest of activities, went unresolved for almost three weeks. Finally Prokofiev asked Rostropovich and Vedernikov to decide between the two versions. Unsurprisingly, they chose his. The issue settled, Prokofiev orchestrated the aria and consigned the opera to posterity, leaving it to future artists to restore to life. He managed, against all odds, to bring his career to a close with a masterpiece—battle-scarred and ragged, but a masterpiece nonetheless.

The life of the opera ended up being true to the life of its source text (between 1866 and 1886, Tolstoy published six editions of his ever-expanding novel under his own supervision). For all the reworking, the music maintains remarkable cohesiveness, robustly enduring sanctioned and nonsanctioned interventions. The porousness of its construction exposes a beguiling contradiction in Prokofiev's creativity: his meticulous attention to detail, manifest in his emblematic defense of the middle section of Kutuzov's aria, but also his pragmatism, his acceptance that the opera would inevitably be altered, even at the expense of his own favorite passages.

The End and the Beginning

In late February and early March, Mira began to notice a change in Prokofiev's mood. He complained that his "soul hurt" and did not respond when she assured him that they would be together "until age ninety."[122] Instead, he urged her to put his affairs in order. His caregiver, physician-therapist, and driver also sensed the change. On March 5, Prokofiev omitted his usual morning stroll in the neighborhood surrounding the Moscow apartment and asked to be taken to the Central (Russian) State Archive of Literature and Art to retrieve a manuscript from his personal holdings there. He also sent a copy of the revised version of his Fifth Piano Sonata to Muzfond, requesting that the score be entrusted to the same copyist who had worked on the original version. Until the end, his fastidious precision did not waver. In the early evening, between 6 and 8, Mira read to him from a collection of reminiscences about Gogol. He went to his room to rest, but then reemerged, lurching from side to side in the midst of a cerebral hemorrhage. Mira summoned his caregiver (she was not immediately available) and physician-therapist; her father returned home to help comfort Prokofiev as Mira made additional calls to Syvatoslav and Oleg. "He was on the divan," Abram recalled, "I tried to cover him, since he was feverish....He began to complain of a fierce headache and asked if the doctor was coming soon. He asked for water with lemon and became nauseous."[123] Mira erroneously trusted that an ambulance would soon arrive. By the time Prokofiev's sons came to the apartment, he had died. Friends and colleagues gathered over the course of the evening.

In her account of these events, Mira emphasized that Prokofiev worked even on the last day of his life. His own chronicle of his work ends four days before, on March 1. That afternoon, he wrote, Stuchevsky stopped by the apartment to pester him about "coarsening" the orchestration of *The Tale of the Stone Flower* with additional instruments in the climactic passages. Prokofiev resisted, complaining that the request was nonsensical. Nevertheless he sat down to work and managed to find something positive in the negative task. "At first it was truly offensive," he wrote, "but by the end it became easier and I completed a few pages."[124]

Prokofiev's brief diary ends here.

◆

Prokofiev died on the same day, purportedly within the same evening hour, as did Stalin. This incongruous historical coincidence has a certain mystical appeal, but its accuracy cannot be vouchsafed owing to an absence of documentation about the circumstances of the Soviet ruler's death and the three-day coma that preceded it. The report of Stalin's March 5 demise was greeted as a national disaster by those who viewed him as a benevolent guardian and defender of the nation, and by those who feared the loss of their positions within the totalitarian establishment. Turmoil spread through the Communist Party and the government it operated; tearful throngs gathered inside and outside the Hall of Columns, where Stalin's body rested on a flower-encrusted catafalque for four days. Party leaders, emissaries from the republics, officials from the trade unions, and artists stood in the honor guard. Teachers interrupted their classes with the news; factories came to a halt. People were crushed trying to obtain a glimpse of the bier. According to one account, Rostropovich's sister Veronika, a violinist with the Moscow Philharmonic summarily dispatched to the Hall of Columns to provide background music for the viewing, wept the whole day. "When her comrades tried to calm her, she began to sob even more," protesting, after several hours of agony, " 'Just leave me alone. I'm not weeping for Stalin, but Prokofiev.' "[125]

The State-sponsored, round-the-clock hysteria about Stalin's demise greatly slowed the spread of the news about Prokofiev. *Sovetskoye iskusstvo* published two obituaries on page 4 of its March 18, 1953, issue, thirteen days after the composer's death. The first, titled "An Outstanding Soviet Composer" (Vïdayushchiysya sovetskiy kompozitor), was signed by twenty-seven cultural officials and artists, a precise hierarchical sequence that included the chairman of the recently disbanded Committee on Arts Affairs (Bespalov), the General Secretary of the Union of Soviet Composers (Khrennikov), the editor of *Sovetskaya muzïka*, the principal of the Moscow Conservatory, elder statesmen, and Stalin Prize winners. The second obituary, titled "A Grand Creative Life" (Bol'shaya tvorcheskaya zhizn'), was written by Kabalevsky.[126] The *New York Times* announced Prokofiev's passing earlier, on March 9 (the article is dated March 8), inaccurately stating that Prokofiev died at Nikolina Gora, rather than in the communal apartment of his economist father-in-law.[127] A follow-up article on March 15 misreports the date of Prokofiev's death (March 4) and the year of Zhdanov's ideological crackdown on Soviet music (1946). Deriding Zhdanov for his "monumental folly," the author of this article, Olin Downes, eulogized Prokofiev as "one of the born music-makers whose problem it was to prune the luxuriance of his invention and imagination rather than to stimulate it." Downes asked: "How far did he succeed in his restless explorations, his endless experiments (sometimes quite mad ones), the indubitable masterpieces that resulted from his magnificent research? The future will estimate him as we cannot."[128]

The March 7 memorial service at the House of Composers (Dom kompozitorov) was a modest affair. Khrennikov attended to the logistics. Shostakovich spoke; Oistrakh performed two movements from the 1946 Violin Sonata; the pianist Samuil Feynberg, Oistrakh's accompanist, performed additional pieces by Bach. Fifteen people attended Prokofiev's interment at Novodevichye cemetery. Flowers were in short supply in Moscow; a photograph of the deceased composer preserved at the Russian State Archive of Documentary Film and Photography in Krasnogorsk shows the casket surrounded by potted plants. These had been brought by a sympathetic neighbor to the memorial service from her apartment, the blooms alive rather than dead.[129] The composer Alfred Schnittke reimagined the funeral procession from a later, safer position in the twentieth century: "Along an almost deserted street that ran parallel to the seething mass hysterically mourning the passing of Stalin, there moved in the opposite direction a small group of people bearing on their shoulders the coffin of the greatest Russian composer of the time....I regard this picture as symbolic. To move against the tide in those days was hopeless. Yet even then there was—just as in earlier ages—the possibility of a choice between two decisions, only one of which was right."[130] However fanciful—some of Prokofiev's pallbearers, Atovmyan included, were true political insiders—Schnittke's *glasnost'*-era sentiments are apt. Prokofiev resisted the current in death as in life.

Lavrovsky, one of the last artists to work with Prokofiev, marked the events of early March in his diary as follows: "Thursday, March 5. S. S. Prokofiev has died. He didn't manage to finish his work on his last ballet *The Tale of the Stone Flower*. It's all very, very sorrowful."[131] Two days later the choreographer went to Novodevichye cemetery for Prokofiev's interment and, two days after that, to Red Square to pay respects to Stalin. Work continued on the ballet, although in the composer's absence it became less a paean to the labor of art and more a study, in fairy-tale guise, of creative paralysis. Lavrovsky, whose burdens included a painful divorce, felt listless and morose: "It's all very complicated and irrelevant, but *what a spectacle* has to be staged!" (March 2). "I went to work in the theater. No one there—no news about the apartment and the notification. Trying not to think about it. I'm rushing everything, rushing myself, but *where*?" (March 16). "Can I cope with this work? It will be what it desires to be" (March 27). "Awful weather. Mood likewise. Headache. I pondered Severyan and Katerina's scene" (March 30). "In the evening I staged Severyan's entrance and his attentions to Katerina. Nothing worked out. Tomorrow I could stage Katerina's scene, but it's not ready, I'm behind" (April 2). "I didn't work this evening; I don't feel well" (April 9).[132]

The Tale of the Stone Flower was assessed twice more by the administration of the Bolshoy Theater—on December 30, 1953, and again on February 3, 1954—and twice found wanting. (For his procrastination with the ballet, and for his ineptitude and malfeasance in general, Anisimov would be ousted from the Bolshoy Theater in 1954.) The complaints centered on the amount of repetition, the opacity of the prologue, the "automatic" and "uninspired" betrothal scene, and the emphasis on Katerina over Danila in the finale. Rostislav Zakharov (the choreographer of the 1945 Moscow premiere of *Cinderella* and one of attendees at the 1948 run-through of *A Story of a Real Man*) scorned the perceived sameness of the music in the first act of the ballet and lamented that it had not been rewritten. His opinion was echoed by the conductor Aleksandr Melik-Pashayev, who discussed what he liked and disliked about the score before allowing that Prokofiev stood in the "first rank" of Soviet composers.

"A few changes could be made," he muttered, before conceding that "since Sergey Sergeyevich is unfortunately not among us," it should be performed as is.[133] The ballet was premiered on February 12, 1954, with Fayer conducting.

The paralysis in the Soviet cultural sphere that grievously encumbered *The Tale of the Stone Flower* persisted through Khrushchev's ascent to power and 1956 secret speech denouncing high Stalinism. Prokofiev's *War and Peace* and *A Story of a Real Man* eventually made it to the Soviet stage, albeit in decidedly abbreviated versions. (The October 8, 1960, Bolshoy Theater premiere of *A Story of a Real Man* featured Mira's rewritten, de-Stalinized libretto, massive cuts—the act 1 overture altogether disappeared, as did entire blocks of declamation—and illogically reordered scenes.) Prokofiev's remembrance involved the arrangement of a pension of 700 rubles a month for Mira; the fixing of memorial plaques to his two principal residences in Moscow, the dacha in Nikolina Gora, and his Sontsovka birthplace; the manufacturing of souvenirs bearing his likeness (calendars, posters, postage stamps, and silver coins); the awarding of the Lenin Prize for the Seventh Symphony in 1957; the planning of festivals in his honor in 1961 and 1991 (the former scrapped, the latter hobbled by the collapse of the Soviet Union); and the publication of select works by an editorial commission headed by Kabalevsky between 1955 and 1967.[134] Prokofiev's manuscripts, along with the documentation about his professional and personal life, were distributed into several archives, a typical Soviet practice that prevents a complete picture of his compositional achievement from being readily perceived. Carefully vetted editions of his autobiographical writings and his articles for the Soviet and foreign press appeared in 1961 and 1965; these volumes, which include select correspondence and reminiscences by his colleagues, have been consulted, where appropriate, throughout this book. *Sovetskaya muzïka* devoted a section of the March 1958 issue to the commemoration of the fifth anniversary of Prokofiev's death, parts of issues in 1962, 1963, 1966, 1967, and 1968 "to the study of S. S. Prokofiev's work," parts of the April 1971 and April 1981 issues in honor of his eightieth and ninetieth birthdays, and the entire April 1991 issue in honor of his centennial. Separate editions of the scores for *Eugene Onegin* and *Boris Godunov* were issued in 1973 and 1983 under the editorship of Elizaveta Dattel, who downplayed the crucial role of the discredited Krzhizhanovsky and repressed Meyerhold in attempting to stage them. The composer's legacy was preserved in order to be controlled, the memory of his life and work carefully constructed by those who came after him. During the Khrushchev and Brezhnev periods, Khrennikov did the most to memorialize Prokofiev, including fighting resistant and resentful bureaucrats to ensure that Prokofiev's first wife, Lina, received comparable pension and housing privileges as did his second wife, Mira. In general, cultural officials planned much more than they achieved on Prokofiev's behalf, except when it came to demonstrating their own power.

The full measure of Prokofiev's contribution to twentieth-century music remains to be taken, since some of his output is unpublished, the most obvious examples being his scores for *Kotovsky*, *Lermontov*, *Partisans in the Ukrainian Steppe*, and *Tonya*. Certain works are presumed lost—one can only access the complete score for *Lieutenant Kizhe* by listening to the film; the manuscript, like the title character of that film, is missing—as are numerous source documents, including Nina Sakonskaya's original, rejected verses for *Peter and the Wolf*. The orchestration of the music for *Cinderella* has not been entirely restored to its original, intended state (the current performing edition reflects the alterations made in 1945 for the Bolshoy Theater premiere), nor has the orchestration and ordering of the numbers of either the 1935 or 1938 versions of *Romeo and Juliet*.[135] The two ballets maintain a place in the repertoire despite changes made to the music against the composer's wishes. Perhaps the most crucial need is a *complete* edition of his works, built up from the autograph manuscripts and pinpointing the date and circumstances of their revision, however complex. Regrettably, the quality of recent critical editions, especially *Ivan the Terrible*, leaves the work to be done again.

Prokofiev was not a victim of the Stalinist regime in the sense that his first wife and numerous friends and colleagues were victims: his decision to relocate to Moscow from Paris in 1936 was free and fateful rather than fatal. Hindsight makes the decision difficult to understand, but it bore its own pressured, inopportune logic. Additional details about that move—the specific nature of Atovmyan's relationship to the NKID, and the timeline of Prokofiev's meetings with Potyomkin—will doubtless come to light. As the example of *War and Peace* demonstrates, his talent arguably overcame and sometimes benefited from outside control, undermining the Western musicological assumption that Soviet artists were always passive victims of brutal, crude, and rigid politics. A case could be made for staging the cohesive 1942 score of *War and Peace*, just as it has been made for the original 1869 version of Musorgsky's *Boris Godunov*, but producing the 1942 score would result in the jettisoning of resplendent dance music of markedly apolitical character. Soviet scholars, notably Anatoliy Volkov, recognized what Prokofiev had to accommodate, reconceive, and reconfigure, and their findings should not be casually dismissed.[136] Nor can the fact that Prokofiev responded to political command, wartime dislocation, and declining health with music of great affective power but disquieting messages, *Zdravitsa* being the most blatant example.

The post-1948 works remain obscure. These, more than the pre-1948 works, are witness to a creative decline and penchant for self-censorship that illustrates the extent to which the consciousness of an artist cannot be separated from the consciousness of his surroundings. Thus Prokofiev retreated in the final months of his life, finding musical models in the past. He sought a structural perfection that, in the language of Christian Science, illustrates "Life's spiritual ideal."[137] That ideal, perceived before his relocation to Moscow, manifested itself in the large- and small-scale scores conceived afterward, from the first version of *Romeo and Juliet* to the last version of *The Tale of the Stone Flower*, whose heroes and heroines exit the constraints of their existences, recognizing that "the visible universe and material man are the poor counterfeits of the invisible universe and spiritual man." The simplification of Prokofiev's musical syntax in the 1930s suggests a striving for the harmoniousness that was, in accord with his newfound spiritual outlook, "the truth of being." As Prokofiev expressed it enthusiastically to a Christian Science practitioner in a letter from January 31, 1933, "Christian Science is helping me enormously in my music. To [put it] more exactly, I do not see any more [of] my work outside of Science."[138]

Prokofiev thus joined that long list of astonishingly productive artists who died in dismal circumstances, leaving his work suspended and predestined for incompletion. His greatest creations, those spared the pressures of Committee on Arts Affairs deadlines and Union of Soviet Composers protocols, maintain a place in the orchestral and theatrical repertoire even as that repertoire shrinks, ceding to the popular idioms from which it sprang. Recent performances and recordings of Prokofiev's lesser-known works, the ongoing Russian- and English-language publication of his diaries and autobiographical writings, and continued scholarly attention attest to his enduring appeal. And here one confronts, in all its oddness, the twist of fate that brought a Christian Scientist home to Stalin's Russia. Much as Christian Science urged its believers to look toward the light, so did the positive—or, to invoke a Soviet cliché, "life-affirming"—sentiments of Prokofiev's music privilege exhilarated listener engagement. Even as his career turned tragic, his works celebrated, on their own terms, a state of happiness.

Prokofiev did not want to be like his times; rather, his times wanted to be like him.

Acknowledgments

This book is the product of primary source research conducted in Russia between 2003 and 2008. Indispensable to its realization was the help I received from the staffs of the numerous federal archives I frequented, as well as less formal, nonstop education from friends and colleagues in Moscow. I am enormously indebted to this book's dedicatee, Galina Zlobina, the deputy director of the Russian State Archive of Literature and Art (RGALI), whose sponsorship of the project, specifically my commitment to determining just what happened to Prokofiev after 1936, confirmed my faith that the documentary record can give rise to a living human being. I am also grateful to Yelena Chugunova and Dmitriy Neustroyev, the managers of the reading room at RGALI, for their assistance procuring materials. Although I pestered them endlessly, they only feigned exasperation.

I owe an immense debt to Malcolm Brown, a cherished friend and mentor who donated his remarkable private collection of Prokofiev materials—scores, letters, interview transcripts, and photographs—to me for use in this book. Another scholar whose expertise informs these pages is Leonid Maximenkov, a Russian archival detective without peer, who answered countless questions, tracked down arcane facts and figures, and shared with me his knowledge of the workings of the Russian cultural matrix, past and present. I must also thank Nikolay Sidorov, of the Russian State Archive of Social-Political History, for aiding my search for contextual information about Prokofiev's relocation to Moscow from Paris, and the dance historian Maria Ratanova, for fulfilling requests for specific documents on *Romeo and*

Juliet and *Cinderella* from holdings in St. Petersburg. Nelly Kravetz likewise provided invaluable assistance as I pieced together the puzzle of Prokofiev's Soviet experience.

This book also belongs to my colleague and closest friend Caryl Emerson, who championed it from the outset, and with whom I collaborated on a production of the Pushkin-Meyerhold-Prokofiev *Boris Godunov* at Princeton University in 2005. Noëlle Mann and Fiona McKnight, both of the London Prokofiev Archive, provided indispensable assistance at the opening and closing phases of the research; Laurel Fay and Richard Taruskin gave the manuscript invaluable critical readings; Ksana Blank answered numerous translation questions; and Anna Wittstruck schooled me in the mechanics of the cello. I am also grateful to Elizabeth Bergman, who shared her knowledge of Prokofiev's final trips to the United States with me; and Kara Olive, who proofread the draft. I am also, of course, indebted to the Prokofiev family, especially Serge Prokofiev Jr., for support throughout the years.

For information and inspiration I must also acknowledge Brian Boyd, Chester Dunning, Sibelan Forrester, Marina Frolova-Walker, Natalya Gromova, Naum Kleyman, Rita McAllister, Irina Medvedeva, Inessa Medzhibovskaya, Mark Morris, Natalya Mospanova, Janice Prater, Kim Robinson, Lesley-Anne Sayers, and Gregory Spears. And I must especially thank Paul De Angelis, Lynn Behrendt, Katherine Boone, Erin Clermont, and Christine Dahlin for preparing the manuscript for publication, and my ever-supportive editor Suzanne Ryan for backing the project from start to finish. Finally, I am grateful to Melanie Feilotter for her companionship, counsel, and support.

Appendix A

The Original Scenario of *Romeo and Juliet*

RGALI f. 1929, op. 1, yed. khr. 66, ll. 1–10.

The original scenario, dated May 16, 1935, was written by Prokofiev in consultation with Radlov in Leningrad. The archival file contains the original handwritten scenario with the act 4 happy ending, and then two typewritten revisions, without the happy ending. The text shown in square brackets is from the revisions to the scenario. Strike-throughs designate text from the original version that Prokofiev either reworked or replaced in the revisions. The durations are from both the draft scenario and the draft score.

1. Introduction

    2 minutes and 20 seconds

    Act 1
    Scene 1: The Street

2. Romeo [Early morning. Romeo passes by, very pensive. Perhaps some female passers-by seek to halt him, but he pays no notice.]

    1 minute

3. Entrances, meetings, disputes. Sustained music. [The stragglers return home. The mood is inoffensive. Unexpectedly (on the last chord) someone flings an orange and smashes a window.]

    1 minute and 10 seconds

4. Servants [and citizens] quarrel (not too hotheaded; socks on the jaw). It gets interrupted.

    1½ minutes

5. Brawl (hotheaded). [Knights with weapons; general mayhem.] Toward the end, the Prince of Verona enters [on a horse], and the brawl ceases.

    2½ minutes

6. The Prince's edict [his first gesture]; in response, the weapons are dropped. [His second gesture]; in response, the elders leave to meet [perhaps someone falls to his knees].

    1¼ minutes

7. The Prince departs. Interlude [between the scenes, expressing the Prince's power. Symphonic and military orchestras. Costumed members of the military orchestra could escort the Prince in front of the curtain.]

    1 minute and 20 seconds

    Scene 2: House of the Capulets

8. Servants [preparing for a ball]; a lead5en scherzo.

    1¼–1½ minutes

9. Juliet's entrance with her nursemaid; she dashes in (her C-major theme, but not immediately). [Just fourteen years old, she girlishly jokes and pranks, unwilling to dress for the ball. The nursemaid nevertheless gets her into a gown. Juliet stands before a mirror and sees a young woman. She briefly muses, and then dashes out.]

    2½ minutes

10. Arrival of the guests (a slow, nondance minuet). [The guests arrive, wearing large mantles and shawls. The dance is mounted as they unwrap and remove their shawls. The guests gradually descend into the interior of the room.]

    3 minutes

11. Entrance of Romeo, Benvolio, and Mercutio [in masks]. A march [Mercutio and Benvolio joke]; Romeo is pensive (8 measures).

    2–2¼ minutes

12. In the interior a ~~curtain~~ [portière] is opened: A) a ponderous dance [for the knights, perhaps in armor]; B) Juliet dances with Paris [ceremoniously and indifferently]; C) return of the ponderous dance (in lighter guise, ending heavily). Romeo sees Juliet and pursues her [he is smitten].

    4¼ minutes

13. Mercutio's dance, somewhat buffoonish (certainly in 3/4). [He enlivens the gathering.]

    1¾ to 2 minutes

14.   Romeo and Juliet's madrigal. [Romeo dances amorously, and Juliet playfully. Romeo dances more ardently than before; Juliet remains playful. They dance together, tenderly. Juliet untangles herself from Romeo and teasingly dashes out.]

2½ minutes

15.   Tybalt ~~sees~~ [recognizes] Romeo. [A Capulet subdues Tybalt. He becomes enraged; the Capulet subdues him once more.] Mercutio and the Capulets escort him out.

1½ minutes

16.   Gavotte. The guests disperse. ~~It becomes quiet~~ [The stage clears;] the candles are extinguished.

3–3½ minutes

17.   [The half-darkened, empty hall. Juliet returns, perhaps in her nightclothes, looking for the kerchief or flower she dropped during her encounter with Romeo].

1 minute and 20 seconds

18.   Romeo appears [from behind a column; Juliet blushes]. ~~Adagio~~ [Amorous dance; the nursemaid perhaps appears and advises Romeo to leave.]

4½ minutes

[Nos. 17–18 correspond to Shakespeare's balcony scene. If the theater has the means to change the décor instantly, then these numbers could be offered as a balcony scene.]

Act 2
Scene 1: The Square [The entire scene represents a folk celebration, against which the separate episodes occur.]

19.   Tarantella

3 minutes

20.   Cheerful and animated, Romeo enters [thinking about Juliet] to the first theme of the madrigal (16 measures). Mercutio greets [and teases] Romeo (from Mercutio's dance, No. 13 in act 1).

2 minutes

21.   [The celebration continues.] Dance of the Five Pairs: 1) quickly, in 2/4 meter; [small,] diminutive movements; 2) a march (winds only); [a cheerful procession passes by on the street]; 3) return to the diminutive movements.

3½ minutes

22.   Nursemaid (C major in 4/4 meter). [The Nursemaid seeks out Romeo on Juliet's instruction.]

2 minutes

23. Mercutio, concealing Romeo, exchanges bows with the Nursemaid [and teases her].

55 seconds

24. ~~Romeo receives the ring and runs out (to the theme of the young Juliet).~~ The Nurse gives Romeo Juliet's ring; Romeo, excited, dashes out.

½ minute

25. General dance (including the Nursemaid and Mercutio) based on the Tarantella, though more intoxicated and featuring more varied accentuation, transitioning into the march [(a jocular procession)] from No. 21, but with the complete orchestra. The curtain descends.

2½ minutes

Scene 2: At Friar Laurence's

26. ~~Interlude and arrival at Friar Laurence's (to his music). Romeo enters: "why was I asked here?" Laurence does not immediately answer; Romeo persists. Laurence brings Juliet in (wearing pure white).~~ [Laurence (who walks rather than dances); Romeo enters; Laurence opens the inner doors and admits Juliet. Dressed in pure white, she embodies virginity.]

2 minutes and 10 seconds

27. Romeo and Juliet look each other in the eye; Laurence departs. Romeo and Juliet embrace but scamper back to their places upon Laurence's return. They kneel before him; he conducts the wedding ceremony. [Curtain. The rest of the music in this episode is for the scene change. Pairs of carnival revelers process along the proscenium in front of the descended curtain.]

2 minutes

~~Curtain (1/2 minute interlude from the preceding interlude, and 1/2 minute of the diminutive movements from No. 21).~~
Scene 3: The Square (décor from scene 1 of this act).

28. Dance of the Five Pairs (see No. 21).

1½ minutes [3 minutes including the curtain music]

29. Appearance of Mercutio and Benvolio with girls. The scene begins with a dance comparable to No. 19; the dance breaks off in dramatic fashion when Tybalt enters and bumps up against Mercutio.

1¾ minutes

30. Tybalt's ~~quarrel~~ [duel] with Mercutio and Romeo. 1) Tybalt and Mercutio stare at each other like bulls (a tremolo in the orchestra; their blood boils). The ~~combat~~ [duel] begins. 2) Romeo enters to a theme from the Friar's cell; 3) Tybalt throws down a glove; Romeo returns it to him[, not accepting the challenge]. ~~Tybalt brandishes his sword; Romeo responds in kind.~~ Mercutio throws himself at Tybalt.

1½ minutes

31. Tybalt's ~~combat~~ [duel] with Mercutio (sustained; i.e., the rhythmic underpinning against which Romeo's reactions are depicted is unbroken). [On the last chord of this number] Mercutio is wounded—pathos, a grand pause.

1 minute and 20 seconds

32. [Tybalt flees.] Mercutio dying (the death theme perhaps as a minor-key trio): 1) Expressive music [he jokes before his death]; 2) The march from No. 11, at times rhythmically formalized. Mercutio dies [at the end of the number]; a brief pause.

2½ minutes

33. Benvolio throws himself at the pensive Romeo with a wail [Romeo decides to avenge Mercutio's death]. ~~Build-up to the combat. Tybalt is killed; this time there is no pause.~~ [Tybalt enters. Romeo combats him. In contrast to Tybalt's duel with Mercutio, where the combatants fail to consider the seriousness of the situation and fight out of youthful ardor, Romeo and Tybalt battle fiercely, to the death. Romeo kills Tybalt.]

2 minutes

34. The stage fills; Benvolio, suddenly energized, wraps Romeo in a cloak and pushes him out[: "flee!"]. The Capulets ~~run in, fall to their knees before Tybalt's body in grief~~ [grieve for Tybalt] and promise vengeance. [A procession with Tybalt's body.] Musically, this number is undivided; it comprises an intensification of the tragic pulsation (the Prince's music is absent here).

1 minute and 25 seconds
TOTAL: 33 minutes

Act 3
Scene 1: Juliet's Bedchamber [Unlike the previous act, which occurs on the square, the third act unfolds in rooms. Accordingly, the orchestration is more chamber-like.]

35. Introduction ~~on the Prince's threatening music~~ [recalling the Prince's power over Romeo's destiny] (see No. 6).

1 minute and 10 seconds

36. Curtain. Predawn haziness. Romeo and Juliet behind the bed curtain (from No. 29). [In order to avoid a misleading impression, the composer attempted to make the music clean and bright.]

1 minute and 20 seconds

37. Pas de deux (the nursemaid at the end). [Romeo and Juliet's farewell before their parting. At the end of the number Romeo departs.]

4½–4¾ minutes

38. The nursemaid forewarns Juliet that her parents and Paris are coming; Juliet goes behind the bed curtain to change. They enter and report to Juliet that Paris is her suitor (he presents her with a bouquet). The music: ½-minute approach to the minuet from No. 10, modestly scored, lasting 1 minute.

2 minutes

39. Juliet's hysteria. ~~Her father shows Paris the door and rushes to her (her father remains to some extent comically good-natured).~~ [Juliet does not want to marry Paris; she weeps; she becomes angry. She is small, powerless, and despondent. During this scene her parents gingerly move Paris away. Juliet's father orders her to marry Paris, "or you are not my daughter." Her parents exit.] The music: 1 minute hysteria; 1 minute of Juliet with her father.

2 minutes

40. ~~Juliet's father and mother (and the nursemaid) exit.~~ [Juliet alone. She decides to go to Laurence. Curtain.]

1½ minutes

41. ~~The room is vacated (½ minute); interlude (1 minute); Juliet goes to Laurence; she wants to stab herself (½ minute).~~ [Interlude for change of decor.]

1 minute and 20 seconds

Scene 2: At Friar Laurence's

42. Laurence suggests the sleeping potion (No. 26). Juliet's preparedness, calmness, even elation. [Juliet leaves, having become a tragic figure.]

3¾ minutes

43. Interlude [for change of decor].

1 minute and 20 seconds

Scene 3: Juliet's Bedchamber Again

44. [Juliet informs her parents of her preparedness to marry Paris.] Juliet, her mother, and her girlfriends fit the wedding dress. Juliet

dispatches everyone, respectfully kissing her mother's hands (the music from No. 12: Juliet and Paris).

1¼–1½ minutes

45.   Juliet alone with her hourglass: the death theme. [Dance with the poison: "I drink for you, Romeo!"] She ~~drinks the poison, instantly reels~~ [drinks, becomes drowsy, drinks twice more, weakens] and falls onto her bed [(or just short of it)], pulling down the bed curtain (1½ + ½ minutes of expiring and ½ minute with the stage empty).

4 minutes

46.   [The quiet, happy sound of a mandolin orchestra is heard from the wings.] Entrance of Paris and others to (and with) an orchestra of mandolins and trumpets, followed by pizzicato orchestral chords and the trio from No. 10. [According to custom, Paris comes with a gift-bearing retinue to rouse his bride on the day of their wedding.]

1 minute and 25 seconds

47.   [Paris has brought an emerald.] Dance of the four ~~Syrian~~ [Antilles] girls [with an emerald].

1 minute and 50 seconds

48.   [Paris bestows carpets.] Dance of the three Moors [with carpets].

1 minute and 40 seconds

49.   [Paris bestows various contraband goods.] Dance of the two ~~Captains~~ [Pirates] to mandolins. [A small orchestra on the stage: mandolins, trumpets, a clarinet, a violin. The symphonic orchestra supplements it.]

1 minute and 40 seconds

50.   [Worry that Juliet has not reacted.] Juliet's mother and nursemaid attempt to rouse Juliet (½ minute); she is dead (½-minute conclusion).

1–1½ minutes

TOTAL: 23¾–26 minutes

Act 4

51.   Curtain (the music follows the pause). Romeo enters and dispatches the servant (1 minute and 40 seconds). He pulls back the cover on Juliet's bed, looks at her (20 seconds), and dances (1 minute). He wants to stab himself, but Laurence, entering, stops him. Laurence struggles with Romeo after a preparatory chord, during a pause.

4½ minutes

52.   Juliet begins to breathe.

¾–1 minute

53.   Laurence strikes a gong. Romeo at first moves to embrace Laurence, but then embraces Juliet. He carries her into a grove.

½ minute–40 seconds

54.   The stage fills with people. They seek to embrace Laurence, who gestures for them to look toward the lovers.

1½–2 minutes

55.   Entrance of Romeo and Juliet. Juliet slowly comes to herself (1½ minutes for the awakening of Juliet before Romeo's appearance). Romeo begins to dance with the reviving Juliet. Everything in their movement reflects their mood. The music is bright, but it does not attain a forte.

1½–2½ minutes

56.   [Unscripted.]

3 minutes and 20 seconds
TOTAL: 14¼ minutes

Appendix B

The *Tonya* Cue Sheet

RGALI f. 1929, op. 1, yed. khr. 104, ll. 1–4.

l. 1:

The Musical Plan:

Introduction; orchestra and titles/80–45 seconds
Public garden/140–120 seconds
Inset titles/3 × 15 = 45 seconds
Transitions between scenes/3 × 8 = 24 seconds
Accents for the dramatic situation (when Tonya is left at the station)/100–80 seconds
German arrival at the station and Tonya's murder/100–80 seconds
Scene in the Soviet dugout; Vasya on the telephone/60–50 seconds
Destruction of the German tanks; explosions in the public garden and on the square/60–50 seconds
Soviet troops arrive in the town/50 seconds
Tonya's grave/110–90 seconds
The offensive continues; finale/60–50 seconds
Approximate length of the music: 830–680 seconds
It is assumed that all of these approximate durations will be precisely determined in 5–6 days.

l. 2:

Shot Sequences:

The Russian People Abandon the Town/95.5 seconds
Tikhon Petrovich walks out of the station (forgetting the picture of Gorky)/16 seconds
Tikhon Petrovich walks onto the railway platform/8.5 seconds

Tikhon Petrovich says: "We'll be back"/6.5 seconds

Pullback from the railway platform (and the train carriage)/8.5 seconds

Tonya rouses from her fainting spell/4.5 seconds

Tonya goes to the telephone to call Tikhon Petrovich/15.5 seconds

Distant shot: the train departs/6.5 seconds

Tonya telephones Tikhon Petrovich and calls out: "Tikhon Petrovich! Tikhon Petrovich!"/14 seconds

The telephone rings at the empty duty post/2.5 seconds

Tonya, frightened to be alone, rises to leave/14 seconds

96.5 seconds

The Dugout

Vasya asks: "Who's on the telephone?"/3 seconds

Tonya answers: "The operator on duty"/2.5 seconds

Vasya exclaims: "Tonya! Could that be you, Tosha?"/4.5 seconds

The commanders ask in wonder: "Sister, wife?"/2.5 seconds

Vasya continues talking to Tonya: "You're in the office—how can this be? They told me...they told me you'd left."/11 seconds

Tonya (in tears) says: "My Vasik, it's you, and I've been afraid. I thought I was alone."/13 seconds

36.5 seconds

The Soviet Artillery

The cannons are raised/16.5 seconds

The Dugout

Vasya falls tensely silent/3.5 seconds

Tonya says: "The enemy's weapons are situated on the square; they have to be destroyed immediately...do so."/12 seconds

Vasya informs the colonel in the dugout: "I have a report that a German battery has been positioned on the square." Colonel: "Neutralize it." Vasya: "Yes sir."/8.5 seconds

Vasya says to Tonya: "Lie on the floor, you hear?"/9.5 seconds

Tonya remains standing in the shadows/2.5 seconds

Vasya sits down and begins checking coordinates/3.5 seconds

Chief of staff (to the commander): "I think he should be replaced." The commander answers: "Captain Pavlov, fulfill your duty."/9 seconds

l. 20b.:

Vasya checks numbers and takes the telephone receiver/5 seconds

Weapons are shown being readied for use/7 seconds

Vasya closes his eyes and orders: "Fire!"/3 seconds

The weapons are ready to be fired/11.5 seconds

The weapons fire/2 seconds

Tonya stands. The whistle of a flying mortar and a resounding explosion are heard/2.5 seconds

The window shatters/1 second

An explosion near Tonya; she is thrown back/4.5 seconds

Tonya takes the telephone/4.5 seconds

Vasya waits.../1.5 seconds

The weapons fire/1.5 seconds

Rout of the Germans on the square/6.5 seconds

Tonya says to Vasya: "Good, Vasik, well done... Don't fear, nothing will happen to me... Keep beating them!"/18.5 seconds

After Tonya's death:

Vasya cries out: "Tonya!"/2.5 seconds

Vasya cries out again: "Tonya, Tonya..."/2 seconds

Vasya takes the receiver and, with malice and hatred, orders: "Fire!"/2.5 seconds

The weapons fire/2 seconds

A mortar explodes on the square/2 seconds

A German descends the staircase and jots something down on a pad/4.5 seconds

Vasya twice orders "Fire!"/3.5 seconds

The weapons fire twice/3.5 seconds

Introduction to the song

An officer is blown up/4.5 seconds

An officer is killed/3.5 seconds

Song

A series of explosions on the square/6.5 seconds

In the dugout, Vasya reports: "Task completed."/7.5 seconds

Against the background of the military material an inset title appears about the attack

The attack

Another inset title about the town's occupation

The flag is raised on the flagstaff/12 seconds

l. 3:

Farewell from Katya

Katya lays a hand on Tonya's shoulder/11 seconds

Katya departs/4 seconds

Tonya is left alone/22 seconds

Farewell from Anya

Anya kisses Tonya/15 seconds

Anya departs/6.5 seconds

Tonya is left alone a second time; she weeps/6.5 seconds

This music flows intact into the military music of the inset title/8 seconds

Important Notes:

1. For the "Russian People" Episode

The first musical segment should last right up to the beginning of the noise of the departing train carriage, that is, the length of the segment should be 29 seconds.

The second musical segment should flow directly out of the distant signal of the train, seen departing in a distant shot. The second segment lasts 30 seconds (Nos. 8–10).

2. For the "Dugout" Episode

The first musical segment (36 seconds) is required for Vasya and Tonya's encounter (recognition on the telephone). The encounter begins with Vasya's question: "Who's on the telephone?" The music's basic character should suit that of the plot. Vasya's heart fills with joy upon contact with Tonya but at the same time he worries about her fate. Joy. Agitation. Worry.

The music for the second episode in the dugout (84 seconds) begins with Tonya's verbal instruction to detonate the enemy's weapons. (She speaks firmly, but warmly, quietly.) The music concludes after the shattering of the window in the telephone office. The music's character: tension before a decisive, critical moment, agitation, stress, empathy with Tonya. The tension develops and culminates with the shattering of the window in Tonya's room, throwing her back.

The third musical segment (22 seconds) is required for the moment when Tonya, weakened by the incident, goes to the telephone and praises Vasya's attack in a quiet, faint voice.

3. For the "Song" Episode

The song arises out of the din of our exploding mortars.

A pause follows the song, when the flag is shown.

l. 30b.:

4. For the "Tonya's Grave" Episode

The music begins 2–3 seconds before the long shot for the scene at Tonya's grave. It might comprise an accented trumpet overture.

A break in the music occurs between the fifth and sixth segments in the narrative.

The actual musical finale begins 6–7 seconds into the fifth segment.

l. 4:

Tonya's Grave

Long shot: the banner is lowered/15 seconds
Flowers on the grave/6.5 seconds
Grave marker with the inscription: "Tonya Pavlova. 19 years old. Died heroically at her post."/7 seconds
The commanders salute/4.5 seconds
The colonel strides to the grave and affixes a medal to it/9.5 seconds
Vasya stands and salutes/5 seconds
The colonel, having affixed the medal, moves back to the side/13.5 seconds
The large grave marker bearing the inscription, with the honor guard at rear/2.5 seconds
The banner is slowly raised/11.5 seconds
The troops depart. Vasya stands in the foreground/9.5 seconds
Vasya stays behind alone/3 seconds
Vasya approaches the grave/13 seconds
Vasya takes a photograph from his pocket/11 seconds
The photograph comes to life/4.5 seconds
Tonya speaks: "Vasik, you're doing swell, keep beating them, beat them!"/11 seconds
Close-up of Tonya at the end/6.5 seconds
Inset title: "End of the film"/3 seconds

136.5 seconds

Note:
The finale begins 6–7 seconds into the fifteenth segment.
A *break* marks the start of the sixth segment.

Notes for the Song:
At the end of page 2 of the itemized segments, the plan for the song is as follows: it begins after a robust introduction to the segment in which Vasya orders "Fire" and mortars explode in sequence on the square. We will name this segment: "Vasya finishes off the enemy."
The song begins soon after the twelfth segment. The song's length is not shown; it will last as long as needed for the segment.
A "break" occurs in the sixteenth segment during the flag raising.

Notes for "Tonya's Grave":
The music for Tonya's grave begins immediately after the flag is raised.

Notes

ABBREVIATIONS

AVP RF	Archive of External Politics of the Russian Federation (Arkhiv Vneshney Politiki Rossiyskoy Federatsii)
GARF	State Archive of the Russian Federation (Gosudarstvennïy Arkhiv Rossiyskoy Federatsii)
LPA	London Prokofiev Archive
MB	Malcolm Brown
RGAE	Russian State Archive of Economics (Rossiyskiy Gosudarstvennïy Arkhiv Ekonomiki)
RGALI	Russian State Archive of Literature and Art (Rossiyskiy Gosudarstvennïy Arkhiv Literaturï i Iskusstva)
RGASPI	Russian State Archive of Social-Political History (Rossiyskiy Gosudarstvennïy Arkhiv Sotsial'no-Politicheskoy Istorii)
RNB	Russian National Library (Rossiyskaya Natsional'naya Biblioteka)
TsGALI SPb	Central State Archive of Literature and Art of St. Petersburg (Tsentral'nïy Gosudarstvennïy Arkhiv Literaturï i Iskusstva Sankt-Peterburga)

INTRODUCTION

1. V[adim] Gayevskiy, *Dom Petipa* (Moscow: Artist. Rezhissyor. Teatr, 2000), 265; N[ina] Berberova, *Kursiv moy: Avtobiografiya* (Moscow: Soglasiye, 1996), 407. Berberova claims that, during his time in America, Prokofiev often said: " 'There's no place for me here, while Rachmaninoff is still alive, and he will perhaps live for another ten or fifteen years. Europe is inadequate for me; moreover I don't wish to be in America.' "

2. Francis Maes, *A History of Russian Music: From Kamarinskaya to Babi Yar* (Berkeley: University of California Press, 2002), 318.

3. Gayevskiy, *Dom Petipa*, 265.

4. Alfred Schnittke, "On Prokofiev," in *A Schnittke Reader*, ed. Alexander Ivashkin; trans. John Goodliffe (Bloomington: Indiana University Press, 2002), 62–63.

5. Sergey Prokof'yev, *Dnevnik 1907–1933*, ed. Svyatoslav Prokof'yev, 2 vols. (Paris: sprkv, 2002). Part of the 1927 diary has been published in English. See Prokofiev, *Soviet Diary 1927 and Other Writings*, ed. and trans. Oleg Prokofiev (Boston: Northeastern University Press 1991), 3–157.

6. Prokof'yev, *Dnevnik 1907–1933*, 2:275 (July 30, 1924, entry).

7. Ibid., 2:377.

8. David Nice, *Prokofiev: From Russia to the West 1891–1935* (New Haven: Yale University Press, 2003).

9. "Postanovleniye Politbyuro TsK RKP(b) o vozmozhnosti priyezda v SSSR S. S. Prokof'yeva i I. F. Stravinskogo. 21 iyulya 1925 g.," in *Vlast' i khudozhestvennaya intelligentsiya: Dokumentï TsK RKP(b)–VKP(b), VChK–OGPU–NKVD, o kul'turnoy politike. 1917–1953 gg.*, comp. and introd. Andrey Artizov and Oleg Naumov; ed. A. N. Yakovlev (Moscow: Mezhdunarodnïy fond "Demokratiya," 2002), 58.

10. RGASPI f. 142, op. 1, d. 460, ll. 8–9. The letter dates from February 1925.

11. RGALI f. 2009, op. 2, yed. khr. 4. Lunacharsky forwarded his August 3, 1925, instruction to Boleslav Yavorsky (1878–1942), who forwarded it in turn to Bryusova, his disciple. Novitsky (1888–1971) was a theater scholar by training; Yavorsky and Bryusova were music theorists.

12. Prokof'yev, *Dnevnik 1907–1933*, 2:339 (July 12, 1925).

13. Ibid., 2:347.

14. In places the choreography was "expressive and forceful," Prokofiev recalled in his diary, "but in other places it was disagreeable and disrespectful of the music: forte and piano counterpoint in the ballet, but in four or eight [counts], while I avoid square-ness. I essentially see the first act for the first time. The orchestra didn't play badly, but without particular force. The climatic buildup toward the end—devised by Massine, Yakulov, and me—was a success. I go out to bow, unhurriedly (would there be political heckling? There wasn't)." Ibid., 2:566.

15. W. M., "Factory Life Ballet: Music and Machinery," *Daily Mail*, July 6, 1927, p. 9.

16. Prokof'yev, *Dnevnik 1907–1933*, 2:49 (October 30, 1919).

17. "Before going out to play my [Third Piano Concerto of 1921] I begin to get stage-fright. I work at it a bit and manage to calm down. Just the same I cannot take too light a view of the situation: I am in Moscow, where they've been looking forward so intensely to seeing me, and—worst of all—where they know my concerto so intimately I dare not play it badly." Prokofiev, *Soviet Diary 1927 and Other Writings*, 29.

18. Ibid., 79.

19. Ibid., 93.

20. Communist International.

21. From 1935 to 1937, Arens would serve as the Soviet Counsel General in New York, after which he was recalled to Moscow, arrested, charged with espionage and involvement in counterrevolutionary activities, and executed.

22. Prokof'yev, *Dnevnik 1907–1933*, 2:714 (June 22, 1929).

23. Prokofiev, *Soviet Diary 1927 and Other Writings*, 153 (March 22).

24. N[ataliya] P. Savkina, "Nekotorïye materialï o zarubezhnom periode zhizni S. S. Prokof'yeva," in *Russkiye muzïkal'nïye arkhivï za rubezhom/Zarubezhnïye muzïkal'nïye arkhivï v Rossii*, ed. I. V. Brezhneva and G. M. Malinina (Moscow: Moskovskaya gosudarstvennaya konservatoriya, 2000), 52. For further details, including quotations from Prokofiev's letters to his relatives, see Nice, *Prokofiev: From Russia to the West 1891–1935*, 233–34, 251–52, and 301.

25. Savkina, "Nekotorïye materialï o zarubezhnom periode zhizni S. S. Prokof'yeva," 52.

26. Ibid., 53.

27. Information from Robert Le Cabec, of the Préfecture de Police in Paris, as related to MB on November 7, 1969. Le Cabec supplied the details of Prokofiev's and his wife's residences in France, their French *certificats d'identité*, and their Soviet passports.

28. Yelena Pol'dyayeva, "Prokof'yev i russkaya emigratsiya v Parizhe 20–x godov," in *Sergey Prokof'yev: Pis'ma, vospominaniya, stat'i*, ed. M. P. Rakhmanova (Moscow: Gosudarst-vennïy tsentral'nïy muzey muzïkal'noy kul'turï im. M. I. Glinki, 2007), 263.

29. Letter from Nikolay Myaskovsky to Prokofiev dated May 30, 1928, in *S. S. Prokof'yev i N. Ya. Myaskovskiy: Perepiska*, ed. D. B. Kabalevskiy (Moscow: Izdatel'stvo "Sovetskiy kompozitor," 1977), 279.

30. Amy Nelson, "The Struggle for Proletarian Music: RAPM and the Cultural Revolution," *Slavic Review* 59:1 (Spring 2000): 129.

31. Yu. Keldïsh, "Balet 'Stal'noy skok' i yego avtor—Prokof'yev," *Proletarskiy muzïkant* 6 (1929): 12–19.

32. D. Gachev, "O 'Stal'nom skoke' i direktorskom naskoke," 1929, excerpted in *Sergey Prokof'yev 1891–1991: Dnevnik, pis'ma, besedï, vospominaniya*, ed. M. E. Tarakanov (Moscow: Izdatel'stvo "Sovetskiy kompozitor," 1991), 200.

33. Ibid., 201.

34. The opera, which concerns demonic possession and religious persecution, was not staged in Prokofiev's lifetime. He found the work difficult to compose. In the midst of a 1926 overhaul of the ostinato-driven score, he confessed: "With Christian Science I have become entirely detached from this storyline, and hysteria and devilry no longer attract me" (*Dnevnik 1907–1933*, 2:425). Two months afterward, he reached a creative impasse, half-seriously joking that he either had to abandon his religion or abandon the opera that had subverted it: "Conclusion? Toss *The Fiery Angel* into the stove" (ibid., 2:439). Placing hopes for a 1927 production on Bruno Walter, the director of the Berlin Städtische Oper, he turned warily back to the now sacrilegious score, but the task of reshaping the scenario, having the text translated, and orchestrating the music extended past the contractual dead-line. Walter, under pressure to reduce the foreign content of his repertoire, used the delay as a pretext to cancel the staging, and then accused Prokofiev of failing to support him in his battle against dilettante nationalism. Upon hearing about the cancellation from his agent, Prokofiev "became distressed, even bitter, but Christian Science soon calmed me down and dispelled my ire" (ibid., 2:596). His suspicion that *The Fiery Angel* was somehow cursed increased in 1930, when Giulio Gatti-Casazza, the director of the Metropolitan Opera, changed his mind about producing it (ibid., 2:764).

35. Ibid., 2:731 (November 11) and 733 (November 14).

36. Ibid., 2:736.

37. On the origins of the Union of Soviet Composers, see Kiril Tomoff, *Creative Union: The Professional Organization of Soviet Composers, 1939–1953* (Ithaca, N.Y.: Cornell University Press, 2006), 13–26.

38. *S. S. Prokof'yev i N. Ya. Myaskovskiy: Perepiska*, 393; also quoted in Nice, *Prokofiev: From Russia to the West 1891–1935*, 303.

39. Prokof'yev, *Dnevnik 1907–1933*, 2:829.

40. Stephen D. Press, *Prokofiev's Ballets for Diaghilev* (Aldershot, U.K.: Ashgate, 2006), 71, 206, and 229–30.

41. Prokof'yev, *Dnevnik 1907–1933*, 2:817.

42. Aleksandr Afinogenov, "Yevropa nashikh dney," RGALI f. 2172, op. 1, yed. khr. 114.

43. One such Proletkult figure was Aleksandr Tarasov-Rodionov (1885–1938), a dilettantish Soviet writer known primarily for *Chocolate* (*Shokolad*, 1922), a parable of ideological purification. Following service in the Revolution and civil war, Tarasov-Rodionov became a strident member of the Russian Association of Proletarian Writers. The Parisian newspaper *Vozrozhdeniye* and Berlin newspaper *Nash vek* place him in Berlin in early December 1931, where he arranged an interview with Vladimir Nabokov. The interview turned into a courtship, with Tarasov-Rodionov extolling the virtues of Soviet life. Nabokov rebuffed the overture, but he claimed that Tarasov-Rodionov had success courting Prokofiev. See Brian Boyd, *Vladimir Nabokov: The Russian Years* (Princeton: Princeton University Press, 1990), 375; and Vladimir Nabokov, *Strong Opinions* (New York: McGraw-Hill, 1973), 97–98. However, there exists no primary source evidence of contact between Tarasov-Rodionov and Prokofiev in Berlin or anywhere else, with the remotely possible exception of a note to the composer from June 13, 1929, in the hand of "A. Tarasoff": it concerns the viewing of an apartment in Paris (LPA binder 21, p. 41). It is extremely unlikely that Stalinist officials would have dispatched such a minor figure to broker Prokofiev's return. The task fell to others.

44. This and the following quotations in the paragraph from Prokof'yev, *Dnevnik 1907–1933*, 2:803.

45. Ibid., 2:810 (July 5, 1932).

46. RGALI f. 2172, op. 1, yed. khr. 114, l. 65.

47. Information in this paragraph from "Prokofiev and Atovmyan: Correspondence, 1933–1952," comp. and introd. Nelly Kravetz, in *Prokofiev and His World*, ed. Simon Morrison (Princeton: Princeton University Press, 2008), 190–91.

48. Levon Atovm'yan, *Vospominaniya* [typescript], chap. 1, p. 33. I am grateful to Nelly Kravetz for introducing me to the author's daughter, Svetlana Merzhanova-Atovmyan (1926–2007), and for allowing me to quote from this document, which she is preparing for Russian-language publication along with other Atovmyan family materials. Those sections concerning Shostakovich have been published under the title "Iz vospominaniy," *Muzïkal'naya akademiya* 4 (1997): 67–77.

49. Atovm'yan, *Vospominaniya* [typescript], chap. 1, p. 33.

50. Prokof'yev, *Dnevnik 1907–1933*, 2:815.

51. Atovm'yan, *Vospominaniya* [typescript], chap. 1, p. 39.

52. LPA binder 34, p. 3.

53. Besides the Bolshoy Theater and Belgoskino, Gusman worked for the official Central Committee newspaper *Pravda* and the film production company Mezhrabpom-Rus, which was funded out of the Comintern budget. From 1934 to 1937 he served as a repertoire programmer for the All-Union Radio Committee and the Committee on Arts Affairs.

54. In 1934, for example, Gusman commissioned a *Collective Farm Suite* (*Kolkhoznaya syuita*), a four-part *Dance Suite* (*Tantseval'naya syuita*), a five-part suite from the score for *Lieutenant Kizhe*, and a seven-part suite from the incidental music for *Egyptian Nights* (*Yegipetskiye nochi*)—all on behalf of the Radio Committee. The first of the potential opera subjects he brought to Prokofiev's attention was *A Story of a Simple Thing* (*Rasskaz o prostoy veshchi*, 1924) by Boris Lavrenyov (real surname Sergeyev, 1891–1959), a civil war adventure about a much-feared Bolshevik who conspires to liberate a town of counterrevolutionaries. In a May 30, 1933, diary entry, Prokofiev recalls Gusman reading the outline of a libretto to him: "[It] is not a bad start (conflict between obligation to the Party and consideration for another person), but there are too few elements. More needs to be brought in about social life and surrounding events. We

sit and improvise for two hours; it comes out better—an operatic subject could be made of it" (*Dnevnik 1907–1933*, 2:836). Prokofiev did not actually compose the opera, but he considered doing so more than once.

55. I. Rummel', a member of the film crew, recalls meeting with Prokofiev at his Leningrad hotel to convince him of the merits of the project, claiming that the composer at first refused to take part in it, since "his time was booked long in advance and he had never written for film." Rummel' claims that he needed "to 'seduce' Sergey Sergeyevich with details of the scenario and persuaded him to read the text. In a day or two he agreed to meet with the filmmakers—the scenario interested him." "Iz istorii 'Poruchika Kizhe,'" *Sovetskaya muzïka* 11 (1964): 69.

56. Prokof'yev, *Dnevnik 1907–1933*, 2:816–17.

57. Before writing the novella, which is titled *Second Lieutenant Kizhe* (*Podporuchik Kizhe*), Tinyanov wrote a silent film script on the subject for the director Sergey Yutkevich (1904–85). This film was not made.

58. Yury Tynyanov [Tinyanov], *Lieutenant Kijé/Young Vitushishnikov*, trans. and introd. Mirra Ginsburg (Boston: Eridanos Press, 1990), xxi.

59. See M. B. Yampol'skiy, "'Poruchik Kizhe' kak teoreticheskiy fil'm," in *Tinyanovskiy sbornik: Vtorïye Tinyanovskiye chteniya* (Riga: Zinatne, 1986), 28–43.

60. Prokof'yev, *Dnevnik 1907–1933*, 2:826.

61. The song is titled "The Little Gray Dove Sighs" (Stonet sizïy golubochek).

62. Prokof'yev, *Dnevnik 1907–1933*, 2:835 (May 27, 1933).

63. The three parcels in question are dated July 13, August 22, and September 13, 1933. In the cover letters, Prokofiev describes the structure and scoring of the now-lost score in minute detail. His outline of the music for the opening shot sequence is typical: "The drumming at the beginning comprises three parts. Part 1—32 seconds of drumming, *pianissimo*. Part 2—40 seconds, flutes with drums, then military music in the distance, then flutes and drums again. Part 3—16 seconds, drums alone. They start a little louder and decline to nothing. 88 seconds in all. If it needs to be lengthened or shortened, this can be done in two places, the first before number [2], where one and the same figure repeats over a span of four measures. It can be repeated twice instead of four times, or from 5–8 times. The second place is in part 3, number [5]; here too a few measures can be lengthened or shortened. The tempo is [quarter note] = 120; in other words each measure lasts 2 seconds, thus it won't be hard for you to calculate an extension or abbreviation. Drums of the Pavel-era type, old and new, must be played with wooden sticks. The entrance of the piccolo and flute is marked *piano*; they don't actually play as such, but sound, as it were, from the distance. The brass orchestra, number 3, sounds in particular from the distance." LPA binder 34, p. 210.

64. Grigoriy Kozintsev describes one of the changes: "The scenario of 'Second Lieutenant Kizhe' included a scene of Pavel I horseback riding. Rumors of the autocrat's departure flew around the city. Shops closed, frightened passers-by dashed behind gates. Locks clicked in doors, windows were curtained. The city deadened. And then the emperor came charging up the empty avenues of St. Petersburg, furiously spurring his horse.

The scene did not have a direct bearing on the plotline. The director calculated the length of footage and, explaining that the scenario was too long, decided to abbreviate the riding shots." "Tinyanov v kino," in *Vospominaniya o Yu. Tinyanove: Portretï i vstrechi*, ed. Veniamin Kaverin (Moscow: Sovetskiy pisatel', 1983), 263.

65. See "Otchyot predsedatelya kinokomissii Orgbyuro TsK VKP(b) A. I. Stetskogo o rabote kinokomissii. 7 oktyabrya [1933 g.]," in *Kremlyovskiy kinoteatr 1928–1953. Dokumentï*, comp. K. M. Anderson, L. V. Maksimenkov, L. P. Kosheleva, and L. A. Rogovaya; introd.

L. V. Maksimenkov; ed. G. L. Bondareva (Moscow: ROSSPEN, 2005), 218. The film created political tensions within Belgoskino. The scenarist B. Brodyansky accused Tinyanov of loading *Lieutenant Kizhe* with "formalist" artifices (A-va, "'Skromnitsï' iz Belgoskino," *Kino [Moskva]*, February 10, 1934, p. 2).

66. Prokofiev, *Soviet Diary 1927 and Other Writings*, 296. This quotation comes from a short autobiography written by Prokofiev in 1941 at the request of the journal *Sovetskaya muzïka*.

67. LPA binder 36, p. 222.

68. N. Otten, "Poruchik Kizhe," *Kino (Moskva)*, January 10, 1934, p. 3. The review is based on a closed showing of the film, which opened to the public on March 7, 1934.

69. A. Petrovich, "'Poruchik Kizhe' (Novïy fil'm Belgoskino)," *Izvestiya*, March 11, 1934, p. 4.

70. M. Bleyman and Il. Trauberg, "'Poruchik Kizhe,'" *Leningradskaya pravda*, March 9, 1934, p. 4. The authors tersely declare that "S. Prokofiev's piquant and expressive music [for the film] is written with insufficient clarity."

71. Prokof'yev, *Dnevnik 1907–1933*, 2:826 (April 21, 1933).

72. RGALI f. 1929, op. 1, yed. khr. 332.

73. Ye. Dolinskaya, "Tema s variatsiyami–puteshestviyami (iz arkhivov Moskovskoy konservatorii)," in *Otechestvennaya muzïkal'naya kul'tura XX veka. K itogam i perspektivam. Nauchno-publitsisticheskiy sbornik*, ed. M. E. Tarakanov (Moscow: Moskovskaya gosudarstvennaya konservatoriya im. Chaykovskogo, 1993), 77.

74. See, for example, Vadim Baranov, "Mnogo gor'kogo: Zhizn' i smert' velikogo pisatelya na televizionnom ekrane," *Literaturnaya gazeta*, December 10–16, 2003, p. 10.

75. RGALI f. 1929, op. 3, yed. khr. 32, l. 1; "On Gorky," in *S. Prokofiev: Autobiography, Articles, Reminiscences*, ed. S. Shlifstein; trans. Rose Prokofieva (Moscow: Foreign Languages Publishing House, n. d.), 102.

76. RGALI f. 1929, op. 2, yed. khr. 87, l. 6.

77. "The Path [*sic*] of Soviet Music" (Puti sovetskoy muzïki), in *S. Prokofiev: Autobiography, Articles, Reminiscences*, 99–100; Nice, *Prokofiev: From Russia to the West 1891–1935*, 320–21.

78. Leo Tolstoy, *What Is Art?* trans. Richard Pevear and Larissa Volokhonsky (London: Penguin Books, 1995), 164. Tolstoy, who was something of a musicophobe, would not have been satisfied with Prokofiev's "new simplicity"; he polemicized in Rousseau-like fashion for a direct return to folksong.

79. Prokof'yev, *Dnevnik 1907–1933*, 2:828.

80. Atovm'yan, *Vospominaniya* [typescript], chap. 1, p. 60.

81. Prokof'yev, *Dnevnik 1907–1933*, 2:827 (April 23–27, 1933).

82. Ibid., 2:834.

CHAPTER 1

1. N. Zhukovskiy, *Na diplomaticheskom postu* (Moscow: Politizdat, 1973), 257–59.

2. Lina Prokofiev, interview with MB, July 18, 1968. In a trifling 1961 memoir, Lina added that "In Paris, we often visited the Potyomkins at the Soviet Embassy, attending dinners and receptions with very interesting people." Lina Prokof'yeva, "Iz vospominaniy," in *Sergey Prokof'yev: Stat'i i materiali*, ed. I. V. Nest'yev and G. Ya. Edel'man (Moscow: Muzïka, 1965), 217.

3. Prokofiev's Soviet passport requests were initially handled by the Commission for Academic Theaters (Komissiya po akademicheskim teatram). Following the dismantling of the Commission in the early 1930s, the applications were handled by the theaters themselves. The Bolshoy Theater requested passports for Prokofiev on September 21 and December 29, 1935, explaining to the Foreign Department of the Moscow Regional Administration

(Mosoblispolkom) that the composer was scheduled to perform abroad; a similar request was made on June 5, 1935, for a passport for Lina to travel to Paris to "settle affairs." During the entire period Prokofiev was working on *Romeo and Juliet* for the Bolshoy Theater. See RGALI f. 648, op. 2, yed. khr. 982, ll. 19, 34, and 68.

4. His status caused him problems at European checkpoints. On April 3, 1934, for example, a border official at Strasbourg sent a letter to the Préfecture de Police in Paris reporting that when Prokofiev crossed the border into Germany he presented a Soviet passport issued in Moscow on October 14, 1933, valid for a year, which contained British, Italian, German, and Swiss visas. The official noted the date of Prokofiev's *certificat d'identité*—December 20, 1933—and the fact that it bore a notice indicating its invalidation the moment the bearer entered the Soviet Union. The official suggested that because Prokofiev was known in several nations he should perhaps be investigated by the French authorities. (Information from Robert Le Cabec, of the Préfecture de Police, as related to MB on November 7, 1969.)

5. Gabriel (Gavriil Grigorovich) Paitchadze to MB, unpublished letter of December 24, 1962.

6. Ibid.

7. Ibid.

8. For a description of Prokofiev's life in Polenovo, see Sviatoslav Prokofiev, "The House in Which *Romeo and Juliet* Was Born," *Three Oranges: The Journal of the Serge Prokofiev Foundation* 11 (May 2006): 24–27.

9. The most thorough discussion of the conception and reception of the ballet is by Deborah Annette Wilson, "Prokofiev's *Romeo and Juliet*: History of a Compromise" (Ph. D. diss., Ohio State University, 2003). I am grateful to the author for recently sending a copy of her work, which goes into much more specific technical detail about the ballet than what is given here.

10. The theater would soon be renamed, after Sergey Kirov, Secretary of the Leningrad City and Regional Committees of the Communist Party, who was assassinated on December 1, 1934. The crime was crudely carried out by a disaffected former Party member, Leonid Nikolayev, with suspected covert backing from the Kremlin. Claiming that the crime was part of a Trotskyite scheme to topple his government, Stalin made it pretext for a campaign of political persecution.

11. Prokofiev's hopes for a staging of these two operas were misplaced. Myaskovsky essentially ruled out the possibility in a January 24, 1935, letter: "Asafyev came over recently. I inquired about your Leningrad dealings. He's pessimistic. He believes that, within the ranks of the Leningrad [Composers'] Union (and everywhere it—the Union—can exert influence: the Philharmonic and, principally, the theaters), they are terribly afraid of you and will do everything possible to exclude you. He reckons, moreover, that your projects for the [Mariinsky] Theater are built on sand, and that you are further spoiling things by insisting on a staging of your various earlier works (*Le Pas d'Acier*)." *S. S. Prokof'yev i N. Ya. Myaskovskiy: Perepiska*, 434; partly quoted in Nice, *Prokofiev: From Russia to the West 1891–1935*, 323.

12. RGALI f. 1929, op. 3, yed. khr. 44, l. 3.

13. RGALI f. 1929, op. 3, yed. khr. 21 (Prokof'yev and M[ira] A[bramovna] Mendel'son, *Notograficheskiy spravochnik proizvedeniy S. Prokof'yeva*, 1951–52), l. 21. There are several different versions of the work list at RGALI. These were typed and annotated by Prokofiev's second wife on Atovmyan's suggestion. They include Prokofiev's occasional handwritten remarks.

14. Noëlle Mann, "Background to *Romeo and Juliet*," *Three Oranges: The Journal of the Serge Prokofiev Foundation* 8 (November 2004): 25.

15. Communist Union of Youth.

16. The statement is translated by Edward Morgan in "Prokofiev's Shakespearian Period," *Three Oranges: The Journal of the Serge Prokofiev Foundation* 10 (November 2005): 5.

17. Radlov's letter requesting the termination of his employment, sent to the Director of the State Theaters, reads: "Since I neither consider it a moral obligation nor a practical benefit to work in the atmosphere of overt and shameless persecution that has been created for me within the walls of the Theater of Opera and Ballet, I ask to be released from work in the Theater." RNB f. 625, yed. khr. 351, l. 1.

18. Mutnïkh was a career military officer, heading, before his January 23, 1935, appointment to the Bolshoy Theater, the Central (Cultural) House of the Red Army (Tsentral'nïy dom Krasnoy Armii). His commissioning of *Romeo and Juliet*, together with another ballet by Asafyev (*Spartak*) and two operas, was announced at a June 17, 1935, meeting of the Bolshoy Theater repertoire board. RGALI f. 648, op. 1, yed. khr. 995, l. 117.

19. RGALI f. 1929, op. 4.

20. Prokof'yev and V[era] V[ladimirovna] Alpers, "Perepiska," in *Muzïkal'noye nasledstvo: Sborniki po istorii muzïkal'noy kul'turï SSSR*, vol. 1, ed. G. B. Bernandt, V. A. Kiselyov, and M. S. Pekelis (Moscow: Gosudarstvennoye muzïkal'noye izdatel'stvo, 1962), 427. The letter is dated July 8, 1935. The draft score (RGALI f. 1929, op. 1, yed. khr. 58) contains 56 numbers. Prokofiev indicates when he completed act 2 (July 22), act 3 (August 29), act 4 (September 7), and the introduction (September 8). The published score contains 52 numbers; act 4 was reduced in length from 6 numbers to 2.

21. *S. S. Prokof'yev i N. Ya. Myaskovskiy: Perepiska*, 440. The letter is dated September 11, 1935.

22. The plot of *The Fountain of Bakhchisaray*, an Orientalist ballet based on a Pushkin poem, unfolds in a Crimean kingdom whose despondent ruler cannot appreciate the splendor of his surroundings or his variegated harem. Besides the maudlin orchestration, Prokofiev blanched at Asafyev's implausible inclusion of a waltz in the harem scene.

23. Atovm'yan, *Vospominaniya* [typescript], chap. 1, p. 60.

24. Mann, "Background to *Romeo and Juliet*," 26.

25. Yuriy Fayer, *O sebe, o muzïke, o balete* (Moscow: Vsesoyuznoye izdatel'stvo sovetskiy kompozitor, 1970), 354.

26. Sergey Radlov, "Yunost'" teatra," *Teatr i dramaturgiya* (June 1935): 23. A variation of this same quotation is included in David Zolotnitsky, *Sergei Radlov: The Shakespearian Fate of a Soviet Director*, trans. Tatania Ganf and Natalia Egunova (New York: Harwood Academic Publishers, 1995), 115.

27. Like Piotrovsky, Dinamov became a victim of the purges.

28. RGALI f. 1929, op. 4.

29. RGALI f. 1929, op. 1, yed. khr. 66, ll. 1–2. S[vetlana] A. Petukhova reproduces the scenario largely intact in "Pervaya avtorskaya redaktsiya baleta Prokof'yeva 'Romeo i Dzhul'yetta.' Istochnikovedcheskiye problemï izucheniya" (Ph. D. diss., MGK. im. P. I. Chaykovskogo, 1997), app. 1, pp. 23–28.

30. Aleksandr Afinogenov, *Izbrannoye*, ed. K. N. Kirilenko and V. P. Koshunova, 2 vols. (Moscow: Iskusstvo, 1977), 2:318.

31. RGALI f. 1929, op. 3, yed. khr. 267, l. 1 (October 4, 1935, diary entry).

32. RNB f. 625, yed. khr. 465, l. 3.

33. RGALI f. 1929, op. 1, yed. khr. 932, no. 108 (A. Kut [Aleksandr Kutuzov], "Balet 'Romeo i Dzhul'yetta' na soveshchanii v 'Sovetskom iskusstve,'" *Sovetskoye iskusstvo*, January 29, 1936).

34. RGASPI f. 82, op. 2, d. 951, l. 1.

35. The director of the Malïy Theater in Moscow, which is located adjacent to the Bolshoy Theater, was also arrested on April 20, 1937. See *Bol'shaya tsenzura: Pisateli i zhurnalistï v Strane Sovetov. 1917–1956*, comp. L. V. Maksimenkov; ed. A. N. Yakovlev (Moscow: Mezhdunarodnïy fond "Demokratiya," 2005), 462–63.

36. Prokofiev, *Soviet Diary 1927 and Other Writings*, 299. The argument that "living people can dance, the dying cannot" came from Radlov. The director stressed that "in a ballet the most essential, expressive, and content–bearing elements must be embodied in dance and only in dance, and we, the designers of this spectacle, firmly hope that Juliet's and Romeo's parts will be ranked among the very best in our ballet repertoire." "Balet 'Romeo i Dzhul'yetta,'" *Sovetskoye iskusstvo*, June 23, 1935, p. 3.

37. "Pis'ma S. S. Prokof'yeva k P. A. Lammu," in *Sergey Prokof'yev: Vospominaniya. Pis'ma. Stat'i*, ed. M. P. Rakhmanova (Moscow: Izdatel'stvo "Deka–VS," 2004), 283 and 290: "Enclosed is act III of *Romeo* (your score, my original and additional pages with references). I'd be grateful if you filled in the holes [those sections of the piano score for which Prokofiev did not dictate the orchestration], which I stopped up with the exception of the part for the mandolin. Please also do the page with No. 51, that is, the beginning of act IV" (August 6, 1936); "Three numbers remain to be done up: two dances with mandolins (Nos. 46 and 49) and the ending—Juliet's death, No. 52" (July 27, 1938).

38. Petukhova, "Pervaya autorskaya redaktsiya baleta Prokof'yeva 'Romeo i Dzhul'yetta.' Istochnikovedcheskiye problemï izucheniya," 89–90.

39. Mary Baker Eddy, *Science and Health with Key to the Scriptures* (Boston: First Church of Christ, Scientist, 1994), 256.

40. William Shakespeare, *The Tragedy of Romeo and Juliet*, ed. Barbara A. Mowat and Paul Werstine (New York: Washington Square Press, 2004), 203.

41. It was intended for the Metropolitan Opera in New York. Prokofiev proposed revising both the libretto of the music of the 1927 version of *The Fiery Angel* in an effort to enliven the visual action. The Metropolitan Opera did not, in the end, contract the revision.

42. In the second of the three draft scenarios preserved at RGALI, the "Dance of the Two Captains" is renamed the "Dance of the Two Pirates." It was part of a trio of exotic dances associated with Paris's wooing of Juliet. "According to custom," the scenario reads, "Paris comes with a gift-bearing retinue to rouse his bride on the day of their wedding." The gifts include Syrian emeralds, Moorish carpets, and "various contraband goods." RGALI f. 1929, op. 1, yed. khr. 66, l. 6.

43. *Music for Children* (*Detskaya muzïka*). Prokofiev premiered the twelve pieces in 1936 and scored seven of them for youth orchestra in 1941 under the title *Summer Day* (*Letniy den'*). The collection is a creative riposte to the children's music composed by Schumann and Chaikovsky. See G. Shestakov, "Detskaya muzïka," in *Sergey Sergeyevich Prokof'yev*, ed. O[l'ga] Ochakovskaya (Moscow: Muzïka, 1990), 121–23.

44. The collection did not enamor the adjudicators; neither, however, did any of the other 2,186 submissions. The results from the contest were published in *Pravda* on March 29, 1936. One of Prokofiev's songs earned a second prize; another received an honorable mention. The collection comprises two songs for chorus and piano, "Partisan Zheleznyak" and "Anyutka," and four songs for solo voice and piano or unison chorus and piano: "The Country Is Growing" (Rastyot strana), "Through Snow and Fog" (Skvoz' snega i tumanï), "Beyond the Mountain" (Za goroyu), and "Song of Voroshilov" (Pesnya o Voroshilove). "Anyutka" earned the second prize award, "The Country Is Growing" honorable mention. "Partisan Zheleznyak" was performed at the March 18, 1936, opening of the Moscow Folk Arts Theater, with Prokofiev in attendance. See "Nevidannoye zrelishche," in *Prokof'yev*

o *Prokof'yeve: Stat'i, interv'yu*, ed. V. P. Varunts (Moscow: Sovetskiy kompozitor, 1991), 137.

45. Lina Prokof'yeva, "Iz vospominaniy," 218–19.

46. "Sumbur vmesto muzïki: ob opere 'Ledi Makbet Mtsenskogo uyezda' D. Shostakovicha," *Pravda*, January 28, 1936, p. 3. Leonid Maksimenkov has determined that the article was almost undoubtedly written by Kerzhentsev. See his *Sumbur vmesto muzïki: Stalinskaya kul'turnaya revolyutsiya 1936–1938* (Moscow: Yuridicheskaya Kniga, 1997), 89–112.

47. "Baletnaya fal'sh'" (Balletic Falseness), *Pravda*, February 6, 1936, p. 3.

48. The fallout from the attacks seemed to ensure that none of the composers who participated in the *Pravda* song contest earned a first-prize award. In a February 20, 1936, letter to Prokofiev, Myaskovsky speculates that the adjudicators "perhaps became scared by the uproar around the articles in *Pravda* about Shostakovich (*Lady* and *Limpid Stream*)." *S. S. Prokof'yev i N. Ya. Myaskovskiy: Perepiska*, 446.

49. Unsigned, "Na sobranii moskovskikh kompozitorov," *Pravda*, February 17, 1936, p. 3.

50. RGALI f. 1929, op. 1, yed. khr. 655, l. 1.

51. Ibid., l. 10b.

52. Ibid., l. 3.

53. Ibid., l. 2.

54. Ibid.

55. This information from a July 25, 1936, letter. See Prokof'yev and Alpers, "Perepiska," 428.

56. After the famous airman Valeriy Chkalov (1904–38), who completed a series of record–breaking flights, including a trip in 1937 from Russia to the United States over the North Pole.

57. RGALI f. 1929, op. 1, yed. khr. 655, l. 4.

58. Ibid.

59. RGALI f. 1929, op. 3, yed. khr. 21 (*Notograficheskiy spravochnik*), l. 22; Yu. Slonimskiy, "Vstrechi s Prokof'yevïm," in *Prokof'yev o Prokof'yeve: Stat'i, interv'yu*, 130.

60. Atovmyan relates: "One evening with Derzhanovsky we discussed the article 'Muddle Instead of Music.' Prokofiev asked me to obtain a copy of the piano and orchestral scores of *Lady Macbeth* for him, which I gladly did. In ten days Prokofiev returned them to me and declared: 'I looked closely at it all. The opera's dramaturgy is wonderful: each scene is constructed very successfully. Your friend orchestrated the opera splendidly and inventively. When the opportunity arises please convey my opinion to him.'" "Iz vospominaniy," 74.

61. RGALI f. 1929, op. 2, yed. khr. 87, l. 190b.

62. Atovm'yan, *Vospominaniya* [typescript], chap. 1, p. 60. Lina often sang Prokofiev's *The Ugly Duckling* (*Gadkiy utyonok*, 1914) when the two of them performed together.

63. Valentina Chemberdzhi, *V dome muzïka zhila: Memuarï o muzïkantakh* (Moscow: Agraf, 2002), 101.

64. RGALI f. 1929, op. 2, yed. khr. 208, l. 1 (letter of September 20, 1936, to Ol'ga Vasil'yevna Codina).

65. Catriona Kelly, "At Peace with the Wolf? Prokofiev's 'Official' Soviet Works for Children," *Three Oranges: The Journal of the Serge Prokofiev Foundation* 12 (November 2006): 6.

66. Natalia Sats, *Sketches from My Life*, trans. Sergei Syrovatkin (Moscow: Raduga Publishers, 1985), 218. See pp. 210–27 for a fuller description of the origins and creation of *Peter and the Wolf*.

67. RGALI f. 1929, op. 1, yed. khr. 241, l. 4.

68. Kelly, "At Peace with the Wolf? Prokofiev's 'Official' Soviet Works for Children," 7–8.

69. Linda J. Ivanits, *Russian Folk Belief* (Armonk, N.Y.: M. E. Sharpe, 1989), 68.

70. RGALI f. 1929, op. 1, yed. khr. 287, l. 160b.

71. The performance also included "The Chatterbox" (Boltun'ya), the first of Prokofiev's *Three Songs for Children* (*Tri detskiye pesni,* 1939).

72. On the following, see Nelly Kravetz, "S. Prokofiev and E. Senkar: The First Performance of the *Russian Overture* op. 72 in Israel in 1938," *Min-Ad: Israel Studies in Musicology Online* 1 (2006). Available at http://www.biu.ac.il/HU/mu/min-ad/06/Kravitz_final.pdf.

73. RGALI f. 1929, op. 3, yed. khr. 267, l. 2 (October 27, 1936, diary entry).

74. Ibid (October 31, 1936). The reason for Prokofiev's absence is unknown.

75. V[alerian] Bogdanov–Berezovskiy, "Kontsert S. Prokof'yeva," *Krasnaya gazeta,* April 17, 1937, p. 4.

76. Mark Bičurin, the director of the Regional Theater in Brno, approached Prokofiev about staging the ballet on June 15, 1937. The January 19, 1938, contract called for the theater to receive the piano score on April 1, the scenario on June 1, and the orchestral score on July 1, 1938. The production, which Prokofiev did not see, extended from December 30, 1938 to May 5, 1939 (seven performances). It was choreographed by Ivo Váňa-Psota (1908–52), who took the part of Romeo. For details of the production and its sociopolitical context, see Rudolf Pečman, "Licht im Dunkel: Zur Brünner Uraufführung von Prokofjews Ballett *Romeo and Julia,*" in *Bericht über das Internationale Symposion "Sergej Prokofjew—Aspekte seines Werkes und der Biographie." Köln 1991,* ed. Klaus Wolfgang Niemöller (Regensburg: Gustav Bosse Verlag: 1992), 251–68. The correspondence between Bičurin and Prokofiev is housed at RGALI f. 1929, op. 1, yed. khr. 852; f. 1929, op. 2, yed. khr. 155; and f. 1929, op. 3, yed. khr. 222.

77. Prokofiev received the commission from the Union of Soviet Composers for the First Suite in 1935 and the Second Suite in 1936 (he completed them both that year). The Third Suite dates from 1946.

78. RGASPI f. 82, op. 2, d. 952, l. 75.

79. RGALI f. 1929, op. 3, yed. khr. 123, l. 1; "V stengazetu Soyuza kompozitorov," in *Prokof'yev o Prokof'yeve: Stat'i, interv'yu,* 139.

80. "Vistupleniye po Bryussel'skomu radio," in *Prokof'yev o Prokof'yeve: Stat'i, interv'yu,* 146.

81. Letter of December 24, 1936, in *Selected Letters of Sergei Prokofiev,* ed. and trans. Harlow Robinson (Boston: Northeastern University Press, 1998), 320.

82. Edward Barry, "Ovation Given Prokofieff at Concert Here," *Chicago Daily Tribune,* January 22, 1937, p. 23.

83. Ibid.

84. L. A. B. et al., "What's Going On in the Arts," *Christian Science Monitor,* February 6, 1937, p. 10.

85. Vernon Duke, *Passport to Paris* (Boston: Little, Brown, 1955), 344–45.

86. In a June 19, 1937, letter from Moscow to New York, Prokofiev informs Duke: "The automobile has arrived, and—with a good chauffeur—makes life much easier, especially when spring comes and one has the opportunity to go out *ins grüne*" (*Selected Letters of Sergei Prokofiev,* 156). A RGALI record suggests that Prokofiev did not receive his own Moscow driver's license until July 16, 1938.

87. Jessie Ash Arndt, "Soviet Envoy Entertains at Musicale in Embassy," *Washington Post,* February 9, 1937, p. 12.

88. The following discussion of the Cantata uses text from Simon Morrison and Kravetz, "The *Cantata for the Twentieth Anniversary of October,* or How the Specter of Communism Haunted Prokofiev," *Journal of Musicology* 23:2 (May 2006): 227–62. This essay offers a much more comprehensive discussion of the libretto and music of the work than given here.

89. Lina Prokof'yeva, "Iz vospominaniy," 214.

90. RGALI f. 2172, op. 1, yed. khr. 191, l. 1 (letter of September 10, 1932).

91. Glinka State Central Museum of Musical Culture (Gosudarstvennïy Tsentral'nïy Muzey Muzïkal'noy Kul'turï im. M. I. Glinki), f. 33, yed. khr. 1299.

92. RGALI f. 1929, op. 1, yed. khr. 806, ll. 2–3.

93. Izraíl' Nest'yev, "O Leninskoy kantate (Iz istorii muzïkal'noy leninianï," *Sovetskaya muzïka* 4 (1970): 96. The letter dates from January 26, 1970.

94. Pierre Souvtchinsky to MB, letter of March 6, 1975.

95. RGALI f. 1929, op. 1, yed. khr. 245, l. 2. Page 4 of this file includes, recto, a portion of the Cantata libretto and, verso, Afinogenov's text for "Gennadiy's Song" (Pesnya Gennadiya), which Prokofiev renamed "The Country Is Growing" for use in his 1935 collection of mass songs.

96. Ibid., l. 1.

97. Ibid., l. 1–10b.

98. These words do not appear in the actual score of the Cantata.

99. RGALI f. 1929, op. 1, yed. khr. 245, ll. 10–13.

100. *Stenogramma soveshchaniya kompozitorov i khoduzhestvennïkh rukovoditeley muz. teatrov o podgotovke muz. proiz. k 20 letiyu Oktyabr'skoy Revolyutsii;* RGALI f. 962, op. 3, yed. khr. 270, l. 9.

101. *Planï, programmï kontsertov v svyazi s podgotovkoy k 20-letiyu Oktyabr'skoy Revolyutsii;* RGALI f. 962, op. 5, yed. khr. 74, ll. 22–23.

102. See L. Danilevich, "Porazheniye kompozitora," *Sovetskoye iskusstvo,* October 5, 1937, p. 4. I am grateful to Marina Frolova-Walker for this reference.

103. "Putevïye zametki muzïkanta," in *Prokof'yev o Prokof'yeve: Stat'i, interv'yu,* 132.

104. "Moi planï," in ibid., 142.

105. Maksimenkov, *Sumbur vmesto muzïki: Stalinskaya kul'turnaya revolyutsiya 1936–1938,* 232–35.

106. Quoted in ibid., 234.

107. P[laton] Kerzhentsev, *Zhizn' Lenina 1870–1924* (Moscow: Partizdat TsK VKPb, 1937).

108. Quoted in Maksimenkov, *Sumbur vmesto muzïki: Stalinskaya kul'turnaya revolyutsiya 1936–1938,* 235. Molotov's remark, written across the front of Kerzhentsev's letter to Tukhachevsky, is dated May 17, 1936 (RGALI f. 962, op. 10, yed. khr. 9, l. 4).

109. Marina Nest'yeva, *Sergey Prokof'yev* (Chelyabinsk: Arkaim, 2003), 146–47.

110. Quotations in this and the next paragraph from RGALI f. 1929, op. 2, yed. khr. 413, ll. 1–2.

111. Demchinsky quotes a famous slogan from a speech Stalin gave on November 17, 1935, to the First All-Union Conference of Stakhanovites.

112. RGALI f. 1929, op. 2, yed. khr. 182, l. 1.

113. Ibid.

114. The passage in question was sketched by Prokofiev in 1930, long before the commissioning of the Cantata. See RGALI f. 1929, op. 1, yed. khr. 285, l. 24.

115. Aleksandr Vasil'yevich Gauk, *Memuarï. Izbrannïye stat'i. Vospominaniya sovremennikov* (Moscow: Sovetskiy kompozitor, 1975), 94.

116. Maksimenkov, *Sumbur vmesto muzïki: Stalinskaya kul'turnaya revolyutsiya 1936–1938,* 235.

117. RGALI f. 1929, op. 2, yed. khr. 87, l. 190b. In his diary, which is preserved in fragments in the Prokofiev holdings at RGALI, Myaskovsky claims that he heard the Cantata a day earlier, on June 18, and found it "a little naive (harmonically)" (RGALI f. 1929, op. 3, yed. khr. 267, l. 2). In another, published excerpt from the diary, he writes: "Prokofiev showed the *Cantata for the Twentieth Anniversary of October*...—terrific" (O[l'ga]

P[avlovna] Lamm, *Stranitsï tvorcheskoy biografii Myaskovskogo* [Moscow: Sovetskiy kompozitor, 1989], 259).

118. "Redaktsionnïye besedï: 'Nedelya sovetskoy muzïki,'" *Sovetskaya muzïka* 1 (1968): 21.

119. Prokof'yev and Alpers, "Perepiska," 430.

120. RGALI f. 1929, op. 3, yed. khr. 24 (*Notograficheskiy spravochnik*), l. 33.

121. "Shlyu Vam staro–druzheskiy privet," comp. and ed. Galina Kopïtova, *Sovetskaya muzïka* 4 (1991): 99–100.

122. RGALI f. 1929, op. 2, yed. khr. 327, l. 5 (Western Union telegram).

123. RGALI f. 1929, op. 3, yed. khr. 24 (*Notograficheskiy spravochnik*), l. 33. The piano score of the Cantata is dated June 5, 1937, and the orchestral score September 21.

124. RGALI f. 1929, op. 2, yed. khr. 327, l. 6 (Western Union telegram).

125. RGALI f. 1929, op. 2, yed. khr. 87, l. 41.

126. RGALI f. 1929, op. 3, yed. khr. 267, ll. 2–3 (December 15, 1937, and November 29, 1938, entries).

127. "Rastsvet iskusstva," in *Prokof'yev o Prokof'yeve: Stat'i, interv'yu*, 157.

128. RGALI f. 1929, op. 2, yed. khr. 107, ll. 1–2.

129. "Yest' chelovek za stenami Kremlya, / Znayet i lyubit yego vsya zemlya / Radost' i schast'ye tvoyo ot nego / Stalin! Velikoye imya yego!"

130. "O Staline mudrom, rodnom i lyubimom, / Prekrasnuyu pesnyu slagayet narod"; "Mï Rodine sluzhim v porïve yedinom / Zatem, shtob mechta vekovaya sbïlas'."

131. In two brief reviews, praise was accorded the fifth number in the suite, "Brother for Brother" (Brat za brata), a ballad to words by Lebedev-Kumach about the death of a soldier and the pledge of his two brothers to replace him in defense of the nation. See RGALI f. 1929, op. 1, yed. khr. 943, no. 128 (A. Gal'skiy, "Pesni nashey rodinï," *Krasnaya gazeta*, November 20, 1938) and no. 129 (V. Vladimirov, "Pesni o rodine," *Sovetskoye iskusstvo*, November 20, 1938).

132. Unsigned, "Dekada sovetskoy muzïki," *Pravda*, November 30, 1938, p. 6; and unsigned, "Zaklyuchitel'nïy kontsert dekadï sovetskoy muzïki," *Pravda*, December 1, 1938, p. 6.

133. These events are related in the memoirs of her daughter, the actress Roksana Sats, in *Put' k sebe: O mame Natalii Sats, lyubvi, iskaniyakh, teatre: Povest'* (Moscow: Voskresen'ye, 1998).

134. Lina Prokofiev, interview with MB, December 20, 1982.

135. Valentina Chemberdzhi, *XX vek Linï Prokof'yevoy* (Moscow: Izdatel'skiy dom "Klassika XXI," 2008), 186. This book, a biography of Lina, includes select quotations from interviews and private letters kept at the Prokofiev family archive in Paris. The poorly edited narrative is biased against Prokofiev's second wife, Mira Mendelson, and it contains various factual errors—for example, that Prokofiev's Pushkin romances were premiered on "experimental television" in 1937, a technological impossibility (p. 184). The author, the daughter of the composer Nikolay Chemberdzhi (1903–48), befriended Lina after 1956 but remembers Mira from 1944.

136. Lina learned the news in London. "We received a letter from the children," she wrote to her mother on January 29, 1938. "It seems that the English school was closed down unexpectedly—it is most annoying and I feel rather upset about it. Now they will have to go to a Russian one" (unpublished postcard; photocopy in the possession of MB).

137. Quoted in Ekaterina Chernysheva, "Sergei Prokofiev—'Soviet' Composer," *Three Oranges: The Journal of the Serge Prokofiev Foundation* 4 (November 2002): 11–12. The letter is dated December 23, 1937. One sentence is excluded from Chernysheva's quotation: "Besides this, Heifetz is playing my Second Violin Concerto everywhere, Toscanini is conducting my *Russian* Overture, and the New York League of Composers,

the University of Chicago, and the Prokofiev Society of the University of New Hampshire have expressed a desire to greet me" (*Prokof'yev o Prokof'yeve: Stat'i, interv'yu,* 158 n. 6).

138. Of biggest concern was a long-planned performance on February 15 at the Chicago Renaissance Society. Judith Cass, "Friends Await Russian News of Prokofieff," *Chicago Daily Tribune,* January 5, 1938, p. 15.

139. AVP RF f. 162, op. 13, papka 68, d. 28, l. 25.

140. Maysky to Voroshilov, letter of February 3, 1938, in *Ivan Mikhaylovich Mayskiy: Izbrannaya perepiska s rossiyskimi korrespondentami,* ed. V. S. Myasnikov et al., 2 vols. (Moscow: Nauka, 2005), 2:68. The actual contract for the "Song of Voroshilov" is dated April 17, 1938. It specifies a work for chorus and orchestra of no longer than eight minutes, to be submitted to the Committee on Arts Affairs by April 28. Prokofiev received a hefty 3,000 rubles for the task (RGALI f. 1929, op. 1, yed. khr. 806, l. 26).

141. AVP RF f. 162, op. 13, papka 68, d. 28, l. 56.

142. "Musicale at Soviet Embassy," *Evening Star,* March 22, 1938, p. B4. Hope Ridings Miller sets the number at 300 ("Troyanovskys Present Two Soviet Musicians," *Washington Post,* March 22, 1918, p. X12).

143. "Her voice, although rich and mellow in quality, lacked in proper production." Vernon Duke to MB, unpublished letter of September 5, 1962.

144. Prokofiev drafted the March 21 Washington program in Hollywood, sending it a week in advance to the Soviet Embassy for review.

145. Miller, "Troyanovskys Present Two Soviet Musicians."

146. Warren Storey Smith, "Prokofieff Dominates Symphony," *Boston Post,* March 26, 1938, p. 8.

147. Unsigned, "Young Russia," *Time,* April 4, 1938, p. 46.

148. AVP RF f. 192, op. 5, papka 44, d. 59, l. 19. The press kit was compiled by the Haensel & Jones firm in New York.

149. Unsigned, "Prokofieff Hails Life of Artist in Soviet; With 4 Incomes, He Is Here for Concerts," *New York Times,* February 6, 1938, p. 43.

150. Arlynn Nellhaus, "Jean Cranmer Hosted Earliest DSO Artists," *Denver Post,* Roundup Section, February 26, 1978, p. 16.

151. Frances Wayne, "Prokofiev, at Piano, Moves Too Fast for Symphony Musicians," *Denver Post,* February 19, 1938, p. 7. Another review, by Anne Stein Roth, was much more generous: "Prokofieff's Work Pleases," *Rocky Mountain News,* February 19, 1938, p. 5.

152. Nellhaus, "Jean Cranmer Hosted Earliest DSO Artists," p. 16. Another critic recalled "Prokofieff's bad manners out-wolfing the wolf in *Peter and the Wolf*" (Childe Herald, "Ideas and Comment," *Rocky Mountain Herald,* December 26, 1953, p. 1).

153. Unpublished letter of March 30, 1938; photocopy in the possession of MB. The phrase "false pride" comes from Christian Science.

154. Serge Koussevitzky Archive, Music Division, box 50, folder 20, Library of Congress, Washington, D.C.

155. Unpublished letter; photocopy in the possession of MB.

156. Elizabeth Bergman, "Prokofiev on the LA Limited," in *Sergey Prokofiev and His World,* 442.

157. Lina Prokof'yeva, "Iz vospominaniy," 221.

158. She and Prokofiev also attended a tea at the home of the actor Edward G. Robinson and his wife on March 15.

159. Information from Russell Merritt ("Recharging *Alexander Nevsky:* Tracking the Eisenstein–Prokofiev War Horse," *Film Quarterly* 48:2 [Winter 1994]: 46–47 n. 11), as

corrected by Dave Smith, director of the Walt Disney Archives, in a November 29, 2005, personal communication.

160. Letter of March 7, 1938, in *Sergey Prokof'yev: Stat'i i materialï*, 222–23.

161. Letter of March 2, 1938, in *S. S. Prokof'yev i N. Ya. Myaskovskiy: Perepiska*, 456–57.

162. Ibid., 458.

163. Paitchadze to MB, unpublished letter of December 24, 1962.

164. In the aforementioned letter from Polk to Koussevitzky, Polk notes that, in 1939, he "succeeding in rekindling [Disney's] interest in the matter and received an offer from him of $1,500.00 for the use of *Peter and the Wolf*. I might add that compared to other prices paid for *Sorcerer's Apprentice*, etc., this offer was not unreasonable."

165. Duke, *Passport to Paris*, 367. In the 1968 Russian-language edition of this memoir, the final lines are adjusted: "'You know, Dima, it just occurred to me that I won't soon return to your parts…Don't you think it would be good for you to come to Russia?' 'No, I don't think so,' [I responded], smiling bravely in order to mask a strange feeling of foreboding." Dukel'skiy, *Ob odnoy prervannoy druzhbe*, 1968, quoted in Igor' Vishnevetskiy, "Pamyatka vozvrashchayushchimsya v SSSR, ili o chyom govorili Prokof'yev i Dukel'skiy vesnoy 1937 i zimoy 1938 v N'yu–Yorke," in *Sergey Prokof'yev: Vospominaniya. Pis'ma. Stat'i*, 391.

166. Berthe Malko, "Prokof'yev," unpublished 1982 typescript in the possession of MB.

167. "The two—Sergei and Lina—argued and fought continually, these arguments and fights usually ending in a flood of tears on L. I.'s part, with me in the middle." Duke to MB, unpublished letter of September 5, 1962.

168. A document filed with the Préfecture de Police in Paris on May 3, 1938, indicates that Lina resided at the Hotel Astor between April 6 and May 7 (information from Le Cabec, as related to MB, November 19, 1969).

CHAPTER 2

1. *Selected Letters of Sergei Prokofiev*, 158; translation slightly adjusted.

2. Duke, *Passport to Paris*, 436.

3. Prokof'yev, *Dnevnik 1907–1933*, 2:756.

4. Ibid., 2:755–57.

5. RGALI f. 1929, op. 1, yed. khr. 332, l.44.

6. Unpublished letter; photocopy in the possession of MB. The lesson cited is from Mary Baker Eddy's *Science and Health with Key to the Scriptures*.

7. Unsigned, "800 kopiy fil'ma 'Aleksandr Nevskiy,'" *Izvestiya*, November 29, 1938, p. 4.

8. Zdeněk Stříbrny, *Shakespeare and Eastern Europe* (Oxford: Oxford University Press, 2000), 84. The author does not identify the critic.

9. Radlov, "Nasha rabota nad 'Gamletom,'" *Krasnaya gazeta*, May 9, 1938, p. 3.

10. Eleanor Rowe, *Hamlet: A Window on Russia* (New York: New York University Press, 1976), 128.

11. Quoted in Morgan, "Prokofiev's Shakespearean Period," 8.

12. "I enclose the five songs for *Hamlet* that I orchestrated on the ship," he wrote on February 2. "Please get them into shape and send them to Radlov's theater in Leningrad." And on February 4: "I'm sending you the final march for Radlov's theater. The orchestration of the *songs* has to reach him quickly, the march less so." "Pis'ma S. S. Prokof'yeva k P. A. Lammu," 288–89.

13. This and the following quotations in the paragraph come from "O muzïke k 'Gamletu' V. Shekspira," in *Prokof'yev o Prokof'yeve: Stat'i, interv'yu*, 158. For an English-language

translation of Prokofiev's program notes, see "On the Music for Shakespeare's *Hamlet*," in *Sergei Prokofiev: Materials, Articles, Interviews*, ed. Vladimir Blok (Moscow: Progress Publishers, 1978), 33–34.

14. In a letter dated December 21, 1937, Prokofiev told Radlov: "I am sending you the songs of Ophelia and the gravedigger. I hope that they won't be difficult [to perform]. In the Ophelia songs (excluding the first) I used folk material. In the second [Ophelia] shouldn't dance during the postlude, but during the song; the postlude should be mimed. I have provided metronomic indications for the tempos: see that they are maintained" (quoted in *Prokof'yev o Prokof'yeve: Stat'i, interv'yu*, 159 n. 1). In his work list, Prokofiev reports that "part of the music of Ophelia's songs came from an English songbook (the name of the songbook is lost)." RGALI f. 1929, op. 3, yed. khr. 24 (*Notograficheskiy spravochnik*), l. 36.

15. "O muzike k 'Gamletu' V. Shekspira," 159.

16. Radlov could not depict Hamlet as a tragic hero. As Rowe argues, "To the extent that mystery and enigma play a part in any great and tragic representation of life, a Soviet tragic hero may be deemed, on purely ideological grounds, a contradiction in terms" (*Hamlet: A Window on Russia*, 127).

17. Quoted in Morgan, "Prokofiev's Shakespearean Period," 8.

18. Leonid Pinsky observes in this context: "For the Soviet researcher or director, viewer or reader, it was obvious, as a rule, that the tragic collisions in Shakespeare are 'the current age' of the bourgeois society colliding with the 'past century' of knighthood." "The Tragic in Shakespeare's Works," in *Russian Essays on Shakespeare and His Contemporaries*, ed. Alexander Parfenov and Joseph G. Price (Newark: University of Delaware Press, 1998), 40.

19. S. Tsimbal wrote, for example: "An enormous role in the drama's success belonged to the composer S. Prokofiev and the artist V. Dmitriyev. Both of them took active parts in the organization of the scenic action, and both of them can be regarded in a broad sense of the term as the co-authors of the spectacle. Prokofiev's theatrical, energetic, and satiating music became an integral part of the scenic action. [He] provided a true example of how one ought to write music for a dramatic spectacle, without appending distracting musical excerpts onto it." RGALI f. 1929, op. 1, yed. khr. 943, no. 15 ("Muzhestvo Gamleta," *Sovetskoye iskusstvo*, June 4, 1938).

20. I. Berezark, *"Gamlet" v Teatre imeni Leningradskogo Soveta. Opit analiza spektaklya* (Leningrad: L[eningradskoye] O[tdeleniye] V[serossiyskogo] T[eatral'nogo] O[bshchestva]), 56–57 and 75–76.

21. David Shearer, "Elements Near and Alien: Passportization, Policing, and Identity in the Stalinist State, 1932–1952," *Journal of Modern History* 76 (December 2004): 847.

22. Letter of May 14, 1938; RGALI f. 1929, op. 1, yed. khr. 655, l. 16.

23. Katerina Clark, *The Soviet Novel* (Bloomington: Indiana University Press, 2000).

24. Abram Tertz, "On Socialist Realism," in *The Trial Begins and On Socialist Realism*, trans. George Dennis; introd. Czeslaw Milosz (Berkeley: University of California Press, 1982), 215.

25. Gitta Hammerburg, *From the Idyll to the Novel: Karamzin's Sentimentalist Prose* (Cambridge: Cambridge University Press, 1991), 7–8. Sentimentalism informed Socialist Realism.

26. RGALI f. 1929, op. 3, yed. khr. 24 (*Notograficheskiy spravochnik*), l. 41.

27. L[yudmila] Skorino, *Pisatel' i yego vremya: Zhizn' i tvorchestvo V. P. Katayeva* (Moscow: Sovetskiy pisatel', 1965), 300.

28. P. A. Borozdina, *A. N. Tolstoy i teatr* (Voronezh: Izdatel'stvo voronezhskogo universiteta, 1974), 166–73. The play is titled *Path to Victory* (*Put' k pobede*).

29. Prokof'yev, *Dnevnik 1907–1933*, 2:520.

30. Tolstoy edited the libretto of Bedřich Smetana's 1866 opera *The Bartered Bride* (*Prodana nevěsta*) for Soviet consumption. Borozdina, *A. N. Tolstoy i teatr*, 165–66.

31. RGALI f. 1929, op. 2, yed. khr. 150, l. 14 (letter of December 15, 1938).

32. Morgan, "A Soldier Came from the Front: New Light on the Literary Sources of Prokof-iev's First 'Soviet' Opera *Semyon Kotko*," *Three Oranges: The Journal of the Serge Prokofiev Foundation* 6 (November 2003): 8. For details on Prokofiev and Katayev's literary collaboration, see pp. 9–11.

33. RGALI f. 1929, op. 3, yed. khr. 30, l. 1. The quotation comes from the typescript of an interview published in *Vechernyaya Moskva* on December 6, 1932. It merits noting that, besides Prokofiev, Makarov-Rakitin based an opera on the novella, but it does not seem to have been staged. It was adjudicated by the Committee on Arts Affairs on June 22, 1940, just one day before the premiere of Prokofiev's opera.

34. Skorino, *Pisatel' i yego vremya: Zhizn' i tvorchestvo V. P. Katayeva*, 290.

35. Ibid., 291.

36. Valentin Katayev, *Ya, sïn trudovogo naroda* (Moscow: Khudozhestvennaya literatura, 1938), 18.

37. RGALI f. 1929, op. 2, yed. khr. 87, l. 37.

38. These and the following quotations in the paragraph from Prokofiev, "Semyon Kotko," in *Materials, Articles, Interviews*, 36–38.

39. Here he mentions the "letter" scene in Chaikovsky's *Eugene Onegin*.

40. The latter occurs in the act 3 "mad" scene, and involves the end-to-end repetition of phrases in the keys of G minor and C-sharp minor. The tritone-partitioning signifies the breakdown of rational thought.

41. Zinaida Raykh (1894–1939), Meyerhold's wife and lead actress, drafted a petition on her husband's behalf about the closing of the theater to Stalin; Meyerhold, however, advised her against mailing it. See T. S. Esenina, *O V. E. Meyerkhol'de i Z. N. Raykh: Pis'ma K. L. Rudnitskomu* (Moscow: Novoye izdatel'stvo, 2003), 228.

42. Ibid., 226.

43. Skorino, *Pisatel' i yego vremya: Zhizn' i tvorchestvo V. P. Katayeva*, 306.

44. Caryl Emerson, "Surviving in the Belly of the Beast: Four Paradoxes about Great Music under Stalin," unpublished paper given at the symposium "Music and Dictatorship: Russia Under Stalin," Carnegie Hall, New York City, February 22, 2003.

45. Kerzhentsev lost his post to Nazarov on January 19, 1938, just days after the liquidation of Meyerhold's Theater. Khrapchenko became the acting chairman of the Committee on April 1, 1938, and chairman on January 4, 1939. He held the position until 1948.

46. Irina Medvedeva, "'Chornoye leto' 1939 goda," in *Sergey Prokof'yev: Vospominaniya. Pis'ma. Stat'i*, 320.

47. Ibid., 321.

48. A. Fevral'skiy, "Prokof'yev i Meyerkhol'd," in *Sergey Prokof'yev: Stat'i i materialï*, 116.

49. RGALI f. 1929, op. 3, yed. khr. 267, l. 3 (April 12, 1939, entry).

50. RGALI f. 1929, op. 3, yed. khr. 283. Although Myaskovsky was a member of the Stalin Prize Committee, his nomination of Prokofiev was rebuffed. Khrapchenko remained unconvinced of Prokofiev's commitment to "the service of the people." At a December 30, 1940, meeting of the Committee, Khrapchenko declared: "I'm not planning to pass judgment on Prokofiev's

talent, but it seems to me that the Stalin Prize is granted not just for talent, but for talent placed in the service of the people, talent used in such a way that the people feel joy, strength, more powerful....If from this point of view one approaches Prokofiev's creativity, then it seems to me that his works do not merit a Stalin Prize, in spite of his talent." *Deyateli russkogo iskusstva i M. B. Khrapchenko, predsedatel' Vsesoyuznogo komiteta po delam iskusstv: aprel' 1939-yanvar' 1948*, comp., ed., and introd. V. V. Perkhin (Moscow: Nauka, 2007), 582–53 n. 11.

51. On the composer's text-setting technique, see Richard Taruskin, "Tone, Style, and Form in Prokofiev's Soviet Operas: Some Preliminary Observations," in *Studies in the History of Music, Vol. 2: Music and Drama* (New York: Broude Brothers, 1988), 215–39.

52. M[arina] Sabinina, *"Semyon Kotko" i problemï opernoy dramaturgii Prokof'yeva* (Moscow: Sovetskiy kompozitor, 1963), 224.

53. This term and its opposite, "nondiegetic," come from film scholarship. See Claudia Gorbman, *Unheard Melodies: Narrative Film Music* (Bloomington: Indiana University Press, 1987), 11–30.

54. Carolyn Abbate, *Unsung Voices: Opera and Musical Narrative in the Nineteenth Century* (Princeton: Princeton University Press, 1991), 4–10.

55. Maksimenkov, *Sumbur vmesto muzïki: Stalinskaya kul'turnaya revolyutsiya 1936–1938*, 67.

56. Skorino, *Pisatel' i yego vremya: Zhizn' i tvorchestvo V. P. Katayeva*, 301. This passage is also translated by Morgan in "A Soldier Came from the Front: New Light on the Literary Sources of Prokofiev's First 'Soviet' Opera *Semyon Kotko*," 9.

57. M[argarita] Aliger, "Dnevniki," in *Uzel. Poetï: Druzhbï i razrïvï. Iz literaturnogo bïta kontsa 20–x—30–x godov*, ed. Natal'ya Gromova (Moscow: Ellis Lak, 2006), 604 (March 31, 1939, diary entry). There is a sarcastic second meaning to Katayev's comment: "Our" (*Nash*) in post-revolutionary parlance meant "Soviet," but the description of Prokofiev as an "acquisition" (*priobreteniye*) suggests that he was not in fact entirely Soviet, that he still needed to adapt.

58. RGALI f. 1929, op. 3, yed. khr. 24 (*Notograficheskiy spravochnik*), l. 42: "Prokofiev had to abbreviate Katayev's libretto and redo those parts that were not in accord with operatic specifics. Disagreements arose between S. Prokofiev and V. Katayev over the makeup of the playbill, since Katayev considered himself to be the sole author of the libretto and did not want Prokofiev's involvement"; RGALI f. 1929, op. 3, yed. khr. 27, l. 260b.: "Katayev considered himself to be the sole author of the libretto and did not want to recognize Prokofiev as the co-author. Prokofiev did not desire payment; rather, he wanted the billboard to recognize that the libretto was by Katayev and Prokofiev based on Katayev's story."

59. Prokof'yev and Alpers, "Perepiska," 432.

60. *The Little Boots* (*Cherevichki*, 1885).

61. The borrowings are identified by A. Klimovitskiy, *Opera Prokof'yeva "Semyon Kotko" (Poyasneniye)* (Moscow: Sovetskiy kompozitor, 1961), 32 and 37. Prokofiev and Katayev also decided to include a quotation from the Ukrainian nationalist poet Taras Shevchenko (1814–61) in the opera. Shevchenko's poem "When I die, then make my grave" (Kak umru, to pokhovayte, 1845) is included in the act 4, scene 1 choral lament for the victims of the German assault on the village. References to Shevchenko typify socialist realist literature about Ukraine, chiefly because in 1847 the poet invoked the wrath of Tsar Nikolay I for writing anti-imperialist poems.

62. The 1872 collection of folksongs with accompaniment was assembled by Aleksandr Rubets (1837–1913).

63. "Elders, elders, why just sit there...?"(Shto vï, starostï, starostï, sidite...?)

64. Sabinina, *"Semyon Kotko" i problemï opernoy dramaturgii Prokof'yeva*, 155.

65. Tertz, "On Socialist Realism," 190.

66. Information in this and the next paragraph from Medvedeva, "'Chornoye leto' 1939 goda," 318–66, and Fevral'skiy, "Prokof'yev i Meyerkhol'd," 118–20.

67. Medvedeva, "'Chornoye leto' 1939 goda," 340. The last word in the quotation, "champagne," is Medvedeva's assumption: the manuscript is difficult to decipher. If "champagne" is accurate, Prokofiev was perhaps thinking of Johann Strauss: "In [Strauss's] waltzes," one of his contemporaries wrote, "a profusion of melodies effervesce and bubble, fizz and froth, dash and sweep like the five hundred thousand devils in the champagne, slipping their bonds and flinging one cork after another into the air." Quoted in Peter Kemp, "Strauss: (1) Johann Strauss (I): Works," in *The New Grove Dictionary of Music and Musicians*, ed. Stanley Sadie and John Tyrell, 29 vols. (Oxford: Oxford University Press, 2001), 24:477.

68. Medvedeva, "'Chornoye leto' 1939 goda," 333.

69. Ibid., 340.

70. Ibid., 327–28. The quotations are from Prokofiev's May 28 and 29 letters to Feldman, which Medvedeva transcribes.

71. G[rigoriy] Shneyerson, "Vstrechi s Prokof'yevïm," in *Sergey Prokof'yev: Stat'i i materialï*, 254.

72. Tishler, "Tri vstrechi s Meyerkhol'dom," quoted in Medvedeva, "'Chornoye leto' 1939 goda," 322.

73. *"Vernite mne svobodu!": Deyateli literaturï i iskusstva Rossii i Germanii—zhertvï stalinskogo terrora*, ed. V. F. Kolyazin (Moscow: Medium, 1997), 220–40. For a chronicle of the events that preceded and followed Meyerhold's arrest, see Edward Braun, "Vsevolod Meyerhold: The Final Act," in *Enemies of the People: The Destruction of the Soviet Literary, Theater, and Film Arts in the 1930s*, ed. Katherine Bliss Eaton (Evanston, Ill.: Northwestern University Press, 2002), 145–62.

74. In a notebook entry dated "1938/9," Prokofiev mentions snubbing Kerzhentsev. "In the [Kislovodsk] sanatorium, Kerzhentsev invited me to play chess. I graciously turned him down." "Following [Kerzhentsev's] resignation," Prokofiev appends, "everyone turned their backs on him." RGALI f. 1929, op. 2, yed. khr. 87, l. 36ob.

75. RGALI f. 1929, op. 1, yed. khr. 655, l. 26ob.

76. Chemberdzhi, *XX vek Linï Prokof'yevoy*, 199.

77. RGALI f. 1929, op. 1, yed. khr. 334, l. 70b. Prokofiev enlisted Lamm and Derzhanovsky to realize the orchestration from his annotations on the expanded piano score. Between April 22 and June 12, 1940, Prokofiev fashioned a plan for extracting an orchestral suite from the opera. This suite was not finished, however, until June 1, 1943, near the end of Prokofiev's wartime stay in Alma-Ata, Kazakhstan (RGALI f. 1929, op. 1, yed. khr. 134–36).

78. "Iz perepiski S. S. Prokof'yeva i S. M. Eyzenshteyna," in *Sergey Prokof'yev: Stat'i i materialï*, 342–44. The letters are dated July 27 (Eisenstein to Prokofiev about the film) and July 30 (Prokofiev to Eisenstein about the opera). For a translation, see *Selected Letters of Sergei Prokofiev*, 210–13.

79. RGALI f. 2046, op. 1, yed. khr. 260.

80. Ibid. Gorodinsky served as editor in chief of the State Music Publisher (Muzgiz) from 1946 to 1948.

81. Information and quotations in this paragraph from a transcript of the discussion of the performance; RGALI f. 2046 op. 1, yed. khr. 259, ll. 1–4.

82. Serafima Birman, "On ves' otdal sebya muzïke" (He gave all of himself to music), in *S. S Prokof'yev: Materialï, dokumentï, vospominaniya*, 500–505. This essay dates from the

summer of 1955; an almost identical typescript, dated July 6, 1954, is preserved in RGALI (f. 1929, op. 1, yed. khr. 994) under the title "I predalsya odnoy muzïke" (He abandoned himself only to music).

83. M[ira] A[bramovna] Mendel'son-Prokof'yeva, "Iz vospominaniy," in *Sergey Prokof'yev 1891–1991: Dnevnik, pis'ma, besedï, vospominaniya*, 249–50.

84. Birman, *Sud'boy darovannïye vstrechi*, 1971, quoted in *Prokof'yev o Prokof'yeve: Stat'i, interv'yu*, 184 n. 2.

85. Birman, "On ves' otdal sebya muzïke," 502–3.

86. To abet negotiations with the Third Reich, Molotov in May 1939 replaced Maksim Litvinov (1876–1951), who was Jewish, as foreign minister, while Stalin assumed the chairmanship of the Council of People's Commissars. Molotov became deputy chairman; he was also a Politburo member.

87. Skorino, *Pisatel' i yego vremya: Zhizn' i tvorchestvo V. P. Katayeva*, 306–7.

88. Nest'yeva, *Sergey Prokof'yev*, 152.

89. Shostakovich commented on the fiasco in a June 29, 1940, letter to the musicologist Ivan Sollertinsky (1902–44): "I planned, being in Moscow on April 26, to see the premiere of Sergey Prokofiev's *Semyon Kotko*. I didn't succeed, however, since the repertory committee still hasn't given permission for the performance, evidently on the basis of a mechanical substitution of Germans with Austrians. Such is how the opera's author explained it to me in a telephone conversation." D[mitriy] D[mitriyevich] Shostakovich, *Pis'ma I. I. Sollertinskomu* (St. Petersburg: Kompozitor, 2006), 215.

90. This and the following quotations from *Deyateli russkogo iskusstva i M. B. Khrapchenko, predsedatel' Vsesoyuznogo komiteta po delam iskusstv: aprel' 1939-yanvar' 1948*, 607–8 n. 4. Solomon Lozovsky (1878–1952) was Deputy Foreign Affairs Minister; Shcheglov was a diplomat.

91. RGASPI f. 82, op. 2, d. 950, l. 99.

92. Oleg Prokofiev, "Papers from the Attic: My Father, His Music, and I," *Three Oranges: The Journal of the Serge Prokofiev Foundation* 9 (May 2005): 30.

93. The protocols of the 1940–41 season of the Stanislavsky Theater are preserved in RGALI f. 2482, op. 1, yed. khr. 239–40.

94. The most positive review was the first: S[emyon] Shlifshteyn, "Semyon Kotko," *Sovetskoye iskusstvo*, June 29, 1940, p. 3.

95. Indeed, an entire page of the November 14, 1939, issue of *Sovetskoye iskusstvo* addressed the "stormy disputes" (burnïye sporï) surrounding *Into the Storm*. The conflict was reflected in two articles, Ivan Dzherzhinsky's "A Creative Success" (Tvorcheskaya udacha) and Shlifshteyn's "Big Ideas and Small Emotions" (Bol'shiye idei i malen'kiye chuvstva). A third article, Georgiy Kreytner's "A New Soviet Opera" (Novaya sovetskaya opera) reconciled the opposing views in Hegelian fashion.

96. Tikhon Khrennikov, *O vremeni, o muzïke i muzïkantakh, o sebe* (Moscow: Kompozitor, 2003), 121–22.

97. Khrennikov, *Tak eto bïlo* (Moscow: Muzïka, 1994), 70. The critic refers to Musorgsky's experimental, prose-based opera *Zhenit'ba* (1868, incomplete).

98. V[iktor] Tsukkerman, "Neskol'ko mïsley o sovetskoy opere," *Sovetskaya muzïka* 12 (1940): 67.

99. Khrennikov, *O vremeni, o muzïke i muzïkantakh, o sebe*, 121.

100. Kravets, "Prokofiev and Sherman: The First Soviet Production of *Romeo and Juliet*," *Three Oranges: The Journal of the Serge Prokofiev Foundation* 8 (November 2004): 19. The original source of this quotation is I[say] E. Sherman, "Vospominaniya o Sergeye

Sergeyeviche Prokof'yeve," in *Dirizhor I. E. Sherman: Stat'i, pis'ma, vospominaniya* (St. Petersburg: Rossiyskiy institut istorii iskusstv, 2002), 55.

101. In Romeo's variation, Prokofiev reused music from the discarded happy ending of the ballet; the passage at rehearsal number 377 of the happy ending recurs intact at rehearsal number 140 of the variation.

102. Letter of November 16, 1939, quoted in Kravetz, "Prokofiev and Sherman: The First Soviet Production of *Romeo and Juliet*," 19. Kravetz points out that the words "so that even Romeo won't be able to milk applause" read, at first, "so that even [Konstantin] Sergeyev won't manage to milk applause"—a jab at the theatrics of the male lead of the Kirov Ballet.

103. Ibid., 19–20.

104. Sherman, "Vospominaniya o Sergeye Sergeyeviche Prokof'yeve," 55.

105. Kravetz, "Prokofiev and Sherman: The First Soviet Production of *Romeo and Juliet*," 20; Sherman, "Vospominaniya o Sergeye Sergeyeviche Prokof'yeve," 57–58.

106. Gayevskiy, *Dom Petipa*, 254.

107. Before Lavrovsky's proposed alterations to the scenario were enacted, Prokofiev down-played them in a February 21, 1939, letter to Radlov: "So far nothing to fear: he [Lavrovsky] wants Romeo to stand pensively in Mantua to the music of the entr'acte, and in a different place for him to kill the [Moorish] merchant with the carpets" (RNB f. 625, yed. khr. 465, l. 4). Prokofiev adds that he had to "*put a stop*" to Lavrovsky's "feeble" requests for additional changes, but these changes, notably the inclusion of the solo varia-tions for Romeo and Juliet, obviously ended up being made.

108. Gayevskiy, *Dom Petipa*, 256–57.

109. Galina Ulanova, "The Author of My Favorite Ballets," in *Sergei Prokofiev: Materials, Articles, Interviews*, 234.

110. Sherman, "Vospominaniya o Sergeye Sergeyeviche Prokof'yeve," 57.

111. Kravetz reveals that "the handwritten score, on which Prokofiev had made pencil cor-rections, was subsequently mutilated in a barbaric fashion. When Sherman conducted *Romeo and Juliet* at the Shakespeare festival in Leningrad (1964), many handwritten sheets had been torn out and replaced with printed ones and orchestral markings in the composer's hand had disappeared without a trace. As a result a complete, authorized score of the second version is unavailable in the Russian archives. In the Glinka Museum there are separate pages from the first and second acts, but it is not known whether they belonged to the composer. The score—published in 1961 (Moskva: Muzgiz) in the Com-plete Works of Prokofiev (volumes 8A and B)—gives no indication of the source from which the score was published." "Prokofiev and Sherman: The First Soviet Production of *Romeo and Juliet*," 21 n. 29.

112. Letter of April 30, 1940, quoted in ibid., 20; translation adjusted.

113. Letter of November 15, 1972, from Boris Khaykin to Mikhaíl Khrapchenko, in *Deyateli russkogo iskusstva i M. B. Khrapchenko, predsedatel' Vsesoyuznogo komiteta po delam iskusstv: aprel' 1939-yanvar' 1948*, 549.

114. RGASPI f. 17, op. 163, d. 1257, l. 87.

115. RGALI f. 1929, op. 2, yed. khr. 111, l. 1; *Prokof'yev o Prokof'yeve: Stat'i, interv'yu*, 174.

116. RGALI f. 1929, op. 2, yed. khr. 150, l. 14.

117. Unsigned, "Reviewer's Notebook," *Los Angeles Times*, August 7, 1938, p. C5.

118. RGALI f. 1929, op. 2, yed. khr. 273, l. 2.

119. RGALI f. 1929, op. 1, yed. khr. 354, l. 41 (letter of June 7, 1939).

120. RGALI f. 1929, op. 2, yed. khr. 150, l. 23.

121. Unsigned, "Prokofieff Unable to Come to America," *New York Times*, January 10, 1940, p. 24.

122. *Tvorchestvo narodov SSSR. XX let Velikoy Oktyabr'skoy sotsialisticheskoy revolyutsii v SSSR. 1917–1937*, ed. A. M. Gor'kiy and L. Z. Mekhlis (Moscow: Izd. Redaktsii "Pravdï," 1937), 105–6, 121–22, and 130.

123. Ibid., 100–104.

124. RGALI f. 1929, op. 1, yed. khr. 835, l. 5; Grigoriy Pantiyelev, "Prokof'yev: razmïshleniya, svidetel'stva, sporï. Beseda s Gennadiyem Rozhdestvenskim," *Sovetskaya muzïka* 4 (1991): 11 and 13.

125. *Bol'shaya tsenzura: Pisateli i zhurnalistï v strane sovetov 1917–1956*, comp. and introd. L. V. Maksimenkov; ed. A. N. Yakovlev (Moscow: Mezhdunarodnïy fond "Demokratiya," 2005), 9.

126. "Prokofiev and Atovmyan: Correspondence, 1933–1952," 235. Prokofiev refers to Andrew Steiger's translation of the *Alexander Nevsky* libretto.

127. Mashistov wrote two opera librettos for the composer Aleksandr Kholminov (b. 1925), *An Optimistic Tragedy* (*Optimisticheskaya tragediya*, 1965, after Vsevolod Vishnevsky's play) and *Anna Snegina* (1967, after Sergey Esenin's poem).

128. Mashistov revised the text of the *Cantata for the Thirtieth Anniversary of October* for the 1962 edition.

129. "Nikogda tak ne bïlo / Pole zeleno / Nebïvaloy radosti / Vsyo selo polno / Nikogda nam ne bïla / Zhizn' tak vesela / Nikogda dosel' u nas / Rozh' tak ne tsvela."

130. RGALI f. 1929, op. 1, yed. khr. 255.

131. Most *chastushki* are lewd four-line rhymes, but in the Soviet period their subject matter expanded to include Communist slogans and anti-religious propaganda.

132. The collection in question, comprising seven songs, was premiered on March 15, 1939, on State Radio.

133. "S. Prokofiev's *Zdravitsa*, a masterfully written composition for chorus and orchestra, fresh and uplifting in its musical language, serves as an artistic expression of the multinational Soviet people's feelings of pride and joy in their newfound happiness"; "S. S. Prokofiev's *Zdravitsa*...made a magnificent impression in the first concert. The composition is unusually clear, bright in color and noble in simplicity." RGALI f. 1929, op. 1, yed. khr. 948, no. 196 (unsigned, "Prazdnichnïy kontsert v Bol'shom zale konservatorii," *Vechernyaya Moskva*, December 22, 1939), and no. 203 (unsigned, "Yubileynïye kontsertï," *Sovetskoye iskusstvo*, December 29, 1939).

134. T[amara] Livanova and Yu[riy] Keldïsh, "Obraz Stalina v muzïke," *Sovetskaya muzïka* 12 (1949): 20.

135. RGALI f. 1929, op. 1, yed. khr. 806, l. 8.

136. Oleg Prokofiev, "Papers from the Attic: My Father, His Music, and I," 28.

137. Vladimir Zak, "Prokof'yev obnimayet mir," *Muzeynïy listok: Prilozheniye k rossiyskoy muzïkal'noy gazete* 40 (November 2003), p. 2.

138. Ibid.

CHAPTER 3

1. "Editorial Eulogy of A. S. Pushkin, 'The Glory of the Russian People,' *Pravda* 10 February 1937," in *Epic Revisionism: Russian History and Literature as Stalinist Propaganda*, ed.

Kevin M. F. Platt and David Brandenberger (Madison: University of Wisconsin Press, 2006), 215–16.

2. Stephanie Sandler, "The 1937 Pushkin Jubilee as Epic Trauma," in *Epic Revisionism: Russian History and Literature as Stalinist Propaganda*, 199. For an account of the centennial's realization, see pp. 193–213. The deposed Comintern leader Karl Radek (1885–1939) died in prison; he was not actually executed. Yuriy Pyatakov (1890–1937) was Deputy Heavy Industry Minister.

3. Prokof'yev and Alpers, "Perepiska," 428.

4. "Postanovleniye Politbyuro TsK VKP(b) ob uchrezhdenii Vsesoyuznogo Pushkinskogo Komiteta," in *Vlast' i khudozhestvennaya intelligentsiya: Dokumentï TsK RKP(b)-VKP(b), VChK–OGPU–NKVD, o kul'turnoy politike. 1917–1953 gg.*, 218–19.

5. Prokofiev, *Soviet Diary 1927 and Other Writings*, 301.

6. Ibid.

7. "Iz vospominaniy O. Litovskogo 'Tak i bïlo,'" in *Prokof'yev o Prokof'yeve: Stat'i, interv'yu*, 133.

8. Ibid.

9. Vadim Perel'muter, "'Traktat o tom, kak nevïgodno bït' talantlivïm,'" in Sigizmund Krzhizhanovskiy, *Vospominaniya o budushchem: Izbrannoye iz neizdannogo* (Moscow: Moskovskiy rabochiy, 1989), 14–15.

10. This and the next quotation from "Iz besedï s rezhissyorami-vïpusknikami Gosudarstvennogo instituta teatral'nogo iskusstva imeni A. V. Lunacharskogo," in A. Ya. Tairov, *Zapiski rezhissyora. Stat'i. Besedï. Rechi. Pis'ma*, ed. P. Markov (Moscow: Izdaniye Vserossiyskogo teatral'nogo obshchestva, 1970), 252–53. The "Decembrist" reading did not spring from Tairov's imagination. Pushkin contemplated ending *Eugene Onegin* with Onegin either dying in the Caucasus or joining the Decembrist movement. This is the content of the "burnt" book 10. Scholars of the Stalinist period used the extant lines from this book, and the contents of an 1829 letter from the author to his brother, to refute the "anti-historical" supposition that Pushkin regarded the Decembrist movement unfavorably. See, for example, N. L. Brodskiy, *Yevgeniy Onegin: Roman A. S. Pushkina. Posobiye dlya uchiteley sredney shkolï* (Moscow: Gosudarstvennoye uchebno-pedagogicheskoye izdatel'stvo ministerstva prosveshcheniya RSFSR, 1950), 351–84.

11. Alexander Pushkin, *Eugene Onegin*, trans. and commentary by Vladimir Nabokov, 4 vols. (Princeton: Princeton University Press, 1975), 1:117.

12. E[lizaveta] Dattel', "'Yevgeniy Onegin' S. Prokof'yeva (neosushchestvlyonnïy muzïkal'no-dramaticheskiy spektakl' v Kamernom teatre)," in *Muzïkal'nïy sovremennik*, vol. 2, ed. L. V. Danilevich (Moscow: Sovetskiy kompozitor, 1977), 10. An earlier version of this essay is reproduced in Prokof'yev, *Yevgeniy Onegin. Muzïkal'no-dramaticheskaya kompozitsiya po odnoimennomu romanu A. S. Pushkina dlya chtetsa, aktyorov i simfonicheskogo orkestra. Partitura i avtorskoye perelozheniye dlya fortepiano* (Moscow: Sovetskiy kompozitor, 1973), 231–44. This version of the score was edited by Dattel with the composer G. S. Zinger, who completed the orchestration based on Prokofiev's annotations.

13. The commission included Sergey Bondi (1891–1983), Leonid Grossman (1888–1965), Mstislav Tsyavlovsky (1883–1947), Tatyana Tsyavlovskaya-Zenger (1897–1978), Vikentiy Veresayev (1867–1945), and Grigoriy Vinokur (1896–1947)—pioneering textologists who devoted their careers to assembling and annotating the Pushkin corpus.

14. "Kalendar 'Onegina,'" RGALI f. 1929, op. 1, yed. khr. 86; f. 1929, op. 3, yed. khr. 253.

15. RGALI f. 1929, op. 1, yed. khr. 85. The autograph originally contained 44 numbers, but three of them (Nos. 38–40) went missing, only to turn up at a Christie's auction. See Clive Bennett, "Prokofiev and Eugene Onegin," *Musical Times* (April 1980): 231. No. 26, a Stravinsky-inspired chorus titled "Mummers" (Ryazhenïye), exists in two versions: the first for voice and piano, the second for voice, violins, oboe, and tambourine. The autograph also includes sketches of two mass songs, "The Soldier's [Fighter's] Sweetheart" (Podruga boytsa) and "Fritz," which Prokofiev included in his *Seven Mass Songs (Sem' massovïkh pesen)* of 1942. Another, complete piano score, in Lamm's hand, survives in the RGALI holding of the theatrical designer and collector Vasiliy Fyodorov (1891–1973): f. 2579, op. 1, yed. khr. 991. It became the basis of the 2005 recording by Jurowski, Capriccio 67 149/50.

16. RGALI f. 1929, op. 1, yed. khr. 85, l. 6.

17. Caryl Emerson, "The Krzhizhanovsky-Prokofiev Collaboration on *Eugene Onegin,* 1936 (A Lesser-Known Casualty of the Pushkin Death Jubilee)," in *Sergey Prokofiev and His World,* 71–72.

18. A. S., "'Yevgeniy Onegin'—dramaticheskiy spektakl'. Beseda s nar. art. resp. A. Ya. Tairovïm," *Krasnaya gazeta,* April 20, 1936, p. 2; unsigned, "'Yevgeniy Onegin' v drame. Beseda s nar. artistom A. Ya. Tairovïm," *Vechernyaya Moskva,* April 23, 1936, p. 3. The last line of the quoted passage is not included in the second source.

19. Prokofiev, *Soviet Diary 1927 and Other Writings,* 301.

20. "Kompozitor v dramaticheskom teatre: Beseda s S. S. Prokof'yevïm," in *S. S. Prokof'yev: Materialï, dokumentï, vospominaniya,* 219.

21. Pushkin, *Eugene Onegin,* 1: 262.

22. See Taruskin, "*Yevgeny Onegin,*" in *The New Grove Dictionary of Opera,* ed. Stanley Sadie, 4 vols. (London: Macmillan, 1994), 4:1193–94.

23. Pushkin, *Eugene Onegin,* 1:294.

24. Olga Peters Hasty, *Pushkin's Tatiana* (Madison: University of Wisconsin Press, 1999), 10.

25. She apparently sought advice on her work from Mira Mendelson, Prokofiev's second wife. See Medvedeva, "Elizaveta Dattel' in Memoriam," in *Sergey Prokof'yev: Pis'ma, vospominaniya, stat'i,* 311–12.

26. Dattel', "'Yevgeniy Onegin' S. Prokof'yeva (neosushchestvlyonnïy muzïkal'no-dramaticheskiy spektakl' v Kamernom teatre)," 9.

27. I am grateful to Daniil Zavlunov for these and other details about the edition.

28. RGALI f. 1929, op. 1, yed. khr. 86, l. 38.

29. Pushkin, *Eugene Onegin,* 1:262.

30. Malfilâtre's words make up the epigraph to book 3 of *Eugene Onegin.*

31. RGALI f. 1929, op. 3, yed. khr. 21 (*Notograficheskiy spravochnik*), l. 260b. The contract specified an 8,000-ruble payment and an August 15, 1936, deadline for the piano score. A separate "work agreement" (*trudovoye soglasheniye*) specified another 8,000-ruble payment for the orchestration—due October 1, 1936—and for Prokofiev's presence during the rehearsals, with the caveat that he would be away from Moscow between December 1 and February 10, 1937 (RGALI f. 1929, op. 1, yed. khr. 814, ll. 21–22). The cancellation of the production resulted in a breach of contract; as late as June 14, 1938, Prokofiev had still not been paid for the orchestration. On that day, he submitted a complaint to the Chamber Theater (RGALI f. 1929, op. 2, yed. khr. 333).

32. Information in this paragraph from A. M. Dubrovsky, "Chronicle of a Poet's Downfall: Dem'ian Bednyi, Russian History, and *The Epic Heroes,*" in *Epic Revisionism: Russian History and Literature as Stalinist Propaganda,* 77–98.

33. *Bol'shaya tsenzura: Pisateli i zhurnalistï v Strane Sovetov. 1917–1956*, 286 n. 11.

34. Quoted in Dubrovsky, "Chronicle of a Poet's Downfall: Dem'ian Bednyi, Russian History, and *The Epic Heroes*," 93. On the Politburo–Committee on Arts Affairs decision, see Maksimenkov, *Sumbur vmesto muzïki: Stalinskaya kul'turnaya revolyutsiya 1936–1938*, 220–21.

35. "The Reaction of Writers and Artists to the Banning of D. Bednyi's Comic Opera," in *Epic Revisionism: Russian History and Literature as Stalinist Propaganda*, 100–101; translation adjusted.

36. Malcolm H. Brown identifies the other quotations from *Eugene Onegin* in the opera in "Prokofiev's *War and Peace*: A Chronicle," *Musical Quarterly* 43:3 (July 1977): 317.

37. For the list, see Tamara Sergeyeva, "'Pikovaya dama': Shto snitsya cheloveku...," *Kinovedcheskiye zapiski* 42 (1999): 220–21.

38. Anatoly Vishevsky, "'The Queen of Spades' Revisited, Revisited, and Revisited...: How Time Changed Accents," *Russian Studies in Literature* 40:2 (Spring 2004): 21.

39. Mikhail Romm, *Izbrannïye proizvedeniya v 3-x tomakh*, ed. L. I. Belova et al. (Moscow: Iskusstvo, 1981), 2:159; also quoted in Vishevsky, "'The Queen of Spades' Revisited, Revisited, and Revisited...: How Time Changed Accents," 22.

40. Romm, *Izbrannïye proizvedeniya v 3-x tomakh*, 2:159.

41. Ibid., 2:157.

42. Ibid., 2:156.

43. Ibid.

44. Ibid., 2:157. Romm bases this claim on Pushkin's 1830 poem "My Genealogy" (Moya rodoslovnaya), in which the poet declares petit bourgeois origins. The poem, however, is parodic.

45. Unsigned, "'Pikovaya dama' v tsvetnom kino," *Kino (Moskva)*, February 11, 1937, p. 2.

46. Romm lauded Pushkin's story for what he considered to be its proto-cinematic traits, arguing, for instance, that the writer experimented with the verbal equivalent of visual montage. See Romm, *Besedï o kino* (Moscow: Iskusstvo, 1964), 116–21.

47. "Rabota i planï S. Prokof'yeva," in *Prokof'yev o Prokof'yeve: Stat'i, interv'yu*, 135.

48. RGALI f. 1929, op. 1, yed. khr. 814, l. 3. The contract specified a total payment of 15,000 rubles for the score, with the first draft of the music to be delivered by June 10.

49. Romm, *Izbrannïye proizvedeniya v 3-x tomakh*, 2:144–45. Sokolovskaya sought advice on the scenario from a Central Committee member, Yan Gamarnik (1894–1937), who ensured its prohibition. For additional details about this period in Romm's career, see his "Avtobiografiya," in *Kremlyovskiy kinoteatr 1928–1953. Dokumentï*, 1063–65.

50. Unsigned, "'Pikovaya dama' v kino," *Kino (Moskva)*, June 4, 1937, p. 4.

51. Unsigned, "Planirovat' ekranizatsiyu klassikov," *Kino (Moskva)*, June 28, 1937, p. 3.

52. Pentslin completed the preparatory work on *The Queen of Spades* in Romm's place.

53. For the history of this film and an overview of Mosfilm's activities in 1937, see Maya Turovskaya "'Mosfil'm'—1937," *Kinovedcheskiye zapiski* 50 (2001): 198–218.

54. RGALI f. 1929, op. 1, yed. khr. 93. The episodes are: (1) Overture; (2) Wandering; (3) Wandering (Hermann in front of the Countess's residence); (4) Liza; (5) Hermann at home; (6) Morning; (7) Hermann sees Liza; (8) Hermann delivers a letter to Liza; (9) Liza reads the letter; (10) Liza muses and writes a reply; (11) Liza enters with the letter for Hermann; (12) Hermann reads the letter (Hermann in front of the Countess's residence); (13) Hermann in Liza's room; (14) Ball; (15) Liza alone in her room; (16) Hermann playing cards alone; (17) The Countess's visit; (18) Hermann makes a note, conceals it, and

comes to the casino; (19) First win; (20) Hermann goes to the casino a second time; (21) Second win; (22) Hermann goes to the casino a third time; (23) Hermann loses; (24) Final encounter.

55. Romm, *Izbrannïye proizvedeniya v 3-x tomakh*, 2: 159.

56. Ibid. for Prokofiev's comments; Romm did not explain why Prokofiev scorned the opera. Elsewhere, the composer observed that "Chaikovsky departed further from the Pushkin original in *The Queen of Spades* than in *Eugene Onegin*. To take just one example: for Chaikovsky, the central figure, Hermann, is lyrically and passionately in love with Liza; for Pushkin, he is a gambler who casually latches on to the Countess's very young ward and transforms her into a tool for the achievement of his aims" ("Moi planï," 142).

57. Letter of July 26, 1936, in *S. S. Prokof'yev i N. Ya. Myaskovskiy: Perepiska*, 449.

58. Pushkin, "Pikovaya dama," in *Polnoye sobraniye sochineniy v desyati tomakh*, 3rd ed. (Moscow: Nauka, 1962–66), 6:355.

59. The manuscript is RGALI f. 1929, op. 1, yed. khr. 95.

60. "Dokladnaya zapiska S. S. Dukel'skogo V. M. Molotovu o tematicheskom plane proizvodstva kinokartin na 1938 g.," in *Kremlyovskiy kinoteatr 1928–1953. Dokumentï*, 489–90.

61. Romm, *Izbrannïye proizvedeniya v 3-x tomakh*, 2:163.

62. RGALI f. 1929, op. 3, yed. khr. 24 (*Notograficheskiy spravochnik*), l. 31.

63. See *Meyerkhol'd repetiruet*, ed. M. M. Sitkovetskaya, 2 vols. (Moscow: Artist. Rezhissyor. Teatr, 1993), 2:218: "Not only external events, but also the internal situation at GosTIM [the State Meyerhold Theater] interfered with the realization of the conception. The situation inside the theater became increasingly difficult. Z[inaida] N. Raykh often irritably rebuked the actors who refused to accept the director's suggestions, further poisoning the atmosphere."

64. Ibid., 2:217. The year 1937 was not only the Pushkin centennial but also the twentieth anniversary of the Revolution, in tribute to which Meyerhold began work on a production of *One Life* (*Odna zhizn'*), based on Nikolay Ostrovsky's novel *How the Steel Was Tempered* (*Kak zakalyalas' stal'*, 1934). The Committee on Arts Affairs curtailed the production on account of its anti-doctrinaire "naturalism" and "pessimism" (Maksimenkov, *Sumbur vmesto muzïki: Stalinskaya kul'turnaya revolyutsiya 1936–1938*, 270–72).

65. See *Bol'shaya tsenzura: Pisateli i zhurnalistï v Strane Sovetov. 1917–1956*, 463–65.

66. Meyerhold was indirectly targeted in the *Pravda* editorial "Muddle Instead of Music." Following his denunciation in a December 17, 1937, article in the same newspaper, Meyerhold expressed remorse for his approach to *Boris Godunov*: "The entire composition should have been subordinated to a painstaking study of the internal world [of the heroes]." *Meyerkhol'd repetiruet*, 2:218.

67. "O likvidatsii teatra im. Vs. Meyerkhol'da," in *Vlast' i khudozhestvennaya intelligentsiya: Dokumentï TsK RKP(b)–VKP(b), VChK–OGPU–NKVD, o kul'turnoy politike. 1917–1953 gg.*, 385–86.

68. Pushkin's drama features two of the poet's forebears, one (Gavrila) who collaborated with the Pretender and another (Afanasiy) who opposed the Tsar domestically.

69. Esenina, *O V. E. Meyerkhol'de i Z. N. Raykh: Pis'ma K. L. Rudnitskomu*, 129. The fact that Esenina was abroad in 1936 attests to the exceptional privileges accorded Meyerhold in 1936. Prokofiev traveled abroad as well in 1936, but he was not allowed to bring his children with him.

70. Pushkin, *Boris Godunov*, trans. Philip L. Barbour (Westport, Conn.: Greenwood Press, 1976), 59; italics added. The translation has been adjusted to make it more literal.

71. During the *Boris Godunov* rehearsals, construction was under way on Triumphal (Mayakovsky) Square for a permanent home for the Meyerhold Theater. In 1937 construction

was delayed and, in 1938, halted following the Politburo decision to terminate Meyerhold's activities. Triumphant Square instead became the home of the Chaikovsky Concert Hall and the Satiric Theater. Neither of these buildings approaches the radicalism of Meyerhold's architectural plan, which envisioned a multi-purpose, multi-tiered space that would absorb the audience into the stage action and bear the look and feel of a marketplace.

72. From a discussion with members of the Vakhtangov Theater, quoted in *Meyerkhol'd i khudozhniki*, ed. A. A. Mikhaylova (Moscow: Galart, 1995), 275.

73. *Meyerkhol'd repetiruet*, 2: 213.

74. Emerson argues that the scene of the "Evil Monk" ("Ograda monastïrskaya [Zloy chernets]"), like that of the "stock-in-trade but crucial figures of Varlaam and Misail," reflects Pushkin's conception of the drama as a historical comedy. Pushkin, Emerson writes, infused the text with "gossip, slander, rumor, [and] cynical realism," which operate "not merely as comic relief from the 'real' tragic plot but as an agent *in* that plot, as an instigator of genuine historical change." "Tragedy, Comedy, Carnival, and History on Stage," in Chester Dunning with Caryl Emerson, Sergei Fomichev, Lidiia Lotman, and Antony Wood, *The Uncensored Boris Godunov* (Madison: University of Wisconsin Press, 2006), 175.

75. V. A. Pyast, "K stsene so zlïm chernetsom," RGALI f. 1929, op. 2, yed. khr. 591, l. 5.

76. Anthony Wood observes that, when divided mid-line, trochaic octometer resembles stylized folk epic, the implication being that the dream is a manifestation of ancestral poetic memory. "Translator's Preface," in *The Uncensored Boris Godunov*, 240.

77. Prokofiev had qualms about the project at first, as evidenced by a September 8, 1934, letter he wrote to Meyerhold from the South of France: "I was very disturbed by your claim that I'd promised to write music for your 'Boris.' On the other hand, the project does sound interesting, if I could figure out how to approach it. So far I haven't figured that out, and especially with all your instruments I'm not sure how to proceed—I don't know how they would sound." *Selected Letters of Sergei Prokofiev*, 85.

78. I. Glikman, *Meyerkhol'd i muzïkal'nïy teatr* (Leningrad: Sovetskiy kompozitor, 1989), 328.

79. Emerson, *Boris Godunov: Transpositions of a Russian Theme* (Bloomington: Indiana University Press, 1986), 101. The embedded quotations come from V[alentin] S. Nepomnyashchiy, *Poeziya i sud'ba*, 1983.

80. Emerson, "Tragedy, Comedy, Carnival, and History on Stage," 176.

81. *Meyerhold at Work*, ed. Paul Schmidt (Austin: University of Texas Press, 1980), 115.

82. Prokofiev did, however, reuse the opening of the battle scene music in act 3, scene 7 of *Semyon Kotko* (rehearsal number 284). In the opera, the music sounds behind the scenes to signal the arrival of a German brigade.

83. In Pushkin's text, Mnishek comments about the resplendent gathering: "We old men no longer dance; we are not drawn to the thundering of music." Pushkin, *Boris Godunov*, 85; translation adjusted.

84. Gorbman, *Unheard Melodies: Narrative Film Music*, 22–23.

85. *Meyerkhol'd repetiruet*, 2:300.

86. Ibid., 2:241. This statement is from an August 4, 1936, rehearsal.

87. The quotation is from p. 102 of Prokofiev's annotated copy of *Dramaticheskiye proizvedeniya A. S. Pushkina* (Moscow: Goslitizdat, 1935), preserved in RGALI, fond 1929, op. 2, yed. khr. 37. The composer repaginated the publication to accommodate Meyerhold's insertions.

88. Ibid., p. 108.

89. See Taruskin, *Stravinsky and the Russian Traditions*, 2 vols. (Berkeley: University of California Press, 1996), 1:856–57.
90. The letter is reproduced in V. Gromov, "Zamïsel postanovki," in *Tvorcheskoye naslediye V. E. Meyerkhol'da*, ed. L. D. Vendrovskaya and A. V. Fevral'skiy (Moscow: Vserossiyskoye teatral'noye obshchestvo, 1978), 399. The author dates the letter "August or September 1936."
91. Fevral'skiy, "Prokof'yev i Meyerkhol'd," 113.
92. Ibid., 113–14.
93. Prokofiev described the structure of the chorus in the manuscript of the piano-vocal score as follows: "The organizing principles of this episode are: 8 measures, of which the 7th and 8th exist in two versions. The first version modulates a tone higher (the mood intensifies); the second version modulates a tone lower (the mood falls). These eight-measure groups can be combined as necessary. In the present instance there is a rise of three scale degrees, then a fall of three scale degrees, but it can be otherwise. Now and again a theme appears above (two variants), but it should not be situated in two successive eight-measure groups" (RGALI f. 1929, op. 1, yed. khr. 87, l. 6). This same description appears in the published conductor's score, which was orchestrated by Lamm according to Prokofiev's instructions.
94. Emerson, *Boris Godunov: Transpositions of a Russian Theme*, 97.
95. RGALI f. 1929, op. 2, yed. khr. 37, l. 34.
96. Meyerhold staged *Tristan und Isolde* in St. Petersburg in 1909.
97. Schmidt, *Meyerhold at Work*, 114.
98. RGALI f. 1929, op. 2, yed. khr. 37, l. 113. Meyerhold is obviously referring here to the delirium suffered by the dying Prince Andrey in Tolstoy's *War and Peace*. The director prefigures what Prokofiev would achieve in his operatic treatment of the novel.
99. Schmidt, *Meyerhold at Work*, 114: "In this part we will hear leitmotifs from the ball scene and other bits. We will get Grigoriy's dream."
100. During a November 27, 1936, rehearsal Meyerhold quipped: "What was it in this subject [Boris Godunov] that so frightened Nicholas I and the censors? Because a presentation of historical events was so much more terrifying from Pushkin that it would have been from any other writer of the period." Schmidt, *Meyerhold at Work*, 126.
101. RGALI f. 1929, op. 1, yed. khr. 87, l. 30b.
102. Emerson, *Boris Godunov: Transpositions of a Russian Theme*, 63.
103. Kerzhentsev, "Chuzhoy teatr," quoted in Maksimenkov, *Sumbur vmesto muzïki: Stalinskaya kul'turnaya revolyutsiya 1936–1938*, 276.
104. Emerson and Robert William Oldani, *Modest Musorgsky and Boris Godunov: Myths, Realities, Reconsiderations* (Cambridge: Cambridge University Press, 1994), 191: "In 1568 Ivan the Terrible, at the height of his reign of terror, forbade the writing of chronicles, a ban that lingered by inertia until 1630."
105. Schmidt, *Meyerhold at Work*, 101.

Chapter 4

1. Information in this paragraph from Mendel'son-Prokof'yeva, "Iz vospominaniy," 236–41.
2. Lina Prokofiev, interview with MB, November 1967.
3. Lina Prokofiev, interview with MB, April 1–2, 1985.
4. The RGAE catalog describes Mendelson (1885–1968) as an "economist, specialist in the sphere of political economy, doctor of economic science, member of the Presidium of

USSR Gosplan [State Planning Commission], board member of the TsSU [Central Statistics Agency], director of the balance sector of the Institute of Economics of the AN [Academy of Sciences], Professor." His personal file (*lichnoye delo*), fills in the details of his youth and early adulthood. Born in Kiev, he was arrested in 1905 and 1906 for participating in student protests and expelled from the Law Faculty at Kiev University. He relocated in 1914 to Moscow, where he became a member of the General Jewish Labor Union (Bund) and the Menshevik movement, a faction of the Russian revolutionary movement aligned with Julius Martov rather than Vladimir Lenin. He renounced his ties with these organizations in April 1920, when he joined the Communist Party. In 1921 he entered the Red Professorial Institute (Institut Krasnoy Professurï), which trained its students in the propagation of Marxist-Leninist dogma. A 1933 commission charged with purging the Party rank and file deemed Mendelson "trustworthy" on the basis of his active political work (RGASPI f. 17, op. 100, d. 74112, l. 8). His RGAE holding includes four letters written by Prokofiev and six by Mira, dated from October 20, 1942, to April 16, 1945.

5. The first award, bestowed in November 1933, dubbed her a "leading activist of socialist construction, actively showing her worth in the effort to fulfill, on the residential and domestic front, the six objectives of the 1st and 2nd years of Comrade Stalin's Five-Year Plan"; the second award, from June 1935, was for "active social work." RGAE f. 168, op. 1, d. 176, ll. 29 and 43.

6. Mira's Gorky Institute records are located in RGALI f. 632, op. 1, yed. khr. 1917. Page 20 shows that she applied in July 1936 for a transfer into the second year of the program of studies, but, owing to the weakness of her sample work, which included a March 1936 translation "from Hebrew" of a poem titled "A Letter to Voroshilov" (Pis'mo Voroshilovu), she was placed in the first year. Her grades matched those of her peers. According to the records of the State Examination Commission, her final exams at the Institute, taken on October 31 and November 3, 1939, involved translating poems by Robert Burns and W. H. Auden and producing essays on Gavrila Derzhavin's works, Aleksandr Ostrovsky's dramaturgy, and Vladimir Mayakovsky's satire (RGALI f. 632, op. 1, yed. khr. 142, ll. 31 and 33).

7. Mendel'son-Prokof'yeva, "Iz vospominaniy," 241; RGALI f. 1929, op. 2, yed. khr. 669.

8. Mira was by most accounts a dutiful, serious, and withdrawn individual, the antithesis of Prokofiev's vivacious, quick-witted, outgoing wife. Valentina Chemberdzhi remembers Mira habitually "dressed in black, which accentuated the thinness and frailness of her figure even more. At the time I saw and knew her, she was the embodiment of goodness and meekness" (*V dome muzïka zhila: Memuarï o muzïkantakh*, 100).

9. Mendel'son-Prokof'yeva, "Iz vospominaniy," 240.

10. RGALI f. 1929, op. 2, yed. khr. 465, l. 10b.

11. Mendel'son-Prokof'yeva, "Iz vospominaniy," 244.

12. Ibid., 245–46; RGALI f. 1929, op. 1, yed. khr. 393, l. 4.

13. Mendel'son-Prokof'yeva, "Iz vospominaniy," 252.

14. RGALI f. 1929, op. 1, yed. khr. 655, l. 260b.

15. Prokofiev put a cheerful face on the situation in an English-language letter to Ephraim Gottlieb, a Chicago-based insurance agent and longtime (from 1920) acquaintance who served as Prokofiev's de facto representative in the United States: "Madam Prokofieff spends a month in Crimea: she likes the sea and is not afraid of the heat, while I prefer the mountains where it is cooler. The children are in a country place, on a lake between Moscow and Leningrad enjoying swimming, fishing, etc." Unpublished letter of August 16, 1939; photocopy in the possession of MB.

16. RGALI f. 1929, op. 1, yed. khr. 655, l. 260b.

17. Lina Prokofiev, interview with MB, November 1967.

18. RGALI f. 1929, op. 2, yed. khr. 464, l. 15; English-language portion of the quotation italicized.

19. Ibid., l. 16.

20. Eddy, *Science and Health with Key to the Scriptures*, 102; RGALI f. 1929, op. 2, yed. khr. 464, l. 17.

21. Mendel'son-Prokof'yeva, "Iz vospominaniy," 253.

22. Lina Prokofiev, interviews with MB, April 1–2, 1985 and November 1967.

23. Mendel'son-Prokof'yeva, "Iz vospominaniy," 247.

24. Romain Rolland, *Beethoven the Creator*, trans. Ernest Newman (1929; repr., New York: Dover, 1964), 147.

25. RGALI f. 1929, op. 3, yed. khr. 267, l. 3 (March 8, 1940, diary entry).

26. See Chia–Hui Tsai, "Sonata Form Innovations in Prokofiev's Nine Piano Sonatas" (D.M.A. thesis, University of Cincinnati, 2003), 57–63.

27. RGALI f. 1929, op. 1, yed. khr. 986, ll. 1–3. Prokofiev seemed relieved that the work had been well received, humbly informing the gathering (there were eight adjudicators in all) that "I chose a somewhat more complex language and feared that it would be less accessible." He added, with a nod to Abramsky, that he sought to "substitute figuration with contrapuntal material or a texture formed with different principles" (ibid., l. 19).

28. Sviatoslav Richter [Rikhter], *Notebooks and Conversations*, ed. and introd. Bruno Monsaingeon, trans. Stewart Spencer (Princeton: Princeton University Press, 2001), 73–74.

29. RGALI f. 1929, op. 1, yed. khr. 219.

30. Material for the Sixth Sonata appears on p. 22 of a sketchbook begun on May 14, 1935 (RGALI f. 1929, op. 1, yed. khr. 287); additional material for this and the other two sonatas appears on pp. 16, 19, 21, and 24 in a sketchbook begun on May 31, 1936 (RGALI f. 1929, op. 1, yed. khr. 288).

31. RGALI f. 1929, op. 1, yed. khr. 217.

32. Deborah Anne Rifkin, "Tonal Coherence in Prokofiev's Music: A Study of the Interrelationships of Structure, Motives, and Design" (Ph. D. diss., University of Rochester, 2000), 77–83.

33. Richter, *Notebooks and Conversations*, 81.

34. RGALI f. 1929, op. 3, yed. khr. 375, l. 57. Prokofiev learned of the award on March 22, 1943.

35. Taruskin, "*Betrothal in a Monastery*," in *The New Grove Dictionary of Opera*, 1:459; quoted words from Mendel'son-Prokof'yeva, "Iz vospominaniy," 248.

36. Taruskin, "*Betrothal in a Monastery*," 1:460.

37. Mendel'son-Prokof'yeva, "Iz vospominaniy," 246–48. The composer also considered setting Shakespeare.

38. The following synopsis from Hugh McLean, *Nikolai Leskov: The Man and His Art* (Cambridge, Mass.: Harvard University Press, 1977), 166–72.

39. The following information and quotations from Prokofiev's autograph scenario for *The Spendthrift* (RGALI f. 1929, op. 1, yed. khr. 16, ll. 1–3).

40. RGALI f. 1929, op. 2, yed. khr. 182, l. 3.

41. The following information from Mendel'son-Prokof'yeva, "Iz vospominaniy," 248–51.

42. RGALI f. 1929, op. 2, yed. khr. 87, l. 20.

43. RGALI f. 2484, op. 1, yed. khr. 237a, l. 10.

44. RGALI f. 1929, op. 1, yed. khr. 806, ll. 4–5.

45. "Radio reportazh," in *Prokof'yev o Prokof'yeve: Stat'i, interv'yu*, 186. Prokofiev felt that Sheridan's title, *The Duenna*, would sound strange in Russian, and so he decided to retitle the opera *Betrothal in a Monastery*; both titles are now habitually used.

46. Mendel'son-Prokof'yeva, "Iz vospominaniy," 249.

47. For an overview, see L[arisa] G[eyorgyevna] Dan'ko, *Teatr Prokof'yeva v Peterburge* (St. Petersburg: Akademicheskiy proyekt, 2003), 76–85.

48. "Prokof'yev rasskazïvayet o svoyey posledney opere po 'Duen'ye' Sheridana," in *Prokof'yev o Prokof'yeve: Stat'i, interv'yu*, 187.

49. RGALI f. 1929, op. 2, yed. khr. 12 (11 pages) and 19 (75 pages).

50. "The breath of morn bids hence the night," sung by Antonio in tableau 1, scene 4; "If a daughter you have, it's the plague of your life," sung by Jerome in tableau 2, scene 5; "When sable night," sung by Clara in tableau 3, scene 3; "Gentle maid, ah! Why suspect me?" sung by Don Carlos in tableau 3, scene 6; "When a tender maid is first essay'd," sung by the duenna in tableau 4, scene 3; and "This bottle's the sun of our table," sung by the monks in tableau 8, scene 1. Taruskin, "*Betrothal in a Monastery*," 1:459.

51. For a thorough discussion of the writing of the libretto, see Dan'ko, *Teatr Prokof'yeva v Peterburge*, 43–75.

52. Prokof'yev, *Duen'ya (Obrucheniye v monastïre): Liriko-komicheskaya opera v 4-x deystviyakh, 9-ti kartinakh* (Moscow: Sovetskiy kompozitor, 1960), 79.

53. "Obrucheniye v monastïre," in *Prokof'yev o Prokof'yeve: Stat'i, interv'yu*, 189. The article is dated January 17, 1941.

54. D[mitriy] Shostakovich, "Zhizneradostnïy spektakl'," *Sovetskoye iskusstvo*, January 17, 1947, p. 4.

55. Lina Prokof'yeva, "Iz vospominaniy," 224.

56. RGALI f. 1929, op. 3, yed. khr. 375, l. 20b.

57. The history of the project is detailed by I. Rayskin, "Kak teatr Kirova ne stal teatrom Shostakovicha: dokumental'noye povestvovaniye," *Ars Peterburg: Rossiyskiy zhurnal iskusstv* 1 (1993): 94–98.

58. RGALI f. 1929, op. 3, yed. khr. 375, l. 1.

59. RGALI f. 1929, op. 1, yed. khr. 751, l. 1 (letter of January 14, 1941). The phrase "If a claw is caught, the whole bird is lost" (Kogotok uvyaz—vsey ptichke propast') is the epigram, perhaps even the alternate title, to Tolstoy's 1888 drama *The Power of Darkness* (*Vlast' t'mï*).

60. TsGALI SPb f. 337, op. 1, d. 206, l. 21 (act I, scene 2 of the opera).

61. RGALI f. 1929, op. 3, yed. khr. 375, l. 1.

62. Atovm'yan, *Vospominaniya* [typescript], chap. 3, p. 7.

63. RGALI f. 1929, op. 3, yed. khr. 375, l. 4. "Song of the Brave" (Pesnya smelïkh) and the Mayakovsky-based song, "Admiral's Trash" (Dryan' admiral'skaya), composed in Kratovo in July 1941, became the second and first songs of Prokofiev's *Seven Mass Songs* of 1942. The collection contains simply rhymed, strophic settings that evince, now and again, signs of Prokofiev's melodic cleverness. Songs three and four, "The Tankman's Oath" (Klyatva tankista) and "The Son of Kabarda" (Sïn Kabardï), set to texts by Mira, date from November 1941. They fulfilled a commission for 1,000 rubles from the Radio Committee in Nalchik for a literary and musical program about Kabardino-Balkarian heroes of the war. Songs five and six, "The Soldier's [Fighter's] Sweetheart" and "Fritz," also to texts by Mira, date from May 1942. They fulfilled a commission, also for 1,000 rubles, from the Red Army Song and Dance Ensemble in Tbilisi. The final song of the collection is taken from the score of the film *Tonya*. RGALI f. 1929, op. 3, yed. khr. 22 (*Notograficheskiy spravochnik*), l. 1.

64. For some of the evacuees' names, see O[l'ga] Lamm, "Druz'ya Pavla Aleksandrovicha Lamma. V evakuatsii (1941–1943)," in *Iz proshlogo sovetskoy muzïkal'noy kul'turï*, vol. 2, ed. T. N. Livanova (Moscow: Izdatel'stvo "Sovetskiy kompozitor," 1976), 99–100.

65. Lina Prokofiev, interview with MB, April 1–2, 1985.

66. Letter of March 8, 1942, in "Prokofiev and Atovmyan: Correspondence, 1933–1952," 201.

67. RGALI f. 1929, op. 3, yed. khr. 375, l. 15: "Seryozha played through the Fifth and Sixth Scenes for me. Pierre is just as Tolstoy portrays him, which is astonishing, since he is so difficult to convert into an opera character without confusion or recourse to simplification. As usual, Natasha appears just as you see her in the pages of the novel."

68. Atovm'yan, *Vospominaniya* [typescript], chap. 3, p. 9.

69. The suite was premiered on January 21, 1943, in Sverdlovsk (Yekaterinburg) by the State Radio Orchestra under the direction of Nikolay Rabinovich (1908–72).

70. RGALI f. 1929, op. 1, yed. khr. 806, l. 19. Prokofiev composed two string quartets in his career; the first (1930) was a commission from the Library of Congress.

71. Lina Prokofiev worked from home as a translator for the agency during the war; Afinogenov helped her to obtain the part-time position.

72. "Khudozhnik i voyna," in *Prokof'yev o Prokof'yeve: Stat'i, interv'yu*, 206.

73. S. I. Taneyev, "O muzïke gorskikh tatar," in *Pamyati Sergeya Ivanovicha Taneyeva 1856–1946. Sbornik statey i materialov k 90-letiyu so dnya rozhdeniya*, ed. Vl. Protopopov (Moscow and Leningrad: Muzgiz, 1947), 205.

74. Ibid., 204. According to Taneyev, the song is played by "shepherds on a pipe in order to settle down their sheep at night. The shepherd plays; the sheep gather together."

75. RGALI f. 1929, op. 3, yed. khr. 267, l. 4 (April 17, 1943, entry); letter of April 24, 1943, in *S. S. Prokof'yev i N. Ya. Myaskovskiy: Perepiska*, 467.

76. *Deyateli russkogo iskusstva i M. B. Khrapchenko, predsedatel' Vsesoyuznogo komiteta po delam iskusstv: aprel' 1939-yanvar' 1948*, 596–97.

77. In a letter dated September 23, 1942, Myaskovsky informed Prokofiev that "I only just received a postcard from Derzhanovsky: in Moscow they played your 2nd quartet and it made an excellent impression, even the 'Scythian' (his word) 1st movement and motley finale" (*S. S. Prokof'yev i N. Ya. Myaskovskiy: Perepiska*, 460). The published reviews of the work were neutral. G. Kovrov, for example, commented, "The quartet was written in a manner typical for Prokofiev in recent years. In the elucidation of the musical language we find here his typically harsh, 'granite' sounds (especially in the first movement), tender lyricism (the second, slow movement), and an original, perhaps questionable but clearly individual approach to the treatment of folksong material." "Kontsertï kvarteta im. Betkhovena," *Literatura i iskusstvo*, September 12, 1942, p. 4.

78. RGALI f. 1929, op. 1, yed. khr. 189 and 190. The tempo shifts from 96 to 104 beats per minute.

79. RGALI f. 1929, op. 3, yed. khr. 375, l. 15 (December 23, 1941, entry).

80. Brown, "Prokofiev's *War and Peace*: A Chronicle," 302.

81. These characters are described by Tolstoy in Book 4, pt. 1, chap. 11 of his novel.

82. The composer Vasiliy Nechayev (1895–1956) and his wife, the conductor Aleksandr Gauk (1893–1963) and his wife, the composer Anatoliy Aleksandrov (1888–1982) and his wife, the actress Valeriya Massalitinova (1878–1945), and Nikolay Myaskovsky and his second sister Valentina (1886–1965).

83. RGALI f. 1929, op. 3, yed. khr. 375, ll. 10–17. Information and quotations in the following paragraphs from ll. 18–23.

84. His duties included gathering scores for evaluation by the Stalin Prize Committee.

85. RGALI f. 1929, op. 3, yed. khr. 375, ll. 26–27 (April 9, 1942): "I had an interesting conversation with Seryozha about Mozart's *Don Giovanni*. In this opera musical numbers alternate with spoken scenes. In some theaters these scenes comprise *secco* recitative with sparse chordal accompaniment on the clavichord. The music of these scenes does not attract interest and does not even seem to be written by Mozart. Seryozha said that he had wanted for a long time to write music for these scenes in the style of (and using material belonging to) Mozart's musical numbers. 'My experience with the Classical Symphony gives me cause to hope for a successful outcome.' Seryozha finds the libretto of *Don Giovanni* ramshackle: when it is staged, some numbers and (especially) recitatives are omitted. The opera would be even greater if musical numbers replaced the fast-paced conversations. For this reason he expressed a desire for me to look over the piano score of *Don Giovanni* and think about potential reductions."

86. Prokofiev's letters to Atovmyan during the war contain urgent requests for manuscript paper of different sizes. See, for example, "Prokofiev and Atovmyan: Correspondence, 1933–1952," 210–11.

87. On March 31, 1942, Mira records: "Seryozha was tortured all day yesterday with a headache. He couldn't work. I read Aleksey Tolstoy's tales 'Incident on Basseynaya Street' [Sluchay na Basseynoy ulitse, 1926], 'The Viper' [Gadyuka, 1928], 'Frozen Night' [Moroznaya noch', 1928], and others aloud to him. The reading takes his thoughts away from the pain. He listens very attentively." RGALI f. 1929, op. 3, yed. khr. 375, l. 25.

88. Ibid., l. 23. The film opened in New York on March 23, 1939; the article, commissioned by VOKS, was intended for the re-release.

89. In his diary, Myaskovsky records: "May 28, 1942. The Prokofievs came by to say goodbye. Tomorrow they are leaving for Alma-Ata" (Lamm, *Stranitsï tvorcheskoy biografii Myaskovskogo*, 287). The trip was delayed; Prokofiev had planned to leave eleven days earlier. In a May 17 letter to Atovmyan, he stated: "Tomorrow I am relocating from Tbilisi to Alma-Ata to work on the film *Ivan the Terrible*. Address: Central Film Studio, me. Please write to me with what you've heard about *War and Peace*; that is, the impressions it made on those who heard it, the perspectives on staging it, and so on. Let me also know if the suite *The Year 1941* and the Quartet on Kabardino-Balkarian Themes are simply sitting on the shelf, or if something will be done with them. And more: did Shlifshteyn pass along to you my two songs about the Kabardino-Balkarian heroes of the war? I would really like 1) these songs to be sung, 2) to be published, and 3) for the SSK [Union of Soviet Composers] to pay me the honorarium for them. I have written two more songs, which I'll send to you when the occasion arises." "Prokofiev and Atovmyan: Correspondence, 1933–1952," 202–3.

90. Richard Pevear, "Preface" to Tolstoy, *What Is Art?* xi.

91. Bessarabia stems from "Basarab," the name of the Romanian, or Wallachian dynastic clan that controlled part of the area in the fourteenth century. The Molotov-Ribbentrop Nonaggression Pact of 1939 gave Stalin a free hand over the entire region.

92. The other two anniversary films were *Leningraders* (*Leningradtsï*), directed by Sergey Gerasimov and Mikhaíl Kolotozov, and *Secretary of the District Committee* (*Sekretar' raykoma*), directed by Ivan Pïryev.

93. E. Vishnevetskaya, "Kinomuzïka S. S. Prokof'yeva voyennïkh let," in *Iz proshlogo sovetskoy muzïkal'noy kulturï*, vol. 1, ed. T. N. Livanova (Moscow: Izdatel'stvo "Sovetskiy kompozitor," 1975), 49.

94. The extant pages of the score are in RGALI f. 1929, op. 1, yed. khr. 105 and 106. The four items in yed. khr. 105—"Song" (Pesnya), "Gallop" (Skachka), "Revolution"

(Revolutsiya), and "Waltz" (Val's)—exist in piano score in the composer's hand; the three items in yed. khr. 106—"Intervention" (Interventsiya), "Kharitonov's Death (incomplete)" (Smert' Kharitonova [bez kontsa]), and "Germans before the Naked Attack" (Nemtsï pered goloy atakoy)—are orchestrated in another hand. Four items from the score are missing. Facsimile pages of much of the extant music from the film are provided in Vishnevetskaya, "Kinomuzïka S. S. Prokof'yeva voyennïkh let," 391–40; see pp. 47–56 for a substantive discussion of the music.

95. This latter song, which dates from 1863, is associated with both Polish and Russian worker causes.

96. Vishnevetskaya, "Kinomuzïka S. S. Prokof'yeva voyennïkh let," 54.

97. *S. S. Prokof'yev i N. Ya. Myaskovskiy: Perepiska*, 461. The cantata, *Ballad of an Unknown Boy*, is discussed later in the chapter. Based almost exclusively on preexisting melodic material from his sketchbooks, the Flute Sonata, a peaceful Mozartian diversion from his brooding wartime projects, received its premiere in Moscow on December 7, 1943. Prokofiev received the contract for the score in Alma-Ata in September 1942, and completed it a year later in Perm. "The Flute Sonata is almost finished," he wrote to Atovmyan on August 12, 1943. "The reprise of the finale remains to be written up. It ended up being quite substantial: four movements, nearly 40 pages, in a word worth all 8,000 rubles" ("Prokofiev and Atovmyan: Correspondence, 1933–1952," 222). Prokofiev converted the Flute Sonata into his Second Violin Sonata on the suggestion of the violinist David Oistrakh (1908–74). It was premiered in Moscow on June 17, 1944.

98. The following information from M[iral'da] G[eyorgyevna] Kozlova, "S. S. Prokof'yev pishet muzïku k fil'mu," *Muzïkal'naya zhizn'* 16 (August 1983): 18–19.

99. I. Tyurin, "Pochemu zapazdïvayet fil'm 'Lermontov'?" *Kino (Moskva)*, June 13, 1941, p. 4.

100. For an example of the criticism see Mikh[aíl] Levidov, "Lozhnaya kontseptsiya," *Kino (Moskva)*, October 18, 1940, p. 3. Noting the pathos-ridden representation of the poet in the first draft of the script, Levidov complains: "A tale about a great man never incorporates that which 'happened' to him, what 'was taking place' around him, what others 'were doing' to him. It must first of all be a tale about what he did. For action is the dominant of each great man, and it is what leaves a mark in history."

101. L. Barn, "Fil'm o Lermontove," *Literatura i iskusstvo*, July 17, 1943, p. 2.

102. RGALI f. 1929, op. 1, yed. khr. 101.

103. The original version of the score (RGALI f. 1929, op.1, yed. khr. 99) comprised a polonaise, a quadrille, three waltzes, a marching song, and an opera excerpt. Lamm orchestrated the polonaise, the "Mephisto" Waltz, and some additional background music associated with the "regime of Nikolay I" (RGALI f. 1929, op. 1, yed. khr. 100).

104. The song resurfaces in Prokofiev's 1948 opera *A Story of a Real Man* (*Povest' o nastoyashchem cheloveke*).

105. RGALI f. 1929, op. 1, yed. khr. 101, l. 2.

106. Konstantin Paustovskiy, "Poruchik Lermontov (Stsenï iz zhizni Lermontova)," in *Sobraniye sochineniy*, ed. N. Kryuchkova, 6 vols. (Moscow: Gosudarstvennoye izdatel'stvo khudozhestvennoy literaturï, 1958), 6:23.

107. Kozlova, "S. S. Prokof'yev pishet muzïku k fil'mu," 18; RGALI f. 1929, op. 3, yed. khr. 61, l. 1.

108. Kozlova, "S. S. Prokof'yev pishet muzïku k fil'mu," 18.

109. Ibid., 19 (letter of July 8, 1942).

110. Ibid.

111. Ibid.

112. Ibid (letter of August 26, 1942).

113. Ibid.

114. Vishnevetskaya, "Kinomuzïka S. S. Prokof'yeva voyennïkh let," 63–64.

115. For a transcription of the folksong—"Oh you, Galya" (Oy tï, Galya)—and an extensive discussion of its use in the film, see ibid., 58–63.

116. Facsimile pages of much of the extant music from the film are provided in ibid., 402–8.

117. Clark, *The Soviet Novel*, 181. The phrase "more alive than the living" comes from the 1924 Mayakovsky elegy "Vladimir Il'yich Lenin." For context on the final point in this paragraph, see pp. 178–82.

118. RGALI f. 2372, op. 5, yed. khr. 7, l. 3.

119. Ibid., l. 9.

120. Ibid., l. 24.

121. Ibid., l. 30.

122. Ibid., l. 32.

123. This quotation and the information in the preceding and following sentences from Jerry T. Heil, *No List of Political Assets: The Collaboration of Iurii Olesha and Abram Room on 'Strogii Iunosha' (A Strict Youth [1936])* (Munich: Verlag Otto Sagner, 1989), 120–21.

124. The psychological content of Room's films is the primary subject of "K 100-letiyu Abrama Rooma: 'Kruglïy stol' v Muzee kino (fragmentï)," *Kinovedcheskiye zapiski* 25 (1994/95): 163–74.

125. Room's 1927 film *Third Meshchanskaya Street*, for example, has been described "as one of the earliest feminist films." Peter Kenez, *Cinema and Soviet Society from the Revolution to the Death of Stalin* (London: I. B. Tauris, 2001), 52–53.

126. RGALI f. 1929, op. 2, yed. khr. 40, l. 1.

127. It is also used in *A Story of a Real Man*, in the scene where the injured fighter pilot Aleksey Maresyev remembers his faraway sweetheart.

128. RGAE f. 168, op. 1, d. 161, l. 4.

129. I am grateful to Laura Hedden for her transcription and annotation of the melodic material in the score.

130. It bears noting, however, that the harmony, phrasing, and scoring of the illustrative music is richer than that of the song. For example, the melody of the third number, "The Park Path," ascends through the upper registers of the orchestra, the E-flat major backdrop suffused by wayward D-flats and G-flats. Harps strum between measures 3 and 5, their tonal stasis answered between measures 8 and 10 by chromatic sequences in the strings and brasses. Prokofiev's musical narrative matches the cause-and-effect motion of the visual narrative: the Germans are on the doorstep of the Soviet town, thus the halcyon ambience of "The Park Path" has to be dispelled.

131. RGALI f. 1929, op. 1, yed. khr. 102, l. 3. The text refers to Field Marshal Aleksandr Suvorov (1729–1800), an iconic figure in Russian history, reputed never to have lost a battle.

132. RGALI f. 1929, op. 2, yed. khr. 339, l. 8.

133. RGALI f. 1929, op. 1, yed. khr. 814, l. 13.

134. *Istoriya sovremennoy otechestvennoy muzïki. Tom. 2 (1941–48)*, ed. M. E. Tarakanov (Moscow: Muzïka, 1999), 453–55.

135. Denise J. Youngblood, *Russian War Films: On the Cinema Front, 1914–2005* (Lawrence: University Press of Kansas, 2007), 59.

136. RGALI f. 1929, op. 1, yed. khr. 522, l. 2.

137. RGALI f. 1929, op. 2, yed. khr. 184, l. 3 (letter of September 4, 1943).

138. RGALI f. 1929, op. 1, yed. khr. 806, l. 21.

139. "Prokofiev and Atovmyan: Correspondence, 1933–1952," 202. On June 10, 1943, Prokofiev sent Atovmyan a follow-up note: "I've almost finished the *Semyon Kotko* Suite. Since you asked in one of your letters what commission I'd like to receive from Muzfond, I'd be grateful if you sent me a contract for the suite. The deadline for completing it can be July 1 of this year. It's turning out to be quite large, eight movements, almost 120 pages of scoring in small hand. This is so the contract won't be too meager" (218–19).

140. Letter of November 1, 1942, reproduced in RGALI f. 1929, op. 3, yed. khr. 375, ll. 47–48.

141. *Deyateli russkogo iskusstva i M. B. Khrapchenko, predsedatel' Vsesoyuznogo komiteta po delam iskusstv: aprel' 1939-yanvar' 1948*, 607.

142. Information from Pavel Antokol'skiy, *Stikhotvoreniya i poemï* (Moscow: Gosudarstvennoye izdatel'stvo khudozhestvennoy literaturï, 1958), 10.

143. "Khudozhnik i voyna," 207.

144. RGALI f. 1929, op. 3, yed. khr. 267, l. 4 (February 19 and 21, 1944, diary entries).

145. Shostakovich, "Sovetskaya muzïka v dni voynï," *Literatura i iskusstvo*, April 1, 1944, p. 2.

146. "Oni proshli po gryazi gruzno, za manekenom maneken."

147. Medvedeva, "Istoriya prokof'yevskogo avtografa, ili GURK v deystvii," in *Sergey Prokof'yev: K 110-letiyu so dnya rozhdeniya: Pis'ma, vospominaniya, stat'i*, ed. M. P. Rakhmanova (Moscow: Gosudarstvennïy tsentral'nïy muzey muzïkal'noy kul'turï imeni M. I. Glinki, 2001), 223–24; *Deyateli russkogo iskusstva i M. B. Khrapchenko, predsedatel' Vsesoyuznogo komiteta po delam iskusstv: aprel' 1939-yanvar' 1948*, 600–601.

148. Medvedeva, "Istoriya prokof'yevskogo avtografa, ili GURK v deystvii," 226–27.

149. Taruskin, "New Life for an Opera Hater's Masterpiece as…an Opera," *New York Times*, Arts & Leisure Section, September 9, 2001, pp. 63 and 68: "Tolstoy describes what would now be diagnosed as a case of tinnitus, a symptom of Andrey's wound that causes him to hear 'a soft, whispering voice repeating over and over again in a steady rhythm: "piti-piti-piti," and then "ti-ti," and again "piti-piti-piti," and "ti-ti." ' "

150. The manuscript of the original piano score of *War and Peace* shows, in the form of pencil inserts, several of the changes made to it between 1943 and 1949. See RGALI f. 1929, op. 1, yed. khr. 36.

151. Medvedeva, "Istoriya prokof'yevskogo avtografa, ili GURK v deystvii," 228 and 230.

152. RGALI f. 1929, op. 3, yed. khr. 375, l. 46.

153. *Deyateli russkogo iskusstva i M. B. Khrapchenko, predsedatel' Vsesoyuznogo komiteta po delam iskusstv: aprel' 1939-yanvar' 1948*, 604.

154. Ibid., 605. The epigraph would eventually be relocated from the start of the first half of the opera to the start of the second (scene 8 in the final version).

155. His travel plans changed. Prokofiev instead left Alma-Ata in late November, stopping en route to Moscow in Semipalatinsk to work on *Partisans in the Ukrainian Steppe*.

156. Collotyping, a printing technique invented in the nineteenth century, involves coating a glass plate with chromate gelatin and exposing it to light under a photographic negative of an image, creating a photographic positive.

157. Richter, *Notebooks and Conversations*, 79.

158. RGALI f. 1929, op. 3, yed. khr. 375, l. 53.

159. Prokofiev did not compose the polonaise specifically for *Lermontov*. It came from his incidental music to the unrealized *Boris Godunov*, and it was later included in the score of *Ivan the Terrible* Part II. Arrangements of the famous "Mephisto" Waltz, an original

contribution to the soundtrack, became part of the Three Pieces for Piano (1942) and Waltz Suite for Orchestra (1946).

160. "Pis'ma S. S. Prokof'yeva k P. A. Lammu," 295 n. 1.

161. "Dokladnaya zapiska G. F. Aleksandrova o neudovletvoritel'nom rukovodstve khudo-zhestvennoy kinematografiyey Komitetom po delam kinematografii pri SNK SSSR," in *Kremlyovskiy kinoteatr 1928–1953. Dokumentï*, 675.

162. RGALI f. 562, op. 1, yed. khr. 171, l. 3. Shklovsky's review is titled "Pages Torn from a Biography and Badly Read" (Listï, vïrvannïye iz biografii i plokho prochtyonnïye).

163. Taruskin, *Defining Russia Musically* (Princeton: Princeton University Press, 1997), 282–84.

164. Atovm'yan, *Vospominaniya* [typescript], chap. 3, p. 19.

165. Eddy, *Science and Health with Key to the Scriptures*, 385.

166. Atovm'yan, *Vospominaniya* [typescript], chap. 3, p. 19.

167. On August 12, 1943, Prokofiev informed Atovmyan: "The question of my trip to Moscow remains uncertain in view of the fact that Eisenstein expects me in Alma-Ata at the end of September to finish the music for *Ivan the Terrible* Part I." "Prokofiev and Atovmyan: Correspondence, 1933–1952," 222–23.

168. The organs of the government transferred to the Volga River city of Kuybïshev (now Samara) beginning on October 15, 1941.

169. Information in this paragraph from Medvedeva, "O 'gimnakh' Prokof'yeva," in *Sergey Prokof'yev: K 110-letiyu so dnya rozhdeniya: Pis'ma, vospominaniya, stat'i*, 212; and from Laurel E. Fay, *Shostakovich: A Life* (Oxford: Oxford University Press, 2000), 139.

170. N. A. Sidorov, "'Gimn bol'shevikov pererastayet u nas v gosudarstvennïy': Dokumentï rossiyskikh arkhivov ob istorii sozdaniya Gosudarstvennogo gimna SSSR: 1943–1946 gg.," *Istoriya v dokumentakh. Rossiya XX vek* (2007). Available at http://www.idf .ru/documents/info.jsp?p=20&set=66230. Mikhalkov and El-Registan's letter is dated September 28, 1943.

171. Medvedeva, "O 'gimnakh' Prokof'yeva," 212.

172. Caroline Brooke, "Changing Identities: The Russian and Soviet National Anthems," *Slavonica* 13:1 (April 2007): 32.

173. This second hymn, to words by Stepan Shchipachyov (1899–1980), is included in fac-simile in Medvedeva, "O 'gimnakh' Prokof'yeva," 214–15.

174. Prokofiev reported the proposal to Atovmyan in a September 16, 1943, letter: "The Kirov Theater has scheduled a staging of my ballet *The Buffoon*, and soon at that. Since I don't have the piano score here, and don't know where mine is, I implore you without haste to make a copy of it. It can be obtained from Nik[olay] Yak[ovlevich Myaskovsky], or perhaps from Ye. V. Derzhanovskaya or the Conservatory library. The Kirov Theater will pay for the copy. Instruct the copyist to carefully write out the comments concerning the visual action, and likewise the indications for the instrumentation (fl., cl., and so forth). Second: To become familiar with the sound of *The Buffoon*, the theater wants to run through the suite in a closed rehearsal. Please send the orchestral score and parts to the theater's chairman, who will deliver them here and return them immediately after the run-through." "Prokofiev and Atovmyan: Correspondence, 1933–1952," 226.

175. D[mitriy] R[omanovich] Rogal'-Levitskiy, "'Mimolyotnïye svyazi': K 70-letiyu so dnya rozhdeniya Sergeya Prokof'yeva," in *Sergey Prokof'yev: K 110-letiyu so dnya rozhdeniya: Pis'ma, vospominaniya, stat'i*, 172.

176. Ibid., 188.

177. Information in this paragraph from RGALI f. 1929, op.3, yed. khr. 375, ll. 60–61.

CHAPTER 5

1. See Maksimenkov, *Sumbur vmesto muzïki: Stalinskaya kul'turnaya revolyutsiya 1936–1938*, 241–53.

2. "Pis'mo S. M. Eyzenshteyna B. Z. Shumyatskomu o svoyey dal'neyshey rabote v kino," in *Kremlyovskiy kinoteatr 1928–1953. Dokumentï*, 417.

3. "Dokladnaya zapiska B. Z. Shumyatskogo I. V. Stalinu o dal'neyshey rabote S. M. Eyzenshteyna," in ibid., 419.

4. "Postanovleniye TsK VKP(b)," in ibid., 419–20.

5. "Dokladnaya zapiska zam. zav. Otdelom kul'turno-prosvetitel'noy rabotï TsK VKP(b) A. I. Angarova I. V. Stalinu i A. A. Andreyevu s predlozheniyem poruchit' S. M. Eyzenshteynu postanovku novoy kinokartinï," in ibid., 424.

6. Ibid., 420 n. 2.

7. "Prilozheniye," in ibid., 425. In a July 6, 1938, letter, Vishnevsky praised *Alexander Nevsky* while expressing regret that he had been unable to collaborate with Eisenstein: "With just a touch of grief I thought about how things would have turned out if we had made *We, the Russian People* together." Vs[evolod] Vishnevskiy, *Stat'i, dnevniki, pis'ma o literature i iskusstve* (Moscow: Sovetskiy pisatel', 1961), 523.

8. The practice of using long-past historical events to allegorize the present day did not end with Stalin. The 2007 film *1612*, directed by Vladimir Khotinenko, suggests parallels between the early seventeenth-century Time of Troubles and the late twentieth-century collapse of the Soviet Union. The film emphasizes the importance of strong Russian leadership and patriotism. The stable, prosperous reign of Tsar Mikhaíl Romanov is likened to Vladimir Putin's rule.

9. Merritt, "Recharging *Alexander Nevsky*: Tracking the Eisenstein–Prokofiev War Horse," 36.

10. Sergei Eisenstein [Sergey Eyzenshteyn], "Alexander Nevsky and the Rout of the Germans" [Aleksandr Nevskiy i razgrom nemtsev], in *The Eisenstein Reader*, ed. Richard Taylor (London: British Film Institute, 1998), 141.

11. Ibid., 144.

12. P. Yevstaf'yev, "O stsenarii 'Rus' ': Blizhe k istoricheskoy pravde," *Literaturnaya gazeta*, April 26, 1938, p. 6.

13. Eyzenshteyn, "Otvet tov. P. Yevstaf'yevu," *Literaturnaya gazeta*, April 26, 1938, p. 6.

14. Quoted in David Brandenberger, "The Popular Reception of S. M. Eisenstein's *Aleksandr Nevskii*," in *Epic Revisionism: Russian History and Literature as Stalinist Propaganda*, 235.

15. Eyzenshteyn, "Aleksandr Nevskiy [final rannego varianta literaturnogo stsenariya]," in *Izbrannïye proizvedeniya*, ed. S. I. Yutkevich, 6 vols. (Moscow: Izdatel'stvo "Iskusstvo," 1964–71), 6:453–55.

16. Eyzenshteyn, *Memuarï*, ed. N. I. Kleyman, 2 vols. (Moscow: Redaktsiya gazetï "Trud"/ Muzey kino, 1997), 2:289.

17. Maksimenkov, "Vvedeniye," in *Kremlyovskiy kinoteatr 1928–1953. Dokumentï*, 11.

18. "Fil'm-kontsert 'Aleksandr Nevskiy' v Bol'shom teatre. Pervïye vpechatleniya. 'Kruglïy stol' v Muzee kino," *Kinovedcheskiye zapiski* 70 (2004): 12.

19. Ibid., 12–13.

20. RGALI f. 1929, op. 1, yed. khr. 814, ll. 7–8.

21. Unsigned, "Fil'm o Ledovom poboishche," *Pravda*, April 21, 1938, p. 6; unsigned, "Kinos'yomki 'Ledovogo poboishcha,'" *Pravda*, July 8, 1938, p. 6.

22. Kevin Bartig notes that part of the overlong Battle on the Ice footage was made into a short for the "Battle Film Album" series. See his "Composing for the Red Screen: Sergei Proko-fiev's Film Music" (Ph. D. diss., University of North Carolina at Chapel Hill, 2008), 162.

23. Information in this paragraph provided by Naum Kleyman in a January 13, 2007, personal communication.

24. Eisenstein, "P–R–K–F–V," in *Notes of a Film Director* (New York: Dover, 1970), 158.

25. Ibid., 149.

26. "Moi novïye rabotï," in *Prokof'yev o Prokof'yeve: Stat'i, interv'yu*, 165.

27. Prokof'yev and Alpers, "Perepiska," 431. Prokofiev sketched his Cello Concerto in E Minor during the summer of 1933 in Paris and completed it, after great delay, on September 18, 1938, in Nikolina Gora. It was premiered in Moscow on November 26, 1938, with Lev Ber-ezovsky (1898–1960) as soloist, during the second *dekada* of Soviet music. Despite positive advance notice in *Sovetskoye iskusstvo*, the three-movement score came in for stinging cri-tique in *Sovetskaya muzïka* for its diffuseness. Pyatigorsky, the cellist with whom Prokofiev conceived the Concerto, unveiled it in Boston on March 8, 1940, thereafter sending the com-poser a list of proposed changes. Like Berezovsky, he found the score unwieldy, and solicited and received (terse) permission from Prokofiev to adjust it.

28. Ibid., 432.

29. B[oris] Vol'skiy, "Vospominaniya o S. S. Prokof'yeve," in *S. S Prokof'yev: Materialï, doku-mentï, vospominaniya*, 526–31.

30. See Merritt, "Recharging *Alexander Nevsky*: Tracking the Eisenstein–Prokofiev War Horse," 44.

31. The scenario also provides a complete cast list, noteworthy for its folkloric doubling of char-acter types: Aleksandr Yaroslavich Nevskiy, Novgorod Prince in conflict with Novgorodi-ans living in Pereyaslav; Aleksandra Bryachislavovna, his wife; Gavrilo Oleksich and Vasiliy Buslay, Novgorod warriors who participated in Aleksandr's victory over the Swedes; Amelfa Timofeyevna, Buslay's widowed mother; Vasilisa, maid of Pskov; Ol'ga, Novgorod maiden; Domash Tverdilovich, Novgorod boyar; a Novgorod merchant; Mikula, leader of the peasant militia; Pegusiy, a monk who participated in Aleksandr's victory over the Swedes; Mikhalka, friend of Aleksandr; Ignat, Novgorod maker of chain armor; Savka, a princeling; Nikita, an old fisherman; Pavsha, an old Pskov commander; Tverdilo, Pskov traitor; Ananiy, Tverdilo's monastic assistant; Avvakum, an old Pskov beggar; Graf German von Balk, master of the Teutonic Order; a Bishop; Brother Hubertus and Brother Dietlieb, Teutonic knights; a Black Monk; Khubilay, the Hun ambassador to Rus'. RGALI f. 1929, op. 1, yed. khr. 98, l. 6.

32. Ibid., l. 5.

33. RGALI f. 1929, op. 1, yed. khr. 97 (cover sheet).

34. Prokofiev received an 8,000-ruble commission from the Committee on Arts Affairs for the Cantata, with the agreement stipulating completion in 1939 (RGALI f. 1929, op. 1, yed. khr. 806, ll. 16–17). "The music for the film *Alexander Nevsky* is the basis of the Cantata," the composer explained. "All of the musical material was subject to funda-mental reworking; the Cantata was significantly expanded by excerpts written for the film, but not included within it." RGALI f. 1929, op. 3, yed. khr. 21 (*Notograficheskiy spravochnik*), l. 29.

35. Vol'skiy, "Vospominaniya o S. S. Prokof'yeve," 530.

36. Bartig, "Composing for the Red Screen: Sergei Prokofiev's Film Music," 146–50.

37. A. Postnikov, "Vsyo li blagopoluchno u poeta Lugovskogo? Pis'mo v redaktsiyu," *Lit-eraturnaya gazeta*, April 26, 1937, p. 5; Valentin Katayev, "Vïdokhi i vdokhi," *Pravda*, November 5, 1938, p. 4.

38. RGALI f. 1929, op. 3, yed. khr. 22 (*Notograficheskiy spravochnik*), l. 13.

39. On January 5, 1950, Lugovskoy sent the following note to Prokofiev: "Here are the outlines of my opus. For now it's been conditionally approved at Muzgiz. I simply dashed off the 8th stanza, which wouldn't otherwise come out" (RGALI f. 1929, op. 1, yed. khr. 599, l. 2).

40. Svyatoslav Prokof'yev, "O moikh roditelyakh: Beseda sïna kompozitora (S. P.) s muzïkovedom Nataliyey Savkinoy (N. S.)," in *Sergey Prokof'yev 1891–1991: Dnevnik, pis'ma besedï, vospominaniya, 229.*

41. In the sketches, "patres mei" (my fathers) substitutes for "pedes meos." See RGALI f. 1929, op. 1, yed. khr. 97, l. 8.

42. "Muzïka k 'Aleksandru Nevskomu,' " in *Prokof'yev o Prokof'yeve: Stat'i, interv'yu, 168.*

43. The source was first identified in print by Morag G. Kerr, "Prokofiev and His Cymbals," *Musical Times* 135 (October 1994): 608–9.

44. Movement 1, a setting of verses 13–14 of Psalm 39, includes the phrase "Quoniam advena sum apud te, et *peregrinus*" (For I am a stranger with Thee, and a *sojourner*); Movement 2, from verses 2–4 of Psalm 40, includes the phrases "*Expectans expectavi* Dominum et intendit mihi" (*I waited* patiently for the Lord, and He inclined unto me) and "Et statuit super petram *pedes meos*" (And He set *my feet* on rock); Movement 3, from Psalm 150 in its entirety, includes the phrase "Laudate eum *in cymbalis* bene sonantibus" (Praise Him *with* the well-tuned *cymbals*).

45. The original title of his ballet *Le Pas d'Acier*, for example, was "Ursignol," a conflation of two abbreviations: "URSS"—the French for USSR—and "gnol" from the end of *rossignol*. The reference is to Stravinsky's opera *Le Rossignol*, which was produced by Diaghilev in 1914, as well as to Stravinsky's symphonic poem *Le Chant du Rossignol*, premiered in 1919 and staged as a ballet in 1925. "Ros" is also the first syllable of "Rossiya."

46. RGALI f. 1929, op. 3, yed. khr. 21 (*Notograficheskiy spravochnik*), l. 29.

47. For a scene-by-scene taxonomy of the battle music, one that accords with Prokofiev's intensions as outlined in the sketches, see Michael Stegemann, "Klang. Geste. Raum. Prokofjews Filmmusik zu Sergej Eisensteins *Alexander Newski*," in *Bericht über das Internationale Symposion "Sergej Prokofjew—Aspekte seines Werkes und der Biographie." Köln 1991, 349–61.*

48. Philip D. Roberts, "Prokofiev's Score and Cantata for Eisenstein's *Alexander Nevsky*," *Semiotica* 21: 1/2 (1977): 161.

49. Moreover, Nevsky rides a white horse, his Teutonic counterpart a black one.

50. Roberts, "Prokofiev's Score and Cantata for Eisenstein's *Alexander Nevsky*," 164–65.

51. Eisenstein, *The Film Sense*, trans. and ed. Jay Leyda (New York: Harcourt Brace, 1975), 161.

52. Gilles Deleuze, *Cinema 2: The Time Image*, trans. Hugh Tomlinson and Robert Galeta (Minneapolis: University of Minnesota Press, 1989), 239.

53. Eisenstein, *The Film Sense*, 172–73.

54. See Brandenberger, "The Popular Reception of S. M. Eisenstein's *Aleksandr Nevskii*," 236–46.

55. Ibid., 238.

56. Ibid., 252 n. 59.

57. *Deyateli russkogo iskusstva i M. B. Khrapchenko, predsedatel' Vsesoyuznogo komiteta po delam iskusstv: aprel' 1939-yanvar' 1948, 53.*

58. See, for example, Joan Neuberger, *Ivan the Terrible* (London: I. B. Tauris, 2003); and Yuri Tsivian, *Ivan the Terrible* (London: British Film Institute, 2002).

59. Eyzenshteyn, "Fil'm ob Ivane Groznom," *Izvestiya*, April 30, 1941, p. 3.

60. For the official account, see Brandenberger and Kevin M. F. Platt, "Terribly Pragmatic: Rewriting the History of Ivan IV's Reign, 1937–1956," in *Epic Revisionism: Russian History and Literature as Stalinist Propaganda*, 157–78.

61. Eyzenshteyn, "Fil'm ob Ivane Groznom."

62. Romm, *Besedï o kino*, 91.

63. Neuberger, *Ivan the Terrible*, 31.

64. "And Tsar Ivan descends to the waves, casting a spell. And the sea is subdued. The waves slowly bow, lapping at the feet of the absolute ruler of the Russian lands." Eyzenshteyn, "Ivan Groznïy [kinostsenariy]," in *Izbrannïye proizvedeniya*, 6:418.

65. For the history, see L. M. Roshal', "'Ya uzhe ne mal'chik i na avantyuru ne poydu...': Perepiska S. M. Eyzenshteyna s kinematograficheskim rukovodstvom po stsenariyu i fil'mu 'Ivan Groznïy,'" *Kinovedcheskiye zapiski* 38 (1998): 142–67.

66. "Iz perepiski S. S. Prokof'yeva i S. M. Eyzenshteyna," in *Sergey Prokof'yev: Stat'i i materialï*, 345. For an English-language translation of the bulk of their correspondence about the film, see *Selected Letters of Sergei Prokofiev*, 213–21.

67. Ibid. (letter of March 3, 1942).

68. Ibid., 346.

69. RGALI f. 1929, op. 3, yed. khr. 375, l. 37.

70. Neuberger, *Ivan the Terrible*, 14. Stalin offered his opinion on the scenario on September 13, 1943: "The scenario turned out not badly. Comrade Eisenstein coped with the task. Ivan the Terrible, as a progressive force for his time, and the *oprichnina*, as his effective instrument, came out not badly. The scenario, it follows, should be quickly realized." "Zapiska I. V. Stalina I. G. Bol'shakovu o stsenarii S. M. Eyzenshteyna 'Ivan Groznïy,'" in *Kremlyovskiy kinoteatr 1928–1953. Dokumentï*, 685.

71. The "extra one" was the sung text "Rejoice the Tsar Is Crowned" for the Uspensky Cathedral coronation scene.

72. V[ladimir] Zabrodin, "S. M. Eyzenshteyn: Iz arkhiva," *Kinograf* 8 (2000): 134.

73. Versions of the song are included in Aleksandr Ostrovsky's play *The Snow Maiden* (*Snegurochka*, 1873) and Rimsky-Korsakov's 1881 opera of the same name.

74. Tatiana K. Egorova, *Soviet Film Music: An Historical Survey*, trans. Tatiana A. Ganf and Natalia A. Egunova (Amsterdam: Harwood Academic Publishers, 1997), 106.

75. Avril Pyman, *A History of Russian Symbolism* (Cambridge: Cambridge University Press, 1994), 256.

76. Information in this and the following paragraphs from the English-language translation of the thematic plan in Prokof'yev, *Muzïka k fil'mu Sergeya Eyzenshteyna Ivan Groznïy. Soch. 116. Partitura. Avtorskiy tekst* (Moscow and Hamburg: Glinka State Central Museum of Musical Culture/Musikverlag Hans Sikorski, 1997), 28–29. Henceforth, this source is listed as the Sikorski Edition.

77. Leonid Kozlov, "'Ivan Groznïy.' Muzïkal'no-tematicheskoye stroyeniye," in *Proizvedeniye vo vremeni: Stat'i, issledovaniya, besedï* (Moscow: Eyzenshteynovskiy tsentr issledovaniy kinokul'turï, 2005), 45.

78. Ibid., 36–44.

79. "Zapiska I. G. Bol'shakova A. S. Shcherbakovu o pros'be S. M. Eyzenshteyna utverdit' na rol' Yefrosin'i v fil'me 'Ivan Groznïy' 'imeyushchuyu semitskiye chertï' aktrisu F. G. Ranevskuyu. 24 oktyabrya 1942 g.," in *Kremlyovskiy kinoteatr 1928–1953. Dokumentï*, 646. See also Kozlov, "Yeshcho o 'kazuse Ranevskoy,'" in *Kinovedcheskiye zapiski* 38 (1998): 168–72. Bolshakov replaced Dukelsky as chairman of the Committee on Cinema Affairs on June 3, 1939.

80. Information in this paragraph from Neuberger, *Ivan the Terrible,* 17–19.

81. The Sikorski Edition offers the detail, from Mira's memoirs, that, on September 6, 1944, a priest was present at the Mosfilm studios for the recording of the liturgical music in the coronation scene. On September 12, Prokofiev and Eisenstein went to the Bolshoy Theater to listen to the bells that had been deposited there following their government-ordered confiscation from Moscow churches (30–31 n. 4).

82. See *Bol'shaya tsenzura: Pisateli i zhurnalisti v Strane Sovetov. 1917–1956,* 541–42. Preparation for the rehabilitation of the Orthodox Church (which included the granting of permission for the election of the Patriarch, something that had not occurred since the time of Peter the Great) began as early as mid-1940, so when Eisenstein received the commission to make *Ivan the Terrible* in 1941, he could already count on including religious music in it.

83. The following list of the contents of the piano score comes from RGALI f. 1929, op. 1, yed. khr. 108–9; and the Sikorski Edition, 234–35:

> *Part I:* Overture (1944); Ocean–Sea [given twice in the score, first in pen without instrumental indications, then in pencil with instrumental indications] (1943); Shuysky and the Huntsmen; The Entrance of Ivan; Mnogo-letiye ["Many Years," a celebratory greeting]; Young Ivan's March; Swan [a choral round dance, or *khorovod,* that Prokofiev would reuse in his ballet *The Tale of the Stone Flower*]; Song of Praise; Riot; Holy Fool; Tatars; Entrance of the Tatars; Ivan's Tent; Attack; Cannoneers; Cannons Move to Kazan; Kazan Is Taken; Malyuta's Jealousy; Ivan Entreats the Boyars; Poisoning; Anastasiya's Illness; Ivan at the Coffin; The Oath of the *Oprichniki* [on poorly preserved paper] (November 18, 1942); Return!; *Part II:* The Furnace Play; The Song of the Beaver; Dances of the *Oprichniki:* 1) Chaotic Dance; 2) Orderly Dance (1945); *Oprichniki* Verses; The *Oprichniki* and Vladimir: Chorus No. 1 (hummed a cappella); Chorus No. 2 (hummed) [with the instruction "the 2nd basses on a separate microphone," doubtless to strengthen the bottom register, which includes a low C].

84. Sikorski Edition, 232–33. The numbers are "The Death of Glinskaya," a portion of the film's original prologue depicting the poisoning of Ivan's mother by the boyars; and "'Wondrous is God' (Conversation of the Ambassadors)," Prokofiev's rearrangement of the ending of the sacred concerto *May God Arise (Da voskresnet Bog)* by Dmitriy Bortnyansky (1751–1825). The Glinka Museum editors posit that Prokofiev intended this number for Part II of the film (the liturgical drama "The Fiery Furnace"), but the film itself features Bortnyansky's original work. The phrase "Conversation of the Ambassadors," moreover, indicates that the number was intended for the Part I coronation scene, not the Part II liturgical drama. During the coronation scene, the ill-willed Livonian ambassador to Moscow tries to sow foment by asking Prince Andrey Kurbsky why he, rather than the young Ivan, did not become tsar.

85. "Iz perepiski S. S. Prokof'yeva i S. M. Eyzenshteyna," 347; the italicized words were written in English.

86. In a June 19, 1942, letter to Prokofiev, Shlifshteyn writes: "You are planning to begin work with Eisenstein on the film *Ivan the Terrible.* Is it not the case that by embarking on Terrible you are hindering the now-realized Kutuzov? My advice is to finish *War and Peace* before taking on *Ivan the Terrible.*" Quoted in RGALI f. 1929, op. 3, yed. khr. 375, l. 40.

87. "Iz perepiski S. S. Prokof'yeva i S. M. Eyzenshteyna," 348. "The Furnace Play" serves a symbolic function in *Ivan the Terrible* Part II. The Metropolitan of Moscow stages the drama in an effort to force Ivan into submitting to the authority of the Church. It recounts the tale, from the Old Testament Book of Daniel, of the three boys—Hananiah, Mishael, and Azariah—who are put in a furnace by King Nebuchadnezzar during his persecution of Jews in Babylon. In defiance of the King, the lads praise God. Following the performance, a small child points to Ivan and declares that he resembles the evil King.

88. Sikorski Edition, 229.

89. Ibid., 165–66. The various other problems with the sacred music in the edition are expertly discussed by Katya Ermolaev Ossorgin in her paper "Liturgical Borrowings as Film Music in Eisenstein's *Ivan the Terrible*," American Association for the Advancement of Slavic Studies National Convention, Washington, D.C., November 19, 2006.

90. "Iz perepiski S. S. Prokof'yeva i S. M. Eyzenshteyna," 349.

91. Ibid., 350. So much time had passed that the original 40,000-ruble contract for *Ivan the Terrible*, signed on November 12, 1942, in Alma-Ata, had expired. Prokofiev signed another contract on September 14, 1944, in Moscow (RGALI f. 1929, op. 1, yed. khr. 814, ll. 16 and 18–19).

92. Unimpressively, the extant recording reveals.

93. Sikorski Edition, 29; translation slightly adjusted.

94. "Iz perepiski S. S. Prokof'yeva i S. M. Eyzenshteyna," 350.

95. Kozlov, "Ten' Groznogo i khudozhnik," 70; Vishnevskiy, "Fil'm 'Ivan Groznïy,'" *Pravda*, January 28, 1945, p. 3.

96. Lamm, *Stranitsï tvorcheskoy biografii Myaskovskogo*, 310 (January 10, 1945, diary entry).

97. Ibid.

98. "Iz perepiski S. S. Prokof'yeva i S. M. Eyzenshteyna," 351.

99. Ibid., 352.

100. RGALI f. 1929, op. 3, yed. khr. 375, l. 98.

101. Eisenstein, "From Lectures on Music and Color in *Ivan the Terrible*," in *The Eisenstein Reader*, 170.

102. Vol'skiy, "Vospominaniya o S. S. Prokof'yeve," 536.

103. Neuberger, *Ivan the Terrible*, 22–23.

104. "Postanovleniye Sekretariata TsK VKP(b) o vtoroy serii fil'ma 'Ivan Groznïy,'" in *Kremlyovskiy kinoteatr 1928–1953. Dokumentï*, 723.

105. "Stalin, Molotov and Zhdanov on *Ivan the Terrible* Part Two," in *The Eisenstein Reader*, 162. The transcript is by Eisenstein and Cherkasov.

106. Thus on November 22, 1952, toward the end of his life, Stalin approved the filming of new versions of the exploits of Alexander Nevsky and Ivan the Terrible, to be directed by Aleksandr Ivanov (1898–1984) and Ivan Pïryev (1901–68), respectively. Scheduled for production in 1953, these films went unrealized. "Proyekt postanovleniya Byuro Prezidiuma TsK KPSS ob utverzhdenii spiska khudozhestvennïkh kinofil'mov dlya proizvodstva v 1953 g.," in *Kremlyovskiy kinoteatr 1928–1953. Dokumentï*, 904.

CHAPTER 6

1. "Prokofiev and Atovmyan: Correspondence, 1933–1952," 223.

2. RGALI f. 1929, op. 3, yed. khr. 375, l. 92.

3. In a letter dated June 29, 1950, Atovmyan reminds Prokofiev that he needs a document facilitating his use of the room: "I asked Mira Aleksandrovna to copy the letter about the room on Mozhayka (with its transfer on the instruction of the Arts Committee). It's very important that this be done, especially for the publishing business" ("Prokofiev and Atovmyan: Correspondence, 1933–1952," 251).

4. Elizabeth Wilson, *Shostakovich: A Life Remembered* (Princeton: Princeton University Press, 2006), 221.

5. RGAE f. 168, op. 1, d. 161, l. 6.

6. Prokofiev to Boris Radin, an employee of the Union of Soviet Composers, letter of June 8, 1944, RGAE f. 168, op. 1, d. 176, l. 31.

7. On September 18, 1944, Prokofiev wrote to Lamm about *Ivan the Terrible* on the Mozhayskoye Shosse stationery, but provided the Hotel Moscow as his address ("Pis'ma S. S. Prokof'yeva k P. A. Lammu," 309).

8. RGALI f. 1929, op. 3, yed. khr. 375, l. 87.

9. RGALI f. 1929, op. 3, yed. khr. 282, ll. 1–2. The two letters, the first an overview of the activities of the Ivanovo composers, the second focused on the Fifth Symphony, are dated August 27, 1944.

10. *Prokof'yev o Prokof'yeve: Stat'i, interv'yu*, 209.

11. Ibid.; "[O moikh rabotakh za godï voynï]," in *S. S. Prokof'yev: Materialï, dokumentï, vospominaniya*, 252.

12. Unsigned, "Composer, Soviet-Style," *Time*, November 19, 1945, p. 57.

13. "Vïstupleniye na zasedanii plenuma Soyuza kompozitorov SSSR," in *Prokof'yev o Prokof'yeve: Stat'i, interv'yu*, 202.

14. See, for example, RGALI f. 1929, op. 1, yed. khr. 290 (Sketchbook No. 10), ll. 2, 80b., and 16; and f. 1929, op. 1, yed. khr. 291 (Sketchbook No. 11), ll. 7 and 8. This latter source is remarkably informative, since it contains sketches for his Fifth Symphony, Sixth Symphony, and revisions of his Second and Fourth Symphonies. On l. 23, Prokofiev identifies a theme as "6–ya simf., II ch., 3–ya tem" (6th Symphony, movement 2, 3rd theme); on ll. 27 and 29 he wrote "dlya 2–oy simf" (for the 2nd Symphony) and "IV smf. III ch." (4th Symphony, movement 3) above reworked melodic material. Prokofiev did not complete the revision of the Second Symphony; the revision of the Fourth Symphony dates from 1947.

15. William W. Austin, "Prokofiev's Fifth Symphony," *Music Review* 17:3 (August 1956): 220.

16. Prokofiev, who remained in intermittent contact with Koussevitzky throughout the war, sent a grateful telegram in English to the conductor on November 6, 1945, three days before the American premiere (RGALI f. 1929, op. 5, yed. khr. 9, l. 45). Like the Soviet media, the American media interpreted the work in bellicose emotional terms. Noel Straus's review is characteristic: "Here Prokofieff comes to grips with humanity in its tremendous struggle, and does so with telling sympathy in music of extraordinary vitality. Not suffering and sorrow dominate the work, however, but the sense of power felt by his race and the overwhelming joy experienced in its realization of certain victory over its foes and the forces of evil." "Prokofieff Fifth in Premiere Here; Composer's New Symphony Is Presented by Koussevitzky and Boston Orchestra," *New York Times*, November 15, 1945, p. 24.

17. Richter, *Notebooks and Conversations*, 89.

18. Oleg Prokofiev, interview with MB, July 18, 1968.

19. Dm[itriy] Kabalevskiy, "O Sergeye Prokof'yeve," in *S. S. Prokof'yev: Materialï, dokumentï, vospominaniya*, 420.

20. RGALI f. 1929, op. 3, yed. khr. 265, ll. 5–6.

21. RGALI f. 1929, op. 3, yed. khr. 267, l. 4.

22. V[ladimir] A[leksandrovich] Vlasov, "Vstrechi s S. S. Prokof'yevïm," in *S. S. Prokof'yev: Materialï, dokumentï, vospominaniya*, 430.

23. RGAE f. 168, op. 1, d. 161, l. 11.

24. Brown, "Prokofiev's *War and Peace*: A Chronicle," 310.

25. An overture on Johnson's behalf came from Ephraim Gottlieb, Prokofiev's de facto representative in the United States. On May 2, 1943, Gottlieb wrote the following to Maksim Litvinov, then the Soviet ambassador in Washington: "In a recent conversation we had in Chicago, Mr. Edward Johnson, Director of the Metropolitan Opera Association, expressed great interest in Serge Prokofieff's new opera 'War and Peace.' He felt that a production of the opera in New York next season would be a valuable means of further cementing cultural relations between the United States and the Union of Soviet Socialist Republics, and he asked me to cable Mr. Prokofieff, who has been a close friend for many years, asking him to send a score of his opera." AVP RF f. 192, op. 10, papka 73, d. 50, l. 4.

   Also on May 2, Prokofiev dispatched a telegram to Khrapchenko from Alma-Ata, reporting: "The American Metropolitan Theater telegraphs its immediate intention to produce *War and Peace*. Please advise." Khrapchenko replied on May 7: "I would advise you to respond to the Metropolitan Theater to the effect that a production of the opera *War and Peace* ought to occur there after a production on the Soviet stage. Let me take this opportunity to sincerely congratulate you on the awarding of a Stalin Prize [for the Seventh Piano Sonata]." Prokofiev responded to Khrapchenko on May 10, but not about the opera: "My heartfelt gratitude to you for the congratulations." *Deyateli russkogo iskusstva i M. B. Khrapchenko, predsedatel' Vsesoyuznogo komiteta po delam iskusstv: aprel' 1939- yanvar' 1948*, 605–6.

26. Prokofiev made this remark in a July 6, 1943, letter to Grigoriy Shneyerson, then the head of the musical division of VOKS ("Vstrechi s Prokof'yevïm," 267). VOKS engaged in tentative discussions with the Metropolitan Opera, and even accommodated Prokofiev's request to have the libretto of *War and Peace* translated into English, but the effort was moot. Prokofiev, for his part, rejected the translation as "imprecise and superficial" (271). Shneyerson empathized with Prokofiev concerning the absence of activity at the Bolshoy Theater: "Unfortunately, your suggestion about the B. Theater is close to the truth," he acknowledged on July 22, 1943. "I had a special conversation on this subject with Shlifshteyn and he said to me that work on staging *War and Peace* is obviously dragging" (RGALI f. 1929, op. 1, yed. khr. 750, l. 3).

27. Shneyerson to Prokofiev, letter of August 16, 1943, RGALI f. 1929, op. 1, yed. khr. 750, l. 4.

28. The reasons for the dismissal are outlined in a June 10, 1943, letter from Khrapchenko to Stalin and Molotov (RGASPI f. 82, op. 2, d. 951, ll. 79–80). Khrapchenko cites poor organization, slow preparation of new productions, and a loss of discipline among the Bolshoy Theater artists and staff. "The Committee on Arts Affairs," he reports, "has repeatedly pointed out to S. A. Samosud the serious deficiencies of his work. Despite formally accepting the criticism and instructions of the Committee, S. A. Samosud has not, in effect, taken any serious measures toward improving the work of the Bolshoy Theater." In conclusion, Khrapchenko recommended reappointing Samosud to a smaller Moscow, Leningrad, or Sverdlovsk theater. Samosud resurfaced after his dismissal as the artistic director of the Stanislavsky Theater.

29. Atovmyan had published the vocal score in collotype in the spring and summer of 1943 in anticipation of a Bolshoy Theater staging; revisions to the end of scene 11, errors on the proofs, and logistical problems related to Prokofiev's wartime relocations slowed the publication process. Prokofiev's April 24, 1943, letter to Atovmyan (sent from Alma-Ata to Moscow) is illustrative: "How annoying that the piano score of *War and Peace* has to be copied anew. Work on the opera at the Bolshoy Theater must be delayed. Did you receive the piano score of the end of scene 11?" ("Prokofiev and Atovmyan: Correspondence, 1933–1952," 217). Samosud's dismissal from the Bolshoy Theater resulted in the cancellation of the planned staging.

30. Letter of July 12, 1945, in Mariya Yudina, *Vïsokiy stoykiy dukh. Perepiska 1918–1945 gg.*, ed. A. M. Kuznetsov (Moscow: Rossiyskaya politicheskaya entsiklopediya, 2006), 499.

31. Ibid., 499–500. For a listing of the Prokofiev works in Yudina's repertoire, see pp. 597–98. Her esteem for Prokofiev can be gleaned from the forty-six letters and telegrams she sent to him from 1938 to 1952.

32. Georgiy Polyanovskiy, "'Voyna i mir.' Novaya opera S. Prokof'yeva," *Vechernyaya Moskva*, July 3, 1945, p. 3.

33. M[ira] A[bramovna] Mendel'son-Prokof'yeva, "Vospominaniya o Sergeye Prokof'yeve. Fragment: 1946–1950 godï," in *Sergey Prokof'yev: Vospominaniya. Pis'ma. Stat'i*, 28–29.

34. Taruskin, "War and Peace," in *The New Grove Dictionary of Opera*, 4:1102.

35. Mendel'son-Prokof'yeva, "Vospominaniya o Sergeye Prokof'yeve. Fragment: 1946–1950 godï," 18; RGALI f. 1929, op. 3, yed. khr. 375, l. 104.

36. Brown, "Prokofiev's *War and Peace*: A Chronicle," 313.

37. Yelena Krivtsova, "Prokof'yev i Shostakovich: 'memuarnoye prikosnoveniye,'" in *Shostakovich—Urtext*, ed. M. P. Rakhmanova (Moscow: Izdatel'stvo "Deka-VS," 2006), 122.

38. These are scored for tenor and baritone with piano accompaniment. The first of them, "How delightful the Moscow road," is heard in *A Story of a Real Man*.

39. RGAE f. 168, op. 1, d. 161, l. 9. The letter is undated.

40. Ulanova, "The Author of My Favorite Ballets," 237–38.

41. Slonimskiy, "Vstrechi s Prokof'yevïm," in *Prokof'yev o Prokof'yeve: Stat'i, interv'yu*, 191.

42. TsGALI SPb f. 337, op. 1, d. 200, l. 3.

43. "Obrucheniye v monastïre," 189.

44. The film was recommended for production by Bolshakov, the chairman of the Committee on Cinema Affairs, in an August 7, 1939, report to Molotov. See *Kremlyovskiy kinoteatr 1928–1953. Dokumentï*, 550–61, esp. 559.

45. N[ikolay] D. Volkhov, *Teatral'nïye vechera* (Moscow: Izdatel'stvo "Iskusstvo," 1966), 397.

46. Volkhov, "Skazka dlya baleta," *Za sovetskoye iskusstvo*, April 12, 1946, p. 4.

47. TsGALI SPb f. 337, op. 1, d. 200, ll. 8 and 11.

48. RNB f. 617, op. 1, yed. khr. 11, l. 2.

49. Ibid., l. 3ob.

50. "Zolushka," in *Prokof'yev o Prokof'yeve: Stat'i, interv'yu*, 192.

51. Volkhov, *Teatral'nïye vechera*, 398.

52. TsGALI SPb f. 337, op. 1, d. 200, l. 21.

53. On February 11, 1943, Radin summoned Chabukiani to Perm from Tbilisi (TsGALI SPb f. 337, op. 1, d. 200, l. 33). The choreographer had fallen ill, however, and decided that he needed to stay in the warm Tbilisi climate in order to recover, which forced Radin to enlist another choreographer.

54. Sherman, "Vospominaniya o Sergeye Sergeyeviche Prokof'yeve," 59–60.

55. RGALI f. 1929, op. 1, yed. khr. 68.

56. V. Prokhorova, *Konstantin Sergeyev* (Leningrad: Iskusstvo, 1974), 84–85.

57. "Vïstupleniye po Moskovskomu radio," in *Prokof'yev o Prokof'yeve: Stat'i, interv'yu*, 200.

58. "O 'Zolushke,' " in *Prokof'yev o Prokof'yeve: Stat'i, interv'yu*, 211–12.

59. Prokofiev specifically recycled—with enriched harmonies—a portion of No. 41 of *Eugene Onegin*, "The Meeting of Onegin and Tatyana in St. Petersburg."

60. Volkhov, *Teatral'nïye vechera*, 399.

61. Ibid.

62. RGALI f. 962 op. 3. yed. khr. 1391, ll. 3 and 5.

63. Pantiyelev, "Prokof'yev: razmïshleniya, svidetel'stva, sporï. Beseda s Gennadiyem Rozhdestvenskim," 16.

64. Ibid. Fayer first approached Rogal-Levitsky to undertake the reorchestration, but the latter refused, emphasizing his unwillingness to jeopardize his relationship with Prokofiev ("'Mimolyotnïye svyazi': K 70-letiyu so dnya rozhdeniya Sergeya Prokof'yeva," 196–99).

65. RGALI f. 1929, op. 3, yed. khr. 27 (*Notograficheskiy spravochnik*), l. 280b.

66. RNB f. 617, op. 1, yed. khr. 11, l. 7.

67. Ibid.

68. B. L'vov-Anokhin, *Galina Ulanova* (Moscow: Iskusstvo, 1984), 148.

69. B. Valerianov [V. Bogdanov-Berezovskiy], " 'Zolushka' na leningradskoy akademicheskoy stsene," *Trud (Moskva)*, April 12, 1946, p. 4.

70. Letter of March 17, 1946, quoted in Mendel'son-Prokof'yeva, "Vospominaniya o Sergeye Prokof'yeve. Fragment: 1946–1950 godï," 93–94.

71. Shostakovich, "Zolushka," *Pravda*, November 29, 1945, p. 2.

72. Arlene Croce, "The Search for *Cinderella*," in *Writing in the Dark, Dancing in the New Yorker* (New York: Farrar, Straus and Giroux, 2000), 481.

73. Ibid., 482.

74. Sem. Rosenfel'd, " 'Zolushka.' Prem'yera novogo baleta v Teatre imeni S. M. Kirova," *Smena*, April 18, 1946, p. 4; A. Vaganova, " 'Zolushka.' Prem'yera v Teatre operï i baleta imeni S. M. Kirova," *Leningradskaya pravda*, April 14, 1946, p. 3.

75. RNB f. 617, op. 1, yed. khr. 12, l. 15.

76. Quoted in Mendel'son-Prokof'yeva, "Vospominaniya o Sergeye Prokof'yeve. Fragment: 1946–1950 godï," 16.

77. T[amara] Tsïtovich, "Zolushka. Balet Prokof'yeva," *Sovetskaya muzïka* 8–9 (1946): 50.

78. The First and Second Suites were published in 1976 and 1977, the Third Suite in 1954.

79. Prokofiev was not, however, registered as a tenant of the apartment until November 15, 1947.

80. His previous car, the blue Ford, was confiscated during the war (Chemberdzhi, *XX vek Linï Prokof'yevoy*, 214).

81. The Committee on Arts Affairs authorization for the trip (*komandirovochnoye udostovereniye*) is preserved in RGAE f. 168, op. 1, d. 176, l. 14.

82. S[amuil] Samosud, "Vstrechi s Prokof'yevïm," in *Sergey Prokof'yev: Stat'i i materialï*, 147–48.

83. Brown, "Prokofiev's *War and Peace*: A Chronicle," 314.

84. RGALI f. 1929, op. 3, yed. khr. 123, l. 6.

85. Mendel'son-Prokof'yeva, "Vospominaniya o Sergeye Prokof'yeve. Fragment: 1946–1950 godï," 33.

86. Corwin worked for CBS Radio, whose administration had been in contact with Prokofiev during the war, approaching him, in a letter dated May 7, 1943, about composing a fifteen-minute orchestral work for broadcast in the fall of 1944. Prokofiev expressed his willingness to take on the task, but it went unrealized (GARF f. 5283, op. 14, yed. khr. 176, l. 14; f. 5283, op. 14, yed. khr. 124, l. 52).

87. Shneyerson, "Vstrechi s Prokof'yevïm," 274.

88. Quoted in Lee Bland to MB, letter of July 18, 1975.

89. For his efforts on behalf of international cultural and political relations, Corwin was blacklisted by Senator Joseph McCarthy and the U.S. House of Representatives Committee on Un-American Activities.

90. According to Kozlova ("Poslesloviye," in Prokof'yev, *Avtobiografiya* [Moscow: Izdatel'skiy dom "Klassika-XXI," 2007], 434–36), the composer first began work on an autobiography on June 1, 1937, finishing forty-seven chapters of the "childhood" section—his birth up to 1904—on October 17, 1939 (notebook 1). In 1941, Kabalevsky, then the general editor of *Sovetskaya muzïka*, solicited an autobiographical essay from him in recognition of his fiftieth birthday. Prokofiev responded with a "short" autobiography comprising three chapters: "Youth" (Yunïye godï), "After the Conservatory" (Po okonchanii konservatorii), and "Years spent abroad and after returning to the motherland" (Godï prebïvaniya za granitsey i posle vozvrashcheniya na rodinu). The first and second chapters were published by *Sovetskaya muzïka* in 1941 and 1946, respectively; the entire essay appeared in 1956 in the first edition of *S. S. Prokof'yev: Materialï, dokumentï, vospominaniya*. In 1945, following his hospitalization and convalescence, Prokofiev resumed writing his "long" autobiography. At the time of his death, he had completed eight notebooks with an elaborate, entertainingly written chronicle of his conservatory experiences up to July 6, 1909. The dates of these notebooks, which are in Mira's hand with Prokofiev's annotations (he dictated them to her and then corrected them), accord with periods of stability in his personal and professional life: May 10, 1945, to July 23, 1945 (notebook 2); July 23, 1945, to September 18, 1945 (notebook 3); September 19, 1945, to July 21, 1946 (notebook 4); July 23, 1946, to [?] and [?] to June 7, 1949 (notebook 5); June 10, 1949, to November 16, 1949 (notebook 6); November 16, 1949, to June 19, 1950 (notebook 7); June 19, 1950, to August 26, 1950 (notebook 8); and August 28, 1950, to [?] (notebook 9). During 1948, a period of crisis, he suspended work on his autobiography altogether.

91. The letter, to Mariya Belkina, is included in Natal'ya Gromova, *Vse v chuzhoye glyadyat okno* (Moscow: Kollektsiya "Sovershenno sekretno," 2002), 177.

92. Mira's notes from the essay, by Mukhtar Auezov and Leonid Sobolev, are included with the typescript of the libretto (RGALI f. 1929, op. 2, yed. khr. 23, l. 50).

93. Sabinina, "Ob opere, kotoraya ne bïla napisana," *Sovetskaya muzïka* 8 (1962): 43.

94. RGALI f. 1929, op. 2, yed. khr. 23, l. 48ob.

95. Information in this paragraph from Sabinina, "Ob opere, kotoraya ne bïla napisana," 44–48.

96. Prokofiev clarifies that he broke up the libretto "into separate moments, like shots in a film, selecting for each shot the musical material that seemed suited to it." *Prokof'yev o Prokof'yeve: Stat'i, interv'yu*, 214–15.

97. It specified 20,000 rubles for the music, 8,000 rubles for the libretto (RGALI f. 1929, op. 1, yed, khr. 806, ll. 22–23).

98. *Prokof'yev o Prokof'yeve: Stat'i, interv'yu*, 215 n.8.

99. *S. S. Prokof'yev i N. Ya. Myaskovskiy: Perepiska*, 471.

100. RGALI f. 1929, op. 3, yed. khr. 24 (*Notograficheskiy spravochnik*), l. 40; see also D[avid] Oystrakh, "O dorogom i nezabvennom (iz vospominaniy o S. S. Prokof'yeve)," in *S. S. Prokof'yev: Materialï, dokumentï, vospominaniya*, 453.

101. Oystrakh, "O dorogom i nezabvennom (iz vospominaniy o S. S. Prokof'yeve)," 452.

102. Prokofiev received a First Class Stalin Prize for the Violin Sonata. The award was announced in the June 7, 1947, issue of *Pravda* and the June 13, 1947, issue of *Sovetskoye iskusstvo*, and discussed in an article titled "The Pride of Soviet Music": "The spirit of contemporary life also envelops works of so-called pure instrumental music. S. Prokofiev's Sonata for Violin and Piano is an outstanding achievement of splendid, glorious Russian craftsmanship as well as an outstanding contribution to Soviet chamber music. Prokofiev's penchant for bold innovation and his constant search for new musical elements harmonically merge in the Sonata with the Russian classical music traditions." A. Samoylov, "Gordost' sovetskoy muzïki," *Sovetskoye iskusstvo*, June 13, 1947, p. 3.

103. Mendel'son-Prokof'yeva, "Vospominaniya o Sergeye Prokof'yeve. Fragment: 1946–1950 godï," 43.

104. Nest'yev, "Proizvedeniya Sergeya Prokof'yeva," *Pravda*, November 21, 1946, p. 4.

105. Mendel'son-Prokof'yeva, "Vospominaniya o Sergeye Prokof'yeve. Fragment: 1946–1950 godï," 45.

106. Ibid., 87.

107. Letter of November 10, quoted in ibid.

108. "Postanovleniye Orgbyuro TsK VKP(b) o zhurnalakh 'Zvezda' i 'Leningrad' " and "Postanovleniye Orgbyuro TsK VKP(b) 'O repertuare dramaticheskikh teatrov i merakh po yego uluchsheniyu,' " in *Vlast' i khudozhestvennaya intelligentsiya: Dokumentï TsK RKP(b)-VKP(b), VChK-OGPU-NKVD, o kul'turnoy politike. 1917–1953 gg.*, 587–96.

109. Information and quotations in this paragraph from Mendel'son-Prokof'yeva, "Vospominaniya o Sergeye Prokof'yeve. Fragment: 1946–1950 godï," 88–90.

110. Samosud, "Vstrechi s Prokof'yevïm," 154–58; Brown, "Prokofiev's *War and Peace*: A Chronicle," 314–17. It merits noting that Prokofiev signed a contract for the "war council" scene of Part II at the same time as the "ball" scene of Part I—on September 19, 1945. The 40,000-ruble agreement with Malegot specified a January 1, 1946, deadline for the "war council" scene and a September 25, 1945, deadline for the "ball" scene (RGALI f. 1929, op. 1, yed. khr. 814, l. 28).

111. Prokof'yev and Alpers, "Perepiska," 434. In the same letter, from February 22, 1947, Prokofiev pressed Alpers for her opinion of the Kirov Theater staging of *The Duenna*.

112. Mendel'son-Prokof'yeva, "Vospominaniya o Sergeye Prokof'yeve. Fragment: 1946–1950 godï," 67.

113. The score of *Romeo and Juliet*, like that of *Cinderella*, continued to be manipulated without Prokofiev's permission. Rozhdestvensky recalls that, for the Bolshoy staging, "a 'Mantua' scene, which is not in the piano score, was written, and all of the graceful folk dances (in 6/8) became thunderous—because a mass of people, the entire corps de ballet, was dancing." Rozhdestvensky adds that "Aleksandr Davïdovich Tseytlin, the pianist concertmaster of the ballet, created 'Mantua.' " Pantiyelev, "Prokof'yev: razmïshleniya, svidetel'stva, sporï. Beseda s Gennadiyem Rozhdestvenskim," 16.

114. "Prokofiev and Atovmyan: Correspondence, 1933–1952," 215.

115. Prokofiev received notice of the award while he was in Perm—he was unable to attend the August 10, 1943, award ceremony at the Kremlin. Atovmyan gushed about it in an August 4 letter: "The [July 27] resolution concerning your award was welcomed by everyone with great joy. I'm not exaggerating—it was a festive occasion (with much drinking),

no less so than the resolution of April 23, 1932 (on the liquidation of RAPM)." "Proko-fiev and Atovmyan: Correspondence, 1933–1952," 221.

116. Information from a biographical questionnaire completed by Prokofiev on January 20, 1953, for the second edition of the *Great Soviet Encyclopedia (Bol'shaya Sovetskaya Entsiklopediya)* (RGALI f. 1929, op. 2, yed. khr. 99, l. 3).

117. "Prokofiev and Atovmyan: Correspondence, 1933–1952," 216.

118. GARF f. 5283, op. 21, yed. khr. 74, l. 68. Prokofiev was also, according to this source, vice president of the Musical Sector of VOKS and a member of the Orgkomitet of the Union of Soviet Composers. The two Prokofiev societies were located in Hanover, New Hampshire (Dartmouth College), and Wheaton, Illinois (Wheaton College). Prokofiev corresponded with the former between 1937 and 1939.

119. RGASPI f. 17, op. 125, d. 571, l. 62. The memorandum, from VOKS Chairman Vladimir Kemenov (1908–88) to Georgiy Aleksandrov (1908–61), reads: "I am sending a draft TASS report about the selection of composer S. Prokofiev as an honorary member of the Swedish Musical Academy. Comrade A. Ya. Vïshinsky approves this draft, so long as there are no objections from the Propaganda and Agitation Department." The August 1, 1947, inscription on the memorandum, in the hand of Polikarp Lebedev, reads: "For the archive. Kemenov is notified that this information can be published in the newspaper *Sovetskoye iskusstvo*." The draft TASS report consists of a single sentence: "Composer Sergey Prokofiev, Stalin Prize laureate, has been named a member of the Royal Swedish Academy of Music" (RGASPI f. 17, op. 125, d. 571, l. 63).

120. For an exemplary discussion of the similarities and dissimilarities between the ballet, the simultaneously composed Fourth Symphony, and the 1947 revision of the Symphony, along with a consideration of the politics behind the revision, see Marina Frolova-Walker, "Between Two Aesthetics: The Revision of Pilnyak's *Mahogany* and Prokofiev's Fourth Symphony," in *Sergey Prokofiev and His World*, 452–92.

121. Brown, "The Symphonies of Sergei Prokofiev" (Ph. D. diss., Florida State University, 1967), 322. Additional information in this paragraph from pp. 292–93.

122. Mendel'son-Prokof'yeva, "Vospominaniya o Sergeye Prokof'yeve. Fragment: 1946–1950 godï," 58 (June 16, 1947).

123. Rita McAllister, "Prokofiev" (unpublished typescript, 1984), 187–88.

124. Rifkin, "Tonal Coherence in Prokofiev's Music: A Study of the Interrelationships of Struc-ture, Motives, and Design," 130.

125. Richter, *Notebooks and Conversations*, 83–84.

126. Ibid., 87.

127. RGALI f. 1929, op. 1, yed, khr. 163.

128. RGALI f. 1929, op. 2, yed. khr. 62.

129. Mendel'son-Prokof'yeva, "Vospominaniya o Sergeye Prokof'yeve. Fragment: 1946–1950 godï," 85.

130. "Stalin leads us forward, / The people follow behind their leader. / We travel Lenin's path, / We follow behind our party, / We sing the glory of the party" (Stalin nas vedyot vperyod, / Za vozhdem idyot narod. / Idyom mï Leninskim putyom, / Za nashey partiyey idyom, / Mï slavu partii poyom).

131. Brown, "The Symphonies of Sergei Prokofiev," 442–43.

132. Mendel'son-Prokof'yeva, "Vospominaniya o Sergeye Prokof'yeve. Fragment: 1946–1950 godï," 69 and 73.

133. RGALI f. 1929, op. 1, yed. khr. 122. These dates call into question the veracity of an anecdote from Shneyerson (as related to the musicologist Daniil Zhitomirsky) regarding

Prokofiev's "first meeting" with Shostakovich in Ivanovo in the summer of 1945. According to the anecdote, Prokofiev eagerly reported to the disinterested, tight-lipped Shostakovich that he had written—rather than just begun to sketch—the first movement of the Sixth Symphony and had begun working on the second. Shostakovich responded to Prokofiev's detailed description of the first movement form with the question: "So, is the weather always like this here?" Daniil Zhitomirskiy, "Shostakovich," *Muzïkal'naya akademiya* 3 (1993): 26–27; Taruskin, *Defining Russia Musically* (Princeton: Princeton University Press, 1997), 482.

134. Mendel'son-Prokof'yeva, "Vospominaniya o Sergeye Prokof'yeve. Fragment: 1946–1950 godï," 50.

135. Ibid., 77.

136. Nest'yev, "Shestaya simfoniya S. Prokof'yeva," *Sovetskoye iskusstvo*, October 18, 1947, p. 4.

137. Besides publishing in *Pravda, Sovetskoye iskusstvo,* and *Sovetskaya muzïka,* Nestyev served from 1945 to 1948 as chief editor for the music division of the Radio Committee; before that he taught at the College for Military Choir Directors (Vïsshee uchilishche voyennïkh kapel'meysterov) of the Military Faculty of the Moscow Conservatory. The turnaround in his relationship with Prokofiev centered on the publication in the United States of his monograph *Sergey Prokofiev: His Musical Life* (New York: Alfred A. Knopf, 1946), an elaboration of information in his dissertation "Tvorcheskiy put' S. S. Prokof'yeva," which he defended on June 1, 1945. In the midst of the anti-Formalism, anti-cosmopolitanism campaign of 1949, Nestyev was attacked by the Committee on Arts Affairs as a Prokofiev "apologist" whose writings were replete with "formalist mistakes." The "anti-patriotic fact—about which comrade Nestyev himself reported—of the publication of his book about Prokofiev in America before it came out in the Soviet Union demands even sterner renunciation" (unsigned, "Protiv kosmopolitizma i formalizma v muzïkal'noy teorii i kritike," *Sovetskoye iskusstvo,* February 26, 1949, p. 3). To rescue his career, Nestyev changed course; his later writings on Prokofiev betray his earlier ones, prompting the composer to nickname him "Judas" (Mendel'son-Prokof'yeva, "Vospominaniya o Sergeye Prokof'yeve. Fragment: 1946–1950 godï," 147). Nestyev's changed attitude to Prokofiev is reflected in his essay "Nasushchnïye voprosï opernogo tvorchestva," *Sovetskaya muzïka* 8 (1949): 17–26, esp. 20: "The modernist direction with particular conviction evinces its inability to embody true-life images when adjoined to the realistic subjects of the civil war (*Semyon Kotko),* heroic Russian history (*War and Peace*) and present-day conflict (*A Story of a Real Man).* Naturalist principles, rejecting beautiful vocal melody, ignoring traditional operatic laws and conventions, in all of these cases enter into unresolvable conflict with true-life images. Namely for this reason S. Prokofiev's operas have not been retained in the music theater repertoire."

138. Shneyerson, "Vstrechi s Prokof'yevïm," 278.

139. Mendel'son-Prokof'yeva, "Vospominaniya o Sergeye Prokof'yeve. Fragment: 1946–1950 godï," 78.

140. "Oda na okonchaniye voynï," in *Prokof'yev o Prokof'yeve: Stat'i, interv'yu,* 211.

141. RGALI f. 1929, op. 3, yed. khr. 22 (*Notograficheskiy spravochnik*), l. 7: "The idea for the makeup of the orchestra came to Prokofiev during the writing of the *Ode.* It was borrowed in part from Stravinsky's *Svadebka* [*Les Noces*]."

142. Nestyev's review of the November 12, 1945, premiere is illuminating in this regard: "As always after a Prokofiev premiere," he writes, "there was much argument. Some were

delighted; others reproached the author for intentionally avoiding complex symphonic development, for his somewhat mechanical construction of the sonorous episodes." RGALI f. 1929, op. 1, yed. khr. 966, no. 25 ("Oda na okonchaniye voynï," *Sovetskoye iskusstvo*, November 23, 1945).

143. RGALI f. 1929, op. 1, yed. khr. 335, l. 140b. For purposes of clarity, the complete title of the *Cantata* has been added to the outline, and the word *number* replaced with *part*.

144. RGALI f. 1929, op. 1, yed. khr. 162.

145. Mendel'son-Prokof'yeva, "Vospominaniya o Sergeye Prokof'yeve. Fragment: 1946–1950 godï," 87.

146. *The Extraordinary Commissar (Chrezvïchaynïy kommissar)* was the original title of *The Great Friendship (Velikaya druzhba)*. For his service to the regime, Ordzhonikidze was in 1926 elected to the Politburo. At the time of his mysterious death he had fallen out of favor with Stalin, who questioned his loyalty, but he was still buried with full Party and Soviet government honors.

147. Konstantin Aleksandrovich Uchitel', *Leningradskiy Malïy opernïy teatr (1927–1948): organizatsiya i tvorchestvo* (St. Petersburg: Gosudarstvennaya akademiya teatral'nogo iskusstva, 2005), 20. Malegot did not stage *War and Peace* Part II during Prokofiev's lifetime. The theater mounted a greatly abridged eleven-scene version of the entire opera on April 1, 1955.

148. RGALI f. 1929, op. 1, yed. khr. 814, l. 29. The contract is dated November 27, 1947.

149. Mendel'son-Prokof'yeva, "Vospominaniya o Sergeye Prokof'yeve. Fragment: 1946–1950 godï," 67.

Chapter 7

1. Prokof'yev, *Dnevnik 1907–1933*, 1:751.

2. The Fifth Symphony and Eighth Piano Sonata were jointly cited for a single award in the 1943–44 competition period.

3. The draft of Prokofiev's letter to Molotov reads:

> Each year, Muzgiz publishes 2–3 of my large works, whereas I am compos-
> ing more than that. At present, more than 15 large opuses are preserved
> in manuscript; I attach a list of them to this letter. When I presented this
> list to Muzgiz for inclusion in its 1948 work plan, Muzgiz reported that it
> could only in essence accommodate one of my works (while also reprinting
> several works that had already been engraved). The basis for this decision
> rests on the fact that its allotment of paper had been reduced from 700 to
> 400 tons in 1948.
>
> I always correct my works myself while making final corrections and
> finishing touches, which takes on average 1–2 months for each work. In
> view of this I would like all of my works to be published during my life-
> time, if possible. I am 56, and if the list of manuscripts continues to grow
> at the same rate, this dream will not, it seems, be realized.
>
> VOKS has forwarded offers to me from French, English, and Ameri-
> can firms to print all of my works, including opera scores, but I would
> consider it unacceptable [corrected by Prokofiev to read: but for me it
> would be extremely unpleasant] for them [my works] to appear some-
> where abroad, rather than with us.

I greatly request your assistance with this matter, if possible. (RGALI
f. 1929, op. 2, yed. khr. 315, l. 1.)

4. GARF f. A-385, op. 18, yed. khr. 2346, ll. 1–7. I am grateful to Leonid Maximenkov for providing a copy of this document.

5. G. Aleksandrov, "Proyekt zapiski Upravleniya propagandï i agitatsii TsK VKP(b) sekretaryu TsK VKP(b) A. A. Zhdanovu o zapreshchyonii postanovki operï V. I. Muradeli 'Velikaya druzhba,'" in *Vlast' i khudozhestvennaya intelligentsiya: Dokumentï TsK RKP(b)-VKP(b), VChK-OGPU-NKVD, o kul'turnoy politike. 1917–1953 gg.*, 627–28.

6. "Postanovleniye Politbyuro TsK VKP(b) 'Ob opere "Velikaya druzhba" V. Muradeli,'" in *Vlast' i khudozhestvennaya intelligentsiya: Dokumentï TSK RKP(b)-VKP(b), VChK-OGPU-NKVD, o kul'turnoy politike. 1917–1953 gg.*, 630–31.

7. Ibid., 631.

8. Kees Boterbloem, *Partner in Crime: The Life and Times of Andrei Zhdanov, 1896–1948* (Montreal and Kingston: McGill-Queen's University Press, 2004), 323.

9. In a memoir, Shepilov downplayed his involvement in the formation of the Resolution. Concerning the December 1947 report that he assembled for his benefactor Zhdanov about "inadequacies in the development of Soviet music," a report that informed the Resolution, Shepilov wrote: "It seems to me that, evidently on Stalin's order, Aleksandr Nikolayevich Kuznetsov, Zhdanov's chief aide, corrected our text to reflect Stalin's predilection for cruel characterizations, for taking matters to his favorite extreme—branding someone an enemy of the people. And when, from Zhdanov's report, the whole procedure unfolded, I was in shock: this was an entirely different approach from what we had discussed. Scathing accusations of antipopulism…and against whom!? Against those we took pride in: Prokofiev, Myaskovsky, and Shostakovich." *I primknuvshiy k nim Shepilov: Pravda o cheloveke, uchyonom, voine, politike*, ed. Tamara Tolchanova and Mikhaíl Lozhnikov (Moscow: Zvonnitsa-MG, 1998), 145.

10. "Zapis' soveshchaniya tov. Zhdanova s avtorami i ispolnitelyami operï 'Velikaya druzhba.' 6 yanvarya 1948 g.," in Khrennikov, *Tak eto bïlo*, 196.

11. Ibid., 198.

12. Tomoff, *Creative Union: The Professional Organization of Soviet Composers, 1939–1953*, 125–29 and 137. For broader context on the political events of 1948, see pp. 122–51.

13. According to Mikhaíl Chulaki (1908–89), a composer who would twice serve as director of the Bolshoy Theater between 1955 and 1970, "on the second day they apparently fetched Prokofiev directly from his dacha, as witnessed by his attire: an everyday work suit of some inconceivable brownish color and baggy-kneed trousers tucked into felt boots." M. I. Chulaki, *Ya bïl direktorom Bol'shogo teatra* (Moscow: Muzïka, 1994), 79.

14. Oleg Prokofiev, interview with MB, July 18, 1968.

15. M[stislav] L[eopol'dovich] Rostropovich, "Iz vospominaniy," in *Sergey Prokof'yev 1891–1991: Dnevnik, pis'ma, besedï, vospominaniya*, 256–57.

16. Khrennikov, *Tak eto bïlo*, 125.

17. Tomoff, *Creative Union: The Professional Organization of Soviet Composers, 1939–1953*, 123.

18. Maximenkov, "Stalin and Shostakovich: Letters to a 'Friend,'" in *Shostakovich and His World*, ed. Laurel E. Fay (Princeton: Princeton University Press, 2004), 52.

19. Atovm'yan, *Vospominaniya* [typescript], chap. 4, p. 8.

20. Ibid., p. 13.

21. O[l'ga] P[avlovna] Lamm, "Vospominaniya. Fragment: 1948–1951 godï," in *Sergey Prokof'yev: Vospominaniya. Pis'ma. Stat'i*, 240–44.

22. Ibid., 242.

23. Ibid., 240.

24. The essay is included in Eyzenshteyn, *Metod*, ed. N. I. Kleyman, 2 vols. (Moscow: Muzey kino/Eyzenshteyn-tsentr, 2002), 2:305–15.

25. Oksana Bulgakowa, *Sergei Eisenstein: A Biography*, trans. Anne Dwyer (Berlin: Potemkin, 2001), 231–32.

26. Mendel'son-Prokof'yeva, "Vospominaniya o Sergeye Prokof'yeve. Fragment: 1946–1950 godï," 104.

27. "Pis'mo I. G. Bol'shakova E. K. Voroshilovu o nagrazhdenii S. M. Eyzenshteyna ordenom Lenina," in *Kremlyovskiy kinoteatr 1928–1953. Dokumentï*, 800.

28. Mendel'son-Prokof'yeva, "Vospominaniya o Sergeye Prokof'yeve. Fragment: 1946–1950 godï," 103–5; RGALI f. 1929, op. 3, yed. khr. 375, ll. 154–55.

29. Lamm, "Vospominaniya. Fragment: 1948–1951 godï," 245.

30. RGASPI f. 77, op. 3-s, d. 142, l. 7. I am grateful to Leonid Maximenkov for providing a copy of this document.

31. Ibid., l. 8.

32. "Postanovleniye politbyuro TsK VKP(b) 'Ob opere "Velikaya druzhba" V. Muradeli,'" 631.

33. Kabalevsky was thinking only of himself. Seemingly managing to have his name struck from the list of "formalist" composers—Popov took his place—he did not wish to be associated with an unrepentant one.

34. Lamm, "Vospominaniya. Fragment: 1948–1951 godï," 245.

35. "Response of Sergei Prokofiev to the Resolution of February 10, 1948," in Jonathan Walker and Marina Frolova-Walker, *Newly Translated Source Documents*, program booklet for the symposium "Music and Dictatorship: Russia under Stalin," Carnegie Hall, New York City, February 22, 2003, pp. 20–22. The version of this document that appeared in *Sovetskaya muzïka* in 1948 excluded the reference to *Zdravitsa*. See "Pis'mo Prokof'yeva Sobraniyu moskovskikh kompozitorov i muzïkovedov," in *Prokof'yev o Prokof'yeve: Stat'i, interv'yu*, 220.

36. "Response of Dmitri Shostakovich to the Resolution of February 10, 1948," in Walker and Frolova-Walker, *Newly Translated Source Documents*, p. 18.

37. Oleg Prokofiev, interview with MB, July 18, 1968.

38. Mendel'son-Prokof'yeva, "Vospominaniya o Sergeye Prokof'yeve. Fragment: 1946–1950 godï," 66; RGALI f. 1929, op. 3, yed. khr. 375, l. 131.

39. Svyatoslav Prokof'yev, "O moikh roditelyakh: Beseda sïna kompozitora (S. P.) s muzïkovedom Nataliyey Savkinoy (N. S.)," 225–26.

40. RGALI f. 1929, op. 2, yed. khr. 560 (Opredeleniya sudebnoy kollegii po grazhdanskim delam gorsuda Sverdlovskogo rayona gor. Moskvï i Verkhovnogo suda RSFSR o nedeystvitel'nosti 1-go braka S. S. Prokof'yeva s L. I. Kodinoy), l. 1.

41. According to Svyatoslav, "When father decided to legalize his new marriage, to his enormous surprise the court told him that a divorce was entirely unnecessary; they considered the marriage, concluded on October 1, 1923, in Ettal (Germany), was now invalid, since it had not been registered in a Soviet consulate. Mama, entering the USSR as his wife, at some mysterious point ceased to be so. Father, being certain of the legality of his marriage to Mother, approached a higher court, but there he was told the same thing—thus he was able to register his new marriage without a divorce. Lawyers later told me that the 'Prokofiev case' was famous in Soviet legal practice." Svyatoslav Prokof'yev, "O moikh roditelyakh: Beseda sïna kompozitora (S. P.) s muzïkovedom Nataliyey Savkinoy (N. S.)," 226.

42. RGALI f. 1929, op. 2, yed. khr. 561.

43. Anna Holdcroft to MB, unpublished letter of October 10, 1964.

44. Frederick Reinhardt to MB, unpublished letter of March 4, 1963.

45. Svyatoslav Prokof'yev, "O moikh roditelyakh: Beseda s ïna kompozitora (S. P.) s muzïkove-dom Nataliyey Savkinoy (N. S.)," 227.

46. Ibid., 226–27.

47. Ibid., 228.

48. Chemberdzhi, *XX vek Linï Prokof'yevoy*, 252–53. Lina provides the surnames of five of her Lefortovo torturers in her petition: "Zubov, Malikov, Belov, and Ryumin, who concluded [the investigation]." "Kulishov," she adds, "headed the [MGB] investigation department." The RGASPI files on two of these horrendous, uneducated individuals, Pyotr Andreyev-ich Malikov (1901–?) and Nikolay Arsentyevich Kuleshov (1909–?), show "disciplined" work as junior and senior investigators in factory, institute, and prison settings.

49. Inna Chernitskaya and Nelli Kravets, "Zhertvï stalinskikh repressiy: O lagernoy zhizni Linï Ivanovnï Prokof'yevoy i sobstvennoy sud'be," *Muzïkal'naya akademiya* 2 (2000): 237.

50. Ye[vgeniya] A[leksandrovna] Taratuta, "Iz vospominaniy," in *Sergey Prokof'yev 1891–1991: Dnevnik, pis'ma, besedï, vospominaniya*, 235.

51. Chernitskaya and Kravets, "Zhertvï stalinskikh repressiy: O lagernoy zhizni Linï Ivanovnï Prokof'yevoy i sobstvennoy sud'be," 239.

52. Taratuta, "Iz vospominaniy," 236.

53. Svyatoslav Prokof'yev, "O moikh roditelyakh: Beseda s ïna kompozitora (S. P.) s muzïkove-dom Nataliyey Savkinoy (N. S.)," 231. The certificate is dated June 15, 1956; the decision by the Military Collegium of the Supreme Court of the USSR to release Lina came on June 13. She was fully rehabilitated, and provided, like Mira, with a pension of 700 rubles a month.

54. RGALI f. 1929, op. 2, yed. khr. 560, ll. 2–6.

55. Unsigned, "Pamyati ushedshikh," *Sovetskaya muzïka* 8 (1968): 159.

56. *Pervïy vsesoyuznïy s'yezd sovetskikh kompozitorov: Stenograficheskiy otchyot* (Moscow: Izdaniye soyuza sovetskikh kompozitorov SSSR, 1948), 13.

57. Ibid., 16–17.

58. Asafyev writes: "In Stravinsky's 1945 [*sic*] book *Musical Poetics* we find an idealization of the medieval—entirely in the spirit of fascist 'aesthetics' and philosophy—and Tartuffe-like sighs about the fact that 'the spirit of our time is ailing and, because of this, music is marked with symptoms of a pathologic blemish that facilitates the further spread of sinfulness in human con-sciousness'" (ibid., 17). In context, the actual quotation reads: "Modern man is progressively losing his understanding of values and his sense of proportions.... In the domain of music, the consequences of this misunderstanding are these: on one hand there is a tendency to turn the mind away from what I shall call the higher mathematics of music in order to degrade music to servile employment, and to vulgarize it by adapting it to the requirements of an elementary utili-tarianism—as we shall soon see on examining Soviet music. On the other hand, since the mind itself is ailing, the music of our time, and particularly the music that calls itself and believes itself *pure*, carries within the symptoms of a pathologic blemish and spreads the germs of a new original sin." Igor Stravinsky, *Poetics of Music in the Form of Six Lessons*, trans. Arthur Knodel and Ingolf Dahl (Cambridge, Mass.: Harvard University Press, 1979), 47.

59. *Pervïy vsesoyuznïy s'yezd sovetskikh kompozitorov: Stenograficheskiy otchyot*, 38–39.

60. Ibid., 39. *The Duenna* was branded a formalist opera in several articles in 1948, including the newspaper summaries of repertoire discussions at the Kirov Theater. See "Sozdadim pol-notsennïye muzïkal'nïye spektakli (Na sobranii rabotnikov Teatra operï i baleta im. S. M. Kirova)," *Leningradskaya pravda*, March 21, 1948; and "Zritel' pred'yavlyayet schyot (Na konferentsii v Teatre operï i baleta im. S. M. Kirova)," *Vecherniy Leningrad*, July 8, 1948.

61. *Perviy vsesoyuzniy s'yezd sovetskikh kompozitorov: Stenograficheskiy otchyot*, 40.

62. Ibid., 45.

63. In 1994, Khrennikov declared that "a group of people wrote the speech. Some of them are still alive today. I don't want to give their names. Yarustovsky oversaw the basic writing of the speech. V. Gorodinsky, S. Shlifshteyn, and someone else wrote the international section" (*Tak eto bïlo*, 130). Boris Yarustovsky (1911–78) was head of the music sector of the Central Committee Propaganda and Agitation Department; Viktor Gorodinsky (1902–59) served as chief editor at Muzgiz.

64. Mendel'son-Prokof'yeva, "Vospominaniya o Sergeye Prokof'yeve. Fragment: 1946–1950 godï," 108–9; RGALI f. 1929, op. 3, yed. khr. 375, l. 157.

65. Fay, *Shostakovich: A Life*, 161–62.

66. *Perviy vsesoyuzniy s'yezd sovetskikh kompozitorov: Stenograficheskiy otchyot*, 380.

67. Tomoff, *Creative Union: The Professional Organization of Soviet Composers, 1939–1953*, 148–50.

68. The list, provided in a February 14, 1948, "Excerpt" from Glavrepertkom "Order No. 17," is published in facsimile in *Sovetskaya muzïka* 4 (1991): 17.

69. RGALI f. 1929, op. 3, yed. khr. 123, l. 7. The letter is dated June 25, 1948.

70. Lamm, "Vospominaniya. Fragment: 1948–1951 godï," 248. Mira repaid the loan to Lamm's widow in 1960.

71. RGALI f. 1929, op. 3, yed. khr. 267, l. 5 (August 17, 1948).

72. Stalin overturned the "unlawful" prohibition in a March 16, 1949, memorandum to the Committee on Arts Affairs (a copy went to Prokofiev). It is published in facsimile in *Sovetskaya muzïka* 4 (1991): 17.

73. S. A. Balasanyan. *Stat'i. Vospominaniya. Pis'ma. K 100-letiyu so dnya rozhdeniya kompozitora*, ed. K. S. Balasanyan (Moscow: Kompozitor, 2003), 97.

74. RGALI f. 1929, op. 2, yed. khr. 315, l. 11.

75. RGALI f. 2040, op. 2, yed. khr. 224, l. 16.

76. Mendel'son-Prokof'yeva, "Vospominaniya o Sergeye Prokof'yeve. Fragment: 1946–1950 godï," 109; RGALI f. 1929, op. 3, yed. khr. 375, l. 157.

77. In the novella, the surname is spelled Meresyev.

78. Boris Polevoi, *A Story about a Real Man*, trans. Joe Fineberg (Moscow: Progress Publishers, 1979), 120.

79. The first phrase, "Lyotchik bez nog—eto ptitsa bez krïl'yev," occurs in scene 5 at rehearsal 123; the second, "A ved' tï zhe sovetskiy chelovek," occurs at rehearsal 173. On the semitonal transpositions of the second phrase, see Taruskin, *"Story of a Real Man, The,"* in *The New Grove Dictionary of Opera*, 4:556.

80. Polevoi, *A Story about a Real Man*, 226–27.

81. Emerson, "Shklovsky's *ostranenie*, Bakhtin's *vnenakhodimost'* (How Distance Serves an Aesthetics of Arousal Differently from an Aesthetics Based on Pain)," *Poetics Today* 26:4 (Winter 2005): 660.

82. Clark, *The Soviet Novel*, 103.

83. The libretto in the original 1947–48 piano score has several passages that broach the fantastic. The opera becomes a series of delusions and counterdelusions, with the recitative passages offering a distorted version of everyday existence, and the songs, dances, and choruses denoting Stalinist super-existence. Scene 7 is the most far-fetched. Here the surgeon, his superior, and a lieutenant announce that the pilots at the sanatorium have been summoned to defend the city of Stalingrad. The pilots celebrate; a farewell dance is organized in their honor. Aleksey has not, however, been recalled, despite near-readiness to return

to service. By way of demonstration, he dances a waltz with Anyuta. It saps his strength. Anyuta, standing alone, expresses her joy at being secretly engaged to Gvozdyov, but frets what awaits him at the front. The dancing flows into the next room. Donning party masks, Andrey and Kukushkin tease Anyuta's secret out of her in a witty jingle. The dancers return, and Aleksey joins them in a rumba. His performance persuades his minders that he will be able to fly again. Aleksey contentedly bids Andrey and the other pilots farewell. They march off, suitcases in hand. RGALI f. 1929, op. 1, yed. khr. 20–22 (photocopy provided by Nelly Kravetz).

84. Information on the quotations in the opera from Shlifshteyn, "S. Prokof'yev i yego opera 'Povest' o nastoyashchem cheloveke,' " in *Izbrannïye stat'i* (Moscow: Sovetskiy kompozitor, 1977), 112 and 116.

85. *Obrabotki russkikh narodnïkh pesen dlya golosa s f-p.* (1944).

86. L. Aleksandrovskiy, "Muzïkal'naya dramaturgiya operï S. Prokof'yeva 'Povest' o nastoyashchem cheloveke,' " in *Iz istorii russkoy i sovetskoy muzïki*, ed. A. Kandinskiy (Moscow: Muzïka, 1971), 193. Polevoy's novella was adapted for the screen. The eponymous film, which starred Pavel Kadochnikov (1915–88, perhaps best known as the Pretender Vladimir in *Ivan the Terrible*) and included music by Kryukov, was released by Mosfilm on October 22, 1949—just ten months after the private hearing of Prokofiev's opera.

87. The linkage calls to mind the sentiments of the arch-patriotic World War II song "Wait for Me and I'll Come Back" (Zhdi menya i ya vernus'), by Konstantin Simonov (1915–79) and Matvey Blanter (1903–90).

88. RGALI f. 1929, op. 3, yed. khr. 267, l. 5 (May 14, 1948).

89. Prokof'yev, "Povest' o chelovecheskom muzhestve," reproduced from the October 30, 1947, edition of *Vechernyaya Moskva*, in *S. S. Prokof'yev: Materialï, dokumentï, vospominaniya*, 253.

90. Egorova, *Soviet Film Music: An Historical Survey*, 117.

91. The document is preserved in RGALI f. 1929, op. 2, yed. khr. 32. Although *Taymïr Calls You* never became an opera, the play was adapted for Soviet television in 1970.

92. Dïkhovichnïy (1911–63) wrote satirical poems, stories, and stage plays. Many of the plays were co-authored with Moris Slobodskoy (1913–91), and feature merciless punning. *A Fakir for an Hour* (1945), for example, concerns a group of vaudeville performers who sing and dance their way into a booked-up hotel. "You have numbers for us," the hotel manager informs them, "but we don't have rooms [nomera] for you." "Fakir na chas," in Vl. Dïkhovichnïy and M. Slobodskoy, *Raznïye komedii* (Moscow: Sovetskiy pisatel', 1965), 8. Even the title of the play is a double entendre. "Fakir na chas" is Russian slang for a minstrel, but the play features an actual fakir.

93. RGALI f. 1929, op. 2, yed. khr. 31, l. 6. This source contains extracts from the libretto, text-setting schema, and information about marine biology.

94. RGALI f. 1929, op. 3, yed. khr. 16, ll. 13–22.

95. RGALI f. 1929, op. 3, yed. khr. 135, l. 3 (letter of July 24, 1948).

96. Ibid., l. 5 (letter of July 17, 1952).

97. Ibid. The two compositions are *On Guard for Peace* and *The Meeting of the Volga and the Don*, discussed in chapter 8.

98. Kostik performs the vaudeville routine for the seemingly despondent Mark. Having taken a cab home, three drunkards enter their building. Two of them prop the third against a wall and go to ring the doorbell. Their comrade falls down. They stand him up, and go again to ring the doorbell, but he falls down again. And again. Vexed, they turn to the cabbie: "See

what happens if you drink too much?" "Truly awful," the cabbie replies, "You've stood him on his head three times!" (Condensed excerpt from the libretto, RGALI f. 1929, op. 1, yed. khr. 29, ll. 170b.–180b.)

99. RGALI f. 1929, op. 3, yed. khr. 269, l. 6.

100. L. Polyakova, " 'Dalyokiye morya': O poslednem opernom zamïsle S. Prokof'yeva," *Sovetskaya muzïka* 3 (1963): 56.

101. Mendel'son-Prokof'yeva, "Vospominaniya o Sergeye Prokof'yeve. Fragment: 1946–1950 godï," 112–13; RGALI f. 1929, op. 3, yed. khr. 375, l. 160.

102. B[oris] Khaykin, *Besedï o dirizhorskom remesle. Stat'i* (Moscow: Sovetskiy kompozitor, 1984), 79.

103. This and subsequent quotations in the paragraph from a letter to Prokofiev from Khaykin, as transcribed in RGALI f. 1929, op. 3, yed. khr. 375, l. 163 (September 24, 1948).

104. Samosud, "Vstrechi s Prokof'yevïm," 165.

105. Lamm, "Vospominaniya. Fragment: 1948–1951 godï," 249.

106. Information and quotations in this and the next three paragraphs from Mendel'son-Prokof'yeva, "Vospominaniya o Sergeye Prokof'yeve. Fragment: 1946–1950 godï," 120–25; and RGALI f. 1929, op. 3, yed. khr. 375, ll. 166–68.

107. Khaykin, *Besedï o dirizhorskom remesle. Stat'i.* 80. Khaykin lamented the end of his friendship with Prokofiev. He declared that his "conscience was clean" with respect to *A Story of a Real Man*, and that he had defended rather than denounced the opera before cultural officials. "I listened to the reproaches and accusations in silence, and when asked directly [about the opera], I answered that I first and foremost consider Prokofiev to be a brilliant composer." He regretted only that he had not "stopped working" on the opera and "advised Prokofiev to wait for better times. But I could not possibly have foreseen that the composer would endure such harsh attacks" (80–81).

108. Quotations in this and the next paragraph from Vas[iliy] Kukharskiy, "Vazhnaya zadacha sovetskikh kompozitorov," *Izvestiya*, January 13, 1949, p. 3.

109. RGALI f. 1929, op. 2, yed. khr. 315, l. 14.

110. RGALI f. 1929, op. 3, yed. khr. 123, l. 9.

111. This and the previous quotations in the paragraph from Mendel'son-Prokof'yeva, "Vospominaniya o Sergeye Prokof'yeve. Fragment: 1946–1950 godï," 125; and RGALI f. 1929, op. 3, yed. khr. 375, l. 168.

112. The transcript is reproduced, with corrections, in Mendel'son-Prokof'yeva, "Vospominaniya o Sergeye Prokof'yeve. Fragment: 1946–1950 godï," 126–36; and RGALI f. 1929, op. 3, yed. khr. 375, ll. 169–78.

113. RGALI f. 1929, op. 2, yed. khr. 98 (Prokof'yev, *Konspekt dlya dnevnika ili kratkiy dnevnik*), l. 9 (November 3, 1952, entry).

114. Mendel'son-Prokof'yeva, "Vospominaniya o Sergeye Prokof'yeve. Fragment: 1946–1950 godï," 129; RGALI f. 1929, op. 3, yed. khr. 375, l. 171.

115. Samosud, "Vstrechi s Prokof'yevïm," 166. See also Taruskin, "*War and Peace*," 4:1103.

116. Information and quotations in this and the next two paragraphs from Mendel'son-Prokof'yeva, "Vospominaniya o Sergeye Prokof'yeve. Fragment: 1946–1950 godï," 137–39; and RGALI f. 1929, op. 3, yed. khr. 375, ll. 178–79.

117. Khrennikov does not recall this incident in his two sets of memoirs. He claims in general that his appointment as head of the Union of Soviet Composers came as a shocking surprise that rattled him to the core. His efforts to distance himself from the regime while also justifying his actions on behalf of the regime are sometimes bewildering, as the following quotations attest:

When in 1948 Stalin named me to the post [of General Secretary of the Union of Soviet Composers], I considered the appointment a personal tragedy. Beforehand I was occupied with music alone; then suddenly I found myself in a mishmash of political dirt and slander. (*O vremeni, o muzïke i muzïkantakh, o sebe*, 131)

But I think that my election to the post in the USSR Union of Composers was perhaps the best outcome of the situation in those years. For, naturally, I tried both then and afterward to soften all of the blows that rained down on our...organization and its individual members. (*Tak eto bïlo*, 131)

118. Lamm, "Vospominaniya. Fragment: 1948–1951 godï," 235. These points from Marina Rakhmanova's introduction.

119. Ibid., 255–56.

120. RGALI f. 1929, op. 2, yed. khr. 87, l. 400b.

121. Lamm, "Vospominaniya. Fragment: 1948–1951 godï," 255.

122. RGALI f. 2658, op. 1, yed. khr. 460, ll. 1–3.

123. Lamm, "Vospominaniya. Fragment: 1948–1951 godï," 241.

CHAPTER 8

1. The history of the commission is sketched by Kabalevsky in his editorial commentary to *S. S. Prokof'yev i N. Ya. Myaskovskiy: Perepiska*, 543 n. 3 to letter 385.

2. "Prokofiev and Atovmyan: Correspondence, 1933–1952," 252.

3. Rostropovich, "Vstrechi s S. S. Prokof'yevïm," in *S. S. Prokof'yev: Materialï, dokumentï, vospominaniya*, 471; RGALI f. 1929, op. 1, yed. khr. 906, no. 127.

4. RGALI f. 1929, op. 1, yed. khr. 673, l. 1.

5. Ibid, l. 3. The town of Ruza is situated in the western outskirts of Moscow.

6. Mendel'son-Prokof'yeva, "Vospominaniya o Sergeye Prokof'yeve. Fragment: 1946–1950 godï," 165.

7. Boris Schwarz, *Music and Musical Life in Soviet Russia* (Bloomington: Indiana University Press, 1983), 236.

8. "Prokofiev and Atovmyan: Correspondence, 1933–1952," 250.

9. Ibid., 250–51.

10. Ibid., 279. Sometime in 1952 or 1953, the three-volume edition became a four-volume edition. In a recollection titled "The Last Days," Mira writes: "Sergey Sergeyevich discussed all of the details concerning the publication of the four-volume edition with Muzgiz and the editor L. T. Atovmyan, expressing his desires in detail." M. Prokof'yeva, "Posledniye dni," in *Sergey Prokof'yev: Stat'i i materialï*, 283.

11. December 29, 1952, entry, RGALI f. 1929, op. 2, yed. khr. 98, ll. 14–15.

12. RGALI f. 1929, op. 1, yed. khr. 231 and 232.

13. Volkhov, *Teatral'nïye vechera*, 399. The Russian version of the Psyche and Eros myth, which Volkhov hoped to convert into a scenario, was written in 1783 by Ippolit Bogdanovich (1744–1803). It bears the title *Dushenka. An Ancient Tale in Free Verse* (*Dushen'ka. Drevnyaya povest' v vol'nïkh stikhakh*).

14. A devoted Leninist and veteran of the civil war, Bazhov nonetheless came in for attack in 1938 during the anti-Trotskyite campaign. He was expelled for just over a year from the Communist Party.

15. There exists an operatic version of the same tale, composed by Kirill Molchanov (1922–82) in 1949, the year he graduated from the Moscow Conservatory. The opera, which bears Rimsky-Korsakov's influence, was produced in 1951, and incorporated the suggestions for alterations recommended by the Union of Soviet Composers on August 13, 1949. See RGALI f. 2077, op. 1, yed. khr. 355 for a transcript of the adjudication.

16. RGALI f. 3045, op. 1, yed. khr. 120, l. 40.

17. Ibid., l. 73.

18. RGALI f. 1929, op. 1, yed. khr. 979, no. 40 (unsigned, "Teatral'naya khronika: Novïye baletnïye spektakli v Bol'shom teatre," *Teatral'naya Moskva* 48 [November 26–December 2, 1952]).

19. Information and quotations in the preceding paragraphs from RGALI f. 3045, op. 1, yed. khr. 120, ll. 17–24.

20. RGALI f. 1929, op. 1, yed. khr. 84. The outline is dated September 6, 1948.

21. This and the following quotations in the paragraph from L[eonid] Lavrovskiy, "'Seyf' tvorcheskogo dara (iz vospominaniy o Sergeye Prokof'yeve)," in *S. S Prokof'yev: Materialï, dokumentï, vospominaniya*, 520–23.

22. His views on the relationship between ballet and folk dance can be fruitfully contrasted with those of Lev Tolstoy. For Tolstoy, in the Russian literature scholar Sibelan Forrester's summation, "folk dance is to ballet as sex within marriage is to prostitution and as a good death is to a public execution" (personal communication, November 21, 2007). For Prokofiev, the opposite clearly seems to be the case.

23. Igor' Moiseyev, "Balet i deystvitel'nost'," *Literaturnaya gazeta*, April 2, 1952, p. 2.

24. RGALI f. 1929, op. 2, yed. khr. 92, l. 100b.

25. RGALI f. 1929, op. 2, yed. khr. 98, l. 16 (January 14, 1953). The reference is to Ludwig (Léon) Minkus (1826–1917), habitually denigrated for the triteness of his ballet scores.

26. Ibid., l. 14 (December 18, 1952); RGALI f. 1929, op. 2, yed. khr. 87, l. 60.

27. RGALI f. 1929, op. 1, yed. khr. 84, l. 30b.

28. Croce, "Theory and Practice in the Russian Ballet," in *Writing in the Dark, Dancing in The New Yorker*, 277.

29. Information in this paragraph from S[vetlana] Katonova, *Muzïka sovetskogo baleta: Ocherki istorii i teorii* (Leningrad: Sovetskiy kompozitor, 1990), 98–108.

30. "Neurotic" and "brooding": Croce, "The Search for *Cinderella*," 481; "to choose between": "Theory and Practice in the Russian Ballet," 277.

31. "Prokofiev and Atovmyan: Correspondence, 1933–1952," 243. Getting the music to Zïbtsev was the biggest headache, since it was in Richter's possession. On June 15 and 16, Prokofiev, virtually incapacitated in Nikolina Gora, sent a pair of urgent letters to Lavrovsky in Moscow, beseeching him to obtain the score and arrange for Zïbtsev to travel to Nikolina Gora to review it (RGALI f. 3045, op. 1, yed. khr. 259, ll. 1–2).

32. Mendel'son-Prokof'yeva, "Vospominaniya o Sergeye Prokof'yeve. Fragment: 1946–1950 godï," 159.

33. Ibid., 161. The official in question was Nikolay Goryainov, former director of Malegot.

34. RGALI f. 1929, op. 2, yed. khr. 92, l. 27.

35. Lamm, "Vospominaniya. Fragment: 1948–1951 godï," 257.

36. Mendel'son-Prokof'yeva, "Vospominaniya o Sergeye Prokof'yeve. Fragment: 1946–1950 godï," 163.

37. Lamm, "Vospominaniya. Fragment: 1948–1951 godï," 257.

38. Ibid., 258.

39. RGASPI f. 82, op. 2, d. 1464, l. 63. "Lechsanupr" is the abbreviation for "lechebno-sanitarnoye upravleniye ministerstva zdravookhraneniya SSSR" (Medical Facility Administration of the Ministry of Health of the USSR).

40. Mendel'son-Prokof'yeva, "Vospominaniya o Sergeye Prokof'yeve. Fragment: 1946–1950 godï," 170. The note in question is dated February 21, 1950.

41. Rikhter, "O Prokof'yeve," in S. S. Prokof'yev: Materialï, dokumentï, vospominaniya, 468.

42. Mendel'son-Prokof'yeva, "Vospominaniya o Sergeye Prokof'yeve. Fragment: 1946–1950 godï," 196; RGALI f. 1929, op. 3, yed. khr. 375, l. 214 (April 20, 1950). The "failure" of Ruslan and Lyudmila related to a shift in operatic taste in St. Petersburg against indigenous repertoire in favor of Italian operas. It also endured criticism for its anti-realist musical complexities and extravagances (Taruskin, "Ruslan and Lyudmila," in The New Grove Dictionary of Opera, 4:94).

43. Prokofiev to Balasanyan, letter of July 2, 1950, in S. A. Balasanyan. Stat'i. Vospominaniya. Pis'ma. K 100-letiyu so dnya rozhdeniya kompozitora, 252.

44. The commission was facilitated by Olga Ochakovskaya, a State Radio employee who apparently introduced Prokofiev and Marshak to each other. See her "Prokof'yev na detskom radioveshchanii," in Sergey Sergeyevich Prokof'yev, 38–41. The contract, signed by Ivan Andreyev, specifies a six-movement score that "must be accessible for children," due on February 28, 1950, for a fee of 12,000 rubles (RGALI f. 1929, op. 1, yed. khr. 806, l. 6).

45. Before On Guard for Peace, the oratorio bore the working titles Glory to Peace (Slava miru), War for Peace (Voyna za mir), and Song [Word] of Peace (Slovo o mire).

46. Stanley D. Krebs, Soviet Composers and the Development of Soviet Music (London: George Allen and Unwin, 1970), 163 n. 2.

47. Mendel'son-Prokof'yeva, "Vospominaniya o Sergeye Prokof'yeve. Fragment: 1946–1950 godï," 199–201; RGALI f. 1929, op. 3, yed. khr. 375, l. 216 (May 11, 1950).

48. Il'ya Erenburg, Na tsokole istoriy…Pis'ma 1931–1967, ed. B. Ya. Frezinskiy (Moscow: Agraf, 2004), 357; Bol'shaya tsenzura: Pisateli i zhurnalistï v Strane Sovetov. 1917–1956, 620–22.

49. Mendel'son-Prokof'yeva, "Vospominaniya o Sergeye Prokof'yeve. Fragment: 1946–1950," 206.

50. Letter of August 11, 1950, as transcribed in ibid., 217.

51. Ibid., 218.

52. The following information from Lamm, "Vospominaniya. Fragment: 1948–1951 godï," 254–55, 260–61.

53. RGALI f. 1929, op. 2, yed. khr. 98, l. 11 (November 23, 1952).

54. Mendel'son-Prokof'yeva, "Vospominaniya o Sergeye Prokof'yeve. Fragment: 1946–1950," 218–20.

55. Tertz, "On Socialist Realism," 154.

56. Reminiscence of the musicologist Vera Sukharevskaya (1903–77), in S. A. Samosud: Stat'i, vospominaniya, pis'ma, 159.

57. RGALI f. 1929, op. 3, yed. khr. 375, l. 236 (undated).

58. Mendel'son-Prokof'yeva, "O Sergeye Sergeyeviche Prokof'yeve," in S. S. Prokof'yev: Materialï, dokumentï, vospominaniya, 383; Prokof'yeva, "Kak sozdavalas' oratoriya 'Na strazhe mira,'" Sovetskaya muzïka 3 (1962): 108.

59. Mendel'son-Prokof'yeva, "Vospominaniya o Sergeye Prokof'yeve. Fragment: 1946–1950 godï," 226; RGALI f. 1929, op. 3, yed. khr. 375, l. 237.

60. Mendel'son-Prokof'yeva, "Vospominaniya o Sergeye Prokof'yeve. Fragment: 1946–1950 godï," 226.

61. RGALI f. 1929, op. 3, yed. khr. 375, l. 236.

62. Mendel'son-Prokof'yeva, "Vospominaniya o Sergeye Prokof'yeve. Fragment: 1946–1950 godï," 226; RGALI f. 1929, op. 3, yed. khr. 375, l. 237.

63. The award was announced in the March 17, 1951, issue of *Sovetskoye iskusstvo*.

64. Unsigned, "New Wolf," *Time*, August 28, 1950, p. 58.

65. Fay, *Shostakovich: A Life*, 175. The anecdote comes from the composer Galina Ustvolskaya (1919–2006).

66. Lavrovskiy, " 'Seyf' tvorcheskogo dara (iz vospominaniy o Sergeye Prokof'yeve)," 524.

67. RGALI f. 648, op. 5, yed. khr. 249, l. 4. Prokofiev dictated the letter to Mira.

68. Ibid., l. 19. This letter is undated. From another it emerges that, as late as November 30, 1952, Prokofiev had still not received payment for the 594-page score (ibid., l. 18).

69. RGASPI f. 17, op. 133, d. 368, l. 28.

70. RGASPI f. 17, op. 133, d. 368, l. 30.

71. RGALI f. 1929, op. 2, yed. khr. 98, l. 3.

72. Ibid., l. 10 (November 6, 1952). Prokofiev refers to Shostakovich's *The Sun Shines over Our Motherland* (*Nad Rodinoy nashey solntse siyayet*).

73. Ibid., l. 5.

74. Ibid., l. 14.

75. Rostropovich provided this information to the filmmaker Mariya Yatskova in an April 2004 interview; he also recalls going to the Radio Committee with Vedernikov to present the Symphony for approval. Vedernikov played the piano score of the first three movements alone; Rostropovich assisted him with the glissandi in the fourth movement. Rostropovich adds that "the old ladies" on the Radio Committee editorial staff "went into rapture" over the score. I am grateful to Ms. Yatskova for providing a copy of the transcript of the interview.

76. RGALI f. 1929, op. 2, yed. khr. 98, l. 2.

77. Ibid., l. 5 (September 28, 1952).

78. Ibid., l. 7.

79. Ibid., l. 8 (October 27, 1952).

80. *Prokof'yev o Prokof'yeve: Stat'i, interv'yu*, 230. The bulletin is dated December 26, 1952.

81. Brown, "The Symphonies of Sergei Prokofiev," 456.

82. *Prokof'yev o Prokof'yeve: Stat'i, interv'yu*, 230 n. 1. For a translation of Kabalevsky's entire recollection of his meeting with Prokofiev regarding the Symphony, see Brown, "The Symphonies of Sergei Prokofiev," 457–58.

83. Brown, "The Symphonies of Sergei Prokofiev," 462.

84. Ibid., 463–64.

85. RGALI f. 1929, op. 2, yed. khr. 98, l. 18 (February 4, 1953).

86. The construction of the waterway was largely carried out by prisoners.

87. RGALI f. 1929, op. 1, yed. khr. 168. In a 2001 memoir, Rostropovich takes credit for managing "to convince [Prokofiev] to compose [*The Meeting of the Volga and the Don*], for which Radio immediately provided the funds that he greatly needed at the time"; Rostropovich adds that he found it difficult to conceal from Prokofiev that the commission was essentially an act of charity. "It was all done with the consent of Balasanyan who, despite his high rank in the management of music at Radio, took an undoubted risk, seeking neither to compromise his conscience nor his respect for Prokofiev's genius" (Rostropovich, "Vospominaniya," in *S. A. Balasanyan. Stat'i. Vospominaniya. Pis'ma. K 100-letiyu so dnya rozhdeniya kompozitora*, 97–98).

88. Rostropovich, "Vstrechi s S. S. Prokof'yevïm," 472. One of the various potential sources of inspiration for the score was the article by M. Mikhaylov, "Stroyki kommunizma—vsenarodnoye delo Volgo–Don," *Sovetskoye iskusstvo*, March 6, 1951, p. 1.

89. "Muzïka i zhizn'," in *S. S. Prokof'yev: Materialï, dokumentï, vospominaniya*, 256.

90. Prokof'yev, "'Vstrecha Volgi s Donom,'" *Sovetskoye iskusstvo*, November 17, 1951, p. 2; *S. S. Prokof'yev: Materialï, dokumentï, vospominaniya*, 257.

91. P. A. Warneck, "The Volga–Don Navigation Canal," *Russian Review* 13:4 (October 1954): 286 and 290.

92. For example, "VOLGO-DON POSTROILI! Uallstritovtsev rasstroili" (roughly: "Volga-Don Constructed! Wall Street Disrupted").

93. Information in this paragraph from unsigned articles in two issues: "Rabotniki iskusstv na trasse kanala," *Sovetskoye iskusstvo*, July 12, 1952, p. 1; and "Na Volgo–Done," *Sovetskoye iskusstvo*, July 16, 1952, p. 1.

94. RGALI f. 1929, op. 1, yed. khr. 806, l. 25.

95. The report comes from the column "News in the Arts" (Novosti iskusstv) on p. 1 of the January 12, 1952, *Sovetskoye iskusstvo*. Framed by comments about rehearsals for a high school drama called "Right to Happiness" (Pravo na schast'ye), a professional production of *King Lear*, and a Soviet photography exhibition, the report reads: "Sergey Prokofiev worked with great intensity on his Concerto for Violoncello and Orchestra. In his composition the author made wide use of Russian folksong material. The Concerto was created in close kinship with the violoncellist Mstislav Rostropovich, to whom it is dedicated. This collaboration allowed the composer to bring out more fully the richest melodic and technical possibilities of the instrument. The Concerto was completed at the start of 1952. S. Prokofiev's new work will be premiered in the near future. In the photograph: S. Prokofiev discusses one of the passages of the Concerto with M. Rostropovich."

96. "Prokofiev and Atovmyan: Correspondence, 1933–1952," 264.

97. Ibid., 265.

98. Ibid., 268.

99. V. Dukhovskaya, "Zametki iz dnevnika," *Sovetskaya muzïka* 4 (1981): 96. Dukhovskaya notes Prokofiev being unable to recall his Moscow telephone number when she asked him for it after the performance: "'I don't know, I don't know,' he answered with great suffering in his voice, 'I don't remember. Everything in the past I remember, but everything in the present I don't remember, I don't remember.'"

100. Rostropovich, CD liner notes to *Rostropovich: The Russian Years 1950–1974*, EMI 72016, p. 28. The cellist recapitulated his point about "the gap between the mundane and the sublime" in another anecdotal account of his collaboration with Prokofiev, this one provided to Claude Samuel:

> [Prokofiev] would ask your opinion of each note, each bar, but it couldn't be you who went to him with a question!…From time to time, he would tell me, 'Here, play me a rapid passage on the cello—anything at all, as long as it's fast.' You can imagine how I'd put my mind to it, all the more since I had taken some composition courses. So, I would offer a passage in which I tried to match his own style and really give my very best. In that two-bar passage, there may have been as many as sixty-four notes!
>
> He would look at the passage in silence, think about it, then pick up a little eraser, get rid of one of the sixty-four notes, and replace it with another note. By then I'd be ready to jump out the window, because it would be

precisely that new note which added the touch of genius to the passage. And I'd wonder: Why couldn't *I* find the right note? One note in sixty-four was enough to make the difference between an ungifted lout and a genius! (Claude Samuel, *Mstislav Rostropovich and Galina Vishnevskaya: Russia, Music, and Liberty*, trans. E. Thomas Glasow [Portland, Ore.: Amadeus Press, 1995], 59)

101. Accordingly, Rostropovich's 1959 piano score of the Sinfonia Concertante contains two versions of the third movement, but in a confusing way: in the middle section, the top systems of the pages show the original version, the bottom systems the revision. The 1959 orchestral score places the revision in an appendix.

102. Atovmyan provides the details in a June 24, 1952, letter ("Prokofiev and Atovmyan: Correspondence, 1933–1952," 270).

103. RGALI f. 1929, op. 2, yed. khr. 98, l. 4.

104. *V. Ya. Shebalin: Zhizn' i tvorchestvo*, comp. V. I. Razheva; introd. T. N. Khrennikov (Moscow: Molodaya gvardiya, 2003), 207.

105. RGALI f. 1929, op. 2, yed. khr. 98, l. 5.

106. *Prokof'yev o Prokof'yeve: Stat'i, interv'yu*, 228.

107. Steven Isserlis, "Prokofiev's Unfinished Concertino—A Twisted Tale," *Three Oranges: The Journal of the Serge Prokofiev Foundation* 3 (May 2002): 32.

108. Ibid.

109. *Prokof'yev o Prokof'yeve: Stat'i, interv'yu*, 228.

110. RGALI f. 1929, op. 1, yed. khr. 179.

111. Prokof'yeva, "Posledniye dni," 288.

112. Prokofiev is referring here to the duet between Natasha and Sonya and Prince Andrey's arioso about the oak tree in scene 1 of the opera. The duet appears to be modeled on that sung by Tatyana and Olga in Chaikovsky's *Eugene Onegin*, and by Liza and Paulina in his *Queen of Spades*.

113. RGALI f. 1929, op. 2, yed. khr. 316, ll. 10b.–2. Prokofiev wrote again to Grikurov on October 27, 1949, for a progress report on the opera: "I would very much like to know if you have received the complete piano score of *War and Peace*, if you have looked it over, and what plans have arisen for it. When is the theater thinking of beginning work on the opera?" (l. 50b.).

114. Mendel'son-Prokof'yeva, "Vospominaniya o Sergeye Prokof'yeve. Fragment: 1946–1950 godï," 167.

115. "Prokofiev and Atovmyan: Correspondence, 1933–1952," 251–52.

116. Brown, "Prokofiev's *War and Peace*: A Chronicle," 321; see also Prokof'yeva, "Posledniye dni," 281.

117. RGALI f. 1929, op. 2, yed. khr. 98, l. 7.

118. Ibid., l. 8 (October 18, 1952).

119. Ibid., l. 9 (November 3 and 4).

120. Samosud, "Vstrechi s Prokof'yevïm," 169.

121. RGALI f. 1929, op. 2, yed. khr. 98, ll. 10–11 (November 9, 16, and 27).

122. Prokof'yeva, "Posledniye dni," 289. Additional information in this paragraph from pp. 290–92.

123. RGALI f. 1929, op. 3, yed. khr. 265, l. 24.

124. RGALI f. 1929, op. 2, yed. khr. 98, l. 21.

125. Khaykin to Khrapchenko, letter of November 15, 1972, in *Deyateli russkogo iskusstva i M. B. Khrapchenko, predsedatel' Vsesoyuznogo komiteta po delam iskusstv: aprel' 1939-yanvar' 1948*, 548.

126. The preceding information from Maximenkov, "Prokofiev's Immortalization," in *Sergey Prokofiev and His World*, 296–97.

127. Unsigned, "Prokofieff, Soviet Composer, Dies; In Favor after Communist Rebuke," *New York Times*, March 9, 1953, pp. 1 and 29.

128. Olin Downes, "A Great Composer; Prokofieff at His Best Was a Modern Master," *New York Times*, March 15, 1953, p. X7.

129. Svyatoslav Prokof'yev, "O moikh roditelyakh: Beseda sïna kompozitora (S. P.) s muzïkovedom Nataliyey Savkinoy (N. S.)," 230. The catalog number of the photograph is 0–305236.

130. Schnittke, "On Prokofiev," 65–66.

131. RGALI f. 2045 op. 1, yed. khr. 171, l. 8.

132. Ibid., ll. 8–9.

133. RGALI f. 648, op. 5, yed. khr. 301, ll. 1–11.

134. For the precise details, see Maximenkov, "Prokofiev's Immortalization," 298–328.

135. A critical edition of the 1935 score is in preparation.

136. A. Volkov, *'Voyna i mir' Prokof'yeva: Opït analiza variantov operï* (Moscow: Muzïka, 1976).

137. This and the next two quotations in the paragraph from Eddy, *Science and Health with Key to the Scriptures*, 337.

138. Series SF, Folder ID Prokofiev, Mary Baker Eddy Library. The letter, written by Prokofiev on the stationery of the St. Moritz Hotel in New York, is addressed to Miss Crain, a longtime Christian Science practitioner with whom he and Lina had consulted in Paris.

Glossary

Glavlit (Glavnoye upravleniye po delam literaturï i izdatelstv), Chief Directorate for Literary and Publishing Affairs. Oversaw the protection of official interests through the censorship and regulation of printed media.

◆

Glavrepertkom (Glavnoye upravleniye po kontrolyu za zrelishchami i repertuarom), Chief Directorate for the Control of Stage Performance and Repertory. Censored and regulated the content of ballet, opera, and theater productions for public viewing. (Film, in contrast, was overseen by the Central Committee.)

◆

Gosplan (Gosudarstvennaya planovaya komissiya), State Planning Commission. Oversaw Soviet economic activity until 1991, including the formation, legislation, and enactment of the Five-Year Plans. Abram Mendelson was a member of its executive committee.

◆

Muzfond (Muzïkal'nïy fond), financial division of the Union of Soviet Composers. Created in 1939, with Levon Atovmyan serving as administrative director and deputy chairman from 1940 to 1948, Muzfond provided financial and material assistance to composers, ensembles, and theaters; subsidized the editing, arranging, and printing of scores; and funded the building and management of composers' residences in, among other places, Ivanovo.

◆

NKID (Narodnïy Komissariat Inostrannïkh Del), People's Commissariat for Foreign Affairs. Also abbreviated as Narkomindel. Directed Soviet external politics from 1917 to 1946, with Vyacheslav Molotov as head from 1939 until two years after it became the Ministry of Foreign Affairs (Ministerstvo inostrannïkh del).

◆

NKVD (Narodnïy Komissariat Vnutrennikh Del), People's Commissariat for Internal Affairs. Established in 1934 to protect the security of the Soviet State through political repression, intelligence gathering, and the management of the massive Gulag prison system. The NKVD was reorganized before, during, and after World War II. The Ministry of State Security (Ministerstvo Gosudarstvennoy Bezopasnosti, or MGB), which came into being in 1946, was one of its successors.

◆

Orgkomitet, Organizing Committee of the Union of Soviet Composers. Established in 1939 to oversee the administration of Muzfond, arrange for the expansion of the Union into the Soviet Republics, and manage membership rosters. It was dissolved at the First Congress of the Union in 1948. The Orgkomitet was chaired by Reinhold Glier, with Aram Khachaturyan serving as deputy chairman.

◆

Sovinformbyuro (Sovetskoye informatsionnoye byuro), Soviet Information Bureau. Established by order of Sovnarkom and the Central Committee in 1941 to dispatch military situation reports to the public as part of its broader function as an international propaganda organization. Lina Prokofiev occasionally translated for the literature division, 1941–43. In 1961 Sovinformbyuro was transformed into the Novosti press agency, the second-largest Soviet news service.

◆

Sovnarkom (Sovet narodnïkh komissarov), Council of People's Commissars. The principal governing body of the Soviet Union from its founding until the end of World War II. In 1946, renamed the Council of Ministers (Sovet ministrov).

◆

Soyuz sovetskikh kompozitorov SSSR, USSR Union of Soviet Composers. Established by Central Committee resolution in 1932 following the dissolution of the Russian Association of Proletarian Musicians and the Association of Contemporary Music, the Union managed the Soviet music profession, from the commissioning and financing of individual works to their adjudication, performance, and publication. The Orgkomitet was dissolved in 1948 at the First Congress of the Union; Tikhon Khrennikov was thereafter installed as the Union's general secretary (later first secretary), a position he held until 1991.

◆

VOKS (Vsesoyuznoye obshchestvo kul'turnïkh svyazey zagranitsey), All-Union Society for Cultural Ties Abroad. Founded in 1925 and dissolved in 1958; propagandized the cultural and scientific achievements of the peoples of the Soviet Union abroad and facilitated international exchanges. Organized exhibitions, published an English-language bulletin, and arranged concerts and festivals. In 1938, Prokofiev performed at a VOKS event in London.

◆

Vsesoyuznïy komitet po delam iskusstv, All-Union Committee on Arts Affairs. Established in 1936 as a subdivision of Sovnarkom to define and enforce official policy in the arts. Platon

Kerzhentsev served as its first chairman, followed after 1938 by Aleksey Nazarov, Mikhaíl Khrapchenko, Polikarp Lebedev, and Nikolay Bespalov. In 1953, the Committee was dissolved and replaced, along with several other branches of the Stalinist cultural apparatus, by the Ministry of Culture (Ministerstvo kulturï).

◆

Vsesoyuznïy komitet po radiofikatsii i radioveshchaniyu, All-Union Radio Committee. Established in 1933, with Platon Kerzhentsev as head until 1936. Before that part of the People's Communications Commissariat (Narodnïy komissariat svyazi). Housed cultural divisions dedicated to literature, music, and children's programs. During World War II the music division was supervised by Dmitriy Kabalevsky. Sergey Balasanyan served as deputy director of the Radio Committee and, during the period of Prokofiev's acquaintanceship with him, the officer responsible for music programming.

Index

THE
NEW
TESTAMENT

God's Word to the Nations
(GWN)

*Spreading and teaching
our Lord's message of
Law and Gospel
to all people!*

BIBLION PUBLISHING
Cleveland

THE NEW TESTAMENT: God's Word to the Nations (GWN)

Biblion Publishing
P.O. Box 26343
21472 Lorain Road
Cleveland, Ohio 44126-0343
(216) 333-4114

For centuries the two major portions of the Bible have been divided by the designations *Old Testament* and *New Testament*. How appropriate! The Old contained the *promises*; the New witnesses the *fulfillments*. Fulfillment in the New Testament spells *completeness* and stands in sharp contrast to the *incompleteness* of the Old Testament.

The Old Testament's covenant-promise to Abraham came to fulfillment in the birth, death, and resurrection of Jesus Christ. Jesus fulfilled the Old Testament promise by putting His "*new* 'last will and *testament*'" into effect through His own blood-shedding death (1 Cor. 11:23-26; Heb. 9:16). This *new testament* offers the *inheritance* of everlasting life and calls every human being to believe that Jesus the Testator is the Messiah or the CHRIST (Jn. 3:16; 4:25,26).

The *chi-rho* emblem on GWN's cover reminds us of the great importance that the New Testament gives to Jesus the Christ, to His "new" message and His "testamental" work. This emblem is composed of two Greek letters (*chi*="ch" and *rho*="r"), which are superimposed on each other, and form an abbreviation of the Name "*CHRIST*." *Chi-rho* emblems also stand in the columns of GWN's New Testament translation, indicating passages which directly quote those Old Testament promises which were fulfilled *in relation to* or *through* the work of the CHRIST (Gal. 4:4; Jn. 1:1,14; 1 Tim. 3:16)!

Because of the centrality of His *new testament*, this present GWN New Testament translation is distributed. It is designed to tell people everywhere of the eternal inheritance won for them by Him who is Jesus the CHRIST.

TABLE OF CONTENTS

MAPS

ILLUSTRATIONS

BIBLICAL HELPS

TO THE READER

This present edition of **THE NEW TESTAMENT** is your introduction to a newly translated and revised version of the Scriptures, which will be entitled: **THE HOLY BIBLE: God's Word to the Nations (GWN)**. The printing of **THE NEW TESTAMENT** portion of this GWN version testifies to the completion of the first phase of the project. It is designed to accomplish two major things: acquaint the Bible reading public with the progress being made toward the final publication of the entire GWN translation of the Bible; and, give a preview of the GWN's textual accuracy, clarity of meaning, and readability. This edition also displays various Scriptural helps for the reader that include informative footnotes and related articles pertaining to all types of Scriptural matters.

It is hoped that this Bible work will encourage you to become involved with the GWN project which is being carried on under the auspices of the LUTHER BIBLE SOCIETY by means of the input and aid of Christians from many different areas of the Christian church. With this in mind you are asked to read the Preface carefully, examine the text thoughtfully, and note the Appendixes at the back. Our prayer is that our Triune God will move your heart toward a positive response of involvement as you do these *three* things. Write today for more information as to how you can become a part of this exciting and vital project. Write: BIBLION PUBLISHING, P.O. Box 26343, 21472 Lorain Road, Fairview Park, OH 44126.

BIBLION PUBLISHING has also prepared an article on page xix ("SPECIAL FEATURES: TEXT, NOTES, AND FORMAT"), which will prove helpful in many ways to you the reader.

May the God of heaven—Father, Son, and Holy Spirit—bless *you* in the best of ways as you study, meditate on, and put into use in your life "**God's Word to the Nations**."

PREFACE

to

THE NEW TESTAMENT
God's Word to the Nations
(GWN)

in preparation for the publication of

THE HOLY BIBLE
God's Word to the Nations
of the Twenty-first Century
(GWN)

It has been said of God's Holy Word, the Bible:

"Sin will keep you from this Book.
This Book will keep you from sin."
—Dwight L. Moody

God's Word! God's Word! His *Word* created all things. "His *Word* became flesh and lived among us...full of grace and truth" (Jn. 1:14). His written and spoken *Word* has "the power to save everyone who believes it" (Rom. 1:16). His *Word* penetrates stony hearts of pride and leads sinners to repentance and to the forgiveness of sins. And His *Word* moves believers to proclaim the saving Word to the nations, to every living person—and in their language, in the language of today.

Primarily, God's Word is to be communicated for understanding, so that all people may "come to know the truth" and be saved.

Yes, God wants to be understood. He is the Great Communicator. For centuries He has communicated through His creation. Throughout the New Testament era He has continuously communicated through His Son (Heb. 1:1,2). This has been done whenever His written Word was read and spoken. In this way God the Communicator has also clearly spoken through the work of His Spirit. Long ago the Spirit inspired the Holy Scriptures to be written (2 Tim 3:16). Today the Spirit still motivates and helps men to produce accurate and easy-to-understand Bible translations, which communicate the same life-giving Word.

In this way the Old Testament Scriptures came to be translated into Greek already in the second and third centuries before Christ. Initially, this translation, called the Septuagint (LXX), was completed so that non-Hebrew and non-Aramaic speaking Jews who lived outside of Palestine could "come to know the truth" and be saved.

By the time of Christ, Greek had become the major language of communication in the Mediterranean world. It is quite natural, then, that our God would use Greek to communicate with people in the New Testament era.

As time passed, the status and importance of particular nations and languages changed. So during the centuries following Christ's death and

resurrection, Latin replaced Greek as the most important language for written communication in the Roman Empire. Therefore, the Old and New Testaments were translated into Latin in order that God's communication could be clearly understood. One Latin version—Jerome's Vulgate—rose to prominence and became the most generally used translation for over 1,000 years.

But the world did not stand still. The centers of political power changed. Languages also continued to change. As a result, both Greek and Latin fell from common use. However, the church did not keep up with the ears of the people. By the time of the Middle Ages God's Word had become virtually meaningless to the average listener. Clear communication was cut off as large numbers of people could no longer understand the Vulgate in Latin; and at that time no substitute translation in the language of the people had come into existence.

It was into this world of religious darkness that men like Bede, Wycliffe, and Luther came. The translations of Bede (d. 735) and Wycliffe (1384) were pioneer efforts. The usage of their work was only temporary, because God's time had not yet come.

God's time finally did come between 1454 and 1534. During those years three significant events took place that changed the whole picture. These events opened the way for the renewal of God's clear communication to mankind and for the worldwide spreading of His Word.

The first of these events was the introduction of movable type. This took place in 1454. The Bible—God's Word—was the first book off Gutenberg's press.

The second event was the renewal of interest in the original languages of the Bible—Hebrew and Greek. In 1516 Erasmus issued the first published Greek New Testament. It also contained a parallel, up-to-date Latin translation.

The third event was Martin Luther's accurate and easy-to-understand translation. It was taken from the original Biblical languages and was put into the German language of his day. Luther completed his New Testament translation in 1522. His translation of the entire Bible was finished by 1534. Luther's German translation immediately became the *norm* for all German translations for 400 years.

William Tyndale used Luther's German translation when he himself translated the New Testament into English. In fact, Tyndale personally consulted Luther and enrolled at the University of Wittenberg in order to spend an academic year learning from Luther and his colleague Melanchthon. (The latter was a professor of Greek at the university.) The first edition of Tyndale's English New Testament was published in 1526. Because it could not be published in England, it was printed in Worms, Germany, a situation made possible because of Tyndale's close relationship with Luther.

During the next 85 years several English translations of the Bible came into existence, for example, Coverdale's Bible, Matthew's Bible, the Great Bible, the Geneva Bible, and the Bishop's Bible. These translations culminated in the King James Version of the Bible (1611). This English translation was finally confirmed and offically recognized in 1662.

We interject these facts: Fifty-four scholars worked on the King James

Version (KJV). (Forty-seven of them are known to us by name.) The background to the KJV translation effort is interesting, but of greater interest (and also to the glory of God who prepared the way for the KJV through the work of former translators) is the textual make-up of the KJV. Most Bible students will be flabbergasted to know that the KJV scholars were just as much revisers as they were translators. Though they worked from the original Hebrew and Greek, they also consulted the various former English versions in an effort to communicate in an accurate, clear, and readable way.

In the final analysis, and we are indebted to Charles C. Butterworth's *Literary Lineage of the King James Bible 1340-1611* (Philadelphia: University of Pennsylvania Press, 1941), the KJV contained much wording taken directly from former English versions: 4% from the Wycliffe versions; 18% from Tyndale's, which included the Matthew's Bible; 13% from the Coverdale/Great Bible versions; 19% from the Geneva Bible (the favorite of the KJV translators); 4% from the Bishop's Bible (the favorite of King James of England); and 3% from all other existing English translations. This, then, leaves 39% of the King James Version as original, and most of those passages followed a revision as well as a translation process. Surprised?

Now back to our specific Preface remarks.

For 350 to 400 years Luther's Bible and the King James Version served as the *norm* for the written Word of God in the German- and English-speaking worlds.

Once again, language did not stand still. The German and English expressions of the sixteenth and seventeenth centuries fell from use, except in the religious arena. There they survived as a kind of special or "church language" for the "insider." Year by year the Word of God became more and more obscure. God's Word in an outdated language no longer communicated to the masses who had not yet come to know Christ as their personal Savior.

In time, God the Great Communicator acted. He once again used language in such a way that His Word might be presented accurately and clearly to the peoples of that day. He did this through a series of significant events.

The first of these significant events occurred at the end of the 1700s. At that time spiritual revival called for a specific mission outreach to all parts of the world. With men like William Carey in India (1793) and the Bible Societies' movement, the "pentecostal principle" was established: the giving of God's Word in a form that can be easily understood by the people.

The second event concerned the major advances made in the fields of archaeology and the study of the text of the Bible in its original languages. Older Biblical materials, inscribed stones, and cuneiform tablets that provided Biblical scholars with new insights into Scriptural meaning were found and made available. When the accuracy of the Biblical text came under attack from rationalists, God also provided faithful Biblical scholars with numerous Greek manuscripts that were 600 to 800 years older than those reflected in the King James Version. Later the 1947 discoveries at Qumran pushed the knowledge of some of the Hebrew textual manuscripts back further, some 1,000 years. This second event gave testimony to the fact that

God the Holy Spirit had originally guided the writing of the Biblical text and since that time had preserved it for His saving purpose.

These first two events set the context for God's timetable to be enacted once again. Parallel to the time of Martin Luther, the context for a new breakthrough in communicating God's Word would not have been fruitful without God's people. People like Luther and his faithful reviewers at Wittenberg were: (1) ready to step out in faith, (2) willing to work deliberately and courageously in the face of criticism, and yet (3) able to push on to give the Word of God to people in an everyday language that they could easily understand.

Dr. William F. Beck became one of the people whom God chose for this new task. Already in 1936 Beck of his own volition started the task of diligently searching and studying the best available manuscripts of the Old and New Testaments in the original languages. He did this in order to hear the voice of God clearly and thereby arrive at the right meaning. Once he comprehended the text, he made every effort to express its meaning in a way that communicated God's thoughts in an unambiguous and easy-to-understand form.

Beck's aim was accuracy of meaning and the absolutely clear expression of that meaning for *all* the English readers of his day. One of his primary concerns was that the Word of God should communicate to all English-speaking peoples, so that all would have the opportunity to hear, understand, believe, and respond with a life of faith and witness. He envisioned that newly converted believers would immediately be equipped with God's living Word at *a level of language* that was easy to understand and also easy to share with others.

At the same time Beck was a faithful Christian who was determined to make sure that Christ and His full truth were preserved on the pages of Scripture. He believed in the Scriptures as the inspired Word of God which tells us of Christ, our only hope for salvation. That tells a great story to any true Christian, for above all else a translator needs to know Christ as Savior and to accept His Word as the truth that makes us free. This, then, explains why Beck was particularly concerned that the Messianic prophecies of the Old Testament be carefully guarded through meticulous translation research and that the fulfillments in the New Testament be handled ever so carefully. In line with this view, the present translators see the *chi-rho* emblem (see "cover" explanation, p. iii) as a significant indicator of the connection of the OLD TESTAMENT with the NEW TESTAMENT; the *promises* of the OLD with the *fulfillments* of the NEW.

In the context of this overall setting Beck was one of the pioneers in the field of modern Bible translation. Already in his time he sensed that English, modern English—not Latin or German or even Shakespearean English—was fast becoming the most common language in the world. The Great Communicator was at work again. For 30 years (1936-1966) Beck translated the entire Bible into modern English.

But language tends to change even within the lifetime of translators. For example, Beck's favorite word for "happy" was "gay." It was a much used word back in the 1940s—but in a totally different sense than today. So when

Beck's New Testament was published in 1963, those passages which related that "so-and-so was very 'gay'" had to be changed because of newer connotations in modern society.

The entirety of Beck's translation was put on the market in 1976, eleven years after his death. For ten of those years Beck's Old Testament was being polished by two hand-picked scholars. When it appeared in print, it was entitled: *THE HOLY BIBLE: An American Translation* (AAT). (Since that time it has been sensed that the term "American" carries too much negative baggage in nations outside America to use it as a title in other countries and on the foreign mission field. It's a great patriotic title in America, but even in Canada it does not communicate the concept of "North American English" minus all political connotations. Thus, a new title has been deemed wise. See below.)

It has now been over 50 years since Beck began his monumental work, which was one of the first of the many modern English translations to have appeared within the last four decades. But already in 1978 the question had arisen: Should Beck's translation just remain a pioneer effort or is it worthy of an updated revision? A team of Bible scholars and pastors of the Evangelical Lutheran Synod (ELS), The Lutheran Church—Missouri Synod (LCMS), and the Wisconsin Evangelical Lutheran Synod (WELS) felt that the translation of Beck was worth the hours of time needed to revise it in order to produce a superior product. Input has also been received from scholars and pastors of the Evangelical Lutheran Church in America (ELCA) and from various other sections of the Christian church, including scholars in touch with schools like Westminster Theological Seminary in Philadelphia and organizations like *Frontiers*, which is doing evangelism work among the world's 800 million Muslims.

Prior to and simultaneous to the building of this team of workers came the clamor and encouragement of other pastors and laypersons to revise Beck's masterful work in a most thorough manner. Such a venture takes dedication, sacrifice, organizational structure, procedural principles, funding, and legal guidance. So in time an organization was set up to supervise all aspects of this mammoth translation/revision task. That organization is the LUTHER BIBLE SOCIETY (LBS) of Fairview Park, Ohio.

As work progressed the revisers became convinced of three main things: (1) the revision had to place accuracy and clarity of communication at the top of the list of priorities; (2) the revision work had to be accompanied with Bible helps for professional church workers and laypersons alike; and (3) there is a market niche for such a translation, and it is waiting to be filled. That niche is the large area that lies between those more recent English translations on one end of the spectrum, which still cling partly or wholly to certain King James Version terminology for the security of the "old familiar," and those versions on the opposite end of the spectrum that have wandered into the area of basic paraphrase, leaving too much of the literal behind. In other words, the question becomes: How modern is too modern or not modern enough? The answer calls for a fine balance, a balance that demands an *accurate* translation in the *common* language of today. This is why a new title has been envisioned for the ultimate, newly revised product: **THE HOLY BIBLE: God's Word to the Nations of the Twenty-first Century (GWN).**

Let us now look at the three major concerns of the GWN translators, as mentioned above.

The concern for accuracy was addressed by engaging scholars who were most proficient in the original languages of Scripture. Data concerning their approach to the Greek text of THE NEW TESTAMENT is given in the article "SPECIAL FEATURES: TEXT, NOTES, AND FORMAT" on page xix.

The revisers also realized that the English of the higher levels of academic achievement is not easily understood by those who are less educated. A lower level of vocabulary can readily communicate to a much wider spectrum of people. With this in mind, educators and laypersons were also asked for their evaluations of revision sections. One opinion became unanimous: No baseball player today would yell, "Throw thou thine ball into mine mitt," and no basketball player would say, "Slam-dunk thou thine basketball into yonder hoop." Shakespeare was out and modern, communicating English had to be in.

The Hebrew and Greek grammar proved easy to handle when contrasted with the difficulty of communicating God's Word accurately, especially in the common language of today. As to the revisers' second concern, the extra Bible helps in the footnotes and appendixes flowed from the text in a most natural way and in an easy-to-communicate manner once the text communicated certain grammatical points clearly.

The third concern in some ways became the most difficult of all. It is deeply related to the first concern, the accuracy/clarity priority. But it also runs much deeper.

The revisers perceived certain strengths as well as weaknesses in Beck's overall work, as well as in themselves. As one of the revisers put it, "We need to do for Beck's translation what Jerome did for the many, previous Latin versions and what the King James Version also did for the Tyndale and Coverdale versions." That says it well! We simply add: "The GWN revisers are simply attempting to make a good translation into an even more excellent one."

Some have lavished praise on Beck's textual methods and style, while others have not been as exuberant. Nevertheless, no matter what their strengths or shortcomings, it is a known fact that one-man translations do not have a long-term mass appeal on the Bible market. They have a life expectancy of roughly 15 years.

With this in mind, the GWN revisers have worked to make the new product more flowing, rhythmic, and consistent—and yet within the parameters of Beck's own translation principles.

For example, Beck was the master of the narrative. His choppy style, for the most part, relates Bible stories very well. On the other hand, Beck was often inconsistent—overly paraphrastic here or overly literal there. Remember, this is a fine line; it was simply felt that more consistency had to be incorporated into the text.

Beck was also very talented when it came to using simple, one-syllable words as well as employing contractions. These both communicate well in certain contexts. Yet too many "gets" and "don'ts" stick out after a while, and their sounds from the lectern in church do not always lend themselves to a worshipful atmosphere, though in certain instances they do.

In this connection the revisers sought to use current, idiomatic English, giving the edge neither to Shakespeare nor to modern colloquialisms. For example, they continued to have Jesus' disciples communicate with contractions in everyday, Bible-conversation narratives. Even Jesus asks questions that contain contractions. It just sounds much more natural in English for Jesus to ask: "Didn't I choose the twelve of you...?" On the other hand, there are times of formality, as when Jesus stands before a government or church official where respect or the emphatic is demanded. In those contexts contractions do not seem quite as appropriate—at least in terms of communication.

As to one-syllable words, these simple forms cannot carry the load as often as Beck chose to use them. This is especially true in doctrinal contexts where meaning, limited in one passage or all-inclusive in another, must be communicated in a most precise way and sometimes by means of more technical terms—but at the same time readable terms.

Where Beck's contributions were many, and the features of accuracy, readability, and narrative his most significant, the highlights of the present GWN translation portray a sharper clarity *via* English sentence structure and a more flowing, rhythmic pattern in relation to prose in general, and to poetry in particular.

Many more twists and turns could be mentioned. But the one that relates to what the King James Version did for the Tyndale and Coverdale versions continues to stand out. As explained above, these two latter versions formed much of the base for the King James Version (KJV) of 1611, but in turn the KJV translators very often incorporated the contents of these versions and others into their new 1611 translation. Though working from the original Hebrew and Greek, the KJV translators also kept a close eye on the many former English versions. We repeat: They retained those portions that were both faithful to the originals as well as quite communicative in English. Other passages were salvaged by means of the *revision* process. Still other segments were translated from scratch. As such, much of the Tyndale/Coverdale/Geneva versions were retained and improved.

The revisers of the GWN also pray that their work, coupled with Beck's solid base, will produce a translation that will reach many for Christ in our day—from nations everywhere—in the English language of today.

In retrospect, therefore, this present revised translation and the helps that accompany it on the following pages form part of the long history of translation that started with the Septuagint and then continued with the Jeromes, the Wycliffes, the Luthers, the Tyndales, the King James translators, the Becks, and the many others known to translation history.

As in the case of the King James translators of old, the names of the scholars who are working on GWN will not be included in any printing of this translation. Later, after the whole GWN Bible is printed, a separate booklet will be prepared in which the procedures followed will be stated, the translators and various personnel involved will be listed, and certain data pertinent to various other matters will be given. Such information at this time would take us far beyond the space permitted in this Preface.

With the introductory comments above, the LUTHER BIBLE SOCIETY

enters into print with its revision of **THE NEW TESTAMENT: God's Word to the Nations (GWN)**. It is hoped that it will accomplish *three* major things:

First, we pray that you the reader will see a great need for the completed type of translation that you now hold in your hands. Today the world's population stands at 5 billion (5,000,000,000). It is estimated that only one and a half billion (1,500,000,000) of these persons are Christian—at least in name. Of that number, perhaps 500 million (500,000,000) persons are *practicing* Christians. This means that many nations need to be reached for Christ in the language of today.

Second, it is urgent for you the reader to realize that 350 million (350,000,000) persons throughout the world now use English as their first language. Also, 700 million (700,000,000) other persons utilize English as a second language. This confirms the great need for an *accurate, clear,* and *easy* version of an English Bible that can reach these people in the language of today. Such a version is essential in the service of our God who desperately wants His Word communicated to the nations.

There is a fervor for English that has people on fire in America as well as in the Orient and elsewhere. Many are the persons who are fleeing to the Americas and are learning English as their second language. Let's have them learn of Christ from the GWN!

What a tool the GWN can become! Just think what the Beck version already has done overseas. In Japan, for instance, children come to the various missionary schools. Why? To learn of Christ? Not always! Many come simply to learn to read English. So some missionaries take advantage of this opportunity. They lead people to Christ through the back door. When the children come to read English, they then teach them to read from Beck's Bible since it is translated on an easy reading level. Thus, English is taught and Christ is communicated at the same time. Brilliant! Can you imagine the possibilities for the completed GWN?

Third, in this confused, pluralistic, humanistic world, a world filled with fear, uncertainty, sin, and destruction, it is hoped that you will also see the need to spread the healing, assuring, friendly, and forgiving Word of Scripture in a most effective, accurate, and clear way.

You can do this by becoming part of our GWN revision effort. **God's Word to the Nations (GWN)** is a Bible version that promises to be an effective tool, both in *reaching* and *teaching*. Its clarity makes it a marvelous God-directed instrument for evangelism and missionary outreach, while its accuracy, clarity, and extra helps make it an invaluable tool for Bible study. It can benefit you and your loved ones as well as reach souls for Christ all over the world.

You can have "ownership" in this marvelous Bible venture by becoming a charter member of the LUTHER BIBLE SOCIETY through your contribution on behalf of GWN's translation work. You will be part of God's translation history in this era. Many were those who helped the Tyndales and Luthers in days past. Now God wishes to use you.

You have a tremendous opportunity under Christ! Some modern English translations of the Bible have not given laypersons much opportunity to

participate in their translation efforts. But our present LBS project does, and you are needed as part of the team effort if the nations are to be reached for Jesus!

THE NEW TESTAMENT: God's Word to the Nations (GWN) now stands in print. Only the lack of funding stands between it and a distribution to persons whose souls need to be reached for Christ. Funding is also needed so that the work on the translation of the Old Testament portion can continue. Therefore, God has seen fit to put this NEW TESTAMENT into your hands, in order to whet your appetite and to ask for your help.

Please look the translation over; view its many helps; and evaluate how it can help pastors, teachers, and laypersons reach all types of people for Christ. (Send your suggestions for improvements.)

Need we say more? This printing of **THE NEW TESTAMENT** is your preview. LBS hopes it also becomes an incentive for you to help this GWN project in Christ's Name with your assistance. LBS also hopes that congregations, pastors, Sunday School teachers and children, grade school teachers and students, Christian ladies groups, Bible class members, youth groups, and Christians everywhere will support this urgent translation effort.

THE NEW TESTAMENT: God's Word to the Nations (GWN) will truly communicate God's Word, which offers forgiveness and hope to all human beings, including the millions of English-speaking peoples.

May this printing of **THE NEW TESTAMENT** be a personal blessing to you and many others.

Luther Bible Society and the GWN Revision Committee

NOTES

SPECIAL FEATURES:
TEXT, NOTES, AND FORMAT

I. Textual Variants in the GWN New Testament

Because the books of the New Testament were copied by hand for over 1,400 years prior to the discovery of the printing press, variants (i.e., more than one reading for a verse) inevitably came into the text. A variant is the result of a copyist's *hand* or *eye* or *ear* leading him to write something other than what was written in the text from which a copy was being made.

Most of those who made copies did so very carefully, out of respect for the Word of God. But in spite of great care, their hands at times wrote something slightly different from what their brain was thinking, their eyes sometimes read something a little different from what was written, or their ears heard something slightly different from what was being read orally. (Copies were often made as one person read out loud while those around him copied down what was being read.)

As a result, all of our written "witnesses" to the New Testament text have variants, which came about through handcopying. However, God has preserved so many of the "witnesses" for us that we can easily eliminate most of these variants. The witnesses we have fall into two basic groups:

A. *Greek manuscripts and Greek quotations*
  1. Papyri (less than one hundred copies made in capital Greek letters on papyrus from A.D. 100-400)
  2. Uncials (several hundred copies made in capital Greek letters mostly on parchment from A.D. 300-900)
  3. Minuscules (several thousand copies made in small Greek letters on parchment from A.D. 800-1500)
  4. Lectionaries (several thousand copies of the Gospel and Epistle lections made in small Greek letters on parchment from A.D. 800-1500)
  5. Church Fathers (quotations found in the writings of church leaders in the first six centuries after Christ)
B. *Translations* (several thousand copies in a number of languages: Latin, Syriac, Coptic (Egypt), Gothic (SE Europe), Ethiopic, Georgian, etc.)

Most of the variants are insignificant. If a variant does not appear in any of the copies of the New Testament by the year A.D. 600, it could not have been part of the *original* New Testament; otherwise, at least one or more of the copies from the first 600 years would have included it. Also, if a variant appears in only one area of the Early Church, it could not have been part of the *original* New Testament; otherwise, at least one or more of the copies made in one or two other areas of the church would have included it.

The only variants worth noting are those which have the following characteristics: (1) both of the readings of the variant are found in copies made *early* in the history of the church; and (2) both of the readings of the variant are found in copies made *in more than one area* of the church (i.e., in two or more of these basic areas of the Early Church, such as Egypt, Palestine, Syria, Asia Minor, SE Europe, Italy and France, Western North Africa).

In variants of this type, it is not easy to decide which reading should be put in the text, because both readings of the variant are early and widespread. In this case, GWN chooses the earlier and the more widespread reading. It puts this reading in the text, while the other reading is indicated in a footnote.

If the footnote says, "*Some* of the older manuscripts and early translations read...," this indicates that the reading in the footnote is not nearly as well supported as the one in the text, because it is not as early or as widespread; but it was at least worth noting. If the footnote says, "*Many* of the older manuscripts and early translations read...," it indicates that although the reading in the footnote is not quite as well supported as the one in the text, it does have enough early and widespread support to make it a close rival to the one in the text.

In the case of these latter and more difficult variants, it is important to note that the decision concerning which reading to use in the text does not in any way affect any doctrine of Scripture. This needs to be emphasized because some people may ask, "How can you speak of an *inspired* and *inerrant* Bible if there are variants in it?"

We can and should answer: It is a fact, to the best of our knowledge, that God did not preserve any of the *original* texts written by the inspired writers. Why He chose not to do this, we do not know. However, God did do something special! He preserved a large number of copies which are in agreement in over 99% of the text; this leaves no doubt that today we have exactly what the original writers said. In regard to the few variants affecting less than 1% of the text, two things are true: First, in every variant there are two readings (one of which is the original reading!) *rather than a blank* in the text. These two definite options prevent readers from filling in whatever they please. Second, *neither* of the readings contained in *any* of those few variants that are harder to decide affects *any* doctrine in *any* way.

Therefore, in spite of the few variants that exist as a result of the New Testament being hand-copied, we can say along with the hymnwriter:

> We have a *sure* prophetic Word
> By inspiration of the Lord;
> And tho' assailed on every hand,
> Jehovah's Word shall ever stand.

> *Abiding, steadfast, firm and sure,*
> *The teachings of the Word endure.*
> Blest he who trusts this steadfast Word;
> His anchor holds in Christ, the Lord.
> —*Emanuel Cronenwett, 1880*

II. Footnotes and Other Helps in the GWN New Testament

In accordance with Acts 17:10-14, where we are told that the Bereans "...were very eager to receive the word, and every day...studied the Scriptures...," it is the prayer of all connected with GWN's translation work that every reader will desire to grow deeply in the Word of God. To that end, GWN wishes to aid both the casual reader as well as the in-depth student of Holy Scripture. Primarily, this has been done through the careful translation of the Biblical text, which permits our Lord's Word to speak accurately, clearly, and understandably. In addition to that finished text, *educational* footnotes, articles, and Biblical listings (glossary and concordance) and charts are included in this present GWN edition.

Footnote indicators in the Biblical text are easily connected to their counterparts at the bottom of the same page where they occur. In turn, an indicator connected with a footnote, for example, *b*- 16, relates that its note goes with the "*b*" indicator of verse 16 in the text above. (A 3*a*- 6 means that this is the first note of chapter 3 and is connected with verse 6 where the *a* indicator is located.) The reader's eye can easily move between text and notes from either starting point.

GWN's readers will also find the comments and helps in the front and strategically placed throughout this translation to be very useful. Likewise, the Appendixes in the back of the volume will prove most valuable. (GWN footnotes make frequent reference to the articles in these Appendixes.)

Please scan pages iii-xxiii and 519-593 to note these special features mentioned above.

III. Special Format Features in the GWN New Testament

GWN's New Testament uses a very spacious page layout; its every feature has been carefully planned for the benefit of the reader.

Each new book of this version begins on a right hand page. This leaves the possibility open for publishing this same edition in notebook form (8 1/2" x 11"), thereby allowing individual books to be removed in units for study and note taking.

GWN has also experimented with large, freestanding numbers at the beginning of chapters, resulting in the only translation able to number the first verse of a chapter with a "1." This allows Bible students to make notes in that area of the page which is normally filled in other Bibles with the beginning verses of the text.

Prose sections are set in a larger type than are the poetic portions. This contrast adds beauty to the page and was done so that more poetic words could be placed per line, preventing "wrapping" of lines that would destroy Biblical parallelisms (see GRAMMATIC/POETIC STRUCTURES THAT CONVEY TEXTUAL MEANINGS on page 558). GWN has consistently refused to split units of poetry at inappropriate places in order to fill pages to the fullest degree. Rather, some pages have "air" at the end of text. This procedure safeguards the *unified* meaning of the text, both technically and visually.

As a rule, GWN pages are divided into three parts: text, cross-references, and footnotes. The text is comprised of God's Word. In this study edition certain indicators and helps are interspersed throughout the text at various places. These indicators include *chapter numbers*, *verse numbers*, *a built-in outline* that divides the whole book into larger subject units, and *headers* that divide smaller story/topic units. (Many *headers* in the Gospels contain cross-references that cite the locations of parallel Gospel accounts. This is a valuable aid in Bible study and in the preparation of sermons and devotions.)

Four other items are present in the textual portion of the page: italics, brackets, half-brackets, and *chi-rho* emblems. Italics indicate words that are cross-referenced to particular Old Testament references; full brackets indicate parallel meanings; half-brackets indicate words that have been added to the text to help it flow and/or communicate in a better way; and the *chi-rho* emblems signal verses where Jesus fulfills Old Testament prophecies concerning Himself.

Special attention should also be given to GWN's *capitalization system*; see GWN CAPITALIZATION on page 521.

All maps in GWN are original. Their placement directly corresponds to Scriptural texts where they will offer the greatest help. Some of the maps appear more than once. This saves much paging back and forth by the reader.

Each of these features is meant to aid understanding of God's Word to the fullest. Expanded explanations of several of these format features are given on pages 521-546, 558-565. Please take time to read this section. It will significantly enhance comprehension.

Finally, we call attention to the Book of *Revelation* that is entirely set in poetic form. For further information, see THE *KAI* STRUCTURE on page 565.

THE NEW TESTAMENT IN CHRONOLOGICAL ORDER

Originally, the books of the New Testament were written on individual scrolls. With the invention of the printing press, all 27 books were able to be consolidated into one volume. This meant they had to be arranged in some kind of order. The arrangement chosen was partially by topic and partially by author, but generally not by the chronological order in which the books were written.

The logic behind this arrangement was fivefold: (1) to emphasize the life of Christ (the Four *Gospels*); (2) to make a smooth transition from the Gospels to the era of the Christian church *via* the spreading of Christ's message (the *Acts* of the Apostles); (3) to group the writings of Paul, the New Testament's most prolific writer (the 13 "Pauline Epistles"); (4) to group the eight remaining New Testament letters by various authors (the "General Epistles"); and (5) to close the New Testament with John's apocalyptic Epistle (*Revelation*).

Some have requested a *chronological* listing of the 27 New Testament books, that is, a listing in sequence as to the time of their individual writing. Such a listing has value, but at best—because specific dates are not given in the New Testament books themselves—that listing is very subjective and should be used only in a *general* way since all dating conclusions are drawn by various deductions. However, certain *internal* clues from the books themselves, as well as *external* comments from the fathers of the Early Church permit certain conclusions to be drawn.

No individual New Testament book can claim a date of composition to which all Bible students agree. Yet there is general agreement that is acceptable to the majority.

The areas of most disagreement revolve around whether the Gospel of *Mark* was written before or after *Matthew* and *Luke*, and whether Paul's four "Prison Epistles" were written from Ephesus around A.D. 53-55 or from Rome around A.D. 61. As to the *Gospels*, we have listed them in one possible sequence; both possibilities have been given for the "Prison Epistles."

CHRONOLOGICAL LISTING OF NEW TESTAMENT BOOKS:

A.D.		A.D.	
45	*James*	62	*1 Peter*
48	*Galatians*	62-63	*1 Timothy*
50	*1 Thessalonians*	63	*Titus*
50	*2 Thessalonians*	64	*Acts*
53-55	*Colossians, Philemon, Ephesians, Philippians* (if written from Ephesus)	64	*2 Timothy*
		64	*2 Peter*
55	*1 Corinthians*	60-70	*Jude*
55	*2 Corinthians*	65-70	*Hebrews*
56	*Romans*	90s	*John*
(?)	*Matthew* (early 50s to early 60s)	90s	*1 John*
(?)	*Luke* (late 50s to early 60s)	90s	*2 John*
(?)	*Mark* (late 50s to late 60s)	90s	*3 John*
61	*Colossians, Philemon, Ephesians, Philippians* (if written from Rome)	90s	*Revelation*

THE
NEW
TESTAMENT

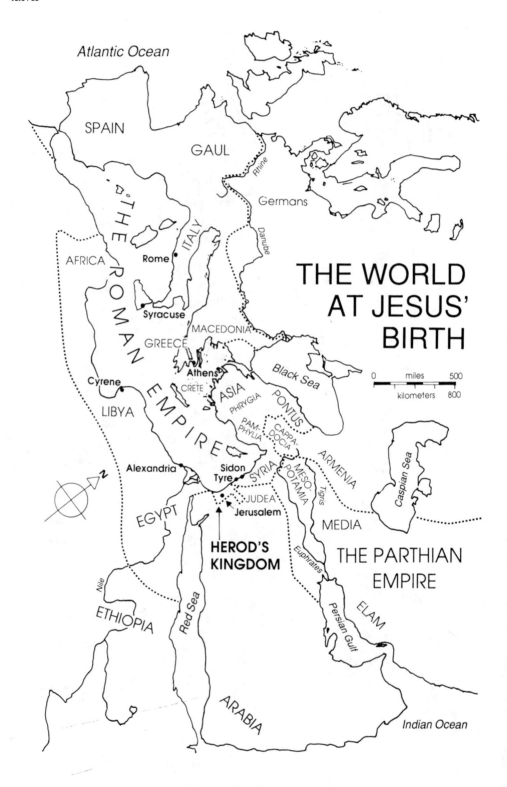

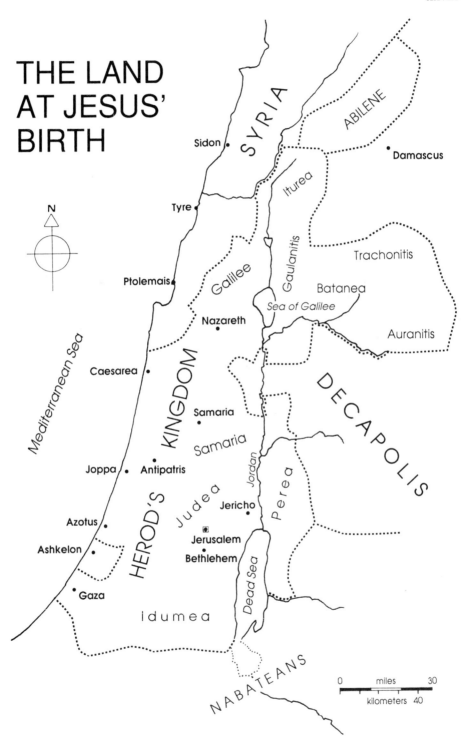

THE LAND
AT JESUS'
BIRTH

N

SYRIA

ABILENE

Sidon

Damascus

Iturea

Tyre

Gaulanitis

Trachonitis

Ptolemais

Galilee

Batanea

Sea of Galilee

Nazareth

Auranitis

Mediterranean Sea

Caesarea

KINGDOM

DECAPOLIS

Samaria

Samaria

Jordan

Joppa

Antipatris

HEROD'S

Judea

Jericho

Perea

Azotus

Ashkelon

Jerusalem

Bethlehem

Gaza

Idumea

Dead Sea

NABATEANS

0   miles   30

kilometers 40

THE GOOD NEWS [GOSPEL] AS TOLD BY
MATTHEW[a]

1ST CHAPTER

A. Jesus' genealogy and infancy (1:1–2:23)

The Family Line Of Jesus Christ—*Luke 3:24-38*[b]

¹ A record of the family history[c] of Jesus Christ, a descendant of David ⌊and⌋ a descendant of Abraham:

²   **Abraham** was the father of Isaac,
    Isaac was the father of Jacob,
    Jacob was the father of Judah and his brothers.
³   **Judah** was the father of Perez and Zerah
      by Tamar ⌊who was their mother⌋.
    Perez was the father of Hezron,
    Hezron was the father of Ram,
⁴   **Ram** was the father of Aminadab,
    Aminadab was the father of Nahshon,
    Nahshon was the father of Salmon,
⁵   **Salmon** was the father of Boaz
      by Rahab ⌊who was his mother⌋.
    Boaz was the father of Obed
      by Ruth ⌊who was his mother⌋.
    Obed was the father of Jesse,
⁶   **Jesse** was the father of King **David**.

SPECIAL NOTE: This translation contains certain unique features and educational aids. The article SPECIAL FEATURES: TEXT, NOTES, AND FORMAT on page xix will help comprehension.

1 *a*   Matthew, also called Levi (Mk. 2:14), leaves his imprint as the author at 9:9-13 and 10:3.
    b   See THE FAMILY LINE OF JESUS CHRIST on page 547 and the "Time line" of Biblical persons and events on page 9.
  c- 1 Greek: "*geneseōs*," as here used by Matthew, is meant to remind the reader of the Hebrew "*tōledōth*" of the Old Testament book of *Genesis*. That Hebrew term is accurately translated as "history" or "family history" in Genesis 2:4a; 5:1; 6:9; 10:1; 11:10,27; 25:12,19; 36:1,9; 37:2 and forms a structural outline for *Genesis* at those eleven points in the book.

David was the father of Solomon
      by her ˎwho had been the wifeˏ of Uriah.
7 **Solomon** was the father of Rehoboam,
Rehoboam was the father of Abijah,
Abijah was the father of Asa,
8 **Asa** was the father of Jehoshaphat,
Jehoshaphat was the father of Joram,
Joram was the father of Uzziah,
9 **Uzziah** was the father of Jotham,
Jotham was the father of Ahaz,
Ahaz was the father of Hezekiah,
10 **Hezekiah** was the father of Manasseh,
Manasseh was the father of Amon,
Amon was the father of Josiah,
11 **Josiah** was the father of **Jechoniah** and his brothers
      when the people were taken away to Babylon.

12 After they had been taken away to Babylon,
      Jechoniah was the father of Shealtiel.
Shealtiel was the father of Zerubbabel,
13 **Zerubbabel** was the father of Abiud,
Abiud was the father of Eliakim,
Eliakim was the father of Azor,
14 **Azor** was the father of Zadok,
Zadok was the father of Achim,
Achim was the father of Eliud,
15 **Eliud** was the father of Eleazar,
Eleazar was the father of Matthan,
Matthan was the father of Jacob,
16 **Jacob** was the father of **Joseph**, the husband of Mary;
      she was the mother of **JESUS**[d] who is called CHRIST. [e]

17 So there are in all
      14 generations from Abraham to David,
      14 generations from David to the Babylonian Captivity,
      14 generations from the Babylonian Captivity to Christ.

An Angel Comes To Joseph

18 This is how Jesus Christ was born.

---

d- 16 Literally: "of whom was born Jesus"; the Greek-based English name "Jesus" and its
      Hebrew-based counterpart "Joshua" both mean "Savior, Helper, the LORD saves, YAHWEH
      helps."
e- 16 The Greek-based English name "Christ" and its Hebrew-based counterpart "Messiah" both
      mean the "Anointed One" or the "Chosen One."

His mother Mary had been promised to Joseph to be his wife. But before they came together, she was found to be with Child by the Holy Spirit.*f*
19 Joseph, her husband, was an honorable man and did not want to disgrace her. So he decided to divorce her secretly.

20 After Joseph had thought about it, an angel of the Lord appeared to him in a dream and said, "Joseph son of David, do not be afraid to take your wife Mary home with you; for her Child*g* is from the Holy Spirit. **21** She will have a son, and you will name Him JESUS,*h* because He will save His people from their sins." **22** All this happened so that what the Lord said through the prophet would be fulfilled: **23** *"Look! The virgin will conceive and have a son, and they will name Him Immanuel,"* which means "God With Us."

24 When Joseph awoke, he did what the Lord's angel had commanded. He took his wife home with him **25** but did not have relations [sexual relations] with her until she had a son.*i* And he named Him JESUS.

2ND CHAPTER

The Wise Men [Magi]

1 Jesus was born in Bethlehem in Judea when Herod was king. Then Wise Men came from the east to Jerusalem. **2** "Where is the Child who was born King of the Jews?" they asked. "We saw His star in the east*a* and have come to worship Him."

3 When King Herod heard about it, he became alarmed and all Jerusalem with him. **4** He called together all the ruling priests and scribes*b* of the people and tried to find out from them where the Christ [Messiah] was to be born.

5 "In Bethlehem in Judea," they told him, "because the prophet has written:

6   *And you, Bethlehem,* in the land of Judah,
         are by no means *the least among the leading towns of Judah,*
           since from you will come a Leader
             who will shepherd My people Israel."

7 Then Herod secretly called the Wise Men and found out from them the exact time the star appeared. **8** As he sent them to Bethlehem, he said, "Go and

---

23 *Is 7:14; 8:8,10*   **6** *2 Sam 5:2; Mic 5:2,4*

f- 18 More literally: "When His mother Mary was betrothed to Joseph, before they came together, she was found to have conceived by the Holy Spirit."

g- 20 Literally: "for what is begotten in her."

h - 21 See 1:16 and its accompanying footnote. "d."

i - 25 Some of the older manuscripts and early translations read: "firstborn son." See Luke 2:7 where the inclusion of "firstborn" is certain.

2 *a*- 2 Or "star rise."

   b- 4 These were the Bible scholars of Jesus' day. Their work and responsibilities varied greatly from one to another. These areas included making handwritten copies of the Old Testament, interpreting and following the Mosaic guidelines of the Pentateuch (Five Books of Moses), formulating oral laws, teaching God's people in classroom situations, etc. In short, the scribes were considered authorities on the Jewish religion. Compare Ezra 7:6,10.

search carefully for the little Child, and when you find Him, report to me so that I too may go and bow down before Him."

9 After hearing the king, they started out. And there was the star they had seen in the east![c] It led them on until it came to a stop over the place where the Child was. **10** They were extremely happy to see the star. **11** They went into the house and saw the little Child with His mother Mary. They knelt and worshiped Him. Then they opened their treasure chests and offered Him *gifts: gold, frankincense,[d]* and myrrh.

12 But God warned them in a dream not to go back to Herod. So they went back to their country by another road.

To Egypt

13 After the Wise Men left, Joseph in a dream saw an angel of the Lord, who said, "Get up, take the little Child and His mother, and flee to Egypt. Stay there until I tell you, for Herod is going to search for the Child to kill Him."

14 Joseph got up at night, took the little Child and His mother, and went to Egypt. **15** He stayed there until the death of Herod. In this way what the Lord said through the prophet was fulfilled: *"I called My Son out of Egypt."*

16 When Herod saw that the Wise Men had tricked him, he became very angry and sent men to kill all the boys in Bethlehem and in all the country around it, up to two years old,[e] according to the exact time which he had determined from the Wise Men. **17** Then what was said through the prophet Jeremiah was fulfilled:

18   *A cry is heard in Rama!*
        Weeping and loud wailing:
           Rachel crying over her children
           and refusing to be comforted,
             because they are gone.

19 But when Herod died, an angel of the Lord appeared in a dream to Joseph in Egypt **20** and told him, "Get up, take the little Child and His mother, and go to the land of Israel. Those who tried to kill the little Child are dead."

21 Joseph got up, took the little Child and His mother, and came to the land of Israel. **22** But when he heard that Archelaus had succeeded his father Herod as king of Judea, he was afraid to go there. And being warned in a dream, he went to Galilee. **23** He came and made his home in a town by the name of Nazareth. And so what the prophets said was fulfilled: "He will be called a Nazarene."[f]

---

11 Ps 72:10,15; Is 60:6   15 Hos 11:1   18 Jer 31:15

---

c- 9 Or "seen when it rose."

d- 11 See Leviticus 2:1 and its accompanying footnote.

e- 16 Some believe that this might be understood to mean "up to *one* year old"; this is based on the idea that Judaism already spoke of infants at birth as being one year old.

f- 23 A wordplay; according to Isaiah 11:1 the Savior would be a *"Netzēr,"* a Branch, growing from the roots of the tree or family of David. See also Judges 13:5,7.

5

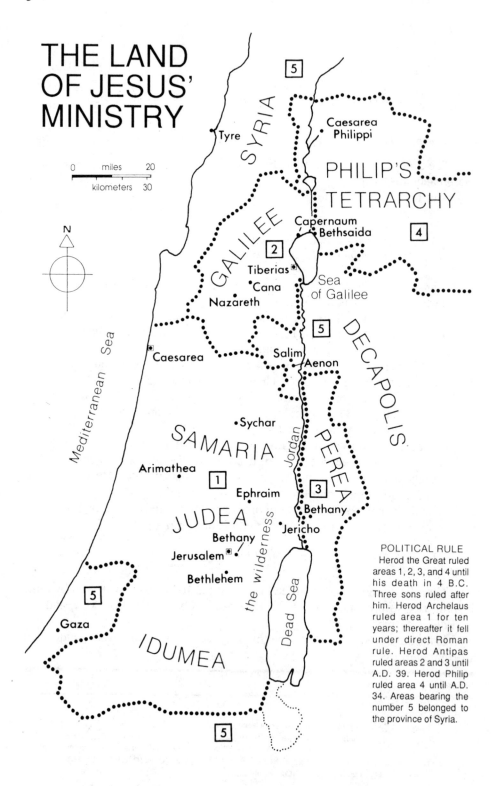

THE LAND OF JESUS' MINISTRY

miles 0 — 20
kilometers 30

N

Tyre

SYRIA

Caesarea Philippi

⑤

PHILIP'S TETRARCHY

④

GALILEE

Capernaum
Bethsaida

②

Tiberias

Cana

Nazareth

Sea of Galilee

DECAPOLIS

⑤

Salim
Aenon

Caesarea

Mediterranean Sea

Sychar

SAMARIA

Jordan

PEREA

Arimathea

①

Ephraim

③

JUDEA

Bethany

Jericho

the wilderness

Bethany

Jerusalem

Bethlehem

Dead Sea

⑤

Gaza

IDUMEA

⑤

POLITICAL RULE
Herod the Great ruled areas 1, 2, 3, and 4 until his death in 4 B.C. Three sons ruled after him. Herod Archelaus ruled area 1 for ten years; thereafter it fell under direct Roman rule. Herod Antipas ruled areas 2 and 3 until A.D. 39. Herod Philip ruled area 4 until A.D. 34. Areas bearing the number 5 belonged to the province of Syria.

3RD CHAPTER

B. Five booklets, a parallel to Moses' fivefold Torah (3:1–25:46)
1. First booklet (3:1–7:29)
a. Narrative and deeds: Galilean ministry begins (3:1–4:25)

John Prepares The Way—*Mark 1:1-8; Luke 3:1-18; John 1:19-28*

1 The time came when John the Baptizer appeared in the wilderness of Judea and preached: **2** "Repent, for the Kingdom of heaven is near." **3** He was the one of whom the prophet Isaiah said:

> *A voice is calling out^a in the wilderness:*
> *"Prepare the way for the Lord;*
> *make the paths straight for Him."*

4 John wore clothes of camel's hair and had a leather belt around his waist. And he lived on locusts and wild honey.
5 Then Jerusalem, all Judea, and the whole Jordan Valley came out to him.
6 As they confessed their sins, he baptized them in the Jordan River.
7 He also saw many Pharisees and Sadducees coming for baptism. He said to them, "You brood of poisonous snakes, who warned you to run away from the punishment waiting for you? **8** Therefore, produce the works that show you have repented. **9** Do not think that you can tell yourselves, 'Abraham is our father.' For I tell you, God can raise up children for Abraham from these stones. **10** The ax is now ready to strike at the root of the trees, and any tree that does not produce good fruit will be cut down and thrown into the fire. **11** I baptize you with water to bring about a change of heart.^b But the One who is coming after me is mightier than I. I am not worthy to carry His sandals.^c He will baptize you with the Holy Spirit and fire. **12** He has the winnowing shovel in His hand, and He will clean up His threshing floor. He will gather His wheat into the barn, but the chaff He will burn^d in a fire that cannot be put out."

John Baptizes Jesus—*Mark 1:9-11; Luke 3:21,22; compare John 1:29-34*

13 Then Jesus came from Galilee to John at the Jordan to be baptized by him. **14** John tried to prevent Him. He said, "I need to be baptized by You, and yet You come to me?"
15 Jesus answered him, "Let it be this way now; that is how we should fulfill all righteousness."

---

3 Is 40:3

---

3 *a-* 3 Or "shouting."
   b- 11 Literally: "with water for the purpose of repentance."
   c- 11 Or "take off His sandals." This was ordinarily a slave's duty.
   d- 12 This word order shows a *chiasmatic* A-B-B-A ("gather-wheat-chaff-burn") arrangement, which is so common to Hebrew structure. See GRAMMATIC/POETIC STRUCTURES THAT CONVEY TEXTUAL MEANINGS on page 558.

Then John gave in to Him. **16** As soon as Jesus was baptized, He came out of the water, and immediately the heavens were opened, and He*ᵉ* saw the Spirit of God coming down on Him as a dove. **17** And a voice from heaven said, "*This is My Son*, whom I love*ᶠ* and in whom I *delight*."

4TH CHAPTER

The Devil Tempts Jesus— *Mark 1:12,13; Luke 4:1-13*

1 Then the Spirit led Jesus into the wilderness to be tempted by the devil. **2** He did not eat anything for 40 days and 40 nights, and at the end of that time He was ˻very˼ hungry.

3 The Tempter came to Him and said, "If You are the Son of God, tell these stones to become loaves of bread."

4 Jesus answered, "It is written: '*A person will not be kept alive by bread alone but by every word that God speaks.*' "

5 Then the devil took Him into the Holy City and had Him stand on the ledge of the Temple. **6** He told Him, "If You are the Son of God, jump down. For it is written: '*He will order His angels to help you. They will carry you in their hands* and *never let you stub your foot against a stone.*' "

7 "It is also written," Jesus answered him, " '*Do not put the Lord your God to a test.*' "*ᵃ*

8 Then the devil took Him to a very high mountain and showed Him all the kingdoms in the world and their glory. **9** The devil told Him, "All this I will give to You if You will bow down and worship me."

10 Then Jesus answered him, "Go away, Satan! For it is written: 'Worship *the Lord your God* and *serve Him* only.' "

11 Then the devil left Him, and angels came and took care of Him.

At Home In Capernaum

12 When Jesus heard that John had been put in prison, He went back to Galilee. **13** Leaving Nazareth, He went and made His home in Capernaum by the sea in the area of Zebulun and Naphtali. **14** And so what the prophet Isaiah said was fulfilled:

15   *Land of Zebulun and land of Naphtali,*
              the way to the sea, across the Jordan, Galilee of the Gentiles!
16   *The people sitting in darkness have seen a great Light;ᵇ*
              for those sitting in the land of the shadow of death, a Light has risen.

---

17 *Ps 2:7; Is 42:1*   **4** *Deut 8:3*   **6** *Ps 91:11,12*   **7** *Deut 6:16*   **10** *Deut 6:13*
15,16 *Is 9:1,2*

---

e- 16 Or "he," if a reference to John the Baptizer (cf. Jn. 1:32,33).
f- 17 Or "This My Son, the Beloved" (also at 17:5; Mk. 1:11; 9:7; Lk. 3:22).
4 *a-* 7 Or "Do not tempt the Lord your God."
b- 16 A reference to the "Gospel"; some would say a reference to "Christ."

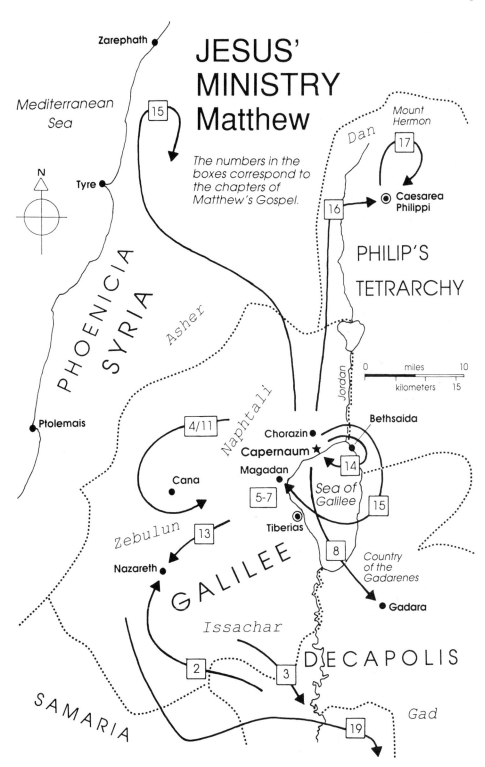

JESUS' MINISTRY
Matthew

Mediterranean
Sea

Zarephath

Tyre

Ptolemais

N

PHOENICIA

SYRIA

Asher

The numbers in the boxes correspond to the chapters of Matthew's Gospel.

15

Dan

Mount Hermon

17

⊙ Caesarea Philippi

16

PHILIP'S

TETRARCHY

Jordan

0   miles   10

kilometers   15

4/11

Cana

Naphtali

Chorazin ●

Capernaum ★

Magadan ●

Bethsaida

14

Sea of Galilee

15

5-7

Tiberias ⊙

Zebulun

13

Nazareth ●

8

Country of the Gadarenes

GALILEE

Issachar

● Gadara

2

3

DECAPOLIS

SAMARIA

19

Gad

17 From then on Jesus began to preach: "Repent, for the Kingdom of heaven is near!"

"Come, Follow Me"—*Mark 1:14-20; Luke 5:1-11; John 1:35-51*

18 As He was walking along the shore of the Sea of Galilee, He saw two brothers, Simon (called Peter) and his brother Andrew, throwing a net into the sea, for they were fishermen. **19** Jesus told them, "Come, follow Me, and I will make you fishers of men." **20** Immediately they left their nets and followed Him.

21 He went on and saw two other brothers, James the ₍son₎ of Zebedee and his brother John. They were in the boat with their father Zebedee, mending their nets. He called them, **22** and immediately they left the boat and their father and followed Him.

Preaching In Galilee—*Mark 1:35-39; Luke 4:42-44*

23 Jesus went around everywhere in Galilee, teaching in their synagogs, preaching the Good News of the Kingdom, and healing every kind of disease and sickness among the people.

24 The news about Him spread all over Syria. And the people brought to Him all who were suffering from various diseases and who were in great pain, the demon-possessed, the epileptics, *c* and the paralyzed; and He made them well. **25** Large crowds followed Him from Galilee, and the Decapolis [Ten Towns], *d* and from Jerusalem, Judea, and the other side of the Jordan.

---

c- 24 Literally: "moonstruck"; what kind of disease is meant is not quite clear.
d- 25 A federation of some ten Greek cities.

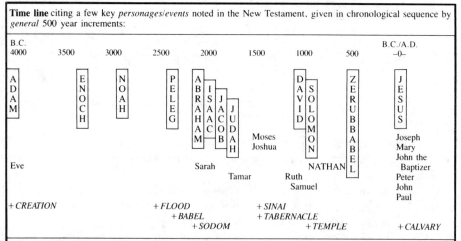

Time line citing a few key *personages/events* noted in the New Testament, given in chronological sequence by *general* 500 year increments:

Note: "NATHAN" is *not* Nathan the prophet who confronted David with his sins of murder and adultery; rather, this Nathan is the brother of Solomon. In the present time line, compactness prevents placing "NATHAN" next to "SOLOMON" since that would overly distort the chronological appearance. In essence both Nathan and Solomon are direct ancestors of Christ (Lk. 3:31). THE FAMILY LINE OF JESUS CHRIST on page 547 explains the significance of this whole ancestry.

5TH CHAPTER

b. Words: Sermon on the Mount (5:1–7:29)

The Sermon On The Mount

1 When Jesus saw the crowds, He went up on the mountainside. And when He sat down, His disciples came to Him. **2** Then He began to teach them:

The Beatitudes

3   "Blessed are those who are *poor in spirit,*
       for the Kingdom of heaven belongs to them.
4   Blessed are *those who mourn,*
       for they will be comforted.
5   Blessed are *those who are gentle,*[a]
       for they will possess the earth.
6   Blessed are those who hunger and thirst for righteousness,
       for they will be satisfied.
7   Blessed are those who are merciful,
       for they will find mercy.
8   Blessed are *those whose hearts are pure,*
       for they will see God.
9   Blessed are those who make peace,
       for they will be called the children of God.
10   Blessed are those who are persecuted for doing right,
       for the Kingdom of heaven belongs to them.

11   "Blessed are you when people
       insult you,
       persecute you,
       lie and speak only evil about you,
         on account of Me.
12   Continue to rejoice and be glad,
       for you have a great reward in heaven.
   Yes, in the same way they persecuted the prophets
       who lived before you."

A Salt and a Light
Mark 4:21-23; Luke 11:33

13 "You are the salt of the earth. If salt loses its taste, how will it be made salty again? It is no longer good for anything but to be thrown out and trampled on by people.

14 "You are the light of the world. A town cannot be hidden when it is located on a hill. **15** And you do not light a lamp and put it under a container but on a lampstand, where it gives light to everyone in the house. **16** So let your light shine before people that they may see the good you do and praise your Father in heaven."

---

3 Is 57:15 (cf. 61:1)   *4 Is 61:2*   *5 Ps 37:11*   *8 Ps 24:4; 51:10; 73:1*

5 *a-* 5 Or "humble."

Jesus Fulfills the Old Testament Scriptures

17 "Do not think that I came to set aside the Law or the Prophets. *b* I did not come to set them aside but to fulfill them. **18** I tell you the truth, until heaven and earth pass away not an *i* or the dot of an *i* will pass away from the Law until everything is done. **19** Anyone, therefore, who sets aside one of the least of these commandments and teaches others to do the same will be called the least in the Kingdom of heaven. But anyone who does and teaches what they say will be called great in the Kingdom of heaven. **20** For I tell you, unless your righteousness is much better than that of the scribes and Pharisees, you will never enter the Kingdom of heaven."

Do Not Murder

21 "You have heard that long ago the people were told: '*Do not murder. Whoever murders must answer for it in court.*' **22** But I tell you that anyone who is angry with his brother without a cause*c* will have to answer for it in court. Anyone who calls his brother a 'numbskull'*d* will have to answer for it before the highest court. *e* Anyone who calls him a 'fool' will have to answer for it in hellfire.*f*

23 "So if you are bringing your gift to the altar and remember there that your brother has something against you, **24** leave your gift there before the altar. First go away and make up*g* with your brother; then come back and offer your gift. *h*

25 "If someone wants to sue you, be quick to solve the problem with him while you are still on the way with him, so that your accuser may not hand you over to the judge, and the judge may not hand you over to the officer, and you may not be thrown into prison. **26** I tell you the truth, you will never get out until you pay the last cent."

Do Not Lust

27 "You have heard that it was said: '*Do not commit adultery.*' **28** But I tell you

---

21 Ex 20:13; Deut 5:17   *27* Ex 20:14; Deut 5:18

---

b- 17 "Law or the Prophets" is a Hebrew idiom referring to the Old Testament Scriptures as a whole. See THE OLD TESTAMENT CANON on page 551 in order to see the individual breakdown of the books under each category of the threefold Old Testament division.
Here Jesus' comment is meant to be broader than a mere reference to His keeping of the Ten Commandments. As He revealed God's *word* and emulated the *actions* of the ancient prophets and sacred ceremonies, He brought the Old Testament Scriptures to fulfillment. In this way Jesus was our Prophet both in "*word and deed.*"
"Law" (v. 18) also must be seen in its broadest sense. It also involves everything that had been commanded in the Old Testament, including all the demands of the Ceremonial Law which pointed to Christ's obedience to the Ten Commandments as well as His *Person* and His *Work* of forgiveness.
c- 22 Some manuscripts and early translations omit: "without a cause."
d- 22 Literally: "empty-one."
e- 22 Literally: "Sanhedrin," the highest Jewish court.
f- 22 Greek: "*gehenna tou puros*" ("hell of fire" - cf. 18:9); see *HADES/GEHENNA* on page 540. "*Gehenna*" is also used at 5:29,30; 10:28; 23:15,33.
g- 24 Literally: "be reconciled."
h- 24 The Greek tense implies "offer as many gifts as you wish."

that anyone who looks at a woman to lust after her has already committed adultery with her in his heart.

29 "If your right eye causes you to stumble ˻in your faith˼,[i] tear it out and throw it away. It is better for you to lose a part of your body than to have all of it thrown into hell. **30** And if your right hand causes you to stumble ˻in your faith˼, cut it off and throw it away. It is better for you to lose a part of your body than to have all of it go into hell.

31 "It was said: 'Whoever divorces his wife *must give her a divorce paper*,' **32** but I tell you that everyone who divorces his wife, except for the fact that she has been sexually unfaithful, causes her to be looked upon as an adulteress, and whoever marries a divorced woman is looked upon as an adulterer."[j]

Do Not Swear

33 "Again, you have heard that long ago the people were told: '*Do not swear falsely*,[k] *but give to the Lord what you swear to give Him*.' **34** But I tell you, do not swear at all, not by *heaven, for it is God's throne*; **35** nor by *earth*, for it is *His footstool*; nor by Jerusalem, for it is *the city of the great King*. **36** And do not swear by your head, because you cannot make one hair white or black. **37** Just say, 'Yes, yes'; 'No, no.' Anything more than this comes from the Evil One."

Love Your Enemies
Luke 6:27-36

38 "You have heard that it was said: '*An eye for an eye, and a tooth for a tooth*.' **39** But I tell you, do not oppose an evil man. If anyone slaps you on your right cheek, turn to him the other also. **40** If someone wants to sue you for your shirt, let him also have your coat. **41** If anyone makes you go one mile, go two miles with him. **42** If someone asks you for anything, give it to him; and if someone wants to borrow anything from you, do not turn away from him.

43 "You have heard that it was said: '*Love your neighbor*, and hate your enemy.'[l] **44** But I tell you, always love your enemies and always pray for those who persecute you. **45** In this way you will show that you are children[m] of your Father in heaven. He makes His sun rise on people whether they are evil or good, and lets rain fall on them whether they are just or unjust. **46** For if you love those who love you, do you deserve a reward for it? Even the tax collectors do that, don't they? **47** If you treat only your brothers kindly, are you doing anything

---

31 Deut 24:1   *33* Lev 19:12; Num 30:2; Deut 23:21; Ps 50:14   *34,35* Is 66:1   *35* Ps 48:2
38 Ex 21:24; Lev 24:20; Deut 19:21   *43* Lev 19:18

---

i- 29 See *SKANDALON* on page 545 (same applies to v. 30).
j- 32 See THE MATTHEW 5:31,32 PASSAGE on page 548.
k- 33 Greek may also mean "Do not commit perjury" or "Do not break your oath."
l- 43 The phrase "and hate your enemy" is not found in the Old Testament; it is, however, found in the writings of the Jewish community of Qumran, known for the Dead Sea Scrolls.
m- 45 Literally: "sons."

extraordinary? Even the people of the world[n] do that, don't they? **48** Therefore *be perfect* as your Father in heaven is perfect."

6TH CHAPTER

Don't Blow Your Own Horn

1 "Be careful not to do your good works[a] before people in order to be seen by them. If you do, your Father in heaven will not reward you. **2** So when you give to the poor, don't blow your own horn as hypocrites[b] do in the synagogs and on the streets, to be praised by people. I tell you the truth, that is all the reward they will have. **3** When you give to the poor, do not let your left hand know what your right hand is doing, **4** that your giving may be in secret. Then your Father, who sees what is done in secret, will reward you."

The Lord's Prayer
Luke 11:2-4

5 "When you pray, do not be like hypocrites who like to stand praying in synagogs and on street corners in order to be seen by people. I tell you the truth, that is all the reward they will have. **6** But when you pray, *go into your own room, shut your door, and pray* to your Father, who is with you in private; and your Father, who sees what you do in private, will reward you.

7 "When you pray, do not babble like the Gentiles, for they think they will be heard if they talk a lot. **8** Do not be like them. For your Father knows what you need before you ask Him.

9 "This is how you should pray:

> Our Father in heaven
>> may Your Name be kept holy,
>
10 > may Your Kingdom come,
>> may Your will be done,
>>> on earth as it is in heaven;[c]
>
11 > give us today our daily bread;
>
12 > and forgive us our sins
>> as we have forgiven those who sin against us;
>
13 > and do not lead us into temptation,
>> but deliver us from evil.[d]

---

48 Deut 18:13   *6 2 Kgs 4:33; Is 26:20*

---

n- 47 Or "the Gentiles."
6 *a*- 1 Literally: "righteous acts."
 b- 2 Literally: "stage actors."
 c- 10 The commas at the end of each of the three former lines indicate that this phrase "on earth as it is in heaven" is to be seen as part of *each* of the three former lines.
 d- 13 The Greek may mean "evil" or "the Evil One." Some manuscripts and early translations add the doxology: "You are the King who rules with power and glory forever. Amen." It is based on Daniel 7:14; 1 Chronicles 29:11.

14 "For if you forgive the sins of others, your Father in heaven also will forgive you. 15 But if you do not forgive the sins of*e* others, your Father will not forgive your sins."

Fasting

16 "When you fast, stop looking sad like hypocrites, because they put on the kind of face which indicates to people that they are fasting. I tell you the truth, that is all the reward they will have. 17 But when you fast, anoint your head and wash your face 18 so that no one will see you fasting except your Father, who is with you in private, and your Father, who sees what you do in private, will reward you."

Treasures

19 "Do not continue to store up for yourselves treasures on earth, where moth and rust destroy and thieves break in and steal. 20 But continue to store up for yourselves treasures in heaven, where moth and rust do not destroy and thieves do not break in and steal. 21 For where your treasure is, there your heart will be also.

22 "The eye is the lamp of the body. Therefore if your eye is healthy, you will have light for your whole body. 23 But if your eye is bad, your whole body will be dark. How dark it is when the light in you is dark!

24 "No one can serve two masters. Either he will hate the one and love the other, or he will be loyal to the one and despise the other. You cannot serve God and money."*f*

Stop Worrying
Luke 12:22-34

25 "So I tell you, stop worrying about what you will eat or drink to keep alive or what you will wear on your bodies. Is not life more than food, and the body more than clothing?

26 "Look at the birds in the air. They do not sow or reap or gather into barns; but your Father in heaven continues to feed them. Aren't you worth more than they?

27 "Can any of you add a single hour to your life*g* by worrying?

28 "And why worry about clothing? Notice how the flowers*h* grow in the field. They do not work or spin. 29 Yet I tell you, even Solomon in all his glory was not dressed like one of these. 30 If that is how God clothes the grass in the field, which is alive today and tomorrow is thrown into an oven, how much more certainly will He put clothing on you—you who trust Him so little?

---

e - 15 Some manuscripts and early translations omit: "the sins of."

f - 24 Literally: "mammon" ("*mamōna*"), including all material things, such as wealth, possessions, property, etc.

g - 27 Or "add a single cubit [18"] to your height."

h - 28 Literally: "lilies."

31 "Do not worry then and say, 'What are we going to eat?' or 'What are we going to drink?' or 'What are we going to wear?' 32 The people of the world*i* run after all these things. Your heavenly Father knows you need them all. 33 Above all, continue to be eager for God's rule*j* and His righteousness, and all these other things will also be given to you.

34 "So do not worry about tomorrow, for tomorrow will take care of itself. Each day has enough trouble of its own."

7TH CHAPTER

Take a Look at Yourself First
Luke 6:37-42

1 "Stop judging, so that you may not be judged. 2 By the standards with which you judge others, you will be judged, and the measure with which you measure will be used for you.

3 "Why do you look at the speck in your brother's eye and do not notice the log in your own eye? 4 Or how can you say to your brother, 'Let me take the speck out of your eye,' when you have that log in your own eye? 5 You hypocrite, first remove the log from your own eye. Then you will see clearly enough to remove the speck from your brother's eye."

Do Not Throw Pearls to Hogs

6 "Do not give what is holy to dogs nor throw your pearls to hogs, or they will trample them underfoot and then turn and tear you to pieces."

Pray
Luke 11:5-13

7 "Keep asking, and it will be given to you. Keep searching, and you will find. Keep knocking, and the door will be opened to you. 8 For anyone who continues to ask receives; anyone who continues to search finds; and to anyone who continues to knock, the door will be opened.

9 "If your son asks you for bread, will any of you give him a stone? 10 Or if he asks for a fish, will you give him a snake? 11 If you, then, as wicked as you are, know how to give your children good gifts, how much more will your Father in heaven give good things to those who ask Him?"

---

i- 32 Literally: "Gentiles."
j- 33 Literally: "Kingdom," that is, God's gracious rule in believers' hearts and lives.

The Golden Rule
Luke 6:31

12 "Therefore, always do for others everything you want them to do for you. That is the Law and the Prophets."

The Narrow Gate

13 "Go through the narrow gate because the gate is wide and the way is broad that leads to destruction, and many are going that way. **14** But the gate is narrow and the way is difficult that leads to life, and only a few are finding it."

False Prophets
Luke 6:43-46

15 "Always beware of false prophets. They come to you disguised as sheep, but in their hearts they are greedy wolves.
16 "You will know them by what they produce.[a] Surely people cannot pick grapes from thornbushes or figs from thistles, can they? **17** In the same way every good tree continues to bear good fruit, and a bad tree bad fruit. **18** A good tree cannot bear bad fruit, or a bad tree good fruit. **19** Any tree that does not bear good fruit is cut down and thrown into the fire. **20** So you will know them by what they produce.
21 "Not everyone who says to Me, 'Lord, Lord,' will enter the Kingdom of heaven, only he who continues to do the will of My Father who is in heaven. **22** Many will say to Me on that Day, 'Lord, Lord, did we not *prophesy in Your Name*, drive out demons in Your Name, and work many miracles[b] in Your Name?' **23** Then I will tell them frankly, 'I never knew you. *Get away from Me, you who are doing what is evil.*' "

Build on the Rock
Luke 6:47-49

24 "Therefore, everyone who hears these words of Mine and continues to follow them is like a man who had sense enough to build his house on the rock. **25** The rain poured down, the floods came, the winds blew and beat against that house. But it did not fall, because its foundation was on the rock.
26 "Everyone who hears these words of Mine but does not continue to follow them is like a man who was so foolish that he built his house on the sand. **27** The rain poured down, the floods came, the winds blew and struck that house. And it went down with a loud crash."
28 When Jesus finished speaking, the crowds were amazed at His teaching, **29** for He taught them with authority and not like their scribes.

---

22 Jer 14:14; 27:15   23 Ps 6:8

---

7 *a*- 16 Compare Deuteronomy 13:1-3; Acts 17:11.
  b- 22 See MIRACULOUS SIGNS, WONDERFUL PROOFS, and MIRACLES on page 527.

8TH CHAPTER

2. Second booklet (8:1–11:1)
a. Narrative and deeds: Ten Messianic miracles of power (8:1–9:35)

Jesus Heals A Leper—*Mark 1:40-44; Luke 5:12-14*

1 When He came down from the mountain, large crowds followed Him.
2 There was a leper, who went to Him and bowed down before Him. "Lord, if You want to," he said, "You can make me clean."
3 Jesus stretched out His hand and touched him. "I want to," He said. "Be clean!" Immediately the leprosy left him, and he was clean.
4 Jesus said to him, "Be careful not to tell anyone, but go, *show yourself to the priest,*[a] and offer the sacrifice Moses commanded, to show them that you are well."

A Believing Captain—*Luke 7:1-10*

5 He went to Capernaum. There a captain approached Him and begged Him:
6 "Lord, my slave is lying at home paralyzed and is suffering terribly."
7 "I will come and make him well," Jesus said.
8 The captain answered, "Lord, I am not worthy for You to come under my roof. But just say a word, and my slave will be made well. **9** For I also am a man under authority who has soldiers under me. I tell one of them, 'Go!' and he goes; and another, 'Come!' and he comes; and my slave, 'Do this!' and he does it."
10 When Jesus heard this, He was surprised and said to the people who were following Him, "I tell you the truth, nowhere in Israel have I found such faith. **11** I also tell you, many will come *from the east and the west* and will eat with Abraham, Isaac, and Jacob in the Kingdom of heaven, **12** but those who were born to be heirs of the Kingdom[b] will be thrown out into the outer darkness where they will weep and grind their teeth.
13 "Go," Jesus told the captain. "Let it be done to you as you believed." And the slave was made well in that same hour.

Peter's Mother-In-Law—*Mark 1:29-34; Luke 4:38-41*

14 Jesus went into Peter's home, and there He saw Peter's[c] mother-in-law lying in bed with a fever. **15** He touched her hand, and the fever left her. She got up and began to wait on Him.
16 In the evening the people brought Him many who were possessed by

---

4 Lev 13:7,49   11 Mal 1:11

---

8 *a-* 4 That is, the healed leper was to show himself to the priest so that he could be examined and then be declared "clean."
   b- 12 Literally: "but the sons of the Kingdom."
   c- 14 Literally: "his."

demons. He drove out the spirits by speaking to them,^{d} and all who were sick He made well. **17** In this way what the prophet Isaiah said was fulfilled: *"He took away our sicknesses and carried our diseases."*

18 When Jesus saw a crowd around Him, He gave orders to cross to the other side.

"I Will Follow You, But . . ."—Luke 9:57-62

19 A scribe came to Him and said, "Teacher, I will follow You anywhere You go."

20 Jesus told him, "Foxes have holes and birds of the air have nests, but the Son of Man^e does not have a place to lay His head."

21 Another disciple said to Him, "Lord, first let me go and bury my father."

22 But Jesus told him, "Follow Me, and let the dead bury their own dead."

Wind And Water Obey Him—Mark 4:35-41; Luke 8:22-25

23 Jesus stepped into a boat, and His disciples went with Him. **24** Suddenly a severe storm churned the sea so that the waves were higher than the boat. But He was sleeping.

25 So they went and woke Him up. "Lord, save us!" they said. "We're going to drown!"

26 "Why are you afraid?" He asked them. "You trust Me so little!" Then He got up and ordered the winds and the sea to be quiet, and they became very calm.

27 The men were amazed and asked, "What kind of a person is He? Even the winds and the sea obey Him!"

The Gergesenes—Mark 5:1-20; Luke 8:26-39

28 He went to the region of the Gergesenes^f on the other side of the sea. There two men with demons in them came out of the burial caves and met Him. They were so savage that no one could go along that road.

29 They shouted, "What do we have in common, Son of God! Did You come here to torture us before it is time?"

30 Far away a herd of many hogs was feeding. **31** "If You mean to drive us out," the demons begged Jesus, "send us into that herd of hogs."

32 "Go," He told them. They came out and went into the hogs. Then the whole herd stampeded down the cliff into the sea and drowned.

33 Those who had taken care of the hogs ran away and went into the town,

---

17 Is 53:4

---

d- 16 Literally: "He expelled the spirits with a word."

e- 20 See "Son of Man" in Glossary.

f- 28 Gergesa was a small village in the territory of Hippus, north of the city of Hippus. It was a part of the area of the Decapolis [Ten Towns], a federation of *Greek* towns. Some of the older manuscripts and early translations have *Gadarenes*; and some early translations have *Gerasenes*.

where they told everything, including the part about the men who were possessed by demons.

34 Then the whole town came out to meet Jesus. When they saw Him, they urged Him to leave their territory.

9TH CHAPTER

Jesus Forgives Sins—Mark 2:1-12; Luke 5:17-26

1 He stepped into a boat, crossed over, and came to His own town. **2** There people brought Him a paralyzed man, lying on a bed.

When Jesus saw their faith, He said to the paralytic, "Cheer up, son! Your sins are forgiven."

3 Then some of the scribes said to themselves, "He is blaspheming."

4 Jesus knew what they were thinking. He asked them, "Why do you think evil in your hearts? **5** Is it easier to say, 'Your sins are forgiven,' or to say, 'Get up and walk'? **6** I want you to know that the Son of Man has authority on earth to forgive sins." Then He said to the paralyzed man, "Get up, take your bed, and go home."

7 He got up and went home. **8** When the crowd saw this, they were filled with awe and praised God, who had given such authority to men.

Matthew—Mark 2:13-17; Luke 5:27-32

9 When Jesus was on His way after leaving that place, He saw a man by the name of Matthew sitting in the tax booth. "Follow Me," He told him. He got up and followed Him.

10 As Jesus was reclining at the table in the house,*ᵃ* many tax collectors and sinners came and ate with Jesus and His disciples. **11** When the Pharisees saw this, they asked His disciples, "For what reason does your Teacher eat with tax collectors and sinners?"

12 Jesus heard them and said, "Those who are healthy do not need a doctor, but those who are sick. **13** Go and learn what this means '*I want mercy and not sacrifice.*' For I did not come to call righteous people, but sinners."*ᵇ*

Jesus Is Questioned About Fasting—Mark 2:18-22; Luke 5:33-39

14 Then John's disciples came to Jesus. They said, "We and the Pharisees fast. Why is it that Your disciples do not fast?"

15 Jesus asked them, "The friends of the bridegroom cannot mourn while the

---

13 Hos 6:6

---

9 *a*- 10 Or "in *my* house"; a reference to Matthew's house (cf. Mk. 2:13-15; Lk. 5:27-29).

  b- 13 Some of the older manuscripts and early translations add: "to repentance." See Luke 5:32 where the inclusion of these words is certain.

bridegroom is with them, can they? The time will come when the bridegroom will be taken away from them; then they will fast.

16 "No one sews a piece of unshrunk cloth on an old garment, for the patch will tear away some of the garment, and the hole will become worse. **17** Neither do people pour new wine into old wineskins;*c* otherwise, the skins burst, the wine runs out, and the skins are ruined. Rather, they pour new wine into fresh skins; then both are preserved."

The Daughter Of Jairus And
A Woman Who Was Continuously Bleeding—*Mark 5:21-43; Luke 8:40-56*

18 While He was talking to the people, an important official came to Him and bowed down before Him. "My daughter just died," he said, "but come, lay Your hand on her, and she will live."

19 Jesus and His disciples got up and followed him.

20 Now there was a woman who had been suffering from a flow of blood for twelve years. She came to Him from behind and touched the tassel of His garment. **21** "If I only touch His garment," she said to herself, "I'll get well."

22 Jesus turned and saw her. "Cheer up, daughter," He said, "your faith has made you well." At that moment the woman was made well.

23 When Jesus came to the official's home and saw the flute players and the noisy crowd, **24** He said, "Go away! The little girl is not dead; she is sleeping." But they laughed at Him.

25 When the crowd had been put outside, He went in and took her hand, and the little girl got up.

26 The news about this spread all over that part of the country.

Two Blind Men

27 When Jesus left that place, two blind men followed Him and shouted: "Have pity on us, Son of David."

28 He went into a house, and there the blind men came to Him. "Do you believe that I can do this?" Jesus asked them.

"Yes, Lord," they replied.

29 Then He touched their eyes and said, "As you believed, so let it be done to you!" **30** Then their sight was restored.

He sternly ordered them: "See that no one finds out about this!" **31** But they went out and spread the news about Him all over that part of the country.

A Man Who Could Not Talk

32 As they were going out, a man who was unable to talk because he had a demon in him was brought to Jesus. **33** But as soon as the demon was driven out, the man who was unable to talk began to speak.

---

c- 17 Containers made from the skins of certain animals.

The crowds were amazed and said, "We have never seen anything like this in Israel."

34 But the Pharisees declared, "The ruler of the demons helps Him drive out the demons."

35 Then Jesus traveled through all the towns and villages, teaching in their synagogs, preaching the Good News of the Kingdom, and healing every kind of disease and sickness.

b. Words: Mission discourse (9:36–11:1)

Pray For Workers

36 As He saw the crowds of people, He felt sorry for them, because they were troubled and helpless *like sheep without a shepherd.* **37** Then He said to His disciples, "There is much grain to be harvested, but there are only a few workers. **38** Therefore, ask the Lord of the harvest to send out workers to bring in His grain."

10TH CHAPTER

Twelve Apostles—*Mark 3:13-19; Luke 6:13-16*

1 Jesus called His twelve disciples and gave them authority to drive out unclean spirits and heal every kind of disease and sickness.

2 These are the names of the twelve apostles: first, Simon (who is called Peter) and his brother Andrew; James the ˻son˼ of Zebedee and his brother John; **3** Philip and Bartholomew; Thomas and Matthew the tax collector; James the ˻son˼ of Alphaeus and Thaddaeus; **4** Simon the Zealot and Judas the man from Kerioth,*ᵃ* who also betrayed Him.

Jesus Sends Out The Twelve—*Mark 6:7-13; Luke 9:1-6*

5 Jesus sent these Twelve out with the following instructions: "Do not go among the Gentiles or into any town of the Samaritans. **6** But go to the lost sheep of Israel. **7** As you go, preach, 'The Kingdom of heaven is near.' **8** Heal people who are sick, raise those who are dead, cleanse lepers, drive out demons. Give these things as you received them—without pay.*ᵇ*

9 "Do not take any gold, silver, or copper money along in your pockets,

---

36 Num 27:17; 1 Kgs 22:17; Ezek 34:5

---

10 *a-* 4 Literally: "Judas Iscariot"; see "*Iscariot*" in Glossary.

   b- 8 Compare 2 Kings 5:16-27, noting that Elisha refused payment when healing Naaman of his leprosy; Gehazi, on the other hand, was greedy, took money from Naaman, and was punished with Naaman's leprosy.

10 nor a bag for the way, nor a spare tunic, nor sandals, nor a staff*c*—a worker deserves to have his needs provided.

11 "When you go into any town or village, look for a person there who is deserving and stay with him until you leave. 12 When you go into a home, greet it. 13 If the home is deserving, let your peace come upon it. But if it is unworthy, let your peace return to you. 14 If anyone does not welcome you or listen to what you say, leave that house or town and shake the dust off your feet. 15 I tell you the truth, on Judgment Day it will be easier for the land of Sodom and Gomorrah than for that town.

16 "You see, I am sending you like sheep among wolves. So be shrewd as snakes and innocent as doves. 17 Be on your guard against men, because they will hand you over to their courts and whip you in their places of worship. 18 On My account you will be brought before governors and kings to testify to them and to the Gentiles. 19 But when they hand you over to the authorities, do not worry how you will speak or what you will say. When the time comes, you will be given what to say. 20 It will not be you speaking*d* but the Spirit of your Father speaking through you.

21 "A brother will betray his brother to death, and a father his child. Children will *turn against* their parents and kill them. 22 Everybody will hate you because of My Name. But the person who is faithful to the end will be saved. 23 When they hunt you in one town, flee to another. I tell you the truth, before you have gone through all the towns of Israel, the Son of Man will come.

24 "A pupil is not above his teacher, nor a slave above his master. 25 A pupil should be satisfied to be like his teacher, and a slave to be like his master. If the master of the house was called Beelzebul, how much more certainly the members of his household! 26 So, do not be afraid of them. For all that is covered will be uncovered, and all that is hidden will be made known. 27 What I say to you in the dark, tell in the daylight; and what you hear whispered in your ear, preach from the housetops. 28 Stop being afraid of those who kill the body but cannot kill the soul, but fear Him who can destroy both soul and body in hell.

29 "Are not two sparrows sold for a cent? And not one of them will fall to the ground without your Father's permission. 30 As for you, even the hairs on your head are all counted. 31 So stop being afraid. You are worth more than many sparrows.

32 "Whoever will confess Me before others, him will I confess before My Father in heaven. 33 Whoever will deny Me before others, him will I deny before My Father in heaven.

34 "Do not think that I came to bring peace to the earth. I did not come to bring peace but a sword. 35 For I came to turn *a man against his father, a daughter against her mother, a daughter-in-law against her mother-in-law.* 36 *A person's enemies will be those in his own home.* 37 Anyone who loves father or mother more than Me is not worthy of Me; and anyone who loves son or daughter more

---

21 Mic 7:6   *35,36 Mic 7:6*

c- 10 Among other things a staff was used for protection and as an aid for walking.
d- 20 Literally: "For not are you the ones speaking."

than Me is not worthy of Me. **38** The person who does not take his cross and follow Me is not worthy of Me. **39** The one who finds his life will lose it, but the one who loses his life for Me will find it.

40 "Anyone who welcomes you welcomes Me; and anyone who welcomes Me welcomes Him who sent Me. **41** Anyone who welcomes a prophet because he is a prophet will receive a prophet's reward. Anyone who welcomes a righteous man because he is righteous will receive a righteous man's reward. **42** Anyone who gives one of these little ones just a cup of cold water because he is My disciple, I tell you the truth, he certainly will never lose his reward."

11TH CHAPTER

1 After Jesus finished giving His twelve disciples these instructions, He went on from there to teach and preach in their towns.

3. Third booklet (11:2–13:53)
a. Narrative and deeds (11:2–12:50)

About John—Luke 7:18-35

2 When John, who was in prison, heard about the works of Christ, he sent his disciples **3** to ask Him, "Are You the One who is coming, or should we look for someone else?"

4 "Go," Jesus answered them, "tell John what you hear and see: **5** *Blind people see* and those who were lame are walking; lepers are made clean and *deaf people hear*; those who were dead are raised and *poor people hear the Gospel*; **6** and blessed is anyone who does not stumble*a* in ⌐his evaluation of⌐ Me."

7 When they were leaving, Jesus began to talk to the crowds about John: "What did you go out into the wilderness to see—a reed shaken by the wind? **8** What did you go out to see—a man dressed in soft robes? Those who wear soft robes are in the palaces of kings.

9 "What did you go out to see—a prophet? Let Me assure you, he is even more than a prophet. **10** This is the one of whom it is written:

I am sending My messenger ahead of You
to prepare Your way before You.

11 I tell you the truth, there never has appeared among all of those born to women anyone greater than John the Baptizer. Yet the least in the Kingdom of heaven is greater than John. **12** From the time of John the Baptizer until now the Kingdom of heaven has been advancing with triumphant force*b* and intense men

---

5 *Is 29:18; 35:5; 61:1*   10 *Mal 3:1 (cf. Ex 23:20)*

---

11 *a-* 6 See *SKANDALON* on page 545.
  b- 12 Or "has been suffering violence."

grasp it quickly. *c* **13** For all the Prophets and the Law *d* prophesied up to the time of John, **14** but he (are you willing to accept it?) is the Elijah who was to come. **15** The one who has ears, let him listen!

16 "How should I picture the people of this generation? They are like little children sitting in the marketplaces and calling to others:

17   'We played a tune on the flute for you,
            but you did not dance.
       We sang a funeral song,
            but you did not mourn.'

18 For John ˌthe Baptizerˌ has come; he does not eat or drink, and people say, 'There is a demon in him!' **19** The Son of Man has come; He eats and drinks, and people say, 'Look at the glutton and drunkard, a friend of tax collectors and sinners!' And yet wisdom is proved right by what it accomplishes." *e*

Woe!

20 Then He began to denounce the cities where He had worked most of His miracles, because they had not repented: **21** "Woe to you, Chorazin! Woe to you, Bethsaida! If the miracles worked in you had been worked in Tyre and Sidon, they would have repented long ago in sackcloth and ashes. **22** I tell you, on Judgment Day it will be easier for Tyre and Sidon than for you. **23** And you, Capernaum, will you be *lifted up to heaven*? No, *you will go down to hell [hades]*! *f* If the miracles that had been worked in you had been worked in Sodom, it would still be there today. **24** I tell you, on Judgment Day it will be easier for the land of Sodom than for you."

"Come To Me!"

25 At that time Jesus said, "I praise You, Father, Lord of heaven and earth, for hiding these things from wise and intelligent people and revealing them to little children. **26** Yes, Father, I praise You for wanting it to be that way.

27 "My Father put everything in My hands. Only the Father knows the Son. And only the Son—and anyone to whom the Son wants to reveal Him—knows the Father.

---

23 *Is 14:13,15*

---

c- 12 A reference to men who act decisively on something they know or believe to be true. The next verse indicates the reason these men acted decisively, namely, because the Law and the prophets were beginning to convince them that the Messianic Age had come. An alternative translation might be: "and violent men take it by force."

d- 13 "Prophets and the Law" is a Hebrew idiom referring to the Old Testament as a whole. See applicable portion of footnote at 5:17.

e- 19 Literally: "wisdom is justified by her works."

f- 23 Meaning "the place of/receptacle for disembodied souls"; see *HADES/GEHENNA* on page 540.

28   "Come to Me, all you who are working hard
           and carrying a heavy burden,
           and I will give you rest.
29   Take My yoke upon you and learn from Me,
           for I am gentle and humble-minded;
           then *you will find rest* for *your* souls—
30   for My yoke is easy,
           and My burden is light."

12TH CHAPTER

Lord Of The Sabbath—Mark 2:23-28; Luke 6:1-5

1 At that time Jesus walked through the grainfields on a Sabbath. His disciples were hungry and began to pick the heads of grain and eat them.

2 When the Pharisees saw this, they said to Him, "Look, Your disciples are doing something which is not right to do on the Sabbath."

3 But He asked them, "Haven't you read what David did when he and his men were hungry—**4** how he went into the House of God and ate the *loaves set out ᵢbefore Godᵢ*, which he and his men had no right to eat, but only the priests? **5** Or have you not read in the book of the Law*a* that the priests in the Temple work on a Sabbath as on other days and yet do no wrong? **6** I tell you, here is something*b* greater than the Temple. **7** If you had known what this means: '*I want mercy and not sacrifice,*' you would not have condemned the innocent. **8** For the Son of Man is Lord of the Sabbath."

The Shriveled Hand—Mark 3:1-6; Luke 6:6-11

9 He went on to another place and went into their synagog, **10** and there was a man with a shriveled hand.

"Is it right to heal on a Sabbath?" they asked Him in an attempt to find something of which to accuse Him.

11 Jesus asked them, "If anyone of you has only one sheep and it falls into a pit on a Sabbath, will you not take hold of it and lift it out? **12** Now how much more valuable is a human being than a sheep? Therefore it is right to do good on the Sabbath!"

13 Then He told the man, "Stretch out your hand." He stretched it out, and it was restored as healthy as the other.

14 But the Pharisees left and plotted against Him to kill Him. **15** Jesus knew about this, and so He left.

The Servant Of The Lord

Many followed Him, and He healed them all, **16** but He ordered them not

---

29 Jer 6:16   *4 Lev 24:5-8; 1 Sam 21:6*   *7 Hos 6:6*

---

12 *a*-   5 See *NOMOS* on page 544.
    b-   6 Some of the older manuscripts and early translations read: "Someone."

to tell people who He was. **17** In this way what the prophet Isaiah said was fulfilled:

18   *Here is My Servant*
            whom I have chosen,
            whom I love,
            and in whom My soul delights.
         I will put My Spirit upon Him
            and He will announce justice to the Gentiles.
19   *He will not quarrel or shout,*
            nor will anyone hear His voice in the streets.
20   *He will not crush a bruised reed*
            nor put out a smoking wick,
               until He has made justice victorious.
21   *His Name will be the hope of the Gentiles.*

Power Over A Demon—*Mark 3:20-30; Luke 11:14-23*

22 At that time some people brought to Him a man who had a demon which made him blind and unable to speak. Jesus healed him so that he could talk and see.

23 The people were all amazed and said, "Certainly this Fellow is not the Son of David, is He?" **24** When the Pharisees heard this, they said, "He can drive out the demons only with the help of Beelzebul, who rules over the demons."

25 Since He knew what they were thinking, Jesus said to them, "Every kingdom divided against itself is ruined. And every town or home divided against itself will not stand. **26** If Satan drives out Satan, he is divided against himself. How then will his kingdom stand? **27** Now if Beelzebul helps Me drive out the demons, who helps your sons drive them out? Therefore, your sons themselves will be your judges. **28** But if the Spirit of God helps Me drive out the demons, then the Kingdom of God has come to you. **29** How can anyone go into a strong man's house and take away his goods without first tying up*c* the strong man? After that he will rob his house.

30 "Anyone*d* who is not with Me is against Me, and anyone who does not join Me in gathering, scatters. **31** So I tell you, people will be forgiven any sin or slander, but slandering the Spirit will not be forgiven. **32** Anyone who speaks a word against the Son of Man will be forgiven, but anyone who speaks against the Holy Spirit will not be forgiven in this world or the next.

33 "Make a tree good, and then its fruit is good, or make a tree bad, and then its fruit is bad. One can recognize a tree by its fruit. **34** Brood of poisonous snakes, how can you who are evil say anything good? What your mouth says flows from your hearts. **35** A good person produces good things from the good stored in him, but an evil person produces evil from the evil stored in him.

36 "I tell you, on Judgment Day people will have to give an account of every

---

18-21 Is 41:8,9; 42:1-4; Hab 1:4

---

c - 29 Literally: "except he first bind" (cf. Rev. 20:2).
d - 30 Literally: "The one/the person" (twice in verse).

careless word they say. **37** By your words you will be acquitted [justified], and by your words you will be condemned."

The Sign Of Jonah—*Luke 11:29-32*

38 Then some scribes and Pharisees said, "Teacher, we want You to show us a miraculous sign."*e*

39 He answered them, "A wicked and unfaithful generation looks for a miraculous sign, but the only sign it will get is that of the prophet Jonah. **40** As *Jonah was in the belly of the huge fish three days* and three nights, so the Son of Man will be in the heart of the earth three days and three nights. **41** The men of Nineveh will come to life along with this generation at the time of Judgment and will condemn it, because they repented when Jonah preached—but something*f* greater than Jonah is here! **42** The queen from the south will be raised up along with this generation at the time of Judgment and will condemn it, because she came from the ends of the earth to hear Solomon's wisdom—but something greater than Solomon is here!

43 "When an unclean spirit comes out of a person, he goes through dry places looking for a place to rest but does not find any. **44** Then he says, 'I will go back to the home I left.' He comes and finds it empty, swept, and decorated. **45** Then he goes and takes home with him seven other spirits worse than himself, and they go in and live there. In the end the condition of that person is worse than it was before. That is what will happen to this wicked generation."

The Mother And Brothers Of Jesus—*Mark 3:31-35; Luke 8:19-21*

46 He was still talking to the people when His mother and brothers were standing outside wanting to talk to Him. **47** Someone told Him, "Look, Your mother and Your brothers are standing outside, and they want to talk to You."

48 He asked the man speaking to Him, "Who is My mother and who are My brothers?" **49** Pointing with His hand to His disciples, He said, "Here are My mother and My brothers. **50** For whoever does the will of My Father in heaven is ᵢin realityᴊ My brother and sister and mother."

13TH CHAPTER

b. Words: Seven Kingdom parables (13:1-53)

The Sower—*Mark 4:1-20; Luke 8:4-15*

1 That same day Jesus left the house and sat down by the sea. **2** But so many people gathered around Him that He stepped into a boat and sat there while all

---

40 Jonah 1:17

---

e - 38 See MIRACULOUS SIGNS, WONDERFUL PROOFS, and MIRACLES on page 527.
f - 41 Here and in the next verse Jesus uses the *neuter* to refer to the Kingdom (cf. v. 28).

"The Sower"

the people stood on the shore. **3** Then He told them many things in parables.

"A sower went out to sow," He said. **4** "As he was sowing, some seed fell along the road, and the birds came and devoured it. **5** Some seed fell on rocky ground, where it did not have much soil. Because the soil was not deep, the seed came up quickly. **6** But when the sun rose, it was scorched, and because its roots were not deep enough, it withered. **7** Some seed fell among thorns, and the thorns grew up and choked it. **8** But some seed fell on good ground and produced grain, some a hundred, some sixty, and some thirty times as much as was sown. **9** The one who has ears, let him listen!"

10 The disciples came to Him. "For what reason do You speak to them in parables?" they asked Him.

11 He answered, "You have been given the privilege of knowing the secrets of the Kingdom of heaven, but to them it has not been given. **12** For whoever has something will be given more, and he will have more than enough. Whoever does not have what he should have, even what he has will be taken from him. **13** For this reason I speak to them in parables because they see and yet do not see, hear and yet do not hear or understand. **14** In them Isaiah's prophecy is being fulfilled:

> *You will hear clearly but never understand;*
> *you will see clearly but never comprehend,*
> **15**   because *these people have become dull at heart*
> *and hard of hearing*
> *and have shut their eyes,*
> *so that their eyes never see,*
> *their ears never hear,*
> *their hearts never understand,* [a]
> *and they never turn to Me for healing.*

16 "Blessed are your eyes because they see and your ears because they hear. **17** I tell you the truth, many prophets and righteous people longed to see what you see and did not see it, to hear what you hear and did not hear it.

18 "Listen to what the parable of the sower means. **19** When anyone hears the word [message] of the Kingdom but does not understand it, the Evil One comes and snatches away what was sown in his heart. This is what was sown along the road. **20** In another person the seed fell on rocky ground. He is one who welcomes the word with joy as soon as he hears it, **21** but it does not take root in him. He believes for a while, but as soon as trouble or persecution comes his way because of the word, he falls ˌfrom faithˌ. [b] **22** In another person the seed was sown among thorns. He is one who hears the word, but the worry of the world and the deceitful pleasure of riches choke the word, and it cannot produce anything. **23** In another person the seed was sown on good ground. He is one who continues to hear and understand the word and so goes on producing good

---

14,15 Is 6:9,10

---

13 *a* - 15 See GRAMMATIC/POETIC STRUCTURES THAT CONVEY TEXTUAL MEANINGS on
       page 558.
   b - 21 See *SKANDALON* on page 545.

things: some a hundred, some sixty, some thirty times as much as was sown."

Weeds In The Wheat

24 He told them another parable: "The Kingdom of heaven is like a man who sowed good seed in his field. **25** But while people were sleeping, his enemy came and sowed weeds*c* among the wheat and went away. **26** When the wheat came up and formed kernels, then the weeds also appeared.

27 "The owner's slaves came to him and asked him, 'Master, didn't you sow good seed in your field? Where did the weeds come from?'

28 " 'An enemy did that,' he told them.

" 'Do you want us to go and pull them out?' the slaves asked him.

29 " 'No,' he said, 'if you pull out the weeds, you may pull up the wheat with them. **30** Let both grow together until the harvest. When the grain is cut, I will tell the reapers, "Gather the weeds first and tie them in bundles to be burned, but bring the wheat into my barn." ' "

A Mustard Seed And Yeast—*Mark 4:30-34; Luke 13:18-21*

31 He told them another parable: "The Kingdom of heaven is like a mustard seed that a man took and sowed in his field. **32** It is a very small seed*d* among all the seeds ͺthat are sown‚; but when it has grown, it is the largest of the garden plants; it becomes a tree big enough for *the birds of the air* to come and *nest in its branches*."

33 He spoke another parable to them: "The Kingdom of heaven is like yeast that a woman took and mixed into three measures*e* of flour until the yeast worked through the whole batch of dough."

34 Jesus used parables to tell the crowds all these things. He did not tell them anything without a parable, **35** so that what the prophet said would be fulfilled:

> *I will open My mouth to speak in parables;*
> *I will tell what has been hidden since the world was made.*

The Meaning Of The Weeds In The Wheat

36 When Jesus had dismissed the people and gone into the house, His disciples came to Him and said, "Tell us what the parable of the weeds in the field means."

37 He answered, "The sower who sows the good seed is the Son of Man. **38** The field is the world. The good seed are the sons of the Kingdom. The weeds are the sons of the Evil One. **39** The enemy who sowed them is the devil. The harvest is the end of the world. The reapers are the angels. **40** As the weeds are

---

32 Ps 104:12; Ezek 17:23; 31:6   35 Ps 78:2

c- 25 Or "darnel," a troublesome weed which looked like wheat until the heads began to form.
d- 32 Literally: "the smaller"; in Greek the comparative is used at times for the superlative, which implies the adverb "very" with the adjective.
e- 33 See MONEY, WEIGHTS, and MEASURES on page 328.

gathered and burned with fire, so it will be at the end of the world. **41** The Son
of Man will send His angels, and they will take out of His Kingdom everything
which causes *people to sin as well as those people who continue to do evil*,
42 and they will throw them into the fiery furnace, where they will weep and
grind their teeth. **43** Then *the righteous will shine like* the sun in their Father's
Kingdom. The one who has ears, let him listen!"

The Treasure, The Pearl, And The Fish

44 "The Kingdom of heaven is like a treasure buried in a field. When a man
found it, he buried it again and was so delighted with it that he went away and
sold everything he had and bought that field.

45 "Again, the Kingdom of heaven is like a dealer who was looking for fine
pearls. **46** When he found a very expensive pearl, he went away and sold everything he had and bought it.

47 "Again, the Kingdom of heaven is like a dragnet that was thrown into the
sea and gathered all kinds of fish. **48** When it was full, they pulled it on the
shore, sat down, and picked out the good fish and put them in containers, but
they threw the bad ones away. **49** So it will be at the end of the world. The angels
will go out and separate the wicked from the righteous **50** and throw them into
the fiery furnace, where they will weep and grind their teeth.

51 "Have you understood all this?"

"Yes," they answered.

52 He said to them, "Therefore, every student of the Scriptures who is trained
for the Kingdom of heaven is like the owner of a house who continues to bring
new and old things out of his treasure chest."

53 When Jesus had finished these parables, He left that place.

4. Fourth booklet (13:54–18:35)
a. Narrative and deeds (13:54–17:27)

His Last Visit To Nazareth—Mark 6:1-6; Luke 4:16-30

54 He went to His hometown and taught the people in their synagog in such
a way that they were amazed. "Where did He get this wisdom and the power to
do these miracles?" they asked. **55** Isn't He the carpenter's son? Isn't His
mother's name Mary; and aren't James, Joseph, Simon, and Judas His brothers?
56 And aren't all His sisters here with us? Where then did this Man get all these
things?" **57** This caused them to stumble*f* in ˌtheir evaluation ofˌ Him.

But Jesus told them, "The only place a prophet is not honored is in his
hometown and in his family."

58 He did not work many miracles there because of their unbelief.

---

41 Job 12:16; Zeph 1:3   43 Dan 12:3

---

f- 57 See *SKANDALON* on page 545.

14TH CHAPTER

The Recalling Of John's Death—Mark 6:14-29; Luke 9:7-9

1 At that time Herod the ruler*ᵃ* heard the news about Jesus. 2 "This is John the Baptizer!" he told his servants. "He is risen from the dead, and that is why these powers are at work in him."*ᵇ*

3 You see, Herod had arrested John, bound him, and put him in prison on account of Herodias, the wife of his brother Philip,*ᶜ* 4 because John kept telling him, "It is not right for you to have her." 5 Herod wanted to kill him but was afraid of the people because they regarded John as a prophet.

6 When Herod's birthday was celebrated, the daughter of Herodias danced before the guests. Herod was so delighted with her that 7 he swore to give her whatever she might ask.

8 Urged on by her mother, she said, "Bring the head of John the Baptizer to me here on a platter."

9 Although the king felt sorry, ⌐yet⌐ because of his oath and because of the guests he ordered it to be brought. 10 He sent and had John beheaded in prison. 11 And his head was brought on a platter and given to the girl, who took it to her mother.

12 John's disciples came and took his body away and buried it. Then they went and told Jesus.

Jesus Feeds 5,000—Mark 6:30-44; Luke 9:10-17; John 6:1-14

13 When Jesus heard about John, He left in a boat and went to a deserted place to be alone. The people heard of it and followed Him on foot from the towns. 14 When Jesus stepped out of the boat, He saw a large crowd. He felt sorry for them and healed their sick.

15 In the evening the disciples came to Him. They said, "This is a deserted place and it's late. Send the crowds away to the villages to buy themselves some food."

16 Jesus answered them, "They do not need to go away. You give them something to eat."

17 "All we have here are five loaves and two fish," they told Him.

18 "Let Me have them," He said.

19 He ordered the people to sit down on the grass. After He took the five loaves and the two fish, He looked up to heaven and gave thanks.*ᵈ* He broke the loaves apart, gave them to the disciples, and they gave them to the people. 20 All of them ate and had enough. They picked up the pieces that were left over—twelve baskets full.

21 Some 5,000 men had eaten, besides women and children.

---

14 *a-* 1 Literally: "the tetrarch," one who ruled over one-fourth of the kingdom of Herod the Great.
b- 2 Or "Him."
c- 3 This Philip is not to be confused with the Philip who was the governor of the area east of the Jordan Valley and of the upper half of the Sea of Galilee; rather, this Philip was a private citizen.
d- 19 Or "and spoke a blessing" if the text means to call upon God to bless a person or thing.

Jesus Walks On Water—Mark 6:45-52; John 6:15-21

22 Jesus quickly made the disciples get into the boat and go on ahead to the other side while He dismissed the people. 23 After sending them away, He went up into the hills to be alone and to pray. When evening came, He was there alone.

24 The boat, now many hundred yards from the shore, was troubled by the waves because there was a headwind.

25 Toward morning He came to them, walking on the sea. 26 When the disciples saw Him walking on the sea, they were terrified. "It's a ghost!" they said, and they cried out in terror.

27 Immediately He talked to them. "Be courageous," He said, "it is I. Stop being afraid."

28 Peter answered, "Lord, if it is You, order me to come to You on the water."

29 "Come," He said. So Peter got out of the boat, walked on the water, and went toward Jesus. 30 But when he saw the wind, he was frightened and started to sink. "Lord, save me!" he cried.

31 Quickly Jesus stretched out His hand and caught him. "How little you trust Me!" He said to him. "Why did you doubt?"

32 When they stepped into the boat, the wind stopped. 33 And the men in the boat bowed down before Him and said, "You certainly are the Son of God."

34 They crossed over and came to the shore at Gennesaret. 35 The men of that place recognized Jesus and sent messengers all around that country. The people brought Him all the sick ones, 36 and they begged Him just to let them touch the tassel of His garment. All who touched it were made well.

15TH CHAPTER

Unclean Hands—Mark 7:1-23

1 Then some Pharisees and scribes came to Him from Jerusalem. 2 "Why do Your disciples sin against the traditions*a* of our fathers?" they asked. "They do not wash their hands when they eat."

3 He asked them, "Why do you sin against the commandments*b* of God for the sake of your own traditions? 4 For example, God has said: '*Honor* your *father and* your *mother*' and '*Put to death the person who speaks evil of father or mother.*' 5 But you say, 'Whoever tells his father or mother, "I'm giving God whatever I might have used to help you," 6 does not have to honor his father.' For the sake of your own traditions you have disregarded the word of God. 7 You hypocrites, Isaiah was right when he prophesied about you: 8 '*These people honor Me*c *with their lips, but their hearts are far from Me.* 9 *They*

---

4 *Ex 20:12; 21:17; Lev 20:9; Deut 5:16*   8,9 *Is 29:13*

---

15 *a-* 2 Greek is singular (also in vv. 3,6).
   b- 3 Greek is singular.
   c- 8 Literally: "This people honors Me."

worship Me in vain, since what they *teach for doctrines* are *rules laid down by men.'*"

10 Then He called the people and told them: "Listen to Me and understand this: 11 What enters into a person's mouth does not make him unclean, but what comes out of his mouth makes him unclean."

12 Then the disciples came to Him. They asked Him, "Do You realize that when the Pharisees heard Your statement it was a stumbling block*d* ⌊for them⌋?"

13 He answered, "Any plant which My Father in heaven did not plant will be torn out by the roots. 14 Let them go; they are blind leaders. When one blind man leads another, both will fall into a ditch."

15 Peter said to Him, "Tell us what You mean by this parable."

16 Jesus said, "Are you still as dense as the others? 17 Do you not know that everything which goes into the mouth goes into the stomach and is expelled ⌊from the body⌋?*e* 18 But what goes out of the mouth comes from the heart, and that makes a person unclean. 19 Yes, out of the heart come evil thoughts, murders, adulteries, sexual sins, stealing, lies, slanders. 20 These are the things that make a person unclean. But eating without washing one's hands does not make one unclean."

The Faith Of A Canaanite Woman—*Mark 7:24-30*

21 Leaving that place, Jesus went away to the neighborhood of Tyre and Sidon.

22 There was a Canaanite woman of that territory who came out and began to shout: "Have pity on me, Lord, Son of David! A demon is severely tormenting my daughter."

23 But He did not answer her a word. Then His disciples came to Him and urged Him, "Send her away. She's yelling after us."

24 "I was sent only to the lost sheep of Israel," He answered.

25 She came and bowed down before Him. "Lord, help me!" she said.

26 He answered, "It is not good to take the children's bread and throw it to the dogs."*f*

27 "You are right, Lord," she said, "but even the dogs eat some of the crumbs that drop from their masters' table."

28 Then Jesus answered her, "O woman, you have a strong faith! Let it be done for you as you wish." At that moment her daughter was made well.

29 Jesus left that place and went along the shore of the Sea of Galilee. Then He went up into the hills and sat there.

30 A large crowd came to Him, bringing the lame, blind, crippled, those unable to talk, and many others, and laid them at His feet; and He healed them. 31 As a result, the people were amazed to see those unable to talk speaking, the crippled being cured, the lame walking, and the blind seeing.

---

d- 12 See *SKANDALON* on page 545.
e- 17 Literally: "and is expelled into a drain [toilet]?"
f- 26 The Greek indicates a household pet.

Jesus Feeds 4,000—Mark 8:1-9

32 Jesus called His disciples and said, "I feel sorry for the people. They have been with Me three days now and have nothing to eat. I do not want to let them go without eating; they may become exhausted on the way."

33 His disciples asked Him, "Where could we get enough bread in a wilderness to feed such a crowd?"

34 Jesus asked them, "How many loaves do you have?"

"Seven," they said, "and a few small fish."

35 He ordered the people to sit down on the ground. **36** Then He took the seven loaves and the fish, gave thanks, broke them, and gave them to the disciples, and they gave them to the people.

37 All of them ate and had enough. They picked up the pieces that were left over—seven baskets full. **38** Four thousand men had eaten, besides women and children.

39 After He dismissed the people, He stepped into the boat and came into the area of Magadan.

16TH CHAPTER

A Sign From Heaven—Mark 8:10-12

1 The Pharisees and Sadducees came, and to test Him they asked Him to show them some miraculous sign from heaven.

2 He answered them, "In the evening you say, 'The weather will be fine, because the sky is red'; **3** and in the morning, 'There will be a storm today, because the sky is red and gloomy.' You know how to judge the appearance of the sky, but you cannot judge the signs of the times. *a*

4 "A wicked and unfaithful kind of people demand a miraculous sign, but the only sign they will be given is that of Jonah."

Then He left them and went away.

The Yeast Of The Pharisees—Mark 8:13b-21

5 When the disciples started out for the other side, they forgot to take bread.

6 "Be on guard!" Jesus said to them. "Beware of the yeast of the Pharisees and Sadducees!"

7 And they were discussing ⌊Jesus' comment⌋ among themselves. They said, "⌊He mentioned yeast⌋ because we have not brought any bread."

8 Since He was aware of what was going on, Jesus asked, "Why are you discussing among yourselves the fact that you do not have any bread? You have so little faith! **9** Do you still not understand or remember the five loaves for the five thousand and how many baskets full you picked up? **10** Or the seven loaves for the four thousand and how many baskets full you picked up? **11** How is it that

---

16 *a*- 3 Jesus' words in verses 2 and 3 are lacking in some of the older manuscripts and early translations.

you do not understand that I was not talking to you about bread?—but that you should beware of the yeast of the Pharisees and Sadducees!"

12 Then they understood that He was not warning them against the yeast in bread but against the teaching of the Pharisees and Sadducees.

"You Are The Christ [Messiah]"—Mark 8:27-30; Luke 9:18-21

13 When Jesus came to the area of Caesarea Philippi, He asked His disciples, "Who do people say the Son of Man is?"

14 "Some say John the Baptizer," they answered; "others Elijah; still others, Jeremiah or one of the prophets."

15 "But you, who do you say I am?" He asked them.

16 "You are the Christ, the Son of the living God!"[b] Simon Peter answered.

17 "Blessed are you, Simon son of John," Jesus answered him, "because this was revealed to you not by flesh and blood but by My Father in heaven. **18** I tell you, you are Peter, and on this rock[c] I will build My church, and the forces of hell[d] will not overpower it. **19** I will give you the keys of the Kingdom of heaven. Whatever you[e] bind on earth will be bound in heaven; and whatever you set free on earth will be set free in heaven."[f]

20 Then He warned the disciples not to tell anyone that He was the Christ.

"I Will Die And Rise"—Mark 8:31-33; Luke 9:22

21 From that time on Jesus Christ began to point out to His disciples that He had to go to Jerusalem, suffer much from the elders, ruling priests, and scribes, be killed, and then rise on the third day.

22 But Peter took Him aside and began to correct Him, "God be merciful to You, Lord! This must never happen to You!"

23 He turned and said to Peter, "Get behind Me, Satan! You are a stumbling block[g] to Me because you are not thinking what God thinks but what men think."

Take Up The Cross—Mark 8:34–9:1; Luke 9:23-27

24 Then Jesus said to His disciples, "If you want to follow Me, deny yourself, take up your cross, and come with Me. **25** For if anyone wants to save his life, he will lose it. But if anyone loses his life for Me, he will find it. **26** What good

---

b- 16 See THE EARLIEST CHRISTIAN CREEDS on page 547.

c- 18 "Peter" is *"Petros"* in Greek, while "rock" is *"petra."* It is crucial to note that the masculine *"petros"* means "rock" in the sense of a stone or pebble, while the feminine *"petra"* indicates an immovable boulder or a portion of the earth's crust. As such, "rock" does not refer to "Peter" but to his *confession.* Thus Christ's church is built on the *truth* of Peter's confession, not on Peter.

d- 18 Literally: "gates of *hades*"; see *HADES/GEHENNA* on page 540.

e- 19 Greek is singular.

f- 19 Literally: "will have been bound in heaven" and "will have been set free in heaven"; the Greek here is the future perfect tense which indicates an immediate and certain future state resulting from a completed action.

g- 23 See *SKANDALON* on page 545.

will it do a person to win the whole world and lose his soul? Or what would a person give to buy back his soul? **27** For the Son of Man is going to come with His angels in His Father's glory, and then *He will give each according to what he has done.* **28** I tell you the truth, there are some standing here who will never taste death until they see the Son of Man coming in His Kingdom."[h]

17TH CHAPTER

Jesus Shows His Glory (The Transfiguration)—Mark 9:2-13; Luke 9:28-36

1 After six days Jesus took with Him Peter, James, and John the brother of James, and led them up a high mountain to be alone with them.

2 He was transfigured[a] before them, His face shone like the sun, and His clothing became as white as light. **3** And suddenly Moses and Elijah appeared to them and were talking with Him.

4 Peter said to Jesus, "Lord, it's good for us to be here. If You wish, I'll put up three shelters[b] here, one for You, one for Moses, and one for Elijah."

5 He was still speaking when a bright cloud suddenly overshadowed them, and a voice came out of the cloud: *"This is My Son,* whom I love ₍and₎ in whom I *delight. Listen to Him!"*

6 When the disciples heard it, they fell facedown; they were terrified. **7** But Jesus came, and as He touched them He said, "Get up and don't continue to be afraid." **8** Then they looked up and saw no one but Jesus.

9 On their way down the mountain Jesus ordered them, "Do not tell anyone what you have seen until the Son of Man has risen from the dead."

10 So the disciples asked Him, "Why then do the scribes say, 'First Elijah has to come'?"

11 Jesus answered, *"Elijah* is coming and *will put* everything *in order again.* **12** But I tell you that Elijah has already come, and people did not know him but treated him as they pleased. In the same way they are going to make the Son of Man suffer."

13 Then the disciples understood that He was talking about John the Baptizer.

The Boy With A Demon—Mark 9:14-29; Luke 9:37-43a

14 When they came to the people, a man came to Jesus and knelt before Him. **15** "Lord," he said, "have pity on my son because he's an epileptic[c] and very sick. Often he falls into fire or into water. **16** I brought him to Your disciples, but they could not make him well."

17 Jesus answered, "O you unbelieving and perverted kind of people! How

---

27 *Ps 62:12; Prov 24:12*   5 *Deut 18:15; Ps 2:7; Is 42:1*   11 *Mal 4:5,6*

---

h- 28 Meaning "coming to rule as King."
17 *a*- 2 Meaning "His appearance changed" as He was transformed.
   b- 4 Or "tabernacles, tents," suggesting that Peter had the Festival of Booths (Tabernacles) on his mind.
   c- 15 See 4:24 and its accompanying footnote.

long must I be with you? How long must I put up with you? Bring him here to Me."

18 Jesus spoke sharply to the demon, and he came out of the boy, and from that time on the boy was well.

19 Then the disciples came to Jesus privately and asked, "Why couldn't we drive out the demon?"

20 "Because you have so little faith," He told them. "I tell you the truth, if you have faith no bigger than a mustard seed, you could say to this mountain, 'Move from here to there,' and it will move. Then nothing will be impossible for you. **21** This kind ͵of demon͵ goes out only by prayer and fasting."*d*

"I Will Die And Rise"—*Mark 9:30-32; Luke 9:43b-45*

22 While they were coming together as a group in Galilee, Jesus told them, "The Son of Man is going to be betrayed into the hands of men, **23** and they will kill Him, but on the third day He will rise." Then they became very sad.

A Coin In A Fish's Mouth

24 When they came to Capernaum, the collectors of the Temple tax came to Peter. "Doesn't your Teacher pay the Temple tax?" they asked.

25 "Certainly," he answered.

Peter went into the house, but before he could speak, Jesus asked him, "What do you think, Simon? From whom do the kings of the world collect toll or tax—from their children or from other people?"

26 When he answered, "From other people," Jesus said to him: "Then the children are certainly free; **27** but in order that we may not become a stumbling block*e* to them, go to the sea and throw in a hook. Take the first fish that comes up, open its mouth, and you will find a coin.*f* Take that and give it to them for Me and for you."

18TH CHAPTER

b. Words: Rules for the new church (people of God) [ekklesia] (18:1-35)

Who Is The Greatest?—*Mark 9:33-37; Luke 9:46-48*

1 At that time the disciples came to Jesus and asked, "Who is really the greatest in the Kingdom of heaven?"

2 He called a little child and had him stand in front of*a* them. **3** "I tell you the truth," He said to them, "if you do not change and become like little children, you will never enter the Kingdom of heaven. **4** Whoever humbles

---

d- 21 Some of the older manuscripts and early translations omit verse 21.

e- 27 See *SKANDALON* on page 545.

f- 27 See MONEY, WEIGHTS, and MEASURES on page 328.

18 *a-* 2 Or "in the middle of."

himself like this little child is the greatest in the Kingdom of heaven. **5** And whoever welcomes one child like this in My Name welcomes Me."

Do I Cause Others To Stumble In Their Faith?—*Mark 9:42-48; Luke 17:1,2*

6 "Whoever causes one of these little ones who believe in Me to stumble ‚in his faith‚,*b* it would be better for him to have a large millstone hung around his neck and to be drowned in the deepest part of the sea. **7** Woe to the world when it causes people to stumble ‚in their faith‚. Things must come which cause people to stumble, but woe to that man who causes others to stumble ‚in their faith‚!

8 "If your hand or your foot causes you to stumble ‚in your faith‚, cut it off and throw it away. It is better for you to go into life without a hand or a foot than to have two hands or two feet and be thrown into the everlasting fire. **9** If your eye causes you to stumble ‚in your faith‚, tear it out and throw it away. It is better for you to go into life with one eye than to have two eyes and be thrown into hellfire.

10 "Be careful not to despise one of these little ones, for I tell you that their angels in heaven always see the face of My Father, who is in heaven. **11** For the Son of Man came to save the lost."*c*

The Lost Sheep—*Luke 15:1-7*

12 "What do you think? If a man has a hundred sheep and one of them strays away, will he not leave the ninety-nine in the hills and go and look for the straying sheep? **13** And if he finds it, I tell you the truth, he is happier about it than about the ninety-nine that have not strayed away. **14** In the same way your Father in heaven does not want one of these little ones to be lost."

Tell Him His Fault

15 "If your brother sins against you, go and point out his sin to him when you are alone with him. If he listens to you, you have won your brother. **16** But if he will not listen, take one or two others with you so that *you have two or three witnesses to verify every word.* **17** If he will not listen to them, tell it to the church. But if he will not listen even to the church, treat him like a heathen and a tax collector. **18** I tell you the truth, whatever you bind on earth will be bound in heaven; and whatever you set free on earth will be set free in heaven.*d*

19 "Again I tell you, if two of you here on earth agree to ask for anything, My Father in heaven will do it for you. **20** For where two or three have come together in My Name, there I am among them."

---

16 Deut 19:15

---

b- 6 See *SKANDALON* on page 545. The same applies to verses 7-9.

c- 11 Some of the older manuscripts and early translations omit verse 11. See also Luke 19:10 where the inclusion of these words is certain.

d- 18 See 16:19 and its accompanying footnote "f."

Forgive!

21 Then Peter came to Jesus and asked Him, "Lord, how often shall I forgive my brother who sins against me? Seven times?"

22 Jesus answered him, "I tell you, not seven times, but seventy times seven times.

23 "That is why the Kingdom of heaven is like a king who wanted to settle accounts with his slaves. **24** When he began to do so, there was brought to him one who owed him ten thousand talents.*e* **25** When this slave could not pay the debt, the master ordered him, his wife, his children, and all he had to be sold in order to settle the account. **26** Then the slave fell on his knees and, bowing low before him, begged: 'Be patient with me, and I will repay you everything!'

27 "The master felt sorry for his slave, freed him, and canceled his debt. **28** But when that slave went away, he found one of his fellow slaves who owed him a hundred denarii.*f* He grabbed him and began to choke him. 'Pay what you owe!' he said.

29 "Then his fellow slave fell on his knees and begged him, 'Be patient with me, and I will repay you.' **30** But he refused. Instead, he turned away and had him put in prison until he would pay what he owed.

31 "When his fellow slaves saw what had happened, they felt very sad and came and told their master the whole story.

32 "Then his master sent for him and said to him: 'You wicked slave! I canceled all you owed me, because you begged me. **33** Shouldn't you also have treated your fellow slave as mercifully as I treated you?' **34** His master was so angry that he handed him over to the torturers until he should pay all that he owed.

35 "That is what My Father in heaven will do to you if each of you will not heartily forgive his brother."

19TH CHAPTER

5. Fifth booklet (19:1–25:46)
a. Narrative and deeds: Judean ministry (19:1–22:46)

Husband And Wife—Mark 10:1-12

1 When Jesus finished these sayings, He left Galilee and went to the territory of Judea*a* on the other side of the Jordan. **2** Large crowds followed Him, and He healed them there.

3 Some Pharisees came to Him to test Him. They asked Him, "Is it right for a man to divorce his wife for any reason?"

4 Jesus replied, "Have you not read that He who created them from the

---

e- 24 See MONEY, WEIGHTS, and MEASURES on page 328.
f- 28 One denarius was a day's pay. See MONEY, WEIGHTS, and MEASURES on page 328.
19 *a-* 1 In the wider sense meaning "Palestine."

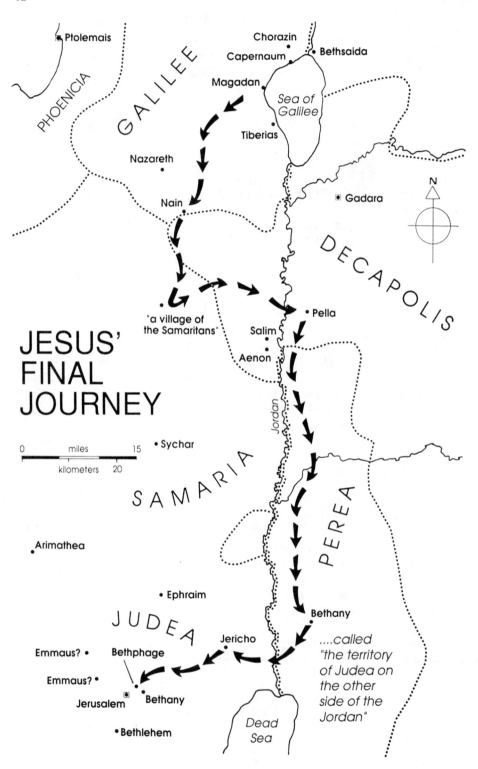

JESUS' FINAL JOURNEY

PHOENICIA

GALILEE

Ptolemais

Chorazin

Capernaum

Bethsaida

Magadan

Sea of Galilee

Tiberias

Nazareth

Nain

Gadara

DECAPOLIS

"a village of the Samaritans"

Salim

Pella

Aenon

Jordan

Sychar

SAMARIA

PEREA

Arimathea

Ephraim

Bethany

JUDEA

Jericho

Emmaus?

Bethphage

Emmaus?

Jerusalem

Bethany

Bethlehem

Dead Sea

....called "the territory of Judea on the other side of the Jordan"

0 miles 15

kilometers 20

N

beginning *made them male and female?*" **5** And He added: *"That is why a man shall leave his father and mother and shall remain united with his wife, and the two shall be one flesh.* **6** And so they are no longer two, but one flesh. Therefore, let no one separate what God has joined together."

7 "Why then," they asked Him, "did Moses order a man *to file a divorce paper and divorce his wife?"*

8 He answered them, "Because your minds are closed,*b* Moses allowed you to divorce your wives, but originally there was no such thing. **9** I tell you, if anyone divorces his wife, except for adultery, and marries another, he is living in adultery."

10 The disciples said to Him, "If a man has to have such grounds in dealing with his wife, it is of no advantage to marry."

11 He answered them, "Not all can do what you suggest, but only those to whom it has been given. **12** For some cannot marry because they were born that way, and others because they have been mutilated by men. And still others have decided to remain unmarried because of the Kingdom of heaven.*c* If anyone can do it, let him do it."

Jesus Loves Children—*Mark 10:13-16; Luke 18:15-17*

13 Then some people brought little children to Jesus to have Him lay His hands on them and pray. But the disciples sternly told them not to do it.

14 Jesus said, "Let the little children come to Me and do not try to keep them away, for the Kingdom of heaven is made up of such as these." **15** After He laid His hands on them, He went away from there.

The Rich Young Leader—*Mark 10:17-31; Luke 18:18-30*

16 There was one who came and asked Him, "Teacher, what good thing shall I do to gain everlasting life?"

17 "Why do you ask Me about what is good? Only One is good. If you want to enter into life, keep the commandments."

18 "Which commandments?" he asked Him.

Jesus said, *"Do not murder. Do not commit adultery. Do not steal. Do not lie.*d* **19** Honor your father and mother. Love your neighbor as yourself."*

20 "I have kept all these," the young man told Him. "What else do I need to do?"

21 "If you want to be perfect," Jesus told him, "go, sell what you have, give

---

4 *Gen 1:27; 5:2*   5 *Gen 2:24*   7 *Deut 24:1*   **18,19** *Ex 20:12-16; Deut 5:16-20*
19 *Lev 19:18*

---

b- 8 Literally: "hardness of your hearts"; a hardened heart leads to a closed or stubborn mind (cf. Ex. 4:21).

c- 12 Literally: "There are eunuchs who were born that way from their mother's womb, and there are eunuchs who were made eunuchs by men, and there are eunuchs who made themselves eunuchs for the sake of the Kingdom of heaven."

d- 18 Or "Do not give false witness."

the money to the poor, and you will have treasure in heaven. Then come and follow Me."

22 When the young man heard this, he went away sad because he was very rich.

23 Jesus said to His disciples, "I tell you the truth, it is hard for a rich man to enter the Kingdom of heaven. **24** Again I tell you, it is easier for a camel to go through the eye of a needle than for a rich person to enter the Kingdom of God."

25 When the disciples heard this, they were dumbfounded. "Who then can be saved?" they asked.

26 Jesus looked at them and said: "For men this is impossible to do, but *for God everything is possible.*"

27 Then Peter spoke up and said to Him: "Look! We gave up everything and followed You. So what will we get out of it?"

28 "I tell you the truth," Jesus said to them, "in the new world, when the Son of Man sits on His throne of glory, you who followed Me will also sit on twelve thrones, ruling*e* the twelve tribes of Israel. **29** And everyone who gave up homes, or brothers or sisters, or father or mother, or children, or fields for the sake of My Name will receive many times as much and will inherit everlasting life. **30** Many who are first will be last, and many who are last will be first."

20TH CHAPTER

"The Last Will Be First"

1 "For the Kingdom of heaven is like the ⸢rich⸣ landowner who went out early in the morning to hire men to work in his vineyard. **2** He agreed with the workers to pay them a denarius*a* a day and sent them into his vineyard. **3** About the third hour [9 a.m.] he went out and saw others standing in the marketplace doing nothing. **4** 'You also go into the vineyard,' he told them, 'and I shall pay you whatever is right.' So they went.

5 "He went out again about the sixth hour [noon] and the ninth hour [3 p.m.] and did the same thing. **6** About the eleventh hour [5 p.m.] he went out and found some others standing around. 'Why are you standing here all day long doing nothing?' he asked them.

7 " 'Nobody has hired us,' they answered him.

" 'You also go into the vineyard,' he told them.

8 "When evening came, the owner of the vineyard told his manager, 'Call the men and give them their pay. Start with the last and go on to the first.'

9 "Those who started working about the eleventh hour [5 p.m.] came, and each received a denarius. **10** When the first ones came, they expected to receive more, but each of them also received a denarius. **11** Although they took it, they

---

26 Gen 18:14; Job 42:2; Zech 8:6

---

e- 28 Or "judging" (cf. Lk. 22:29,30).
20 *a-* 2 See MONEY, WEIGHTS, and MEASURES on page 328.

began grumbling against the owner: **12** 'These last men worked only one hour, and you have treated them exactly as you treated us who have endured the burden and the blazing heat of the day.'

13 " 'Friend, I am doing you no wrong,' he answered one of them. 'You agreed with me on a denarius, didn't you? **14** Take your money and go. I want to give this last man as much as I give you. **15** Don't I have the right to do as I please with what is mine? Or are you critical of me because I am generous?'

16 "In this way the last will be first and the first last."

The Cup Of Suffering—Mark 10:32-45

17 When Jesus was going up to Jerusalem, He took the Twelve by themselves and said to them on the way: **18** "Look, we are going up to Jerusalem, and the Son of Man will be betrayed to the ruling priests and scribes. They will condemn Him to die **19** and hand Him over to the Gentiles to be made fun of, whipped, and crucified, but on the third day He will rise."

20 Then the mother of Zebedee's sons came to Jesus with her sons and bowed before Him to make a request of Him.

21 "What do you want?" He asked her.

She told Him, "Promise that one of my two sons will sit at Your right and the other at Your left in Your Kingdom."

22 Jesus answered, "You do not realize what you are asking. Can you drink the cup which I am about to drink?"

"We can," they told Him.

23 He told them, "You will drink My cup, but to sit at My right and at My left I can grant only to those for whom My Father has prepared these positions."*b*

24 When the other ten heard about it, they became angry with the two brothers. **25** Jesus called them and said: "You know that the rulers of the Gentiles are lords over them, and their great men are tyrants over them. **26** But it is not to be that way among you. Anyone who wants to become great among you, let him be your servant;*c* **27** and anyone who wants to be first among you, let him be your slave,*d* **28** just as the Son of Man did not come to be served but to serve and give His life as a ransom for many."*e*

Two Blind Men

29 As they were leaving Jericho, a large crowd followed Him. **30** There were two blind men sitting by the road. When they heard that Jesus was passing by, they shouted: "Lord, have pity on us, Son of David!"

---

b- 23 Literally: "for whom it has been prepared by My Father."

c- 26 Literally: "shall be your servant"; in Greek the future is used at times as an imperative.

d- 27 Literally: "shall be your slave"; in Greek the future is used at times as an imperative.

e- 28 Greek: "*pollōn*," meaning "a large number of," a Hebrew idiom which at times means "all" (Is. 53:11,12), as we see from Romans 5:19. That the meaning "all" is to be applied to the present passage and to Mark 10:45 should become evident from a comparison with 2 Corinthians 5:15 which uses the Greek word "*panton*" ("all").

31 The crowd urged them to be quiet. But they shouted even louder: "Lord, have pity on us, Son of David!"

32 Jesus stopped and called them. "What do you want Me to do for you?" He asked.

33 "Lord, we want our eyes to be opened," they told Him.

34 Because Jesus felt sorry for them, He touched their eyes, and immediately their sight was restored and they followed Him.

21ST CHAPTER

The King Comes To Jerusalem—*Mark 11:1-11; Luke 19:29-44; John 12:12-19*

1 When they came near Jerusalem and had reached Bethphage ₍and₎ the Mount of Olives, Jesus sent two disciples. **2** He told them, "Go into the village ahead of you, and at once you will find a donkey tied up and a colt with her. Untie them and bring them to Me. **3** If anyone says anything to you, you are to say, 'The Lord needs them,' and immediately he will send them."

4 This happened so that what the prophet said would be fulfilled:

5   *Tell the daughter of Zion:*
        "Look! Your King is coming to you,
            gentle,
            riding on a donkey,
                even on a colt, the foal of a beast of burden." ᵃ

6 The disciples went and did as Jesus had directed them. **7** They brought the donkey and the colt and laid their garments on them; and Jesus sat on them. ᵇ **8** Most of the people spread their garments on the road. Others cut branches from the trees and spread them on the road. **9** The crowds that went ahead of Him and that followed Him were shouting:

    "*Hosanna*ᶜ *to the Son of David!*
        Blessed is He who is coming in the Name of the Lord!
    Hosanna in the highest heavens!"

10 When He came into Jerusalem, the whole city was in an uproar, asking, "Who is this?"

11 The crowds answered, "This is Jesus the Prophet who is from Nazareth in Galilee."

---

5 *Is 62:11; Zech 9:9*   **9** *Ps 118:25,26*

---

21 *a*- 5 This description emphasizes the *humble* nature of the Messiah's rule.
  b- 7 Jesus rode only on the colt (Mk. 11:2,7; Lk. 19:30,35; Jn. 12:14). Therefore, "laid their garments on *them*" implies "on the animals," while "sat on *them*" infers "on the garments."
  c- 9 A Hebrew word meaning "Save now, we pray!" It became an expression of praise.

Cleansing The Temple—Mark 11:15-19; Luke 19:45-48

12 Jesus went into the Temple and drove out all those who were selling and buying in the Temple, and He upset the tables of the moneychangers and the chairs of those who sold pigeons. 13 He told them, "It is written: *'My House shall be called a house of prayer*, but you are turning it into *a den of robbers*!'"

14 Blind and lame persons came to Him in the Temple, and He made them well.

15 When the ruling priests and the scribes saw the wonderful things He did and the children shouting in the Temple, *"Hosanna^d* to the Son of David!" they did not like it at all. 16 "Do You hear what they are saying?" they asked Him.

"Yes," Jesus answered them. "Have you never read: *'You have made little children and infants sing Your praises'*?"

17 He left them and went out of the city to Bethany and spent the night there.

Nothing But Leaves—Mark 11:12-14, 20-25

18 In the morning as He went back to the city, Jesus became hungry. 19 When He saw a fig tree by the road, He went up to it and found nothing on it but leaves. "May no fruit ever grow on you again!" Jesus said to it. And immediately the fig tree dried up.

20 The disciples were surprised to see this. "How did the fig tree dry up so quickly?" they asked.

21 "I tell you the truth," Jesus answered them, "if you believe and do not doubt, not only will you do what I did to the fig tree, but also if you say to this mountain, 'Be lifted up and be thrown into the sea,' it will be done. 22 Whatever you ask for in prayer, believing, you will receive."

From Heaven—Mark 11:27-33; Luke 20:1-8

23 When He came to the Temple and was teaching, the ruling priests and the elders of the people came to Him. They asked, "By what authority are You doing these things?" and "Who gave You this authority to do them?"

24 Jesus answered them, "I shall also ask you one question. If you answer it for Me, I will tell you by what authority I am doing these things. 25 John's baptism—was it from heaven or from men?"

They argued among themselves, "If we say, 'From heaven,' He will ask us, 'Then why didn't you believe him?' 26 But if we say, 'From men,' we're afraid of the people; they all think of John as a prophet." 27 So they answered Jesus, "We do not know."

Then Jesus also told them, "Neither will I tell you by what authority I am doing these things."

---

13 Is 56:7; Jer 7:11   *15 Ps 118:25,26*   *16 Ps 8:2*

d- 15 See footnote at 21:9.

Two Sons

28 "What do you think of this? A man had two sons. He went to the first and said, 'Son, go and work in the vineyard today.'

29 "He answered, 'I will not!' Later he changed his mind and went.

30 "The father went to the other one and told him the same thing. He answered, 'I will, sir,' but he did not go.

31 "Which of the two did what the father wanted?"

"The first," they answered.

Jesus said to them, "I tell you the truth, tax collectors and prostitutes are going into the Kingdom of God ahead of you. 32 For John came to you teaching you the way of righteousness,*e* but you did not believe him; the tax collectors and prostitutes believed him. But even when you had seen that, you did not later change your minds and believe him."

God's Vineyard—Mark 12:1-12; Luke 20:9-19

33 "Listen to another parable: A man who owned property *planted a vineyard. He put a wall around it, dug a winepress in it, and built a watchtower.* Then he leased it out to workers and left home.

34 "When the grapes were getting ripe, he sent his servants to the workers to obtain his share of the grapes. 35 The workers took his servants and beat one, killed another, and stoned a third. 36 Then he sent other servants, this time a larger number, and they treated them the same way.

37 "Finally he sent his son to them, saying, 'They will respect my son.'

38 "When the workers saw the son, they said to one another, 'This is the heir. Come, let's kill him and take possession of his inheritance.' 39 So they took him, threw him out of the vineyard, and killed him.

40 "Now when the owner of the vineyard comes, what will he do to those workers?"

41 They [the priests and elders] answered, "He will make those scoundrels die a miserable death and lease out the vineyard to other workers who will give him his share of the grapes when they are ripe."

42 Jesus asked them, "Have you never read in the Scriptures:

> *The very Stone*
>> *which the builders rejected*
>>> *has become the Cornerstone.*
> *The Lord has done it,*
>> *and it is marvelous for us to see?*

43 That is why I tell you, the Kingdom of God will be taken away from you and be given to a people who continue to do its works. 44 Anyone who falls on this Stone will be dashed in pieces, and if It falls on anyone, It will scatter him like dust."

---

33 Is 5:1,2   42 Ps 118:22,23

---

e- 32 Literally: "came to you in a way of righteousness."

45 When the ruling priests and Pharisees heard His parables, they knew He was talking about them. 46 They wanted to arrest Him but were afraid because the people thought He was a prophet.

22ND CHAPTER

Come To The Wedding!

1 Again Jesus used parables in speaking to them. He said: 2 "The Kingdom of heaven is like a king who prepared a wedding for his son. 3 He sent his servants*a* to call those who had been invited to the wedding, but they refused to come. 4 Then he sent other servants and said to them, 'Tell the people who are invited, "Look here! I have prepared my dinner. My bulls and fattened calves have been killed, and everything is ready. Come to the wedding." '

5 "But they paid no attention and went away, one to his farm, another to his business; 6 and the rest took his servants, shamefully mistreated them, and murdered them.

7 "The king became angry. He sent his soldiers, killed those murderers, and burned their city.

8 "Then he said to his servants: 'The wedding is ready, but the people who were invited did not deserve the honor. 9 Now go where the highways leave the city, and invite everyone you find there to the wedding.' 10 Those servants went out on the highways and brought in all the people they found, both bad and good. And the wedding hall was filled with guests.

11 "When the king came in to observe the guests, he saw a man there without a wedding garment. 12 He asked him, 'Friend, how did you get in here without a wedding garment?'

"The man could not say a thing. 13 Then the king told the servants, 'Tie him hand and foot and throw him out into the outer darkness where he will weep and grind his teeth.'

14 "Yes, many are invited, but few are chosen."

Taxes—Mark 12:13-17; Luke 20:20-26

15 Then the Pharisees went away and plotted to trap Him with a question. 16 They sent their disciples with Herod's supporters*b* to say to Him: "Teacher, we know that You are honest, that You teach the way of God faithfully, since You do not favor any individuals because of who they are.*c* 17 Now tell us: What do You think? Is it right to pay a tax to Caesar or not?"

18 Because Jesus recognized their wicked plot, He asked, "Why do you test Me, you hypocrites? 19 Show Me the coin with which the tax is paid."

---

22 *a-* 3 Literally: "slaves," which in Greek reflects total subjection (also in vv. 4,6,8,10).

b- 16 Or "Herodians"; not a religious sect like the Pharisees or Sadducees (v. 23), rather a political faction that supported the Herods; however, all these groups opposed Jesus.

c- 16 Literally: "since it does not matter to You concerning anyone, for You do not look on the face of men."

They brought Him a denarius. *d* **20** "Whose head is this and whose inscription?" He asked them.

21 "Caesar's," they said.

Then He told them, "Therefore give to Caesar what is Caesar's and to God what is God's."

22 They were surprised to hear this. Then they let Him alone and went away.

The Dead Live—*Mark 12:18-27; Luke 20:27-40*

23 On that day some Sadducees, who say that there is no resurrection, came to Him with this question: **24** "Teacher, Moses said: *'If anyone dies childless, his brother should marry his widow and have children for his brother.'* **25** Now there were seven brothers among us. The first married and died, and since he had no children, he left his widow to his brother. **26** The second brother did the same, and so did the third and the rest of the seven. **27** Last of all, the woman died. **28** Now in the resurrection, whose wife will she be of the seven, since they all had married her?"

29 "You are wrong," Jesus answered, "because you do not know the Scriptures or the power of God. **30** In the resurrection people do not marry nor are they given in marriage but are like the angels in heaven. **31** And concerning the resurrection of the dead—have you not read what God told you: **32** *'I am the God of Abraham, the God of Isaac, and the God of Jacob'*? He is not the God of the dead but of the living."

33 His teaching amazed the crowds who heard Him.

Love God And Your Neighbor—*Mark 12:28-34*

34 When the Pharisees heard that He had silenced the Sadducees, they got together. **35** One of them, an expert in the Law, tested Him by asking, **36** "Teacher, which is the greatest commandment in the Law?"

37 Jesus answered him, " *'Love the Lord your God with all your heart, with all your soul, and with all your mind.'* **38** This is the greatest and most important commandment. **39** The next is like it: *'Love your neighbor as yourself.'* **40** All the Law and the Prophets*e* depend on these two commandments."

David's Son—*Mark 12:35-37a; Luke 20:41-44*

41 While the Pharisees were still together, Jesus asked them, **42** "What do you think of the Christ [Messiah]? Whose son is He?"

"David's," they answered Him.

43 He asked them, "Then how can David, moved by the Spirit, call Him 'Lord'? For he says,

---

24 *Gen 38:8; Deut 25:5,6*   **32** *Ex 3:6*   **37** *Deut 6:5*   **39** *Lev 19:18*

d- 19 See MONEY, WEIGHTS, and MEASURES on page 328.
e- 40 See initial portion of footnote at 5:17.

44   *The Lord said to my Lord:*
      'Sit at My right hand
            until I put Your enemies under Your feet.'

45 Now if David calls Him 'Lord,' how can He be his son?"

46 No one could answer Him a word, and from that time on no one dared to ask Him another question.

23RD CHAPTER

b. Words: Seven woes and the last things [eschatology] (23:1–25:46)

Beware!—*Mark 12:37b-40; Luke 20:45-47*

1 Then Jesus said to the crowds and to His disciples: 2 "The scribes and the Pharisees sit in Moses' seat. 3 Do everything they tell you, and follow it; but do not do what they do, because they do not do what they say. 4 They tie together heavy loads that are hard to carry and lay them on the shoulders of the people, but they are not willing to raise a finger to move them.

5 "They do everything in order to be seen by the people. They make their phylacteries broad and the tassels of their garments long. *ᵃ* 6 They like the places of honor at dinners and the front seats in synagogs. 7 They like to be greeted in the marketplaces and to have people call them 'Rabbi' ['Teacher']. 8 But as for you, do not have others call you 'Rabbi,' because you have only one Teacher, and you are all brothers. 9 And do not call anyone on earth 'Father'; you have only one Father, and He is in heaven. 10 Do not have others call you 'Leaders'; you have only one Leader, and that is Christ. 11 The greatest among you will be one who serves you. 12 If someone honors himself, he will be humbled, but if someone humbles himself, he will be honored."

Woes And Warnings—*Luke 11:37-54*

13 "Woe to you, scribes and Pharisees, you hypocrites! You lock people out of the Kingdom of heaven, for you do not go in yourselves, nor do you permit others to go in when they try to do so. *ᵇ*

15 "Woe to you, scribes and Pharisees, you hypocrites! You go across sea and

---

44 Ps 110:1

---

23 *a-* 5 A phylactery was a small leather box fastened by a leather strap on the forehead or on the left arm. In the box were pieces of parchment on which were written the words of Exodus 13:1-10, 11-16; Deuteronomy 6:4-9; 11:13-21. An Israelite wore a tassel on each of the four corners of his outer garment. See Numbers 15:37-40; Deuteronomy 22:12.

b- 13 Many of the older manuscripts and early translations omit verse 14: "Woe to you, scribes and Pharisees, you hypocrites! You swallow the widows' houses and then, to cover up, make long prayers. Their sentence will be more severe." The addition of this verse would break the sevenfold pattern so often evident in Matthew's Gospel. Without this verse there are seven "woes." These words are included at Mark 12:40 and Luke 20:47 where their authenticity is certain.

land to convert a single person, and when he is converted, you make him twice as fit for hell as you are.

16 "Woe to you, blind guides! You say, 'If anyone swears by^c the Temple, that is nothing. But if anyone swears by the gold in the Temple, he must keep his oath.' **17** Blind fools! Which is greater, the gold or the Temple that made the gold holy? **18** Or again, 'If anyone swears by the altar, that is nothing. But if anyone swears by the gift that is on it, he must keep his oath.' **19** You blind men! Which is greater, the gift or the altar that makes the gift holy? **20** If you swear by the altar, you swear by it and by everything on it. **21** If you swear by the Temple, you swear by it and by the One who lives there. **22** And if you swear by heaven, you swear by God's throne and the One who sits on it.

23 "Woe to you, scribes and Pharisees, you hypocrites! You give a tenth of mint and dill and cummin, but you have neglected the more important things of the Law: to be just, merciful, and trustworthy. You should have done the one without neglecting the other. **24** Blind guides! You strain out the gnat but swallow the camel.

25 "Woe to you, scribes and Pharisees, you hypocrites! You clean the outside of a cup and of a dish, but inside they are full of greed and uncontrolled desires. **26** You blind Pharisee! First clean the inside of the cup and of the dish in order that the outside also may be clean.

27 "Woe to you, scribes and Pharisees, you hypocrites! You are like white-washed graves that look beautiful on the outside but inside are full of dead men's bones and every kind of decay. **28** So on the outside you look righteous to people, but inside you are full of hypocrisy and lawlessness.

29 "Woe to you, scribes and Pharisees, you hypocrites! You build the tombs of the prophets and decorate the graves of the righteous, **30** and you say, 'If we had lived at the time of our fathers, we would not have shared in the murder of the prophets.' **31** And so you testify against yourselves that you are the sons of those who murdered the prophets. **32** Go on, finish what your fathers started!

33 "You snakes! Brood of poisonous snakes! How can you escape being condemned to hell? **34** That is why I am sending you prophets, wise men, and teachers of the Scriptures.^{d} Some of them you will kill and crucify. Others you will whip in your synagogs and persecute from town to town. **35** In this way all the innocent blood shed on the earth will come upon you, from the blood of righteous Abel to the blood of Zechariah ˻the˼ son of Barachiah, whom you murdered between the sanctuary and the altar.^{e} **36** I tell you the truth, all these things will come upon this generation.

37 "Jerusalem, Jerusalem, you who murdered the prophets and stoned those who were sent to you, how often I wanted to bring your children together as a hen gathers her chicks under her wings, but you were not willing! **38** Now your

---

c- 16 In verses 16-19 the Greek preposition used here seems to imply more than just swearing "by" something. As verses 20-22 explain, swearing "by" something means that anything connected with that item is also included in the oath.

d- 34 Literally: "and scribes"; see 2:4 and its accompanying footnote.

e- 35 See Diagram #1 on page 430. The "sanctuary" included the Most Holy Place and the Holy Place. The "altar" is a reference to the "altar for burnt offering." Compare 2 Chronicles 24:20-22.

house will be left to you *a deserted place.* **39** For I tell you, you will never see Me again until you say, *'Blessed is He who comes in the Name of the Lord.' "*

24TH CHAPTER

The Destruction Of Jerusalem And The World—Mark 13:1-31; Luke 21:5-33

1 When Jesus left the Temple and was walking away, His disciples came to Him to show Him the buildings of the Temple. **2** Jesus said to them, "You see all these things, do you not? I tell you the truth, not one stone will be left on another here; every one will be torn down."

3 As Jesus was sitting on the Mount of Olives, His disciples came to Him privately and said, "Tell us, when will these things happen and what will be the miraculous sign which will tell us when You are coming back and when the world will come to an end?"

4 Jesus answered them, "Be careful not to let anyone deceive you. **5** For many will come using My Name and saying, 'I am the Christ [Messiah],' and will deceive many.

6 "You are going to hear of wars and rumors of wars. See that you do not become alarmed. It *must happen*, but that is not yet the end. **7** *Nation will fight against nation* and *kingdom against kingdom*, and there will be famines and earthquakes in various places. **8** But all these are only the beginning pains of childbirth. *a*

9 "Then they will hand you over to those who will make you suffer, and they will kill you, and all nations will hate you on account of My Name. **10** Then *many will fall* ₍from faith₎, *b* and they will betray one another and hate one another. **11** Many false prophets will arise and lead many people astray. **12** And because there will be more and more lawlessness, the love of most people will grow cold. **13** But that person who endures to the end will be saved.

14 "This Good News of the Kingdom will be preached all over the world as a testimony to all nations, and then the end will come.

15 "Daniel the prophet spoke of *the devastating abomination* *c* which would stand *in the sacred place.* *d* When you see it—let the reader take note *e* —**16** then let those in Judea flee to the mountains. **17** He who is on the roof should not come down to take things out of his house. **18** He who is in the field should not turn back to get his coat.

19 "Woe to the women who are pregnant and to those who are nursing babies in those days. **20** Pray that it may not be winter or a Sabbath when you flee.

---

38 Jer 12:7; 22:5   *39* Ps 118:25,26   *6* Dan 2:28   *7* 2 Chr 15:6; Is 19:2   *10* Dan 11:41
15 Dan 9:27; 11:31; 12:11

---

24 *a-* 8 The Greek word denotes "labor pains." As in childbirth, sharper pains will follow before the Savior comes in glory.

b- 10 See *SKANDALON* on page 545.

c- 15 A reference to Daniel 9:27 and 12:11, but not 11:31.

d- 15 Meaning the "Temple"; see Diagram #1 on page 430 and compare Exodus 25:8,9.

e- 15 Or "let the reader read with understanding."

21 For it will be a time of great *misery, such as has not happened from the beginning* of the world *until now*—and surely will never happen again. **22** And if that time had not been cut short, no one would be saved. But that time will be cut short for the sake of those whom He has chosen.

23 "At that time if anyone tells you, 'Look, here is Christ!' or 'There He is!' do not believe it, **24** because false christs [messiahs] and false *prophets* will *come and work* great *miraculous signs and wonderful proofs*[f] to deceive, if possible, even those whom God has chosen. **25** You see, I have told you this before it happens. **26** So when you are told, 'There He is in the wilderness!' do not go out; or 'Here He is in the inner rooms!' do not believe it. **27** For the coming of the Son of Man will be like lightning which starts in the east and flashes ⌊across the whole sky⌋ to the west. **28** Where the dead body is, there the vultures[g] will gather.

29 "Right after the misery of that time *the sun will turn dark, the moon will not give its light, the stars will fall from the sky*, and *the powers of heaven* will be shaken. **30** Then the miraculous sign announcing the Son of Man will appear in the sky, and then *all the groups of people on earth*[h] *will mourn* when they see *the Son of Man coming on the clouds in the sky* with power and great glory. **31** And He will send His angels[i] *with a loud trumpet call*, and they *will gather* His chosen ones *from the north, south, east, and west*,[j] *from one end of the sky to the other*.

32 "Learn from the illustration[k] of the fig tree: When its branch becomes tender and it sprouts leaves, you know summer is near. **33** So also, when you see all these things, you know that He is near, at your door.

34 "I tell you the truth, this kind of people[l] will not pass away until all these things take place. **35** Heaven and earth will pass away, but My words will never pass away."

Watch And Be Ready!—*Compare Mark 13:32-37; Luke 21:34-48*

36 "No one knows about that Day or Hour, not the angels in heaven, not even the Son, but only the Father.

37 "When the Son of Man comes, it will be exactly like the time of Noah. **38** For in the days before the flood people were eating and drinking, marrying and being married until the day that *Noah went into the ark*. **39** They did not become aware ⌊of what was happening⌋ until *the flood came* and swept them all away. That is how it will be when the Son of Man comes.

40 "At that time there will be two men in the field; one will be taken and the

---

21 *Dan 12:1*   **24** *Deut 13:1*   **29** *Is 13:10; 34:4; Ezek 32:7,8*   **30** *Dan 7:13; Zech 12:10,12*
31 *Deut 30:4; Is 27:13; Zech 2:6*   **38,39** *Gen 7:6,7*

---

f- 24 See MIRACULOUS SIGNS, WONDERFUL PROOFS, and MIRACLES on page 527.
g- 28 Or "eagles" (also at Lk. 17:37).
h- 30 Literally: "all the tribes of the land."
i- 31 Or "messengers."
j- 31 Literally: "from the four winds."
k- 32 Or "parable."
l- 34 Or "this generation."

other left. **41** Two women will be grinding at a mill; one will be taken and the other left.

42 "Therefore watch, because you do not know on which day your Lord is coming. **43** You are aware of the fact that if the homeowner had known at what time of the night the burglar was coming, he would have stayed awake and would not have let anyone break into his house. **44** Therefore you be ready also, because the Son of Man is coming when you do not expect Him.

45 "Who then is the faithful and sensible servant, whom the master has put in charge of his household slaves to give them their food at the right time? **46** Blessed is that servant whom his master finds doing this when he comes. **47** I tell you the truth, he will put him in charge of all his property. **48** But if that servant is wicked and says to himself, 'My master is staying away a long time,' **49** and he begins to beat his fellow servants and eats and drinks with the drunkards, **50** the master of that servant will come on a day when he is not expecting him and at a time unknown to him. **51** His master will cut him in pieces and assign him a place with the hypocrites. There they will weep and grind their teeth."

25TH CHAPTER

The Bridegroom Is Coming

1 "Then the Kingdom of heaven will be like ten bridesmaids*a* who took their lamps and went out to meet the bridegroom. **2** Five of them were foolish, and five were wise. **3** The foolish ⌊bridesmaids⌋ brought their lamps, but they took no ⌊olive⌋ oil. **4** The wise took flasks of oil with their lamps. **5** But the bridegroom delayed, and so the ⌊bridesmaids⌋ all dozed off to sleep.

6 "At midnight there was a shout: 'The bridegroom is here! Come out to meet him!' **7** Then all those bridesmaids woke up and got their lamps ready.

8 "The foolish said to the wise, 'Give us some of your oil because our lamps are going out.'

9 "But the wise ⌊bridesmaids⌋ answered, 'There will never be enough for us and for you. Rather, go to the dealers and buy some for yourselves.'

10 "While they were away buying it, the bridegroom came. The ⌊bridesmaids⌋ who were ready went in with him to the wedding, and the door was locked.

11 "Later the other bridesmaids also came and said, 'Lord, lord, open the door for us!'

12 " 'I tell you the truth,' he answered them, 'I do not know you!'

13 "Therefore keep awake, because you do not know the Day or the Hour."

Three Kinds Of Workers And Their Talents

14 "For ⌊the Kingdom of heaven is⌋ like a man going on a trip. He called his

---

25 *a*- 1 Literally: "virgins" (also in vv. 7 and 11).

servants and put his money into their hands. **15** He gave one man five talents,*b* another two talents, and another one talent, each according to his ability. Then he left.

"Immediately*c* **16** the one who received five talents went out and put them to work and made another five talents. **17** The one who had two talents did the same and made another two talents. **18** But the one who received one talent went out and dug a hole in the ground and hid his master's money.

19 "After a long time the master of those servants came and had them give an account. **20** The one who received five talents came and brought an additional five talents. 'Master,' he said, 'you gave me five talents. Look, I've made another five talents.'

21 " 'Well done, good and faithful servant!' his master replied. 'You proved you could be trusted with a few things; I will put you in charge of many things. Come and share your master's happiness.'

22 "The one who received two talents came and said, 'Master, you gave me two talents. Look, I've made another two talents.'

23 " 'Well done, good and faithful servant!' his master replied. 'You proved you could be trusted with a few things; I will put you in charge of many things. Come and share your master's happiness.'

24 "Then came also the one who had received the one talent. 'Master,' he said, 'I knew that you are a hard man. You harvest where you have not sown and gather where you have not scattered. **25** I was afraid, so I went out and hid your talent in the ground. Here is your money!'

26 " 'You wicked and lazy servant!' his master responded. 'So you knew that I harvest where I have not sown and gather where I have not scattered? **27** Then you should have invested my money with the bankers; and on my return, I would have received my money back with interest. **28** Take the talent away from him, and give it to the one who has the ten talents. **29** Whoever has anything will receive, and he will have more and more. And from him who does not have ⌊what he should have⌋, even what he has will be taken away. **30** Throw this good-for-nothing servant out into the outer darkness where there will be weeping and grinding of teeth.' "

Jesus Will Judge The World

31 "When the Son of Man *comes* in His glory *and all the* angels *with Him*, then He will sit on His throne of glory. **32** And all nations will be gathered before Him, and He will separate them from one another, as a shepherd separates the sheep from the goats, **33** and He will have the sheep stand at His right but the goats at His left.*d*

34 "Then the King will say to those at His right, 'Come, you whom My Father

---

31 Zech 14:5

---

b- 15 See MONEY, WEIGHTS, and MEASURES on page 328. In this parable the talents and their value are *not* the main point; the way in which one puts them to work is the primary point of the parable.

c- 15 Some English translations place "immediately" with the preceding verb in verse 15.

d- 33 Literally: "at His right but the goats at the left."

has blessed, inherit the Kingdom prepared for you from the time the world was created. **35** For I was hungry, and you gave Me something to eat; I was thirsty, and you gave Me a drink; I was a stranger, and you took Me into your homes; **36** naked, and you gave Me something to wear; sick, and you looked after Me; in prison, and you visited Me.'

37 "Then the righteous will ask Him, 'Lord, when did we see You hungry and · feed You, or thirsty and give You a drink? **38** When did we see You a stranger and take You into our homes, or naked and give You something to wear? **39** When did we see You sick or in prison and visit You?'

40 "And the King will answer them, 'I tell you the truth, anything you did for one of My brothers here, even the least important of them, you did for Me.'

41 "Then He will say to those at His left,*e* 'Go away from Me, you cursed ones, into the everlasting fire prepared for the devil and his angels. **42** For I was hungry, and you gave Me nothing to eat; thirsty, and you did not give Me a drink; **43** a stranger, and you did not take Me into your homes; naked, and you did not give Me anything to wear; sick and in prison, and you did not look after Me.'

44 "Then they also will ask, 'Lord, when did we see You hungry or thirsty or a stranger or naked or sick or in prison and didn't help You?'

45 "Then He will answer them, 'I tell you the truth, anything you did not do for one of these, even the least important of them, you did not do for Me.'

46 "Then *these* will go away to *everlasting* punishment, but the righteous *to everlasting life.*"

26TH CHAPTER

C. Passion, death, and resurrection (26:1–28:20)

The Plot—Mark 14:1,2; Luke 22:1,2; John 11:45-57

1 When Jesus finished saying all these things, He told His disciples, **2** "You know that after two days the Passover will be celebrated, and the Son of Man will be handed over to be crucified."

3 Then the ruling priests and the elders of the people met in the palace of the high priest, whose name was Caiaphas. **4** They plotted to arrest Jesus in an underhanded way and kill Him. **5** But they said, "Not during the festival, or there may be a riot among the people."

Mary Anoints Jesus—Mark 14:3-9; John 12:1-8

6 Jesus came to Bethany and went into the home of Simon the leper. **7** There

---

46 Dan 12:2

e- 41 Literally: "those at the left."

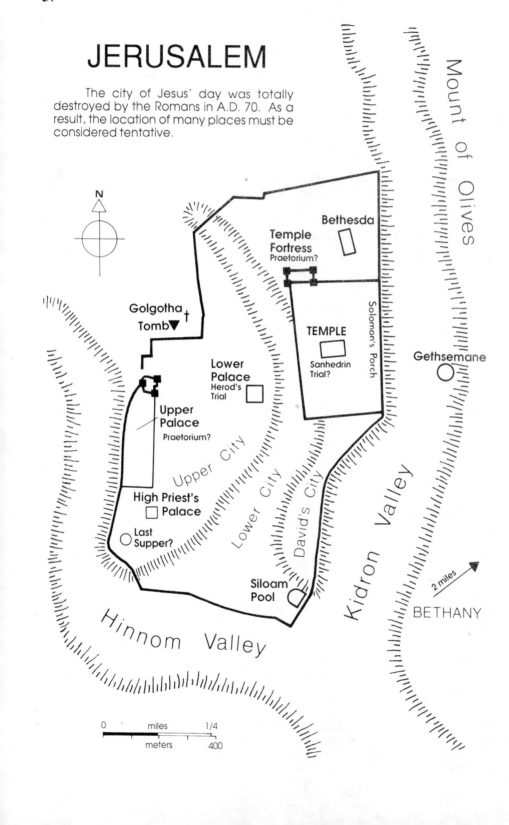

JERUSALEM

The city of Jesus' day was totally destroyed by the Romans in A.D. 70. As a result, the location of many places must be considered tentative.

N

Mount of Olives

Golgotha
Tomb ▼ †

Temple
Fortress
Praetorium?

Bethesda

Solomon's Porch

TEMPLE

Sanhedrin
Trial?

Gethsemane

Lower
Palace
Herod's
Trial

Upper
Palace
Praetorium?

Upper City

High Priest's
Palace

Lower City

David's City

Last
Supper?

Siloam
Pool

Kidron Valley

2 miles

BETHANY

Hinnom Valley

0   miles   1/4

meters   400

a woman came to Him with an alabaster jar of expensive perfume, and she poured it on His head while He was reclining at the table.

8 The disciples saw it and did not like it. They asked, "Why should there be such a waste? 9 This could have been sold for a high price and the money given to the poor."

10 Since He knew what was going on, Jesus asked them, "Why do you trouble the woman? She has done a beautiful thing*a* to Me. 11 For the poor you always have with you, but you are not always going to have Me. 12 She poured this perfume on My body to prepare Me for My burial. 13 I tell you the truth, wherever this Gospel is preached in the whole world, what this woman has done will also be told in memory of her."

Judas Plans To Betray Jesus—*Mark 14:10,11; Luke 22:3-6*

14 Then one of the Twelve, the one called Judas the man from Kerioth,*b* went to the high priests. 15 "What will you give me if I hand Him over to you?" he asked.

They *offered* him *30 pieces of silver.c* 16 And from then on he kept looking for a chance to betray Him.

The Passover—*Mark 14:12-17; Luke 22:7-17*

17 On the first of the Passover days of the Festival of Unleavened Bread, the disciples came to Jesus. "Where do You want us to get things ready for You to eat the Passover?" they asked.

18 He said, "Go into the city to a certain man and tell him: 'The Teacher says, "My time is near. I am going to celebrate the Passover with My disciples at your house." ' "

19 The disciples did as Jesus directed them and prepared the Passover.

20 When evening came He reclined at the table with the Twelve.

Who Is The Betrayer?—*Mark 14:18-21; Luke 22:21-23; John 13:21-30*

21 While they were eating, He said: "I tell you the truth, one of you is going to betray Me!"

22 Feeling deeply hurt, they asked Him one by one, "You don't mean me, do You, Lord?"

23 Jesus answered, "He who dips his hand into the bowl with Me is the one who will betray Me! 24 The Son of Man is going away as the Scriptures say He

---

15 *Zech 11:12*

---

26 *a*- 10 Literally: "a good work."

   b- 14 Literally: "Judas Iscariot"; see "*Iscariot*" in Glossary.

   c - 15 This particular amount represents the standard price for a slave who was gored (cf. Ex. 21:32) and was equivalent to the wages that a slave received for a six month period. In Zechariah 11:12,13 it represents a sum that is chintzy, demeaning, and insulting.

will, but woe to that man by whom the Son of Man is betrayed! It would be better for that man if he had never been born."

25 "You do not mean me, do You, Rabbi?" asked Judas, the one who was betraying Him.

"Yes, I do!"*d* He told him.

The Lord's Supper—Mark 14:22-26; Luke 22:18-20; 1 Corinthians 11:23-25

26 While they were eating, Jesus took bread and gave thanks.*e* He broke it and gave it to the disciples and said, "Take and eat; this is My body."

27 Then He took a cup and spoke a prayer of thanks. He gave it to them, saying, "Drink of it, all of you. **28** For this is My *blood of the 'last will and testament,'f* which is being poured out for many for the forgiveness of sins.

29 "I tell you, from now on I will not drink of this fruit of the vine until that day when I drink it in a new way with you in My Father's Kingdom."

30 After they sang a hymn,*g* they started out for the Mount of Olives.

"You Will Deny Me"—Mark 14:27-31; Luke 22:31-34; John 13:36-38

31 Then Jesus said to them, "Tonight you will all stumble ˌin your faithˌ*h* because of ˌwhat is going to happen toˌ Me. For it is written: 'I will *strike down the Shepherd, and the sheep of the flock will be scattered.*' **32** But after I have risen, I will go ahead of you to Galilee."

33 Peter answered Him, "Even if they all stumble ˌin their faith, because of ˌwhat happens toˌ You, I will never stumble."

34 "I tell you the truth," Jesus told him, "tonight before the rooster crows, you will deny Me three times."

35 Peter told Him, "Even if I have to die with You, I will never deny You!" All the other disciples said the same thing.

Gethsemane—Mark 14:32-42; Luke 22:39-46

36 Then Jesus went with the disciples to a place called Gethsemane and told them, "Sit down here while I go over there and pray."

37 Taking Peter and Zebedee's two sons with Him, He began to feel sad and troubled. **38** Then He said to them, "*My soul is so full of sorrow* that I am at the point of death. Remain here and stay awake with Me."

39 Going ahead a little, He fell down with His face to the ground and prayed, "My Father, if it is possible, let this cup pass away from Me, but let it not be as I want it but as You want it."

40 When He came back to the disciples, He found them asleep. He said to

---

28 Ex 24:8; Jer 31:32; Zech 9:11   31 Zech 13:7   38 Ps 42:5; 43:5

---

d- 25 Literally: "You have said it!"

e- 26 Or "spoke a blessing" if the text means to call upon God to bless a person or thing.

f- 28 See *DIATHĒKĒ* on page 531.

g- 30 Psalms 115 through 118.

h- 31 See *SKANDALON* on page 545. Occurs twice in verse 33.

Peter, "So you could not stay awake with Me one hour! [i] **41** Stay awake and pray that you may not be tempted. [j] The spirit is willing, but the flesh is weak."

42 Then He went away a second time and prayed, "My Father, if this ⌐cup⌐ cannot pass by without My drinking it, Your will be done."

43 He came again and found them asleep because they could not keep their eyes open.

44 After leaving them again, He went away and prayed the same prayer a third time. **45** Then He came back to the disciples and said [k] to them, "Are you going to sleep on now and take your rest? Now the time has come, and the Son of Man is being betrayed into the hands of sinners. **46** Get up, let us go. Look, here comes the one who is betraying Me!"

The Arrest—Mark 14:43-52; Luke 22:47-54a; John 18:1-14

47 While Jesus was still talking, Judas, one of the Twelve, came; and with him was a large crowd from the ruling priests and elders of the people. They were carrying swords and clubs, **48** and the traitor had given them a signal. He said, "The One I kiss is the Man. Grab Him."

49 Then Judas quickly stepped up to Jesus and said, "Greetings, Rabbi!" and kissed Him.

50 "Friend, why are you here?" [l] Jesus asked him.

Then the others came forward, took hold of Jesus, and arrested Him. **51** One of the men with Jesus reached for his sword and drew it. He struck the high priest's slave and cut off his ear. **52** Then Jesus told him, "Put your sword back in its place. For all who take the sword will die by the sword. **53** Or do you think I could not call on My Father to send right now more than 72,000 [twelve legions of] [m] angels to help Me? **54** How then are the Scriptures to be fulfilled which say that this must happen?"

55 At that time Jesus said to the crowd, "You came out to arrest Me with swords and clubs as if I were a robber! Day after day I sat and taught in the Temple, and you did not arrest Me. **56** But all this has happened so that what the prophets have written would be fulfilled."

Then all the disciples left Him and ran away.

The First Trial Before The Jewish Court—Mark 14:53-65

57 Those who arrested Jesus took Him to Caiaphas the high priest, where the scribes and the elders had been called together. **58** Peter followed Him at a distance until he came to the high priest's courtyard. He went inside and sat with the Temple guards to see how this would end.

---

i- 40 See footnote at verse 45.

j- 41 Literally: "that you do not come into temptation," that is, "that you do not fall prey to temptation" (also at Mk. 14:38; Lk. 22:40,46).

k - 45 Literally: "comes back . . . and says"; in verse 40 "came, found, said" literally read: "comes, finds, says," respectively. Compare Mark 14:37,41 where the same applies.

l- 50 Or "Friend, do what you have come for!"

m- 53 There were 6,000 troops in a Roman legion when it was at full strength; the text could then imply a figure as large as 72,000 angels.

59 The ruling priests and the whole Jewish council [Sanhedrin] kept on searching for false testimony against Jesus in order to kill Him, **60** but they did not find any, although many came forward with false testimony. At last two men came forward, **61** saying, "He said, 'I can tear down God's Temple and build it in three days.' "

62 The high priest stood up and asked Him, "Don't You have anything to say to this? What are these men testifying against You?"

63 But Jesus was silent.

Then the high priest said to Him, "Swear by the living God and tell us, are You the Christ, the Son of God?"

64 Jesus answered him, "I am,*ⁿ* but I tell you, from now on you will see *the Son of Man sitting at the right hand* of power and *coming on the clouds of heaven.*"

65 Then the high priest tore his robes and said, "He has blasphemed! Why do we need any more witnesses? You just heard the blasphemy. **66** What is your verdict?"

"He is guilty and deserves to die!" they answered.

67 Then they *spit* in His face and struck Him with their fists, and some slapped Him, **68** saying, "Prophesy, You Christ, and tell us: Who hit You?"

Peter Denies Jesus—Mark 14:66-72; Luke 22:54b-62; John 18:15-18, 25-27

69 Now Peter was sitting out in the courtyard. A maid came to him, saying, "You too were with Jesus the Galilean."

70 But he denied it in front of them all by saying, "I don't know what you're talking about."

71 As he went out to the entrance, another maid saw him, "He was with Jesus from Nazareth," she told those who were there.

72 Again Peter denied and swore, "I don't know the Man!"

73 After a little while the men who were standing there approached Peter and said, "It's obvious you're also one of them. Why, your accent gives you away!"

74 Then he began to curse and swear, "I don't know the Man!" Just then the rooster crowed, **75** and Peter remembered that Jesus had said, "Before the rooster crows, you will deny Me three times." And he went outside and wept bitterly.

27TH CHAPTER

The End Of Judas

1 Early in the morning all the ruling priests and the elders of the people decided to kill Jesus. **2** They bound Him, led Him away, and handed Him over to Pilate the governor.

3 When Judas, who betrayed Him, saw that Jesus was condemned, he felt

---

64 Ps 110:1; Dan 7:13　　　*67 Is 50:6*

n- 64 Literally: "You say."

sorry and brought the 30 pieces^a of silver back to the high priests and elders. 4 He said, "I have sinned by betraying innocent blood."

They said, "What do we care? That's your problem."

5 Then he threw the money into the Temple and went away and hanged himself.

6 When the high priests took the money, they said, "It is not right to put it into the Temple treasury since it is blood money." 7 So they decided to use it to buy the potter's field for the burial of strangers. 8 That is why that field has ever since been called the Field of Blood. 9 Then what the prophet Jeremiah said was fulfilled: "They *took the thirty shekels of silver, the price of Him on whom* the children of Israel *had set a value,*^{b} 10 *and* they *gave them for the potter's field, as the Lord directed me.*"

Before Pilate—*Mark 15:1-5; Luke 23:1-4; John 18:28-38*

11 Jesus stood before the governor. "Are You the King of the Jews?" the governor asked Him.

"Yes, I am,"^{c} Jesus answered.

12 While the ruling priests and elders were accusing Him, He said nothing. 13 Then Pilate asked Him, "Don't You hear how many charges they are bringing against You?"

14 But Jesus did not answer him in regard to a single thing that was said, so that the governor was very much surprised.

Barabbas—*Mark 15:6-15; Luke 23:17-25; John 18:39,40*

15 Now at every festival the governor used to free one prisoner whom the crowd wanted. 16 At that time there was a well-known prisoner by the name of Barabbas. 17 So when the people had gathered, Pilate asked them, "Whom do you want me to set free for you: Barabbas, or Jesus who is called Christ?" 18 For he knew that they had handed Jesus over to him because they were jealous.

19 While he was sitting on the judgment seat, his wife sent someone to tell him, "Let that righteous Man alone, because I suffered much in a dream last night^d on account of Him."

20 But the ruling priests and elders persuaded the people to ask for Barabbas and to have Jesus killed.

21 The governor asked them, "Which of the two do you want me to set free for you?"

They said, "Barabbas."^{e}

9,10 Jer 32:6-9; Zech 11:12,13

---

27 *a-* 3 See footnote at 26:15.
   b- 9 Literally: "whom they priced from the sons of Israel."
   c- 11 Literally: "You say it!"
   d- 19 Literally: "today"; the previous night was considered part of that day.
   e- 21 Made up of two Aramaic words: "*bar*" ("son") and "*abba*" ("father"), meaning "son of the father." Could the presence of one named *Barabbas* imply that the "sons (and daughters) of the heavenly Father" went free as the "Son of the heavenly Father" went to the cross for them?

22 "Then what should I do with Jesus who is called Christ?" Pilate asked them.

"Crucify Him!"*f* they all said.

23 "Why, what wrong has He done?" he asked.

But they began to shout even louder: "Crucify Him!"

24 When he saw that he was not getting anywhere, but that a riot was breaking out instead, Pilate took water and washed his hands before the crowd. "I am innocent of this Man's blood,"*g* he said. "See to it yourselves!"

25 And all the people answered, "His blood be on us and on our children."

26 Then he released Barabbas to them, but Jesus he whipped*h* and handed over to be crucified.*i*

"Hail, King!"—Mark 15:16-19; John 19:1-3

27 Then the governor's soldiers took Jesus into the palace*j* and gathered the whole troop of soldiers around Him. **28** They took off His clothes and put a scarlet robe on Him. **29** They twisted some thorns into a crown, placed it on His head, and put a stick in His right hand. Then they knelt before Him and made fun of Him by saying: "Hail, King of the Jews!" **30** After having *spit* on Him, they took the stick and began to beat Him on the head.

"They Crucified Him"—Mark 15:20-32; Luke 23:26-38; John 19:16b-24

31 After they had made fun of Him, they took off the robe and put His own clothes on Him. Then they took Him away to crucify Him.

32 As they were going out, they found a man from Cyrene by the name of Simon. They forced him to carry His cross.

33 They came to a place called Golgotha,*k* which means "Place of the Skull." **34** *They offered Him a drink* of wine mixed with *gall*, but when He tasted it, He refused to drink it. **35** After they had crucified Him, *they divided His clothes among them by throwing dice.*l* **36** Then they sat down there and kept watch over Him. **37** Above His head they placed the accusation that had been written against Him. It read:

THIS IS JESUS
THE KING OF THE JEWS.

---

30 Is 50:6   34 Ps 69:21   35 Ps 22:18

---

f- 22 Literally: "Let Him be crucified!" (also in v. 23).

g- 24 Some manuscripts read: "of the blood of this just Man."

h- 26 Literally: "scourged," that is, a severe beating with a whip which could cause extensive bleeding and often led to death; the same applies to John 19:1, for example, where a different Greek word is used.

i- 26 The Greek word order is preserved to represent Matthew's *chiasmatic* arrangement, that is, an A-B-B-A structure ("released-Barabbas-Jesus-whipped"). See GRAMMATIC/POETIC STRUCTURES THAT CONVEY TEXTUAL MEANINGS on page 558.

j- 27 Greek: "*praitōrion*" (Latin: "*praetorium*"); exact location uncertain. See Map of JERUSALEM on page 57.

k- 33 "*Golgotha*" is Aramaic; its Latin form is "*Calvary*."

l- 35 Literally: "lots."

38 At that time they crucified two robbers with Him, one at His right and the other at His left. *m*

D
⚹ **39** Those who passed by *ridiculed* Him, *shaking their heads* **40** and saying, "You who are going to tear down the Temple and build it in three days—save Yourself. If You are the Son of God, come down from the cross." **41** The ruling priests together with the scribes and elders *made fun of* Him in the same way, saying, **42** "He saved others—He cannot save Himself. He is Israel's King—He
D
⚹ should come down from the cross now, and we shall believe Him. **43** *He has put His trust in God—let God rescue Him now* if He so wishes, for He said, 'I am the Son of God.' " **44** In the same way the robbers who were crucified with Him also were *insulting* Him.

Jesus Dies—Mark 15:33-41; Luke 23:44-49; John 19:28-30

45 At noon darkness came over the whole land and lasted until three in the
D
⚹ afternoon. **46** About three o'clock Jesus cried out with a loud voice, saying, *"Eli, Eli, lema sabachthani?"* which means, "My God, My God, why did You forsake Me?" **47** When they heard Him say that, some of those standing there said, "He's calling Elijah." **48** Immediately one of the men ran, took a sponge,
D
⚹ soaked it in *sour wine*, put it on a stick, *n* and *offered Him a drink.* **49** The others said, "Let's see if Elijah comes to save Him."

50 Then Jesus cried out once again with a loud voice and gave up His spirit.

51 Just then the ⌊inner⌋ curtain in the Temple*o* was torn in two from top to bottom. The earth shook and the rocks were split. **52** The tombs were opened, and the bodies of many believers [saints] who had been sleeping were brought back to life. **53** They came out of the tombs after He had risen and went into the Holy City where they appeared to many people.

54 Now when the captain and those watching Jesus with him saw the earthquake and the other things happening, they were terrified. "Certainly this was the Son of God!" they said.

55 Many women were there watching *from a distance.* They had followed Jesus from Galilee to support*p* Him. **56** Among them were Mary from Magdala, Mary the mother of James and Joseph, and the mother*q* of Zebedee's sons.

Jesus Is Buried—Mark 15:42-47; Luke 23:50-56; John 19:38-42

57 In the evening there came a rich man from Arimathea by the name of Joseph, who had also become a disciple of Jesus. **58** He went to Pilate and asked for the body of Jesus. Then Pilate ordered that it be given to him.

59 Joseph took the body, wrapped it in a clean linen cloth, **60** and laid it in his

---

39 Ps 22:7; 109:25   *41 Ps 22:6,7*   *43 Ps 22:8*   *44 Ps 22:6,7*   *46 Ps 22:1*   *48 Ps 69:21*
55 Ps 38:11

---

m- 38 See Mark 15:27 and its accompanying footnote.
n- 48 Literally: "reed."
o- 51 See Diagram #2 on page 438.
p- 55 Compare Luke 8:3.
q- 56 Some suggest that this may have been Salome (cf. Mk. 15:40).

own new tomb that he had cut in the rock. After rolling a large stone against the door of the tomb, he went away. **61** Mary from Magdala and the other Mary were there, sitting opposite the tomb.

The Guard

62 The next day—the Saturday after the day of preparation*ʳ*—the ruling priests and Pharisees met with Pilate. **63** They said, "Sir, we remember how that imposter said while He was still alive, 'After three days I will rise.' **64** Therefore order the tomb to be made secure until the third day, to keep His disciples from coming to steal Him and saying to the people, 'He rose from the dead.' And so the last deception will be worse than the first."

65 "Take a guard," Pilate told them; "go and make it as secure as you know how."

66 So they went out and secured the tomb by sealing the stone and setting the guard.

28TH CHAPTER

The Easter Resurrection—Mark 16:1-8; Luke 24:1-12; John 20:1-10

1 After the Sabbath, as Sunday*ᵃ* was dawning, Mary from Magdala and the other Mary went to look at the tomb.

2 There was a great earthquake, for an angel of the Lord came down from heaven, went ˌto the tombˌ, rolled the stone away, and sat on it. **3** He was as bright as lightning, and his clothes were as white as snow. **4** The guards were so afraid of him that they shook and became like dead men.

5 The angel said to the women, "Don't be afraid any longer; I know you are looking for Jesus, who was crucified. **6** He is not here. He has risen as He said. Come, see the place where He was lying. **7** And go quickly, tell His disciples, 'He has risen from the dead. To be sure, He is going ahead of you into Galilee. There you will see Him.' Take note that I have told you."

8 They hurried away from the tomb*ᵇ* and ran with fear and great joy to tell His disciples.

9 Just then Jesus met them and said, "Good morning!" They went up to Him, took hold of His feet, and worshiped Him.

10 Then Jesus said to them, "Don't be afraid any longer! Go, tell My brothers to go to Galilee, and there they will see Me."

The Guards

11 While the women were on their way, some of the guards went into the city and told the high priests everything that had happened.

---

r- 62 Literally: "And the next day, which is after the preparation"; the next day—a reference to the most solemn Sabbath of the Jewish religious year; for an explanation of "the day of preparation" see John 19:31 and its accompanying footnote.

28 *a-* 1 Literally: "the first day of the week."

b- 8 Literally: "they went away quickly" (cf. v. 7).

12 These men met with the elders and agreed on a plan. They gave the soldiers a large sum of money 13 and told them, "You are to say, 'His disciples came at night and stole Him while we were sleeping.' 14 And if the governor hears about it, we will persuade him and see that you have nothing to worry about."

15 They took the money and did as they were told. And their story has been spread among the Jews to this day.

"Go And Make Disciples!"

16 The eleven disciples went to the mountain in Galilee where Jesus had told them to go. 17 When they saw Him, they worshiped Him; but some doubted.

18 When Jesus came near, He spoke to them. He said, "All authority has been given to Me in heaven and on earth. 19 Go and make disciples of all people by baptizing them in the Name of the Father and of the Son and of the Holy Spirit 20 and, by teaching them to pay close attention to everything I have commanded you. And remember—I am with you always, until the end of time."*c*

---

c- 20 Literally: "until the end of this age."

THE GOOD NEWS [GOSPEL] AS TOLD BY
MARK[a]

1ST CHAPTER

A. Theme (1:1) and introduction (1:2-13)

John Prepares The Way—*Matthew 3:1-12; Luke 3:1-18; John 1:19-28*

1 The beginning of the Good News of Jesus Christ,[b] the Son of God.
2 It is written in the prophet Isaiah:[c]

> Look! I am sending My messenger ahead of You
>   to prepare the way for You.
> **3** A voice is calling out[d] in the wilderness:
>   "Prepare the way for the Lord;
>   make the paths straight for Him."

4 John the Baptizer lived in the wilderness and preached that people should repent and be baptized for the forgiveness of sins. **5** All Judea and all the people of Jerusalem kept coming out to him. As they confessed their sins, he baptized them in the Jordan River.

6 John was dressed in camel's hair and wore a leather belt around his waist, and he ate locusts and wild honey.

7 He preached: "The One who is mightier than I is coming after me. I am not worthy to bend down and untie His sandal straps.[e] **8** I have baptized you with water. He will baptize you with the Holy Spirit."

John Baptizes Jesus—*Matthew 3:13-17; Luke 3:21,22; compare John 1:29-34*

9 It was in those days that Jesus came from Nazareth in Galilee and was

---

2 Mal 3:1   3 Is 40:3

---

1 *a*   Mark, the author, possibly leaves his signature at 14:51, 52. (Cf. also Col. 4:10; 2 Tim. 4:11.) Mark is often referred to as John Mark.

  b- 1 The Greek-based English name "Jesus" and its Hebrew-based counterpart "Joshua" both mean "Savior, Helper, the LORD saves, YAHWEH helps." The Greek-based English name "Christ" and its Hebrew-based counterpart "Messiah" both mean the "Anointed One" or the "Chosen One." In essence the name CHRIST JESUS means the "Chosen Savior."

  c- 2 A combined prophecy, found partly in Isaiah 40:3 and partly in Malachi 3:1.

  d- 3 Or "shouting."

  e- 7 This was ordinarily a slave's duty.

baptized by John in the Jordan. **10** Just as He came out of the water, He *f* saw heaven torn open and the Spirit coming down on Him as a dove. **11** And a voice from heaven said, "You are *My Son*, whom I love. *I am delighted* with You."

The Devil Tempts Jesus—Matthew 4:1-11; Luke 4:1-13

12 Then the Spirit drove Him out into the wilderness, **13** and He was in the wilderness for 40 days while Satan continued to tempt Him. He was there with the wild animals, and the angels took care of Him.

B. Galilean period (1:14–9:50)
1. Around the Sea of Galilee (1:14–5:43)

"Come, Follow Me"—Matthew 4:18-22; Luke 5:1-11; John 1:35-51

14 After John had been put in prison, Jesus went to Galilee and preached the Good News of God: **15** "The time has come, and the Kingdom of God is near. Repent, and believe the Gospel."

16 As He was walking along the Sea of Galilee, He saw Simon and Simon's brother Andrew throwing a net into the sea, for they were fishermen. **17** Jesus told them, "Come, follow Me, and I will make you fishers of men." **18** Immediately they left their nets and followed Him.

19 Going on a little farther, He saw James the ⌊son⌋ of Zebedee and his brother John in their boat, mending the nets. **20** And immediately He called them, and they left their father Zebedee with the hired men in the boat and followed Him.

Jesus Drives Out A Demon—Luke 4:31-37

21 Then they went to Capernaum. The next Sabbath Jesus went into the synagog and began to teach. **22** The people were amazed at the way He taught, because He continued to teach them as one who had authority and not as the scribes *g* taught.

23 At that time there was a man in their synagog with an unclean spirit, and he cried out, **24** "What do we have in common with You, Jesus from Nazareth! Have You come to destroy us? I know who You are—the Holy One of God."

25 Jesus spoke sharply to him: "Be quiet, and come out of him." **26** The unclean spirit threw the man into convulsions and with a loud shriek came out of him.

---

11 Ps 2:7; Is 42:1

f- 10 Or "he," if a reference to John the Baptizer (cf. Jn. 1:32,33).

g- 22 These were the Bible scholars of Jesus' day. Their work and responsibilities varied greatly from one to another. These areas included making handwritten copies of the Old Testament, interpreting and following the Mosaic guidelines of the Pentateuch (Five Books of Moses), formulating oral laws, teaching God's people in classroom situations, etc. In short, the scribes were considered authorities on the Jewish religion. Compare Ezra 7:6,10.

27 They were all so amazed that they debated with one another: "What is this? This is a new teaching which has authority behind it! He gives orders to the unclean spirits, and they obey Him."

28 The news about Him spread quickly everywhere throughout the surrounding region of Galilee.

Simon Peter's Mother-In-Law—*Matthew 8:14-18; Luke 4:38-41*

29 Immediately after leaving the synagog they went into the home of Simon and Andrew. James and John went with them. 30 Simon's mother-in-law was down in bed with a fever, and the first thing they did was to tell Him about her. 31 He went to her, took her hand, and helped her get up. The fever left her,*h* and she began to wait on them.

32 In the evening when the sun had set, the people brought to Him all the sick and those possessed by demons. 33 The whole town had gathered at His door. 34 He healed many who were suffering from various sicknesses and drove out many demons, but He would not allow the demons to speak, because they knew who He was.

Preaching In Galilee—*Matthew 4:23-25; Luke 4:42-44*

35 In the morning, long before daylight, Jesus got up and went out to a lonely place, and there He prayed. 36 Simon and those who were with him searched for Him. 37 When they found Him, they told Him, "Everyone is looking for You."

38 "Let us go somewhere else," He told them, "to the small towns that are near, so that I may preach there also, since this is why I have come."

39 He went and preached in their synagogs everywhere in Galilee and drove out the demons.

Jesus Heals A Leper—*Matthew 8:1-4; Luke 5:12-14*

40 Then a leper came to Him, begging Him on his knees, and saying, "If You want to, You can make me clean."

41 Jesus felt sorry for him, and stretching out His hand He touched him. "I want to," He said to him. "Be clean!"

42 Immediately the leprosy left him, and he was made clean.

43 Then Jesus sent him away quickly with a stern warning: 44 "Be careful not to say anything to anyone, but go, *show yourself to the priest,i* and offer the sacrifices for your cleansing which Moses commanded, to show them that you are well."

45 But when he had left, he began to talk so much and to spread the news so widely that, as a result, Jesus could no longer go openly into a town. Instead He

---

44 Lev 13:7,49

---

h- 31 Some of the older manuscripts and early translations read: "Immediately the fever left her."
i- 44 That is, the healed leper was to show himself to the priest so that he could be examined and then be declared "clean."

stayed out in lonely places, and still the people kept coming to Him from everywhere.

2ND CHAPTER

Jesus Forgives Sins—Matthew 9:1-8; Luke 5:17-26

1 Later Jesus came back to Capernaum, and after a few days people heard that He was home. 2 Such a large number of people gathered*a* that there was no room, not even in front of the door. He was speaking the word to them.

3 Then some people came and brought Him a paralyzed man, carried by four men. 4 But since they could not bring him to Jesus because of the crowd, they opened up the roof over the place where Jesus was. And after they had dug an opening, they let down the bed on which the paralytic was lying.

5 When He saw their faith, Jesus said to the paralytic, "Son, your sins are forgiven."

6 There were some scribes sitting there, and they thought to themselves: 7 "Why does He talk this way? He is blaspheming. Who but God alone can forgive sins?"

8 Immediately Jesus knew in His spirit what they were thinking. He asked them, "Why do you have these thoughts in your hearts? 9 Is it easier to say to this paralyzed man, 'Your sins are forgiven,' or to say, 'Get up, take your bed, and walk'? 10 I want you to know that the Son of Man*b* has authority on earth to forgive sins." Then He said to the paralyzed man, 11 "I tell you, get up, take your bed, and go home."

12 The man got up, immediately took his bed, and walked out before all of them, so that they were all amazed and praised God. "Never have we seen anything like this," they said.

Matthew [Levi]—Matthew 9:9-13; Luke 5:27-32

13 Again Jesus went out to the seashore. All the people continued coming to Him, and He continued teaching them.

14 As He passed by, He saw Levi the ₁son₁ of Alphaeus, sitting in the tax booth. "Follow Me," He told him. He got up and followed Him.

15 Later, as Jesus was reclining at the table in Matthew's*c* home, many tax collectors and sinners were eating with Jesus and His disciples, because there were many who followed Him. 16 When the scribes who were Pharisees saw Him eating with sinners and tax collectors, they asked His disciples, "Why in the world does He eat with tax collectors and sinners?"

17 Jesus heard them and answered: "Those who are healthy do not need a

---

2 *a-* 2 Some of the older manuscripts and early translations read: "Immediately such a large number of people gathered . . . ."

b- 10 See "Son of Man" in Glossary.

c- 15 Literally: "his."

doctor, but those who are sick. I did not come to call righteous people, but sinners."

Jesus Is Questioned About Fasting—*Matthew 9:14-17; Luke 5:33-39*

18 John's disciples and the Pharisees, who fasted regularly, came to Jesus. They said to Him, "John's disciples and the disciples of the Pharisees fast. Why is it that Your disciples do not fast?"

19 Jesus said to them, "The friends of the bridegroom cannot fast while the bridegroom is with them, can they? As long as they have the bridegroom with them, they cannot fast. 20 But the time will come when the bridegroom will be taken away from them, and then at that time they will fast.

21 "No one sews a piece of unshrunk cloth on an old garment; otherwise, the new patch will tear away some of the old cloth, and the hole will become worse. 22 No one pours new wine into old wineskins;*d* otherwise, the wine will burst the skins, and both the wine and the skins will be lost. Rather, new wine has to be poured into fresh skins."

Lord Of The Sabbath—*Matthew 12:1-8; Luke 6:1-5*

23 Once Jesus was going through the grainfields on a Sabbath. As the disciples walked along, they began to pick the heads of grain.

24 The Pharisees asked Him, "Look, why are they doing something which is not right to do on the Sabbath?"

25 Jesus asked them, "Haven't you ever read what David did when he and his companions were in need and became hungry—26 how he went into the House of God when Abiathar was high priest, and ate the *loaves set out ⌊before God⌋*, which only the priests had the right to eat, and how he also gave some to his companions?"

27 Then He added, "The Sabbath was made for man, not man for the Sabbath. 28 For this reason the Son of Man is Lord also of the Sabbath."

3RD CHAPTER

The Shriveled Hand—*Matthew 12:9-15a; Luke 6:6-11*

1 Then He went again into a synagog, and there was a man with a shriveled hand. 2 They were watching Him closely to see whether He would heal him on a Sabbath, because they were attempting to find something of which to accuse Him.

3 He told the man with the shriveled hand, "Stand up and come forward." 4 Then He asked them, "Is it right on the Sabbath to do good or to do evil, to save a life or to kill?"

---

26 *Lev 24:5-8; 1 Sam 21:6*

---

d- 22 Containers made from the skins of certain animals.

But they remained silent. **5** When He looked around at them, He felt angry as well as sorry because their minds were closed.[a] Then He told the man, "Stretch out your hand." He stretched it out, and his hand was made normal again.

6 Then the Pharisees left and immediately started plotting with Herod's supporters[b] against Jesus as to how they might kill Him.

Many Are Healed—*Luke 6:17-19*

7 Jesus went away with His disciples to the seashore. A large crowd from Galilee followed Him. There was also a large crowd from Judea, **8** from Jerusalem, from Idumea, from the other side of the Jordan, and from the area of Tyre and Sidon who heard about everything that He was doing and came to Him. **9** To keep the crowd from crushing Him He told His disciples to have a small boat ready for Him. **10** He healed so many that all who had diseases rushed up to Him in order to touch Him. **11** Whenever the unclean spirits saw Him, they would fall down before Him and shout, "You are the Son of God!" **12** But He gave them strict orders not to reveal who He was.

Twelve Apostles—*Matthew 10:1-4; Luke 6:13-16*

13 He went up into the hills and called those whom He wanted, and they came to Him. **14** He appointed twelve[c] to be with Him and to be sent out by Him to preach **15** and to have authority to drive out demons.

16 He appointed the Twelve: Simon (to whom He gave the name Peter); **17** James the ⌞son⌟ of Zebedee and John the brother of James (to them He gave the name Boanerges, which means "Thunderbolts"[d]); **18** Andrew, Philip, Bartholomew, Matthew, Thomas, James the ⌞son⌟ of Alphaeus, Thaddaeus, Simon the Zealot, **19** and Judas the man from Kerioth,[e] who also betrayed Him.

Power Over A Demon—*Matthew 12:22-32; Luke 11:14-23*

20 Then Jesus came into a house. Again such a crowd gathered that Jesus and those with Him could not eat. **21** When His family heard about it, they went to take charge of Him, because they were saying, "He's out of His mind!"

22 The scribes who had come down from Jerusalem said, "Beelzebul is in Him," and "The ruler of the demons helps Him drive out demons."

23 He called them and said to them by way of illustration:[f] "How can Satan

---

3 *a*- 5 Literally: "because of the hardness of their heart"; a hardened heart leads to a closed or stubborn mind (cf. Ex. 4:21).

b- 6 See Matthew 22:16 and its accompanying footnote "b."

c- 14 Some manuscripts and early translations add: "whom He called apostles."

d- 17 Literally: "Sons of Thunder."

e- 19 Literally: "Judas Iscariot"; see *Iscariot* in Glossary.

f- 23 Literally: "said to them in parables."

drive out Satan? **24** If a kingdom is divided against itself, that kingdom cannot stand. **25** And if a house is divided against itself, that house can never stand. **26** And so if Satan rebels against himself and is divided, he cannot stand, but his end has come.

27 "No one can go into a strong man's house and take away his goods without first tying up*g* the strong man. After that he will rob his house.

28 "I tell you the truth, anything that people do will be forgiven, even their sinful slanders, though they be ever so many. **29** But anyone who slanders the Holy Spirit will never be forgiven. Yes, he is guilty of an everlasting sin." **30** He said this because they had said, "He has an unclean spirit."

The Mother And Brothers Of Jesus—*Matthew 12:46-50; Luke 8:19-21*

31 Just then*h* His mother and His brothers came. They stood outside and sent someone to Him to ask Him to come out. **32** The crowd sitting around Jesus told Him, "Look, Your mother and Your brothers are outside looking for You."

33 "Who are My mother and My brothers?" He asked them. **34** Then looking around at those who sat in a circle around Him, He said, "Look, here are My mother and My brothers. **35** Whoever does God's will, that person is ⌊in reality⌋ My brother and sister and mother."

4TH CHAPTER

The Sower—*Matthew 13:1-23; Luke 8:4-15*

1 Again Jesus began to teach by the seashore. The crowd that gathered around Him was so very large that He stepped into a boat and sat in it on the sea, while all the people were on the shore, facing the sea. **2** Then He used parables to teach them many things.

In His teaching He said to them: **3** "Listen! A sower went out to sow. **4** As he was sowing, some seed fell along the road, and the birds came and devoured it. **5** Some seed fell on rocky ground, where it did not have much soil. Because the soil was not deep, the seed came up quickly. **6** When the sun rose, it was scorched, and—because it did not have deep roots—it withered. **7** Some seed fell among thorns. The thorns grew up and choked it, and it produced no grain. **8** But some seed fell on good ground. It came up, grew, and produced grain, thirty, sixty, and a hundred times as much as was sown." **9** He added, "The one who has ears to hear, let him listen!"

10 When He was alone, the Twelve and the others around Him asked Him about the parables.

11 He answered them, "You are given the privilege of knowing the secret of the Kingdom of God, but to those on the outside everything comes in parables—

---

g - 27 Literally: "except he first bind" (cf. Rev. 20:2).

h - 31 Meaning that the two events recorded in verses 21-30 and 31-35 were taking place at the same time.

12   *with the result that they may*
            see clearly and yet not comprehend,
            hear clearly and yet not understand,
            so that they never turn to Me
            and so are never forgiven.

13 "Don't you understand this parable?" He asked them. "Then how will you understand any of the parables?

14 "The sower sows the word. 15 And these are the ones along the road where the word is sown: as soon as they hear it, Satan comes and takes away the word that was sown in them. 16 These are the ones who are sown on rocky ground where the same thing happens: as soon as they hear the word, they immediately welcome it with joy, 17 but it does not take deep root in them. They believe for a while. But when the word brings them trouble or persecution, they immediately fall ⌊from faith⌋.*a* 18 The others are the ones who are sown among the thorns: they hear the word, 19 but the worries of the world, the deceitful pleasure of riches, and the desires for other things come in and choke the word, and it produces nothing. 20 The rest are the ones who are sown on good ground: they continue to hear the word, welcome it, and go on producing good things, thirty, sixty, and a hundred times as much as was sown."

A Lamp And A Lampstand—Matthew 5:14-16; Luke 11:33

21 He said to them: "You do not get out a lamp to put it under a container or under a bed, do you? Shouldn't it ⌊rather⌋ be put on a lampstand? 22 For something is secret only to be revealed and hidden only to come into the open. 23 The one who has ears to hear, let him listen!"

24 He continued to tell them: "Be careful what you hear! The measure with which you measure will be used for you. Yes, you will receive even more. 25 For if a person has something, he will be given more. But if he does not have what he should have, even what he has will be taken away from him."

Seed Growing By Itself

26 He said, "The Kingdom of God is like this: A man scatters seed on the ground. 27 While he sleeps by night and is awake by day, the seed sprouts and grows, although he does not know how. 28 The ground produces grain by itself, first the green blade, then the head, then the full wheat in the head. 29 As soon as the grain is ready, he *swings the sickle, because harvesttime has come.*"

The Mustard Seed—Matthew 13:31,32; Luke 13:18,19

30 He asked, "To what can we compare the Kingdom of God, or how should we picture it? 31 It is like a mustard seed, which when sown on the ground is a

---

12 *Is 6:9,10*   29 *Joel 3:13*

4 *a*- 17 See *SKANDALON* on page 545.

very small seed[b] among all the seeds on earth. **32** But when it is sown, it comes up and becomes the largest of all the garden plants. It grows such large branches that *the birds of the air can nest in* its *shade."*

33 He used many parables like these to speak as much of the word as they were able to understand. **34** He did not speak to them without using a parable. But when He was alone with His disciples, He fully explained everything to them.

Wind And Water Obey Him—*Matthew 8:23-27; Luke 8:22-25*

35 In the evening of that day Jesus said to His disciples, "Let us cross over to the other side."

36 Then after dismissing the crowd,[c] they took Jesus, just as He was, with them in the boat. There were other boats with Him.

37 Then a violent storm came up, and the waves dashed into the boat so that it was quickly filling up. **38** Meanwhile, He was in the back of the boat, sleeping on the cushion.

They woke Him and said to Him, "Teacher, don't You care that we're going to drown?"

39 He got up and ordered the wind to stop. "Hush!" He said to the sea. "Be still!" And the wind quieted down, and it became very calm.

40 He asked them, "Why are you so afraid? Have you still not learned to trust?"

41 They were struck with great awe, and they asked one another, "Who then is this Person? Even the wind and the sea obey Him."

5TH CHAPTER

The Gergesenes—*Matthew 8:28-34; Luke 8:26-39*

1 Then they came to the other side of the sea into the region of the Gergesenes.[a] **2** Just as He stepped out of the boat, a man with an unclean spirit came out of the burial caves and met Him. **3** He lived in these burial caves. No one could bind him any longer, not even with a chain. **4** He had often been bound with chains on ¸his¸ hands and feet, but he had torn the handcuffs apart and had ground to pieces the chains on his feet, and nobody was strong enough to control him. **5** Continually, night and day, he was shrieking in the burial caves and in the hills and bruising himself with stones.

6 When he saw Jesus at a distance, he ran, bowed down before Him, **7** and shouted at the top of his voice, "What do we have in common, Jesus, Son of the Most High God! Swear to me by God that You will not torture me." **8** (For

---

32 Ps 104:12; Ezek 17:23; 31:6

---

b- 31 See Matthew 13:32 and its accompanying footnote.

c- 36 Or "Leaving the crowd behind."

5 *a*- 1 Gergesa was a small village in the territory of Hippus, north of the city of Hippus. It was a part of the area of the Decapolis [Ten Towns], a federation of *Greek* towns. Some of the older manuscripts and early translations have *Gadarenes*; others *Gerasenes*.

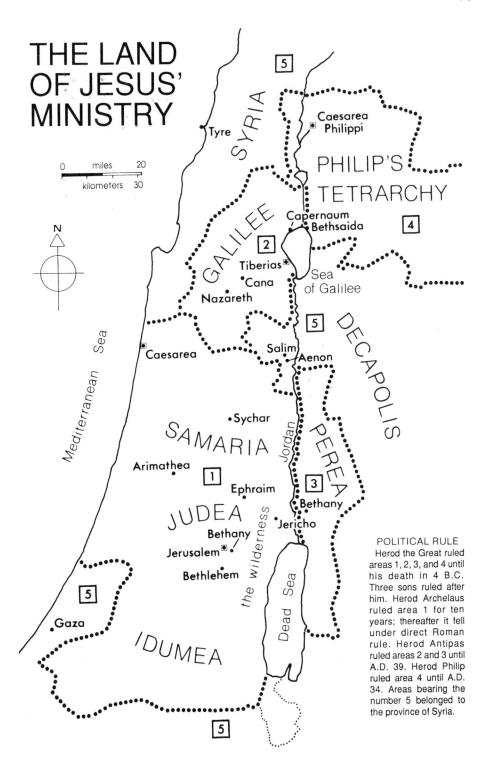

THE LAND OF JESUS' MINISTRY

0 miles 20

kilometers 30

N

Tyre

SYRIA

Caesarea Philippi

PHILIP'S TETRARCHY

5

Capernaum
Bethsaida

GALILEE

4

2

Tiberias

Cana

Nazareth

Sea of Galilee

DECAPOLIS

Mediterranean Sea

Caesarea

Salim

Aenon

5

Sychar

SAMARIA

Jordan

PEREA

Arimathea

1

Ephraim

JUDEA

3

Bethany

Jericho

Bethany

Jerusalem

Bethlehem

the wilderness

Dead Sea

5

Gaza

IDUMEA

5

POLITICAL RULE
Herod the Great ruled areas 1, 2, 3, and 4 until his death in 4 B.C. Three sons ruled after him. Herod Archelaus ruled area 1 for ten years; thereafter it fell under direct Roman rule. Herod Antipas ruled areas 2 and 3 until A.D. 39. Herod Philip ruled area 4 until A.D. 34. Areas bearing the number 5 belonged to the province of Syria.

Jesus had begun to tell him, "You unclean spirit, come out of the man.")

9 Jesus asked him, "What is your name?"

He told Him, "My name is Legion [Six Thousand],*b* because we are many." **10** They begged Him earnestly not to send them out of the country.

11 There was a large herd of hogs feeding on the hillside. **12** "Send us to the hogs," they begged Him, "so that we may enter into them."

13 He let them do this.*c* The unclean spirits came out and went into the hogs; and the herd, about 2,000 hogs, stampeded down the cliff into the sea and was drowned.

14 Those who had taken care of them ran away and reported it in the town and in the country, and the people came to see what had happened. **15** They came to Jesus and saw that the man who had been possessed by the legion of demons was sitting there dressed and in his right mind; and they were frightened.*d* **16** Those who had seen it told them what had happened to the man possessed by demons, and ⌊they told them⌋ about the hogs ⌊also⌋. **17** Then the people began to urge Jesus to leave their country.

18 As He was stepping into the boat, the man who had been possessed by the demons begged Jesus to let him go with Him. **19** But Jesus did not let him. "Instead," Jesus told him, "go home to your people and tell them how much the Lord has done for you and how merciful He has been to you."

20 So the man left and began to tell publicly in the Decapolis [Ten Towns] how much Jesus had done for him. And all were amazed.

The Daughter Of Jairus And
A Woman Who Was Continuously Bleeding—*Matthew 9:18-26; Luke 8:40-56*

21 When Jesus had again crossed over in the boat to the other side of the sea, a large crowd gathered around Him by the seashore.

22 A synagog leader by the name of Jairus came, and when he saw Jesus, he knelt at His feet. **23** He pleaded earnestly with Jesus: "My little daughter is dying. Come and lay your hands on her that she may get well and live."

24 Jesus went with the man, and a huge crowd followed Him and pressed Him on all sides.

25 There was a woman who had a flow of blood for twelve years. **26** She had suffered much under the care of many doctors and had spent all she had. She had not been helped at all but had actually become worse. **27** Since she had heard about Jesus, she came from behind in the crowd and touched His garment. **28** She said, "If I only touch His clothes, I'll get well." **29** Immediately her bleeding stopped, and she felt in her body that she had been healed from her suffering.

30 At that moment Jesus felt within Himself that power had gone from Him. He turned around in the crowd and asked, "Who touched My clothes?"

---

b- 9 There were 6,000 soldiers in a Roman legion, that is, when it was at full strength (see v. 15 also).

c- 13 Some of the older manuscripts and early translations read: "Immediately He let them do this."

d- 15 Or "overawed."

31 "You see how the crowd is pressing You on all sides," His disciples said to Him, "and You ask, 'Who touched Me?' "

32 But He kept looking around to see the woman who had done this. 33 The woman, trembling with fear because she knew what had happened to her, came and bowed down before Him and told Him the whole truth.

34 He told her, "Daughter, your faith has made you well. Go in peace; be healed from your suffering."

35 While He was still talking, some men came from the home of the synagog leader. "Your daughter has died," they said. "Why trouble the Teacher anymore?"

36 When*e* Jesus heard what they said,*f* He told the synagog leader, "Do not continue to be afraid! Only believe!"

37 He allowed no one to go with Him except Peter, James, and John the brother of James. 38 So they came to the home of the synagog leader. There He saw a noisy crowd, with people weeping and wailing loudly. 39 When He came into the house, He asked them, "Why do you go on making such a noise and weeping? The child is not dead; she is sleeping."

40 They laughed at Him. But He put them all outside, took the child's father and mother and those who were with Him, and went in where the child was. 41 He took the child's hand and said to her, "Talitha, koum!" which means, "Little girl, I tell you, get up!"

42 Immediately the girl got up and walked around. (She was twelve years old.) Then the others were completely amazed.

43 He gave them strict orders not to let anyone know about this. And He told them to give her something to eat.

6TH CHAPTER

2. In Galilee (6:1–9:50)

His Last Visit To Nazareth—*Matthew 13:54-58; Luke 4:16-30*

1 Leaving that place, Jesus went to His hometown, and His disciples went with Him. 2 When the Sabbath came, He began to teach in the synagog. Many who heard Him were amazed. "Where did He learn this?" they asked. "What is this wisdom given to Him that He is able to do such great miracles?*a* 3 Isn't He the carpenter, the son of Mary, and a brother of James, Joseph, Judas, and Simon? And aren't His sisters here with us?" This caused them to stumble*b* in their evaluation of Him.

4 But Jesus told them, "The only place a prophet is not honored is in his hometown, among his relatives, and in his family." 5 He could not work any

---

e- 36 Some of the older manuscripts and early translations read: "Immediately when . . . ."
f- 36 A few of the older manuscripts read: "Paying no attention to what they said, ..."
6 a- 2 See MIRACULOUS SIGNS, WONDERFUL PROOFS, and MIRACLES on page 527.
b- 3 See *SKANDALON* on page 545.

miracle there except lay His hands on a few sick people and make them well. **6** Their unbelief amazed Him.

Then He went around in the villages and taught.

Jesus Sends Out The Twelve—*Matthew 10:1-42; Luke 9:1-6*

7 Jesus called the Twelve, began to send them out two by two, and gave them authority over the unclean spirits. **8** He gave them these instructions: "Do not take anything with you on the way except a staff*c*—no bread, no bag, no copper money in your pocket, **9** but wear sandals and do not put on two tunics."

10 He also told them, "Wherever you go into a home, stay there until you leave that place. **11** If people anywhere do not welcome you or listen to you,*d* leave that place and shake the dust off the soles of your feet as a warning to them."

12 They left and preached that people should repent. **13** They also drove out many demons and poured oil on many who were sick and made them well.

The Recalling Of John's Death—*Matthew 14:1-12; Luke 9:7-9*

14 King Herod heard about Jesus, because Jesus' Name was now well known. "John the Baptizer has risen from the dead and that is why these powers are at work in him,"*e* Herod said.*f* **15** Others said, "He is Elijah." Still others said, "He is a prophet like one of the other prophets." **16** But when Herod heard about it, he said, "John, whom I beheaded, has been raised!"

17 You see, Herod himself had sent men who had arrested John, bound him, and put him in prison, because Herod had married Herodias, the wife of his brother Philip.*g* **18** For John had told Herod, "It is not right for you to have your brother's wife."

19 Herodias continued to hold a grudge against John and wanted to kill him, but she could not do it, **20** because Herod was afraid of John since he knew John was a just and holy man. So he protected him. When he listened to John, he was very much disturbed, and yet he liked to hear him.

21 An opportunity came on Herod's birthday, when he gave a dinner for his noblemen, the tribunes, and the leading men of Galilee. **22** His daughter, that is, the daughter of Herodias, came in and danced, and Herod and his guests were delighted with her. The king told the girl, "Ask me for anything you want and I will give it to you." **23** And he solemnly swore to her: "I will give you anything *you ask, up to half of my kingdom.*"

---

23 Esther 5:3; 7:2

---

c- 8 Among other things a staff was used for protection and as an aid for walking.
d- 11 Literally: "And whatever place does not receive you or hear you."
e- 14 Or "Him."
f- 14 Literally: "he said" (cf. Matt. 14:2); a few of the older manuscripts and early translations read: "they said" (cf. Lk. 9:7).
g- 17 See Matthew 14:3 and its accompanying footnote.

24 She went out and asked her mother, "What should I ask for?"

"The head of John the Baptizer," her mother said. *h*

25 So she hurried right back to the king and made her request: "I want you to give me at once the head of John the Baptizer on a platter."

26 Although the king felt very sorry, ⌊yet⌋ because of his oaths and because of the guests he did not want to refuse her. **27** Immediately the king sent a guard and ordered him to bring John's head. He went and beheaded John in prison. **28** Then he brought the head on a platter and gave it to the girl, and the girl gave it to her mother.

29 When John's disciples heard about it, they came and took his body and laid it in a grave.

Jesus Feeds 5,000—Matthew 14:13-21; Luke 9:10-17; John 6:1-14

30 The apostles gathered around Jesus and reported to Him everything they had done and taught. **31** He told them, "Now come away to some deserted place where you can be alone, and rest a little." So many were coming and going that there was not even time to eat.

32 So they went away in the boat to a deserted place to be alone. **33** But many saw them leave and recognized them. And they ran there from all the towns and arrived ahead of them. **34** When Jesus stepped out of the boat, He saw a large crowd and felt sorry for them because they were *like sheep without a shepherd.* Then He began to teach them many things.

35 When it was quite late, His disciples came to Him. "This is a deserted place," they said, "and it's late. **36** Send them away to the farms and villages around here in order to buy themselves something to eat."

37 Jesus answered them, "You give them something to eat."

"Should we go and buy bread for two hundred denarii," *i* they asked Him, "and give it to them to eat?"

38 He said to them, "How many loaves do you have? Go and see."

They found out and said, "Five, and two fish."

39 He ordered them all to sit down in groups on the green grass. **40** They sat down in groups *j* of hundreds and fifties.

41 After He took the five loaves and the two fish, He looked up to heaven and gave thanks. *k* He broke the loaves apart and kept giving them to the disciples to give to the people. He also gave pieces of the two fish to everybody. **42** All of them ate and had enough. **43** They picked up pieces of bread and of the fish—twelve baskets full. **44** There were 5,000 men who had eaten the bread.

---

34 Num 27:17; 1 Kgs 22:17; Ezek 34:5

---

h- 24 Literally: "she said."

i- 37 See MONEY, WEIGHTS, and MEASURES on page 328.

j- 40 This *second* use of the word "groups" (cf. v. 39) literally means "garden plots," a picturesque concept. If this is the intended meaning, it would imply that the *colorful* garments of the crowd made the "groups" look like a series of flower beds.

k- 41 See Matthew 14:19 and its accompanying footnote.

Jesus Walks On Water—Matthew 14:22-33; John 6:15-21

45 He quickly made His disciples get into the boat and cross over to Bethsaida ahead of Him, while He sent the people away. **46** After saying good-bye to them, He went up into the hills to pray. **47** When evening came, the boat was in the middle of the sea, and He was alone on the land.

48 Jesus saw that they were in great trouble as they rowed, because the wind was against them. Toward morning He came to them, walking on the sea. He wanted to pass by them. **49** They saw Him walking on the sea, and thinking He was a ghost, they cried out, **50** because they all saw Him and were terrified.

Immediately He spoke to them. "Be courageous," He said, "it is I. Stop being afraid." **51** He came into the boat with them, and the wind died down. The disciples were completely dumbfounded. **52** They had not understood about the loaves. Instead, their minds were closed.*

53 They crossed over and came to the shore at Gennesaret and anchored there.

54 As soon as they stepped out of the boat, the people recognized Him. **55** They ran all over that part of the country and began to carry the sick on their beds to any place where they heard He was. **56** And wherever He came—to villages, towns, or farms—they would lay down the sick in the public places and beg Him just to let them touch the tassel of His garment. And all who touched it were made well.

7TH CHAPTER

Unclean Hands—Matthew 15:1-20

1 The Pharisees and some scribes who had come from Jerusalem gathered around Jesus. **2** They saw some of His disciples eat with unclean hands, that is, without washing them. **3** (Now the Pharisees, like all other Jews, do not eat without washing their hands up to the wrist—to follow the tradition of their fathers. **4** When they come from* the marketplace, they do not eat without first washing; and there are many other rules they have been taught to follow, such as washing* cups, huge wine jars, brass pots, and dining couches.)*

5 The Pharisees and the scribes asked Him: "What is the reason that Your disciples do not live according to the traditions handed down by our fathers?* They eat with unclean hands!"

6 He told them, "Isaiah was right when he prophesied about you hypocrites, as it is written: *'These people honor Me* with their lips, but their hearts are far*

6,7 Is 29:13

---

l- 52 See 3:5 and its accompanying footnote.
7 *a*- 4 Or "whatever comes from."
   b- 4 Note that "washing" is the English translation in *three* instances in verses 3 and 4. In verse 3 the word is "*nipsō*," but in the first part of verse 4 it is the Greek verb "*baptizō*" and in the last part of the verse it is the noun "*baptismos*."
   c- 4 A few of the older manuscripts and early translations omit: "and dining couches."
   d- 5 Literally: "tradition of the fathers."
   e- 6 Literally: "This people honors Me."

from Me. **7** *They worship Me in vain, since what they teach for doctrines are rules laid down by men.'* **8** You abandon the commandments of God, but you hold on to the traditions of men."*f* **9** He added: "You have a fine way of setting aside the commandments of God in order to keep*g* your own traditions! **10** For example, Moses said: *'Honor your father and your mother'* and *'Put to death the person who speaks evil of father or mother.'* **11** But you say, 'If anyone says to his father or mother, "Anything by which I might help you is Corban (that is, a gift to God)," ' **12** then you do not let him do anything for his father or his mother anymore. **13** In this way, by the traditions you have taught, you disregard the word of God. And you are doing many things like that."

14 Then He called the people again and said to them, "Listen to Me, all of you, and understand this: **15** Nothing that comes into a person from the outside can make him unclean, but what comes out of a person makes him unclean. **16** The one who has ears to hear, let him listen!"*h*

17 When He had left the people and gone home, His disciples asked Him about this illustration.*i*

18 He asked them, "Are you as dense as the others? Aren't you aware that nothing which comes into a person from the outside can make him unclean, **19** because it does not go into his heart but into his stomach and so passes out ⌊of the body⌋,*j* thus making all foods clean?" **20** He added: "What comes out of a person makes him unclean. **21** For from within, out of people's hearts, come evil thoughts, sexual sins, stealing, murders, adulteries, **22** greed, wickedness, cheating, shameless lust, a jealous eye, slander, pride, foolishness. **23** All these evils come from within and make a person unclean."

The Faith Of A Gentile Woman—*Matthew 15:21-31*

24 Leaving that place, Jesus went away to the neighborhood of Tyre. He went into a house not wanting anyone to know it, but it could not be kept a secret.

25 There was a woman in whose little daughter there was an unclean spirit. As soon as she heard about Him, she came and bowed down at His feet. **26** The woman was a Greek, a Phoenician from Syria by birth. She asked Him to drive the demon out of her daughter.

27 He answered her, "First let the children eat all they want. It is not good to take the children's bread and throw it to the dogs."*k*

28 She answered Him, "You are right, Lord, but even the dogs under the table eat some of the children's crumbs."

29 "Because you said this, go!" Jesus told her. "The demon has gone out of your daughter."

---

10 Ex 20:12; 21:17; Lev 20:9; Deut 5:16

---

f- 8 The words "commandments" (vv. 8,9) and "traditions" (vv. 8,9,13) are all singular in the Greek.

g- 9 Some of the older manuscripts and early translations read: "establish."

h- 16 Some of the older manuscripts and early translations omit this verse.

i- 17 Greek: "*parabolēn*" ("parable").

j- 19 Literally: "and goes out into the drain [toilet]."

k- 27 The Greek indicates a household pet.

30 The woman went home and found the little child lying on the bed and the demon gone.

"Ephphatha!" ["Be Opened!"]

31 Jesus again left the country of Tyre and went through Sidon and the country of the Decapolis[l] to the Sea of Galilee.

32 Some people brought to Him a man who was deaf and had a speech defect, and they urged Jesus to lay His hand on him. **33** After Jesus took him away from the crowd to be alone with him, He put His fingers into the man's ears. He spit and touched his tongue **34** and looked up to heaven and sighed. Then He said to him, "Ephphatha!" which means, "Be opened!" **35** And immediately his ears were opened, his tongue was set free to speak, and he talked naturally.

36 Jesus ordered the people not to tell anyone. But the more He forbade them, the more widely they spread the news. **37** They were dumbfounded. "He has done everything well," they said. "He even makes the deaf hear and the speechless speak."

8TH CHAPTER

Jesus Feeds 4,000—Matthew 15:32-39

1 Again at that time there was a large crowd of people gathered together. And since they had nothing to eat, Jesus called the disciples to His side and said to them: **2** "I feel sorry for the people. They have been with Me three days now and have nothing to eat. **3** If I let them go home without eating, they will become exhausted on the road. Some of them have come a long way."

4 His disciples asked Him, "Where could anyone get enough bread here in the wilderness to feed these people?"

5 "How many loaves do you have?" Jesus asked them.

"Seven," they answered.

6 He ordered the people to sit down on the ground. Then He took the seven loaves, gave thanks, broke them, and gave them to His disciples to hand out, and they handed them out to the people. **7** They also had a few small fish. He spoke a blessing over them and asked that these also be handed out. **8** They ate and had enough, and they picked up the pieces that were left over—seven baskets. **9** About 4,000 people were there.

Then He dismissed the people.

A Sign From Heaven—Matthew 16:1-4

10 Right after that Jesus and His disciples got into the boat and came into the area of Dalmanutha.[a]

---

l- 31 See footnote at 5:1.

8 *a*- 10 Dalmanutha is difficult to identify. Some ancient sources propose that it is identical to Magdala on the western side of the Sea of Galilee. Compare Matthew 15:39.

11 The Pharisees came and began to argue with Him. To test Him, they asked Him for some miraculous sign[b] from heaven.

12 With a deep sigh from His spirit He asked, "Why does this kind of people want a sign? I tell you the truth, this kind of people will be given no sign!"

13 Then He left them.

The Yeast Of The Pharisees—*Matthew 16:5-12*

He got into the boat again and started to cross to the other side. 14 But they forgot to take bread and had only one loaf with them in the boat.

15 "Be on guard!" Jesus commanded them. "Watch out for the yeast of the Pharisees and the yeast of Herod!"

16 And as they were discussing this with one another, they said, "He said this because we do not have any bread."

17 Since He was aware of what was going on, Jesus asked them, "Why are you discussing the fact that you do not have any bread? Do you still not see or understand? Are your minds closed?[c] 18 *You have eyes—do you not see? You have ears—do you not hear?* And do you not remember? 19 When I broke the five loaves for the five thousand, how many baskets full of pieces did you pick up?"

"Twelve," they told Him.

20 "And the seven loaves for the four thousand—how many baskets full of pieces did you pick up?"

"Seven," they answered Him.

21 He asked them, "Do you still not understand?"

A Blind Man

22 So they came to Bethsaida. There people brought a blind man to Jesus and begged Him to touch him. 23 He took the blind man's hand and led him out of the village. Then He spit on his eyes and laid His hands on him. He asked him, "Can you see anything?"

24 He looked up. "I see the people," he said. "They look to me like trees walking around."

25 When Jesus again laid His hands on his eyes, he saw distinctly; his sight was restored, and he saw everything clearly. 26 Jesus sent him home, saying, "But do not go into the village."

"You Are The Christ [Messiah]"—*Matthew 16:13-20; Luke 9:18-21*

27 Then Jesus and His disciples went to the villages around Caesarea Philippi. On the way He asked His disciples, "Who do people say I am?"

---

18 Jer 5:21; Ezek 12:2

b- 11 See MIRACULOUS SIGNS, WONDERFUL PROOFS, and MIRACLES on page 527.
c- 17 See 3:5 and its accompanying footnote.

28 "John the Baptizer," they answered Him; "others say Elijah; and still others, one of the prophets."

29 "But you, who do you say I am?" He asked them.

"You are the Christ!" Peter answered Him.

30 He warned them not to tell anyone about Him.

"I Will Die And Rise"—Matthew 16:21-23; Luke 9:22

31 Then He began to teach them: "The Son of Man has to suffer much. He has to be rejected by the elders, the ruling priests, and the scribes, be killed, and then rise after three days." **32** He was speaking this fact quite frankly.

But Peter took Him aside and began to correct Him. **33** When Jesus turned and looked at His disciples, He corrected Peter. "Get behind Me, Satan!" He said. "You are not thinking what God thinks but what men think."

Take Up The Cross—Matthew 16:24-28; Luke 9:23-27

34 Now when He had called the people, as well as His disciples, He said: "If anyone wants to follow Me, let him deny himself, take up his cross, and follow Me. **35** Whoever wants to save his life will lose it; but whoever will lose his life for Me and for the Gospel, he will save it. **36** What good is it if a person wins the whole world yet loses his own soul? **37** Or what would a person give in exchange for his own soul? **38** For whoever is ashamed of Me and My words in this unfaithful and sinful generation, the Son of Man will also be ashamed of him when He comes with the holy angels in His Father's glory."

9TH CHAPTER

1 "I tell you the truth," He told them, "there are some standing here who will never taste death until they see that the Kingdom of God has come with power."

Jesus Shows His Glory (The Transfiguration)—Matthew 17:1-8; Luke 9:28-36

2 After six days Jesus took Peter, James, and John with Him and led them up a high mountain to be alone with them.

There He was transfigured*a* before them, **3** and His clothes became dazzling white—no one on earth could bleach them so white. **4** Then Elijah and Moses appeared to them and were talking with Jesus.

5 Peter said to Jesus, "Rabbi [Teacher], it's good for us to be here. Let's put up three shelters,*b* one for You, one for Moses, and one for Elijah." **6** He really did not realize what he was saying because they were so terrified.

---

9 *a-* 2 Meaning "His appearance was changed" as He was transformed.

   b- 5 See Matthew 17:4 and its accompanying footnote.

7 A cloud came and overshadowed them, and a voice came out of the cloud: *"This is My Son,* whom I love. *Listen to Him!"*

8 Suddenly, as they looked around, they no longer saw anyone with them except Jesus.

9 On their way down the mountain Jesus ordered them not to tell anyone what they had seen until the Son of Man had risen from the dead. **10** They kept in mind what He said, but they continued to discuss the question among themselves as to what He meant by "rising from the dead." **11** And they asked Him, "Why do the scribes say, 'First Elijah has to come'?"

12 He told them, "First *Elijah* is coming and he *will put* everything *in order again.ᶜ* And what is written about the Son of Man? Namely, that He must suffer much and be treated shamefully. **13** But I tell you, Elijah has come, and people treated him as they pleased, just as it is written about him."

The Boy With An Evil Spirit—Matthew 17:14-20; Luke 9:37-43a

14 When they got back to the other disciples, they saw a large crowd around them and some scribes in discussion with them. **15** And immediately, when all the people saw Jesus, they were amazed and ran and welcomed Him.

16 He asked them, "What are you discussing with them?"

17 "Teacher," someone in the crowd answered, "I brought You my son. There is a speechless spirit in him. **18** Whenever it takes hold of him, it throws him down; he foams at the mouth and grinds his teeth and becomes rigid. I asked Your disciples to drive out the spirit, but they could not do it."

19 "O you unbelieving kind of people!" Jesus answered. "How long must I be with you? How long must I put up with you? Bring him to Me."

20 They brought the boy to Him. As soon as the spirit saw Jesus, it threw the boy into convulsions. He fell on the ground and rolled around and foamed at the mouth.

21 Jesus asked his father, "How long has he been like this?"

"Since he was a child," he said. **22** "It often threw him into fire or into water to kill him. But, if You can do anything, have pity on us and help us."

23 Jesus answered him, "You say, 'If You can'! Anything can be done for one who believes."

24 Immediately the child's father cried out, "I do believe; help me with my unbelief."

25 When Jesus saw a crowd quickly gather around Him, He spoke sharply to the unclean spirit: "You speechless and deaf spirit, I order you, 'Come out of him, and do not go into him again.' "

26 It screamed and wrenched him violently and came out. The boy became like a corpse, so that everybody said, "He's dead."

27 Jesus took his hand, helped him get up, and he stood up.

28 When He went into a house and His disciples were alone with Him, they asked Him, "Why couldn't we drive out the spirit?"

---

7 Deut 18:15; Ps 2:7   *12 Mal 4:5,6*

---

c- 12 Literally: "After Elijah has first come, he restores all things."

29 He told them, "This kind can be driven out only by prayer and fasting."

"I Will Die And Rise"—Matthew 17:22,23; Luke 9:43b-45

30 They left that place and were passing through Galilee. Jesus did not want anyone to know about it, **31** because He was teaching His disciples and telling them: "The Son of Man is going to be betrayed into the hands of men, and they will kill Him, but three days after He is killed, He will rise."

32 They did not understand what He said and were afraid to ask Him.

Who Is The Greatest?—Matthew 18:1-5; Luke 9:46-48

33 Then they came to Capernaum. When He came home, He asked the disciples, "What were you discussing on the way?" **34** They were silent because on the way they had discussed who was the greatest.

35 He sat down and called the Twelve. He told them, "If anyone wants to be first, he will have to take last place and be a servant to everyone else." **36** Then He took a little child and had him stand in front of[d] them. He put His arms around him and said to them, **37** "Whoever welcomes a child like this in My Name welcomes Me. And whoever welcomes Me welcomes not Me but the One who sent Me."

"He Is For Us"—Luke 9:49,50

38 John said to Jesus, "Teacher, we saw someone who is not one of us driving out demons in Your Name. We tried to stop him because he was not one of us."

39 Jesus said, "Do not try to stop him. Anyone who works a miracle in My Name cannot turn right around and speak evil of Me. **40** For anyone who is not against us is for us. **41** I tell you the truth, anyone who gives you a cup of water to drink because you belong to Christ will certainly not lose his reward."

Do I Cause Others To Stumble In Faith?—Matthew 18:6-10; Luke 17:1,2

42 "And, if anyone causes one of these little ones who believe in Me to stumble ⌞in his faith⌟,[e] it would be better for him to have a large millstone hung around his neck and to be thrown into the sea.

43 "Again, if your hand causes you to stumble ⌞in your faith⌟, cut it off. It is better for you to go into life without a hand than to have two hands and go to hell,[f] where the fire cannot be put out.[g] **45** If your foot causes you to stumble ⌞in your faith⌟, cut it off. It is better for you to go into life without a foot than to have two feet and be thrown into hell. **47** If your eye causes you to stumble ⌞in your faith⌟, tear it out. It is better for you to enter the Kingdom of God with

---

d- 36 Or "in the middle of."

e- 42 See *SKANDALON* on page 545. The same applies to verses 43,45,47.

f- 43 Greek: *"gehenna"* (also in vv. 45 and 47); see *HADES/GEHENNA* on page 540.

g- 43 Some of the older manuscripts and early translations omit verses 44 and 46: "Where their worm does not die and the fire is not put out." See verse 48 where the inclusion of these words is certain.

one eye than to have two eyes and be thrown into hell, **48** where *their worm does not die and the fire is not put out.* **49** For everyone will be salted with fire. **50** Salt is good. But if salt loses its taste, how will you make it taste salty again? Keep salt within you, and live in peace with one another."

10TH CHAPTER

> *C. Judean period (10:1–16:8)*
> *1. Pre-passion (10:1–13:37)*

Husband And Wife—Matthew 19:1-12

1 Jesus left that place and went into the territory of Judea,*ᵃ* which was on the other side of the Jordan; and again the crowds gathered around Him. And again He taught them as was His custom.

2 Some Pharisees came to Him. "Is it right for a man to divorce his wife?" they asked Him in order to test Him.

3 He asked them, "What did Moses order you to do?"

4 They said, "Moses allowed a man to *write out a divorce paper and divorce his wife.*"

5 Jesus told them, "He wrote this law for you because of your closed minds.*ᵇ* **6** But when God made the world in the beginning, He *made them male and female.* **7** *That is why a man shall leave his father and mother,* **8** *and the two shall be one flesh.* And so they are no longer two, but one flesh. **9** Therefore, let no person separate what God has joined together."

10 When they were in the house, the disciples asked Him about this again.*ᶜ* **11** He answered them, "If anyone divorces his wife and marries another, he is living in adultery with her. **12** And if a wife divorces her husband and marries another man, she is living in adultery."

Jesus Loves Children—Matthew 19:13-15; Luke 18:15-17

13 Some people were bringing little children to Jesus to have Him touch them, but the disciples sternly told them not to do it.

14 Now when Jesus saw this, He became angry. He told them, "Let the little children come to Me and do not try to keep them away, for the Kingdom of God is made up of such as these. **15** I tell you the truth, whoever does not receive the Kingdom of God in the same manner as a little child ˌreceives itˌ, he will never enter it."

---

48 *Is 66:24*   **4** *Deut 24:1*   **6** *Gen 1:27; 5:2*   **7,8** *Gen 2:24*

---

10 *a*- 1 In the wider sense meaning "Palestine."
  b- 5 See 3:5 and its accompanying footnote.
  c- 10 Or "When they were in the house *again*, the disciples asked Him about this."

16 He took them in His arms, laid His hands on them, and blessed them. *d*

The Rich Young Leader—*Matthew 19:16-30; Luke 18:18-30*

17 As Jesus was coming out to the road, a man came running to Him and knelt before Him. "Good Teacher," he asked Him, "what shall I do to inherit everlasting life?"

18 "Why do you call Me good?" Jesus asked him. "No one is good except One, namely, God. **19** You know the commandments: *Do not murder. Do not commit adultery. Do not steal. Do not lie.* *e* Do not cheat. *Honor your father and mother.*"

20 "Teacher," he told Him, "I have kept all these since I was a child."

21 Jesus looked at him and loved him. "You lack one thing," Jesus told him. "Go, sell everything you have, and give the money to the poor, and you will have treasure in heaven. Then come and follow Me."

22 When he heard that, he looked unhappy and went away sad, because he was very rich. **23** Jesus looked around and said to His disciples, "How hard it will be for those who are rich to enter the Kingdom of God!"

24 The disciples were surprised at His words. But Jesus said to them again, "Children, how hard it is to enter into the Kingdom of God! **25** It is easier for a camel to go through the eye of a needle than for a rich person to enter the Kingdom of God."

26 They were more amazed than ever. They asked one another, "Who then can be saved?"

27 As He looked at them, Jesus said: "For men it is impossible, but not for God, because *everything is possible for God.*"

28 Then Peter spoke up: "Look! We gave up everything and followed You."

29 "I tell you the truth," Jesus said, "everyone who gave up his home, brothers or sisters, mother, father, or children, or fields for Me and for the Gospel **30** will certainly receive a hundred times as much here in this life: houses and brothers and sisters and mothers and children and fields, along with persecutions; and in the coming world: everlasting life. **31** But many who are first will be last, and the last first."

The Cup Of Suffering—*Matthew 20:17-28*

32 As they were on their way up to Jerusalem, Jesus walked ahead of them. They were amazed, and the others who were following Him were afraid. So once again He took the Twelve with Him, and He began to tell them what was going to happen to Him: **33** "Look, we are going up to Jerusalem, and the Son

---

19 Ex 20:12-16; Deut 5:16-20   27 Gen 18:14; Job 42:2; Zech 8:6

---

d- 16 Literally: "After He placed His hands on them, He began to (or 'continued to') bless them." The Greek tense indicates either that an action began or that it was continued. Perhaps in this present context it refers to Jesus blessing the children one by one.

e- 19 Literally: "Do not give false witness."

of Man will be betrayed to the ruling priests and the scribes. They will condemn Him to die and hand Him over to the Gentiles. 34 They will make fun of Him and spit on Him, whip Him and kill Him. But after three days He will rise."

35 James and John, the sons of Zebedee, came to Him. "Teacher," they said to Him, "we want You to do for us whatever we ask."

36 "What do you want Me to do for you?" He asked them.

37 They told Him, "Let one of us sit at Your right and the other at Your left in Your glory."

38 Jesus answered them, "You do not realize what you are asking. Can you drink the cup which I am drinking or be baptized with the baptism with which I am being baptized?"

39 "We can," they told Him.

"You will drink the cup which I am drinking," Jesus told them, "and be baptized with the baptism with which I am being baptized, 40 but to sit at My right or at My left ˌare positions thatˌ I can grant only to those for whom they have been prepared."ᶠ

41 When the other ten heard about it, they became angry with James and John. 42 Then Jesus called them and told them, "You know that those who are considered rulers of the Gentiles are lords over them, and their great men are tyrants over them. 43 But it is not to be that way among you. Anyone who wants to become great among you, let him be your servant;ᵍ 44 and anyone who wants to be first among you, let him be slave of all.ʰ 45 Why, even the Son of Man did not come to be served but to serve and to give His life as a ransom for many."ⁱ

Blind Bartimaeus—Luke 18:35-43

46 Then they came to Jericho. As Jesus and His disciples and many people were leaving Jericho, Bartimaeus the son of Timaeus, a blind beggar, was sitting by the roadside. 47 When he heard that it was Jesus from Nazareth, he began to shout, "Son of David, Jesus, have pity on me!"

48 Many were urging him to be quiet. But he shouted even louder, "Son of David, have pity on me!"

49 Jesus stopped and said, "Call him!" They called the blind man and told him, "Cheer up! Get up! He's calling for you." 50 He laid aside his outer garment, jumped up, and went to Jesus.

51 Jesus asked him, "What do you want Me to do for you?"

"Rabboni,ʲ I want to see again," the blind man told Him.

52 Jesus told him, "Go, your faith has made you well."

Immediately he could see, and he began to follow Him on the road.

---

f- 40 Literally: "for whom it has been prepared."

g- 43 Literally: "shall be your servant"; in Greek the future is used at times as an imperative.

h- 44 Literally: "shall be slave of all"; in Greek the future is used at times as an imperative.

i- 45 This verse is usually regarded as the theme of Mark's Gospel. Concerning the term "many" ("polloi") see Matthew 20:28 and its accompanying footnote.

j- 51 Literally: "My Rabbi," meaning "my Teacher" or "my Master."

11TH CHAPTER

The King Comes To Jerusalem—Matthew 21:1-11; Luke 19:29-44; John 12:12-19

1 When they were approaching Jerusalem and came to Bethphage and Bethany, at the Mount of Olives, Jesus sent two of His disciples. **2** He told them, "Go into the village ahead of you, and just as you enter it, you will find a young donkey tied up there on which no one has ever sat. Untie it and bring it to Me. **3** And if anybody asks you, 'Why are you doing that?' say, 'The Lord needs it,' and that person will promptly send it back here."

4 They went and found the colt tied to a gate, outside in the street, and they began to untie it.

5 "What are you doing, untying that colt?" some of the men standing there asked them. **6** They answered them just as Jesus had told them, and the men let them go.

7 So they brought the colt to Jesus, put their garments on it, and He sat on it. **8** Many spread their garments on the road, and others spread leafy branches that they had cut in the fields. **9** Those who went ahead and those who followed Him were shouting:

> "*Hosanna!*[a]
> *Blessed is He who is coming in the Name of the Lord!*
> **10** Blessed is the coming Kingdom of our father David!
> Hosanna in the highest heavens!"

11 He came into Jerusalem and went into the Temple where He looked around at everything. Since it was already late, He went with the Twelve out to Bethany.

Nothing But Leaves—Matthew 21:18-22

12 The next day when they left Bethany, Jesus became hungry. **13** In the distance He saw a fig tree with leaves, and He went to see if He could find anything on it. When He came to it, He found nothing but leaves, because it was not the season for figs. **14** Then He said to the tree, and His disciples heard Him: "May no one ever eat fruit from you again!"

Cleansing The Temple—Matthew 21:12-17; Luke 19:45-48

15 When they came to Jerusalem, He went into the Temple and began to drive out those who were selling and buying in the Temple. He upset the tables of the

---

9 Ps 118:25,26

---

11 *a-* 9 See Matthew 21:9 and its accompanying footnote.

moneychangers and the chairs of those who sold pigeons. 16 He would not let anyone carry an item ‚for sale‚ across the Temple court.

17 Then He taught: "It is written, '*My House shall be called a house of prayer for all nations,*' is it not? But you have made it *a den of robbers.*"

18 When the ruling priests and scribes heard Him, they tried to find a way to kill Him. They were afraid of Him, because He amazed all the people with His teaching.

19 Whenever evening came, they [Jesus and His disciples] would leave the city. [b]

The Fig Tree Is Withered—*Matthew 21:18-22; Mark 11:12-14*

20 When they walked by early in the morning, they saw the fig tree withered from the roots. 21 Peter, remembering, said to Him, "Rabbi, look! The fig tree You cursed is dried up."

22 "Believe in God!" Jesus answered them. 23 "I tell you the truth, whoever says to this mountain, 'Be lifted up and be thrown into the sea,' and has no doubt in his mind but believes what he says will be done, it will be done for him. 24 That is why I tell you, anything you ask for in prayer, believe that you have already received it, and you will have it. 25 When you stand and pray, if you have anything against anyone, forgive him, so that your Father in heaven may forgive you your sins. 26 But if you do not forgive, your Father in heaven will not forgive your sins." [c]

From Heaven—*Matthew 21:23-27; Luke 20:1-8*

27 They came again to Jerusalem. As He was walking in the Temple, the ruling priests, the scribes, and the elders came to Him. 28 They asked Him, "By what authority are You doing these things? Or who gave You this authority to do these things?"

29 Jesus answered them, "I will ask you one question. You answer Me, and then I will tell you by what authority I am doing these things. 30 John's baptism—was it from heaven or from men? Answer Me."

31 They argued among themselves, "If we say, 'From heaven,' He will ask, 'Then why didn't you believe him?' 32 But if we say, 'From men'—"; they were afraid of the people because everyone thought John certainly was a prophet. 33 So they answered Jesus, "We do not know."

Then Jesus told them, "Neither will I tell you by what authority I am doing these things."

---

17 Is 56:7; Jer 7:11

b- 19 Apparently this remark applies to the activity of Jesus during the first days of Holy Week (Sunday through Wednesday).

c- 26 Some of the older manuscripts and early translations omit verse 26. See also Matthew 6:15 where the inclusion of these words is certain.

12TH CHAPTER

God's Vineyard—*Matthew 21:33-46; Luke 20:9-19*

1 Then He began to speak to them in parables: "A man *planted a vineyard.* He *put a wall around it, dug a pit for the winepress, and built a watchtower.* Then he leased it out to workers and left home.

2 "At the right time he sent a slave to the workers to obtain from them a share of the fruit of the vineyard. **3** But they took him, beat him, and sent him back empty-handed. **4** Again, he sent another slave to them. They hit him on the head and treated him shamefully. **5** He sent another, and that one they killed. Then many others. Some of these they beat, and others they killed.

6 "He had one more, a son, whom he loved. Finally he sent him to them saying, 'They will respect my son.'

7 "But those workers said to one another, 'This is the heir. Come, let's kill him, and the inheritance will be ours.' **8** They took him, killed him, and threw him out of the vineyard.

9 "What will the owner of the vineyard do? He will come and kill the workers and give the vineyard to others. **10** Haven't you read this Scripture passage:

> *The very Stone*
> > *which the builders rejected*
> > > *has become the Cornerstone.*
> **11** *The Lord has done it,*
> > *and it is marvelous for us to see?"*

12 They wanted to arrest Him, because they knew His parable was aimed at them; but they were afraid of the crowd. So they let Him alone and went away.

Taxes—*Matthew 22:15-22; Luke 20:20-26*

13 Next, they sent some Pharisees and some of Herod's supporters[a] to Him in order to trap Him with a question. **14** When they came to Him, they said, "Teacher, we know that You are honest and do not favor any individuals because of who they are;[b] rather, You teach the way of God faithfully. Is it right to pay a tax to Caesar or not? Should we pay it, or not?"

15 Because Jesus recognized their deceptive intent, He asked them, "Why do you test Me? Bring Me a denarius[c] so I can look at it."

16 They brought it. "Whose head is this and whose inscription?" He asked them.

"Caesar's," they told Him.

---

1 Is 5:1,2   ***10,11** Ps 118:22,23*

---

12 *a* - 13 See Matthew 22:16 and its accompanying footnote "b."
   b- 14 Literally: "and it does not matter to You concerning anyone, for You do not look on the face of men."
   c- 15 See MONEY, WEIGHTS, and MEASURES on page 328.

17 Jesus told them, "Give to Caesar what is Caesar's and to God what is God's." He amazed them.

The Dead Live—*Matthew 22:23-33; Luke 20:27-40*

18 Next, some Sadducees, who say that there is no resurrection, came to Him with this question: **19** "Teacher, Moses wrote for us: *'If anyone dies and leaves a wife but no child, his brother should marry his widow and have children for his brother.'* **20** Now there were seven brothers. The first took a wife, died, and left no children. **21** The second married her, died, and left no children. So did the third. **22** None of the seven left any children. Last of all the woman died too. **23** When they rise*d* in the resurrection, whose wife will she be since the seven had her as wife?"

24 Jesus asked them, "Isn't this the reason you are mistaken, because you do not know the Scriptures or the power of God? **25** When they rise from the dead, they neither marry nor are they given in marriage but are like the angels in heaven. **26** Concerning the resurrection of the dead, have you not read in the book of Moses, in the passage about the 'bush,' how God told him: *'I am the God of Abraham, the God of Isaac, and the God of Jacob'?* **27** He is not the God of the dead but of the living. You are badly mistaken!"

Love God And Your Neighbor—*Matthew 22:34-40*

28 One of the scribes came to Him. When he heard the others argue with Him and saw how well Jesus answered them, he asked Him, "Which is the most important of all the commandments?"

29 Jesus answered, "The most important is: *'Listen, Israel, the Lord our God, the Lord is One.'e* **30** *Then love the Lord your God with all your heart, with all your soul, with all your mind, and with all your strength.'* **31** The next is: *'Love your neighbor as yourself.'* No other commandment is greater than these."

32 "Right, Teacher!" the scribe said to Him. "You told the truth: *'He is One, and there is no other besides Him,* **33** and *loving Him with all your heart*, with all your understanding, *and with all your strength*, and, *loving your neighbor as yourself* is more than all the *burnt offerings and sacrifices.'* "

34 When Jesus saw how sensibly he answered, He told him, "You are not far away from the Kingdom of God."

After that no one dared to ask Him another question.

David's Son—*Matthew 22:41-46; Luke 20:41-44*

35 While Jesus was teaching in the Temple, He asked, "How can the scribes

---

19 Gen 38:8; Deut 25:5,6   26 Ex 3:6   29,30 Deut 6:4,5   31 Lev 19:18   32,33 Deut 4:35; 6:4,5   33 Lev 19:18; 1 Sam 15:22

d- 23 Some of the older manuscripts and early translations omit these first three words of the verse.

e- 29 Or "the Lord our God is one Lord." See Deuteronomy 6:4.

say that the Christ [Messiah] is David's son? **36** David himself said by the Holy
Spirit:

> *The Lord said to my Lord:*
>   *'Sit at My right hand*
>   *until I put Your enemies under Your feet.'*

37 David himself calls Him 'Lord'; then how can He be his son?"

Beware!—*Matthew 23:1-12; Luke 20:45-47*

The large crowd liked to hear Him. **38** As He taught, He said, "Beware of
the scribes, who like to parade around in long robes, to be greeted in the
marketplaces, **39** to sit in the front seats in synagogs, and to have the places of
honor at dinners. **40** They swallow up the houses of widows and then, to put on
a good appearance, they make long prayers. They will receive a more severe
punishment."

The Widow's Coins—*Luke 21:1-4*

41 As Jesus sat facing the contribution boxes,*ƒ* He was watching how people
put money into them. Many rich people put in much; **42** a poor widow also came
and dropped in two small coins, worth about one cent.*ᵍ*

43 He called His disciples. "I tell you the truth," He said to them, "this poor
widow has contributed more than all the others who are putting money into the
treasury. **44** For all of them have taken some of what they have extra and dropped
it in; but she put in what she needed for herself—all she had, in fact, everything
she had to live on."

13TH CHAPTER

The Destruction Of Jerusalem And The World—*Matthew 24:1-35; Luke 21:5-33*

1 As He was going out of the Temple, one of His disciples said to Him,
"Teacher, look at those magnificent stone buildings!"*ᵃ*

2 Jesus asked him, "Do you see these great buildings? Not one stone will be
left on another; every one will be torn down."

3 As Jesus was sitting on the Mount of Olives, facing the Temple, Peter,
James, John, and Andrew asked Him privately: **4** "Tell us, when will these
things be, and what will be the miraculous sign which will tell us when all these
things are going to happen?"

---

36 Ps 110:1

ƒ- 41 Or "the treasury."

  ᵍ- 42 Compare Matthew 10:29; Luke 12:6; see MONEY, WEIGHTS, and MEASURES on page 328.

13 *a*- 1 Literally: "magnificent stones and magnificent buildings."

5 Jesus began to say to them, "Be careful not to let anyone deceive you.
6 Many will come using My Name and saying, 'I am He,' and will deceive many.

7 "When you hear of wars and rumors of wars, do not become alarmed. It *must happen*, but that is not yet the end. 8 *Nation will fight against nation* and *kingdom against kingdom*. There will be earthquakes in various places, and there will be famines. These are only the beginning pains of childbirth. [b]

9 "Be on your guard! Men will hand you over to their courts and whip you in their synagogs. You will be brought before governors and kings for My sake in order to testify to them. [c] 10 Before the end comes, the Gospel must be preached to all nations. 11 When they are taking you away to hand you over to the authorities, do not worry ahead of time about what you will say. But say whatever is given you to say when the time comes; for you will not be the ones who speak, but the Holy Spirit.

12 "A brother will betray his brother to death, and a father his child. *Children will rebel against their parents* and kill them. 13 Everyone will hate you because of My Name. But that person who endures to the end will be saved.

14 "When you see *the devastating abomination* standing where it should not be—let the reader take note[d]—then let those in Judea flee to the mountains. 15 He who is on the roof ⌊of his house⌋ should not come down nor go into his house to take anything out. 16 He who is in the field should not turn back to get his coat.

17 "Woe to the women who are pregnant and to those who are nursing babies in those days. 18 Pray that it will not happen in winter. 19 For *it will be a time of misery, such as has not happened from the beginning* of God's created world *until now*—and surely will never happen again. 20 And if the Lord had not shortened that time, no one would be saved. But for the sake of the elect whom He has chosen, He has shortened the time.

21 "At that time if anyone tells you, 'Look, here is Christ!' or 'There He is!' do not believe it. 22 False christs [messiahs] and false *prophets* will *come and work miraculous signs and wonderful proofs*[e] to deceive, if possible, those whom God has chosen. 23 Be on your guard; I have told you everything before it happens.

24 "Now, after the misery of that time *the sun will turn dark, the moon will not give its light,* 25 and *the stars will be falling from the sky.* And *the powers of heaven* will be shaken. 26 Then people[f] will see *the Son of Man coming in clouds* with great power and glory. 27 And then He will send the angels[g] and

---

7 Dan 2:28	*8 2 Chr 15:6; Is 19:2*	*12 Mic 7:6*	*14 Dan 9:27; 11:31; 12:11*	*19 Dan 12:1*
22 Deut 13:1	*24,25 Is 13:10; 34:4; Ezek 32:7,8*	*26 Dan 7:13*		

---

b- 8 The Greek word denotes "labor pains." As in childbirth, sharper pains will follow before the Savior comes in glory.

c- 9 Or "in order to witness to them."

d- 14 Or "let the reader understand."

e- 22 See MIRACULOUS SIGNS, WONDERFUL PROOFS, and MIRACLES on page 527.

f- 26 Literally: "they."

g- 27 Or "messengers."

gather His chosen ones *from the north, south, east, and west,* [h] *and from one end of the world to the other.* [i]

28 "Learn from the illustration[j] of the fig tree: When its branch becomes tender and it sprouts leaves, you know summer is near. **29** So also, when you see these things happen, you know He is near, at your door.

30 "I tell you the truth, this kind of people[k] will not pass away until these things all take place. **31** Heaven and earth will pass away, but My words will not pass away."

Be Careful And Watch!—*Compare Matthew 24:36-51; Luke 21:34-38*

32 "No one knows about that Day or Hour, neither the angels in heaven, nor the Son, but only the Father. **33** Be careful and watch, because you do not know when it will happen. **34** It is like a man who went on a trip. As he left home, he put his slaves in charge, assigned work to each one, and ordered the doorkeeper to watch. **35** Therefore watch, because you do not know when the master of the house is coming, whether in the evening, at midnight, at the time when the rooster crows, or early in the morning. **36** Make sure he does not come suddenly and find you asleep. **37** What I tell you, I tell everyone: 'Watch!' "

14TH CHAPTER

2. Passion and resurrection (14:1–16:8)

The Plot—*Matthew 26:1-5; Luke 22:1,2; John 11:45-57*

1 It was two days before the Passover and the Festival of Unleavened Bread. The ruling priests and the scribes were looking for some underhanded way to arrest Jesus and kill Him. **2** But they said, "Not during the festival or there will be a riot among the people."

Mary Anoints Jesus—*Matthew 26:6-13; John 12:1-8*

3 While Jesus was in Bethany in the home of Simon the leper and was reclining at the table, a woman came with an alabaster jar of perfume, real nard and very expensive. She broke the jar[a] and poured the perfume on His head.

4 But some who were there felt annoyed and said to one another, "Why was the perfume wasted like this? **5** This perfume could have been sold for more than

---

27 Deut 30:4; Zech 2:6

---

  h- 27 Literally: "from the four winds."
  i- 27 Literally: "from the end of the earth to the end of the sky."
  j- 28 Or "parable."
  k- 30 Or "this generation."
14 *a-* 3 The neck of this kind of container had to be broken to release its content, which was a substance called "nard"; see "nard" in Glossary.

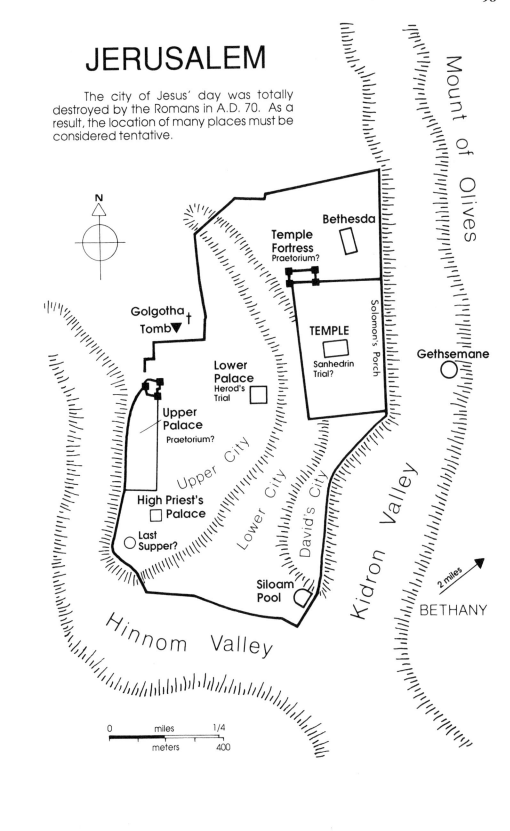

JERUSALEM

The city of Jesus' day was totally destroyed by the Romans in A.D. 70. As a result, the location of many places must be considered tentative.

N

Mount of Olives

Bethesda

Temple Fortress
Praetorium?

Golgotha
Tomb †

TEMPLE

Solomon's Porch

Gethsemane

Lower Palace
Herod's Trial

Sanhedrin Trial?

Upper Palace
Praetorium?

Upper City

Lower City

David's City

Kidron Valley

High Priest's Palace

Last Supper?

Siloam Pool

2 miles

BETHANY

Hinnom Valley

0   miles   1/4
meters   400

three hundred denarii[b] and the money given to the poor." And they were grumbling at her.

6 Jesus said, "Let her alone. Why are you bothering her? She has done a beautiful thing[c] to Me. **7** For the poor you always have with you, and you can help them whenever you want to, but you are not always going to have Me. **8** She has done what she could. She came ahead of time to pour perfume on My body to prepare it for burial. **9** I tell you the truth, wherever the Gospel is preached in the whole world, what she has done will also be told in memory of her."

Judas Plans To Betray Jesus—*Matthew 26:14-16; Luke 22:3-6*

10 Judas the man from Kerioth,[d] one of the Twelve, went to the high priests to betray Jesus to them. **11** They were delighted to hear it and promised to give him money.[e] So he kept looking for a chance to betray Him.

The Passover—*Matthew 26:17-20; Luke 22:7-17*

12 On the first of the Passover days of the Festival of Unleavened Bread, when it was customary to kill the Passover lamb, the disciples asked Jesus, "Where do You want us to go and get things ready for You to eat the Passover?"

13 He sent two of His disciples and told them: "Go into the city, and you will meet a man carrying a jar of water. Follow him, **14** and when he goes into a house, tell the owner: 'The Teacher asks, "Where is My room in which I can eat the Passover with My disciples?" ' **15** Then he will show you a large room upstairs, furnished and ready. Make preparations for us there."

16 The disciples left, went into the city, and found everything as He had told them. And so they prepared the Passover.

17 When evening came He arrived with the Twelve.

Who Is The Betrayer?—*Matthew 26:21-25; Luke 22:21-23; John 13:21-30*

18 While they were reclining at the table and eating, Jesus said, "I tell you the truth, one of you is going to betray Me, one who is *eating with Me!*"

19 This made them sad and they began to ask Him one after another, "I'm not the one, am I?"

20 He told them, "It is one of the Twelve, the one who is dipping into the bowl with Me. **21** The Son of Man is going away as it is written about Him, but woe to that man by whom the Son of Man is betrayed! It would be better for that man if he had never been born."

---

18 Ps 41:9

---

b- 5 See MONEY, WEIGHTS, and MEASURES on page 328.
c- 6 Literally: "a good work."
d- 10 Literally: "Judas Iscariot"; see *"Iscariot"* in Glossary.
e- 11 Literally: "silver."

The Lord's Supper—Matthew 26:26-30; Luke 22:18-20; 1 Corinthians 11:23-25

22 While they were eating, Jesus took bread, gave thanks,*f* broke it, and gave it to them and said, "Take it; this is My body."

23 Then He took a cup, spoke a prayer of thanks, and gave it to them. And they all drank of it. **24** He told them, "This is My *blood of the 'last will and testament,' g* which is being poured out for many.

25 "I tell you the truth, I will never again drink of the fruit of the vine until that day when I drink it in a new way in the Kingdom of God."

26 After they sang a hymn,*h* they started out for the Mount of Olives.

"You Will Deny Me"—Matthew 26:31-35; Luke 22:31-34; John 13:36-38

27 Then*i* Jesus told them, "You will all stumble ˌin your faithˌ,*j* because it is written: 'I will *strike down the Shepherd, and the sheep will be scattered.*' **28** But after I have risen, I will go ahead of you to Galilee."

29 Peter answered Him, "Even if they all stumble ˌin their faithˌ, I will not."

30 "I tell you the truth," Jesus told him, "today, this very night, before the rooster crows twice, you will deny Me three times."

31 But he kept insisting even more strongly, "If I have to die with You, I will never deny You." All the others said the same thing.

Gethsemane—Matthew 26:36-46; Luke 22:39-46

32 Then they came to a place called Gethsemane, and He said to His disciples, "Sit down here while I pray."

33 He took Peter, James, and John with Him, and He began to feel terror and grief. **34** He told them, "*My soul is so full of sorrow* that I am at the point of death. Remain here and stay awake."

35 Going ahead a little, He fell to the ground and prayed that if it were possible He might not have to suffer what was ahead of Him.*k* **36** He said, "Abba!*l* Father! You can do anything. Take this cup away from Me. But let it not be what I want but what You want."

37 He came and found them asleep. He asked*m* Peter, "Simon, are you sleeping? Could you not stay awake one hour? **38** Stay awake and pray that you may not be tempted. The spirit is willing, but the flesh is weak."

39 He went away again and prayed the same as before. **40** He came again and found them asleep—they could not keep their eyes open, and they did not know what to say to Him.

---

24 Ex 24:8; Jer 31:32; Zech 9:11   27 Zech 13:7   34 Ps 42:5; 43:5

---

f- 22 See Matthew 26:26 and its accompanying footnote.

g- 24 See *DIATHĒKĒ* on page 531.

h- 26 Psalms 115 through 118.

i- 27 Verses 27-31 very likely took place in the Upper Room.

j- 27 See *SKANDALON* on page 545. The same applies to verse 29.

k- 35 Literally: "that if it is possible the hour might pass from Him."

l- 36 The Aramaic word for "father."

m- 37 Compare Matthew 26:45 and its accompanying footnote.

41 He came back a third time and said to them, "Are you going to sleep on now and take your rest? It is enough. The time has come. Now the Son of Man is being betrayed into the hands of sinners. **42** Get up, let us go. Look, here comes the one who is betraying Me!"

The Arrest—Matthew 26:47-56; Luke 22:47-54a; John 18:1-14

43 Just then, while Jesus was still talking, Judas, one of the Twelve, arrived; and with him was a crowd of men from the ruling priests, the scribes, and the elders. They were carrying swords and clubs, and **44** the traitor had given them a signal. He said, "The One I kiss is the Man. Grab Him, take Him away, and do not let Him escape."

45 When he came there, he quickly stepped up to Jesus and said, "Rabbi!" and kissed Him.

46 Then the men took hold of Jesus and arrested Him. **47** One of those who were standing nearby drew his sword, struck the high priest's slave, and cut off his ear.

48 Jesus asked them, "Did you come out to take Me prisoner with swords and clubs as if I were a robber? **49** Day after day I was with you as I taught in the Temple, and you did not arrest Me. But what the Scriptures say has to be fulfilled."

50 Then all the disciples left Him and ran away. **51** A certain young man who also was following Him had nothing on but a linen cloth. They tried to grab him, **52** but he left the linen cloth and ran away naked.

The First Trial Before The Jewish Court—*Matthew 26:57-68*

53 The men took Jesus to the high priest, and all the ruling priests, elders, and scribes were coming together. **54** Peter followed Him at a distance, even into the courtyard of the high priest; he was sitting with the Temple guards and warming himself by the fire.

55 The ruling priests and the whole Jewish council [Sanhedrin] tried to get some testimony against Jesus in order to kill Him, but they could not find any. **56** While many gave false testimony against Him, their statements did not agree.

57 Then some stood up and gave this false testimony against Him: **58** "We heard Him say, 'I will tear down this Temple, made by human hands, and in three days build another not made by human hands.' " **59** But even on this point their statements did not agree.

60 Then the high priest stepped forward and asked Jesus, "Are You not going to reply to what these men are testifying against You?"

61 But He was silent and did not answer.

Again the high priest asked Him, "Are You the Christ, the Son of the Blessed One?"

62 "I am," Jesus said. "And you will see *the Son of Man sitting at the right hand* of power and *coming with the clouds of heaven.*"

---

62 Ps 110:1; Dan 7:1

63 Then the high priest tore his clothes, saying, "Why do we need any more witnesses? **64** You have heard the blasphemy. What do you think?"

Then they all condemned Him, saying that He was guilty and deserved to die. **65** Some of them began to *spit* on Him. They covered His face, struck Him with their fists, and told Him, "Prophesy!" Even the Temple guards took Him and slapped Him.[n]

Peter Denies Jesus—Matthew 26:69-75; Luke 22:54b-62; John 18:15-18,25-27

66 While Peter was down in the courtyard, one of the maids of the high priest came, **67** and seeing Peter warming himself, she looked at him and said, "You too were with the Man from Nazareth, this Jesus!"

68 But he denied it by saying: "I don't know Him, and I don't know what you're talking about."

He went out to the entrance. Then a rooster crowed.

69 The maid saw him. Once again she began to say to those who were standing around, "This is one of them!" **70** Again he denied it.

After a little while those who stood near told Peter again, "It's obvious you're one of them. Why, you're a Galilean!"

71 Then he began to curse and swear: "I don't know this Man whom you're talking about." **72** Just then a rooster crowed a second time, and Peter remembered Jesus telling him: "Before the rooster crows twice, you will deny Me three times." And he broke down and wept.

15TH CHAPTER

Before Pilate—Matthew 27:11-14; Luke 23:1-4; John 18:28-38

1 As soon as it was morning, the ruling priests, the elders, and the scribes, that is, the whole Jewish council [Sanhedrin], came to a decision. They bound Jesus, took Him away, and handed Him over to Pilate.

2 Pilate then asked Him, "Are You the King of the Jews?"

"Yes," Jesus answered him.

3 The ruling priests were accusing Him of many things.

4 "Don't You have anything to say to this?" Pilate asked Him again. "See how many accusations they are bringing against You!"

5 But Jesus did not answer him anymore, so that Pilate was surprised.

Barabbas—Matthew 27:15-26; Luke 23:17-25; John 18:39,40

6 Now at every festival Pilate used to free a prisoner whom the people

---

65 *Is 50:6*

n- 65 Or "guards took Him and beat Him."

requested. **7** There was a man by the name of Barabbas. *a* He was in prison with the rebels who in their revolt had committed a murder. **8** And the crowd came up and asked Pilate to do for them as he had done before. **9** Pilate answered them by asking, "Do you want me to free the King of the Jews for you?" **10** For he knew the ruling priests had handed Jesus over to him because they were jealous.

11 The ruling priests stirred up the people so that Pilate would release Barabbas to them instead.

12 So Pilate again asked them, "What then should I do with Him whom you call the King of the Jews?"

13 "Crucify Him!" they shouted back.

14 "Why, what wrong has He done?" Pilate asked them.

But they shouted even louder, "Crucify Him!"

15 Then Pilate, wanting to satisfy the people, released Barabbas to them, but he whipped *b* Jesus and handed Him over to be crucified.

16 The soldiers took Him into the palace (which is the Praetorium), and they called together the whole troop of soldiers. **17** They put a purple robe on Him, twisted some thorns into a crown and placed it on His head, **18** and began to greet Him: "Hail, King of the Jews!" **19** They hit Him on the head with a stick, *spit* on Him, and knelt and worshiped Him.

"They Crucified Him"—*Matthew 27:31-44; Luke 23:26-38; John 19:16b-24*

20 After they had made fun of Him, the soldiers *c* took off the purple robe and put His own clothes on Him. Then they took Him out to crucify Him. **21** A certain man, Simon from Cyrene, the father of Alexander and Rufus, was on his way in from the country, and as he was about to pass by, they forced him to carry the cross of Jesus.

22 They took Jesus to Golgotha, *d* which means "Place of the Skull." **23** They tried to give Him wine mixed with myrrh, but He did not take it. **24** They crucified Him. And *they divided His clothes among them by throwing dice e for them* to see what each one should get. **25** It was nine in the morning when they crucified Him. **26** There was a written notice of the accusation against Him. It read:

THE KING OF THE JEWS.

---

19 Is 50:6   *24 Ps 22:18*

---

15 *a*- 7 Made up of two Aramaic words: *"bar"* ("son") and *"abba"* ("father"), meaning "son of the father." Could the presence of one named *Barabbas* imply that the "sons (and daughters) of the heavenly Father" went free as the "Son of the heavenly Father" went to the cross for them?

b - 15 See Matthew 27:26 and its accompanying footnote "h."

c- 20 Literally: "they."

d- 22 Literally: "to the place Golgotha"; *"Golgotha"* is Aramaic; its Latin form is *"Calvary."*

e- 24 Literally: "lots."

Ɒ
X
27 With Him they crucified two robbers, one at His right hand and the other at His left.*f*

Ɒ
X
29 Those who passed by *ridiculed* Him, *shaking their heads* and saying, "Ha! You who are going to tear down the Temple and build it in three days—**30** come down from the cross, and save Yourself!" **31** In the same way the ruling priests

Ɒ
X
and the scribes *made fun of* Him among themselves and said, "He saved others—He cannot save Himself. **32** Let the Christ, the King of Israel, now come

Ɒ
X
down from the cross in order that we may see and believe." Even those crucified with Him were *insulting* Him.

Jesus Dies—Matthew 27:45-56; Luke 23:44-49; John 19:28-30

33 When noon came, darkness fell over the whole land and lasted until three

Ɒ
X
in the afternoon. **34** At three o'clock Jesus cried out in a loud voice, *"Eloi, Eloi, lama sabachthani?"* which means, "My God, My God, why did You forsake Me?"

35 When they heard Him say that, some of those standing nearby said, "Lis-

Ɒ
X
ten! He's calling Elijah." **36** Someone ran, soaked a sponge in *sour wine*, put it on a stick,*g* and *offered Him a drink.* He said, "Let's see if Elijah comes to take Him down."

37 Then Jesus cried out in a loud voice and died. **38** And the ⌐inner¬ curtain in the Temple*h* was torn in two from top to bottom.

39 When the captain who stood facing Jesus saw how He gave up His spirit, he said, "Certainly this Man was the Son of God!"

40 There were also women watching *from a distance.* Among them were Mary from Magdala and Mary the mother of James the Younger and of Joseph, and Salome. **41** While He was in Galilee, they had followed Him and supported*i* Him. There were also many other women who had come up to Jerusalem with Him.

Jesus Is Buried—Matthew 27:57-61; Luke 23:50-56; John 19:38-42

42 Since it was already evening on the day of preparation, which is the day before the Sabbath,*j* **43** Joseph from Arimathea, an important member of the Jewish council [Sanhedrin] who also was waiting for the Kingdom of God, dared to go to Pilate and ask for the body of Jesus.

44 Pilate wondered whether Jesus was already dead. So he called the captain and asked him, "Has He died already?" **45** And when he was assured of this by the captain, Pilate let Joseph have the body.

---

29 Ps 22:7; 109:25   *31,32 Ps 22:6-8*   *34 Ps 22:1*   *36 Ps 69:21*   *40 Ps 38:11*

f- 27 Some of the older manuscripts and early translations add verse 28: "And what the Scriptures said was fulfilled: 'He was counted among criminals.'" See the parallel thought in Luke 22:37 where its inclusion is certain; also note the prophetic source of these words in Isaiah 53:9,12.

g- 36 Literally: "reed."

h- 38 See Diagram #2 on page 438.

i- 41 Compare Luke 8:3.

j- 42 Literally: "And now evening having come, since it was the preparation, which is the day before the Sabbath"; see fuller explanation at John 19:31 and its accompanying footnote.

46 Joseph bought some linen, took the body down, wrapped it in the linen, and laid it in a tomb that had been cut in the rock, and rolled a stone against the door of the tomb. **47** Mary from Magdala and Mary the mother of Joses watched where He was laid.

16TH CHAPTER

The Easter Resurrection—Matthew 28:1-10; Luke 24:1-12; John 20:1-10

1 When the Sabbath was over, Mary from Magdala, Mary the mother of James, and Salome bought spices to go and anoint Jesus.

2 On Sunday*ᵃ* they were coming to the tomb very early when the sun had just come up. **3** They asked one another, "Who is going to roll away the stone for us from the door of the tomb?" **4** But when they looked up, they saw that the stone had been rolled back, even though it was very large. **5** As they went into the tomb, they saw a young man, dressed in a white robe, sitting at the right side. And they were amazed.

6 He told them, "Don't be amazed any longer. You are looking for Jesus from Nazareth, who was crucified. He has risen. He is not here. See the place where He was laid. **7** But go and tell His disciples and Peter, 'He is going ahead of you to Galilee. There you will see Him, just as He told you.' "

8 They went out and hurried away from the tomb, because they were trembling and bewildered; and they said nothing to anyone, because they were afraid.*ᵇ*

D. Postscript (16:9-20)

The Living Savior

9 After Jesus rose early on Sunday, He showed Himself first to Mary from Magdala, out of whom He had driven seven demons. **10** She went and told the news to those who had been with Him and were now mourning and crying. **11** When they heard He was alive and had been seen by her, they did not believe it.

12 Later He appeared in a different form to two of them as they were walking into the country. **13** They went back and told the others, but they did not believe them either. **14** Still later He showed Himself to the Eleven while they were reclining at the table. He scolded them for their unbelief and stubbornness because they did not believe those who had seen Him after He had been raised.

15 Then He told them, "Go everywhere in the world and preach the Gospel to the whole creation. **16** He who believes and is baptized will be saved, but he who does not believe will be damned.

17 "These are the miraculous signs that will accompany the believers: In My

---

16 *a-* 2 Literally: "On the first day of the week" (also in v. 9).
  b- 8 A few of the older manuscripts and early translations omit Mark 16:9-20.

Name they will drive out demons; they will speak new languages; **18** they will pick up snakes; if they drink any deadly poison, it will not hurt them. They will lay their hands on the sick, and these will get well."

19 After talking with them, the Lord was *taken up to heaven and sat down at the right hand of God.*

20 They went out and preached everywhere, and the Lord worked with them and confirmed the word by the miraculous signs that accompanied their preaching.

---

19 2 Kgs 2:11; Ps 110:1

THE GOOD NEWS [GOSPEL] AS TOLD BY
LUKE[a]

1ST CHAPTER

A. Preface (1:1-4)

Luke's Research

1 Many have undertaken to plan and write an account of what has been done among us, **2** just as we heard it from those who from the first became eyewitnesses and servants of the word. **3** For this reason I too decided to check everything carefully from the beginning and to write it down in the proper order for you, excellent Theophilus, **4** so that you will be sure that what you have been told is completely dependable.

B. Beginnings: Infancy of John the Baptizer and Jesus through the temptation of Jesus (1:5–4:13)

The Angel Gabriel Comes To Zacharias

5 In the days of King Herod of Judea,[b] there was a priest by the name of Zacharias. He belonged to the division of priests named after Abijah. His wife was a descendant of Aaron, and her name was Elizabeth. **6** Both were righteous before God, living blamelessly according to all the commandments and regulations of the Lord.

7 But they had no children, because Elizabeth was barren and both were getting old.[c]

8 Once when Zacharias was on duty with his division, serving as a priest before God, **9** he was chosen by lot—according to the custom of the priesthood—to go into the Lord's Temple to burn incense. **10** All the people were praying outside while he was burning incense.

11 Then he saw an angel of the Lord standing at the right side of the altar of incense. **12** Zacharias was startled to see him and was terrified.

---

1 *a* Luke was a Gentile by birth and a physician by occupation (cf. Col. 4:14; Phlm. 24; and 2 Tim. 4:11). The many medical references in Luke (e.g., 7:11-17; 10:25-37; 22:44,51) substantiate the tradition that Luke the physician is the author.

b- 5 In the wider sense indicating "Palestine" (also in 4:44; 6:17; 7:17; 23:5).

c- 7 Literally: "both having advanced in their days."

13 *"Stop being afraid*, Zacharias," the angel told him. *"Your prayer has been heard. You and your wife* Elizabeth *will have a son, and you are to name him* John. **14** He will be your joy and delight, and many will be glad he was born.

15 "For he will be a great man in the sight of the Lord. *He will drink no wine or other intoxicating drink.* He will be filled with the Holy Spirit while he is still in his mother's womb. **16** And he will bring many in Israel back to the Lord their God. **17** He will go ahead of Him with the spirit and power of *Elijah, to turn the hearts of the fathers to the children*, and the disobedient to the wise thinking of righteous men—and so make ready a people who are thoroughly prepared for the Lord."

18 Zacharias asked the angel, "How can I be sure of this? I am an old man, and my wife is old."

19 The angel answered him, "I am Gabriel! I stand before God and was sent to speak to you and tell you this good news. **20** And now, you will be silent and not able to talk until the day this happens, because you did not believe what I said. But it will be fulfilled at the right time."

21 Meanwhile, the people were waiting for Zacharias and were surprised that he was staying so long in the Holy Place. *d* **22** When he did come out, he could not speak to them. Then they realized that he had seen a vision in the Holy Place. He kept motioning to them and remained unable to talk.

23 When the days of his service were over, he went home. **24** After this time his wife Elizabeth conceived and for five months did not show herself in public. She said, **25** "The Lord did this for me at a time when He was concerned about removing the feeling of shame that I had among people."

The Angel Gabriel Comes To Mary

26 In the sixth month God sent the angel Gabriel to a town in Galilee called Nazareth, **27** to a virgin engaged to a man by the name of Joseph, a descendant of David. The virgin's name was Mary.

28 When the angel entered her home, he said, "Greetings, you who are greatly blessed. The Lord is with you."

29 She was startled by what he said and tried to figure out what such a greeting might mean.

30 The angel told her, "Stop being afraid, Mary. God has chosen to bless you. *e* **31** *You see:*

> *You will conceive and give birth to a Son,*
> *and you will name Him* JESUS;*f*
> **32** He will be great
> and will be called *the Son* of the Most High.

---

13 Gen 17:19; Dan 10:12   *15 Num 6:3; Judg 13:4*   *17 Mal 4:5,6*   *31 Is 7:14*

---

d- 21 See Diagram #1 on page 430.

e- 30 Literally: "You have obtained favor in the sight of God."

f- 31 The Greek-based English name "Jesus" and its Hebrew-based counterpart "Joshua" both mean "Savior, Helper, the LORD saves, YAHWEH helps."

And the Lord God will give Him
    the throne of His ancestor *David*;
33 *He will be King over* the people of Jacob *forever*,
    and His Kingdom will never end."

34 Mary asked the angel, "How can this be? I have had no relations [sexual relations] with a man."

35 The angel answered her, "The Holy Spirit will come over you, and the power of the Most High will overshadow you. And for that reason the Holy Being[g] to be born ₒof youᵤ will be called the Son of God. **36** Also consider the fact that even Elizabeth, your relative, has conceived a son in her old age. People call her childless, but she is now in her sixth month. **37** *There is nothing that God will not be able to do.*"

38 "I am the Lord's servant," Mary answered. "Let it happen to me as you said."

Then the angel left her.

Mary Visits Elizabeth; Her Song

39 At this time Mary hurried away to the hill country to a town of Judah. **40** There she went into the home of Zacharias and greeted Elizabeth.

41 When Elizabeth heard Mary's greeting, the baby leaped in her womb. Then Elizabeth was filled with the Holy Spirit, **42** and she cried out in a loud voice, "Blessed are you among women, and blessed is the Child who will come from your womb.[h] **43** But how does this happen to me that the mother of my Lord comes to me? **44** As soon as I heard your greeting, the baby leaped with delight in my womb. **45** And blessed is she who believed that the Lord will accomplish what He promised to do for her."

46 Mary said:

"*My soul* magnifies[i] *the Lord,*
47   and my spirit *delights in God, my Savior,*
48   because *He has looked kindly at His humble servant.*
    Yes, from now on—throughout all generations—
    people will call me blessed
49   because He has done great things to me—
            He who is mighty,
            whose Name is holy,
50   and *who is merciful from generation to generation*
            to those who fear Him.

32,33 *2 Sam 7:12-14,16; 1 Chr 17:12-14; Is 9:7; Mic 4:7*   **37** *Gen 18:14; Job 42:2; Zech 8:6*
46,47 *1 Sam 2:1; Hab 3:18*   **48** *1 Sam 1:11*   **49** *Ps 111:9; Is 57:15*   **50** *Ps 103:17*

---

g- 35 In Greek this word is in the neuter gender.
h- 42 Literally: "blessed is the Fruit of your womb."
i- 46 This Latin-based English term indicates why the church refers to Mary's song (vv. 46-55) as the *Magnificat* (*Magnifies*).

51 "Mighty are the deeds He has done *with His arm*:
    He has scattered those who think so proudly in their hearts;
52   *He has pulled down strong rulers* from their thrones
        and *lifted up lowly people.*
53   *Those who were hungry He has filled with good things,*
        and the rich He has sent away empty-handed.
54   *He has come to help His servant Israel;*
    He *remembered His mercy*[j]
55   (as *He promised our fathers*),
          the mercy He has for Abraham
            and his descendants[k] *forever.*"

56 Mary stayed with Elizabeth about three months and then went back home.

John Is Born

57 Now the time came for Elizabeth to have her baby, and she gave birth to a son. 58 Her neighbors and relatives heard how the Lord had been unusually kind to her; and they shared her joy.

59 On the eighth day they came to circumcise the baby. They were going to call him Zacharias because that was his father's name. 60 But his mother spoke up and said, "No, he will be named John."

61 "But there is no one among your relatives who has that name," they told her.

62 Then they motioned[l] to his father to see what name he might want him to have. 63 He asked for a writing tablet and wrote, saying, "His name is John." They were all surprised.

64 At once Zacharias' speech was restored,[m] and he began to speak, praising God.

65 Everyone who lived around them was overawed. And throughout the hill country of Judea people kept talking about all these things. 66 All who heard about it thought it over[n] and asked, "What is this child going to be?" For it was clear that the Lord's hand was with him.

67 His father Zacharias was filled with the Holy Spirit, and he prophesied:

68   *"Praise the Lord,*[o] *the God of Israel,*
        because He has visited[p] *His people,*
        and has prepared *a ransom for them.*

---

51 *Ps 89:10*   **52** *Job 12:19; 5:11; Ezek 21:26*   **53** *Ps 107:9*   **54** *Ps 98:3; Is 41:8,9*
55 *Gen 17:7; Mic 7:20*   **68** *Ps 41:13; 72:18; 89:52; 106:48; 111:9*

---

j- 54 Literally: "in order to remember His mercy."

k- 55 Literally: "seed," meaning either "descendants" (Gen. 13:15,16; 22:17, referring to the *descendants* of Abraham) or "Descendant" (Gen. 22:18; Gal. 3:16, indicating the "*Messiah*").

l- 62 Luke may be telling his readers that Zacharias had become both deaf and unable to talk.

m- 64 Or "organs of speech were restored"; literally: "And his mouth was opened instantly and his tongue."

n- 66 Literally: "All who had heard put these things in their heart."

o- 68 Literally: "Blessed ‚be the‚ Lord"; this Latin-based English word "blessed" indicates why the church refers to Zacharias' song (vv. 68-79) as the *Benedictus* (*Blessing*).

p- 68 "Visited" is an important term which is *inclusive* of the ideas of looking over a situation and being concerned about it as well as doing something about it.

69 He has *raised* up a *Horn of salvation* for us
    in the family of His servant David,
70   as He said long ago through His holy prophets
71   that *He would save* us *from* our *enemies*
      and *from the power* of all *who hate* us.
72 He wanted to be *merciful to our fathers*
    and *remember His* holy *covenant*q
73   *the oath He swore to* our father *Abraham*—
74   to rescue us from our *enemies*
      and to let us serve Him without fear
75   in holiness and righteousness
        before Him all our life.

76 "And you, child, will be called a prophet of the Most High.
    For you will go *ahead of the Lord*
      to prepare His ways—
77   to make known to His people that they can be saved
      by the forgiveness of their sins,
78   because our God is merciful
        and will let a heavenly *Sun rise* upon us—
79   *to shine on those who sit in darkness*
          and in the shadow of death,
      to guide our feet into *the way of peace.*"

80 The child John grew and became strong in spirit. He lived in the wilderness until he appeared in public before Israel.

2ND CHAPTER

Jesus Is Born

1 In those days Caesar Augustus ordered that a census be taken of the whole world. 2 (This was the first census while Quirinius was governing Syria.)*a*
3 Everyone went to register, each to his own town.

4 Joseph also went up from the town of Nazareth in Galilee to David's town in Judea, which is called Bethlehem, because he was one of the descendants of David, 5 to register with Mary, his fiancee,*b* who was going to have a child.

6 Now while they were there, the time came for her to have her baby, 7 and she gave birth to her firstborn son. She wrapped Him in baby clothes*c* and laid Him in a manger because there was no room for them in the inn.

---

69 *1 Sam 2:10; Ps 18:2; 132:17*   **71** *Ps 106:10*   **72** *Mic 7:20*   **72-74** *Gen 22:16,17;*
Lev 26:42; Ps 105:8,9; 106:45   **76** *Mal 3:1*   **78** *Mal 4:2*   **79** *Ps 107:10; Is 9:2; 59:8*

q- 72 Compare Genesis 15:1-18; see *DIATHĒKĒ* on page 531.
2 a- 2 Or "This took place as a census before Quirinius was ruling Syria."
  b- 5 Literally: "who was promised to him in marriage."
  c- 7 The "baby clothes" (also in v. 12) of Jesus' day consisted of long strips of cloth that were wrapped around an infant's body, thus binding it in the style of a mummy. In this way the body was kept warm and the bones were aided in growing straight.

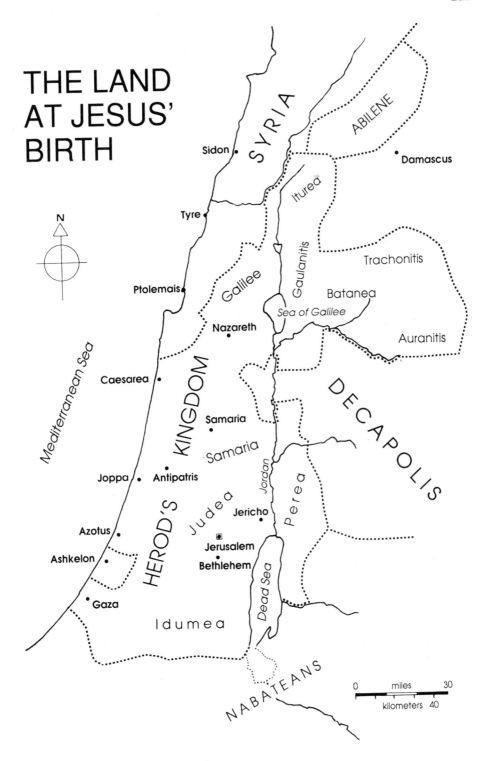

THE LAND
AT JESUS'
BIRTH

N

Sidon

SYRIA

ABILENE

Damascus

Iturea

Tyre

Galilee

Gaulanitis

Trachonitis

Batanea

Ptolemais

Sea of Galilee

Auranitis

Nazareth

Mediterranean Sea

Caesarea

KINGDOM

DECAPOLIS

Samaria

Samaria

Joppa

Antipatris

Jordan

Judea

Perea

HEROD'S

Jericho

Azotus

Jerusalem

Ashkelon

Bethlehem

Dead Sea

Gaza

Idumea

NABATEANS

0   miles   30
kilometers 40

The Shepherds

8 And there were shepherds living out in the countryside nearby. They were taking turns watching their flocks at night.

9 Then an angel of the Lord appeared to them, and the glory of the Lord shone all around them. They were terrified. **10** "Stop being afraid," the angel said to them, "for look, I have good news for you. A great joy will come to all the people, **11** because the Savior, who is Christ the Lord, was born for you today in David's town. **12** And this is how you will know Him: you will find an Infant wrapped in baby clothes and lying in a manger."

13 Suddenly there was with the angel a large number of the angels of heaven, *d* who were praising God and saying:

14   "Glory to God in the highest heavens, *e*
          and on earth peace to people who have His good will!"

15 When the angels had left them and gone to heaven, the shepherds said to one another, "The Lord has told us what has happened. Let's go to Bethlehem and see it."

16 Then they came in a hurry and found Mary and Joseph, and the Baby lying in the manger. **17** When they had seen Him, they told others what they had been told about this Child. **18** And everyone was surprised to hear the story that the shepherds told.

19 But Mary treasured all these things in her heart and kept thinking about them.

20 The shepherds went back, glorifying and praising God for everything they had heard and seen. It was just as they had been told.

In The Temple

21 On the eighth day when the time had come to circumcise the Child, He was named JESUS, *f* the Name the angel had given Him before He was conceived in the womb.

22 When *the time came* for them *to be purified* according to the Law *g* of Moses, Joseph and Mary took Jesus up to Jerusalem to present Him to the Lord **23** (as it is written in the Law of the Lord: *"Every firstborn boy shall be* called *'holy to the Lord' "h*). **24** They also went to offer a sacrifice according to what the Law of the Lord states: *"a pair of turtledoves or two young pigeons."*

25 Now, there was a man in Jerusalem by the name of Simeon. He was a

---

22 *Lev 12:6*   23 *Ex 13:12*   24 *Lev 5:7,11; 12:8; Num 6:10*

d- 13 Literally: "a multitude of a heavenly army."

e- 14 The Latin-based English of "Glory . . . in the highest heavens" indicates why the church refers to the song of the angels (v. 14) as the *Gloria in Excelsis.*

f- 21 See 1:31 and its accompanying footnote.

g- 22 Greek: *"nomos"*; here a reference to the laws and regulations which Moses received from God. Compare verses 23 and 24 where "Law of the Lord" also refers to the Five Books of Moses. See *NOMOS* on page 544 for an overview of this concept with its various meanings in the New Testament.

h- 23 Meaning "shall be set aside to serve the Lord."

righteous man, who feared God and was waiting for the One who would comfort Israel. The Holy Spirit was upon him. 26 The Holy Spirit had told him that before he would die he would see the Christ [Messiah]*i* sent by the Lord.

27 Moved by the Spirit, he went into the Temple. When the parents brought in the Child Jesus to do for Him what was customary according to the Law, 28 Simeon took Him in his arms, praised God, and said:

29   "Lord, now You are letting Your servant depart*j* in peace as You promised,
30   because my eyes have *seen Your Salvation*
31   which You prepared for all people to see—
32   *a Light to shine on the Gentiles,*
                    and the *Glory of* Your people *Israel.*"

33 His father and mother*k* were surprised at the things that were being said about Him. 34 Then Simeon blessed them and said to His mother Mary, "Here is what this Child is appointed for: Many in Israel will fall and rise again because of Him; and He will be a Sign*l* that many will speak against 35 to show what they are thinking in their hearts. And a sword will pierce your own soul too."

36 Anna, a prophetess, was also there. She was a daughter of Phanuel, of the tribe of Asher. She was now very old; when she was young, she had married a man and lived with him seven years.*m* 37 After that she was a widow until she was 84. She never left the Temple but worshiped day and night, fasting and praying. 38 Just then she too came forward, thanked God, and talked about the Child to all who were looking for Jerusalem to be redeemed.

39 When Joseph and Mary had done everything the Law of the Lord commanded them to do, they went back to Galilee to their town of Nazareth.

The Boy Jesus

40 The little Child grew and became strong, being filled with wisdom; and God's favor was with Him.

41 Every year His parents would go to Jerusalem to celebrate the Passover. 42 And so when He was twelve years old, they went up for the festival as usual.

43 When the festival days were over and they started for home, the boy Jesus stayed behind in Jerusalem. But His parents*n* did not know it. 44 They thought He was with the others who were traveling with them. After traveling a day,

---

30 *Is 40:5; 52:10*   32 *Is 42:6; 46:13; 49:6*

i- 26 The Greek-based English name "Christ" and its Hebrew-based counterpart "Messiah" both mean the "Anointed One" or the "Chosen One."

j- 29 The Latin-based English of the words "now are letting depart" (or "now are dismissing") indicates why the church refers to Simeon's song (vv. 29-32) as the *Nunc Dimittis* (*Now Dismissing*).

k- 33 Some manuscripts and early translations read: "Joseph and his mother."

l- 34 Or "Miraculous Sign," the regular translation of the Greek "semeion" in this GWN version; compare MIRACULOUS SIGNS, WONDERFUL PROOFS, and MIRACLES on page 527.

m- 36 Literally: "She being advanced in many days and having lived with a husband seven years from her virginity . . . ."

n- 43 Some of the older manuscripts and early translations read: "Joseph and his mother."

they started to look for Him among their relatives and friends. **45** When they did not find Him, they went back to Jerusalem, looking for Him.

46 Three days later they found Him in the Temple, sitting among the teachers, listening to them and asking them questions. **47** His understanding and His answers surprised all who heard Him.

48 When His parents saw Him, they were amazed. His mother asked Him, "Son, why did You do this to us? See how anxiously Your father and I have been looking for You!"

49 "Why were you looking for Me?" He asked them. "Didn't you realize that I must be in My Father's House?"*o* **50** But they did not understand what His reply meant.*p*

51 Then He went back with them to Nazareth. And He was always obedient to them.

His mother kept all these things in her heart. **52** And Jesus grew wiser and taller and *won the approval of God and of people.*

3RD CHAPTER

John Prepares The Way—Matthew 3:1-12; Mark 1:1-8; John 1:19-28

1 In the fifteenth year of the rule of Emperor Tiberius, Pontius Pilate was governor of Judea, Herod ruled Galilee,*a* his brother Philip ruled Iturea and Trachonitis, Lysanias ruled Abilene, **2** and Annas and Caiaphas were the high priests. Then God spoke to John the ͺsonͺ of Zacharias in the wilderness. **3** He went into the whole Jordan Valley and preached the baptism of repentance for the forgiveness of sins. **4** This was what the prophet Isaiah had said in his book:

> *A voice is calling out*^b *in the wilderness:*
> *"Prepare the way for the Lord;*
> *make the paths straight for Him.*
> 5   *Every ravine will be filled;*
> *every mountain and hill will be leveled;*
> *the crooked will be made straight*
> *and the rough roads smooth;*
> 6   *and all people will see that God has saved them."*

7 So he would say to the crowds who were coming out to be baptized by him, "You brood of poisonous snakes, who warned you to run away from the punishment waiting for you? **8** Therefore, produce works which show that you have repented.*c* And do not start telling yourselves, 'Abraham is our father,' for I tell

---

52 1 Sam 2:26   4-6 Is 40:3-5

---

o- 49 Or "about My Father's affairs?" Greek is close to English: "in My Father's."
p- 50 Literally: "did not understand the saying which He spoke to them."
3 a- 1 Literally: "ruling as tetrarch of Galilee" (three times in this verse); see ahead at verse 19 and its accompanying footnote.
b- 4 Or "shouting."
c- 8 Literally: "Produce therefore fruits worthy of repentance."

you that God can raise children for Abraham from these stones. **9** The ax is now ready to strike at the root of the trees. Therefore, every tree that does not produce good fruit will be cut down and thrown into the fire."

10 "What should we do?" the crowds asked him.

11 He answered them, "The person who has two garments should share with him who has none, and the person who has food should do the same."

12 Some tax collectors also came to be baptized. "Teacher," they asked him, "what should we do?"

13 "Stop collecting more money than you are ordered to collect," he told them.

14 Some soldiers also asked him, "And what should we do?"

He told them, "Do not use threats or blackmail to get money from anyone, but be satisfied with your pay."

15 The people were expecting something and all were wondering in their hearts whether John was perhaps the Christ [Messiah]. **16** John answered them all: "I baptize you with water. But the One who is mightier than I is coming. I am not worthy to untie His sandal straps.*d* He will baptize you with the Holy Spirit and with fire. **17** He has the winnowing shovel in His hand to clean up His threshing floor and to gather the wheat into His barn, but the chaff He will burn*e* in a fire that cannot be put out."

18 And so with many other challenging words he was telling the people the Gospel [Good News].

In Prison

19 When John was showing Herod the ruler*f* how wrong he was in regard to his brother's wife Herodias and in regard to all his other wicked deeds, **20** Herod—on top of everything else—locked John up in prison.

The Baptism Of Jesus—*Matthew 3:13-17; Mark 1:9-11; compare John 1:29-34*

21 When all the people were being baptized, Jesus was also baptized. While He was praying, heaven opened, **22** and the Holy Spirit came down on Him in bodily form as a dove. And a voice from heaven said, "You are *My Son*, whom I love. *I am delighted* with You."

23 Jesus was about 30 years old when He began His ministry.

The Family Line Of Jesus—*Matthew 1:1-17g*

Jesus was the son (so it was thought) of Joseph, of Eli, **24** of Matthat, of

---

22 *Ps 2:7; Is 42:1*

---

d- 16 This was ordinarily a slave's duty.

e- 17 See Matthew 3:12 and its accompanying footnote.

f- 19 Literally: "the tetrarch," one who ruled over one-fourth of the kingdom of Herod the Great (also in 9:7).

g See THE FAMILY LINE OF JESUS CHRIST on page 547 and the "Time line" of Biblical persons and events on page 9.

Levi, of Melchi, of Jannai, of Joseph, 25 of Mattathias, of Amos, of Nahum, of Esli, of Naggai, 26 of Maath, of Mattathias, of Semein, of Josech, of Joda, 27 of Joanan, of Rhesa, of Zerubbabel, of Shealtiel, of Neri, 28 of Melchi, of Addi, of Cosam, of Elmadam, of Er, 29 of Jesus,*h* of Eliezer, of Jorim, of Matthat, of Levi, 30 of Simeon, of Judas, of Joseph, of Jonam, of Eliakim, 31 of Melea, of Menna, of Mattatha, of Nathan, of David, 32 of Jesse, of Obed, of Boaz, of Salmon, of Nahshon, 33 of Amminadab, of Ram, of Admin, of Arni, of Hezron, of Perez, of Judah, 34 of Jacob, of Isaac, of Abraham, of Terah, of Nahor, 35 of Serug, of Reu, of Peleg, of Eber, of Shelah, 36 of Cainan, of Arphaxad, of Shem, of Noah, of Lamech, 37 of Methuselah, of Enoch, of Jared, of Mahalaleel, of Cainan, 38 of Enos, of Seth, of Adam, of God.

4TH CHAPTER

The Devil Tempts Jesus—Matthew 4:1-11; Mark 1:12,13

1 Jesus, full of the Holy Spirit, left the Jordan and was led by the Spirit into the wilderness 2 where the devil continued to tempt Him for 40 days. He ate nothing during those days, and when they were over, He was ˌveryˌ hungry.

3 The devil said to Him, "If you are the Son of God, tell this stone to become a loaf of bread."

4 Jesus answered him, "It is written, '*A person will not be kept alive by bread alone but by every word of God.*' "*a*

5 The devil took Him up and in a moment showed Him all the kingdoms of the world. 6 "I will give You all this authority and glory," the devil told Him, "because it was given to me and I give it to anyone I please. 7 So, if You will worship me,*b* all this will be Yours."

8 Jesus answered him,*c* "It is written, 'Worship *the Lord your God and serve Him* only.' "

9 The devil took Him into Jerusalem and had Him stand on the ledge of the Temple. "If You are the Son of God," he told Him, "jump down from here. 10 For it is written: '*He will order His angels to watch over you carefully.* 11 *They will carry you in their hands* and *never let you stub your foot against a stone.*' "

12 Jesus answered him, "It is written, '*Do not put the Lord your God to a test.*' "*d*

---

4 *Deut 8:3*   8 *Deut 6:13*   **10,11** *Ps 91:11,12*   **12** *Deut 6:16*

---

h- 29 Or "Joshua," the Hebrew-based English form of "Jesus," which is the Greek-based English form of the textual "*Iēsous.*"

4 *a*- 4 A few of the older manuscripts and early translations omit: "but by every word of God."

   b- 7 Or "bow down to me."

   c- 8 Some manuscripts and early translations add: "Get behind Me, Satan!" See Matthew 4:10 where the inclusion of the words "Go away, Satan!" is certain.

   d- 12 Or "Do not tempt the Lord your God."

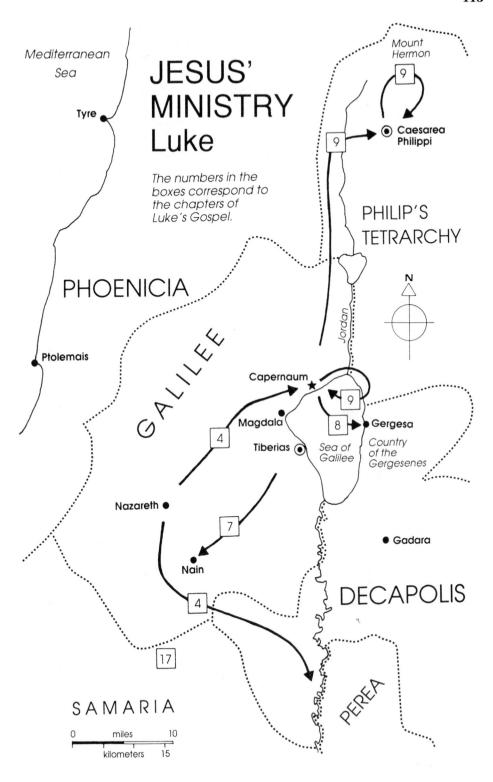

Mediterranean
Sea

JESUS' MINISTRY Luke

The numbers in the boxes correspond to the chapters of Luke's Gospel.

Mount Hermon

9

9 → Caesarea Philippi

Tyre

PHILIP'S TETRARCHY

PHOENICIA

N

Ptolemais

Jordan

GALILEE

Capernaum ★

9

Magdala

8 → Gergesa

4

Tiberias

Sea of Galilee

Country of the Gergesenes

Nazareth

7

Nain

Gadara

DECAPOLIS

4

17

PEREA

SAMARIA

0   miles   10

kilometers   15

13 When the devil had finished every way of tempting Him, he left Him until another opportunity would present itself. *e*

C. Jesus' ministry in Galilee (4:14–9:50)

Nazareth Rejects Jesus—Matthew 13:54-58; Mark 6:1-6

14 In the power of the Spirit Jesus went back to Galilee. The news about Him spread all over the surrounding country. 15 He continued to teach in their synagogs, and everybody praised Him.

16 Then Jesus came to Nazareth where He had been brought up. On the Sabbath He went into the synagog as was His custom. He stood up to read 17 and was given the scroll of the prophet Isaiah. Unrolling the scroll, He found the place where it says:

18   *The Spirit of the Lord is upon Me because—*
             He anointed Me
                 to preach the Gospel to the poor.
             *He sent Me*ᶠ
                 to announce freedom to prisoners,
                 ₁to announce₁ the restoring of sight to the blind,
                 to set free those who have been oppressed,
19   *to announce an acceptable year of the Lord.*ᵍ

20 He rolled up the scroll, gave it back to the attendant, and sat down. Everyone in the synagog was watching Him closely 21 as He said, "Today, while you are listening, this Scripture passage is fulfilled."

22 All spoke well of Him and were surprised to hear the gracious words flowing from His lips. "Isn't this the son of Joseph?" they were asking.

23 He answered them: "You will undoubtedly quote to Me this proverb, 'Doctor, heal yourself!' and say, 'We have heard about all the things You did in Capernaum. Do the same here in Your hometown.' " 24 He added, "I tell you the truth, no prophet is accepted in his hometown.

25 "But I tell you this truth: There were many widows in Israel in the days of Elijah, when it did not rainʰ for three years and six months and there was a severe famine all over the land. 26 But Elijah was not sent to anyone except *a widow at Zarephath in the territory of Sidon.* 27 And there were many lepers in

---

18,19 Is 58:6; 61:1,2   *26 1 Kgs 17:9*   *27 2 Kgs 5:14*

---

e- 13 Literally: "until a favorable time."

f- 18 Some of the older manuscripts and early translations at this point add the words: "to heal those who are brokenhearted."

g- 19 A reference to the Old Testament "Year of Jubilee" (Lev. 25:8-55), the time when the Lord frees His people and accepts them.

h- 25 Literally: "when the sky was closed."

Israel at the time of the prophet Elisha. But no one except *Naaman* from Syria *was made clean.*"

28 As they were listening, all in the synagog became furious. **29** They got up, forced Him out of town, and led Him to a cliff of the hill on which their town was built, in order to throw Him over ⌊the cliff⌋. **30** But He walked right through them and went away.

Jesus Drives Out A Demon—*Mark 1:21-28*

31 He went down to Capernaum, a town in Galilee, and was teaching people on a Sabbath. **32** The people were amazed at the way He taught, because He spoke with authority.

33 In the synagog there was a man with a spirit of an unclean demon. He cried out with a loud voice, **34** "Oh, what do we have in common with You, Jesus from Nazareth! You have come to destroy us! I know who You are—the Holy One of God."

35 Jesus spoke sharply to him: "Be quiet, and come out of him." The demon threw him down in the middle ⌊of the crowd⌋ and then came out of him without doing him any harm.*ⁱ*

36 They were all amazed and said to one another, "What kind of command is this? With authority and power He gives orders to the unclean spirits, and they come out."

37 So the news about Him spread to every place throughout the surrounding region.

Simon Peter's Mother-In-Law—*Matthew 8:14-18; Mark 1:29-34*

38 Leaving the synagog, Jesus went to Simon's home. Simon's mother-in-law was sick with a high fever, and they asked Him to help her. **39** He bent over her, ordered the fever to leave, and it left. She got up immediately and began to wait on them.

40 When the sun was going down, all who had sick ones suffering from various diseases brought them to Him. He laid His hands on each of them and made them well. **41** The demons went out of many, shouting, "You are the Son of God," but He spoke sharply to them and would not allow them to speak, because they knew He was the Christ.*ʲ*

42 In the morning He went out to a lonely place. The crowds continued to look for Him. When they came to Him, they tried to keep Him from leaving them. **43** But He said to them, "I have to preach the Good News of the Kingdom of God also in other towns, because that is what I was sent to do."

44 Then He kept on preaching in the synagogs of Judea.*ᵏ*

---

i- 35 An act of exorcism, that is, the driving out of an evil spirit.
j- 41 Since the older manuscripts did not contain punctuation, this sentence could also be rendered: "He . . . would not let them go on saying that they knew He was the Christ."
k- 44 In the wider sense of "Palestine," including "Galilee" in particular in this context and indicating the synagogs of northern Palestine.

5TH CHAPTER

Fishers Of Men—Matthew 4:18-22; Mark 1:14-20; John 1:35-51

1 One day Jesus was standing by the Lake of Gennesaret,*ᵃ* and the people were crowding Him as they were listening to God's word. **2** He saw two boats on the shore of the lake. The fishermen had stepped out of them and were washing their nets. **3** So Jesus got into one of the boats, the one which was Simon's, and asked him to go out a little way from the shore. Then He sat down and taught the people from the boat.

4 When He had stopped speaking, He told Simon, "Take the boat out where the water is deep, and let down your nets for a catch."

5 "Master," Simon answered, "we worked hard all night and caught nothing. But if You tell me to,*ᵇ* I will let down the nets."

6 When the men had done this, they caught a very large number of fish, and their nets began to tear. **7** So they waved to their partners in the other boat to come and help them. They came, and they filled both boats so that they began to sink.

8 When Simon Peter saw this, he fell down at Jesus' knees. "Leave me, Lord," he said. "I am a sinful man." **9** He and all who were with him were amazed to see the fish they had caught, **10** and so were James and John, the sons of Zebedee, who were Simon's partners.

Jesus told Simon, "Stop being afraid. From now on you are going to catch men."

11 When they had brought the boats to the shore, they left everything and followed Him.

Jesus Heals A Leper—Matthew 8:1-4; Mark 1:40-44

12 One day Jesus was in a town where there was a man who was covered with leprosy. When he saw Jesus, he bowed down with his face to the ground. "Lord," he begged Him, "if You want to, You can make me clean."

13 Jesus stretched out His hand and touched him. "I want to," He said. "Be clean!" Immediately the leprosy left him.

14 "Do not tell anyone," Jesus ordered him, "but go, *show yourself to the priest,ᶜ* and offer the sacrifice for your cleansing which Moses commanded, to show them that you are well."

15 But the news about Jesus spread even more, and large crowds were gathering to hear Him and have their diseases healed. **16** But He continually went away to lonely places and prayed.

---

14 Lev 13:7,49

---

5 *a-* 1 Alternate name for the Sea of Galilee.
  b- 5 Literally: "but on the basis of [because of] the word of Yours."
  c- 14 That is, the healed leper was to show himself to the priest so that he could be examined and then be declared "clean."

Jesus Forgives Sins—Matthew 9:1-8; Mark 2:1-12

17 One day as Jesus was teaching, some Pharisees and teachers of the Law were sitting there. They had come from every village in Galilee and Judea and from Jerusalem. And He had the power of the Lord*d* to heal.

18 Then some men brought a paralyzed man on a bed and tried to take him in and place him in front of Jesus. 19 But when they could not find a way to get him in because of the crowd, they went up on the roof and through the tiles let him and the bed down among the people, right in front of Jesus.

20 When Jesus saw their faith, He said, "Man, your sins are forgiven." 21 Then the scribes*e* and the Pharisees began to argue, saying, "Who is this Fellow who speaks blasphemies? Who but God alone can forgive sins?"

22 Jesus knew what they were thinking. He asked them, "Why do you have such thoughts in your hearts? 23 Is it easier to say, 'Your sins are forgiven,' or to say, 'Get up and walk'? 24 I want you to know that the Son of Man*f* has authority on earth to forgive sins"—then He said to the paralyzed man, "I tell you, get up, take your bed, and go home."

25 Immediately the man stood up in front of them, took the bed he had been lying on, and went home, praising God.

26 They were all amazed and praised God. They were filled with awe and declared, "We can't believe what we have seen today!"

Matthew [Levi]—Matthew 9:9-13; Mark 2:13-17

27 After that He went out and saw a tax collector by the name of Levi sitting in the tax booth. He told him, "Come with Me." 28 Levi got up, left everything, and went with Him.

29 Then Levi gave a large banquet for Jesus at his home, and there was a big crowd of tax collectors and others who were eating with them.

30 The Pharisees and their scribes complained to His disciples: "For what reason do you eat and drink with tax collectors and sinners?"

31 Jesus answered them, "Those who are healthy do not need a doctor, but those who are sick. 32 I have not come to call righteous people, but sinners to repentance."

Jesus Is Questioned About Fasting—Matthew 9:14-17; Mark 2:18-22

33 They said to Him, "John's disciples, as well as the disciples of the Pharisees, often fast and say prayers; but Yours eat and drink."

34 Jesus asked them, "You cannot make the friends of the bridegroom fast while the bridegroom is with them, can you? 35 The time will come when the bridegroom will be taken away from them, and in those days they will fast."

---

d- 17 That is, "the power of God."

e- 21 These were the Bible scholars of Jesus' day. Their work and responsibilities varied greatly from one to another. These areas included making handwritten copies of the Old Testament, interpreting and following the Mosaic guidelines of the Pentateuch (Five Books of Moses), formulating oral laws, teaching God's people in classroom situations, etc. In short, the scribes were considered authorities on the Jewish religion. Compare Ezra 7:6,10.

f- 24 See "Son of Man" in Glossary.

36 He also pictured it for them in this way: "No one tears a piece of cloth from a new garment and sews it on an old one; otherwise, the new cloth also will tear ⌊the old⌋,[g] and the patch from the new will not match the old. **37** No one pours new wine into old wineskins;[h] otherwise, the new wine will burst the skins and run out, and the skins will be ruined. **38** Rather, new wine has to be poured into fresh skins.

39 "No one who has drunk old wine[i] wants the new; for he says, 'The old is good enough!' "

6TH CHAPTER

Lord Of The Sabbath—Matthew 12:1-8; Mark 2:23-28

1 While Jesus was walking through grainfields on a Sabbath, His disciples were picking the heads of grain, rubbing them in their hands, and eating them.

2 Some of the Pharisees asked, "Why are you doing something you have no right to do on the Sabbath?"

3 Jesus asked them, "Haven't you read what David did when he and his men were hungry—**4** how he went into the House of God and took the *loaves set out* ⌊*before God*⌋, which only the priests had the right to eat, and ate of them and gave some to the men with him?" **5** Then He added, "The Son of Man is Lord of the Sabbath."

The Shriveled Hand—Matthew 12:9-15a; Mark 3:1-6

6 On another Sabbath Jesus went into the synagog and taught. And there was a man whose right hand was shriveled. **7** The scribes and the Pharisees were watching Jesus closely to see whether He would heal him on a Sabbath. They wanted to find something of which to accuse Him.

8 But He knew what they were thinking; so He said to the man with the shriveled hand, "Get up and come forward." The man got up and stood there. **9** Then Jesus said to them, "I ask you, is it right on a Sabbath to do good or to do evil, to save a life or to kill?" **10** After looking around at all of them, He told the man, "Stretch out your hand." He did, and his hand was made normal again.

11 They were furious and began to discuss with one another what they could do to Jesus.

Twelve Apostles—Matthew 10:1-4; Mark 3:13-19

12 In those days Jesus went up into the hills to pray, and He continued to pray to God all night.

---

4 Lev 24:5-8; 1 Sam 21:6

---

g- 36 Compare Matthew 9:16 and Mark 2:21.
h- 37 Containers made from the skins of certain animals.
i- 39 Some of the older manuscripts and early translations add the word "immediately" at this point.

13 When it was day, He called His disciples. He chose twelve of them whom He also called apostles: **14** Simon (whom He also named Peter) and his brother Andrew; James and John; Philip and Bartholomew; **15** Matthew and Thomas; James ˻the son˼ of Alphaeus; Simon, the one called Zealot; **16** Judas ˻the son˼ of James; and Judas the man from Kerioth,*a* who became a traitor.

Many Are Healed—Mark 3:7-12

17 He went down with them and stood on a level place with a large crowd of His disciples and a great many people from all over Judea, Jerusalem, and the seacoast of Tyre and Sidon. **18** They had come to hear Him and be healed of their diseases. And those who were plagued by unclean spirits were made well. **19** All the people were trying to touch Him, because power was coming from Him and healing them all.

Blessing And Woe

20 Jesus looked at His disciples and said:

> "Blessed are you who are *poor*,
> > for the Kingdom of God is yours.

21
> Blessed are you who are hungry now,
> > for you will be satisfied.
> *Blessed are you who are crying now,*
> > *for you will laugh.*

22
> Blessed are you when
> > people hate you and exclude you ˻from their company˼,
> > insult you and reject your name as evil,
> > > because you believe in the Son of Man.*b*

23
> "Rejoice in that day and leap for joy,
> > for, you see, you have a great reward in heaven.
> That is just the way their fathers treated the prophets,

24
> > but—

> "Woe to you who are rich,
> > for you have had your comfort.

25
> Woe to you who are well fed now,
> > for you will be hungry.
> Woe to you who are laughing now,
> > for you will mourn and cry aloud.

26
> Woe to you when everyone speaks well of you,
> > for that is how their fathers treated the false prophets."*c*

---

20 Is 57:15 (cf. 61:1)   *21 Is 61:2,3; Ps 126:5,6*

---

6 *a*- 16 Literally: "Judas Iscariot"; see "*Iscariot*" in Glossary.
  b- 22 Literally: "on account of the Son of Man."
  c - 26 Compare the "Blessing"/"Woe" format with Deuteronomy 27:11–28:14.

Love Your Enemies—Matthew 5:38-48

27 "But I tell you who are listening: Love your enemies, be kind to those who hate you, 28 bless those who curse you, and pray for those who insult you. 29 If someone strikes you on the cheek, offer him the other also. If someone takes your coat, do not stop him from taking your shirt. 30 Give to everyone who asks you for something, and if someone takes what is yours, do not insist on getting it back.

31 "Treat others in exactly the same way that you want them to treat you.

32 "If you love those who love you, do you deserve any thanks for that? Even sinners love those who love them. 33 If you help those who help you, do you deserve any thanks for that? Sinners do that too. 34 If you lend anything to those from whom you expect to get something, do you deserve any thanks for that? Sinners also lend to sinners to get back what they lend. 35 Rather, always love your enemies, help them, and lend to them without expecting to get anything back. Then you will have a great reward and will be the sons of the Most High, since He is kind to unthankful and wicked people. 36 Be merciful as your Father is merciful."

Take A Look At Yourself First—Matthew 7:1-5

37 "Stop judging, and you will not be judged. Stop condemning, and you will not be condemned. Forgive, and you will be forgiven. 38 Give, and it will be given to you. A good measure, pressed together, shaken down, and running over, will be put into your lap. You see, the measure you use will be used for you."

39 And He also spoke a parable to them: "A blind man cannot lead a blind man, can he? Won't both fall into a ditch? 40 A pupil is not above his teacher. But everyone who is well trained will be like his teacher.

41 "Why do you look at the speck in your brother's eye and do not notice the log in your own eye? 42 How can you say to your brother, 'Brother, let me take the speck out of your eye,' as long as you do not see the log in your own eye? You hypocrite, first remove the log from your own eye. Then you will see clearly enough to remove the speck from your brother's eye."

Hear And Do!—Matthew 7:15-23

43 "A good tree does not produce bad fruit, or a bad tree produce good fruit. 44 To be sure, each tree is known by its fruit. For you do not pick figs from thornbushes, or grapes from brambles. 45 A good person brings that which is good out of the good stored in his heart, and an evil person brings that which is evil out of the evil that is stored there. What a person says with his mouth flows from his heart.

46 "Why do you call Me 'Lord, Lord,' but do not do what I tell you?

47 "I will show you what everyone is like who comes to Me and who hears My words and continues to follow them. 48 He is like a person who in building a house dug deep and laid the foundation on the rock. When a flood came, the floodwaters dashed against that house but could not move it, because it was well

built. **49** The one who hears ⌊My words⌋ but does not follow them is like a person who built a house on the ground without a foundation. When the floodwaters dashed against it, that house immediately collapsed and went down with a loud crash."

7 TH CHAPTER

A Believing Captain—Matthew 8:5-13

1 When Jesus had finished all He had to say to the people who heard Him, He went to Capernaum. **2** There the slave of a certain captain was sick. He was dear to the captain and now he was dying. **3** The captain heard about Jesus and sent some Jewish elders to ask Him to come and save the life of his slave. **4** They came to Jesus and earnestly pleaded with Him, "He deserves to have You do this for him, **5** because he loves our people and built the synagog for us."

6 Jesus went with them. He was not far from the house when the captain sent friends to tell Him, "Lord, do not bother. For I am not worthy to have You come under my roof. **7** And so I did not think I was fit to come to You either. But just say a word, and my servant will be made well. **8** For I also am a man under authority who has soldiers under me. I tell one of them, 'Go!' and he goes; and another, 'Come!' and he comes; and my slave, 'Do this!' and he does it."

9 When Jesus heard these words, He was amazed at the captain. He turned to the crowd following Him and said, "I tell you, not even in Israel have I found such faith."

10 When the men who had been sent returned to the house, they found the slave well again.

Jesus Raises A Widow's Son

11 Soon after this, Jesus went to a town called Nain, and His disciples and a large crowd went with Him. **12** As He came near the gate of the town, a dead man was carried out. He was his mother's only[a] son, and she was a widow. A large crowd from the town was with her.

13 When the Lord saw her, He felt sorry for her. "Stop crying," He told her.

14 He went up to the open coffin and touched it, and the men who were carrying it stood still. He said, "Young man, I tell you, wake up." **15** The dead man sat up and began to talk. And Jesus *gave him to his mother*.

16 They were all overawed and praised God. They said, "A great prophet has risen among us," and "God has come to help His people."[b] **17** This report about Jesus spread throughout Judea and all the surrounding region.

---

15 1 Kgs 17:23

---

7 *a*- 12 See *MONOGENĒS* on page 542.
  b- 16 Literally: "and God has visited His people"; see 1:68 and its accompanying footnote "p."

John Sends Two Disciples—Matthew 11:2-6

18 The disciples of John told him about all these things. **19** Then John called two of his disciples and sent them to ask the Lord, "Are You the One who is coming, or should we look for someone else?"

20 The men came to Jesus and said, "John the Baptizer sent us to ask You, 'Are You the One who is coming, or should we look for someone else?' "

21 Right at that time He healed many people of their diseases, ailments, and evil spirits, and He gave sight to many who were blind.

22 Jesus answered, "Go, tell John what you have seen and heard: *Blind people see* and those who were lame are walking; lepers are made clean and *deaf people hear*; those who were dead are raised and *poor people hear the Gospel*; **23** and blessed is anyone who does not stumble*c* in ˻his evaluation of˼ Me."

About John—Matthew 11:7-19

24 When the messengers of John had left, Jesus began to speak to the crowds about John: "What did you go out into the wilderness to see—a reed shaken by the wind? **25** What did you go out to see—a man dressed in soft robes? Those who wear fine clothes and live in luxury are found in the palaces of kings. **26** What did you go out to see—a prophet? Let Me assure you, far more than a prophet. **27** This is the one of whom it is written:

> *I am sending My messenger ahead of You*
> *to prepare* Your *way before* You.

28 I tell you, of all those born to women, none is greater than John, and yet the least in the Kingdom of God is greater than he.

29 "By letting John baptize them, all the people who heard him, even the tax collectors, admitted that God was right. *d* **30** But the Pharisees and the experts in the Law, by not letting John baptize them, rejected what God had planned for them.

31 "How should I picture the people of this generation? What are they like? **32** They are like little children sitting in the marketplace and calling to one another:

> 'We played a tune on the flute for you,
>   but you did not dance.
> We sang a funeral song,
>   but you did not weep.'

33 For John the Baptizer has come; he does not eat bread or drink wine, and you say, 'There's a demon in him!' **34** The Son of Man has come; He eats and drinks,

---

22 *Is 29:18; 35:5; 61:1*   27 *Mal 3:1 (cf. Ex 23:20)*

---

c- 23 See *SKANDALON* on page 545.
d- 29 Literally: "even the tax collectors justified God"; compare verse 35.

and you say, 'Look at the glutton and drunkard, a friend of tax collectors and sinners!'

35 "And yet wisdom is proved right*e* by all her children."

"Her Love Is Great"

36 One of the Pharisees invited Jesus to eat with him. Jesus went into the Pharisee's home and reclined at the table.

37 In the town there was a sinful woman. When she found out He was eating at the Pharisee's home, she brought an alabaster jar of perfume **38** and stood behind Him at His feet. She was weeping and began to wet his feet with her tears. Then with the hair of her head she dried His feet, kissed them, and poured perfume on them.

39 The Pharisee who had invited Jesus saw this and said to himself, "If He were a prophet, He would know who is touching Him and what kind of woman she is, for she is a sinner."

40 Jesus answered him, "Simon, I have something to say to you."

"Say it, Teacher," he said.

41 "Two men owed a moneylender some money: One owed him five hundred denarii,*f* and the other fifty. **42** When they could not pay it back, he was kind enough to cancel the debt for both of them. Now, which of them will love him more?"

43 Simon answered, "I suppose the one who had the bigger debt canceled."

"You are right," Jesus told him. **44** Then, turning to the woman, He said to Simon, "Do you see this woman? I came into your home, and you gave Me no water for My feet, but she wet My feet with her tears and dried them with her hair. **45** You gave Me no kiss, but ever since I came in, she has not stopped kissing My feet. **46** You poured no olive oil on My head, but she poured perfume on My feet. **47** That is why I tell you that her many sins have been forgiven—for she loved very much. But he who has little forgiven loves little."

48 Then He said to her, "Your sins are forgiven." **49** His fellow guests began to ask among themselves, "Who is this Person who even forgives sins?"

50 Jesus said to the woman, "Your faith saved you. Go in peace!"

8TH CHAPTER

Through Galilee

1 After this Jesus traveled from one town and village to another, preaching and telling the Good News of God's Kingdom. The Twelve were with Him, **2** and some women who had been healed of evil spirits and diseases: Mary, also called the woman from Magdala (seven demons had gone out of her); **3** Joanna the wife of Chusa, Herod's manager; Susanna; and many other women. They supported Jesus and His disciples with their property.

---

e- 35 Literally: "is justified"; compare verse 29.
f- 41 See MONEY, WEIGHTS, and MEASURES on page 328.

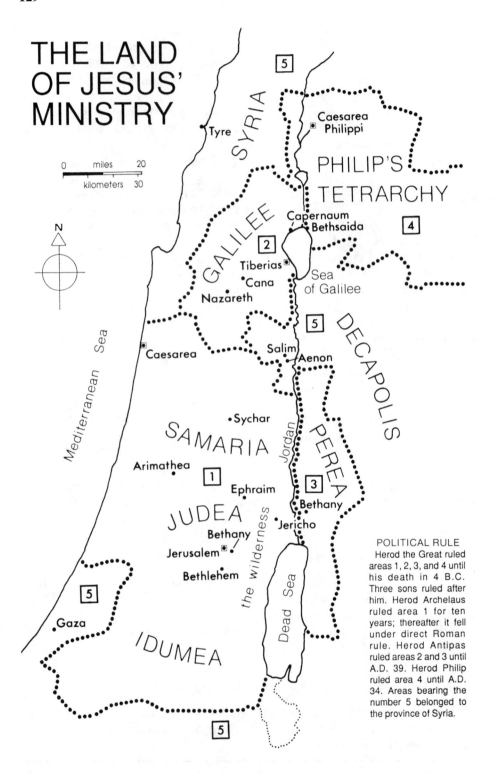

THE LAND OF JESUS' MINISTRY

0 miles 20
kilometers 30

N

SYRIA

Tyre

Caesarea
Philippi

PHILIP'S
TETRARCHY

GALILEE

Capernaum
Bethsaida

5

4

2

Tiberias

Cana

Nazareth

Sea
of Galilee

DECAPOLIS

Caesarea

Salim

Aenon

5

Mediterranean Sea

Jordan

Sychar

SAMARIA

PEREA

Arimathea

1

Ephraim

3

Bethany

JUDEA

Jericho

Bethany

the wilderness

Jerusalem

Bethlehem

Dead Sea

5

Gaza

IDUMEA

5

POLITICAL RULE
Herod the Great ruled
areas 1, 2, 3, and 4 until
his death in 4 B.C.
Three sons ruled after
him. Herod Archelaus
ruled area 1 for ten
years; thereafter it fell
under direct Roman
rule. Herod Antipas
ruled areas 2 and 3 until
A.D. 39. Herod Philip
ruled area 4 until A.D.
34. Areas bearing the
number 5 belonged to
the province of Syria.

The Sower—Matthew 13:1-23; Mark 4:1-20

4 When a large crowd was gathering and people were coming to Him from every town, He told them a parable: **5** "A sower went out to sow his seed. As he was sowing, some seed fell along the road and was trampled on, and the birds in the air devoured it. **6** Some fell on rocky soil. When it came up, it withered because it had no moisture. **7** Some seed fell among thorns, and the thorns grew up with it and choked it. **8** But some seed fell on good ground, and it came up and produced a hundred times as much as was sown."

When He had said this, He called out, "The one who has ears to hear, let him listen!"

9 His disciples asked Him what this parable meant. **10** He answered, "You are given the privilege of knowing the secrets of the Kingdom of God, but to the others they are given in parables—with the result that *they see and yet do not see, they hear and yet do not understand.*

11 "This is what the parable means: The seed is God's word. **12** The people along the road are those who hear it. Then the devil comes and takes the word out of their hearts to keep them from believing and being saved. **13** The people on rocky soil are those who welcome the word with joy as soon as they hear it, but it does not take root in them. They believe for a while, but in time of temptation, they fall away. **14** In others the seed fell among thorns. They hear ⌊the word⌋, but as they go along, worries, riches, and pleasures of life choke them, and they do not produce anything good. **15** But in others the seed fell on good ground. They are the ones who hear the word and keep it in a good and honest heart, and who go on in patient endurance producing good things.

16 "No one lights a lamp and hides it under a jar or puts it under a bed. No, you put it on a lampstand so that those who come in will see the light. **17** Everything hidden will be uncovered, and every secret certainly will be known and come to the light.

18 "Be careful therefore how you listen! For whoever has something will be given more. But whoever does not have what he should have, even what he thinks he has will be taken away from him."

The Mother And Brothers Of Jesus—Matthew 12:46-50; Mark 3:31-35

19 His mother and His brothers came to Him but could not get near Him because of the crowd. **20** Jesus was told, "Your mother and Your brothers are standing outside and want to see You."

21 He answered them, "My mother and My brothers are those who continue to hear God's word and follow it."

Wind And Water Obey Him—Matthew 8:23-27; Mark 4:35-41

22 One day He and His disciples stepped into a boat. "Let us cross over to the other side of the sea," He said to them. They started out. **23** And as they were sailing along, He fell asleep.

---

10 Is 6:9

A violent storm hit the sea, the boat was filling with water, and they were in danger. **24** They went to Him and woke Him. "Master, Master!" they called. "We're going to drown!"

He got up and ordered the winds and the waves to stop. They stopped and it became calm. **25** "Where is your trust?" He asked them.

They were frightened and amazed, and they asked one another, "Who then is this Person? He gives orders even to the winds and the water, and they obey Him!"

The Gergesenes—Matthew 8:28-34; Mark 5:1-20

26 They landed in the region of the Gergesenes,*a* which is opposite Galilee. **27** When He stepped out on the shore, a man from the town who had demons in him met Him. He had not worn clothes for a long time. He would not stay in a house but in the burial caves. **28** When he saw Jesus, he cried out and fell down before Him and in a loud voice said, "What do we have in common, Jesus, Son of the Most High God! I beg You, do not torture me!" **29** For Jesus had begun to order the unclean spirit to come out of the man. For a long time it had taken control of him. He had been bound with chains on ˎhisˎ hands and feet and had been kept under guard, but he would tear the chains and be driven by the demon into lonely places.

30 Jesus asked him, "What is your name?"

"Legion [Six Thousand],"*b* he answered, because many demons had gone into him. **31** They begged Him not to order them to go into the bottomless pit.

32 There was a herd of many hogs feeding on the hillside. So they begged Him to let them go into these. He let them. **33** The demons came out of the man and went into the hogs; and the herd stampeded down the cliff into the sea and was drowned.

34 But when those who had taken care of the hogs saw what had happened, they ran away and reported it in the town and in the country. **35** The people went out to see what had happened. They came to Jesus and found the man from whom the demons had gone out. He was now sitting at Jesus' feet, dressed and in his right mind; and the people were frightened. *c* **36** Those who had seen it told them how the man plagued by demons had been made well.

37 Then all the people of the surrounding region of the Gergesenes asked Jesus to leave them, because terror had gripped them. *d*

He got into a boat and started back. **38** Now the man from whom the demons had gone out begged Jesus to let him be with Him. But He sent him away and told him, **39** "Go home and tell how much God has done for you." So the man left and preached all over the town how much Jesus had done for him.

---

8 *a-* 26 Gergesa was a small village in the territory of Hippus, north of the city of Hippus. It was a part of the area of the Decapolis [Ten Towns], a federation of *Greek* towns. Some of the older manuscripts and early translations have *Gadarenes*; others *Gerasenes*.

b- 30 There were 6,000 soldiers in a Roman legion, that is, when it was at full strength.

c- 35 Or "overawed."

d- 37 Or "because they were overcome with awe."

The Daughter Of Jairus And
A Woman Who Was Continuously Bleeding—*Matthew 9:18-26; Mark 5:21-43*

40 When Jesus came back, the people welcomed Him, because they were all expecting Him.

41 A man named Jairus, who was a leader of the synagog, came and kneeled at Jesus' feet. He begged Jesus to come to his home, **42** because his only*e* daughter who was about twelve years old was dying. As He went, the crowd almost crushed Him.

43 There was a woman who had a flow of blood for twelve years. No one could cure her, even though she had spent all she had on doctors.*f* **44** She came to Him from behind and touched the tassel of His garment, and immediately her bleeding stopped.

45 Jesus asked, "Who touched Me?"

When everyone denied having touched Him, Peter said, "Master, the people are crowding You and pressing against You."

46 Jesus said, "Someone did touch Me, for I know that power went out from Me."

47 When the woman saw she was discovered, she came trembling, bowed down before Him, and in front of all the people told why she touched Him and how she was made well immediately.

48 He told her, "Daughter, your faith has made you well. Go in peace!"

49 While He was still speaking, someone came from the home of the leader of the synagog. "Your daughter is dead," he said. "Don't trouble the Teacher anymore."

50 When Jesus heard this, He told the synagog leader,*g* "Stop being afraid. Only believe, and she will get well."

51 When He came into the house, He permitted no one to go in with Him except Peter, John, James, and the child's father and mother. **52** And they were all weeping and mourning for her.*h* He said, "Do not go on weeping. She's not dead; she is sleeping."

53 They laughed at Him, because they knew she had died. **54** He took her hand and called, "Girl, get up!" **55** Her spirit returned, and she got up immediately. Jesus ordered that she be given something to eat. **56** And her parents were amazed. But He ordered them not to tell anyone what had happened.

9TH CHAPTER

Jesus Sends Out The Twelve—*Matthew 10:1-42; Mark 6:7-13*

1 Jesus called the Twelve together and gave them power and authority over

---

e- 42 See *MONOGENĒS* on page 542.

f- 43 Some of the older manuscripts and early translations omit: "even though she had spent all she had on doctors."

g- 50 Literally: "him."

h- 52 Literally: "and bewailing her."

all the demons and to heal diseases. **2** He sent them to preach the Kingdom of God and to heal the sick.

3 He told them, "Do not take anything with you on the way, no staff,[a] no bag, no bread, no money. Do not take two tunics. **4** When you go into a home, stay there, and from there go out. **5** If people do not welcome you, leave that town, and shake the dust off your feet as a warning to them."

6 They left and went from village to village, preaching the Gospel and healing the sick everywhere.

Has John Come Back?—*Matthew 14:1-12; Mark 6:14-29*

7 Herod the ruler[b] heard about everything Jesus was doing and did not know what to make of it, because some people were saying, "John has risen from the dead"; **8** others were saying, "Elijah has appeared"; still others were saying, "One of the ancient prophets has risen."

9 Herod said, "I beheaded John. Now then, who is this about whom I hear such things?" And he wanted to see Jesus.

Jesus Feeds 5,000—*Matthew 14:13-21; Mark 6:30-44; John 6:1-14*

10 The apostles came back and told Jesus all they had done. He took them away with Him to a town called Bethsaida in order to be alone. **11** But the crowds found out about it and followed Him. He welcomed them, talked to them about God's Kingdom, and healed those who needed healing.

12 Toward the end of the day the Twelve came to Him and told Him, "Send the crowd away to the villages and farms around here so that they may find lodging and food, because here we are in a deserted place."

13 He told them, "You give them something to eat."

They answered, "All we have are five loaves and two fish, unless perhaps we go and buy food for all these people." **14** There were about 5,000 men.

Then He told His disciples, "Have them sit down in groups of about fifty." **15** They did this and got them all seated.

16 After He took the five loaves and the two fish, He looked up to heaven, gave thanks[c] for them, broke them, and kept giving them to the disciples to give to the people. **17** All of them ate and had enough. And they picked up the pieces that were left over—twelve baskets full.

You Are The Christ [Messiah]—*Matthew 16:13-20; Mark 8:27-30*

18 Once when He was praying and only His disciples were with Him, He asked them, "Who do people say I am?"

19 "John the Baptizer," they answered Him; "others say Elijah; and still others, that one of the ancient prophets has come back to life."

20 "But you, who do you say I am?" He asked them.

---

9 *a*- 3 Among other things a staff was used for protection and as an aid for walking.

  b- 7 Literally: "the tetrarch," one who ruled over one-fourth of the kingdom of Herod the Great.

  c- 16 See Matthew 14:19 and its accompanying footnote.

"The Christ whom God has sent," Peter answered.

21 But He gave them strict orders to tell this to no one.

Take Up Your Cross—Matthew 16:24-28; Mark 8:34–9:1

22 Jesus said, "The Son of Man has to suffer much. He has to be rejected by the elders, ruling priests, and scribes, be killed, and then be raised on the third day."

23 And He told all of them, "If you want to follow Me, deny yourself, take up your cross every day, and come with Me. 24 For whoever wants to save his life will lose it, but whoever loses his life for Me will save it. 25 For what good does it do a person to win the whole world and destroy or lose himself? 26 For whoever is ashamed of Me and My words, of that person the Son of Man will be ashamed when He comes in the glory which He shares with the Father and the holy angels.

27 "Let me assure you, there are some standing here who will never taste death until they see the Kingdom of God."

Jesus Shows His Glory (The Transfiguration)—Matthew 17:1-8; Mark 9:2-13

28 About a week*d* after He said this, Jesus took Peter, John, and James with Him and went up the mountain to pray. 29 While He was praying, the appearance of His face changed*e* and His clothing became dazzling white. 30 And there were two men talking with Him; they were Moses and Elijah. 31 They appeared in glory and were talking about His leaving this world,*f* which was about to happen at Jerusalem.

32 But Peter and the men with him had been overcome by sleep. When they woke up, they saw His glory and the two men standing with Him. 33 When these were leaving Him, Peter said to Jesus, "Master, it's good for us to be here. Let's put up three shelters,*g* one for You, one for Moses, and one for Elijah." He did not realize what he was saying.

34 While he was saying this, a cloud came and overshadowed them. They were frightened as they went into the cloud. 35 Then a voice came out of the cloud: *"This is My Son, whom I have chosen. Listen to Him!"* 36 When the voice had spoken, they saw that Jesus was alone.

They kept silent, and in those days they told no one about anything they had seen.

The Boy With An Evil Spirit—Matthew 17:14-20; Mark 9:14-29

37 The next day, when they had come down from the mountain, He met a large crowd. 38 Then a man in the crowd called, "Teacher, I beg You to take a

---

35 *Deut 18:15; Ps 2:7; Is 42:1*

---

d - 28 Literally: "About eight days."
e - 29 That is, Jesus was transfigured; see Matthew 17:2; Mark 9:2.
f - 31 Literally: "His departure," that is, His suffering and death.
g - 33 See Matthew 17:4 and its accompanying footnote.

look at my son, because he is my only[h] child. **39** A spirit keeps taking hold of him, and suddenly he shrieks. It throws him into convulsions, and he foams at the mouth. It hardly ever stops mistreating him. **40** I asked Your disciples to drive out the spirit, but they could not do it."

41 Jesus answered, "O you unbelieving and perverted kind of people! How long must I be with you and put up with you! Bring your son here."

42 While the boy was coming, the demon knocked him to the ground and threw him into convulsions.

Jesus spoke sharply to the unclean spirit, made the boy well, and gave him back to his father. **43** All were amazed to see God's wonderful power.

The Son Of Man Will Be Betrayed—*Matthew 17:22,23; 18:1-5; Mark 9:30-37*

While everybody was amazed at all the things that Jesus was doing, He said to His disciples, **44** "Listen carefully to what I say. The Son of Man is going to be betrayed into the hands of men."

45 But they did not know what He meant. It was hidden from them so that they did not understand it. And they were afraid to ask Him about it.

46 A discussion started among them as to which of them would be the greatest. **47** But Jesus knew what they were thinking. He took a little child, had him stand by Him, **48** and said to them, "Whoever welcomes this little child in My Name welcomes Me. And whoever welcomes Me welcomes the One who sent Me. You see, the one who is least among all of you, this is the one who is great."

"He Is For Us"—*Mark 9:38-41*

49 John said, "Master, we saw a man driving out demons in Your Name, and we tried to stop him, because he's not one of us."

50 "Do not try to stop him," Jesus told him, "for anyone who is not against you is for you."

D. Jesus' journey from Galilee to Jerusalem (9:51–19:27)

To Jerusalem

51 As the time was coming nearer for Jesus to be taken up to heaven, He showed that He was determined to go to Jerusalem. **52** He sent messengers ahead of Him. They went and entered into a village of the Samaritans to arrange a place for Him to stay. **53** But the people did not welcome Him, because He was headed for Jerusalem. **54** When His disciples James and John saw this, they asked, "Lord, do You want us to order *fire to come down from heaven and burn* them up?"

---

54 2 Kgs 1:10,12

---

h- 38 See *MONOGENĒS* on page 542.

55 But He turned and sternly corrected them. *i* 56 So they went on to another village.

"I Will Follow, But . . ."—Matthew 8:19-22

57 As they were walking along the road, a man said to Him, "I will follow You anywhere You go."

58 Jesus told him, "Foxes have holes and birds of the air have nests, but the Son of Man does not have a place to lay His head."

59 He told another man, "Follow Me."

But he said, "Lord, first let me go and bury my father."

60 But Jesus told him, "Let the dead bury their own dead. But you go and tell about the Kingdom of God."

61 Another said, "I will follow You, Lord, but first let me say good-bye to those at home."

62 Jesus answered him, "Anyone who puts his hand to a plow and keeps looking back is not fit for the Kingdom of God."

10TH CHAPTER

72 Missionaries

1 After this the Lord appointed 72*a* others and sent them out two by two to go ahead of Him to every town and place where He intended to go.

2 He told them, "There is much grain to be harvested, but there are only a few workers. Ask the Lord of the harvest to send out workers to bring in His harvest. 3 Go! I am sending you like lambs among wolves. 4 Do not carry a purse, a bag, or sandals; and do not stop to greet anyone on the way. 5 Whenever you go into a house, say first, 'May there be peace in this house.' 6 If a man of peace lives there, your peace will rest on him; but if not, it will come back to you. 7 Stay in that house and eat and drink whatever they have, since a worker earns his pay. Do not move around from one house to another. 8 Whenever you go into a town and the people welcome you, eat what they serve you. 9 Heal the sick that are there, and tell the people, 'The Kingdom of God has come close to you!'

10 "But whenever you go into a town and they do not welcome you, go out on its streets and say, 11 'The dust of your town has clung to our feet—we are wiping it off in protest against you! But realize this: The Kingdom of God has come near you!' 12 I tell you, on that Day it will be easier for Sodom than for that town.

13 "Woe to you, Chorazin! Woe to you, Bethsaida! If the miracles*b* worked in you had been worked in Tyre and Sidon, they would long ago have repented,

---

i- 55 Some of the older manuscripts and early translations add: " 'You do not know the kind of spirit that is influencing you. The Son of Man did not come to destroy men's lives but to save them,' He said."

10 *a*- 1 Or "70" (also in v. 17). See JESUS SENDS THE 72 MISSIONARIES on page 554.

b- 13 See MIRACULOUS SIGNS, WONDERFUL PROOFS, and MIRACLES on page 527.

sitting in sackcloth and ashes. **14** In the Judgment it will be easier for Tyre and Sidon than for you. **15** And you, Capernaum, you will not be *lifted up to heaven*, will you? No, *you will go down to hell [hades].*^c

16 "The person who hears you hears Me, and the person who rejects you rejects Me. And the person who rejects Me rejects the One who sent Me."

17 The 72 came back delighted. They said, "Lord, even the demons do what we tell them in Your Name."

18 He said to them, "I watched^d Satan fall from heaven like lightning. **19** Take note! I have given you the authority to *step on snakes* and scorpions and to trample on all the enemy's power, and nothing will hurt you. **20** However, do not rejoice over the fact that the spirits obey you, but rejoice that your names are written in heaven."

21 In that hour the Holy Spirit filled Jesus with joy. He said, "I praise You, Father, Lord of heaven and earth, for hiding these things from wise and intelligent people and revealing them to little children. Yes, Father, I praise You for wanting it to be that way.

22 "My Father has put everything in My hands. Only the Father knows the Son, and only the Son—and anyone to whom the Son wants to reveal Him —knows the Father."

23 He turned to His disciples and said to them alone, "Blessed are the eyes that see what you see. **24** For I tell you, many prophets and kings longed to see what you see but did not see it, and hear what you hear but did not hear it."

The Good Samaritan

25 Then an expert in the Law came forward to test Jesus. He asked, "Teacher, what should I do to inherit everlasting life?"

26 Jesus in turn asked him, "What is written in the Scriptures?^e What do you read there?"

27 He answered, " 'Love the Lord your God with all your heart and with all your soul and with all your strength and with all your mind, and your neighbor as yourself.' "

28 Jesus told him, "You are right. *Continue to do this and you will live.*"

29 But he wanted to justify himself. So he asked Jesus, "And who is my neighbor?"

30 Jesus replied and said: "A man went from Jerusalem down to Jericho and fell into the hands of robbers. They stripped him, struck him blow after blow, and went away leaving him half dead.

31 "Now it so happened that a priest came down that road, but when he saw him, he passed by on the other side. **32** A Levite who came to the place did the same thing: he looked at him and passed by on the other side.

33 "Then a Samaritan, as he was traveling, came near him, and when he saw

---

15 Is 14:13,15   *19 Ps 91:13*   *27 Lev 19:18; Deut 6:5*   *28 Lev 18:5*

---

c- 15 Meaning "the place of/receptacle for disembodied souls"; see *HADES/GEHENNA* on page 540.
d- 18 Or "I was watching."
e- 26 Literally: "Law"; see 2:22 and its accompanying footnote.

him, he felt sorry for him. **34** He went to him and bandaged his wounds, pouring on ͺolive͵ oil and wine. Then he put him on his own animal, brought him to an inn, and took care of him. **35** The next day he took out two denarii*f* and gave them to the innkeeper. 'Take care of him,' he said, 'and anything else you spend on him I will pay back to you when I return.'

36 "Which of those three, do you think, was a neighbor to the man who had fallen into the hands of the robbers?"

37 He said, "The one who was kind enough to help him."

Jesus told him, "Go and do as he did."

Mary Listens To Jesus

38 As they were walking along, Jesus came to a village where a woman by the name of Martha welcomed Him into her home. **39** She had a sister by the name of Mary who continually sat at the Lord's feet and listened to His word.

40 But Martha was worried about all she had to do for them. She came and asked, "Lord, don't You care that my sister has left me and I have to do the work alone? Now tell her to help me."

41 The Lord answered her, "Martha, Martha, you worry and fuss about a lot of things. **42** But there is only one thing you need.*g* Mary has made the right choice, and it will not be taken away from her."

11TH CHAPTER

The Lord's Prayer—Matthew 6:9-13

1 Once Jesus was praying in a certain place. When He stopped, one of His disciples said to Him, "Lord, teach us to pray as John taught his disciples."

2 He told them, "When you pray, say:

> Our Father in heaven*a*
> > may Your Name be kept holy,
> > may Your Kingdom come,
> > may Your will be done,
> > > on earth as it is in heaven;*b*
>
> **3** give us every day our daily bread;
> **4** forgive us our sins
> > as we, too, forgive everyone who sins against us;
> and do not lead us into temptation,
> but deliver us from evil."*c*

---

f- 35 See MONEY, WEIGHTS, and MEASURES on page 328.

g- 42 Some of the older manuscripts and early translations read: "But of the few things ͺworth worrying about͵ there is only one thing you need."

11 *a-* 2 Some of the older manuscripts and early translations omit: "Our" and "in heaven."

b- 2 Some of the older manuscripts and early translations omit: "may Your will be done on earth as it is in heaven." The commas at the end of each of the three former lines indicate that this phrase "on earth as it is in heaven" is to be seen as part of *each* of the three former lines.

c- 4 Some of the older manuscripts and early translations omit: "but deliver us from evil" or "from the Evil One." The doxology "You are the King who rules with power and glory forever. Amen." is found in later manuscripts. It is based on Daniel 7:14; 1 Chronicles 29:11.

Pray—*Matthew 7:7-11*

5 Jesus said to His disciples, "Suppose one of you has a friend, and you go to him at midnight and say to him, 'Friend, lend me three loaves. 6 A friend of mine on a trip has dropped in on me, and I have nothing to serve him.' 7 And suppose he answers you from within: 'Stop bothering me! The door is already locked, and my children are with me in bed. I can't get up and give you anything.' 8 I tell you, although he will not get up and give you anything even though he is your friend, yet because you persist, he will get up and give you anything you need.

9 "So I tell you: Keep asking, and it will be given to you. Keep searching, and you will find. Keep knocking, and the door will be opened to you. 10 For anyone who continues to ask receives; anyone who continues to search finds; and to anyone who continues to knock, the door will be opened.

11 "If your son asks you, his father, for a fish, you wouldn't give him a snake instead of a fish, would you? 12 Or if he should ask for an egg, would you give him a scorpion? 13 Now if you, wicked as you are, know enough to give your children good gifts, how much more will your Father in heaven give the Holy Spirit to those who ask Him?"

Power Over A Demon—*Matthew 12:22-32; Mark 3:20-30*

14 He was driving out a demon who was unable to talk. When the demon had gone out, the man who was unable to talk began to speak.

The people were amazed. 15 But some of them said, "He drives out the demons with the help of Beelzebul, who rules over the demons." 16 Others, meaning to test Him, demanded that He show them some miraculous sign[d] from heaven.

17 Since He knew what they were thinking, He said to them, "If any kingdom is divided against itself, it is ruined, and a house divided against itself[e] falls. 18 If Satan is divided against himself, how can his kingdom stand? I say this because you say Beelzebul helps Me drive out the demons. 19 But if Beelzebul helps Me drive out the demons, who helps your sons drive them out? That is why they will be your judges. 20 But if I with the finger of God drive out the demons, then the Kingdom of God has come to you.

21 "When a strong man, fully armed, guards his palace, his property is not disturbed. 22 But when someone stronger than he attacks him and defeats him, he will take away his whole armor in which he trusted, and divide the plunder.

23 "Anyone[f] who is not with Me is against Me, and anyone who does not join Me in gathering, scatters.

24 "When an unclean spirit comes out of a person, he goes through dry places looking for rest but does not find any. Then he says, 'I will go back to the home I left.' 25 He comes and finds it swept and decorated. 26 Then he goes and brings seven other spirits worse than himself, and they go in and live there. In the end that person is worse off than he was before."

---

d- 16 See MIRACULOUS SIGNS, WONDERFUL PROOFS, and MIRACLES on page 527.

e- 17 Literally: "a house against a house."

f- 23 Literally: "the one/the person" (twice in verse).

The Sign Of Jonah—Matthew 12:38-42

27 When Jesus said this, a woman in the crowd raised her voice and called out to Him, "Blessed is the mother who gave birth to You and the breasts which nursed You."

28 "Yes," He said, "but blessed are those who continue to listen to God's word and keep it."

29 As the people were crowding around Him, He said: "This generation is a wicked one. It is looking for a miraculous sign, but the only sign it will receive is that of Jonah. 30 As Jonah became a miraculous sign to the people of Nineveh, so the Son of Man will be to this generation. 31 The queen of the south will be raised up along with the men of this generation at the time of Judgment and will condemn them, because she came from the ends of the earth to hear Solomon's wisdom—but something*g* greater than Solomon is here! 32 The men of Nineveh will come to life along with this generation at the time of Judgment and will condemn it, because they repented when Jonah preached—but something greater than Jonah is here!"

Your Light—Matthew 5:14-16; Mark 4:21-23

33 "No one lights a lamp and puts it in a cellar or under a container but on the lampstand, so that those who come in will see it shine.

34 "Your eye is the lamp of your body. When your eye is healthy, you have light for your whole body. But when your eye is bad, your body is dark! 35 Then see to it that the light in you is not dark. 36 Now if you have light for your whole body and no part of it is dark, it will all have light just as when a lamp shines brightly on you."

Warnings And Woes—Matthew 23:13-39

37 During the time that Jesus spoke, a Pharisee invited Him to eat at his home. So He went in and reclined at the table. 38 But the Pharisee was surprised to see that He did not wash before the meal.

39 The Lord said to him, "You Pharisees keep cleaning the outside of the cup and of the dish, but inside you are full of greed and wickedness. 40 You fools, didn't the One who made the outside make the inside too? 41 Give what is inside as a gift to help the poor, and then everything will be clean for you.

42 "But woe to you Pharisees! You give a tenth of mint, rue, and every garden herb, but you fail to be just and to love God. You should have done these without neglecting the others.

43 "And woe to you Pharisees! You like to have the seats of honor in the synagogs and to be greeted in the marketplaces. 44 Woe to you! You are like the unmarked graves that people walk over without knowing what they are."

45 One of the experts in the Law said to Him, "Teacher, when You say that, You insult us also."

---

g- 31 Here and in the next verse Jesus uses the *neuter* to refer to the Kingdom (cf. v. 20).

46 He said, "Woe also to you experts in the Law! You load people with burdens they can hardly carry, but you yourselves will not touch these burdens with one of your fingers. **47** Woe to you! You build monuments for the prophets whom your fathers murdered. **48** So you are witnesses and approve of what your fathers did, because they murdered the prophets, and you build ˌtheir monumentsˌ. **49** That is why the wisdom of God said:*ʰ* 'I will send them prophets and apostles, and they will murder or persecute some of them **50** so that this generation may be punished for the blood of all the prophets shed since the world was made, **51** from the blood of Abel to the blood of Zachariah, who was killed between the altar and the Temple.' Yes, I tell you, this generation will be punished for it.

52 "Woe to you experts in the Law! You have taken away the key to knowledge. You yourselves did not go in, and you kept out those who tried to go in."

53 When Jesus went outside, the scribes and the Pharisees began to oppose Him fiercely and cross-examine Him about many things, **54** watching Him closely to trap Him in something He might say.

12TH CHAPTER

Do Not Be Afraid Of Men

1 When so many thousands of people came together that they trampled on one another, Jesus began to speak first to His disciples: "Beware of the yeast of the Pharisees—I mean, their hypocrisy. **2** Everything that is covered will be uncovered, and every secret will be known. **3** Everything you said in the dark will be heard in the light, and what you whispered in the ear in the inner rooms will be announced from the rooftops. **4** But I tell you, My friends, do not be afraid of those who kill the body and then cannot do any more. **5** I will point out the One you should fear. Fear Him who after He has killed you has the authority to cast you into hell.*ᵃ* Yes, I tell you, fear Him!

6 "Are not five sparrows sold for two cents? And God does not forget any one of them. **7** Why, even the hairs on your head are all counted! Stop being afraid—you are worth more than many sparrows! **8** I tell you, whoever will confess Me before others, him the Son of Man will confess before the angels of God. **9** The person who denies Me before other people will be denied before the angels of God. **10** Anyone who will speak against the Son of Man will be forgiven. But he who slanders the Holy Spirit will not be forgiven.

11 "When they bring you before synagogs, rulers, and authorities, do not

---

h - 49 That is, "God in His wisdom" (cf. 7:35): God's intention as interpreted by Jesus. The statement by Jesus which follows (vv. 49-51) does not quote any one specific passage of the Old Testament. A portion of it refers to something known only within the Godhead Itself; the substance of the rest is to be found throughout various places of the Old Testament. Note that Jesus does the "sending" in Matthew 23:34, but the "wisdom of God" does it here in Luke (cf. Prov. 8). This can denote the Trinity in action.

12 *a* - 5 Greek: "*gehenna*"; see *HADES/GEHENNA* on page 540.

worry about how you will defend yourselves or what you will say. **12** When that time comes, the Holy Spirit will teach you what to say."

Guard Against Greed

13 Someone in the crowd said to Him, "Teacher, tell my brother to give me my share of the property ⌊that our father left us⌋."

14 "Man," He asked him, "who appointed Me to be your judge or a divider over ⌊your property⌋?"

15 He told the people, "Be careful and guard against every kind of greed, because even if a person has more than enough, his property does not make his life secure."[b]

16 Then He told them a parable: "A rich man had good crops on his land. **17** He thought to himself, 'What am I going to do? I have no place to store my crops.' **18** He said, 'This is what I will do: I will tear down my barns and build bigger ones and store all my grain and goods in them. **19** Then I'll say to myself, "You have a lot of good things stored up for many years. Take life easy, eat, drink, and enjoy yourself." '

20 "But God said to him, 'You fool, tonight you will die.[c] And what you have prepared—who will get it?' **21** That is how it is when a person stores up goods for himself and is not rich toward God."

Stop Worrying—Matthew 6:25-34

22 He said to His disciples: "That is why I tell you: Stop worrying about what you will eat to keep alive or what you will wear on your bodies. **23** For life is more than food, and the body more than clothing. **24** Look at the ravens. They do not sow or reap; they have no storeroom or barn; yet God continues to feed them. You are worth much more than birds.

25 "Can any of you add an hour to your life[d] by worrying? **26** So if you cannot do even the smallest thing, why worry about the rest? **27** Consider how the flowers[e] grow; they do not work or spin. Yet I tell you, even Solomon in all his glory was not dressed like one of them. **28** If that is how God clothes the grass which lives in the field today and tomorrow is thrown into an oven, how much more certainly will He put clothing on you—who trust Him so little?

29 "Stop thinking about what you will eat or drink, and stop worrying. **30** For all the heathen in the world run after these things, but your Father knows you need them. **31** Rather, continue to be eager for God's rule,[f] and these other things will also be given to you. **32** Don't be afraid any longer, little flock, because it has pleased your Father to give you the Kingdom.

33 "Sell what you have and give the money to the poor. Make yourselves

b- 15 Jesus is here warning against the Satanic delusion that a person's life consists in owning more and more property, and, as such Jesus is denouncing the belief which says that when a person has enough property then his life is truly secure.

c- 20 Literally: "tonight your life will be demanded of you."

d- 25 Or "add a cubit [18"] to your height."

e- 27 Literally: "lilies."

f- 31 Literally: "His Kingdom," that is, God's gracious rule in believers' hearts and lives.

purses that do not wear out, a treasure that will never be used up—in heaven, where no thief can come near it and no moth destroy it. **34** For where your treasure is, there also your heart will be."

Be Ready—*Matthew 24:36-51; Mark 13:32-37*

35 "Be dressed for action*g* and have your lamps burning, **36** like men waiting for their master when he comes back from the wedding, so that they can open the door for him the moment he comes and knocks. **37** Blessed are those slaves whom the master finds watching when he comes. I tell you the truth, he will prepare himself for the task,*h* have them recline at the table, and come and serve them. **38** Even if he comes in the middle of the night or toward morning and finds them that way, blessed are they.

39 "You know that if the owner of a house had known just when the burglar was coming, he would not have let anyone break into his house. **40** You also get ready, because the Son of Man is coming when you do not expect Him."

41 Peter asked, "Lord, by this parable do you mean to warn us—or everybody else too?"

42 The Lord asked, "Who do you suppose the trustworthy and sensible manager is whom the master will put in charge of his servants, to give them their share of food at the right time? **43** Blessed is that slave whom his master will find doing just this when he comes. **44** I tell you the truth, he will make him manager over all his property. **45** But if that slave says to himself, 'My master is not coming back for some time,' and he begins to beat the young male and female servants and to eat, drink, and get drunk, **46** the master of that slave will come one day when he is not expecting him and at a time he does not know and will cut him in pieces and assign him a place with the unfaithful.

47 "That slave who knew what his master wanted and did not prepare himself or do what he wanted will be beaten with many blows. **48** But he who did not know and did things for which he deserved to be beaten will receive few blows. If anyone was given much, much will be expected of him; and if a person was entrusted with much, all the more will be demanded of him."

Sorrow Ahead

49 "I have come to bring fire on earth, and how glad I would be if it were already started! **50** I must be baptized with a baptism, and how I am troubled until it is done!

51 "Do you think I came to bring peace on earth? No, I tell you, but rather to bring division. **52** Yes, from now on five in one family will be divided, three against two and two against three. **53** A father will be against a son and *a son against a father*, a mother against a daughter and *a daughter against her mother*,

---

53 *Mic 7:6*

---

g - 35 Literally: "Let your loins be girded."
h - 37 Literally: "he will gird himself."

a mother-in-law against her daughter-in-law and *a daughter-in-law against her mother-in-law*."

This Is Your Opportunity

54 Jesus said to the people, "When you see a cloud coming up in the west, you immediately say, 'There's going to be a heavy rain,' and it happens as you expected. **55** And when you see a wind blowing from the south, you say, 'It's going to be hot,' and that is what happens. **56** You hypocrites! You know what the appearance of the earth and of the sky means. How is it that you fail to interpret this present time? **57** Why don't you judge for yourselves what is right?

58 "When you go with your opponent to be tried before a ruler, do your best to settle with him on the way; or he may drag you before the judge, and the judge will hand you over to the officer, and the officer will throw you into prison. **59** I tell you, you will never get out until you pay the last cent."

13TH CHAPTER

Repent

1 At that time some men were there to tell Him about the Galileans whose blood Pilate had mixed with their sacrifices. **2** Jesus asked them, "Do you think that those Galileans were worse sinners than all the other Galileans because this happened to them? **3** I tell you, no; but unless you repent, you will all perish as they did! **4** Or those eighteen on whom the tower at Siloam fell and killed them—do you think they were worse sinners than all the other people living in Jerusalem? **5** I tell you, no; but unless you repent, you will all perish as they did!"

Another Year

6 He told them this parable: "A man had a fig tree growing in his vineyard. He came looking for fruit on it but did not find any. **7** He said to the man who worked the vineyard, 'Look here! For the last three years I have come looking for figs on this fig tree and haven't found any. Cut it down. Why should it use up the ground?'

8 " 'Master,' he answered him, 'let it stand one more year. Let me dig around it*a* and fertilize it; **9** it may have figs next year. If not, cut it down.' "

Sick For Eighteen Years

10 Jesus was teaching in one of the synagogs on a Sabbath, **11** and there was a woman whom a spirit had crippled for eighteen years. She was bent over and could not stand up straight. **12** When Jesus saw her, He called her and said,

---

13 *a-* 8 Literally: "until I dig around it," meaning "wait until I have a chance to dig around it."

"Woman, you are rid of your trouble." 13 He laid His hands on her, and immediately she stood up straight and began praising God.

14 But the synagog leader was annoyed with Jesus for healing on the Sabbath. He told the people, "There are six days to do your work. Come on those days and be healed but not on the day of rest."

15 The Lord answered him, "You hypocrites! Doesn't each of you untie his ox or donkey from the manger on the Sabbath and take it out to water? 16 Now here is this daughter of Abraham, whom Satan has bound these eighteen years; is it not right for her to be freed from her bond on the day of rest?"

17 As He said this, all His enemies had to feel ashamed, but all the common people were happy over the wonderful things He was doing.

Mustard Seed And Yeast—*Matthew 13:31-33; Mark 4:30-32*

18 He asked, "What is the Kingdom of God like, and with what shall I compare it? 19 It is like a mustard seed that a man took and planted in his garden. It grew to be a tree, and *the birds in the air nested in its branches.*"[b]

20 He asked again, "With what shall I compare the Kingdom of God? 21 It is like yeast that a woman mixed into three measures[c] of flour until the yeast worked through the whole batch of dough."

The Narrow Door

22 Then Jesus went and taught in one town and village after another on His way to Jerusalem.

23 Someone asked Him, "Lord, are only a few people going to be saved?"

He told them: 24 "Struggle to enter through the narrow door. I tell you, many will try to enter and not succeed. 25 After the Owner of the house gets up and closes the door, you will begin to stand outside and to knock at the door and say, 'Lord, open up for us!' But He will answer you, 'I do not know where you are from.' 26 Then you will say, 'We ate and drank with You, and You taught in our streets.' 27 But He will tell you, 'I do not know where you are from. *Get away from Me, all you who do wrong.*' 28 Then you will weep and grind your teeth when you see Abraham, Isaac, Jacob, and all the prophets in the Kingdom of God, while you are being thrown out. 29 People will come *from the east and the west*, the north and the south, and will recline at the table in the Kingdom of God. 30 Take note! Some who are last will be first, and some who are first will be last."

Jesus Warns Jerusalem

31 Right at that time some Pharisees came and told Him, "Leave here and go somewhere else, because Herod wants to kill You."

---

19 Ps 104:12; Ezek 17:23; 31:6   *27 Ps 6:8*   *29 Mal 1:11*

---

b- 19 Compare Daniel 4:12.
c- 21 See MONEY, WEIGHTS, and MEASURES on page 328.

32 He answered them, "Go, and tell that fox, 'Listen, today and tomorrow I will drive out demons and work healings, and on the third day I will finish.' **33** But I must be on My way today, tomorrow, and the next day; for it is not acceptable for a prophet to die outside Jerusalem.

34 "Jerusalem, Jerusalem, you murder the prophets and stone those sent to you! How often I wanted to gather your children the way a hen gathers her chicks under her wings, but you were not willing! **35** Look, now your *house is forsaken.* I tell you, you certainly will not see Me until ⌞the time⌟ comes when you say,*d* *'Blessed is He who comes in the Name of the Lord.'* "

14TH CHAPTER

Dinner Is Ready!

1 Once on a Sabbath Jesus went to the home of a leader of the Pharisees to eat a meal, and they were watching Him carefully.

2 In front of Him was a man who had dropsy. **3** This led Jesus to ask the experts in the Law and the Pharisees, "Is it right to heal on the Sabbath or not?" **4** But they did not say anything.

So Jesus took hold of the man, made him well, and sent him away. **5** He asked them, "If your son or your ox falls into a well, which of you will not immediately pull him out on a Sabbath?" **6** They could not answer this.

7 He spoke a parable to those who had been invited, since He kept noticing how the guests were trying to get the places of honor: **8** "When anyone invites you to a wedding, do not take the place of honor in case he has invited someone more important than you. **9** Then he who invited both of you will come and tell you, 'Give this man your place.' Then you will feel ashamed when you have to take the lowest place. **10** No, when you are invited, go and take the lowest place, so that when your host comes he will tell you, 'Friend, move up higher.' Then all your fellow guests will see how you are honored. **11** For everyone who honors himself will be humbled, but the person who humbles himself will be honored."

12 Then He told the man who had invited Him, "When you give a dinner or a supper, do not invite your friends, your brothers, your relatives, or rich neighbors. Otherwise they will also invite you and pay you back. **13** No, when you give a banquet, invite the poor, the crippled, the lame, and the blind. **14** Then you will be happy because they have nothing with which to pay you back. You will be paid back when the righteous rise from the dead."

15 When one of those eating with Him heard this, he said to Jesus, "Blessed is he who will eat bread in the Kingdom of God."

16 Jesus said to him: "A man once gave a banquet and invited many. **17** When it was time for the dinner, he sent his slave to tell those who were invited, 'Come, everything is ready now!'

18 "Then they all alike began to excuse themselves. 'I bought a field,' the first

---

35 Ps 118:26; Jer 12:7; 22:5

d- 35 Literally: "until shall come when you say."

told him, 'and I have to go out and see it. Please excuse me.' **19** Another said, 'I bought five teams of oxen, and I'm on my way to try them out. Please excuse me.' **20** And another said, 'I just got married, and that's why I can't come.'

21 "The slave went back and reported this to his master. Then the master of the house became angry. 'Go out quickly into the streets and alleys of the city,' he told his slave, 'and bring in here the poor, the crippled, the blind, and the lame.'

22 "And the slave said, 'Master, it is done as you ordered, and there still is room.'

23 "Then the master told the slave, 'Go out to the roads and stone fences, and make them come in! I want my house to be full. **24** I tell you, none of those men who were invited will taste my dinner.' "

Leave Everything

25 Large crowds were going with Jesus. He turned to them and said, **26** "If anyone comes to Me and does not hate his father, mother, wife, children, brothers, and sisters, and even his own life, he cannot be My disciple. **27** Whoever does not carry his cross and follow Me cannot be My disciple.

28 "If anyone of you wants to build a tower, won't he first sit down and figure out what it costs, to see if he has enough to finish it? **29** Otherwise, when he has laid a foundation but cannot finish the building, all who watch him will make fun of him **30** and say, 'This fellow started to build but could not finish it.'

31 "Or suppose a king is going into battle against another king. Will he not first sit down and consider if with ten thousand men he can oppose the other coming against him with twenty thousand? **32** If he cannot, then, while the other is still far away, he sends ambassadors to ask for terms of peace. **33** In the same way anyone of you who does not give up everything he has cannot be My disciple.

34 "Now, salt is good. But if the salt loses its taste, how will it be made salty again? **35** It is not any good for the ground or for the manure pile. People throw it away.

"The one who has ears to hear, let him listen!"

15TH CHAPTER

Lost—A Sheep—Matthew 18:12-14

1 All the tax collectors and sinners were coming to Jesus to hear Him. **2** But the Pharisees and the scribes grumbled and said, "This Man welcomes sinners and eats with them."

3 So He told them this parable: **4** "If a person has a hundred sheep and loses one of them, does he not leave the ninety-nine in the wilderness and go after the lost one until he finds it? **5** When he finds it, he lays it on his shoulders and is glad. **6** He goes home and calls his friends and neighbors together and says to them, 'Be happy with me. I found my lost sheep!' **7** So, I tell you, there will be

more joy in heaven over one sinner who repents than over ninety-nine good people who do not need to repent.''

Lost—A Coin

8 ''Or suppose a woman has ten coins*a* and loses one. Does she not light a lamp and sweep the house and look for it carefully until she finds it? **9** When she finds it, she calls her friends and neighbors together and says, 'Be happy with me. I found the coin I lost.' **10** So, I tell you, the angels of God are made happy over one sinner who repents.''

Lost—A Son

11 Then Jesus said: ''A man had two sons. **12** The younger of them said to his father, 'Father, give me my share of the property.' So he divided his property between them.

13 ''After a few days the younger son gathered everything together,*b* left home for a distant country, and there squandered all he had in wild living. **14** When he had spent it all, a severe famine came over that country, and he started to be in need. **15** He went and attached himself to one*c* of the citizens of that country, who sent him to his fields to feed hogs. **16** And he would have been glad to fill up on the pods that the hogs were eating, but no one would give him any.

17 ''When he came to his senses, he said, 'How many of my father's hired men have more food than they can eat, and here I am starving to death. **18** I shall get up and go to my father and tell him, "Father, I have sinned against heaven and against you. **19** I do not deserve to be called your son anymore. Make me one of your hired men.'' '

20 ''So he got up and went to his father. While he was still far away, his father saw him and felt sorry for him. He ran and put his arms around him and kissed him. **21** 'Father,' the son told him, 'I have sinned against heaven and against you. I do not deserve to be called your son anymore.'*d*

22 ''The father told his slaves, 'Quickly, bring out a robe—the best—and put it on him and put a ring on his finger and sandals on his feet. **23** And bring the fattened calf, kill it, and let's eat and begin to celebrate. **24** For this son of mine was dead and has come to life again. He was lost and has been found.' And they began to celebrate.

25 ''Now, his older son was out in the field. As he was coming in and approaching the house—he heard music and dancing! **26** After he called one of the servants, he asked, 'What's going on here?'

27 '' 'Your brother has come home,' he was told, 'and your father has killed the fattened calf because he has him back safe and sound.'

28 ''Then he became angry and would not go in. So his father came out and begged him. **29** But he answered his father, 'All these years I've been working

---

15 *a-* 8 Or ''ten silver coins''; Greek: ''*drachmas*''; one ''*drachma*'' was equivalent to a total day's wage. See MONEY, WEIGHTS, and MEASURES on page 328.

b- 13 This younger son most likely had received his share in the form of cash.

c- 15 Or ''and joined himself to one.''

d- 21 Some of the older manuscripts and early translations add: ''Make me one of your hired men.''

like a slave for you and have never disobeyed a command of yours, but you never gave me even a little goat to celebrate with my friends. **30** But as soon as this son of yours came back, who devoured your property with prostitutes, you killed the fattened calf for him.'

31 " 'Son,' the father said to him, 'you are always with me, and everything I have is yours. **32** But we had to celebrate and be glad. This brother of yours was dead and has come to life. He was lost and has been found.' "

16TH CHAPTER

The Dishonest Manager

1 Then Jesus said to His disciples: "There was a rich man whose manager was accused of squandering the man's property. **2** He called the manager and asked him, 'What is this that I hear about you? Give an account of your management, because you cannot manage my property any longer.'

3 "The manager said to himself, 'What will I do? My master is taking my job away from me. I'm not strong enough to dig; I'm ashamed to beg. **4** I know what I'll do so that, when I have lost my job, people will welcome me into their homes.'

5 "After calling each one of his master's debtors, he asked the first one, 'How much do you owe my master?'

6 " 'Eight hundred gallons of ˌolive, oil,' he answered.

" 'Take your note,' he said, 'and sit down quickly and write "four hundred." '

7 "Then he asked another, 'How much do you owe?'

"He answered, 'A thousand bushels of wheat.'

"He told him, 'Take your note and write "eight hundred." '

8 "And the master praised the dishonest manager for acting so shrewdly. For in dealing with their own kind of people the men of this world are more shrewd than those who are in the light.

9 "And I tell you: Win friends for yourselves with the worldly wealth that is often used in wrong ways,[a] so that when it is gone, you will be welcomed into the everlasting homes. **10** The person who can be trusted with very little can be trusted with much. And the person who is dishonest with very little is dishonest with much. **11** Therefore, if you cannot be trusted with worldly wealth that is often used in wrong ways, who will trust you with that which is really[b] good? **12** And if you could not be trusted with someone else's things, who will give you your own?

13 "No slave can serve two masters. For either he will hate the one and love the other, or he will be loyal to the one and despise the other. You cannot serve God and money."[c]

---

16 *a*- 9 Literally: "Win friends for yourselves with the mammon of unrighteousness" (cf. v. 11).

   b- 11 See *ALĒTHINOS* COMPARED WITH *ALĒTHĒS* on page 530.

   c- 13 Literally: "mammon" (*"mamōna"*), including all material things, such as wealth, possessions, property, etc.

14 The money-loving Pharisees heard all this and turned up their noses at Him. **15** Then He said to them, "You try to make people think that you are good,[d] but God knows your hearts. What people consider valuable is detested by God.

16 "The Law and the Prophets[e] were until John. Since then the Good News of the Kingdom of God is being preached, and everyone tries to force his way into it.[f] **17** It is easier for heaven and earth to disappear than for one dot of an *i* to drop from the Law.

18 "Anyone who divorces his wife and marries another is living in adultery. And the man who marries a woman divorced from her husband is living in adultery."[g]

The Rich Man And Lazarus

19 "Now there was a rich man who dressed in purple and fine linen and lived in luxury every day. **20** And a beggar by the name of Lazarus was laid regularly at his gate. He was covered with sores **21** and longed to satisfy his hunger with anything that might fall from the rich man's table. And the dogs would even come and lick his sores.

22 "One day the beggar died, and the angels carried him to Abraham's side.[h] The rich man also died and was buried. **23** As he was being tormented in hell [*hades*],[i] he looked up and saw Abraham far away, and Lazarus at his side. **24** 'Father Abraham,' he called, 'have pity on me and send Lazarus to dip the tip of his finger in water and cool off my tongue, because I am suffering in this fire.'

25 "But Abraham said, 'Remember, son, you had your good things in your life, while Lazarus had his misery. Now he is comforted here, while you are suffering. **26** And besides all these things, there is a wide chasm fixed between us and you, so that those who might want to cross from here over to you cannot do it, nor do any from there come over to us.'

27 " 'Then I ask you, father,' he said, 'send him to my father's home—**28** for I have five brothers—to warn them so that they also do not come to this place of torture.'

29 "Abraham said, 'They have Moses and the prophets.[j] They should listen to them.'

30 " 'No, Father Abraham,' he said, 'but if someone comes to them from the dead, they will repent.'

31 "He answered him, 'If they do not listen to Moses and the prophets, they will not be convinced even if someone should rise from the dead.' "

---

d- 15 Literally: "You justify yourselves before men."

e- 16 See initial portion of footnote at Matthew 5:17.

f- 16 Everyone wanted to enter the Messianic Kingdom; but the exact meaning of "force" here is disputed; it could refer to the people's eagerness.

g - 18 Compare THE MATTHEW 5:31,32 PASSAGE on page 548.

h - 22 Literally: "bosom/chest" (also in v. 23).

i - 23 Meaning "the place of/receptacle for disembodied souls"; see *HADES/GEHENNA* on page 540.

j - 29 Or "Moses and the Prophets" (also in v. 31; cf. v. 16 and Matt. 5:17 and its accompanying footnote).

17TH CHAPTER

When Others Sin—*Matthew 18:6-10; Mark 9:42-48*

1 Jesus told His disciples, "Things which cause people to stumble in their faith,ᵃ are sure to come, but woe to him through whom they come. **2** It would be better for him to have a large millstone hung around his neck and to be thrown into the sea than to cause one of these little ones to stumble in his faith. **3** Watch yourselves.

"If your brother sins, correct him; and if he repents, forgive him. **4** Even if he sins against you seven times in one day and seven times comes back to you and says, 'I'm sorry,'ᵇ forgive him."

Faith And Duty

5 Then the apostles said to the Lord, "Give us more faith."

6 The Lord said, "If you had faith like a mustard seed, you could say to this mulberry tree, 'Be pulled up by the roots, and be planted in the sea,' and it would obey you.

7 "If your slave is plowing or watching sheep and comes in from the field, will any of you say to him, 'Come quickly and eat'? **8** Won't youᶜ rather say to him, 'Prepare something for me to eat, and after you have gotten yourself ready,ᵈ serve me while I eat and drink, and after that you can eat and drink'? **9** You will not thank the slave for doing what he was ordered to do, will you? **10** So you too, when you have done all you were ordered to do, say, 'We are slaves who can claim no credit. We have only done our duty.' "

The Ten Lepers (Only One Thanks God)

11 On His way to Jerusalem, Jesus traveled through the middle of Samaria and Galilee.ᵉ **12** As He came to a village, ten lepers came toward Him. They stopped at a distance **13** and raised their voices, calling out, "Jesus, Master, have pity on us!"

14 When He saw them, He told them, "Go, *show yourselves to the priests.*"ᶠ

And this is what happened: As they went, they were cleansed of their leprosy. **15** One of them, seeing he was healed, turned back, and with a loud voice praised God. **16** He bowed down at Jesus' feet and thanked Him. And he was a Samaritan.

---

14 Lev 13:7,49

---

17 *a-* 1 See *SKANDALON* on page 545. The same applies to verse 2.
  b- 4 Literally: "I repent" (see v. 3).
  c- 8 Literally: "he."
  d- 8 Literally: "and having girded yourself."
  e- 11 Or "through the area between," that is, "along the border between Samaria and Galilee."
  f- 14 See 5:14 and its accompanying footnote.

17 Jesus asked, "Were there not ten cleansed? But the nine—where are they? **18** Didn't any of them come back to give God glory except this foreigner?" **19** And He told him, "Get up; go! Your faith has made you well."

Where Is The Kingdom Of God?

20 The Pharisees asked Jesus, "When will the Kingdom of God come?"

He answered them, "People cannot observe the coming of the Kingdom of God. **21** They will not say, 'Look, here it is!' or 'There it is!' For you see, the Kingdom of God is within you."*g*

Jesus Is Coming

22 He told the disciples, "The time will come when you will long to see one of the days of the Son of Man and will not see it. **23** People will say, 'Look, there He is!' or 'Here He is!' Do not go off and run after them. **24** For the Son of Man in His Day*h* will be exactly like the lightning that flashes and lights up the sky from one end to the other. **25** But first He must suffer much and be rejected by this kind of people.

26 "When the Son of Man comes, it will be as it was at the time of Noah: **27** They were eating and drinking as well as marrying and being given in marriage until the day that *Noah went into the ark*, and *the flood came* and destroyed them all.

28 "Likewise, it will be just as it was in the time of Lot: They were eating and drinking, buying and selling, planting and building. **29** But on the day that Lot left Sodom, *fire and sulfur rained from heaven and destroyed* them all. **30** That is how it will be on the Day when the Son of Man is revealed.

31 "On that Day, the person who is on the roof and has his goods in the house should not go down to get them. Likewise, the person who is in the field should not *turn back*. **32** Remember *Lot's wife!* **33** Whoever tries to save his life will lose it; whoever loses it will save it.

34 "I tell you, that night there will be two people in one bed; one will be taken and the other left. **35** Two women will be grinding together; one will be taken and the other left."*i* **37** They asked Him, "Where, Lord?"

He told them, "Where there is a ⌐dead⌐ body, there the vultures*j* will gather."

---

27 Gen 7:6,7   **29** Gen 19:24,25   **31,32** Gen 19:17,26

g- 21 The Greek can also mean "is ⌐now⌐ among you." Here the word "you" may be used in a *general*, not definite, sense. *Unbelieving* Pharisees would *not* be included in the phrase "within you."

h - 24 Some of the older manuscripts and early translations omit: "in His Day." Concerning the capitalization of "Day" (also in vv. 30 and 31), see "Last Day" on page 523.

i- 35 Many older manuscripts and early translations omit verse 36: "Two will be in a field; one will be taken and the other left." See Matthew 24:40 where the inclusion of these words is certain.

j- 37 Or "eagles" (also at Matt. 24:28).

18TH CHAPTER

God Hears

1 Jesus told them a parable to show that they should always pray and not give up: **2** "In a town there was a judge who did not fear God or care what people thought. **3** In that town there was also a widow who kept coming to him and saying, 'Help me receive justice against my enemy!'

4 "For a while he refused to do anything, but then he said to himself, 'Even though I do not fear God or care what people think, **5** yet because this widow keeps bothering me, I will have to see to it that she receives justice, or she will keep coming until she wears me out.' "

6 The Lord added, "Listen to what the unjust judge says. **7** And will God not see to it that His chosen ones, who cry to Him day and night, receive justice? Is He slow to help them? **8** I tell you, He will quickly see to it that they receive justice. But when the Son of Man comes, will He find faith on earth?"

The Pharisee And The Tax Collector

9 Jesus told this parable to some who were sure they were righteous and so looked down on everybody else: **10** "Two men went up to the Temple to pray. One was a Pharisee and the other a tax collector. **11** The Pharisee stood and prayed in reference to himself: 'God, I thank You that I am not like the rest of the people: robbers, wrongdoers, adulterers, or even like that tax collector. **12** I fast twice a week and give a tenth of all my income.'

13 "But the tax collector, standing at a distance, would not even look up to heaven but was beating his breast and saying, 'God, be merciful to me, the sinner!'

14 "I tell you, this man, and not the other, went home justified [declared free from his sin]. For everyone who honors himself will be humbled; but he who humbles himself will be honored."

Jesus Loves Children—Matthew 19:13-15; Mark 10:13-16

15 Some people were bringing babies to Jesus to have Him touch them. When the disciples saw them, they sternly told them not to do it.

16 But Jesus called them [the babies] to Him and said, "Let the little children come to Me, and do not try to keep them away, for the Kingdom of God is made up of such as these. **17** I tell you the truth, whoever does not receive the Kingdom of God in the same manner as a little child ‚receives it‚, he will never enter it."

The Rich Young Leader—Matthew 19:16-30; Mark 10:17-31

18 An official asked Him, "Good Teacher, what shall I do to inherit everlasting life?"

19 "Why do you call Me good?" Jesus asked him. "Nobody is good except One—God. **20** You know the commandments: *Do not commit adultery. Do not murder. Do not steal. Do not lie.*ᵃ *Honor your father and mother.*"

21 "I have kept all these since I was a child," he said.

22 When Jesus heard this, He told him, "You still lack one thing: Sell everything you have, distribute the money among the poor, and you will have treasure in heaven. Then come and follow Me."

23 When he heard this, he became very sad, because he was very rich. **24** Jesus watched him and said, "How hard it is for those who are rich to enter the Kingdom of God! **25** Indeed, it is easier for a camel to go through the eye of a needle than for a rich person to enter the Kingdom of God."

26 Those who heard Him asked, "Who then can be saved?"

27 He answered, "The things that are impossible for men to do *are possible for God to do.*"

28 Then Peter said, "Look, we have left our possessions and followed You."

29 "I tell you the truth," He answered them, "everyone who gave up his home or wife, brothers, parents, or children for the Kingdom of God **30** will certainly receive many times as much in this life, and, in the coming world, everlasting life."

The Shadow Of The Cross

31 He took the Twelve aside and said to them: "Look, we are going up to Jerusalem, and everything that the prophets wrote about the Son of Man will be done: **32** He will be handed over to the Gentiles. They will make fun of Him and insult Him, spit on Him, **33** whip Him, and kill Him. And on the third day He will rise."

34 But they understood none of this. What He said was a mystery to them, and they did not know what He meant.

A Blind Man—Mark 10:46-52

35 As He came near Jericho, a blind man was sitting by the road begging. **36** When he heard a crowd going by, he tried to find out what it was all about. **37** "Jesus from Nazareth is passing by," they told him. **38** He shouted, "Jesus, Son of David, have pity on me!" **39** Those who went ahead were urging him to be quiet. But he shouted even louder, "Son of David, have pity on me!"

40 Jesus stopped and ordered the man to be brought to Him. When he came near, Jesus asked him, **41** "What do you want Me to do for you?"

"Lord, I want to see," he said.

42 Jesus told him, "Receive your sight! Your faith has made you well." **43** Immediately he could see, and he began to follow Jesus, praising God. And all the people who saw this praised God.

---

20 *Ex 20:12-16; Deut 5:16-20*   **27** *Gen 18:14; Job 42:2; Zech 8:6*

18 *a*- 20 Literally: "Do not give false witness."

19TH CHAPTER

Zacchaeus

1 He went into Jericho and was passing through it. **2** Here was a man by the name of Zacchaeus. He was an overseer of tax collectors, and he was rich. **3** He was trying to see who Jesus was, but being a small man, he could not see Him because of the crowd. **4** So he ran ahead and climbed up a sycamore-fig*ª* tree to see Him, because Jesus was coming that way.

5 When Jesus came to the place, He looked up. "Zacchaeus, hurry down," He told him, "for today I must stay at your home."

6 He hurried down and was happy to welcome Him. **7** But all who saw this began to grumble: "He went to be the guest of a sinful man."

8 But Zacchaeus stood and said to the Lord, "Look, Lord, half of my property I am giving to the poor, and if I have cheated anyone in any way, I am paying him back four times as much."

9 Jesus told him, "Today salvation has come to this home, since he too is a son of Abraham. **10** The Son of Man has come to *seek* and to save *the lost*."

Use God's Gifts

11 While they were listening to this, Jesus went on to tell them a parable, because He was near Jerusalem and they thought the Kingdom of God was about to appear immediately. **12** Therefore He said, "A man of noble birth went to a distant country to become a king and to return. **13** He called ten of his slaves, gave them ten minas,*ᵇ* and told them, 'Trade with these till I come.'

14 "But the men of his own country hated him and sent representatives after him to say, 'We do not want this man to be our king.'

15 "After he became king, he came back. Then he said, 'Call those slaves to whom I gave the money, so that I may know what each one has gained by trading.'

16 "The first came and said, 'Master, your mina has made ten minas.'

17 "'Well done, my good slave!' he told him. 'You proved you could be trusted in a very small matter. Take charge of ten cities.'

18 "The second came and said, 'Your mina, master, has made five minas.'

19 "He told this one, 'You be in charge of five cities.'

20 "Then another came and said, 'Master, here is your mina. I put it away in a cloth and kept it there because **21** I was afraid of you. You are a hard man. You take what you have not deposited, and you harvest what you have not sown.'

22 "'I will judge you by what you say, you wicked slave!' he told him. 'You knew that I am a hard man, taking what I have not deposited and harvesting what

---

10 Ezek 34:16

---

19 *a-* 4 A tree with sturdy, spreading branches, the lowest of which was closer to the ground than those of most trees and which easily extended over paths when planted near them (cf. Amos 7:14).

   b- 13 A mina was worth 100 denarii, the equivalent of the wages for 100 days' worth of labor. See MONEY, WEIGHTS, and MEASURES on page 328.

I have not sown. 23 Why did you not put my money in the bank? Then, when I came back, I could have collected it with interest.' 24 He told his men, 'Take his mina away and give it to the man who has ten.'

25 " 'Master,' they answered him, 'he has ten minas.'

26 " 'I tell you, everyone who has something will be given more, and anyone who does not have ˌwhat he should haveˌ, even what he has will be taken away. 27 But those enemies of mine who did not want me to be their king—bring them here and kill them in front of me.' "

E. Jesus' last days in and around Jerusalem:
Holy Week (His passion, death, resurrection) to the ascension (19:28–24:53)

The King Is Coming!—*Matthew 21:1-11; Mark 11:1-11; John 12:12-19*

28 After Jesus had said this, He continued on His way up to Jerusalem.

29 When He came near Bethphage and Bethany at the Mount of Olives, as it was called, He sent two of His disciples. 30 He said, "Go into the village ahead of you, and as you enter, you will find a colt tied up on which no one has ever sat. Untie it and bring it. 31 And if anyone asks you, 'Why are you untying it?' say, 'The Lord needs it.' "

32 The men whom He sent went and found it just as He had told them. 33 While they were untying the colt, its owners asked them, "Why are you untying the colt?"

34 "The Lord needs it," they said.

35 So they brought the colt to Jesus, put their garments on it, and sat Jesus on it. 36 As He was riding along, people spread their garments on the road. 37 And as He was coming near the place where the road goes down the Mount of Olives, the whole crowd of the disciples began to praise God joyfully and loudly[c] for all the miracles they had seen. 38 They said:

> "*Blessed is* the King *who is coming in the Name of the Lord*!
> In heaven peace, and glory in the highest ˌheavensˌ."

39 Some of the Pharisees in the crowd said to Him, "Teacher, order Your disciples to be quiet."

40 "I tell you," He answered them, "if these are quiet, the stones will cry out."

41 When He came near and saw the city, He wept over it 42 and said, "If today you only knew—yes, you—the way to peace! But now it is hidden so that you cannot see it. 43 The time will come for you when your enemies will put up ramparts against you and surround you and press against you from every side. 44 They will *dash* you and *your children* to the *ground* and not leave one stone on another in you, because you did not know the time in which help came to you."

---

38 Ps 118:26   44 Ps 137:9

c- 37 Literally: "while rejoicing began to praise God with a loud voice."

Cleansing The Temple—Matthew 21:12-17; Mark 11:15-19

45 Jesus went into the Temple and began to drive out the men who were selling things there. 46 He said to them, "It is written, '*My House shall be a house of prayer*, but you have made it *a den of robbers.*' "

47 Every day He was teaching in the Temple. The ruling priests, the scribes, and the leaders of the people were trying to kill Him, 48 but they could not find a way to do it, because the people were all eager to hear Him.

20TH CHAPTER

From Heaven—Matthew 21:23-27; Mark 11:27-33

1 One day, as He was teaching the people in the Temple and telling them the Gospel, the ruling priests, scribes, and elders came to Him. 2 "Tell us," they asked Him, "by what authority are You doing these things? Or who is the One who gave You this authority?"

3 Jesus answered them, "I also shall ask you a question. Tell Me, 4 John's baptism—was it from heaven or from men?"

5 They argued among themselves, "If we say, 'From heaven,' He will ask, 'Why didn't you believe him?' 6 But if we say, 'From men,' all the people will stone us, for they are convinced that John was a prophet." 7 So they answered that they did not know from where it came.

8 Then Jesus told them, "Neither will I tell you by what authority I am doing these things."

God's Vineyard—Matthew 21:33-46; Mark 12:1-12

9 Then He began telling the people this parable: "A man *planted a vineyard*, leased it out to workers, and left home for a long time.

10 "At the right time he sent a servant to the workers to obtain from them a share of the products of the vineyard. But the workers beat him and sent him back empty-handed. 11 He sent another servant; they also beat him, treated him shamefully, and sent him back empty-handed. 12 Then he sent a third; they also wounded this one and threw him out.

13 "Then the owner of the vineyard said, 'What shall I do? I will send my son, whom I love. Maybe they will respect him.'

14 "When the workers saw him, they talked it over among themselves. 'This is the heir,' they said. 'Let's kill him so the inheritance may be ours.' 15 And they threw him out of the vineyard and killed him.

"Now, what will the owner of the vineyard do to them? 16 He will come and kill those workers and give the vineyard to others."

"That must never happen!" said those who heard Him.

17 Jesus looked at them and asked, "What then does this mean in the Scriptures:

---

46 Is 56:7; Jer 7:11   9 Is 5:2

The very Stone
which the builders rejected
has become the Cornerstone?

18 Everyone who falls on that Stone will be dashed in pieces, and if that Stone falls on anyone, It will scatter him like dust."

19 The scribes and the ruling priests wanted to arrest Him then and there, because they knew He had aimed this parable at them; but they were afraid of the people.

Taxes—Matthew 22:15-22; Mark 12:13-17

20 They watched for an opportunity and sent spies ˌto pretend to be righteous menˌ in order to catch Him in what He would say. They wanted to hand Him over to the governor's control and authority. **21** They had a question for Him. "Teacher," they said, "we know that You are right in what You say and teach, and that You do not favor any special individuals; rather, You teach the way of God faithfully. **22** Is it right for us to pay a tax to Caesar or not?"

23 Because He saw through their trickery, He told them, **24** "Show Me a denarius.*ᵃ* Whose head is on it and whose inscription?"

"Caesar's," they answered.

25 He told them, "Well then, give to Caesar what is Caesar's, and to God what is God's."

26 They could not catch Him before the people in anything He said, and since His answer surprised them, they became silent.

The Dead Live—Matthew 22:23-33; Mark 12:18-27

27 Some of the Sadducees, who say that there is no resurrection, came to Him with this question: **28** "Teacher, Moses wrote for us, *'If any married man dies and has no children, his brother should marry the widow and have children for his brother.'* **29** Now there were seven brothers. The first married and died childless. **30** Then the second brother married the widow, **31** and so did the third. In the same way all seven died and left no children. **32** Finally, the woman also died. **33** Now, in the resurrection, whose wife will she be since the seven had her as wife?"

34 Jesus told them: "In this world people marry and are given in marriage, **35** but those who are considered worthy to rise from the dead and live in that world neither marry nor are they given in marriage; **36** nor can they die anymore, because they are like the angels. They are God's children since they share in the resurrection.

37 "Even Moses showed in the passage about the 'bush' that the dead are raised, when he says that the 'LORD' is *'the God of Abraham, the God of Isaac,*

---

17 Ps 118:22   28 Gen 38:8; Deut 25:5,6   37 Ex 3:6

20 *a*- 24 See MONEY, WEIGHTS, and MEASURES on page 328.

and the God of Jacob.' **38** He is not the God of the dead but of the living. For all who are His are alive."

39 Some scribes told Him, "Teacher, that is well said." **40** For no one dared to ask Him another question.

David's Son—*Matthew 22:41-46; Mark 12:35-37a*

41 "How can people say that the Christ [Messiah] is David's son?" He asked them. **42** "For David himself says in the book of Psalms:

> The Lord said to my Lord,
>   'Sit at My right hand
> **43**   until I make Your enemies Your footstool.'

44 David therefore calls Him 'Lord'; then how can He be his son?"

Beware!—*Matthew 23:1-12; Mark 12:37b-40*

45 While all the people were listening, He said to the disciples: **46** "Beware of the scribes! They like to parade around in long robes and love to be greeted in the marketplaces, to sit in the front seats in the synagogs, and to have the places of honor at dinners. **47** They swallow up the houses of widows, and then—to put on a good appearance—they make long prayers. They will receive a more severe punishment."

21ST CHAPTER

The Widow's Coins—*Mark 12:41-44*

1 Looking up, He saw rich people dropping their gifts into the contribution boxes.*a* **2** Then He noticed a certain poor widow drop in two small coins.*b* **3** He said, "I tell you the truth, this poor widow has put in more than all the others. **4** For all the others have taken some of what they have extra and dropped it in among the gifts, but she—even though she did not have enough for herself—put in everything she had to live on."*c*

The Destruction Of Jerusalem And The World—*Matthew 24:1-35; Mark 13:1-31*

5 Some were saying about the Temple, "It is beautifully constructed with fine stones and gifts."

He said: **6** "About these things that you see, the time will come when not one stone will be left on another; every one will be torn down."

42,43 Ps 110:1

---

21 *a-* 1 Or "the treasury."
  b- 2 Compare Mark 12:42.
  c- 4 Literally: "she put in some of what she needed, everything she had to live on."

7 "Teacher," they asked Him, "when will these things be, and what will be the miraculous sign which will tell us when these things are going to happen?"

8 Jesus said, "Be careful not to let anyone deceive you. For many will come using My Name and saying, 'I am He!' and 'The time has come.' Do not follow them.

9 "When you hear of wars and revolutions, do not become alarmed. For these things *must happen* first, but the end will not come right away."

10 Then He told them, *"Nation will fight against nation* and *kingdom against kingdom.* **11** There will be great earthquakes and famines and plagues in various places, terrible sights and great miraculous signs coming from heaven.

12 "Before all these things happen, men will arrest you and persecute you, hand you over to church councils, and put you in prisons. They will bring you before kings and governors on account of My Name. **13** It will be your chance to testify to them.*d* **14** So make up your minds not to worry beforehand how you will defend yourselves. **15** For I will give you such speech and wisdom that none of your enemies will be able to oppose it or talk against it.

16 "Even parents, brothers, relatives, and friends will betray you and kill some of you, **17** and everybody will hate you because of My Name. **18** But not a hair on your head will be lost. **19** Patiently endure, and you will gain your lives.*e*

20 "When you see Jerusalem surrounded by an army, then know the time has come for her to be destroyed. **21** Then let those in Judea flee to the mountains. Those in Jerusalem should leave it. Those in the country should not go into the city, **22** because that will be a *time of vengeance* when everything will be fulfilled as it is written.

23 "Woe to the women who are pregnant and to those who are nursing babies in those days. For there will be great distress in this country, and God will punish this nation.*f* **24** The sword will cut them down, and they will be taken away as prisoners among all nations; and *Jerusalem will be trampled on by the Gentiles* until the times of the Gentiles are fulfilled.*g*

25 "There will be miraculous signs in the sun, the moon, and the stars, and on the earth *nations* will be in distress, not knowing which way to turn from *the roaring and tossing of the sea.* **26** People will faint as they fearfully wait for what will happen to the world. *The powers of the heavens* will be shaken.

27 "Then they will see *the Son of Man coming in a cloud* with power and great glory.

28 "When these things begin to happen, stand ready and lift your heads, because your redemption*h* is drawing near."

29 He gave an illustration to them:*i* "Look at the fig tree or any of the trees. **30** As soon as leaves grow on them, you see and know without being told that

---

9 Dan 2:28   *10 2 Chr 15:6; Is 19:2*   *22 Deut 32:35; Hos 9:7*   *24 Is 63:18; Zech 12:3*
25 Ps 65:7; Ezek 32:7,8   *26 Is 34:4*   *27 Dan 7:13*

d- 13 Or "It will result in your being a witness to them."
e- 19 Or "souls."
f- 23 Literally: "and wrath on this people."
g- 24 Or "are completely over."
h- 28 Meaning "your time to be set free."
i- 29 Or "He told them a parable."

summer is near. **31** So also, when you see these things happen, you know that the Kingdom of God is near.

32 "I tell you the truth, this kind of people*ʲ* will not pass away until all these things take place. **33** Heaven and earth will pass away, but My words will never pass away."

Watch And Pray!—Compare Matthew 24:36-51; Mark 13:32-37

34 "Be careful that your hearts never become burdened with carousing*ᵏ* and drunkenness and worries about this life, or that Day will take you by surprise like *a trap*. **35** For it will surprise all people wherever they *live on the earth*. **36** But always watch and pray that you may be able to escape all these things that are going to happen and to stand before the Son of Man."

37 During the day He would teach in the Temple, but at night He would go out to the Mount of Olives, as it was called, and stay there for the night; **38** and all the people got up early and went to the Temple to hear Him.

22ND CHAPTER

The Plot—Matthew 26:1-5; Mark 14:1, 2; John 11:45-57

1 The Festival of Unleavened Bread, called the Passover, was near. **2** The ruling priests and the scribes were looking for some ⌊underhanded⌋ way to kill Him, because they were afraid of the people.

3 Then Satan entered into Judas, called the man from Kerioth,*ᵃ* one of the Twelve. **4** He went to the high priests and the captains of the Temple and discussed with them how he might betray Jesus to them. **5** They were delighted and agreed to give him some money. **6** He promised to do it and kept looking for a chance to betray Him when He was away from the crowd.

The Passover—Matthew 26:17-20; Mark 14:12-17

7 Then came the day of the Festival of Unleavened Bread, when the Passover ⌊lamb⌋ had to be killed. **8** Jesus sent Peter and John, saying, "Go, prepare the Passover ⌊lamb⌋ for us to eat."

9 They asked Him, "Where do You want us to prepare it?"

10 He told them, "Go into the city and you will meet a man carrying a jar of water. **11** Follow him into the house he enters, and tell the owner of the house: 'The Teacher asks you, "Where is the room in which I can eat the Passover with

---

34,35 Is 24:17

---

j- 32 Or "this generation."
k- 34 The Greek word "*kraipalē*" indicates a carousing that includes excess drinking as well as nausea and any other accompanying symptoms.
22 *a-* 3 Literally: "Judas . . . Iscariot"; see "*Iscariot*" in Glossary.

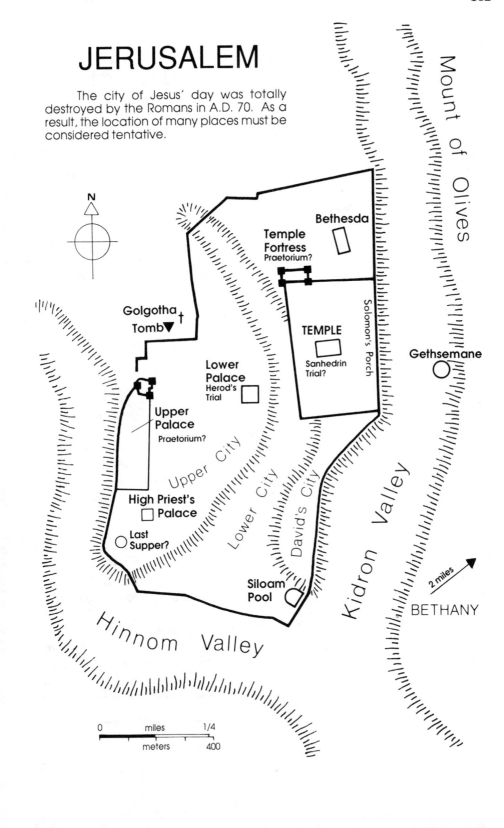

JERUSALEM

The city of Jesus' day was totally destroyed by the Romans in A.D. 70. As a result, the location of many places must be considered tentative.

N

Mount of Olives

Bethesda

Temple Fortress
Praetorium?

Golgotha
Tomb ▼ †

TEMPLE

Solomon's Porch

Gethsemane

Sanhedrin Trial?

Lower Palace
Herod's Trial

Upper Palace
Praetorium?

Upper City

Lower City

David's City

Kidron Valley

2 miles

High Priest's Palace

Last Supper?

Siloam Pool

BETHANY

Hinnom Valley

0   miles   1/4
meters   400

My disciples?" ' **12** He will show you a large, furnished room upstairs. Get things ready there."

13 They went and found it as He had told them, and they prepared the Passover.

14 When the hour had come, He and the apostles reclined at the table. **15** He said to them, "I have longed very much to eat this Passover with you before I suffer. **16** For I tell you, I will not eat it again until it finds its fulfillment in the Kingdom of God." **17** Then He took a cup and spoke a prayer of thanks. He said, "Take this and share it."

The Lord's Supper—*Matthew 26:26-30; Mark 14:22-26; 1 Corinthians 11:23-25*

18 "I tell you, from now on I will not drink of the product of the vine until the Kingdom of God comes."

19 Jesus took bread, spoke a prayer of thanks, broke it, and gave it to them, saying, "This is My body, which is given for you. Do this to remember Me."

20 He did the same with the cup when the supper was over, saying, "This cup is *the new 'last will and testament'* [b] in My *blood*, which is being poured out for you."

Who Is The Betrayer?—*Matthew 26:21-25; Mark 14:18-21; John 13:21-30*

21 "But look, the hand of him who is betraying Me is with Me on the table. **22** The Son of Man is following the course that has been determined,[c] but woe to that man by whom He is betrayed."

23 Then they began to discuss with one another which of them it might be who was going to do this.

Who Is The Greatest?

24 Then the disciples started to quarrel among themselves as to which of them was considered the greatest.

25 He told them, "The kings of the Gentiles lord it over them, and their rulers call themselves benefactors. **26** With you it should be different. Rather, the greatest among you should become like the youngest, and one who leads should be like one who serves. **27** For who is greater, the one who reclines at the table or the one who serves? Is it not the one who reclines at the table? But I am among you as one who serves.

28 "You have stood by Me in the troubles that have tested Me. **29** I give you the right to rule, just as My Father did to Me **30** in order that you may eat and drink at My table in My Kingdom; and you will sit on thrones, ruling[d] the twelve tribes of Israel."

---

20 *Ex 24:8; Jer 31:32; Zech 9:11*

---

b- 20 See *DIATHĒKĒ* on page 531.
c- 22 Literally: "is going according to what has been determined."
d- 30 Or "judging" (cf. Matt. 19:28).

You Will Be Tested—Matthew 26:31-35; Mark 14:27-31; John 13:36-38

31 "Simon, Simon," ˌsaid the Lordˌ, "you know that Satan has begged to have all of you to sift you like wheat. **32** But I prayed for you, Simon, that your faith may not fail. And when you come back, strengthen your fellow disciples."

33 "Lord," he told Him, "I am ready to go to prison and to die with You."

34 "I tell you, Peter," He said, "the rooster will not crow tonight until you deny three times that you know Me."

35 Then He asked them, "When I sent you out without purse, bag, or sandals, you did not lack anything, did you?"

"Not a thing!" they answered.

36 He told them, "But now the person who has a purse should take it, and also a bag. And the person who does not have a sword should sell his garment and buy one. **37** For it is written: *'He was counted with criminals,'* and I tell you, this must find fulfillment in Me. Yes, whatever is written about Me is being fulfilled."

38 "Lord, look, here are two swords!" they said.

"It is enough!" He told them.

Gethsemane—Matthew 26:36-46; Mark 14:32-42

39 Jesus went out and as usual came to the Mount of Olives. The disciples went with Him. **40** When He came to the place, He told them, "Pray that you may not be tempted."

41 He withdrew from them about a stone's throw, knelt down and prayed: **42** "Father, if You wish, take this cup away from Me; however, do not let My will but Your will be done."

43 An angel from heaven appeared to Him and gave Him strength. **44** And as He began to struggle inwardly, He prayed more earnestly, and His sweat became like drops*ᵉ* of blood falling on the ground.*ᶠ*

45 After praying, He got up, went to the disciples, and found them sleeping because they were feeling sad. **46** "Why are you sleeping?" He asked them. "Get up and pray that you may not be tempted."

The Arrest—Matthew 26:47-56; Mark 14:43-52; John 18:1-14

47 While He was still talking, the crowd came. The one called Judas, one of the Twelve, was leading them; and he came close to Jesus to kiss Him.

48 Jesus asked him, "Judas, are you betraying the Son of Man with a kiss?"

49 The men around Jesus, seeing what was going to happen, asked, "Lord,

---

37 *Is 53:9,12*

e- 44 This noun can also mean "clots." Some feel that the text suggests a mixing of sweat with blood. If so, this would indicate that a most unique medical phenomenon is being reported by Luke the physician (cf. Col. 4:14).

f- 44 Some older manuscripts and early translations omit verses 43 and 44.

should we strike with our swords?" **50** And one of them struck the high priest's slave and cut off his right ear.

51 But Jesus said, "Let them do it. No more of this!" And, touching the ear, He healed him.

52 Then Jesus said to the ruling priests, captains of the Temple, and elders who had come for Him, "You came out for Me with swords and clubs as if I were a robber! **53** Day after day I was with you in the Temple, and you laid no hands on Me. But this is your time when darkness rules."

54 They arrested Him, led Him away, and took Him to the high priest's palace.

Peter Denies Jesus—Matthew 26:69-75; Mark 14:66-72; John 18:15-18,25-27

Now Peter followed at a distance.

55 The men had lit a fire in the middle of the courtyard, and as they sat together, Peter sat among them. **56** A maid saw him sitting in the light of the fire, and looking straight at him, she said, "He, too, was with Him."

57 But he denied it. "I don't know Him, woman," he said.

58 A little later someone else looked at him and said, "You are one of them."

Peter said, "Man, I am not!"

59 About an hour later another insisted: "It's obvious that this man was also with Him. Why, he's a Galilean!"

60 Peter said, "Man, I don't know what you're talking about."

Just then, while he was still speaking, a rooster crowed. **61** Then the Lord turned and looked at Peter, and Peter remembered the Lord telling him, "Before the rooster crows today, you will deny Me three times." **62** So he went outside and wept bitterly.

The Jewish Court Condemns Jesus

63 The men who were holding Jesus were *making fun of* Him as they struck Him. **64** They covered His face and kept asking Him: "Prophesy! Who hit You?" **65** And they went on *insulting* Him in many other ways.

66 In the morning all the elders of the people, ruling priests, and scribes had a meeting. They brought Jesus before their council [Sanhedrin] and asked, **67** "Are You the Christ? Tell us."

He said to them, "If I tell you, you will not believe Me. **68** And if I ask you a question, you will not answer. **69** But from now on *the Son of Man* will be *sitting at the right hand* of the power *of God*."

70 "Are You then the Son of God?" all of them asked.

He answered them, "As you say: I am He."

71 "Why do we need any more testimony?" they asked. "We ourselves have heard Him say it."

---

63 Ps 22:7   *65 Ps 22:7; Is 50:6*   *69 Dan 7:13; Ps 110:1*

23RD CHAPTER

Before Pilate—Matthew 27:11-14; Mark 15:1-5; John 18:28-38

1 Then the entire assembly stood up and took Him to Pilate.

2 Then they began to accuse Him: "We found that He makes our people disloyal, keeps them from paying taxes to the emperor, and says He is Christ, a King."

3 Pilate asked Him, "Are You the King of the Jews?"

"Yes," He answered him.

4 Pilate told the ruling priests and the crowd, "In no way do I find this Man guilty."

Before Herod

5 The priests and the crowd kept urging him: "He stirs up the people by teaching all over Judea,*a* beginning in Galilee and coming here."

6 When Pilate heard that, he asked, "Is the Man from Galilee?" 7 And when he found out that Jesus came from the country ruled by Herod, he sent Him to Herod, who also was in Jerusalem at that time.

8 Herod was very glad to see Jesus. For a long time he wanted to see Him because he was hearing about Him, and he was hoping to see Jesus work some miraculous sign. 9 He asked Him many questions, but Jesus did not answer him. 10 The ruling priests and the scribes were standing there and accusing Him vehemently.

11 Herod and his soldiers treated Jesus with contempt and made fun of Him. They put a splendid garment on Him and then sent Him back to Pilate. 12 On that day Herod and Pilate became friends. Before this they had been enemies.

13 Then Pilate called the ruling priests, the other leaders, and the people together. 14 He told them, "You brought me this Man as one who turns the people against the government. And now look, I have examined this Man before you and found Him innocent of the things of which you accuse Him. 15 And Herod did too, because he sent Him back to us. You see, He has not done anything to deserve death. 16 So I am going to have him whipped and let Him go."

Barabbas—Matthew 27:15-26; Mark 15:6-15; John 18:39,40

17 Now at every festival he [the governor] had to set someone free for them.*b*

18 The whole crowd then shouted ₁in a loud voice₁: "Away with Him. Free Barabbas*c* for us." 19 Barabbas had been thrown into prison for a revolt that had taken place in the city and for murder.

---

23 *a-* 5 In the wider sense indicating Palestine.

b- 17 Some of the older manuscripts and early translations omit verse 17. See Matthew 27:15 and Mark 15:6 where the inclusion of these words is certain.

c- 18 Made up of two Aramaic words: "*bar*" ("son") and "*abba*" ("father"), meaning "son of the father." Could the presence of one named *Barabbas* imply that the "sons (and daughters) of the heavenly Father" went free as the "Son of the heavenly Father" went to the cross for them?

20 But because Pilate wanted to let Jesus go, he called out to the people again. **21** But they kept yelling: "Crucify, crucify Him!"

22 And Pilate spoke to them a third time: "Why, what wrong has He done? I have found nothing in Him that deserves death. So I am going to teach Him a lesson and let Him go."

23 But they kept pressing him with loud shouts, demanding that He be crucified, and their shouts were overpowering Pilate. **24** Then Pilate decided that what they demanded should be done: **25** he let them have Barabbas, who had been put in prison for revolt and murder, for whom they were asking, and he handed Jesus over to them in line with their wishes.

On The Way

26 As they led Jesus away, they took hold of Simon, a man from Cyrene, who was coming in from the country, and they laid the cross on him, to carry it behind Jesus.

27 A large crowd of the people followed Him. The women in the crowd were beating their breasts and weeping over Him. **28** He turned to them and said, "Daughters of Jerusalem, do not continue to cry over Me; rather, cry over yourselves and your children, **29** because the time is coming when people will say:

> 'Blessed are
> the women who could not have children,
> the wombs that did not bear, and
> the breasts that did not nurse.'

30 Then

> *people will say*
> *to the mountains: 'Fall on us!' and*
> *to the hills: 'Cover us!'*

31 For if this is done to the green tree, what will be done to a dry one?"

32 Two others, who were criminals, were also taken away to be executed with Him.

"They Crucified Him"—*Matthew 27:31-44; Mark 15:20-32; John 19:16b-24*

33 When they came to the place called Skull,*d* they crucified Him there with the criminals, one at His right and the other at His left.*e*

---

30 Hos 10:8

---

d - 33 In Aramaic this place was called "*Golgotha*"; its Latin form is "*Calvary*." See Matthew 27:33; Mark 15:22.

e - 33 See Mark 15:27 and its accompanying footnote.

34 Then Jesus said, "Father, forgive them, for they do not know what they are doing."*f*

They divided His clothes among them by throwing dice.g

35 The people stood there *watching*. The rulers were *sneering*, "He saved others; He should save Himself if He is the Christ whom God has chosen." **36** The soldiers also made fun of Him when they went up to Him and *offered Him sour wine*. **37** They said, "If You are the King of the Jews, save Yourself."

38 There was a written notice placed above Him:

THIS IS THE KING OF THE JEWS.

A Criminal Turns To Jesus

39 One of the criminals who were hanging there was mocking Him: "Aren't You the Christ? Save Yourself and us!"

40 But the other, warning him, asked, "Aren't you afraid of God? You are condemned just as He is. **41** Our punishment is just, for we are getting what we deserve for what we've done, but this One has done nothing wrong."

42 Then he said, "Jesus, remember me when You come into Your Kingdom."

43 "I tell you the truth," Jesus said to him, "today you will be with Me in Paradise."

Jesus Dies—*Matthew 27:45-56; Mark 15:33-41; John 19:28-30*

44 It was about noon when darkness came over the whole land—lasting until three in the afternoon, **45** because the sun stopped shining. The ⌐inner⌐ curtain in the Temple*h* was torn in two.

46 And Jesus cried out with a loud voice, "Father, *into Your hands I entrust My spirit*." After He said this, He died.

47 When the captain saw what had happened, he praised God and said, "Certainly this Man was righteous!" **48** When all the people who had gathered to view this incident saw what was happening, they beat their breasts and turned back. **49** All *His friends*, including the women who had followed Him from Galilee, *stood at a distance* and watched these things.

Jesus Is Buried—*Matthew 27:57-61; Mark 15:42-47; John 19:38-42*

50 There was a man by the name of Joseph, a member of the Jewish council [Sanhedrin], a good and righteous man **51** who had not voted for their plan and action. He was from Arimathea, a Jewish town, and he was waiting for the Kingdom of God.

52 He went to Pilate and asked for the body of Jesus. **53** Then He took it down,

---

34 Ps 22:18   *35 Ps 22:7*   *36 Ps 69:21*   *46 Ps 31:5*   *49 Ps 38:11*

---

f- 34 Some of the older manuscripts and early translations omit this first saying from the cross.
g- 34 Literally: "lots."
h- 45 See Diagram #2 on page 438.

wrapped it in some linen, and laid it in a tomb cut in the rock, in which no one had yet been laid. **54** It was the day of preparation,^{i} and the Sabbath was just beginning.

55 The women who had come with Him from Galilee followed closely behind. They observed the tomb and how His body was laid. **56** Then they went back and prepared spices and perfumes. But on the Sabbath they rested according to the commandment.

24TH CHAPTER

The Easter Resurrection—Matthew 28:1-10; Mark 16:1-8; John 20:1-10

1 Very early on Sunday morning^a the women came to the tomb, bringing the spices which they had prepared. **2** They found the stone rolled back from the tomb, **3** but when they went in, they did not find the body of the Lord Jesus. **4** While they were troubled about this, suddenly two men stood beside them in clothes that were shining with the brightness of lightning. **5** The women were terrified, and they bowed their faces to the ground.

They asked the women, "Why do you look among the dead for Him who is alive? **6** He is not here; He has risen! Remember what He told you while He was still in Galilee: **7** 'The Son of Man must be handed over to sinful men, be crucified, and rise on the third day.' " **8** They remembered what He had told them.

9 Having returned from the tomb, they reported all this to the Eleven and all the others. **10** It was Mary from Magdala, Joanna, Mary the mother of James, and the other women with them who told the apostles about these things.

11 The apostles thought that what the women said was nonsense, and they would not believe them.

12 But Peter started out and ran to the tomb. He bent down and saw only the linen cloths. Then he went away, amazed at what had happened.

On The Way To Emmaus

13 On the same day, two of them were going to a village called Emmaus, about seven miles^b from Jerusalem. **14** They were talking with one another about everything that had happened.

15 While they were talking and discussing, Jesus Himself caught up to them and walked along with them. **16** They saw Him but were kept from knowing who He was.

17 He asked them, "What are you discussing with one another as you are walking along?"

They stood still; their faces were sad. **18** The one by the name of Cleopas

---

i- 54 See explanation at John 19:31 and its accompanying footnote.
24 *a-* 1 Literally: "On the first day of the week while still very early."
 b- 13 Literally: "60 stadia." See MONEY, WEIGHTS, and MEASURES on page 328.

asked Him, "Are you the only stranger living in Jerusalem who does not know what things happened there these days?"

19 He asked, "What sort of things?"

"The things about Jesus from Nazareth," they told Him, "who was a Prophet, mighty in what He did and said before God and all the people, 20 and how our high priests and rulers handed Him over to be condemned to death and crucified Him. 21 But we were hoping He would be the One who was going to free Israel. What is more, this is now the third day since these things happened. 22 But then some of our women startled us. They went to the tomb early this morning 23 and did not find His body. They came and told us that they had even seen a vision of angels who said He is alive! 24 Some of our men went to the tomb and found it as the women had said, but they did not see Him."

25 He told them, "How unthinking you are, and how slow you are in your heart to believe everything the prophets said! 26 Did not the Christ [Messiah] have to suffer these things and enter into His glory?" 27 Then starting with Moses and all the prophets He explained to them what was said about Him in all the Scriptures.

28 They came near the village where they were going, and He acted as if He were going farther. 29 "Stay with us," they urged Him. "It's getting late, and the day is almost gone." So He went in to stay with them.

30 While He was at the table with them, He took the bread and gave thanks. c He broke it and gave it to them. 31 Then their eyes were opened, and they knew who He was. But He vanished from them.

32 They said to each other, "Didn't our hearts glow as He was talking to us on the way and explaining the Scriptures to us?"

33 That same hour they started out and went back to Jerusalem. They found the Eleven and those who were with them all gathered together. 34 They were saying, "The Lord really did rise and has appeared to Simon."

35 Then the two men told what had happened on the way and how they had recognized Him while He was breaking the bread.

Behind Locked Doors—*John 20:19-23*

36 While they were talking about what had happened, Jesus stood among them. "Peace to you!" He said to them. 37 They were startled and terrified and thought they were seeing a ghost.

38 He asked them, "Why are you troubled? And why do doubts come into your minds? 39 Look at My hands and My feet: it is I Myself. Feel Me and see. A ghost does not have flesh and bones as you see Me have." 40 As He said this, He showed them His hands and His feet.

41 While they were still so overwhelmed with joy that they could not believe it, He asked them, "Do you have anything here to eat?" 42 They gave Him a piece of broiled fish. d 43 He took it and ate it while they watched Him.

44 He said to them, "These are the very words I spoke to you while I was still with you, namely, that everything written about Me in the Law of Moses, the

---

c- 30 Or "spoke a blessing."
d- 42 Some manuscripts and early translations add: "and a piece of honeycomb."

Prophets, and the Psalms*e* must be fulfilled." **45** Then He opened their minds to understand the Scriptures. **46** He told them, "This is what is written: The Christ [Messiah] will suffer and rise from the dead on the third day; **47** and on the basis of His Name,*f* repentance and forgiveness of sins will be preached to all nations, beginning at Jerusalem. **48** You will testify to these things."

Jesus Goes Up To Heaven

49 "I am sending you what My Father promised. Wait here in the city until you are armed with power from above."

50 He took them out to a place where Bethany lay ahead of them. Then He raised His hands and blessed them. **51** While He was blessing them, He parted from them and was taken up to heaven.

52 And having knelt in worship of Him, they went back to Jerusalem with great joy. **53** And they were always in the Temple, praising God.

---

e- 44 See THE OLD TESTAMENT CANON on page 551.

f - 47 That is, on the basis of who Jesus was and what He did for the human race.

RESURRECTION AND POST-RESURRECTION EVENTS

as related to

Jesus' Actions and Appearances

(1 Cor. 15:13,14)

1. Jesus rises from the dead (cf. 1 Cor. 15:4).*
2. Jesus descends into hell (cf. 1 Pet. 3:19; Is. 63:1-6).
3. The angel rolls away the stone from the grave and the guards flee (Matt. 28:2).
4. Women see from a distance that the stone is moved (Mk. 16:1-4).
5. Mary runs to tell the disciples that the stone has been moved (Jn. 20:1).
6. The women enter the grave and see two angels who tell them that Jesus is alive (Lk. 24:2-6).
7. Jesus appears to several women (Matt. 28:8-10; cf. Lk. 24:10).
8. Peter and John arrive at the grave and see folded burial clothes (Jn. 20:2-10).
9. Jesus appears to Mary who had returned to the Garden-grave (Jn. 20:11-18; cf. Mk. 16:9).
10. The guards report the empty grave to the high priests (Matt. 28:11-15).
11. Jesus appears to Peter (1 Cor. 15:5; Lk. 24:34).
12. Jesus walks with two disciples on the road to Emmaus and reveals Himself at supper (Lk. 24:13-35; Mk. 16:12).
13. Jesus appears to His disciples behind closed doors on Easter evening; Thomas is absent (Jn. 20:19-24).
14. A week later Jesus appears again to the disciples when Thomas is present (Jn. 20:26-29; cf. Mk. 16:14).
15. Jesus has breakfast with the disciples in Galilee (Jn. 21:1-14).
16. Jesus appears to 500 disciples at one time (1 Cor. 15:6).
17. Jesus appears to James (1 Cor. 15:7).
18. Jesus meets the Eleven on a mountain in Galilee and issues The Great Commission (Matt. 28:16-20).
19. Jesus ascends to heaven from the Mount of Olives (Acts 1:3-12).
20. Jesus appears to Stephen (Acts 7:55).
21. Jesus appears to Paul (1 Cor. 15:8; cf. Acts 9:3-5; 22:17,18; Gal. 1:12).
22. Jesus appears to John in the vision of *Revelation* (Rev. 1:12-19).

*Anytime after 6:00 p.m. Holy Saturday evening, which according to Jewish time was already Sunday. (A Jewish day went from 6:00 p.m.–6:00 p.m.)

THE GOOD NEWS [GOSPEL] AS TOLD BY
JOHN[a]

1ST CHAPTER

A. Prolog: Jesus—the WORD [Logos]—becomes flesh (1:1-18)

The Word Becomes Flesh

[1] In the beginning was the Word,[b] and the Word was with God, and the Word was God. [2] He was in the beginning with God.

[3] Everything was made by Him, and not one thing that was made was made without Him.

[4] In Him was life, and the Life was the Light of mankind. [5] The Light is shining in the dark, and the darkness has not put it out.

[6] A man came—God sent him—his name was John. [7] He came to testify, that is, to testify about the Light so that through him[c] everyone might believe. [8] He was not the Light but came to witness about the Light.

[9] The genuine[d] Light that gives light to everyone was coming into the world. [10] He was in the world, and He made the world, and the world did not know Him. [11] He came to His own, and His own people did not welcome Him. [12] But to all who welcomed Him, who believe in His Name, He gave the right to become the children of God. [13] They have been born not of blood, nor of an urge of the flesh, nor of a husband's desire, but of God.

[14] And the Word became flesh and lived among us,[e] and we saw His glory, the glory of the Father's one-and-only Son[f]—He is full of grace and truth.

[15] John testified about Him when he cried out: "This is the One of whom I said, 'He who is coming after me ranks above me because He existed before me.' " [16] For all of us have received one gift of grace after another[g] from the fullness of His grace. [17] For the Law was given through Moses, but grace and truth came through Jesus Christ. [18] No one has ever seen God; the one-and-only

---

1 *a*   John wrote this Gospel toward the end of the first century A.D. to Christians around Ephesus
           who were acquainted with the other three Gospels.
   b-   1   A reference to Jesus Christ, as climaxed in verse 14.
   c-   7   Or "Him."
   d-   9   Greek: "*alēthinos*"; see *ALĒTHINOS* COMPARED WITH *ALĒTHĒS* on page 530.
   e-   14   Literally: "tented [tabernacled] among us."
   f-   14   This means His "one-of-a-kind Son" or "only-begotten Son"; see *MONOGENĒS* on page 542.
   g-   16   Literally: "grace upon grace."

Son who is God,[h] who is close to the Father's heart,[i] has made Him known.[j]

B. The WORD reveals Himself to Israel (1:19–4:54)

John Prepares The Way—Matthew 3:1-12; Mark 1:1-8; Luke 3:1-18

19 This was John's testimony when the Jews in Jerusalem sent priests and Levites to ask him, "Who are you?" **20** He confessed and did not deny. He confessed: "I am not the Christ [Messiah]."[k]

21 They asked him, "Who are you then? Are you Elijah?"

"I am not," he said.

"Are you the Prophet?"[l]

"No," he answered.

22 Then they asked him, "Who are you? We want to bring an answer to those who sent us. What do you say about yourself?"

23 He said: "I am *a voice calling out*[m] *in the wilderness*: '*Make the way straight for the Lord,*' as the prophet Isaiah said."

24 Some who had been sent belonged to the Pharisees. **25** They asked him, "Why then do you baptize if you are not the Christ or Elijah or the Prophet?"

26 "I baptize with water," John answered them. "There is One standing among you whom you do not know, **27** the One who is coming after me. I am not worthy to untie His sandal strap."[n]

28 This happened at Bethany on the other side of the Jordan, where John was baptizing.

The Lamb Of God—Compare Matthew 3:13-17; Mark 1:9-11; Luke 3:21,22

29 The next day John saw Jesus coming toward him and he said, "Look! The Lamb of God who takes away the sin of the world. **30** He is the One I meant when I said, 'A Man is coming after me who ranks above me because He existed before me.' **31** Even I did not know who He was, but I came and baptized with water to show Him to Israel."

32 John testified: "I saw the Spirit come down from heaven as a dove and stay on Him. **33** I did not know who He was, but He who sent me to baptize with

---

23 Is 40:3

h- 18 Some of the older manuscripts and early translations read: "the only God." The Greek words for "one-and-only Son" mean "one-of-a-kind Son" or "only-begotten Son"; see *MONOGENĒS* on page 542.

i- 18 Literally: "who is in the Father's bosom."

j- 18 Literally: "has revealed Him."

k- 20 See ahead at 1:41.

l- 21 Or "the prophet"; some Jews felt the "Prophet" ("prophet") of Deuteronomy 18:15,18 referred to a second Moses, others to a second Elijah or Jeremiah, and still others to the coming Messiah (cf. Mal. 4:5; Matt. 16:14; Jn. 7:40). With one voice the Early Christian Church identified "the Prophet" with Christ on the basis of Acts 3:22 and 7:37.

m- 23 Or "shouting."

n- 27 This was ordinarily a slave's duty.

water told me, 'When you see the Spirit come down on Someone and stay on Him, He is the One who baptizes with the Holy Spirit.' **34** I have seen it and have testified, 'This is the Son of God.' "

The First Disciples—Matthew 4:18-22; Mark 1:14-20; Luke 5:1-11

35 The next day, while John was again standing with two of his disciples, **36** he saw Jesus passing by. He said, "Look, the Lamb of God!" **37** When the two disciples heard him say this, they followed Jesus.

38 Jesus turned around and saw them following. He asked them, "What are you looking for?"

They said to Him, "Rabbi" (which means "Teacher"), "where are You staying?"

39 He told them, "Come, and you will see." So they came and saw where He was staying, and they stayed with Him that day. It was about ten in the morning. *o*

40 Andrew, Simon Peter's brother, was one of the two who heard John and then followed Jesus. **41** He first found his own brother Simon and told him, "We have found the Messiah" (which means "Christ"). *p* **42** He brought him to Jesus.

Looking at him, Jesus said, "You are Simon the son of John. Your name will be Cephas" (which means "Peter"). *q*

43 The next day Jesus wanted to go to Galilee. He found Philip. Jesus told him, "Follow Me!" **44** Philip was from Bethsaida, the hometown of Andrew and Peter.

45 Philip found Nathanael and told him, "We have found the One about whom Moses wrote in the Law*r* and about whom the prophets also wrote*s*—Jesus, Joseph's son from Nazareth."

46 Nathanael asked him, "Nazareth—can anything good come from there?"

"Come and see!" Philip told him.

47 Jesus saw Nathanael coming toward Him. He said of him, "Here is a true Israelite in whom there is no deceit."

48 Nathanael asked Him, "Where did You get to know me?"

Jesus answered him, "Before Philip called you, when you were under the fig tree, I saw you."

---

o- 39 Literally: "the tenth hour"; the text represents Roman time; Jewish time would be 4 p.m. John follows the Roman time system throughout his Gospel (cf. 4:6,52; 19:14). The Romans began a new day at 12 a.m. (midnight).

p- 41 The Greek-based English name "Christ" and its Hebrew-based counterpart "Messiah" both mean the "Anointed One" or the "Chosen One." See also 4:25.

q- 42 "Cephas" ("Kepha") is of Aramaic origin, while "Peter" ("Petros") is from the Greek; both forms are masculine and mean "rock" in the sense of stone or pebble. See Matthew 16:18 and its accompanying footnote "c."

r- 45 Greek: "nomos"; here a reference to the first division of the Old Testament canon. This division is called the "Law" (Hebrew: "Tōrāh"). See THE OLD TESTAMENT CANON as well as NOMOS on pages 551 and 544, respectively.

s- 45 Here the text makes reference to *all* the various Old Testament personages who were known as writing prophets. As such, Philip would also have reference to prophecies made in the "Writings" section, not only the "Prophets" portion of the Old Testament canon. For example, David the *prophet* (Acts 2:29-31) *wrote* many psalms in the "Writings" section. See THE OLD TESTAMENT CANON on page 551.

49 "Rabbi," Nathanael answered Him, "You are the Son of God! You are the King of Israel!"

50 Jesus answered him, "You believe because I told you that I saw you under the fig tree. You will see greater things than that." **51** And He said to him, "I tell you the absolute truth, you will see *heaven* opened *and the angels of God going up and coming down* on the Son of Man."[t]

2ND CHAPTER

Jesus Changes Water Into Wine

1 On the third day there was a wedding in Cana in Galilee, and Jesus' mother was there. **2** Jesus and His disciples had also been invited to the wedding.

3 When they were out of wine, Jesus' mother said to Him, "They do not have any wine."

4 Jesus asked her, "What do we have in common, woman?[a] My time has not yet come."

5 His mother told the waiters, *"Do anything He tells you."*

6 Six stone water jars were standing there for the religious washings of the Jews. Each jar held 18 to 27 gallons.

7 "Fill the jars with water," Jesus told them. And they filled them to the top. **8** He said to them, "Now dip some of it out and take it to the manager of the dinner." Then they took it to him.

9 When the manager tasted the water that had been changed to wine and did not know where it had come from (but the waiters who had dipped the water knew), the manager called the groom **10** and said to him, "Everybody serves his good wine first, and when people have drunk much, then the poorer wine. You have kept the good wine until now."

11 Jesus worked this, the first of His miraculous signs,[b] in Cana in Galilee. He showed His glory, and His disciples believed in Him.

12 After this He, His mother, His brothers, and His disciples went down to Capernaum and stayed there a few days.

Jesus Clears Out The Temple

13 The Jewish Passover was near, so Jesus went up to Jerusalem.

14 In the Temple He found those who were selling cattle and sheep and pigeons, as well as the moneychangers sitting there. **15** He made a whip of small ropes and drove them all out of the Temple, together with their sheep and cattle. He scattered the coins of the moneychangers and upset their tables.

---

51 Gen 28:12   *5 Gen 41:55*

t- 51 See "Son of Man" in Glossary.
2 *a-* 4 Literally: "What is it to Me and to you?"
    b- 11 See MIRACULOUS SIGNS, WONDERFUL PROOFS, and MIRACLES on page 527.

16 He told those who sold pigeons, "Take these away! Stop making My Father's House a place of business!"

17 His disciples remembered that it is written: *"The zeal for Your House will consume Me."*

18 So the Jews spoke up and asked, "By what miraculous sign can You prove to us that You may do this?"

19 Jesus answered them, "Tear down this Temple and I will raise it in three days."

20 "It took forty-six years to build this Temple," said the Jews, "and will You raise it in three days?"

21 But the Temple He spoke of was His own body. **22** So after He rose from the dead, His disciples remembered that He had said this; and they believed the Scripture and this statement which Jesus had made.

23 Now, while He was in the crowd at the Passover in Jerusalem, many believed in His Name when they saw the miraculous signs which He was working. **24** Jesus, however, did not take them entirely into His confidence,*c* because He fully understood all people. **25** He did not need to be told about human nature since He knew what mankind was really like.*d*

3RD CHAPTER

Nicodemus

1 Now, there was a Pharisee by the name of Nicodemus, a member of the Jewish council.*a* **2** He came to Jesus one night and said to Him, "Rabbi, we know You are a Teacher who has come from God. For no one can work these miraculous signs that You work unless God is with him."

3 "I tell you the absolute truth," Jesus answered him, "if anyone is not born again,*b* he cannot see the Kingdom of God."

4 Nicodemus asked Him, "How can anyone be born when he is old? He cannot go back into his mother's womb and be born a second time, can he?"

5 Jesus answered him, "I tell you the absolute truth, if anyone is not born of water and the Spirit, he cannot enter the Kingdom of God. **6** What is born of the flesh is flesh, but what is born of the Spirit is spirit. **7** Do not be surprised when I tell you that you must all be born again. **8** The wind blows where it pleases and you hear the sound of it, but you do not know where it is coming from or where it is going. So it is with everyone born of the Spirit."

9 Nicodemus asked Him, "How can these things be?"

10 "You are the teacher of Israel," Jesus said to him, "and you don't know

---

17 Ps 69:9

---

c - 24 Literally: "Jesus, however, did not entrust Himself to them, ..."

d- 25 Literally: "And because He had no need that anyone should witness [tell Him] about mankind for He knew what was in mankind."

3 a- 1 Literally: "a ruler of the Jews," meaning a member of the Sanhedrin.

b- 3 Or "born from above"; the Greek word can mean either "again" or "from above." Some interpreters feel it means both here (also in v. 7; cf. "from above" in v. 31; 19:11).

these things? 11 I tell you the absolute truth, We speak what We know, and We testify to what We have seen. But you people do not accept Our testimony. *c* 12 If you do not believe the earthly things I told you, how will you believe Me if I tell you heavenly things? 13 No one has gone up to heaven except the One who came down from heaven—the Son of Man who is in heaven. *d*

14 "As Moses *lifted up the snake* in the wilderness, so the Son of Man must be lifted up 15 so that everyone who believes in Him would have everlasting life.

16 "For God loved the world so much that He gave His one-and-only Son, *e* so that everyone who believes in Him would not perish but have everlasting life. 17 You see, God did not send His Son into the world to condemn the world but that the world would be saved through Him. 18 The person who believes in Him is not condemned, but the person who does not believe is already condemned because he does not believe in the Name of God's one-and-only Son. *f* 19 This is why people are condemned: The Light came into the world, but people have loved darkness rather than the Light because they have been doing wrong. 20 For everyone who does wrong hates the Light and will not come to the Light—he does not want his works to be seen in the light. 21 But the person who lives in the truth comes to the Light so that his works may be seen to have been done in God." *g*

John's Explanation Of Christ

22 After this, Jesus and His disciples went into the country of Judea, and there He was spending some time with them and baptizing.

23 John, too, was baptizing in Aenon, near Salim, because water was plentiful there. People came and were baptized, 24 for John had not yet been put in prison.

25 John's disciples began a discussion with a Jew about religious cleansing 26 and they came to John. "Rabbi," they told him, "He who was with you on the other side of the Jordan and to whom you gave your testimony—look, He is baptizing and everyone is going to Him!"

27 John answered, "A person cannot receive anything unless it has been given to him from heaven. 28 You yourselves are witnesses that I said, 'I am not the Christ but am sent ahead of Him.'

29 "The One who has the bride is the Bridegroom. The Bridegroom's friend stands and listens to Him. And when the Bridegroom speaks, He makes His

---

14 Num 21:8

c- 11 The five capitalized pronouns of this verse certainly are inclusive of Jesus. Thus, their capitalization! The plural pronouns could associate others with Jesus, such as His disciples, John the Baptizer, etc. (cf. 17:21,22). See GWN CAPITALIZATION on page 521. Also compare Jesus' "We" as contrasted to Nicodemus' "we" in verse 2.

d- 13 Some of the older manuscripts and early translations omit: "who is in heaven."

e - 16 See 1:14 and its accompanying footnote "f."

f - 18 See 1:14 and its accompanying footnote "f."

g- 21 Many view verses 16-21 as being words of theological explanation by John the Apostle, not the words of Jesus. Some would end Jesus' words already at verse 10. A more critical question involves whether the words of verses 14 and 15 or 14-21 were spoken to Nicodemus or spoken on another occasion. We know too little to be dogmatic.

friend very happy. Now, this is my happiness, and it is complete. 30 He must become greater, but I must become less ⌊significant⌋.

31 "The One who comes from above is above all. The one who comes from the earth is earthly and talks about earthly things. The One who comes from heaven is above all others. *h* 32 He testifies to what He has seen and heard, but no one accepts His testimony. 33 The person who has accepted His testimony has certified that God tells the truth. 34 For the One whom God has sent speaks God's words because God gives Him His Spirit without limit. 35 The Father loves the Son and has put everything in His hands. 36 The person who believes in the Son has everlasting life, but the one who rejects the Son will not see life; instead, the wrath of God rests on him." *i*

4TH CHAPTER

The Samaritan Woman

1 When the Lord *a* found out that the Pharisees had heard that He was making and baptizing more disciples than John, 2 although Jesus Himself was not baptizing but His disciples were, 3 He left Judea and went back again toward Galilee.

4 Now Jesus had to go through Samaria. 5 So He came to a town in Samaria by the name of Sychar, near the piece of land which Jacob gave to his son Joseph. 6 Jacob's Well was there; so Jesus, tired as He was from traveling, sat down by the well. It was about six in the evening. *b*

7 A woman of Samaria came to draw water. Jesus said to her, "Give Me a drink." 8 (His disciples had gone into the town to buy food.)

9 The Samaritan woman asked Him: "How is it that You, a Jew, ask me, a Samaritan woman, for a drink?" (Jews, you see, do not associate with Samaritans.) *c*

10 Jesus answered her, "If you knew what God's gift is and who it is that says to you, 'Give Me a drink,' you would have asked Him, and He would have given you living water."

11 "Sir, You have nothing to draw water with," she told Him, "and the well is deep. Where, then, can You get this living water? 12 You are not greater than Jacob, our ancestor, are You? He gave us the well and he himself drank from it—also his sons and his animals."

13 Jesus answered her, "Everyone who drinks this water will become thirsty again. 14 Anyone who drinks the water that I will give him will never become thirsty again. But the water I will give him will become in him a spring of water bubbling up to everlasting life."

15 "Sir, give me this water," the woman told Him. "Then I won't get thirsty or have to come out here to draw water."

---

h- 31 Some manuscripts omit: "is above all others."
i- 36 Many view verses 31-36 as being the words of theological explanation by John the Apostle, not the words of John the Baptizer.
4 *a*- 1 Many of the older manuscripts and early translations read: "Jesus."
 b- 6 Literally: "the sixth hour." See 1:39 and its accompanying footnote.
 c- 9 See JEWS AND SAMARITANS on page 553.

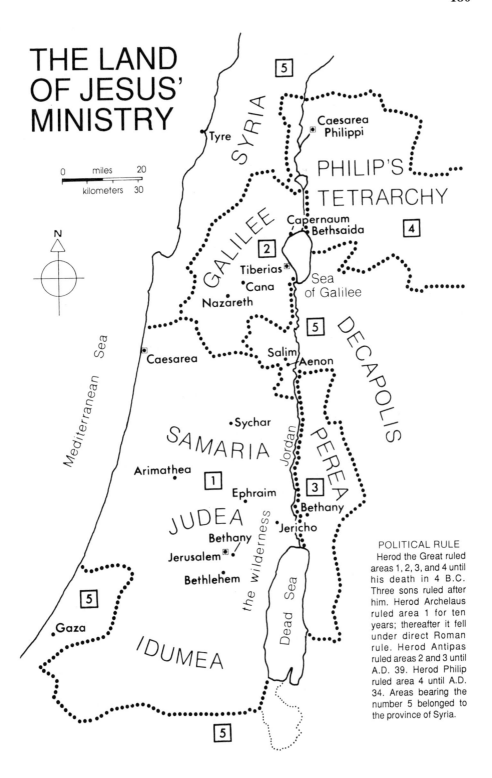

THE LAND OF JESUS' MINISTRY

0 miles 20

kilometers 30

N

SYRIA

Tyre

Caesarea Philippi

PHILIP'S TETRARCHY

GALILEE

Capernaum
Bethsaida

4

2

Tiberias

Cana

Sea of Galilee

Nazareth

DECAPOLIS

Mediterranean Sea

Caesarea

Salim

Aenon

5

Sychar

Jordan

PEREA

SAMARIA

Arimathea

1

Ephraim

3

Bethany

JUDEA

the wilderness

Jericho

Bethany

Jerusalem

Bethlehem

Dead Sea

5

Gaza

IDUMEA

5

POLITICAL RULE
Herod the Great ruled areas 1, 2, 3, and 4 until his death in 4 B.C. Three sons ruled after him. Herod Archelaus ruled area 1 for ten years; thereafter it fell under direct Roman rule. Herod Antipas ruled areas 2 and 3 until A.D. 39. Herod Philip ruled area 4 until A.D. 34. Areas bearing the number 5 belonged to the province of Syria.

16 Jesus told her, "Go, call your husband and come back here."

17 "I don't have a husband," the woman answered Him.

Jesus told her, "You are right when you say, 'I don't have a husband.' 18 You have had five husbands, and the man you have now is not your husband. You have told the truth!"

19 "Sir," the woman said to Him, "I see that You are a prophet! 20 Our ancestors worshiped on this mountain, but You say, 'The place where people must worship is in Jerusalem.' "

21 Jesus told her, "Believe Me, woman, the time is coming when you will not be worshiping the Father on this mountain or in Jerusalem. 22 You do not know what you are worshiping. We ˌJewsˌ know what we are worshiping, because salvation comes from the Jews. 23 But the time is coming, and it is now here, when the genuine*d* worshipers will worship the Father in spirit and in truth. You see, the Father is looking for such people to worship Him. 24 God is a spirit, and those who worship Him must worship in spirit and in truth."

25 The woman said to Him, "I know that the Messiah" (who is called Christ)*e* "is coming. When He comes, He will tell us everything."

26 Jesus told her, "I, the One who speaks to you, am He."

27 Just then His disciples came and were surprised that He was talking to a woman. But none of them asked, "What do You want?" or "Why are You talking to her?"

28 Then the woman left her water jar and went back into the town. 29 "Come," she told the people, "see a Man who told me everything I have done. Could He be the Christ?" 30 They left the town and were coming to Him.

31 Meanwhile the disciples were urging Him, "Rabbi, eat."

32 He told them, "I have food to eat that you do not know about."

33 The disciples asked one another, "Did anyone bring Him something to eat?"

34 Jesus told them, "My food is to do the will of Him who sent Me and to finish His work.

35 "Do you not say, 'Four more months and the harvest will be here'? I tell you, look and see how the fields are white and ready to be harvested. 36 Already the reaper is getting paid and is gathering grain for everlasting life, so that the sower and the reaper may be glad together. 37 For in this respect the proverb [saying] is true,*f* 'One sows, and another reaps.' 38 I sent you to reap where you had not worked before. Others have done the hard work, and you have succeeded them in their work."

39 Many Samaritans in that town believed in Him because of the statement of the woman who testified: "He told me everything I have done." 40 So when the Samaritans came to Him, they asked Him to stay with them. And He stayed there two days. 41 Then many more believed because of what He said. 42 They told the woman, "We no longer believe because of what you said, for we heard Him ourselves and we know He really is the Savior of the world."

---

d- 23 Greek: "*alēthinos*"; see ALĒTHINOS COMPARED WITH *ALĒTHĒS* on page 530.

e- 25 See 1:41 and its accompanying footnote. Compare Deuteronomy 18:18; Psalm 2:2.

f- 37 Greek: "*alēthinos*"; see ALĒTHINOS COMPARED WITH *ALĒTHĒS* on page 530.

Jesus Heals An Officer's Son

43 After two days He left and went to Galilee. **44** (Remember, Jesus Himself declared that a prophet is not honored in his own country.)

45 Now when He came to Galilee, the people in Galilee welcomed Him. They had seen all He did at the festival in Jerusalem since they, too, had gone to the festival.

46 In view of this, Jesus again came to Cana in Galilee, where He had changed water to wine.

There was a certain king's officer whose son was sick at Capernaum. **47** When he heard Jesus had come from Judea to Galilee, he went to Him and asked Him to come down and heal his son since he was about to die.

48 Jesus told him, "If you do not see miraculous signs and wonderful proofs,[g] you certainly will not believe."

49 "Lord," the officer said to Him, "come down before my little boy dies."

50 "Go," Jesus told him, "your son is well." The man believed what Jesus told him and left.

51 Already while he was on his way back, his slaves met him and told him that his boy was well. **52** So he asked them at what time he had become better. They told him, "Yesterday at seven in the evening[h] the fever left him." **53** Then the father knew it was the same hour when Jesus had told him, "Your son is well." And he and everyone in his house believed.

54 This was the second miraculous sign that Jesus worked after He had come from Judea to Galilee.

5TH CHAPTER

C. The WORD is rejected by Israel (5:1–12:50)

Sick For 38 Years

1 After this there was a Jewish festival, and Jesus went up to Jerusalem.

2 Near the Sheep Gate in Jerusalem there is a pool which in Aramaic[a] is called Bethesda. It has five porches.[b] **3** In them there used to lie a crowd of people who were sick, blind, lame, and paralyzed.[c] **5** One man who was there had been sick 38 years. **6** Jesus saw him lying there and knew that he had been sick a long time. "Would you like to get well?" He asked him.

---

g- 48 See MIRACULOUS SIGNS, WONDERFUL PROOFS, and MIRACLES on page 527.

h- 52 Literally: "the seventh hour." See 1:39 and its accompanying footnote.

5 a- 2 Literally: "Hebrew"; Aramaic was the related Semitic language that Jesus and His fellow Jews ordinarily spoke in New Testament times. See also 19:13,17,20; 20:16. (Note use of Aramaic word at Rom. 8:15.)

b- 2 Literally: "five colonnades."

c- 3 Many of the older manuscripts and early translations omit verses 3b,4: "waiting for the water to be stirred. At a certain time the Lord's angel would come down into the pool and stir the water. After the stirring of the water, the first to step in was healed from whatever disease he was suffering." However, the statement in verse 7 that the water was stirred (and that healing took place at this time) is certain.

7 "Lord," the sick man answered Him, "I don't have anybody to put me into the pool when the water is stirred. And while I am trying to get there, somebody else steps in ahead of me."

8 "Get up," Jesus told him, "pick up your bed, and walk." 9 Immediately the man was healed, picked up his bed, and walked.

That day was a Sabbath, 10 so the Jews told the man who had been healed, "Today is the Sabbath. It is wrong for you to carry your bed."

11 He answered them, "The One who made me well told me, 'Pick up your bed and walk.' "

12 They asked him, "Who is the Man who told you, 'Pick up your bed and walk'?" 13 But the man who had been healed did not know who He was, because Jesus had withdrawn from the crowd that was there.

14 Later Jesus found him in the Temple and said to him, "Look, you are well now. Do not sin anymore or something worse may happen to you."

15 The man went back and told the Jews that it was Jesus who had made him well.

God's Son

16 So the Jews began to persecute Jesus because He was doing such things on the Sabbath. 17 But Jesus answered them, "My Father has been working until now, and so I am working."d

18 As a result, the Jews were all the more eager to kill Him, since He was not only breaking the Sabbath but was even calling God His own Father, making Himself equal to God.

19 "I tell you the absolute truth," Jesus answered them, "the Son can do nothing by Himself, but only what He sees the Father doing. Indeed, the Son does exactly what the Father does. 20 For the Father loves the Son and shows Him everything He is doing. And He will show Him even greater works than these so that you will be amazed. 21 As the Father raises the dead and gives them life, so also the Son gives life to whom He wishes.

22 "For the Father does not judge anyone but has entrusted the judgment entirely to the Son 23 so that all might honor the Son as they honor the Father. The person who does not honor the Son does not honor the Father who sent Him. 24 I tell you the absolute truth, the person who listens to My word and believes Him who sent Me has everlasting life and will not be judged but has crossed over from death to life.

25 "I tell you the absolute truth, the hour is coming and is now here when the dead will hear the voice of the Son of God, and those who listen to it will live. 26 As the Father has ⌊the source of⌋ life in Himself, so He has granted also the Son to have ⌊the source of⌋ life in Himself.

27 "He has also given Him authority to execute judgment because He is the Son of Man. 28 This should not surprise you, because the hour is coming when all who are in their graves will hear His voice 29 and will come out. Those who have done good will rise to live; those who have done evil will rise to be condemned. 30 I can do nothing by Myself. I judge only as I am told to do, and

---

d- 17 See Isaiah 43:10.

My judgment is just, because I am not trying to do My will but the will of Him who sent Me.

31 "If I ₍alone₎ testify about Myself, My testimony is not dependable. **32** There is Someone else testifying about Me, and I know that what He testifies about Me is true. **33** You sent to John, and he testified to the Truth. **34** Not that I receive My testimony from a man, but I say this to save you. **35** John was a lighted lamp that was shining, and for a while you wanted to enjoy his light. **36** But I have a greater testimony than John had. For the works that the Father gave Me to carry out, these works which I do, testify that the Father sent Me. **37** The Father who sent Me—He testified about Me. You never heard His voice or saw His form. **38** You do not keep His word within you, because you do not believe Him whom He sent. **39** You search the Scriptures since you think you have everlasting life in them. They testify about Me! **40** And yet you do not want to come to Me in order to have life.

41 "I do not receive glory from men. **42** But I know you; I know that in your hearts you do not love God. **43** I have come in My Father's Name, and you do not accept Me. If someone else comes in his own name, you will accept him. **44** How can you believe while you accept honor from one another, and yet you are not eagerly seeking the honor that comes from the only God?

45 "Do not continue to think that I will accuse you before the Father. There is already one who accuses you—Moses, on whom you have rested your hope. **46** If you really believed Moses, you would believe Me, because he wrote about Me. **47** But if you do not believe what he wrote, how will you believe what I say?"

6TH CHAPTER

Jesus Feeds 5,000—Matthew 14:13-21; Mark 6:30-44; Luke 9:10-17

1 Some time later Jesus crossed over to the other side of the Sea of Galilee, which is the Sea of Tiberias. **2** A large crowd was following Him because they saw the miraculous signs which He worked on the sick. **3** Jesus went up on the hillside and sat down there with His disciples. **4** The Jewish Festival of the Passover was near.

5 As Jesus looked up and saw a large crowd coming to Him, He said to Philip, "Where should we buy bread for these people to eat?" **6** He asked this to test him, since He knew what He was going to do.

7 Philip answered, "Two hundred denarii*ᵃ* would not buy enough bread for each of them to have just a little."

8 One of His disciples, Andrew, Simon Peter's brother, told Him, **9** "There's a boy here who has five barley loaves and two fish; but what's that among so many?"

10 "Have the people sit down," Jesus said. Since there was plenty of grass there, they sat down. There were about 5,000 men.

11 Jesus took the loaves, gave thanks, and distributed them to the people who

---

6 *a-* **7** A denarius was a day's pay. See MONEY, WEIGHTS, and MEASURES on page 328.

were sitting down—and in the same way as much of the fish as they wanted.
¹² When they had enough, He told His disciples, "Gather the leftover pieces so that nothing will be wasted." ¹³ So they gathered them and filled twelve baskets with pieces of the five barley loaves that were left over by those who had eaten.

¹⁴ When the people saw the miraculous sign which He worked, they said, "This certainly is the *Prophet* who is coming into the world."

Jesus Walks On Water—*Matthew 14:22-33; Mark 6:45-52*

¹⁵ When Jesus realized that the people intended to come and take Him by force to make Him king, He went back again into the hills by Himself. ¹⁶ When evening came, His disciples went down to the sea, ¹⁷ stepped into a boat, and were on their way across the sea to Capernaum. By this time it was dark, and Jesus had not yet come to them. ¹⁸ A strong wind started to blow and stir up the sea.

¹⁹ After they had rowed three or four miles, they saw Jesus walking on the sea and coming near the boat, and they were terrified.

²⁰ He told them, "It is I. Stop being afraid!"

²¹ They were willing to take Him into the boat, and in a moment the boat reached the shore where they were going.

Bread From Heaven

²² The next day the people were still lingering on the other side of the sea. They had noticed that only one boat was there and that Jesus had not stepped into that boat with His disciples, but they had gone away without Him. ²³ Other boats came from Tiberias near the place where they had eaten the bread after the Lord gave thanks. ²⁴ When the people saw that neither Jesus nor His disciples were there, they stepped into these boats and came to Capernaum, looking for Jesus. ²⁵ They found Him on the other side of the sea and asked Him, "Rabbi, when did You get here?"

²⁶ "I tell you the absolute truth," Jesus answered them, "you are not looking for Me because you have seen miraculous signs but because you have eaten of the loaves of bread and been well fed. ²⁷ Do not continue to work for the food that spoils but for the food that keeps until everlasting life, which the Son of Man will give you because God the Father has placed His seal of approval on Him."

²⁸ They asked Him, "What are the works that God wants us to do?"

²⁹ Jesus answered them, "This is the work of God—that you believe in Him whom He sent."

³⁰ They asked Him, "What miraculous sign are You going to work? Let us see it and we will believe You. What are You going to do? ³¹ Our fathers ate the manna in the wilderness, as it is written: '*He gave them bread from heaven to eat.*'"

³² "I tell you the absolute truth," Jesus said to them, "Moses did not give you

---

14 Deut 18:18   31 Ex 16:4,15; Ps 78:24

the bread from heaven, but My Father gives you the real[b] Bread from heaven. 33 For God's Bread is the One who comes down from heaven and gives life to the world."

34 "Lord," they said to Him, "always give us this bread."

35 "I am the Bread of Life," Jesus told them. "The person who comes to Me will never be hungry and the person who believes in Me will never be thirsty. 36 But I have said to you that you have even seen Me and yet you do not believe! 37 All that the Father gives Me will come to Me; and the person who comes to Me I will never turn away, 38 because I came down from heaven not to do My will but to do the will of Him who sent Me. 39 And this is the will of the One who sent Me, that I do not lose any of those He gave Me, but that I raise them on the Last Day. 40 Yes, My Father wants everyone who sees the Son and believes in Him to have everlasting life, and He wants Me to raise him on the Last Day."

41 The Jews therefore grumbled because He said, "I am the Bread that came down from heaven." 42 They asked, "Isn't this Jesus, Joseph's son, whose father and mother we know? How can He now say, 'I came down from heaven'?"

43 Jesus answered them, "Stop grumbling among yourselves. 44 A person can come to Me only if the Father who sent Me draws him; and I will raise him on the Last Day. 45 The prophets wrote: *'God will teach everyone.'* Everyone who listens to the Father and learns from Him comes to Me. 46 Not that anyone has seen the Father; only He who comes from God has seen the Father. 47 I tell you the absolute truth, the one who believes in Me[c] has everlasting life.

48 "I am the Bread of Life. 49 Your fathers ate the manna in the wilderness, and they died. 50 This is the Bread coming down from heaven so that anyone may eat it and not die. 51 I am the living Bread that came down from heaven. If anyone eats this Bread, he will live forever. The Bread I will give to bring life to the world is My flesh."

52 The Jews argued with one another: "How can He give us His flesh to eat?"

53 "I tell you the absolute truth," Jesus answered them, "unless you eat the flesh of the Son of Man and drink His blood, you do not have any life in you. 54 The person who eats My flesh and drinks My blood has everlasting life, and I will raise him on the Last Day. 55 My flesh is true food, and My blood is true drink. 56 The person who eats My flesh and drinks My blood remains in Me and I in him. 57 As the living Father sent Me, and I live because of the Father, so the person who feeds on Me will live because of Me. 58 This is the Bread that came down from heaven. It is not like the bread the fathers ate; they died. The person who eats this Bread will live forever."

59 He said this while He was teaching in a synagog in Capernaum. 60 When they heard it, many of His disciples said, "This teaching is hard to understand. Who is able to accept it?"

61 Since He was inwardly aware that His disciples were complaining about

---

45 *Is 54:13*

b- 32 Greek: "*alēthinos*"; see *ALĒTHINOS* COMPARED WITH *ALĒTHĒS* on page 530.
c- 47 Some of the older manuscripts and early translations omit: "in Me."

this, Jesus asked them, "Does this cause you to stumble ⌐in your faith⌐?*d* **62** What if you see the Son of Man go up where He was before? **63** The Spirit is the One who gives life; the flesh is of no help whatsoever. The words I have spoken to you are spirit and they are life. **64** But some of you do not believe." Jesus knew from the beginning those who would not believe and the one who would betray Him. **65** And He added, "That is why I told you that a person can come to Me only if the Father gives him ⌐the power to come⌐."

66 After this many of His disciples went back to their old life and did not go with Him anymore. **67** So Jesus asked the Twelve, "Do you also want to leave Me?"

68 Simon Peter answered Him, "Lord, to whom shall we go? You have words of everlasting life. **69** And we have come to believe and know that You are the Holy One of God."*e*

70 Jesus asked, "Didn't I choose the twelve of you? Yet, one of you is a devil!" **71** He meant Judas ⌐the son⌐ of Simon the man from Kerioth,*f* for he was going to betray Him, even though he was one of the Twelve.

7TH CHAPTER

To Jerusalem

1 Later Jesus went around in Galilee. He did not want to travel in Judea because the Jews were trying to kill Him.

2 The Jewish Festival of Booths*a* was near. **3** So His brothers told Jesus, "Leave this place, go to Judea, and there let Your disciples see the works You are doing. **4** For no one goes on doing things secretly when he wants to be known publicly. If You do these things, let the world see You." **5** For even His brothers did not believe in Him.

6 Jesus told them, "It is not the right time for Me yet, but any time is right for you. **7** The world cannot hate you, but it hates Me because I testify about it, that it is doing wrong. **8** You go up to the Festival.*b* I am not going up to this Festival ⌐right now⌐, because the right time has not yet arrived for Me."

9 After telling them this, He stayed in Galilee. **10** But after His brothers had gone up to the Festival, He also went up, not publicly but without being seen.

At The Festival Of Booths [Tabernacles, Gathering-In]*c*

11 The Jews were looking for Jesus in the crowd at the Festival. They kept asking, "Where is He?" **12** And there was much whispering about Him in the

---

d- 61 See *SKANDALON* on page 545.

e- 69 Many manuscripts and early translations include words similar to Matthew 16:16: "You are the Christ, the Son of the living God." However, textual evidence seems to favor omission.

f- 71 Literally: "Judas Iscariot"; see *"Iscariot"* in Glossary.

7 *a-* 2 The Hebrew for "Booths" is *"Succoth"*; also sometimes translated as "Tabernacles" (cf. Lev. 23:33-43).

b- 8 Compare 1 Kings 8:2.

c This Festival, along with Passover and Pentecost, was one of the three main religious festivals that the Jews celebrated each year.

crowds. "He is a good Man," some said; but others said, "No, He deceives the people." 13 Yet no one would talk about Him in public because everyone was afraid of the Jews.

14 But when the Festival was already half over, Jesus went up to the Temple and started to teach. 15 The Jews were surprised and asked, "How can He know so much when He has not been someone's disciple?"*d*

16 Jesus answered them, "What I teach does not come from Me but from Him who sent Me. 17 If anyone wants to do His will, he will know whether My teaching is from God or if I speak My own thoughts.*e* 18 He who speaks his own thoughts tries to glorify himself. But He who wants to glorify the One who sent Him tells the truth, and there is no unrighteousness in Him. 19 Didn't Moses give you the Law? Yet none of you does what the Law tells you. Why do you want to kill Me?"

20 "There's a demon in You," the crowd answered. "Who wants to kill You?"

21 Jesus answered them, "I did one thing and you are all surprised about it. 22 Because Moses gave you circumcision (not that it came from Moses, but from our ancestors), you also circumcise a male on a Sabbath. 23 If a male is circumcised on a Sabbath to keep the Law of Moses, are you angry with Me because I made a man entirely well on a Sabbath? 24 Stop judging by outward appearance; rather, make a judgment which is right."

25 Some of the men from Jerusalem said, "Isn't He the man they want to kill? 26 But here He speaks in public, and they do not say a thing to Him! Surely the rulers have not found out that He is the Christ [Messiah], have they? 27 However, we know where this One comes from. But when the Christ comes, no one is going to know where He is from."

28 Jesus called out as He was teaching in the Temple, "You know Me and you know where I come from. I did not decide to come on My own, but He who sent Me is true.*f* You do not know Him. 29 I know Him because I come from Him and He sent Me."

30 They therefore tried to arrest Him, but no one laid a hand on Him, because His time had not yet come.

31 But many in the crowd believed in Him and asked, "When the Christ [Messiah] comes, will He work ⌊even⌋ more miraculous signs than this One has worked?"

32 The Pharisees heard the people muttering such things about Him, and ⌊so⌋ the ruling priests as well as the Pharisees sent Temple guards to arrest Him.

33 Jesus said, "I will be with you just a little while longer, then I am going to Him who sent Me. 34 You will be looking for Me and will not find Me; and where I am, you cannot come."

35 The Jews asked one another, "Where is He intending to go, saying that we

---

d- 15 Literally: "How knows this Man letters, not having been discipled?" The leaders of the Jews reasoned that Jesus could not know so much unless He first had been the disciple of a master teacher.

e- 17 Jesus here claims to be God's certified Agent. In doing so He forces the authorities to make a decision they cannot avoid under their legal system. Either He is God's certified Agent and must be believed, or else He is not and must be punished as a blasphemer. No middle ground is open.

f- 28 Greek: "*alēthinos*"; see ALĒTHINOS COMPARED WITH ALĒTHĒS on page 530.

will not find Him? He does not intend to go to the Jews scattered among the Greeks and teach the Greeks, does He? **36** What does He mean by saying, 'You will be looking for Me and will not find Me,' and 'Where I am, you cannot come'?"

37 On the last day, the great day of the Festival, *g* as Jesus was standing there, He called out, "If anyone is thirsty, let him come to Me and drink. **38** As the Scripture has said, 'From deep within *h* the person who believes in Me streams of *living water* will flow.' " **39** By this He meant the Spirit, whom those who believed in Him were going to receive. For the Spirit had not yet come, because Jesus had not yet been glorified.

40 After they heard Him speak these words, some of the people said, "This is certainly the *Prophet*." **41** Others said, "This is the Christ [Messiah]." Still others asked, "What! The Christ does not come from Galilee, does He? **42** Does the Scripture not say: 'The Christ *will come from the descendants of David* and *from* the little town of *Bethlehem,* where David lived'?" **43** So the people were divided over Him. **44** Some of them wanted to arrest Him, but no one laid hands on Him.

45 When the Temple guards went back to the ruling priests and Pharisees, these asked them, "Why didn't you bring Him?"

46 The Temple guards answered, "No one ever spoke like this Man."

47 The Pharisees asked them, "Have you also been deceived? **48** Has any ruler or Pharisee believed in Him? **49** But this crowd, which does not know the Scriptures, *i* is cursed."

50 One of them, Nicodemus, who had once come to Jesus, asked them, **51** "Does our Law condemn anyone without first hearing what he has to say and finding out what he is doing?"

52 They asked him, "Are you also from Galilee? Search and see; the Prophet does not come from Galilee." *j*

53 Then each of them went home.

8TH CHAPTER

The Adulteress

1 But Jesus went to the Mount of Olives. **2** Early in the morning He came back into the Temple. All the people came to Him, and He sat down and taught them.

---

38 Zech 14:8   40 Deut 18:18   42 2 Sam 7:12; Mic 5:2

---

g- 37 See verses 2 and 8 of this chapter.

h- 38 Literally: "from his belly."

i- 49 Greek: "*nomos*" (lit. "Law, Instruction"); since the quotes in the text would include references to the books of 2 Samuel and Micah, the term "*nomos*" is used here in its wider sense to encompass the whole Old Testament Scriptures. See THE OLD TESTAMENT CANON as well as *NOMOS* on pages 551 and 544, respectively.

j- 52 Many of the older manuscripts and early translations omit verses 7:53–8:11, the story of the adulteress.

3 The scribes[a] and the Pharisees brought a woman who had been caught in adultery, and they had her stand in the middle ˻of the group˼. **4** "Teacher," they told Him, "this woman was caught in the act of adultery. **5** In the Law Moses ordered us to stone such women. Now, what do You say?" **6** They asked this to test Him, in order to find something of which they could accuse Him.

Jesus bent down and wrote on the ground with His finger. **7** But when they kept on asking Him, He stood up and said, "The person who is without sin among you should be the first to throw a stone at her." **8** Then He bent down again and wrote on the ground.

9 Those who heard Jesus were convicted by their conscience and went out one by one, beginning with the older men, until all had gone. Jesus was left alone with the woman in the middle ˻of the place˼. **10** Jesus stood up. "Woman, where are they?" He asked her. "Did no one condemn you?"

11 She said, "No one, Lord."

Jesus said, "I do not condemn you either. Go, ˻and˼ from now on do not sin anymore."

Jesus Argues With The Jews

12 Jesus spoke to them again: "I am the Light of the world. The person who follows Me will never wander in the darkness but will have the Light of Life."

13 The Pharisees said to Him, "You testify about Yourself. Your testimony is not true."

14 Jesus answered them, "Even if I testify about Myself, My testimony is true because I know where I came from and where I am going; but you do not know where I came from or where I am going. **15** You judge in a human way; I do not judge anyone. **16** But whenever I judge, My judgment is valid[b] because I am not alone, but I am with the Father who sent Me. **17** In your own Law it is written that the testimony of two people is true. **18** I testify about Myself, and the Father who sent Me testifies about Me."

19 They asked Him, "Where is Your Father?"

Jesus answered, "You do not know Me or My Father. If you knew Me, you would know My Father also."

20 He spoke these words in the room of the treasury while He was teaching in the Temple; no one arrested Him, because His time had not yet come.

21 He said to them again, "I am going away and you will be looking for Me, but you will die in your sin. Where I am going, you cannot come."

22 The Jews asked, "Is He going to kill Himself? Is that what He means when He says, 'Where I am going, you cannot come'?"

23 He told them, "You are from below; I am from above. Your home is in this world; My home is not in this world.[c] **24** That is why I told you, 'You will die

---

8 *a*- 3 These were the Bible scholars of Jesus' day. Their work and responsibilities varied greatly from one to another. These areas included making handwritten copies of the Old Testament, interpreting and following the Mosaic guidelines of the Pentateuch (Five Books of Moses), formulating oral laws, teaching God's people in classroom situations, etc. In short, the scribes were considered authorities on the Jewish religion. Compare Ezra 7:6,10.

b- 16 Greek: "*alēthinos*"; see *ALĒTHINOS* COMPARED WITH *ALĒTHĒS* on page 530.

c- 23 Literally: "You are of this world; I am not of this world."

in your sins'; for if you do not believe that I am the One,*d* you will die in your sins."

25 "Who are You?" they asked Him.

"What should I tell you first?"*e* Jesus asked them. **26** "I have much to say, even to condemn, concerning you. But I tell the world only what I heard from Him who sent Me, and He tells the truth." **27** They did not understand that He was talking to them about the Father.

28 So Jesus told them, "When you have lifted up the Son of Man, you will know that I am the One and I do nothing by Myself, but I speak exactly as My Father taught Me. **29** And He who sent Me is with Me and has not left Me alone, because I always do what pleases Him."

30 As He was saying this, many believed in Him. **31** Therefore, Jesus said to those Jews who believed in Him, "If you remain in My word, you are really My disciples, **32** and you will know the truth, and the truth will set you free."

33 They answered Him, "We are Abraham's descendants and have never been anyone's slaves. How can You say, 'You will be set free'?"

34 "I tell you the absolute truth," Jesus answered them, "everyone who keeps on sinning is a slave to sin. **35** A slave does not stay in the home forever; a son stays forever. **36** If, then, the Son sets you free, you will certainly be free. **37** I know you are Abraham's descendants. But you want to kill Me because there is no room for My word in you. **38** What I am saying is what I have seen at My Father's side; you are doing what you have heard from your father."

39 They answered Him, "Abraham is our father."

"If you were Abraham's children," Jesus told them, "you would do what Abraham did. **40** But now you want to kill Me, a Man who told you the truth, which I heard from God. Abraham did not do that. **41** You are doing what your father does."

They said, "We were not born as illegitimate children.*f* God alone is our Father."

42 Jesus told them, "If God were your Father, you would love Me because I came from God and I am here. I did not decide to come on My own, but He sent Me. **43** For what reason do you fail to grasp what I say? It is because you are not able to understand My word. **44** Your father is the devil, and you want to do what your father desires. From the beginning he has been murdering people and has not stayed in the truth, because there is no truth in him. Whenever he tells a lie, he is telling it from his heart,*g* because he is a liar and the father of lies. **45** Now, because I tell the truth, you do not believe Me. **46** Which of you can prove Me guilty of a sin? If I tell the truth, why is it that you do not believe Me? **47** The person who belongs to God listens to God's words. You do not listen to Him because you do not belong to God."

48 The Jews answered Him, "Are we not right when we say that You are a Samaritan and there is a demon in You?"

---

d- 24 Literally: "I am ˌHeˌ"; compare with this same expression in 8:58 and 18:5,6,8. This expression recalls the self-description of God in Deuteronomy 32:39; Isaiah 41:4; 43:10; 46:4; etc. See also verse 28.

e- 25 Or "What have I told you from the beginning?"

f- 41 Literally: "not born of fornication."

g- 44 Literally: "from his own."

49 "There is no demon in Me," Jesus answered. "No, I honor My Father, but you dishonor Me. **50** I am not trying to obtain glory for Myself. There is One who wants Me to have it, and He is the Judge. **51** I tell you the absolute truth, if anyone keeps My word, he will never see death."

52 The Jews told Him, "Now we know that there is a demon in You. Abraham died, and so did the prophets, but You say, 'If anyone keeps My word, he will never taste death.' **53** Are You greater than our father Abraham? He died and the prophets died. Who do You think You are?"

54 Jesus said, "If I glorify Myself, My glory is nothing. It is My Father who glorifies Me, He of whom you say, 'He is our God.' **55** Yet you do not know Him, but I know Him. And if I would say that I do not know Him, I would be a liar like you. But I do know Him, and I obey His word. **56** Your father Abraham was delighted that he would see My day; he saw it and was glad."

57 The Jews said to Him, "You are not yet fifty years old and You have seen Abraham?"

58 "I tell you the absolute truth," Jesus told them, "before Abraham came into being, *I AM*."*h*

59 They therefore picked up stones to throw at Him; but Jesus hid Himself and left the Temple.

9TH CHAPTER

A Blind Man Sees

1 As Jesus was passing by, He saw a man who had been blind from his birth. **2** His disciples asked Him, "Rabbi, why was he born blind? Did he sin or his parents?"

3 Jesus answered, "Neither this man nor his parents sinned. Rather, he is blind so that God can show what He can do in this man's case.*a* **4** We must do the works of Him who sent Me while it is day. The night is coming when no one can work. **5** As long as I am in the world, I am the Light of the world."

6 After He said this, He spit on the ground and with the spit made some mud and put the mud on the man's eyes. **7** "Go," He told him, "wash in the pool of Siloam" (the name means "Sent"). He went and washed; and as he came back, he could see.

8 His neighbors, then, and those who used to see him as a beggar asked, "Isn't this the man who used to sit and beg?"

9 Some said, "It is he." Others said, "No, but he does look like him." But he himself said, "I am the one."

10 So they asked him, "How did you receive your sight?"

---

58 Ex 3:14; Is 43:13

---

h- 58 Literally: "before Abraham was, I AM"; see Exodus 3:14; Isaiah 43:13 (cf. Jn. 5:17).
9 *a-* 3 Literally: "in him."

11 He answered, "The man they call Jesus made some mud and put it on my eyes and told me, 'Go to Siloam and wash.' So I went and washed, and then I could see."

12 They asked him, "Where is he?"

"I don't know," he answered.

13 They brought him who had been blind to the Pharisees. **14** Now it was a Sabbath when Jesus made the mud and gave him his sight. **15** So the Pharisees also asked him how he received his sight.

"He put mud on my eyes," the man told them, "and I washed them, and I am able to see."

16 "This man is not from God," said some of the Pharisees, "because he does not keep the Sabbath." Others asked, "How can a man who is a sinner work such miraculous signs?" So they disagreed.

17 They therefore asked the blind man again, "What do you say about him, since he opened your eyes?"

"He is a prophet," he answered.

18 The Jews did not believe that the man had been blind and had received his sight until they called the parents of the man who had received his sight. **19** They asked them, "Is this your son who you say was born blind? How does it happen that he is now able to see?"

20 "We know he is our son," his parents answered, "and that he was born blind. **21** But we do not know how it is that he is now able to see or who has opened his eyes. Ask him; he is of age. He will tell you about himself." **22** His parents said this because they were afraid of the Jews, for the Jews had already agreed to put out of the synagog anyone who confessed that Jesus was the Christ [Messiah]. **23** That is why his parents said, "He is of age; ask him."

24 So once again they called the man who had been blind. They told him, "Give glory to God. We know this man is a sinner."

25 "I do not know if he is a sinner," he answered. "I know only one thing—I was blind, but now I can see."

26 They asked him, "What did he do to you? How did he open your eyes?"

27 "I have already told you," he answered them, "and you did not listen. Why do you want to hear it again? You do not want to become his disciples too, do you?"

28 They answered him scornfully, "You are his disciple, but we are Moses' disciples. **29** We know God spoke to Moses, but this fellow—we do not know where he is from."

30 The man answered them, "Well, that is amazing! You do not know where he is from, yet he opened my eyes. **31** We know that God does not hear sinners but hears anyone who worships God and does what He wants. **32** Since the beginning of time no one has ever heard of anyone opening the eyes of a person born blind. **33** If this one were not from God, he could not do anything."

34 They answered him, "You were completely born in sins—and ₍now₎ you are trying to teach us?" Then they put him out ₍of the synagog₎.*b*

---

b- 34 Meaning "they excommunicated him."

35 Jesus heard that they had put him out. When He found him, He asked, "Do you believe in the Son of Man?"*c*

36 He asked, "Sir, who is he, so that I may believe in him?"

37 Jesus told him, "You have seen Him. He is the One who is now talking with you."

38 "I do believe, Lord," he said and bowed down to worship Him.

39 Then Jesus said, "I have come into this world to judge people, so that those who do not see may see and those who see may become blind."

40 Some Pharisees who were near Him heard this. They asked Him, "We are not blind, are we?"

41 Jesus told them, "If you were blind you would not have continued to cling to sin. But now you say, 'We see,' ⌊so⌋ your sin remains."

10TH CHAPTER

The Good Shepherd

1 "I tell you the absolute truth, the man who does not come into the sheepfold through the door but climbs over somewhere else is a thief and a robber. **2** But the one who comes in through the door is the shepherd of the sheep. **3** The doorkeeper opens the door for him, and the sheep listen to his voice. He calls his own sheep by name and leads them out. **4** When he has brought out all his own sheep, he walks ahead of them, and the sheep follow him because they know his voice. **5** They will not follow a stranger but will run away from him because they do not know the voice of strangers."

6 This was the illustration Jesus used in talking to them, but they did not understand what He meant. **7** So Jesus spoke again: "I tell you the absolute truth, I am the Door for the sheep. **8** All who came before Me*a* were thieves and robbers, but the sheep did not listen to them. **9** I am the Door. If anyone comes in through Me, he will be saved and will go in and out and find pasture.

10 "A thief comes only to steal and kill and destroy. I came so that they will have life and have it abundantly in them. **11** I am the Good Shepherd. The Good Shepherd gives His life for the sheep. **12** When a hired man, who is not a shepherd and does not own the sheep, sees a wolf coming, he leaves the sheep and runs away—and the wolf carries them off and scatters them—**13** because he works for money and does not care about the sheep. **14** I am the Good Shepherd, and I know My own and My own know Me, **15** as the Father knows Me and I know the Father. And I give up My life for the sheep. **16** I also have other sheep which are not in this fold. I must also lead them. They too will listen to My voice, and so they will become one flock with *one Shepherd.* **17** The Father loves Me because I give up My life in order to take it back again. **18** No

---

16 Ezek 34:23

c- 35 Many manuscripts and early translations read: "Son of God." However, on the basis of equally reliable texts, the weight of evidence seems to favor "Son of Man."

10 *a-* 8 Meaning "all who came claiming to be 'the Door.' "

one takes it from Me. No, of My own free will I am giving it up. I have the authority to give it up, and I have the authority to take it back again. This is what My Father ordered Me to do."

19 These words again caused a split among the Jews. **20** Many of them said, "There's a demon in Him and He's out of His mind. Why do you listen to Him?" **21** Others said, "No one talks like this when there is a demon in him. Certainly a demon cannot open the eyes of the blind, can he?"

"I And The Father Are One"

22 Then came the Festival of Dedication in Jerusalem. It was winter, **23** and Jesus was walking in Solomon's porch*b* in the Temple.

24 The Jews surrounded Him. They asked Him, "How long will You keep us in suspense? If You are the Christ [Messiah], tell us frankly."

25 Jesus answered them, "I did tell you, but you do not believe it. The works I do in the Name of My Father testify about Me. **26** But you do not believe, because you are not My sheep. **27** My sheep listen to My voice, and I know them, and they follow Me, **28** and I give them everlasting life. They will never be lost, and no one will tear them out of My hand. **29** My Father, who gave them to Me, is greater than all others, and no one can tear them out of My Father's hand. **30** I and the Father are one."

31 Again the Jews picked up stones to stone Him. **32** Jesus answered them, "I have shown you many good works that come from the Father. For which of these works are you going to stone Me?"

33 The Jews answered Him, "We are going to stone You, not for a good work but for blasphemy, because You claim to be God, although You are only a man."

34 Jesus said to them, "Is it not written in your Scriptures:*c* *'I said, "You are gods"* '? **35** If He called them 'gods' to whom God's word came—and the Scripture cannot be set aside*d*—**36** do you say to Me, whom the Father appointed ⌊for His holy purpose⌋ and sent into the world, 'You are blaspheming,' because I said, 'I am the Son of God'? **37** If I am not doing My Father's works, do not believe in Me. **38** But if I do them, even if you do not believe in Me, believe in My works so that you might learn and understand that the Father is in Me and I am in the Father."

39 Again they tried to arrest Him, but He escaped from their hands. **40** He went back across the Jordan to the place where John had been baptizing earlier, and He stayed there.

41 Many came to Him. They said, "John worked no miraculous sign, but everything John said about this Man is true." **42** And many believed in Him there.

---

34 Ps 82:6

---

b- 23 Literally: "Solomon's colonnade."
c- 34 See 7:49 and its accompanying footnote.
d- 35 Literally: "cannot be untied" or "cannot be broken."

11TH CHAPTER

Jesus Raises Lazarus

1 A man named Lazarus was sick. He was in Bethany, the village where Mary and her sister Martha were living. 2 (Mary was the one who poured perfume on the Lord and wiped His feet with her hair. It was her brother Lazarus who was sick.)

3 So the sisters sent someone to tell Jesus, "Lord, the one You love is sick."

4 When Jesus heard it, He said, "This sickness is not meant to cause death, but to show the glory of God*a* in order that the Son of God may be glorified by it."

5 Jesus loved Martha and her sister and Lazarus. 6 Yet when He heard that Lazarus was sick, He stayed two days where He was. 7 After that He said to His disciples, "Let us go back to Judea."

8 The disciples said to Him, "Rabbi, recently the Jews have been trying to stone You, and You are going back there?"

9 Jesus answered, "Are there not twelve hours in a day? If anyone walks during the day, he does not stumble, because he sees the light of this world. 10 But if anyone walks at night, he stumbles because he has no light."

11 After He said this, He told them, "Our friend Lazarus is asleep, but I am going there to wake him up."

12 His disciples said to Him, "Lord, if he is asleep, he will get well."

13 Jesus meant he was dead, but they thought He meant he was only sleeping. 14 Then Jesus told them in plain words, "Lazarus has died, 15 and I am glad that I was not there; it will help you believe. But let us go to him."

16 Thomas, who was called Didymus [Twin], said to his fellow disciples, "Let us also go that we may die with Him."

17 When Jesus arrived, He found that Lazarus had already been in the tomb four days.

18 Bethany was near Jerusalem, not quite two miles away, 19 and many Jews had come to Martha and Mary to comfort them about their brother.

20 So when Martha heard that Jesus was coming, she went to meet Him, while Mary stayed at home. 21 Martha told Jesus, "Lord, if You had been here, my brother would not have died. 22 But now I know God will give You anything You ask Him."

23 Jesus told her, "Your brother will rise again."

24 Martha answered Him, "I know he will rise again in the resurrection on the Last Day."

25 Jesus said to her, "I am the Resurrection and the Life. The person who believes in Me will live even if he dies. 26 Yes, everyone who lives and believes in Me will never die. Do you believe that?"

27 "Yes, Lord," she told Him, "I believe You are the Christ, the Son of God, who was to come into the world."

---

11 *a-* 4 Literally: "sickness is not to death, but in behalf of the glory of God."

28 After she said this, she went to call her sister Mary. "The Teacher is here," she whispered, "and is calling for you."

29 When Mary heard it, she got up quickly to go to Him. **30** Jesus had not yet come to the village but was still where Martha had met Him. **31** The Jews, who were in the house with Mary and comforting her, saw her get up quickly and leave. So they followed her, thinking she was going to the tomb to weep. **32** When Mary came where Jesus was and saw Him, she fell at His feet and said, "Lord, if You had been here, my brother would not have died."

33 When Jesus saw her weeping, and the Jews weeping who came with her, He groaned deeply and was troubled.

34 He asked, "Where did you lay him?"

"Lord, come and see," they answered Him.

35 Jesus wept. **36** The Jews said, "See how He loved him." **37** But some of them asked, "He opened the eyes of the blind man—could He not have kept this man from dying?"

38 Groaning deeply again, Jesus came to the tomb. It was a cave, and a stone was laid against it. **39** Jesus said, "Move the stone away."

Martha, the dead man's sister, told Him, "Lord, he smells already. He has been dead four days."

40 Jesus said to her, "Did I not tell you, 'If you believe, you will see the glory of God'?" **41** So they moved the stone away.

Jesus looked up and said, "Father, I thank You for hearing Me. **42** I knew that You always hear Me, but I spoke so that the people standing around Me will believe that You sent Me." **43** After He had said this, He called out with a loud voice, "Lazarus, come out!"

44 The dead man came out, his feet and hands wrapped in bandages and his face wrapped in a cloth. Jesus told them, "Unwrap him and let him go."

The Plot—Matthew 26:1-5; Mark 14:1,2; Luke 22:1-6

45 Therefore many of the Jews who had come to Mary, and had seen what He did, believed in Him. **46** But some of them went to the Pharisees and told them what Jesus had done. **47** So the ruling priests and the Pharisees called a meeting of the council. They asked, "What are we doing? This Man is working many miraculous signs. **48** If we let Him go on like this, everyone will believe in Him, and then the Romans will come and take away our place*b* and our nation."

49 But one of them, Caiaphas, who was high priest that year, told them, "You do not know anything, **50** and you do not consider that it is better for you*c* that one Man should die for the people, and that the whole nation should not perish." **51** He did not think of this himself, but being high priest that year, he prophesied that Jesus was going to die for the nation, **52** and not only for this nation, but also to bring God's scattered children together and make them one.

53 From that day on they planned to kill Him. **54** So Jesus no longer walked in public among the Jews; instead, He left there and went into the country near

---

b- 48 Meaning "our 'position' or 'Temple.' "

c- 50 Many of the older manuscripts and early translations read: "for us." However, textual evidence seems to favor "for you."

the wilderness, to a town called Ephraim. There He stayed with His disciples.

55 The Jewish Passover was near, and many came from the country to Jerusalem before the Passover to purify themselves. **56** They were looking for Jesus and asking one another as they stood in the Temple, "What do you think? He is not coming to the festival, is He?" **57** The ruling priests and the Pharisees had given orders that, if anyone found out where He was, he should report it so that they might arrest Him.

12TH CHAPTER

Mary Anoints Jesus—Matthew 26:6-13; Mark 14:3-9

1 Six days before the Passover, Jesus came to Bethany, where Lazarus was, whom Jesus had raised from the dead. **2** There a dinner was prepared for Him. Martha served, and Lazarus was one of those eating with Him.

3 Now Mary took a pound of perfume, real nard*a* and very expensive, and poured it on Jesus' feet and dried His feet with her hair. The fragrance of the perfume filled the house.

4 Judas (the man from Kerioth, one of His disciples, who was going to betray Him) asked, **5** "Why wasn't this perfume sold for three hundred denarii*b* and the money given to the poor?" **6** He did not say this because he cared about the poor but because he was a thief and used to steal what was put in the money bag which he carried.

7 Jesus said, "Let her do it for the day of My burial. **8** For the poor you always have with you, but you are not always going to have Me."

9 A large crowd of the Jews found out that He was there, and they came, not only on account of Jesus but also to see Lazarus, whom He had raised from the dead. **10** But the ruling priests decided to kill Lazarus too, **11** because he was the reason why many Jews were going over to Jesus and believing in Him.

The King Comes To Jerusalem—Matthew 21:1-11; Mark 11:1-11; Luke 19:29-44

12 The next day the large crowd that had come to the festival, hearing that Jesus was coming to Jerusalem, **13** took branches from the palm trees and went out to meet Him, shouting:

> "*Hosanna!c*
>   *Blessed is He who is coming in the Name of the Lord,*
>   the King of Israel!*"

14 Jesus found a donkey and sat on it, as it is written:

---

13 Ps 118:25,26

---

12 *a-*   3 Literally: "a litra of ointment, real nard"; see "litra" in MONEY, WEIGHTS, and MEASURES on page 328 and "nard" in Glossary.
    b-   5 See MONEY, WEIGHTS, and MEASURES on page 328.
    c- 13 A Hebrew word meaning "Save now, we pray!" It became an expression of praise.

15 *Do not continue to be afraid, daughter of Zion!*
   Look! Your King is coming,
    riding on a donkey's colt.[d]

16 At first His disciples did not know what it meant, but when Jesus was glorified, then they remembered that these things had been written about Him and were done to Him.

17 The people who had been with Him when He called Lazarus out of the tomb and raised him from the dead were telling what they had seen. 18 Because the crowd heard that He had worked this miraculous sign, it came to meet Him.

19 The Pharisees therefore said to one another, "You see, you're not getting anywhere. Look! The world is running after Him."

Death And Glory

20 Among those who came up to worship at the festival were some Greeks. 21 They went to Philip (who was from Bethsaida in Galilee) and told him, "Sir, we want to see Jesus." 22 Philip went and told Andrew; Andrew and Philip went and told Jesus.

23 Jesus answered them, "The time has come for the Son of Man to be glorified. 24 I tell you the absolute truth, if a kernel of wheat does not fall into the ground and die, it will be just one kernel. But if it dies, it produces much grain. 25 The person who loves his life loses it, and the person who hates his life in this world will secure it for everlasting life. 26 If anyone serves Me, let him follow Me; and where I am, there My servant will be. If anyone serves Me, the Father will honor him.

27 "*I am deeply troubled* now. But what should I say? Father, save Me from this time ⌊of suffering⌋? No! I came just because of this time. 28 Father, glorify Your Name."

A voice came from heaven: "I have glorified My Name and will glorify it again."

29 The crowd, which stood there and heard it, said it had thundered. Others said, "An angel talked to Him." 30 Jesus explained: "That voice did not come for My benefit but for yours.

31 "Now this world is being judged; now the ruler of this world will be thrown out. 32 And once I have been lifted up from the earth, I will draw all people to Myself." 33 He said this to indicate how He was going to die.

34 The crowd answered Him, "We have heard from the Scriptures[e] that the Christ is going to remain forever. How then can You say, 'The Son of Man must be lifted up'? Who is this 'Son of Man'?"

35 Jesus answered them, "The Light will be with you just a little longer. Walk while you have the Light, so that darkness will not overtake you. The person

---

15 Is 40:9; 62:11; Zech 9:9 27 Ps 6:3

---

d- 15 This description emphasizes the humble and suffering nature of the Messiah's rule.

e- 34 See 7:49 and its accompanying footnote. The reference back to the Old Testament could include passages such as 2 Samuel 7:13,16; Psalm 89:36,37; 110:4.

who walks in the dark does not know where he is going. **36** While you have the Light, believe in the Light so that you become children of light."

After Jesus had said this, He went away and hid from them. **37** Although they had seen Him work so many miraculous signs, they did not believe in Him. **38** In this way what the prophet Isaiah had said was fulfilled:

> *Lord, who has believed what they heard from us?*
> *And to whom has the arm of the Lord been revealed?*

39 And so they could not believe, because Isaiah also said:

> **40** *He blinded their eyes*
> *and hardened their hearts,*
> *so that their eyes do not see*
> *and their hearts do not understand,*
> *and they do not turn to Me for healing.*

41 Isaiah said this because he saw His [Jesus'] glory and spoke of Him. **42** And yet even many of the rulers believed in Him but would not confess it publicly, because the Pharisees would have put them out of the synagog. **43** Yes, they loved to be praised by people more than by God.

44 Then Jesus called out, "The person who believes in Me does not believe ₌only₌ in Me but in Him who sent Me. **45** And the person who sees Me sees Him who sent Me. **46** I have come as a Light into the world so that everyone who believes in Me will not remain in darkness. **47** If anyone hears My words but does not keep them, I do not condemn him; because I did not come to condemn the world but to save the world. **48** The person who rejects Me and does not take to heart what I say has one that is condemning him; the word that I spoke will condemn him on the Last Day, **49** because what I said did not come from Me, but the Father Himself who sent Me gave Me a command to say and tell it.*ᶠ* **50** I know that His command gives*ᵍ* everlasting life. And so, whatever I say, I say it just as the Father told Me."

13TH CHAPTER

D. The WORD is received by the disciples (13:1–17:26)

Jesus Washes The Disciples' Feet

1 (Before the Festival of the Passover Jesus knew the time had come for Him to leave this world and go to the Father. He had loved His own who were in the world, and He loved them to the end.)

---

38 Is 53:1   40 Is 6:10

f- 49 See 7:17 and its accompanying footnote.
g- 50 Literally: "is."

2 The supper was taking place, and the devil had already put the idea of betraying Jesus into the mind of Judas ͺthe sonͺ of Simon the man from Kerioth.

3 Jesus knew that the Father had put everything in His hands and that He had come from God and was going back to God. **4** Jesus rose from supper, laid aside His outer garment, took a towel, and tied it around Himself. **5** Then He poured water into a basin and began to wash the disciples' feet and to dry them with the towel that was tied around Him.

6 He came to Simon Peter. "Lord," Peter asked Him, "are You going to wash my feet?"

7 Jesus answered him, "You do not know what I am doing, but later you will understand."

8 "No!" Peter told Him. "You will never wash my feet."

"If I do not wash you," Jesus answered him, "you have no share with Me."

9 "Lord," Simon Peter told Him, "not only my feet but also my hands and my head!"

10 Jesus told him, "The person who has bathed needs only to have his feet washed—he is completely clean. You are clean, but not every one of you." **11** For He knew who was betraying Him. That is why He said, "Not all of you are clean."

12 After He had washed their feet and put on His garment, He reclined at the table again. He asked them, "Do you know what I have done to you? **13** You call Me 'Teacher' and 'Lord,' and you are right because I am. **14** Now if I, the Lord and the Teacher, have washed your feet, you also ought to wash one another's feet. **15** For I have given you an example so that you also will do as I did to you. **16** I tell you the absolute truth, a slave is no greater than his master, and one who is sent is no greater than the One who sent him. **17** If you know these things, you are blessed if you do them.

18 "I am not talking about all of you. I know whom I have chosen. But in this way the Scripture is fulfilled which says: *'He who eats My bread lifts up his heel against Me.'* *a* **19** From now on I am telling you these things before they happen so that when they happen you may believe that I am the One.

20 "I tell you the absolute truth, the person who receives anyone I send receives Me, and the person who receives Me receives Him who sent Me."

Who Is The Betrayer?—*Matthew 26:21-25; Mark 14:18-21; Luke 22:21-23*

21 After saying this, Jesus was deeply troubled. He declared, "I tell you the absolute truth, one of you is going to betray Me!"

22 The disciples started to look at one another, wondering whom Jesus meant.

23 One of His disciples, the one whom Jesus loved, was lying close to Him. **24** Simon Peter motioned to him and said, "Ask Him who it is that He is talking about!"

---

18 Ps 41:9

---

13 *a*- 18 The imagery is that of kicking someone; thus the modern idiom: "give a person a swift kick"; the identical wording in Psalm 41:9 reminds one of an animal kicking out its heel at its master; in short, the idiom portrays a person being unsuspectingly betrayed by one regarded as a friend.

25 Leaning over so that he was against His chest, he asked Jesus, "Lord, who is it?"

26 Jesus answered, "I will dip this piece of bread*b* and give it to him. He is the one." So He dipped it and gave it to Judas ⌊the son⌋ of Simon the man from Kerioth.

27 Then, after Judas took the piece of bread, Satan entered into him. So Jesus told him, "What you are doing, do quickly." 28 No one at the table knew why Jesus said this to him. 29 Since Judas had the money bag, some thought that Jesus was telling him, "Buy what we need for the festival"; or that he should give something to the poor.

30 After Judas took the piece of bread, he immediately went outside. And it was night.

31 When Judas had gone out, Jesus said, "Now the Son of Man is glorified, and in Him God is glorified. 32 If God is glorified in Him,*c* God will also glorify Him in Himself; yes, He will glorify Him now."

Jesus Warns Peter—Matthew 26:31-35; Mark 14:27-31; Luke 22:31-38

33 "Children," Jesus said, "I will be with you just a little longer. You will look for Me, but as I told the Jews, so I tell you now: Where I am going, you cannot come.

34 "I am giving you a new commandment: Love one another! Love one another as I have loved you. 35 By your loving one another everyone will know that you are My disciples."

36 Simon Peter asked Him, "Lord, where are You going?"

Jesus answered him, "Where I am going you cannot follow Me now, but you will follow Me later."

37 "Lord, why can't I follow You now?" Peter asked Him. "I will give up my life for You."

38 Jesus asked, "Will you give up your life for Me? I tell you the absolute truth, the rooster will not crow until you have denied Me three times."

14TH CHAPTER

"I Am Going Away"

1 "Do not feel troubled. Believe in God and believe in Me. 2 In My Father's house there are many rooms. If it were not so, I would have told you, because I am going to prepare a place for you. 3 And if I go to prepare a place for you, I will come again and take you home with Me so that you will be where I am. 4 You know the way to the place where I am going."

5 Thomas said to Him, "Lord, we do not know where You are going, so how can we know the way?"

6 Jesus answered him, "I am the Way, the Truth, and the Life. No one comes

---

b- 26 Not a reference to the breaking of the bread which came later in the Lord's Supper.
c- 32 Some of the older manuscripts and early translations omit: "If God is glorified in Him. . . ."

to the Father except by Me. **7** If you have learned to know Me, you will know My Father also. From now on you know Him and have seen Him."

8 Philip said to Him, "Lord, show us the Father, and that will be enough for us."

9 "Have I been with you for so long," Jesus answered him, "and you still do not know Me, Philip? The person who has seen Me has seen the Father. How can you say, 'Show us the Father'? **10** Do you not believe that I am in the Father and the Father is in Me? These words which I am telling you do not come from Me; but the Father, who remains in Me, is doing His works. **11** Believe Me, I am in the Father, and the Father is in Me. Or else believe Me on account of My works.

12 "I tell you the absolute truth, the person who believes in Me will do the works that I am doing; and he will do greater works than these, because I am going to the Father, **13** and I will do anything you ask in My Name in order that the Father may be glorified in the Son. **14** If you ask Me for anything in My Name, I will do it.

15 "If you love Me, you will obey My commandments. **16** And I will ask the Father, and He will give you another Comforter [Helper] to be with you forever. **17** He is the Spirit of Truth, whom the world cannot receive, because it does not see or know Him. You know Him, because He remains with you and will be in you.

18 "I will not leave you as orphans; I am coming back to you. **19** Only a little while longer and the world will not see Me anymore, but you will see Me. Because I live, you also will live. **20** On that day you will know that I am in My Father and you in Me and I in you. **21** The person who has My commandments and obeys them, he is the one who loves Me. And the person who loves Me, My Father will love him, and I will love him and show Myself to him."

22 Judas (not the man from Kerioth) asked Him, "Lord, what has happened that You are going to show Yourself to us and not to the world?"

23 Jesus answered him, "If anyone loves Me, he will obey My word, and My Father will love him, and We will come to him and make Our home with him. **24** A person who does not love Me does not obey My words. The word which you hear is not Mine but the Father's who sent Me.

25 "I have told you this while I am still with you. **26** But the Comforter, the Holy Spirit, whom the Father will send in My Name, He will teach you everything and remind you of everything I told you.

27 "Peace I leave with you; My peace I give to you. I do not give it to you as the world gives it. Do not let your heart be troubled or afraid. **28** You heard Me tell you, 'I am going away, but I am coming back to you.' If you loved Me, you would be glad that I am going to the Father, because the Father is greater than I.

29 "I have told you this now before it happens, so that when it happens, you might believe. **30** I will not say much to you anymore, because the ruler of the world is coming. He has no claim on Me. **31** But I want the world to know that I love the Father and am doing exactly what the Father has ordered Me to do.

"Come, let us go away."

15TH CHAPTER

The Vine And The Branches

1 "I am the genuine[a] Vine, and My Father is the Caretaker of the vineyard. 2 He cuts away every branch of Mine that bears no fruit, and He trims every branch that bears fruit to make it bear more fruit.

3 "The word which I have spoken to you has already made you clean. 4 Remain in Me, and I will remain in you. A branch cannot bear any fruit by itself unless it remains on the vine. In exactly the same way, you cannot bear fruit, unless you remain in Me.

5 "I am the Vine; you are the branches. The person who remains in Me and I in him, he bears much fruit; for without Me you can do nothing. 6 If anyone does not remain in Me, he is thrown away like a branch and dries up. Such branches are gathered, thrown into the fire, and burned. 7 If you remain in Me and My words remain in you, ask for anything you want, and it will be done for you. 8 You glorify My Father when you bear much fruit and show yourselves to be[b] My disciples.

9 "As the Father has loved Me, so I have loved you. Remain in My love. 10 If you obey My commandments, you will remain in My love, just as I have obeyed My Father's commandments and remain in His love. 11 I have told you this so that My joy will be in you and that your joy will be complete. 12 This is My commandment, that you love one another as I have loved you. 13 No one has greater love than this, that a person lay down his life for his friends. 14 You are My friends if you continue to do what I command you to do. 15 I do not call you slaves anymore, because a slave does not know what his master is doing. But I have called you friends because I have made known to you everything that I have heard from My Father. 16 You did not choose Me, but I chose you and appointed you to go and bear fruit, and your fruit should remain so that the Father might give you whatever you ask in My Name. 17 This is what I command you to do: Love one another.

18 "If the world hates you, you know that it hated Me first. 19 If you had anything in common with the world, the world would love you as its own. But you do not have anything in common with the world; I chose to separate you from the world. That is why the world hates you. 20 Remember the word which I spoke to you: 'A slave is not greater than his master.' If they persecuted Me, they will also persecute you. If they obey My word, they will also obey yours. 21 Now they will do all this to you on account of Me,[c] because they do not know Him who sent Me. 22 If I had not come and spoken to them, they would have no sin, but now they have no excuse for their sin. 23 The person who hates Me also hates My Father. 24 If I had not done the works among them that no one else

---

15 *a* - 1 Greek: "*alēthinos*"; see *ALĒTHINOS* COMPARED WITH *ALĒTHĒS* on page 530.

   b - 8 The present translation handles this verb as an aorist subjunctive. John's reading reflects a Hebraic manner of speech in which two parallel ideas (i.e., "you bear much fruit" and "you show yourselves to be My disciples") are understood as communicating a single idea. The meaning of verse 8, then, is that the Father is glorified only when Jesus' disciples are *fruitful* disciples.

   c - 21 Literally: "on account of My Name."

has done, they would have no sin. But now they have seen and hated both Me and My Father. **25** In this way the word is fulfilled which is written in their Scriptures:*d* *'They hate Me without any reason.'*

26 "When the Comforter [Helper] comes, whom I shall send you from the Father, the Spirit of Truth, who goes out [proceeds] from the Father, He will testify about Me. **27** And you also will testify, because you have been with Me from the beginning."

16TH CHAPTER

Sorrow Will Turn To Joy

1 "I have spoken these things to you so that you will not stumble in your faith.*a* **2** You will be put out of the synagog. Yes, the time is coming when anyone who murders you will think that he is serving God. **3** People will do these things because they did not know the Father or Me. **4** But I told you this so that when it happens you will remember that I told you about it. I did not tell you this at first, because I was with you.

5 "Now I am going to Him who sent Me, and none of you asks Me, 'Where are You going?' **6** But because I told you this, your hearts are filled with sadness. **7** But I tell you the truth, it is good for you that I go away. For if I do not go away, the Comforter will not come to you. But if I go, I will send Him to you. **8** He will come and convict the world of sin, righteousness, and judgment: **9** of sin, because they do not believe in Me; **10** of righteousness, because I am going to the Father and you will not see Me anymore; **11** of judgment, because the ruler of this world is judged.

12 "I have much more to tell you, but it would be too much for you now. **13** When the Spirit of Truth comes, He will lead you into the whole truth.*b* For what He will say will not come from Himself, but He will speak what He hears and tell you what is coming. **14** He will glorify Me, because He will take from what is Mine and tell it to you. **15** Everything the Father has is Mine. That is why I said, 'He takes from what is Mine and will tell it to you.'

16 "A little while and you will not see Me anymore; and again a little while and you will see Me."

17 Some of His disciples asked one another, "What does He mean when He tells us, 'A little while and you will not see Me; and again a little while and you will see Me,' and 'I am going to the Father'?" **18** So they were asking, "What does He mean when He says, 'A little while'? We do not know what He means."

19 Jesus knew they wanted to ask Him something. He asked them, "Are you trying to find out from one another what I meant by saying, 'A little while and you will not see Me; and again a little while and you will see Me'? **20** I tell you

---

25 *Ps 35:19; 69:4*

d- 25 See 7:49 and its accompanying footnote.
16 *a*- 1 See *SKANDALON* on page 545.
  b- 13 Some of the older manuscripts and early translations read: "lead you *by* the whole truth."

the absolute truth, you will cry and mourn, but the world will be glad. You will have sorrow, but your sorrow will turn to joy. **21** When a woman is giving birth to a child, she has pains because her time has come. But after the child is born, she does not remember her pains anymore because she is so happy that a human being has been born into the world.

22 "You, too, are sad now; but I will see you again, *and your heart will be glad*, and no one will take your joy away from you. **23** In that day you will not ask Me any questions. I tell you the absolute truth, if you ask the Father for anything, He will give it to you in My Name. **24** So far you have not asked for anything in My Name. Ask and you will receive so that your joy might be complete.

25 "I have used figurative language in speaking to you about these things. The time is coming when I will no longer speak to you in figurative language. Rather, I will tell you about the Father in plain words. **26** In that day you will ask in My Name, and I do not say that I will pray to the Father for you. **27** For the Father Himself loves you because you have loved Me and believe that I came from the Father. **28** I left the Father and came into the world; again I am leaving the world and going to the Father."

29 His disciples said, "Yes, now You are talking in plain words and are not using figurative language. **30** Now we know that You know everything and do not need to have anyone ask You anything. That is why we believe that You have come from God."

31 Jesus answered them, "Do you now believe? **32** The hour is coming, in fact, it is here, when you will be scattered, everyone to his home, and you will leave Me alone. And yet I am not alone, because the Father is with Me. **33** I told you this so you will have peace in Me. In the world you have trouble. But have courage; I have conquered the world."

17TH CHAPTER

Jesus' High Priestly Prayer (A Personal Request)

1 After saying this, Jesus looked up to heaven and said: "Father, the time has come. Glorify Your Son so that Your Son will glorify You, **2** since You have given Him authority over all people, to give everlasting life to all whom You gave Him. **3** This is everlasting life—to know You, the only true*a* God, and Jesus Christ, whom You sent. **4** I have glorified You on earth by finishing the work You gave Me to do. **5** And now, Father, glorify Me at Your side with the glory I had with You before the world existed."

---

22 Is 66:14

17 a- 3 Greek: "alēthinos"; see ALĒTHINOS COMPARED WITH ALĒTHĒS on page 530.

Jesus' High Priestly Prayer (A Request For His Apostles)

6 "I made Your Name known to the people You gave Me out of the world. They were Yours, and You gave them to Me, and they have kept Your word. 7 Now they know that everything You gave Me comes from You, 8 because I gave them the words that You gave Me. And they have accepted them and learned the truth that I came from You, and they have believed that You sent Me.

9 "I pray for them. I do not pray for the world but for those You gave Me, because they are Yours. 10 All that is Mine is Yours, and what is Yours is Mine. And I am glorified in them. 11 I am no longer in the world, but they are in the world, and I am coming to You. Holy Father, keep them in Your Name, ⌐the Name⌐ which You gave Me, so that they will be one as We are one. 12 While I was with them, I kept them safe in Your Name, which You gave Me. I watched over them, and none of them was lost except that lost one, so that the Scripture might be fulfilled.

13 "But now I am coming to You, and I say this while I am in the world so that they will feel My complete joy in their hearts. 14 I gave them Your word. But the world has hated them because they do not belong to the world any more than I belong to the world. 15 I am not asking You to take them out of the world but to keep them from the Evil One. 16 They do not belong to the world any more than I belong to the world.

17 "Make them holy in the truth; Your word is truth. 18 As You sent Me into the world, I have sent them into the world. 19 In this holy way I give Myself for them, so that they also might be made holy in the truth."

Jesus' High Priestly Prayer (A Request For His Church For All Time)

20 "I am not asking for them only, but also for those who through their word will believe in Me, 21 that they all may be one. As You, Father, are in Me and I in You, let them also be in Us[b] so that the world may believe that You have sent Me. 22 I have given them the glory that You gave Me, so that they may be one, just as We are one. 23 I am in them, and You are in Me. Let them be completely one so that the world may know that You have sent Me and You have loved them just as You loved Me.

24 "Father, I want those You have given Me to be with Me where I am, so that they may see My glory which You gave Me, because You loved Me before the world was made. 25 Righteous Father, the world did not know You, but I knew You, and these have learned to know that You sent Me. 26 I have made Your Name known to them, and I will continue to make it known; so that the love You have for Me will be in them and I will be in them."

---

b- 21 Many manuscripts and early translations read: "let them be *one* in Us"; also, "let them be" (here and in v. 23) could be translated "in order that they may be."

18TH CHAPTER

E. The WORD brings grace and truth
through His passion, death, and resurrection (18:1–20:31)

The Arrest—Matthew 26:47-56; Mark 14:43-52; Luke 22:47-54a

1 After Jesus said this, He took His disciples to the other side of the Kidron Valley where there was a garden. He and His disciples went into it.

2 Judas, who was betraying Him, also knew the place because Jesus and His disciples often gathered there. 3 So Judas took the troop of soldiers and Temple guards from the ruling priests and Pharisees and came there with lanterns and torches and weapons.

4 Now Jesus went out, knowing exactly what was going to happen to Him. "Who is it that you are looking for?" He asked them.

5 "Jesus from Nazareth," they answered Him.

"I am He,"*a* Jesus told them.

Judas, who was betraying Him, was standing with them. 6 When Jesus told them, "I am He," they backed away and fell to the ground.

7 He asked them again, "Who is it that you are looking for?"

"Jesus from Nazareth," they said.

8 Jesus answered, "I told you that I am He. So if I am the One you want, let these others go." 9 In this way the statement which He had made was fulfilled: "I lost none of those You gave Me."

10 Simon Peter, who had a sword, drew it, struck the high priest's slave, and cut off his right ear. The slave's name was Malchus.

11 Jesus told Peter, "Put your sword into its scabbard. The cup My Father gave Me—should I not drink it?"

12 So the troop of soldiers, the tribune, and the Jewish Temple guards arrested Jesus, bound Him, 13 and took Him first to Annas, because he was the father-in-law of Caiaphas, who was high priest that year. 14 It was Caiaphas who had advised the Jews, "It is better that one Man should die for the people."

Peter Denies Jesus—Matthew 26:69-75; Mark 14:66-72; Luke 22:54b-62;
John 18:25-27

15 Now, Simon Peter and another disciple were following Jesus. The other disciple was known to the high priest and went with Jesus into the high priest's courtyard. 16 But Peter was standing outside the door. So the other disciple, whom the high priest knew, went out and talked to the girl watching the door and brought Peter in.

17 This doorkeeper asked Peter, "You aren't one of this Man's disciples too, are you?"

"I am not," he answered.

---

18 *a-* 5 See 8:24 and its accompanying footnote; this strong self-designation of deity caught the Pharisees totally by surprise (v. 6).

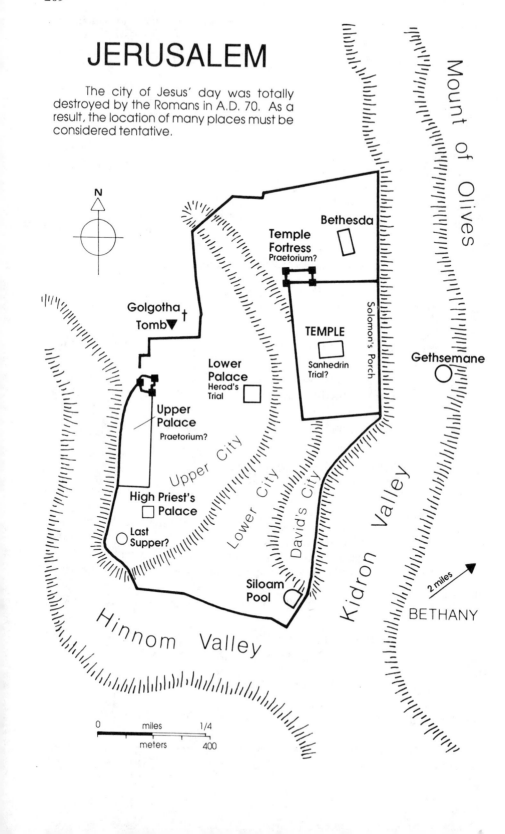

JERUSALEM

The city of Jesus' day was totally destroyed by the Romans in A.D. 70. As a result, the location of many places must be considered tentative.

N

Mount of Olives

Bethesda

Temple Fortress
Praetorium?

Golgotha
Tomb▼ †

TEMPLE

Solomon's Porch

Gethsemane

Lower
Palace
Herod's
Trial

Sanhedrin
Trial?

Upper
Palace
Praetorium?

Upper City

High Priest's
Palace

Lower City

David's City

Kidron Valley

Last
Supper?

Siloam
Pool

2 miles

BETHANY

Hinnom Valley

0   miles   1/4
meters   400

18 The slaves and the Temple guards were standing around and had made a heap of burning coals because it was cold, and they were warming themselves. Peter was also standing with them and warming himself.

Before Annas

19 The high priest asked Jesus about His disciples and His teaching.

20 Jesus answered him, "I have spoken publicly to the world. I have always taught in a synagog or in the Temple, where all the Jews gather, and I have not said anything in secret. **21** Why do you ask Me? Ask those who heard Me what I said to them; they know what I said."

22 When He said this, one of the Temple guards standing near Jesus slapped His face. "Is that how You answer the high priest?" he asked.

23 Jesus answered him, "If I said anything wrong, tell us what was wrong. But if I told the truth, why do you hit Me?"

24 Annas sent Him, still bound, to Caiaphas the high priest.

Peter Denies Again—*Matthew 26:69-75; Mark 14:66-72; Luke 22:54b-62; John 18:15-18*

25 Simon Peter continued to stand and warm himself. So the men asked him, "You aren't one of His disciples too, are you?"

He denied saying, "I am not!"

26 One of the slaves of the high priest, a relative of the man whose ear Peter had cut off, asked, "Didn't I see you with Him in the garden?"

27 Again Peter denied, and just then a rooster crowed.

Before Pilate—*Matthew 27:11-14; Mark 15:1-5; Luke 23:1-4*

28 The Jews took Jesus from Caiaphas to the palace.^{b} It was early in the morning.

To keep from becoming unclean (they wanted to celebrate the Passover), the Jews themselves did not go into the palace. **29** So Pilate came out to them and asked, "What accusation are you bringing against this Man?"

30 They answered him, "If He were not a criminal, we would not have handed Him over to you."

31 Pilate therefore told them, "Take Him yourselves and judge Him according to your law."

The Jews answered him, "We are not permitted to execute anyone." **32** In this way the statement that Jesus made when He predicted how He would die was fulfilled.

33 Pilate went back into the palace and called for Jesus. He asked Him, "Are You the King of the Jews?"

34 "Did you think of that yourself," Jesus asked, "or did others tell you about Me?"

---

b- 28 Greek: *"praitōrion"* (Latin: *"praetorium"*), also in verse 33 and 19:9; exact location uncertain. See Map of JERUSALEM on page 209.

35 "Am I a Jew?" Pilate asked. "Your own people and the ruling priests handed You over to me. What did You do?"

36 Jesus answered, "My Kingdom does not belong to this world. If My Kingdom belonged to this world, My helpers would fight to keep Me from being handed over to the Jews. But now My Kingdom is not of this world."*c*

37 "Then You are a king?" Pilate asked Him.

Jesus answered, "You are correct in saying that I am a king. I was born and came into the world for this very reason, that I might testify to the truth. Everyone who lives in the truth listens to Me."

38 Pilate said to Him, "What is truth?" After saying this, he went out to the Jews again and told them, "I do not find this Man guilty of anything.

39 "You have a custom that I set one person free for you at the Passover. So would you like me to set the King of the Jews free for you?"

40 Then they shouted: "Not this One but Barabbas!"*d* Now Barabbas was a revolutionary.*e*

19TH CHAPTER

"Look At The Man!"— *Matthew 27:27-30; Mark 15:16-19*

1 Then Pilate took Jesus and had Him whipped. **2** The soldiers twisted some thorns into a crown and placed it on His head and put a purple robe on Him. **3** They went up to Him and said, "Hail, King of the Jews!" and slapped His face.

4 Pilate went outside again and told them, "I am bringing Him out to you to let you know that I find no guilt in Him." **5** Jesus came outside wearing the crown of thorns and the purple robe. Pilate said to them, "Look at the Man!"

6 When the ruling priests and the servants saw Him, they shouted, "Crucify, crucify Him!"

Pilate told them, "Take Him yourselves and crucify Him, for I do not find Him guilty of anything."

7 The Jews answered him, "We have a law, and according to the law He deserves to die because He has claimed to be the Son of God."

8 When Pilate heard them say that, he was frightened more than ever. **9** He went into the palace again and asked Jesus, "Where are You from?" But Jesus did not give him an answer.

10 Pilate then asked Him, "Aren't You going to speak to me? Don't You know that I have the authority to free You or the authority to crucify You?"

11 Jesus answered him, "You would not have any authority over Me if it had not been given to you from above. That is why the man who handed Me over to you is guilty of a greater sin."

---

c- 36 Literally: "is not from here."

d- 40 Made up of two Aramaic words: "*bar*" ("son") and "*abba*" ("father"), meaning "son of the father." Could the presence of one named *Barabbas* imply that the "sons (and daughters) of the heavenly Father" went free as the "Son of the heavenly Father" went to the cross for them?

e- 40 See Luke 23:19.

12 This made Pilate anxious to let Him go, but the Jews shouted, "If you let Him go, you are no friend of Caesar. Anyone who makes himself a king is speaking against Caesar."

13 When Pilate heard these words, he took Jesus outside and sat in the judge's seat at a place called Stone Pavement, or Gabbatha in Aramaic.^a **14** It was the day of the preparation of the Passover^b and about six in the morning.^c

He said to the Jews, "Look at your King!"

15 Then they shouted, "Away with Him! Kill Him! Crucify Him!"

Pilate asked them, "Should I crucify your King?"

"We have no king but Caesar," the ruling priests answered.

16 Then Pilate handed Jesus over to them to be crucified.

"They Crucified Him"—Matthew 27:31-44; Mark 15:20-32; Luke 23:26-38

So they took Jesus; **17** and carrying His own cross, He went out to what was called Place of the Skull, which in Aramaic^d is called Golgotha.^e **18** There they crucified Him with two others, one on each side and Jesus in the middle.

19 Pilate also wrote a notice and put it on the cross. It read:

JESUS FROM NAZARETH
THE KING OF THE JEWS.

20 Many Jews read this notice, because the place where Jesus was crucified was near the city, and it was written in Aramaic, Latin, and Greek.

21 Therefore the high priests of the Jews told Pilate, "Do not write: 'The King of the Jews,' but: 'He said, "I am the King of the Jews."'"

22 Pilate answered, "What I have written I have written."

23 When the soldiers had crucified Jesus, they took His clothes and divided them into four parts, one for each soldier, and the tunic was left over. The tunic was without a seam, woven in one piece from top to bottom. **24** They said to one another, "Let's not tear it, but let's throw dice^f and see who gets it"—in this way what the Scripture said was fulfilled: *"They divided My clothes among them, and for My garment they threw dice."* So that is what the soldiers did.

Mary

25 Now, His mother and His mother's sister, Mary the wife of Clopas, and

---

24 Ps 22:18

---

19 *a*- 13 See 5:2 and its accompanying footnote "a."
   b- 14 Meaning "Friday"; *not* a reference to preparing to celebrate the Passover but rather the preparation day to celebrate the most solemn *Sabbath* which followed the Passover celebration. See ahead at verse 31 and its accompanying footnote.
   c- 14 Literally: "the sixth hour." See 1:39 and its accompanying footnote.
   d - 17 See 5:2 and its accompanying footnote "a" (also applies to v. 20).
   e- 17 The Latin form is *"Calvary."*
   f- 24 Literally: "lots" (twice in verse).

Mary from Magdala were standing near the cross of Jesus. [g]

26 Jesus saw His mother and the disciple whom He loved standing near. "Woman," He said to His mother, "there is your son!" 27 Then He said to the disciple, "There is your mother!"

From that time on this disciple took her into his own home.

Jesus Dies—*Matthew 27:45-56; Mark 15:33-41; Luke 23:44-49*

28 After this, knowing that everything had now been finished, and to have the words of the Scripture come true, Jesus said, *"I am thirsty."*

29 A jar full of *sour wine* was standing there. So they put a sponge soaked in the *sour wine* on a hyssop stem and held it to His mouth.

30 When Jesus had taken the wine, He said, *"It is finished!"*

Then He bowed His head and gave up His spirit.

No Bone Was Broken

31 Since it was the day of preparation[h] and the Jews did not want the bodies to stay on the crosses on the Sabbath, because that Sabbath was an important day, they asked Pilate to have the legs of the men broken and the bodies taken away. 32 So the soldiers came and broke the legs of the first man and then of the other who had been crucified with Him.

33 But when they came to Jesus and saw that He was dead already, they did not break His legs; 34 but one of the soldiers stuck a spear into His side, and immediately blood and water came out. 35 He who saw it has testified about it, and his testimony is true,[i] and he knows he is telling the truth so that you also will believe.

36 In this way what the Scripture said was fulfilled: *"None of His bones shall be broken."* 37 And another Scripture passage says: *"They will look at Him whom they pierced."*

Jesus Is Buried—*Matthew 27:57-61; Mark 15:42-47; Luke 23:50-56*

38 Later Joseph from Arimathea—who was a disciple of Jesus, but secretly because he was afraid of the Jews—asked Pilate to let him take away the body of Jesus. Pilate allowed him to take it. So he came and took His body away.

28,29 Ps 69:21   *30 Ps 22:31*   *36 Ex 12:46; Num 9:12; Ps 34:20*   *37 Zech 12:10*

---

g- 25 It is difficult to determine whether John indicates *three* or *four* women in this passage. The punctuation used leaves the question open.
If three women are indicated, then Mary's *sister* is a sister-in-law named Mary, and her husband Clopas would be Jesus' uncle on His mother's or father Joseph's side.
If four women are indicated, then Mary's *sister* would possibly be Salome, the mother of John the Gospel writer and aunt of Jesus (cf. Mk. 15:40).

h- 31 The common designation for the more modern term "Friday"; in the instance of our text it refers to that particular Friday when the Jews prepared for this most solemn Sabbath which followed the Passover celebration (also in v. 42).

i- 35 Greek: "*alēthinos*"; see ALĒTHINOS COMPARED WITH ALĒTHĒS on page 530.

39 Nicodemus also came, the one who had first come to Jesus at night. He brought a mixture of myrrh and aloes, about 75 pounds.*j*

40 They took the body of Jesus and wrapped it with the spices in linen wrappings according to the Jewish custom of burying the dead.

41 There was a garden at the place where Jesus was crucified, and in the garden was a new tomb, in which no one had yet been laid. 42 So they laid Jesus there, because it was the Jewish day of preparation and the tomb was near.

20TH CHAPTER

The Easter Resurrection— Matthew 28:1-10; Mark 16:1-8; Luke 24:1-12

1 Early on Sunday*a* morning, while it was still dark, Mary from Magdala went to the tomb and saw that the stone had been taken away from the tomb. 2 So she ran and came to Simon Peter and the other disciple whom Jesus loved. "They have taken the Lord out of the tomb," she told them, "and we don't know where they laid Him."

3 So Peter and the other disciple started out for the tomb. 4 The two were running side by side, but the other disciple ran faster than Peter and came to the tomb first. 5 He bent over and looked in. He saw the linen wrappings lying there, but he did not go in.

6 Now Simon Peter arrived after him and went into the tomb. He saw the linen wrappings lying there, 7 also the cloth that had been on the head of Jesus, not lying with the linen wrappings but rolled up in a place by itself. 8 Then the other disciple, who got to the tomb first, also went in, saw it, and believed. 9 For they did not yet know what the Scripture meant when it said He had to rise from the dead.

10 So the disciples went home again.

"Mary!"

11 Mary stood outside, facing the tomb and crying. As she cried, she looked into the tomb 12 and saw two angels in white clothes sitting where the body of Jesus had been lying, one at the head and the other at the feet. 13 They asked her, "Woman, why are you crying?"

She told them, "They have taken my Lord away, and I don't know where they laid Him."

14 After she said this, she turned around and saw Jesus standing there, but she did not know it was Jesus. 15 Jesus asked her, "Woman, why are you crying? Who is it that you are looking for?"

"Sir," she said to Him, thinking He was the gardener, "if you carried Him away, tell me where you laid Him, and I will take Him away."

16 Jesus said to her, "Mary!"

---

j- 39 Literally: "about 100 *litras*."
20 *a-* 1 Literally: "on the first day of the week."

She turned. "Rabboni!" she said to Him in Aramaic.[b] (The word means "Teacher.")

17 Jesus told her, "Stop holding on to Me, for I have not yet gone up [ascended] to the Father. But go to My brothers and tell them, 'I am going up to My Father and your Father, to My God and your God.' "

18 Mary from Magdala went and told the disciples, "I saw the Lord," and that He said these things to her.

Behind Locked Doors—Luke 24:36-48

19 That Sunday evening the doors were locked where the disciples were, because they were afraid of the Jews. Then Jesus came and stood among them and said to them, "Peace be with you!" **20** When He said this, He showed them His hands and His side. So the disciples were delighted to see the Lord.

21 "Peace be with you!" Jesus said to them again. "As the Father sent Me, so I am sending you." **22** When He had said this, He breathed on them and said, "Receive the Holy Spirit. **23** Whenever you forgive people's sins, they are forgiven; whenever you do not forgive them, they are not forgiven."[c]

Thomas Sees Jesus

24 But Thomas, one of the Twelve, who was called Didymus [Twin], was not with them when Jesus came. **25** So the other disciples told him, "We saw the Lord."

He told them, "Unless I see the mark of the nails in His hands and put my finger in the mark of the nails and put my hand in His side, I will never believe."

26 A week later His disciples were again in the house, and Thomas was with them. The doors were locked, but Jesus came and stood among them. "Peace be with you!" He said. **27** Then He told Thomas, "Put your finger here, and look at My hands—and take your hand and put it in My side. And do not go on doubting but believe."

28 Thomas answered Him, "My Lord and my God!"

29 "Do you believe because you have seen Me?" Jesus asked him. "Blessed are those who have not seen and still have believed."

Much More

30 His disciples saw Jesus work many other miraculous signs that are not written in this book. **31** But these things are written that you may believe that Jesus is the Christ, the Son of God, and that by believing you may have life in His Name.

---

b- 16 See 5:2 and its accompanying footnote "a."

c- 23 Literally: "they have not been forgiven"; the Greek uses a perfect tense here to indicate action which is completed with continuing results.

21ST CHAPTER

F. Appendix (21:1-25)

Breakfast With The Lord (Jesus)

1 After this, Jesus showed Himself again to the disciples at the Sea of Tiberias.*a* This is how He showed Himself: **2** Simon Peter, Thomas called Didymus [Twin], Nathanael from Cana in Galilee, the sons of Zebedee, and two other disciples of Jesus were together. **3** Simon Peter said to the others, "I'm going fishing."

They told him, "We're going with you."

They went out and got into the boat. But that night they caught nothing. **4** When morning came, Jesus stood on the shore. But the disciples did not know that it was Jesus.

5 Jesus asked them, "Friends,*b* you do not have any fish, do you?"

"No," they answered Him.

6 He told them, "Throw the net out on the right side of the boat and you will find some." So they threw it out, and then they could not pull it in, because there were so many fish.

7 The disciple whom Jesus loved said to Peter, "It is the Lord." When Simon Peter heard him say, "It is the Lord," he put on the outer garment he had taken off, fastened it with his belt, and jumped into the sea. **8** But the other disciples, who were not far from the shore, only about 100 yards,*c* came in the small boat, dragging the net full of fish.

9 As they stepped out on the shore, they saw burning coals there with fish lying on them, and bread.

10 "Bring some of the fish you just caught," Jesus told them. **11** Simon Peter got into the small boat and pulled the net on the shore. It was filled with 153 large fish. Although there were so many, the net was not torn.

12 Jesus told them, "Come, have breakfast." None of the disciples dared to ask Him, "Who are You?" They knew it was the Lord. **13** Jesus came and took the bread and gave it to them, and also the fish.

14 This was now the third time Jesus showed Himself to the disciples after He rose from the dead.

"Do You Love Me?"

15 When they had eaten breakfast, Jesus asked Simon Peter, "Simon ˻son˼ of John, do you love Me more than these do?"

"Yes, Lord," he answered Him, "You know I love You."

"Feed My lambs," Jesus told him.

16 He asked him a second time, "Simon ˻son˼ of John, do you love Me?"

---

21 *a-* 1 Alternate name for the Sea of Galilee.
   b- 5 Literally: "Little children," which was a term of endearment when addressing someone.
   c- 8 Literally: "about 200 cubits"; see MONEY, WEIGHTS, and MEASURES on page 328.

"Yes, Lord," he answered Him, "You know I love You."

Jesus told him, "Be a shepherd of My sheep."

17 "Simon ⌊son⌋ of John," He asked him a third time, "do you love Me?" Peter felt sad because He asked him a third time, "Do you love Me?" He answered Him, "Lord, You know everything. You know I love You."

Jesus told him, "Feed My sheep. 18 I tell you the absolute truth, when you were younger, you used to fasten your belt and go where you wanted. But when you are old, you will stretch out your hands, and someone else will tie you and take you where you do not want to go." 19 He said this to show by what kind of death Peter would glorify God. After saying this, He told him, "Follow Me."

20 Peter turned and saw the disciple whom Jesus loved following them. He was the one who at the supper leaned against Jesus' chest and asked, "Lord, who is going to betray You?" 21 When Peter saw him, he asked Jesus, "Lord, what about him?"

22 "If I want him to stay alive until I come," Jesus asked him, "what is that to you? You follow Me." 23 And so it was said among the brothers [Christians]: "That disciple will not die." But Jesus did not say, "He will not die," but, "If I want him to stay alive until I come, what is that to you?"

24 This is the disciple who testified about these things and wrote this. And we know that what he testifies is true.

Much More

25 Jesus also did many other things. If every one of these were written down, I suppose the world would not have room for the books that would be written.

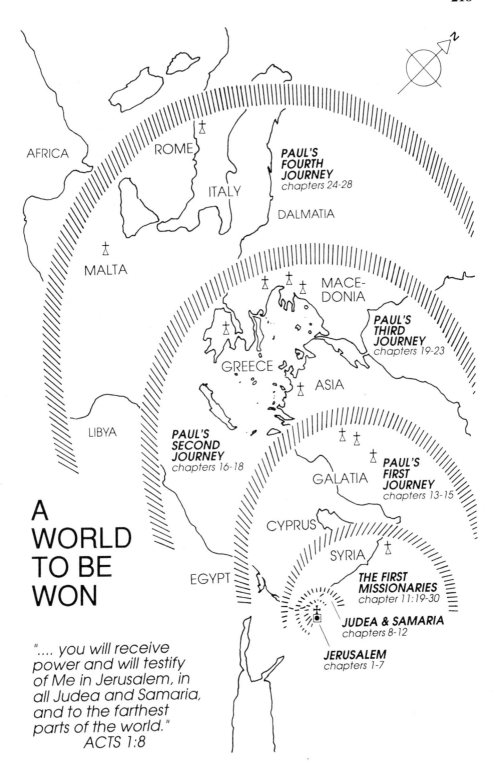

AFRICA

ROME

ITALY

**PAUL'S
FOURTH
JOURNEY**
chapters 24-28

DALMATIA

MALTA

MACE-
DONIA

**PAUL'S
THIRD
JOURNEY**
chapters 19-23

GREECE

ASIA

LIBYA

**PAUL'S
SECOND
JOURNEY**
chapters 16-18

GALATIA

**PAUL'S
FIRST
JOURNEY**
chapters 13-15

CYPRUS

SYRIA

A
WORLD
TO BE
WON

EGYPT

**THE FIRST
MISSIONARIES**
chapter 11:19-30

JUDEA & SAMARIA
chapters 8-12

JERUSALEM
chapters 1-7

*".... you will receive
power and will testify
of Me in Jerusalem, in
all Judea and Samaria,
and to the farthest
parts of the world."*
ACTS 1:8

ACTS OF THE APOSTLES[a]

1ST CHAPTER

A. Introduction (1:1-7) and theme (1:8)

[1] In my first book, Theophilus, I wrote about everything that Jesus began to do and to teach [2] until the day He was taken up to heaven after having given instructions by the Holy Spirit to the apostles whom He had chosen.

Jesus Ascends To Heaven

[3] After His suffering Jesus also showed the apostles through many convincing proofs that He was alive; He was seen by them for 40 days and spoke with them about the Kingdom of God.

[4] When He met with them, He ordered them not to leave Jerusalem but to wait for what the Father had promised, "which," ⌊He said,⌋ "you have heard from Me; [5] for John baptized with water, but in a few days you will be baptized with the Holy Spirit."

[6] When they came together, they asked Him, "Lord, are You now going to reestablish the kingdom of Israel?"

[7] He told them, "It is not for you to know what times or periods the Father has set by His own authority. [8] But when the Holy Spirit comes upon you, you will receive power and will testify of Me in Jerusalem, in all Judea and Samaria, and to the farthest parts of the world."

B. The Gospel in Jerusalem (1:9–7:60)

[9] When He had said this and while they were watching Him, He was lifted up, and a cloud took Him away so they could no longer see Him.

---

1 *a*   This book, often called the *Acts of the Apostles*, reports the earliest history of the New Testament Church when apostles like Peter and Paul were beginning to spread the Gospel or Good News of Jesus everywhere (cf. Acts 1:8). Luke wrote *Acts* as a second volume (or scroll) to his Gospel (cf. Lk. 1:1-4; Acts 1:1-3).

10 As He was going up and they were gazing into the sky, two men in white clothes were standing right beside them. 11 They asked, "Men of Galilee, why are you standing here looking up into the sky? This Jesus, who was taken away from you to heaven, will come back in the same way that you saw Him go to heaven."

12 Then they went back to Jerusalem from the mountain called Olivet,[b] which is near Jerusalem, a Sabbath day's walk away.[c]

There Must Be Twelve

13 When they came into the city, they went to the second-floor room where they were staying—Peter, John, James, and Andrew; Philip and Thomas; Bartholomew and Matthew; James ⌊the son⌋ of Alphaeus, Simon the Zealot, and Judas ⌊the son⌋ of James.

14 With one mind these all kept praying together. With them were the women, including Mary the mother of Jesus, and His brothers.

15 In those days Peter stood up among the disciples[d] (the total number of persons was about 120), and he said, 16 "Brothers,[e] long ago the Holy Spirit spoke through the mouth of David about Judas, who led the men that arrested Jesus. And what Scripture said had to be fulfilled.

17 "Judas was counted as one of us and was given a share in this ministry of ours. 18 With the money obtained through his wrongdoing, he bought a piece of land;[f] and falling headfirst, he burst in the middle, and all his intestines poured out. 19 Everyone living in Jerusalem heard about it. And so that piece of land is called Akeldama in their language; the word means 'Field of Blood.' 20 For it is written in the book of Psalms: *'Let his home be deserted and let there be no one who lives there,'* and *'Let someone else take his office.'* Therefore someone must be added to our number as a witness of His resurrection. 21 He should be one of the men who went with us the entire time that the Lord Jesus went in and out among us, 22 beginning with John's baptism to the day He was taken up from us."

23 The disciples established that two were qualified: Joseph called Barsabbas (who was also known as Justus) and Matthias. 24 Then they prayed, "Lord, You know the hearts of all. Show us which of these two You have chosen 25 to serve in this apostolic ministry, which Judas abandoned to go where he belonged."

26 They provided lots for ⌊both of⌋ them, and the lot fell to Matthias; and he was chosen ⌊by vote⌋ to be added to the eleven apostles.

---

20 *Ps 69:25; 109:8*

---

b- 12 Or "the Mount of Olives."

c- 12 Less than a mile away.

d- 15 Literally: "brothers"; throughout *Acts* and the rest of the New Testament this Greek term for "brothers" is translated with various terms, such as "brothers, disciples, fellow disciples, Christians, fellow Christians, fellow Jews." This is helpful for ease of reading and in making the text more meaningful. It is to be noted that the choice of terms in each context carefully distinguishes between Christian and non-Christian audiences.

e- 16 Literally: "Men, brothers."

f- 18 Literally: "Now this one [Judas] bought a field *from the reward of unrighteousness* . . . ."

2ND CHAPTER

The Holy Spirit Comes

1 The day of Pentecost*a* came, and they were all gathered in one place.
2 Suddenly a sound like a violent blast of wind came from heaven and filled the
whole house where they were sitting. **3** They saw tongues like flames that
separated,*b* and one rested on each of them. **4** They were all filled with the Holy
Spirit and began to speak in other languages*c* as the Spirit gave them the ability
to speak.

5 Jews who feared God—from every nation under heaven—were living in
Jerusalem. **6** When that sound took place, the crowd gathered and was dumbfounded because each one heard the disciples speak his own language. **7** Amazed
and wondering, they asked, "Aren't all these who are speaking Galileans? **8** And
how does every one of us hear his own native language—**9** Parthians, Medes,
and Elamites; people living in Mesopotamia, Judea and Cappadocia, Pontus and
the province of Asia, **10** Phrygia and Pamphilia, Egypt and the country near
Cyrene in Libya; visitors from Rome, Jews as well as proselytes;*d* **11** people
from Crete and Arabia? In our own languages we hear them tell about the
wonders which God has done." **12** They were all amazed and puzzled. They
asked one another, "What can this mean?" **13** Others sneered: "They're full of
new wine."

Peter's Pentecost Sermon

14 Then Peter stood up with the Eleven, raised his voice, and addressed them:
"Jews*e* and all you who live in Jerusalem, understand this, and listen closely to
what I say. **15** These men are not drunk, as you suppose, for it is only nine in
the morning.*f* **16** Rather, this is what the prophet Joel spoke about:

17   In the last days, *God says,*
       *I will pour out My Spirit*g *on all people.*
          *Then your sons and your daughters will speak God's word,*h
          your young men will see visions, and
          your old men will dream dreams.

17-21 Joel 2:28-32

---

2 *a*- 1 A festival on the 50th day after Passover when the Jews celebrated the wheat harvest and
           perhaps commemorated the giving of the Law to Moses on Mount Sinai.
 b- 3 The Greek for "separated" may indicate either "divided" tongues (flames) or the "distribution"
           of the tongues of fire.
 c- 4 Or "other tongues"; compare ahead at 1 Corinthians 12:10 and its accompanying footnote.
 d- 10 Meaning "Jews and also Gentiles who had accepted the Jewish religion."
 e- 14 Or "Men of Judea."
 f- 15 Literally: "the third hour"; the Jewish system of reckoning time, not the Roman, is used by
           Luke in the book of *Acts*.
 g- 17 Literally: "from My Spirit" (also in v. 18).
 h- 17 Literally: "will prophesy" (also in v. 18).

18   *Yes, in those days—even on My slaves, both men and women—*
        I will pour out My Spirit,
            and they will speak God's word.

19   *I will give you wonderful proofs in the sky above*
        and miraculous signs[i] *on the earth* below:
            blood and fire and a cloud of smoke;

20   *the sun will turn dark and the moon to blood*
            before the coming of the great and splendid day of the Lord.

21   *And everyone who calls on the Name of the Lord will be saved.*

22 "Men of Israel, listen to what I have to say: When Jesus from Nazareth was among you, He was a Man whom God commended to you—as you well know—by the miracles, wonderful proofs, and miraculous signs[j] which God worked through Him. **23** Although God definitely planned and intended to have Him betrayed, you ˌwere the ones whoˌ had wicked men nail Him to a cross, and you killed Him. **24** But God set aside the pains of death and raised Him, because it was not possible for death to hold Him. **25** For David says of Him:

     I always see the Lord before Me.
        He is at My right hand
            so that I will not be shaken.

26   *And so My heart is glad,*
        and My tongue rejoices,
            yes, even My body will rest in hope,

27   *because You will not leave Me in the grave [hades][k]*
            or allow Your Holy One to experience decay.

28   *You made the way of life known to Me,*
        You will fill Me with joy by being with Me.

29 "Fellow Jews,[l] I can tell you frankly that our ancestor David died and was buried, and his grave is here to this day. **30** Therefore, it was because he was a prophet and knew that *God had sworn to him[m] to place one of his descendants on his throne,* **31** that David saw what was coming and said concerning the resurrection of the Christ [Messiah][n] that *He would not be left in the grave [hades],[o]* and His body *would not experience decay.*

32 "God has raised this Jesus—of that we are all witnesses. **33** Therefore, having been lifted up to God's right hand and having received the promised Holy Spirit from the Father, He has poured out what you see and hear. **34** For David did not go up to heaven, but he says:

25-28 *Ps 16:8-11*   **30** *Ps 89:3,4; 132:11*   **31** *Ps 16:10*

i- 19 See MIRACULOUS SIGNS, WONDERFUL PROOFS, and MIRACLES on page 527.
j- 22 See MIRACULOUS SIGNS, WONDERFUL PROOFS, and MIRACLES on page 527.
k- 27 Literally: "You will not abandon My soul to *hades*"; see *HADES/GEHENNA* on page 540.
l- 29 Literally: "Men, brothers" (also in v. 37).
m- 30 Some manuscripts and early translations add: "to raise Christ according to the flesh."
n- 31 The Greek-based English name "Christ" and its Hebrew-based counterpart "Messiah" both mean the "Anointed One" or the "Chosen One."
o- 31 Literally: "neither was He abandoned in *hades*"; see footnote at 2:27.

> *The Lord said to my Lord:*
> *'Sit at My right hand*
35   *until I make Your enemies a footstool for Your feet.'*

36 "So all the people of Israel should know that it is true that God made Him Lord and Christ—this Jesus whom you crucified."

37 When the people heard this, they were cut to the heart. They asked Peter and the other apostles, "Fellow Jews, what should we do?"

38 Peter answered them, "Repent and be baptized, every one of you, in the Name of Jesus Christ*p* so that your sins will be forgiven, and you will receive the gift of the Holy Spirit. **39** For this promise is made to you and to your children and to all *who are far away*, all *whom the Lord* our God *will call*."

40 He said much more to warn them. He urged them, "Be saved from this crooked kind of people." **41** Those who accepted what he said were baptized. And that day about 3,000 persons were added.

How Christians Lived

42 They continued to hold firmly to the teaching of the apostles and to the fellowship, to the breaking of the bread,*q* and to the prayers. **43** Awe came on everybody—the apostles were working many wonderful proofs and miraculous signs. **44** All who believed were together and shared everything with one another; **45** from time to time they sold their lands and other possessions and then distributed the money to all ⌊the needy⌋ in proportion to each one's need.*r* **46** All were one at heart as they continued to go to the Temple every day; and breaking bread*s* from house to house, they shared their food with glad and simple hearts, **47** praising God and having the good will of all the people. And every day the Lord added to their number those who were being saved.

3RD CHAPTER

The Cripple

1 Peter and John were going up to the Temple for the hour of prayer at three in the afternoon. **2** Now there was a man who had been a cripple from his birth. Men would carry him and lay him every day at the Temple gate called the Beautiful Gate, so that he could beg for gifts from those going into the Temple. **3** When he saw that Peter and John were about to go into the Temple, he asked them for a gift.

34,35 Ps 110:1   39 Is 57:19; Joel 2:32

---

p- 38 Literally: "on the basis of the Name of Jesus Christ."
q- 42 "Breaking of the bread" can refer to the common practice of eating an ordinary meal
   -   (Lk. 24:30,35) or to the special practice of participating in the Lord's Supper (1 Cor. 10:16).
r - 45 Literally: "and they kept on selling . . . and kept on distributing them [*via* money] to all ⌊the needy⌋ to whatever degree each one had a need."
s- 46 See 2:42 and its accompanying footnote.

4 Peter and John stared at him. "Look at us!" Peter said. 5 He paid close attention to them, expecting to receive something from them. 6 Peter said, "I do not have any silver or gold, but I will give you what I have. In the Name of Jesus Christ from Nazareth, walk!" 7 He took hold of his right hand and raised him up. Immediately his feet and ankles were made strong. 8 He jumped up, stood, and started to walk. And he went with them into the Temple, walking, jumping, and praising God.

9 When all the people saw him walking and praising God, 10 they knew that he was the man who used to sit and beg at the Beautiful Gate of the Temple. They were very much surprised and amazed to see what had happened to him. 11 As he clung to Peter and John, all the people came running together to them at Solomon's Porch,*a* as it was called. They were dumbfounded.

12 When Peter saw the people, he said to them, "Men of Israel, why are you wondering about this, or why are you staring at us as if by our own power or piety we had made him walk? 13 *The God of Abraham, Isaac, and Jacob*, the God of our fathers, has *glorified His Servant* Jesus, whom you delivered and denied before Pilate when he had decided to let Him go. 14 You denied the Holy and Righteous One, and asked to have a murderer given to you. 15 You killed the Author*b* of life. But God raised Him from the dead—we are witnesses of that. 16 And when he believed in Jesus' Name, that Name strengthened the limbs of this man whom you see and know. The faith that Jesus worked*c* has given him this perfect health in front of all of you.

17 "And now, fellow Jews,*d* I know that like your rulers you did not know what you were doing. 18 But in this way God fulfilled what He predicted by the mouth of all the prophets—His Christ would suffer. 19 Repent then, and turn, to have your sins wiped away, 20 so that times may come when the Lord refreshes you and sends Him whom He appointed to be Christ, namely, Jesus, 21 whom heaven must receive*e* until the times when everything will be restored, as God said long ago by the mouth of His holy prophets.

22 "Moses said: *'The Lord your God will raise up a Prophet for you from among your brothers who is like me. Listen to everything He tells* you. 23 *And every person who will not listen to that Prophet will be completely cut off from the people.'* 24 Samuel and all the prophets after him, as many as have spoken, told about these days. 25 You are the heirs of the prophets and of the covenant ['last will and testament']*f* that God made with our fathers when He said to Abraham: *'And in your Descendant all the people on earth*g* will be blessed.'*

---

13 *Ex 3:6; Is 52:13*   22 *Deut 18:15,18,19*   23 *Lev 23:29; Deut 18:19*   25 *Gen 12:3; 18:18;*
22:18; 26:4; 28:14

---

3 *a*- 11 Literally: "Solomon's colonnade."
  b- 15 Or "Prince."
  c- 16 Or "that this Name worked."
  d- 17 Literally: "brothers."
  e- 21 Another translation, favored by Luther and Chemnitz, reads: "Jesus, who must take possession of heaven . . . ." Either translation ultimately conveys the same thing, namely, that Christ now rules over all things in heaven and on earth also according to His human nature.
  f- 25 See *DIATHĒKĒ* on page 531.
  g- 25 Literally: "families of the earth."

26 Now that God has raised His Servant, He sent Him first to you to bless you by turning every one of you from your wicked ways."

4TH CHAPTER

In Court

1 The priests, the captain of the Temple, and the Sadducees approached them while they were speaking to the people. 2 They were greatly annoyed because Peter and John were teaching the people and preaching the resurrection of the dead through Jesus. 3 They arrested them, and since it was already evening, they put them in prison until the next day.

4 But many of those who had heard the word believed, and the number of the men grew to about 5,000.

5 The next day their rulers, elders, and scribes*a* met in Jerusalem 6 with Annas the high priest, Caiaphas, John, Alexander, and all the rest of the high priest's family. 7 They had the two men stand before them, and they began to ask, "By what power or Name did you do this?"

8 Then Peter was filled with the Holy Spirit. He said to them, "Rulers of the people and elders, 9 if we are being cross-examined today about the good we did for a crippled man, how he was made well, 10 all of you and all the people of Israel should know that this man stands before you healed by the Name of Jesus Christ from Nazareth, whom you crucified but God raised from the dead. 11 This One is

> the very Stone
> *rejected* by you *builders*
> which has become the Cornerstone.

12 No one else can save us, because in all the world there is no other NAME given among mankind by which we must be saved."

13 When they found out that Peter and John had no special education or training, they were surprised to see how boldly they spoke. Then they realized that these men had been with Jesus. 14 And seeing the healed man standing with them, they could not say anything against them. 15 So they ordered them to leave the courtroom and talked the matter over among themselves: 16 "What should we do with these men? They have worked a miraculous sign which is widely known; everyone living in Jerusalem can see it clearly, and we cannot deny it.

---

11 Ps 118:22

---

4 *a*- 5 These were the Bible scholars of Jesus' day. Their work and responsibilities varied greatly from one to another. These areas included making handwritten copies of the Old Testament, interpreting and following the Mosaic guidelines of the Pentateuch (Five Books of Moses), formulating oral laws, teaching God's people in classroom situations, etc. In short, the scribes were considered authorities on the Jewish religion. Compare Ezra 7:6,10.

17 However, in order that it *b* may spread no further among the people, let's warn them never again to speak to anyone using this Name."

18 They called Peter and John and ordered them not to say or teach anything using the Name of Jesus.

19 Peter and John answered them, "Whether God considers it right to listen to you rather than to Him, you may judge ʟfor yourselvesˌ. 20 For we cannot stop telling what we have seen and heard."

21 Once more they threatened them and then let them go. They could not find any way to punish them, because all the people were praising God for what had happened. 22 For the man who had been healed by this miraculous sign was over 40 years old.

The Church Prays

23 When Peter and John were released, they went to their friends and told them everything the high priests and elders had said. 24 When they heard it, they all raised their voices together to God and said, "Master, You *made heaven and earth, the sea, and everything in them.* 25 You said by the Holy Spirit through the mouth *c* of David, Your servant, our father:

> *Why do the nations rage*
> *and the peoples plot to no avail?*
> 26 *The kings of the earth stand ready,*
> *and the rulers join their forces*
> *against the Lord*
> *and against His Anointed.* *d*

27 "Herod and Pontius Pilate *indeed joined forces* with *the Gentiles and the people* of Israel in this city against Your holy Servant Jesus, *whom You anointed.* 28 They did everything that You by Your will and power long ago decided should be done.

29 "And now, Lord, see how they are threatening us, and grant that Your servants may continue to speak Your word with all boldness, 30 as You stretch out Your hand to heal and work miraculous signs and wonderful proofs by the Name of Your holy Servant Jesus."

31 When they had prayed, the place where they were meeting was shaken. They were all filled with the Holy Spirit and continued to speak the word of God with boldness.

Sharing

32 The whole group of believers was one in heart and soul. And no one called

---

24 Ex 20:11; Neh 9:6; Ps 146:6   25-27 Ps 2:1,2

b- 17 In this context "it" could refer to the news of the miracle or the Name in which the miracle was done (cf. the last part of the verse).

c - 25 Literally: "through the Holy Spirit's mouth"; also, the later Greek manuscripts omit: "Holy Spirit."

d- 26 Or "Christ" ["Messiah"].

any of his possessions his own, but they shared everything.

33 With great power the apostles continued to testify that the Lord Jesus had risen, and much good will[e] rested on all of them. **34** For none of the people was in need, because all who had land or houses sold them from time to time and brought the money from the things which were sold. **35** They laid it at the apostles' feet, and then it was distributed to each one in proportion to his need.[f]

36 Joseph (the one the apostles called Barnabas, which means "Son of Comfort"), a descendant of Levi, born on Cyprus, **37** had some land and sold it. He brought the money and laid it at the apostles' feet.

5TH CHAPTER

Ananias And Sapphira

1 A man by the name of Ananias and his wife Sapphira sold some property; **2** he held back some of the money for himself—and his wife knew about it—and he brought some of it and laid it at the feet of the apostles.

3 "Ananias," Peter asked, "for what reason did Satan fill your heart so that you tried to make the Holy Spirit a liar by holding back some of the money you received for the land? **4** While you had the land, wasn't it your own? And after it was sold, couldn't you have done as you pleased with the money? How could you think of doing such a thing? You did not lie to men but to God!"

5 When Ananias heard him say this, he fell down and died. And all who heard of it were terrified. **6** The young men got up, wrapped his body in a sheet, carried him out, and buried him.

7 About three hours later his wife came in. She did not know what had happened. **8** "Tell me," Peter asked her, "did you sell the land for that price?"

She answered, "Yes, that was the price."

9 Then Peter said to her, "How could you two agree to put the Spirit of the Lord to a test? There at the door are the feet of those who buried your husband, and they will carry you out."

10 Immediately she fell down at his feet and died. When the young men came in, they found her dead and carried her out and buried her beside her husband. **11** The whole church and all others who heard about it were terrified.

Many Miracles

12 Many miraculous signs and wonderful proofs were worked among the people by the apostles. And the Christians[a] were all together in Solomon's Porch.[b] **13** None of the others dared to join with them, but the people thought

---

e- 33 Or "grace."
f- 35 Compare 2:45 and its accompanying footnote.
5 *a*- 12 Literally: "they."
  b- 12 Literally: "Solomon's colonnade."

very highly of them; **14** and still more believers, a large number of men and women, were added to the Lord. **15** As a result people carried their sick out into the streets and laid them down on cots and mats, so that at least Peter's shadow might fall on one or the other of them as he went by. **16** Crowds would gather even from the towns around Jerusalem, bringing their sick and those who were troubled by unclean spirits, and they were all made well.

In Court

17 Then the high priest and all those with him, who made up the party of the Sadducees, became very jealous. **18** They arrested the apostles and put them in the public prison. **19** But at night the angel of the Lord opened the prison doors and brought them out. **20** "Go," he said, "stand in the Temple, and keep on telling the people everything about the Life ⌞in Christ⌟."*c*

21 After they had heard him, they went into the Temple early in the morning and began to teach.

The high priest and those who were with him came and called the Jewish council [Sanhedrin] and all the elders of Israel together. They also sent men to the prison to get the apostles. **22** But when the Temple guards arrived, they did not find them in prison. They came back and reported, **23** "We found the prison very securely locked and the guards standing at the doors, but when we opened them, we found no one inside." **24** When the captain of the Temple and the high priests heard this, they were puzzled as to what could have happened to them.

25 Then someone came and told them, "The men you put in prison are standing in the Temple teaching the people."

26 Then the captain went with the Temple guards and got them, but without using force, because they were afraid the people would stone them. **27** They brought them and had them stand before the council.

The high priest questioned them **28** and said, "We gave you strict orders not to teach using this Name, and here you have filled Jerusalem with your teaching. You want to take revenge on us for putting this Man to death."*d*

29 Peter and the other apostles answered, "We must obey God rather than men. **30** *You hanged* Jesus *on a cross* and murdered Him. But the God of our fathers raised Him **31** and took Him up to His right hand as Leader and Savior in order to give the people of Israel repentance and forgiveness of sins. **32** We are witnesses of these things—we and the Holy Spirit, whom God has given to those who obey Him."

33 When they heard this, they became furious and wanted to kill them. **34** But a Pharisee in the Jewish council by the name of Gamaliel, a teacher of the Law, highly respected by all the people, stood up and ordered the men taken outside a little while.

35 He said to them, "Men of Israel, consider carefully what you are going to do with these men. **36** Some time ago Theudas appeared, claiming to be some-

---

30 Deut 21:22

c- 20 Literally: "about this Life."
d- 28 Literally: "You want to bring this Man's blood on us."

body, and about four hundred men joined him. He was killed, and all who followed him were scattered, and they disappeared.

37 "After him, Judas from Galilee appeared at the time of the census and led people in a revolt. He also perished, and all who followed him were scattered.

38 "And now I tell you, keep away from these men and let them alone. If it is men planning or doing this, it will fail, **39** but if it is from God, you will not be able to stop them. You may even discover that you are fighting against God."

40 They took his advice. They called the apostles, beat them, ordered them not to speak using the Name of Jesus, and let them go. **41** The apostles left the council, happy to have been thought worthy to suffer shame for the NAME. *e* **42** And every day, in the Temple and from house to house, they kept right on teaching and telling the Good News that Jesus is the Christ [Messiah].

6TH CHAPTER

Seven Helpers

1 In those days, as the number of the disciples grew larger and larger, a complaint was brought against those who spoke Aramaic by those who spoke Greek*a* that every day, when the food was handed out, their widows were being neglected.

2 The Twelve called the whole group of disciples together and said, "It is not right for us to give up teaching God's word in order to serve at tables. **3** Now, fellow disciples,*b* select seven men from among you of whom people speak well, who are full of the Spirit and wisdom, and we will put them in charge of this work. **4** Then we will devote ourselves to praying and to serving by speaking the word."

5 The idea pleased the whole group. So they chose Stephen, a man full of faith and of the Holy Spirit, Philip, Prochorus, Nicanor, Timon, Parmenas, and Nicolaus, who had become a Jew in Antioch. **6** They had these men stand before the apostles, who prayed and laid their hands on them.

7 The word of God kept on spreading, and the number of disciples in Jerusalem was growing very large. Even a large number of the priests came to believe and obey the word.*c*

Stephen Is Arrested

8 Stephen, full of God's grace*d* and power, was working wonderful proofs and great miraculous signs among the people. **9** Some men of the Synagog of the

---

e- 41 Meaning "for Jesus."

6 *a-* 1 Literally: "there was a murmuring of the Hellenists (Greeks) against the Hebrews"; refers to a disagreement between Greek-speaking Jews and Hebrew-speaking Jews; Aramaic, a language similar to Hebrew, was spoken by the Jews of Paul's day.

b- 3 Literally: "brothers."

c- 7 Literally: ". . . and a great crowd of the priests obeyed the faith," that is, the teachings of the faith.

d- 8 "Grace" here in the sense of God's gift.

Freedmen, as it was called, and men from Cyrene and Alexandria, and men from Cilicia and Asia rose up to argue with Stephen. 10 But they could not match the wisdom and the Spirit by whom he spoke.

11 Then they secretly got some men to say, "We heard him speak slanderous things against Moses and God." 12 They stirred up the people, the elders, and the scribes, and rushing at him, took him by force and brought him before the Jewish council [Sanhedrin]. 13 There they had witnesses stand up and lie, "This man never stops talking against the sacred place*e* and the Law. 14 For we have heard him say, 'This Jesus from Nazareth will tear this place down and change the customs that Moses gave us.' "

15 All who sat in the council stared at him and saw his face—it was like the face of an angel.

7TH CHAPTER

Stephen Defends Himself

1 Then the high priest asked, "Is this so?"

2 He answered, "Fellow Jews*a* and fathers, listen. *The God of glory* appeared to our father Abraham while he was in Mesopotamia before he lived in Haran. 3 *'Leave your land and your relatives,'* God told him, *'and come to the land that I will show you.'*

4 "Then Abraham left the country of the Chaldeans and lived in Haran. After his father died, God had him move from there to this land where you live now.

5 "He *gave* him nothing to call his own,*b* *not even enough to set his foot on,* but promised *to give it to him as a possession and to his descendants after him,* although he had no child. 6 And God spoke in this way—that *His descendants would be strangers in a foreign country, and its people would make slaves of them and mistreat them four hundred years.* 7 *'But I will punish the people whom they will serve,'* God said, *'and after that they will leave and worship Me in this* place.'

8 "He gave him the *covenant* of *circumcision.* And so, when his son Isaac was born, *he circumcised him on the eighth day.* Isaac did the same to his son Jacob, and Jacob to his twelve sons, the ancestors of our tribes.

9 "These ancestors *were jealous of Joseph and sold him into Egypt,* but *God was with him.* 10 He rescued him from all his troubles *and gave him the good will of Pharaoh, the king of Egypt, and wisdom as he stood before him*—Pharaoh made him ruler *of Egypt and of his whole palace.* 11 But a *famine* with much misery *came over* all Egypt and *Canaan,* and our ancestors could not find any food. 12 When *Jacob heard that there was grain in Egypt,* he sent our ancestors

---

2 *Ps 29:3*   **3** *Gen 12:1*   **5** *Gen 12:7; 13:15; 17:8; 48:4; Deut 2:5*
6,7 *Gen 15:13,14; Ex 2:22; 3:12; 12:40*   **8** *Gen 17:10; 21:4*   **9** *Gen 37:11,28; 39:2,3,21; 45:4*
10 *Gen 39:21; 41:40,41,43,46; Ps 105:21*   **11** *Gen 41:54; 42:5*   **12** *Gen 42:2*

---

e - 13 See Diagram #1 on page 430.

7 *a*- 2 Literally: "Men, brothers."

  b- 5 Literally: "gave not to him an inheritance."

on their first trip. 13 On the second, *Joseph told his brothers who he was*, and Pharaoh learned about the family from which Joseph came. 14 Joseph sent and had his father Jacob come to him, and all his relatives—*seventy-five persons.* 15 So *Jacob went down to Egypt.* He and our ancestors died 16 and *were brought* to *Shechem* and *laid* in the burial place which *Abraham bought* for a sum of money *from the sons of Hamor at Shechem.*

17 "When the time that God set in His promise to Abraham had almost come, the people *had grown and their number had become very large* in Egypt. 18 And now *a different king who knew nothing of Joseph became ruler of Egypt.* 19 He *was shrewd in scheming against* our people, and he *mistreated* our fathers by making them abandon*ᶜ* their babies so they would not live.

20 "At that time Moses was born, and he was a very *beautiful* child.*ᵈ* For *three months* he was cared for in his father's home. 21 When he was abandoned, *Pharaoh's daughter took him*ᵉ and raised him *as her son.* 22 Moses was educated in all the wisdom of the Egyptians and became a great man in what he said and did. 23 When he was forty years old, he thought he would *visit his own people, the Israelites.* 24 When he saw a man being wronged, he defended him. He avenged the man who was mistreated by *striking down the Egyptian.* 25 He thought his own people would understand that he was the one by whom God was going to give them freedom, but they did not understand. 26 *The next day he came* to them *as they were fighting*, and he tried to make peace between them. 'Men, you are brothers,' he said. 'Why are you doing wrong to one another?'

27 "But *the man who was doing wrong to his neighbor* pushed Moses away. *'Who made you ruler and judge over us?'* he asked. 28 *'Do you want to kill me as you killed the Egyptian yesterday?'* 29 When he said that, *Moses fled and became a stranger living in the land of Midian.* There he had *two sons.*

30 "After forty years had passed, *an Angel appeared to him in the flames of a burning thornbush in the wilderness* of Mount Sinai. 31 When Moses saw it, the sight amazed him. As *he went closer to examine it,* the voice of *the Lord spoke* to him, 32 *'I am the God of your fathers, the God of Abraham, Isaac, and Jacob.'* Moses started to tremble and *did not dare to look.* 33 *The Lord told him,* 'Take off your sandals, for the place where you are standing is holy ground. 34 I have clearly seen how My people are mistreated in Egypt. I have heard their groaning and have come down to rescue them. And now come, I will send you to Egypt.'

35 "This Moses whom they rejected by saying, *'Who made you ruler and judge?'* this one God sent to rule and free them with the help of the Angel who appeared to him in the thornbush. 36 He led them out, working *wonderful proofs and miraculous signs in Egypt*, at the Red Sea, and *for forty years in the wilderness.* 37 It was this same Moses who told the Israelites: *'God will raise up*

---

13 Gen 45:1   **14,15** Gen 46:6,27; Ex 1:5; Deut 10:22   **16** Gen 50:13; Josh 24:32   **17-19** Ex 1:7,8,10,11   **20** Ex 2:2   **21** Ex 2:5,10   **23-26** Ex 2:11,12   **27-29** Ex 2:13-15,22; 18:3   **30-34** Ex 2:24; 3:1-8,10; 4:19   **35** Ex 2:14   **36** Ex 7:3; Num 14:33   **37** Deut 18:15,18

---

c- 19 Meaning "set out to die," (also in v. 21); a reference to a form of infanticide practiced by the Egyptians by which a child was placed out in the desert sun to die.

d- 20 Or "he was fair in the sight of God."

e- 21 Or "adopted him."

a Prophet for you from among your brothers who is like me.' **38** Moses was in the congregation in the wilderness with the Angel who spoke to him on Mount Sinai and with our fathers. He received living messages to give to us, **39** but our fathers were not willing to obey him. Yes, they rejected him,*ᶠ* and their hearts *turned away to Egypt.* **40** *'Make gods for us who will lead us,'* they told Aaron, *'because this Moses who took us out of Egypt—we do not know what has happened to him.'* **41** That was the time *they made a calf, brought a sacrifice* to the idol, *and delighted* in what their hands had made.

42 "So God turned away from them and abandoned them to worship *the sun, the moon, and the stars,ᵍ* as it is written in the book of the Prophets:*ʰ 'People of Israel, you did not offer Me slaughtered animals and sacrifices during the forty years in the wilderness, did you?* **43** *You even took along the tent of Moloch, the star of the god Rephan, and the images you made* in order to worship them. *And so I will send you away to live on the other side* of Babylon.'

44 "In the wilderness our fathers had the Tabernacle *in which God spoke to His people.ⁱ* It was built ⌐exactly⌐ *like the model Moses had seen,ʲ* just as He who *spoke to Moses* had ordered him *to make* it. **45** From him our fathers received it, and they brought it here under Joshua when they took the land from the nations whom God drove out before our fathers, and ⌐here it was⌐ until the time of David. **46** He found that God was kind to him and asked that *he might find a home for the Godᵏ of Jacob.* **47** And *Solomon built Him a Temple.*

48 "But the Most High does not live in things made by human hands, as the prophet says:

49   *Heaven is My throne,*
            and the earth is My footstool.
        What kind of house will you build Me? the Lord asks, or
        What place is there where I can rest?
50   *Did My hand* not *make all these things?*

51 *"How stubborn you are and pagan at heart and deaf to the truth!ˡ* You are always *opposing the Holy Spirit.* Your fathers did it, and so do you! **52** Was there ever a prophet your fathers did not persecute? They killed those who announced, 'The Righteous One will come!' and now you have become His betrayers and murderers. **53** You were the people who received the Law through the directions of ⌐God's⌐ angels, but you did not keep it."

---

39 *Num 14:3,4*   **40,41** *Ex 32:1,4,6,23*   **42** *Jer 7:18; 19:13*   **42,43** *Amos 5:25-27*
44 *Ex 25:1,40; 27:21*   **46** *Ps 132:5*   **47** *1 Kgs 6:1*   **49,50** *Is 66:1,2*
51 *Ex 33:3,5; Lev 26:41; Num 27:14; Is 63:10; Jer 9:26; 6:10*

---

f- 39 Or "pushed him aside."
g- 42 Literally: "worship the heavenly bodies."
h- 42 A reference to the *second* division of the Old Testament Scriptures. See THE OLD TESTAMENT CANON on page 551. Also compare Matthew 5:17 and its accompanying footnote.
i- 44 Literally: "Tent of Testimony."
j- 44 Compare Exodus 25:9.
k- 46 Some of the older manuscripts and early translations read "house of Jacob," but the context as well as Psalm 132:5 seem to favor the above reading.
l- 51 Literally: "You stiffnecked and uncircumcised in heart and ears."

The Stoning Of Stephen

54 As they heard these things, they [the members of the council] became furious and ground their teeth at him. **55** But he, full of the Holy Spirit, gazed up to heaven and saw God's glory and Jesus standing at God's right hand. **56** He said, "Look, I see heaven opened and the Son of Man[m] standing at the right hand of God!"[n]

57 But they shouted at the top of their voices and held their ears shut. They rushed at him with one purpose, **58** threw him out of the city, and began to stone him. The witnesses had laid their outer clothes at the feet of a young man named Saul.

59 While they were stoning him, Stephen called out, "Lord Jesus, receive my spirit." **60** Then, kneeling, he shouted, "Lord, do not hold this sin against them." When he had said this, he fell asleep.

8TH CHAPTER

C. The Gospel in Judea and Samaria (8:1–12:25)

1 Saul also approved of putting him to death.

On that day a great persecution broke out against the church in Jerusalem, and everyone, except the apostles, was scattered throughout the open country of Judea and Samaria.

2 God-fearing men buried Stephen as they mourned loudly over him.

The Samaritans Believe

3 Saul began to destroy the church. Going into one house after another and dragging off men and women, he put them in prison.

4 The people who were scattered went from place to place preaching the word. **5** Philip went down to the city of Samaria and proclaimed Christ to the people. **6** The crowds listened eagerly to what Philip had to say when they heard his words and saw the miraculous signs that he continued to work. **7** For there were those who were plagued by unclean spirits which were screaming as they came out of them. And many who were paralyzed and lame were made well. **8** So there was great joy in that city.

9 There was a certain man by the name of Simon who previously was practicing witchcraft in the city and astonished the people of Samaria. He claimed to be a great man, **10** and everybody from the least to the greatest listened eagerly to him, saying, "This man is the power of God, the power called Great." **11** They were so fascinated by him because he had astonished them for a long time by his witchcraft. **12** But when Philip preached the Good News about the Kingdom of God and about the Name of Jesus Christ, men and women believed him and

---

m- 56 See "Son of Man" in Glossary.

n- 56 Compare Matthew 26:63-68; Mark 14:61-65. The same leaders had recently heard a similar description of the "Son of Man" from Jesus Himself, provoking a similar reaction; see "Son of Man" in Glossary.

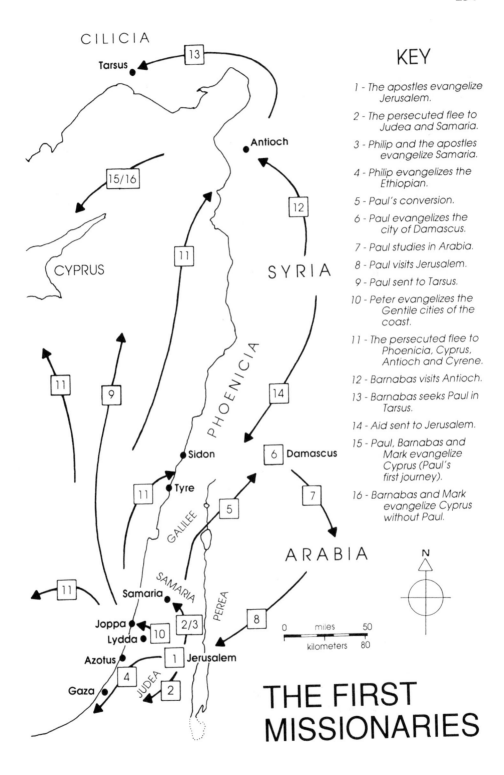

KEY

1 - The apostles evangelize Jerusalem.

2 - The persecuted flee to Judea and Samaria.

3 - Philip and the apostles evangelize Samaria.

4 - Philip evangelizes the Ethiopian.

5 - Paul's conversion.

6 - Paul evangelizes the city of Damascus.

7 - Paul studies in Arabia.

8 - Paul visits Jerusalem.

9 - Paul sent to Tarsus.

10 - Peter evangelizes the Gentile cities of the coast.

11 - The persecuted flee to Phoenicia, Cyprus, Antioch and Cyrene.

12 - Barnabas visits Antioch.

13 - Barnabas seeks Paul in Tarsus.

14 - Aid sent to Jerusalem.

15 - Paul, Barnabas and Mark evangelize Cyprus (Paul's first journey).

16 - Barnabas and Mark evangelize Cyprus without Paul.

THE FIRST MISSIONARIES

were baptized. **13** Even Simon believed, and when he was baptized, he stayed with Philip. He was amazed to see the miraculous signs and great miracles that were taking place.

14 When the apostles in Jerusalem heard that Samaria had accepted the word of God, they sent Peter and John to them. **15** These two went down and prayed that the people would receive the Holy Spirit, **16** for He had not yet come upon any of them; but they had only been baptized into the Name of the Lord Jesus. **17** Then Peter and John laid their hands on them, and they received the Holy Spirit.

18 When Simon saw that the Spirit was given by the laying on of the apostles' hands, he offered them money. **19** "Give me this authority also," he said, "so that anyone on whom I lay my hands may receive the Holy Spirit."

20 "May your money perish with you," Peter told him, "because you thought you could buy God's gift with money. **21** You have no part or share in this matter, because your *heart is not right with God.* **22** Now repent of this wickedness of yours, and ask the Lord if He will perhaps forgive you for thinking such a thing. **23** For I see that you are filled with a *bitter poison* and have been *chained by wickedness."* *a*

24 Simon answered, "Pray to the Lord for me that none of the things you said may happen to me."

25 After they had testified and spoken the word of the Lord, they also brought the Gospel [Good News] to many Samaritan villages on their way back to Jerusalem.

The Treasurer From Ethiopia

26 An angel of the Lord said to Philip, "Get up and go south to the road that goes down from Jerusalem to Gaza." (This is a desert area.)

27 He got up and went. Here there was a man from Ethiopia, a eunuch who was a high official in charge of all the treasures of Candace, queen of the Ethiopians. He had come to Jerusalem to worship **28** and was on his way home, sitting in his chariot and reading the prophet Isaiah.

29 The Spirit said to Philip, "Go over to that chariot and stay close to it."

30 Philip ran up to it and there heard him reading the prophet Isaiah. "Do you understand what you are reading?" he asked.

31 And the eunuch answered, "How can I unless someone guides me?" So he urged Philip to come up and sit with him.

32 This was the part of the Scripture he was reading:

> *He was led away like a sheep to be slaughtered,*
> *and as a lamb is dumb before the man who cuts off its wool,*
> *so He does not open His mouth.*
> **33** *When He humbled Himself,*
> *His condemnation was taken away.*

---

21 Ps 78:37   *23 Deut 29:18; Is 58:6*   *32,33 Is 53:7,8*

---

8 *a*- 23 See Deuteronomy 29:18.

Who will describe His descendants,
because His life is cut off from the earth?

34 The eunuch said to Philip, "I ask you, of whom is the prophet speaking —himself or someone else?" 35 Then Philip spoke. Starting with that statement of the Scriptures, he told him the Good News of Jesus.

36 As they were going along the road, they came to some water. The eunuch said, "Here is water. What is there to keep me from being baptized?"*b* 38 He ordered the chariot to stop, and both Philip and the eunuch stepped down into the water, and Philip baptized him. 39 When they had stepped out of the water, the Spirit of the Lord suddenly took Philip away, and the eunuch, going happily on his way, did not see him again.

40 But Philip found himself in Ashdod. He went through all the towns, preaching the Gospel until he came to Caesarea.

9TH CHAPTER

Jesus Changes Saul [Paul]

1 And Saul, still breathing threats and murder against the Lord's disciples, went to the high priest 2 and asked him for letters to the synagogs in Damascus, in order to bring any of the followers of Jesus*a* whom he might find there, men or women, back to Jerusalem in chains.

3 On his way, as he was coming near Damascus, suddenly a light from heaven flashed around him. 4 He fell to the ground and heard a voice saying to him, "Saul! Saul! Why are you persecuting Me?"

5 "Who are You, Lord?" he asked.

"I am Jesus," He said, "whom you are persecuting. 6 But get up, go into the city, and you will be told what you should do."

7 Meanwhile the men traveling with him were standing speechless. They heard the voice but did not see anyone.

8 Saul got up from the ground. When he opened his eyes, he could not see anything. So they took him by the hand and led him into Damascus. 9 For three days he could not see and did not eat or drink.

Ananias Comes To Saul [Paul]

10 In Damascus there was a disciple by the name of Ananias. The Lord said to him in a vision: "Ananias!"

"Yes, Lord," he answered.

11 The Lord told him, "Get up, go to the street called Straight, and in the home of Judas look for a man from Tarsus by the name of Saul. For at this very

---

b- 36 All of the older manuscripts and most of the earlier translations omit verse 37: "If you believe with all your heart," Philip said, "you may." He answered, "I believe Jesus Christ is the Son of God."

9 *a*- 2 Literally: "those who were of the Way."

moment he is praying. **12** And in a vision he has seen a man by the name of Ananias come in and place his hands on him to restore his sight."

13 "Lord," Ananias answered, "I have heard many tell how much wrong this man has done to Your believers [saints] in Jerusalem, **14** and he is here with authority from the high priests to put in chains all who call on Your Name."

15 "Go," the Lord told him, "for this man is My chosen instrument to bring My Name before the Gentiles and kings and before the people of Israel. **16** Indeed, I will show him how much he has to suffer for the sake of My Name."

17 Ananias went and came to the house. After he laid his hands on Saul, he said, "Brother Saul, the Lord sent me—Jesus, whom you saw on your way here—so that you may see again and be filled with the Holy Spirit."

18 Immediately something like scales fell from his eyes, and he saw again. He got up and was baptized. **19** Then he had something to eat and was strengthened.

Saul [Paul] Preaches Jesus

While Saul was with the disciples in Damascus several days, **20** he immediately started to preach in the synagogs: "Jesus is the Son of God." **21** All who heard him were amazed and asked, "Isn't this the man who destroyed those in Jerusalem who call on this Name, and didn't he come here to bring them in chains to the high priests?"

22 But Saul grew more and more powerful and bewildered the Jews living in Damascus by proving that Jesus is the Christ [Messiah]. **23** After some time the Jews plotted to murder him, **24** but Saul was told about their plot. Since they were watching the gates day and night to murder him, **25** his disciples took him at night and let him down through an opening in the wall by lowering him in a basket.

26 After he arrived in Jerusalem, he tried to join the disciples. But they were all afraid of him because they would not believe that he was a disciple.

27 Then Barnabas took him, brought him to the apostles, and told them how Saul saw the Lord on the road and that the Lord spoke to him and how in Damascus Saul boldly preached in the Name of Jesus. **28** Then he went in and out among them in Jerusalem, **29** preaching boldly in the Name of the Lord.

He kept on talking and arguing with the Greek-speaking Jews. But they were trying to kill him. **30** As soon as the disciples *b* found out about it, they took him down to Caesarea and sent him away to Tarsus.

31 Then the church all over Judea, Galilee, and Samaria had peace and was built up. The church lived in the fear of the Lord and in the comfort of the Holy Spirit, and it grew larger and larger in number.

Aeneas—Tabitha

32 Now when Peter was going around among all the disciples, he also came down to the believers living in Lydda. **33** There he found a man by the name of Aeneas who was paralyzed and had been lying on a mat for eight years.

---

b- 30 Literally: "brothers."

34 "Aeneas," Peter said to him, "Jesus Christ makes you well. Get up and make your bed." And immediately he got up.

35 All who lived in Lydda and Sharon saw him and turned to the Lord.

36 In Joppa there was a woman disciple by the name of Tabitha (which when translated into Greek, is Dorcas). *c* She was always doing good works and giving things to the poor. **37** Just at that time she became sick and died; so she was washed and laid in a room upstairs.

38 Lydda is near Joppa. When the disciples heard that Peter was in Lydda, they sent two men to him and urged him: "Come to us without delay!"

39 Peter went with them. When he came there, they took him upstairs. There all the widows stood around him; they were crying and showing all the inner and outer garments that Dorcas made while she was still with them.

40 But Peter made them all leave the room.

He knelt and prayed. Then, turning toward the body, he said, "Tabitha, get up!"

She opened her eyes, and seeing Peter, she sat up. **41** He gave her his hand and helped her stand. After he called the believers, especially the widows, he presented her to them alive.

42 The news spread all over Joppa, and many believed in the Lord.

43 Peter stayed in Joppa for many days with Simon, a tanner.

10TH CHAPTER

Cornelius Sees A Vision

1 Now in Caesarea there was a man by the name of Cornelius, a captain in the troop called the Italian Regiment. **2** He was a religious man, who feared God together with all those in his home. He gave much to the poor among the people and was continually praying to God.

3 One day about three in the afternoon he had a vision in which he clearly saw an angel of God come to him and say to him, "Cornelius!"

4 He stared at the angel and was terrified. He asked him, "What is it, Lord?"

The angel answered him, "Your prayers and your gifts to the poor have gone up before God as your memorial-offering. *a* **5** And now send men to Joppa, and get a man named Simon, who is also called Peter. **6** He is a guest of Simon, a tanner, whose house is by the sea."

7 When the angel who was speaking to him had left, he called two of his household servants and a God-fearing soldier, one of those who served him regularly. **8** After explaining everything to them, he sent them to Joppa.

---

c- 36 Luke here uses the Greek word "*Dorcas*" which means "gazelle" (as does the Aramaic name "*Tabitha*").

10 *a* - 4 This refers to a sacrifice which asks God to remember the giver (Lev. 2:2; 24:7) or to a gift which serves as a memorial of the giver (Mk. 14:9).

Peter Sees A Vision

9 The next day about noon, while they were on their way and coming close to the town, Peter went up on the roof to pray. **10** But he became hungry and wanted to eat. While the food was being prepared, he fell into a trance. **11** He saw heaven opened and something like a large linen sheet coming down, being let down by its four corners to the ground. **12** In it were all kinds of four-footed animals, wild animals, reptiles that crawled along the ground, and birds of the air.

13 A voice told him, "Get up, Peter, kill and eat."

14 "Oh, no, Lord!" Peter answered, "I have never eaten anything which is ⌞ceremonially⌟ impure or unclean."*b*

15 A voice spoke to him a second time: "You should not continue to call unclean what God has made clean."

16 This happened three times, then the sheet was quickly taken up to the sky.

17 While Peter was still puzzling over the meaning of the vision he had seen, the men sent by Cornelius asked for Simon's house and came to the gate. **18** They called and asked, "Is Simon, who is called Peter, staying here?" **19** Peter was still thinking about the vision when the Spirit said, "There are three men looking for you. **20** Now get up, go down, and do not hesitate to go with them, for I have sent them."

21 So Peter went down to the men. He said, "I'm the man you are looking for. What brings you here?"

22 They answered, "Cornelius is a captain, a righteous man who fears God, and all the Jewish people speak well of him. He was instructed by a holy angel to summon you to his home and hear what you have to say."

23 Peter asked them to come in, and they were his guests.

Peter And Cornelius

The next day he left with them, and some of the fellow disciples*c* from Joppa went along. **24** The following day he came to Caesarea. Cornelius was expecting them and had called his relatives and close friends together.

25 When Peter was about to go in, Cornelius met him, bowed down at his feet, and worshiped him. **26** But Peter made him stand up. "Get up," he said. "I am only a man."

27 While he was talking with him, he went in and found that many people had gathered. **28** He said to them, "You understand how wrong it is for a Jew to mingle with or visit anyone who is not a Jew. But God has demonstrated to me not to call anyone ⌞ceremonially⌟ impure or unclean.*d* **29** That is why I did not object to coming here when you sent for me. Now I want to know: Why did you send for me?"

30 Cornelius answered, "Three days ago I was at home praying at this very time, at three in the afternoon, when a man in shining clothes stood in front of

---

b- 14 This refers to foods which were impure and unclean because the laws given at Mt. Sinai forbade Jews to eat them.

c- 23 Literally: "brothers."

d- 28 See 10:14 and its accompanying footnote.

me. **31** 'Cornelius,' he said, 'God has heard your prayer and remembers your gifts to the poor. **32** Now send to Joppa and ask Simon, who is called Peter, to come to you. He is a guest in the home of Simon, a tanner, by the sea.' **33** So I sent to you immediately, and it was good of you to come. We are all here before God now, ready to hear everything the Lord has ordered you to say."

34 Then Peter spoke: "Now I truly realize that *God does not favor one person over another*, **35** but that in every nation the one who fears Him and does what is right is acceptable to Him. **36** *He sent His word* to the people of Israel to *bring the news of peace* through Jesus Christ—He is Lord of all! **37** You know what has happened throughout Judea,*e* beginning in Galilee after the baptism that John preached: **38** *God anointed* Jesus from Nazareth *with the* Holy *Spirit* and power, and Jesus went around doing good and healing all who were under the tyranny of the devil, because God was with Him. **39** We have seen everything He did in the land of the Jews and in Jerusalem, and we can tell about it. Men *hanged Him on a cross* and killed Him. **40** But God raised Him on the third day and showed Him to us—**41** not to all the people but to us whom God has chosen to be witnesses and who ate and drank with Him after He rose from the dead. **42** He ordered us to preach to the people and warn them that God has appointed Him to judge the living and the dead. **43** All the prophets testify about Him that through His Name everyone who believes in Him receives forgiveness for his sins."

44 While Peter was still speaking these words, the Holy Spirit came down on all who heard the word. **45** The believers who insisted on circumcision,*f* namely, all those who had come with Peter, were surprised that the gift of the Holy Spirit also had been poured out on people who were Gentiles. **46** For they heard them speaking in other languages*g* and praising God.

47 Then Peter asked, "Surely no one can refuse water and keep them from being baptized, can he? They have received the Holy Spirit just as we did." **48** And he ordered that they be baptized in the Name of Jesus Christ.

Then they asked him to stay several days.

11TH CHAPTER

Peter Defends Himself

1 The apostles and other disciples*a* in all Judea heard: "The Gentiles too have accepted God's word." **2** But when Peter went up to Jerusalem, those who insisted on circumcision disagreed with him. **3** They said, "You went to visit uncircumcised men and you ate with them."

---

34 Deut 10:17   *36 Ps 107:20; 147:18; Is 52:7; Nah 1:15*   *38 Is 61:1*   *39 Deut 21:22,23*

---

e- 37 In a wider sense meaning "Palestine."
f- 45 These were Christians who insisted that circumcision and the keeping of the Old Testament Law were as necessary for salvation as was believing (faith). The same words are used at Acts 11:2 and Galatians 2:12 (cf. also Acts 15:1,5).
g- 46 Or "other tongues"; see 1 Corinthians 12:10 and its accompanying footnote.
11 *a-* 1 Literally: "brothers" (also in vv. 12,29).

4 Then Peter began to explain to them point by point what had happened. He said, **5** "I was in the town of Joppa praying when in a trance I saw a vision: Something like a large linen sheet was coming down. It was lowered by its four corners from the sky, and came down to me. **6** Looking in, I examined it and saw four-footed animals of the earth, wild animals, reptiles, and birds of the air. **7** I also heard a voice telling me, 'Get up, Peter, kill and eat.'

8 "But I answered, 'Oh, no, Lord! Nothing ⌊ceremonially⌋ impure or unclean[b] has ever come into my mouth.'

9 "A voice spoke from heaven a second time, 'You should not continue to call unclean what God has made clean.' **10** This happened three times. Then all of it was pulled up to the sky again.

11 "At that moment three men, sent to me from Caesarea, came to the house we were in. **12** The Spirit told me to go with them without any hesitation. These six fellow disciples went with me, and we came into this man's home.

13 "He told us how he had seen the angel standing in his home and saying, 'Send to Joppa and ask Simon, who is called Peter, to come. **14** What he will tell you will save you and everyone in your home.'

15 "When I began to speak, the Holy Spirit came down on these people as He originally came on us, **16** and I remembered what the Lord had said: 'John baptized with water, but you will be baptized with the Holy Spirit.' **17** Now if God gave them the same gift that He gave us when we believed in the Lord Jesus Christ, who was I—could I stop God?"

18 When the others heard this, they had no further objections. And they praised God, saying, "Then God has given repentance also to the Gentiles so that they will live."

The New Church In Antioch

19 The people who were scattered by the persecution that broke out following Stephen's death[c] went as far as Phoenicia, Cyprus, and Antioch, and they spoke the word only to Jews. **20** But among them were some men from Cyprus and Cyrene who came to Antioch and started talking also to the Greeks, preaching the Good News of the Lord Jesus. **21** The hand of the Lord was with them, and a large number believed and turned to the Lord.

22 The church in Jerusalem heard the news about them, and they sent Barnabas to Antioch. **23** When he came there, he was delighted to see what God's grace [undeserved love] had done, and he urged them all to be deeply determined to be faithful to the Lord. **24** He was a good man, full of the Holy Spirit and faith. And a large crowd was brought to the Lord.

25 Then Barnabas left for Tarsus to look for Saul. **26** He found him and brought him to Antioch. And it turned out that they met with the church for a whole year and taught a large crowd. It was in Antioch that the disciples were first called "Christians."

27 At that time some prophets came from Jerusalem down to Antioch. **28** One of them by the name of Agabus stood up and by the Spirit predicted that there

---

b- 8 See 10:14 and its accompanying footnote.
c- 19 Literally: "scattered from the affliction occurring to Stephen."

would be a severe famine all over the world (it came while Claudius was emperor). **29** Every one of the disciples decided, as he was able, to send relief to the fellow Christians living in Judea. **30** They did this by sending Barnabas and Saul to bring it to the elders.

12TH CHAPTER

An Angel Frees Peter

1 At that time King Herod[a] arrested some members of the church in order to mistreat them. **2** He killed James the brother of John with a sword. **3** When he saw how this pleased the Jews, he arrested Peter too. It happened during the days of Unleavened Bread. **4** When he arrested Peter, he put him in prison and had sixteen soldiers in squads of four to guard him. He wanted to bring him before the people after the Passover. **5** So Peter was kept in prison.

But the church was earnestly praying to God for him. **6** The night before Herod was going to bring him before the people, Peter, bound with two chains, was sleeping between two soldiers, and guards in front of the door were watching the prison.

7 Suddenly an angel of the Lord stood near him, and a light shone in his cell. He struck Peter on his side, woke him, and said, "Get up! Hurry!" Peter's chains dropped from his wrists.

8 The angel told him, "Fasten your belt and tie on your sandals!" He did this. The angel told him, "Put on your garment and follow me."

9 Peter followed him outside, not realizing the angel was actually doing this. He thought he was seeing a vision. **10** They passed through the first guard and the second guard and came to the iron gate leading into the city. It opened by itself before them, and they went outside and up the street. There the angel suddenly left him.

11 When Peter was himself again, he said, "Now I am sure that the Lord sent His angel and rescued me from Herod and from everything the Jewish people were expecting."

Peter Comes To His Friends

12 When he realized what had happened, He went to the home of Mary (the mother of John—the one called Mark). Many had gathered there and were praying. **13** He knocked at the entrance gate, and a maid by the name of Rhoda came to answer. **14** When she recognized Peter's voice, she was so happy that instead of opening the gate she ran inside and reported, "Peter is standing at the gate!"

15 "You're crazy!" they told her. But she insisted it was so. They said, "It is his angel."

16 But Peter kept on knocking. When they opened the gate, they were surprised to see him. **17** He waved his hand to quiet them down and told them how

---

12 *a-* 1 Herod Agrippa I, grandson of Herod the Great who tried to kill the baby Jesus in Bethlehem.

the Lord had taken him out of the prison. "Tell James and the other Christians[b] about this," he said. Then he left and went to another place.

18 In the morning the soldiers were more than a little upset as they asked, "What happened to Peter?" **19** Herod searched for him but did not find him. So he examined the guards and ordered them executed.

Herod Dies

Then Herod left Judea, went down to Caesarea, and stayed there awhile. **20** He had a violent quarrel with the people of Tyre and Sidon. So they came to him in a group. After they had won over Blastus, who was in charge of the king's bedroom, they asked for peace because the king's country provided food for their country.

21 On a day that was set, Herod put on his royal robe, sat on the platform, and made a speech to them. **22** The people shouted, "A god is speaking, not a man!"

23 Immediately an angel of the Lord struck him because he did not give glory to God. He was eaten by worms, and he died.

24 But God's word continued to spread and win many followers.

On Cyprus

25 After Barnabas and Saul delivered the offering for relief, they came back from Jerusalem, bringing with them John, who was also called Mark.

13TH CHAPTER

D. The Gospel to the ends of the earth (13:1–28:31)

1 The following were prophets and teachers in the church at Antioch: Barnabas; Simeon (called Black);[a] Lucius from Cyrene; Manaen, who had been raised with Herod the ruler;[b] and Saul.

2 While they were worshiping the Lord and fasting, the Holy Spirit said, "Set Barnabas and Saul apart for Me to do the work for which I called them." **3** Then they fasted and prayed, laid their hands on them, and let them go.

4 Barnabas and Saul, sent by the Holy Spirit, went down to Seleucia and from there sailed to Cyprus. **5** They came to Salamis and there started to preach God's word in the synagogs of the Jews. They also had John to help them. **6** They went through the whole island as far as Paphos. There they found a Jewish sorcerer and false prophet by the name of Barjesus, **7** who was with the proconsul Sergius Paulus, an intelligent man. He sent for Barnabas and Saul and wanted to hear the word of God. **8** But Elymas the sorcerer (that was what his name meant) opposed them and tried to turn the proconsul away from the faith.

---

b- 17 Literally: "brothers."
13 a- 1 Greek: "*Niger*," meaning "black" or "dark-skinned."
b- 1 Literally: "the tetrarch," one who ruled over one-fourth of the kingdom of Herod the Great.

Aegean Sea

Black Sea

ASIA

PHRYGIA

Ephesus

PISIDIA
Antioch

GALATIA

PAMPHYLIA

Attalia

Perga

Iconium

Lystra

LACAONIA

Derbe

CILICIA

Tarsus

Paphos

Salamis

Antioch

Seleucia

CYPRUS

Mediterranean Sea

SYRIA

Euphrates

Tyre

Caesarea

Damascus

JUDEA

Jerusalem

N

0   miles   100

kms.   150

PAUL'S
FIRST
JOURNEY
Acts 13-15

9 But Saul (also called Paul),*c* filled with the Holy Spirit, looked steadily at him **10** and said, "O you who are full of every treachery and villainy, you son of the devil, enemy of all that is right! Will you not stop twisting *the straight ways of the Lord*? **11** And now the Lord's hand is on you: You will be blind and not see the sun for a while."

At that moment a mist and a darkness came over him, and he went around looking for people to take his hand and lead him. **12** When the proconsul saw what had happened, he believed. The teaching of the Lord amazed him.

At Antioch Near Pisidia

13 Paul and his men took a ship from Paphos and came to Perga in Pamphylia. There John*d* left them and went back to Jerusalem. **14** But they went on from Perga and came to Antioch near Pisidia. On the Sabbath day they went into the synagog and sat down.

15 After the reading of the Law and the Prophets,*e* the synagog leaders sent ₍a message₎ to them, saying: "Fellow Jews,*f* if you have any word of encouragement for the people, speak."

16 Paul stood up and motioned with his hand. He said, "Men of Israel, and those who fear God, listen to me. **17** The God of this people Israel chose our fathers and made them a great people while they lived as strangers in Egypt, and *with supreme power*ᵍ *He led them out of it.* **18** *He put up with them* for about forty years *in the wilderness.* **19** Then *He destroyed seven nations in the land of Canaan and gave their land* to His people *as an inheritance.* **20** He did all this in about four hundred and fifty years. After that He gave them judges until the time of the prophet Samuel.

21 "Then the people demanded a king, and God gave them Saul for forty years. He was a son of Kish, a man of the tribe of Benjamin. **22** But God took the throne away from him again and made David their king. In regard to him He declared: '*I found David* the ₍son₎ of Jesse *to be a man after My own heart, who will do everything I want him to do.*'

23 "As promised, God had a Savior, Jesus, come to Israel from the descendants of David. **24** When He came into the world, John went ahead of Him as a herald to tell all the people of Israel to repent and to be baptized. **25** As John was finishing his work, he said, 'Who do you think I am? I am not the One. No, there is Someone coming after me, and I am not worthy to untie the sandals on His feet.'*h*

---

10 Hos 14:9   **17** Ex 6:1,6; 14:8   **18** Deut 1:31   **19** Deut 7:1; Josh 14:1
22 1 Sam 13:14; Ps 89:20; Is 44:28

---

c- 9 From this point on his name is always given as Paul; this was important since "Paul" was the Greek counterpart of the Hebrew "Saul"; after this Paul moved on to new lands to do his mission work.

d- 13 That is, Mark, also called John Mark.

e- 15 Meaning "After the appropriate readings for the day, chosen from the Law and the Prophets." See initial portion of footnote at Matthew 5:17.

f- 15 Literally: "Men, brothers" (also in vv. 26,38).

g- 17 Literally: "with uplifted arm"; parallel to the Old Testament phrase "with an outstretched arm" (Deut. 5:15).

h - 25 See John 1:26,27.

26 "Fellow Jews, descendants of Abraham, and those among you who fear God, *the message* of this salvation *was sent* to us. **27** The people in Jerusalem and their rulers did not know who Jesus was, and they did not understand the messages of the prophets which were read every Sabbath. And so by condemning Jesus they fulfilled what the prophets had predicted. **28** Although they found no good reason to kill Him, they asked Pilate to have Him executed. **29** When they had done everything that was written about Him, they took Him down from the cross and laid Him in a grave. **30** But God raised Him from the dead, **31** and for many days He was seen by those who had come with Him from Galilee up to Jerusalem. They are now the ones who are testifying to the people about Him. **32** And we are bringing you the Good News: What God promised the fathers **33** He has fulfilled for us, their children, by raising Jesus, as it is written in the second Psalm:

> *You are My Son;*
> *today I have begotten You.*

34 "He raised Him from the dead, never to suffer *decay*, as He said: 'I will give *you what I gave David—mercies that one can trust.*' **35** Another Psalm says: '*You will not let Your Holy One experience decay.*' **36** When *David* had served the people of his time, he by God's will *fell asleep* and was laid away *with his fathers.* His body decayed, **37** but the body of Him whom God raised did not decay.

38 "And so you should know, my fellowmen—that through this Jesus forgiveness of sins is being announced to you, **39** even for all the sins from which you could not be justified [acquitted] by keeping the Law of Moses. Everyone who believes in this Jesus is justified.

40 "Now be careful, or what the prophets said will happen to you:

41   *Look, you scorners, then wonder and perish,*
>   *because I will do something in your days*
>   *that you would never believe if anyone told you!*"

42 As Paul and Barnabas were going out, the people urged them to speak on the same subject the next Sabbath. **43** When the meeting of the synagog broke up, many Jews and others who had come to fear God followed Paul and Barnabas, who talked to them and urged them to continue in God's grace.

44 The next Sabbath almost the whole city was there to hear God's word. **45** When the Jews saw the crowds, they became very jealous. They opposed what Paul said by slandering him.

46 Paul and Barnabas boldly declared: "We had to speak the word of God to you first, but since you reject it and judge yourselves unworthy of everlasting life, see, we are now turning to the Gentiles. **47** For that is what the Lord has ordered us to do:

---

26 Ps 107:20   *33 Ps 2:7*   *34 Is 55:3*   *35 Ps 16:10*   *36 1 Kgs 2:10*   *41 Hab 1:5*

I have made you a light for the Gentiles,
to save people all over the earth."

48 The Gentiles were delighted to hear what the Lord had said and praised
Him for it, and all who had been appointed for everlasting life believed. **49** The
word of the Lord spread throughout the whole region. **50** But the Jews stirred up
the devout women of high social standing and the leaders of the city. They
started a persecution against Paul and Barnabas and drove them out of their
territory.

51 In protest against them Paul and Barnabas shook the dust off their feet and
went to Iconium. **52** Meanwhile the disciples continued to be full of joy and of
the Holy Spirit.

14TH CHAPTER

In Iconium

1 The same thing happened in Iconium. Paul and Barnabas went into the
synagog of the Jews and spoke in such a way that a large crowd of Jews and
Gentiles believed. **2** But the Jews who refused to believe stirred up the Gentiles
and poisoned their minds against the Christians.*a* **3** For a long time Paul and
Barnabas continued to speak boldly, trusting in the Lord, who affirmed their
message of His grace [undeserved love] by letting their hands work miraculous
signs and wonderful proofs. **4** But the people of the town were divided—some
were with the Jews, others with the apostles.

5 But when Gentiles and Jews with their rulers planned to mistreat and stone
them, **6** they found out about it and escaped to Lystra and Derbe, towns of
Lycaonia, and to the surrounding territory. **7** There they kept on preaching the
Gospel.

In Lystra

8 There was a man in Lystra who was sitting, because his feet were crippled.
He had been lame from his birth and had never walked. **9** He was listening to
Paul as he spoke. Paul watched him, and when he saw that the man believed he
would be made well, **10** he said with a loud voice, *"Stand up* straight *on your
feet."* The man jumped up and walked around.

11 The people who saw what Paul had done shouted in the language of Lycaonia, "The gods have become like men and have come down to us." **12** And they
called Barnabas "Zeus" and Paul "Hermes," because he was the one who did
most of the speaking.*b* **13** The priest of the temple of Zeus at the entrance to the

---

47 Is 49:6   *10 Ezek 2:1,2*

---

14 *a-* 2 Literally: "brothers."

b- 12 Literally: "because he was the chief speaker."

town brought bulls and garlands to the gates. He and the crowd wanted to sacrifice.

14 When the apostles Barnabas and Paul heard of it, they tore their clothes and rushed out into the crowd. **15** "Men, why are you doing this?" they shouted. "We too are just human beings, with experiences like yours, and we are preaching the Gospel to turn you away from these worthless idols to the living God, *who made heaven and earth, the sea, and everything in them.* **16** In the ages that have gone by He let all people go their own ways; **17** yet He did not fail to give evidence of Himself by doing good, giving you rain from heaven and crops in their seasons, filling you with food, and your hearts with happiness."*c* **18** Although they said these things, they could hardly keep the crowd from sacrificing to them.

19 But then some Jews came from Antioch and Iconium and won the people over. They stoned Paul and dragged him out of the town, thinking he was dead. **20** But when the disciples came and stood around him, he got up and went into the town.

Derbe And Back Home

The next day he and Barnabas left for Derbe. **21** As they were preaching the Gospel in that town, they won many disciples. Then they went back to Lystra, Iconium, and Antioch, **22** strengthening the disciples and encouraging them to be loyal to the faith, saying, "It is through many troubles that we must enter into the Kingdom of God." **23** They appointed elders*d* for them in each church. And with prayer and fasting they entrusted them to the Lord in whom they believed.

24 When they had gone through Pisidia, they came to Pamphylia. **25** After they had spoken the word in Perga, they went down to Attalia. **26** From there they took a boat to Antioch, where they had been entrusted to God's grace for the work they now had finished. **27** When they arrived, they called the church together and told them everything God had done with them and how He had opened the door of faith for the Gentiles. **28** Then they spent a long time with the disciples.*e*

15TH CHAPTER

Must Gentiles Be Circumcised?

1 Some men came down from Judea and started to teach the Christians:*a* "If you are not circumcised according to the custom taught by Moses, you cannot be saved." **2** When Paul and Barnabas had no small conflict and argument with

---

15 *Ex 20:11*

c- 17 Literally: "filling your hearts with food and happiness."
d- 23 Or "they had elders elected."
e- 28 At this time, late in A.D. 48, Paul probably wrote his letter to the churches of Galatia which he had founded on his First Missionary Journey.
15 *a-* 1 Literally: "brothers" (also in vv. 3,22,23,32,33,36,40).

them, Paul and Barnabas and some of the others were appointed to go up to Jerusalem and see the apostles and elders about this question.

3 The church sent them on their way. As they were going through Phoenicia and Samaria, they told the whole story of how the Gentiles were turning to God, and they brought great joy to all the Christians.

4 When they came to Jerusalem, they were welcomed by the church, the apostles, and the elders. They reported everything that God had done with them. **5** But some believers of the party of the Pharisees stood up and said, "We must circumcise people and order them to keep the Law of Moses."

6 The apostles and elders met to look into this matter. **7** After much discussion Peter stood up and said to them, "Brothers,[b] you know that in the early days God chose me to be the one among you to preach the Gospel to the Gentiles so that they would hear it and believe. **8** And God, who knows our hearts, showed that He approved by giving them the Holy Spirit as He gave Him to us. **9** And by cleansing their hearts by faith He has declared that we are not different from them. **10** Now then, why do you test God by putting a yoke on the neck of the disciples which neither our fathers nor we could bear? **11** No, we believe that we are saved by the grace [undeserved love] of the Lord Jesus, and so are they."

12 The whole crowd was silent. Then they heard Barnabas and Paul tell about all the miraculous signs and wonderful proofs that God had worked among the Gentiles through them.

13 After they finished speaking, James said, "Fellow Christians, listen to me. **14** Simon[c] has explained how God first came to the Gentiles to take from them a people for His Name. **15** This agrees with what the prophets said. It is written:

16 *Afterwards I will come back*
  and rebuild the tent of David
    that has fallen down,
  and its ruins I will rebuild and set up again,
17   *so that the rest of the people,*
    yes, all the Gentiles
    whom I have made My own,[d]
      may search for the Lord.
  The Lord says this and does this
18   *which was made known long ago.*

19 So it is my judgment that we should not trouble these Gentiles who are turning to God, **20** but we should write a letter telling them to keep away from things polluted by idols[e] and from sexual sin and not eat anything strangled or any blood. **21** Since Moses is read in the synagogs every Sabbath, from ancient times he has had those who preach him in every city."

---

16 Jer 12:15   *16-18 Is 45:21; Amos 9:11,12*

---

b- 7 Literally: "Men, brothers" (also in v. 13).

c- 14 Greek: "Simeon"; apparently a name of endearment for Simon Peter among his Jewish associates in Palestine; see 2 Peter 1:1.

d- 17 Literally: "among whom My Name has been called."

e- 20 This refers to anything which is polluted because it has something to do with idols (e.g., food offered to idols).

22 Then the apostles, the elders, and the whole church decided to choose some men of their group and send them with Paul and Barnabas to Antioch: Judas, called Barsabas, and Silas—leaders among the Christians. 23 And they wrote this letter for them to deliver:

> The apostles and elders, your brothers, send greetings to their Gentile fellow Christians in Antioch, Syria, and Cilicia:
>
> 24 Since we heard that some men, coming from us without our instructions, have said things to trouble you, and they continue to upset you, 25 it seemed best to us—since we were all agreed—to choose men and send them to you with our dear Barnabas and Paul, 26 who have devoted their lives to the Name of our Lord Jesus Christ. 27 So we are sending Judas and Silas to talk to you and tell you the same things. 28 The Holy Spirit and we have decided not to burden you more than is necessary: 29 Keep away from food sacrificed to idols, from blood, from the meat of strangled animals, and from sexual sin. Be careful to avoid these and you will be doing right.
>
> Farewell!

30 After they were sent on their way, they came to Antioch where they gathered the congregation together and delivered the letter. 31 The people read it and were delighted with the encouragement it brought them. 32 And Judas and Silas, who also were prophets, said much to encourage and strengthen the Christians.

33 After they had stayed for some time, the Christians let Judas and Silas go back with a friendly greeting to those who had sent them.*f* 35 But Paul and Barnabas stayed in Antioch, and along with many others they taught and preached the word of the Lord.

Paul Takes Silas With Him

36 After a while Paul said to Barnabas, "Let's go back and visit our fellow Christians in every city where we have preached the word of the Lord, and let's see how they are."

37 Barnabas also wanted to take John, called Mark, along with them. 38 But Paul thought it best not to take him, because he had deserted them in Pamphylia and had not gone with them into the work. 39 They disagreed so sharply that they separated, and Barnabas, taking Mark along, sailed away to Cyprus. 40 But Paul chose Silas and, after his fellow Christians entrusted him to the Lord's grace, he departed.

41 He went through Syria and Cilicia, strengthening the churches.

---

f- 33 Many of the older manuscripts and early translations omit verse 34: "But Silas decided to stay there, and Judas departed alone."

16TH CHAPTER

Timothy Joins Paul In Lystra

1 He came down to Derbe, then to Lystra. Here there was a disciple by the name of Timothy. His mother was a Jewish believer, but his father was a Greek. 2 The Christians*a* in Lystra and Iconium spoke well of him. 3 Paul wanted him to go with him, so he took him and circumcised him on account of the Jews who were in those places, because everybody knew his father was a Greek.

4 As they went through the towns, they delivered the decisions that the apostles and elders in Jerusalem had made for the people to keep. 5 So the churches were strengthened in the faith and grew in number more and more every day.

The Call To Europe

6 They went through the region of Phrygia and Galatia, but then the Holy Spirit kept them from speaking the word in the province of Asia. 7 They went down to Mysia and tried to go into Bithynia, but the Spirit of Jesus did not permit it. 8 After they passed through Mysia, they went down to Troas.

9 One night Paul saw a vision—a man from Macedonia was standing there and continued to urge him, "Come over to Macedonia and help us!"

10 As soon as he had seen the vision, we immediately looked for a way to get to Macedonia, since we concluded that God had called us to preach the Gospel to them.

At Philippi

11 After we sailed from Troas, we went straight to Samothrace, the next day to Neapolis, 12 and from there to Philippi, a leading city in that part of Macedonia and a colony of Rome. We stayed in that city for some days.

13 On the Sabbath day we went out of the gate and along the river, where we thought there was a place of prayer. We sat down and began to talk to the women gathered there. 14 There was a woman by the name of Lydia, a dealer in purple goods, who came from the town of Thyatira. She worshiped God. As she listened, the Lord opened her heart to accept what Paul said. 15 When she and her family were baptized, she urged us, "If you are convinced that I believe in the Lord, come and stay at my home." And she made us come.

16 One day when we were going to the place of prayer, we met a slave girl with a spirit of fortunetelling in her; she made much money for her owners by telling fortunes. 17 She would follow Paul and us and cry out, "These men are servants of the Most High God and are telling you how to be saved." 18 She kept on doing this for many days until Paul, very much annoyed, turned to the spirit and said, "In the Name of Jesus Christ I command you to go out of her!"

Then and there the spirit went out of her. 19 When her owners realized that

---

16 *a*- 2 Literally: "brothers" (also in v. 40).

MACEDONIA

Danube

Thessalonica
Apollonia
Berea
Amphipolis
GREECE
Philippi
Neapolis

Samo-
thrace
THRACE

Black Sea

Corinth
Cenchrae
Athens
Troas

MYSIA

BITHYNIA

Ephesus

ASIA
PHRYGIA
GALATIA

PONTUS

CRETE

Antioch
Lystra
Iconium

Mediterranean Sea

Derbe

CILICIA

CYPRUS
Antioch

Euphrates

Alexandria

SYRIA

EGYPT

Caesarea

Nile
Jerusalem

PAUL'S SECOND JOURNEY

Acts 16-18

0   miles   150

kms.   200

their hope of making money was gone, they grabbed Paul and Silas. Then they dragged them before the officers in the marketplace, **20** and brought them before the highest Roman officials. They said, "These men are stirring up a lot of trouble in our city. They are Jews, **21** and they are teaching customs that we as Romans are not allowed to adopt or practice."

22 The crowd also joined in attacking them. Then the officials tore the clothes off Paul and Silas and ordered them beaten with rods. **23** After striking them many times, the men put them in prison and ordered the jailer to keep a close watch on them. **24** Since he received such a strict order, the jailer put them into the innermost cell and fastened their feet in the stocks.

25 About midnight Paul and Silas were praying and singing hymns of praise to God, and the other prisoners were listening to them. **26** Suddenly the earth quaked so violently that the foundations of the prison were shaken, all the doors immediately flew open, and everyone's chains were unfastened.

27 The jailer woke up and saw the prison doors open. Thinking the prisoners had escaped, he drew his sword and was about to kill himself. **28** But Paul shouted out in a loud voice, "Don't harm yourself! We are all here!"

29 The jailer asked for lights, rushed in, and fell down trembling before Paul and Silas. **30** Then he took them outside and asked, "Sirs, what do I have to do to be saved?"

31 They answered, "Believe in the Lord Jesus and you and your family will be saved." **32** They spoke the Lord's word to him and everyone in his home.

33 At that hour of the night he took them with him and washed their wounds. And he and all who were with him were baptized immediately. **34** He took them up into his home and gave them a meal. He and everyone in his home were very happy to have found faith in God.

35 In the morning the officials sent attendants and said, "Let those men go."

36 The jailer reported the message to Paul. He said, "The officials sent word to let you go. Come out now and *go in peace.*"

37 But Paul told them, "They have beaten us publicly without a trial, even though we are Roman citizens, and have thrown us into prison. And now they are trying to release us secretly? I should say not! Rather, let them come themselves and escort us out."

38 The attendants reported to the officials what Paul said. When they heard that Paul and Silas were Roman citizens, they were frightened. **39** So they came; and as they escorted them out they pleaded with them, asking them to leave the city.

40 After Paul and Silas left the prison,*ᵇ* they went to Lydia, saw the Christians and encouraged them, and then left.

---

36 Judg 18:6

---

b- 40 Literally: "Having departed from the prison."

17TH CHAPTER

In Thessalonica

1 Paul and Silas traveled through Amphipolis and Apollonia and came to Thessalonica. Here the Jews had a synagog. **2** Paul went in as usual and on three Sabbaths had discussions with them on the basis of the Scriptures. **3** He explained and showed them that the Christ [Messiah] had to suffer and rise from the dead. ⌊He said,⌋ "The One who is the Christ is this Jesus whom I am telling you about."

4 Some of the Jews were persuaded and joined Paul and Silas, as did a large crowd of the God-fearing Greeks and more than a few of the wives of the leaders.[a]

5 Then the Jews became jealous, took some wicked men from the marketplace, formed a mob, and started a riot in the city. When they arrived at Jason's home, they searched for Paul and Silas in order to bring them out to the people. **6** When they did not find them, they dragged Jason and some other Christians[b] before the city officials, shouting, "Those men who have made trouble all over the world are now here **7** and are Jason's guests. They are all going against Caesar's decrees by saying that there is another King—Jesus!"

8 Hearing this, the crowd and the officials were upset. **9** But after they made Jason and the others post bond, they let them go.

10 Immediately that night the Christians sent Paul and Silas away to Berea.

At Berea

When they came there, they went into the synagog of the Jews. **11** These people were more noble than those at Thessalonica—they were very eager to receive the word, and every day they studied the Scriptures to see if those things were so. **12** And many of them believed, and more than a few of them were prominent Greeks, both women and men.

13 But when the Jews at Thessalonica found out that Paul was preaching God's word also in Berea, they came there to stir up trouble among the people. **14** Immediately the Christians sent Paul away to the sea, but Silas and Timothy stayed there.

In Athens

15 Those who escorted Paul took him all the way to Athens. When they left, they took instructions to Silas and Timothy to come to him as soon as possible.

16 While Paul was waiting for them in Athens, he was stirred inwardly when he saw that the city was full of idols. **17** He had discussions in the synagog with Jews and others who feared God, and in the marketplace every day with those who happened to be there. **18** Some Epicurean and Stoic philosophers also debated with him, but some asked, "What is this fellow with his scraps of learn-

---

17 *a-* 4 Or "the wives of the prominent men."
b- 6 Literally: "brothers" (also in vv. 10,14).

ing^c trying to say?" Others said, "He seems to be telling about foreign gods" —because he was preaching the Gospel [Good News] of Jesus and the resurrection.

19 Then they took him and brought him before the court of Mars' Hill [Areopagus] and asked, "Could we know, what is this new thing you teach? **20** For you bring some things that sound strange to our ears, and we want to know what they mean."

21 Now everyone in Athens, also the visitors staying there, did nothing else other than spend their time telling or hearing something new.

22 Paul stood before the court of Mars' Hill and said, "Men of Athens, I see how very religious you are in every way. **23** As I went through your city and carefully observed the things you worship, I found an altar with the inscription: TO AN UNKNOWN GOD. Now I am telling you about what you worship, even though you don't know ˌanything about itˌ. **24** *The God who made* the world and everything in it is the Lord of *heaven and earth*. He does not live in temples made by human hands, **25** and He is not served by human hands as if He needed anything. He Himself *gives* everyone life and breath and everything ˌthey haveˌ. **26** From one man^d He made every nation of mankind to live all over the earth. He set the times allotted to them and the boundaries within which they live, **27** that they should look for God and perhaps feel their way to Him and find Him. He is never far from any one of us, **28** because in Him we live and move and exist; as some of your poets^e have said, 'You see, we also are His children.' **29** Now, if we are God's children,^f we should not think that God is like gold, silver, or stone, an image formed by the art and imagination of a human being.

30 "While God overlooked the times when people were ignorant, He now tells all of them everywhere to repent of their sins, **31** because He has set a Day when *He is going to judge the world with justice*, by a Man whom He has appointed to do this. And by raising Him from the dead He has given everyone a good reason to believe."

32 When they heard about a resurrection of the dead, some started to mock, while others said, "We will hear you again about this."

33 And so Paul left the meeting. **34** Some men joined him and believed. Among them were Dionysius, a member of the court, and a woman by the name of Damaris, and some others with them.

18TH CHAPTER

In Corinth

1 After that he left Athens and came to Corinth. **2** There he found a Jew by

---

24,25 Is 42:5   31 Ps 9:8; 96:13; 98:9

---

c- 18 Literally: "this seed-picker," an expression used to refer to a babbler.
d- 26 Many of the older manuscripts and early translations read: "From one blood."
e- 28 Aratus and Cleanthes wrote this about 270 B.C.
f- 29 Literally: "offspring" or "descendants" (also in v. 28).

the name of Aquila, born in Pontus, and his wife Priscilla. They had recently come from Italy because Claudius had ordered all Jews to leave Rome.[a] Paul went to them; 3 and because they made tents for a living just as he did, he stayed with them and they worked together.

4 Every Sabbath he would discuss ⌊Scripture⌋ in the synagog and try to win Jews and Greeks. 5 But when Silas and Timothy came down from Macedonia, Paul devoted himself entirely to teaching the word, solemnly assuring the Jews, "Jesus is the Christ [Messiah]!"[b] 6 But they opposed him and slandered him. In protest he shook the dust from his clothes and told them, "Your blood be on your own heads. I am innocent. From now on I will go to the Gentiles."

7 Then he left the place and went to the home of a man by the name of Titius Justus, who worshiped God. His house was right beside the synagog. 8 Now Crispus the synagog leader and all who were in his home believed in the Lord. And many other people in Corinth who heard Paul believed and were baptized.

9 One night the Lord spoke to Paul in a vision, *"Stop being afraid! But speak, and do not be silent—*10 *I am with you, and no one will attack you to harm you,* because I have many people in this city."

11 He stayed there a year and six months and taught the word of God among them.[c]

12 But when Gallio was proconsul of Greece, the Jews united in an attack on Paul and brought him into court. 13 They said, "This man is persuading people to worship God in ways that are against the Law."

14 Just as Paul was going to answer, Gallio said to the Jews, "If this were a crime or vicious wrong, it would be only fair that I listen to you Jews. 15 But since we have questions here about words, names, and your own Law, see to it yourselves. I do not want to be a judge of those things." 16 And he drove them out of his court.

17 Then all of them took Sosthenes the synagog leader and beat him in front of the court. But Gallio paid no attention to it.

Home

18 After staying there quite a while longer, Paul said good-bye to the Christians.[d] Priscilla and Aquila went with him. At Cenchrea he had his hair cut, since he had been under a vow. They took a boat for Syria 19 and came to Ephesus, where Paul left Priscilla and Aquila. There he went into the synagog and had a discussion with the Jews. 20 They asked him to stay longer, but he refused. 21 As he said good-bye to them, he told them, "I will come back to you if God wants me to."

He sailed from Ephesus 22 and landed at Caesarea. He went up,[e] greeted the church, and went down to Antioch.

9,10 Ex 3:12; Josh 1:5; Is 41:10; 43:5; Jer 1:8

---

18 *a-* 2 This decree was issued in A.D. 49.
  b- 5 See THE EARLIEST CHRISTIAN CREEDS on page 557.
  c- 11 Paul wrote the two letters to the Thessalonians in A.D. 50 from Corinth.
  d- 18 Literally: "brothers" (also in v. 27).
  e- 22 That is, he went to Jerusalem, which lay at a higher altitude.

Apollos

23 After staying there for some time, Paul left and went from place to place through the Galatian country and through Phrygia, strengthening all the disciples.

24 A Jew by the name of Apollos, who was born in Alexandria, came to Ephesus. He was a learned*f* man and mighty in the Scriptures. **25** After he had been instructed in the Lord's way, he spoke with a glowing enthusiasm and taught correctly about Jesus but knew only the baptism of John. **26** He started to speak boldly in the synagog. When Priscilla and Aquila heard him, they took him with them and explained God's way to him more accurately.

27 As he wanted to cross over to Greece, the Christians wrote to the disciples there urging them to welcome him. When he arrived, he gave much help to those who by God's grace [undeserved love] were now believers. **28** Publicly and vigorously he proved that the Jews were wrong, by showing from the Scriptures that Jesus is the Christ [Messiah].

19TH CHAPTER

Paul In Ephesus

1 While Apollos was in Corinth, Paul traveled over the mountainous country to get to Ephesus. He met some disciples there **2** and asked them, "Did you receive the Holy Spirit when you became believers?"

"No," they answered him, "we have not even heard that there is a Holy Spirit."

3 He asked them, "Into what then were you baptized?"

"Into John's baptism," they answered.

4 Paul said, "John baptized with the baptism of repentance and told the people to believe in the One coming after him, that is, in Jesus."

5 When they heard this, they were baptized into the Name of the Lord Jesus. **6** And when Paul laid his hands on them, the Holy Spirit came on them, and they started to talk in other languages*a* and to speak God's word.*b* **7** There were about twelve men in the group.

8 He went into the synagog and spoke there boldly for three months, discussing and trying to convince people about God's Kingdom. **9** When some became stubborn, refused to believe, and slandered the Christian religion*c* before the crowd, he left them, took his disciples away from them, and had daily discussions in the lecture hall of Tyrannus. **10** This went on for two years so that all who lived in the province of Asia, Jews and Greeks, heard the word of the Lord.

11 God worked extraordinary miracles by Paul's hands. **12** When handkerchiefs and aprons that had touched his skin were taken to the sick, their sicknesses left them, and the evil spirits went out of them.

---

f- 24 Or "an eloquent."

19 *a*- 6 Or "other tongues"; see 1 Corinthians 12:10 and its accompanying footnote.

  b- 6 Literally: "and prophesied."

  c- 9 Literally: "slandered the Way."

MACEDONIA

Danube

Berea

Thessalonica

Philippi

Black Sea

Corinth

Troas

Assos

Mitylene

GREECE

Chios

ASIA

Samos

Ephesus

PHRYGIA

Miletus

Cos

GALATIA

CRETE

Antioch

Rhodes

Patara

Iconium

Lystra

Mediterranean Sea

Derbe

CILICIA

CYPRUS

Antioch

Alexandria

SYRIA

Ptolemais

Tyre

Caesarea

EGYPT

Jerusalem

Nile

0   miles   150

kms.   200

PAUL'S
THIRD
JOURNEY
Acts 19-23

13 Some Jews who went around and drove out evil spirits tried to use the Name of the Lord Jesus over those who had evil spirits. They said, "I order you ⎡to come out⎤ by that Jesus whom Paul preaches." **14** Seven sons of Sceva, a Jewish ruling priest, were doing this.

15 But the evil spirit answered them, "I know Jesus, and I know Paul, but who are you?" **16** Then the man with the evil spirit jumped on them, got the better of them, and overpowered them all so that they fled naked and bruised out of that house.

17 All the Jews and Greeks living in Ephesus heard about it. They were all frightened and started to think very highly of the Name of the Lord Jesus. **18** Many of those who believed came and confessed, admitting their former practices. **19** Many of those who had practiced magic gathered their books and burned them in front of everybody. They added up the cost of these books and found they were worth 50,000 denarii. *d* **20** In that way the word of the Lord grew mightily and triumphed. *e*

21 After all these things had happened, Paul decided to go through Macedonia and Greece and then to Jerusalem. He said, "After I have been there, I must also see Rome." **22** But he sent two of his helpers, Timothy and Erastus, to Macedonia, while he himself stayed in the province of Asia a while longer.

The Riot

23 During that time there was more than a small disturbance about the Christian religion. *f*

24 A silversmith by the name of Demetrius provided a large income for the skilled workers by making silver shrines of Artemis. **25** He called a meeting of these and others who did similar work. "Men," he said, "you know that we are earning a fine income from this business, **26** and you see and hear that this Paul has won and taken away a large crowd, not only in Ephesus but almost all over the province of Asia by telling them, 'Gods made by human hands are not gods.' **27** There is a danger that people will not only reject our line of business but will also think nothing of the temple of the great goddess Artemis, and then she whom all Asia and the world worship will be robbed of her glory."

28 When they heard this, they became furious and they began shouting, "Great is Artemis of the Ephesians!" **29** The confusion spread all over the city. And they all rushed into the theater together, dragging with them Gaius and Aristarchus, Paul's fellow travelers from Macedonia.

30 Paul wanted to go into the crowd, but the disciples would not let him. **31** Even some officials of the province of Asia who were his friends sent men to him and urged him not to risk going into the theater.

---

d- 19 "*Drachma*," a Greek word for denarius; a denarius was one day's pay. See MONEY, WEIGHTS, and MEASURES on page 328.

e- 20 Paul wrote his first letter to the Corinthians from Ephesus c. A.D. 55. Some scholars believe that he also wrote the four "captivity letters" or "prison epistles" from Ephesus, namely, *Philippians, Philemon, Colossians*, and *Ephesians*. Others, however, feel that these particular letters were written during Paul's Roman imprisonment at the end of *Acts* in the early 60's A.D.

f- 23 Literally: "concerning the Way."

32 Some were shouting one thing, some another, because the crowd was confused, and most of them did not know why they had come together. **33** Then the Jews pushed Alexander to the front, and some of the crowd told him what to do. Alexander waved his hand to quiet them and wanted to make a defense before the people. **34** But when they found out he was a Jew, they all started to shout in unison and kept it up for about two hours, "Great is Artemis of the Ephesians!"

35 After the city clerk had quieted the crowd, he spoke: "Men of Ephesus, who in the world does not know that this city of the Ephesians is the keeper of the temple of the great Artemis and of the statue that fell down ˌfrom Zeusˌ? **36** Since no one can deny this, you must be quiet and not do anything reckless. **37** For the men you brought here do not rob temples or insult our goddess. **38** Now if Demetrius and his workers have something against anyone, we have special days and proconsuls to hold court; there they should accuse one another. **39** And if you want anything else, it must be settled in a legal meeting. **40** Indeed, we are in danger of being accused of a riot today for which there is no good reason. We will not be able to explain this mob." **41** After saying this, he dismissed the assembly.

20TH CHAPTER

1 When the uproar had died down, Paul sent for the disciples, encouraged them, and after saying good-bye to them left to go to Macedonia.ᵃ **2** He went through those parts of the country and spoke many words of encouragement to the people, and then he went to Greece **3** and stayed there three months.ᵇ

At Troas

Just as Paul was going to sail for Syria, the Jews plotted against him, so he decided to go back through Macedonia. **4** Sopater ˌthe sonˌ of Pyrrhus from Berea went with him, as well as Aristarchus and Secundus from Thessalonica; and Gaius from Derbe, and Timothy; also Tychicus and Trophimus from the province of Asia; **5** they went ahead and were waiting for us in Troas. **6** After the days of Unleavened Bread we sailed from Philippi and in five days came to them in Troas and stayed there seven days.

7 On Sunday, when we met for a meal, Paul spoke to the people. Since he intended to leave the next day, he went on talking until midnight. **8** There were many lamps in the upstairs room where we were meeting.

9 A young man by the name of Eutychus, sitting in the window, was dropping off into a deep sleep as Paul talked on and on. Finally, overcome by sleep, he fell down from the third story and was picked up dead. **10** But Paul went down, lay on him, and took him into his arms. "Don't be alarmed any longer," he said. "He's alive!" **11** Then he went upstairs again, broke the bread, and ate. And after a long talk that lasted until sunrise, he left.

---

20 *a-* 1 Paul wrote his second letter to the Corinthians from Macedonia about A.D. 55.
   b- 3 Paul wrote his letter to the Romans from Corinth in the winter of A.D. 55-56.

12 The people took the boy away alive and were very much comforted.

From Troas To Miletus

13 We went ahead to the boat and sailed to Assos. There we were going to take Paul on board the boat; he had arranged it that way, since he had planned to go there on foot. 14 When we met him in Assos, we took him on board and went on to Mitylene. 15 We sailed from there and on the following day came opposite Chios. The next day we crossed over to Samos and on the next day came to Miletus. 16 Paul had decided to sail past Ephesus to avoid spending time in the province of Asia; he was in a hurry to get to Jerusalem, if possible, for the day of Pentecost.

With The Pastors Of Ephesus

17 From Miletus he sent men to Ephesus and asked the pastors *c* of the church to come to him. 18 When they came to him, he said to them: "You know how I lived with you all the time from the first day I came into the province of Asia; 19 how I served the Lord very humbly, with tears, and in trials which I endured as the Jews plotted against me; 20 how I did not shrink from telling you anything that would help you or from teaching you publicly and from house to house; 21 and how I earnestly warned Jews and Greeks to turn from sin to God and to believe in our Lord Jesus. 22 And now, you see, the Spirit compels me to go to Jerusalem. I do not know what will happen to me there, 23 except that in every town the Holy Spirit keeps warning me that chains and troubles are waiting for me. 24 However, I do not count my life worth anything. I just want to finish running my race and carrying out the ministry that the Lord Jesus entrusted to me, testifying to the Gospel of the grace [undeserved love] of God.

25 "I went around among you preaching the Kingdom, and now I know that none of you will see me again. 26 That is why I declare to you today that I am innocent of the blood of any of you, 27 because I did not shrink from telling you the whole plan of God.

28 "Take care of yourselves and the whole *flock* among whom the Holy Spirit has made you overseers. *d* You are to shepherd *the church of God which He bought* with His own blood. 29 I know that when I am gone fierce wolves will come in among you and not spare the flock. 30 And even some of your own men will stand up and say things which are perversions of the truth in order to draw away disciples after themselves. 31 So be on your guard! Remember that for three years, day and night, it was with tears that I continued to warn each and every one of you. *e* 32 And now I entrust you to God and to the word of His grace, which can build you up and give you *the inheritance shared by all who are made holy.*

---

28 Ps 74:1,2   32 Deut 33:3,4

---

c- 17 Literally: "elders"; see footnote ahead at 1 Timothy 4:14.
d- 28 Or "bishops" or "pastors"; see footnote ahead at Philippians 1:1.
e- 31 Literally: "I did not stop warning every one of you with tears."

33 "I did not want anyone's silver or gold or clothes. **34** You yourselves know that these hands worked for my own needs and for ⌊the needs of⌋ the men who were with me. **35** In every way I showed you that by this kind of hard work we should help the weak and remember the words that the Lord Jesus Himself said: 'It is more blessed to give than to receive.' "

36 When he had said this, he knelt down with all of them and prayed. **37** They wept very much, put their arms around Paul, and kissed him. **38** It hurt them most of all that he had said they would not see him again. Then they took him to the ship.

21ST CHAPTER

At Tyre

1 When we had broken away from them, we sailed and followed a straight course to Cos and the next day to Rhodes and from there to Patara. **2** We found a ship going across to Phoenicia, went on board, and sailed. **3** We came in sight of Cyprus, and leaving it on our left, sailed on to Syria and landed at Tyre because there the ship unloaded its cargo.

4 We looked up the disciples and stayed there seven days. By the Spirit they told Paul not to go up to Jerusalem. **5** When our time was up, we started on our way. All of them with their wives and children accompanied us out of the city. There we knelt on the beach and prayed **6** and said good-bye to one another. Then we went on board the ship, and they went back home.

At Caesarea

7 We continued our sailing, going from Tyre to Ptolemais. There we greeted our fellow Christians*a* and spent a day with them. **8** The next day we left and came to Caesarea. We went into the home of Philip the evangelist, one of the seven, and stayed with him. **9** He had four unmarried daughters who prophesied.

10 While we were staying there longer than we had expected, a prophet by the name of Agabus came down from Judea. **11** He came to us, took Paul's belt, tied his own feet and hands, and said, "The Holy Spirit says, 'This is how the Jews in Jerusalem will tie the man to whom this belt belongs and hand him over to the Gentiles.' "

12 When we heard this, we and those living there urged him not to go up to Jerusalem.

13 Then Paul answered, "What are you doing—crying and breaking my heart? For I am ready not only to be bound but even to die in Jerusalem for the Name of the Lord Jesus."

14 When he would not be persuaded, we were silent and could only say, "May the Lord's will be done."

---

21 *a-* 7 Literally: "brothers" (also in v. 17).

In Jerusalem

15 After those days we got ready and went up to Jerusalem. **16** Some of the disciples from Caesarea came with us and took us to the home of Mnason to be his guests. He was from Cyprus and was one of the first disciples. **17** When we came to Jerusalem, our fellow Christians gave us a warm welcome.

18 The next day we went with Paul to James, and all the elders were there. **19** After greeting them, Paul related in order each of the things which God had done among the Gentiles through his ministry.

20 When they heard about it, they praised God. They told him, "You see, brother, how many tens of thousands among the Jews now believe, and all are zealous for the Law. **21** They have been told that you teach all the Jews living among the Gentiles to turn away from Moses, telling them not to circumcise their children or follow the customs. **22** What should we do about it? They will certainly hear that you have come. **23** So do what we tell you. We have four men who are under a vow. **24** Take them, purify yourself with them, and pay their expenses so that they may *shave their heads*. Then everybody will know that there is no truth in what they have been told about you, but that you yourself are also living in a way which keeps the Law. **25** About the Gentiles who now believe, we wrote in a letter that we decided they should keep away from food sacrificed to idols, from blood, from the meat of strangled animals, and from sexual sin."

26 Then Paul took the men and the next day purified himself with them and went to the Temple to announce the time *when* the purification would be *over* and the sacrifice would be offered for each of them.

27 When the seven days were almost over, the Jews from the province of Asia, seeing him in the Temple, stirred up the whole crowd. They grabbed him, **28** shouting, "Men of Israel, help! This is the man who in teaching all people everywhere turns them against our people, the Law, and this place. And now he has even brought Greeks into the Temple and made this sacred place[b] unclean." **29** They had seen Trophimus from Ephesus with him in the city and thought Paul had taken him into the Temple.

30 The whole city was aroused and the people rushed together. They took Paul, dragged him out of the Temple, and immediately the doors were shut.

31 They were trying to kill him when it was reported to the tribune who was in charge of about 600 soldiers:[c] "All Jerusalem is stirred up!" **32** Immediately he took soldiers and captains and ran down to them. When they saw the tribune and the soldiers, they stopped hitting Paul. **33** Then the tribune went to him, arrested him, and ordered him bound with two chains.

He asked who he was and what he had done. **34** Some in the crowd shouted this and some that. There was such a noisy confusion that he could not get the facts, so he ordered Paul to be taken to the barracks. **35** When Paul came to the stairs, the crowd was so violent the soldiers had to carry him. **36** The mob was right behind them and kept shouting, "Away with him!"

---

24 Num 6:9,18,19   *26 Num 6:13*

---

b - 28 See Diagram #1 on page 430.
c - 31 Literally: "the chiliarch of the cohort."

Paul Defends Himself

37 Just as he was going to be taken into the barracks, Paul asked the tribune, "May I say something to you?"

"Can you speak Greek?" he asked. 38 "Aren't you the Egyptian who some time ago stirred up four thousand dagger-men to rebel and follow him into the wilderness?"

39 Paul answered, "I am a Jew from Tarsus in Cilicia, a citizen of an important city. Now I am asking you, let me talk to the people."

40 When the tribune permitted him to do so, Paul stood on the stairs and motioned with his hand to quiet the people. When there was a hush all around, he spoke to them in Aramaic:*d*

22ND CHAPTER

1 "Brothers*a* and fathers, listen as I now defend myself before you."

2 When they heard him call to them in Aramaic, they quieted down still more.

3 Then he said: "I am a Jew, born in Tarsus in Cilicia and raised in this city, trained at the feet of Gamaliel in the strict ways of the Law of our fathers, as zealous for God as all of you are today. 4 I hunted to their death those who belong to the Christian religion,*b* tying up men and women and putting them in prisons, 5 as the high priest and the whole council of elders can testify about me. From them I received letters against the Christians*c* in Damascus and was going there to bind those who were there and bring them to Jerusalem to be punished. 6 But as I was on my way and coming near Damascus about noon, suddenly a bright light from heaven flashed around me. 7 I fell to the ground and heard a voice asking me, 'Saul! Saul! Why are you persecuting Me?'

8 "I asked, 'Who are You, Lord?'

" 'I am Jesus from Nazareth,' He told me, 'whom you are persecuting.'

9 "The men who were with me saw the light but did not understand the voice of Him who was speaking to me.

10 "Then I asked, 'What should I do, Lord?'

"The Lord told me, 'Get up, go into Damascus, and there you will be told everything you are ordered to do.'

11 "That light was so bright that I could not see anything. So the men who were with me took me by the hand and led me into Damascus.

12 "Ananias was there, a man who feared God according to the Law, and all the Jews living there spoke well of him. 13 He came to me and stood by me. 'Brother Saul,' he said to me, 'receive your sight!' At that very moment I could see him.

---

d- 40 Literally: "Hebrew"; Aramaic was the related Semitic language that Jesus and His fellow Jews ordinarily spoke in New Testament times. See also 22:2; 26:14; John 5:2 and its accompanying footnote.

22 *a*- 1 Literally: "Men, brothers."

   b- 4 Literally: "I persecuted this Way to their death . . . ."

   c- 5 Literally: "brothers."

14 "He said, 'The God of our fathers chose you to know what He wants, to see the Righteous One and hear Him speak to you, 15 because you must be His witness and tell all people what you have seen and heard. 16 And now, what are you waiting for? Get up, and calling on His Name, be baptized and have your sins washed away.'

17 "I came back to Jerusalem and while I was praying in the Temple, I fell into a trance 18 and saw Him. 'Hurry,' He told me, 'and get out of Jerusalem quickly because they will not accept your testimony about Me.'

19 " 'Lord,' I said, 'they know I went from synagog to synagog to imprison and beat those who believe in You. 20 And when the blood of Your witness*d* Stephen was being poured out, I myself was standing by, approving, and guarding the clothes of those who were murdering him.'

21 " 'Go,' He told me. 'I will send you far away to the Gentiles.' "

22 They listened to him until he said that. Then they shouted, "Rid the world of such a person! He's not fit to live!"

23 While they were yelling, tossing their clothes around, and throwing dust in the air, 24 the tribune ordered Paul to be taken into the barracks and told his men to examine him by whipping him. He wanted to find out why the people were yelling at him like this. 25 But when his men had stretched him out with the straps, Paul asked the captain standing near, "Is it right for you to whip a Roman citizen who has not been condemned?"

26 When the captain heard this, he went and told the tribune about it. He asked, "What are you going to do? This man is a Roman citizen."

27 The tribune went and asked Paul, "Tell me, are you a Roman citizen?"

"Yes," he said.

28 The tribune declared, "I had to pay a lot of money to be a citizen."

"But I was born a citizen," Paul said.

29 Immediately those who were going to examine him withdrew from him. When the tribune found out that Paul was a Roman citizen, he was frightened because he had tied him up.

Paul Before The Council

30 The next day, since he wanted to find out exactly what the Jews were accusing Paul of, he released him and ordered the high priests and the whole Jewish council [Sanhedrin] to meet. Then he brought Paul down and had him stand before them.

23RD CHAPTER

1 Paul fixed his eyes on the Jewish council and said, "Fellow Jews,*a* I have lived before God with a very good conscience to this very day."

2 The high priest Ananias ordered the men standing near him to strike him on the mouth. 3 Then Paul said to him, "God is going to strike you, you

---

d- 20 The Greek word for "witness" is "*martyros*" from which we get our word "martyr."
23 *a*- 1 Literally: "Men, brothers" (also in v. 6).

whitewashed wall! Do you sit there to judge me according to the Law and yet break the Law by ordering them to strike me?"

4 The men standing near him asked, "Do you insult God's high priest?"

5 Paul answered, "Fellow Jews, [b] I did not know that he is the high priest. For it is written: *'Do not speak evil of a ruler of your people.'* "

6 When Paul saw that some of them were Sadducees and others Pharisees, he called out in the council, "Fellow Jews, I am a Pharisee ˌandˏ a son of Pharisees. I am on trial for my hope that the dead will rise."

7 When he said that, the Pharisees and Sadducees started to quarrel, and the men in the meeting were divided. **8** The Sadducees say that the dead do not rise and that there is no angel or spirit, while the Pharisees believe in all these things. **9** There was some loud shouting and some of the scribes who belonged to the party of the Pharisees stood up and argued vehemently: "We find nothing wrong with this man. Suppose a spirit spoke to him, or an angel—."

10 The quarrel was getting violent, and the tribune was afraid they would tear Paul to pieces. So he ordered the soldiers to go down, take him away from them by force, and bring him to the soldiers' quarters.

11 That night the Lord stood near him and said, "Keep up your courage! As you have told the truth about Me in Jerusalem, so you must also tell it in Rome."

The Plot To Kill Paul

12 In the morning the Jews plotted together and vowed that God should punish them if they ate or drank anything before they had killed Paul. **13** There were more than forty who swore to carry out this plot.

14 They went to the high priests and elders and said, "We have vowed that God should punish us if we taste any food before we have killed Paul. **15** Now then, you and the council tell the tribune to bring him down to you as if you meant to obtain more exact information about him. We are ready to kill him before he gets to you."

16 But the son of Paul's sister heard about the ambush. He came and entered the barracks and told Paul. **17** Then Paul called one of the captains and told him, "Take this young man to the tribune. He has something to tell him."

18 He took him to the tribune and said, "The prisoner Paul called me and asked me to bring this young man to you. He has something to tell you."

19 The tribune took him by the arm and stepping aside to be alone with him, he asked him, "What do you have to tell me?"

20 He answered, "The Jews have agreed to ask you to bring Paul down to the Jewish council [Sanhedrin] tomorrow as if they meant to obtain more information about him. **21** Now, do not listen to them. For more than forty of them are planning to ambush him. They have vowed that God should punish them if they eat or drink anything before they have murdered him. They are ready now, just waiting for your promise ˌto bring Paulˏ."

---

5 Ex 22:28

b- 5 Literally: "Brothers."

22 The tribune dismissed the young man. "Do not tell anyone that you reported this to me," he ordered.

23 Then he called two of his captains and said, "Get two hundred soldiers to go to Caesarea, and seventy on horses, and two hundred with spears, and have them ready to start at nine tonight." **24** They were also to provide animals for Paul to ride on and so to take him safely to Governor Felix. **25** The tribune wrote a letter with this message:

26 Claudius Lysias sends greetings to the excellent Governor Felix:

27 The Jews had seized this man and were going to murder him, but when I found out that he was a Roman citizen, I came with the soldiers and rescued him. **28** I wanted to know what they had against him; so I took him down to their Jewish council [Sanhedrin] **29** and found their accusations had to do with questions about their Law, but there was none for which he deserved to die or be in chains. **30** Since I am informed that they are plotting against the man, I am quickly sending him to you and also ordering his accusers to state before you what they have against him.

31 So the foot soldiers, as they were ordered, took Paul and brought him to Antipatris during the night. **32** The next day they returned to their barracks, letting the men on horses ride on with him. **33** When these came to Caesarea, they delivered the letter to the governor and handed Paul over to him.

34 After he read the letter, he asked which province he was from and found out he was from Cilicia. **35** He said, "I will hear your case when your accusers come." And he ordered him to be kept in Herod's palace. *c*

24TH CHAPTER

Before Felix

1 Five days later the high priest Ananias came down with some elders and Tertullus, an attorney, and they reported to the governor what they had against Paul.

2 When Paul had been called, Tertullus began to accuse him, saying, "Excellent Felix, you have brought us much peace, and your foresight has given these people reforms **3** in every way and in every place. We appreciate them and thank you very much. **4** Not to keep you too long—I ask you to listen in your kindly way to what we briefly have to say. **5** We have found this man a pest who starts quarrels among all the Jews in the world, and he is a ringleader of the sect of the Nazarenes. **6** He even tried to pollute the Temple, and so we arrested him. We wanted to try him under our Law. **7** But Tribune Lysias came and used force

---

c- 35 Greek: *"praitōrion"* (Latin: *"praetorium"*).

to take him out of our hands, **8** ordering his accusers to come before you.*a* When you examine him yourself, you will be able to find out from him everything of which we accuse him."

9 The Jews supported his attack by declaring that these things were so.

10 The governor nodded to Paul to speak, and he answered, "For many years you have been a judge of this nation. Knowing that, I am glad to defend myself. **11** No more than twelve days ago, as you can verify for yourself, I went up to Jerusalem to worship. **12** They did not find me arguing with anyone in the Temple or stirring up a crowd in the synagogs or in the city; **13** and they cannot prove to you the things of which they are now accusing me. **14** But I confess to you that according to the Christian religion,*b* which they call a sect, I worship the God of our fathers. I believe everything written in the Law and the Prophets **15** and trust God for the same thing they are looking for, that the dead will rise, both the righteous and the wicked. **16** That is why I am doing my best always to have a clear conscience before God and men. **17** After some years I came to my people to bring gifts for the poor and offerings. **18** They found me busy with these things and purified in the Temple, but there was no crowd or noisy mob. **19** There were some Jews from the province of Asia, who should be here before you to accuse me if they have anything against me. **20** Or these men should tell what wrong they found in me as I stood before their council, **21** unless it is the one thing I shouted when I stood among them: 'I am on trial before you today in regard to the resurrection of the dead.' "

22 But Felix, who knew the Christian religion*c* rather well, told them to wait for a decision. He said, "When Tribune Lysias comes down, I will decide your case." **23** He ordered the captain to guard him but to let him have some liberty and not keep any of his friends from attending to his needs.*d*

24 Some days later Felix came again. His wife Drusilla, who was a Jewess, was with him. He sent for Paul and heard him tell about faith in Christ Jesus. **25** As he spoke of righteousness, self-control, and the coming judgment, Felix was frightened and answered, "You can leave now. When I have a chance, I will send for you." **26** At the same time he expected Paul to give him money. And so he used to send for him often and talk with him.

27 Two whole years passed. Then Porcius Festus succeeded Felix. Since Felix wanted to do the Jews a favor, he left Paul in prison.

25TH CHAPTER

Paul Appeals To The Emperor

1 Three days after Festus took over his duties in the province of Judea he went from Caesarea up to Jerusalem. **2** The high priests and the leaders of the

---

24 *a-* 8 Some of the older manuscripts and early translations omit verses 6b-8a.
    b- 14 Literally: "according to the Way."
    c- 22 Literally: "knew the things concerning the Way."
    d- 23 Paul was put under house arrest, the so-called "*custodia libera*" or "free custody."

Jews reported to Festus what they had against Paul. They urged **3** and begged him to do them a favor and have Paul brought to Jerusalem. They were laying an ambush to kill him on the way.

4 But Festus answered that Paul would be kept in Caesarea and he himself would be going there soon. **5** He said, "Those of you who have the authority come down with me, and if the man has done anything wrong, accuse him."

6 He stayed with them no more than eight or ten days and then went down to Caesarea. The next day he sat on the judge's seat*a* and ordered Paul to be brought in.

7 When Paul came in, the Jews who had come down from Jerusalem surrounded him and were accusing him of many serious wrongs that they could not prove. **8** Paul defended himself: "I have in no way sinned against the Law of the Jews or the Temple or Caesar."

9 But Festus wanted to do the Jews a favor. So he asked Paul, "Do you want to go up to Jerusalem to be tried there before me in regard to these things?"

10 Paul said, "I am standing before Caesar's judgment seat and there I must be tried. I have not done anything wrong to the Jews, as you also very well know. **11** Now if I am guilty and have done something for which I deserve the death penalty, I do not refuse to die. But if their accusations are untrue,*b* no one can hand me over to them. I appeal to Caesar!"

12 Festus talked it over with his council and then answered, "You appealed to Caesar; to Caesar you will go!"

13 Some time later King Agrippa and Bernice came down to Caesarea to welcome Festus. **14** When they stayed there a number of days, Festus laid Paul's case before the king.

He said, "There is a man here whom Felix left in prison. **15** When I went up to Jerusalem, the high priests and elders of the Jews informed me about him and asked me to condemn him.

16 "I answered them, 'It is not customary for Romans to hand over a man before he has faced his accusers and had a chance to defend himself against their accusation.'

17 "They came here with me, and the next day without any delay I sat down on the judge's seat and ordered the man to be brought. **18** When his accusers stood up, they did not accuse him of the crimes I was suspecting. **19** But they disagreed with him about their own religion and about a certain Jesus who died; Paul claimed He is alive. **20** Their debate about these things left me puzzled, so I asked if he would like to go to Jerusalem and be tried there in regard to these things. **21** But Paul appealed. He asked to be held in custody and to have his majesty the Emperor*c* decide his case. So I ordered him to be held in prison until I send him to Caesar."

22 Agrippa told Festus, "I myself would like to hear the man."

He answered, "Tomorrow you will hear him."

---

25 *a-* 6 A portable chair that could be moved from place to place.
  b- 11 Literally: "nothing."
  c- 21 Literally: "the 'revered' or 'venerated' one" (also in v. 25).

Before Agrippa

23 The next day Agrippa and Bernice came with great pomp and went with the tribunes and leading men of the city into the hall. Then Festus gave the order, and Paul was brought in.

24 Festus said, "King Agrippa and all you men here with us, you see this man about whom all the Jewish people in Jerusalem and here have appealed to me, shouting that he must not live any longer. 25 I found that he has not done anything to deserve to die, but when he appealed to his majesty the Emperor, I decided to send him. 26 I have nothing reliable to write our lord about him. So I have brought him before you, and especially before you, King Agrippa, so that after we examine him, I might have something to write. 27 It makes no sense to me to send a prisoner without indicating the charges against him."

26TH CHAPTER

1 Agrippa said to Paul, "You may speak for yourself."

Then Paul, stretching out his hand, began to defend himself: 2 "King Agrippa, I think I am fortunate in that I am going to defend myself today before you in regard to everything of which the Jews accuse me, 3 especially since you are so very familiar with all the Jewish customs and problems. So I ask you to listen to me patiently.

4 "The Jews all know how I lived from my youth, from my earliest days, among my own people and in Jerusalem. 5 They have known me for a long time and could testify, if they were willing, that I lived the life of a Pharisee, the strictest party of our religion.

6 "And now I am on trial here because I trust the promise God made to our fathers. 7 Our twelve tribes, worshiping zealously day and night, expect to see this promise come true. This is the hope, O King, in regard to which some Jews accuse me. 8 Why do you think it is so incredible that God raises the dead?

9 "Once I believed that I had to work hard against the Name of Jesus from Nazareth. 10 I did that in Jerusalem. By the authority I received from the high priests, I locked up many of the believers [saints] in prison, and when they were to be killed, I voted against them. 11 As I went to all the synagogs, one by one, I often punished the believers, and in this way I tried to force them to blaspheme. In my furious rage against them, I hunted them down even to foreign cities.

12 "That is how I came to be traveling to Damascus, authorized and appointed by the high priests, 13 when on the way, O King, at noon I saw a light brighter than the sun, flashing from heaven around me and around those who were traveling with me. 14 All of us fell to the ground, and I heard a voice asking me in Aramaic, 'Saul, Saul! Why are you persecuting Me? You are only hurting yourself by kicking against the goads.'

15 "I asked, 'Who are You, Lord?'

" 'I am Jesus,' the Lord answered, 'whom you are persecuting. 16 But get

up and *stand on your feet*. I showed Myself to you to appoint you to serve Me as a witness of what you have seen about Me and of what will be shown to you by Me. **17** *I will rescue you* from your people and *from the Gentiles to whom I am sending you,* **18** in order *to open their eyes* and to turn them *from darkness to light* and from Satan's control to God, so that they may receive the forgiveness of sins and a share ⌊in the inheritance⌋ of those who are made holy by believing in Me.'

19 "And so, King Agrippa, I did not disobey what I saw from heaven, **20** but first I told the people in Damascus and Jerusalem, then the whole country of Judea, and the Gentiles that they should turn from sin to God and do the works that show they have repented. **21** For this the Jews took me prisoner in the Temple and tried to murder me.

22 "God has helped me to this day, and so I have been standing and testifying to high and low, stating only what the prophets and Moses said would happen, **23** that Christ had to suffer and by being the first to rise from the dead He would announce light to our people and to the Gentiles."

24 As he was defending himself in this way, Festus shouted, "You are insane, Paul! Your great learning is driving you out of your mind."

25 "I am not insane, excellent Festus," Paul said, "but what I am saying is both true and sensible. **26** Yes, the king knows about these things, and I am talking boldly to him. I am sure he has not missed any of them, since this was not done in a corner. **27** King Agrippa, do you believe the prophets?[a] I know you believe them!"

28 Agrippa said to Paul: "You almost persuade me to be a Christian!"

29 Paul said, "I wish to God that not only you but all those listening to me today would become both almost and completely the same as I am—except for these chains."

30 The king, the governor, Bernice, and those who sat with them stood up **31** and left and said to one another, "This man is not doing anything for which he deserves to die or to be in chains."

32 Agrippa told Festus, "This man could be set free if he had not appealed to Caesar."

27TH CHAPTER

Paul Sails For Rome

1 When it was decided that we should sail to Italy, Paul and some other prisoners were turned over to a captain by the name of Julius, of the troop of Augustus. **2** We boarded a ship from Adramyttium that was going to sail to the ports on the coast of the province of Asia, and we started out. Aristarchus, a Macedonian from Thessalonica, went with us.

3 The next day we landed at Sidon, where Julius treated Paul kindly and let

---

16 Ezek 2:1,2   17 1 Chr 16:35; Jer 1:7,8   18 Is 35:5; 42:7,16

26 a- 27 Or "Prophets"; see THE OLD TESTAMENT CANON on page 551.

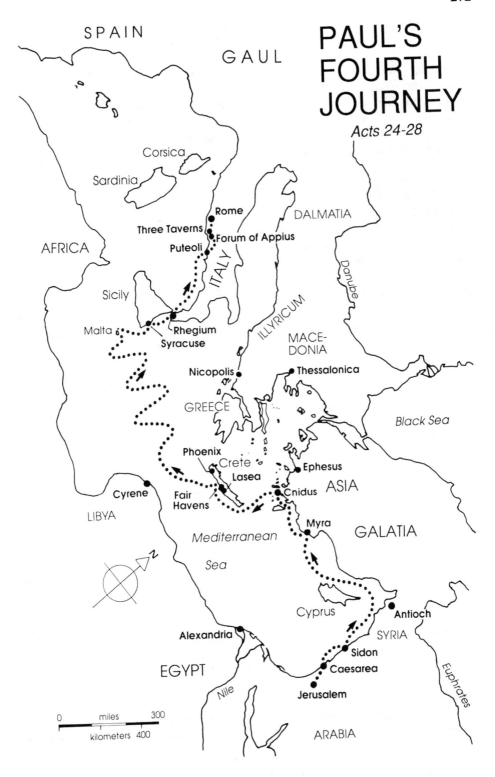

PAUL'S FOURTH JOURNEY

Acts 24-28

SPAIN

GAUL

Corsica

Sardinia

DALMATIA

Rome

Three Taverns

Forum of Appius

Puteoli

AFRICA

ITALY

Danube

Sicily

ILLYRICUM

Malta

Rhegium

Syracuse

Nicopolis

MACE-
DONIA

Thessalonica

Black Sea

GREECE

Phoenix

Crete

Lasea

Ephesus

Cyrene

Fair
Havens

Cnidus

ASIA

LIBYA

Myra

GALATIA

Mediterranean

Sea

Cyprus

Antioch

Alexandria

SYRIA

EGYPT

Sidon

Caesarea

Nile

Jerusalem

Euphrates

ARABIA

0   miles   300

kilometers   400

him go to his friends to receive any care he needed. **4** Leaving Sidon, we sailed on the sheltered side of Cyprus because the winds were against us. **5** We crossed the sea off Cilicia and Pamphylia and landed at Myra in Lycia. **6** There the captain of the soldiers found a ship from Alexandria sailing to Italy and put us on it. **7** We were sailing slowly for a number of days and had some difficulty getting near Cnidus. The wind would not let us go on, and so, starting at Cape Salmone, we sailed on the sheltered side of Crete. **8** Hugging the coast, we struggled on to a place called Fair Havens, near the town of Lasea.

9 We had lost a lot of time. Even the day of fasting *a* had already gone by, and sailing was now dangerous. So Paul advised them, **10** saying: "Men, I see that on this voyage we are going to suffer hardship and a heavy loss, not only of the cargo and ship but also of our lives." **11** But the captain of the soldiers listened to the pilot and the captain of the ship and not to what Paul said. **12** Since that harbor was not a good place to spend the winter, the majority decided to sail on, hoping they could somehow reach Phoenix to spend the winter there. It is a harbor of Crete facing southwest and northwest. **13** When a gentle breeze blew from the south, they felt they could easily make it. They took up the anchor and sailed close to the shore of Crete.

14 But after a little while a hurricane, called a northeaster, dashed down. **15** It caught the ship so that it could not face the wind, and we gave up and were swept along. **16** As we ran into the shelter of a small island called Clauda, we managed with a struggle to get hold of the lifeboat. **17** They pulled it up on deck. Then they passed ropes around the ship to reinforce it. Fearing that they would run on the great sandbank near Africa, they lowered the sail and so drifted along. **18** We continued to be tossed so violently by the storm that the next day the men began to throw the cargo overboard, **19** and on the third ˌdayˌ they threw the ship's tackle overboard with their own hands. **20** For a number of days we could not see any sun or stars. We were in a great storm until at last we began to give up all hope of coming through alive.

21 Since hardly anyone wanted to eat, Paul stepped before them and said, "Men, you should have listened to me and not have sailed from Crete. You would have avoided this hardship and damage. **22** But now I urge you to cheer up because you will lose no lives but only the ship. **23** For an angel stood by me last night, an angel of the God to whom I belong and whom I also serve. **24** He said, 'Stop being afraid, Paul! You must stand before Caesar, and now God has given you all who are sailing with you.' **25** So, cheer up, men, because I trust God that it will be just as He told me. **26** But we must run aground on some island."

The Shipwreck

27 It was the fourteenth night and we were drifting through the Adriatic Sea *b* when about midnight the sailors suspected land was coming closer. **28** They took soundings and found that the water was 120 feet deep. A little farther they took

---

27 *a*- 9 A reference to the Day of Atonement (cf. Lev. 16).

   b- 27 At that time the "Adriatic" Sea included the present Adriatic, plus a large part of the Mediterranean Sea south of it.

soundings again and found that it was 90 feet. 29 Fearing we might run on rocks, they dropped four anchors from the back of the ship and prayed for morning to come.

30 The sailors tried to escape from the ship. They let the lifeboat down into the sea, pretending they were going to take out the anchors from the front of the ship and let them down. 31 But Paul told the captain of the soldiers and his men, "If these men do not stay with the ship, you cannot be rescued." 32 Then the soldiers cut the ropes that held the boat and let it drift away.

33 Just before daybreak Paul was urging all of them to eat something. "This is the fourteenth day you have waited and gone hungry and not eaten a thing. 34 So I urge you to eat something. It will help you come through this safely. None of you will lose a hair of his head." 35 After saying this, he took some bread, thanked God in front of everybody, broke it, and began to eat. 36 They were all cheered up, and they too had something to eat. 37 There were 276 of us on the ship. 38 After they had eaten all they wanted, they lightened the ship by dumping the wheat into the sea.

39 In the morning they could not tell what land it was but gradually could see a bay with a beach on which they planned, if possible, to run the ship ashore. 40 They cut off the anchors and left them in the sea. At the same time they untied the ropes that held up the steering oars, spread out the foresail to catch the wind, and steered the ship to the shore. 41 They struck a bank in the water and ran the ship aground. The front of the ship stuck and could not be moved, while the back was being pounded to pieces by the sea.

42 To keep any of the prisoners from swimming away and escaping, the soldiers planned to kill them, 43 but the captain of the soldiers wanted to save Paul, so he kept them from doing this. He ordered those who could swim to jump out first and get to the shore, 44 and the rest to follow, some on planks and some on other pieces from the ship. In this way all of them came safely to the shore.

28TH CHAPTER

Safe On Malta

1 Once safely on shore, we found out that the island was called Malta. 2 The natives were unusually kind to us. It had started to rain and was cold, and so they made a fire and welcomed all of us around it.

3 Paul gathered an armful of dry branches and put them on the fire. The heat made a poisonous snake come out, and it bit his hand. 4 When the natives saw the snake hanging from his hand, they said to one another, "This man certainly is a murderer! He did escape from the sea, but justice did not let him live."

5 Paul shook the snake into the fire and suffered no harm. 6 They were waiting for him to swell up or suddenly fall down dead. They waited a long time, but they saw nothing unusual happen to him. Then they changed their minds and said he was a god.

7 The governor of the island, whose name was Publius, had property around that place. He welcomed us and treated us kindly while we were his guests for three days. **8** The father of Publius happened to be sick in bed with fever and dysentery. Paul went to him, prayed, and laid his hands on him, and made him well.

9 After that had happened, the other sick people on the island also came to him and were made well. **10** They honored us in many ways, and when we were going to sail, they put on board whatever we needed.

From Malta To Rome

11 After three months we sailed on a ship from Alexandria that had stopped at the island for the winter. In front it had a figure of the Twin Sons of Zeus.[a] **12** We stopped at Syracuse and stayed there three days. **13** From there we sailed around and came to Rhegium. On the second day a south wind started blowing, and on the second day we came to Puteoli. **14** There we found fellow Christians[b] who urged us to stay seven days with them.

And so we came to Rome. **15** The fellow Christians there, having heard about us, came as far as the Market [Forum] of Appius and the Three Taverns to meet us. When Paul saw them, he thanked God and felt encouraged.

In Rome

16 When we came into Rome, Paul was allowed to live by himself, with a soldier who was guarding him. **17** After three days he called the leaders of the Jews together. When they came, he said to them, "Fellow Jews,[c] although I have not done anything against our people or the customs of our fathers, I am a prisoner from Jerusalem who was handed over to the Romans. **18** They examined me and wanted to let me go because I had done no wrong for which I deserve to die. **19** But the Jews objected and forced me to appeal to Caesar—not that I am accusing my people of anything. **20** That is why I asked to see you and speak with you, since it is for the hope of Israel that I wear this chain."

21 They told him, "We have had no letters from Judea about you, and no Jewish person coming here has reported or said anything bad about you. **22** We would like to hear from you what you think, because we know that everywhere people are talking against this sect."

23 They set a day to meet with him, and more of them came to him where he was staying. From morning until evening he explained and declared the truth about the Kingdom of God to them and tried to convince them about Jesus from the Law of Moses and the Prophets.[d] **24** Some of them were convinced by what he said, but others continued in unbelief.

25 They disagreed with one another as they were leaving, and Paul added one

---

28 *a*- 11 Castor and Pollux, the guardian gods of sailors.
   b- 14 Literally: "brothers" (also in vv. 15,21).
   c- 17 Literally: "Men, brothers."
   d- 23 See initial portion of footnote at Matthew 5:17.

more statement: "The Holy Spirit spoke the truth to your fathers through the prophet Isaiah 26 when he said: *'Go to these people and say:*

> *You will hear clearly but never understand;*
> *you will see clearly but never comprehend,*
> 27   *because these people have become dull at heart*
>   *and hard of hearing*
>   *and have shut their eyes,*
>   *so that their eyes never see,*
>   *their ears never hear,*
>   *their hearts never understand,*
>   *and they never turn to Me for healing.'*

28 "You should know that *the salvation which comes from God* has been sent out *to the Gentiles*, and they will listen." 29 After he said this, the Jews left, arguing vigorously among themselves.[e]

30 For two whole years he lived in his own rented place and welcomed all who came to him. 31 He preached God's Kingdom and very boldly taught the truth about the Lord Jesus Christ, and no one stopped him.

26,27 Is 6:9,10   *28 Ps 67:2; 98:2,3*

---

e- 29 Some of the older manuscripts and early translations omit verse 29.

ROMANS[a]

1ST CHAPTER

A. Introduction (1:1-15) and theme (1:16,17)

Paul Greets The Roman Christians

1 Paul, a servant of Jesus Christ, called to be an apostle and appointed to preach the Gospel [Good News] of God

> (**2** He promised this Good News, in advance through His prophets in the Holy Scriptures. **3** It is about His Son, who according to flesh[b] was born a descendant of David, **4** but according to spirit—a spirit of holiness[c]—was declared by His resurrection from the dead to be the powerful Son of God. And He is our Lord Jesus Christ, **5** through whom we have received the grace of holding the apostolic office[d] to make Him known[e] among the Gentiles, so that they may listen and come to faith.[f] **6** These Gentiles include you who[g] have been called to belong to Jesus Christ.)

7 to all in Rome whom God loves and has called to be His believers [saints]: Grace to you and peace from God our Father and the Lord Jesus Christ.[h]

I Want To See You

8 First, I thank my God through Jesus Christ for all of you because the news

---

1 *a* The Apostle Paul wrote to the Christians in Rome on his Third Missionary Journey (c. A.D. 56) just before he left Corinth with the collection for the poor in Jerusalem (cf. 15:25).

b- 3 Or "according to a fleshly [physical] state"; a reference to Christ's state of humiliation (cf. 1 Tim. 3:16; 1 Pet. 3:18; 4:6 and the corresponding footnotes; also note 1 Cor. 15:44-49).

c- 4 Or "according to a spiritual state characterized by holiness"; a reference to Christ's state of exaltation (cf. 1 Tim. 3:16; 1 Pet. 3:18; 4:6 and the corresponding footnotes; also note 1 Cor. 15:44-49).

d- 5 Literally: "grace and the apostolic office."

e- 5 Literally: "in behalf of His Name."

f- 5 Literally: "for obedience of faith among all the nations [Gentiles]."

g- 6 Literally: "Among whom you also."

h- 7 Verse 7 grammatically follows verse 1, making verses 2-6 parenthetical.

of your faith is spreading all over the world. **9** God, whom I serve in my spirit by preaching the Gospel of His Son, knows how I never fail to mention you **10** whenever I pray, as I keep asking that—somehow by the will of God—I will now at last succeed in coming to you. **11** For I long to see you, so that I may share a spiritual gift with you in order to strengthen you. **12** What I mean is that when I am with you I will be encouraged by your faith and you by mine.

13 I do not want you to be unaware, fellow Christians,*i* that I often planned to come to you (but have been hindered up to now), in order to enjoy some of the results of working among you as I have enjoyed such results among the other Gentiles. **14** I have an obligation both to Greeks and non-Greeks, to the wise and the foolish. **15** So I am eager to preach the Gospel also to you in Rome.

16 For I am not ashamed of the Gospel,*j* for it is God's power to save everyone who believes it, the Jew first and also the Greek. **17** For it reveals the righteousness which comes from God by faith so that people may come to faith,*k* as it is written: *"The righteous will live by faith."*

B. Justification:
By works or by Christ's atonement (1:18–4:25)?
1. The "anger of God" as related to the Law (1:18–3:20)

God Is Angry

18 For the anger of God is being revealed from heaven against all the ungodliness and unrighteousness of people who suppress the truth by their unrighteousness. **19** What can be known about God is clear to them, because God has made it clear to them. **20** For since the creation of the world, they have seen the unseen things of God. From the things He created, they can tell that He has everlasting power and is God. Therefore they have no excuse, **21** since they knew God but did not honor Him as God, nor did they thank Him. Instead, their thoughts became total nonsense, and their ignorant hearts were darkened.

22 While claiming to be wise, they became fools; **23** they exchanged *the glory* of the immortal God *for the likeness of an image* of mortals, and of birds, and of four-footed animals, and of crawling creatures. **24** And so, as they followed the lusts of their hearts, God handed them over to live immorally by dishonoring their bodies with one another. **25** He did this because they traded the truth of God for a lie, that is, they worshiped and served what was created instead of the Creator, who is blessed forever. Amen!

26 That is why God gave them up to shameful lusts. Their women have even exchanged natural relations for the unnatural. **27** And men likewise have given up the natural relations with a woman and burned with lust for one another, men doing shameful acts with men and suffering in themselves the punishment they deserve for their perversion.

---

17 Hab 2:4   *23 Ps 106:20*

i- 13 Literally: "brothers."
j- 16 Many manuscripts from the Middle Ages add: "of Christ."
k- 17 Literally: "the righteousness from faith to faith" or "the righteousness by faith for faith."

28 And since[l] they regarded it as worthless to hold on to the true knowledge of God, God handed them over to ˌthe control ofˌ a mind that is worthless, to live immorally. **29** Their lives are full of all kinds of unrighteousness, wickedness, greed, malice. They are full of envy, murder, quarreling, deceit, viciousness, gossip. **30** They slander and are hated by God. They are haughty, proud, boastful. They invent new evils. They disobey parents. **31** They are foolish. They break their promises. They are loveless and show no mercy. **32** Although they know God's righteous decree that those who do such things deserve to die, they not only continue to do them but approve of others who do them.

2ND CHAPTER

God Will Judge The Jews

1 So, whoever you are, if you condemn anyone, you have no excuse. For when you condemn anyone else, you condemn yourself, since you as the judge are doing the same things. **2** We know God is right when He condemns people for doing such things. **3** When you condemn people for doing such things but do them yourself, do you think you will escape being condemned by God? **4** Or do you think lightly of God, who is very kind to you, puts up with you, and deals patiently with you? ˌThis could happen only if you doˌ not realize that it is the kindness of God which leads you to repent of your sins.

5 But you stubbornly refuse to turn from sin, and so you are ensuring that God will be more and more angry with you on the Day of His Anger, when God will show how right His judgment is:

6	*He will give every person according to what he has done—*
7	everlasting life to those
	who by patient endurance in working good are seeking
	for glory, honor, and immortality;
8	but anger and fury to those
	who are selfish, and
	who disobey the truth, and
	who follow unrighteousness;
9	sorrow and anguish for every human being
	who does evil,
	for the Jew first and also the Greek;
10	but glory, honor, and peace for every person
	who does good,
	for the Jew first and also the Greek;
11	for God does not favor one person over another.[a]

6 Ps 62:12; Prov 24:12

l- 28 Literally: "And in the same way as."

2 a- 11 The prose of Paul's argumentation in verses 6-11 has been set in a poetic format to aid the reader. Paul uses a grammatical structure, called a chiasm, to communicate. In this A-B-B-A structure verses 7 and 10 form one thought parallel and verses 8 and 9 the other. Verses 6 and 11 constitute the introduction and conclusion, respectively. See GRAMMATIC/POETIC STRUCTURES THAT CONVEY TEXTUAL MEANINGS on page 558.

12 All who sin without having the Law will also perish without the Law. And all who sin having the Law will be judged by the Law. 13 For it is not those who only hear the Law who are righteous before God, but it is those who do what the Law says who will be justified [declared righteous]

> (14 Yes, when Gentiles—who do not have the Law—do by nature what the Law says, they are a law to themselves even though they do not have the Law. 15 They show that what the Law requires them to do is written in their hearts. Their conscience tells the same truth, and their thoughts accuse them on one occasion or defend them on another.)

16 on the Day when, according to the Gospel which I preach, God through Christ Jesus will judge the secrets of people. *b*

Who Is A Jew?

17 If you call yourself a Jew and rest comfortably in the Law and boast about your God, 18 if you know what He wants and approve of the better things since you are instructed by the Law, 19 if you feel sure that you are a guide to the blind and a light to those in darkness, 20 that you can train the foolish and teach children because you have in the Law the embodiment of knowledge and truth—21 now then, while you are teaching someone else, do you fail to teach yourself? You preach, "Do not steal," but are you stealing? 22 You say, "Do not commit adultery," but are you committing adultery? You are disgusted with idols, but are you robbing temples? 23 You boast about the Law, but by breaking the Law you are dishonoring God. 24 Yes, as it is written: *"Because of you the Gentiles speak evil of God's Name."*

25 Circumcision benefits you only if you do what the Law says. If you are breaking the Law, your circumcision is changed into uncircumcision. 26 So if an uncircumcised man does what the Law demands, will he not be considered circumcised? 27 If a man who has never been circumcised really does what the Law says, he will condemn you for breaking the Law, you who have the written Law and circumcision. 28 For he is not a Jew who is merely one outwardly, nor is circumcision that which is only visible and physical. *c* 29 Rather, a real Jew is one who is a Jew inwardly, and a real circumcision is a circumcision of the heart. It consists of an inward, not just an outward, change. *d* A real Jew *e* is one who is praised by God, not one praised by men.

---

24 Is 52:5

---

b- 16 Verse 16 grammatically follows verse 13, making verses 14 and 15 parenthetical.
c- 28 Literally: "nor is circumcision in the open in the flesh."
d- 29 Literally: "a circumcision of the heart in spirit not in letter [or '. . . by the Spirit, not by something written']."
e- 29 The word "Jew," coming from the Hebrew word for "Judah," may mean "Praised" (cf. Gen. 49:8); if so, note the play on words that follows.

3RD CHAPTER

The Advantage Of Being A Jew

1 What is the advantage then of being a Jew? Or what benefit is there in being circumcised? **2** Much in every way! The most important advantage is that God entrusted His word to the Jews.

God Is Faithful

3 What if some were unbelieving? Will their unbelief make God untrustworthy? **4** Never! Let God be true and *every man a liar*, as it is written:

> *That You may be declared right^a when You speak*
> *and win the case when You are in court.*

5 But if our unrighteousness shows how right God is, what shall we say? Shall we say (I am talking like a man) that God is wrong when He is angry and punishes? **6** Never! Otherwise how could God judge the world? **7** But if my lie honors God by showing how much truth there is in Him, why am I still condemned as a sinner? **8** Or shall we say, "Let's do evil that good may come of it"? Some slander us and claim that we say this. Their condemnation is what they deserve.

All Are Sinners

9 What then? Are we any better off? Not at all. We have already charged that both Jews and Greeks are all under ˌthe power ofˌ sin, **10** as it is written:

> *No one is righteous, no, not one—*
>
> **11** *no one understands—*
> *no one is searching for God:^{b}*
>
> **12** *All have turned away*
> *and together have become worthless;*
> *no one is doing anything good,*
> *not a single one.*
>
> **13** *Their throats are an open grave;*
> *they have spoken to deceive;*
> *their lips hide the poison of serpents;*
> **14** *their mouths are full of cursing and bitterness.*
> **15** *Their feet are quick to spill blood;*
> **16** *wherever they go, there is destruction and misery;*
> **17** *they have not learned the way of peace;*
> **18** *they have no fear of God.^{c}*

---

4 *Ps 51:4; 116:11*   **10-12** *Ps 14:1-3; 53:1-3; Eccl 7:20*   **13** *Ps 5:9; 140:3*   **14** *Ps 10:7*
15-17 *Is 59:7,8*   **18** *Ps 36:1*

---

3 *a*- 4 Or "be justified."
   b- 11 See GRAMMATIC/POETIC STRUCTURES THAT CONVEY TEXTUAL MEANINGS on page 558.
   c- 18 Literally: "There is not fear of God before their eyes."

19 Now we know that whatever the Law says, it says to those who are under the Law, so that every mouth may become silent and the whole world may stand guilty before God. 20 Therefore, *not one person will be justified [declared righteous]*d *before God* by doing what the Law says, because the Law teaches us to recognize sin.

2. The "righteousness of God" as based on the Gospel (3:21–4:25)

God Justifies Us

21 But now God has shown a righteousness that comes from Him—a righteousness apart from the Law. The Law and the Prophetse tell about it. 22 This righteousness comes from God to all who believe, just by their believing [by having faith] in Jesus Christ.

There is no difference, 23 for all have sinned and are without the praise that God gives.f 24 They are justified [declared righteous]g freely by His grace, through the ransom Christ Jesus paid. 25 God publicly displayed Him as the *Atonement Cover*h through faith in His blood. God did this to show that He is just, even though in His patience He had left unpunished those sins which had been done in the past. 26 He wanted to show His justice at the present time, so that He might be righteous and the One who justifies [acquits] the person who believes in Jesus.

27 What then becomes of our pride? It is excluded. On what principle? On the principle of works? No, rather it is excluded on the principle of faith! 28 For we conclude that a person is justified [declared righteous] by faith—apart from the works of the Law.

29 Or is God only the God of the Jews? Is He not also the God of the Gentiles? Certainly also of the Gentiles, 30 since it is one and the same God who will justify [acquit] the circumcised by faith and the uncircumcised through the same faith.

31 Do we then by faith cancel the Law? Never! Rather, we uphold the Law.

---

20 *Ps 143:2*   25 *Lev 16:2*

---

d- 20 See ahead at 3:24 and its accompanying footnote.

e- 21 See Matthew 5:17 and its accompanying footnote.

f- 23 Compare 2:29 where Paul speaks of a "real Jew" as one who is "praised" by God.

g- 24 God declares us "not guilty," that is, He "acquits" us in His role as our Judge, and by believing His verdict we receive the righteousness of Christ by grace through faith ("grace" and "faith" concepts follow in vv. 24a and 28, respectively). This "justification" concept is also found in verses 26,28,30; compare also 4:5.

h- 25 Greek: "*hilastērion*," meaning "mercy-seat" or "propitiation," parallel to the Hebrew "*kapporeth*," both referring to the "lid" or "covering" on top of the ark of the covenant which sat in the Most Holy Place in the Old Testament Tabernacle, but which here is applied to Christ, who became our Covering or Atonement Cover for sin. As such, Christ's blood became the means or provided the "propitiatory power" by which our sins were forgiven. See Diagram #2 on page 438.

4TH CHAPTER

We Are Justified By Faith

1 What shall we say that Abraham, our ancestor, found as a result of his efforts?[a] **2** For if he was justified [declared righteous] by what he did, he had something to boast about. But he could not boast before God. **3** For what does the Scripture say? *"Abraham believed God and it was credited to his account as righteousness."*

4 Now when a person works, his pay is not considered a gift but a debt. **5** But for the person who, instead of working, believes in Him who justifies [acquits] the ungodly,[b] his faith is credited to his account as righteousness. **6** In the same way David also calls the person "blessed" to whom God credits righteousness apart from works:

7   *Blessed are those whose wrongs are forgiven*
         and whose sins are covered.[c]
8   *Blessed is the person*
         against whose account the Lord never charges sin.

9 Now then, is this blessing only for the circumcised person, or is it also for the uncircumcised? For we say, *"Abraham's faith was credited to his account as righteousness."* **10** What was the situation when it was credited to his account? Was he circumcised at that time, or not? He was not circumcised but was uncircumcised. **11** And he received *circumcision as a mark* to confirm that righteousness ˻which he earlier had received˼ by faith[d] *when he was still uncircumcised.* He was to be the father of all who believe but who were not circumcised, *so that they might be credited in their account as righteous.* **12** He is also the father of the circumcised who not only are circumcised but who also follow in the footsteps of our father Abraham by believing as he did when he was still uncircumcised.

13 It was not by the Law that Abraham or his descendants received the promise that he would inherit the world, but it was by the righteousness of faith. **14** Because if the Law is the way to inherit, then faith has been made worthless and the promise has been made powerless. **15** For the Law brings God's anger on us;[e] but where there is no Law, there is no breaking of the Law. **16** Therefore, the promise is by faith that it might come to us as a free gift [by grace], so that the promise might be sure to all the descendants, not only to those who live by the Law but also to those who only believe as Abraham did. He is the father of all of us, **17** as it is written: *"I have made you a father of many nations."*

---

3 Gen 15:6   **7,8** Ps 32:1,2   **9** Gen 15:6   **11** Gen 15:6; 17:11   **17** Gen 17:5

---

4 *a-* 1 Literally: "according to flesh" (cf. Gal. 3:3).
  b- 5 "Ungodly," a very strong term, equivalent to "unbeliever."
  c- 7 See 3:25 and its accompanying footnote (also applies to vv. 5,25).
  d- 11 Literally: "the sign of circumcision, a seal of the righteousness of faith."
  e- 15 Literally: "the Law produces wrath," meaning that our breaking of the Law causes God to become angry with us.

Standing before God, Abraham believed that God makes the dead live and that He⌋ calls into being that which does not exist. **18** ⌈Abraham,⌋ hoping contrary to what he could expect, believed and so became *a father of many nations*, as he had been told: *"That is how many descendants you will have."* **19** He did not become weak in faith—although he realized that since he was about a hundred years old he could not have children anymore; and Sarah could not have any either.*f* **20** There was no unbelief to make him doubt what God promised, but his faith was made strong and he gave glory to God. **21** He was fully convinced that what God promised, He could also do. **22** That is why it [his faith] *was credited to his account as righteousness.*

23 But the words *"it was credited to his account"* were written not only for him **24** but also for us. Already then, God also had in mind *to credit* it [our faith] to us *who believe* in Him who raised our Lord Jesus from the dead. **25** It was He who was *handed over to death* because of our failures*g* and then was raised because of our justification [acquittal].*h*

5TH CHAPTER

C. Christian freedom—
from God's anger, from sin, from the Law, from death (5:1–8:39)

Our Hope

1 Now that we are justified [declared righteous] by faith,*a* we have peace with God through our Lord Jesus Christ, **2** who provided us with the way*b* to come into this grace in which we stand. And our boast is based on our hope for God's glory.

3 More than that, we also boast of our sufferings, because we know that suffering produces patient endurance; **4** and patient endurance produces a genuine Christian character; and a genuine Christian character produces hope. **5** In this *hope we will not be disappointed*, because the Holy Spirit, who has been given to us, has poured God's love into our hearts.

6 To be sure, at the set time, while we were still helpless, Christ died for the ungodly. **7** You see, it is a rare thing that a person would die for someone who is righteous, though perhaps a person might be brave enough to die for someone who has been good to him.*c* **8** But God shows His love for us by this: While we were still sinners Christ died for us.

---

18 Gen 15:5; 17:5   *22-24* Gen 15:6   *25* Is 53:12   *5* Ps 22:5; 25:3,20

f- 19 Literally: "he considered his own body ⌈now⌋ dead; and the deadness of Sarah's womb."

g- 25 The Greek word used here indicates the act of "falling to the side" or "going astray," that is, the failure to follow a straight path (also in 5:15-18,20).

h- 25 The meaning is that it was because of our sins that God delivered Jesus into death, and it is because Christ's death justified us that God raised Him from the dead.

5 *a-* 1 See 3:24 and its accompanying footnote (also applies to vv. 9,16,18).

b- 2 Literally: "Christ, through whom we have access."

c- 7 Literally: "for the good person."

9 Now that His blood has justified [acquitted] us, we are even more certain that He will save us from the wrath of God. **10** For if we were reconciled to God by the death of His Son when we were still His enemies, we are even more certain—now that we have this changed relationship*d*—that He will save us by His life. **11** More than that, our boast is only in God through our Lord Jesus Christ, who has now given us this changed relationship.

Adam And Christ

12 So then, just as sin came into the world through one man, and death through sin, so death also spread to all people, since all sinned. **13** For ˌevenˌ before the Law,*e* sin was in the world. But sin is not charged against anyone's account when there is no Law. **14** Yet, death ruled from Adam to Moses, also over those who did not sin in the same way as Adam did in his disobedience. (Adam was a type [picture] of Him who was to come.)

15 But the free gift is not at all like the failure. Since multitudes*f* died as the result of one man's failure, God's grace and the gracious gift of the One Man, Jesus Christ, have overflowed even more on the multitudes.

16 And ˌthe effect ofˌ this undeserved gift is not the same as ˌthe effect ofˌ the one who sinned. For the sentence which followed the one ˌfailureˌ resulted in condemnation, but the free gift which followed many failures resulted in justification [acquittal]. **17** Yes, if death ruled through one man as a result of his failure, we who have received God's overflowing grace and His gift of righteousness will live and rule*g* even more through the One Man, Jesus Christ.

18 So therefore, as through one failure, condemnation came to all people, so also through one righteous act,*h* justification [acquittal] which brings life came to all people. **19** For in the same way, as through the disobedience of one man, multitudes were proclaimed to be sinful, so also through the obedience of the One Man, multitudes will be proclaimed righteous. **20** The Law was added to multiply the failure. But when*i* sin multiplied, God's grace overflowed even more. **21** ˌThis happenedˌ so that in the same way as sin ruled, resulting in death, so also His grace would rule through righteousness, resulting in our living forever through our Lord Jesus Christ.

6TH CHAPTER

Live For God

1 Therefore what shall we say? Shall we say, "Let's go on sinning so that

---

d- 10 The Greek word for "changed relationship" (also in v. 11) is the same as that translated "reconciled" in this same verse.

e- 13 Literally: "For until Law."

f- 15 Greek: "*hoi polloi*," the Greek expression which stresses that the number of people involved is very large. In verse 18 Paul indicates that this includes all people (also in v. 19).

g- 17 Or "righteousness by His life will rule."

h- 18 Or "So therefore, as through the failure of one man, condemnation came to all people, so also through the righteous act of One Man."

i- 20 Or "where."

God may be more gracious to us"?[a] 2 Certainly not! We died to sin. How can we ˌthenˌ live in it any longer?

3 Or do you not know that all of us who were baptized into Christ Jesus were baptized into His death? 4 Now when we were baptized into His death, we were buried with Him so that, as Christ was raised from the dead with the same glory as the Father's, we too will live a new life. 5 If we were united with Him in this likeness of His death, then we will be united with Him also in the likeness of His resurrection. 6 We know that our old self was nailed with Him to the cross to render our sinful body powerless in order that we might not be slaves to sin any longer; 7 for the one who has died has been justified [declared free][b] from sin.

8 But if we died with Christ, we believe that we will also live with Him, 9 because we know that Christ, since He was raised from the dead, will not die again. Death no longer has any hold on Him. 10 For when He died, He died to sin once, never to die again, and the life He lives He lives for God. 11 So you too, because you are in Christ Jesus, think of yourselves as dead to sin and living for God.

12 Therefore, do not let sin go on ruling in your dying body so that you do what it wants. 13 Do not go on presenting the members of your body to sin, as tools for doing wrong. But as people who have come back from the dead and are alive, present yourselves to God, and let God use the members of your body as tools for doing what is right. 14 Indeed, sin will not rule over you, because you are not under law but under grace.

15 What then? Are we going to sin because we are not under law but under grace? Certainly not! 16 Do you not know that if you present yourselves to obey someone as slaves, you are slaves of the person you obey—either of sin which results in death or of obedience that results in righteousness? 17 But thanks be to God that, although you once were the slaves of sin, you have heartily obeyed the pattern of teaching to which you were committed. 18 Freed from sin, you were made the slaves of righteousness.

19 I am speaking in a human way because you are naturally weak. Indeed, just as you once presented the members of your body as slaves to impurity and wickedness to do wrong, so now present your members as slaves to righteousness in order to live in a holy way. 20 For when you were slaves of sin, you were not free to serve righteousness as your master.

21 What was the result[c] then of doing the things that make you blush now? To be sure, they end in death. 22 But now that you have been made free from sin and have been made slaves of God, the result is that you live in a holy way[d] and finally have everlasting life. 23 The wages paid by sin is death, but the gift given freely by God in Christ Jesus our Lord is everlasting life.

---

6 a- 1 Literally: "in order that grace may increase."
b- 7 See 3:24 and its accompanying footnote.
c - 21 Literally: "What fruit do you have?"
d - 22 Literally: "You have your fruit to sanctification [holiness]."

7TH CHAPTER

¹ Or do you not know, my fellow Christians*ᵃ*—for I am speaking to people who know the Law—that you have to obey the Law only as long as you live? ² The Law, for example, binds a married woman to her husband while he is living, but if her husband dies, the Law does not bind her to her husband any longer. ³ So, while her husband is living, she will be called an adulteress if she lives with another man. But if her husband dies, she is free from the Law, and so she is not an adulteress if she marries another man.

⁴ So you too, my fellow Christians, have through Christ's body died to the Law to marry Another—Him who rose from the dead so that we might produce fruit for God. ⁵ While we were living in the flesh, the sinful lusts, ˌstirred upˌ by the Law, worked in the members of our bodies to produce fruit for death. ⁶ But now that we have died to the Law which bound us, we are freed from it, to serve in a new spiritual way, not in the old way of outward obedience.*ᵇ*

The Law Shows What Sin Is

⁷ What then shall we say to all this? Is the Law ˌthe cause ofˌ sin? Certainly not! Rather, only by the Law did I learn what sin is. For example, I would not have understood that wrong desires are sinful,*ᶜ* if the Law had not said: *"Do not wrongfully desire."* ⁸ But sin took the opportunity*ᵈ* provided by this commandment and worked in me every kind of wrong desire. For without the Law sin is dead. ⁹ Once I was alive without the Law, but when the commandment came, sin became alive, and I died. ¹⁰ And the commandment which was intended to bring me life actually brought me death. ¹¹ For by taking the commandment as a challenge, sin seduced me and used the commandment to kill me.

¹² So the Law itself is holy, and the commandment is holy, right, and good. ¹³ Now, did this good thing kill me? Certainly not! But sin, in order to be recognized as sin, clearly used this good thing to kill me, so that sin through the commandment would become extremely sinful.

Struggling With Sin

¹⁴ We know that the Law is spiritual, but I am unspiritual,*ᵉ* sold into the slavery of sin. ¹⁵ For I am acting in a way that I do not understand. For instead of doing what I want to do, I do what I hate. ¹⁶ And if I do what I do not want to do, I agree that the Law is good. ¹⁷ Now it is not really I who am doing this,

---

7 Ex 20:17; Deut 5:21

---

7 *a*- 1 Literally: "brothers" (also in v. 4).
  b- 6 Literally: "in newness of spirit, not in oldness of letter" (cf. 2:29).
  c- 7 Literally: "I would not have understood the nature of sinful desire."
  d- 8 The Greek word refers to the "starting point" or "base of operations" for a military expedition. Paul says sin used this commandment (see v. 7) as an "occasion" or "pretext" to do just the opposite of what the commandment demanded. (This same Greek word is translated "launching pad" at Galatians 5:13.)
  e- 14 Literally: "fleshly," that is, weak and sinful.

rather it is sin living in me. **18** Yes, I know that nothing good lives in me, that is, in my flesh. For I want to do what is right, but I just do not do it. **19** I do not do the good I want to do; instead, I do the evil that I do not want to do. **20** Now, if I am doing what I do not want to do, it is not really I who am doing this, rather it is sin living in me.

21 So I find this to be the rule: When I want to do what is right, evil is there with me. **22** In my inner being I delight in God's Law, **23** but all through the members of my body I see another law fighting against the Law in my mind and making me a prisoner to the law of sin which exists in the members of my body. **24** What a miserable person I am! Who will rescue me from this body which brings death? **25** Thanks be to God—He does it through our Lord Jesus Christ! So on the one hand I serve the Law of God with my mind,*f* but on the other ⌐I serve⌐ the law of sin with my flesh.*g*

8TH CHAPTER

The Spirit Gives Life

1 So now no condemnation remains for those who are in Christ Jesus. **2** The law of the spiritual life that we have in Christ Jesus has set you free from the law of sin and death. **3** For what the Law could not do, because it is weakened by the flesh, God has done by sending His Son to be like sinful flesh. God sent Him to be a sacrifice for sin and condemned sin in His flesh, **4** so that we who do not follow the flesh*a* but ⌐who follow⌐ the spirit*b* might be as righteous as the Law demands.

5 Those who follow the flesh have their minds set on the things of the flesh, but those who follow the spirit have their minds set on the things of the spirit. **6** For what the flesh has in mind kills; what the spirit has in mind gives life and peace. **7** This is so because the fleshly mind hates God.*c* Yes, it refuses to be subordinate*d* to God's Law because it cannot obey it. **8** Those who live in the flesh*e* cannot please God. **9** You, however, are not living in the flesh but in the spirit if God's Spirit lives in you.

Anyone who does not have the Spirit of Christ does not belong to Him. **10** But if Christ is in you, even though your bodies are dead because of sin, your spirits are alive because you are righteous. **11** And if the Spirit of Him who raised Jesus from the dead lives in you, He who raised Christ Jesus from the dead will also make your dying bodies alive by His Spirit living in you.

---

f- 25 Or "my new converted nature and attitude."

g- 25 Or "my old unconverted nature and attitude."

8 *a-* 4 That is, our old unconverted nature and attitude.

b- 4 That is, our new converted nature and attitude. Verse 16 makes it very clear that in this whole context Paul uses the word "spirit" in two different senses, namely, of our "converted nature" and of the "Third Person of the Trinity," who creates our new nature. Compare Galatians 5:16 and its accompanying footnote.

c- 7 Or "the fleshly attitude is hatred toward God."

d- 7 A Greek term which indicates the placing of one person under the authority of another; see *HUPOTASSO* on page 541.

e- 8 Literally: "Those who are in flesh" (cf. also v. 9).

12 And so, fellow Christians,*f* we do not owe it to the flesh to live according to the flesh. **13** Yes, if you live according to the flesh, you will die. But if by the Spirit you kill the activities of the body, you will live. **14** For all who are moved by God's Spirit are God's children. **15** For you did not receive the spirit of slaves to make you feel afraid again, but you received the spirit of God's adopted children by which we call out, "Abba, Father!"*g* **16** The Spirit Himself testifies with our spirit that we are God's children, **17** and if children, then heirs, God's heirs, and joint heirs with Christ since we share in His suffering in order that we may also share in His glory.

We Want To Be Free

18 I consider our present sufferings to be unimportant when I compare them with the glory soon to be revealed to us. **19** For the created world is waiting on tiptoe to see the unveiling of God's children. **20** For this created world must waste away,*h* not because it wants to but because its Master would have it so; but it does so with hope, **21** because this created world also will be freed from the slavery of decay in order to share the freedom of glory with the children of God. **22** For we know that all creation has been groaning with the pains of childbirth until now.

23 And what is more, also we, who have the Spirit as our first taste of heaven,*i* groan inwardly as we look forward to being adopted as His children; then our body will be set free. **24** For we are saved, and so we hope for this. But if we hope for something we see, it is not really hope. Who hopes for what he sees? **25** But if we hope for what we do not see, we patiently wait for it with eager expectation.

26 In the same way the Spirit also helps us in our weakness, because we do not know how we should pray, but the Spirit Himself pleads for us with sighs for which we cannot find the words.*j* **27** But He who searches our hearts knows what the Spirit has in mind, for He is pleading for the believers [saints] in God's own way.

God Gives Us Glory

28 We know that all things work together for good for those who love God, those whom He called according to His plan. **29** This is true because those whom He knew from the first He also appointed long ago to have a form that is the same as the likeness of His Son, so He would be the Firstborn among many brothers. **30** Now those whom He appointed long ago, He also called; those whom He called, He also justified [declared righteous];*k* and those whom He justified, He also glorified.

31 What then shall we say to all this? If God is for us, who can be against us?

---

f- 12 Literally: "brothers."
g- 15 Meaning "Father, Father!" *Abba* is the Aramaic word for "father."
h- 20 Literally: "For this creation was subordinated to futility."
i- 23 Literally: "who have the firstfruits of the Spirit."
j- 26 Namely, to express our yearnings.
k- 30 See 3:24 and its accompanying footnote (also applies to v. 33).

32 He who did not spare His own Son but gave Him up for all of us—won't He certainly also give us all things along with Him? **33** Who will accuse those whom God has chosen? It is God *who justifies [acquits]* us. **34** *Who will condemn?* It is Christ who died, and more than that, He rose; He is at the right hand of God, and He prays for us. **35** Who will separate us from the love of Christ? Will sorrow, hardship or persecution, hunger or nakedness, danger or sword? **36** As it is written:

> *For you we are being killed all the day long.*
> *We are considered as sheep to be slaughtered.*

37 But in all this He who loved us helps us win an overwhelming victory. **38** Yes, I am convinced that neither death nor life, neither angels nor rulers, neither anything in the present nor in the future, no powers, **39** nothing above or below, nor any other creature can ever separate us from the love God has for us in Christ Jesus our Lord.

9TH CHAPTER

D. Eternal predestination/election,
as illustrated by the example of the Jews and Gentiles (9:1–11:36)

God's People

1 I am telling the truth in Christ; I am not lying, as my conscience assures me by the Holy Spirit, **2** when I say that I have great sorrow and continuous pain in my heart. **3** To be sure, I could wish myself cut off from Christ and damned for my fellow Jews,*a* ⌊those who are⌋ my own flesh and blood. **4** They are the people of Israel. They were made God's children. They have the glory, the covenants,*b* the Law, the worship, and the promises. **5** They have the ancestors, and from them, according to His human nature,*c* came Christ, who is God over everything, blessed forever. Amen.

6 This does not mean that God failed to keep His word. For not all who are descended from Israel are the real Israel,*d* **7** and not all who are descended from Abraham are for that reason his real children. No, *"Isaac's children will be called your descendants."* **8** This means that ⌊Abraham's⌋ children who are born in a natural way*e* are not counted as the children of God. Only the children of the promise are counted as his descendants.

33,34 *Is 50:8*   36 *Ps 44:22*   7 *Gen 21:12*

---

9 *a-* 3 Literally: "brothers."
  b- 4 See *DIATHĒKĒ* on page 531.
  c- 5 Literally: "according to flesh."
  d- 6 Compare 2:28,29.
  e- 8 Literally: "of the flesh."

God's Right To Choose

9 This is how the promise was worded: *"I will come back at the right time, and Sarah will have a son."* **10** The same thing happened to Rebekah. She was about to bear children for our ancestor Isaac. **11** They had not yet been born nor had they done anything good or bad. Even then—in order that God might carry out His purpose according to His choice, which does not depend on anything that we do but on Him who calls us—**12** she was told: *"The older will serve the younger."* **13** And so it is written:

> Jacob I loved,
>> but Esau I hated.

14 Does this mean, then, that God is unjust? Never! **15** For He says to Moses:

> *I will be merciful to anyone to whom I wish to be merciful;*
> *I will pity anyone whom I wish to pity.*

16 Therefore, it [God's choosing] does not depend on anyone's desire or on anyone's effort;*f* rather, it depends on God's mercy. **17** For example, the Scripture says to Pharoah: *"I raised you to the throne to demonstrate My power through you and to spread My Name over all the earth."* **18** So He pities whom He wishes to pity and *makes stubborn* whom He wishes to make stubborn.

19 You will ask me, "Why does He still find fault with anyone? Who can resist His will?" **20** But now, who are you, man, to talk back to God? *Will the thing which is formed say to the one who formed it*, "Why did you make me like this?" **21** Does not *a potter* have the right over *his clay* to make out of the same lump of clay one thing for a noble purpose and another for a lowly purpose?

22 What if God, wanting to show people His anger and to let them know His power, waited very patiently before He *punished those who deserved it*, those who had prepared themselves *for destruction*? **23** What if He also did this to show the riches of the glory that He has in store for those to whom He is merciful and whom He long ago prepared for glory, **24** namely, us whom He called, not only from the Jews but also from the Gentiles?

God Chooses Gentiles [Non-Jews]

25 So He says in Hosea:

> Those who are not My people
>> I will call "My people,"
> and those who are not loved
>> I will call "My loved ones";
26 and where they were told,

---

9 Gen 18:10,14   **12** Gen 25:23   **13** Mal 1:2,3   **15** Ex 33:19   **17** Ex 9:16
18 Ex 4:21; 7:3; 9:12; 14:4,17   **20** Is 29:16; 45:9   **21** Jer 18:6   **22** Is 13:5; Jer 50:25
25,26 Hos 2:1,23; 1:10

---

f- 16 Literally: "running."

> *"You are not My people,"*
> *they will be called sons of the living God.*

27 Isaiah exclaims in regard to Israel:

> *Though the people of Israel are as many as the sand by the sea,*
> *only a remnant will be saved.*
> **28** *For the Lord will execute His sentence on the land,*
> *completely and decisively.*

29 So Isaiah said long ago:

> *If the Lord of armies [hosts]ᵍ had not left us some survivors,ʰ*
> *we would have become like Sodom and ended like Gomorrah.*

30 What we are saying then is this: The Gentiles who were not pursuing righteousness found it, namely, a righteousness which is received by believing. **31** On the other hand, Israel—by pursuing the Law to gain righteousness—did not reach their goal.ⁱ **32** Why? They did not pursue it by faith but by works. They stumbled over *the stumbling block,* **33** as it is written:

> *See, I am putting in Zion*
> *a Stone which will cause them to stumble*
> *and*
> *a Rock which will cause them to fall.ʲ*
> *But the person who believes in Him will not be disappointed.*

10TH CHAPTER

Jews Should Believe

1 Fellow Christians,ᵃ my heart's desire and my prayer to God is to save the Israelites. **2** I can testify that they are zealous for God, but without understanding. **3** Not knowing the righteousness which God gives, and trying to set up their own, they have not become subordinateᵇ to God's righteousness. **4** You see, Christ is the end of the Law to give righteousness to everyone who believes.

5 Moses writes: *"If you have done* the righteous things demanded by the Law, *you will find life in them."* **6** But the righteousness obtained by faith says this: *"Do not ask yourself, 'Who will go up to heaven?'* (which means, to bring Christ down) **7** or *'Who will go down into the depths?'* (which means, to bring Christ

---

27,28 Is 10:22,23; 28:22   29 Is 1:9   32,33 Is 8:14; 28:16   5 Lev 18:5   6 Deut 9:4
6-8 Deut 30:12,14; Ps 107:26

---

g- 29 Greek: "sabaōth," from the Hebrew "tsābā" ("host," "army").
h- 29 Literally: "seed."
i- 31 Literally: "by pursuing a Law of righteousness did not come up to the Law."
j- 33 See *SKANDALON* on page 545.
10 *a-* 1 Literally: "brothers."
b- 3 See *HUPOTASSŌ* on page 541.

up from the dead)." **8** But what does it say? *"The word is near you, in your mouth and in your heart."* This is the word of faith which we preach. **9** We preach that if you confess with your mouth, "Jesus is Lord," and believe in your heart that "God raised Him from the dead," you will be saved. **10** For with the heart a person believes and is justified [declared righteous], and with the mouth a person confesses and is saved. **11** For the Scripture says, *"Anyone who believes in Him will not be disappointed."*

12 There is no difference between Jew and Greek, because they all have the same Lord, who gives His riches to all who call on Him. **13** Yes, *everyone who calls on the Name of the Lord will be saved.*

14   But how can they call on Him
         if they have not believed in Him?
     How can they believe in Him
         if they have not heard of Him?
     How can they hear
         if no one preaches?
15   How can they preach
         if they are not sent?

Just as it is written:

     How beautiful are the feet of the messengers who bring good news!

16 But not all have obeyed^c the Good News [Gospel]. Isaiah asks:

     Lord, who has believed our message?

17 So then faith comes from hearing the message, and the message comes through the word of Christ.

18 But I ask, "They certainly have heard, have they not?" Indeed they have!

     Their voice has gone all over the earth
       and their words to the farthest parts of the world.

19 Again I ask, "Israel certainly knew, did they not?" Moses was the first to say:

     I will make you jealous of those who are not a nation;
     I will make you angry with a people who do not understand.

20 Then Isaiah boldly says:

     I was found by those who were not looking for Me;
     I was revealed to those who were not asking for Me.

---

11 *Is 28:16*   **13** *Joel 2:32*   **15** *Is 52:7*   **16** *Is 53:1*   **18** *Ps 19:4*   **19** *Deut 32:21*
20,21 *Is 65:1,2*

---

c- 16 That is, "embraced" or "accepted."

21 And He says concerning Israel:

> All day long I have stretched out My hands to a people,
> although they disobeyed and opposed Me.

11TH CHAPTER

The Remnant

1 So I ask, *"God did not reject His people, did He?"* Certainly not—I am an Israelite myself, a descendant of Abraham and of the tribe of Benjamin. 2 *God has not rejected His people* whom He chose long ago. Or do you not know what the Scripture says in the passage about Elijah when he pleads with God against Israel: 3 *"Lord, they have killed Your prophets, they have torn down Your altars, I am the only one left, and they are trying to kill me"*? 4 *But* what did *God answer him*? *"I have kept for Myself seven thousand men who have not bowed their knees to Baal."* 5 So then, there is also right now a remnant that God has chosen by His grace. 6 But if they were chosen by grace, it could not have been because of what they had done; otherwise grace [undeserved love] would no longer be grace.

7 What then? Israel did not receive what it wanted, but those whom God chose did receive it.

God's Way Of Saving "All Israel"

And the minds of the others were dulled, 8 as it is written:

> God has given them a spirit of deep sleep,
> eyes that should not see
> and ears that should not hear;
> and so it has been until this day!

9 And David says:

> Let their table be a snare and a trap
> to make them fall and receive what they deserve.
> 10 Let their eyes have no light so they cannot see.
> Let their backs be bent forever.ᵃ

11 So I ask, "They did not stumble in order to be lost, did they?" Certainly not! Rather, by their fall, salvation has come to the Gentiles *to make the Jews jealous.* 12 And if their fall made the world rich and their loss made the Gentiles rich, how much more their [the Jews'] fullness will do this also! 13 Now, I am

---

1,2 1 Sam 12:22; Ps 94:14   *3,4 1 Kgs 19:10,14,15,18*   *8 Deut 29:4; Is 29:10*
9,10 Ps 69:22,23   *11 Deut 32:21*

11 *a*- 10 That is, load them with burdens difficult to bear.

speaking to you Gentiles. Therefore, I will continue to glorify my ministry for as long as I am sent to the Gentiles. **14** Perhaps I can *make* my fellow Jews *jealous* and save some of them. **15** For when God rejects them, the world is reconciled to God;*b* when God accepts them, what can it mean but that the dead will come to life?

16 If the first handful of dough is holy, so is the whole dough. If the root is holy, so are the branches. **17** But if some of the branches have been broken off, and you ⌊a Gentile⌋, a wild olive, have been grafted in among them, and the rich sap from the root of the olive tree nourishes you too, **18** do not boast of being more than the other branches. If you boast, remember that you do not support the root, but the root supports you. **19** You will then say: "Branches were cut off to graft me in." **20** Right! They were broken off because they did not believe, but you stand by faith. Do not feel proud, but be afraid. **21** For if God did not spare the natural branches, He will not spare you. **22** Now see how kind and how severe God can be—severe to those who fell, but kind to you if you cling to His kindness; otherwise you too will be cut off.

23 And if the Jews do not continue in their unbelief, they will be grafted back ⌊into their place⌋, because God is able to graft them in again. **24** Yes, since you have been cut from an olive tree that grows wild and have been unnaturally grafted into a cultivated olive tree, how much more likely it is that these natural branches will be grafted back into their own olive tree!

25 To keep you from thinking too highly of yourselves, my fellow Christians,*c* I want you to know this mystery:*d* The minds of a part of the Jews were closed until the full number of the Gentiles comes in. **26** And in this way all Israel will be saved, as it is written:

> *The Savior will come from Zion;*
> *He will get rid of ungodliness in Jacob.*
> 27 *And this will be My "last will and testament"* *e* *with them*
> *when I take away their sins.*

28 From the viewpoint of the Gospel they are treated as enemies for your benefit, but from the viewpoint of God's choice they are loved on account of their fathers. **29** For God never changes His mind when He gives anything or calls anyone. **30** Once you disobeyed God, but now that the Jews have disobeyed, He has been merciful to you. **31** So they also have disobeyed now—while you enjoy mercy—that they also might receive mercy. **32** You see, God has put all people in a prison of disobedience in order to be merciful to all.

---

14 Deut 32:21   *26,27 Is 27:9; 59:20,21*

---

b- 15 Reconciliation places a person into a *changed relationship* with God.
c- 25 Literally: "brothers."
d- 25 The Greek word here used refers to a *secret* that is hidden from human understanding and cannot be grasped by those outside the Christian faith. The same Greek word is used, for example, in 16:25; 1 Corinthians 15:51; Ephesians 1:9; 1 Timothy 3:16.
e- 27 See *DIATHĒKĒ* on page 531.

33 How deep are God's riches, wisdom, and knowledge;
   how impossible it is to figure out His decisions and to trace His ways!

34 *Who has found out how the Lord thinks?*
   Or who has become His adviser?

35   *Or who has first given Him something*
      for which he must *be paid back?*

36 Everything is from Him and by Him and for Him.
To Him be glory forever. Amen.

12TH CHAPTER

E. Practical Christian ethics/morality (12:1–15:13)

Live For God

1 Therefore I appeal to you, fellow Christians,*a* by the mercies of God, to offer your bodies as a living sacrifice, holy and pleasing to God. In doing this you will be worshiping in a spiritual way. 2 Do not follow the pattern of this world, but let yourselves be transformed by a renewing of your minds so that you can test and be sure of what God wants, namely, what is good and pleasing and perfect.

3 As God gave me His gift of grace, I say to everyone of you: Do not let your thoughts about your value go beyond what is proper. Rather, as you think about this, keep your thoughts in bounds. Consider how God has given a measure of faith to each of you. 4 For we have many parts in one body, and these parts do not all do the same thing. 5 In the very same way, many as we are, we are one body in Christ and individually parts of one another. 6 We have gifts that are different according to what His grace gave us. If a person's gift is speaking God's word, let him speak it in complete agreement with the faith.*b* 7 If a person's gift is serving, then let him serve. If it is teaching, let him teach. 8 If it is encouraging others, let him encourage. If a person's gift is sharing, let him be generous. If it is managing, let him do it eagerly. If it is helping people in need, let him do it cheerfully.

Love

9 Love sincerely. Hate evil; cling to what is good. 10 Love one another tenderly as fellow Christians.*c* Outdo one another in showing respect. 11 Do not be timid in your zeal, but let your spirit glow, and serve the Lord. 12 Be happy

---

34 *Is 40:13*   35 *Job 35:7; 41:11*

---

12 *a-* 1 Literally: "brothers."
   b- 6 Meaning "If a person can prophesy, let what he says be, in complete conformity with the standard [Greek: '*analogia*' ('analogy')] of the faith." The Greek word for "standard" refers to the equality that must exist between the two parts of an equation or between the members of a proportion.
   c- 10 Literally: "in brotherly love."

in your hope, be patient in trouble, and continue in prayer. 13 Share what you have with the believers [saints] who are in need. Eagerly welcome strangers as guests.

14 Bless those who persecute you; bless and do not curse them. 15 Be happy with those who are happy; weep with those who weep. 16 Live in harmony with one another. Do not have your mind set on high things, but follow the humble ways of others. *Do not think that you are wise.*

17 Do not pay back evil for evil. *Let your mind dwell on those things that everyone considers noble.* 18 Do as much as you can to live in peace with everybody. 19 Do not take revenge, dear friends, but let God punish, *d* because it is written: *"I alone have the right to avenge. I will pay back,"* says the Lord. 20 Rather:

> *If your enemy is hungry, feed him.*
> *If he is thirsty, give him a drink.*
> *If you do this, you will heap burning coals on his head.*

21 Do not let evil conquer you, but conquer evil with good.

13TH CHAPTER

Obey Your Government

1 Let everyone be subordinate *a* to government officials, because no government exists unless God has permitted it, and the governments which do exist have been established by God. 2 Therefore, anyone who resists the authority of the government opposes what God has established, and those who do this will bring judgment on themselves.

3 You do not have to be afraid of those who rule if you do right, only if you do wrong. Would you like to live without being afraid of your government? Do what is right, and it will praise you; 4 for it is God's servant to help you. If you do wrong, you should be afraid, because the government carries the sword for a purpose. *b* It is God's servant, an avenger who is there to punish anyone doing wrong. 5 Therefore it is necessary ⌐for you⌐ to be subordinate, not only because of the punishment but also because your conscience tells you to obey. *c*

---

16 Prov 3:7   17 Prov 3:4 (Greek)   19 Deut 32:35   20 Prov 25:21,22

---

d- 19 Literally: "Do not avenge yourselves, beloved, but give an opportunity for the anger ⌐of God⌐."

13 a- 1 Greek: *"hupotassō."* This Greek term speaks of persons who are placed in an "order" or "rank" below or under the authority of another. In the mind of sinful human beings this is often falsely equated with *inferiority.* However, Jesus taught us that among Christians this is not to be the case. It is not the one in authority who is the greatest but the one who is servant to all (Matt. 20:25-28; Mk. 10:42-45); authority and servitude are always to be used for the benefit of others.

The English "subordinate" captures the totality of this *hupotassō* concept quite well. In the passage before us Paul uses the word in terms of our *everyday relationships within society* (cf. v. 5; Tit. 3:1; 1 Pet. 2:13). See *HUPOTASSO* on page 541.

b- 4 Literally: "the government does not carry the sword in vain."

c- 5 Literally: "because of your conscience."

6 That is why you also pay taxes. People in the government serve God and are busy doing this work. 7 Pay to all whatever you owe them. If you owe anyone tribute, pay tribute; if taxes, then taxes; if respect, then respect; if honor, then honor.

Love One Another

8 Do not owe anyone anything, except to love one another; for the person who loves another has kept the whole Law. 9 To be sure, the commandments, *"Do not commit adultery, Do not murder, Do not steal, Do not wrongfully desire,"* and if there is any other commandment, are summed up in this: *"Love your neighbor as yourself."* 10 Love does nothing which is harmful to another person. Therefore, to love is to keep the whole Law. *d*

11 Do this especially since you know the time ˩in which we are living˩. It is now time for you to wake up from sleep, because our salvation is now nearer than when we ˩first˩ came to faith. 12 The night is almost over, and the day is dawning. So let us put away the works of darkness and put on the armor of light. 13 Let us live decently as is proper in the daytime, not carousing or getting drunk, not sinning sexually or living wildly, not quarreling or being jealous. 14 But put on the Lord Jesus Christ, and do not make plans to satisfy ˩your˩ fleshly desires.

14TH CHAPTER

Weak Christians

1 Welcome the person who is weak in the faith, but do not argue about different opinions. 2 One person believes he can eat anything; another person whose faith is weak eats only vegetables. 3 Let there be no despising of the person who does not eat by the one who does eat. And let there be no criticism of the one who eats by the one who does not eat, because God has accepted that person. 4 Who are you to criticize someone else's servant? It is a matter for his lord to determine whether he succeeds or fails. And he will succeed, because the Lord can make him succeed.

5 One person thinks one day is better than the other; another thinks they are all alike. Let everyone be thoroughly convinced in his own mind. 6 The person who has a special day means to honor the Lord. The person who eats does it for the Lord since he thanks God. And the person who keeps from eating does it for the Lord, and he thanks God. 7 Indeed, none of us lives for himself, and none dies for himself. 8 For if we live, we live for the Lord; and if we die, we die for the Lord. So whether we live or die, we belong to the Lord. 9 For this reason Christ died and became alive again to be the Lord of both the dead and the living.

---

9 *Ex 20:13-15,17; Deut 5:17-19,21; Lev 19:18*

d- 10 Or "Therefore, love is the fulfillment of the Law."

10 I ask one of you, "Why do you criticize your fellow Christian?"*a* Or I ask another, "Why do you despise your fellow Christian?" For we must all stand before God to be judged. **11** It is written:

> As surely as I live, says the Lord,
>> everyone will kneel before Me,
>>> and every tongue will praise God.

12 So each of us will have to give an account of himself to God.

13 Therefore let us stop criticizing one another. Rather, be determined not to lay any stumbling block or death trap*b* in the way of a fellow Christian. **14** I know and am convinced in the Lord Jesus that nothing is unclean in itself; but to the person who thinks anything is unclean, to that person it is unclean. **15** But if what you eat hurts your fellow Christian, you are no longer living according to love anymore. Do not ruin any person for whom Christ died by what you eat. **16** Do not let anyone denounce what you know to be good.

17 God's Kingdom is not a matter of eating and drinking but of righteousness and peace and joy in the Holy Spirit. **18** Yes, the person who serves Christ in this way is accepted by God and approved by people.

19 So we eagerly pursue the things which make for peace and by which we help one another grow. **20** Do not ruin God's work just for food. Everything is clean, but it is wrong for a person to eat it if it causes someone else to stumble. **21** It is not good to eat meat, drink wine, or do anything else that causes your fellow Christian to stumble. **22** Hold on to the faith which you have as your own conviction before God.*c* Blessed is the person who never has to condemn himself in regard to anything he approves. **23** But if a person doubts and still eats, he is condemned because he does not live according to what he believes. Any act that is not based on what a person believes is sin.

15TH CHAPTER

More Concerning Weak Christians

1 But we who are strong have a continuing obligation to be patient with the weaknesses of those who are not strong, and not just go on pleasing ourselves. **2** Let each of us please his neighbor for his ͺneighbor'sͺ good, to help him grow. **3** Even Christ did not please Himself, but ͺit happened to Him, as it is written: *"The insults of those who are insulting You have fallen on Me."*

---

11 Is 45:23,24; 49:18   3 Ps 69:9

---

14 *a-* 10 Literally: "brother" (twice; also in vv. 13,15,21).
   b- 13 See *SKANDALON* on page 545.
   c- 22 Literally: "Hold on to the faith which you have by yourself before God." This verse is difficult. Paul seems to be directing the people of God to do what their faith tells them to do concerning this matter.

Jews And Gentiles [Non-Jews]

4 All that was written long ago was written to teach us, so that we would have hope through the patient endurance and encouragement which the Scriptures give us. **5** May God, who helps you to patiently endure and encourages you, give you such harmony with one another as you follow Christ Jesus, **6** so that with one heart and one voice you might praise the God and Father of our Lord Jesus Christ.

7 Therefore, as Christ has received you, receive one another in order to glorify God. **8** For I tell you that Christ became a Servant to the Jews to do what God promised to the fathers—showing that He tells the truth—**9** and to have the Gentiles praise God for His mercy, as it is written:

> *For this I shall confess You among the Gentiles*
> *by singing praise to Your Name.*

10 And again it says:

> *Be happy, you Gentiles, together with His own people!*

11 And again:

> *Praise the Lord, all you Gentiles,*
> *and let all the people praise Him.*

12 Again, Isaiah says:

> *Jesse will have the Descendant,*[a]
> *who will rise to rule the Gentiles,*
> *and in Him will the Gentiles put their hope.*

13 May the God of hope fill you with perfect happiness and peace as you believe, so that you overflow with hope by the power of the Holy Spirit.

F. Conclusion (15:14–16:27)

New Fields

14 I myself am convinced, my fellow Christians,[b] that you also are full of kindness, fully equipped with every kind of knowledge, and able to correct one another. **15** However, I have written you a letter—parts of which are rather bold—as a reminder to you. I have been bold, because of that special gift of grace that was given to me by God **16** to be a servant of Christ Jesus among the Gentiles. My duty was to work for the Gospel of God as a priest that I might

---

9 2 Sam 22:50; Ps 18:49   10 Deut 32:43   11 Ps 117:1   12 Is 11:1,10

15 *a*- 12 Literally: "There will be a Root of Jesse."
  b- 14 Literally: "brothers."

bring the Gentiles as an acceptable offering made holy by the Holy Spirit. **17** So I can boast in Christ Jesus of what I am doing for God, **18** because I will dare to tell only what Christ has done through me to make the Gentiles obedient. Christ did this by what I said and did, **19** by the power of miraculous signs and wonderful proofs, *c* by the power of God's Spirit, so that I have finished preaching the Gospel of Christ from Jerusalem all the way around to Illyricum.

20 But I was ambitious to preach the Gospel only where the Name of Christ was not known, so as not to build on a foundation which others had laid, **21** but as it is written:

> Those who were never told about Him will see,
> and those who never heard will understand.

I Hope To See You

22 That is why I have so often been kept from coming to you. **23** But now there is no more opportunity for me to work in this territory. For many years I have longed to come to you **24** on my way to Spain. Yes, I hope to see you when I pass through and, after I have enjoyed being with you for a while, to have you send me on my way there.

25 Right now I am going to Jerusalem to bring help to the believers [saints] there. **26** You see, Macedonia and Greece decided to share their goods with the poor among the believers in Jerusalem. **27** That was their decision, and they owe something to the Jews. For if the Jews have shared their spiritual goods with the Gentiles, the Gentiles owe it to them to serve them with their earthly goods.

28 When that is done and I have certified this fruit to the Jews in this way, *d* I will come to you on my way to Spain. **29** I know that when I come to you I will bring the full blessing of Christ.

30 By our Lord Jesus Christ and by the love of the Spirit, I urge you to join me in my struggle by praying to God for me. **31** Pray that I may be rescued from those in Judea who refuse to believe and that the believers in Jerusalem may welcome the help I bring, **32** so that by the will of God I may come to you with joy and be refreshed in your company.

33 May the God of peace be with you all. Amen.

16TH CHAPTER

Farewell

1 I am introducing Phoebe, our fellow Christian, *a* to you. She is a worker in the church in Cenchreae. **2** Welcome her in the Lord in a way which is worthy

---

21 Is 52:15

---

c- 19 See MIRACULOUS SIGNS, WONDERFUL PROOFS, and MIRACLES on page 527.
d- 28 Paul wanted the Jews to recognize that this gift was a product ("fruit") that flowed from the Gentiles' faith.
16 *a-* 1 Literally: "sister."

of believers [saints] and give her any help she may need from you, because she has become a protector of many, including me.

3 Greet Prisca and Aquila, my fellow workers in Christ Jesus, 4 who risked their necks to save my life. Not only I but all the churches among the Gentiles are grateful to them. 5 Greet also the church that meets in their house.

Greet my dear Epaenetus, who was the first in the province of Asia to turn to Christ.

6 Greet Mary, who has worked very hard for you.

7 Greet Andronicus and Junias, my fellow Jews, who went to prison with me. They are outstanding among the apostles. They also came to Christ before I did.

8 Greet Ampliatus, who is dear to me in the Lord.

9 Greet Urban our fellow worker in Christ, and my dear Stachys.

10 Greet Apelles, a tried and true Christian.

Greet those who belong to the family of Aristobulus.

11 Greet Herodion my fellow Jew.

Greet those in the family of Narcissus who are in the Lord.

12 Greet Tryphaena and Tryphosa, who have worked hard for the Lord.

Greet dear Persis, who has worked very hard for the Lord.

13 Greet Rufus, the chosen one in the Lord, and his mother—who has been a mother to me too.

14 Greet Asyncritus, Phlegon, Hermes, Patrobas, Hermas, and the fellow Christians*b* who are with them.

15 Greet Philologus, Julia, Nereus, and his sister, and Olympas, and all the believers who are with them.

16 Greet one another with a holy kiss. All the churches of Christ greet you.

17 I urge you, fellow Christians, to take note of those who cause disagreements and cause people to fall ⌊from faith⌋*c* by going against the teaching you learned. Turn completely away from them. 18 Such people are not serving Christ our Lord but their own feelings,*d* and by their smooth words and flattering talk are deceiving innocent people.

19 Everybody has heard how you obey, and so I am happy about you. I want you to be wise concerning what is good, and innocent in respect to what is evil. 20 The God of peace will soon *crush* Satan under your feet.

May the grace of our Lord Jesus be with you!

21 Timothy my fellow worker greets you;
so do Lucius, Jason, and Sosipater, my fellow Jews.

22 I, Tertius, who penned this letter, greet you in the Lord.

---

20 Gen 3:15

b- 14 Literally: "brothers" (also in v. 17; "brother" in v. 23).

c- 17 See *SKANDALON* on page 545.

d- 18 Literally: "belly" which in Greek is often referred to as the source of passions and desires (cf. Phil. 3:19).

23 Gaius, my host and the host of the whole church, greets you.
Erastus the city treasurer greets you,
and Quartus our fellow Christian. *e*

25 Now to Him—

who can make you strong by the Gospel which I bring and by
the preaching of Jesus Christ, by unveiling the mystery*f* that
was veiled in silence for long ages **26** but now has been brought
to light and has been shown to all the Gentiles by means of
what the prophets wrote, as the everlasting God ordered them,
to lead them to believe and obey—

27 to the only wise God through Jesus Christ be glory forever. Amen.

---

e- 23 Some of the older manuscripts and early translations add verse 24: "The grace of our Lord
Jesus Christ be with you all. Amen." Compare verse 20 where these same words appear.
f- 25 See 11:25 and its accompanying footnote "d."

FAMOUS CHAPTERS OF THE NEW TESTAMENT

Matthew	5-7	"The Sermon on the Mount" Chapters
Matthew	13	"Most Parables" Chapter
Matthew	24	"Eschatology" Chapter (cf. Mk. 13; Lk. 21:5-38)
Luke	2	"The Christmas Story" Chapter (cf. Matt. 1 and 2)
Luke	10	"The Good Samaritan" Chapter (vv. 25-37)
Luke	15	"The Lost Chapter" Chapter (Lost sheep, coin, son)
John	10	"The Good Shepherd" Chapter
John	17	"The High Priestly Prayer of Jesus" Chapter
Romans	3	"Justification by Faith" Chapter
Romans	8	"The Greatest Chapter of the Bible" Chapter
1 Corinthians	7	"Marriage" Chapter (cf. Eph. 5:22-33)
1 Corinthians	11	"The Lord's Supper" Chapter (vv. 11-34)
1 Corinthians	13	"Love" Chapter
1 Corinthians	15	"Resurrection" Chapter
2 Corinthians	8,9	"Stewardship" Chapters
Hebrews	11	"Faith" Chapter
Revelation	21	"New Heavens and New Earth" Chapter

GREATEST BIBLE PASSAGES OF THE NEW TESTAMENT

Matthew	28:19	"The Great Commission" Passage
John	3:16	"FAMOUS 'GOSPEL-IN-A-NUTSHELL' " Passage
John	8:31,32	"Study-the-Bible" Passage
John	14:6	"The Only-WAY-to Heaven" Passage
John	15:5	"Jesus-Gives-the-Ability" Passage
Romans	1:16; 3:28	"The Reformation" Passages
Romans	8:28	"God-Will-Work-It-Out" Passage
1 Corinthians	12:3	"Spirit-Gets-All-the-Credit" Passage
2 Corinthians	5:14,15	"From-Sacrifice-to-sacrifice" Passage
2 Corinthians	5:18-21	"The Great Reconciliation" Passage
Ephesians	2:8,9	"The Most Clear 'Way-of-Salvation' " Passage
2 Timothy	3:16	"Bible" Passage
1 John	4:8	"God Is Love" Passage
Revelation	2:10	"The Ultimate Promise" Passage

GREAT PASSAGES OF COMFORT AND HOPE

Matthew 11:28-30; John 10:28; 11:25; Romans 8:38,39; 1 Corinthians 5:7; 10:13; Philippians 1:6; 4:6-7; 1 Timothy 2:4; Hebrews 2:18; 4:15; 12:1-13; 13:5,20,21; 1 John 2:2

GREAT PASSAGES OF GUIDANCE AND WARNING

Matthew 6:15; 7:15; 18:6; Acts 2:38; 4:12; 1 Corinthians 10:12; 2 Corinthians 5:10; Galatians 6:9,10; 2 Thessalonians 3:10; Hebrews 9:27; James 4:7; 1 Peter 5:8; 1 John 1:8,9

1 CORINTHIANS[a]

1ST CHAPTER

A. Congregational problems reported to Paul (1:1–6:20)
1. Factions in the church (1:1–4:21)

1 Paul, called as an apostle of Christ Jesus by the will of God, and Sosthenes my fellow Christian,[b] **2** to the church of God in Corinth, made holy by Christ Jesus and called to be holy,[c] with all who anywhere call on the Name of our Lord Jesus Christ, their Lord and ours—**3** may God our Father and the Lord Jesus Christ give you grace[d] and peace.

4 I am always thanking God for you because of His grace which was given to you in Christ Jesus. **5** For in Him you have been made rich in every way, in speech and knowledge of every kind, **6** just as our testimony concerning Christ was confirmed in you. **7** And so you do not lack any gift as you eagerly look for our Lord Jesus Christ to appear again. **8** He will strengthen you to the end so that no one can accuse you of anything on the Day of our Lord Jesus Christ. **9** You can depend on God, who called you to the fellowship of His Son Jesus Christ our Lord.

Everyone For Christ

10 Fellow Christians,[e] by the Name of our Lord Jesus Christ I urge you all to agree and not to be divided but to be perfectly united in your understanding and judgment. **11** For Chloe's people told me that you are quarreling, my fellow Christians. **12** I mean that each of you says, "I belong to Paul," or "I belong to Apollos," or "I belong to Peter," or "I belong to Christ." **13** Is Christ divided? Was Paul crucified for you? Or were you baptized into Paul's name? **14** I thank God that[f] I did not baptize any of you except Crispus and Gaius, **15** so that no one can say you were baptized into my name. **16** I also baptized the family of

---

1 *a*   The Apostle Paul wrote his first letter to Corinth from Ephesus on his Third Missionary Journey after making arrangements for the collection for the poor in Jerusalem (16:1-4). The date was around A.D. 55.

b- 1 Literally: "brother."

c- 2 Or "saints."

d- 3 Meaning "God's undeserved love."

e- 10 Literally: "brothers" (also in vv. 11,26).

f- 14 A few of the older manuscripts read: "I am thankful that."

Stephanas. I do not know whether I baptized anyone else. **17** For Christ did not send me to baptize but to preach the Gospel [Good News] without using any cleverness in my preaching, for fear that the cross of Christ might lose its power. *g*

The Foolish Things Used By God

18 The story of the cross is foolishness to those who are perishing, but to us who are being saved it is the power of God. **19** For it is written:

> *I will destroy the wisdom of the wise*
> *and defeat the intelligence of the intelligent.*

20 *Where is the wise man? Where is the Bible scholar?* *h* *Where is the debater of our time? Has God not made foolish the wisdom of the world?* **21** Yes, since in the wisdom of God the world by its wisdom did not learn to know God, God gladly decided to use the foolishness of our preaching to save those who believe. **22** For Jews ask for miraculous signs *i* and Greeks look for wisdom, **23** but we preach a crucified Christ. To the Jews this is a stumbling block *j* and to the Greeks it is foolishness, **24** but to those who are called, both Jews and Greeks, He is Christ, God's power and God's wisdom, **25** because ᵢthey have learned to know thatᵢ *k* God's foolishness is wiser than man's wisdom, and God's weakness is stronger than man's strength.

26 For you see what happened, fellow Christians, when God called you. Not many of you are wise from a human point of view, not many are in positions of power, not many are born of noble parents. **27** But God chose the foolish things in the world to put those who are wise to shame. God chose the weak things in the world to put those who are strong to shame. **28** God chose the lowly things in the world, that which it despises, that which is nothing, to do away with that which is something—**29** in order to keep anyone from boasting before God. **30** He gave you your life in Christ Jesus, whom God made our wisdom, righteousness, holiness, and ransom from sin, **31** so that it might be as it is written: *"Let the one who boasts, boast in the Lord."*

2ND CHAPTER

1 When I came to you, fellow Christians, *a* I did not come to proclaim the

---

19 Ps 33:10; Is 29:14   *20 Is 19:12; 33:18; 44:25*   *31 Jer 9:24*

---

g - 17 Or "Gospel, not in words of human [worldly] wisdom, lest the cross of Christ dwindle to nothing."

h - 20 Or "scribe."

i - 22 See MIRACULOUS SIGNS, WONDERFUL PROOFS, and MIRACLES on page 527.

j - 23 See *SKANDALON* on page 545.

k - 25 Compare verse 21 ("did not learn to know God") and verse 26 ("For . . .").

2 a - 1 Literally: "brothers."

testimony*b* of God with a fancy display of words or wisdom. **2** For while I was with you, I was determined to know only Jesus Christ and Him crucified. **3** I came to you in weakness, in fear, and with much trembling. **4** When I spoke and preached, I did not use clever words to persuade you, but I let the Spirit demonstrate His power, **5** so that your faith might not depend on the wisdom of men but on the power of God.

6 But we speak wisdom to those who are mature, a wisdom unknown to the world today and to its rulers of today who pass away. **7** However, we tell about God's hidden wisdom, *c* wisdom which was concealed but which God planned for our glory before the world began. **8** None of those who rule this world knew it. For if they had known it, they would not have crucified the Lord of glory. **9** But this is exactly what is written:

> *No eye has seen,*
> *no ear has heard,* and
> *no mind has comprehended,*
> *what* God has prepared *for those who* love *Him.*

10 For God has revealed it to us by His Spirit. The Spirit searches out everything, even the deep things of God. **11** For who knows what a person thinks except his own inner spirit? In the same way only God's Spirit knows what God thinks. **12** Now we did not receive the spirit of the world but the Spirit who comes from God, so that we know the things which God has freely given to us. **13** And we speak about them in words not taught by human wisdom but taught by the Spirit, explaining the things of the Spirit to those who have the Spirit. *d*

14 But an unspiritual person does not accept the things of the Spirit of God. He thinks they are foolish, and he cannot know them because one must have the Spirit to judge them correctly. **15** The person who has the Spirit judges everything correctly, but he himself is under no man's judgment.

16   For *who has known the mind of the Lord,*
       that he may teach Him?

But we have the mind of Christ.

3RD CHAPTER

We Plant And Build

1 Fellow Christians, *a* I could not talk to you as spiritual people but as people

---

9 *Is 64:4*   **16** *Is 40:13*

---

b- 1 Some of the older manuscripts and early translations read: "mystery"; see 4:1 and its accompanying footnote.

c- 7 Literally: "about God's wisdom in a mystery"; see 4:1 and its accompanying footnote.

d- 13 Or "as we explain spiritual things in spiritual words."

3 *a*- 1 Literally: "brothers."

of the world, as babies in Christ. **2** I gave you milk to drink, not solid food, because you were not ready for it. Why even now you are not ready for it, **3** because you still are influenced by your sinful flesh!

For when you are jealous, quarreling, and forming different parties, are you not following your flesh and acting like other people? **4** When one of you says, "I belong to Paul" and another, "I belong to Apollos," aren't you acting like ordinary human beings? **5** Now what is Apollos? Or what is Paul? They are servants by whose help you came to believe, and each helped only as the Lord gave him the ability. **6** I planted, Apollos watered, but God made it grow. **7** Now then, neither the one who plants nor the one who waters is anything, but ⌊only⌋ God who makes it grow. **8** The one who plants and the one who waters are one and the same, and each will get paid for his own work. **9** For we are God's co-workers. You are God's field, God's building.

10 In accordance with the grace [undeserved love] that God gave me, I laid a foundation as an expert master builder, and somebody else is continuing to build on it. But everyone should be careful how he builds on it. **11** For no one can lay any other foundation than the one that is already laid, and that is Jesus Christ. **12** If someone builds on this foundation with gold, silver, precious stones, wood, hay, or straw, **13** what each one does will become evident. For that Day will show what it is, because the fire will reveal it and test it to show what kind of work everyone has done. **14** If what a person has built on the foundation stands the test, he will receive a reward. **15** If his work is burned, he will lose something, but he himself will be saved, though it will be like going through a fire.

16 Do you not know that you are the temple of God and that the Spirit of God lives in you? **17** If anyone destroys the temple of God, God will destroy him, because God's temple is holy. And you are that temple.

18 Do not deceive yourself. If any one of you imagines he is wise in the ways of this world, he should become a fool to become really wise. **19** For God considers this world's wisdom to be foolishness, as it is written: *"He catches the wise with their own trickery"*; **20** and again: *"The Lord knows that the planning of the wise is useless."*

21 So let no one boast about people. For everything is yours—**22** whether Paul, Apollos, Peter, the world, life or death, present or future things—everything is yours. **23** And you belong to Christ and Christ to God.

4TH CHAPTER

We Are Managers [Stewards]

1 So let a person think of us as servants of Christ and managers of God's mysteries.*a* **2** Now then, it is demanded of any manager that he be found trustworthy.

---

19 *Job 5:13*   20 *Ps 94:11*

---

4 *a*- 1 The Greek word here used refers to a *secret* that is hidden from human understanding and cannot be grasped by those outside the Christian faith. The same Greek word is used in 2:7; 13:2; 14:2; 15:51 (cf. Rom. 11:25).

³ It means very little to me that you or any human court should examine[b] me. I do not even examine myself. ⁴ I have a clear conscience, but that does not justify me.[c] It is the Lord who examines me. ⁵ So do not judge anything too early. Wait until the Lord comes. He will let the light shine on what is hidden in the darkness and reveal the plans that people have in their hearts. And then everyone will receive his praise from God.

⁶ Fellow Christians,[d] using a special way of speaking for your sakes, I have referred only to myself and Apollos, so that you might learn from us not to go beyond what Scripture says, in order that you might not boast about one man at the expense of another.

Not A King But A Father

⁷ For does anyone see anything special in you? What do you have that you did not receive? And if you received it, why do you boast as if it were not received?

⁸ So you are already satisfied! You have already become rich! You have become kings without us! I only wish you had become kings so that we might be kings with you.

⁹ For I think God has had us apostles come last in the procession, like men condemned to die; because we have become a spectacle for the world, both for angels and people to see. ¹⁰ We are fools for Christ, but you are wise in Christ. We are weak, but you are strong. You are honored, but we are despised. ¹¹ Up to this hour we are hungry, thirsty, poorly dressed, beaten, homeless, ¹² and we wear ourselves out working with our hands. When we are insulted, we bless. When we are persecuted, we put up with it. ¹³ When slandered, we talk kindly. We have come to be the filth of the world, the scum of the earth, and we are that to this day.

¹⁴ I am not writing this to make you feel ashamed, but I am warning you as my dear children. ¹⁵ For you may have 10,000 guardians in Christ, but not many fathers, because in Christ Jesus I became your father by preaching the Gospel to you. ¹⁶ So I urge you to become my imitators. ¹⁷ That is why I sent Timothy to you. He is my dear and dependable son in the Lord. He will help you keep in mind my ways in Christ Jesus, as I teach them everywhere in every church.

¹⁸ Some of you are puffed up as though I were not coming to you. ¹⁹ But I will come to you soon if it is the Lord's will, and then I will find out, not what these puffed-up fellows say but what they can do. ²⁰ For the Kingdom of God is not a matter of what one says but of what one can do.[e]

²¹ Which would you like? Should I come to you with a stick, or with love and a gentle spirit?

---

b- 3 This is a courtroom term; it refers to the *examination* carried on at a trial to get at the facts in the case (also in v. 4).

c- 4 See Romans 3:19,20.

d- 6 Literally: "brothers."

e- 20 Literally: "For the Kingdom of God is not through word but through power."

5TH CHAPTER

2. Immorality (5:1–6:20)

Remove The Wicked Man

1 We actually hear that there is sexual sin among you, such as is not found even among the Gentiles, that a man has his father's wife. **2** And you feel proud of yourselves! Shouldn't you rather have wept so that the man who did this might be removed from among you? **3** Although I am away from you in body, I am with you in spirit and, being with you, I have already made a judgment in regard to the man who did this. **4** Call a meeting. My spirit and the power of our Lord Jesus will be with you. Then in the Name of our Lord Jesus **5** hand such a person over to Satan to destroy his sinful flesh, in order to save his spirit on the Day of the Lord.

6 It is not good for you to feel proud. Do you not know that a little yeast spreads through the whole batch of dough? **7** Get rid of the old yeast in order that you may be a new batch of dough, inasmuch as you are without yeast because Christ, our *Passover* ₍*Lamb*₎, has been *sacrificed.ᵃ* **8** Let us then celebrate our festival, not with old yeast, not with any yeast of vice and wickedness, but with bread that has no yeast, the bread of purity and truth.

9 In my letter to you I wrote*ᵇ* that you are not to associate with those who live in sexual sin. **10** I did not mean that you should altogether keep away from people who live in sexual sin in this world or from those who are greedy, who rob, or who worship idols; then you would have to get out of this world. **11** But now I am writing you: Do not associate with anyone who calls himself a Christian*ᶜ* and ₍yet₎ lives in sexual sin or is greedy, worships idols, slanders, gets drunk, or robs. Do not eat with such a person.

12 For what business is it of mine to judge those who are outside ₍the Christian faith₎?*ᵈ* Do you not judge those who are inside? **13** God judges those who are outside. *Remove the wicked man from among yourselves.*

6TH CHAPTER

Do Not Sue One Another

1 When one of you has a case against another, do you dare to bring it before

---

7 Ex 12:21   *13 Deut 17:7; 19:19; 22:21,24; 24:7*

5 *a -* 7 Some manuscripts and early translations add: "for us."
  b- 9 Greek word could mean "I write" as in verse 11, or "I wrote."
  c- 11 Literally: "brother."
  d- 12 Or "judge the outsiders."

a court of unrighteous people and not before the believers [saints]? **2** Or do you not know that believers will judge the world? And if you judge the world, are you not able to judge trifles? **3** Do you not know that we will judge angels? Should we then not judge things of this life? **4** If then you are having things of this life decided, are you letting people who have no standing *a* in the church be your judges? **5** I say this to make you feel ashamed. Really, are none of you wise enough to decide a matter between Christians?*b* **6** Instead, one Christian sues another—and this happens in front of unbelievers!

7 Suing one another means that you already have completely failed. Why do you not rather suffer wrong? Why do you not rather let yourself be robbed? **8** Instead, you do wrong, and you rob, and you do it to fellow Christians. *c*

You Are God's Temple

9 Or do you not know that wicked people will not be heirs of the Kingdom of God? Do not be misled about this: Nobody who lives in sexual sin or worships idols, no adulterers or people used by homosexuals or homosexuals ⌊themselves⌋, **10** none who steal, are greedy, get drunk, slander, or rob will be heirs of the Kingdom of God. **11** Some of you used to do these things. But you have been washed, you have been made holy, you have been justified [declared righteous] in the Name of the Lord Jesus Christ and in the Spirit of our God.

12 It is permissible for me to do anything, but not everything is beneficial. It is permissible for me to do anything, but I will not allow anything to gain control over my life. **13** Food is for the stomach, and the stomach for food, but God will put an end to both of them. The body is not for sexual sin but for the Lord, and the Lord is for the body.*d* **14** God raised the Lord, and He will also raise us by His power.

15 Do you not know that your bodies are members of Christ? Now, should I take the members of Christ and make them members of a prostitute? Never! **16** Or do you not know that he who joins himself with a prostitute is one in body with her? For God says: *"The two will be one flesh."* **17** But the one who joins himself with the Lord, he is one in spirit with Him.

18 Flee from sexual sin. Every other sin a person may do is outside the body. But the person who sins sexually sins against his own body. **19** Or do you not know that your body is a temple of the Holy Spirit, whom God gives you and who is in you? You do not belong to yourselves **20** because you were bought for a price. Then glorify God in your body.

---

16 Gen 2:24

---

6 *a-* 4 Literally: "who are despised."
  b- 5 Literally: "brothers" (also in v. 8; "brother" in v. 6).
  c- 8 Literally: "rob, and this to brothers."
  d- 13 The Lord's concern for our body is evident in the fact that He redeemed it (v. 20), makes it His temple (v. 19), and will raise it on the Last Day (v. 14).

7TH CHAPTER

B. Questions raised by the Corinthian Christians (7:1–15:58)
1. Marriage and celibacy (7:1-40)

If You Are Married

1 Now concerning the things you wrote: It is good for a man not to touch[a] a woman. **2** To avoid sexual sins, let each man have his own wife and each woman her own husband.

3 Let a husband do for his wife what he owes her, and let a wife do the same for her husband. **4** A wife cannot do as she likes with her body; her husband has a right to it. In the same way a husband cannot do as he likes with his body; his wife has a right to it. **5** Do not deprive one another unless you agree to do so for a while, so that you may take time to pray[b] and to come together again so that Satan may not tempt you because you cannot control yourselves. **6** But this I say by way of concession, not as a command.

7 I would like everyone to be like myself, but each one has the gift God gave him, one this and another that. **8** To those who are not married and to widows I say: It is good for them to stay single as I am myself, **9** but if they cannot control themselves, let them get married; it is better to marry than to burn.[c]

10 If you are married, I command—not I, but the Lord: A wife should not leave her husband. **11** If she does leave him, she should stay single or make up with her husband. And a husband should not divorce his wife.

If You Are Married To An Unbeliever

12 To the rest I say—I, not the Lord: If a Christian man[d] has a wife who does not believe and she agrees to live with him, he should not divorce her. **13** And if a wife has a husband who does not believe and he agrees to live with her, she should not divorce her husband. **14** For an unbelieving husband married to such a wife serves a holy purpose, and an unbelieving wife married to a believer serves a holy purpose. For otherwise your children would be unclean, but now they are holy. **15** But if the unbelieving person leaves, let him leave. In such a case a Christian man or woman[e] is not bound. But God called us to live in peace. **16** For you wife, what do you know—you may save your husband. Or you husband, what do you know—you may save your wife.

---

7 *a-* 1 The Greek word "touch" can mean to touch a woman sexually or to have sexual relations with a woman.
  b- 5 Some manuscripts and translations add: "and to fast."
  c- 9 Greek may mean "burn" (literally) or "burn with passion."
  d- 12 Literally: "a brother."
  e- 15 Literally: "a brother or sister."

Stay As God Called You

17 But everyone should live the life that the Lord assigned to him just as God called him. This is the rule I lay down in all the churches.

18 Were you circumcised when you were called? Do not try to get rid of your circumcision. Were you uncircumcised when you were called? Do not get circumcised. **19** Circumcision is nothing, and the lack of it is nothing; but doing what God commands is everything. **20** Everyone should stay as he was when he was called. **21** Were you a slave when you were called? Do not let that trouble you. On the other hand, if you have a chance to become free, take it. **22** For if you are a slave when you are called in the Lord, you are the Lord's freedman. In the same way, if you are free when you are called, you are Christ's slave. **23** You were bought for a price; do not become the slaves of people. **24** My fellow Christians,*ᶠ* before God everyone should stay just as he was when he was called.

To Marry Or Not To Marry

25 Now concerning virgins I have no command from the Lord, but I am giving you a judgment as a person whom you can trust because of the Lord's mercy. **26** Because the present situation is so full of stress for us, I believe it is good for a person to stay as he is. **27** Are you married to a woman? Do not look for a divorce. Are you divorced from a wife? Do not look for a wife. **28** But if you do get married, it is no sin, and if a virgin gets married, it is no sin. However, I would like to spare you the troubles that such people will have in life.*ᵍ*

29 This is what I am saying, my fellow Christians: the time has been shortened. While it lasts, may those who have wives live as though they had none; **30** those who weep, as though they were not weeping; those who are happy, as though they were not happy; those who purchase, as though they did not possess; **31** and those who use the world, as though they were not misusing it, since this world in its present form is passing away.

32 I do not want you to worry. An unmarried man is concerned about the things of the Lord: how he can please the Lord. **33** But the one who is married worries about earthly things: how he can please his wife; **34** his interests are divided.

An unmarried woman or virgin is concerned about the Lord's things so that she may be holy in body and in spirit. But the one who is married worries about earthly things, how she can please her husband. **35** I am saying this to help you, not to put a restraint on you, but to show you how to live nobly for the Lord without being distracted by other things.

36 If a man thinks he is acting improperly toward his fiancee,*ʰ* and if his passion is very strong and so he ought to get married,*ⁱ* he should do as he wishes—it is no sin—let them get married. **37** But a man who has a strong

---

f- 24 Literally: "brothers" (also in v. 29).
g- 28 Or "that such people will have in their flesh"; compare verses 3,5b,10,11,26a.
h- 36 Literally: "girl" or "virgin" (also in vv. 37, 38); see footnote at end of verse 38.
i- 36 Literally: "and so it ought to be."

character, feeling no dominating passion, but who has willpower[j] and has made up his mind to keep his fiancee as she is,[k] he will be doing right. **38** So then he who marries his fiancee is doing right, but he who does not marry her will be doing better.[l]

39 A wife is bound to her husband as long as he lives. If her husband dies,[m] she is free to marry anyone she wishes, but let it be in the Lord. **40** But she will be happier if she stays as she is. That is my judgment, and I think that I also have the Spirit of God.

8TH CHAPTER

2. Food sacrificed to idols (8:1–10:33)

Weak Consciences

1 Now concerning the meat sacrificed to idols: We know that all of us have some knowledge. Knowledge puffs up, but love builds up. **2** The person who thinks he knows something still has something to learn. **3** But if he loves God, God knows him.

4 Now about eating meat that was sacrificed to idols: We know that there is no idol that is truly alive in the world[a] and that there is no other God except the one God. **5** For even if there are so-called gods in heaven or on earth (as there are many gods and many lords), **6** yet for us there is only one God—the Father, from whom comes everything, and we live for Him. And there is only one Lord—Jesus Christ, through whom all things came into being and through whom we exist.

7 But not everyone knows this. Some are still so conscious of their former idolatrous practice that they think of the meat they eat as having been sacrificed to an idol; and their conscience, being weak, is stained with guilt.

8 Food will not bring us closer to God. We lose nothing by not eating and gain nothing by eating. **9** But be careful, or the weak may fall into sin because you do as you please. **10** For if anyone who has a weak conscience sees you eating in a temple of an idol, you who have this knowledge, will you not be

---

j- 37 Literally: "But the one who stands firm in his heart, not feeling necessity, but has control over his own desire."

k- 37 Meaning "he has decided that the wedding date should not be set for the time being."

l- 38 This passage (vv. 36-38) can be understood in two different ways. Is Paul speaking of a young man's interest in a girl or a father's concern for his daughter? (The translator's answer to this question determines the translation.) Our translation has adopted the first view. The latter view would translate: "If a man [father] thinks that he is acting improperly toward his girl [daughter], if she is beyond the flower of youth and so it must be, let him do as he wishes; it is no sin; let them [daughter and her fiance] get married. But a man [father] who stands firm in his conviction (lit. 'heart'), feeling no compelling reason (lit. 'not feeling necessity'), but who has the courage of his conviction and has decided in his own heart to keep his girl [daughter] as she is, he will be doing right. So then he who gives away his girl [daughter] in marriage is doing right, but he who does not give her away will be doing better."

m- 39 Literally: "falls asleep."

8 *a*- 4 Literally: "We know that an idol is nothing in the world."

encouraging him to eat the meat sacrificed to idols? **11** Then your knowledge is ruining the weak fellow Christian[b] for whom Christ died. **12** But when you sin against your fellow Christians in this way and wound their weak consciences, you sin against Christ.

13 So if food causes my fellow Christian to stumble ⌊in his faith⌋,[c] I will never eat meat, so that I may not make my fellow Christian stumble ⌊in his faith⌋.

9TH CHAPTER

A Pastor's Pay

1 Am I not free? Am I not an apostle? Did I not see Jesus our Lord? Are you not my work in the Lord? **2** If I am not an apostle to others, I certainly am one to you. For you are the seal which proves that I am an apostle in the Lord. **3** That is how I defend myself before those who examine me. **4** Do we not have a right to eat and drink? **5** Do we not have a right to take along a Christian wife[a] like the other apostles and the brothers of the Lord and Peter? **6** Or is it only Barnabas and I who do not have a right to stop working for a living?

7 Does a soldier ever pay his own expenses? Does anyone plant a vineyard and not eat its grapes? Or does anyone take care of a flock and not drink any milk from it? **8** Am I merely stating a man-made rule? Does the Law not say the same thing? **9** For the Law of Moses says: *"Do not muzzle an ox when he is treading out grain."* Certainly God is not concerned about oxen, is He? **10** His words have only us in mind, do they not?[b] This was written to show us that the person who plows or threshes ought to do so with the expectation that he will receive a share of the crop. **11** If we have sown the spiritual life in you, is it too much if we reap your earthly goods? **12** If others enjoy this right over you, do we not have a better claim? But we have not made use of this right. Rather, we put up with anything in order not to hinder the Good News of Christ.

13 Do you not know that the men who work at the Temple receive their food from the Temple? And that those who help at the altar receive their share of what is on the altar? **14** In the same way the Lord has commanded that those who preach the Gospel should receive their living from the Gospel.

15 But I have not used any of these rights. And I am not writing this to have such things done for me. For I would rather die than let anyone take away my boast. **16** If I preach the Gospel, I have nothing to boast about because I am compelled to preach it. Woe to me if I do not preach the Gospel! **17** For if I do it because I want to do it, I receive a reward. But if I do not want to do it, I still have this work entrusted to me.

18 What then is my reward? Just this: When I preach the Gospel, I will not

---

9 Deut 25:4

---

b- 11 Literally: "brother" (also in v. 13; "brothers" in v. 12).
c- 13 See *SKANDALON* on page 545.
9 *a-* 5 Literally: "sister as a wife."
b- 10 Or "Is He not speaking altogether for our benefit?"

let it cost anyone anything, so that I may not take advantage of my right in preaching the Gospel.

Everything To Everyone

19 For although I am free from all people, I have made myself a slave to all of them in order to win more of them. **20** To the Jews I became like a Jew to win Jews; to those under law I became like a man under law—although I am not under law—to win those under law. **21** To those who are without law I became like a man without law—although I am not without God's law but am under Christ's law—to win those who are without law. **22** To weak persons I became weak to win the weak. I have become everything to everyone so that in every way I might save some of them.

23 I am doing everything for the Gospel in order to have a share of what it gives. **24** Do you not know that those who run in a race all run, but only one wins the prize? Like them, run to win! **25** Everyone who enters an athletic contest goes into strict training. Now, they do it to win a wreath that withers, but we do it to win one that never withers. **26** So I run with a clear goal ahead of me. I fight and do not just shadow box. **27** Rather, I beat my body and make it my slave so that, when I have summoned others^c to run the race, I myself may not be disqualified.

10TH CHAPTER

A Warning

1 I want you to know, fellow Christians,^{a} that our fathers were all under the cloud and all went through the sea. **2** By baptism in the cloud and in the sea they were all united with Moses. **3** They all ate the same spiritual food **4** and all drank the same spiritual drink, because they drank from the spiritual Rock that went with them, and that Rock was Christ. **5** Yet God was not pleased with most of them, for *they were killed in the wilderness.*

6 Now, these things happened as lessons for us so that we might not *long for* what is evil as they did. **7** Do not worship idols as some of them did, as it is written: *"The people sat down to eat and drink and got up to play."* **8** Let us not sin sexually as some of them did—23,000 died on one day. **9** Let us not go too far in testing the Lord's patience as some of them did—the snakes killed them. **10** Do not complain as some of them did—the angel of death destroyed them. **11** These things happened to them to make them a lesson to others, and they were written down to warn us, on whom the end of the ages has come. **12** So let the one who thinks he is standing firm be careful that he does not fall.

13 No temptation has taken hold of you other than that which any human being

---

5 *Num 14:16*   6 *Num 11:4,34*   7 *Ex 32:6*

c- 27 Literally: "when having preached to others."
10 a- 1 Literally: "brothers."

can expect. And you can trust God. He will not let you be tested more than you can stand. But when you are tested, He will also give you a way out so that you can bear it.

Meat Sacrificed To Idols

14 And so, my dear friends, flee from the worship of idols.

15 I am talking to sensible people. Judge for yourselves what I say. **16** Is the cup of blessing which we bless*b* not a communion with the blood of Christ? Is the bread which we break not a communion with the body of Christ? **17** Because there is one loaf, we who are many are one body; for all of us partake of the one loaf.

18 Look at the people of Israel in the way that people normally would. Aren't those who eat the sacrifices sharing in the altar? **19** What do I mean by this? That a sacrifice made to an idol is something or that an idol really is something? **20** No, because these *sacrifices* of the Gentiles *are made to demons and not to God.* I do not want you to be partners of demons. **21** You cannot drink the Lord's cup and the cup of demons. You cannot share *the table of the Lord* and the table of demons. **22** Or are we *trying to make the Lord jealous?* Are we stronger than He?

23 It is permissible for us to do anything, but not everything is beneficial. It is permissible for us to do anything, but not everything encourages growth. **24** No one should be seeking his own advantage but rather that of the other person. **25** Eat anything sold in the market and do not ask any questions or let your conscience trouble you, **26** because *the earth with everything in it belongs to the Lord.* **27** If one of the unbelievers invites you and you wish to go, eat anything they serve you and do not ask any questions or let your conscience trouble you. **28** But if someone tells you, "This was sacrificed," do not eat it, keeping in mind both the one who told you and conscience—**29** I do not mean yours but the other person's conscience. Why should my freedom be judged by someone else's conscience? **30** If I give thanks for what I eat, why should I let myself be denounced for eating that for which I thank God? **31** So, whether you eat or drink or do anything else, do everything to glorify God. **32** Do not cause others to sin, whether they are Jews, Greeks, or of God's church, **33** just as I do not. I try to please everyone in every way by not continuing to seek my advantage but that of many people so that they may be saved.

11TH CHAPTER

3. Disorders in public worship (11:1-34)
a. Women's dress (11:1-16)

1 Imitate me as I imitate Christ.

---

20 Deut 32:17; Ps 106:37   *21 Mal 1:7,12*   *22 Deut 32:21*   *26 Ps 24:1*

---

b- 16 Or "over which we speak the blessing."

Long Hair And Hats

2 I praise you for thinking of me in every way and for keeping the Christian teachings[a] as I delivered them to you.

3 I want you to know that the Head of every man is Christ, the head of a woman is the man, and the Head of Christ is God. **4** Every man who keeps his head covered when he prays or when he prophesies dishonors his head. **5** And every woman who prays or prophesies with nothing on her head dishonors her head. For she is exactly like the woman whose head is shaved. **6** For if a woman wears nothing on her head, she should also get her hair cut off. But if it is a disgrace for a woman to get her hair cut or shaved off, she should keep her head covered. **7** For a man does not have a continuing obligation to cover his head, because he is *God's image* and glory; but a woman is a man's glory. **8** For the man was not made from the woman but the woman from the man, **9** and the man was not made for the woman but the woman for the man. **10** That is why a woman has a continuing obligation to wear something on her head to show she is under authority, out of respect for the angels.

11 Yet, in the Lord, woman does not exist apart from man or man apart from woman. **12** For just as woman came into existence from man, so man comes into existence by woman, and it all comes from God.

13 Judge your own situation. Is it proper for a woman to pray to God with nothing on her head? **14** Does not the nature[b] ⌊of the situation⌋ itself teach you that it is disgraceful for a man to have long hair, **15** but that it is a woman's glory to wear her hair long? Her hair is given her in place of a covering. **16** But if anyone means to argue about this, we do not have such a custom—nor do the churches of God.

b. The Lord's Supper (11:17-34)

How To Go To The Lord's Supper

17 As I instruct you in this matter, I am not praising you, because when you come together ⌊to worship⌋ it results in more harm than good. **18** For in the first place I hear that when you gather as a church you are divided, and some of what I hear I believe. **19** Of course there must be divisions among you to indicate which of you are passing the test.

20 When you gather ⌊for worship⌋ in one place, you do not come to eat the Lord's Supper. **21** As a matter of fact, each of you eats his own meal ahead of time; and so one stays hungry and another gets drunk. **22** Surely it is not the case that you do not have homes in which to eat and drink, is it? Or are you trying to despise the church of God and humiliate those who do not have anything?

---

7 Gen 1:27

---

11 a- 2 Literally: "traditions."
   b- 14 The Greek word *"physis"* ("nature") here may indicate the custom of society. In Corinth, custom required the kind of behavior Paul here recommends. Verse 16 makes it very evident that this was only the custom (situation) in Corinth.

What should I say to you? Should I praise you? I will not praise you for this.

23 For I received from the Lord what I also have passed on to you, namely, that the Lord Jesus on the night He was betrayed took bread. **24** He gave thanks, broke it, and said, "This is My body, which is broken*ᶜ* for you. Do this to remember Me." **25** He did the same with the cup after the supper. He said, "This cup is the *new 'last will and testament'ᵈ* in My *blood.* Every time you drink it, do it to remember Me." **26** For every time you eat this bread and drink this cup, you are proclaiming the Lord's death—until He comes.

27 And so anyone who eats the bread or drinks the Lord's cup in an unworthy way is guilty of sinning against the Lord's body and blood. **28** But let a person examine himself and then eat of the bread and drink from the cup. **29** For anyone who eats and drinks without recognizing the Lord's body*ᵉ* brings a judgment on himself as he eats and drinks.

30 That is why many of you are sick and ailing and a number ⌊of you⌋ have died.*ᶠ* **31** But if we were evaluating ourselves, we would not be under judgment. **32** But when the Lord judges us, we are being corrected in order to keep us from being condemned with the world.

33 So then, my fellow Christians,*ᵍ* when you gather to eat, wait for one another. **34** If you are hungry, eat at home so that you may not have a gathering which brings a judgment on you.

I will give directions concerning the other matters when I come.

12TH CHAPTER

4. Spiritual gifts (12:1–14:40)

The Gifts Of The Spirit

1 Now concerning matters involving the Spirit, fellow Christians,*ᵃ* I do not want you to remain uninformed. **2** You know that when you were Gentiles, however you happened to be led, you were drawn to idols that cannot speak. **3** So I tell you that no one who is speaking by God's Spirit will say, "Cursed be Jesus," and no one is able to say, "Jesus is the Lord," except by the Holy Spirit.

4 Now differing spiritual gifts are given to different persons, but the same Spirit gives them. **5** Differing ways of serving are assigned to them, but the same

---

25 *Ex 24:8; Jer 31:31; Zech 9:11*

---

c- 24 A few of the older translations have "given" instead of "broken," while some of the older manuscripts contain neither word.

d- 25 See *DIATHĒKĒ* on page 531.

e- 29 A reference to "the body of Christ" in the Lord's Supper (cf. vv. 24,27); some view "body" as a reference to "the church of Christ" (cf. 1 Cor. 10:17; 12:13,27).

f- 30 Literally: "have fallen asleep."

g- 33 Literally: "brothers."

12 a- 1 Literally: "brothers."

Lord assigns them. **6** Differing powers are given to them, but the same God works everything in all of them. **7** Now the Spirit shows Himself to each one to make him useful. **8** The Spirit gives one person the ability to speak wisely. To another the same Spirit gives the ability to speak with knowledge. **9** To another the same Spirit gives faith. To another that same Spirit gives the ability to heal. **10** Another can work miracles. Another can prophesy. Another can tell the true Spirit from evil spirits. Another can speak in ˌvariousˌ kinds of languages. *b* Another can interpret languages. **11** One and the same Spirit works all these things by giving as He wishes to each individually.

12 For as the body is one and yet has many parts, and all the parts of the body—many as they are—form one body, so also is Christ. **13** Yes, in one Spirit all of us—whether Jews or Greeks, whether slaves or free—were baptized to form one body, and we all were given to drink of that one Spirit.

14 For indeed, the ˌhumanˌ body is not made up of one part, but of many. **15** Suppose a foot says, "I am not a hand and so I am not a part of the body"; it would not on this basis stop being a part of the body. **16** Or suppose an ear says, "I am not an eye and so I am not a part of the body"; it would not on that basis stop being a part of the body. **17** If the whole body were an eye, how could we hear? If it were all hearing, how could we smell? **18** As it is, God arranged the parts, fitting each of them into the body as He wished. **19** If all of it were one part, how could there be a body? **20** As it is, there are many parts but one body.

21 The eye cannot say to the hand, "I do not need you"; or again the head to the feet, "I do not need you." **22** No, we really cannot do without the parts of the body that we think are weaker. **23** The parts of the body that we think less honorable we dress with special honor and our unpresentable parts have greater respectability, **24** which our presentable parts do not need. But God has put the body together and given special honor to the part that lacks it, **25** so that the body might not be divided but rather that the parts might feel the same concern for one another. **26** If one member suffers, all the others suffer with it. If one is honored, all the others are happy with it.

27 Now you are the body of Christ and each of you is an individual part of it. **28** God has appointed in the church first apostles, next preachers, *c* third teachers, then miracle workers, then healers, helpers, managers, and those who can speak in ˌvariousˌ kinds of languages. **29** Certainly not all are apostles, nor preachers, nor teachers, are they? Certainly not all can work miracles **30** nor heal, can they? Certainly not all can speak in other languages nor interpret them, can they? **31** Eagerly desire the better gifts. And now I will show you what is by far the best way.

---

b- 10 Greek: "*glōssa*" means "tongue" or "language." The term may indicate speaking in a *language* that is familiar or unfamiliar (foreign) to the hearer. The concept of speaking in a foreign language (a foreign tongue) fits the context of Acts 2 quite well, and for that reason, the renderings "languages," "other languages," and "another language" have been used in this translation. (The term "tongue" is automatically fitting in 1 Corinthians 14:9.) Some scholars interpret tongues, for example, in 1 Corinthians 12–14, as unintelligible, mysterious utterances (a heavenly type of "angel language," if you will); as a result, they prefer to use the term "tongues" throughout the 1 Corinthians 12–14 context.

c- 28 Literally: "prophets"; also in verse 29.

13TH CHAPTER

Love

1 If I speak in the languages of men and of angels but have no love, I have become a loud gong or a clashing cymbal. **2** Even if I prophesy and understand all mysteries*a* and have all knowledge, even if I have all faith to move mountains but have no love, I am nothing. **3** Even if I give away all that I have to feed the hungry and give up my body to be burned*b* and have no love, it does not help me.

4 Love is patient. Love is kind. Love is not envious. It does not boast or become conceited. **5** It is not indecent. It is not selfish. It is not irritable. It *does not plan to hurt anyone.* **6** It does not delight in wrongdoing but is happy with the truth. **7** It bears everything, believes everything, hopes for everything, endures everything.

8 Love never fails. If there are prophecies, they will be brought to an end; or other languages, they will stop; or knowledge, it will be brought to an end. **9** For we learn only a portion of something and prophesy only a portion. **10** But when the completed thing comes, that which is only a portion will be brought to an end. **11** When I was a child, I used to talk like a child, think like a child, plan like a child. Now that I have become a man, I have given up the ways of a child. **12** Now we see a blurred image in a mirror, but then we will see face to face. Now I learn only in part, but then I shall know as He has known me.

13 And now there remains these three—faith, hope, love—but the greatest of these is love.

14TH CHAPTER

Speak To Be Understood

1 Pursue love and be eager to have the gifts of the Spirit, especially prophecy.*a* **2** When a person speaks in another language, he does not speak to people but to God, because no one understands him; his spirit is speaking mysteries.*b* **3** But when a person prophesies, he speaks to people in order to help them grow, to encourage them, and to comfort them. **4** When a person speaks in another language, he helps himself grow. But when a person prophesies, he helps the church grow. **5** I wish that all of you would speak in other languages, but I would rather have you prophesy. It is more important to prophesy than to speak in other languages, unless you interpret what you say in order to help the church grow.

---

5 *Zech 7:10; 8:17*

---

13 *a*- 2 See 4:1 and its accompanying footnote.
   b- 3 A few manuscripts read: "that I may boast." The Greek word for "boast" differs in only one letter from the Greek word for "burn."
14 *a*- 1 Literally: "be eager to have the things of the Spirit, especially that you may prophesy."
   b- 2 See 4:1 and its accompanying footnote.

6 Now, my fellow Christians,[c] if I come to you and speak in other languages, how can I help you unless I tell you what God has revealed to me or what He has made known or what He is prophesying or teaching?

7 Lifeless instruments such as a flute or a harp produce sounds, but if there is no distinction in the sounds, how can you tell what is being played on the flute or harp? **8** To be sure, if the trumpet does not sound a clear call, who will get ready for battle? **9** In the same way, if you do not give a message with your tongue which is understood, how will anyone know what you are saying? You will be talking into the air. **10** There are, I suppose, ever so many kinds of languages in the world, and none is without meaning. **11** Now if I do not know what a language means, I shall be a foreigner to him who speaks it and he will be a foreigner to me. **12** So you too, since you are eager to have the gifts of the Spirit, try to be rich in them so that you help the church grow. **13** So then let the person who speaks in another language pray that he may be able to interpret what he says.

14 If I pray in another language, my spirit prays but my mind is not productive. **15** So what will I do? I will pray with my spirit and I will also pray with my mind. I will sing praise with my spirit and I will also sing with my mind. **16** Otherwise, if you praise God only with your spirit, how can the person who occupies the place of an "inquiring visitor"[d] say "Amen" to your prayer of thanks? He does not know what you are saying. **17** Yes, it is good that you give thanks, but it does not help the other person grow. **18** I thank God that I speak in other languages more than any of you, **19** but in the church I would rather say 5 words that can be understood, in order to teach others, than 10,000 words in another language.

20 Fellow Christians, do not be childish in the use of your minds. In evil be babies, but in the use of your minds be mature. **21** It is written in the Scripture:[e]

> *In other languages*
> *and through the mouths* of foreigners
> *I will speak to these people,*
> but even then *they will not listen* to Me,

says the Lord. **22** And so, other languages are a miraculous sign, not for believers but for unbelievers, while prophecy is a sign not for unbelievers but for believers. **23** Now if the whole congregation gathers and all speak in other languages, and then some "inquiring visitors" or unbelievers come in, will they not say that you are insane? **24** But if they all prophesy and some unbeliever or

---

21 Is 28:11,12

---

c- 6 Literally: "brothers" (also in vv. 20,26,39).

d- 16 From the Greek *"idiōtēs,"* meaning "layperson, unschooled, untrained"; in this instance an "inquirer" is one who would be classified somewhere between those who were recognized as full-fledged Christians and those who were outright deniers of the Christian faith (cf. v. 23). They attended or visited church services to inquire and learn more about Christian truth. This term is also used in verses 23 and 24.

e- 21 Literally: "Law"; Paul is quoting Isaiah 28:11,12, that is, he is quoting "Law" in the sense of God's revelation, namely, the Old Testament. See Matthew 5:17 and its accompanying footnote.

"inquiring visitor" comes in, all convince him of sin and all call him to account. 25 The secrets of his heart are shown, and so he bows down with his face on the ground, worships God, and declares, *"God is certainly here among you."*

Keep Order In Worship Services

26 What are you doing then, my fellow Christians? When you gather, each is ready with a hymn, a word of instruction, some revelation from God, another language, or an interpretation. Do it all to help one another grow. 27 If anyone speaks in another language, only two should speak or three at the most, one at a time, and someone should interpret. 28 If there is no one to interpret what he says, he should not say anything in church but only speak to himself and to God.

29 Two or three prophets should speak, and the others should decide whether what is being said is right or wrong. 30 If God reveals something to another person who is seated, the first speaker should be silent. 31 For you can all prophesy one after another so that everyone learns something and is encouraged. 32 The spirits of prophets are in continual subordination*f* to prophets. 33 For God is not a God of disorder but of peace (as He is in all the churches of the believers [saints]). 34 Let women keep silent in your churches because they are not allowed to speak. Rather, let them be subordinate,*g* as the Law says. 35 If there is something they desire to know, let them ask their husbands at home. For it is a disgrace for a woman to speak in church.*h*

36 Did God's word first come from you? Or were you the only ones whom it has reached? 37 If anyone thinks he is a prophet or has the Spirit, let him acknowledge that what I write to you is what the Lord commands. 38 But if anyone ignores this, just ignore him.

39 So, my fellow Christians, be eager to prophesy, and do not try to keep someone from speaking in other languages. 40 But everything should be done in a proper and orderly way.

---

25 Is 45:14

---

f- 32 Compare verses 32-34 with Paul's parallel in 1 Timothy 2:11,12. See *HUPOTASSŌ* on page 541.

g- 34 Greek: "*hupotassō.*" This Greek term speaks of persons who are placed in an "order" or "rank" below or under the authority of another. In the mind of sinful human beings this is often falsely equated with *inferiority.* However, Jesus taught us that among Christians this is not to be the case. It is not the one in authority who is the greatest but the one who is servant to all (Matt. 20:25-28; Mk. 10:42-45); authority and servitude are always to be used for the benefit of others.

The English "subordinate" captures the totality of this *hupotassō* concept quite well. In the passage before us Paul applies *hupotassō* to *the lines of authority* which God lays down *for Christian congregations* as they relate to male/female functions (cf. 1 Tim. 2:11). See *HUPOTASSŌ* on page 541.

h - 35 According to 1 Corinthians 11:5,10 a woman could speak aloud together with the other people in public worship if she had her "head covered" as a "sign of authority." Here in chapter 14, however, Paul is speaking of a situation where *judging* what others said was involved (v. 29). If a second person arose to speak, the first was to be silent (v. 30) and so subordinate *himself* (v. 32) to what God revealed to the second person. For a woman to speak in this situation would be contrary to God's will, for the woman was also to be subordinate (v. 34).

15TH CHAPTER

5. Resurrection: Christ's and ours (15:1-58)

Jesus Rose From The Dead

1 My fellow Christians,*ᵃ* I am proclaiming to you the Gospel which I brought to you, which you accepted, on which you now stand, **2** and by which you are saved if you cling to the word I preached to you—unless your faith means nothing. **3** For I brought you what I received—something very important—that Christ died for our sins as the Scriptures said He would, **4** that He was buried, and that He was raised on the third day as the Scriptures said He would. **5** Later Peter saw Him, then the Twelve, **6** then more than 500 Christians at one time; most of whom are still living, but some have fallen asleep ᵢin deathᵢ. **7** Then James saw Him, then all the apostles. **8** Last of all I saw Him, I who was like one born unexpectedly, **9** since I am the least of the apostles and not fit to be called an apostle because I persecuted the church of God. **10** God's grace [undeserved love] made me what I am, and His grace was not wasted on me. But I did far more hard work than all the others—not I but the grace of God that was with me. **11** Now,, whether I did it or they, this is what we preach, and this is what you believed.

We Will Be Raised

12 If we preach that Christ was raised from the dead, how can some of you say, "There is no resurrection of the dead"? **13** If there is no resurrection of the dead, Christ was not raised. **14** And if Christ was not raised, our preaching means nothing and your faith means nothing. **15** Also, we stand there as men who lied about God because we have sworn by God*ᵇ* that He raised Christ, whom He did not raise if it is true that the dead are not raised. **16** To be sure, if the dead are not raised, Christ has not been raised; **17** and if Christ has not been raised, your faith cannot help you; you are still in your sins. **18** Then also those who have fallen asleep in Christ have perished. **19** If Christ is our hope in this life only, we are to be pitied more than all other people.

20 But now Christ was raised from the dead, the first in the harvest of those who have fallen asleep. **21** For since a man brought death, a Man also brought the resurrection of the dead. **22** For as in Adam all die, so in Christ all will be made alive. **23** But each one in his own turn: Christ the Firstfruit; then, when He comes, those who belong to Christ.

24 Then the end will come, when He hands over the Kingdom to God the Father, after He has put an end to every government, authority, and power, **25** since He must rule until *God puts all His enemies under His feet.* **26** The last

---

25 *Ps 110:1*

---

15 *a-* 1 Literally: "brothers" (also in vv. 6,31,50,58).
    b - 15 Literally: "we have given testimony about God."

enemy He will get rid of is death, **27** for *everything is to be subordinated^c under His feet.* When He says *everything is subordinated,* this clearly does not include Him who *subordinates everything.* **28** But when *everything has been subordinated,* then the Son will subordinate Himself to Him who *subordinated everything under* the Son, so that God will be everything in everything.

29 Otherwise, what will they do who are baptized for ⌞the benefit of⌟ the dead?^d Why are they baptized for them if the dead are not raised at all?

30 Why are we in danger every hour? **31** Fellow Christians, I face death every day; I swear it by the pride that I take in you in Christ Jesus our Lord. **32** If I have fought with wild animals in Ephesus from a purely human standpoint,^e what have I gained?

If the dead are not raised,

> Let us eat and drink,
>   for tomorrow we die!

33 Do not let anyone deceive you. "Bad company ruins good habits."^f **34** Come back to a sober and righteous life, and do not sin anymore. For some people do not know God. I say this to make you feel ashamed.

Our Glorified Bodies

35 But someone will ask, "How are the dead raised? And what kind of body will they have when they come?"

36 You fool! The seed you sow has to die before it is made alive. **37** And the body you sow is not the body that it will be, but just a bare kernel, maybe wheat or some other seed. **38** But God gives it the body He wishes it to have, and to each kind of seed its own body. **39** Not all flesh is the same. Human beings have one kind of flesh, animals have another, birds have another, and fish have still another. **40** And so there are heavenly bodies and earthly bodies. But the splendor of the heavenly bodies is different from that of the earthly bodies. **41** The splendor of the sun is different from the splendor of the moon, and the splendor of the stars is different again. Even one star differs in splendor from another star.

42 That is how it will be when the dead are raised. When the body is sown,

---

27,28 Ps 8:6   32 Is 22:13

---

c - 27 Greek: *"hupotassō."* This Greek term speaks of things and persons that are placed in an "order" or "rank" below or under the authority of another. In the mind of sinful human beings this is often falsely equated with *inferiority.* However, Jesus taught us that among Christians this is not to be the case. It is not the one in authority who is the greatest but the one who is servant to all (Matt. 20:25-28; Mk. 10:42-45); authority and servitude are always to be used for the benefit of others.
The English "subordinate" captures the totality of this *hupotassō* concept quite well. Paul here applies *hupotassō* to *everything created* in heaven and on earth and under the earth (vv. 27 and 28; cf. Phil. 2:9-11). Ultimately all stands under the Father and the Son. Compare our present passage with Philippians 3:21 and its accompanying footnote. See HUPOTASSO on page 541.
d - 29 See BAPTISM FOR THE DEAD on page 549.
e - 32 Compare verses 29-31.
f - 33 This saying is attributed to the Greek playwright Menander (342-291 B.C.) in his play *Thais.*

it decays; when it is raised, it cannot decay. **43** When it is sown, it is not glorious; when it is raised, it is glorious. When it is sown, it is weak; when it is raised, it is strong. **44** It is sown a natural body; it is raised a spiritual body. Just as there is a natural body, so there is a spiritual body.

45 As it is written: "The first man *Adam became a natural living being*"; the Second Adam*g* became a life-giving spirit. **46** That which is spiritual does not come first, but the *natural*; then that which is spiritual. **47** The first *man is made of the soil of the earth*; the Second Man is the Lord*h* from heaven. **48** The people of the earth are like the man from the earth; the people of heaven are like the Man from heaven. **49** Just as we have worn the likeness of the man from the earth, we shall also wear the likeness of the Man from heaven. **50** I tell you, fellow Christians, flesh and blood cannot have a share in the Kingdom of God, nor can decaying things share in what does not decay.

51 Now I shall tell you a mystery:*i* We shall not all fall asleep ˌin deathˌ, but we shall all be changed—**52** in a moment, in the twinkling of an eye when the last trumpet sounds. Yes, it will sound, and the dead will be raised immortal and we shall be changed. **53** For it is necessary that what is decaying be clothed with what cannot decay and what is dying be clothed with what cannot die. **54** And when that which is decaying is clothed with what cannot decay and that which is dying is clothed with what cannot die, then this passage of Scripture will come true: *"Death is swallowed up in victory!"*

55   *Death, where is your victory?*
         Death, where is your sting?

56 Sin gives death its sting, and the Law gives sin its power. **57** But thanks be to God who continues to give us the victory through our Lord Jesus Christ.

58 Stand firm, then, my dear fellow Christians, and let nothing move you. Always do more work for the Lord than ever, since you know that in the Lord your hard work is not wasted.

16TH CHAPTER

C. Conclusion (16:1-24)

The Collection

1 Concerning the collection for the believers [saints]—do just as I directed the churches in Galatia to do. **2** Every Sunday*a* let each of you put aside whatever his success provides and save it so that nothing will have to be collected when I come. **3** But when I come, I will have you approve some men, and I will

---

45-47 Gen 2:7   **54** *Is 25:8*   **55** *Hos 13:14*

g- 45 Literally: "the Last Adam"; "Adam" means "Man," referring here to Christ.
h- 47 Some of the older manuscripts and early translations omit: "the Lord."
i- 51 See 4:1 and its accompanying footnote.
16 *a*- 2 Literally: "On the first day of the week."

send them with letters ˌof introductionˌ to take your gift to Jerusalem. **4** If it is worthwhile for me to go also, I shall go with them.

I Am Coming

5 When I go through Macedonia, I will come to you. For I am going through Macedonia, **6** and I probably will stay with you or even spend the winter with you, so that you may send me on my way wherever I may be going. **7** For I do not want to see you now just in passing; because I hope to stay with you for some time, if the Lord will let me. **8** But I will be staying in Ephesus until Pentecost **9** because a door has opened wide for me to do effective work, and many are opposing me.

Timothy, Apollos, And Others

10 If Timothy comes, see to it that he does not have to be afraid while he is with you. He is doing the Lord's work just as I am. **11** Therefore no one should despise him. Send him on his way in peace so that he may come to me, because I am expecting him with the other Christians. *b*

12 As for Apollos our fellow Christian—I tried hard to get him to go to you with the other Christians, but it was not at all his wish to go now. He will come when the time is right.

13 Watch, stand firm in your faith, *be courageous, be strong.* **14** Do everything with love.

15 You know that the family of Stephanas was the first to be won*c* in Greece, and they committed themselves to the service of the believers. I urge you, my fellow Christians, **16** be subordinate*d* to such people and anyone else who works hard with you. **17** I am glad that Stephanas, Fortunatus, and Achaicus came here, because they have made up for your absence. **18** For they have refreshed my spirit and also yours. Therefore appreciate men like that.

Greetings

19 The churches in the province of Asia greet you. Aquila and Prisca*e* and the church at their home send you hearty greetings in the Lord. **20** All the Christians greet you. Greet one another with a holy kiss. **21** Here is the greeting that I, Paul, write with my own hand.

22 If anyone does not love the Lord, a curse on him! Come, Lord!*f*

23 May the grace of the Lord Jesus be with you! **24** My love be with you all in Christ Jesus. Amen.

---

13 Ps 31:24

---

b- 11 Literally: "brothers" (also in vv. 12,15,20; "brother" in v. 12).

c- 15 Literally: "firstfruit."

d- 16 Greek: "*hupotassō.*" See general comments in footnote at 15:27. Particular to our present passage is Paul's application in regard to *the respect that Christians owe to one another.* See *HUPOTASSŌ* on page 541.

e - 19 "Prisca" at Romans 16:3; 2 Timothy 4:19, but "Priscilla" at Acts 18:2,18,26.

f- 22 Paul uses the Aramaic "*Maranatha,*" which means "The Lord is coming."

MONEY, WEIGHTS, and MEASURES

(Measurements are approximate values only)

Greek/Roman	Value	Translation	Reference
assarion	less than a cent	cent	Matt. 10:29
batos	10 gallons	gallon	Lk. 16:6
cubit	18 inches	yard	Jn. 21:8
denarius	one day's pay	denarius	Mk. 6:37
drachma	one day's pay	coin	Lk. 15:8
kodrantes	less than a cent	cent	Matt. 6:37
koinix	one quart	quart	Rev. 6:6
koras	8 bushels	bushel	Lk. 16:7
lepton	1 cent	coin	Mk. 12:42
litra	12 ounces	pound	Jn. 12:3
metretes	10 gallons	gallon	Jn. 2:6
milion	5,000 feet	mile	Matt. 5:41
mina	3 months' pay	mina	Lk. 19:13
orguia	6 feet	feet	Acts 27:28
saton	1 peck	measure	Matt. 13:33
stadion	606 feet	yard mile	Matt. 14:24 Lk. 24:13
talent	100 pounds $30,000 (gold) $ 2,000 (silver)	pound talent	Rev. 16:21 Matt. 18:24

2 CORINTHIANS[a]

1ST CHAPTER

A. Introduction (1:1-7)

1 Paul, an apostle of Christ Jesus by the will of God, and Timothy our fellow Christian,[b] to the church of God in Corinth and to all the believers [saints] everywhere in Greece—**2** may God our Father and the Lord Jesus Christ give you grace[c] and peace!

God Comforts And Rescues Us

3 Let us praise the God and Father of our Lord Jesus Christ, the Father of mercy and the God of all comfort. **4** He comforts us in every trouble to make us able to comfort others in any trouble with the same comfort with which God comforts us. **5** As the sufferings of Christ overflow to us, so Christ makes our comfort overflow. **6** If we suffer, it is for your comfort and salvation. If we are comforted, it helps us to comfort you effectively when you patiently endure the same sufferings that we endure. **7** Our hope for you is firm, because we know that just as you share our sufferings you also share our comfort.

B. The Past: Paul's apostolic authority at Corinth (1:8–7:16)

8 Fellow Christians,[d] we do not want you to be uninformed about our suffering in the province of Asia. It was so extreme, so much more than we could stand, that we even despaired of living. **9** But we experienced this sentence of death within ourselves so that we might learn not to trust in ourselves but in God, who raises the dead. **10** He is the One who rescued us from such a death, and He will ⌐continue to⌐ rescue us. We have placed our hope in Him that He will also rescue us again, **11** since you are also joining in helping us through your

---

1 a   *2 Corinthians* was written by the Apostle Paul from Macedonia in A.D. 55 when the collection
     for the poor in Jerusalem was under way (see chapters 8 and 9).
  b- 1 Literally: "brother."
  c- 2 Meaning "God's undeserved love" (also in 13:14).
  d- 8 Literally: "brothers."

prayers for us. Then many people will thank God on our behalf for the gift which comes to us as a result of the prayers of many people.*e*

We Were Sincere

12 There is something of which we can boast (and our conscience will testify that it is true), namely, that we have conducted ourselves in the world, especially toward you, with God-given openness*f* and sincerity, without human cleverness but with God's grace. **13** For we are writing you only what you read and understand. And I hope you will fully understand, **14** as you have to some extent understood us, because you are our ⌊reason to⌋ boast, just as we will be yours on the Day of our Lord Jesus.

15 Feeling sure of this, I wanted you to have the benefit of a double visit. I planned to come to you first—**16** passing through ⌊on the way⌋ to Macedonia, and then to come back to you again from Macedonia, and ⌊finally⌋ to be sent on by you to Judea.

I Want To Spare You

17 When I made these plans, you certainly do not think that I easily changed my mind,*g* do you? Or, when I make plans, do I make them according to the way that people often do with the result that when I say "yes" or "no" I never change?*h* **18** (However, you can trust God that our message to you is not "yes" and "no." **19** For God's Son Jesus Christ, whom I, Silvanus,*i* and Timothy preached to you, was not "yes" and "no," but in Him "yes" has taken place. **20** For in all the promises of God He is the "Yes" that makes them come true. And so He makes it possible for us to give glory to God by saying, "It is true."*j* **21** It is God who makes both us and you firm in Christ*k* and who also has anointed us **22** and has put His seal on us and given us the Spirit as a guarantee in our hearts.)

23 I call on God and my own life as my witness that I stayed away from Corinth because I wanted to spare you. **24** I do not mean that we are lording it over your faith, but we are working with you to make you happy. For you stand on your own feet by faith.

2ND CHAPTER

1 I made up my mind not to come if I had to bring you grief again. **2** For if

---

e- 11 Literally: "as a result of many people looking ⌊up to God in prayer⌋."
f- 12 Some of the older manuscripts and early translations read: "God-given holiness."
g- 17 Literally: ". . . I acted with fickleness."
h- 17 Literally: "Or, do I make them according to a human pattern [to the flesh] so that with me the 'yes' is 'yes' and the 'no' is 'no'?" Paul is indicating that he would not stubbornly stick to a plan (vv. 15,16) if a change of plans was better for the Corinthians (vv. 23,24). In the intervening verses Paul assures the Corinthians that though *his plans* may change, *the word of God* which he brings never changes.
i- 19 The Roman spelling of Silas, a Roman citizen, who accompanied Paul on his Second Missionary Journey (cf. Acts 15:40).
j- 20 Literally: "Amen."
k- 21 Or the "Anointed One" ["Messiah"].

I make you sad, who is there to make me happy except the person whom I am making sad? **3** This is what I said in my letter. I did not want to come and be made sad by those who ought to make me happy. I am sure about all of you—that what makes me happy also makes all of you happy.

4 I was deeply troubled and in anguish when I wrote to you with much weeping. I did not write to make you sad but to have you realize how very much I love you.

Forgive The Man Who Did Wrong

5 If someone caused grief, he did not do it to me but to some extent (not to make it too strong) to all of you. **6** More and more of you have rebuked him; that is enough for such a person. **7** So now instead, forgive and comfort him, or too much grief may overwhelm someone like that. **8** So I urge you to assure him of your love. **9** For this reason I wrote to see whether you would stand the test and obey in every way.

10 To whom you forgive anything, so do I. Indeed, what I forgave, if I forgave anything, I did so in the presence of Christ to help you, **11** so that we might keep Satan from getting the best of us. For we are not uninformed as to what Satan has in mind.

A Fragrance Of Christ

12 When I went to Troas to tell the Good News [Gospel] of Christ, a door to do the work of the Lord stood wide open for me. **13** But my spirit could not find any relief, because I did not find Titus my fellow Christian.*a* So I said good-bye to the people and went to Macedonia.

14 But thanks be to God! He always leads us in a triumphal procession in Christ and through us spreads the fragrance*b* of knowing Him everywhere. **15** Yes, we are the fragrance of Christ for God among those who are saved and among those who perish—**16** to some an aroma of death as a prelude to death,*c* to others an aroma of life as a prelude to life.*d*

And who is qualified for this? **17** At least we do not peddle an impure word of God like many others, but in Christ we stand before God and speak a message which is both sincere and which comes from God.

3RD CHAPTER

1 Are we beginning to recommend ourselves again? Or do we, like some people, need letters of recommendation to you or from you? **2** You are our letter, written in our hearts, known and read by everybody. **3** Anyone can see that you are Christ's letter, which resulted from our ministry and is written not with ink

---

2 *a*- 13 Literally: "brother."

    b- 14 Paul very likely has in mind the burning of incense in the Roman triumphal parades.

    c- 16 Literally: "from death to death."

    d- 16 Literally: "from life to life."

but with the Spirit *of* the living *God*, not *on stone tablets* but on *tablets of human hearts*.

4 It is Christ who gives us such a confidence as this before God. **5** It is not that we can produce anything by ourselves and claim that the ability to do it was our own, but God gives us our ability. **6** He has made us able ministers of a new "last will and testament,"*a* not of letter*b* but of spirit,*c* because the letter brings death, but the spirit brings life.

The Ministry Of The Spirit And Its Glory

7 Now if that ministry, engraved in letters on stone and bringing death, came with such glory that the people of Israel could not look at *the face of Moses* because it *shone with a glory*—a *glory* which was fading—**8** how much more will the ministry of the spirit*d* have *glory*? **9** For if the ministry that condemns has *glory*, the ministry that gives righteousness overflows much more in *glory*. **10** In fact, that which had *glory* lost it because the other *glory* outshone it. **11** Now, if that ˎministryˌ which was done away with by *glory* ˎwas gloriousˌ, how much more ˎglorious isˌ that ˎministryˌ which remains in *glory*.

12 Therefore, since we have such hope, we are very bold **13** and are not like *Moses*, who *wore a veil over his face* to keep the people of Israel from seeing the last rays of the fading *glory*. **14** But their minds have been closed.*e* To this day the same *veil* is still there at the reading of the old covenant*f* and is not removed,*g* because it is only done away with in Christ. **15** Rather, to this day, when they read Moses, a *veil* covers their hearts. **16** But *whenever anyone turns to the Lord, the veil is taken away*.

17 This Lord*h* is the Spirit, and where the Spirit of the Lord is, there is freedom. **18** And all of us, as we reflect *the Lord's glory* in our unveiled faces, are being changed by that glory into the same likeness, namely, to the very same glory which comes from the Lord, who is the Spirit.

4TH CHAPTER

Treasure In Clay Jars

1 Therefore, we do not become discouraged, since we have this ministry by God's mercy. **2** But we have renounced the secret ways that are shameful. We

---

3 Ex 24:12; 31:18; Prov 3:3; Ezek 11:19; 36:26   *7-16 Ex 34:29,30,33-35*   *18 Ex 16:7,10; 24:17*

---

3 *a*- 6 Compare Jeremiah 31:31-34. See *DIATHĒKĒ* on page 531.

b- 6 The old covenant, at best, could bring about only an outward change and thus could result only in death.

c- 6 The new Gospel testamental covenant brings about an inward, spiritual change that results in life. For another example of this contrast between letter and spirit, compare Romans 2:29 and 7:6.

d- 8 See verse 6 and its accompanying footnote "c."

e- 14 Literally: "minds were hardened" (cf. Mk. 3:5 and its accompanying footnote).

f- 14 See *DIATHĒKĒ* on page 531.

g- 14 Literally: "unveiled."

h- 17 That is, "the Lord" who is mentioned in the previous verse.

are not using trickery, nor are we falsifying God's word. Rather, by clearly revealing the truth, we recommend ourselves to everyone's conscience before God.

3 If the Gospel that we preach is veiled, it is veiled to those who are perishing, **4** whose unbelieving minds the god of this world has blinded to keep them from seeing the light of the Good News of the glory of Christ, who is the image of God.

5 We do not preach ourselves but Jesus Christ as the Lord, and ourselves as your servants for Jesus' sake. **6** For God, who said, *"Let light shine* out of the darkness,"* has shone in our hearts for the purpose of revealing the knowledge of the glory of God in the person of Christ.*a*

7 Now we have this treasure in clay jars to show that its extraordinary power comes from God and not from us. **8** In every way we are hard-pressed but not crushed, in doubt but not in despair, **9** persecuted but not forsaken, struck down but not destroyed. **10** In our bodies we are always carrying around the death of Jesus, so that you can see in our bodies the life of Jesus. **11** While we are living, we are always being given up to die for Jesus so that you can see in our dying flesh the life of Jesus. **12** So death is working in us, but life is working in you.

13 It is written: *"I believed and so I spoke."* Having the same spirit of faith, we also believe and so we speak, **14** because we know that He who raised the Lord Jesus will also raise us with Jesus and bring us with you before Him.

15 All this is to help you so that God's grace, as it spreads, will move more and more people to overflow with thanks so that God will be glorified. **16** That is why we are not discouraged. Rather, our outward person is being destroyed; our inward person is being renewed from day to day. **17** For the light trouble of this moment is producing for us an everlasting weight of glory, greater than anything we can imagine. **18** We do not look at the things that are seen but at the things that are not seen, for what we see lasts only a while, but what we do not see lasts forever.

5TH CHAPTER

We Long For A Heavenly Dwelling

1 If the earthly tent that we live in is torn down, we know that we have one from God, not made by human hands but lasting forever in heaven. **2** To be sure, in our present dwelling we sigh as we long to put on the dwelling we have from heaven, **3** since, after we have put it on, we will not be found naked. **4** So while we are in this tent, we sigh, feeling distressed for this reason—that we do not wish to put off this dwelling, but that we wish to put on the other and have life swallow up our death. **5** It is God who has prepared us for this and who has given us His Spirit as a guarantee.

6 And so we always feel confident. We know that as long as we are living in this body we are living away from the Lord. **7** For we live by faith, not by

---

6 *Gen 1:3*   13 *Ps 116:10*

4 *a* - 6 Literally: "in the face of Christ."

sight. **8** We feel bold and prefer to move out of this body and to move in with the Lord. **9** Now, whether we live here or move out, we make it our goal to please Him. **10** We must all appear before the judgment seat of Christ, each to receive what he deserves according to what he did with his body, whether good or evil.

Christ Compels Us

11 Since we know the fear of the Lord, we are trying to persuade people. God already knows what we really are, and I hope you too are clearly conscious of it. **12** We are not recommending ourselves to you again, but we are giving you an opportunity to boast about us. We are doing this so that you can answer those who boast about what is outward rather than about what is in the heart. **13** If we were crazy, it was for God. If we are sane, it is for you. **14** For the love of Christ compels us because we are convinced that One died for all; therefore they all died.*a* **15** And He died for all so that those who live would no longer live for themselves but for Him who died and rose for them.

16 And so from now on we do not think of anyone from a human point of view.*b* Once we thought of Christ from a human point of view,*c* but not anymore. **17** So if anyone is in Christ, he is a new creation. The old things have passed away; they have become new!

God Reconciled The World To Himself

18 But God has done it all. He reconciled us to Himself, through Christ, and gave us the responsibility of distributing this reconciliation.*d* **19** God did this in this way: In Christ He reconciled the world to Himself by not counting their sins against them, and He put into our hands*e* the message of this reconciliation. **20** Therefore we are ambassadors for Christ. It is as if God were pleading through us. We plead with you in behalf of Christ, "Be reconciled to God." **21** God made Him who did not know sin to be sin for us, that in Him we might become righteous before God.*f*

6TH CHAPTER

1 As men who are working with God we plead with you: Do not let God's grace [undeserved love] be wasted on you. **2** For He says:

---

5 *a*- 14 So completely substitutionary is the atonement!
　b- 16 Literally: "according to the flesh" (that is, "according to their outward appearance").
　c- 16 Literally: "according to the flesh" (that is, "according to His outward appearance").
　d- 18 The words "reconciled" and "reconciliation" are used *five* times in verses 18-20. They indicate a *changed relationship* that has been effected between God and mankind by the work of Christ Jesus, and Paul adds that the responsibility of preaching the message of this *changed relationship* rests upon God's people.
　e- 19 Literally: "He placed in us."
　f- 21 Literally: "that we might become the righteousness of God in Him."

At a favorable time I have heard you;
on the day of salvation I have helped you.
Look, now is *the favorable time!*
Look, now is *the day of salvation!*

So We Endure

3 We are not laying any kind of a stumbling block which would result in the ministry being discredited. **4** Instead, in everything we are showing that we are the ministers of God: in great endurance, in troubles, in need, in hardships; **5** when we are beaten or put in prison, when there are riots, when we work hard and go without sleep and food; **6** by being pure, by knowledge, by patience and kindness; by a spirit of holiness;*a* by sincere love, **7** by telling the truth, by God's power, with the weapons of righteousness in the right hand and the left; **8** when we are honored or dishonored, blamed or praised. Treated as deceivers, we are honest; **9** as unknown, we are well-known; as *dying*, and you see, we go on *living*; as *corrected but not killed*; **10** as sad but always glad; as beggars but making many rich; as having nothing but having everything.

11 We have been very open in speaking to you Corinthians. Our *hearts are wide open.* **12** You are not being crowded out of our feelings, but we are being crowded out of yours. **13** I ask you as my children: Treat me as I treat you, and also open your hearts wide.

Do Not Be Yoked With Unbelievers

14 Do not be yoked together with unbelievers. How can righteousness and wickedness be partners? Or how can light have anything to do with darkness? **15** How can Christ agree with Belial?*b* Or what does a believer have in common with an unbeliever? **16** How can a temple of God agree with idols? For we are the temple of the living God, as God said:

I will live and walk among them,
and I will be their God,
and they will be My people.
17 *So come away from their company,*
and separate yourselves from them, says the Lord,
and do not touch anything unclean.
Then I will welcome you,
18 *and I will be* your *Father,*
and you *will be My sons* and daughters,
says *the Lord Almighty.*

---

2 *Is 49:8*   **9** *Ps 118:17,18*   **11** *Ps 119:32*   **16-18** *Lev 26:11,12; 2 Sam 7:7,14;*
Is 52:11; Jer 32:38; 51:45; Ezek 20:34,41; 37:27; Amos 4:13

---

6 *a-* 6 Or "by the Holy Spirit."
   b- 15 That is, the devil.

7TH CHAPTER

1 Therefore since we have these promises, dear friends, let us cleanse ourselves from everything that defiles body and spirit, and let us continually do what is holy in the fear of God.

You Encouraged Us

2 Make room in your hearts for us. We have not wronged anyone, have not ruined anyone, have not taken advantage of anyone. 3 I am not saying this to condemn you. I have told you before that you are in our hearts to die together and to live together. 4 I have great confidence in you; I have much to boast about to others concerning you; I am very much encouraged; I am overjoyed in all our troubles.

5 Since coming to Macedonia our bodies have had no rest. Rather, we have been afflicted in every way, outwardly faced with fighting and inwardly afraid. 6 But *God*, who *comforts those who feel miserable, comforted* us by the coming of Titus, 7 and not only by his coming but also by the comfort he had received because of you. He told us how you long for me, how sorry you are, and how eager you are on my behalf; and this made me even happier.

8 For I am not sorry if my letter made you sad. Even if I did feel sorry—for I see that the letter made you sad, though only for a while—9 now I am glad, not because you were sad but because your sadness led you to repent of your sin. You were sad in a godly way. And so we have not done you any harm. 10 In fact, godly sorrow produces repentance which leads to salvation, free from regret; but worldly sorrow produces death. 11 Take a close look at ⌐what happened when⌐ you were led to godly sorrow! Note how eager it made you! And not just this, but also how ready to clear yourselves, also how disgusted with wrong, also how alarmed you were, also what longing and zeal you felt, and finally how ready you were to punish ⌐wrongdoing⌐! In every way you have shown that you are innocent in this matter. 12 And so, when I wrote to you, I did not write for the sake of the man who did wrong or him who was wronged, but I wanted you to show before God how zealous you are for us. 13 This is what has comforted us.

While we were comforted, we were much more delighted to see how happy Titus was, because all of you had cheered his spirit. 14 If I have boasted to him about you, you did not disappoint me. But just as everything we told you was true, so our boast to Titus proved to be true. 15 And his deepest feelings go out to you all the more as he recalls how ready all of you were to do what he asked and how you welcomed him with respect and trembling. 16 I am glad that I feel confident about you in every way.

---

6 Is 49:13

8TH CHAPTER

C. The Present: Collection for the Christians at Jerusalem (8:1–9:15)

Finish Your Collection

1 Fellow Christians,*a* we make known to you the grace [undeserved love] of God which He gave to the churches of Macedonia. **2** While they were severely tested by trouble, their overflowing joy and their deep poverty have overflowed into a rich and sincere concern. **3** I assure you that they have given all they could, yes, more than they could give, of their own free will. **4** With much pleading they begged this favor of us that they might share in the help given to the believers [saints]. **5** They did more than we anticipated: through the will of God they gave themselves to the Lord first and then to us.

6 This led us to urge Titus to finish this work of kindness among you in the very same way as he had started it. **7** As you are rich in everything—in faith, in speech, in knowledge, in every kind of zeal, and in the love which you have toward us—we want you also to overflow in this work of kindness.

8 I am not ordering you but testing you by the zeal of others to see how real your love is. **9** For you know the grace of our Lord Jesus Christ—He was rich, yet for you He became poor in order to make you rich through His poverty.

10 I am giving you advice about this, because this will be helpful to you. Last year you were the first not only to do something but to want to do something. **11** Now finish the job so that your eagerness to want to do it might be matched by your completion of it. **12** Do it with what you have, for God accepts ͵a person's gift͵ according to what he has, not according to what he does not have.

13 We do not mean to bring relief to others while we bring hardship to you; rather, we want to strike a balance. **14** Right now your abundance will supply what they need and their abundance will supply what you need, and so things will balance out, **15** just as it is written: *"Anyone who gathered much did not have too much, and anyone who gathered little did not have too little."*

16 We thank God for putting into the heart of Titus the same devotion that I have for you. **17** This is evident both by the fact that he welcomed my request and that he is eagerly coming to you by his own choice.

18 We are sending with him the Christian brother*b* whom all the churches praise for his preaching of the Gospel. **19** More than that, the churches elected him to travel with us in this work of love that we are doing in order to honor the Lord and ͵to show͵ our willingness to help.

20 We are trying to avoid any criticism of the way that we are handling this great gift. **21** To be sure, we *intend to do what is right not only in the sight of the Lord but also in the sight of people.*

---

15 *Ex 16:18*   21 *Prov 3:4*

---

8 *a*- 1 Literally: "brothers" (also in v. 23).
   b- 18 Probably a reference to Luke.

22 We are also sending with them our Christian brother*c* whom we have often tested in many ways and found to be zealous, and now find to be much more zealous than ever because he has so much confidence in you.

23 As for Titus, he is my partner and fellow Christian among you. And our fellow Christians, those*d* who are sent by the churches, are the glory of Christ. 24 Give a clear demonstration of your love and show the congregation how right we were to boast about you to these men.

9TH CHAPTER

How To Give

1 I really do not need to write to you about helping the believers [saints], 2 because I know how eager you are. This is what I am telling the people of Macedonia in boasting about you: "Greece has been ready since last year," and your enthusiasm has stirred up more and more of them. 3 Now I am sending my fellow Christian ⌊workers⌋*a* so that our boast might not prove to be an empty one in this regard, but that—as I said—you may be ready. 4 Otherwise, if any Macedonians come with me and find that you are not ready, you will make us (to say nothing of yourselves) feel ashamed of being so confident. 5 So I thought it necessary to urge these fellow Christians to go to you ahead of me and arrange in advance this promised expression of your praise and thanks, so that it may be ready as an expression of praise and thanks*b* and not of miserliness.

6 Remember this: *The person who plants [sows] sparingly will harvest [reap] sparingly; and the person who plants with expressions of praise and thanks will harvest with expressions of praise and thanks.* 7 Let each person do what he has decided in his heart, not grudgingly or as a result of pressure, because *God loves a cheerful giver.*

God Blesses You

8 God can make every gift of His grace [undeserved love] overflow on you, so that you, since you always have all that you need in every way, may overflow in every good work, 9 as it is written:

> *He*c* scatters his gifts to the poor;*
> *his righteousness lasts forever.*

6,7 Prov 22:8   **9** *Ps 112:9*

---

c- 22 The person referred to is uncertain. Some suggest that it may be Aristarchus (cf. Acts 19:29; 20:4).

d- 23 Probably a reference to those mentioned in Acts 20:4.

9 *a-* 3 Literally: "brothers" (also in v. 5).

b- 5 The phrase "expression of praise and thanks," used twice, is the translation of the word which means "generous gift" in the Greek sentence (cf. v. 6).

c- 9 That is, the righteous person.

10 Now He who provides *seed for the sower* and *bread for eating* will also provide and multiply your seed and increase *the products of your righteousness.* **11** You are being made rich in every way so that you are totally sincere. This moves us to give thanks to God, because **12** this work that you do in serving others does not only supply the needs of the believers, but it also continues to overflow through the many prayers of thanksgiving that are offered to God. **13** By your successful completion of the test which this service provided, you are glorifying God as you show your subordination*d* to the Good News of Christ which you confess. ₍You show this₎ by the sincere concern that you have toward them and toward all with whom you share fellowship. **14** At the same time their deep longing for you is expressed in prayer for you, because they see the extraordinary grace of God that is given to you. **15** Thanks be to God for His indescribable gift.

10TH CHAPTER

D. *The Future: Paul's defense against opponents (10:1–13:10)*

I Am Bold

1 I plead with you, I, Paul, with the gentleness and kindliness of Christ—I who am humble when I am face to face with you but bold toward you when I am away!*a* **2** I beg you that when I come I will not have to be as confident and bold as I think I will dare to be against some men who think we are living according to the flesh. **3** Of course, we are living in the flesh, but we are not fighting in a fleshly way.*b* **4** The weapons with which we fight are not of flesh but have divine power to tear down fortresses. **5** With them we tear down arguments and everything that raises its proud head against the knowledge of God, and we make every thought a prisoner in obedience to Christ. **6** We are ready to punish every act of disobedience when you have become completely obedient.

7 You are looking at things as they appear outwardly.*c* If anyone feels sure that he belongs to Christ, he should consider, as he examines his own position again, that we belong to Christ just as he does. **8** Yes, if I boast a little too much about our authority, which the Lord gave us to build you up and not to tear you down, I will not have to feel ashamed.

9 Let me not be thought of as trying to frighten you with my letters since some say: **10** "His letters are powerful and strong, but when he is with us, he is unimpressive and he is a poor speaker." **11** Such a person should understand that

---

10 Is 55:10; Hos 10:12

---

d- 13 See *HUPOTASSŌ* on page 541.
10 *a-* 1 Paul here is very likely echoing words which his enemies in Corinth used to describe him.
  b- 3 Literally: "according to the flesh."
  c- 7 Or "Look at things as they appear."

when we come we will act in exactly the same way in which we express ourselves in letters when we are absent.

We Are Proud Of Our Work

12 We do not dare to put ourselves in a class or compare ourselves with some of those who speak highly of themselves, but when they measure themselves by their own yardstick and compare themselves with themselves, they do not show good sense. **13** We will not boast about things that are not able to be measured, but we will confine ourselves to those things which are measured by the standard that God laid down for us, namely, our coming to you. **14** We are not going too far in our boasting, as we would be if we had not come to you. The fact is that we were the first to come to you with the Good News of Christ. **15** We are not boasting about unmeasurable things found in the work done by others. We have the hope that, as your faith grows, we will be able to do much more in carrying out our assignment **16** by preaching the Gospel to the regions beyond you. We do not want to boast of things already accomplished by an assignment given to someone else.

17 *If anyone boasts, let him boast in the Lord.* **18** For it is not the person who commends himself who is approved, but he whom the Lord commends.

11TH CHAPTER

I Am Jealous

1 I hope that you have been putting up with a little foolishness from me. But I also hope that you will continue to put up with me. **2** I am jealous of you with a godly jealousy because I promised you in marriage to one Husband, to bring you as a pure virgin to Christ. **3** But I am afraid that as the *snake* by its trickery *deceived* Eve, your minds somehow may be led away from your sincere and pure devotion to Christ. **4** When someone comes along and preaches a different Jesus from the One we preached, or when you receive a different spirit from the One you received before, or when you accept a different gospel from the One you accepted before—you put up with it well enough.

5 I do not think I am in any way less than your "super" apostles. **6** Even if I am not a trained speaker, yet I know what I am talking about. In every way we have made this clear to you on all subjects.

7 I charged you nothing for bringing you the Good News of God. Did I do wrong when I humbled myself in this way, so that you would be lifted up? **8** I robbed other churches, by taking pay from them in order to serve you. **9** When I was with you and needed anything, I did not bother anyone to help me, because our fellow Christians[a] who came from Macedonia supplied everything that I

---

17 *Jer 9:24*   3 *Gen 3:4,13*

---

11 *a-* 9 Literally: "brothers," a reference to Silas and Timothy (cf. Acts 18:5; 2 Cor. 1:19).

needed. I kept myself from being a burden to you in any way, and I will continue to do that.

10 As the truth of Christ is in me, this boast of mine will not be silenced anywhere in Greece. **11** Why? Because I do not love you? God knows I do. **12** But I will go on doing what I am doing, to take away the opportunity of those who want an opportunity to get others to think that they are like us in the work about which they are boasting. **13** Such men are false apostles and deceitful workers, since they masquerade as apostles of Christ. **14** And no wonder, for Satan himself masquerades as an angel of light. **15** So it is not surprising if his servants also masquerade as servants of righteousness. In the end they will get what they deserve for what they are doing.

I Will Boast

16 Again I say no one should think that I am a fool. But if you do, then let me come to you as a fool and also boast a little. **17** What I say when I boast so confidently is not the Lord's way of speaking but that of a fool. **18** Since many boast in a human way,*b* I will too, **19** because you, being wise, gladly put up with fools. **20** For you put up with anyone who makes you his slaves, or who devours what you have, or who traps you, or who lords it over you, or who slaps your face. **21** I am ashamed to admit it, but we have been too weak to do that.

But what anyone else dares to claim—I am talking like a fool—I dare to claim too. **22** Are they Jews? So am I! Do they belong to the people of Israel? So do I! Are they descended from Abraham? So am I! **23** Are they servants of Christ? I am mad to talk like this, but I am a better one! I have done much more hard work, been in prison much more, been beaten very much more, and often faced death. **24** Five times the Jews gave me 39 lashes, **25** three times I was beaten with sticks, once I was stoned, three times I was in a shipwreck, a night and a day I drifted on the sea. **26** I have traveled much and faced dangers from flooded streams and from robbers, dangers from my own people and from Gentiles, dangers in the city, in the wilderness, and on the sea, dangers from false friends.*c* **27** I have toiled and struggled, have often been sleepless, hungry and thirsty, often starving, cold, and naked. **28** Besides everything else, I have a daily burden—I am anxiously concerned about all the churches. **29** When anyone is weak, am I not weak too? When anyone falls ⌊from faith⌋,*d* don't I also feel a burning grief? **30** If I have to boast, I will boast of the things that show how weak I am. **31** The God and Father of the Lord Jesus, who is blessed forever, knows that I am not lying. **32** In Damascus the governor under King Aretas had the city of Damascus watched to catch me, **33** but I was let down in a basket through an opening in the wall, and I escaped from his hands.

---

b- 18 Literally: "according to the flesh."
c- 26 Literally: "false brothers."
d- 29 See *SKANDALON* on page 545.

12TH CHAPTER

Caught Up To Paradise

1 I have to boast. It does not do any good, but I will go on with visions and revelations from the Lord. **2** I know a man in Christ; fourteen years ago— whether in his body or outside it, I do not know, God knows—that man was caught up to the third heaven. **3** I know that such a man—whether in his body or outside it, I do not know, God knows—**4** was caught up to Paradise and heard what no human being is allowed to speak. **5** About such a man I will boast, but I will not boast about myself, except to boast about my weaknesses.

6 If I would want to boast, I would not be a fool, because I would be telling the truth. But I am going to spare you, in order to keep anyone from thinking more of me than what he does when he sees or hears me.

7 To keep me from feeling proud because such wonderful things were revealed to me, I was given a thorn for my flesh, a messenger of Satan to plague me in order to keep me from feeling proud. **8** Three times I begged the Lord that He might rid me of it, **9** but He told me: "My grace is enough for you. For My power is at its best when you are weak." So I will delight all the more to boast of my weaknesses in order to have Christ's power dwell in me. **10** That is why I am glad to be weak and mistreated, to suffer hardships, to be persecuted and hard-pressed for Christ. For when I am weak, then I am strong.

I Will Be No Burden

11 I have spoken foolishly; you have driven me to do it. Really, you should have commended me to others. Even if I am nothing, I was not in any way inferior to your "super" apostles. **12** The signs which prove that I am an apostle were worked among you with much patience: miraculous signs, wonderful proofs, and miracles. *a*

13 How were you treated worse than the other churches, except that I did not burden you? Forgive me this wrong! **14** Here I am ready to come to you a third time, and I am not going to be a burden, because I do not want what you have but I want you. To be sure, children are not obligated to save up for their parents but parents for their children. **15** And I shall be very glad to spend what I have, and also myself, on behalf of your souls. Do you love me less because I love you so much?

16 But if you grant that I was no burden to you, was I a clever fellow who trapped you with some trick? *b* **17** Did I take advantage of you through any of the men I sent you? **18** I urged Titus to go to you, and I sent the fellow Christian ⌊worker⌋ *c* with him. Titus did not take advantage of you, did he? Didn't we act in the same spirit and walk in the same footsteps?

19 Have you been thinking all along that we were only defending ourselves

---

12 *a*- 12 See MIRACULOUS SIGNS, WONDERFUL PROOFS, and MIRACLES on page 527.
  b- 16 Once again Paul seems to echo a criticism voiced by his enemies in Corinth.
  c- 18 Literally: "brother."

before you? We are speaking before God in Christ; and everything, dear friends, is meant to help you grow.

Will There Be No Trouble?

20 I am afraid that I may come and find you different from what I want you to be, and you may find me different from what you want me to be. I am afraid that there may be quarreling, jealousy, angry feelings, selfish ambitions, slander, gossip, pride, and disorderly conduct. **21** I am afraid that when I come again, my God may humble me in regard to you, and I may have to weep over many who formerly lived in sin and have not repented for the unclean, sexual, and lustful things they did.

13TH CHAPTER

1 This is the third time I am coming to you.

Everything must be proved by what two or three witnesses say. **2** I have said it before and I am saying it again ahead of time (as if I were present for the second time, even though I am now absent) to all those who formerly lived in sin and to all the rest: When I come again, I will not spare you—**3** seeing that you want proof that Christ is speaking through me. He is not weak in dealing with you but continues to be able to do something among you. **4** He did indeed die on a cross in weakness, but He lives by God's power. We indeed are weak in Him, but we continue to live with Him when God puts His power to work for you.

5 Examine yourselves to see whether you really believe. Test yourselves. Do you not know that Jesus Christ is in you—unless you fail in your test? **6** I hope that you will realize that we have not failed in our test. **7** We pray to God that you will do no wrong—not to show that we have passed the test, but that you may do what is right even if we may seem to have failed. **8** For we cannot do anything against the truth but only in behalf of it. **9** We are glad when we are weak and you are strong. And what we are praying for is this, that God may make you complete.

10 Here is the reason that I am writing these things while I am not with you: When I come, I do not want to have to be severe in using the authority which the Lord gave me to build you up and not to tear you down.

E. Conclusion (13:11-14)

Farewell

11 Finally, fellow Christians,*ᵃ* farewell! Strive for perfection. Take encour-

---

1 Deut 19:15

---

13 *a-* 11 Literally: "brothers."

agement from me. Agree with one another, live in peace, and the God of love and peace will be with you. **12** Greet one another with a holy kiss. **13** All the believers [saints] greet you. **14** May the grace of the Lord Jesus Christ, the love of God, and the fellowship of the Holy Spirit be with you all!

PAUL WRITES TO THE
GALATIANS[a]

1st CHAPTER

A. Introduction (1:1-5)

1 Paul, an apostle (not sent from men or by any man but by Jesus Christ and by God the Father, who raised Him from the dead), **2** and all the Christians[b] who are with me, to the churches in Galatia—**3** grace[c] and peace to you from God the Father and our Lord Jesus Christ, **4** who gave Himself for our sins so that He might deliver us from this present wicked world according to the will of our God and Father. **5** To Him be glory forever and ever! Amen.

B. Personal argument (1:6–2:21)

You Are Turning Away

6 I am surprised that you are so quickly leaving Him who called you by the grace of Christ and are turning to another kind of gospel, **7** which is really not "gospel" ["good news"] at all.[d] Rather, there are some men who are troubling you by wanting to change the Gospel [Good News] of Christ. **8** But even if we or an angel from heaven would preach any other gospel than the one we preached, a curse be on him! **9** I say again what we said before: If anyone preaches any other gospel than the one you received, a curse be on him!

10 Do I say this now to win the approval of men—or of God? Or am I trying to please men? If I were still trying to please men, I would not be a slave of Christ.

Jesus Gave Me The Good News That I Preach

11 I want you to know, fellow Christians, that the Gospel I preached is not a

---

1 *a*   *Galatians* may be the earliest of the letters of the Apostle Paul (c. A.D. 48). However, some people believe that it was written at the same time as *Romans* in the winter of A.D. 55-56 (cf. Rom. 4 and Gal. 3). *Galatians* is sometimes called "the little *Romans*."
     b-   2 Literally: "brothers" (also in v. 11).
     c-   3 Meaning "God's undeserved love."
     d-   7 Literally: "which is not another."

human message, **12** for I did not receive it from a man nor was I taught it; rather, Jesus Christ revealed it to me.

13 You have heard what I used to do when I still lived according to the Jewish religion,*e* how violently I persecuted God's church and tried to destroy it **14** and how I advanced in the Jewish religion*f* beyond many who were my contemporaries among my people—so extremely zealous I had become for the traditions of my ancestors.

15 But when God (who *separated*ᵍ *me from my mother's womb* and called me by His grace) was pleased **16** to show me His Son so that I would proclaim Him among the Gentiles, I did not immediately talk it over with any human being, **17** nor did I go up to Jerusalem to see those who were apostles before me. Rather, I went to Arabia and then came back to Damascus.

18 Then three years later I went up to Jerusalem to visit Peter, and I stayed with him fifteen days. **19** But I did not see any of the other apostles,*h* except James the Lord's brother. **20** (And I declare before God that I am not lying in what I am writing.) **21** Then I went to the regions of Syria and Cilicia. **22** The churches of Christ in Judea were not acquainted with me personally. **23** The only thing they continued to hear was this: "The man who used to persecute us is now preaching the faith that he once tried to destroy," **24** and they praised God for what had happened to me.

2ND CHAPTER

Fellowship With The Apostles

1 Then fourteen years later I went up to Jerusalem again, this time with Barnabas, and I also took Titus with me. **2** As a result of a revelation ⌞from God⌟, I went up and laid before them the Gospel which I preach among the Gentiles, that is, ⌞I laid it⌟ privately before those who were recognized as leaders; I did so because I did not in any way want to be running or to have run in vain.

3 Titus was with me. Although he was a Greek, no one forced him to be circumcised.

4 Also, there were false Christians*a* who had come in secretly. They sneaked in to spy out the freedom that we have in Christ Jesus so that they might make us slaves. **5** But not for a moment did we let them dictate to us,*b* so that you might always have the true Gospel.

6 Also, the respected leaders—what sort of people they once were really makes no difference to me, since *a person's position in life*ᶜ *does not matter to*

---

15 Is 49:1   6 Deut 10:17

---

  e- 13 Literally: "according to Judaism."
  f- 14 Literally: "advanced in Judaism."
  g- 15 Or "appointed" (cf. Rom. 1:1).
  h- 19 Or "did not see anyone other than the apostles" (cf. Acts 9:27).

2 *a*- 4 Literally: "brothers."
  b- 5 Literally: "to whom we did not yield for an hour by way of subordination"; see *HUPOTASSŌ* on page 541.
  c- 6 Literally: "a person's appearance."

God—indeed, these leaders did not teach me anything new. **7** On the contrary, they saw that I had been entrusted with bringing the Gospel to the uncircumcised [Gentiles] as Peter was to bring it to the circumcised [Jews]. **8** For He who had worked in Peter to make him an apostle to the circumcised [Jews] had also worked in me to make me an apostle to the Gentiles. **9** When James, Peter, and John, who were considered pillars, saw what God's grace had given me, they gave Barnabas and me the right hand of fellowship with the understanding that we would work among the Gentiles and they among the circumcised [Jews]. **10** All they asked was that we keep remembering the poor, the very thing which I was eager to do.

I Criticized Peter

11 When Peter came to Antioch, I opposed him to his face because he was completely wrong. **12** He had been eating with the Gentiles before certain persons came from James. But when they came, he drew back and stayed away from the Gentiles because he was afraid of those who insisted on circumcision. **13** And the other Jews acted just as hypocritically as he did, so that even Barnabas was led astray by their hypocrisy.

14 But when I saw that they were not doing what is right according to the truth of the Gospel, I told Peter in front of everyone: "If you, a Jew, do not live like a Jew but like a Gentile, how can you insist that the Gentiles must live like Jews?"

15 Since we were born Jews and not Gentile sinners, **16** we know that a person cannot be justified [declared righteous]*d* by doing what the Law says, but only by believing in Jesus Christ. So we also believed in Jesus Christ in order to be justified [declared righteous] by faith in Christ and not by the works of the Law, *because not one person will be justified [declared righteous]* by the works of the Law.

17 Now if we who are seeking to be justified [declared righteous] in Christ are found to be sinners ourselves, has Christ then become one who encourages sin? Never! **18** For if I build up again the very things which I have torn down, I make myself a sinner.*e* **19** To be sure, by the Law I died to the Law that I might live to God.*f* I have been crucified with Christ. **20** So, it is no longer I who live, but it is Christ who lives in me. The life I now live in my body I live by believing in the Son of God, who loved me and gave Himself for me. **21** I do not reject the grace of God. For if we could receive righteousness through the Law, then Christ died for nothing.

---

16 Ps 143:2

---

d- 16 See Romans 3:20 as well as 3:24 and accompanying footnotes. Also apply these references from *Romans* to Galatians 2:17; 3:8,11,24; 5:4.

e- 18 The meaning of verse 18 is this: When we seek justification alone by faith in Christ (cf. v. 17), we "tear down" the Law. If, to please the Jews, we try again to be justified by doing what the Law demands and so "build it up," the Law only condemns us as sinners.

f- 19 The context, as well as the appositive which follows, explains that Christians give up on the Law completely ("die to the Law") so that they may be justified before God ("live to God") by faith in Christ (cf. esp. vv. 16 and 21).

3RD CHAPTER

C. Doctrinal argument (3:1–4:31)

The Believer Is Blessed

1 Foolish Galatians! Who has bewitched you—you who saw Jesus Christ so clearly pictured[a] before your eyes as crucified? **2** I want you to tell me just one thing: Did you receive the Spirit by doing what the Law says, or by believing what you heard? **3** Are you so foolish? You started by the Spirit; are you now going to finish by your own effort?[b] **4** Did you experience so much for nothing—if it really was for nothing? **5** Therefore, does God supply you with the Spirit and work miracles among you[c] by your doing what the Law says, or by believing what you are hearing?

6 *Abraham* is a good example: He *believed God, and it was credited to him as righteousness.* **7** You see, then, that those who believe[d] are Abraham's real descendants. **8** Since the Scripture foresaw that God would justify [acquit] the nations by faith, He announced the Gospel to Abraham beforehand: *"Through you all nations will be blessed."* **9** So those who believe are blessed together with Abraham, a man of faith.

10 There is a curse on all who depend on doing what the Law says, because it is written: *"Cursed is everyone who does not continue to do everything written in the book of the Law."* **11** It is clear that no one is justified [declared righteous] before God by doing what the Law says, because *the just [righteous person] will live by faith.*[e] **12** But the Law is not based on faith; rather, it says: *"The person who does these things will find life in them."*

13 Christ paid the price to free us from the curse of the Law by becoming a curse for us, for it is written: *"Cursed is everyone who hangs on a tree [cross]."* **14** ⌊He redeemed us⌋ so that in Jesus Christ the blessing of Abraham might come to the nations, and that we by believing might receive the promised Spirit.

The Promise Was First

15 My fellow Christians,[f] let me use an example from daily life. Once a "last

---

6 Gen 15:6	**8** Gen 12:3; 18:18; 22:18; 26:4; 28:14	**10** Deut 27:26	**11** Hab 2:4
12 Lev 18:5	**13** Deut 21:22,23		

---

3 *a-* 1 The Greek verb means "to portray publicly." Paul is saying that he had presented the message of Christ's Gospel to the Galatians so clearly as if it had been portrayed on a public billboard for all to see.

b- 3 For a similar use of the terms "spirit" and "flesh," compare Romans 2:28,29.

c- 5 Compare Mark 16:20.

d- 7 Literally: "the 'by believing' ⌊people⌋," or "the 'by faith' ⌊people⌋." This expression is also used in verse 9, and a contrasting expression "the 'by the works of the Law' ⌊people⌋" is used in verse 10. Paul seems to be classifying two groups: one that seeks to be justified "by faith"; the other that seeks to be justified "by works" (cf. 2:16,17a; 3:2,5).

e- 11 See Romans 1:17 and its accompanying footnote.

f- 15 Literally: "brothers."

will and testament"[g] is ratified, even if it is only a human will, no one sets it aside or adds to it. **16** Now the promises were spoken in reference to Abraham and in reference to his Descendant. He does not say: "in descendants," as referring to many, but as referring to one: "*in your Descendant*," who is Christ. **17** What I am saying is this: The Law, which came 430 years after God's confirmation of the covenant ["last will and testament"] ⌐made with Abraham⌐,[h] does not make this covenant null and void,[i] and so cancel its promise.[j] **18** For if we receive the inheritance by the Law, we do not receive it by a promise; but God gave it to Abraham by a promise.

Our Guardian

19 Why then was the Law given? It was added to point out[k] trespasses until the Descendant would come to whom the promise referred. And it was given through angels by the hand of a mediator. **20** A mediator deals with more than one, but God is One.[l]

21 Is the Law then opposed to the promises of God? Never! For if a law had been given that could make us alive, then certainly righteousness would become ours by keeping that law. **22** But the Scripture has said that everything is a prisoner of sin, so that the promised blessing might be given[m] to believers through faith in Jesus Christ.

23 Before this faith came, we were kept under guard by the Law, until this faith which was about to come would be revealed.

24 Thus the Law has been our guardian[n] until Christ came, so that we might be justified [declared righteous] by faith. **25** But now that faith has come, we are no longer under a guardian. **26** For you are all God's children by believing in Christ Jesus, **27** because all of you who were baptized into Christ have put on Christ. **28** There is neither Jew nor Greek, slave nor free, male nor female—for

---

16 Gen 22:18; 26:4

---

g - 15 Greek: "*diathēkēn*"; here Paul pictures a "last will and testament" and its quality of unchangeableness in order to set up his argumentation for verses 16-18 where he shows that the *Gospel*-promise which God gave to Abraham could *not* later be negated by the *Law*. See *DIATHĒKĒ* on page 531.

h- 17 Literally: "a covenant having been confirmed by God"; some manuscripts and early translations add: "confirmed of God *in Christ*."

i- 17 Greek: "*akuroō*" ("make null and void"); same word is used at Matthew 15:6 and Mark 7:13.

j- 17 The covenant given to Moses at Mount Sinai (e.g., Ex. 20) came 430 years after the Gospel-promise or testamental covenant (*diathēkē*) had been spoken by God to Abraham, Isaac, and Jacob (cf. Gen. 12:1-3; 22:18; 26:4; 28:14; etc.). See *DIATHĒKĒ* on page 531.

k- 19 Literally: "because of."

l- 20 God gave the Sinaitic covenant through Moses, a mediator who brought it to the people, but God gave His Gospel-promise to Abraham directly. The Law was given through a mediator because it had conditions attached to it, but the Gospel-promise has no conditions attached. The meaning of the expression "God is One" is uncertain in this context. Some take it to mean that God is always the same (cf. Rom. 3:30; Jas. 2:19). This meaning would emphasize that God's Gospel-promise or testamental covenant always remains the same, that is, with no conditions attached.

m- 22 Meaning "might be given as a gift."

n- 24 Greek: "*paidagōgos*," a slave whose duty was similar to that of a modern-day chaperon. Such a slave saw to it that a child under his care was raised properly. He escorted the child to school and reminded the child of who he was and why he was to conduct himself properly.

you are all one in Christ Jesus. **29** If you belong to Christ, then you are Abraham's descendants and heirs, just as God promised.

4TH CHAPTER

God's Sons

1 Now I say that as long as the heir is a child, he is no better than a slave, although he owns everything. **2** Rather, he is under guardians and managers until the day set by his father. **3** So it is with us. When we were children, we were slaves under the elementary rules of the world.*a* **4** But when the time finally came, God sent out*b* His Son to be born of a woman and to be born under law, **5** in order to pay the price to free [redeem] those under law that we might be adopted as His full-fledged sons.*c* **6** And because you are sons, God sent out the Spirit of His Son into our hearts to cry, "Abba! Father!"*d* **7** So you are no longer a slave but a son. And since you are a son, God has also made you an heir.

8 On the other hand, when you did not know God, you were slaves to gods who do not really exist. **9** Now that you know God—or rather, God knows you—how can you turn back again to those elementary rules, so weak and beggarly, and be willing to become slaves to them all over again? **10** You observe days, months, seasons, and years! **11** I am afraid for you that the hard work I did on you may have been wasted.

You Welcomed Me

12 I beg you, my fellow Christians,*e* act as I did because I am acting as you did.*f* You did me no wrong. **13** You know that I brought you the Gospel the first time because I was sick.*g* **14** Though my sick body was a test for you, you did not despise or scorn me, but you welcomed me as if I were a messenger of God or Christ Jesus Himself. **15** Your positive attitude toward me—what has become of that? I can say for a fact that if it had been possible, you would have torn out your eyes and given them to me. **16** Can it be that I have become your enemy by telling you the truth?

17 These men are zealous for you, but not in your interest. They want to cut you off from me so that you will be zealous for them. **18** It is good to be zealous in a good cause always, and not only when I am present with you.

19 My children, I am suffering birth pains for you again until Christ is formed

---

4 *a*- 3 A reference to the provisions of the ceremonial law (cf. v. 9 and Col. 2:20).
  b- 4 As in being "sent out" on a mission (cf. v. 6 also).
  c- 5 Literally: "that we might receive the adoption as sons."
  d- 6 "*Abba*" is the Aramaic word for "father." Thus Paul says, "Father! Father!"
  e- 12 Literally: "brothers" (also in vv. 28,31).
  f- 12 Literally: "become like me, since I am becoming like you."
  g- 13 It may have been malaria that forced Paul to leave the swampy country of Pamphylia and climb up the rugged Taurus Mountains to Antioch near Pisidia, lying 3,600 feet above sea level. Here Paul began his missionary work among the Galatians. See Acts 13:13,14.

in you. **20** I wish I were with you right now and could change my way of speaking to you, because I am puzzled about you.

We Are Like Isaac

21 Tell me, you who want to be under the Law, will you not listen to what the Law says? **22** It is written that Abraham had two sons; one was the son of the slave woman and the other the son of the free woman. **23** Now the son of the slave woman was born in a natural way,[h] but the son of the free woman by the promise.

24 I am going to use these historical events as illustrations.[i] The women are two covenants [two "last wills and testaments"].[j] The children of the covenant given on Mount Sinai are born to be slaves; this is Hagar. **25** Hagar in this sense is Mount Sinai in Arabia and she is like Jerusalem today: she and her children are slaves. **26** But the Jerusalem that is above is free; and she is our mother. **27** It is written:

> Be glad, barren woman,
> > you who do not have any children;
> break into shouting,
> > you who feel no pains of childbirth,
> > > because the deserted woman has many more children
> > > than the one who has the husband.

28 Now you, my fellow Christians, like Isaac, are children of the promise. **29** Furthermore, at that time the son who was born in a natural way[k] persecuted the son born in a spiritual way.[l] And it is exactly the same way now. **30** But what does the Scripture say? *"Get rid of the slave woman and her son, because the son of the slave woman will not be an heir together with the son* of the free woman." **31** Now then, fellow Christians, we are not children of a slave woman but of a free woman.

5TH CHAPTER

D. Practical applications (5:1–6:10)

Christ Has Freed Us

1 Christ has freed us so that we will be free. Stand firm then, and do not get caught again under a yoke of slavery.

---

27 Is 54:1　　　30 Gen 21:10

---

h- 23 Literally: "according to the flesh."
i - 24 Literally: "Which things are being used allegorically." Paul's *allegory* is based on historical events recorded in Genesis 16 and 21. He uses these events in a figurative way and thereby illustrates a spiritual truth.
j- 24 See *DIATHĒKĒ* on page 531.
k- 29 Literally: "according to the flesh."
l- 29 Literally: "according to the spirit."

2 I, Paul, tell you, if you have yourselves circumcised, Christ will be of absolutely no benefit to you. **3** And again I warn everyone who has himself circumcised that he obligates himself to do everything the Law says. **4** You who try to be justified [declared righteous] by law have been cut off from Christ and have fallen from grace. **5** For we through the Spirit eagerly await by faith the righteousness for which we hope. *a* **6** For in Christ Jesus neither circumcision nor the lack of it counts for anything, but what counts is faith that is active in love.

7 You were running well. Who cut in on you so that you are not persuaded by the truth? **8** This persuasion does not come from the One who called you. **9** A little yeast spreads through the whole batch of dough. **10** I am convinced in the Lord that you will think in no other way, but the one who is troubling you will have to take his punishment—whoever he may be. **11** My fellow Christians, *b* if I am still preaching that people have to be circumcised, why am I still being persecuted? In that case the cross would be eliminated as a stumbling block *c* ⌊to the Jews⌋. **12** I wish the men who upset you would castrate themselves. *d*

13 You were indeed called to be free, fellow Christians. Only do not use your freedom as a launching pad *e* for the flesh; rather, by love continue to serve one another, **14** for the whole Law is summarized in a single saying: *"Love your neighbor as yourself."* **15** But if you continue to bite and devour one another, be careful, or you will be destroyed by one another.

16 I say, let the Spirit direct your life, *f* and you will not carry out what your flesh desires. **17** For what the flesh desires is against the Spirit, and what the Spirit desires is against the flesh, because they are opposed to each other, so that you do not do what you want to do. **18** But if you are led by the Spirit, you are not under law.

19 Now you know the works of the flesh. They are: sexual sin, impurity, unrestrained lust, **20** worshiping of idols, witchcraft, hate, bickering, jealousy, anger, selfishness, quarreling, divisions, **21** envy, drunkenness, carousing, and the like. I warn you, as I did before, those who continue to do such things will have no share in the Kingdom of God.

22 But the fruit of the Spirit is love, joy, peace, patience, kindness, goodness, faithfulness, **23** gentleness, and self-control. There is no law against such things.

---

14 Lev 19:18

---

5 *a*- 5 Or "the hope of righteousness."

  b- 11 Literally: "brothers" (also in v. 13).

  c- 11 See *SKANDALON* on page 545.

  d- 12 Or "be completely cut off from you."

  e- 13 The Greek word refers to the "starting point" or "base of operations" for an expedition. Here Paul is warning against the danger of permitting the flesh to launch out into a life of sin or of permitting the flesh to find an "occasion" or "pretext" for sin. (This same Greek word is translated "opportunity" at Romans 7:8.)

  f- 16 Literally: "walk with the Spirit" ("Spirit" also in vv. 17,18,22,25). The Greek word *pneuma* may denote either the "Holy Spirit" or the "spirit" ("new nature") produced in believers by the working of the Holy Spirit. This latter concept is especially brought out in Ephesians 4:24 and Colossians 3:10 where Paul calls this the "new self." In contexts such as the present one it is sometimes difficult to decide whether the word "spirit" should be spelled with a small or a capital "s." Either way the thought of the passage does not change much since no one can have a *new nature* unless the *Holy Spirit* is already present (1 Cor. 12:3) and when the *Holy Spirit* is present a *new nature* always lives within the converted person (Jn. 3:6).

24 But those who belong to Christ Jesus have crucified the flesh with its passions and desires. **25** If we live by the Spirit, let us also keep in step with the Spirit. **26** Let us not become conceited, challenge one another, or become envious of one another.

6TH CHAPTER

When Anyone Sins

1 My fellow Christians,*a* if a person is caught in ˌthe trap ofˌ some sin, let those of you who are spiritual set him right again in a humble manner. At the same time keep an eye on yourself so that you also are not tempted. **2** Help one another bear these burdens, and so you will carry out the law of Christ. **3** For if anyone thinks he is something when he is nothing, he is fooling himself. **4** Let each one test the genuineness of his own work. Then he will have something to boast about in regard to himself alone and not in regard to another person. **5** For everyone will carry his own burden.

We Reap What We Sow

6 Let the person who is taught the word share all good things with his teacher. **7** Make no mistake about this; you can never make a fool of God. For whatever a person sows he will reap, **8** because: the one who sows for his own flesh will from his flesh reap destruction, but the one who sows for his spirit will from his spirit reap everlasting life. **9** Let us not become tired of doing good, because we will reap, each in his own appointed time, if we do not give up. **10** So whenever we have a chance, let us do good to everyone, especially to our family of believers.

E. Conclusion (6:11-18)

The New Life

11 See what large letters I make when I write to you with my own hand.

12 These men who want to make a good showing in an outward way*b* are insisting that you have yourselves circumcised. They do this only to keep themselves from being persecuted for the cross of Christ. **13** Why, these who are having themselves circumcised do not keep the Law themselves, but they want you to have yourselves circumcised so that they can boast of what was done to you physically.*c* **14** May I never boast of anything but the cross of our Lord Jesus Christ, by whom the world is crucified to me and I to the world. **15** It does not matter whether a person is circumcised or not circumcised, but what matters is

---

6 *a-* 1 Literally: "brothers" (also in v. 18).
　 b- 12 Literally: "in the flesh."
　 c- 13 Literally: "in your flesh."

being a new creation. **16** And to all those who follow this rule, may *peace* and mercy be on them, namely, *on* the *Israel* of God.*d*

17 From now on let no one make trouble for me, because I bear on my body the scars of Jesus.

18 May the grace [undeserved love] of our Lord Jesus Christ be with your spirit, my fellow Christians! Amen.

---

16 Ps 125:5; 128:6

---

d- 16 Compare 3:7.

PAUL WRITES TO THE
EPHESIANS*a*

1ST CHAPTER

A. Introduction (1:1,2)

1 Paul, an apostle of Christ Jesus by God's will, to the believers [saints] in Ephesus*b* who trust in Christ Jesus: **2** May God our Father and the Lord Jesus Christ give you grace*c* and peace.

B. Doctrinal section:
The church is God's workmanship created in Christ Jesus (1:3–3:21)

What God Has Done

3 Let us praise the God and Father of our Lord Jesus Christ, who in Christ has blessed us with every spiritual blessing in heaven.

4 Before He made the world, His love led Him to choose us in Christ to be holy and blameless in His sight. **5** In the kindness of His will He appointed [predestined] us long ago to be made His sons by Jesus Christ. **6** He did this in order that the glory of the grace which He bestowed on us in His dear Son might be praised. **7** His dear Son paid our ransom price with his blood;*d* we have forgiveness of our sins as a result of the riches of His grace. **8** He poured out even more of this grace on us by giving us every kind of wisdom and under-

---

1 *a*   Ephesians is one of the four "prison epistles" or "captivity letters" which the Apostle Paul wrote from prison either in Rome about A.D. 61 (cf. 3:1; 4:1; 6:20) or during his three year stay in Ephesus (cf. Acts 20:31) about A.D. 53-55.

   b- 1 A few of the older manuscripts omit: "in Ephesus." The letter was very likely written for all the churches in Asia Minor founded during Paul's Third Missionary Journey. The "letter from Laodicea," spoken of in Colossians 4:16, may very well be this letter.

   c- 2 Meaning "God's undeserved love."

   d- 7 Literally: "in whom we have the redemption through His blood"; by translating "*apolutrōsin*" (redemption) with the words "ransom price" both aspects of the word "redeem" are captured, namely, the concept of "being set free" (ransom) and that of "paying a certain sum" (price).

standing[e] **9** when He made known to us the mystery[f] of His will.

In His kindness it was His purpose in Christ **10** to manage everything in heaven and on earth in such a way that, when the right time would come, all things would be organized under Christ as its Head.

11 He who carries out everything exactly as His will plans it, appointed [predestined] us long ago in Christ and chose us according to His purpose. **12** He did this so that His glory might be praised by us who were the first to hope in Christ. **13** When you heard the message of the truth, the Good News [Gospel] that you were saved, and when you believed in Him, you also were sealed in Him by the Holy Spirit whom He promised. **14** That Holy Spirit is now the guarantee of our inheritance until God frees us to be His people[g] so that His glory might be praised.

I Am Praying For You

15 Therefore, since I heard how you believe in the Lord Jesus and love all the believers, **16** I never stop thanking God for you as I remember you in my prayers. **17** I ask the God of our Lord Jesus Christ, the Father of glory, to give you a spirit of wisdom that will reveal more and more to you as you come to know Him better. **18** Then the eyes of your minds[h] will be enlightened so that you know the hope to which He called you, the rich glory which *His holy people [saints]* will *inherit,* **19** and the vast resources of His power working in the interest of us who believe according to the working of His mighty power.[i] **20** He worked with that same power in Christ when He raised Him from the dead, and *made Him sit at His right hand* in heaven, **21** above all rulers, authorities, powers, lords, and any name that can be mentioned, not only in this age but also in the next. **22** And *He put everything under[j] His feet,* and established Him as the Head of everything for the good of the church, **23** which is His body, completely filled by Him[k] who fills everything in every way.

2ND CHAPTER

God's Grace [Undeserved Love] Saved You

1 You also were once dead in your trespasses and sins. **2** You led your life

---

18 *Deut 33:3,4*   20 *Ps 110:1*   22 *Ps 8:6*

---

e- 8 Literally: "His grace, which He made to abound toward us in all wisdom and understanding."
f- 9 The Greek word here used refers to a *secret* that is hidden from human understanding and cannot be grasped by those outside the Christian faith. This same Greek word is used in 3:3,4,9; 5:32; 6:19 (cf. Rom. 11:25).
g- 14 Or "until He frees us to gain possession of it."
h- 18 Literally: "hearts."
i- 19 Or "His power working with might and strength in the interest of us who believe."
j- 22 See *HUPOTASSŌ* on page 541.
k- 23 Or "body, the fullness of Him."

in those sins, following the ways of this present world and the ruler who governs the air,[a] the spirit who[b] is now working in the people who disobey. **3** All of us once lived among them in our fleshly lusts, doing what our flesh and mind wanted to do. By nature we deserved God's anger[c] just like all the others.

4 But God, who is rich in mercy, because of His deep love for us, **5** also made us who were dead in sins alive with Christ. (You are saved by grace.) **6** And in Christ Jesus He raised us with Him and had us sit with Him in heaven, **7** in order to show in the coming ages the immeasurable riches of His grace by being kind to us in Christ Jesus. **8** Yes, by His grace you are saved through faith. It was not your own doing; it is God's gift. **9** It is not the result of anything you have done; and so no one may boast. **10** For He has made us what we are, creating us in Christ Jesus to do good works, which God prepared in advance for us to do.[d]

Jews and Gentiles

11 Remember, then, that once you were outwardly[e] Gentiles, called "uncircumcised" by those who claimed a physical[f] circumcision for themselves. **12** ⌊Remember⌋ that at that time you were without Christ, excluded from citizenship in Israel and strangers to the covenants ["last wills and testaments"][g] of the promise. You had no hope and were without God in the world.

13 But now in Christ Jesus you who once were *far away* have been brought *near* through the blood of Christ. **14** For He is our *Peace*: In His flesh He has made both ⌊Jew and Gentile⌋ one by breaking down the wall of hostility that kept them apart. **15** He did this when He put away the Law with its commandments and regulations, in order to make the two [Jew and Gentile] one new person in Himself—so making peace. **16** He also reconciled them both to God in one body by His cross,[h] on which He killed the hostility. **17** And He came *preaching peace* ⌊both⌋ *to you who were far away* and to those *who were near*, **18** since by one Spirit He enables both of us to come to the Father.[i]

19 Therefore you are no longer foreigners or strangers but fellow citizens with the believers [saints] and members of God's family. **20** You are built on the *foundation* of the apostles and prophets, and Christ Jesus Himself is the *Cornerstone*. **21** In Him the whole building is fitted together and grows to be a holy temple in the Lord. **22** In Him you also are built up with the others into God's spiritual dwelling place.

13,14 Is 57:19   **17** Is 52:7; 57:19   **20** Is 28:16

---

2 *a-* 2 This refers to the sinful atmosphere of the world, paralleling the preceding thought: "the ways of this present world."

b- 2 Or "which," referring to the sinful atmosphere of the world.

c- 3 Literally: "were children of wrath by nature."

d- 10 Literally: "which God prepared in advance that we should walk [live] in them."

e- 11 Literally: "in the flesh."

f- 11 Literally: "in the flesh."

g- 12 See *DIATHĒKĒ* on page 531.

h- 16 Meaning that through Calvary's cross Jesus put both Jew and Gentile into a *changed relationship* ("reconciled") with His heavenly Father.

i- 18 Or "since He enables both of us to come to the Father in one spirit."

3RD CHAPTER

God's Purpose In Me

1 For this reason I, Paul, the prisoner of Christ Jesus for the sake of you who are Gentiles[a]—

2 (Surely you have heard how God gave me the administration of His grace toward you, **3** how He made the mystery[b] known to me by a revelation, as I have already briefly written. **4** When you read this, you can see that I understand the mystery of Christ, **5** which was not made known to the people of other ages, ˻that is,˼ in the same way as it now has been revealed by the Spirit to His holy apostles and prophets. **6** ˻This mystery is˼ that in Christ Jesus the Gentiles have the same inheritance, belong to the same body, and share the same promise through the Gospel.

7 I was made a servant of this Gospel by the gift of grace which God gave me by the working of His power. **8** To me, though I am less than the least of all His believers [saints], He gave this grace: to preach the Good News of the immeasurable riches of Christ to the Gentiles **9** and to make clear to everyone the administration of the mystery, which through the ages has been hidden in God who created all things.[c] **10** ˻God did this˼ so that through the church His many-sided wisdom would now be shown to the rulers and authorities in the heavens.[d] **11** He planned it through the ages and then carried it out in Christ Jesus our Lord. **12** In Him, by believing in Him, we have confidence and can boldly come to God. **13** So I ask you not to become discouraged by what I suffer for you. It is an honor to you.)

How Christ Loves Me

14 For this reason[e] I kneel before the Father,[f] **15** from whom the whole family[g] in heaven and on earth has its name, **16** and ask Him to give you a gift in proportion to the riches of His glory. I ask that His Spirit will inwardly

---

3 *a-* 1 Here Paul breaks off and does not take up the thought again until verse 14. Thus, verses 2-13 are parenthetical.

b- 3 See 1:9 and its accompanying footnote. This same Greek word is also used in verses 4 and 9.

c- 9 Many later manuscripts add: "through Jesus Christ."

d- 10 This might mean that it is through the church that the evil angels have become aware of God's plan of salvation (Eph. 6:12), or it could refer to the fact that the holy angels only observe God's plan of salvation as it unfolds in the history of the church (cf. 1 Pet. 1:12b).

e- 14 The repetition of these words ("For this reason") continues the thought begun in verse 1, indicating that verses 2-13 have been parenthetical.

f- 14 Many of the older manuscripts and early translations add: "of our Lord Jesus Christ." See 1:3 where this fuller expression is certain.

g- 15 A play on words: the Greek word for father is "*pater*," and the word for family is "*patria*."

strengthen you with power, 17 in order that Christ will live in your hearts by faith, and you will be firmly rooted and built up in love. 18 I ask for this gift, so that you and all the believers can grasp how broad and long and high and deep His love is. 19 Then you will know how much Christ loves us—more than we can know—so that you will be filled with God's full measure.

20 Now to Him who by the power which is working in us can do far, far more than anything we ask or imagine, 21 to Him be glory in the church and in Christ Jesus through all generations, forever and ever. Amen.

4TH CHAPTER

C. Practical section:
The church is created to serve Christ by doing good works (4:1–6:20)

We Are One

1 So I, a prisoner in the Lord, urge you to live in a manner worthy of people whom God has called. 2 Be humble and gentle in every way, be patient, and bear with one another in a loving manner. 3 Do your best to keep the oneness of the Spirit, using peace as your bond. 4 There is one body and one Spirit—even as you have been called to share one hope—5 one Lord, one faith, one baptism, 6 one God and Father of all, who is over all, through all, and in all.

7 But grace has been given to each of us, measured out by Christ who gave it. 8 So it says:

> When He *went up on high,*
> He *took captive those who had captured us*
> and gave *gifts to people.*

9 Now what can "He went up" mean except that He also had gone down to the lower earthly regions?*a* 10 He who went down also "went up" above all the heavens to fill everything. 11 And He gave some to be apostles, some to be prophets, some to be evangelists [preachers of the Gospel], some to be pastors and teachers. 12 His purpose was to prepare believers [saints] for service as workers in building up the body of Christ 13 until all of us become one in our faith and in our knowledge of God's Son, until we become mature, until we reach the full height of Christ. 14 Then we will not be babies any longer, tossed and driven by every doctrinal wind, by the trickery of people and their clever scheming to lead us astray. 15 Rather, as we speak the truth with love, we will grow up into Him who is the Head, namely, Christ. 16 He makes the whole body fit together and unites it by the support of every joint; and to the extent that each and every part is doing its job, He makes the body grow so that it builds itself up in love.

---

8 Ps 68:18

---

4 *a*- 9 A reference to Christ's incarnation.

A New Life

17 So I tell you and call on you in the Lord not to live any longer like the Gentiles. Their minds are set on worthless things. **18** Their understanding is darkened. Their natural state of ignorance, caused by their closed minds,*b* has made them strangers to the life which God gives. **19** Having become callous, they have given themselves over to a life of lust—to practice every kind of vice with a constant desire for more.

20 But that is not what you learned when you came to know Christ, **21** if indeed you have heard Him and have been taught by Him, as the truth is in Jesus. **22** You were taught to strip off your old self,*c* which follows your former ways of living and ruins you as it follows the desires that deceive you. **23** Instead, you were taught to be continually renewed in the spirit of your minds, **24** and to put on the new self,*d* which is created to be like God, truly righteous and holy.

25 So after each of you has stripped off lying, *speak the truth to one another*, because we are members of one another. **26** *Be angry without sinning.e* Do not let the sun go down on your anger, **27** and do not give the devil any opportunity ⌊to work⌋.

28 Let the person who has been stealing steal no longer, but instead let him work hard, doing something good with his own hands, so that he has something to share with anyone in need. **29** Do not let any harmful word come out of your mouth, but only what is good, so that you provide help where it is needed for the benefit of those who hear you.

30 And do not grieve God's Holy Spirit, by whom you were sealed for the Day when you will be set free.

31 Get rid of all bitterness and temper and anger and shouting and slander, along with every way of hurting one another. **32** Be kind to one another and tenderhearted, forgiving one another as God in Christ has forgiven you.

5TH CHAPTER

You Are A Light

1 Therefore imitate God as His dear children, **2** and live in love just as Christ also loved us and gave Himself for us as a *fragrant offering and sacrifice* to God.

3 Do not let sexual sin, impurity, or greed even be mentioned among you. This is the right attitude for believers [saints]. **4** No shameful things, foolish talk, or coarse jokes! These are not proper. Instead, give thanks. **5** Yes, be sure of this, that no one who is immoral, impure, or greedy (such a person worships an idol) has any share in the Kingdom of Christ, who is God. **6** Do not let anyone

---

25 *Zech 8:16*　　26 *Ps 4:4*　　2 *Ps 40:6; Ezek 20:41*

---

b- 18 See Mark 3:5 and its accompanying footnote.
c- 22 Literally: "the old person" or "the old man" (including the "old attitude").
d- 24 Literally: "the new person" or "the new man" (including the "new attitude").
e- 26 Literally: "Be angry and do not sin."

fool you with meaningless words. For these ⌊sins⌋ bring God's anger on disobedient children. **7** Therefore do not be their partners.

8 For once you were darkness, but now you are light in the Lord. Live as children of light, **9** for light produces everything that is good and righteous and true. **10** And test things to see whether they please the Lord. **11** Do not have anything to do with the works of darkness, from which no good can come, but instead continue to expose them as wrong, **12** for it is a shame even to mention what such people do secretly. **13** Everything which is exposed is made clear by the light; **14** yes, anything which shows something clearly is light. So it says:

> Wake up, sleeper!
> Rise from the dead,
> and Christ will shine on you.

15 Be very careful, then, as to how you live. Do not be unwise, but wise. **16** And make the most of your opportunities because these are evil days. **17** So do not be foolish, but understand what the Lord wants. **18** *Do not get drunk on wine*, which leads to wild living. But let the Spirit fill you **19** as you speak psalms, hymns, and spiritual songs to one another, singing with your hearts and making music to the Lord, **20** as you always thank God the Father for everything in the Name of our Lord Jesus Christ, **21** as you are subordinate*a* to one another out of respect for Christ.

Husbands And Wives

22 Wives, be subordinate*b* to your husbands as ⌊you are subordinate⌋ to the Lord, **23** because a husband is the head of his wife as Christ is the Head of the church, His body, of which He is the Savior. **24** Yes, as the church is subordinate*c* to Christ, so let wives ⌊be subordinate⌋ to their husbands in everything.

25 Husbands, love your wives as Christ loved the church and gave Himself for her, **26** to make the church holy by using water together with the word to wash her clean. **27** He did this so that He could present her to Himself as a glorious church, without spot or wrinkle or any such thing; yes, He did this so that she might be holy and without fault. **28** This is how husbands have an obligation to

---

18 Prov 23:31

---

5 *a-* 21 Compare verse 24 and its accompanying footnote.

   b- 22 A few of the older manuscripts omit: "be subordinate." Compare verse 24 and its accompanying footnote.

   c- 24 Greek: "*hupotassō*." This Greek term speaks of persons who are placed in an "order" or "rank" below or under the authority of another. In the mind of sinful human beings this is often falsely equated with *inferiority*. However, Jesus taught us that among Christians this is not to be the case. It is not the one in authority who is the greatest but the one who is servant to all (Matt. 20:25-28; Mk. 10:42-45); authority and servitude are always to be used for the benefit of others.
   The English "subordinate" captures the totality of this *hupotassō* concept quite well. This is here applied to *the church* [the people of God] and to *marriage* by Paul in accordance with the rank or order as laid down by God. This ranking from the top downward is Christ, husbands (men), wives (women), children (cf. Phil. 3:21; Tit. 2:5; 1 Pet. 3:1; 5:5; Jas. 4:7). See *HUPOTASSŌ* on page 541.

love their wives, namely, like their own bodies. A man who loves his wife is loving himself. **29** To be sure, no one ever hated his own body. Rather, everyone feeds his body and treats it tenderly, as Christ does the church **30** because we are parts of His body. **31** *This is why a man will leave his father and mother and remain united with his wife, and the two will be one flesh.* **32** There is a great mystery[d] here—I mean that of Christ and the church. **33** But let each and every one of you ⌊husbands⌋ love his wife as he loves himself. And let a wife respect her husband.

6TH CHAPTER

Children And Parents

1 Children, obey your parents in the Lord, because this is right. **2** *Honor your father and mother*—this is an important[a] commandment with a promise—**3** that *it may be well with you, and you may live long on the earth.*

4 And fathers, do not make your children angry, but bring them up in the *training* and instruction *of the Lord.*

Slaves and Masters

5 Slaves, obey your earthly masters with respect and trembling and be sincere in your heart, just as ⌊you are when⌋ you obey Christ. **6** Do not serve only while you are being watched, as if you merely wanted to please people, but serve like slaves of Christ who are glad to do what God wants them to do. **7** Serve eagerly as you would serve the Lord and not merely men. **8** You know that the Lord will reward each one if he does something useful, whether he is slave or free.

9 And masters, treat your slaves in the same way, and stop threatening them. You know that both they and you have one Master in heaven, and He does not favor one person over another.

Put On The Whole Armor

10 Finally, let the Lord and His mighty power make you strong. **11** Put on God's whole armor, so that you may be able to stand against the tricky ways of the devil, **12** because we are not fighting against flesh and blood but against the powers, against the authorities, against the rulers of this dark world, against the evil spirits that are in the heavens. **13** For this reason take up God's whole armor so that you may be able to resist when things are at their worst and, after you have done everything, to hold your ground.

---

31 Gen 2:24   *2,3* Ex 20:12   *4* Prov 3:11

---

d- 32 See 1:9 and its accompanying footnote.
6 *a-* 2 Literally: "first"; the Greek word can indicate either that a thing came first in time or ranks at the top of a list.

14   Take your stand, then,
>> *having truth as a belt fastened around* your *waist,*
>> *having righteousness covering you as a breastplate,* and

15   *having eagerness for the Gospel of peace* tied to your *feet* as sandals.

16   Besides all these,
>> take faith as the shield
>>> with which you can put out
>>>> all the flaming arrows of the Evil One; and

17   take *salvation as your helmet,*
>> and the *sword* of the Spirit,
>>> which is the word of God.

18 At the same time pray in a spiritual way in every situation, using every kind of prayer and request. For the same reason be alert and keep at it continually as you pray for all the believers [saints]. 19 Pray also for me, so that when I open my mouth ˌto speakˌ I will be given[b] what to say, so that I will boldly make known the mystery[c] of the Gospel 20 (for which I am an ambassador in chains) just as boldly as I must preach it.

D. Conclusion (6:21-24)

Farewell

21 Now Tychicus, our dear fellow Christian[d] and loyal helper in the Lord, will tell you everything, so that you might know what is happening to me and how I am getting along. 22 I am sending him to you to let you know about us and to encourage you.

23 May God the Father and the Lord Jesus Christ give peace and love, together with faith, to our fellow Christians. 24 His grace be with all who have an undying love for our Lord Jesus Christ.

---

14 Is 11:5; 59:17   *15 Is 52:7*   *17 Is 49:2*

---

b- 19 Compare Luke 21:15.
c- 19 See 1:9 and its accompanying footnote.
d- 21 Literally: "brother" ("brothers" in v. 23).

PAUL WRITES TO THE
PHILIPPIANS[a]

1ST CHAPTER

A. Introduction: Greeting and prayer (1:1-11)

1 Paul and Timothy, servants of Christ Jesus, to all the believers [saints] in Christ Jesus at Philippi, together with the pastors[b] and deacons: **2** May God our Father and the Lord Jesus Christ give you grace[c] and peace.

You Are In My Heart

3 Every time I think of you, I thank my God. **4** Every time I pray for all of you, I always do it with joy, **5** because of your partnership in the Gospel [Good News] from the first day until now. **6** I am sure of this very thing, that He who began a good work in you will go on to finish it until the Day of Christ Jesus. **7** And it is right for me to feel like this about all of you, because whether I am in my chains or defending and confirming the Gospel, you are all in my heart as people who share God's grace with me. **8** To be sure, God can testify how I long for all of you with the tenderness of Christ Jesus.

9 And I pray that your love will overflow more and more in knowledge and in every kind of understanding. **10** Then you will approve the better things in order that you may be pure and without blame until the Day of Christ, **11** filled with righteous fruit which Jesus Christ produces ⌊in your lives⌋ to the glory and praise of God.

B. Personal news (1:12-26)

If Only Christ Is Preached

12 I want you to know, my fellow Christians,[d] that what happened to me

---

1 *a*   *Philippians* is another of the "prison epistles" or "captivity letters" written toward the close of the Apostle Paul's imprisonment either in Rome about A.D. 61 (cf. 1:13,14,17,25,26) or during his three year stay in Ephesus (Acts 20:31) about A.D. 53-55.

b - 1   The Greek word means "overseers" ("*episkopos*"). This Greek word, along with the Greek term for "presbyters" or "elders" ("*presbuteros*" - 1 Tim. 4:14), was a term used to refer to pastors of local congregations.

c - 2   Meaning "God's undeserved love" (also in v. 7).

d - 12   Literally: "brothers."

actually has helped spread the Gospel, [13] so that it has become clear to the whole Praetorium[e] and all the others that I am in chains for Christ. [14] And so my chains have given most of our Christian friends[f] confidence in the Lord to speak God's word more boldly and fearlessly than ever.

[15] Some people are moved by jealousy and rivalry to preach Christ, but others are moved by good will. [16] Those who preach out of love for Him know that God has put me here[g] for the defense of the Gospel. [17] But the others preach Christ selfishly, without a pure motive, and intend to stir up trouble for me even while I am in chains. [18] But what does it matter? Only this, that in one way or another, whether with motives that are honest or dishonest, Christ is being preached—and I am glad of that.

To Live Is Christ; To Die Is Gain

Yes, I will also continue to be happy, [19] because I know that through your prayer and the help of the Spirit of Jesus Christ *this will result in my deliverance*, [20] as I eagerly expect and hope that there will be nothing of which I will be ashamed. But by speaking very boldly I will now as always glorify Christ in my body by living or by dying, [21] since for me to live is Christ and to die is gain. [22] If I live here in my body, that will mean more results from my work. And which of the two would I choose? I do not know. [23] I find it hard to choose between the two. I want to leave and be with Christ; that is much better. [24] But for your benefit it is more necessary that I remain in my body. [25] And since I feel convinced of this, I know that I shall live and be with all of you to help you grow and be joyful in your faith. [26] And so by coming to you again I want to give you even more reason to glory in Christ Jesus.

C. Plea for unity (1:27–2:18)

Fighting For The Faith

[27] But live as citizens worthy of the Good News of Christ so that, whether I come and see you or stay away, I may hear that you are standing firm, one in spirit, and fighting side by side with one mind for faith in the Gospel. [28] Do not let your enemies frighten you in any way. This is how you prove to them that they will be destroyed and you will be saved, and this proof is from God. [29] For it is God's gift to you, not only to believe in Christ but also to suffer on His behalf, [30] since you are involved in the same struggle that you once saw me in and now hear that I am in.

---

[19] Job 13:16

e- 13 A reference either to the Praetorian Guard in Rome or to the staff of the official residence of the Roman governor either in Ephesus or Caesarea.

f- 14 Literally: "brothers."

g- 16 Literally: "that I am set."

2ND CHAPTER

Live In Harmony

1 Now if you are encouraged in any way in Christ, moved by any comforting words of love, if you have any fellowship of the Spirit, if you are tender and sympathetic in any way, **2** make my happiness complete—be one in thought and in love, live in harmony, keep one purpose in mind. **3** Do not act out of selfish ambition or with conceit, but in humility think of others as being better than yourselves, **4** while at the same time not being concerned about your own things, but rather about the things of others.

Jesus Christ Is The Exalted Lord!

5 Have the same attitude that Christ Jesus had. **6** Although He was God, He did not consider His being equal with God as a prize to be displayed, **7** but He emptied Himself, made Himself a slave, became like other human beings, **8** and when He appeared in the form of a man, He became obedient and humbled Himself even to the point of death, yes, death on a cross. **9** That is why God also very highly exalted Him and gave Him the Name which is above every other name, **10** that at the Name of JESUS *everyone* in heaven and on earth and under the earth *should kneel*, **11** and that *everyone should confess* that "JESUS CHRIST IS LORD"*a* *to the glory of God* the Father.

Work Out Your Salvation

12 My dear friends, you have always obeyed, not only when I was with you but even more now that I am absent. In the same way continue to work out your salvation with fear and trembling, **13** since it is God who continues to work in you, both to be willing and to be doing what is pleasing to Him.

14 Do everything without complaining or arguing, **15** so that you will be blameless and innocent, *God's children without blame* in *a generation of crooked and perverse people*, among whom you shine like stars*b* in the world, **16** as you cling to the word of life. Then I can boast on the Day of Christ that I did not run in vain or *work in vain*. **17** But even if my life is poured out as a part of the sacrifice and service ⌊offered to God⌋ in behalf of your faith, I am glad, and I share my joy with all of you. **18** So you also be glad and share your joy with me.

D. Two praiseworthy workers (2:19-30)

Timothy And Epaphroditus

19 I hope in the Lord Jesus to send Timothy to you soon so that I may receive

---

10,11 Is 45:23,24   *15 Deut 32:5*   *16 Is 49:4; 65:23*

---

2 *a*- 11 See THE EARLIEST CHRISTIAN CREEDS on page 557.
  b- 15 Compare Daniel 12:3.

news about you that will cheer me up. **20** You see, I do not have anyone else who will take as genuine an interest in your welfare. **21** For all look after their own interests, not after those of Jesus Christ. **22** But you know how he has stood the test, how like a son helping his father he worked hard with me to preach the Gospel. **23** So I expect to send him as soon as I see what is going to happen to me. **24** And I have been given confidence by the Lord that I will be coming soon.

25 I think that I must send you Epaphroditus my fellow Christian,^{c} fellow worker, and fellow soldier, whom you sent to help me in my need, **26** since he has been longing to see all of you and is deeply troubled because you heard that he was sick. **27** Yes, he was so sick that he almost died, but God had pity on him—not only on him but also on me, to keep me from having one sorrow after another. **28** So I am especially eager to send him in order to give you the joy of seeing him again and to feel more relief myself. **29** So give him a very happy welcome in the Lord, and honor such men highly, **30** because he risked his life and almost died for the work of Christ in order to make up for the service you could not give me.

3RD CHAPTER

E. Warning against false teachers (3:1-21)

Only Christ

1 Now then, my fellow Christians,^{a} be happy in the Lord. It is no trouble to write the same things to you, and it is necessary for your safety. **2** Look out for those dogs, look out for those who do evil, look out for those who cut ˌthe bodyˌ.^{b} **3** For we are really the circumcised people—we who worship God spiritually and boast of Christ Jesus instead of placing our confidence in a physical act,^{c} **4** although I, too, could have such confidence. If anyone else supposes that he can trust in something physical, I could claim more. **5** I was circumcised on the eighth day, a descendant of Israel, of the tribe of Benjamin, a Hebrew son of Hebrew parents;^{d} as far as the Law is concerned, a Pharisee; **6** as far as zeal is concerned, a persecutor of the church; as far as righteousness is concerned, namely, the righteousness that comes from keeping the Law, I was blameless.

7 But those things which I counted as gain I now consider as a loss for Christ.^{e} **8** Yes, I would even say that I consider everything as a loss because it is so much better to know Christ Jesus my Lord. For Him I have lost everything

---

c- 25 Literally: "brother."

3 a- 1 Literally: "brothers" (also in vv. 13,17).

b- 2 Very likely a reference to circumcision (cf. vv. 3-6).

c- 3 Literally: "in the flesh"; a possible reference to circumcision.

d- 5 Literally: "a Hebrew of Hebrews," indicating that Hebrew, not Greek, was the language in the home of Paul's parents, especially in their worship life.

e- 7 Paul is saying that he now has his priorities straight. He now realizes that what he had formerly put in life's "gain column" really belongs in the "loss column." Verses 8b-11 find Paul placing Christ and the things of Christ into the real "gain column."

and consider it rubbish*f* in order to gain Christ **9** and to be found in Him, not having my own righteousness which comes from keeping the Law but having the righteousness which is through faith in Christ and which comes from God on the basis of faith. **10** I want to know Him, both the power of His resurrection and the close relationship that we have with His suffering, as we are made like Him in His death, **11** if somehow I may join those who rise from the dead.

12 I do not mean that I have already reached the goal or have already completed the course, but I eagerly strive to lay claim to that for which Jesus Christ also claimed me. **13** Fellow Christians, I do not think I have it in my hands. But one thing I do: I forget what is behind; I reach for what is ahead; **14** and with my eyes on the mark I go after the heavenly prize to which God has called us in Christ Jesus.

15 Let as many of us as are mature think this way. But if you think differently about anything, God will also reveal this to you. **16** Only be guided by what we have learned so far.

Citizens Of Heaven

17 My fellow Christians, keep on imitating me and taking note of those who live according to the example we are giving you. **18** For I have often told you and now tell you with tears, many live as the enemies of the cross of Christ. **19** In the end they will be destroyed. Their own feelings*g* are their god; they glory in their shame; and their mind is on earthly things. **20** For we are citizens of heaven and look for the Lord Jesus Christ to come from heaven as the Savior, **21** who will change our humble bodies and make them like His glorified body because He has the power by which He can make everything subordinate*h* to Himself.

4TH CHAPTER

F. Godly advice (4:1-9)

1 And so, my fellow Christians,*a* whom I love and for whom I long, my joy and crown, stand firm in the Lord, dear friends.

---

f- 8 Or "dung."

g- 19 Literally: "Their belly"; used in a figurative way to denote man's lower and even lowest nature—as parallel to Paul's usage of "belly" in Romans 16:18 and of "*kakon*" (that which is "evil, base, of inferior morality") in Romans 16:19—which is parallel to "shame" and "earthly things" in the present verse.

h- 21 Greek: "*hupotassō*." This Greek term speaks of things and persons that are placed in an "order" or "rank" below or under the authority of another. In the mind of sinful human beings this is often falsely equated with *inferiority*. However, Jesus taught us that among Christians this is not to be the case. It is not the one in authority who is the greatest but the one who is servant to all (Matt. 20:25-28; Mk. 10:42-45); authority and servitude are always to be used for the benefit of others.
The English "subordinate" captures the totality of this *hupotassō* concept quite well. This is here applied by Paul to *everything that is created* and which as a result is "subordinate" to Christ, its Creator and Lord. See *HUPOTASSŌ* on page 541.

4 *a-* 1 Literally: "brothers" (also in vv. 8,21).

Two Women

2 I urge Euodia and I urge Syntyche to agree in the Lord. 3 Yes, I also beg you, my loyal fellow worker,*b* to help these women. In proclaiming the Gospel they fought side by side with me as well as with Clement and the rest of my fellow workers, whose names are in *the Book of Life*.

Be Happy

4 Be happy in the Lord always! I will say it again: Be happy! 5 Let everyone know how gentle you can be. The Lord is near. 6 Do not worry about anything, but in every concern thankfully make known your requests to God in prayer. 7 Then the peace of God which is beyond all understanding will guard your hearts and minds in Christ Jesus.

8 Finally, my fellow Christians, keep your minds on all that is true, all that is noble, all that is right, all that is pure, all that is lovely, all that is appealing—on anything that is excellent or that deserves praise. 9 Continue to do what you have learned and received and heard from me, and what you saw me do. Then the God of peace will be with you.

G. Thanks for gifts (4:10-20)

Your Gift

10 It made me very happy in the Lord that now again you showed a fresh interest in me. You were interested but did not have an opportunity to show it. 11 I am not saying that I need anything, for I have learned to be content in any situation. 12 I know how to live with too little or too much. In every way and in everything I have learned the secret of being fully satisfied and of being hungry, of having too much and having too little. 13 I can do everything through Him who gives me strength. 14 But it was kind of you to share my trouble.

15 You people of Philippi also know that in the early days of the Gospel, when I left Macedonia, you were the only church to share with me in a balancing of giving and receiving. 16 Even while I was in Thessalonica, you sent help more than once for my needs. 17 What I seek is not the gift but the growing profit in your account. 18 You have paid me in full, and I have more than enough. I am fully supplied, now that I received from Epaphroditus what you sent. It is *a sweet fragrance*, a sacrifice that God accepts and with which He is pleased. 19 My God will give you everything you need according to His riches, in His glory, and in Christ Jesus. 20 To our God and Father be glory forever and ever. Amen.

---

3 Ps 69:28   *18 Ezek 20:41*

b- 3 Or "my loyal Syzygus."

H. Conclusion: Greetings (4:21-23)

21 Greet all the believers [saints] in Christ Jesus. The Christians who are with me greet you. 22 All the believers greet you, especially those of Caesar's household. 23 The grace [undeserved love] of our Lord Jesus Christ be with your spirit. Amen.

PAUL WRITES TO THE
COLOSSIANS[a]

1st CHAPTER

A. Introduction (1:1-12)

1 Paul, an apostle of Christ Jesus by God's will, and our fellow Christian[b] Timothy, **2** to the believers [saints] and faithful Christians who believe in Christ at Colossae: May God our Father give you grace[c] and peace.

We Are Praying For You

3 In our prayers for you we are always thanking God, the Father of our Lord Jesus Christ, **4** since we have heard how you believe in Christ Jesus and love all the believers **5** because of the hope which is stored up for you in heaven. You heard of it before in the word of truth, the Gospel [Good News], **6** which continues to come to you. As it is producing fruit and growing all over the world, so it did among you from the day you heard it and came to know what the grace of God truly means. **7** It is the same Gospel that you learned from Epaphras our dear fellow servant, who is loyally serving Christ in your place. **8** And he is also the one who told us about your love in the Spirit.

9 That is why, since the day we heard of it, we have not stopped praying for you and asking God to fill you with a clear knowledge of His will by giving you every kind of spiritual wisdom and understanding. **10** We ask this so that you live worthy of the Lord, aiming to please Him in every way as you produce every kind of good work and grow in the knowledge of God. **11** We ask Him to strengthen you according to His wonderful might with all the power that you need to patiently endure whatever comes, as you joyfully **12** thank the Father, who made you fit to share the believer's inheritance in the light.

---

1 *a*   *Colossians* is another of the "prison epistles" or "captivity letters" of the Apostle Paul and was written at the same time as *Ephesians* and *Philemon* (cf. 4:7-9; Eph. 6:21) either in Rome about A.D. 61 or during his three year stay in Ephesus about A.D. 53-55.
b - 1 Literally: "brother" ("brothers" in v. 2).
c - 2 Meaning "God's undeserved love."

B. Christ is all-sufficient (1:13-23)

God's Son Brought Peace

13 He rescued us from the power of darkness and transferred us into the Kingdom of the Son whom He loves. **14** In His Son we have redemption, namely, the forgiveness of sins. **15** He is the image of the invisible God, the Firstborn of all creation, **16** since in Him was created everything in heaven and on earth, things visible and invisible, whether thrones or lords or powers; everything was created by Him and for Him. **17** He was before everything, and He holds everything together. **18** He is also the Head of the church, which is His body. He is the Beginning, the first from the dead to become alive that He may be first in everything. **19** ⌊This is true⌋ because God decided to have His whole Being live in Him **20** and by Him to reconcile to Himself everything on earth and in heaven in a peace made by the blood of His cross.

21 Once you were strangers to God, and in your mind you were His enemies, doing wicked things. **22** But now He has reconciled you by dying in His human body in order to have you stand before Him without sin or fault or blame—**23** if, of course, you continue in your faith to stand firm on the foundation and are not moved from the hope of the Gospel which you heard. This Gospel, of which I, Paul, was made a servant, has been preached to every creature under heaven.

C. Paul's ministry (1:24–2:7)

Our Work Among You

24 I am now happy to suffer for you, and in my body I am enduring whatever afflictions of Christ need to be endured in behalf of His body, the church. **25** God made me a servant of the church when He gave me this work among you in order to fulfill the word of God. **26** This is the mystery*d* hidden for ages and generations but now shown to His believers, **27** to whom God wished to make known the glorious riches of this mystery among the Gentiles. This mystery is Christ in you, the Hope of glory.

28 Him we preach, warning everyone and teaching everyone, using every kind of wisdom, in order to present everyone perfect in Christ. **29** This is what I am working for, struggling like an athlete by His power which is effectively at work in me.

2ND CHAPTER

1 I want you to know how much I am struggling for you and for the people of Laodicea and for all who have not seen me face to face. **2** ⌊I say this⌋ so that your hearts may be encouraged to be bound together by love and to be richly

---

d- 26 The Greek word here used refers to a *secret* that is hidden from human understanding and cannot be grasped by those outside the Christian faith. The same Greek word is used in verse 27; 2:2; 4:3 (cf. Rom. 11:25).

convinced in your understanding, so that you recognize the mystery[a] of God, namely, Christ, 3 in whom are hidden all the treasures of wisdom and knowledge. 4 I say this so that no one will mislead you by fine-sounding arguments. 5 Although I am absent from you physically, I am with you in spirit and delight to see how orderly and firm you are in your faith in Christ.

6 Just as you accepted Christ Jesus as your Lord, so live in Him. 7 Be rooted and built up in Him, and be strengthened in your faith, just as you were taught—overflowing all the while with thanksgiving.

D. The false teaching (2:8–3:4)

8 Be careful or someone will capture you through an empty and foolish philosophy, as he follows the traditions of men and the principles of this world rather than Christ.

9 In Him, that is, in His body, lives all the fullness of the Deity. 10 And in Him, who is the Head of all rulers and powers, you are complete. 11 In Him you also were circumcised, not by human hands but by putting away the sinful body[b] by the circumcision of Christ, 12 since you were buried with Him in baptism and raised with Him through faith produced by God, who raised Him from the dead.

13 Although you were dead in sins and in your uncircumcised flesh, God made you alive with Christ when He forgave us all our sins. 14 He did this by wiping out the debt which was recorded against us because of the Law's demands. He took it out of the way by nailing it to the cross. 15 He stripped rulers and powers of their armor and made a public show of them as He celebrated His victory in Christ.

Man-Made Rules

16 Let no one then say that you are wrong in what you eat or drink or do on a festival, on the first of the month,[c] or on a Sabbath. 17 These are a shadow of the things to come, but the body itself is Christ.[d]

18 Let no one defraud you by delighting in false humility and in the worship of angels. Such a person goes on searching his visions; for no reason he is puffed up by his fleshly mind. 19 Such a person does not cling to the Head, who—by being in touch with the whole body which is supported and bound together by ligaments and sinews—makes it grow as God gives it growth.

20 If you have died with Christ to the basic principles of this world, then why (as though you were living with the world) do you let others dictate to you:

---

2 a- 2 See 1:26 and its accompanying footnote.

b- 11 Literally: "the putting off of the body of the flesh."

c- 16 Literally: "at the time of the new moon," which coincided with the first day of each month.

d- 17 The picture is this: At times a person is only able to see the shadow of someone who is coming, but when that person arrives the body itself can be seen. In Biblical terms the Old Testament ceremonies were but mere shadows of or types which foreshadowed the coming of Christ physically. Note that Paul is saying that the shadows were important to watch in Old Testament times, but now we must keep our eyes on Christ rather than on the Old Testament ceremonies which lost their reason for existence when Christ came and fulfilled them.

21 "Do not take hold, do not taste, do not touch"? 22 All these principles concern themselves with things that are used up and pass away. You are doing *what men order and teach*; 23 this looks like wisdom, with its self-imposed worship, humble attitude, and harsh treatment of the body. But it is of no real value to anyone in curbing the constant desires of the flesh.

3RD CHAPTER

With Christ In Glory

1 Now if you were raised with Christ, be eager for the things that are above, where Christ is *sitting at the right hand of God.* 2 Keep your mind on things above, not on earthly things. 3 For you have died, and your life is hidden with Christ in God. 4 When Christ, your Life, appears, then you too will appear with Him in glory.

E. The life in Christ (3:5–4:6)

Be Like Him

5 Therefore kill what is earthly in you: sexual sin, impurity, passion, evil lust, and greed, which is idol worship; 6 these bring down the anger of God. 7 Once when you lived in them, you also practiced them. 8 But now also get rid of all such things as anger, fury, malice, slander, and filthy talk. 9 Do not lie to one another, since you have put away your old self[a] and its ways 10 and have put on the new self,[b] which is continually renewed in knowledge *to be like Him who created him.* 11 Here there is no Greek or Jew, circumcised or uncircumcised, barbarian, Scythian, slave or free, but Christ is everything in all of you.

Live As God's People

12 As believers, then, whom God has chosen and loved, dress yourselves with tenderheartedness, kindness, humility, gentleness, patience; 13 bear with one another and forgive one another if you have any complaint against anyone. Forgive just as the Lord forgave you. 14 On top of all these ˌvirtuesˌ put on love, which binds it all together to make it perfect. 15 Also let the peace of Christ, to which you were called as one body, rule in your hearts—and continue to be thankful! 16 Let Christ's word live richly among you, as with all wisdom you teach and warn one another by singing psalms, hymns, and spiritual songs to God with thankful hearts. 17 And everything you say or do, do it in the Name of the Lord Jesus. In this way continue to give thanks to God the Father through Him.

---

22 *Is 29:13*   1 *Ps 110:1*   10 *Gen 1:26,27*

3 *a-* 9 Literally: "the old person" or "the old man" (cf. Eph. 4:22), including "the old attitude."
b- 10 Literally: "the new person" or "the new man" (cf. Eph. 4:24), including "the new attitude."

Parents, Children, And Slaves

18 Wives, be subordinate[c] to your husbands as is right in the Lord. **19** Husbands, love your wives, and do not be harsh with them.

20 Children, obey your parents in everything, for this is pleasing to the Lord. **21** Fathers, do not irritate your children, or they will become discouraged.

22 Slaves, obey your earthly masters in everything. Do not serve them only when they are watching you, as if you meant only to please them, but ⌊serve them⌋ with a sincere heart out of respect for the Lord. **23** Whatever you do, work heartily as for the Lord and not for people, **24** because you know the Lord will give you the inheritance as your reward. It is the Lord Christ whom you are serving. **25** To be sure, the person who does wrong will be paid back for the wrong he has done, and there will be no favoritism ⌊shown⌋.

4TH CHAPTER

1 Masters, be just and fair to your slaves because you know that you also have a Master in heaven.

Winning The Others

2 Be persistent in prayer; and as you pray, be both alert and thankful. **3** At the same time pray for us also, that God will open a door for the word so that we may tell the mystery[a] of Christ, for which I am in chains, **4** ⌊and⌋ that I may make it as clearly known as I should.

5 Be wise in the way you live with those who are outside ⌊the Christian faith⌋,[b] and make the most of your opportunities.

6 Always talk pleasantly, season your speech with salt,[c] so that you will know how you should answer each individual.

F. Conclusion (4:7-18)

Tychicus And Onesimus

7 Tychicus a dear fellow Christian,[d] loyal helper, and fellow servant in the Lord, will tell you all about me. **8** I am sending him to you specifically to bring

---

c- 18 Greek: "*hupotassō*." See general comments in footnote at Ephesians 5:24. Particular to our present passage is Paul's application in regard to *marriage* according to the rank or order laid down by God (cf. Tit. 2:5 and 1 Pet. 3:1). See *HUPOTASSŌ* on page 541.

4 a- 3 See 1:26 and its accompanying footnote.

b- 5 Literally: "outsiders."

c- 6 "Season your speech with salt" may communicate one of two things. It may mean that Christians are to prepare what they are going to say in a most careful manner just as cooks should carefully use *salt* in the preparation of food. This interpretation beautifully flows into the second half of the 6th verse.

From another point of view Paul could be suggesting that our words are to breathe friendliness. This interpretation would relate to a custom in Paul's day when the sharing of *salt* served as an expression of friendship. This view beautifully complements verse 5.

d- 7 Literally: "brother" (also in v. 9).

you the news about us and to comfort your hearts. 9 Onesimus, our loyal and dear fellow Christian who is one of you, is with him. They will tell you about everything that is happening here.

Greetings

10 Aristarchus my fellow prisoner sends greetings. So does Mark the cousin of Barnabas (concerning whom you received instructions to welcome him, if he comes to you). 11 Jesus, called Justus, also greets you. They are the only Jews working with me for God's Kingdom. They have been a comfort to me. 12 Epaphras, one of you, a servant of Christ Jesus, greets you. He is always wrestling in prayer for you, so that you will stand mature and be fully convinced in everything that God wants. 13 I assure you that he works hard for you and the people in Laodicea and Hierapolis. 14 Luke, the physician whom we love, and Demas greet you. 15 Greet the fellow Christians*e* in Laodicea, also Nympha and the church that meets in her house.

16 When this letter has been read to you, have it read also in the church at Laodicea, and see that you also read the letter from Laodicea.

17 Tell Archippus, "See that you do all the work you undertook as the Lord's servant."

18 I, Paul, am writing this greeting with my own hand. Remember that I am in chains. Grace be with you.

e- 15 Literally: "brothers."

1 THESSALONIANS[a]

1ST CHAPTER

A. Opening greeting (1:1)

1 Paul, Silas, and Timothy to the church of the Thessalonians, which is in God the Father and the Lord Jesus Christ: May grace[b] and peace be yours!

B. Summary remarks on the church in Thessalonica (1:2–3:13)

The Gospel [Good News]

2 We always thank God for all of you and mention you in our prayers, **3** never forgetting before our God and Father how your faith is working, your love is toiling, and your hope in our Lord Jesus Christ is patiently enduring. **4** Fellow Christians,[c] loved by God, we know that He has chosen you, **5** because the Gospel we preached did not come to you with mere words, but with power, with the Holy Spirit, and with conviction—just as you know what kind of men we proved to be among you for your good. **6** And you became imitators of us and of the Lord as you welcomed the word, in spite of much suffering. You did that with such joy in the Holy Spirit **7** that you became a model for all the believers in Macedonia and Greece. **8** To be sure, not only has the Lord's word spread from you through Macedonia and Greece, but people everywhere have heard of your faith in God so that we do not need to say anything. **9** For they themselves report the kind of reception that you gave us. They report how you turned from idols to God in order to serve a God who lives and is real[d] **10** and to wait for His Son to come from heaven, the Son He raised from the dead, namely, Jesus, who rescues us from the coming anger ⌊of God⌋.

---

1 *a*   *1 Thessalonians* is an early letter of the Apostle Paul, written from Corinth about A.D. 50 on his Second Missionary Journey.

    b-   1 Meaning "God's undeserved love" (also in 5:28).

    c-   4 Literally: "brothers."

    d-   9 See *ALĒTHINOS* COMPARED WITH *ALĒTHĒS* on page 530.

2ND CHAPTER

1 You know, fellow Christians,^a that our coming to you has not been in vain. 2 We had suffered and been shamefully mistreated in Philippi, as you know. But our God gave us the courage to tell you the Good News of God, ˌevenˌ in the face of much conflict.

3 Our encouragement does not contain any error or impurity, and we are not deceiving you. 4 Rather, just as we have God's approval to be entrusted with the Gospel, so we preach it, not to please people but ˌto pleaseˌ God, *who tests our hearts*. 5 For we never flattered, as you know, nor found excuses to make money, as God knows, 6 nor did we seek praise from people, either from you or from others, 7 although we had a right as apostles of Christ to make demands on you.

You Are Dear To Us

But we were gentle when we were with you, like a mother^b tenderly caring for her children. 8 We longed for you so much that we were determined to share with you not only the Good News of God but even our own lives—so dear you had become to us. 9 For you remember, fellow Christians, how hard we worked and struggled. While we worked night and day so that we would not burden any of you, we preached the Good News of God to you. 10 You are witnesses, and so is God; how holy, righteous, and blameless we proved to be in our dealings with you who believe. 11 As you know, like a father urging his children, we used to urge, encourage, and warn every one of you 12 to live worthy of God, who is calling you into His Kingdom and glory.

13 There is another reason why we always thank God: When you received the word of God, which you heard from us, what you accepted was not the word of men; rather ˌyou acceptedˌ, as it was in truth, the word of God, which is also at work in you who believe.

14 You, fellow Christians, became just like the churches of God in Christ Jesus that are in Judea, since you suffered the same things from the people of your own country as they did from the Jews. 15 These Jews killed both the Lord Jesus and the prophets; they also drove us out. They do not please God, and they are opposed to everybody, 16 even trying to keep us from speaking to the Gentiles so that they may be saved. The result is that they keep *the cup of* their *sins filled* at all times. ˌGod'sˌ anger has come upon them forever.^c

17 Fellow Christians, when we were torn from you like orphans for a little while—you were out of sight but not out of mind—we were all the more eagerly and intensely longing to see you. 18 Therefore we wanted to come to you—I, Paul, wanted to ˌcomeˌ more than once—but Satan placed a barrier in our way.

---

4 *Jer 11:20*   16 *Gen 15:16*

---

2 *a-* 1 Literally: "brothers" (also in vv. 9,14,17).
  b- 7 Greek "*trophos*" ("nurse"), parallel in our day to one who cares for young children in a day-care center.
  c- 16 The Greek for "forever" could also mean "at last" or "fully."

[19] After all, who is our hope or joy or crown of glory in the presence of our Lord Jesus when He comes? Are you not that? [20] Yes, you are our glory and joy!

3RD CHAPTER

We Long To See You

[1] When we could not stand it any longer, we thought it best to be left alone in Athens. [2] We sent Timothy, our fellow Christian[a] who serves God[b] in preaching the Good News of Christ, to strengthen you and encourage you in your faith, [3] so that these troubles will not disturb anyone, because you know we are destined to suffer them. [4] In fact, when we were with you, we warned you, "We are going to suffer." And so it happened, as you know. [5] That is why I could not stand it any longer, and I sent to find out about your faith. I was afraid the Tempter had in some way tempted you and our work might be wasted.

[6] But now Timothy has come back to us from you and has told us the good news of your faith and love, also that you continually have a fond memory of us and long to see us, just as we long to see you. [7] So fellow Christians, you by your faith have encouraged us in all our distress and trouble. [8] For now we live if you stand firm in the Lord.

[9] How can we ever return thanks to God for all the joy you give us before our God, [10] as we earnestly pray day and night to see you face to face and to supply whatever is lacking in your faith? [11] May our God and Father Himself and the Lord Jesus clear the way for us to come to you.

[12] May the Lord make you grow in love and overflow with it for one another and for everybody, just as we love you. [13] As a result, may He give you inward strength to be holy and without fault before our God and Father when our Lord Jesus comes with all His holy ones![c]

4TH CHAPTER

C. Instruction and encouragement (4:1–5:22)

Live To Please God

[1] And now, fellow Christians,[a] this is what we ask and urge you to do in the Lord Jesus. You learned from us how God wants you to live in order to please Him, and that is how you are living. But now we urge you to do this more and more. [2] For you know what instructions we gave you by the Lord Jesus. [3] God wants you to be holy and keep away from sexual sin. [4] He wants you to know

---

3 a- 2 Literally: "brother" ("brothers" in v. 7).
  b- 2 Some of the older manuscripts and early translations add or substitute the words: "and who works with us."
  c- 13 Literally: "saints"; a reference to "people" or to "angels" or probably to both.
4 a- 1 Literally: "brothers" (also in vv. 10,13; "brother" in v. 6).

how to obtain a husband or wife[b] in a holy and honorable way, 5 and not in the way of passionate lust like *the Gentiles who do not know God*. 6 No one should sin by taking advantage of his fellow Christian in this matter, because *the Lord avenges* all these things, as we told you and warned you before. 7 For God did not call us to be unclean, but holy. 8 Therefore, if anyone rejects this, he does not reject a man but God, *who gives you His* Holy *Spirit*.

9 You do not need anyone to write to you about brotherly love, because God has taught you to love one another. 10 In fact, you are practicing it toward all the Christians throughout Macedonia. But we urge you, fellow Christians, grow ⌞in love⌟ more and more: 11 Make it your ambition to live quietly, to mind your own business, and to work with your hands, as we taught you to do. 12 Do this so that your way of life may win the respect of those outside ⌞the Christian faith⌟,[c] and so that you do not have to depend on others for anything.

Comfort One Another With These Words!

13 We do not want you to be uninformed about those who fall asleep,[d] fellow Christians, so that you do not grieve like the others who have no hope. 14 For since we believe that Jesus died and rose again, we also believe that in the same way God will bring with Him those who have fallen asleep in Jesus.[e] 15 To be sure, we tell you only what the Lord has told us: We who remain and are still living when the Lord comes will not arrive ahead of those who have fallen asleep. 16 For the Lord Himself will come down from heaven with a loud command, with the voice of the archangel,[f] and with the trumpet ⌞sound⌟ of God, and the dead who are in Christ will rise first. 17 Then we who remain and are still living will be caught up together with them in the clouds to meet the Lord in the air, and so we shall always be with the Lord. 18 Now then, comfort one another with these words!

5TH CHAPTER

Watch

1 Fellow Christians,[a] you do not need anyone to write to you about the passing of time and God's plans for the future,[b] 2 because you know very well that the Day of the Lord will come just as a thief in the night. 3 When people say, "All's well and safe!" then destruction will come on them suddenly like

---

5 *Ps 79:6; Jer 10:25*   6 *Ps 94:1*   8 *Ezek 36:27; 37:14*

b- 4 Literally: "to obtain his own vessel"; some translate: "to know how to control his body" or "to know how to live with his wife."

c- 12 Literally: "of the outsiders."

d- 13 A euphemistic expression for "die."

e- 14 Or "God through Jesus will bring with Him those who have fallen asleep."

f- 16 Possibly "Archangel"; the only archangel named in Scripture is Michael (cf. Jude 9); see MICHAEL THE ARCHANGEL on page 555.

5 a- 1 Literally: "brothers" (also in vv. 4,12,14,25,26,27).

b- 1 Literally: "the times ⌞of the calendar⌟ and the times ⌞which are appropriate⌟."

labor pains on a woman who is going to have a baby, and they will not escape. 4 But you, fellow Christians, are not in darkness that you should let that Day take you by surprise as a thief would do. 5 For you are all children of light and children of day. We have nothing to do with night and darkness. 6 Let us not sleep then, like the others, but be awake and sober. 7 For people who sleep, sleep at night, and those who get drunk, get drunk at night. 8 But let us who live in the daylight continue to be sober by *putting on* faith and love *as a breastplate* and the hope of *salvation as a helmet*. 9 For God did not appoint us to be punished by His righteous anger, *c* but to obtain salvation through our Lord Jesus Christ. 10 He died for us so that, whether we are awake or alseep, we may live with Him. 11 Therefore, encourage one another and strengthen one another just as you are doing.

Some Last Words

12 We ask you, fellow Christians, to appreciate those who work with you and who lead you in the Lord and who warn you. 13 Love them and think very highly of them on account of the work they are doing. Live in peace with one another.

14 We urge you, fellow Christians, warn those who are disorderly, cheer up those who are discouraged, help the weak, be patient with everyone else. 15 See to it that no one pays back wrong for wrong, but always be eager to help each other and everyone else also.

16 Always be joyful. 17 Always keep on praying. 18 Whatever happens, give thanks, because it is God's will that you do this.

19 Do not put out the fire of the Spirit. 20 Do not despise God's word when anyone speaks it. *d* 21 But test everything. Cling to what is good. 22 *Keep away from every* kind of *evil*.

D. Conclusion (5:23-28)

23 May the God of peace make you holy in every way and keep your spirit, soul, and body sound and without fault when our Lord Jesus Christ comes. 24 You can depend on Him who calls you—He will do it.

25 Fellow Christians, pray for us.

26 Greet all the Christians with a holy kiss.

27 I put you under solemn obligation before the Lord to read this letter to all the Christians.

28 May the grace of our Lord Jesus Christ be with you! Amen.

---

8 *Is 59:17*   22 *Job 1:1,8; 2:3*

---

c- 9 Literally: "appoint us to wrath."

d- 20 Literally: "Do not despise prophecies"; see 1 Corinthians 12:10,28; 13:2; 14:1-40; Ephesians 4:11.

2 THESSALONIANS[a]

1ST CHAPTER

A. Opening greeting (1:1,2)

1 Paul, Silas, and Timothy to the church of the Thessalonians in God our Father and the Lord Jesus Christ: **2** May God our Father and the Lord Jesus Christ give you grace[b] and peace!

B. Thanksgiving and encouragement (1:3-12)

Look To God In Suffering

3 We have a continuing obligation to thank God for you, fellow Christians.[c] It is the right thing to do because your faith is growing much stronger and the love of every one of you for one another is increasing. **4** As a result we are boasting in God's churches about your patient endurance and your faith in all the persecutions and trials which you are suffering. **5** It shows how God judges righteously so that you are counted worthy of His Kingdom, for which you are suffering. **6** It really is right for God to pay back suffering to those who make you suffer **7** and to give relief to you who suffer, and also to us. He will do this when the Lord Jesus will be revealed from heaven with His mighty angels *in a blazing fire,* **8** *taking vengeance on those who do not know God and on those who will not obey* the Good News [Gospel] of our Lord Jesus. **9** They will be punished with an eternal destruction, separated *from the presence of the Lord and from the glory of His power.* **10** ⌊This will happen⌋ when He comes *on that Day* to *be glorified among His holy ones[d]* and *admired* by all who have come to believe. (You did believe the truth we told you.) **11** With this in mind, we are always praying for you that our God will make you worthy of His calling and will powerfully accomplish every good thing you decide to do and every work

---

7,8 Ps 79:6; Is 66:4,15; Jer 10:25   **9** Is 2:10,19,21   **10** Ps 68:35; Is 2:11,17; 49:3

---

1 *a*   *2 Thessalonians* was written from Corinth about A.D. 50 by the Apostle Paul on his Second Missionary Journey.

b- 2 Meaning "God's undeserved love" (also in 3:18).

c- 3 Literally: "brothers."

d- 10 Literally: "saints"; a reference to "people" or to "angels" or probably to both.

of faith. **12** We pray this *so that the Name of our Lord* Jesus *may be glorified* among you, and you in Him, according to the grace [undeserved love] of our God and Lord Jesus Christ.

2ND CHAPTER

C. Instructions about the "last times" and Christ's return (2:1-17)

The "Man Of Sin"

1 Our Lord Jesus Christ is coming, and we will be gathered to meet Him. But we ask you, fellow Christians,*a* **2** not to lose your heads quickly or become alarmed either by a "spirit" message or by a word or by a letter that supposedly comes from us, saying, "The Day of the Lord has already come!" **3** Do not let anyone deceive you in any way. For the revolt must first take place, and the "man of sin" who is doomed to destruction must be revealed. **4** He opposes and *sets himself above everyone* who is *God's representative* or to whom honor is due,*b* so that *he sits in God's temple* and proclaims that *he is God.*

5 Do you not remember that I told you this when I was still with you? **6** And now you know what is holding him back, so that he will be revealed when his time comes. **7** For this rebellious thing is already working secretly, but only until he who is now holding it back gets out of the way. **8** Then the rebellious one will be revealed, and the Lord Jesus *will destroy him with the breath of His mouth* and make him powerless at His return appearance.

9 The coming of this rebellious one is the work of Satan, who uses all types of misleading miracles, miraculous signs, and wonderful proofs,*c* **10** and every kind of wrongdoing which deceives those who are perishing, because they refused to love the truth and so be saved. **11** That is why God sends a deception which works effectively, so that they might believe the lie **12** and all might be condemned who did not believe the truth but delighted in wrongdoing.

God Has Chosen You

13 But we have a continuing obligation to thank God for you, fellow Christians, whom *the Lord loves*, because in the beginning God chose you to be made holy by the Spirit, to believe the truth, and so to be saved. **14** For this purpose also He called you by the Gospel which we preach; He wants you to have the glory of our Lord Jesus Christ.

---

12 Is 66:5   *4 Ezek 28:2; Dan 11:36*   *8 Job 4:9; Is 11:4*   *13 Deut 33:12*

---

2 *a-* 1 Literally: "brothers" (also in vv. 13,15).

    b- 4 Literally: "over everyone who is called God or is to be shown reverence"; these words refer to everyone who was God's representative whether in the church, in the family, or in government, and so were to be highly honored.

    c- 9 See MIRACULOUS SIGNS, WONDERFUL PROOFS, and MIRACLES on page 527.

15 Stand then, fellow Christians, and cling to the instructions we handed down to you when we spoke to you or wrote to you.

16 Now may our Lord Jesus Christ Himself and God our Father, who loved us and by His grace gave us everlasting comfort and good hope, **17** comfort you inwardly and strengthen you to do and say everything that is good.

3RD CHAPTER

D. Prayer and discipline (3:1-15)

Pray For Us

1 Finally, fellow Christians,*a* pray for us that the Lord's word may spread rapidly and gain glory as it did among you **2** and that we may be rescued from wicked and evil people. For not everybody is trustworthy, **3** but the Lord is!*b* He will strengthen you and protect you against the Evil One. **4** We are certain in the Lord that you are doing and will be doing what we instructed you to do. **5** May the Lord direct your hearts to the love of God and the patient endurance of Christ.

Work

6 Now we instruct you, fellow Christians, in the Name of our Lord Jesus Christ not to associate with any Christian who lives out of line with the instructions you received from us. **7** For you know what is necessary for you to do to imitate us, because we were not idle when we were with you. **8** We took no free meals from anyone but worked hard and struggled day and night in order not to burden any of you. **9** It is not as though we did not have a right to receive support; rather, we wanted to give you an example to imitate. **10** For while we were with you, we gave you the instruction: "If anyone does not want to work, neither should he eat."

11 We hear that some of you are living a lazy life, not doing any work, but being busybodies. **12** Such people we instruct and encourage by the Lord Jesus Christ to work quietly and eat their own bread. **13** And you, fellow Christians, do not become tired of doing good.

14 If anyone will not listen to what we say in this letter, take note of him, and do not have anything to do with him, so that he will feel ashamed. **15** Yet, do not treat him like an enemy, but warn him like a brother.

E. Conclusion (3:16-18)

Farewell

16 May the Lord of peace Himself give you His peace in every way. The Lord

---

3 *a*- 1 Literally: "brothers" (also in vv. 6,13; "brother" in v. 6).
  b- 3 Or "For not all have faith, but the Lord is faithful."

be with you all.

17 I, Paul, am writing this greeting with my own hand, which is a distinguishing mark in every letter [epistle]: this is my handwriting.

18 May the grace of our Lord Jesus Christ be with you all!

PAUL WRITES

1 TIMOTHY[a]

1ST CHAPTER

A. Introduction and false teaching (1:1-20)

1 Paul, an apostle of Christ Jesus by the command of God our Savior and of Christ Jesus our Hope, **2** to Timothy, my real son by faith: May God the Father and Christ Jesus our Lord, give you grace,[b] mercy, and peace!

Warning Against False Teachers And Their Doctrine

3 When I was going to Macedonia, I urged you to stay in Ephesus, so that you might order certain men not to teach any wrong doctrine **4** nor to busy themselves with myths and endless genealogies that give rise to speculations rather than presenting God's plan ₎of salvation₎ which centers in faith.[c]

5 The goal of our instruction is love flowing from a pure heart, from a good conscience, and from a sincere faith. **6** Certain people have wandered off course and have turned to silly talk. **7** They want to be teachers of the Law, but they understand neither the things they say nor the things about which they are so sure.

8 But we know the Law is good if it is used as it was meant to be used. **9** We need to keep in mind that the Law is not meant for a righteous person but for those who break the Law and those who rebel against it, for the ungodly and sinners, for those who live unholy lives and for those who insult holy things; for those who kill their fathers and for those who kill their mothers, for those who are murderers, **10** for those who are sexually immoral, for those who are homosexuals, for kidnappers, for those who lie, for those who swear falsely ₎under oath,[d]—as well as anything else that is found to be contrary to sound teaching **11** when judged according to the glorious Gospel [Good News] of the blessed God, which was entrusted to me.

---

1 *a* *1 Timothy* is the first of the so-called "pastoral letters." The Apostle Paul wrote it to give his disciple Timothy, who was at Ephesus, further instruction regarding the administration of the office of a pastor.

b - 2 Meaning "God's undeserved love."

c - 4 Literally: "rather than God's plan which is through faith."

d - 10 For an explanation of Paul's chiasm in verses 9 and 10 see GRAMMATIC/POETIC STRUCTURES THAT CONVEY TEXTUAL MEANINGS on page 558.

God's Mercy Toward Paul

12 I thank Christ Jesus our Lord, who made me strong. He considered me to be trustworthy and appointed me to do His work, 13 although I used to be a blasphemer, a persecuter, and a violent person. However, I received mercy because I acted ignorantly in unbelief. 14 Our Lord poured His grace [undeserved love] on me abundantly, along with faith and love in Christ Jesus.

15 This is a statement we can trust and it is worthy of whole-hearted acceptance: Christ Jesus came into the world to save sinners—of whom I am the worst. 16 But for this reason God was merciful to me in order that Jesus Christ might demonstrate in me, the worst ,of sinners,, all His patience as an example to those who are going to believe in Him and live forever. 17 To the everlasting King, the immortal, invisible, and only God, be honor and glory forever and ever! Amen.

Fight And Pray

18 I am giving you this instruction, my son Timothy, according to the prophecies made earlier about you, so that with them in mind you might fight a good fight, 19 while ,still, holding on to faith and a good conscience. Some refused to listen to their conscience and suffered shipwreck in their faith. 20 Among them are Hymenaeus and Alexander, whom I turned over to Satan to teach them not to blaspheme.

2ND CHAPTER

B. Public worship (2:1-15)

Guidelines For Worship

1 Therefore I urge you, first of all, that petitions, prayers, intercessions, and thanksgivings be made for all people—2 for kings and all who are over us, so that we may live quietly and peacefully and be godly and reverent in every way. 3 This is good and pleases God our Savior, 4 who wants all people to be saved and to come to know the truth.

5 There is one God. There is also one Mediator between God and men, the Man Christ Jesus, 6 who gave Himself as a ransom for all people, the proof that God's appointed time had come. *a* 7 For this purpose I was appointed a preacher and an apostle—I am telling the truth and not lying—a teacher of faith and truth *b* to the Gentiles.

8 So I want the men to pray everywhere, lifting up holy hands, without anger or argument.

9 Similarly, I want women to dress in decent clothes, modestly, and with good judgment. Their adornment is not a matter of attractive hair-styling, gold,

---

2 *a-* 6 Or "the testimony given at the appropriate time."
 b- 7 Or "a teacher of the true faith."

pearls, or expensive clothes, but of good works, **10** as is proper for women who claim to worship God.

11 Let a woman learn in quietness, being completely subordinate. *c* **12** I do not allow a woman to teach in such a way as to have authority over a man; rather, she is to conduct herself quietly. **13** For Adam was formed first, then Eve. **14** And Adam was not deceived; but the woman *d* by being deceived fell into sin. **15** However, women will be saved as they have children, if they live in faith and love and holiness, while using good judgment.

3RD CHAPTER

C. Qualifications for pastors (3:1-16)

Church Workers

1 This is a statement we can trust: If anyone sets his heart on being a pastor, *a* he desires to do a noble work. **2** Now, a pastor must be blameless, the husband of one wife, not drinking too much wine, ₍a man₎ of good judgment and fine behavior, kind to guests, able to teach, **3** no drunkard, not violent but gentle, not quarrelsome, not one who loves money. **4** He must manage his own family well and have his children obey *b* him with proper respect. **5** (If anyone does not know how to manage his own family, how can he take care of God's church?) **6** He must not be a new convert, in order that he will not become proud and fall into the judgment of the devil. **7** The people outside the church must speak well of him, so that he does not fall into disgrace and the devil's snare.

8 In the same way the deacons in the church must be serious, not using doubletalk, not drinking a lot of wine, not greedy. **9** With a clear conscience they must hold on to the mystery *c* of the faith. **10** Let these men be tested first; then if no fault is found in them, let them serve. **11** In the same way the women *d* must be serious, not slandering, not drinking too much wine, but trustworthy in every

---

c- 11 Greek: "*hupotassō.*" This Greek term speaks of persons who are placed in an "order" or "rank" below or under the authority of another. In the mind of sinful human beings this is often falsely equated with *inferiority.* However, Jesus taught us that among Christians this is not to be the case. It is not the one in authority who is the greatest but the one who is servant to all (Matt. 20:25-28; Mk. 10:42-45); authority and servitude are always to be used for the benefit of others.

The English "subordinate" captures the totality of this *hupotassō* concept quite well. In the passage before us Paul applies *hupotassō* to *the lines of authority* which God lays down *for Christian congregations* as they relate to male/female functions (cf. 1 Cor. 14:34). Note verse 13 which says that God's creation established this order in ranking. Compare Genesis 2:20-23; 3:16. This identical Greek word is translated "obey" in 3:4. See *HUPOTASSō* on page 541.

d- 14 Or "womankind." This noun is also the subject of the verb "will be saved" in verse 15 where the reference is to womankind.

3 *a-* 1 Greek: "*episkopēs*"; see footnote at Philippians 1:1 or 1 Timothy 4:14.

b- 4 See *HUPOTASSō* on page 541.

c- 9 The Greek word here used refers to a *secret* that is hidden from human understanding and cannot be grasped by those outside the Christian faith. This same word is used in verse 16; 1 Corinthians 15:51; Ephesians 1:9 (cf. Rom. 11:25).

d- 11 Or "wives"; Paul refers either to *deaconesses* (trained female church workers) or to the *wives of deacons.*

way. **12** Let deacons be the husbands of one wife. At the same time let them manage their children and their own households well. **13** For when they have served well as deacons, they gain a noble standing for themselves and great confidence in their faith in Christ Jesus.

We Bring The Truth

14 I hope to come to you soon but am writing you this **15** so that, if I am delayed, you may know how God wants people to behave within His family, which is the church of the living God, the pillar and support of the truth. **16** There is no doubt about it: Deep*e* is the mystery*f* of our religion—

> He*g* appeared in flesh,*h*
> Was justified in spirit,*i*
> Was seen by angels,
> Was preached among nations,
> Was believed in the world,
> Was taken up in glory.

4TH CHAPTER

D. False teachers (4:1-16)

Danger Ahead

1 The Spirit says clearly that in later times some will turn away from the faith as they listen to spirits who deceive and to things taught by demons. **2** They are led astray by the hypocrisy of liars, whose consciences have been branded as with a red-hot iron.*a* **3** These liars order people not to marry and to keep away from foods which God created to be received with thanks by those who believe and know the truth. **4** For everything God created is good. Nothing is to be rejected if it is received with thanksgiving, **5** because the word of God and prayer make it holy.

How To Serve Christ

6 Point these things out to our fellow Christians,*b* and you will be a good servant of Christ Jesus, nourished by the words of the faith and of the sound

---

e- 16 Literally: "Great."
f- 16 See 3:9 and its accompanying footnote.
g- 16 Some of the later manuscripts read: "God."
h- 16 Or "in a fleshly [physical] state," referring to Christ's state of humiliation (cf. Rom. 1:3; 1 Pet. 3:18; 4:6 and the corresponding footnotes; also note 1 Cor. 15:44-49).
i- 16 Or "in a spiritual state," referring to Christ's state of exaltation (cf. Rom. 1:4; 1 Pet. 3:18; 4:6 and the corresponding footnotes; also note 1 Cor. 15:44-49).
4 *a*- 2 The meaning is either that they have an accusing conscience or a conscience which no longer has any feeling.
b- 6 Literally: "brothers."

teaching you have followed. **7** Do not have anything to do with worldly old wives' tales.^c Rather, train yourself for a godly life. **8** For training the body helps a little, but godliness helps in every way since it has a promise for life here and hereafter. **9** That statement you can trust and accept absolutely. **10** Yes, that is the reason we work and struggle, because our hope is in the living God, who is the Savior of all people, especially of those who believe.

11 Insist on these things and keep on teaching them. **12** Do not let anyone look down on you because you are young, but be an example to those who believe: in speech, behavior, love, faith, and purity. **13** Until I come, devote yourself to the public reading ˻of Scripture˼, encouragement, and teaching. **14** Do not neglect the gift you have which was given to you by prophecy when the pastors^d laid their hands on you. **15** Practice these things; continue in them, so that everyone can see your progress. **16** Watch yourself and your teaching. Continue in these things. For if you do so, you will save both yourself and those who hear you.

5TH CHAPTER

E. Attitude toward various groups (5:1–6:2a)

1 Do not be harsh with an older man, but encourage him as a father, younger men as brothers, **2** older women as mothers, younger women as sisters, keeping yourself altogether pure.

Take Care of Widows^a

3 Honor widows who are all alone.^b **4** If any widow has children or grandchildren, let them first of all learn to respect their own family and repay their parents, because that pleases God. **5** The widow who is all alone and forsaken puts her hope in the Lord and keeps on asking and praying day and night. **6** But one who lives for pleasure is dead while she lives. **7** Insist that they also do these things so that they cannot be criticized. **8** If anyone does not take care of his own relatives, especially his family, he has denied the faith and is worse than an unbeliever.

9 Put a widow on your list ˻of widows˼ if she is not under 60, if she was the wife of one husband,^c **10** if people tell about the good she has done, if she raised children, welcomed strangers, washed the feet of believers [saints], helped the suffering, and was busy doing every kind of good work. **11** But do not put

---

c- 7 Or "worldly myths and old wives' tales."

d- 14 The Greek word means "presbyters" or "elders" (*"presbuteros"*). This Greek word, along with the Greek term for "overseers" or "bishops" (*"episkopos"* - Phil. 1:1), was a term used to refer to pastors of local congregations.

5 *a* This section speaks of three classes of widows: 1) those who have relatives to look after them (v. 4); 2) those who have no one to look after them ("all alone" or "truly widowed" - vv. 3,5, cf. v. 16); 3) those, whether helped by the church or not, who are to carry out certain church functions and meet certain regulations (vv. 9-15).

b- 3 Or "really widowed" (also in vv. 5,16).

c- 9 Note the probable implication here for the interpretation of "husband of one wife" in 3:2,12; Titus 1:6.

younger widows on the list. For when their natural desires become stronger than their devotion to Christ, they want to marry, **12** and so they become guilty of breaking the pledge that they originally made. **13** At the same time they learn to be idle and to go around from house to house. And they are not only idle but gossiping and meddling, saying things they should not say.

14 So I want younger women to marry, have children, manage their homes, and give the enemy no chance to slander them. **15** For some have already turned away to follow Satan. **16** If any believing woman has relatives who are widows, let her help them and not allow them to become a burden to the church, so that the church may help those widows who are all alone.

Pastors

17 Let pastors*d* who are good leaders be considered worthy of double honor, especially if their work is preaching and teaching, **18** because the Scripture says: *"When an ox is treading out the grain, do not muzzle him,"* and *"A worker deserves his pay."*

19 Do not accept an accusation against a pastor unless *it is supported by two or three witnesses.* **20** Those who keep on sinning, correct before everyone in order that the others may be made aware ‚of the seriousness of sin‚.*e*

21 I solemnly call on you before God and Christ Jesus and the chosen angels to keep these things without prejudice and without preference for anyone in anything you do.

22 Do not be in a hurry to ordain*f* anyone. Do not share in the sins of others. Keep yourself pure.

23 Do not drink only water, but use a little wine for your stomach because you are often sick.

24 The sins of some people are obvious as they go ahead of them to judgment, but the sins of others follow them there. **25** Similarly, anyone can also see good works, and even when they cannot be seen, they cannot stay hidden.

6TH CHAPTER

Slaves and Masters

1 All who are under the yoke of slavery should think of their own masters as men who deserve every respect, so that God's Name and what we teach is not blasphemed. **2** If you have masters who believe, do not think less of them because they are fellow Christians,*a* but serve them all the better because those who receive the benefit of your work are believers and are dear to you.

---

18 Deut 25:4   *19 Deut 19:15*

---

d- 17 See 4:14 and its accompanying footnote; also applies to 5:19.
e- 20 Or "that others may be made afraid" or "that others may take warning."
f- 22 Literally: "Lay hands quickly on no one."
6 *a-* 2 Literally: "brothers."

F. Final warnings against false teachers and advice to Timothy (6:2b-21)

Religion And Contentment

Teach and urge them to do these things. 3 If anyone teaches anything else and does not agree with the sound words of our Lord Jesus Christ and godly teaching, 4 he is proud and does not know anything; he has a morbid craving for debates and arguments, which produce jealousy, quarreling, abusive insults, evil suspicions, 5 and the continued wrangling of people whose minds are corrupt, who have lost the truth and think that religion is a way to make a profit.

6 Religion, of course, does bring a large profit—to those who are satisfied with what they have. 7 For we did not bring anything into the world, and we cannot take anything out. 8 As long as we have food and clothing, let us be satisfied with that.

9 But people who want to get rich fall into temptation and a snare and many foolish and harmful desires, which drown them in destruction and ruin. 10 For the love of money is the root of all evils; and some people, eager to get rich, have wandered away from the faith and pierced themselves with many pains.

Fight The Good Fight

11 But you, man of God, flee from these things. Pursue righteousness, godliness, faith, love, patient endurance, gentleness. 12 Fight the good fight of faith; take hold of the everlasting life to which you were called and which you confessed so beautifully before many witnesses.

13 I insist on this before God, from whom comes all life, and before Christ Jesus, who testified with a beautiful confession before Pontius Pilate, 14 that you keep this command without spot or blame until our Lord Jesus Christ appears. 15 At His own right time God will show Him to us—He, the blessed and only Ruler, the King of kings and Lord of lords, 16 who alone has immortality, who lives in a light to which no one can come near, whom no one has ever seen or can see. To Him be honor and power forever! Amen.

17 Tell those who are rich in this world not to feel proud and not to trust anything as uncertain as riches—but to trust God, who richly provides us with everything to enjoy. 18 Tell them to do good, to be rich in good works, to be glad to give to others, and to share. 19 In this way they are storing up for themselves a treasure, as a good foundation for the future, that they may take hold of the life that is really life.

20 Timothy, guard what has been entrusted to you. Turn away from empty, worldly talk and contradictory statements of what is falsely called "knowledge." 21 Although some claim to have it, they have lost their faith.

Grace be with you!*b*

---

b- 21 In Greek the word "you" is in the plural, indicating that this letter was to be read to the church (believers) at Ephesus.

2 TIMOTHY*a*

1ST CHAPTER

A. Introduction (1:1-5)

1 Paul, an apostle of Christ Jesus, by the will of God who has promised life in Christ Jesus,*b* **2** to Timothy, my dear son—may God the Father and Christ Jesus our Lord, give you grace,*c* mercy, and peace!

3 I thank God—whom I serve with a clear conscience, like my fathers did—when I remember you in my prayers, as I never fail to do, day and night. **4** As I remember your tears, I long to see you that I might be filled with happiness. **5** I recall how sincere your faith was; just as it lived in your grandmother Lois and your mother Eunice before you, so I am convinced it is also in you.

B. Appeal to remain loyal and guard the truth (1:6-18)

The Gift Of God In You

6 That is why I remind you to fan into a flame the gift of God which is in you through the laying on of my hands. **7** For God did not give us a cowardly spirit but a spirit of power and love and good judgment. **8** So do not be ashamed to witness about our Lord; and do not be ashamed of me, His prisoner, but with God's power to support us, join me in suffering for the Gospel [Good News]. **9** He saved us and called us to be holy, not because of what we had done but because He planned to give us His grace [undeserved love]. This grace He gave us in Christ Jesus before the world began; **10** it has now come to light by the coming of our Savior Christ Jesus. He took away the power of death and by the Gospel brought into the light the life which cannot be destroyed.*d* **11** I was

---

1 *a*   *2 Timothy* is the last of the letters of the Apostle Paul. It was written from prison in Rome when Paul was expecting to be executed for his preaching of the Gospel.

b- 1 Literally: "by the will of God according to the promise of life in Christ Jesus."

c- 2 Meaning "God's undeserved love."

d - 10 Literally: "brought to light life and immortality through the Gospel"; Paul uses a hendiadys, a grammatical structure which expresses one idea through two nouns connected by "and," instead of by a noun and an adjective—namely, "life" and "immortality" for "immortal life."

appointed a preacher, apostle, and teacher of this Gospel.

12 That is why I suffer as I do, but I am not ashamed, because I know Him in whom I trust, and I am sure that He can keep for that Day what I have entrusted to Him.

13 With faith and love in Christ Jesus keep what you heard me say as an example of sound teaching. **14** With the help of the Holy Spirit living in us, guard the good thing entrusted to you.

Onesiphorus

15 You know how everyone in the province of Asia deserted me, including Phygelus and Hermogenes.

16 The Lord be merciful to the family of Onesiphorus because he often cheered me up. He did not feel ashamed of my being a prisoner, **17** but coming to Rome, he searched hard for me and found me. **18** May the Lord let him find mercy from the Lord on that Day. And you know very well all that he did to help me in Ephesus.

2ND CHAPTER

C. Encouragement to face hardships (2:1-13)

Be A Good Soldier

1 You, my son, let God's grace [undeserved love] in Christ Jesus make you strong, **2** and what you heard me say before many witnesses entrust to faithful men who will also be able to teach others.

3 Share hardships with me like a good soldier of Christ Jesus. **4** No one who becomes a soldier will get mixed up with the affairs of everyday life because he wants to please the one who enlisted him. **5** And if a person enters a contest, he wins a prize only if he competes according to the rules. **6** The hard-working farmer should be the first to get a share of the crops. **7** Try to understand what I say, because the Lord will give you understanding in everything.

8 Keep in mind Jesus Christ, who is risen from the dead, a descendant of David—this is the Gospel I preach. *a* **9** For this I am suffering, even chained like a criminal. But the word of God is not chained. **10** That is why I can patiently endure anything for those who have been chosen, that they may receive salvation in Christ Jesus and everlasting glory. **11** You can depend on this:

> If we have died with Him,
>> we shall also live with Him.
>
> **12** If we patiently endure,
>> we shall also rule with Him.
>
> If we disown Him,
>> He will also disown us.

---

2 *a-* 8 Literally: "according to my Gospel."

13   If we do not believe,
            He remains faithful
                because He cannot disown Himself.

D. Charge to combat false teachers (2:14-26)

14 Remind them of these things and warn them in the presence of God not to fight about words; it does not do any good but only ruins those who are listening. **15** Be eager to come before God as one whom He approves, a worker who does not have to feel ashamed because he teaches the word of truth in the correct way.*b* **16** Keep away from empty, worldly discussions, because they will lead more and more to impiety, **17** and such talk will spread like a cancer. Among them are Hymenaeus and Philetus, **18** who have departed from the truth by saying that the resurrection has already taken place. They are upsetting the faith of some people.

19 But there stands God's solid foundation, and it has this seal: *"The Lord knows those who are His own,"* and *"Let everyone who calls on the Name of the Lord* give up wrongdoing."

20 In a large house there are not only things of gold and silver, but also of wood and clay. Some are used in an honorable way and others in a dishonorable way. **21** Now if anyone will cleanse himself from the latter, he will be a tool which is ready for an honorable purpose, purified, useful to the Master, and prepared to do every good work.

22 Flee from the lusts of young people and pursue righteousness, faith, love, and peace, along with those who call on the Lord with a pure heart. **23** Do not have anything to do with foolish and unintelligent arguments; you know they breed quarrels. **24** A servant of the Lord must not quarrel, but he must be kind to everyone. He must be a good teacher, willing to suffer wrong, **25** and gentle in correcting those who oppose him. Perhaps God will change their hearts and lead them to know the truth. **26** Then they will come to their senses and escape the snare of the devil, who trapped them into doing what he desires.

3RD CHAPTER

E. Dangers of the "last days" (3:1-17)

The Last Days

1 Understand this, that in the last days there will come times of trouble. **2** People will love themselves and money. They will brag and be proud. They will blaspheme. They will disobey parents. They will be ungrateful and unholy, **3** without love, never forgiving an enemy, slanderous. They will be without self-control, without mercy, without love for what is good. **4** They will be treacherous, reckless, proud. They will love pleasure rather than God. **5** They

---

19 Num 16:5; Is 26:13

---

b- 15 Literally: "because he takes the word of truth along a straight path."

will have the appearance of godliness but refuse to let it be a power. Keep away from such people.

6 Some of them make their way into homes and captivate weak women, who are loaded with sins and are driven by all kinds of desires. 7 These women are always learning and never able to understand the truth.

8 Just as Jannes and Jambres opposed Moses, so those people oppose the truth. Their minds are corrupt, and they are rejected in regard to their faith. 9 But they will not get very far; like Jannes and Jambres,*a* they will be seen by everybody to be the plain fools they are.

Teach The Truth

10 But you have closely followed my teaching, my way of living, my purpose, my faith, my patience, my love, my patient endurance, 11 my persecutions, my sufferings—which happened to me in Antioch, Iconium, and Lystra—those persecutions which I endured. The Lord rescued me from everything. 12 All who want to live a godly life in Christ Jesus will be persecuted.

13 But evil people and religious quacks will become worse as they deceive and are deceived. 14 But you continue in what you have learned and found to be true. You know from whom you learned it 15 and that since childhood you have known the Holy Scriptures, which are able to make you wise so that you may be saved through faith in Christ Jesus. 16 All Scripture is inspired by God*b* and is useful for teaching, for pointing out error, for correcting, for training in righteousness, 17 so that the person who belongs to God is ready, equipped for every good work.

4TH CHAPTER

F. Correction of error (4:1-8)

1 In the presence of God and Christ Jesus, who is going to judge the living and the dead, and in view of His coming and His ruling over us, I solemnly charge you: 2 Preach the word, be ready whether it is convenient or not convenient,*a* correct, rebuke, encourage, being very patient and thorough in your teaching.

3 A time will come when people will not listen to sound teaching but, following their own desires, they will surround themselves more and more with teachers who say what they want to hear. 4 They will refuse to listen to the truth and will turn to myths.

5 But you keep a clear head in everything, endure hardship, do the work of one who preaches the Gospel, do everything else that God desires you to do as a pastor.*b*

---

3 *a*- 9 Literally: "like those."
   b- 16 Or "All Scripture is God-breathed."
4 *a*- 2 Literally: "in season or out of season."
   b- 5 Literally: "fulfill your ministry."

⁶ I am now being poured out as a drink offering,ᶜ and the time of my departure has come. ⁷ I have fought the good fight; I have completed the race; I have kept the faith. ⁸ Now there is waiting for me the crown of righteousness which the Lord, the righteous Judge, will give me on that Day, and not only to me but also to all who are longing to see Him come again.ᵈ

G. Personal items (4:9-18)

⁹ Do your best to come to me soon. ¹⁰ For Demas fell in love with this world, deserted me, and went to Thessalonica. Crescens went to Galatia, ˏandˌ Titus went to Dalmatia. ¹¹ Only Luke is with me. Get Mark and bring him with you, because he is helpful to me in my work. ¹² I sent Tychicus to Ephesus.

¹³ When you come, bring the warm coat I left with Carpus in Troas, and the scrolls, especially the parchments.ᵉ

¹⁴ Alexander the metalworker did me much harm. *The Lord will pay him back for what he did.* ¹⁵ Be on your guard against him, because he was very much opposed to what we said.

¹⁶ At my first hearing no one stood up in my defense, but everybody deserted me—may it not be held against them. ¹⁷ But the Lord stood by me and gave me strength, that the full message would be preached by me and all the Gentiles would hear it; and *I was rescued from the lion's mouth.*

The Lord Will Deliver Me

¹⁸ The Lord will rescue me from all harm and will take me safely to His heavenly Kingdom. To Him be glory forever. Amen.

H. Conclusion (4:19-22)

Final Greetings

¹⁹ Greet Prisca and Aquila and the family of Onesiphorus. ²⁰ Erastus stayed in Corinth. I left Trophimus sick in Miletus. ²¹ Do your best to come before winter. Eubulus and Pudens and Linus and Claudia and all the fellow Christiansᶠ greet you.

²² The Lord be with your spirit! Grace be with you!ᵍ

---

14 Ps 62:12; Prov 24:12   *17* Ps 22:21; Dan 6:20,27

---

c- 6 Compare Paul's comment with Exodus 29:40,41.
d- 8 Literally: "all who have loved His appearing."
e- 13 Parchments were made from the skins of animals and were used as one type of writing material in ancient times.
f- 21 Literally: "brothers."
g- 22 In Greek the word "you" is in the plural, indicating that this letter was to be read to the church (believers) at Ephesus.

TITUS^a

1ST CHAPTER

A. Introduction (1:1-4)

1 Paul, a servant^b of God and an apostle of Jesus Christ—sent to help God's chosen people to believe and to know the truth which promotes godliness. **2** This belief and knowledge is based on the hope of everlasting life, which God, who never lies, promised before time began, **3** and which at His own right time He revealed in His word through the preaching entrusted to me by the command of God our Savior—**4** to Titus, my real son by the faith we share: May God the Father and Christ Jesus our Savior give you grace^c and peace!

B. Requirements for pastors (1:5-16)

Appoint Good Pastors

5 I left you behind in Crete to make the improvements still needed and to appoint pastors^d in every town as I directed you. **6** A pastor must be one who is blameless; he must have only one wife; his children must be believers who are not accused of wild living or disobedience. **7** As a manager appointed by God, a pastor^e must be blameless. He must not insist on always having his own way,^f not become angry easily, not drink too much, not be quick to strike anyone, and not be greedy for more money. **8** Rather, he is to welcome guests, love what is good, use good judgment, live right, be holy, and have self-control. **9** He is to be one who clings to the word which he can depend on, just as he was taught, so that by sound teaching he can encourage people and correct those who oppose him.

---

1 *a*   *Titus* is one of the three "pastoral letters" and was written to Titus, Paul's associate in bringing the Gospel to the people of Crete.

b-   1 Literally: "slave," reflecting Paul's total subjection to God.

c-   4 Meaning "God's undeserved love" (also in 3:15).

d-   5 Greek: *"presbuteros"*; see footnote at 1 Timothy 4:14 (cf. footnote at Phil. 1:1).

e-   7 Greek: *"episkopon"*; see footnote at Philippians 1:1.

f-   7 Greek may also mean: "arrogant."

Correct Your Opponents

10 There are many who are rebellious, who talk foolishly and deceive, especially those who came out of Judaism.*g* 11 They must be silenced because they are ruining whole families by teaching what they must not teach; they do this for the shameful purpose of making money.

12 One of their own men, their own prophet, said, "Men of Crete are always liars, savage animals, lazy gluttons."*h* 13 That statement is true. For that reason correct them sharply so that they may be sound in their faith, 14 not paying attention to Jewish myths or commands given by people who reject the truth. 15 Everything is pure to those who are pure. But nothing is pure to those who are corrupt and who do not believe—rather, both their mind and their conscience are corrupt. 16 They openly claim to know God, but they deny Him by what they do. They are abominable, disobedient, and not fit to do anything good.

2ND CHAPTER

C. Moral instruction for various groups (2:1-15)

Guidelines

1 But as for you, tell people what is right according to sound teaching. 2 Tell older men: Be sober, serious, sensible, and sound in faith, love, and patient endurance.

3 Similarly, tell older women: Behave in a way which is fitting for holy women. Do not slander. Do not be slaves to much wine. Teach what is good 4 in order to train young women to love their husbands and their children, 5 to use good judgment, to be pure, to keep house, to be helpful, to be subordinate*a* to their husbands, so that people may not speak evil of God's word.

6 In the same way urge the young men to use good judgment. 7 In everything be an example of good works. Do not let anything corrupt your teaching. But be dignified 8 and give a sound message that cannot be condemned, so that anyone who opposes us will be ashamed because he cannot say anything bad about us.

9 Tell slaves: Obey your masters in everything, please them, and do not talk back. 10 Do not steal, but show that you can be trusted in every way, so that in everything you show the beauty of the teaching of God our Savior.

11 For the grace [undeserved love] of God has appeared. It brings salvation to all people 12 and trains us to say "No" to ungodliness and worldly lusts, that we

---

g- 10 Literally: "especially the ones from the circumcision."

h- 12 This quotation is attributed to the Cretan poet Epimenides of Knossos (500 B.C.).

2 *a*- 5 Greek: "*hupotassō*." See general comments in footnote at Ephesians 5:24. Particular to our present passage is Paul's application of *hupotassō* in regard to *marriage* according to the rank or order laid down by God (cf. Col. 3:18; 1 Pet. 3:1). Also, cite 1 Timothy 2:11,13, noting the references to Genesis as they are indicated in the accompanying footnote. This identical Greek word is translated "obey" in verse 9. See *HUPOTASSŌ* on page 541.

might live sensibly and uprightly and godly in the present world **13** as we look for our blessed hope, namely, the glorious appearance of our great God and Savior, Jesus Christ. **14** He gave Himself as *a payment* for us *to free* us *from all wickedness* and cleanse us *to be His own people*, eager to do good works.

15 These are the things you are to say. Continue to encourage and correct with full authority—let no one ignore you!

3RD CHAPTER

D. Christian morality in general (3:1-8a)

1 Remind people to be subordinate[a] to governments and authorities, to obey, to be ready to do any good work, **2** not to speak evil of anyone or fight, but to yield and show kindness to everyone.

What God Did For Us

3 For we too were once foolish, disobedient, deceived. We were enslaved to many kinds of passions and pleasures. We lived in resentment and jealousy, being hated and hating one another.

4 But when God our Savior showed how kind He is and how He loves us,[b] **5** He saved us, not because of any righteous works[c] which we have done, but because of His mercy. He saved us by the washing in which the Holy Spirit gives us a new birth and a new life. **6** He poured a rich measure of this Spirit on us through Jesus Christ our Savior, **7** so that we who were justified [acquitted][d] by His grace might become heirs in keeping with the hope of everlasting life. **8** You can depend on this statement.

E. Advice to Titus (3:8b-11)

And I want you to insist on these things so that those who believe in God have their minds set on being busy with good works. This is good, and it helps other people.

---

14 Ex 19:5; Deut 14:2; Ps 130:8

---

3 a- 1 Greek: "*hupotassō*." This Greek term speaks of persons who are placed in an "order" or "rank" below or under the authority of another. In the mind of sinful human beings this is often falsely equated with *inferiority*. However, Jesus taught us that among Christians this is not to be the case. It is not the one in authority who is the greatest but the one who is servant to all (Matt. 20:25-28; Mk. 10:42-45); authority and servitude are always to be used for the benefit of others.

The English "subordinate" captures the totality of this *hupotassō* concept quite well. In the passage before us Paul uses the word in terms of our *everyday relationships within society* (cf. Rom. 13:1; 1 Pet. 2:13,18). See *HUPOTASSŌ* on page 541.

b- 4 Literally: "But when God our Savior's kindness and love of mankind appeared."

c- 5 Literally: "because of works of righteousness."

d- 7 That is, "to declare righteous, not guilty, innocent."

9 But keep away from foolish arguments, genealogies, quarreling, and fighting about the Law, for these help no one and are worthless. **10** Give a warning to a person who chooses to be different in his teaching; then warn him a second time; and after that do not have anything more to do with him, **11** because you know such a person is set in his wrong way and is a sinner who condemns himself.

F. Conclusion (3:12-15)

Farewell

12 When I send Artemas or Tychicus to you, hurry to come to me at Nicopolis, for I have decided to stay there for the winter. **13** Do your best to help Zenas the lawyer and Apollos to get on their way so that they have everything they need.

14 Our people should learn to be busy with ⌞good⌟ works in order to help in cases of real need, so that they do not waste their lives.

15 All who are here with me send greetings. Greet those who love us as fellow believers.

Grace be with you all!

PAUL WRITES TO
PHILEMON*a*

A. Opening greeting (1-3)

1 Paul, a prisoner of Christ Jesus, and Timothy our fellow Christian,*b* to Philemon our dear fellow worker, **2** to Apphia our sister ⌊in the faith⌋, to Archippus our fellow soldier, and to the church*c* that meets in your house: **3** May God our Father and the Lord Jesus Christ give you grace*d* and peace!

B. Philemon's love and faith (4-7)

4 I am always thanking my God when I mention you in my prayers, **5** because I hear how you believe in the Lord Jesus and love Him and all the believers [saints]. **6** I pray that the sharing of your faith may be effective in this way that you fully understand every good thing which we have in Christ. **7** Yes, your love delighted and encouraged me very much because you, my fellow Christian, have refreshed the hearts of the believers.

C. Plea in behalf of Onesimus (8-22)

8 For that reason, although I feel bold enough in Christ to order you to do what is right, **9** I prefer to make an appeal on the basis of love. I am appealing as*e* Paul, an old man and now a prisoner of Christ Jesus. **10** My appeal to you concerns my child Onesimus, who became my son while I was in chains. **11** Once he was useless to you, but now he is quite useful*f* both to you and to me.

12 I am sending him back to you—and my heart goes with him. **13** I would have liked to keep him with me in order to have him serve me in your place

---

a   *Philemon* is one of the Apostle Paul's "prison epistles" or "captivity letters"; it was written at the same time as *Colossians* and *Ephesians* (cf. Col. 4:7-9; Eph. 6:21) either in Rome about A.D. 61 or during his three year stay in Ephesus (cf. Acts 20:31) about A.D. 53-55.

b- 1 Literally: "brother" (also in vv. 7,16,20).

c- 2 Meaning "Christian people."

d- 3 Meaning "God's undeserved love" (also in v. 25).

e- 9 Literally: "Being such a one as."

f- 11 A play on words on the name Onesimus which means "useful."

while I am in chains for the Gospel [Good News], 14 but I do not want to do anything without your approval. I do not want you to be kind because you have to be but because you want to be.

15 Perhaps Onesimus left you for a while only to be yours again forever, 16 no longer as a slave but more than a slave, a fellow Christian, who is especially dear to me, but even more so to you, both as a fellow human being and as a brother in the Lord.*g*

17 Now if you think of me as your partner, welcome him as you would welcome me. 18 If he wronged you or owes you anything, charge it to me. 19 I, Paul, am writing this with my own hand—I will pay it back. I do not want to mention that you owe me more than that—your own self. 20 Yes, my fellow Christian, I would like to have some benefit from you in the Lord. Refresh my heart in Christ. 21 As I write to you, I am sure you will do this since I know that you will do even more than I ask.

22 One thing more: Have a guest room ready for me, because I hope by the prayers of all of you to be given back to you.

D. Conclusion (23-25)

23 Greetings to you from Epaphras my fellow prisoner in Christ Jesus, 24 and from my fellow workers: Mark, Aristarchus, Demas, Luke.

25 May the grace of the Lord Jesus Christ be with the spirit of all of you!*h* Amen.

---

g- 16 Literally: "both in the flesh and in the Lord."
h- 25 Literally: "with your spirit."

THE LETTER TO THE
HEBREWS[a]

1ST CHAPTER

A. Christ's superiority (1:1–3:6)
1. Christ is superior to the prophets (1:1-3)

1 At many times and in various ways, God—who long ago spoke to our fathers by the prophets—**2** has in these last days spoken to us by His Son, whom He made the Heir of everything and by whom He also made the world. **3** He who shines with God's glory and is the perfect copy of His Being maintains everything by His mighty word. After He had made a cleansing from sins, He *sat down at the right hand* of the Majesty in heaven.

2. Christ is superior to the angels (1:4–2:18)

4 Since He became so much better than the angels, He also inherited a Name that is more excellent than theirs. **5** For to which of the angels did God ever say:

> *"You are My Son;*
> *today I have begotten You"*?[b]

Or again:

> *"I will be His Father,*
> *and He will be My Son"*?

6 And again when He brings the firstborn Son into the world, He says:

> Let *all the angels of God worship Him.*

---

3 *Ps 110:1*   **5** *2 Sam 7:14; Ps 2:7*   **6** *Deut 32:43; Ps 97:7*

---

1 *a*   *Hebrews* was written by an *unknown* author to urge Jewish Christians to remain faithful to Christianity. The reason: The theme is that Christianity is "better" or "more excellent" (two key words of the letter) than what they had had in Judaism.

b - **5** Contrary to GWN's usual format of *not* using quotation marks around indented quotes, they are used here in verse 5 and also in verse 13 so that the *question marks* can stand *outside* and indicate that they do not go with the quote but rather with the introductory statements.

7 Of the angels He says:

> *He makes His angels winds*
> *and His servants fiery flames.*

8 But of the Son He says:

> *Your throne, O God, is forever and ever,*
> *and You rule Your Kingdom with a scepter of righteousness.*
> 9   *You have loved righteousness and hated lawlessness,*
> *that is why God, Your God, has put You above Your companions*
> *by anointing You with the Oil of Joy.*

10 And:

> *Lord, in the beginning You laid the foundation of the earth,*
> *and the heavens are the works of Your hands!*
> 11   *They will perish, but You continue.*
> *They will all become old like a garment,*
> 12   *You will roll them up like a blanket,*
> *and like a garment they will be changed;*
> *but You are the same,*
> *and Your years will never end.*

13 To which of the angels did He ever say:

> *"Sit at My right hand*
> *until I make Your enemies a footstool for Your feet"*?

14 Are not all angels spirits who serve, being sent to help those who are going to inherit salvation?

2ND CHAPTER

Do Not Neglect Your Salvation

1 That is why it is necessary that we listen all the more carefully to what we have been told, so that we do not drift away. 2 For if the word spoken through angels*a* was valid, and every trespass and disobedience received a just punishment, 3 how shall we escape if we neglect a salvation as great as this? First the Lord spoke of it, and then those who heard Him guaranteed its truth to us, 4 while God added His testimony by both miraculous signs and wonderful proofs, by different kinds of miracles,*b* and by distributing gifts of the Holy Spirit as He wished.

---

7 *Ps 104:4*   **8,9** *Ps 45:6,7*   **10-12** *Ps 102:25-27; Is 50:9; 51:6*   **13** *Ps 110:1*

---

2 *a-* 2 Compare Deuteronomy 33:2; Acts 7:53; Galatians 3:19.
   b - 4 See MIRACULOUS SIGNS, WONDERFUL PROOFS, and MIRACLES on page 527.

Lord Of Everything

5 He did not put the coming world about which we are talking under the control of angels. **6** But somewhere someone has declared:

> What is man that You should think of him,
>   or a son of man that You should care for him?^c

7 You made Him lower than the angels for a little while,
>   then crowned Him with glory and honor
>   and made Him Ruler over what Your hands have made^d
>   and put everything under His feet.^e

8

When *God put everything under His feet*, He left nothing outside His control.

Jesus Died For Us

At the present time we do not yet see *everything put under Him.*^f **9** But we do perceive that Jesus, who *for a little while was made lower than the angels, is now crowned with glory and honor* because He suffered death, so that by God's grace [undeserved love] He might taste death on behalf of everyone. **10** Yes, it fitted God well, for whom and by whom everything exists, that in leading many sons to glory He should make the Leader of their salvation perfect through suffering.

11 He who makes people holy and those who are made holy all have one father.^g That is why He is not ashamed to call them *brothers.* **12** He says:

> I will proclaim Your Name to My brothers;
>   in the congregation I will sing Your praise.

13 And again:

> I will trust Him.

And again:

> Here am I
>   and the children God has given Me.

6-9 *Ps 8:4-6*   **11,12** *Ps 22:22*   **13** *2 Sam 22:3; Ps 18:2; Is 8:17,18*

---

c- 6 Or "What is Man that You should think of Him,
>   or a Son of Man that You should care for Him?"
d- 7 A number of manuscripts omit this line.
e- 8 Or "You made him lower than the angels for a little while,
>   then crowned him with glory and honor
>   and made him ruler over what Your hands have made
>   and put everything under his feet."
f- 8 See 12:9 and its accompanying footnote in relation to the concept "put . . . under" in verses 5 and 8.
g- 11 The writer very likely is referring to Adam.

14 Now since all these *children* share flesh and blood, He also took on flesh and blood to be like them, so that by His death He might take away all the power of him who had the power of death (that is, the devil), **15** and thus He might free those who were subjected to slavery all their lives by their fear of death. **16** It is clear that He did not *come to help* angels. Rather, He *helps the descendants of Abraham.* **17** And so in every way He had the obligation to become like His brothers, so that He might be a merciful and faithful High Priest in representing them before God[h] and thus pay for the sins[i] of the people. **18** Furthermore, because He Himself experienced testing when He suffered, He is able to help others when they are tested.

3RD CHAPTER

3. Christ is superior to Moses (3:1-6)

1 Therefore, fellow Christians,[a] who are holy and share the heavenly calling, consider Jesus, the Apostle and High Priest whom we confess. **2** He was faithful to Him who appointed Him, just as *Moses was faithful in God's whole house.* **3** To be sure, He deserves greater glory than Moses, just as the builder of a house is honored more than the house. **4** You see, every house is built by someone, but He who built everything is God.

5 Now, *Moses was faithful in God's whole house* as *a servant* who was to testify of what would be said later, **6** but Christ is faithful as a Son in charge of *God's house.* We are His house if we continue unshaken in our courage and in the hope of which we boast.

(Warning about unbelief, 3:7–4:13)

Do Not Make Your Hearts Stubborn

7 And so, as the Holy Spirit says:

> *Today, if you hear Him speak,*
> **8**   *do not make your hearts stubborn[b]*
>   *as happened when the people rebelled*
>   *at the time they tested Me in the wilderness,*
> **9**   *where your fathers put Me to a test*
>   *when they saw My works for forty years.[c]*

14-16 Is 41:8,9   *2-6 Num 12:7*   *7-18 Num 14:22,29; Ps 95:7-11*

h- 17 Literally: "in respect to the things before God" (cf. Ex. 18:19 where the high priest represented the people before God).

i- 17 Jesus covers our sins with His blood and thus appeases the anger of God.

3 a- 1 Literally: "brothers" (also in v. 12).

b- 8 Literally: "do not harden your hearts" (similarly in 3:13,15; 4:7); compare Mark 3:5 and its accompanying footnote as well as Exodus 4:21.

c- 9 The traditional verse division would start verse 10 with the words: "For forty years . . . ."

10 That was why I was angry with those people, and I said:

> *In their hearts they are always going astray,*
> *and they have not known My ways.*
> 11   *So because I was angry, I swore*
> *that they would never come to My place of rest!*

12 See to it, fellow Christians, that none of you has a wicked heart which in unbelief turns away from the living God. 13 Rather, encourage one another day by day, as long as *"today"* lasts, that none of you *may become stubborn* through the deception of sin. 14 For we share in Christ only if we keep our first confidence unshaken to the end.

15 When it says:

> *Today, if you hear Him speak,*
> *do not make your hearts stubborn*
> *as the people did when they rebelled—*

16 who were those that heard Him and *rebelled*? Were they not all those whom Moses led out of Egypt? 17 With whom was He *angry for 40 years*? Was it not with those who sinned and whose *bodies dropped dead in the wilderness*? 18 To whom did He *swear that they would not come to His place of rest* if not to those who were unbelieving? 19 So we see that they could not come there since they did not believe.

4TH CHAPTER

There Is A Rest For Us

1 We should be aware of the situation then, that although we still have the promise of coming to His place of rest, one or the other of you may imagine that he is excluded. 2 The fact is that we have the same Gospel [Good News] preached to us as they did, but the message they heard did not help them because those who heard it did not combine their hearing with faith.

3 We who have believed *are coming to His place of rest*, just as He has said:

> *So I swore in My anger*
> *that they would never come to My place of rest.*

And yet God finished His work when He made the world, 4 because somewhere He spoke thus concerning the seventh day:

> *On the seventh day*
> *God rested from all His work.*

5 And in this passage again:

---

3 Num 14:23; Ps 95:7-11   4 Gen 2:2

> They will never come
> to My place of rest.

6 Now, it is still true that some *are coming to His place of rest*, although those who once had the Gospel preached to them did not come *into it* because they did not believe; 7 so He again sets another day—"*today*"—when long afterwards He says in David's words, already quoted:

> Today, if you hear Him speak,
> do not make your hearts stubborn.

8 For if Joshua had given them rest, God would not later[a] have spoken of another day. 9 So there is still a Sabbath rest for the people of God, 10 since anyone who *comes to His rest finds rest from his work* as God did *from His.*

11 Let us be diligent then to *come to* that *rest,* so that no one may fall by following the same pattern of unbelief.

The Living Word

12 You see, the word of God is living and active. It cuts better than any two-edged sword; it penetrates until it divides soul and spirit, joints and marrow. And it can judge the inner thoughts and intentions of the heart. 13 No creature can hide from Him. Everything is uncovered and exposed to the eyes of Him to whom we must give an account.

B. Christ's priesthood is superior to the Levitical priesthood (4:14–7:28)

Our High Priest

14 Now that we have a great High Priest who has gone through the heavens, Jesus the Son of God, let us cling to what we confess. 15 For we do not have a High Priest who is unable to sympathize with our weaknesses. He was tempted in every way just as we are—⌐yet He remained¬ without sin. 16 So let us come boldly to the throne of grace to receive mercy and find grace to help us when we need it.

5TH CHAPTER

Christ Our High Priest Compared To Melchizedek

1 Any high priest selected from men is appointed to represent them before God, that he may bring gifts and sacrifices on behalf of their sins. 2 He can be gentle with ignorant and erring people, because he too is troubled with weak-

---

5-10 Num 14:23; Ps 95:7-11   *10 Gen 2:2*   *11 Num 14:22; Ps 95:7-11*

4 *a-* 8 David lived around 400 years after Joshua's time.

ness; **3** and for that reason he has an obligation to bring sacrifices for his own sins, just as he does for the sins of his people.

4 No one takes the honor of this office for himself, but God calls him as He called Aaron. **5** So also Christ did not take the glory of being a High Priest for Himself, but it was given to Him by the One who said to Him:

> You are My Son;
>> today I have begotten You.

6 So He also said in another place:

> You are a Priest forever
>> according to the nature of Melchizedek's priesthood. *a*

7 During His life on earth*b* Jesus—while crying loudly with tears—offered prayers and pleas to Him who could save Him from death; and because He feared God, He was heard. **8** Although Jesus was the Son, *c* He learned obedience from the things which He suffered. **9** And when He was made perfect, He became the Source who gives *everlasting salvation* to all who obey Him, *d* **10** being proclaimed by God a High *Priest "according to the nature of Melchizedek's priesthood."*

More Than ABC's

11 We have much to say about this, but it is difficult to explain, because you have become so lazy in listening ˻to God's word˼. **12** At a time when you in fact ought to be teachers you need someone to teach you the ABC's of God's word;*e* you have come to need milk instead of solid food. **13** Everyone who lives on milk is not acquainted with the message of righteousness, for he is still a baby. **14** But solid food is for mature people, whose senses are trained by practice to distinguish good from evil.

6TH CHAPTER

1 Let us leave behind the ABC's of Christ's teaching, and let us rush on to maturity. Let us not again repeat the fundamental teachings: of turning away from dead works, of faith in God, **2** of teaching about baptisms, of laying on of hands, of the rising of the dead, and of everlasting judgment—**3** and if God permits we will do this.

---

5 Ps 2:7   6 Ps 110:4   9 Is 45:17   10 Ps 110:4

---

5 *a-* 6 Literally: "in the order of Melchizedek" (also in v. 10; 6:20; 7:11,17).
 b- 7 Literally: "in the days of His flesh" (cf. Rom. 1:3; 1 Pet. 3:18).
 c- 8 Or "Although Jesus was a son"; this alternate reading would see our present verse as a reference to verse 7a, emphasizing Jesus as a human being; the reading in the text would relate to verse 5 where Jesus is called "Son."
 d- 9 Meaning "the obedience created by faith" (cf. Rom. 1:5).
 e- 12 Or "the elementary truths of the words of God" (cf. 6:1).

4 It is impossible for those who once had the light and tasted the gift from heaven, who had the Holy Spirit just as others did **5** and tasted the goodness of the word of God and the powers of the coming age—**6** ˌit is impossibleˌ when they fall away to bring them back to repentance. ˌIt is impossibleˌ because they to their own undoing crucify the Son of God again and hold Him up to mockery. **7** For when the *earth* drinks in the rain that often falls on it and when it *produces plants* that can be used by those for whom it is worked, it is blessed by God. **8** But if *it produces thorns and thistles*, it is worthless and a *curse* hangs over it; its end is destruction by fire.

9 Although we say this, we are convinced, dear friends, that there are better things in store for you, things which mean salvation. **10** For God is not so unjust as to forget your work and the love you showed for His Name as you helped His believers [saints] and still continue to help them. **11** We want every one of you to show the same zeal, so that your hope may be certain until the end. **12** We want you to do this so that you do not become lazy but imitate those who by believing and being patient are inheriting what is promised.

13 God made a promise to Abraham, and since He had no one greater to swear by, He *swore by Himself* **14** and said:

> *I will certainly bless you*
> *and make you a great people.*

15 And so, after waiting patiently, Abraham received what God promised.

16 People swear by someone greater, and their oath guarantees what they say and brings an end to every dispute. **17** When God wanted to make it perfectly clear to those who were the heirs of His promise,[a] ˌnamely,ˌ that He would not change His plan, He bound Himself with an oath. **18** ˌHe did thisˌ so that we, who have found safety in Him, would have two unalterable things in which God cannot lie,[b] to give us strong encouragement toˊtake hold of the hope set before us. **19** We have this hope like an anchor for our souls, ˌa hopeˌ which is sure and strong and which *goes behind the curtain,*[c] **20** where Jesus, as a Forerunner on our behalf, has entered in, having become a High *Priest forever* "*according to the nature of Melchizedek's priesthood.*"

7TH CHAPTER

A Priest Forever

1 This *Melchizedek, king of Salem* and *priest of the Most High God*, met

---

7 *Gen 1:11,12*   8 *Gen 3:17,18*   **13,14** *Gen 22:16,17*   **19** *Lev 16:2,12*   **20** *Ps 110:4*
1,2 *Gen 14:17-20*

---

6 *a-* 17 Literally: "to the heirs of the promise."
 b- 18 That is, the promise and the oath of God, "who never lies" (Tit. 1:2).
 c- 19 A reference to the "curtain" in the Tabernacle behind which God symbolically hid His presence. In Christ we can reach behind the curtain and by faith be close to Him. See Diagram #1 on page 430.

Abraham coming back from defeating the kings. He blessed Abraham. 2 *And Abraham gave him a tenth of everything.* His name, in the first place, means *"king of righteousness,"* but then he is also called *"king of Salem,"* that is, *"king of peace."* 3 There is no record of his, father, mother, or line of ancestors, of the beginning of his days or the end of his life. *a* But since he is compared to the Son of God, *b* he continues *a priest forever.* *c*

4 See how great he was! *Abraham gave him a tenth* from the best of the spoils, even Abraham who was the father *d* of the chosen people! 5 And the Law orders those descendants of Levi who become priests to receive a tenth from the people, that is, from other Israelites, *e* although they, too, are descendants of Abraham. 6 But this man, who was outside their line of descent, received *a tenth* from *Abraham* and *blessed him* who had the promises. 7 No one can deny that the higher [better] one blesses the lower.

8 Also in the one case people who die receive a tenth, but in the other case the tenth is received by him who is declared as still living. 9 And we may say that Levi, who receives a tenth, in *Abraham gave a tenth*, 10 since he was still in the body of his ancestor when *Melchizedek* met him.

11 Levi's descendants were the priests; on this basis the Law was given to the people. Now, if the priests who descended from Levi could have given us perfection, why did God say another *Priest* still needed to come *"according to the nature of Melchizedek's priesthood,"f* rather than according to Aaron's priesthood? 12 Now when the priesthood is changed, the Law also has to be changed. 13 For the One of whom these things are said belongs to a different tribe which has never had a priest serving at the altar. 14 For everyone knows our Lord descended from Judah, but Moses said nothing about priests in regard to this tribe. 15 That point is much clearer still when we see a different *Priest* appear exactly *like Melchizedek,* 16 not appointed because He fulfills a certain, regulation that says He must be someone's descendant, but because He has the power of a life that cannot be destroyed. 17 For this declaration is made about Him: "You are a *Priest forever 'according to the nature of Melchizedek's priest-hood.'"* 18 The foregoing rule is canceled since it is weak and cannot help us because 19 the Law made nothing perfect; there is also the introduction of a better hope by which we continue to come close to God.

---

3 Ps 110:4   *4-10 Gen 14:17-20*   *11-28 Ps 2:7*

---

7 *a-* 3 All these records served as credentials for the person who held the position of high priest (cf. Ezra 2:62f.; Neh. 7:63f.).

 b- 3 Melchizedek is able to be compared to Jesus on the basis that Scripture does not contain any record of his coming into existence or of his death, just as Jesus' Person is eternal and supercedes human records. As such, both Melchizedek and Jesus are priests who have different qualifications than those priests descended from the tribe of Levi (cf. Ps. 110 and vv. 4-10 of our present chapter).

 c- 3 The concept of a priesthood that lasts beyond death is a New Testament concept already present in the Old Testament when the Israelites are called a nation of priests. This concept is emphasized especially in the book of *Revelation* (20:6).

 d- 4 Literally: "Abraham was the patriarch." (The word "patriarch" has an emphatic position in the Greek.)

 e- 5 Literally: "brothers."

 f- 11 See 5:6 and its accompanying footnote.

20 Since this priesthood was not established without an oath—

> For when those men [the Levites] were made priests, there was no oath. **21** But when Jesus was appointed, God took an oath, as He said to Him: *"The Lord has sworn and will not change His mind: 'You are a Priest forever.' "*

22 —therefore Jesus is established as the Guarantee of a better "last will and testament."[g]

23 Once many were made priests because death did not let them continue as priests. **24** But because Jesus lives forever, His is an *unchanging priesthood.* **25** And so He can forever save those who come to God by Him, because He always lives to pray for them.

26 Here is the High Priest we needed—holy, innocent, spotless, separated from sinners, and made higher than the heavens. **27** He does not need to bring sacrifices every day like those high priests, first for His own sins, then for the sins of the people. For He did this once and for all when He sacrificed Himself. **28** For the Law appointed weak men to be high priests, but God's *oath,*[h] which came after the Law, appointed the *Son,* who was made perfect *forever.*

8TH CHAPTER

C. Christ's sacrifice is superior
to the animals sacrificed by the Levitical priests (8:1–10:39)

A New And Better "Last Will And Testament"

1 Now, this is my main point. We have such a High Priest, and He *sat down at the right hand* of the throne of the Majesty in heaven **2** to serve as Priest of the SACRED PLACE[a] and of the true[b] TABERNACLE *set up by the Lord,* not by men. **3** To be sure, as every high priest is appointed to offer gifts and sacrifices, this One also had to bring some sacrifice.

4 If He were on earth, He would not even be a priest, because there are priests who offer the gifts according to the Law. **5** They serve as a pattern and a shadow of what is in heaven, as God warned Moses when he was going to make the Tabernacle: *"Be careful to make* all of it ˴exactly˴ *like*[c] *the model you were shown on the mountain."*

6 Now, just as the priestly work that Jesus was given to do is more excellent, so also the "last will and testament"[d] of which He is the Mediator is a better one, because God has based it on better promises. **7** Indeed, if that first ˴covenant˴

---

28 *Ps 110:4*   1 *Ps 110:1*   2 *Num 24:5,6*   5 *Ex 25:9,40; 26:30; 27:8*

g - 22 See *DIATHĒKĒ* on page 531.
h - 28 Literally: "but the word of the oath" (cf. v. 21).
8 a - 2 See THE HOLY PLACES on page 550 and compare "the sacred place" (Diagram #1 on page 430) with its heavenly counterpart in the present text.
b - 2 Literally: "*alēthinēs*"; see *ALĒTHINOS* COMPARED WITH *ALĒTHĒS* on page 530.
c - 5 Compare Exodus 25:9.
d - 6 See *DIATHĒKĒ* on page 531. This also applies to verses 7,8,10, and 13.

had been without fault, no one would have wanted to make room for a second one. **8** But God is finding fault with them when He says:

> *See! The time is coming, says the Lord, when I will set up a new "last will and testament" [new covenant] for the people of Israel and the people of Judah,* **9** *not like the covenant[e] that I made with their fathers when I took them by the hand to lead them out of Egypt, because they did not continue in My covenant. And so I turned away from them, says the Lord.* **10** *The "last will and testament" [covenant] that I will decree for the people of Israel after those days, says the Lord, is this: I will put My laws into their minds and write them on their hearts, and I will be their God, and they will be My people.* **11** *No more will each one teach his fellow citizen or his brother and say, "Know the Lord!" For they will all know Me from the least to the greatest of them,* **12** *because I will forgive their wrongdoing and no longer remember their sins.*

13 By calling it a "'new' ⌊last will and testament⌋," He has made the first ⌊covenant⌋ "old." What is "old" and is growing older is at the point of disappearing.

9TH CHAPTER

The Tabernacle

1 The first ⌊covenant⌋ had its regulations for worship and for the earthly sacred place.[a] **2** A Tabernacle was set up. In the first part were the lampstand, the table, and the bread set out ⌊before God⌋; this is called the Holy Place.[b] **3** Behind the second curtain was the part of the Tabernacle called the Most Holy Place[c] **4** with the golden altar of incense and the ark of the covenant, completely covered with gold. In the ark were the golden jar containing the manna, Aaron's rod that had budded, and the tablets on which the covenant[d] was written. **5** Above it were the angels [cherubim] of glory overshadowing the "*atonement cover*"[e]—I cannot at this time go into detail about these.

6 But that is how it was arranged. The priests are always going into the first

---

8-12 *Jer 31:31-34*   5 *Lev 16:2*

---

e- 9 See *DIATHĒKĒ* on page 531.
9 *a*- 1 See THE HOLY PLACES on page 550, and compare "the sacred place" of Diagram #1 on page 430.
b- 2 See this area as referred to on Diagram #1 on page 430.
c- 3 See this area as referred to on Diagram #1 on page 430.
d- 4 See *DIATHĒKĒ* on page 531.
e- 5 See Diagram #1 on page 430 and Diagram #2 on page 438. Blood was sprinkled on the "atonement cover" to cover sin.

part of the Tabernacle to carry out the worship of God, **7** but only the high priest goes into the second part once a year, ⌊but⌋ not without blood, which he offers for himself and for the sins which the people have done in ignorance. **8** By this the Holy Spirit clearly tells us that the way into the MOST HOLY PLACE*f* had not yet been thrown open as long as the first Tabernacle was still standing.

9 This is a picture which pointed to the time in which we live. Because it is only a picture, the gifts and sacrifices which are brought cannot make the worshiper feel perfect in his conscience; **10** they concern only food and drink and various baptisms, which are regulations imposed upon the body until the time of the new order.

Jesus' Blood

11 But Christ came as a High Priest of the good things that have come; He went through that greater and more perfect TABERNACLE not made by human hands (that is, not a part of our created world). **12** And He did not use the blood of goats and calves, but with His own blood He entered once and for all into the MOST HOLY PLACE*g* and paid a price that frees us forever.*h* **13** Now, if sprinkling the blood of goats and bulls and the ashes of a calf on unclean people makes them outwardly holy and clean, **14** how much more will the blood of Christ, who by the everlasting Spirit offered Himself without spot to God, wash our consciences clean from dead works so that we may worship the living God?

15 For this reason He is the Mediator of a " 'new' last will and testament."*i* By dying He paid the ransom to free people from the sins under the first covenant.*j* He did this so that those who are called might receive the promise of an eternal inheritance. **16** For where there is a "last will and testament," it must be shown that the one who made it has died, **17** since a "last will and testament" takes effect only when a person is dead. It is not in force as long as the one who made it is still living. **18** That is why even the first ⌊covenant⌋ was not dedicated without blood. **19** Yes, when *Moses* had told all the people every commandment of the Law, he *took the blood* of calves and goats together with some water, scarlet wool, and hyssop, *and he sprinkled* the scroll and *all the people*. **20** He said:

> This is the blood of the covenant
> which God has ordered you to keep.

21 In the same way he sprinkled blood on the Tabernacle and on everything used in the worship. **22** According to the Law almost everything is cleansed by blood, and if no blood is poured out, no sins are forgiven.

19,20 Ex 24:8

f - 8 See THE HOLY PLACES on page 550, and compare the "Most Holy Place" (Diagram #1 on page 430) with its heavenly counterpart in the present text.

g - 12 See THE HOLY PLACES on page 550, and compare the "Most Holy Place" (Diagram #1 on page 430) with its heavenly counterpart in the present text.

h - 12 Or "PLACE, having obtained eternal redemption."

i - 15 See *DIATHĒKĒ* on page 531. This also applies to verses 16 and 17.

j - 15 See *DIATHĒKĒ* on page 531. This also applies to verse 20.

One Perfect Sacrifice

23 Now the patterns of the things in heaven had to be cleansed by these sacrifices, but the heavenly things themselves needed better sacrifices. **24** For Christ did not go into sacred places[k] made by human hands, which are a representation of the real[l] thing, but into heaven itself, to appear now before God for us. **25** He did not go there to sacrifice Himself over and over again like the high priest who every year goes into the Most Holy Place[m] with blood that is not his own. **26** Otherwise, He would have had to suffer many times since the world was made. But now He has appeared once at the end of the ages to set aside sin by His sacrifice. **27** And just as people are appointed to die once and after that comes judgment, **28** so Christ also was sacrificed once to *take away the sins of many people*. And to those who eagerly look for Him, He will appear a second time, not to deal with sin but to bring salvation to them.

10TH CHAPTER

The Ineffectiveness Of Animal Sacrifices

1 The Law, which has only a dim outline of the good things in the future and not their substance, can never—by the same sacrifices repeatedly offered year after year—make perfect those who worship. **2** Otherwise would they not have stopped bringing sacrifices? Once cleansed, the worshipers would no longer be aware of any sins. **3** Instead, year after year these sacrifices reminded people of their sins. **4** For the blood of bulls and goats cannot take away sins.

5 That is why He [Christ] says when He comes into the world:

> *You did not want sacrifice and offering,*
> *but You prepared a body for Me.*

6   *Burnt offerings and sacrifices for sin did not please You.*
7   *Then I said: Look! I have come.*[a]
> *(The writing in the scroll of the book tells about Me.)*
> ⌊*I am here*⌋ *to do Your "will," O God.*

8 First He [Christ] says: "*You did not want and You were not* pleased *with sacrifices, offerings, burnt offerings, and sacrifices for sin* which are offered according to the Law." **9** Then He adds: "*Look! I have come to do Your 'will.' "* He does away with the first in order to establish the second. **10** It is because of

---

28 *Is 53:12*   5-10 *Ps 40:6-8 (Greek)*

---

k- 24 See THE HOLY PLACES on page 550.
l- 24 See *ALĒTHINOS* COMPARED WITH *ALĒTHĒS* on page 530.
m- 25 See THE HOLY PLACES on page 550, and note the "Most Holy Place" on Diagram #1 on page 430.
10 *a-* 7 Note that these words continue the quote of Psalm 40, as Jesus Himself says: "Then I said: Look! I have come."

this *"will"* that we are made holy by the *sacrifice* of the *body* of Jesus Christ once and for all.

11 Every other priest stands and serves day after day, and over and over again brings the same sacrifices, which can never take away sins. **12** But He made one sacrifice for sins, which is good forever, and then *sat down at the right hand of God*. **13** Since that time, He is waiting *for His enemies to be made a footstool for His feet*. **14** For by one sacrifice He made perfect forever those who are being made holy.

15 The Holy Spirit assures us of this. For after He says:

16   *This is the "last will and testament" [covenant]*[b] *that*
        I will make with them after those days, says the Lord:
        I will put My laws on their hearts
        and write them on their minds;

17 then He adds:

    I will not remember their sins
        and their rebellious actions anymore.

18 Now, where sins are forgiven, there is no more sacrificing for sin.

19 Fellow Christians,[c] with the blood of Jesus we can now go boldly into the MOST HOLY PLACE[d] **20** by the new, living way that He opened for us through the curtain, that is, through His body, **21** and we have a *great Priest* in charge of *God's house*.[e] **22** Let us then go in, with a heart filled with the genuine[f] conviction of faith, because our hearts were sprinkled to take away our guilty feelings, and our bodies were washed with clean water. **23** Let us cling to the confession of our hope without wavering, for He who made the promise is faithful.

Give Up Sin

24 And let us consider how we can stimulate one another to love and to do good works. **25** We do this not by staying away from our worship services,[g] as some are regularly doing, but by continuing to encourage one another—and this all the more as you see the Day coming nearer.

26 If we willfully go on sinning after we have learned the truth, there is no longer a sacrifice which remains ⌊to be made⌋ for sin, **27** only a terrible waiting for judgment and *an eager fire that will devour the enemies* of God. **28** Anyone who violated the Law of Moses *died* without pity *on the testimony of two or*

12,13 Ps 110:1   *16,17 Jer 31:33,34*   *21 Zech 6:11-13*   *27 Is 26:11*   *28 Deut 17:6*

---

b- 16 See *DIATHĒKĒ* on page 531. This also applies to verse 29.
c- 19 Literally: "brothers."
d- 19 See THE HOLY PLACES on page 550.
e- 21 Meaning that Christ is in charge of the house and its family of believers who inhabit it by faith.
f- 22 See *ALĒTHINOS* COMPARED WITH *ALĒTHĒS* on page 530.
g- 25 Literally: "not forsaking the meeting together of ourselves."

three witnesses. **29** How much greater a punishment do you think that person will deserve who tramples on God's Son, treats as an unholy thing *the blood of the "last will and testament"* that made him holy, and insults the Spirit of grace? **30** For we know Him who said:

> *I have the right to punish;*
> *I will pay back;*

and again:

> *The Lord will judge His people.*

31 It is terrifying to fall into the hands of the living God.

Endure

32 Remember those earlier days, when, after you had received the light, you patiently endured a hard and painful struggle. **33** Mocked at times and mistreated, you were made a public spectacle; at times you shared the life of those who were treated that way. **34** For example, you sympathized with the prisoners, and when you were robbed of your property, you took it cheerfully because you know you have better and permanent possessions. *h*

35 Therefore, do not lose your courage. There is a great reward for it. **36** To be sure, you need patient endurance *i* so that after you have done the will of God you might receive what He promised.

> **37**   *For soon, so very soon—He who is coming will come and will not delay,*
> **38**   *and by faith My righteous one will live;*
>   *but if he shrinks back, I will not be pleased with him.*

39 Now, we are not a part of those who *shrink back* and so are lost, but of those who have *faith* and so are saved.

11 TH CHAPTER

D. The triumphs of faith (11:1-40)

God's Men And Women Of Faith

1 Faith is being sure of the things we hope for, being convinced of the things we cannot see. **2** For it was on the basis of this kind of faith that the men of long ago won ⌊God's⌋ approval.

---

29 Ex 24:8   *30 Deut 32:35,36; Ps 135:14*   *37 Is 26:20*   *37-39 Hab 2:3,4*

h- 34 Some of the older manuscripts and early translations add: "in heaven."
i - 36 Compare Romans 15:4; 2 Corinthians 6:4-10.

3 By faith we know that God created the world by His word so that what we see was not made from what can be seen.

4 By faith *Abel offered* a richer sacrifice to God than Cain, and by faith he was approved as righteous when *God* approved of *his offerings.* He died, but through his faith he is still speaking to us.

5 By faith *Enoch* was taken away so that he would not face death, and he *could not be found, because God had taken him.* For before he was taken, it was declared that *God was pleased with him.* **6** It is impossible to *please* God without faith. Yes, if anyone comes to God, he must believe that God exists and rewards those who search for Him.

7 By faith Noah, when he was warned about the things that no one could foresee, respected God and built an ark to save his family. By this faith he condemned the world and became an heir of the righteousness that comes by faith. *a*

8 By faith *Abraham* obeyed when he was called to *go* to a place that he would receive as an inheritance, and he went without knowing where he was going. **9** By faith he *lived as a stranger* in the Promised Land, as though it belonged to someone else. He lived in tents with Isaac and Jacob, who were heirs together with him of the same promise. **10** He did all this because he was looking for the city with foundations, the one designed and built by God. **11** By faith Sarah, even though she was too old, was given the ability to have a child because she believed she could trust Him who had promised. *b* **12** And so, although he was physically unable to have a child, one man had *many* descendants, *as many as the stars in the sky and the sand on the seashore which no one can count.*

13 One by one these all died in faith without having received what was promised. But they saw it far ahead and welcomed it, and they confessed that they were *strangers and pilgrims* on earth. **14** To be sure, those who talk that way show that they are looking for a land of their own. **15** If their hearts had been in the land which they had left, they could have found an opportunity to go back. **16** Instead, they were longing for a better land—I mean heaven. That is why God is not ashamed to be called their God, because He has prepared a city for them.

17 By faith *Abraham,* when he was *tested, offered* Isaac. Yes, this man, who received the promises, was offering *his only son* *c* **18** about whom God had said: *"Isaac's children will be called your descendants."* **19** He was thinking: "God can even raise him from the dead." And so, figuratively speaking, he did get him back from the dead.

20 By faith Isaac blessed Jacob and Esau in regard to their future. **21** By faith a dying Jacob blessed each of Joseph's sons and *worshiped, leaning on the top of his staff.* **22** By faith Joseph, when his end was near, remembered how the

---

4 Gen 4:4   5,6 Gen 5:24   8,9 Gen 12:1,4; 23:4; 47:9   12 Gen 15:5; 22:17; 32:12
13 Gen 12:1,4; 23:4; 47:9   17 Gen 22:1,2,10,12   18 Gen 21:12   21 Gen 47:31

---

11 *a*- 7 Literally: "and became heir of the righteousness that is according to faith."
   b- 11 This verse can also be translated: "By faith he [Abraham] was given the ability to have a child, even though he was too old and Sarah was unable to bear a child, because he believed he could trust Him who had promised."
   c- 17 See *MONOGENES* on page 542.

Israelites would leave Egypt, and he gave directions as to what they should do with his bones. *d*

23 By faith, when Moses was born, his parents *hid him three months* because *they saw that he was a fine baby*, and they were not afraid of the king's order. 24 By faith *Moses, when he grew up*, refused to be called a son of Pharaoh's daughter 25 and preferred being mistreated with God's people rather than enjoying the short-lived pleasures of sin. 26 He considered the *abuse* suffered for *Christ* greater riches than the treasures of Egypt, because he was looking ahead to the reward.

27 By faith he left Egypt without fearing the king's anger; for he persisted as one who was constantly seeing Him who cannot be seen. 28 By faith he celebrated the *Passover* and sprinkled the *bloode* to keep him who *destroyed* the firstborn from touching his people. 29 By faith they went through the Red Sea as if it were dry land. The Egyptians tried it also, but they were drowned.

30 By faith the walls of Jericho fell after the people marched around them seven days. 31 By faith the prostitute Rahab welcomed the spies as friends and so did not perish with the disobedient people.

32 And what more should I say? There will not be time enough for me to tell about Gideon, Barak, Samson, Jephthah, David, Samuel, and the prophets, 33 who by faith conquered kingdoms, did righteous works, received what was promised, shut the mouths of lions, 34 put out raging fires, escaped death by the sword, found strength when weak, proved to be mighty in battle, put foreign armies to flight. 35 Women received their dead back alive. Some were tortured; they refused their release in order to rise to a better life. 36 Others suffered mocking and whipping and were even put in chains and in prison. 37 They were stoned, tempted,*f* sawed in half,*g* murdered with a sword. They went around in sheepskins and goatskins, needy, oppressed, mistreated. 38 The world was not worthy of them as they wandered around in deserts and in the hills, in caves and holes in the ground.

39 By faith all these won approval, but they did not receive what was promised, 40 since God planned something better for us, in order that they might not reach their goal without us.

12TH CHAPTER

E. The application to the present trials (12:1-29)

Run The Race

1 Now then, with all these witnesses around us like a cloud, let us also rid ourselves of every burden and the sin into which we easily fall and with patient

---

23 Ex 2:2   *24 Ex 2:11*   *26 Ps 69:9; 89:50,51*   *28 Ex 12:12,13*

---

d- 22 Literally: "and gave orders concerning his bones."
e- 28 That is, on the doorposts.
f- 37 A papyrus and some of the early translations omit: "tempted."
g- 37 Tradition says that this happened to Isaiah the prophet.

endurance run the race that is laid out before us, [2] looking to Jesus, who gives us our faith from start to finish.[a] For the joy that was set before Him, He endured the cross, thinking nothing of its shame, and *sat down at the right hand of God's throne.*

[3] Consider Him who patiently endured such opposition from sinners, so that you do not grow tired and give up. [4] In your struggle against sin you have not yet resisted to the point of shedding your blood. [5] And you have forgotten the encouragement spoken to you as sons:

> *My son, do not think lightly of the Lord's discipline*[b]
> *or give up when He corrects you.*
>
> 6 *For whom the Lord loves He disciplines,*
> *and He gives punishment to everyone whom He accepts as His son.*

[7] Endure ₍suffering₎ as a *discipline.* God is treating you *as* His *sons.* For is there *a son* whom his father does not *discipline?* [8] All sons are *disciplined;* if you are not given discipline you are *not sons* but are illegitimate. [9] Furthermore, our natural fathers used to discipline us, and we respected them. Should we not much more be subordinate[c] to the Father of spirits and live? [10] They disciplined us for a short time as it seemed best to them. But He disciplines us for our good, to have us share His holiness. [11] While we are being disciplined, it always seems painful, rather than joyful. But for those who have gone through it,[d] discipline gives a return of the peaceful fruit of righteousness.

[12] And so, *if your hands are letting go, take a firm hold; if you feel weak in your knees, stand firm,* [13] and *smooth out the paths for your feet.* Do this so that the crippled limb will not be dislocated, but will be made well.

[14] *Keep on striving to live in peace* with everybody and to do what is holy. Without this no one will see the Lord. [15] See to it that no one loses God's grace, *that no root with bitter fruit grows up to trouble you* and so defiles many of you, [16] that no one lives in sexual sin or is unholy like *Esau,* who for one meal *sold his rights as the firstborn.* [17] For you know that later, when he wanted to inherit

---

2 Ps 110:1   **5-8** Job 5:17; Prov 3:11,12   **12,13** Prov 4:26; Is 35:3   **14** Ps 34:14
15 Deut 29:18   **16** Gen 25:33,34

---

12 a- 2 Literally: "Jesus, the Author and Finisher of our faith."

b- 5 The Greek word *"paideia"* includes all that a parent does in bringing up a child in a proper way. It includes instruction, guidance, and discipline when necessary. The writer of *Hebrews* uses this term throughout verses 5-11.

c- 9 Greek: *"hupotassō."* This Greek term speaks of persons who are placed in an "order" or "rank" below or under the authority of another. In the mind of sinful human beings this is often falsely equated with *inferiority.* However, Jesus taught us that among Christians this is not to be the case. It is not the one in authority who is the greatest but the one who is servant to all (Matt. 20:25-28; Mk. 10:42-45); authority and servitude are always to be used for the benefit of others.
The English "subordinate" captures the totality of this *hupotassō* concept quite well. In the passage before us the writer of *Hebrews* uses the word in terms of *all Christians* as they are placed under the Father into a lower rank or order. Compare 2:5,8 where the Greek term is used *three* times and is translated "put . . . under." Another form of the same Greek word is translated "outside His control" in 2:8. See *HUPOTASSO* on page 541.

d- 11 Literally: "who have been trained in it."

the blessing, he was rejected. To be sure, he had no chance to bring about a change of mind,[e] although he begged for it with tears.

You Have Come To God

18 *You did not come to ˌa mountainˌ[f] that you could touch, blazing with fire, covered by darkness, gloomy and stormy,* 19 *to the blast of a trumpet, or the speaking of a voice.* Those who heard that voice begged to hear no more, 20 because they could not endure the order that was given: *"Even an animal, if it touches the mountain, must be stoned."* 21 The sight was so terrible that even Moses said, *"I am terrified and trembling."*

22 Rather, you have come to MOUNT ZION, the CITY of the living God, the heavenly JERUSALEM. Here are tens of thousands of angels, the whole festival gathering 23 and an assembly of God's firstborn people whose names are written in heaven. Here is the Judge, the God of all. Here are the spirits of the righteous who have been made perfect. 24 And here is Jesus, the Mediator of the new "last will and testament,"[g] and here is the sprinkled blood that has better things to say than Abel's.

25 See that you do not refuse to listen to Him who is speaking. For if they[h] did not escape when they refused to listen to Him who was warning them on earth, much less will we if we turn away from Him who warns us from heaven. 26 At that time His voice shook the earth. But now He has promised:

> *Once more I will shake* not only the *earth*
> but also *heaven.*

27 The words *"once more"* show clearly that He will take away what is *shaken,* seeing He made it, leaving what is not *shaken* as permanent. 28 Since we have received a Kingdom that cannot be *shaken,* let us be thankful and so serve Him in a way that pleases Him, with fear and awe, 29 because our *God is a consuming fire.*

13TH CHAPTER

F. Concluding advice and encouragement (13:1-25)

Live As Christians

1 Let brotherly love continue. 2 Do not forget to show hospitality, for this is how some entertained angels without ˌevenˌ knowing it. 3 Remember those in

---

18-20 Ex 19:12,13,16; Deut 4:11   *21 Deut 9:19*   *26-28 Hag 2:6*   *29 Deut 4:24; 9:3*

---

e- 17 That is, Esau was not able to change his father's mind.
f- 18 Implied from verse 22.
g- 24 See *DIATHĒKĒ* on page 531.
h- 25 That is, the Israelites to whom the Law was given.

prison as if you were in chains with them, and those who are mistreated as if you could feel it.

4 Let everyone think highly of marriage and be sexually faithful ˌto one's own marriage partnerˌ,*a* because God will judge those who sin sexually—whether single or married.

5 Let your way of life be free from a love for money. Be satisfied with what you have, because He said: *"I will never leave you or desert you."* 6 And so we may say with confidence:

> *The Lord is my Helper.*
> *I will not be afraid.*
> *What can man do to me?*

Follow Your Teachers

7 Remember your leaders who have spoken the word of God to you. Consider how their lives ended,*b* and imitate their faith.

8 Jesus Christ is the same yesterday, today, and forever.

9 Do not be carried away with different kinds of strange teachings. For it is good to be inwardly strengthened by God's grace, not by foods, which have not helped those who make them a way of life.

10 We have an altar, and those who still worship at the Jewish Tabernacle have no right to eat from this altar.

11 For when the high priest *brings the blood* of animals *into the holy places*°c for sin,*d* the bodies of those animals are *burned outside the camp.* 12 And so Jesus suffered outside the gate*e* to make the people holy by His own blood. 13 Then let us go out to ˌjoinˌ Him *outside the camp* and bear the abuse He suffered.*f* 14 You see, we do not have a permanent city here, but we look for the one that is coming. 15 Through Jesus, then, let us always *bring to God a sacrifice of praise*, that is, *the fruit of our lips* praising His Name. 16 And do not forget to do good and to share; for such sacrifices are pleasing to God.

17 Obey your leaders and submit to them, for they must give an account of how they watch over your souls. Obey them so that they may be happy in their work and do not have to complain about you, for that would not be to your advantage.

18 Pray for us, for we are sure that we have a good conscience since we want to behave honorably in every way. 19 I urge you all the more to do this that I may be brought back to you sooner.

---

5 *Deut 31:6,8; Josh 1:5; 1 Chr 28:20*   6 *Ps 56:4,11; 118:6*
11-13 *Ex 29:14; Lev 4:12,21; 8:17; 9:11; 16:27; Num 19:3,5*   15 *Ps 50:14,23; Hos 14:2*

---

13 *a-* 4 Literally: "and the marriage bed kept pure."
  b- 7 Or "Consider the outcome of their behavior."
  c- 11 See THE HOLY PLACES on page 550.
  d- 11 This was done when the sacrifice was made for all the people or for the high priest, who was a representative of the nation before God. It was not done if the sacrifice was for an individual Jew or for a secular ruler (Lev. 4:3-31).
  e- 12 Thus indicating the removal of sin.
  f- 13 That is, sever our fellowship with the apostate church of Judaism.

Farewell

20 May the God of peace—who *brought back* from the dead our Lord Jesus, the Great *Shepherd of the sheep* who by His *blood made an everlasting "last will and testament"* ᵍ—**21** equip you with every good thing that you need, to do what He wants you to do, working in us through Jesus Christ that which pleases Him. To Him be glory forever. Amen.

22 I urge you, fellow Christians, ʰ listen patiently to what I say to encourage you, because I have written you a short letter. **23** You should know that Timothy our fellow Christian is free again. If he comes here soon, he and I will see you.

24 Greet all your leaders and all the believers [saints]. Those with us who are from Italy greet you.

25 Grace be with all of you.

---

20 Is 55:3; 63:11,12; Jer 32:40; 50:5; Ezek 16:60; 37:26; Zech 9:11

g- 20 See *DIATHĒKĒ* on page 531.
h- 22 Literally: "brothers" ("brother" in v. 23).

DIAGRAM #1

430

THE TABERNACLE and OUTER COURT

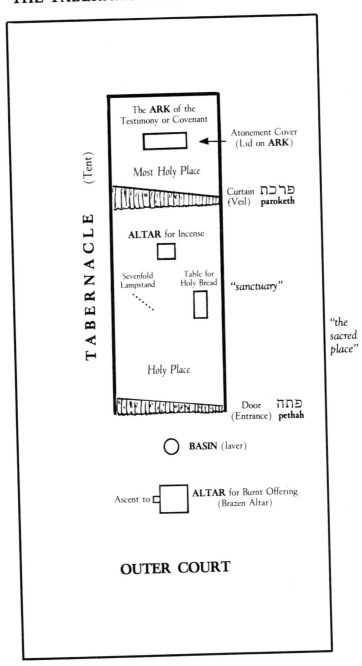

WILDERNESS

THE LETTER OF
JAMES[a]

1ST CHAPTER

A. Introduction (1:1)

1 James, a servant of God and of the Lord Jesus Christ, to the twelve tribes who are scattered throughout the world:[b] Greetings.

B. Turn to your God, the good Giver of perfect gifts (1:2-27)

Cheer Up

2 When you are tested in different ways, my fellow Christians,[c] consider it pure joy, **3** because you know that the testing of your faith produces patient endurance. **4** Now let patient endurance finish its work so that you may be perfect and complete, lacking nothing.

5 If anyone lacks wisdom, let him ask God, who gives to everyone with an open hand and who does not keep on reminding a person of what he owes, and He will give it to him. **6** But let that person ask in faith, having no doubts. For anyone who doubts is like a wave of the sea, driven and tossed by the wind. **7** To be sure, such a person should not expect to receive anything from the Lord. **8** He is indecisive[d]—wavering in everything he does.

9 Let the lowly Christian be proud of his high position, **10** and a rich one of his lowliness, because he will pass away *like a flower on a plant.* **11** The sun comes up with a burning heat and *dries up the plant; its flower drops off* and its beauty is gone. In the same way the rich person will fade away in whatever he undertakes.

Our Desires Tempt Us

12 *Blessed is* the person *who patiently endures* when he is tested. When he

---

10,11 Is 40:6-8   **12** Dan 12:12; Zech 6:14

---

1 a   *James*, probably written by James the brother of the Lord, encourages Jewish Christians to live their faith.

b-   1 Literally: "tribes in the dispersion"; this refers to those Jews who did not live in Palestine. The scattering of the Jews was known as the *"diaspora."* Such Jews had been scattered *via* the beginnings of the Assyrian Exile (723 B.C., 2 Kgs. 17:23), the Babylonian Exile (599-588 B.C., 2 Kgs. 24 and 25), and Alexander the Great's foreign policies (332-323 B.C.).

c-   2 Literally: "brothers" (also in vv. 16,19; "brother" in v. 9).

d-   8 Literally: "a double-minded person."

passes the test, *he will receive the crown of life* which God promised to those who love Him. **13** Let no one say when he is tempted, "God is tempting me." For God cannot be tempted to do wrong, and He does not tempt anyone. **14** Each person is tempted by his own desire when it draws him away and tries to trap him. **15** When desire conceives, it gives birth to sin, and when sin becomes full-grown, it gives birth to death.

God's Children

16 Do not make a mistake, my dear Christian friends. **17** Every act of giving that is good and every gift that is perfect comes down from above, from the Father of lights, with whom there is no shifting nor suggestion of change.*e*

18 As He planned, He gave birth to us by the word of truth, so we would be the first and best of His creatures.*f*

19 My dear fellow Christians, remember this: Let everyone be quick to listen, slow to speak, and slow to get angry. **20** For an angry person does not do what is right before God. **21** So get rid of everything filthy and all the evil that is so prevalent around you, and with a gentle spirit welcome the word that is planted in you, which can save your souls.

22 Do what the word says; do not merely listen to it and so deceive yourselves. **23** If anyone listens to the word but does not do what it says, he is like a person who in a mirror sees the face that he was born with. **24** He looks at himself, goes away, and immediately forgets what he looked like. **25** But if a person looks into God's perfect word which makes him free,*g* and continues to do so—if a person does not merely listen and then forget but does what it says, he will be happy as he does it. **26** Someone may think that he is religious, but if he does not control his tongue, he is deceiving himself—his religion is worthless. **27** Religion is pure and unstained before God the Father if people look after orphans and widows in their troubles and keep themselves unspotted from the world.

2ND CHAPTER

C. Turn to true and active faith (2:1-26)

Do Not Prefer The Rich

1 My fellow Christians,*a* believing as you do in Jesus Christ, our Lord of glory, do not favor one person over another. **2** For example, if a man wearing gold rings and fine clothes comes into your worship service and a poor man in

---

e- 17 Literally: "nor shadow of change."

f- 18 Literally: "so that we should be a kind of firstfruits of His creatures."

g- 25 Literally: "if a person looks into the perfect 'law' of freedom." For a Jew the word "law" (Greek: "*nomos*"; Hebrew: "*tōrāh*") basically meant "instruction" or "teaching." The reference here is to "law" in the wider sense, as a name for the whole "word" or "instruction" of God; see NOMOS on page 544.

2 *a*- 1 Literally: "brothers" (also in vv. 5,14; "brother or sister" in v. 15).

dirty clothes also comes in **3** and you give special attention to the one wearing fine clothes and say, "Please take this good seat," but you say to the poor man, "Stand there," or "Sit on the floor by my footstool"—**4** have you not shown favoritism and become judges who give corrupt opinions? **5** Listen, my dear fellow Christians, did God not choose those who are poor in the world to be rich in faith and to inherit the Kingdom that He promised to those who love Him? **6** But you have insulted the poor man. Do not the rich oppress you and drag you into court? **7** Do they not slander the beautiful Name by which you were called? **8** If you really do everything the Royal Law demands, as it is written: *"Love your neighbor as yourself,"* you are doing right. **9** But if you favor one over the other, you are committing a sin, and the Law convicts you of being lawbreakers.

Keep The Whole Law

10 Whoever keeps the whole Law but fails in one point, that person is guilty of breaking all of it. **11** For the One who said: *"Do not commit adultery,"* also said: *"Do not murder."* If you *do not commit adultery* but you *murder*, you are a lawbreaker. **12** Talk and act as people who are going to be judged by the word that brings liberty. *b* **13** For anyone who shows no mercy will be judged without mercy. Mercy triumphs over judgment.

Faith Is Active

14 What good does it do, my fellow Christians, if you say you have faith but do not have any works? Can such a faith save you? **15** If a Christian man or woman is going without clothes or daily food **16** and one of you tells them, "Go in peace, keep warm, and eat heartily," but does not give them what the body needs, what good does it do? **17** So faith, if it is not accompanied by works, is dead for that very reason. *c*

18 But someone will say, "You have faith, and I have works. Prove to me that you have faith without any works, and by my works I will prove to you that I have faith." **19** You believe that *"God is One." d* That's fine! The demons also believe that—and shudder.

20 Do you want proof, you foolish person, that faith without works is dead? **21** Wasn't our father Abraham considered justified [declared righteous] in what he did when he *offered his son Isaac on the altar?* **22** You see his faith was active with works, and by works was made complete. **23** And what the Scripture said was fulfilled: *"Abraham believed God, and it was credited to his account as righteousness,"* and he was called *the friend of God.* **24** You see a person is justified by works, and not by faith alone. **25** The same is true of the prostitute

---

8 *Lev 19:18*   11 *Ex 20:13,14; Deut 5:17,18*   19 *Deut 6:4; Zech 14:9; Mal 2:10*   21 *Gen 22:2,9*
23 *Gen 15:6; 2 Chr 20:7; Is 41:8*

b- 12 Literally: "the law of freedom" (cf. 1:25).
c- 17 Literally: "if it does not have works, is dead by itself."
d- 19 May be a quote from Deuteronomy 6:4: "The LORD our God, the LORD is One"; or it could be translated: "God is always the same." See Galatians 3:20 and its accompanying footnote; also Romans 3:30.

Rahab. Was she not justified by works when she welcomed the messengers and sent them away on a different road? **26** To be sure, just as the body without the spirit is dead, so faith without works is dead.

3RD CHAPTER

D. Turn, teachers, to God-given wisdom (3:1-18)

Control Your Tongue

1 Not many of you should become teachers, my fellow Christians,*a* because you know that we who teach will be judged more severely.

2 All of us make many mistakes. If anyone does not make a mistake in what he says, he is a perfect person who can also control his whole body. **3** If we put bits into the mouths of horses to make them obey us, we direct their whole bodies. **4** Look at the ships—even though they are so large and are driven by strong winds, yet a very small rudder steers them anywhere the pilot wants them to go. **5** So also the tongue is a small part, but it can boast of big things.

You know how a large forest is set on fire by just a little spark. **6** The tongue is also a fire. It stands among the members of our body as a world of wickedness: it soils the whole body, it sets on fire the whole course of our life, and it is set on fire by hell. **7** A human being can tame and has tamed all kinds of animals, birds, reptiles, and creatures in the sea. **8** But not one person can tame the tongue—a restless evil, full of deadly poison.

9 We praise the Lord and Father with our tongue, and with it we ₗalsoᵤ curse other people, who have been *made in God's likeness*. **10** From the very same mouth come both praise and cursing. Such a thing should not happen, my fellow Christians. **11** Does a spring pour out both fresh and bitter water from the same opening? **12** My fellow Christians, can a fig tree produce olives, or a grapevine figs? Neither can a salt spring produce fresh water.

Wisdom From Above

13 Who among you is wise and intelligent? Let that person show this by his noble life, namely, that what he does is an expression of a gentle spirit of wisdom. **14** But if you feel bitter jealousy and selfish ambition in your hearts, do not boast and lie against the truth. **15** Such wisdom does not come from above, but from this earth, from this life, and from the devil. **16** For where there is jealousy and selfishness, there is confusion and every kind of evil.

17 The wisdom that comes from above is first of all pure, then peaceful, gentle, willing to obey, full of mercy and good works, impartial, and without

---

9 Gen 1:27; 5:1

3 *a*- 1 Literally: "brothers" (also in vv. 10,12).

hypocrisy. **18** And those who continually bring about peace are sowing a harvest of righteousness in ˌthe field ofˌ peace. *b*

4TH CHAPTER

E. Turn to God, the Giver of the Spirit and of all grace (4:1-12)

Do Not Love The World

1 Why is there fighting and quarreling among you? Is it not because of your cravings for pleasure which are fighting in your bodies? **2** You want something but do not get it. You kill and try to get something, but you cannot lay your hands on it. You quarrel and fight. You do not receive things, because you do not ask for them. **3** Or you ask for something but do not get it because you want it for a wrong purpose—to spend it on your pleasures.

4 Adulterous people, do you not know that to love the world is to hate God? Whoever wants to be a friend of the world makes himself an enemy of God. **5** Or do you think the Scripture says in vain: "The Spirit who dwells in us strongly opposes envy"?

6 But *He gives grace* more generously. And so it says:

> God opposes the proud
> but gives grace to the humble.

7 Therefore be subordinate*a* to God:

> Resist the devil,
> and he will run away from you.
> **8** Come close to God,
> and He will come close to you.
> Wash your hands, you sinners,
> and purify your hearts, you doubters.
> **9** Be miserable, mourn, and cry;
> turn your laughter into mourning
> and your joy into gloom.
> **10** Humble yourselves before the Lord,
> and He will lift you up.

Do Not Talk Against One Another

11 Stop talking against one another, my fellow Christians. *b* Anyone who talks against his fellow Christian*c* or judges him, talks against the Law and judges the

---

6 *Prov 3:34*

---

b- 18 Literally: "The fruit of righteousness is sown in ˌthe sphere ofˌ peace by those who constantly practice peace."

4 *a-* 7 See *HUPOTASSŌ* on page 541.

b- 11 Literally: "brothers."

c- 11 Literally: "brother."

Law. If you judge the Law, you are not a doer of the Law, but a judge of it.
12 There is only one Lawgiver and Judge, the One who is able to save and
destroy. And who are you to judge your neighbor?

F. Turn from the world's self-assurance (4:13–5:6)

"If The Lord Is Willing"

13 Come now, you who say, "Today or tomorrow we will go into this city,
stay there a year, do business, and make money." 14 You do not know about
tomorrow! For what is your life? You are a mist which is seen for a little while,
then vanishes. 15 Instead say: "If the Lord is willing, we will live and do this or
that." 16 But instead, you boast in your pride. All such boasting is wrong.

17 If a person knows what is right but does not do it, he is sinning.

5TH CHAPTER

Woe To The Rich

1 Come now, you rich people, cry and howl over the miseries that are coming
to you. 2 Your riches are rotten and your clothes are eaten by moths. 3 Your gold
and silver are tarnished, and their tarnish will be evidence against you and will
eat your flesh like *fire*. You have *piled up treasures* in these last days. 4 But now
the wages that you never paid to the workers who reaped your fields cry out.
And the *groans* of those who cut the grain *have come to the ears of the Lord
of armies [hosts].* ᵃ 5 You have lived here on earth in luxury and pleasure. You
have fattened yourselves in *the day of slaughter*. 6 You have condemned and
murdered the person who is righteous—he does not resist you.

G. Turn to the returning Lord (5:7-20)

Be Patient

7 Be patient, fellow Christians, ᵇ until the Lord comes. See how the farmer
looks for the precious crop of the ground and waits patiently for it to receive *the
fall and the spring rains*. 8 Be patient also, and keep your courage, because the
Lord will soon be here. 9 Do not blame your troubles on one another, fellow
Christians, or you will be judged. You know, the Judge is standing at the door.

10 Fellow Christians, as an example of patiently suffering wrong, take the

---

3 *Ps 21:9; Prov 16:27*   4 *Ex 2:23; 3:9; Lev 19:13; 2 Sam 22:7; Ps 18:6; Is 5:9; Mal 3:5*
5 *Jer 12:3*   7 *Deut 11:14*

---

5 *a-* 4 Greek: "*sabaōth*," from the Hebrew "*tsābā*" ("host," "army").
 b- 7 Literally: "brothers" (also in vv. 9,10,12,19).

prophets who spoke in the Name of the Lord. 11 Remember, *we call those "blessed" who patiently endured.* You have heard how Job patiently endured, and you saw how the Lord finally treated him, because *the Lord is tenderhearted and merciful.*

Do Not Swear

12 Above all things, my fellow Christians, do not swear by heaven or by the earth or by any other oath, but let your "yes" be "yes" and your "no" be "no," so that you will not be condemned.

The Power Of Prayer

13 Is anyone among you suffering? Let him pray! Is anyone among you happy? Let him sing a song of praise! 14 Is anyone among you sick? Let him call for the elders of the church, and let them pray over him, anointing him with olive oil in the Name of the Lord. 15 Your prayer offered in faith will save the sick person. The Lord will raise him up, and if he has committed sins, he will be forgiven. 16 So confess your sins to one another, and pray for one another to be healed.

The earnest prayer of a righteous person accomplishes much. 17 Elijah was a man just like us, and he prayed earnestly that there should be no rain, and no rain fell on the ground for three years and six months. 18 Then he prayed again, and the sky gave rain, and the ground produced its crops.

Bring Back The Lost

19 My fellow Christians, if one of you wanders away from the truth and someone brings him back, 20 you should know that whoever brings a sinner back from his wrong way will save his soul from death and will *cover many sins.*

11 Ex 34:6; 2 Chr 30:9; Ps 86:15; 103:8; 111:4; 112:4; 145:8; Dan 12:12; Joel 2:13; Jonah 4:2; Neh 9:17,31   20 Prov 10:12

DIAGRAM #2   **438**

CHRISTIAN CHURCH STRUCTURE

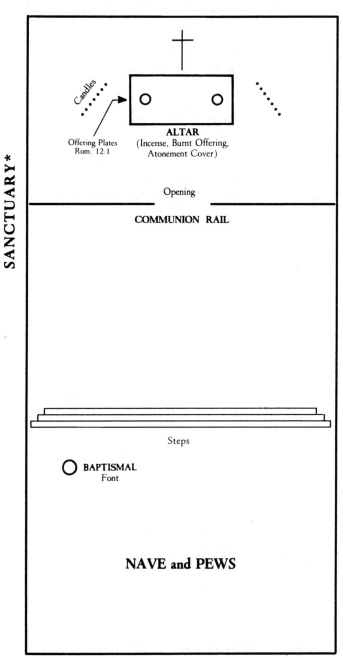

SANCTUARY*

Candles

Offering Plates
Rom. 12:1

ALTAR
(Incense, Burnt Offering,
Atonement Cover)

Opening

COMMUNION RAIL

Steps

○ **BAPTISMAL**
Font

NAVE and PEWS

*Note: Sanctuary comes from **sanctus,** meaning "holy", as in "holy place" and "most holy place." See Leviticus 16:3.

1 PETER ^a

1ST CHAPTER

A. Opening greeting (1:1,2)

1 Peter, an apostle of Jesus Christ, to the chosen people who are living as strangers scattered in Pontus, Galatia, Cappadocia, Asia,*b* and Bithynia, **2** chosen according to the foreknowledge of God the Father to be made holy by the Spirit, so that you might obey Jesus Christ and be *sprinkled with* His *blood:c* May *you* have *more and more* grace*d* and *peace.e*

B. Hope through Christ (1:3-12)

Christ Saves You

3 Let us praise the God and Father of our Lord Jesus Christ, who by raising Jesus Christ from the dead has in His great mercy given us a new birth. Now we have a living hope, **4** which awaits an inheritance that cannot be destroyed or defiled and never fades away, reserved for you in heaven. **5** And through faith, you are protected by God's power until you come to the salvation that is ready to be revealed at the end of time. **6** This brings you great joy, even though now for a little while you may have to suffer various trials. **7** Your faith is tested for its genuineness through this suffering, ⌐just as⌐ gold is tested for its genuineness by fire. When your faith passes this test and is proven to be more precious than gold which perishes, it results in praise and glory and honor when Jesus Christ appears again.

8 You never saw Him, but you love Him. You do not see Him now, but you believe in Him. And a joy, unspeakable and wonderful, fills you with delight,

---

2 Ex 24:6,8; Lev 16:14,15; Dan 6:25

---

1 *a*   The Apostle Peter wrote this letter to Christians in Asia Minor in order to strengthen them, particularly encouraging them to remain faithful in a time of persecution. *1 Peter* is called "the epistle of hope."

b- 1 Referring to the Roman province of Asia, the western part of Asia Minor.

c- 2 Literally: "Spirit, for obedience to Jesus Christ and sprinkling by the blood."

d- 2 Meaning "God's undeserved love."

e- 2 See Romans 1:7.

9 because you receive by faith what you are looking for, namely, the salvation of your souls.

10 The prophets, who wrote beforehand concerning what God's grace [undeserved love] would do for you, made a thorough search to learn all they could about this salvation. 11 They tried to find out what Person or what time the Spirit of Christ in them was pointing out when He predicted the sufferings of Christ and the glories that would follow. 12 God told them that they were not serving themselves but you in these things. And now the Holy Spirit, who is sent from heaven, gave these men the Gospel [Good News] to preach to you, announcing to you the things of which the angels long to catch a glimpse.

C. Hope with holiness of life (1:13–2:10)

Be Holy

13 Now then, get ready mentally for action; keep a clear head; and be perfectly sure of what God's grace is bringing you when Jesus Christ appears. 14 Being children who obey, do not live according to your lusts as you once did when you did not know any better. 15 Rather, as the One who called you is holy, so you also be holy in all your ways, 16 since it is written: *"Be holy, because I am holy."* 17 And if you *call on* Him as your *Father*, who judges each person according to what he has done, without favoring one over another, live reverently as you spend your time here as strangers. 18 Do this because *you* know that you were *freed [ransomed]* from the worthless life you inherited from your fathers, *not by a payment of silver* or gold, which perish, 19 but by the precious blood of Christ, the Lamb without blemish or spot. 20 He is the Lamb who was appointed before the world was made, and He was revealed in the last period of time to help you. 21 Through Him you believe in God, who raised Him from the dead and gave Him glory; and so your faith and hope rest in God.

The Ever-Living Word

22 You have purified yourselves by obeying the truth, with the result that the love you have for your fellow Christians*f* is not insincere. Therefore, love one another intensely with a pure heart. 23 Do this because you were born again, not by a seed that perishes, but by one that cannot perish, namely, *God's ever-living* word, because:

24   *All people are like grass,*
        and all their glory like the flower of the grass.
    The grass withers and the flower drops off,
25   *but the word of the Lord remains forever.*

This *word* is the *Gospel [Good News]* which was *preached* to you.

---

16 *Lev 11:44,45; 19:2; 20:7,26*   17 *Ps 89:26*   18 *Is 52:3*   23 *Dan 6:26; 12:7*
24,25 *Is 40:6-9*

f- 22 Literally: "brothers."

2ND CHAPTER

1 Therefore get rid of every kind of wickedness and deceit, hypocrisy, jealousy, and every kind of slander; 2 and, like newborn babies, thirst for the pure milk of the word in order that it may cause you to grow so that you are saved. 3 Surely *you have tasted that the Lord is good*!

The Living Stone

4 As you keep coming to Him who is the living *Stone*, whom men rejected but whom God *selected* as *precious*, 5 you also are being built as living stones into a spiritual temple. As such you are holy priests who bring spiritual sacrifices that God gladly accepts through Jesus Christ. 6 As the Scripture states:

> *I am laying in Zion a Cornerstone,*
> *chosen and precious,*
> *and the person who believes in Him*
> *will never be disappointed.*

7 This position of honor belongs to you who believe, but to those who do not believe *He is*

> *the very Stone—rejected by the builders—*
> *who has become the Cornerstone,*
> 8   *a Stone which makes them stumble*
>   *and*
>   *a Rock which causes them to fall.*[a]

Because they disobey the word, they stumble over it; that is the end appointed for them.

God's People

9 But you are *a chosen people, a royal priesthood, a holy nation, a people who are His own, that you may tell others about the wonderful deeds* of Him who called you out of darkness into His marvelous light. 10 Once you were *no people*, but now you are *God's people*. Once you had *received no mercy*, but now you have *received mercy*.

D. Hope in spite of suffering (2:11–4:11)

11 Dear friends, I urge you, as *guests and strangers* in this world: Keep your distance from the desires of your flesh which constantly attack your soul. 12 Live a noble life among the Gentiles, so that *when they observe you,*[b] instead of accusing you of doing wrong, they may see the good you do and so glorify God.

---

3 Ps 34:8   **4** Is 28:16   **6,7** Is 28:16   **7** Ps 118:22   **8** Is 8:14   **9** Ex 19:5,6; Deut 7:6; 14:2; Is 42:12; 43:20,21   **10** Hos 1:6,8-10; 2:1,23   **11** Gen 23:4; Lev 25:23; 1 Chr 29:15; Ps 39:12   **12** Is 10:3

---

2 *a*- 8 See *SKANDALON* on page 545.
   b- 12 Or "so that when God comes to visit."

Being Under The Authority Of Others

13 Be subordinate[c] to every human authority to please the Lord: to the emperor as one who is the top authority, **14** or to governors as men whom he sent to punish those who do wrong and to praise those who do right. **15** For God wants you to silence ignorant and foolish people by doing what is right. **16** Act as free people, but do not use your freedom as a cover-up to do wrong; instead, be God's slaves. **17** Honor everyone; love your fellow believers;[d] *fear God*; honor the *emperor*.

18 Servants, be subordinate to your masters, showing every respect, not only when they are good and kind, but also when they are unfair.

Suffer Patiently

19 It is a fine thing if, moved by his conscience to please God, a person patiently bears the pains of unjust suffering. **20** For what credit ˌdo you deserveˌ if you are beaten for sinning and you patiently endure it? But if you suffer for doing good and you patiently endure it, God is pleased with you.

21 This is what you were called for, seeing that Christ also suffered for you and left you an example so that you might follow in His steps. **22** *He never sinned nor was found to be deceitful when He spoke.* **23** When others abused Him, He did not abuse them in return; when He suffered, He did not threaten but left it in the hands of Him who judges fairly. **24** *He Himself carried our sins* in His body on the cross, so that we might die to sins and live for righteousness. *His wounds have healed you.* **25** For you were *like lost sheep*, but now you have come back to the Shepherd and Caretaker of your souls.

3RD CHAPTER

Wives And Husbands

1 In the same way, you wives, be subordinate[a] to your husbands. Then even

---

17 Prov 24:21   *22 Ps 32:2; Ps 53:9; Zeph 3:13*   *24 Is 53:4,12*   *24,25 Is 53:5,6; Ezek 34:5*

---

c- 13 Greek: "*hupotassō.*" This Greek term speaks of persons who are placed in an "order" or "rank" below or under the authority of another. In the mind of sinful human beings this is often falsely equated with *inferiority*. However, Jesus taught us that among Christians this is not to be the case. It is not the one in authority who is the greatest but the one who is servant to all (Matt. 20:25-28; Mk. 10:42-45); authority and servitude are always to be used for the benefit of others.
The English "subordinate" captures the totality of this *hupotassō* concept quite well. In the passage before us Peter uses the word in terms of our *everyday relationships within society* (cf. Rom. 13:1; Tit. 3:1). This applies to verse 18 also. See *HUPOTASSŌ* on page 541.

d- 17 Literally: "love the brotherhood."

3 a- 1 Greek: "*hupotassō.*" See general comments in footnote at Ephesians 5:24. Particular to our present passage is Peter's application in regard to *marriage* according to the rank or order laid down by God (cf. Col. 3:18; Tit. 2:5). This also applies to verse 5. See *HUPOTASSŌ* on page 541.

if some of them refuse to listen to the word, you will win them, without talking about it, by the way you live as wives, 2 when they see how you are pure and reverent in your lives.

3 Do not let your beauty[b] be something outward, such as braiding the hair, putting on gold ornaments and dresses, 4 but let your beauty be the hidden person that you are in your heart, with the imperishable quality of a gentle and quiet spirit; this is very precious to God. 5 For this is how the holy women of long ago, whose hope rested in God, used to make themselves beautiful: They were subordinate to their husbands, 6 like *Sarah* who obeyed Abraham and *called* him "*lord.*" You are her daughters if you do good and *let nothing terrify you.*

7 Likewise, you husbands, live with your wives in a way which shows that you understand that as a woman she is weaker than you are. Honor them as those who share the gift of life with you—so that nothing will interfere with your prayers.

When You Are Wronged

8 Finally, all of you, live in harmony, be sympathetic, love your fellow Christians,[c] be tenderhearted and humble. 9 Do not pay back evil for evil, insult for insult, but speak a blessing instead. That is what you were called to do—so that you might inherit a blessing.

10	*If a person wants to love life and enjoy happy days,*
	let him stop speaking evil
	or saying anything deceitful;
11	*let him turn away from wrong*
	and do good;
	let him be eager for peace
	and pursue it.
12	*For the Lord watches the righteous*
	and hears their prayer,
	but the Lord is against those who do wrong.

13 Who will harm you if you are eager to do good? 14 But even if you should suffer because you are righteous, you would be blessed. *Do not fear what they fear and do not be intimidated.* 15 *But* in your hearts *have deep respect* for Christ as Lord. Always be ready to answer anyone who asks you to explain the hope you have, but be gentle and respectful. 16 Keep a good conscience so that those who make fun of your good life in Christ will feel ashamed of their slander. 17 It is better, if God wants it that way, to suffer for doing right than for doing wrong.

The Righteous One Died

18 For Christ died once for our sins, the Righteous One for the unrighteous,

---

6 Gen 18:12; Prov 3:25   *10-12 Ps 34:12-16*   *14,15 Is 8:12,13*

---

b- 3 Greek: "*kosmos,*" the basis for the English word "cosmetic"; see also verse 5 ("beautiful").
c- 8 Literally: "brothers."

to bring us to God. He was put to death in flesh[d] but made alive in spirit,[e] 19 in which He also went and preached to the spirits kept in prison, 20 who disobeyed long ago in the days of Noah when God waited patiently while the ark was being built. In this ark a few, that is, eight persons, were saved by water. 21 In the same way also, baptism now saves us, not by washing dirt from the body, but by guaranteeing us a good conscience before God by the resurrection of Jesus Christ, 22 who has gone to heaven and is at the right hand of God, where angels, rulers, and powers have been put under Him.[f]

4TH CHAPTER

You Have Given Up Sin

1 Since, therefore, Christ has suffered for us[a] in His body, arm yourselves with the same attitude that He had (for when He suffered in His body He was done with sin), 2 so that you no longer live the rest of your time in the body in the lusts of men but in the will of God. 3 For you spent enough time in the past doing what the Gentiles like to do, when you lived in unbridled immorality, lusts, drunkenness, wild celebrations, drinking parties, and the abominable worship of idols. 4 They are surprised now because you do not plunge into the same flood of wild living with them, and they slander you. 5 They will have to give an account to Him who is ready to judge the living and the dead. 6 Yes, it was for this reason that the dead also once heard the Gospel, so that they might be judged like human beings in the flesh,[b]—but then live like God in the spirit.[c]

Love Fervently

7 The end of everything is near. So be sensible and keep your heads clear for your prayers. 8 Above all, continue to love one another fervently, because *love covers many sins.* 9 Welcome one another as guests without grumbling. 10 Serve one another, each with the gift that he has received, as good managers of the various gifts of God. 11 If a person speaks, let him say what God says. If a person serves, let him do it with the strength God gives, so that in every way God is glorified through Jesus Christ. His is the glory and the power forever and ever! Amen.

---

8 Prov 10:12

d- 18 Or "in a fleshly [physical] state," referring to Christ's state of humiliation and meaning He was put to death in a humbled state. When flesh and spirit are used as opposites in connection with Christ, they refer to His humbled state and His exalted state (cf. Rom. 1:3; 1 Tim. 3:16; 1 Pet. 4:6 and the corresponding footnotes; also note 1 Cor. 15:44-49).

e- 18 Or "in a spiritual state," referring to Christ's state of exaltation (cf. Rom. 1:4; 1 Tim. 3:16; 1 Pet. 4:6 and the corresponding footnotes; also note 1 Cor. 15:44-49), meaning He was made alive in an exalted state (cf. preceding footnote).

f- 22 See Hebrews 12:9 and its accompanying footnote.

4 a- 1 Some of the older manuscripts and early translations omit: "for us."

b- 6 Or "in their fleshly [physical] state," meaning while they live in their natural body here on earth (cf. 1 Cor. 15:44-49).

c- 6 Or "in their spiritual state," meaning while they live in their spiritual body in heaven (cf. 1 Cor. 15:44-49).

E. Advice for the persecuted (4:12–5:11)

You Share Christ's Sufferings

12 Dear friends, do not be surprised by this fiery trial by which you are being tested, as though something strange were happening to you. **13** But whenever you share Christ's sufferings, be happy—so that you may also be overjoyed when His glory will be revealed. **14** If you are insulted now for the Name of Christ, you are fortunate because the Spirit of glory and power,[d] *the Spirit of God*, is resting on you.

15 Of course, none of you should suffer as a murderer, a thief, a criminal, or one who meddles in the affairs of others. **16** But if you suffer for being called a Christian, do not feel ashamed, but praise God for that name. **17** For it is time for the judgment to *start in the household of God*. But if it is starting with us, how will it end for those who refuse to listen to the Good News of God?

18   *If it is hard for a righteous person to be saved,*
         what will happen to the ungodly and the sinner?

19 So you also who are suffering according to the will of God, entrust your souls to Him—you can trust Him who created you—and keep on doing what is right.

5TH CHAPTER

To The Pastors

1 I appeal to you pastors,[a] I who also am a pastor. I saw Christ suffer, and I share in the glory that is to be revealed. **2** Be shepherds of God's flock that is with you, watching over it, not because you have to but because you want to, as is God's will; **3** not greedily but eagerly; not lording it over the people entrusted to you but being examples to the flock. **4** And when the Head Shepherd appears, you will win the unfading crown of glory.

Humble Yourselves

5 In a similar way, you young people, be subordinate[b] to those who are older.

 All of you, wear humility as a sign of service to one another, because

---

14 *Is 11:2*   **17** *Ezek 9:6*   **18** *Prov 11:31*   **5** *Prov 3:34*

---

d- 14 Some of the older manuscripts and early translations omit: "power."
5 a- 1 Greek: "*presbuteros*"; see footnote at 1 Timothy 4:14.
   b- 5 Greek: "*hupotassō*." Compare 2:13 and its accompanying footnote. This Greek term is here *applied* by Peter *to everyday relationships within society* where God has ranked young people *under* older people. See HUPOTASSŌ on page 541.

> God opposes the proud
> but gives grace to the humble.

6 Therefore, be humbled under the mighty hand of God, so that He may honor you at the right time.

Watch

7 *Throw all your worry on Him* because *He* cares for *you.* **8** Keep a clear head and watch! Your enemy, the devil, is prowling around like a roaring lion, looking for someone to devour. **9** Be strong in your faith and resist him, knowing that your fellow Christians[c] in the world are undergoing the same kind of suffering. **10** After you have suffered a little while, the God of all grace, who called you in Christ Jesus to His everlasting glory, will restore you, firm you up, make you strong, and give you a good foundation. **11** He has the power forever and ever. Amen.

F. Conclusion (5:12-14)

Farewell

12 With the help of Silvanus,[d] whom I consider a faithful fellow Christian,[e] I am writing you this short letter to encourage you and testify that this is the true grace of God. Stand firm in it.
13 Your sister church in Babylon,[f] chosen by God, greets you; and so does Mark my son. **14** Greet one another with a kiss of love. Peace to you all in Christ!

---

7 Ps 55:22

c- 9 Literally: "your brotherhood."
d- 12 The Roman spelling of *Silas*, a Roman citizen who accompanied Paul on his Second Missionary Journey (cf. Acts 15:40).
e- 12 Literally: "brother."
f- 13 By the term "Babylon" some think that Peter may be referring to Rome.

THE LETTER OF
2 PETER[a]

1ST CHAPTER

A. *True knowledge (1:1-21)*

1 Simon Peter, a servant and an apostle of Jesus Christ, to the people who by the righteousness of our God and Savior Jesus Christ were given a faith as precious as ours: **2** Along with your knowledge of God and our Lord Jesus, *may you enjoy more and more* of His grace[b] and peace.

Grow

3 His divine power has given to us everything needed for life and godliness. This He did by leading us to a full knowledge of Him who called us to His own glory and excellence. **4** Thus He has given us His precious and very great promises, so that after you have escaped the corruption that lust brought into the world, you might by these promises share in the divine nature.

5 In view of that, by using every bit of your energy, to your faith add excellence, to excellence knowledge, **6** to knowledge self-control, to self-control patient endurance, to patient endurance godliness, **7** to godliness brotherly kindness, to brotherly kindness love. **8** For if you have these and they are increasing, they will demonstrate that knowing our Lord Jesus Christ has not made you useless and unproductive. **9** If anyone does not have these, he is blind, short-sighted, and has forgotten that his old sins were washed away.

10 Be all the more eager then, fellow Christians,[c] to make sure that your calling and choosing are secure. If you do this, you will never fall away. **11** For then you will be welcomed richly into the everlasting Kingdom of our Lord and Savior Jesus Christ.

12 And so I am always going to remind you of this, although you already know it and are well-grounded in the truth that you have. **13** I think it is right,

---

2 *Dan* 6:25

1 *a* The Apostle Peter wrote this letter to warn his readers against false teachers. *2 Peter* is often called "the epistle of knowledge."
   b- 2 Meaning "God's undeserved love" (also in 3:18).
   c- 10 Literally: "brothers."

as long as I am in the tent of this body, to refresh your memory, **14** because I know that soon I am going to lay aside my tent, as our Lord Jesus Christ has told me. **15** And I will do my best to see to it that you have a constant reminder of these things after I am gone.*d*

God's Word

16 We were not following any clever myths when we told you about the power of our Lord Jesus Christ and His coming. Rather, with our own eyes we saw His majesty. **17** For He received honor and glory from the Father when a voice spoke these words to Him while He was covered by sublime glory: "This is My Son, whom I love and *with whom I am delighted*."*e* **18** We heard that voice speak to Him from heaven when we were with Him on the holy mountain.

19 We have, as something more sure, the prophetic word. Please look to it as to a light shining in a gloomy place until the day dawns and the *Morning Star rises* in your hearts. **20** Understand this first, that no prophetic utterance of Scripture comes as a result of a human explanation, **21** for no prophecy was ever spoken because a man decided to prophesy, but men said what God gave them to say as they were directed*f* by the Holy Spirit.

2ND CHAPTER

B. False teachers (2:1-22)

False Teachers

1 But there were also false prophets among the people, just as there will also be false teachers among you. They will secretly bring in their own destructive teachings. Since they deny the Lord who has bought them, they are bringing quick destruction on themselves. **2** And many will follow their immoral ways and *cause* people *to slander* the way of truth. **3** In their greed they will twist the meaning of words to make a profit. A just punishment has been preparing itself for them for a long time, and their destruction is not sleeping.*a*

4 God did not spare angels who sinned but put them into the gloomy dungeons of hell to be kept for judgment. **5** And He did not spare the ancient world but protected eight people, including Noah who was a preacher of righteousness,

---

17 2 Sam 7:14; Ps 2:7; Is 42:1   **19** *Is 14:12*   *2 Is 52:5*

---

d- 15 This came true through Mark's Gospel, traditionally associated with Peter.
e- 17 Compare Matthew 17:5; Luke 9:34,35.
f- 21 The verb that is used here is used of a divine utterance in verses 17 ("spoke"), 18 ("speak"), and 21a ("spoken"). Literally: "carried along" or "moved by."
2 *a-* 3 A picturesque way of saying that their destruction will not fail to come.

when He brought a flood on a world of ungodly people. **6** And He condemned the towns of Sodom and Gomorrah, destroyed them by burning them to ashes, and made them a warning to those who are going to be ungodly. *b* **7** But He rescued righteous Lot, whom the wicked people vexed with their immoral life. **8** For as he saw and heard the wicked things they were doing, this righteous man tortured his righteous soul day after day as he lived among them.

9 The Lord knows how to rescue godly people when they are tested and to keep the wicked under punishment for the Day of Judgment, **10** especially those who go lusting after sinful flesh to defile themselves and who despise the Lord's authority.

Being bold and headstrong, they do not tremble when they slander God's splendor. *c* **11** They do this before the Lord, where even angels—although they are greater in strength and power—do not condemn and abuse such people. **12** But like unthinking animals which by nature are born to be caught and killed, they slander what they do not understand, and like animals they will be destroyed—**13** and so lose what they hoped to gain by their wrongdoing.

Their idea of pleasure is to live it up in broad daylight. They are spots and blemishes who in their lusts are obsessed with wild drinking parties *d* while they feast with you. **14** They have eyes for nothing else except an adulterous woman and eyes that are restlessly looking for sin. They try to trap weak souls.

Since their hearts are trained to be greedy, they are going to be cursed. *e* **15** They left the straight way and wandered off to follow the way of Balaam the son of Beor, who loved the reward he would get for doing wrong. **16** But he was rebuked for his defiance: A donkey which cannot speak spoke with a human voice and did not let the prophet go on in his insane way.

17 They are dried-up springs, fogs driven by a storm. Dark gloom is reserved for them. **18** For by talking high-sounding nonsense and by using physical cravings, they set traps baited with lusts for the people who are just escaping from those who live in error. **19** Although they promise others freedom, they are themselves slaves of corruption—anyone is a slave of that which has defeated him.

20 If by knowing the Lord and Savior Jesus Christ they escaped the world's corruptions, but then are entangled and conquered by them again, these people are worse off in the end than they were before. **21** It would have been better for them never to have known the way of righteousness than to learn it and then turn their backs on the holy commandment that was given them. **22** The proverb is true that tells what happened to them: *"A dog goes back to what he has vomited,"* and *"A sow that has been washed goes back to roll around in the mud."*

---

22 Prov 26:11

b- 6 Some of the older manuscripts and early translations read: "warning of the things which are going to happen to the ungodly."
c- 10 Literally: "glories"; the meaning is unclear. It could refer to the despising of: 1) authority; 2) leaders in the church; 3) glorious angelic beings (cf. Jude 8); or 4) Christ in His exalted state (cf. 1 Pet. 1:11).
d- 13 Literally: "reveling (or 'carousing') in their lusts."
e- 14 Literally: "accursed children."

3RD CHAPTER

C. Christ's return (3:1-18)

The World Will Be Destroyed

1 Dear friends, this is now the second letter I am writing to you. In both of them I stir up your pure minds by reminding you **2** to think of the words spoken in the past by the holy prophets and of what the Lord and Savior commanded through your apostles.

3 First of all you should know that in the last days mockers, following their own impulses, will come with their mockery **4** and say: "He promised to come. What has happened? From the time the fathers fell asleep everything has remained as it was since the world was first created."

5 What they deliberately forgot is that a long time ago by the word of God the heavens existed and the earth was formed out of water and by water. *a* **6** Then those waters flooded the world and destroyed the form it had at that time. **7** And the same word has reserved the present heavens and the earth for fire and keeps them for the Day when the ungodly will be judged and destroyed.

8 Do not forget, dear friends, with the Lord one day is like a thousand years, and *a thousand years are like one day.* **9** The Lord is not slow to do what He promised, as some people think. Rather, He is patient with you because He does not want any to perish but wants all to come to repentance.

10 The Lord's Day will come like a thief. On that Day the heavens will pass away with a roar, the elements will be destroyed by heat, and the earth and what was done on it will become evident.

11 Since all these things will be destroyed in this way, think how necessary it is for you to continue living in a holy and godly way, **12** as you wait for and earnestly desire the coming of the Day of God, which will destroy the heavens with fire and melt the elements with heat. **13** But according to His promise we expect *new heavens and a new earth* where righteousness lives. **14** With this to look forward to, dear friends, make every effort to have Him find you without spot or blemish and at peace.

15 Keep in mind that the patience of our Lord is for our salvation, just as our dear brother Paul wrote to you according to the wisdom given him. **16** He talks about this in all his letters. Some things in these letters are hard to understand, and those who are ignorant and not well-grounded twist their meaning, as they do with the rest of the Scriptures, and so they destroy themselves.

---

8 Ps 90:4   13 Is 65:17; 66:22

---

3 a- 5 That is, the waters on earth were separated from the waters of the heavens, and then the mountains appeared, causing the earthly waters to be gathered together into oceans (cf. Gen. 1:6-10). An alternate translation would read: "What they choose to forget is that the word of God caused the heavens to exist for a long time and preserved the earth separate from the water and between water."
The words "and by water" (second reference to "water" in the text) refer either to the water *above the expanse* ("between water" - Gen. 1:6,7) or to the water that God used *to preserve plant life* ("by water" - Gen. 2:5,6).

[17] Now you, dear friends, although you already know this, be on your guard so that you are not swept away by the error of unprincipled men and so lose your firm grip. [18] But grow in God's grace and in knowing our Lord and Savior Jesus Christ. To Him be glory now and forever. Amen.

THE LETTER OF
1 JOHN[a]

1st CHAPTER

A. Introduction: The revelation (1:1-4)

The Word Of Life

1 That which was from the beginning, which we have heard, which we have seen with our eyes, which we have looked at and our hands have touched, this is what we are speaking about, namely, the Word who is the Life.[b] **2** This Life was revealed; we have seen It and we testify to It, and we proclaim to you the eternal Life, which was with the Father and which was revealed to us. **3** What we have seen and heard we proclaim also to you, so that you too may have fellowship with us. And our fellowship is with the Father and with His Son Jesus Christ. **4** We are writing these things so that our joy may be complete.

B. The first standard: "God is Light and in Him . . . no darkness" (1:5–2:28)

5 This is the message we heard from Him and which we are telling you: God is Light and in Him there is no darkness. **6** If we say that we have fellowship with Him and ⌐yet⌐ live in darkness, we are lying and not living the truth.

The Blood Of Jesus

7 But if we live in the light as He is in the light, we have fellowship with one another, and the blood of Jesus His Son washes us clean from every sin. **8** If we say that we are not sinful, we deceive ourselves, and the truth is not in us. **9** If we confess our sins, He will keep His promise and do what He obligated Himself to do:[c] He will forgive our sins and wash away all unrighteousness. **10** If we say we have not sinned, we make Him a liar and His word is not in us.

---

1 *a* This letter by the Apostle John is often called "the epistle of love."
 b- 1 Or "the Word of Life."
 c- 9 Literally: "He is faithful and just." In this verse His "faithfulness" refers to His promise in regard to our sins, and His being "just" refers to His obligation "to do what is right," namely, to do what He said He would do with our sins, both of which are explained by the clause which follows.

2ND CHAPTER

1 My little children, I am writing this to you to keep you from sinning. If anyone sins, we have One to plead for us with the Father—Jesus Christ, who is righteous. **2** He is the atoning sacrifice [the covering] for our sins,*a* and not only ours, but also for ˌthe sins ofˌ the whole world.

Live And Love

3 We are sure that we know Him if we keep His commandments. **4** Anyone who says, "I know Him," but does not keep His commandments is a liar, and there is no truth in him. **5** But whoever does what He says,*b* God's love has really accomplished in that person what He wants. That is how we know that we are in Him. **6** If a person says, "I remain in Him," he has an obligation to live in the same way as He lived.

7 Dear friends, I am not writing you a new commandment, but an old one which you had from the beginning. This old commandment is the word which you have heard. **8** On the other hand, I am writing you a new commandment, one that is verified*c* in Him and in you, because the darkness is passing away and the genuine*d* light is already shining.

9 Anyone who says, "I am in the light," but hates his brother is still in darkness. **10** Anyone who loves his brother remains in the light, and there is nothing in him that causes someone else to stumble ˌin his faithˌ.*e* **11** Anyone who hates his brother is in darkness and walks in darkness and does not know where he is going, because the darkness has blinded his eyes.

Do Not Love The World

12   I am writing to you, little children,
        because your sins are forgiven for His Name's sake.*f*

13   I am writing to you, fathers,
        because you know Him who has been from the beginning.
    I am writing to you, young men,
        because you have conquered the Evil One.
    I am writing to you, children,
        because you know the Father.

14   I am writing to you, fathers,
        because you know Him who has been from the beginning.
    I am writing to you, young men,
        because you are strong,
        God's word remains in you,
        and you have conquered the Evil One.

2 *a -* 2 Greek: "*hilasmos*"; compare Leviticus 16:15 and Roman 3:25 and its accompanying footnote, noting, however, that the Greek terms in Romans 3:25 and in our present passage are not identical.
   b- 5 Or "whoever keeps His word."
   c- 8 See *ALĒTHINOS* COMPARED WITH *ALĒTHĒS* on page 530.
   d- 8 See *ALĒTHINOS* COMPARED WITH *ALĒTHĒS* on page 530.
   e- 10 See *SKANDALON* on page 545.
   f- 12 Meaning "your sins are forgiven on account of Jesus Christ"; Jesus' Name includes both *who* He is and *what* He did for sinful humankind.

15 Do not love the world or the things in the world. If anyone loves the world, he does not love the Father, 16 because everything in the world—the lust of the flesh, the lust of the eyes, and the vain display of property—does not come from the Father but from the world. 17 And the world with its lust is passing away. But the person who does the will of God remains forever.

Antichrist And Antichrists

18 Children, it is the last hour. You heard that an antichrist[g] is coming. And now many antichrists have come. That is how we know it is the last hour. 19 They left us, but they never really belonged to us. If they had been a part of us, they would have remained with us. But their leaving showed that they really do not all belong to us.

20 The Holy One has anointed you, and all of you have knowledge. 21 I am writing to you, not as though you do not know the truth, but because you know it and no lie comes from the truth.

22 Who is a liar but he who denies that Jesus is the Christ [Messiah]? The one who is the antichrist is he who denies the Father and the Son. 23 Everyone who denies the Son does not have the Father. The one who confesses the Son also has the Father. 24 Let that which you have heard from the beginning remain in you. If that which you have heard from the beginning remains in you, you also will remain in the Son and in the Father. 25 And this is what He promised us—everlasting life!

26 I am writing these things to you about those who are trying to lead you astray. 27 You received the anointing from Him, and that anointing remains in you, and you do not need anyone to teach you. But since His anointing teaches you everything—and since it is true and no lie, just as He also has taught you—remain in Him.

28 And now, little children, remain in Him so that when He appears we may be bold and not shrink from Him in shame when He comes.

C. The second standard: "We are now God's children" (2:29—4:6)

God's Children

29 If you know that He is righteous, you know that everyone who keeps on doing what is right has been given birth by Him.

3RD CHAPTER

1 See how greatly the Father has loved us—we are called God's children, and that is what we are. The world does not know us, because it did not know Him. 2 Dear friends, we are now God's children, but it has not yet been shown what we are going to be. We know that when it will be shown, we will be like

---

g- 18 The "anti" in "antichrist" means "against."

Him because we will see Him as He is. ³ And everyone who puts his hope in Him purifies himself, just as Christ is pure.

⁴ Everyone who sins also breaks the Law, for sin is the breaking of the Law. ⁵ And you know that He appeared in order to take away our sins. There is no sin in Him. ⁶ Anyone who remains in Him does not keep on sinning. Anyone who keeps on sinning has not seen Him or known Him. ⁷ Little children, do not let anybody deceive you. Whoever does right is righteous, just as He is righteous.

⁸ Anyone who lives in sin is the devil's child, because the devil has been sinning from the beginning. The reason that the Son of God appeared was to undo the works of the devil. ⁹ Everyone who has been given birth by God does not keep on sinning, because God's new life*ᵃ* is in him, and he cannot keep on sinning, because he has been given birth by God. ¹⁰ In this way you can see who the children of God are and who the children of the devil are, namely, everyone who does not do right or love his brother is not God's child.

Love One Another

¹¹ This is the message that you have heard from the beginning: Love one another. ¹² Do not be like Cain. He was a son of the Evil One and murdered his brother. And why did he murder him? Because his works were evil and his brother's were righteous. ¹³ Do not be surprised, my fellow Christians,*ᵇ* if the world hates you.

¹⁴ We know that we have come from death into life, because we love our brothers. Anyone who does not love remains in death. ¹⁵ Everyone who hates his brother is a murderer, and you know that no murderer has everlasting life awaiting him.

¹⁶ This is how we learned what love is: He gave His life for us. We also have an obligation to give our lives for our brothers. ¹⁷ If anyone has this world's goods and sees his brother in need but shuts his heart against him, how can he still be loving God?*ᶜ* ¹⁸ Little children, let us not only love in words or in talk, but let us put our love into action and make it real.*ᵈ*

¹⁹ This is how we will know that we are living in the truth and how we will reassure our consciences*ᵉ* before Him: ²⁰ Whenever our conscience condemns us, God is greater than our conscience, and He knows everything. ²¹ Dear friends, if our conscience does not condemn us, we can talk boldly to God ²² and receive from Him anything we ask, because we keep His commandments and

---

3 *a-* 9 Literally: "His seed." Because of this "new life," a Christian will no more practice a life-style of immorality, impurity, etc. (cf. Gal. 5:19-22) than a green plant will grow toward the darkness away from the light of the sun (cf. 1 Jn 1:6,7). The Christian, like a fragile plant in need of God's care, may not always be strong or always stand tall against the forces of darkness within and without, but the direction of his life will always be toward the light of God's love and away from the darkness of sin.

b- 13 Literally: "brothers."

c- 17 Literally: "how does the love of God remain in him?"; the Greek for "love of God" could mean either the love God has for us or the love we have for God; either interpretation could fit this text.

d- 18 Literally: "in action and in truth."

e- 19 Literally: "heart" (also in vv. 20,21).

do what pleases Him. **23** And this is His commandment, that we believe in the Name of His Son Jesus Christ and love one another as He has commanded us. **24** Anyone who does what He commands remains in God and God in him. And this is how we know that He remains in us—by the Spirit whom He has given us.

4TH CHAPTER

False Prophets

1 Dear friends, do not believe every spirit, but test the spirits to see whether they are from God, because many false prophets have gone out into the world. **2** This is how you can recognize God's Spirit: Every spirit who confesses that Jesus Christ has come in the flesh is from God. **3** And any spirit who does not confess that Jesus Christ has come in the flesh*a* is not from God. This is the spirit of the Antichrist, which you have heard is coming and which already now is in the world.

4 Little children, you are God's family,*b* and you have won a victory over these people, because He who is in you is greater than he who is in the world. **5** These people belong to the world. That is why they speak the thoughts of the world, and the world listens to them. **6** We are God's children.*c* Anyone who knows God listens to us. Anyone who is not God's child*d* does not listen to us. In this way we can tell what is the "spirit of truth" and what is the "spirit of error."

D. The third standard: "God is Love" (4:7–5:12)

God's Love In Us

7 Dear friends, let us love one another because love comes from God, and everyone who loves has been given birth by God and knows God. **8** The one who does not love does not know God, because God is Love. **9** God has shown us His love by sending His one-and-only Son*e* into the world, so that we might live through Him. **10** This is real love, not that we have loved God, but that He loved us and sent His Son to be the atoning sacrifice [the covering] for our sins.*f* **11** Dear friends, if that is how God loved us, then we have an obligation to love one another. **12** No one has ever seen God. If we love one another, God remains in us, and His love has been brought to maturity in us. **13** This is how we know that we remain in Him and He in us: He has shared His Spirit with us.*g*

14 We have seen and can witness to the fact that the Father sent His Son as

---

4 *a-* 3 Some of the older manuscripts and early translations omit: "Christ has come in the flesh."
b- 4 Literally: "from God."
c- 6 Literally: "from God."
d- 6 Literally: "not from God."
e- 9 This means His "one-of-a-kind Son" or "only-begotten Son"; see *MONOGENĒS* on page 542.
f- 10 Compare Leviticus 16:15; Romans 3:25.
g- 13 Literally: "He has given us of His Spirit."

the Savior of the world. **15** If anyone confesses that Jesus is God's Son, God remains in him and he in God. **16** And we have come to know and believe the love which God has for us. God is Love; whoever remains in His love remains in God and God remains in him.

17 His love has been brought to maturity when we can look ahead confidently to the Day of Judgment, because we are exactly what He is in this world. **18** There is no fear where His love is; but His mature love throws out fear, because fear involves punishment. The person who fears has not been brought to maturity in His love.

19 We love because He first loved us. **20** If anyone says, "I love God," but hates his brother, he is a liar. For if anyone does not love his brother whom he has seen, he cannot love God whom he has not seen. **21** And this is the commandment that He gave us: Let the person who loves God also love his brother.

5TH CHAPTER

Faith In The Son Of God

1 Everyone who believes that Jesus is the Christ [Messiah] has been given birth by God. And everyone who loves the One who gave birth loves the person who has been given birth by God.*a* **2** We know that we love God's children when we love God and do what He commands us to do. **3** For loving God means that we carry out His commandments. And His commands are not burdensome. **4** For everyone who has been given birth by God conquers the world, and our faith is the victorious conqueror over the world. **5** Who is the one who conquers the world but he who believes that Jesus is the Son of God?

6 This is He who came by water and blood—Jesus Christ—not by water only, but by water and by blood. And the Spirit is the One who testifies, because the Spirit is the Truth. **7** There are three who testify:*b* **8** the Spirit, the water, and the blood, and these three have one purpose.

9 If we accept the testimony of men, God's testimony is greater because it is God's own testimony which He has given about His Son. **10** The person who believes in the Son of God has the testimony of God in him. If a person does not believe God, he has made God a liar, because he has not believed the testimony which God has given about His Son.

11 This is the testimony of God: He has given us everlasting life and this life is in His Son. **12** The person who has the Son has life. The person who does not

---

5 *a*- 1 Literally: "And everyone who loves Him who gave birth loves the one who was given birth by Him."

b- 7 All of the older manuscripts lack verses 7b-8a: "in heaven: the Father, the Word, and the Holy Spirit, and these Three are One. And there are three testifying on earth." Early in the 16th century a translator apparently took these words from Latin manuscripts and inserted them in his Greek New Testament. Erasmus took them from this Greek New Testament and inserted them in the third edition (1522) of his Greek New Testament. Luther used the text prepared by Erasmus. But even though the inserted words taught the Trinity, Luther ruled them out and never included them in his translation. In 1550 Bugenhagen objected to these words "on account of the truth." In 1574 Feyerabend, a printer, added them to Luther's text, and in 1596 they appeared in the Wittenberg copies.

have the Son of God does not have life.

E. Conclusion: The great certainties to which we hold (5:13-20)

[13] I am writing this to you so that you who believe in the Name of the Son of God may know that you have everlasting life.

[14] We have confidence in God that if we ask for anything according to His will, He listens to us. [15] And if we know that He listens to whatever requests we make, then we know that we are given those requests which we make of Him. [16] If someone sees his brother committing a sin which does not lead to death, let him ask and God will give him life—⌊this is true⌋ for those who commit sins which do not lead to death. There is sin which leads to death; I do not tell you to pray about that. [17] Every kind of wrongdoing is sin, and there is sin which does not lead to death.

[18] We know that no one who has been given birth by God goes on sinning, but the One born of God keeps a close watch on him,[c] and the Evil One does not touch him. [19] We know that we are God's children, and that the whole world is in the power of the Evil One.

[20] We know that the Son of God came and gave us the understanding to know Him who is true,[d] and we are in Him who is true, in His Son Jesus Christ. He is the true God and everlasting life.

F. Closing admonition (5:21)

[21] Little children, keep away from idols.

---

c- 18 Or "the person born of God keeps a close watch on himself."
d- 20 Greek: "alēthinos" (twice more in verse); see *ALĒTHINOS* COMPARED WITH *ALĒTHĒS* on page 530.

THE LETTER OF
2 JOHN[a]

A. Opening greeting (1-3)

1 The Elder to the chosen lady and her children, whom I love in the truth, and not I alone, but all who know the truth, **2** because the truth remains in us and will be with us forever. **3** God the Father and Jesus Christ, the Father's Son, will give us grace,[b] mercy, and peace in truth and love.

B. Walking in the truth (4-6)

4 I was very happy to find some of your children living in the truth, as the Father has commanded us. **5** And now I ask, dear lady—not as if I were writing you a new commandment, but one which we have had from the beginning—that we love one another. **6** And this is love, that we live according to His commandments. This is the same commandment as you have heard from the beginning: Live in love.

C. Erroneous teachers (7-11)

7 Many deceivers have gone out into the world. They do not confess Jesus Christ as One who comes in the flesh. That is the mark of the deceiver and the Antichrist. **8** Watch yourselves so you will not lose what you worked for, but that you may receive your full reward.

9 Everyone who goes beyond and does not stay with what Christ has taught does not have God. The person who stays with what He taught has both the Father and the Son. **10** If anyone comes to you and does not bring what Christ taught, do not take him into your home or greet him. **11** For the person who greets him shares the wicked things he does.

D. Conclusion: Plan to visit and a greeting (12,13)

12 While I have much to write to you, I do not want to do it with paper and

---

a   *2 John* is the Apostle John's letter written either to a Christian lady or to a church (v. 1), since the Greek word for "church" is a feminine noun. "Elder" (v. 1) can be viewed as a proper title for John (equivalent to "the venerable John") since he apparently outlived all of Jesus' original disciples by some 25 years.

b- 3 Meaning "God's undeserved love."

ink, but I hope to come to you and talk with you face to face, so that we^c may be very happy.

13 The children of your sister, whom God has chosen, greet you.

---

c- 12 Some of the older manuscripts and earlier translations read: "you."

THE LETTER OF
3 JOHN[a]

A. Opening greeting (1)

1 The Elder to my dear Gaius, whom I love in truth.

B. About Gaius (2-8)

2 Dear friend, I pray that you are doing well in every way and are healthy, just as your soul is doing well. **3** I was delighted when some fellow Christians[b] came and told me about the truth you have—how you continue to live in it. **4** Nothing gives me greater joy than to hear that my children continue to live in the truth.

5 Dear friend, you are exercising your faith in what you are doing for your fellow Christians, even though they are strangers. **6** They have publicly told the church about your love. Please help them on their way, as it is right before God, **7** because they went out for the Name ⸤of Jesus⸥, taking nothing from the Gentiles. **8** We have an obligation to support such people in order to work with them for the truth.

C. Criticism of Diotrephes (9,10)

9 I wrote something to the church, but Diotrephes, who loves to be in charge, will not listen to us. **10** For this reason, if I come, I will bring up what he is doing when he talks such wicked nonsense about us. Not satisfied with that, he refuses to welcome the fellow Christians as guests; he also attempts to stop those who want to welcome them and tries to put them out of the church.

D. About Demetrius (11,12)

11 Dear friend, do not imitate what is wrong but what is right. The one who does what is right is the child of God.[c] The one who does wrong has not seen God.

---

a   *3 John* is a letter to Gaius, evidently a member of one of the congregations under the Apostle John's supervision. "Elder" (v. 1) can be viewed as a proper title for John (equivalent to "the venerable John") since he apparently outlived all of Jesus' disciples by some 25 years.

b- 3 Literally: "brothers" (also in vv. 5,10).

c- 11 Literally: "is from God."

12 Everyone speaks well of Demetrius, and so does the truth itself. We also speak well of him, and you know that our testimony is true.

E. Conclusion: Plan to visit and greetings (13-15)

13 I have much to write to you, but I do not want to do it with pen and ink. 14 I hope to see you very soon and talk with you face to face.
15 Peace to you! The friends here send you their greetings. Greet each of our friends by name.

THE LETTER OF
JUDE^a

A. *Opening greeting (1,2)*

1 Jude, a servant^b of Jesus Christ and a brother of James, to you who have been called, who are loved in God the Father and kept for Jesus Christ: **2** *May more and more* mercy, *peace*, and love *be yours!*

B. *Purpose of letter (3,4)*

Fight For The Faith

3 While I have been very eager to write to you, dear friends, about the salvation we share, now it is necessary that I write to you and urge you to fight for the faith once entrusted to the believers [saints].

4 There are some people who have sneaked in among you—some time ago it was written that they were headed for this condemnation—ungodly persons who turn the grace [undeserved love] that our God has for us into unrestrained lust and who disown our only Master and Lord, Jesus Christ.

C. *Examples of God's judgment (5-7)*

5 You already know all this, but I want to remind you how the Lord saved His people from Egypt but afterwards destroyed those who did not believe. **6** And there were angels who did not keep their position of authority but left their estate. He put them in everlasting chains and gloom to be kept for the judgment of the great Day—**7** just like Sodom and Gomorrah and the towns around them, who in the exact same way committed sexual sins and gave themselves over to unnatural vice. As they suffer their judgment, they lie before us as a warning concerning everlasting fire.

D. *Description of false teachers (8-16)*

8 Yet in the same way these men with their dreams defile the body, reject the Lord's authority, and slander God's splendor. ^c **9** When *the archangel Michael*^d

---

2 Dan 4:1; 6:25   *9 Dan 10:13,21; 12:1*

---

a   *Jude* probably was written by Jude "the brother of James," who very likely was "the brother of the Lord" (see Matt. 13:55; Mk. 6:3; and especially the footnote on the title to the book of *James). Jude* is very similar to the second chapter of *2 Peter* in warning against false teachers.

b- 1 Literally: "slave," reflecting Jude's total subjection to God.

c- 8 Literally: "glories"; see 2 Peter 2:10 and its accompanying footnote.

d- 9 Or "Archangel Michael"—if it is a reference to Christ. Compare Revelation 12:7 and see MICHAEL THE ARCHANGEL on page 555.

was debating with the devil and arguing about the body of Moses, he did not dare to bring a charge of slander against him, but said, *"The Lord rebuke you!"* 10 But whatever these men do not understand, they slander; and whatever they, like unthinking animals, know by instinct, they use to destroy themselves. 11 Woe to them! They have gone the way of Cain; for a profit they have rushed into the error of Balaam; they have rebelled like Korah and perished.

12 They are a blot on your love meals, where they are feasting together with you without fear, shepherds who take care of ₍only₎ themselves; clouds driven along by the winds without giving rain; trees that in late fall have no fruit but are torn up by the roots, and so they are twice dead; 13 wild waves of the sea, foaming out their own shame; wandering stars for whom the gloom of darkness is reserved forever.

14 Enoch, the seventh ₍in descent₎ from Adam, prophesied about them. He said, "The Lord has come with ten thousands of His holy ones, *e* 15 in order to bring judgment on all of them and to convict all the ungodly of all the ungodly things that they have done in their ungodliness and of all the defiant things that ungodly sinners have said against Him."

16 They grumble, constantly complain, follow their lusts, brag, and flatter people in order to take advantage of them.

E. Advice (17-23)

17 But you, dear friends, remember what the apostles of our Lord Jesus Christ predicted. 18 They told you, "In the last time there will be scoffers, following their own ungodly lusts." 19 They are causing divisions. They are worldly because they do not have the Spirit.

Build Yourselves Up

20 But you, dear friends, while you build yourselves up in your most holy faith and pray in the Holy Spirit, 21 keep yourselves in God's love, as you look for the mercy of our Lord Jesus Christ to give you everlasting life.

22 Some people are in doubt—show mercy to them; 23 save others *by snatching them from the fire*; be careful as you show mercy to still others detesting their clothing which has been stained by their flesh.

F. Closing doxology (24,25)

Praising God

24 Now to Him who is able to keep you from falling and have you stand without fault and with great joy in the presence of His glory, 25 to the only God, who saves us through Jesus Christ our Lord—to Him be glory, majesty, power, and authority—as it was from everlasting, so be it now and forever. Amen.

---

23 Zech 3:2

---

e- 14 That is, the angels who accompany Him on Judgment Day.

REVELATION[a]

1ST CHAPTER

A. Introduction (1:1-20)

1 This is the revelation[b] of JESUS CHRIST which God gave Him
   to show His servants *the things that must happen* without delay;
   and He sent this revelation by way of symbols[c]
   through His angel to His servant John.

2 John testifies about what he saw;
   it is God's word
   and the testimony of Jesus Christ.[d]

3 Blessed is the one who reads
   and those who hear the words of this prophecy
   and keep what is written in it—because the time is near.

---

1 Is 48:6; Dan 2:28-30,45

SPECIAL NOTE: Our present Bible version has chosen to set the entire book of *Revelation* in
poetic style. In this book units of poetic thought are held together with "ands," the number of
which relates to the particular number of thoughts contained in the unit. The sum total of
these thoughts within a unit indicates the subject matter that is being communicated. The
grouping of *running* "ands" *via* poetic set helps the reader identify units. For this reason
GWN refuses to split units of thought from one page to another since this would interrupt
unified *visual* contact. This refusal has created a very educational format but also has forced
several pages to remain unfilled since the beginning of units often had to be pushed to a new
page since the whole unit would not fit on a former page. See GRAMMATIC/POETIC
STRUCTURES THAT CONVEY TEXTUAL MEANINGS on page 558 and THE *KAI*
STRUCTURE on page 565.

1 a *Revelation* is the Apostle John's vision of the future victory of Christ's church. John received
   his vision on the island of Patmos toward the close of the first century (before A.D. 96).
 b- 1 Meaning "unveiling."
 c- 1 Literally: "and which He made known by visual signs when He sent it."
 d- 2 Literally: "His servant John [v.1], who testified the word of God and [namely] the testimony of
   Jesus Christ, which things he saw" (cf. 1:9).

To The Seven Churches

4 John to the seven[e] churches in the province of Asia:
  Grace[f] and peace to you from
    the *One-Who-Is* and
    the One-Who-Was and
    the *One-Who-Will-Be,*
  and from the Seven Spirits[g] who are before His throne,
5   and from Jesus Christ—
    He is *the faithful Witness,*
    the First of the dead *to live* again,
    and *the Ruler over the kings of the earth.*
  To Him who loves us
    and by His blood has *freed* us *from* our *sins*
6   and has made us *a kingdom, priests* to God and His Father—
  to Him be glory and power forever ⸤and⸥ ever.[h] Amen.

7 *Look, He is coming in the clouds,*
  and every eye *will see Him,*
  even[i] *the men who pierced Him,*
  and all *the groups of people on earth*[j] *will mourn because of Him.*
    So it will be. Amen.

8 "*I am* the Alpha and the Omega [the A and the Z],"[k] *says*
  God
  the Lord,
    the *One-Who-Is* and
    the One-Who-Was and
    the *One-Who-Will-Be,*
  the Almighty.[l]

---

4 Ex 3:14; Ps 118:26; Is 40:10; Dan 7:13; 9:26; Hab 2:3; Zech 14:10; Mal 3:1   *5 Ps 89:27,37;*
Is 40:2; Jer 42:5   *6 Ex 19:6; Is 61:6; Dan 7:18,22,27*   *7 Dan 7:13; Zech 12:10,12,14*
8 Ex 3:14; Ps 118:26; Is 40:10; Dan 7:13; 9:26; Hab 2:3; Mal 3:1

e- 4 See THE SYMBOLICAL NUMBERS OF *REVELATION* on page 567.

f- 4 Meaning "God's undeserved love" (also in 22:21).

g- 4 A name for the Holy Spirit, probably based on Isaiah 11:2 (also in 3:1; 4:5; 5:6).

h- 6 Literally: "the ages of ages," rendered "forever ⸤and⸥ ever." This phrase also occurs at 4:9,10;
  5:13; 7:12; 10:6; 11:15; 14:11; 15:7; 19:3; 20:10; 22:5. The half-brackets in GWN's text
  signal that the Greek *kai* or "and" is *not* in the text. This is important for readers to note so
  that they do *not* view this "and" as part of John's *kai* structure or "running units of ands."
  See THE *KAI* STRUCTURE on page 565. In other books of the New Testament GWN does
  not put half-brackets around the "and" in the phrase "forever and ever."

i- 7 Greek: "*kai*"; see THE *KAI* STRUCTURE on page 565.

j- 7 Literally: "all the tribes of the land." Compare Matthew 24:30.

k- 8 The Greek says: "I am the *Alpha* and the *Omega,*" that is, "I am the A and the O." These two
  letters are the first and the last letters of the Greek alphabet, respectively, as A and Z are the
  first and the last letters in the English alphabet. If Jesus would have been speaking to English
  speaking people in Revelation 1:8, then He would have stated, as the brackets indicate, "I am
  the A and the Z."

l- 8 The *Septuagint* (*LXX*), the ancient Greek translation of the Old Testament, translates "the
  LORD of armies [hosts]" with "the Lord Almighty" exactly 100 times. Compare 4:8f.; examine
  also 18:8 and its accompanying footnote as well as 19:6 and 21:22.

9 I, John, your fellow Christian[m] and one who shares with you
    in suffering
    and ruling
    and patiently enduring in Jesus,
        was ⌊exiled⌋ on the island called Patmos
           for speaking God's word
           and the testimony of Jesus,[n]

10 I came under the Spirit's power[o] on the Lord's day,
    and I heard a loud voice behind me like a trumpet, **11** saying:

      "Write on a scroll what you see
        and send it to the seven churches—to Ephesus
                  and to Smyrna
                  and to Pergamum
                  and to Thyatira
                  and to Sardis
                  and to Philadelphia
                  and to Laodicea."

12 And I turned to see the voice which was talking to me;
    and when I turned, *I saw* seven golden lampstands
13 and among the lampstands ⌊Someone⌋ *like the Son of Man:*[p]

      He *was clothed with a robe that reached down to His feet*;
      and He wore *a golden belt* around His chest;
14 *His head*
      and *His hair were white like white wool, like snow,*[q]
      and *His eyes were like flames of fire;*
15   and *His feet were like glowing bronze*, refined in a furnace;
      and *His voice was like the sound of many waters;*
16   and in His right hand He held seven stars;
      and out of His mouth came a sharp, double-edged sword;
      and His face was *like the sun* when it shines *in all its brightness.*[r]

17 And when I saw Him, I fell down at His feet as a dead man.
    And He laid His right hand on me, saying:

    "Stop being afraid!

12-15 Ezek 1:24; 9:2,3,11; 43:2; Dan 7:9,13; 10:5,6   **16** Judg 5:31   **17** Is 44:2,6; 48:12

m - 9 Literally: "brother."

n - 9 Meaning "which testifies about Jesus."

o - 10 Literally: "I came to be in spirit," that is, John found himself in a state of heightened spiritual awareness, as in a spiritual trance, a state in which he was able to see and hear things which men ordinarily do not see or hear.

p - 13 Or "like a son of man," meaning "like a human being" (also in 14:14). See "Son of Man" in Glossary.

q - 14 Some of the manuscripts read: "and (Greek: 'kai') like snow"; see THE *KAI* STRUCTURE on page 565.

r - 16 Literally: "strength" or "power"; the poetry is lined up flush to emphasize the *ten* features of Christ here mentioned. The number *ten* (indicating "completion") is one of the numbers used frequently in *Revelation* as an individual number or as a total of the various items within given patterns. See THE SYMBOLICAL NUMBERS OF *REVELATION* on page 567.

> "*I am the First and the Last* **18** and the Living One;
> and I died, and now you see I am alive forever
> and I have the keys of death and of *hades*.*s*

19 "Therefore write down
> what you have seen,
> and what is now,
> and *what is going to happen after these things*.

20 "*The hidden meaning* of the seven stars that you saw in My right hand
> and of the seven golden lampstands is this:

> The seven stars are the angels*t* of the seven churches,
> and the seven lampstands are the seven churches."

2ND CHAPTER

B. First vision: Seven letters (2:1–3:22)

Letter To The Church In Ephesus

1 "To the angel of the church in Ephesus write:

> The One who holds the seven stars in His right hand,
> the One who walks among the seven golden lampstands, says these things:

2
> I know what you have done
> and how hard you have worked
> and how you have patiently endured,
> and I know that you cannot tolerate wicked people;
> and you have tested those who call themselves apostles—
> and are not—
> and you have found them to be liars;
3 > and you have patiently endured
> and have suffered trouble for My Name
> and have not grown weary.

4
> But I have this against you,
> that your love is not what it was at first.

5
> Remember from where you have fallen,
> and repent,
> and do as you did at first;
> or else, if you do not repent,
> I will come to you
> and take your lampstand from its place.

19,20 Is 48:6

s - 18 Literally: "the unseen," meaning "the 'place of/receptacle for' disembodied souls"; see
HADES/GEHENNA on page 540.
t - 20 Or "messengers," that is, pastors.

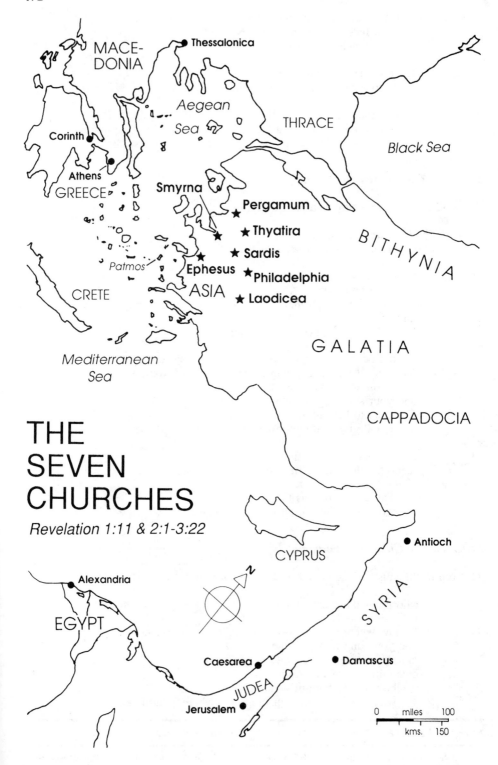

MACE-
DONIA

● Thessalonica

*Aegean
Sea*

THRACE

Black Sea

● Corinth

● Athens

GREECE

Smyrna

Pergamum

★ Thyatira

★ Sardis

BITHYNIA

Patmos

Ephesus

★ Philadelphia

CRETE

ASIA

★ Laodicea

*Mediterranean
Sea*

GALATIA

CAPPADOCIA

THE
SEVEN
CHURCHES

Revelation 1:11 & 2:1-3:22

CYPRUS

● Antioch

● Alexandria

SYRIA

EGYPT

Caesarea ●

● Damascus

JUDEA

Jerusalem ●

0   miles   100

kms.   150

6 But this you have ᵢin your favor¬—
    you hate the actions of the Nicolaitans,
     which I also hate.

7 Let the one who has an ear
    listen to what the Spirit says to the churches:

     'To the one who wins the victory I will give
     the privilege of eating from *the tree of life*
     that stands in the *Paradise* of God.' "

Letter To The Church In Smyrna

8 "And to the angel of the church in Smyrna write:

  The First and the Last,
  who died and became alive, says these things:

9 I know how you are suffering
    and how poor you are (but you are rich!)
    and how you are slandered by those who say that they are Jews—
    and are not—
    but rather are the synagog of Satan.

10 Do not be afraid of what you are going to suffer.
    You see, the devil is going to throw some of you into prison
      in order that you may be *tested*,
    and your suffering will go on for *ten days*.
    Continue to be faithful until death,
    and I will give you the crown of life.

11 Let the one who has an ear
    listen to what the Spirit says to the churches:

     'The one who wins the victory
     will not be hurt at all by the second death.' "

Letter To The Church In Pergamum

12 "And to the angel of the church in Pergamum write:

He who holds the sharp, double-edged sword, says these things:

13 I know where you live—where the throne of Satan is;
    and you cling to My Name
    and did not deny your faith in Me,
    even[a] in the days of Antipas—
     he was My faithful witness,[b]
     who was killed in your presence, where Satan lives.

---

7 Gen 2:9; 3:22,24; Ezek 31:8 **8** *Is 44:6; 48:12* **10** *Dan 1:12,14*

---

2 *a*- 13 Some of the manuscripts omit: "*kai*" ("and" or "even"); see THE *KAI* STRUCTURE on page 565.
  b- 13 Or "martyr."

14   But I have a few things against you
        because you have men there who hold what *Balaam* taught.
    He taught Balak to put a death trap[c] before *the people of Israel,*
        that is, *to eat food sacrificed to idols*
        and *to sin sexually.*[d]

15   So you also[e] have some who hold what the Nicolaitans teach.

16   Repent, then,
        or else I will come to you quickly
            and fight against them with the sword of My mouth.

17   Let the one who has an ear
    listen to what the Spirit says to the churches:

        'To the one who wins the victory
            I will give some of the hidden manna,
            and *I will give him* a white stone,
            and *a new name* written on the white stone,
                ₐa name⌟ that is known only to him who receives it.' "

Letter To The Church In Thyatira

18 "And to the angel of the church in Thyatira write:

    God's Son, whose *eyes are like flames of fire*
    and whose feet *are like glowing bronze*, says these things:

19   I know your works
            and your love
            and your faith
            and your service
            and your patient endurance,
        and that your latest works are more than the first.

20   But I hold it against you
            that you tolerate that woman Jezebel—
                she calls herself a prophetess,
                and teaches
                and misleads My servants[f] *to sin sexually*
                and *to eat food sacrificed to idols*;
21   and I gave her time to repent,
                but[g] she refuses to repent of her sexual sins.

---

14 Num 25:1,2; 31:16   *17* Is 56:5; 62:2; 65:15   *18* Dan 10:6   *20* Num 25:1,2; 31:16

c- 14 See *SKANDALON* on page 545.
d- 14 Compare 2:20.
e- 15 Greek: "*kai*"; see THE *KAI* STRUCTURE on page 565.
f- 20 The translated text has sacrificed English flow and communication at this point in favor of retaining John's string of Greek *kais* ("ands"). Communicatively, the words "and teaches and misleads . . ." mean "and misleads My servants by teaching them . . . ."
g- 21 Greek: "*kai*"; see THE *KAI* STRUCTURE on page 565.

22 Watch Me! I am throwing her into a bed
and those who live in sexual sin with her into great suffering,
  unless they repent of what she is doing;

23 and I will kill her children;
and all the churches will know that I am the One
  who searches *minds and hearts*;
and *I will give each* of you *according to what you have done.*

24 But I say to the rest of you in Thyatira,
all who do not hold this teaching,
who have not learned the 'deep things' of Satan, as they call them:

I am putting no other burden on you;
25 only cling to what you have until I come.

26 And to the one who wins the victory
and continues to do My works to the end
  I will give authority over *the nations*,
    just as I have received it from My Father,
27 and he *will rule them with a rod of iron,*
      shattering them like pottery;
28 and I will give him the Morning Star.

29 Let the one who has an ear
listen to what the Spirit says to the churches."

3RD CHAPTER

Letter To The Church In Sardis

1 "And to the angel of the church in Sardis write:

He who has God's Seven Spirits
and the seven stars, says these things:

I know what you are doing:
  You have a reputation that you are alive,
  but*a* you are dead.

2 Wake up
    and strengthen the remaining things that are about to die,
      for I have found that your works
      are not complete in the sight of My God.
3 So remember how you once accepted and listened ⌊to the truth⌋.
    and hold on to it
      and repent!
If you do not wake up, I will come like a thief,
  and you will certainly not know
    at what time I will come upon you.

---

23 Ps 7:9; 26:2; 62:12; Prov 24:12; Jer 11:20; 17:10; 20:12   **26,27** *Ps 2:8,9*

3 *a-* 1 Greek: "*kai*"; see THE *KAI* STRUCTURE on page 565.

4   But you have a few people^b in Sardis
        who have not soiled their clothes,
   and they will walk with Me in white garments
      because they are worthy.

5   The one who wins the victory in this way
        will be dressed in white garments,
   and I will never *erase* his *name out of the Book of Life*,
   and I will confess his name before My Father and before His angels.

6   Let the one who has an ear
      listen to what the Spirit says to the churches."

Letter To The Church In Philadelphia

7 "And to the angel of the church in Philadelphia write:

   The One who is holy,
    the One who is genuine,^c
    the One who has *the key of David*,
     who opens ⸢a door⸣ and *no one will shut it*,
     who shuts^d ⸢a door⸣ and *no one opens it*, says these things:

8   I know what you are doing
     (see, I have opened a door before you that no one can shut),
      that you have only a little strength,
      and have kept My word,
      and have not denied My Name.

9   Look, I will make those of Satan's synagog,
      who say that they are Jews—
        yet^e are not—but are lying,
    look, I will make them *come*
      and *bow down* at your feet
        and realize that *I have loved you*.

10   Because you have kept My word of patience,^f
      I also will keep you safe at the time of testing
      which is coming upon the whole world
        to test those living on the earth.

---

5 Ex 32:32,33; Ps 69:28   *7* Job 12:14; Is 22:22   *9* Ps 22:27; 86:9; Is 43:4; 45:14;
49:23; 60:14; 66:23; Jer 16:19

---

b- 4 Literally: "names," that is, names which are written in God's Book of Life (cf. v. 5c,d).
c- 7 Greek: "*alēthinos*"; see *ALĒTHINOS* COMPARED WITH *ALĒTHĒS* on page 530.
d- 7 Or "*and* who shuts"; many of the older manuscripts omit: "and," no doubt because only one
    article governs both participles in Greek: "*ho anoigōn . . . kleiōn*" (lit. "the One opening . . .
    shutting").
e- 9 Greek: "*kai*"; see THE *KAI* STRUCTURE on page 565.
f- 10 Meaning that God's word had provided the strength to patiently endure. The idea that the text
    is saying "you have kept My *command* to be patient" is questionable and too limiting. God's
    word does not only command us to be patient, rather, it also provides the strength to develop
    patience. This latter truth seems to fit the present context best.

11   I am coming soon!

         Cling to what you have
         so that no one takes your crown.

12   The one who wins the victory—
         I will make him a pillar in the TEMPLE[g] of My God,
           and he will never leave it again,
             and I will write on him the Name of My God
             and *the name of the city* of My God—
                the NEW JERUSALEM coming down
                out of heaven from My God—
         and My *new Name.*

13   Let the one who has an ear
         listen to what the Spirit says to the churches."

Letter To The Church In Laodicea

14 "And to the angel of the church in Laodicea write:

     The Amen,
     the Witness who is faithful and true,[h]
     the *Source*[i] *of God's creation*, says these things:

15   I know what you are doing,
         that you are neither cold nor hot;
           I wish you were cold or hot.
16   But now that you are lukewarm
         and not hot or cold,
           I am going to spit you out of My mouth.

17   Because you say: '*I'm rich*
                  and *wealthy*
                  and don't need anything';
     and ⌐yet⌐ you do not know that you are
         miserable and pitiful and poor and blind and naked,
18   ⌐therefore⌐ I advise you to
         buy gold from Me which has been purified in fire
           so you may be rich,
         and ⌐buy⌐ white clothes from Me to put on[j]
           so you may keep your shameful nakedness from showing,
         and ⌐buy⌐ salve to put on your eyes
           so you may see.

---

12 *Is 56:5; 62:2; 65:15; Ezek 48:35*   **14** *Ps 89:37; Prov 8:22,23; Jer 42:5*   **17** *Hos 12:8*

---

g- 12 Beginning here and also occurring at 7:15; 11:19; 13:6; 14:15,17; 15:5,6,8; 16:1,17; and
     21:2,3,10,22,23, the terms TEMPLE, NEW JERUSALEM, TENT, ARK of His COVENANT,
     TABERNACLE, SANCTUARY of the TABERNACLE OF THE TESTIMONY, SANCTU-
     ARY, HOLY CITY NEW JERUSALEM, TABERNACLE of God, HOLY CITY JERUSA-
     LEM, GLORY OF GOD, and LAMP appear in all capitals. This style is employed when these
     terms, which ordinarily refer to *earthly* phenomena, are used of their *heavenly* counterparts. This
     was the pattern used in Hebrews 8–13. See THE HOLY PLACES on page 550.

h- 14 Greek: "*alēthinos*"; see *ALĒTHINOS* COMPARED WITH *ALĒTHĒS* on page 530.

i- 14 The Greek word can also mean "Ruler."

j- 18 The Greek has a "*kai*" ("and") at this point. However, the English "and" just does not flow in

19   *I correct and discipline all whom I love*;
          take this seriously then
             and repent.

20   See, I am standing *at the door* and *knocking*.
       If anyone listens to My voice and *opens* the door,
          I will come in to him
          and eat with him,
          and he with Me.

21   To the one who wins the victory
          I will give the privilege of sitting with Me on My throne,
     just as I have won the victory
          and have sat down with my Father on His throne.

22   Let the one who has an ear
     listen to what the Spirit says to the churches."

4TH CHAPTER

C. Second vision: Seven seals (4:1–7:17)

The Heavenly Court In Session Around The Throne

1   After these things I looked,
    and there a door ⌊was standing⌋ open in heaven,
    and I heard the first *voice* like *a trumpet*[a] speaking to me.
      It said:

        "*Come up* here,
          and I will show you *what must happen* after these things."

2   And[b] instantly I came under the Spirit's power;[c]
    and look, a throne was standing in heaven;
    and *Someone was sitting on the throne!*

3   And the *One who sat* there looked like a jasper stone
    and ⌊like⌋ a carnelian stone,
    and there was *a rainbow around* the throne which looked like an emerald.

---

19 Prov 3:12   20 S of S 5:2   1 Ex 19:16,24; Is 48:6; Dan 2:28-30,45
2,3 1 Kgs 22:19; 2 Chr 18:18; Ps 47:9; Is 6:1; Ezek 1:26-28

---

the present context. Nevertheless, it is important to John's structure of *Revelation*; see THE *KAI* STRUCTURE on page 565.

4 *a*- 1 A reference back to 1:10.
  b- 2 Some of the older manuscripts and early translations omit: "and"; see THE *KAI* STRUCTURE on page 565.
  c- 2 See 1:10 and its accompanying footnote.

4 And around the throne were 24 other thrones;
and on these thrones sat 24 elders dressed in white garments;
and there were golden crowns on their heads.

5 And from the throne *came*
flashes of lightning and *rumblings* and peals of thunder;
and seven flaming torches were burning in front of the throne;
these are the Seven Spirits of God.

6 And in front of the throne there was also something
like a sea of glass, like crystal;
and *in the center* near the throne
and around the throne, there *were four living creatures*,
covered with eyes in front and in back.

7 And *the first living creature was like a lion,*
and *the second like a young bull,*
and *the third had a face like that of a human being,*
and *the fourth was like a* flying *eagle*;
8 and *each* of the four living creatures *had six wings*
which *were covered with eyes all around* and under;
and day and night without stopping they were saying:

"*HOLY, HOLY, HOLY is the*
Lord God Almighty,
Who-Was and *Who-Is* and *Who-Will-Be*."[d]

9 And whenever the living creatures *give glory* and honor and thanks
to *Him who is sitting on the throne,*
to Him who *lives forever* ⌐and⌐ ever,
10 the 24 elders *bow down before Him who is sitting on the throne*
and *worship Him who lives forever* ⌐and⌐ ever,
and they place their crowns before the throne, saying:

11 "Our Lord and God, You are worthy
to receive glory and honor and power—
for You created everything,
and because of Your will they came into existence
and were created."

---

5 Ex 19:16; Ezek 1:13   **6** Ezek 1:5,18; 10:12   **7** Ezek 1:10   **8** Ex 3:14; Ps 118:26;
Is 6:2,3; 40:10; Ezek 1:18; 10:12; Dan 7:13; 9:26; Hab 2:3; Mal 3:1
9 1 Kgs 22:19; 2 Chr 18:18; Ps 47:9; Is 6:1; Dan 4:34; 6:26; 12:7   **10** 1 Kgs 22:19; 2 Chr 18:18;
Ps 22:27; 47:9; 86:9; Is 6:1; 45:14; 49:23; 60:14; 66:23; Jer 16:19; Dan 4:34; 6:26; 12:7

---

d- **8** Note that *seven* sets of *threes* are detailed by John in verses 2-8. (*Three* here suggests
trinitarian overtones.) Observe John's usage of "ands" (Greek: "*kai*") as connectives; these will
help the reader detect the sets of *threes*. See THE *KAI* STRUCTURE on page 565. The reader
should especially note that verses 7-8c contain the sixth threesome, while verse 8d-f contains
the seventh threesome. Of great intrigue is the fact that this *seventh* threesome is, of itself,
comprised of *three* additional threesomes. (On this basis some would see *ten* sets of *threes*.)
See THE SYMBOLICAL NUMBERS OF *REVELATION* on page 567.

5TH CHAPTER

The Scroll (With Seven Seals) And The Lamb

1 And in the right hand of *Him who sat on the throne* I saw *a scroll,*
  with writing both on the inside and the outside,
  sealed with seven seals.
2 And I saw a mighty angel, calling out with a loud voice,

  "Who is worthy to open the scroll
  and break the seals on it?"

3 And no one in heaven, on earth, or under the earth
  could open the scroll or look into it.
4 And I cried bitterly because no one was found
  who was worthy to open the scroll or look into it.
5 And one of the elders said to me:

  "Stop crying!
      You see, the *Lion* from the tribe of *Judah,*
      the Root of David, has won the victory.
      He can open the scroll and its seven seals."

6 And in the center near the throne
  and ⸢in the center⸥ of the four living creatures
  and in the center of the elders
      I saw a *Lamb* standing.
          ⸢The Lamb⸥ seemed to have been *slain*;
          ⸢He⸥ had seven horns and *seven eyes,*
              which are the Seven Spirits of God
                  who are sent *all over the world.*

7 And He went
  and took ⸢the scroll⸥ from the right hand of Him who sat *on the throne.*

8 And when He had taken the scroll,
      the four living creatures and the 24 elders
      bowed down before the Lamb.
          (Each held a harp and golden bowls full of *incense*
          which are the *prayers* of the believers. *a)*
9 And they *sang a new song,* saying:

---

1 *1 Kgs 22:19; 2 Chr 18:18; Ps 47:9; Is 6:1; 29:11; Ezek 2:9,10*   **5** *Gen 49:9,10; Is 11:1,10;*
Jer 23:5   **6** *Is 53:7; Zech 4:6 (cf. 3:9)*   **7** *1 Kgs 22:19; 2 Chr 18:18; Ps 47:9; Is 6:1*
8 *Ps 141:2*   **9** *Ps 33:3; Dan 3:4; 7:14*

---

5 *a-* 8 Literally: "saints" (also at 8:3,4; 11:18; 13:7,10; 14:12; 16:6; 17:6; 18:20,24; 19:8; 20:9).

"You are worthy to take the scroll and open the seals on it,
> because You were slain;
and with Your blood You bought us
> from every *tribe* and *language* and *people* and *nation*
> to be God's own;
10   and You made them a *kingdom* and *priests* to our God;
and they will continue to rule as *kings on the earth.*"

11 And I saw and heard—
> the voice of many angels surrounding the throne
> and the four living creatures
> and the elders;

> and their number was *ten thousand times ten thousand*
> and *thousands of thousands.*

12   With a loud voice they were saying:

> "The *Lamb* who was *slain* is worthy to receive
>> power
> and wealth
> and wisdom
> and strength
> and honor
> and glory
> and praise."

13 And I heard every creature
> in heaven and on earth and under the earth and on the sea,
and all that are in them, saying:

> "To *Him who sits on the throne* and to the Lamb be
> praise and honor and glory and might forever ˌandˌ ever."

14 And the four living creatures said, "Amen!"
And the elders *bowed down and worshiped.*

6TH CHAPTER

The Lamb Executes The Initial Verdicts: Six Afflictions

1 And I saw when the Lamb opened the first of the seven seals,
and I heard one of the four living creatures call with a voice like thunder:
> "Come!"

---

10 Ex 19:6; Is 61:6   11 Dan 7:10   12 Is 53:7   13 1 Kgs 22:19; 2 Chr 18:18; Ps 47:9; Is 6:1
14 Ps 22:27; 86:9; Is 45:14; 49:23; 60:14; 66:23; Jer 16:19

2   And I looked, and there ⌐was¬ a *white horse*,
           and its rider[a] had a bow,
           and he was given a crown
           and rode off as a conqueror to conquer.

3   And when He opened the second seal,
   I heard the second living creature call,
      "Come!"

4   And another *horse* came out, fiery *red*,
           and its rider was given the power to take away peace from the earth
           and to have people murder one another,
           and he was given a large sword.

5   And when He opened the third seal,
   I heard the third living creature call,
      "Come!"

           And I looked, and there ⌐was¬ a *black horse*,
              and its rider had a scale in his hand.
6   And I heard what seemed to be a voice,
              ⌐coming¬ from among the four living creatures, saying:

              "A quart of wheat for a day's pay
              and three quarts of barley for a day's pay,
              and do not harm the oil and the wine."

7   And when He opened the fourth seal,
   I heard the voice of the fourth living creature call,
      "Come!"

8   And I looked, and there ⌐was¬ a pale horse,
              and its rider's name was *Plague*,
                 and *Hades*[b] came close behind.

   And they[c] were given power over a fourth of the earth
      to *kill* people *with sword*
      and with *famine*
      and with *plague*
      and by the *beasts* of the earth.

2-5 Zech 6:1,3   *8 Jer 14:12; 15:2; 21:7; Ezek 5:12; 14:21; Hos 13:14*

---

6 a- 2 Or "Rider," if a reference to *Christ* (cf. 19:11); some feel that the "rider" is a reference to the *Gospel*; fitting the sense of the three horsemen who follow (vv. 4,5,8) others feel that this first horseman stands for *oppressive tyranny* (cf. 6:8h).

   b- 8 See 1:18 and its accompanying footnote.

   c- 8 "They" may either refer to "Plague and *Hades*" (v. 8b,c) or to the four horsemen (vv. 2,4,5,8). If the latter is the case note verse 8, lines e, f, g, h. Line e would relate to the second horseman (v. 4 "sword"—*war* and *bloodshed*), line f to the third horseman (v. 5—*famine*), line g to the fourth horseman (v. 8 "Plague"), and line h to the first horseman (v. 2 "conquer"— possibly *tyrannic oppression*, the "beasts" of line h being human oppressors). Such an interpretation makes the "fourth" of line d distributive to each of the four horsemen, meaning a fourth to each. However, this is debatable since one would expect the Greek to say "they were *each* given power over a fourth, etc.," that is, if "a fourth" is meant to be distributive. If the "they" refers to "Plague and *Hades*," then possibly the Greek term translated "Plague" and "plague" in lines b and g, respectively, would best be translated "Death" and "death," respectively.

9 And when He opened the fifth seal,
   I saw under the altar the souls of those who had been slain
        because of God's word
        and His testimony to which they held.
10 And they called out with a loud voice, saying:

> "*Master*, holy and genuine,*d*
> *how long* ˌwill You waitˌ until You judge and *punish*
> those living on the earth because ˌthey shedˌ our blood?"

11 And each of them was given a white robe,
    and they were told to rest a little longer
    until all their fellow servants and fellow Christians*e* who were to be killed,
    even*f* as they had been,
    also*g* would be present.

12 And when He opened the sixth seal, I looked,
    and a great earthquake took place,
    and the *sun turned black* like coarse cloth made of hair,
    and *the* full *moon became* like *blood*,
13 and *the stars fell from the sky* to the earth
        like figs dropping from *a fig tree* when it is shaken by a strong wind,
14 and *the sky* vanished *like a scroll being rolled up*,
    and every mountain and island was moved from its place.

15 And *the kings of the earth*
    and the great men
    and the generals
    and the rich
    and the powerful
    and every slave
    and ˌeveryˌ free man
        hid themselves *in the caves* and *among the rocks* of the mountains,
16   and they kept *saying to the mountains and rocks*:

> "*Fall on us*
> *and hide us*
>   *from the face of the One who sits on the throne*
>   and from the anger of the Lamb,
17   because *the great Day* of Their *Anger has come*,
>   and *who is able to stand?*"

---

10 *Deut 32:43; 2 Kgs 9:7; Ps 79:5*   **12-14** *Is 13:10; 34:4; Ezek 32:7,8; Joel 2:30,31*   **15** *Ps 2:2*
15,16 *Is 2:10,19,21; Jer 4:29; Hos 10:8*   **16** *1 Kgs 22:19; 2 Chr 18:18; Ps 47:9; Is 6:1*
17 *Ps 76:8; Joel 2:11,31; Nah 1:6; Zeph 1:14,15; Mal 3:2; 4:5*

---

d- 10 Greek: "*alēthinos*"; see *ALĒTHINOS* COMPARED WITH *ALĒTHĒS* on page 530.
e- 11 Literally: "brothers."
f- 11 Greek: "*kai*"; see THE *KAI* STRUCTURE on page 565.
g- 11 Greek: "*kai*"; see THE *KAI* STRUCTURE on page 565.

7TH CHAPTER

Believers Sealed For Salvation Before The Seventh Seal Is Opened And The Seven Trumpets Sound

1   After this I saw four angels
     standing at the *four corners* of the earth,
     holding back the *four winds of the earth*
        to keep any of them from blowing
        on the land or on the sea or on any tree.
2   And I saw another angel coming up from the east
     with the seal of the living God,
   and he called out with a loud voice to the four angels
     who had been given power to harm land and sea, **3** saying:

> "Do not harm the land or the sea or the trees
>   until we have put the *seal on the foreheads* of the servants of our God."

4   And I heard the number of those who were sealed: "144,000."

   Those who were sealed were from every tribe of the people of Israel:

5   12,000 from the tribe of Judah sealed,
           12,000 from the tribe of Reuben,
           12,000 from the tribe of Gad,
6   12,000 from the tribe of Asher,
           12,000 from the tribe of Naphtali,
           12,000 from the tribe of Manasseh,
7   12,000 from the tribe of Simeon,
           12,000 from the tribe of Levi,
           12,000 from the tribe of Issachar,
8   12,000 from the tribe of Zebulun,
           12,000 from the tribe of Joseph,
           12,000 from the tribe of Benjamin*a* sealed.

9   After these things I looked,
   and there ⌊was⌋ a large crowd that no one could count,
     from every *nation* and *tribe* and *people* and *language*,
        standing before the throne and before the Lamb,
        wearing white robes and ⌊carrying⌋ palm branches in their hands.

---

1 *Jer 49:36; Ezek 7:2; 37:9; Dan 7:2; Zech 6:5*   **3** *Ezek 9:4,6*   **9** *Dan 3:4; 7:14*

7 *a*- 8 Note that this listing of the *twelve* tribes is unique, as are most of the other Bible listings of the *twelve* tribes. The tribes of Dan and Ephraim are missing. In the Old Testament the tribe of Joseph was divided into the two tribes of Ephraim and Manasseh. The tribe of Levi did not receive any section of land that was located in just one particular area; instead they were spread throughout the land in 48 levitical cities designated for their use (Num. 35:7). The total of the 12,000 sequence in verses 5-8 is 144,000 as indicated in verse 4. For an explanation see THE SYMBOLICAL NUMBERS OF *REVELATION* on page 567.

10 And they called out with a loud voice, saying:

> "We are saved by our *God who sits on the throne*
> and by the Lamb!"

11 And all the angels stood around the throne
>   and ₍around₎ the elders
>   and ₍around₎ the four living creatures;
> and they *bowed down* before the throne, with their faces to the ground
> and *worshiped God*, **12** saying:

> "Amen!
>   Praise
>   and glory
>   and wisdom
>   and thanks
>   and honor
>   and power
>   and strength be to our God forever ₍and₎ ever!
> Amen!"

13 And one of the elders turned to me, saying:

> "These people dressed in white robes—
>   who are they
>   and where did they come from?"

14 I answered him, "My lord, you know."
And he told me:

> "These are the people who have come through the great suffering,[b]
>   and they have *washed* their *robes*
>   and have made them white in *the blood of the Lamb*.
> **15**   Therefore they are before the throne of God
>   and serve Him day and night in His TEMPLE,
>   and *He who sits on the throne* will spread His TENT over them.
> **16**   *They will never be hungry again*
>   *nor will they ever be thirsty again*,
>   *nor will the sun ever overcome them*
>   *nor any burning heat*,[c]
>   because the Lamb in the center near the throne
> **17**   *will be their Shepherd*,
>   and He *will lead them to springs of the water of life*;
>   and *God will wipe every tear from their eyes*."

---

10 *1 Kgs 22:19; 2 Chr 18:18; Ps 47:9; Is 6:1*   **11** *Ex 19:16; Ezek 1:13*   **14** *Gen 49:11; Ex 12:5,7*
15 *1 Kgs 22:19; 2 Chr 18:18; Ps 47:9; Is 6:1*   **16,17** *Ps 23:2; 121:6; Is 49:10; Jer 2:13; Ezek 34:23*
17 *Is 25:8*

---

b- 14 The suffering described in the six seals (6:1-17).
c- 16 Note that *ten* truths are listed in verses 14c-16; see footnote at 1:16.

"The Riders of Revelation" (Rev. 6 and 19)

8TH CHAPTER

D. Third vision: Seven trumpets (8:1–11:19)

Prayers With Incense

1 And when He opened the seventh seal,
  there was silence in heaven for about half an hour.
2 And I saw the seven angels standing before God,
  and they were given seven trumpets.
3 And another angel, with a golden censer, came and *stood at the altar*.
And he was given much *incense* to offer
  with the *prayers* of all the believers
  on the golden altar in front of the throne.
4 And from the angel's hand the smoke of the *incense*
  went up before God with the *prayers* of the believers.
5 And the angel took *the censer*
  and *filled it with fire from the altar*
  and hurled it to the earth.
And there came peals of thunder
  and *rumblings*
    and *flashes of lightning*
      and an earthquake.

The First Six Trumpets Sound Their Verdicts: Six Afflictions

6 And the seven angels who had the seven trumpets prepared to blow them.
7 And the first blew his trumpet,
  and there came *hail and fire* mixed with blood,
  and the mixture was hurled *to the earth*.
And a third of the earth was burned up,
  and a third of the trees were burned up,
  and all the green grass was burned up.

8 And the second angel blew his trumpet,
    and something like a huge *mountain burning* with fire
      was thrown into the sea.
And a third of the sea *turned to blood*,
9   and a third of the creatures living in the sea died,
      and a third of the ships were destroyed.

---

3 Amos 9:1   3,4 Ps 141:2   5 Ex 19:16; Lev 16:12   7 Ex 9:23,24; Ezek 38:22   8 Ex 7:20,21;
Jer 51:25

10 And the third angel blew his trumpet,
   and a huge *star*, flaming like a torch, *fell from the sky*,
   and it fell on a third of the rivers
   and on the springs of water.
11 And that star was called Wormwood;
   and a third of the waters turned to wormwood,
   and many people died from these waters because they had turned bitter.

12 And the fourth angel blew his trumpet,
   and a third of the *sun was struck*,
   and a third of the *moon*,
   and a third of the stars,
      so that a third of them turned dark—
      and there was *no light* for a third of the day
      and for a third of the night.

13 And I saw and heard a single eagle[a] flying in mid-heaven,
      saying with a loud voice:

"Woe, woe, woe to those living on the earth,
   because of the remaining trumpet blasts of the three angels
   who are about to blow their trumpets."

9TH CHAPTER

The First Woe

1 And the fifth angel blew his trumpet,
   and I saw *a star that had fallen out of the sky to the earth.*
   And he was given the key to the shaft of the bottomless pit.
2 And he opened the shaft of the bottomless pit,
   and *smoke went up from the shaft like the smoke from a large furnace,*
   and it *darkened the sun* and the air.
3 And out of the smoke *came locusts on the earth,*
   and they were given power like the power of earthly scorpions.
4 And they were told not to harm
      the grass on the earth or any green plant or tree;
      they could harm only the people
         who do not have the *seal* of God *on their foreheads.*
5 But[a] they were not allowed to kill them,
      only to torture them for five months.

And their torture was like the torture of a scorpion whenever it stings a person.
6 And in those days people will *look for death*
   and *never find it*;
   and they will long to die,
   but[b] death will escape them.

---

10 *Is 14:12; Dan 8:10*   12 *Ezek 32:7,8*   1 *Is 14:12; Dan 8:10*   2 *Gen 19:28; Ex 19:18;*
Joel 2:10   3 *Ex 10:12*   4 *Ezek 9:4,6*   6 *Job 3:21*

---

8 *a*- 13 Or "vulture."
9 *a*- 5 Greek: "*kai*"; see THE *KAI* STRUCTURE on page 565.
   b- 6 Greek: "*kai*"; see THE *KAI* STRUCTURE on page 565.

7 And the locusts looked *like horses* prepared *for battle*;
and on their heads there seemed to be crowns that looked like gold;
and their faces were like human faces;

8 and they had hair like women's hair
and *teeth like lions' teeth*;

9 and they had breastplates like iron;
and the noise of their wings was *like the roar of chariots*
with many horses *rushing into battle*;

10 and they had tails like scorpions;
and stingers;
and in their tails they had the power to hurt people for five months. *c*

11 The king who was over them was the angel of the bottomless pit.

In Hebrew he is called Abaddon,
and in Greek he is called Apollyon. *d*

12 The first woe is past.
Take note that after these things there are two more woes yet to come.

The Second Woe

13 And the sixth angel blew his trumpet.
And I heard a voice from the four*e* horns of the golden altar before God.

14 It said to the sixth angel (he was the one who had the trumpet):

"Free the four angels who are held bound at *the great river Euphrates.*"

15 And the four angels who had been held ready
for that hour and day and month and year were untied
to kill a third of the people.

16 And the number of soldiers on horses was 200,000,000;
I heard how many there were.

17 And this is the way I saw the horses in the vision
and those who were riding on them:

They [the riders] had breastplates that were
fire-red
and pale blue
and sulfur-yellow.

7-9 Joel 1:6; 2:4,5   *14 Gen 15:18; Deut 1:7; 11:24; Josh 1:4*

---

c- 10 Note the *ten*-part description of the locusts in verses 7-10 (cf. another ten-part description in 1:13b-16).

d- 11 Both "*Abaddōn*" and "*Apollyōn*" mean "Destroyer."

e- 13 Many of the older manuscripts omit: "four."

And the horses had heads like lions,
>> and out of their mouths came fire
>> and smoke
>> and sulfur.

18   These three plagues—
>> the fire
>> and smoke
>> and sulfur
>>> which kept coming out of their mouths—killed a third of mankind.

19   For the power of the horses was in their mouths
>> and in their tails;
> for their tails were like serpents, having heads;
>> and with these they caused harm.

20 And the rest of mankind,
>> those who were not killed by these plagues,
>>> did not repent by turning from *what their hands had made*.
> If they had, they would have given up worshiping
>> demons
> and *idols of gold*
> and *silver*
> and *bronze*
> and *stone*
> and *wood*,
>> *things which cannot see or hear* or walk.

21 And they did not repent of their murders,
>> nor of their *witchcraft*,
>>> nor of their *sexual sin*,
>>> nor of their stealing.

10TH CHAPTER

The Mighty Angel And The Little Scroll

1   And I saw another mighty Angel come down from heaven—
>> He was robed in a cloud,
> and there was a rainbow over His head.
> And His face was like the sun,
> and His feet were like pillars of fire.

2   And in His hand He held a little scroll which was unrolled.
> And He set His right foot on the sea and[a] His left on the land.

3   And He cried with a loud voice, as when a lion roars.
> And when He cried, the seven thunders spoke with voices of their own.

4   And when the seven thunders had spoken, I was going to write it down.
> And I heard a voice say from heaven:

---

20 Deut 4:28; Ps 115:4; 135:15-17; Is 2:8,20; 17:8; Jer 1:16; Dan 5:4,23   *21 2 Kgs 9:22*
4 Dan 8:26; 12:4,9

---

10 a- 2 Greek: "*de*," not "*kai*"; see THE *KAI* STRUCTURE on page 565.

> "*Seal up* what the seven thunders have said,
>   and do not write it down."

5 And the Angel whom I saw standing on the sea and on the land
>   *raised His right hand to heaven*
6 and *swore by Him who lives forever* ₎and₎ *ever,*
>   *who created heaven* and what is in it,
>   and *the earth* and *what is in it,*
>   and *the sea and what is in it:*

>   "Time will be no more,
7 >   but in the days of the sound of the seventh angel,
>   whenever he is about to blow his trumpet,
>   indeed[b] *the mystery*[c] *of God* will be completed,
>   *as He had made this Gospel known to His servants the prophets.*"

8 And the voice which I had heard from heaven spoke to me again,
and said:

>   "Go, take the scroll that lies unrolled in the hand of the Angel
>   who is standing on the sea and on the land."

9 And I went to the Angel, telling Him to give me the little scroll,
and *He said to me*:

>   "Take it and *eat it*;
>   and it will be bitter *in your stomach,*
>   but in your mouth it will be *sweet like honey.*"

10 And *I* took the little scroll from the Angel's hand and *ate it,*
>   and *it was sweet like honey in my mouth,*
>   but[d] when *I had eaten it,* it was bitter *in my stomach.*

11 And they told me:

>   "You must prophesy again before many
>   *peoples* and *nations* and *languages* and *kings.*"

11TH CHAPTER

The 42 Months [1,260 Days]; The Two Witnesses [Prophets]

1 And I was given a measuring stick like a rod. He said:

5,6 Gen 14:19; Ex 20:11; Deut 32:40; Neh 9:6; Ps 146:6; Dan 4:34; 6:26; 12:7   *7 Deut 29:27;*
Amos 3:7; Zech 1:6   *9,10 Ezek 2:8,9; 3:1-3*   *11 Dan 3:4; 7:14*

---

b- 7 Greek: "*kai*"; see THE *KAI* STRUCTURE on page 565.
c- 7 The Greek word used here refers to a *secret* that is hidden from human understanding and
cannot be grasped by those outside the Christian faith. This same Greek word is used, for
example, in 1 Corinthians 15:51; Ephesians 1:8; 1 Timothy 3:16. The greatest mystery of all is
the *Gospel* which remains a secret until divine revelation enlightens individual hearts (1 Cor.
2:7-13). See also 17:5,7.
d- 10 Greek: "*kai*"; see THE *KAI* STRUCTURE on page 565.

"Stand up
and measure the Temple of God
and the altar,
and count those who worship there;

2 but^a exclude the outer court of the Temple,
and do not measure it, because it is given to *the Gentiles*,
and they will *trample on the Holy* City for forty-two months.

3 "And I will give ⌐authority⌐ to My two witnesses who are dressed in sackcloth
and they will speak God's word^b for twelve hundred ⌐and⌐ sixty days.

4 *"These are the two olive trees* and the two lampstands
  standing before the Lord of the earth.

5 And if anyone wishes to hurt them,
  fire comes *out of* their *mouths* and *consumes* their *enemies.*
And if anyone should wish to hurt them,
  he must be killed in this manner.

6 "These have the authority to shut up heaven
  in order to keep *rain* from falling during the days
  when they are speaking God's word;^c
and they have authority over the *waters*
  in order to *turn them into blood*,
and ⌐authority⌐ to *strike* the earth *with any plague* as often as they desire.

7 "And whenever they have finished their testimony, *the beast*,
  which *comes up* out of the bottomless pit, *will fight with* them,
and *conquer them*,
and kill them.

8 And their dead bodies will lie on the street of the great city,
  which is called Sodom and Egypt because of its spiritual condition,^d
even^e where their Lord was crucified.

9 And those from the *peoples* and *tribes* and *languages* and *nations* will look
  at their dead bodies for three and a half days
and will not let anyone bury them.

10 And those living on the earth will rejoice over them
and will celebrate
and will send gifts to one another
  because these two prophets tormented those living on the earth.

11 "And after three and a half days a *breath of life* from God *went into them*,
and *they stood up on their feet*,
and a *great fear fell* on those who saw them.

---

2 *Is 63:18; Zech 12:3* **4** *Zech 4:3,11,12,14* **5** *2 Sam 22:9; 2 Kgs 1:10,12; Is 26:11; Jer 5:14*
6 *Ex 7:17,21; 1 Sam 4:8; 1 Kgs 17:1* **7** *Dan 7:3,21* **9** *Dan 3:4; 7:14*
11 *Gen 15:12; Ezek 37:5,10*

---

11 *a-* 2 Greek: "*kai*"; see THE *KAI* STRUCTURE on page 565.
 b- 3 Literally: "will prophesy."
 c- 6 Literally: "are prophesying."
 d- 8 Literally: "which is called spiritually Sodom and Egypt."
 e- 8 Greek: "*kai*"; see THE *KAI* STRUCTURE on page 565.

12   "And they heard a loud voice from heaven calling to them:

'Come up here.'

And they went up to heaven in a cloud
and their enemies watched them;
13   and *at that moment* there was *a great earthquake*
and a tenth of the city *fell*
and seven thousand people were killed by the earthquake,
and the rest were terrified
and they gave glory to the God of heaven."

14   The second woe is past.
Take note that the third woe will soon be here.

The Third Woe

15   And the seventh angel blew his trumpet.
And there were loud voices in heaven, saying:

"The kingdom of the world has become the Kingdom of our *Lord
and of His Christ,*
and *He will rule as King forever* ˻and˼ ever."

16   And the 24 elders, who were sitting on their thrones before God,
fell down on their faces
and worshiped God, 17 saying:

"We thank You, *Lord God Almighty,*
the *One-Who-Is*
and the One-Who-Was,
because You have taken Your great power and *ruled as King.*

18   "And *the nations were angry*;
and Your anger has come;
and it is the time You set to judge the dead
and to give the reward to *Your servants the prophets*
and to the believers, *small and great,*
and to those *who fear* Your Name,
and to destroy those who are destroying the earth."

19   And God's TEMPLE in heaven was opened
and *the ARK of* His *COVENANT [TESTAMENT]f* was seen in His *TEMPLE.*
And there were *flashes of lightning*
and *rumblings*
and peals of thunder
and an earthquake
and *heavy hail.*

---

*13 Ezek 38:19,20; Dan 2:19   15 Ex 15:18; 1 Sam 12:3; Ps 2:2; 10:16; 22:26; Dan 2:44; Obad 21;
Mal 4:7   16 Ps 22:27; 86:9; Is 45:14; 49:23; 60:14; 66:23; Jer 16:19   17 Ex 3:14
17,18 Ps 99:1   18 Ps 115:13; Dan 9:6,10; Amos 3:7; Zech 1:6   19 Ex 9:23; 19:16; 1 Kgs 8:1,6*

f- 19 See *DIATHĒKĒ* on page 531.

12TH CHAPTER

E. Fourth vision: The woman and the dragon (12:1–15:4)

The Woman's Son And The Dragon

1 And a great miraculous sign[a] was seen in heaven[b]—
    a woman with the sun for her garment
and the moon under her feet
and a crown of twelve stars on her head;
2 and she was pregnant,
and she cried out *in pain*
and agony *to give birth.*
3 And another miraculous sign was seen in heaven—
and look, a large fire-red dragon *with* seven heads and *ten horns*
and with seven crowns[c] on his heads;
4 and his tail swept away a third of *the stars in heaven*
and *hurled them to the earth*;
and the dragon stood in front of the woman
    who was going to have a Child
        to devour her Child whenever it was born.

5 And she *gave birth to a Son, a Boy,*
    who is to rule all *the nations with a rod of iron.*
And her Child was taken straight up to God and to His throne.
6 And the woman fled into the wilderness
    where God has prepared a place for her
        so that she might be fed for 1,260 days.

7   And then a war broke out in heaven—
Michael[d] and his angels had to fight with the dragon;
and the dragon fought
and his angels;
8   but[e] he was not strong enough
    nor was there a place for them in heaven any longer;
9   and the great dragon was hurled down—
    the old *serpent*, called *Devil* and *Satan,*[f]
        who *deceives* the whole world,
            was hurled to the earth;
and his angels were hurled down with him.

---

2 Is 66:7; Mal 4:10   **3** Dan 7:7,20,24   **4** Dan 8:10   **5** Ps 2:8,9; Is 66:7; Jer 20:15
8 Dan 2:35   **9** Gen 3:13,15; Zech 3:1

---

12 *a-* 1 See MIRACULOUS SIGNS, WONDERFUL PROOFS, and MIRACLES on page 527.
    b- 1 Or "the sky" (also in vv. 3,4).
    c- 3 Literally: "*diadem*"; this word for "crown" (not the same Greek word as used for "crown" in
        v. 1) has not been used previously. It indicates the type of crown worn by the kings of Persia
        and was a sign that the wearer claimed to be *God*.
    d- 7 See MICHAEL THE ARCHANGEL on page 555.
    e- 8 Greek: "*kai*"; see THE *KAI* STRUCTURE on page 565.
    f- 9 The Greek word "*Diabolos*," translated "Devil," means "deceiver" or "slanderer"; the Greek
        term "*Satanas*," translated "Satan," is a proper noun meaning the "Accuser."

10   And I heard a loud voice in heaven, saying:

> "Now has come the salvation
> and the power
> and the Kingdom of our God
> and the rule of His Christ,
>> because the accuser of our fellow Christians,[g]
>> the one accusing them before our God—day and night—
>> has been thrown out;

11 and they conquered him because of *the blood of the Lamb*
> and because of the word of their testimony;
> and they did not love their life but were willing to die.

12 For this *be glad, you heavens*, and those who live in them.
> Woe to the earth and the sea,
>> because the devil has come down to you with great anger,
>> knowing that he has little time."

The Devil And The Church

13 And when the dragon saw that he had been hurled to the earth,
> he persecuted[h] the woman who had given birth to the Boy.

14 And the woman was given two wings of the great eagle
> to fly to her place in the wilderness away from the serpent,
>> where she would be fed for a *time and times and half a time*.[i]

15 And from his mouth the serpent poured out a stream of water
> after the woman in order to sweep her away like a river.

16 And the earth helped the woman.
> And the earth opened its mouth
>> and swallowed the stream that the dragon poured from his mouth.

17 And the dragon was angry with the woman
> and went away to fight with her other children,
>> those who do what God has commanded
>> and who hold on to the testimony of Jesus.

18 And he stood on the sandy shore of the sea.[j]

---

11 Ex 12:5,7   *12* Is 44:23; 49:13   *14* Dan 7:25; 12:7

---

g- 10 Literally: "brothers."
h- 13 Or "pursued."
i- 14 Meaning "a year, two years, and a half year" (3 and 1/2 years); see 11:2; 13:5 ("forty-two months") and 11:3; 12:6 ("twelve hundred and sixty days"; 360 days were given to a year), that is, *three and a half years* in each case (cf. also Dan. 7:25).
j- 18 Some versions include this sentence in verse 1 of Chapter 13.

13TH CHAPTER

1 And I saw *a beast coming up out of the sea*—
  he had ten horns
 and seven heads,
 and on his horns ten crowns;[a]
 and there were blasphemous names on his heads;
2 and the beast which I saw was *like a leopard*
 and his feet were *like* those of *a bear*
 and his mouth *like a lion's* mouth;
 and the dragon gave him his power
 and his throne
 and great authority.

3 And one of his heads seemed to have been fatally wounded,
 but[b] his fatal wound was healed.

 And the whole world was amazed
 and followed after the beast
4 and worshiped the dragon because he had given authority to the beast;
 and they worshiped the beast, saying:

  "Is there anyone like the beast?
  And is there anyone who can fight with him?"

5 And he was given a mouth *speaking proud* and blasphemous *things*,
 and he was given authority to *act* for 42 months.
6 And he opened his mouth to blaspheme God, to blaspheme His Name
  and His TABERNACLE, those who are living [tabernacling] in heaven.
7 And he was given ⌊authority⌋
  to wage war against the believers
  and *to conquer them*,
 and he was given authority
  over every *tribe* and *people* and *language* and *nation*.
8 And everyone living on the earth will worship him,
  ⌊everyone⌋ whose name *is not written in the Book of Life*,
   ⌊that Book⌋ which belongs to the *Lamb*
    who was *slain* from the beginning of the world.[c]
9 If anyone has an ear, let him listen:

10   *If anyone is to be taken prisoner,*
   to prison he will go.
  If anyone is to be killed with a sword,
   with a sword he must be killed.

 In this situation the believers need patient endurance and confidence.

---

1 Dan 7:3,7,20,24 *2 Dan 7:4-6* **5-7** *Dan 7:8,21; 11:36* **7** *Dan 3:4; 7:14* **8** *Ex 12:6,21;*
32:32,33; Lev 1:11; Ps 69:28; 139:16; Is 4:3; 53:7; Jer 11:19; Dan 12:1; Mal 3:16 **10** *Jer 15:2*

---

13 *a*- 1 See 12:3 and its accompanying footnote.
 b- 3 Greek: "*kai*"; see THE *KAI* STRUCTURE on page 565.
 c- 8 Or "whose name is not written from the beginning of the world in the Book of Life, which
  belongs to the Lamb who was slain" (cf. 17:8).

11 And I saw another beast come up out of the earth;
   and he had two horns like the Lamb,
   and he talked as the dragon.

12 And he exercises all the authority of the first beast before him.
   And he makes the earth
        and those living on it
             worship the first beast,
                  whose fatal wound was healed.
13 And he works great miraculous signs
        so that he even[d] makes fire come down
             from heaven to the earth
                  in front of the people.
14 And he deceives those living on the earth
        because of the miraculous signs that he is given to do in front of the beast,
             telling those living on the earth to make an image
                  for the beast who was wounded by a sword and yet lived.
15 And he was given ˌpowerˌ to put breath into the image of the beast
        so that the image of the beast could both[e] talk and cause
             as many as would not worship the image of the beast to be put to death.
16 And he forces all people,

                  great
             and small
             and rich
             and poor
             and free
             and slave

        to be branded on their right hands
        or on their foreheads,
17   and ˌhe does itˌ so that no one may buy
        or sell,
             unless one has the brand—the beast's name
             or the number of his name.

18 In this situation wisdom is needed.

        Let the person who has insight figure out the number of the beast,
             because it is the number of a man;
        and his number is 666.[f]

---

15 Dan 3:5,6

---

d- 13 Greek: "*kai*"; see THE *KAI* STRUCTURE on page 565.
e- 15 Greek: "*kai*"; see THE *KAI* STRUCTURE on page 565.
f- 18 The number *six* generally indicates something evil; see THE SYMBOLICAL NUMBERS OF *REVELATION* on page 567. The piling up of a possible *three* sets of sixes in the present context suggests the ultimate, highest form of evil that will try to oppose the Trinity. See THE *KAI* STRUCTURE on page 565 for a plausible explanation of the number 666 as based on this observation.

14TH CHAPTER

The New Song

1 And I looked, and there the Lamb ⌊was⌋ standing on Mount Zion;
   and with Him ⌊there were⌋ 144,000 people who had His Name;
   and His Father's Name ⌊was⌋ written on their foreheads.
2 And I heard *a sound* from heaven *like the noise of many waters*
      and the noise of loud thunder.
   And the sound I heard was also like the music of harpists
      playing on their harps.
3 And they were *singing a new song* before the throne
      and before the four living creatures
         and the elders.
   And only the 144,000 who had been bought [redeemed] from the earth
      could learn the song.

4 These are the ones who have not defiled themselves with women,
      for they are virgins.
   These are the ones who follow the Lamb wherever He goes.
   These were bought from among mankind
      as the first ones offered*a* to God and to the Lamb;
5   and *they have never been known to tell a lie*;
            they are without fault.

Seven Judgments From Heaven

6 And I saw another angel flying in mid-heaven with the everlasting Gospel
      to preach to those who live on the earth
   and to every *nation* and *tribe* and *language* and *people*,
      saying with a loud voice:

7   "Fear God
               and give Him glory,
                  because the time has come for Him to judge;
            and worship Him *who made heaven*
               and *the earth*
                  and *the sea*
                     and springs of water."

---

2 *Ezek 1:24; 43:2*   **3** *Ps 33:3; 40:3; 96:1; 98:1; 144:9; 149:1; Is 42:10*   **5** *Ps 32:2; Is 53:9;*
Zeph 3:13   **6** *Dan 3:4; 7:14*   **7** *Gen 14:19,22; Ex 20:11; Ps 146:6; Neh 9:6*

---

14 *a-* 4 Literally: "firstfruits"; *firstfruits* in Biblical times signify that part of the harvest which was
offered to God in the Temple. The rest of that harvest was consumed or used for seed and thus
perished.

8 And a second angel followed him, saying:

> "*Fallen, the great Babylon has fallen*—
> she who has made all *the nations drink of the wine of her* immoral passion!"

9 And a third angel followed them, saying with a loud voice:

> "If *anyone worships the beast* and his *image*
> and is branded on his forehead or on his hand,
> **10** he will also[b] *drink of the wine of God's fury*,
> which has been poured *unmixed into the cup of His anger*.
> And he will be tortured by *fire and sulfur*
> before the holy angels and before the Lamb.
> **11** And *the smoke* of their torture *goes up forever* ⌊and⌋ ever.
> And there is no rest *day and night* for *those*
> *who worship the beast* and his *image*
> and for anyone branded with his name."[c]

12 In this situation the believers need patient endurance,
those who keep God's commandments and their faith in Jesus.

13 And I heard a voice from heaven saying, "Write:
Blessed are the dead who die in the Lord from now on!"
"Yes," says the Spirit, "let them rest from their hard work,
for what they have done accompanies them."

14 And then I looked,
and there ⌊was⌋ a white cloud,
and *on the cloud sat One who was like the Son of Man,*[d]
with a golden crown on His head
and a sharp sickle in His hand.

15 And another angel came out of the TEMPLE,
calling out with a loud voice to the One who sat on the cloud:

> "*Swing Your sickle*
> and reap,
> for *the time has come to reap*,
> because *the harvest on the earth is very ripe*."

16 And the One who sat on the cloud *swung His sickle* over the earth,
and the reaping of the earth was completed.

---

8 Is 21:9; Jer 25:15; 50:2; 51:7,8; Dan 4:30   *9 Dan 3:5,6*   *10 Ps 75:8; Is 51:17; Jer 25:15*
10,11 Gen 19:24; Is 34:10   *11 Dan 3:5,6*   *14 Dan 7:13*   *15 Jer 51:33; Joel 3:13*
16-19 Joel 3:13

---

b- 10 Greek: "*kai*"; literally: "*and* he will drink"; see THE *KAI* STRUCTURE on page 565.
c- 11 Literally: "and anyone who receives the mark of his name."
d- 14 See 1:13 and its accompanying footnote.

17 And another angel came out of the TEMPLE in heaven,
also[e] having a sharp sickle.

18 And another angel came from the altar with authority over the fire;
and he called with a loud voice to the one with the sharp sickle:

"*Swing your* sharp *sickle*
and gather the bunches of grapes from the vine of the earth,
because the grapes on it are ripe."

19 And the angel *swung* his *sickle* on the earth
and gathered the grapes from the vine of the earth
and threw them into the great winepress of *God's anger*.

20 And ⌊*the grapes*⌋ *were trampled in the winepress* outside the city,
and blood flowed out of the winepress,
as deep as the horses' bridles for 1,600 stadia.[f]

15TH CHAPTER

Seven Plagues

1 And I saw another miraculous sign in heaven, great and wonderful—
seven angels with *seven plagues*—the last plagues,
since in them the anger of God was completed.

2 And I saw what looked like a sea of glass mixed with fire.
And those who had won the victory over the beast
and his image
and the number of his name
were standing on the glassy sea, holding God's harps

3 and singing *the song of Moses, God's servant*,
and the song of the Lamb, saying:

"*Great and wonderful are Your works, Lord God Almighty.*
Righteous and dependable[a] are Your ways, King of the nations.[b]

4 *Is there anyone, Lord, who will not fear*
and *glorify Your Name*,
because You alone are holy;
because *all the nations[c] will come and worship You;*
because Your righteous judgments have been revealed?"

19,20 Is 63:2,3   1 Lev 26:21
3 Ex 15:1; 34:10; Deut 32:4; Josh 14:7; Ps 111:2; 139:14; 145:17
4 Ps 22:27; 86:9; Is 66:23; Jer 10:7; Mal 1:11

---

e- 17 Greek: "*kai*"; see THE *KAI* STRUCTURE on page 565.
f- 20 See MONEY, WEIGHTS, and MEASURES on page 328.
15 a- 3 Greek: "*alēthinos*"; see *ALĒTHINOS* COMPARED WITH *ALĒTHĒS* on page 530.
b- 3 Some of the older manuscripts and early translations read: "King of the ages."
c- 4 Or "Gentiles."

F. Fifth vision: Seven bowls (15:5–16:21)

5 And after these things I looked,
  and the SANCTUARY of the *TABERNACLE OF THE TESTIMONY*d
    was opened in heaven;
6 and the seven angels with the *seven plagues* came out of the SANCTUARY,
  clothed in clean, shining linen
 and had golden belts fastened around their chests.
7 And one of the four living creatures gave to the seven angels
   seven golden bowls full of the anger of God,
     who lives forever ⌊and⌋ ever.
8 And *the SANCTUARY was filled with smoke* ⌊that rises⌋
  from *the glory of God* and from His power;
 and no one could go into the SANCTUARY
  until the *seven plagues* of the seven angels were completed.

16TH CHAPTER

1 And I heard a loud *voice from the TEMPLE* saying to the seven angels:

  "Go and *pour out* the seven bowls of *God's anger on the earth.*"

2 And the first went and poured out his bowl on the earth;
 and terrible and *painful sores came on the people*
  who had the brand of the beast
  and who *worshiped his image.*

3 And the second poured out his bowl into the sea,
 and *it turned to blood* like that of a dead man,
 and every living thing in the sea *died.*

4 And the third poured out his bowl into the *rivers* and the springs of water;
 and *they turned to blood.*
5 And I heard the angel of the waters saying:

  "*Just are You,*
    the One-Who-Is and the One-Who-Was, the *Holy One,*
     because You have judged these things,
6   because *they have poured out*
      the blood of believers and prophets;
       and You have given *them blood to drink;*
       they deserve it."

7 And I heard the altar ⌊answer⌋, saying:

---

5 *Ex 38:21; Num 1:50,53; 9:15; 10:11; 17:7,8; 18:2; 2 Chr 24:6*   **6** *Lev 26:21*
7 *Dan 4:34; 6:26; 12:7*   **8** *Ex 40:34,35; Lev 26:21; 1 Kgs 8:10,11; Is 6:1,4; Ezek 44:4*
1 *Ps 69:24; Is 66:6; Jer 10:25; Zeph 3:8*   **2** *Ex 9:10; Deut 28:35; Dan 3:5,6*   **3,4** *Ex 7:17,19-21;*
Ps 78:44   **5** *Ex 3:14; Ps 119:137; 145:17*   **6** *Ps 79:3; Is 49:26*

d- 5 See 3:12 and its accompanying footnote.

"Yes, *Lord God Almighty,*
Your judgments are dependable[a] and just."

8 And the fourth poured out his bowl on the sun;
and it was allowed to burn people with fire;
9 and they were badly burned;
and they blasphemed the Name of God,
the One who had the authority over these plagues;
and they did not repent to give Him glory.

10 And the fifth poured out his bowl on the throne of the beast;
and his kingdom *turned dark;*
and people[b] gnawed their tongues in anguish
11 and cursed the *God of heaven* for their pains and their sores;
and they did not repent of their ,evil, deeds.

12 And the sixth poured out his bowl on *the great river Euphrates.*
And *the water in it dried up* to prepare the road for the kings *from the east.*
13 And I saw three unclean spirits, like frogs,
come out of the mouth of the dragon
and out of the mouth of the beast
and out of the mouth of the false prophet.[c]
14   For they are spirits of demons,
working miraculous signs,
who go out to the kings of the whole world
to gather them for the war on the great Day of the Almighty God.

15   "See, I am coming like a thief.
Blessed is the one who stays awake
and holds onto his clothes,
so that he will not have to go naked
and let others see his shameful parts."

16   And they[d] gathered the kings[e] at the place
which in Hebrew is called Armageddon.[f]

17 And the seventh poured out his bowl over the air;
and a loud *voice* came *from the throne* in the TEMPLE,
saying: "It is done!"
18 And *there were flashes of lightning*
and *rumblings*
and peals of thunder,
and a severe earthquake took place—
such a severe earthquake as *has not happened*
since mankind *has been on the earth.*

---

7 *Ps 19:9*   **10** *Ex 10:22*   **11** *Dan 2:19*   **12** *Is 41:2,25; 44:27; Jer 50:38*   **17** *Is 66:6*
18 *Ex 19:16; Dan 12:1*

---

16 *a-* 7 Greek: "*alēthinos*"; see ALĒTHINOS COMPARED WITH *ALĒTHĒS* on page 530.
b- 10 Literally: "they."
c- 13 The second beast (13:11-18; 19:20; 20:10).
d- 16 Meaning "And 'the spirits' " (cf. v. 14); some manuscripts read: "And *he*."
e- 16 Literally: "them."
f- 16 "The mountain of Megiddo," possibly a reference to Mount Carmel where Elijah fought with the prophets of Baal.

19 And the great city split into three parts
     and the other cities of the nations fell.
     And God remembered to give *the great Babylon*
        the cup of the wine of His fierce *anger.*
20 And every island vanished
     and the mountains could not be seen anymore.
21 And *huge hailstones*, weighing about one hundred pounds[g] each,
        fell from the sky on people;
     and they blasphemed God on account of the plague of hail,
        because the plague it brought was so *terrible.*[h]

17TH CHAPTER

G. Sixth vision: God's final triumph (17:1–20:15)

The Woman And The Beast

1 And one of the seven angels who held the seven bowls came
     and spoke to me, saying:

        "Come,
            I will show you the judgment of the great prostitute
                who sits *on many waters.*
2   *The kings of the earth lived in sexual sin* with her,
                    and *those living on the earth*
                        became drunk on the wine of her sexual sin."

3 And so he carried me into the wilderness in the Spirit.[a]
     And I saw a woman sitting on a scarlet *beast,*
        covered with blasphemous names,
            with seven heads and *ten horns.*
4 And the woman wore purple
        and scarlet
            and ornaments of gold
                and jewels
                    and pearls,
                        holding *a golden cup* in her hand[b] filled with abominations ·
                        and the unclean things of her sexual sin.

5 And on her forehead was written a name:

---

19 *Ps 75:8; Is 21:9; 51:17; Jer 25:15; 50:2; 51:7,8; Dan 4:30*   **21** *Ex 9:24*   **1** *Jer 51:13*
2 *Is 23:17; Jer 51:7*   **3** *Dan 7:7,20,24*   **4** *Jer 51:7*

---

g- 21 Literally: "a talent"; see MONEY, WEIGHTS, and MEASURES on page 328.
h- 21 Verses 17-21 (the seventh bowl) refer to the last judgment.
17 *a-* 3 See 1:10 and its accompanying footnote.
b- 4 Note the *six* items connected with the evil woman; see THE SYMBOLICAL NUMBERS OF
     REVELATION on page 567 and THE *KAI* STRUCTURE on page 565.

MYSTERY
THE GREAT BABYLON
THE MOTHER OF PROSTITUTES
AND OF THE ABOMINATIONS OF THE EARTH.

6 And I saw that the woman was drunk
    with the blood of the believers and
    with the blood of the witnesses of Jesus.
And I was very much surprised when I saw her.

7 And the angel asked me:

    "Why are you surprised?
      I shall tell you the mystery of the woman
      and of the beast on which she sits,
         that *beast which has* the seven heads
         and the *ten horns.*

8   "*The beast* which you saw once was
      and is no longer,
      and he will *come up from* the bottomless pit
      and go to his destruction.

    "And they will be surprised,
    those living on the earth,
    whose names have not been *written in the Book of Life*[c]
      from the beginning of the world,
    when they see the beast,
      because he was
      and is no longer
      and will come again.

9   "In this situation a mind with wisdom is needed.

    "The seven heads are seven hills on which the woman is sitting;
10   and they are also seven kings:
      five have fallen,
        one is ruling now,
          the other has not yet come,
            and whenever he comes, he must stay a little while.

11   And the beast that was
    and is no longer,
    even[d] he is the eighth ⌊king⌋,
    and comes from the seven
    and goes to his destruction.

---

5 *Dan 4:30*   7 *Dan 7:7,20,24*   8 *Ex 32:32,33; Ps 69:28; 139:16; Is 4:3; Dan 7:3; 12:1; Mal 3:16*

---

c- 8 Compare 13:8.
d- 11 Greek: "*kai*"; see THE *KAI* STRUCTURE on page 565.

12   "And the *ten horns* that you saw *are ten kings*
          who have not yet started to rule,
          but they will receive authority ⌊to rule⌋ as kings with the beast for one hour.
13   They have one purpose
          and give their power and authority to the beast.
14   They will go to war against the Lamb,
          and the Lamb will conquer them
              because He is *Lord of lords and King of kings*;
          and those who are with Him are called and chosen and believing."

15   And he told me:

          "The waters you saw, where the prostitute is sitting, are
              peoples and crowds and *nations* and *languages*.
16   And *the ten horns* and the beast you saw will hate the prostitute,
          and they will cause her to be forsaken and naked,
          and they will devour her flesh
          and burn her with fire.
17   For God has put it into their hearts to do what He has decided,
          and to carry out one purpose,
          and to give their kingdom to the beast
              until the words of God will be carried out.
18   And the woman you saw is the great city
          that is ruling over *the kings of the earth*."

18TH CHAPTER

Babylon Has Fallen

1   After these things I saw another angel come down from heaven.
          He had great power,
          and his glory lit up the earth,
2   and he called out with a loud voice:

      "*Fallen! The great Babylon has fallen!*
          And she *has become a home for demons*
          and a dungeon for every unclean spirit
          and a dungeon for every unclean *bird*
          and a dungeon for every unclean and hated beast.*a*
3   For all *the nations* fell by *the wine of her* immoral passion.
          And *the kings of the earth have lived in sexual sin* with her.
          And the wealth of her luxury
              has made the merchants of the earth rich."

4   And I heard another voice call from heaven, saying:

---

12 Dan 7:7,20,24   *14 Deut 10:17; Dan 2:47*   *15 Dan 3:4; 7:14*   *16 Dan 7:7,20,24*
18 Ps 2:2; 89:27   *2 Is 13:20,21; 21:9; 34:11,14; Jer 50:2; 51:7,8; Dan 4:30*   *3 Is 21:9; 23:17;*
Jer 25:15; 50:2; 51:7,8; Dan 4:30

---

18 *a*- 2 Some of the older manuscripts and early translations omit in verse 2: "and a dungeon for every
    unclean and hated beast," and read in the previous line: "a dungeon for every unclean *and*
    hated bird."

"*Come out of her, My people,*
　　so that you will not share her sins
　　and suffer from any of her plagues;
5　　　　for her sins *have reached up to heaven,*
　　　and God has remembered her crimes.

6　Pay her back,
　even[b] *as she has paid,*
　and *pay her back* double *for what she has done.*
　Mix her a double drink in the cup that she mixed for others.
7　Give her as much torture and misery
　　as she *gave* herself glory and *luxury,*
　　　because *in her heart she says*:

　　　　'I am a queen on a throne;
　　　　and I am not a widow,
　　　　and *I will never feel miserable.*'

8　"For that reason her plagues *will come in one day,*
　　　death
　　and misery
　　and hunger,
　　and she will be *burned with fire,* because
　　　God,
　　　the *Lord,*
　　　the One *who is judging* her[c] is *mighty.*

9　"And *the kings of the earth*
　　　who lived in sexual sin and luxury with her
　　　　will weep and mourn over her
　　　　　whenever they see the smoke rise from her burning.
10　Frightened by her torture, they will stand far off, saying:

　　　'Woe, woe to the great city,
　　　　the mighty city of Babylon,
　　　　　for in one moment judgment has come on you!'

11　"And the merchants of the earth weep and mourn over her,
　　because no one buys their loads of goods anymore—

---

4 *Gen 19:14; Is 48:20; 52:11; Jer 50:8; 51:6,45*　　**5** *Jer 51:9*　　**6** *Ps 137:8; Jer 50:29*
7,8 *Is 47:8,9*　　**8** *Jer 50:32,34*　　**9** *Is 23:17*　　**10** *Ezek 26:17*

b-　6 Greek: "*kai*"; see THE *KAI* STRUCTURE on page 565.
c-　8 Literally: "the Lord, the God, the One judging her"; some manuscripts have "Lord" and "God"
　　inverted (the text above has chosen to use that rotation in order to aid English flow); the
　　comma between "God, the Lord" in text is intentional in order to show the *threefold*
　　arrangement. See THE SYMBOLICAL NUMBERS OF *REVELATION* on page 567.

12   their loads of gold and of silver and of jewels and of pearls,
and of fine linen and of purple and of silk and of scarlet cloth,
and all kinds of citrus wood
    and all kinds of ivory goods
        and all kinds of articles made of very costly wood
and of bronze and of iron and of marble,

13   and cinnamon and spice *d* and incense and perfume and frankincense,
and wine and olive oil and fine wheat flour and wheat,
and cattle and sheep, and horses and wagons,
    and bodies and souls of *human beings.* *e*

14   "And the fruit you longed for is gone,
and all your luxuries and your splendor have perished,
and no one will ever find them again.

15   The merchants who were made rich by selling these things—
frightened by her torture—
will stand far off, weeping and mourning, **16** saying:

    'Woe, woe to the great city that wore
        fine linen
    and purple
    and scarlet
    and ornaments of gold
    and jewels
    and pearls, *f*

17   for in one moment all this wealth has been laid waste!'

    "And every ship captain
and all who go anywhere by ship
and *sailors*
and all those who make a living at sea *stood* far off;

18   and they were *crying out*
when they saw the smoke rise from her burning, saying:

    'Was there ever a city as great as this?'

19   "And *they threw dust on their heads*
and cried out, *weeping and mourning*, saying:

    'Woe, woe to the great city, *whose treasures have made* everyone
who had a ship on the sea *rich*,
    for in one hour she has been laid waste!'

---

13 Ezek 27:13   *17-19 Ezek 27:29-33*

---

d- 13 Greek: "*amōmon.*"

e- 13 Note the *seven* classifications listed in verses 12 and 13. *Seven* in this context would indicate "judgment" upon man's perfect idolatry of materialism; see THE SYMBOLICAL NUMBERS OF *REVELATION* on page 567.

f- 16 Note the *six* items connected with the evil city; see THE SYMBOLICAL NUMBERS OF *REVELATION* on page 567.

20   *"Be happy* over her,
            heaven
                and *believers*,
                    and apostles
                        and prophets,
                            because God has judged her
                                for the judgment that you received from her."

21 And a mighty angel lifted up *a stone* like a large millstone
    and *threw it into* the sea, saying:

        "With *such* violence
            will Babylon, the great city, *be hurled down*
        and will never be found again;
22   and the *sound of* harpists and *musicians* and flutists and trumpeters
            will never be heard in you again;
        and no skilled worker
            will ever be found in you again;
        and the sound of a millstone
            will never be heard in you again;
23   and *the light of a lamp*
            will never shine in you again;
        and *the voice of a groom and a bride*
            will never be heard in you again, *ᵍ*
                because your *merchants were the great men of the world*,
                because by your witchcraft all the nations were deceived.
24   And there was found in her the blood of prophets
        and believers
        and of all who had been murdered on the earth."

19TH CHAPTER

Alleluia [Praise The Lord]!

1 After these things I heard
    what seemed to be the loud sound of a large crowd in heaven, saying:

        "Alleluia!ᵃ
            Salvation and glory and power belong to our God
2   because *His judgments are dependableᵇ and just*;
                    for He has sentenced the great prostitute
                        who corrupted the world with her sexual sin,
                            and He *has punished* her
                                for the blood of His servants."

---

20 *Deut 32:43; Is 44:23; Jer 51:48*   **21,22** *Jer 51:63,64; Ezek 26:12,13; Dan 4:30*
23 *Is 23:8; Jer 7:34; 16:9; 25:10*   **1** *Ps 104:35*   **2** *Deut 32:43; 2 Kgs 9:7; Ps 19:9; 119:137*

---

g- 23 Note the *sixfold* use of the word "again" in verses 21-23; see THE SYMBOLICAL NUMBERS
        OF *REVELATION* on page 567.
19 a- 1 Meaning: "Praise the Lord!" This is the *only chapter* in the New Testament in which the
        common Old Testament word "Hallelujah" is found.
    b- 2 Greek: "*alēthinos*"; see *ALĒTHINOS* COMPARED WITH *ALĒTHĒS* on page 530.

3 And a second time they said:

> "*Alleluia!*
> And *the smoke goes up from her forever* ͺand ͺ ever."

4 And the 24 elders and the four living creatures *bowed down*
and *worshiped God*, who was *sitting on the throne*, saying:

> "Amen! Alleluia!"

5 And a voice came from the throne, saying:

> "*Praise* our God, *all His servants,*
> and *you who fear Him, small and great.*"

The Lamb's Wedding

6 And I heard
> what *seemed to be the sound of a* large *crowd*
> and what seemed to be *the sound of many waters*
> and what seemed to be the sound of loud peals of thunder, saying:

> "*Alleluia!*
> For *the Lord, our God, the Almighty* has become *King.*

7 > *Let us rejoice and be delighted* and give Him glory
> because the marriage of the Lamb has come,
> and His bride has prepared herself,

8 > and she has been permitted to put on dazzling and pure linen."
> For the fine linen consists of the verdicts
> of "not guilty"*c* pronounced on the believers.

9 And he [the angel] said to me, "Write:
> Blessed are those who are invited to the Lamb's wedding banquet."
And he told me,
> "These are the genuine*d* words of God."

10 And I *bowed down at his* feet *to worship him.*
And he told me:

> "Be careful!
> Do not do that!
> > I am a fellow servant of yours and of your fellow Christians*e*
> > who have the testimony of Jesus.*f*
> Worship God,
> > for the testimony of*g* Jesus is the spirit of prophecy!"*h*

---

3 *Is 34:10*   4 *1 Kgs 22:19; 2 Chr 18:18; Ps 22:27; 47:9; 86:9; 106:48; Is 6:1; 45:14; 49:23; 60:14;*
66:23; Jer 16:19   5 *Ps 22:23; 115:13; 134:1; 135:1*   6 *Ps 93:1,4; 97:1; 99:1; 104:35; Ezek 1:24;*
43:2; Dan 10:5,6   7 *Ps 118:24*   10 *Ps 22:27; 86:9; Is 45:14; 49:23; 60:14; 66:23; Jer 16:19*

---

c- 8 Or "For the fine linen consists of the righteous acts."
d- 9 Greek: "*alēthinos*"; see ALĒTHINOS COMPARED WITH ALĒTHĒS on page 530.
e- 10 Literally: "brothers."
f- 10 Literally: "who hold to the witness of Jesus."
g- 10 Or "about."
h- 10 That is, "the heart and soul of prophecy."

The King of Kings

11 And *I saw heaven opened*, and look, there was a white horse,
    and its Rider is called Faithful and True,[i]
    and *He is righteous when He judges* and goes to battle.
12   *His eyes are a flame of fire*,
    and on His head are many crowns
       (there is a Name written on Him, but only He knows what it is),
13   and He wears a garment dipped in blood,
    and His Name is called "the Word of God,"
14   and the armies of heaven, dressed in pure, white linen,
      follow Him on white horses;
15   and a sharp sword comes *out of His mouth to strike down* the nations;
    and He *will rule them with a rod of iron*
    and will *tread the winepress of* the fierce *anger* of *Almighty God*;
16   and on His garment
    and on His thigh He has a Name written:

      KING OF KINGS AND LORD OF LORDS![j]

17 And I saw an angel standing in the sun,
    and he called out with a loud voice, saying *to all the birds flying* in mid-heaven:

    "*Come*, gather *together for* the great banquet of God **18** *to eat*
        the flesh of kings
      and the flesh of generals
      and *the flesh of warriors*
      and *the flesh of horses*
      and *their riders*
      and *the flesh of all people*, both free
                and slave,
                and small
                and great."

19 And I saw the beast[k]
    and the *kings of the earth*
    and their armies *gathered* to fight against the Rider on the horse and His army.
20 And the beast was captured
    and with him the false prophet[l]
      who had worked miraculous signs for the beast by which he deceived those
      who had received the brand of the beast and *worshiped his image*;
      both were thrown alive into the fiery lake of *burning sulfur*.
21 And the remainder were killed
      with the sword of the Rider on the horse,
      with the sword that came out of His mouth;
    and all the birds gorged themselves on their flesh.

---

11 *Ps 96:13; Is 11:4,5; Ezek 1:1* **12** *Dan 10:6* **15** *Ps 2:8,9; Is 11:4; 63:2,3; Lam 1:15; Joel 3:13*
16 *Deut 10:17; Dan 2:47* **17,18** *Ezek 39:4,17-20* **19** *Ps 2:2* **20** *Is 30:33; Dan 3:5,6*

i- 11 Greek: "*alēthinos*"; see ALĒTHINOS COMPARED WITH ALĒTHĒS on page 530.
j- 16 Note the *ten* descriptions given of Christ in verses 12-16 and compare them to 1:13b-16 and
    the accompanying footnote "r."
k- 19 That is, "the beast from the sea" (cf. 13:1ff.).
l- 20 That is, "the beast from the ground" (cf. 13:11ff.).

20TH CHAPTER

The Devil's Last Battle

1 And I saw an Angel coming down from heaven, holding
  the key to the bottomless pit and a large chain in His hand;
2 and He overpowered the dragon—
  he is the old *serpent*, which is *Devil* and *Satan*—
  and He bound him[a] for a thousand years,
3 and threw him into the bottomless pit,
  and shut it
  and sealed it over him to keep him from deceiving the Gentiles[b] anymore
    until the thousand years would end;
  after these things he must be set free for a little while.

4 And *I saw thrones*,
  and they sat on them
  and to them was *given authority to judge*;
  and I saw the souls of those who had been beheaded
    because of their testimony of Jesus
    and because of the word of God.
  And they had not *worshiped* the beast nor *his image*
  and were not branded on their foreheads and on their hands;
  and *they lived* and *ruled* with Christ for a thousand years.

5   The rest of the dead did not live until the thousand years came to an end.
    This is the first resurrection.

6   Blessed and holy is the one who shares in the first resurrection.
    The second death has no power over them.
  But they will continue to be *priests of God* and of Christ.
  And they will rule with Him for a thousand years.

The Judgment

7 And whenever the thousand years come to an end,
    Satan will be freed from his prison.
8 And he will go out to deceive the Gentiles in all parts of the world—
    that is, *Gog* and *Magog*—to gather them for battle;
      they will be as many as the sand by the sea.
9 And they came up, *spreading over* the broad expanse of *the earth*,
  and surrounded the camp of the believers and the city He loves.
  And *fire came down from heaven and consumed them.*
10 And the devil who deceived them was thrown into the lake of *fire* and *sulfur*,
    where the beast and the false prophet are,
  and they will be tortured day and night forever ˌandˌ ever.

---

2 *Gen* 3:1,13; *Zech* 3:1   **4** *Dan* 3:5,6; 7:9,22,27   **6** *Is* 61:66   **8** *Ezek* 38:2   **9** *2 Sam* 22:9;
2 *Kgs* 1:10,12; *Is* 26:11; *Jer* 5:14; *Hab* 1:6   **10** *Gen* 19:24

---

20 *a-* 2 See Matthew 12:29; Mark 3:27; and Luke 11:22.
  b- 3 Or "nations" (also in v. 8).

11 And *I saw a* great white *throne*
and *the One sitting on it from whose presence the earth* and the sky fled away,
and *no place was found for them.*
12 And I saw the dead, great and small, standing before the throne.
And *books were opened,*
and another book was opened—*the Book of Life.*
And the dead were judged on the basis of the things
written in the books *according to what they had done.*
13 And the sea gave up the dead who were in it,
and death and *hades^c* gave up the dead who were in them,
and each one was judged *according to what he had done.*
14 And death and *hades* were thrown into the fiery lake.
The fiery lake is the second death.
15 And if anyone was not found *written in the Book of Life,*
he was thrown into the fiery lake.

21ST CHAPTER

H. Seventh vision: God's new world (21:1–22:5)

A New Heaven And A New Earth

1 And I saw *a new heaven and a new earth,*
because the first heaven and the first earth had passed away.
And there was no longer any sea.
2 And I saw the *HOLY CITY,* NEW *JERUSALEM,* coming down from God
out of heaven, *dressed as a bride* ready for her husband.
3 And I heard a loud voice from the throne, saying:

"Look, the *'TABERNACLE of God'* is among the people!
And He will live with them,
and *they will be His people,*
and *God Himself will be with them* as their God;
4 and *He will wipe* every *tear from their eyes*;
and there will be *no* more *death,*
nor will there be grief
nor crying
nor pain,
because the first things have passed away."

5 And *the One seated on the throne* said:
"Look, *I am making* everything *new.*"
And He said:
"Write this because these words are faithful and genuine."*^a*

---

11 *1 Kgs 22:19; 2 Chr 18:18; Ps 47:9; 114:7; Is 6:1; Dan 2:35*   12 *Ex 32:32,33; Ps 69:28; 139:16;*
Is 4:3; Dan 7:10; 12:1; Mal 3:16   12,13 *Ps 28:4; 62:12*   15 *Ex 32:32,33; Ps 69:28; 139:16;*
Is 4:3; Dan 12:1; Mal 3:16   1 *Is 65:17; 66:22*   2 *Is 52:1; 61:10*   3 *Is 7:14; 8:8,10;*
Ezek 37:27; Zech 2:10   4 *Is 25:8*   5 *1 Kgs 22:19; 2 Chr 18:18; Ps 47:9; Is 6:1; 43:19*

---

c- 13 See 1:18 and its accompanying footnote; compare verse 14.
21 a- 5 Greek: "*alēthinos*"; see ALĒTHINOS COMPARED WITH *ALĒTHĒS* on page 530.

6 And He said to me:

"It is done!
I am the Alpha and the Omega [the A and the Z],[b]
the Beginning and the End.
To anyone *who is thirsty* I will give ˌwaterˌ
from the fountain of the *water of life—without cost!*
7 The one who wins the victory will inherit these things,
and *I will be his God,*
and *he will be My son.*

8 "But as for the cowardly
and unfaithful
and abominable people,
and those who murder
and sin sexually
and practice witchcraft
and worship idols,
and all liars—
they will find themselves in the lake *burning with fire* and *sulfur;*
this is the second death."

The New Jerusalem

9 And one of the seven angels
who had the seven bowls full of the *seven* last *plagues* came,
and he spoke to me, saying:

"Come, I will show you the bride, the wife of the Lamb."

10 And he carried me away in the Spirit[c] *to a* large and *high mountain,*
and he showed me *the HOLY CITY, JERUSALEM,*
coming down from God out of heaven,
11 *having the glory of God.*

The ˌsource ofˌ its light was like a very precious stone,
like a jasper stone, clear as crystal.

12 It had a large and high wall with *twelve gates,*
and at the gates twelve angels,
and on the gates were written the names of the twelve tribes of Israel.

13 There were *three gates on the east side*
and *three gates on the north*
and *three gates on the south*
and *three gates on the west.*

---

6 Is 55:1; Zech 14:8   *7 2 Sam 7:14; Zech 8:8*   *8 Is 30:33*   *9 Lev 26:21*   *10 Is 52:1;*
Ezek 40:2   *11 Is 58:8; 60:1,2,19*   *12,13 Ex 28:21; Ezek 48:31-35*

---

b- 6 See 1:8 and its accompanying footnote "k."
c- 10 See 1:10 and its accompanying footnote.

14 And the wall of the city had twelve foundation stones.
And on them were the twelve names of the twelve apostles of the Lamb.

15 And the angel who was talking to me had a golden *measuring rod* to measure
the city
and its gates
and its wall.

16 And the city was *square*;
and it was as wide as it was long;
and he measured the city with the rod at 12,000 stadia*d*—
its length
and width
and height were the same.

17 And he measured its wall; it was 144 cubits,*e*
according to human measurement, which the angel was using.*f*

18 And its wall was made of jasper.

And the city was of pure gold, like clear glass.

19 *The foundations* of the city wall were made beautiful
with all kinds of precious stones:

      the first foundation stone was jasper,
      the second *sapphire*,
      the third agate,
      the fourth emerald,
20   the fifth sardonyx,
      the sixth carnelian,
      the seventh chrysolite,
      the eighth beryl,
      the ninth topaz,
      the tenth chrysoprase,
      the eleventh jacinth,
      the twelfth amethyst.

21 And the twelve gates were twelve pearls;
each gate was made of one pearl.

And the street of the city was of pure gold, like clear glass.

22 And I did not see any Temple in it,
because the *Lord God Almighty*
and the Lamb are its TEMPLE.

---

15 Ezek 40:3,5   *16* Ezek 43:16   *19* Is 54:11   *22* Ex 3:15; Is 40:10; Mal 3:1

d- 16 This seems to be the length of each side. See MONEY, WEIGHTS, and MEASURES on page 328.
e- 17 The measurements in *Revelation* have not been put into modern equivalents because this would cause the *symbolical* significance of the original numbers to be lost. See MONEY, WEIGHTS, and MEASURES on page 328.
f- 17 Literally: "which is the angel's."

23 And the city does not need *any sun or moon to give it light,*
because the *GLORY OF GOD gave it light,*
and the Lamb is its LAMP.

24 And *the nations will walk by* its *light,*
and *the kings* of the earth *will bring* their glory into it.

25 And its *gates will never be shut by day* because *there will be no night* there.

26 And they will bring the glory and wealth of the nations into it.

27 And *nothing unclean,*
and no one who does anything abominable and tells lies *will ever come into it,*
only those who are *written in the Lamb's Book of Life.*^g

22ND CHAPTER

1 And he showed me a river of the *water of life,* clear as crystal,
flowing from the throne of God and of the Lamb.

2 *Between* the street of the city and *the river,*
there *was a tree*^a *of life*
⌊visible⌋^b *from this side and from that;*
it *produces* twelve kinds of *fruit,*
for each month its own fruit;
and *the leaves of the tree are*
for the *healing* of the nations.

3 And *there will be no more curse;*
and the throne of God and of the Lamb will be in the city;
and His servants will worship Him 4 and *see Him,*
and His Name will be on their foreheads;
5 and *there will be no more night,*
and they will not need any lamplight and *sunlight,*
because *the Lord God will shine* on them;
and *they will be kings forever* ⌊and⌋ ever.

---

23 *Is 60:19*   **24,25** *Is 60:3,5,11*   **25** *Zech 14:7*   **27** *Ex 32:32,33; Ps 69:28; 139:16; Is 4:3; 52:1;*
Dan 12:1; Mal 3:16   **1** *Ezek 47:1,12; Joel 3:18; Zech 14:8*   **2** *Gen 2:9; 3:22,24; Ezek 47:7,12*
3 *Zech 14:11*   **4** *Ps 17:15; 42:2*   **5** *Is 60:19; Dan 7:18,22,27; Zech 14:7*

---

g- 27 Note that this section on The New Jerusalem (vv. 9-27) has been structured into *twenty* parts,
each being indicated in the text by a separated paragraph. Of interest is the observation that the
twelve foundation stones are listed at the twelfth paragraph. See THE SYMBOLICAL
NUMBERS OF *REVELATION* on page 567.

22 *a-* 2 The Greek word for "tree" ("*xulon*"), which is used here, is the same word used for "cross."
Some suggest that this is done to lead the reader to think both of the Tree of Life in the
Garden of Eden as well as the *cross* of Christ.

b- 2 One might supply the thought of "equidistant."

I. Conclusion (22:6-21)

I Am Coming Soon

6 And he said to me:

> "These words are faithful and genuine;*c*
> and the Lord, the God of the spirits of the prophets,
>> has sent His angel to show His servants*d the things
>> that must happen* without delay."

7 "And remember, *I am coming* soon!
Blessed is the one who keeps the words of the prophecy of this book."

8 I, John, heard and saw these things,
and when I had heard and seen them,
> I *bowed down to worship* at the feet of the angel
> who had been showing me these things.

9 And he told me:

> "Do not do that!
>> I am a fellow servant of yours
>> and of your fellow Christians*e* the prophets
>> and of those who keep the words of this book.
> Worship God!"

10 And he said to me:

> "*Do not seal up* the words of the prophecy of *this book*,
> because the *time* is near.

11 "Let *the wrongdoer still do wrong*,
> and the filthy one still be filthy,
> and let the righteous one still do right,
> and the holy one still be holy."

12 "See, *I am coming* soon
> and *will have My reward with Me*
>> to *pay everyone according to what he has done*.

---

6 Is 48:6; Dan 2:28-30,45   *7* Is 40:10   *8* Ps 22:27; 86:9; Is 45:14; 49:23; 60:14; 66:23;
Jer 16:19   *10* Dan 8:26; 12:4   *11* Dan 12:10   *12* Ps 28:4; 62:12; Is 40:10

> *c-* 6 Greek: "*alēthinos*"; see *ALĒTHINOS* COMPARED WITH *ALĒTHĒS* on page 530.
> *d-* 6 Meaning that the same God who had created new "spirits" (that is, converted hearts/new
> attitudes/spiritual lives) in the Old Testament prophets and who had used these prophets as His
> revealing instruments is now sending His revealing angel to do the same in terms of things still
> future. God is doing this so that His servants (Christians) when reading *Revelation* might
> understand and believe, as did the believers of the Old Testament.
> *e-* 9 Literally: "brothers."

13 "I am the Alpha and the Omega [the A and the Z],*f*
  the First and the Last,
    the Beginning and the End.

14 "Blessed are those who *wash their robes*
    so that they may have the right to the *tree of life*
      and may go through the gates into the city.

15 "Outside are the dogs
          and the people who practice witchcraft
          and sin sexually
          and murder
          and worship idols
          and everyone who loves lies and tells them.

16 "I, Jesus, have sent My angel to give this testimony to you for the churches.
  I am *David's* Creator
    and *Descendant,g*
      the Bright Morning Star."*h*

17 "And the Spirit and the bride say, 'Come!'
  And the one who hears this, let him say, 'Come!'
  And *the one who is thirsty, let him come!*
  The one who wants it, let him take *the water of life as a free gift.i*

18 "I warn*j* everyone who hears the words of the prophecy of this book:

    If anyone *adds anything to this,*
      God will *add to him* the plagues
        that are *written in this book;*
19   and if anyone *takes away* any words from this book of prophecy,
      God *will take away* his share in *the tree of life* and in the Holy City
        that are described in this book."

20 He who is testifying to these things says:

    "Yes, *I am coming* soon!"

  Amen!
    Come, Lord Jesus!
21   The grace of the Lord Jesus be with all of you.
  Amen!

---

13 *Is* 44:2,6; 48:12   **14** *Gen* 2:9; 3:22,24; 49:11   **16** *Is* 11:1,10; *Jer* 23:5
17 *Is* 55:1; *Zech* 14:8   **18,19** *Deut* 4:2; 13:1; 29:19,20   **19** *Gen* 2:9; 3:22,24
20 *Is* 40:10

---

f- 13 See 1:8 and its accompanying footnote "k."
g- 16 Literally: "the Root and Descendant of David."
h- 16 Literally: "the Star, the Bright, the Morning"; most translate "bright Morning Star."
i- 17 Literally: "water of life freely" or "water of life without cost."
j- 18 Literally: "testify."

APPENDIXES

APPENDIXES

The following Appendixes are meant to lead the reader to a greater understanding of the text of GWN's New Testament. They present several examples of varied Christian educational helps.

APPENDIX 1
UNIQUE GWN STYLISTIC FEATURES

GWN contains major stylistic features, some them unique. Each is aimed at making the text more readily understandable. The following is a list of these features:

- A. GWN capitalization system
- B. Punctuation that aids silent as well as oral reading
- C. Italics to identify parallel quotes in Old and New Testaments
- D. GWN brackets/half-brackets usage
- E. Outlines within each Biblical book
- F. Headers
- G. The *chi-rho* emblem
- H. An initial footnote in each book that explains its title
- I. A Hebraic poetic format that is carefully reflected in the English across-the-page text.

(GWN also contains additional features common to other Bible editions. They include sections of introductory notes, elaborate footnoting, articles, maps, illustrations, a glossary, and a concordance.)

A. GWN CAPITALIZATION

Capitalization in the New Testament text of GWN does not always follow standard English style. At times it goes beyond and sets a standard of its own. Some of its unique features, primarily using examples from the Gospel of *John*, are:

1. *Pronouns* **referring to God—Father, Son (Jesus), or Holy Spirit.** When referring to the true God, pronouns such as "He" (Jn. 1:30), "Him" (Jn. 1:31), "His" (Jn. 2:12), "We" (Jn. 3:11), "Our" (Jn. 3:11), "Me" (Jn. 3:12), and so forth are capitalized. This capitalization is intended to give honor to our God. At the same time it is designed to aid readers in quickly distinguishing between persons in a narrative; this is true especially in sections where pronouns abound and Jesus needs to be distinguished from others, or where pronouns represent proper names that are implied by a former, somewhat removed sentence. (At times the text of GWN replaces a pronoun with the repetition of a proper name, such as "Jesus" for "He," so that the English flows more clearly.)

2. *Indefinite indicators.* Terms such as "One" (Jn. 1:26) or "Man" (Jn. 4:29)—when referring to Jesus—are capitalized if they are *not* used in a totally generic sense (contrast "man" in Jn. 9:11). Also, capitalization of pronouns is employed when God's Name is found on the lips of unbelievers or opponents of Christ (Jn. 8:33).

3. *Titles.* When used concerning Jesus, titles such as "Word" (Jn. 1:1), "Light" (Jn. 9:5), "Door" (Jn. 10:9), "Good Shepherd" (Jn. 10:11), and so forth are capitalized.

4. *The term Word.* It is our custom in English to capitalize "Bible," "Scripture," and even the designations "Word" and "Book" when they refer to the Bible as a whole. But this is our custom today, many years after the Scriptures have been gathered into one body. However, at the time when the Scriptures were being written, years before they were put into book form, the books of the Bible were for the most part individual entities written on individual scrolls. And phrases such as "the word of the Lord came to the prophet, saying" were general references to particular messages from God, rather than specific references to the Bible as a whole.

By Jesus' and Paul's day the books of the Old Testament were already seen to be one united whole (2 Tim. 3:16), but the New Testament certainly was not yet gathered into one unit since not all of it was written down until after A.D. 90. The capitalized form should be used only to refer to the whole *written* Bible, or when it is a title for Jesus (Jn. 1:14). Phrases such as "the word of the Kingdom" (Matt. 13:19) or "remain in My word" (Jn. 8:31) are not references to the Book called the Bible; rather, they are references to God's message in general, and it is only when we apply them, as in a sermon, that they refer to the Bible as a whole.

GWN recognizes this distinction and capitalizes the term "word" only when it is used as a title for Jesus, identical to other Bibles in print.

5. *Kingdom, Name, Temple, etc.* The capitalization of terms such as "Kingdom," "Name," and "Temple" is unique to the text of GWN and should attract attention to these important terms.

When "Kingdom" is capitalized, either its importance (Jn. 3:3) or its contrast to earthly kingdoms or earthly rule (Jn. 18:36) is emphasized.

The capitalization of "Name" is made on the basis of Isaiah 42:8 and the importance of this term (Acts 3:16; 4:12; Phil. 2:10); this importance is often underestimated. Where the term "name" stands as a substitute for a specific title of God, "NAME" in all capitals (Acts 5:41) is used, as parallel to Deuteronomy 12:5.

"Temple" (cf. Jn. 2:15) is viewed in the text of GWN as the *proper* name for the building to which the Jews went for worship in Jerusalem. Therefore, it is

capitalized. (The same applies to the word "House," which is the word for "Temple" in the Old Testament. See Jn. 2:17.)

"Jacob's Well" (Jn. 4:6), treated in the GWN text as a proper name, could be debated. However, its historic designation in New Testament times can justify capitalization, even if only for emphasis.

6. Terms for *Satan*. The words "devil" (Jn. 8:44, "deceiver, liar") and "demon" (Jn. 8:52) are generic terms for the leader of hell and his evil angelic followers. Thus, no capitalization! (Only in Revelation 12:9 and 20:2 is "Devil" used as a proper noun.) However, terms like "Satan" (Jn. 13:27, meaning "Accuser") and "Evil One" (Jn. 17:15) are *proper nouns* and so are capitalized; but no sense of honor is intended.

7. *Last Day*. This term, as in John 12:48, is handled in the text of GWN as a proper noun synonym for "Judgment Day," as is the single term "Day" when it refers to the time of Christ's final coming (Lk. 17:30,31; 21:34).

8. *I AM*. This term in John 8:58 is obviously a reference back to Exodus 3:14. The use of this term as God's Name in both passages validates its fuller capitalization. However, revisers of the text of GWN had reservations concerning the fuller capitalization of several other occurrences of *ego eimi* ("I am") in John's Gospel (e.g., Jn. 14:6; 15:1). Except for the 8:58 passage, all the other usages of *ego eimi* function as linking verbs, not as God's Name. The lack of *ego* with *eimi* at John 9:5 forces one to be cautious so that a translation like GWN does not become unnecessarily interpretive.

9. *Earthly and heavenly counterparts*. At times certain earthly *concepts* ("city, covenant, glory"), *places* ("Jerusalem, sanctuary, Zion"), and *items* ("ark, lamp, Tabernacle") are used in terms of the religious or sacred. As such, they are set aside for a holy purpose by Scripture, and for effective communication can be referred to with an initial capital in written form.

When these same terms, which have already been capitalized in a religious context, are moved by Scripture to a higher level and are made into a heavenly concept, that is, the earthly images are transformed into fulfilled realities that have their counterparts in heaven itself, then the only thing left to do for sake of communication is to capitalize *all* the letters of such words like "CITY, JERUSALEM, LAMP," and so forth. This methodology has been followed in Hebrews 8–13 and in appropriate portions of *Revelation*. For further study see THE HOLY PLACES on page 550 as well as Revelation 3:12 and its accompanying footnote.

The capitalization system of GWN is intended to aid clarity of understanding and to give glory to the Triune God. Obviously, such a capitalization system poses some difficulties and drawbacks at places (see Jn. 3:11, note c), but overall it should be a welcome feature, helpful to Bible readers.

B. GWN'S PUNCTUATION

GWN employs a mixture of two styles of punctuation. At places it follows the more modern trend of fewer commas. In other places commas are used more liberally. This seeming inconsistency was followed for two reasons: to let the text flow naturally and to indicate appropriate pause points to the oral reader. In particular passages where the meaning of the Biblical text is difficult to determine and certain punctuation would favor one varying view over another, GWN has sought to remain neutral by means of the punctuation employed or not employed (cf. Jn. 19:25 and its accompanying footnote).

As a general rule, quotation marks are not placed around poetic sections to indicate their Old Testament origin. They are present, however, when a person, for example, is speaking the words or when a certain section demands them because of unique structure. Example: Hebrews 1:5 needs them to separate a direct statement which sits within a context that asks a direct question.

C. GWN'S ITALICS

Italics in the GWN New Testament are reserved for a special purpose: to indicate that the italicized words are taken directly from the Old Testament. Cross-references toward the bottom of a page show where the Old Testament quotations can be found. These references are listed according to the chronological order of Old Testament books cited, not in order of citation within the New Testament passage itself.

D. GWN BRACKETS/HALF-BRACKETS

GWN's use of *brackets* in the text will prove to be helpful. The data within the brackets will provide handy information, less need to refer to footnotes, greater clarity for the reader of the text, and greater comprehension for the listener when another reads the bracketed material properly.

Words in brackets offer parallel meanings ("Christ"="Messiah," Jn. 1:20), give definitions ("proverb" means "saying," Jn. 4:37), reveal meanings of foreign names and terms ("Didymus" means "Twin," Jn. 11:16), indicate antecedents in relation to pronouns ("His"="Jesus'," Jn. 12:41), provide alternatives[1] between a more common way of saying something as parallel to a more archaic—and maybe even more familiar way of saying the same thing ("goes out"="proceeds," Jn. 15:26), state meanings of terms ("brothers" refers to "Christians," Jn. 21:23), and add extra parallel terms for broader comprehension of Biblical data ("tented"="tabernacled," Jn. 1:14, note e).

---

[1] Brackets do not offer variant reading alternatives. GWN footnotes include such readings.

Religious or lay leaders who are handling bracketed sections orally may do one of *three* things to aid the flow as they read. They may ignore the term in the brackets, substitute the word in the brackets for the appropriate word(s) in the text, or read both renderings. If doing the latter, readers should add the words "which means" or "that is" before the bracketed words (along with a relative pronoun at times). Examples:

1. Mark 9:5, "Rabbi [Teacher]" would read: "Peter said to Jesus, "Rabbi [*which means* Teacher], it's good for us to be here."
2. Mark 11:19, "they [Jesus and His disciples]" would read: "Whenever evening came, they [*that is*, Jesus and His disciples] would leave the city."
3. John 15:26, "who goes out [proceeds]" would read: " . . . I shall send you . . . the Spirit of Truth, who goes out [*that is, who* proceeds] from the Father . . . ."

Half-brackets are used to insert extra words into the text, words that are not in the original Greek but are needed to make the English flow or to complete the thought in English (cf. Jn. 5:12; Rom. 3:25).

In oral reading, the words within the half-brackets are to be read as if they are an actual part of the text. In Biblical study, they are *not* to be viewed as authoritative for determining original meaning.

E. OUTLINES INCORPORATED THROUGHOUT GWN'S TEXT

Useful outlines of all 27 New Testament books appear throughout the New Testament text of GWN. They are used by permission, being adapted for this New Testament printing from Robert G. Hoerber's *Reading the New Testament for Understanding* (St. Louis: Concordia Publishing House, 1986).

F. HEADERS

"Headers" are not to be confused with GWN's "incorporated outlines" (as mentioned directly above). These headers sit flush to the left column and appear throughout the text. They are intended to break the text into small units which contain unified thoughts or narratives. At the same time such headers provide concise summaries of various sections. They help to locate certain stories with greater ease.

G. THE *CHI-RHO* EMBLEM

The *chi-rho* emblem, consisting of two Greek letters, one superimposed on the other, stands in the margin next to passages that are fulfillments of Old

Testament prophecies concerning *Christ*. The *chi* is the Greek letter for the sound "ch" and resembles an "x" in English; the *rho* is the Greek "r," which is written like our English "P." In Greek the name *Christos* begins with a "Chr," as does the English "Christ." Thus, the *chi-rho* emblem is an abbreviation for "Christ" and is appropriately used as a signal for fulfillments of Old Testament prophecies concerning Christ. This emblem may also stand next to passages that imply fulfillments even though a word-for-word passage is not quoted from the Old Testament (cf. Jn. 6:14).

H. INITIAL FOOTNOTES IN THE BIBLICAL BOOKS

All 27 New Testament books begin with a footnote to their respective titles, which gives a brief summary of such information as author, date written, origin and/or destination of the writing, and sometimes the purpose and content of the writing as deemed pertinent for the readers.

I. GWN'S POETIC FORMAT

Some would consider GWN's *poetic format* to be its most unique feature. In terms of importance it may eventually rank second only to its accuracy and ease of understanding, in which this poetic style also plays a major part. This poetic format plays a major role in many sections of the New Testament to say nothing of giant areas of the Old Testament.

In particular to this present printing of the GWN New Testament, we call the reader's attention to several articles. First, John's book of *Revelation* is entirely set in a poetic format—with no prose. The importance of this phenomenon is explained in two articles entitled: GRAMMATIC/POETIC STRUCTURES THAT CONVEY TEXTUAL MEANINGS on page 558 and THE *KAI* STRUCTURE on page 565. Second, the GRAMMATIC/POETIC article deals with several other poetic sections of the New Testament. Third, a few superior examples of Old Testament poetry are given in the following listing: "PREVIEW OF COMING ATTRACTIONS" on page 569.

APPENDIX 2
SPECIAL GWN TRANSLATION FEATURES

GWN seeks to be very faithful to the Greek New Testament text. Such concern for accuracy has led the revisers to give special attention to certain areas of translation that are sometimes overlooked:

  A. GWN emphasizes the special meaning of the present tense, including particularly the Greek present imperative.

B. GWN makes a distinction between three Greek terms which are translated as "miraculous signs," "wonderful proofs," and "miracles."

C. GWN gives special treatment to and explanations of terms such as *alethes, alethinos, amen, diatheke, hades/gehenna, hupotasso, monogenes, nomos, skandalon.*

A. THE GREEK PRESENT TENSE

The Greek present tense at times stresses the *continuation* of an action. The GWN text brings out this emphasis over and over again.

The present tense deserves special attention in the imperative mood. This present tense in Matthew 7:7,8 is pertinent when the translation shows that Jesus means: "*Keep asking*, and it will be given to you. *Keep searching*, and you will find. *Keep knocking*, and the door will be opened to you. For anyone who continues to ask receives; anyone who continues to search finds; and to anyone who continues to knock, the door will be opened."

Readers should also be alert to the fact that a *negative* Greek imperative in the present tense urges that an action *not* be continued. Thus, those translations of John 20:17 which say "Don't touch Me" are misleading in their handling of the present imperative. Mary already was touching Jesus, so He said, "*Stop holding on* to Me" or "*Do not continue to hold on* to Me." The same is true of Zacharias and the virgin Mary. Both of them were already "afraid" when they saw Gabriel, so the angel said, "*Stop being afraid*" (Lk. 1:13,30).

B. MIRACULOUS SIGNS, WONDERFUL PROOFS, and MIRACLES

The New Testament uses several Greek words to talk about Jesus' superhuman acts. Three of these terms are:

1. *dunamis*, translated "miracle";
2. *teras*, translated "wonderful proof";
3. *semeion*, translated "miraculous sign."[2]

These terms are used together in three different passages—Acts 2:22; 2 Corinthians 12:12; 2 Thessalonians 2:9. Thus, simply to translate them all with the identical term "miracle" would not be realistic. It would neither convey the real thought to the reader, nor would it be accurate. Rather, each

---

[2] The term *erga* ("works") also enters into our present discussion. It is a more general term that includes Jesus' whole miraculous activity. Whatever is said about the three terms to be discussed can be said of *erga*, which can be seen as a general substitute for these words.

term indicates a different flavor and seeks to signal a particular truth, but a truth that is only one part of a unified whole. That "whole" of Jesus' miraculous activity is the sum total of the intent of all three terms.

In his original translation Dr. William F. Beck, whose work GWN uses as its solid base, made a distinction between these three Greek terms but not with a repetitive consistency in each text. The present text has made the translation consistent. In this way the English reader will be able to realize which term is used in the Greek text by recalling the meanings of 1, 2, and 3 above.

1. The import of *dunamis*. The word *dunamis* is related to our English word "dynamite." It means "power." Thus GWN's translation renders it "miracle" since in English that term is very much associated with an action that demands superhuman or supernatural *power*.

It could be argued that most of Jesus' supernatural actions were "miracles" (see Matt. 11:21,23; Mk. 6:2; Lk. 19:37). However, the narratives do not call any certain action of Jesus a "miracle" within the report of the individual story; rather, His actions are called "miracles" in a collective sense. One of the narratives that comes close to labeling a supernatural action with the term *dunamis* is in Mark 5:30/Luke 8:46, where "*power* went out" of Him.

The significance of a *dunamis*, however, is easy to detect by viewing "power" or "miracle" passages as a whole. Certain facts should not elude even the most casual Bible reader. For example, the passages which speak about the *power* that is inside Jesus (Lk. 5:17) as well as those which tie "power" and "authority" together in Jesus' healing ministry (Lk. 4:36; 9:1) are most revealing.

By the use of *dunamis* to refer to Jesus' supernatural actions (cf. again Matt. 11:21,23), Scripture encourages its readers to believe that He has divine authority and power to control lives on earth through both physical care and spiritual forgiveness (cf. Matt. 28:18-20). By leaving the individual actions unspecified and not *individually* identifying them as being *dunamis*, Scripture permits the interpreter to view them in two other directions also, in order to comprehend the fuller picture of His ministry of miraculous actions.

2. The import of *teras*. The term *teras* is related to the English word "terrify." Like *dunamis*, *teras* is not applied to particular supernatural actions connected with any one individual character in any given narrative. Likewise, it is used in a collective sense (Mk. 13:22; Jn. 4:48; Acts 5:12). (It can also be observed that *teras* is *always* used in connection with *semeion* in any given context.)

The significance of *teras* is also easy to detect if one considers several aspects. Remembering that a *teras* is the basis for the English word "terrify," one can

visualize people who witnessed one of Jesus' *teras*-type supernatural acts. They would be inclined to become *terrified, jolted,* and *awe-struck,* because any *teras* caused the unexpected to happen. It made the people *wonder.* In other words a *teras* caused all types of reactions at one and the same time: terror, surprise, awe, wonder, favorable impression, suspicion.

Though the concept of *teras* leads off in a direction somewhat different from *dunamis,* it ends up in concert with the overall meaning of the supernatural. *Teras* also calls God's people to faith in the Savior who has "proved" Himself in His earthly ministry. We stand in *terror* of His anger toward sin, in *awe* of His death on the cross, in a state of *surprise* concerning His empty tomb, in *wonderment* at His generous forgiveness, and, being both strong and weak in faith at times, we tend to be both *impressed* and *suspicious* of His Lordship. But He still calls us to believe the "wonderful proofs" of His love (Jn. 10:25,37,38) and to reject any so-called "wonderful proofs" of Satan (2 Thess. 2:9).

3. The import of *semeion*. The word *semeion* ("sign") is a favorite of John in his Gospel. In fact, he reports *seven* superhuman actions that Jesus worked prior to His death and resurrection.

The significance of these supernatural acts of Jesus is also easy to ascertain, though many have overlooked their fuller meaning.

A "sign" obviously points to something outside or beyond itself. The miracles of the Old Testament pointed to a Day when miracles would abound and a Person, even superior to the great Moses, would work such "signs" (cf. Ex. 4:17) in a way far more *numerous* and *superior* to any Old Testament personage.[3] *Semeion* calls us to a reevaluation, for a greater than Jonah or Solomon, in fact, a greater than Moses, Joshua, Elijah, Elisha, John the Baptizer, etc., has come. He is Jesus—and could we expect anyone to come who would do more "miraculous signs" than He Himself worked on earth (see Jn. 7:31)? There were so many "signs" that no one could even keep a count (Jn. 20:30; cf. 21:35)!

The *semeion*-direction is different from that of *dunamis* and *teras*; yet it stands as a solid part of a whole, a whole which forms a picture of the total meaning of Jesus' ministry of superhuman "works." And Peter underscores this truth when he says in Acts 2:22: " . . . listen to what I have to say: When Jesus from Nazareth was among you, He was a Man whom God commended to you—as you well know—by the miracles, wonderful proofs, and miraculous signs which God worked through Him."

---

[3] Richard C. Trench, *Notes on the Miracles of Our Lord* (Westwood, NJ: Fleming H. Revell Company, 1953), p. 38.

No wonder Satan, who wants us to follow him instead of Christ, tries to emulate Christ with "misleading miracles, miraculous signs, and wonderful proofs" (2 Thess. 2:9). But to combat such displays of misleading activity, God worked a counter activity through followers such as Paul (2 Cor. 12:12). And we who believe in Christ can do even greater things than these. See Mark 16:20, *semeion*; Luke 24:49, *dunamin*; Matthew 28:20, [relating to *teras*] "authority" and "I am with you"; John 20:30,31, *semeion* and "that by believing you may have life in His Name."[4] We can forgive one another's sins in the Name of Jesus (Jn. 20:23). That is real miraculous activity!

The Gospel writers give their readers much to consider through their varied usage of several Greek terms for the miraculous activity of Jesus. What we must add when all is said and done, however, is this: Each Gospel writer has his special emphasis within any given narrative, but the reader must realize that any given miracle, though stated under one emphasis, most likely also fits the other two categories in Biblical scope. For example, a *dunamis*-type miracle which emphasizes power should also be seen as one that can have a "sign" aspect and relate to some Old Testament prophet's foreshadowing of Christ's activity. This keeps one from limiting the meaning, for the Gospel writers never intended to subtract from Jesus' miraculous activity by any of their special emphases.

In summary, Jesus' *dunamis*-activity substantiated His Messiahship as these "miracles" demonstrated a divinely endorsed authority and power; His *teras*-activity illustrated "wonderful proofs" of the heavenly endorsement of His Gospel message and ministry; and His *semeion*-activity gave "miraculous signs" that Jesus as Messiah was the fulfillment of all. When these parts are then seen as a *whole*, Bible readers will realize that all three call on them to *believe* that Jesus is the Messiah whose Gospel message fulfills all (Matt. 3:15) by bringing forgiveness to all (Jn. 1:29; Acts 4:12; 10:43; Rom. 10:9-17; 2 Cor. 5:19; 1 Pet. 1:5; 1 Jn. 2:2).

Remember: GWN translates *dunamis* as "miracle," *teras* as "wonderful proof," and *semeion* as "miraculous sign."

C. THE SPECIAL HANDLING OF CERTAIN GREEK TERMS

1. *Alethinos* compared with *alethes*

John carefully distinguishes between the Greek words *alethinos* and *alethes*. Most English translations do not; they render them both with "true." In

---

[4] As in the case of Jesus' three types of miracles, our active faith gives evidence of the fact that we have authority and power in Christ, that the Gospel message is substantiated in us, and that we are authentically in the succession of those who have believed before us.

several cases this is fine; however, in certain contexts the translation "true" for *alethinos* can lead to a false or misleading connotation.

Alethinos (used at Jn. 1:9; 4:23,37; 6:32; 7:28; 8:16; 15:1; 17:3; 19:35) basically means "genuine" or "primary," whereas *alethes* means "true" in contrast to "false." John's use of *alethinos* in John 1:9 emphasizes that John the Baptizer is a *secondary* light, one who receives illumination from Jesus the *primary* Light. It is important to note that John the Gospel writer uses *alethinos*, not *alethes*, since he does *not* wish to leave the impression that John the Baptizer's message was false while Jesus' message was true. (*Alethinos* is the word used in the historic Nicene Creed for the word "very" in the phrase "very God of very God," thus communicating that Jesus is "genuine God.") Note that *alethinos* can be translated "true" when properly understood. It is translated as such on *four* different occasions in the Gospel of *John*. *Alethinos* is also found at Luke 16:11; 1 Thessalonians 1:9; Hebrews 8:2; 9:24; 10:22; 1 John 2:8; 5:20; Revelation 3:7,14; 6:10; 15:3; 16:7; 19:2,9,11; 21:5; 22:6.

2. *Amen, Amen*

Most are familiar with the words "verily, verily" or "truly, truly" in various versions of the English Bible. These words are the translation of the Greek "*amen, amen*." In the Synoptic Gospels the compounding of the term is not employed. This is only done in *John*. With its surrounding formula in the the the Synoptics, one could hear Jesus state: "Verily, I say unto you." The GWN has chosen to translate this formula: "I tell you the truth," "the truth" standing for the single Greek *amen*. When coming to the compounding of *amen* in *John*, one could hardly say in flowing English: "I tell you the truth, the truth." To capture this repetition in *John* the GWN has translated: "I tell you the absolute truth." In this translation "the truth" represents the first *amen*, while "absolute" represents the second *amen*.

Note: The similar wording, for example, in John 16:7 ("I tell you the truth") is not to be confused with the above formula in *John*. John 16:7 contains a different Greek structure.

3. *Diatheke*

Diatheke is one of the most important and fascinating terms in all of Scripture. Its depth and conceptual richness, the history of its translation into English, and the debate over its meaning in several Biblical contexts have demanded as much in-depth research and prayerful decision-making as any other single term translated in GWN.

The Greek *diatheke* (coupled with the Hebrew term *berith*, which is rendered "covenant" in virtually every English Old Testament translation) needs—

almost demands—a volume of explanation. This is illustrated by the many pages that have been written concerning both of these terms in the history of the church. This present article adds another contribution to that ongoing discussion, a discussion, however, which by our day has become quite one-sided. GWN, *via* its particular translation of *diatheke* in various New Testament contexts, hopes to encourage a renewal of discussions that are more willing to look once again at all the evidence available.

The questions are: (1) Should *diatheke* be translated "covenant" or "testament" ("last will and testament")? (2) Are the two English concepts mutually *exclusive*, or do they overlap? (3) How much should the usage and context of given passages influence the translation of the term, exegetically speaking, as one applies the raw Greek lexical data? Related to these questions is the call to examine translation history a bit and to reexamine additional Scripture passages quite a bit. By the fact that GWN variously translates the 33 New Testament occurrences of *diatheke* with "covenant," "last will and testament," or with one of the two terms followed by the other in brackets indicates that GWN does not believe that a simple answer can be given.

Setting the tone. After considerable research of the term *diatheke*, GWN conclusions have sought to avoid polarization toward either opposing position: (1) the almost exclusive usage of "covenant"; or (2) the almost exclusive usage of "testament." This approach reflects the evaluation of much evidence. (In fairness, it is also stated that not every GWN translator had a strong opinion in the matter, and parallel to the discussions-at-large in the field of Biblical scholarship, not all GWN translators saw eye to eye on the final translation of each passage.)

On the one hand, even though *diatheke* was used in the sense of a "last will and testament" from Democritus (c. 400 B.C.) onward, there is no evidence that the term was too narrow to permit its inclusion of "covenant" if New Testament writers wished to use it that way. (Those who see *diatheke* only in terms of a "last will and testament" and/or who also see *berith* ["covenant"] as an independent concept must explain how *diatheke* could have been used to designate the "*berith*" of Exodus 24:8 or Jeremiah 31:32 in passages like Hebrews 8:9 or 9:20, when the two Old Testament *berith* verses could hardly be viewed as "testamental" in their "law" contexts. This is especially true in the light of certain implications given in passages like Romans 4:13-25.)

On the other hand, one cannot help but be impressed with Moulton and Milligan's assertion that " . . . a Hellenist like the *auctor ad Hebraeos* [author of Hebrews], or even a Jew like Paul, with Greek language in the very fibre of his thought, could never have used *d[iatheke]* for *covenant* without the slightest consciousness of its ordinary and invariable contemporary meaning."[5]

---

5 "Diatheke," *The Vocabulary of the Greek Testament*. The words " . . . its ordinary and invariable contemporary meaning" refer to "last will and testament."

Finally, from the Old Testament end of the spectrum, the idea that the Jews of the Old Testament were not accustomed to writing "last wills and testaments" is not decisive. For example, God gave His promises through the *word*; that was His signature. His people signed by *faith*. Thus, Old Testament Jews would not necessarily have had to put personal promissory testaments into writing in their everyday life. As God's people, they were also expected to be as good as their word (Prov. 6:1-3).

Diatheke: Its history of translation. Biblically speaking, the Greek term *diatheke* was first employed to translate the Hebrew *berith* some 250 years before Christ. This was done by the translators of the Septuagint (LXX), the Greek translation of the Hebrew Old Testament. Later, the New Testament used this same term to communicate given messages of the Holy Spirit (cf. 2 Pet. 1:20; 1 Pet. 1:12b).

In time, the entire Bible came to be translated into Latin. The Vulgate became the dominant Latin version. Jerome, its translator, consistently rendered *diatheke* with the term *testamentum* throughout his New Testament. He also used this word quite often in the Old Testament. It was Jerome who entitled Scripture's two distinct units as "Old Testament" and "New Testament," terminology that still holds to this very day.

Martin Luther followed Jerome's *diatheke* or "last will and testament" approach, but not blindly. He knew the writings of the church fathers well. Church fathers, such as Chrysostom, had spoken consistently of Christ's "last will and testament." Reformers like Martin Chemnitz, "the Second Martin (Luther)," continued this tradition. Though such reformers occasionally interchanged *testamentum* (when they wrote in Latin) with *pactum* or *foedus* (the regular words for "covenant"), their writings clearly indicated why they were using *testamentum* in the *narrow* sense in particular contexts. In such passages, they contended, *diatheke* referred to a "last will and testament," not to a "covenant" in the wider sense.

Luther, in his German Bible, displayed amazing insight as he skillfully moved back and forth between *Bund* ("covenant") and *"Testaments"* in his New Testament. (He did, however, consistently use *Bund* to translate *berith* throughout his whole Old Testament.) Luther's writings ably explain his methodology. Whenever the *diatheke* was a mere *promise*, he used *Bund*, that is, when the context implied that the promise had not yet been fulfilled. Whenever a context dealt with the *fulfillment* of a "covenant" promise, especially in terms of Jesus' death and His work as the God-Man, Luther used some form of *Testaments*.

For Luther the *berith* of the Old Testament was, in essence, the Gospel-promise of Jesus Christ, while the *diatheke* was the Gospel-promise *completed* in the Christ who was already born, sacrificed, risen, and who was coming again to give His people the ultimate inheritance: forgiveness of sins in heaven. This is why he writes: "And so that little word 'testament' is a short

summary of all God's wonders and grace, fulfilled in Christ."[6]

Luther knew that every faithful Bible translator also has to be a capable exegete. This means letting "Scripture interpret Scripture." Hebrews 9 and Galatians 3, therefore, settled much of the *diatheke* question for Luther: "Between a testament and a promise there is this difference: a testament is made by someone who is about to die; a promise, however, is made by someone who expects to continue living. . . . Since God in the Scriptures again and again calls his promise a testament he means to announce thereby that he will die; . . . . A testament is nothing but the last will of one who is dying, telling how his heirs are to live with and dispose of his properties after his death. . . . The testator is Christ, who is about to die."[7]

Luther clearly distinguished between the "old covenant" and the "new 'last will and testament'" (cf. Ex. 24:8; Jer. 31:31; 1 Cor. 11:25). The "old" was picturesque, physical, outward, and temporal; the "new" was real, spiritual, inward, and eternal.[8] This comprehension was gained from the whole of Scripture in general and from 2 Corinthians 3:7-15 in particular.

As the Reformation spread, the Scriptures were translated into many different languages.

Following Jerome and Luther, the King James (KJV) or Authorized Version (A.V.) translated *diatheke* with "covenant" and "testament" according to the basic guidelines laid down by Luther.

In time, the pendulum began to swing. Between 1881-1885 the Revised Version (R.V.) of the KJV translated *diatheke* in almost all instances with the term "covenant." The trend continued but was also cautioned against by men of the caliber of Adolf Deissmann (to be quoted below) and Geerhardus Vos. In fact, Vos not only advocated a return to "testament" in certain passages like those of the Lord's Supper, where he said that it "may seem advisable," but he also had a clear concept of the difference between the "old" *diatheke* and the "new" *diatheke*.[9] But the trend to use "covenant" was to continue.

The late 1940s, especially the 1950s, and the years on down to the present all produced writings by such scholars as G. E. Mendenhall, writings which noted various parallels between the *berith* forms of the Bible and those forms of the ancient Near East, forms discovered by archaeologists.

Such a trend has continued to foster a one-sided conclusion. This has caused every modern translation of the past few decades to turn almost exclusively to

---

[6] *Luther's Works* (Philadelphia: Muhlenberg Press, 1960), XXXV, 84.
[7] *Luther's Works* (Philadelphia: Muhlenberg Press, 1959), XXXVI, 179.
[8] *Luther's Works* (Philadelphia: Muhlenberg Press, 1960), XXXV, 84f.
[9] *Biblical Theology; Old and New Testaments* (Grand Rapids: Wm. B. Eerdmans Publishing Company, 1948), pp. 34-36.

"covenant" as its translation of *diatheke*. Even the New King James Version (NKJV) and the Roman Catholic translation known as The Jerusalem Bible have followed this trend. Only in a few selected passages, like Galatians 3:15 and Hebrews 9:16,17, has the term "will" or "testament" been retained.

A choice. THE NEW TESTAMENT: God's Word to the Nations (GWN) makes conspicuous use of "last will and testament" for *diatheke*. What warrants such a bold move? Does it merely reflect an older tradition, or is it a serious call for a renewed and ongoing evaluation?

There can be no doubt that much of the switch to "covenant" was well-intentioned and still is. "Covenant" seems to be a more familiar English word, and it introduces an explicit connection between the Old and New Testaments, a golden thread, if you will, that holds both Testaments together as a unified whole.

But as Deissmann says, the whole *diatheke* decision involves much more than the question of whether we retain the two divisions labeled "Old Testament" and "New Testament," instead of changing to "Old Covenant" and "New Covenant." His words are as relevant today as they were in the 1920s:

> Perhaps the most necessary investigation still waiting to be made is that relating to the word *diatheke*, which so many scholars translate unhesitatingly "covenant" .... To St. Paul the word [*diatheke*] meant what it meant in his Greek Old Testament, "a unilateral enactment," in particular "a will or testament." This one point concerns more than the merely superficial question whether we are to write "New Testament" or "New Covenant" on the title-page of the sacred volume; it becomes ultimately the great question of all religious history: a religion of grace, or a religion of works?[10]

Those who favor "covenant" for *diatheke* see *berith* and *diatheke* as one-sided promises (suzerainty covenants) wherein God the Suzerain makes the promises and keeps all of them in Christ His Son. In many cases—and in line with Scripture—they teach that a person's response to God's covenant is *faith*, a faith that is solely created by God Himself (1 Cor. 12:3).

In defense of scholars like Deissmann, it is true that certain problems have been created by some "covenant" proponents. These problems force us to consider very carefully how we translate the term *diatheke*.

There are some reasons for the above. It is a truism that many church liturgies still retain "new testament" in the words of institution at celebrations of the

---

[10] Adolf Deissmann, *Light from the Ancient East* (Grand Rapids: Baker Book House, 1965), pp. 337f.

Lord's Supper—and without laypersons or even a number of the clergy being aware that modern Bibles exclusively use "covenant," not "testament," in those Supper passages.

Moreover, the concept of "covenant" has been advocated by some and used by others to deny ideas, such as the fact that "God died" to enact His testament (cf. Heb. 2:14; 1 Tim. 3:16), or that salvation is solely by grace (cf. Eph. 2:8,9). Those who know Scripture well and who are subordinate to it are well aware that no text presents the "covenant" concept as a "deal" between God and mankind.

The latter misunderstandings are often permitted or promoted in certain quarters where "covenant theology" is strong. There one finds a significant amount of the mixing of grace with works under the heading of "covenant." Some of these conclusions have been reached most innocently. Unwisely, many proponents—in a zeal to emphasize man's response to God's initial grace—have overstated the human covenant role. (By no means do all advocates of "covenant theology" fall under this particular category.)

It does not seem proper within this article to state the names of those who advocate that which runs so counter to Biblical truth nor to list materials that promote such error. Thus, the avoidance of certain supportive footnotes! Rather, in the spirit of a friendly call toward a reopening of the whole *diatheke* discussion, let it be suggested that those interested read the article entitled "COVENANT" by Leon Morris in his *The Apostolic Preaching of the Cross* (Grand Rapids: Wm. B. Eerdmans Publishing Co., 1960), pp. 60-107. As far as it goes, it is an excellent, unbiased treatment of *diatheke* by a Christian scholar who favors the translation "covenant."

In addition, the present article includes other data to facilitate and encourage renewal of discussion. GWN puts an old choice with new approaches before the Bible-reading public by using both "covenant" and "testament" in a varied format.

The English problem. Some would say that *diatheke* presents more of a problem to translators in English than it did to the writers of Scripture in Greek. It is true that the terms "covenant" and "testament" do not track as well with each other in English; on the surface they seem like two unrelated concepts. We talk of a "baptismal covenant" and a "last will and testament," but never of a "baptismal testament" or a "last will and covenant." Obviously the two concepts were also not totally interchangeable in Latin and German, as is evidenced by the fact that (1) Jerome, who uses *pactum, foedus,* and *testament* rather interchangeably in his Old Testament, does not interchange them for *diatheke* in the New; and (2) Luther, who translated the Bible into very down-to-earth German, often decided to avoid the simpler *Bund* in favor of the more complex *Testaments* in the New Testament portion of his translation.

This would indicate that the "testament" approach, followed for over 1,400

years in the history of New Testament translation, had been used after much thought was given to it. The occurrence of "covenant" in one passage and "testament" in another was not arbitrary.

It should also be stated that proponents of the "covenant" concept, perhaps unwittingly, may have made "covenant" too much of a focal point in their theology. In fact, their view may tend to limit Christ and His work (cf. Jn. 5:39). At times it tends to obscure other Biblical concepts, preventing them from exhibiting their full value. It may be accurate to say that modern Biblical scholarship has become overly enamored with the undeniably beautiful concept of "covenant."

Such shift in interpretation and translation has caused many "covenant" advocates to become less precise in terms of communication. This lack of precision is also a symptom in the "testament" camp. In English the words of Jesus, "This cup is the *new testament* in My blood," easily permit one to think of the New Testament portion of the Bible, not the concept of a "will." This is why GWN uses "new 'last will and testament'" to avoid such miscommunication. Likewise, the average churchgoer and English-speaking person who hears the word "covenant" will usually think of a contract between two parties, each of whom makes concessions, has obligations, and contributes something; "covenant" just sounds like it means "let's make a deal."

These very realities certainly create a dilemma for translators. However, the possibility of communicating two beautifully combined concepts in a meaningful way ought to offer them a positive challenge.

Superimposed concepts that challenge. GWN has faced what every translation faces: the question of primary dictionary meaning, plus or minus considerations that let the translation be shaped by the context. In other words, do exegetical considerations play into translation? In the case of *diatheke* it is hard not to answer in the affirmative, especially when *diatheke* is used to speak of the "old covenant" of Mount Sinai, a covenant that certainly did not promise the death of any type of testator. Sacrificial lambs certainly did not put much of anything into effect, as is the conclusion of Hebrews 9:13 and 10:4 (cf. Ex. 24:5-8).

To be sure, no one should deny the presence of a "covenant" concept on the pages of the Old Testament. At the same time, who can ignore the the various "testamental" components that sit in so many "covenant" contexts? All should agree that from a Gospel point of view Genesis 12 and 15 are the key "covenant" chapters of the Old Testament. Note how chapter 12 contains the threefold promise (land, seed, and blessings) made to Abraham, a promise that for all intents and purposes contains nothing other than an inheritance oath that was never totally attainable until Christ completed His work (Heb. 11:13). Chapter 15 is even more amazing as it speaks of God "cutting" a covenant with Abraham. This is done right in the midst of a context that

contains "testamental" terminology: "heir," "child," "inherit," "property" (vv. 2,3,7,14). Also compare Acts 3:25.

These Genesis examples are so crucial that the adding of other examples of "promissory testaments," like those of Leviticus 24:8 or Deuteronomy 32:48–33:29, seems superfluous.[11]

In short, there is a mixture of two concepts on the pages of Scripture, that of "testament" superimposed over the top of the "covenant" picture, but not vice versa.

This can lead one to believe that the translation **"testamental covenant"** (not "covenantal testament") may be the best possible translation for both *berith* and *diatheke*. This, of course, would not work in a modern translation that aims at simplicity of communication. Possibly the easiest of all would be to translate *berith* or "covenant" as *"promise"* and *diatheke* and its completed "testament" concept as *"fulfilled promise."* But this would also be unacceptable since the original idioms would be lost.

This forces the faithful translator to consider each individual context and to shape his translation accordingly. "Covenant" seems fine in the Old Testament where animals, not God, died (Gen. 15:10). Once again, Luther says it so well. Quoting Jerome, he writes: " . . . Jerome mentions, namely, that in the Hebrew one finds "covenant" rather than "testament." Then Luther explains why: "He who stays alive makes a covenant; he who is about to die makes a testament. Thus Jesus Christ, the immortal God, made a covenant. At the same time He made a testament, because He was going to become mortal. Just as He is both God and man, so He made both a covenant and a testament."[12]

And how things changed at the time of Jesus, "on the night He was betrayed," during the earlier hours of the day on which He would die! Finally God the Testator was ready to make His "last will and testament" (1 Cor. 11:23-25), which would put the inheritance into effect (Heb. 9:16,17). For that reason Paul adds that every time Christians go to the Supper they are "proclaiming the Lord's death—until He comes," that is, they acknowledge that Jesus the God-Man died, that His death has put His testament into effect, and that at His return He will take His people to their ultimate inheritance. This concept cannot be overemphasized!

Let every Bible reader who is interested in the whole *diatheke* question take the time to scan a concordance, looking up words like "adoption," "blessing," "heir," "inherit," "possess," "promise," and "son." One will also be amazed

---

[11] Compare Meredith G. Kline, *Treaty of the Great King* (Grand Rapids: William B. Eerdmans Publishing Company, 1963), pp. 144-149.
[12] *Luther's Works* (St. Louis: Concordia Publishing House, 1964), XXVII, 268.

at how many times "testamental" ideas are present in the *berith* ("covenant") contexts of the Old Testament.

The above conclusions tend to reveal a need for permitting "testament" to overshadow "covenant" in several contexts. The idea of fulfillment or enactment of the "testament" by Christ's death dare not be blurred. Just note how the placement of the word *"new"* within the Lord's Supper accounts indicates the idea of *fulfillment* (Matt. 26:29; Mk. 14:25; Lk. 22:20; 1 Cor. 11:25).

It is in relation to these points that Bible students can do themselves and the church a great favor. They also need to obtain a crystal clear understanding of the "old and new covenants" in relation to the term *diatheke*.[13]

Something else besides! The *blood* emphasis which is so present in the "covenant" picture as well as the *heir/inheritance* thought in the "testament" concept will help students of the Bible endorse an acceptable balance of emphasis. Then books like *Hebrews* will come to life in a new way, as one notices that Hebrews 1:2 mentions Jesus as the "Heir"; that 1:14 and 6:12-14 continue the "testament" emphasis; that 9:11-28 speaks of the Testator Jesus in action; and that chapter 11 on no less than eleven occasions uses words that relate to a "testament." For example, Hebrews 11 speaks of Noah as "an heir of righteousness that comes by faith" (v. 7); of Abraham, Isaac, and Jacob as "heirs . . . of the same promise," who had lived in the "Promised Land" (v. 9); and so forth. Then to top it off, the book ends—as it began—with a *diatheke* reference (13:20), speaking of "the Great Shepherd of the sheep" who died, and who "by His blood [implying both "covenant" and death] of the everlasting *diatheke*" can take care of all needs. Need it be said that the gifts of inheritance take care of all needs?

---

[13] *Luther's Works* (Philadelphia: Muhlenberg Press, 1960), XXXV, 84f.: "Therefore whenever in Scripture God's testament is referred to by the prophets, in that very word the prophets are taught that God would become man and die and rise again, in order that his word, in which he promises such a testament, might be fulfilled and confirmed. For if God is to make a testament, as he promises, then he must die; and if he is to die, then he must be a man. And so that little word 'testament' is a short summary of all God's wonders and grace, fulfilled in Christ . . . .

"The old testament was a promise made through Moses to the people of Israel, to whom was promised the land of Canaan. For this testament God did not die, but the paschal lamb had to die instead of Christ and as a type of Christ. And so this was a temporal testament in the blood of the paschal lamb, which was shed for the obtaining and possessing of the land of Canaan. And as the paschal lamb, which died in the old testament for the land of Canaan, was a temporal and transitory thing, so too the old testament—together with that very possession or land of Canaan allotted and promised therein—was temporal and transitory.

"But Christ, the true paschal lamb [I Cor. 5:7], is an eternal divine Person, who dies to ratify the new testament. Therefore the testament and the possessions therein bequeathed are eternal and abiding. And that is what he means when he contrasts this testament with the other. 'A new testament,' he says, so that the other may become obsolete [Heb. 8:13] and no longer be in effect. 'An eternal testament,' he says, not temporal like that other one; not to dispose of temporal lands and possessions, but of eternal blessings. 'In my blood,' he says, not in the blood of a lamb [Heb. 9:12]. The purpose of all this is that the old should be altogether annulled and should give place to the new alone."

An attention getter—John 3:16. Ask a crowd of believers for the most famous passage in the Bible. "JOHN 3:16!" a large percentage of them will reply. Isn't it interesting that this passage just happens to be in "testamental" form?

When a person goes to an attorney to draw up his "last will and testament," five things are usually involved: (1) *a testator*, the one who makes the will; (2) *heir(s)*; (3) *a method of effectuation*, the way by which a testament goes into effect (by death); (4) *a testator's promissory signature,* which validates—through his word of promise—that which will be given to the heir(s); and (5) *the actual inheritance* to be left behind.[14]

John 3:16: "For God (the Testator) loved the world (the heirs) so much that He gave (into death) His one-and-only Son, so that everyone who believes in Him would not perish (the Testator's signature by word of promise) but have everlasting life (the inheritance)." Amazing!

A pleasant duty. God calls on us not to add or subtract from His Word (Rev. 22:18,19). Christians joyfully comply and seek to be a check, even on themselves. Several generations have now grown up without having heard much of an emphasis on the "last will and testament" concept of Scripture. GWN translators pray that this present translation may play a part in successfully encouraging many leaders and followers to reexamine God's whole *diatheke* truth.

NOTE: GWN has used "last will and testament" where God's "new *diatheke*" stands fulfilled and "covenant" when it has not yet come to fulfillment. In texts which go back and forth between prophetic promise and fulfillment, a system of *brackets* is used to help communication, so that the mind of the reader can better track the thoughts being expressed.

4. Hades/Gehenna

In order to understand the meaning of and distinction between the Greek terms *hades* and *gehenna*, one must be familiar with the Hebrew word *sheol*.

In the Old Testament the word *sheol* is used in two senses: (1) the *state or condition of physical death into which all people eventually pass*, believers and unbelievers alike; as such it may be translated "grave"; and (2) the *abode of the damned* which is "hell," the place of nether (down, under) torment. In each appearance of *sheol* its context and description determine the meaning which should be attached to the particular passage under consideration.

---

14 J. Barton Payne, *The Theology of the Older Testament* (Grand Rapids: Zondervan Publishing House, 1962), p. 87 with modification.

The Septuagint, the Greek translation of the Hebrew Old Testament, uses the word *hades* to translate *sheol*; and thus *hades* carries the same two meanings in the Septuagint as it does in the Old Testament.

In the New Testament *hades* appears ten times, again signifying either the *condition of death* (Acts 2:31) or *hell* itself (cf. Lk. 16:23)—but in the latter case "hell" is specifically conceived of as a *receptacle for the disembodied spirits of the damned*, that is, the place of torment where the damned are consigned during the interval between their physical death and the final resurrection. Depending upon the meaning intended, *hades* is then translated with the term "grave" or "hell," respectively.

In addition to the above, it must be mentioned that the concept of "hell" is also the intended meaning of another Greek term: *gehenna*. When *hell* is referred to as the *abode of the damned in body and spirit after the final resurrection and judgment*, then that place of torture is designated as *gehenna* in the Greek and should always be translated as "hell" or "gehenna" in English translations (cf. Lk. 12:5).

Of significance is the fact that *gehenna* comes from the Hebrew *Ge-Hinnom* which means "Valley of Hinnom." This valley lay south of Jerusalem and was the city garbage dump where fires were always burning. Jesus compared "hell" to this valley by referring in His teaching to the *"gehenna of fire"* (Matt. 5:22; 18:9).

Additional note: In 2 Peter 2:4 the word *Tartarus* is also used for "hell." The Greeks used this word to refer to a place deep within the earth, a place far deeper than even *Hades* itself, where the wicked are forever punished.

5. *Hupotasso*

Unlike the case with several other Greek terms used repeatedly in Scripture, the GWN, through the use of expanded footnotes, chose to explain several of the occurrences of *hupotasso* right at the point where they occur. This was done to pick up the *flavor* of any given context. However, this present article was still deemed necessary as background for rationale in translation.

Our GWN translation has chosen to translate the Greek term *hupotasso* with its English equivalent "be subordinate." The Greek word *hupotasso* simply expresses that a line of authority has been established, with one person being in authority and another being under authority. The English "subordinate" (made up of the Latin terms *sub*, meaning "under," and *ordo*, meaning "order/rank") seems to convey this thought best.

In His love for His people the Lord has carefully spelled out lines of authority in His Word. These are lines of authority regarding the responsibilities of all people with respect to governments, personal relationships, family life, and

church life. In every case God wants to use the person in authority to convey one or more of His blessings to the person or people under authority. In Scripture our Lord has chosen the Greek word *hupotasso* to communicate the lines of authority that He has established for our protection in society as well as for our well being and happiness in general.

When our God tells us to "be subordinate" to the government (Rom. 13:1), or wives to "be subordinate" to their husbands (Eph. 5:24), or children to "be subordinate" to parents or to elders (1 Tim. 3:4; 1 Pet. 5:5), or employees to "be subordinate" to employers (1 Pet. 2:18), He means this for the good of all His people. In so commanding, our Lord also lays a great burden of responsibility on the one in charge, and God holds the one in authority accountable for discharging all authority in a God-pleasing way. The government is God's servant for the good of the people under its authority (Rom. 13:4). The husband is to seek his wife's highest good and happiness (Eph. 5:25-29). Parents are to care for their children's physical and spiritual needs (Eph. 6:4). Employers are to note that their actions are all judged by God (Eph. 6:9).

It is important to remember that even now for our sakes our great Savior according to His human nature is still willing to "be subordinate" to the Father to all eternity (1 Cor. 15:28). This is incentive enough for us to "be subordinate" in line with Scripture's directives, in particular, with those guidelines given in connection with the term *hupotasso*. As Scripture says: *"Always thank God the Father for everything in the Name of our Lord Jesus Christ, as you are subordinate to one another out of respect for Christ"* (Eph. 5:20,21).

6. *Monogenes*

The Greek language has two words which can mean "to beget." The stems of these two words are *genn-* (note the double *n*) and *gin-* (or *gen-* in the past tense).

The first word with the stem *genn-* has only the one meaning: "to beget." The double *n* in this word makes it unlikely that *monogenes* comes from this stem. This word (*genn-*) is used to refer to Jesus being begotten of the Father in Hebrews 1:5 and of Christians being born of the Holy Spirit in 1 John 5:1.

The second word which has the stem *gen-* is more likely the Greek word from which *monogenes* comes. This word with one *n* has two meanings: (1) "to come into existence, to be born *or* begotten"; and (2) "to be, to exist." This stem is used twice as a verb to refer to Jesus' birth as a human being (Rom. 1:3; Gal. 4:4), but it is never used as a verb to refer to Jesus being "begotten" of the Father.

The question arises, therefore, as to which of the two meanings of *gen-* is to be used in the translation of *monogenes*. The prefix *mono-* means "only," but does *-genes* mean "begotten" or "existing"? Several things need to be considered in answering this question.

One point has already been mentioned. In the one passage in which the New Testament uses a verb to refer to Jesus as being "begotten" of the Father (Heb. 1:5), it uses *genn-* with the double *n*, not *gen-* with the single *n*. The latter is used only to refer to Jesus' birth as a human being.

But a more important factor to consider is how the New Testament uses the term *monogenes* (*gen-* with a single *n*) itself. Luke uses this word three times to refer to the *only* child of people whom Jesus helped: the son of the widow of Nain (Lk. 7:12), the daughter of Jairus (Lk. 8:42), and the man's son who was demon-possessed (Lk. 9:38). Each of these children is referred to as a *monogenes* child. In Hebrews 11:17 Isaac is called Abraham's *monogenes* son. In these four passages most of the translations, including the *King James Version*, translate *monogenes* as "only" and not as "only-begotten."

The only other New Testament writer to use *monogenes* is John. He uses it five times (Jn. 1:14,18; 3:16,18; 1 Jn. 4:9). In all of these passages either of the meanings of *monogenes* fits the context. One could translate either "only-begotten" or "only-existing." ("Only-existing" means "the only-one-there-is" or "one-of-a-kind.")

Since John is the only New Testament writer to use this term to refer to Jesus, it is impossible to say conclusively which of the two meanings is the best translation in the five passages in John. If other New Testament writers had used the term *monogenes* to refer to Jesus, or if John had included the incidents of Jairus' daughter, the young man of Nain, and the demon-possessed son, we might have a better idea which of the two translations is preferable.

As it is, Luke (7:12; 8:42; 9:38) and the writer to the Hebrews (11:17) use *monogenes* in the sense of "only-existing." But since they use it of human children and not of Christ, their use of *monogenes* is not exactly the same as John's and so does not prove anything about John's use of this term.

Some people who probably should know better have suggested that a Bible which does not automatically translate *monogenes* as "only-begotten" is thereby showing that it denies the Nicene Creed. Yes, the Nicene Creed confesses that Christians believe that Jesus was "begotten of the Father from all eternity" (the *eternal* generation of Christ). But this truth is taught in Scripture whether or not the five passages from John's writings are translated "only-begotten" or not. Every passage in Scripture which refers to God as the Father of Jesus (e.g., 1 Pet. 1:3; 1 Thess. 1:1) and to Jesus as the Father's Son (e.g., Rom. 1:3; 8:32; 1 Jn. 1:7) teaches that the Son derives His essence from

the Father through the *eternal* generation,[15] not through His human birth.

In addition it should be noted that the term *monogenes* is also used in the Greek of the Apostles' Creed, but it is translated "only" in English, "*unicus*" in Latin, and "*einig*" in German. The German of the Nicene Creed also translates *monogenes* with the word "*einig*" ("only"). From this it is clear that *monogenes* has not always been translated with "only-begotten" in the history of the Christian church.

In this present translation, we have chosen to translate *monogenes* the same way in every passage in order to be consistent. The reader will find the translation "only" in all nine instances where this word is used: three in *Luke*, five in *John*, and one in *Hebrews* (11:17). To call attention to the five passages in John's Gospel where it is used of Jesus, we have footnoted each one to alert the reader to the fact *monogenes* is used of Jesus and that it could mean "the only-existing" ("the only-one-there-is" or "one-of-a-kind"), or that it could have the special meaning of "only-begotten."

7. *Nomos*

Nomos is a Greek word meaning "law" and is used to translate a number of Hebrew words having a similar meaning. It is, therefore, a general term whose precise sense needs to be gained from its context. In the New Testament it may have one of six basic meanings: (1) any "law" of any group, religious or otherwise (Acts 18:15); (2) a "rule, principle, regulation, norm" (Rom. 7:21); (3) the Pentateuch or the Five Books of Moses, known as Genesis through Deuteronomy (Jn. 1:45; 8:5); (4) the Old Testament as a whole (Jn. 7:49; 12:34); (5) the laws and regulations of the Sinai Covenant that were given by God through Moses to Israel (Jn. 1:17; Rom. 4:16; 9:4; Gal. 3:17-21; Heb. 7:11,12); or (6) the moral law of God which applies to all people of all time (Rom. 2:15; 3:19; 8:7; 1 Cor. 15:56; Gal. 3:11; 4:4; 1 Jn. 3:4).

The first two uses above are rare in the New Testament; however, the last four are very common, and of them the fifth and sixth uses are especially prevalent in Paul's writings. One will have to look at the context very carefully to determine which of these two uses Paul intends.

In speaking of the obligation to keep the "law," the New Testament writers stress that Christians are *not* legally bound to the rules and regulations of the Sinai Covenant (i.e., "the Law") as were God's people, Israel, in the Old Testament. That is why Christians do not feel obligated to worship on Saturday, the Old Testament Sabbath, and why they often eat foods forbidden under Mosaic Law. At the same time, God's moral Law, of which the Ten

---

[15] Louis J. Roehm, "The Person of Christ," *The Abiding Word*, ed. Theodore Laetsch (Saint Louis: Concordia Publishing House, 1955), I, 21. This volume also has a brief explanation of the eternal Sonship of Jesus.

Commandments are the sum and essence (Rom. 13:9), applies to *all* human beings in every age of history and requires that they love God and their fellow humans (Matt. 22:34-40; Rom. 13:10; Jas. 2:8).

In speaking of salvation, the New Testament writers insist that nothing a person does in keeping the *law* (whether the Sinai Covenant by the Jew or God's moral law by any human being) contributes anything to being righteous in God's sight (Rom. 3:19,20; Gal. 2:16; 3:10). This is true because God demands of everyone who wants to be righteous on the basis of keeping the law that his obedience be absolutely perfect (Matt. 5:48; Gal 3:10; Jas. 2:10); but every human being is disobedient and guilty of sin (Rom. 3:10-19; Gal. 3:22). The Christian, therefore, does not rely on keeping the *law* to be righteous in God's sight but trusts only in the righteousness Christ won for him by His perfect life and His atoning death (Rom. 4:5; 8:3,4; Phil. 3:8,9; Gal. 5:4-6). In this sense the Christian is also "not under law" (Rom. 6:14; Gal. 5:18).

This, however, does not mean that the Christian despises God's moral law. Rather, he recognizes it as God's holy will for his life (1 Pet. 1:15), and he commits himself to obeying God's law (Rom. 6:13; 12:1,2)—not out of fear of punishment (Rom. 8:1), nor seeking a reward (Lk. 17:10), but as a "thank you" to God for all His gracious gifts (Eph. 5:15,16,20; Col. 3:17). This motivation of thanks in the Christian life is derived from God's Spirit. Christians are motivated to keep the Law, especially by the Spirit-worked gratitude for the love that Christ showed through His keeping of the Law, His earthly ministry, His death on the cross in their behalf, and His ongoing love (1 Jn. 4:19; cf. Jn. 14:15). Christians do, however, need to be told the truth about God's will for their lives; at times this may be a gentle nudge (Phil. 3:1) or be quite harsh (Gal. 1:8,9; 3:1). The central point for Paul is that the Christian life, if it is God-pleasing, is the work of God's Spirit (Gal. 5:22,23,25; Rom. 8:5-14).

8. *Skandalon*

The Greek words *skandalon* (noun) and *skandalizein* (verb) are used very seldom in the Greek language outside the Septuagint (the Greek translation of the Old Testament, also known as the LXX) and the New Testament. However, the Greeks did have a word with the same root (*skandalethron*). It helps us get a feeling for the serious consequences of this family of words in any context in which they are used.

When the Greeks spoke of a *skandalethron*, they referred to the arm or stick to which bait was attached in a death trap. An animal was lured by the bait to move the stick and so cause its own death.

In the Old Testament Septuagint this basic idea of a "death trap" is still retained. Things such as alliances with foreign nations (Josh. 23:13) as well

as success and prosperity (Ps. 69:22) are called "traps" that lead nations or individuals to their ruin. When *skandalon* is used in the sense of a "death trap" in a spiritual context, it refers to a *fall from faith*.

A second meaning was added to the word *skandalon* in Old Testament usage. This meaning of "stumbling block" also speaks of serious consequences. In Leviticus 19:14 the command is given that no one should put a stumbling block before the blind. When *skandalon* is used in this sense in a spiritual context, it often refers to someone or something which causes a person to stumble in faith, that is, become weaker in faith, and so forth.

In the New Testament we need to keep these same *two* meanings in mind in order to get the full implication of what the inspired writer is saying when he uses *skandalon* or *skandalizein*.

In some cases we have simply used the two basic meanings of this word in translation: "death trap" in some instances; "stumble" or "stumbling block" in other instances.

In contexts where the word *skandalon* refers to a person *falling from faith* to his eternal ruin, we have translated "fall ˻from faith˼," or "cause to fall ˻from faith˼." Luke shows us that this is a meaning of the word *skandalon* when he uses the idea of "falling away" (Lk. 8:13) for the parallel word *skandalon* used by Matthew in the same context (Matt. 13:21).

In contexts where the word *skandalon* refers to a person *stumbling in faith* for a time, we have translated "stumble ˻in faith˼," or "cause to stumble ˻in faith˼." Again, Luke shows us that this is a meaning of the word *skandalon* when he uses the idea of "faith failing" (Lk. 22:31) for the parallel word *skandalon* used by Matthew in the same context (Matt. 26:31).

The words in half-brackets are added to remind the reader of the serious nature of the situation to which the writer is referring when he uses *skandalon* or *skandalizein*. In whatever context this word is used, there is one basic point to keep in mind: it always implies dire consequences.

APPENDIX 3
THE FAMILY LINE OF JESUS CHRIST

MATTHEW   **LUKE**

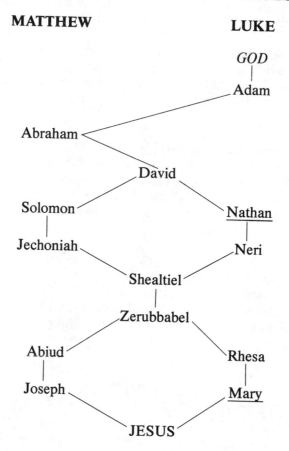

Matthew 1:1-17 traces the family line or genealogy of Jesus from *Abraham* forward, while Luke 3:24-38 reverses the process and trails the lineage from Jesus back to *Adam*, in fact, even to *God* Himself. Two items of importance must be noted and comprehended if one is to derive maximum spiritual benefit from these genealogies.

First, the emphasis of *Matthew* is on *Jesus the Messiah*, especially as He is the fulfillment of many Old Testament prophecies. According to those ancient promises Jesus was to be a descendent of Abraham and David. Initially, therefore, Matthew shows that *Jesus from Nazareth* descended from the right family line. This he did in a most convincing way (Matt. 1:1,2,6; 1:18-2:23). Next, Matthew illustrates that Jesus fulfilled the rest of the prophetic data *via* His life, teaching, and work (Matt. 3-28). When the latter was accepted, then the former genealogy was more than sufficient in going back no farther than *Abraham* to substantiate that Jesus was the Jewish Messiah. The reason for this: Abraham was considered "the father of the Jewish nation" (cf. Gen. 12:2).

The Gospel of *Luke*, on the other hand, was eager to present a *universal Savior*, a Savior who came for all, Jew and Gentile alike. Thus, its genealogy goes all the way back to *Adam*, the first human being, in order to include everyone, all of whom really came from *God* Himself (Lk. 3:38).

Second, the careful Bible reader will note that the vast majority of the names in between "David" and "Jesus" in the Matthew genealogy differ from those between "Jesus" and "David" in the Luke account. Yet there is no contradiction once the two listings are understood. Take a glance at the diagram above.

The key to a correct understanding lies in noting that Luke traces Jesus' lineage from David through David's son <u>Nathan</u> through <u>Mary</u>, Jesus' earthly and biological mother. This accounts for the two divergences, one at David's time and one at Zerubbabel's time. In this way Luke states what Bible students call the "actual" lineage of Jesus. (Note the "Time line" of Biblical persons and events on page 9.)

Matthew, on the other hand, adds to our understanding by showing that Jesus also descended from David through David's son *Solomon* through *Joseph*, Jesus' earthly—though not biological—father (Jn. 6:42). (The doctrine of the Virgin Birth in Matthew 1:16,18-25 and Luke 1:34,35; 3:24 explains the seeming contradiction or mystery of the former statement.) Accordingly, Matthew the author records what Bible students call the "legal" lineage of Jesus.

APPENDIX 4
THE MATTHEW 5:31,32 PASSAGE

In Matthew 5:31,32 Jesus states: "It was said: 'Whoever divorces his wife must give her a divorce paper,' but I tell you that everyone who divorces his wife, except for the fact that she has been sexually unfaithful, causes her to be looked upon as an adulteress, and whoever marries a divorced woman is looked upon as an adulterer."

Let us first deal with the verbal phrase "causes her to be looked upon as an adulteress." If it is translated "causes her to commit adultery," it can leave a wrong impression and give some poor woman today a bad conscience when, in essence, she is the innocent party in a divorce. For Jesus Himself is speaking of a woman who would be an innocent party (except in a case of sexual unfaithfulness).

The verb is a passive infinitive and therefore GWN translates "causes her to be looked upon as an adulteress," meaning that other people ordinarily view a divorced woman as guilty when she is dismissed by her husband.

The second verbal phrase "is looked upon as an adulterer" is often translated "commits adultery." But it can be a Greek passive as GWN has translated it

parallel to the verb form discussed in the previous paragraph. The male in this portion of the verse would be one who marries an innocent female like the one mentioned in the first part of the verse. Under such circumstances other people ordinarily view this man as guilty for having married a woman who had been divorced by her husband.

Some, however, do *not* regard the verb in the second phrase as a passive. Then this latter half of the verse is translated: "and whoever marries a divorced woman commits adultery." In this case the last part of the verse would be stating a general principle, as Jesus does in Luke 16:16, rather than addressing the matter of an innocent party in a divorce.

APPENDIX 5
BAPTISM FOR THE DEAD
1 Corinthians 15:29

The phrase "they . . . who are baptized *for* the dead" has baffled interpreters for centuries. Paul simply mentions this practice without explaining it in detail or indicating whether he endorses it or not, whether it was a proper or improper Christian practice. Since so little is known about it, Christians cannot be dogmatic concerning one view or another. The whole conclusion hinges on how one understands the preposition *hyper* and its accompanying genitive in the text. (Please, note this point carefully.) Four major views have been put forth:

View 1. "They . . . who are baptized *for* the dead" were new converts who were being baptized *in place of* (*hyper*) Christians who had died. This view holds that converts to Christianity were baptized to take "the place of" Christians who had died, meaning that newly baptized Christians replaced those who had died and thereby continued to carry on the Christian church.

As stated above, we do not know for sure if this interpretation catches the meaning of Paul's comment. If so, such a practice would not have run counter to any truth of Scripture.

View 2. "They . . . who are baptized *for* the dead" were Christians who were being baptized a second time, this time *for* (*hyper*: "in behalf of/for the sake of") Christians who had died before being able to be baptized. This would have been for the purpose of permitting departed, unbaptized Christians to share in Christ's baptism, along with other baptized Christians. (Present-day Mormonism teaches this view in expanded form. They endorse "baptism by proxy," the redeeming of the unbaptized dead.)

Once again, we do not know if anyone was practicing this form of baptism in Paul's day or not. If so, it could hardly be endorsed by Paul or the Christian church in view of Acts 2:38, which speaks of people being individually baptized for themselves, not *for* or *in behalf of* (*hyper*) others.

View 3. "They . . . who are baptized *for* the dead" were converts who were being baptized *over* (*hyper*) the graves of other Christians who had already died, thus connecting the faith of believers in the past with the faith of believers in the present.

Again we reiterate that we do not know whether this is what Paul is saying or not. We have no historical record of such a practice. Besides, New Testament Greek never uses the preposition *hyper* with a genitive to indicate "over" in a local sense, as in "being baptized *over* ₗthe graves of, the dead."

View 4. "They . . . who are baptized *for* the dead" were converts who, knowing the reality of their own eventual deaths, were baptized *for* (*hyper*: "for the benefit of") themselves, they *themselves* who would be the "dead" of the future. In this way they affirmed their belief that since Christ rose, they also would rise (1 Cor. 15:22,23; Jn. 14:19), for baptism permits Christians to *be united* in Christ's resurrection, spiritually and physically, and thereby to be assured of their own personal resurrection (Rom. 6:3-11; Mk. 16:16). "Otherwise," why be baptized? Recall the wording of 1 Corinthians 15:29: "Otherwise, what will they (the converts to Christianity) do who are baptized *for* ₗthe benefit of, the dead? Why are they baptized for them if the dead are not raised at all?" (The reference to "them," according to this view, is *inclusive*, referring both to those who were previously baptized and were now dead as well as to those converts who were now being baptized.)

APPENDIX 6
THE HOLY PLACES
(Of Hebrews 8-13)

The book of *Hebrews* is known for its complex Greek and deep theological concepts as well as its demand that the translator and interpreter be very familiar with the Old Testament, especially its Levitical priesthood, Tabernacle, sacrifices, and functions. As such, the understanding of the 10 references to the various holy places and things in Hebrews 8-13 is crucial. Several items must be noted:

A. The basic Greek term involved for consideration is *hagios*, meaning "holy." In particular, we note four varying usages: *hagia* (neuter plural, 9:2,12,24,25; 13:11), *hagion* (adjective neuter used as a substantive, 9:1), *hagion* (genitive plural, 8:2; 9:8; 10:19), and *hagia*

hagion ("holy of holies/most holy place," 9:3).

B. The references could be translated "holy place" (nine times) and "most holy place" (one time) in the 10 instances. Our translation, however, for greatest ease of comprehension, reflects the various flavors and areas of meaning. This is done through the usage of distinguishing terms and interpretive capitalization, based on the individual contexts.

C. The reader must be aware of the various contexts by noting that some of the references refer to the *earthly* Tabernacle and its various areas (9:1-3,24,25; 13:11), while the remaining texts denote its *heavenly, perfect, better* counterpart. (The heavenly designations are distinguished by *total* capitalization in the text.)

D. Carefully note Diagram #1 which depicts the earthly Tabernacle (p. 430). *Eight* of the texts correspond directly to a particular part of the earthly Tabernacle area, whether to its earthly name or its heavenly counterpart. (Observe the various areas and their names carefully.) Both of the two remaining texts refer to *holy places* that were in close proximity to the Tabernacle area. In 9:24 the reference to "sacred places made by human hands" would seem to refer to *all* the various areas *inside* "the sacred place" (Diagram #1, p. 430); 13:11 seems to refer to all types of "holy places" inside and outside "the sacred place" of Diagram #1 (p. 430), as indicated in Exodus 29:14; Leviticus 4:12,21; 8:17; 9:11; 16:27; Numbers 19:3,7.

E. There are three reasons for the plural usage of the terms formed from *hagios*: it permits several areas to be referred to at the same time; it suggests that the "holy things" of the *holy places* are an integral part of the meaning; and in the place of grammatical superlatives it emphasizes the *utter holiness* of given places.

APPENDIX 7
THE OLD TESTAMENT CANON

This article addresses the matter of the Old Testament *canon*. The word "canon" comes from the Hebrew *qaneh* and the Greek *kanon* (basis for our English "cane"), meaning "reed" or "measuring rod," that is, a reed or stick that had measuring marks on it. When applied to the books of Scripture, the word "canon" took on the derivative sense of "that which measures up," meaning "standard" or "rule." In other words a given book had to "measure up" to certain standards in order to make the "canon" of Scripture, that is, if it were to be included in any authoritative listing.

The Old Testament Hebrew canon was divided somewhat differently than we are accustomed to seeing it listed in our English Bibles. However, even though this is the case, the Hebrew division or rotation of books is still of much importance if we wish to understand our Savior's comments concerning the Old Testament writings. Otherwise, we cannot comprehend His statement in Luke 24:44: "the Law of Moses, the Prophets, and the Psalms." Let us therefore note the Hebrew formation and comment on it in relation to a few New Testament texts.

A. Law (*Torah*):[16]

    (Genesis, Exodus, Leviticus, Numbers, Deuteronomy)   5 books

B. Prophets (*Nebhi'im*):

    1. Former Prophets (Joshua, Judges, Samuel, Kings)   4 books
    2. Latter Prophets (Isaiah, Jeremiah, Ezekiel, The Twelve)   4 books

C. Writings or **Scriptures** (*Kethubhim*):

    1. Poetry (Psalms, Job, Proverbs)   3 books
    2. Scrolls (Song of Solomon, [Ruth], [Lamentations],
        Ecclesiastes, Esther)   3 [5] books
    3. History (Daniel, Ezra-Nehemiah, Chronicles)   3 books
                            Total 22 [24] books

This total is in agreement with Josephus' comment that the Jews had 22 books in their Old Testament canon. (Josephus was a famous Jewish historian, a later contemporary of Christ's.) The English reader should realize that the texts of the Old Testament were originally written on "scrolls" or "rolls." Some books, like *Isaiah*, were so long that they took up an entire scroll themselves. Yet, other books were very short; several of them could fit on the same scroll. Note, for example, "B2" above where *The Twelve* refers to the 12 books of *Hosea* to *Malachi*, all 12 of which fit on the same scroll and therefore were counted as only *one* book.

This division explains the comments of Christ and His apostles when they speak of the Old Testament. For instance, in Luke 24:44 Jesus says: " . . . everything written about Me in the Law of Moses, the Prophets, and the Psalms must be fulfilled." Here in a concise statement Christ refers to the

16 Also known as the "Law of Moses," the "Five Books of Moses," the "Pentateuch."

three major divisions of the Old Testament. He says that the Old Testament spoke of Him in the *Law*, the *Prophets*, and the *Psalms*. The term "Psalms" in this context is collective, including all of those books in the third section, the *Writings*. (*Psalms* was the first book in that third section and therefore sometimes is given the role of speaking for all of the other books in this category.) The threefold division is a Hebraism. In English Jesus would say something like: " . . . everything written about Me *in the entire Old Testament* must be fulfilled."

At Jesus' time it was also a custom to refer to the entire Old Testament either by the term "*Law*" or "*Scriptures*" (Lk. 24:27; Jn. 10:34). This is what Paul does when he writes to Timothy and tells him to remain faithful to the entire Old Testament since "all '*Scripture*' is given by inspiration of God."

(It should also be mentioned that in the opinion of some the total number mentioned in the listing above varies between 22 and 24. The reason for this is that it is sometimes said that the book of *Ruth* was not counted with the book of *Judges* as one book or the book of *Lamentations* with *Jeremiah* as one entity. If both *Ruth* and *Lamentations* were counted separately at times, this would expand the total from 22 to 24 books.)

APPENDIX 8
JEWS AND SAMARITANS

The term "Jew" is used in various ways in the Bible. Originally, it referred in the Old Testament to a descendant of the tribe of Judah (see Rom. 2:29 and its accompanying footnote "e").

As time passed "Jew" primarily came to mean an *inhabitant* of Judah (2 Kgs. 16:6; Neh. 1:2; Jer. 32:12). However, after the Fall of the Northern Kingdom in 721 B.C., there was a tendency to refer to all Hebrews (from any tribe or location) as "Jews" (Jer. 34:9). By New Testament times the term "Jew" was used—both by Jews and Gentiles—to refer to any Israelite, regardless of tribal origin or national birth (cf. the remarks of Paul in Acts 21:39 and Phil. 3:5). This development, together with the fact that an increasing number of non-Jews became converts to the Jewish faith during the Intertestamental Period, contributed to an emphasis on "Jew" as a religious category (cf. Jn. 18:35 where the context involves religious background and knowledge).

With the exception of *Acts*, the most frequent and complex use of "Jew" in the New Testament is found in *John* (c. 70 times). At times the term is simply used in a general sense (see Jn. 2:6; 4:22). Most often, however, John used the term "Jew" to refer to the Jewish ecclesiastical leadership centered in Jerusalem. (This is somewhat comparable to the phrase "scribes and Pharisees" in the other three Gospels.) In such cases the term "Jew" takes on a negative connotation, referring to those leading Jews who generally rejected the Savior

(Jn. 5:10-18; 9:18-23). Note that this is not always the case (Jn. 8:31; 11:45).

Much of Jesus' public discourse in *John* takes place in contest with the theological and political leaders of Jerusalem, that is, with "the Jews." This, in turn, explains why *John* contains so little *parabolic* language. Jesus spoke to the general public "in parables," which by their very nature short-circuited discussion. However, the Gospel of *John* presents Jesus discussing His divine, Messianic status quite candidly with Jewish leaders in public, *outside* the circle of His disciples. Jesus could do this since He knew that these leaders would not use His message to incite Messianic fervor of a political nature (cf. Matt. 16:16-20 with Jn. 10:31-39; see also **Christ, Messiah** in Glossary).

It is difficult to trace precisely the origin and historical development of the Samaritan community. Many scholars believe that its roots go back to the Fall of the Northern Kingdom. At this time the Assyrian rulers exiled the leading citizens of Northern Israel, while simultaneously replacing them with many foreigners from other parts of their empire who intermarried with the Jews remaining in Israel (cf. 2 Kgs. 17). According to this view, the resulting descendants became known as *Samaritans*.

In time, these descendants were regarded by Jews as half-Jews, less than Jews, and not worthy to be equated with Jewish heritage. The Samaritans also fostered strong resentment, as becomes apparent from Luke 9:51-56 as well as from the historical events recorded by Josephus the Jewish historian. (It is interesting that both Josephus and the Jewish Talmud and Mishnah remain ambiguous as to attitude toward the *Samaritans*. This may reflect a somewhat favorable viewpoint and a recognition that there was an undeniable connection between Jewish/Samaritan race and religion.)

In spite of the considerable tension between Samaritans and Jews, there were still several fundamental beliefs which the two groups held in common, such as confession of one God, Moses as God's prophet, and the Pentateuch as God's word. A chief bone of contention between them concerned the proper place where God was to be worshiped, Mount Gerizim or in the Temple at Jerusalem (cf. Jn. 4:20).

Jesus denounced any hatred between peoples, using the Jews and Samaritans as an example, when He told of the *Good Samaritan* (Lk. 10:25-37).

APPENDIX 9
JESUS SENDS THE 72 MISSIONARIES

Luke 10:1 and 10:17 are the object of a great deal of discussion among translators. Did Jesus send out "70" or "72" disciples two by two? Any discussion should begin with the manuscript evidence (cf. "Textual Variants

in the GWN New Testament" on page xix). Both readings, "70" and "72," are found early in the history of the church and both are widespread: "70" = Egypt, Palestine, Syria, Asia Minor, and Southeast Europe; "72" = Egypt, Palestine, Syria, Gaul and Italy, and Northwest Africa.

Arguments for a change made by copyists from "72" to "70" (e.g., the 70 elders of Israel in Numbers 11:25; the 70 descendants of Jacob according to the Masoretic text of Exodus 1:5; the 70 members of the Sanhedrin; the LXX [70] title of the Septuagint; the 70 nations in the "Table of Nations" in Genesis 10) or from "70" to "72" (e.g., the 72 translators of the Septuagint; the 72 nations in the "Table of Nations" in Gen. 10; the 72 members of the Sanhedrin) are quite subjective and so prove nothing about why some copyists have "70" and others "72." (For those interested, Genesis 10 contains 70 or 72 names, depending on the counting procedure that one uses.)

Here is one example of those rare instances (mentioned in the article cited above) where we honestly have to admit that we cannot be sure which reading is original. So we have to choose one of the two readings and put the other in a footnote.

No matter which reading we choose, the points we learn from these passages are the same. First, Jesus wanted His disciples to be active in bringing the message of salvation to others. Second, there were quite a few others, besides the Twelve, who were *daily* followers of Jesus whom He trained to be His messengers; in fact, some of them were with Jesus, along with the Twelve, from the time of Jesus' baptism to His ascension. These were also qualified, therefore, to replace Judas after his fall (Acts 1:21,22).

By the above, this article does not imply that Jesus did not convey a certain message in His day *via* the sending of "70" or "72" two by two. We might suspect that it had to do with His injunction, obviously only related to this Luke 10 lesson, *to reach Gentiles and/or Jews* with the Gospel. The reality of the blessing of evangelism success was a lesson then (Lk. 10:17-20), as it is now. Beyond that, time separation from those early days has blocked our ability to determine definitely between the "70" and "72."

From a practical point of view, Jesus has given a valuable evangelism procedure by revealing the two by two method.

APPENDIX 10
MICHAEL THE ARCHANGEL

Interpreters of Holy Scripture are divided concerning the identification of Michael—whether it refers to Jesus Himself or just one of several "ruling angels" of heaven.

The term "archangel" can mean either "ruling" or "leading angel," implying one of several angelic leaders; or it can mean the ultimate, highest ruling angel who is over all other angels. Scripture talks of at least three, possibly four categories of angels: (1) seraphim; (2) cherubim; (3) one Angel called the "Captain of the LORD's army" (Josh. 5:14); and (4) archangels, if there is more than one archangel (if there is only one, then the sole Archangel, even Michael, could be equivalent to the angelic "Captain" in Joshua 5).

Concerning that "Captain," one is compelled on the basis of Scriptural evidence to identify Him as none other than Jesus Christ Himself (compare Ex. 3:5 with Josh. 5:15 and Ex. 24:20,21 with Mal. 3:1, especially noting that "Messenger" and "Angel" represent the same word in Hebrew). Christ as Creator of the angels (Jn. 1:3; cf. vv. 1 and 14 also) certainly fits the position to be the ultimate Leader or Ruler of the angels, thus the ultimate Archangel.

But is He Michael? And is Michael the sole leader of the angels?

Michael appears to be the highest leader of the angels in Revelation 12:9. He also appears to be stronger than Gabriel ("the strong one") in Daniel 10:13, and no complete victory seems possible without the presence of Michael (Dan. 10:21). Also, it is Michael who is called "the great prince" of God's people (Dan. 12:1), and he is one who appears to be able to hold off Satan (Jude 9), even to defeat him (Rev. 12:9).

But can Michael do the things that Jesus the Angel of the LORD can do on the pages of the Old Testament, and do them without the help of others (cf. Is. 63:3)? That mysterious "Angel of the LORD" could even forgive sin (Zech. 3:1,4).

Scripture does not say that Michael can defeat Satan all by himself. Rather, he takes on hell with an army (Rev. 12:9). Jesus, of course, was able to take on Satan single-handedly (Is. 63:3; Heb. 2:14). The best hints of Michael's ability to do this are Jude 9 and Revelation 12:9, where Michael is always chosen as the one to be specifically named in any serious conflict involving Satan.

From another point of view though, Jude 9 would seem to weigh heavily *against* an identification of Michael with Jesus since Michael did not dare to bring "a charge of slander" against Satan. Yet Jude 9 is quite parallel to Zechariah 3:2, where also Jesus the Angel of the LORD does not "rebuke" Satan. Interpreters who equate Michael with Jesus explain both of these episodes in light of the fact that each took place *before* Jesus' death, resurrection victory, and exaltation at the Father's right hand.

The heaviest argument against Michael as being identical to Jesus Christ comes in Daniel 10:13, where Michael is called "one of the leading princes." On the other hand, as stated above, Michael is "the great prince" of Israel in Daniel 12:1.

Since Christians are warned not to add or subtract from Scripture (Deut. 4:2;

Rev. 22:18,19) and since passages can be cited on both sides of the "Michael" question, an interpreter—though he himself may lean to one side or the other on this matter—should not bind consciences. Certainly we do not wish to give Michael glory that belongs to Christ if the two are not the same. But we can be dogmatic in knowing that Satan has met his match when he was taken on by Jesus the Angel of the LORD (Zech. 3) and Michael (Rev. 12:9), whether they be *two* different figures or *one-in-the-same* Person.

APPENDIX 11
THE EARLIEST CHRISTIAN CREEDS

Most Christians are very familiar with the three ecumenical creeds—the Apostles', Nicene, and Athanasian. These were composed in the earliest Christian centuries as a summary, confession, and defense of Christian doctrine.

However, there were three significant Biblical creeds that preceded them.

In the Old Testament a basic creed was given in Deuteronomy 6:4: "The LORD is our God, the LORD alone!"

With the dawn of the Christian era and fuller revelation from God in the Person of His Son Jesus (Heb. 1:1,2), two new creeds came into existence. They expanded the Old Testament declaration and formed a solid base for the three ecumenical creeds that were to follow. As such, they became a link between the Old Testament era and the growth of Christianity throughout the Jewish and Gentile communities.

The first of these two creeds is found in Matthew 16:16. Here (through God the Father's initiative and wisdom, v. 17) Peter confesses concerning Jesus: "You are the Christ [Messiah], the Son of the living God!" Compare Acts 18:5.

This first statement of Christian belief distinguished Jewish Christians from other Jewish people who had not accepted the Christian faith. Both Jews and Christians were zealous concerning the coming Christ [Messiah]. The big difference was that the Jews continued to look for a coming Messiah, while the Christians confessed that He had come in the Person of Jesus of Nazareth. Thus, the earliest believers were called "Christians" (Acts 11:26) since they *identified* the "Christ," *confessed* He had come in the Person of Jesus, and *taught* that He, and He only, must be embraced by faith by anyone who hopes to be saved for eternity (Acts 4:12). (See **Christ, Messiah** in Glossary.)

The second creed of the early Christian era is found in Philippians 2:11: "JESUS CHRIST IS LORD!" The greater context in verses 10 and 11 reads: "... at the Name of JESUS everyone in heaven and on earth and

under the earth should kneel, and everyone should confess that 'JESUS CHRIST IS LORD' to the glory of God the Father."

This second statement of Christian belief distinguished Gentile Christians from other Gentiles who had not accepted the Christian faith. Both of them were zealous to confess the One they called "Lord." The difference is that the non-Christian Gentiles confessed Jupiter or Zeus as Lord, while the Christians confessed that "JESUS CHRIST IS LORD!"

Thus from earliest times the Christians had creeds for use among both Jew and Gentile. With these two statements they upheld and spread their faith in Jesus to a fertile, but hostile, world. Both creeds spelled out the major points of difference between believer and unbeliever. At the same time they signaled a bond between all believers and sounded a clear confession to all who were being confronted with the Christian faith.

APPENDIX 12
GRAMMATIC/POETIC STRUCTURES THAT CONVEY TEXTUAL MEANINGS

This article will speak of the structure and importance of Biblical poetry. Then, on the basis of several Scriptural passages, specific examples will be given which illustrate *how* New Testament meaning (understanding) is beautifully conveyed or aided by a knowledge of its grammatic and poetic structure. Finally, the poetry of the Book of *Revelation* will be treated separately.

A. Biblical Poetry In General

At least a third of the Bible is comprised of poetry or underlying poetic thought forms. In addition, many sections of prose contain elements that fit poetic thought-forms (see Rom. 2:6-11; 16:3-16, prose sections that have been typeset in semi-poetic format for purposes of communication). Bible readers should also realize that almost all poetry of the Bible is based on *Hebrew* structure, not just the poetry of the Old Testament. This is true even of New Testament books written by a Gentile author like Luke. There are two reasons for this: (1) Most of the poetry in the New Testament is taken directly from the Hebrew Old Testament. (2) Even though the authors of the New Testament wrote in Greek, the majority thought in terms of Hebraic style, either because they were Jews themselves or because they were Gentiles who were greatly influenced by their constant and careful study of the Old Testament Scriptures.

Hebrew poetic style revolves around a phenomenon known as *parallelism*. Each line of poetry stands in some relationship to one, two, or three other lines. Twofold, threefold, and fourfold patterns are present all over the Bible and each has a name:

SYNONYMOUS	ANTITHETICAL	CONSTRUCTIVE		CHIASTIC		STAIRLIKE[17]
A	A	A	A	A	A	A
A	B	B	B	B	B	B
			C	B	C	C
				A	C	D
					B	
					A	

A-A (synonymous) means that a second line repeats the first but in different words; A-B (antithetical) indicates that a second line says the opposite of the first; A-B (two-line constructive) and A-B-C (three-line constructive) are used to build ideas as a second and even third line add to the former line; A-B-B-A (chiastic) presents the same idea in the first and fourth lines but in different vocabulary, while lines two and three parallel each other, also in different words, or A-B-C-C-B-A (chiastic) parallels lines one and six, two and five, and three and four; and A-B-C-D (stairlike) moves downward on the page but upward in memory as each line adds a thought to the former. "Stairlike" is a further developed version of the "constructive."

A positioning of the various lines in a *vertical* (synonymous) or *slanted* (antithetical, constructive) or either *vertical* or *slanted* (stairlike) as well as *vertically varied indentations* (chiastic) helps to indicate meanings. The following concrete examples will illustrate this.

Before we do that, however, two additional thoughts must be added.

As the reader will notice, the GWN has chosen to typeset across the entire page rather than divide the page into two columns as is customary in most Bibles. This is crucial if one is going to keep one line of poetry from wrapping onto another line. Nonwrapping is vital so that each line can be seen in parallel to another. In fact, since spacing is so valuable in avoiding wrapping, the GWN has chosen to go with a very wide page format and also to set its *poetry* sections in smaller type than its prose. This has obviously permitted more poetry words per line; the added benefit is that it also has made for a beautiful page format which also assists the reader's understanding.

Biblion Publishing's commitment to superb communication warrants that Scripture's poetry also be presented to God's people in the best way possible, so that Scripture's valuable structures will continue to convey full, rich textual meanings.

---

[17] This is only a partial listing of Hebrew poetry types. Those who wish to pursue study of Hebrew "parallelism" should consult Gleason Archer, *A Survey of Old Testament Introduction* (Chicago: Moody Press, 1964), pp. 418-20.

B. Examples Of Hebrew Parallelism

The reader is encouraged to refer back and forth between the examples below and the descriptions of the various kinds of Hebrew parallelisms presented above. Additional explanations will be given from time to time in relation to unique examples. These explanations will also become more detailed as progression is made from less complex to more complex examples.

1. **A-A** Synonymous Parallelism
(Vertical Lineup)

(a) Matthew 3:3: **A** Prepare the way for the Lord;
A make the paths straight for Him.

(b) Matthew 11:30: **A** for My yoke is easy,
A and My burden is light.

2. **A-B** Antithetical Parallelism
(Slanted Lineup)

(a) Luke 6:21: **A** Blessed are you who are crying now,
B   for you will laugh.

(b) Luke 6:25: **A** Woe to you who are well fed now,
B   for you will be hungry.

(c) Luke 7:32: **A** We played a tune on the flute for you,
B   but you did not dance.
A We sang a funeral song,
B   but you did not weep.

This latter example is a double antithetical.

3. **A-B** or **A-B-C** Constructive Parallelism
(Slanted Lineup)

(a) Mark 12:11: **A** The Lord has done it,
B   and it is marvelous for us to see.

(b) Ephesians 5:14: **A** Wake up, sleeper!
B   Rise from the dead,
C   and Christ will shine on you.

The latter example builds meaning from one line to another, indicated by the slanted lineup, and line by line means: (1) Wake up and realize your sin; (2) stand up in faith; and (3) Christ will bless you.

4. A-B-B-A or A-B-C-C-B-A Chiastic Parallelism
(Vertically Varied Indented Lineup)

(a) Matthew 3:12b: He will *gather* His *wheat* into the barn, but the *chaff* He will *burn* . . . .

> **A** gather
> **B** wheat
> **B** chaff
> **A** burn

A prose section that internally resembles poetic structure! The same applies to Matthew 27:26 ("released-Barabbas-Jesus-whipped").

(b) Matthew 13:15: **A** because these people have become dull at heart
> **B**   and hard of hearing
> **C**   and have shut their eyes,
> **C**   so that their eyes never see,
> **B**   their ears never hear
> **A** their hearts never understand, ..."

Note: "heart/hearts; hearing/hear; eyes/eyes."

(c) Romans 2:7-10 is revealing. Externally it is a prose section, but internally it communicates *via* poetic structure. The GWN has set it in a poetic format (also verses 6 and 11) to help the reader detect meaning. Note the A-B-B-A structure in verses 7-10: (A-A) "everlasting life/glory, honor, peace"; (B-B) "anger and fury/sorrow and anguish."

(d) 1 Timothy 1:8-11 (especially verses 9b-10e and 2 Cor. 6:4-10) are possibly the two most complex prose sections that follow grammatic/poetic thought-form. Because of space considerations only the first of the two passages is here discussed:

[8] But we know the Law is good if it is used as it was meant to be used. [9] We need to keep in mind that the Law is not meant for a righteous person but

> for those who break the Law and for those who rebel against it,
> for the ungodly and for sinners,
> for those who live unholy lives and for those who insult holy things;
> for those who kill their fathers and for those who kill their mothers,

> for those who are murderers,
> [10] for those who are sexually immoral,
> for those who are homosexuals,
> for kidnappers,
> for those who lie,
> for those who swear falsely ₍under oath₎,—

as well as anything else that is found to be contrary to sound teaching [11] when judged according to the glorious Gospel of the blessed God, which was entrusted to me.

Certain things should be noted in this passage. First, Paul basically runs though the Ten Commandments in rotation.

Next, observe that the word "and" (Greek: *kai*) occurs *four* times, tying together *eight* items in the first four indented lines of verse 9. In turn, the next six lines do not contain even one "and"; thus an interlock of an 8/6 as to persons and sins mentioned.

However, when one considers the persons and sins in the first three indented lines of verse 9 and then separates them (the ending semicolon is a human aid) from the persons and sins in the remaining indented lines, one notices a 6/8 flip-flop. Coincidental? It is like having a **B-A** inside an **A-B**, thus making an **A-B-B-A** chiastic. As a result, the grammatic/poetic structure makes the meaning clearer.

5. A-B-C-D Stairlike Parallelism
(Slanted or Vertical Lineup)

(a) Luke 4:18,19: The Spirit of the Lord is upon Me because—
                         He anointed Me
                             to preach the Gospel to the poor.
                         He sent Me

A	to announce freedom to prisoners,
B	ˌto announce ˌ the restoring of sight to the blind,
C	to set free those who have been oppressed,
D	to announce an acceptable year of the Lord.

The structure of this passage is beautiful. Jesus introduces his poetic thought in the first line with a reference to each person of the Trinity. He follows this with an **A-A** (synonymous) in lines two and four. Then in lines five to eight He climbs as He adds thought after thought to the previous thought or thoughts with a stairlike **A-B-C-D**. In this case it is wise to line the stairlike parallelism up in a *vertical* manner since a *slanted* lineup would come off line four and erroneously make lines four to eight appear as a unit, whereas lines five to eight are the unit. (Note how nicely poetic structure serves for a topic or sermon outline. Line one is the Introduction; lines two and four are Parts I and II; line three is a single point under Part I, while lines five to eight serve as four points under Part II.)

(b) ROMANS 3:10b-18:

10 **A**   No one is righteous, no, not one—
11 **B**   no one understands—
   C   no one is searching for God:

```
12 A        All have turned away
    B           and together have become worthless;
       C           no one is doing anything good,
          D           not a single one.
13 A        Their throats are an open grave;
    B           they have spoken to deceive;
       C           their lips hide the poison of serpents;
14     D           their mouths are full of cursing and bitterness.
15 A     Their feet are quick to spill blood;
16   B        wherever they go, there is destruction and misery;
17     C        they have not learned the way of peace;
18       D        they have no fear of God.
```

Here is an astounding poetic thought-form in prose from the pen of the Apostle Paul. It is an **A-B-C** constructive parallelism (vv. 10,11) that is followed by a triple stairlike **A-B-C-D** parallelism that relates back to each of the lines of the **A-B-C** constructive, respectively. The **A-B-C-D** of verse 12 relates back to the **A** of verse 10, reiterating that no human being is sinless, "no, not one." The same is true of how the **A-B-C-D** of the four lines of verses 13 and 14 reiterate the **B** of verse 11a. Ditto for the **A-B-C-D** of verses 15-18 which reiterate the **C** of verse 11b. Of interest is the fact that the Greek translates so effectively into the English positioning of the *last* words of sections one and three. Consider the "one" and "one" reiteration in **A** (v. 10) and **D** (v. 12d); the "God" and "God" reiteration in **C** (v. 11b) and **D** (v. 18); and the "understands" in **B** (v. 11a) as reiterating the general thought that where wrong things come out of the mouth against God and man then there is the absence of *understanding* (vv. 13,14).

6. Smaller and Larger Units of Parallelisms, Grouped

We could add numerous examples to this discussion. Readers will be able to solve most of them if they follow the principles outlined. We simply wish to add two passages for more complete comprehension:

(a) Look up Matthew 12:15b-21 and Luke 1:68-80. They are just two of many poetic passages that have all types of smaller parallelisms within them, being grouped together into a larger whole. For example, in Matthew 12:18b-d we find a stairlike parallelism; verse 19 contains a synonymous parallelism; verse 20 is a threefold constructive parallelism.

The Luke 1 passage is a masterpiece. It would take pages to explain. Try to work through it, but be sure to note the verticals, slants, and indents. Note the larger **A-B-C** at verses 68a, 69a, and 72a which form a larger unit over the top of their own individual smaller units. This can best be illustrated in our examples from *Revelation* below.

(b) Matthew 6:9-13

9This is how you should pray:

> Our Father in heaven
>> may Your Name be kept holy,
10
>> may Your Kingdom come,
>> may Your will be done,
>>> on earth as it is in heaven;
11
>> give us today our daily bread;
12
>> and forgive us our sins
>>> as we have forgiven those who sin against us;
13
>> and do not lead us into temptation,
>> but deliver us from evil.

Whether it is meant to be prose or poetry, this unit lines up nicely for educational purposes. After the Introduction in verse 9b, the next indent level has a sevenfold **A-B-C-D-E-F-G**, which states the Seven Petitions or "Askings" that Christians pray. A great aid to comprehension and memory!

C. The Poetic Parallelisms In *Revelation*

The GWN translation of the Book of *Revelation* is the first time that this entire Epistle has been set in poetic format. Two special *Revelation* articles entitled, THE *KAI* STRUCTURE on page 565 and THE SYMBOLICAL NUMBERS OF *REVELATION* on page 567, will touch upon certain poetic aspects beyond the scope of this article, aspects that are more relevant to *Revelation* in particular than to Hebrew poetry in general.

The present section will state a few unique generalities concerning *Revelation* and print a few concrete examples for the sake of clarity.

As the article THE *KAI* STRUCTURE indicates, much of the structure of *Revelation* revolves around the Greek word "*kai*" ("and"), which serves as the cement or glue that binds units together in sets of twos, threes, fours, fives, sixes, sevens, tens, twelves, or multiples thereof. These *kai*s sit for the most part on the left margins and relate to one another by means of a vertical or slanted lineup. The meaning of the subject matter contained within the *kai* structure relates directly to the number of items listed. At the same time this meaning falls within the parameters of Hebrew parallelism. But in *Revelation* the *stairlike* phenomenon far outnumbers all the other usages, though there are also numerous examples of the synonymous and constructive. (Hebrew parallelisms are also in full array in those lines where *kai*s are absent.) Ironically, *Revelation* contains much more poetry than the rest of the New Testament, as well as types of poetry that are quite superb; yet in most places it is the easiest of all to identify in terms of Hebrew grammatic/poetic distinctions.

1. Revelation 1:3; 1:4b-5d; 4:2-8

(a) Blessed is the one who reads
    and those who hear the words of this prophecy
    and keep what is written in it—because the time is near.

This is a simple **A-B-C** constructive pararallelism.

(b) **A**   Grace and peace to you from
    A   the One-Who-Is and
    A   the One-Who-Was and
    A   the One-Who-Will be,
    B   and from the Seven Spirits who are before His throne,
    C   and from Jesus Christ—
    A   He is the faithful Witness,
    A   the First of the dead to live again,
    A   and the Ruler over the kings of the earth.

This is a Trinitarian section. The Father (first **A-A-A**) and the Son (second **A-A-A**) surround the single line given to the Holy Spirit, signaling three in one and one in three. The outside **A-B-C** constructive relates to Father, Spirit, and Son; while the two inside constructive **A-A-A**'s speak of the Father and Son in threes, whereas the Spirit appears as a cohesive one (cf. Matt. 28:19 and 1 Cor. 8:4).

(c) One choice for the most clever poetic thought-form in all of Scripture has to be Revelation 4:2-8. Look this passage up and carefully absorb its accompanying note d.

2. Revelation 18:11-13; 18:20

The first passage listed is truly striking. It has an inside *stairlike constructive* parallelism surrounded by an outside sevenfold *stairlike* structure.

When the *kai*s are absent in *Revelation*, the lineups are somewhat more difficult to determine. For example, one can know that a given parallelism is *stairlike*, but other conclusions are less definite. Revelation 18:20 is a good case in point.

APPENDIX 13
THE KAI *STRUCTURE*

"*Kai*" is the Greek word for "and," which is how it is generally translated in English versions, though it at times can also be translated as "but, even, both, also, yet, indeed." The term *kai* and its repeated use serve as the glue or cement that bind structures together in the Book of *Revelation*. Each repeated

use of *kai* in a series serves as a connective, tying thoughts together into specific units.

Each *kai*-structured unit is composed of a certain number of thoughts which convey a common meaning or message. The meaning or message varies according to the *number* of parts and ideas present in any given unit. Each unit is called an "arithmelogue." For example, a two-part structure or arithmelogue conveys a different common message than does a four-part or seven-part structure. (These individual meanings, which are consistently linked to each special base number (2,3,4,5,6,7,10,12) of *Revelation*, are explained in THE SYMBOLICAL NUMBERS OF THE BOOK OF *REVELATION* on page 567.)

The *kai*s or "ands" which introduce a *kai*-structured unit are lined up on the left margin of individual lines of poetry in *Revelation*. Please refer to the text and note this arrangement of the text.

It is amazing how these *kai*s run throughout the entire Book of *Revelation*. This phenomenon is known as polysyndeton, meaning "many ands." In a few cases the GWN has also moved *kai*s to the far right side of poetic lines in order to let other identical words line up in a visually effective way on the left (cf. 1:4c-e,8d-f). Left-hand-margin *kai*s are sometimes extensively indented for similar visual effect (cf. 1:10d-j; 15:2b-d; 19:17j-m); often the word(s) of the first line of component subject matter is indented for the same visual reason (cf. 5:12c-i; 7:12b-h; 9:17d-f,h-j; 13:16b-g; 19:17e-j; 21:8a-h).

Other *kai*s are scattered throughout the *interior* portions of various poetic lines. They connect parallel words, words which are generally governed either by a verb that controls two nouns connected by an "and" or by a main noun that has two verbs connected by an "and" (2:8b; 4:11a; 6:6e; 7:15b; 8:3a; 11:5b; 15:4d).

A varying number of *kai*s can bind individual units together. For example, in a seven-part structure there can be six "ands" holding seven ideas together or seven "ands" holding seven ideas together. The running units of "ands" are called *kai*meter. Technically, then, the running "ands" of *kai*meter hold arithmelogue units together. (At times, the grouped ideas of *Revelation* fall together under the category of asyndeton, meaning "no ands," 7:16a-17a; 14:a,c,d; 15:4c-e. When this is the case, the *number-to-structure* relationships are more difficult to detect. In every case these groupings relate to the general *poetic* guidelines laid down in GRAMMATIC/POETIC STRUCTURES THAT CONVEY TEXTUAL MEANINGS on page 558.)

Other books of the New Testament as well as of the Old Testament employ the use of "ands" as unit connectives, but not to John's extent. However, it can be said that Old Testament visionary literature, which falls under the same category as *Revelation*, also uses the word "and" (Hebrew: *waw*) in much the same way as does John.

More detailed information on *kai* structure, *kai* count, *kai*meter, and arithmelogues is offered by Jack M. Cascione, *In Search of the Biblical Order* (Cleveland: Biblion Publishing, 1987), pp. 1-182.

APPENDIX 14
THE SYMBOLICAL NUMBERS OF REVELATION

The vision given to John the Apostle in the Book of *Revelation* came "by way of symbols" (1:1). Therefore, most of the book must be interpreted as *symbolic*, including its numbers. The Holy Spirit revolves the poetic meter of *Revelation* around this symbolic meaning of its numbers.

The detection of this factor, based on the convincing evidence presented by Jack M. Cascione, *In Search of the Biblical Order* (Cleveland: Biblion Publishing, 1987), pp. 1-182, concludes that the various "lists" in *Revelation* which have the *same* number of thoughts repeatedly speak about the *same* general subject matter. The name given to this poetic phenomenon is "arithmelogue." It refers to *a numerically ordered series of thoughts on the same subject*. The correlation of this *number-to-structure* poetic format appears over and over throughout the entire book and is vividly portrayed in GWN by means of its poetic structure. (This is the reason why the GWN translation, for the first time in history, has set the Book of *Revelation* entirely in poetic form instead of prose.) The *number-to-structure* format is as follows:

Two-part structures (e.g., 1:11a,b; 1:2b,c; 19:4a,b) speak about how God's *word* is sent, communicated, confessed, witnessed, testified, described, received, believed, and obeyed. (Together these signal the totality of *worship*, a frequent two-part subject.)

Three-part structures (e.g., 1:8b-d; 14:3a-c; 2:5a-c; 9:18b-d; 1:3; 4:2) speak about *God*: Father, Son, and Holy Spirit. *Heaven*—where God lives—is also described in three-part forms. Responses to God, like *cursings* or *praise*, and responses from God, such as *warnings*, *curses*, and *blessings*, also come in three-part entities.

Four-part structures (e.g., 5:9e; 18:22a; 6:8e-h, note line d also; 5:13b) speak about *mankind, human activity, earth, the creation*, or *created things*.

Five-part structures (e.g., 3:17e; 18:13a) speak about *the entire gamut of human emotions* or *human experiences*, including the five senses.

Six-part structures (e.g., 18:15e-j; 22:15) speak about the *process and results of creating* or characterize *the nature of what is created*.

Seven-part structures (e.g., 11:19; 14:18c,d,f-j; 22:3-5a,b,d; cf. 1:4f) speak about God's *judgment*. Such judgment is double-sided. It ultimately leads

unbelievers to destruction and hell or believers to blessings, heaven, and perfection. (The Spirit is a seven because He already is holy or *perfect*.) Realize that the Book of *Revelation* is divided into a *perfect* seven major parts, The Seven Visions: Seven Letters; Seven Seals; Seven Trumpets; Woman and the Dragon; Seven Bowls; God's Final Triumph; God's New World.

Ten-part structures (e.g., 1:13b-16; 2:2,3) speak about *completion* and comprise *a complete list/description* or *the full scope of a particular subject*.

Twelve-part structures (e.g., 7:5-8; 12:1b-4c) speak about the *church*, the Lord's believing people. Note that *Revelation* speaks of *twelve* stars, gates, angels, tribes, foundation stones, names, apostles, stones, pearls, kinds of fruit, even 24 elders (two sets of 12).

These various "arithmelogues" in *Revelation* are either *negative* or *positive*. This means that a series of *three* thoughts either can relate three negative elements that are under a curse or three positive elements that are giving a blessing. Such negative or positive subject matter may symbolize the forces opposed to God or those forces in accord with God's will.

In addition to the above, as regarding numbers, it should be recognized that larger numbers, such as 1,000 and 144,000, are multiples of smaller symbolic numbers—and are symbolic themselves. For example, 1,000 (10 x 10 x 10) =*completion* times *completion* times *completion*, indicating ultimate completion; 144,000 (12 x 12 x 10 x 10 x 10)=*church* (believers) times *church* (believers) times *completion* times *completion* times *completion,* indicating the ultimate number of believers that will go to heaven. Behind this latter symbolism would be: Old Testament church (12 tribes) times New Testament church (12 apostles and their followers) times their complete number times their complete number times their complete number symbolically equals the total number of Old and New Testament believers who will be saved. The number system is a symbolic code that indicates a spiritual truth. Other larger numbers like 666 may just be the grouping of three 6's together, as may be suggested by the three former six-part structures in the text (13:12-16a, 16b-g, 16h-17d, cf. v. 18).

It is also important to note that most groupings of "arithmelogues" in *Revelation* are connected with the word "and" (Greek: "*kai*"). See THE *KAI* STRUCTURE on page 565. Readers will do themselves a favor if they take time to page through *Revelation* and observe patterns of "ands" lining up on every page. (In order to maintain continuity of thought within the numerically ordered units of poetry, the GWN has been forced to leave gaps at the bottom of many of its pages in *Revelation*. If a whole unit did not fit on a given page, it was moved to the start of another page where it did fit.)

Finally, it is of interest to note that numbers in certain passages of the rest of Scripture also reflect a correlation to the *subject-numbers* of a book like *Revelation*. Using the number *five* as the number of *human emotions* and

experience, consider the *fives* of Luke 16:28; John 5:2; and Matthew 25:2: in the first the *"five* brothers" are experiencing hell; in the next the sick are feeling sickness in the area of the *"five* porches"; and in the third passage there are *"five* bridesmaids" who will experience heaven and *"five"* who will experience hell.

APPENDIX 15
PREVIEW OF COMING ATTRACTIONS

A. OLD TESTAMENT PROSE

GENESIS 1:1:   In the beginning God created the heavens and the earth. The earth was formless and empty; it was also dark on the deep sea, but God's Spirit hovered over the waters. Then God said, "Let there be light!" And there was light.

GENESIS 6:15:   "This is how you should make it: The ark should be three hundred cubits [450'] long, fifty cubits [75'] wide, and thirty cubits [45'] high."

GENESIS 10:6:   Ham's sons were Cush [Ethiopia], Mizraim [Egypt], Put, and Canaan.

GENESIS 10:25:   Eber [Hebrew] had two sons; the name of the one was Peleg [Division], because in his days the earth was divided; and his brother's name was Joktan.

GENESIS 37:3:   Israel loved Joseph best of all his sons because he was born when Israel was old. He made Joseph a coat reaching to the wrists and ankles.[18]

EXODUS 1:16:   "When you help the Hebrew women give birth to a child, and observe it on the 'birthstool,' "[19] he said, "if it is a boy, kill him; if it is a girl, let her live."

RUTH 1:20:   "Don't call me Naomi [Pleasant]," she answered them. "Call me Mara [Bitter]. . . ."

---

[18] The Hebrew can either indicate a coat with long sleeves or a coat of "pieces," that is, one made up of multi-colored pieces. The latter would be a "coat of many colors" which might indicate a "prophet's coat" (cf. Gen. 37:11), while the former indicates "an overseer's coat." In either case jealousy on the part of the brothers prevailed.

[19] A type of a parallel to the modern "birthing chair" or older "delivery table."

B. OLD TESTAMENT POETRY

MICAH 1:10-12

10   Do not tell it in Winepress Town [Gath];
          do not squeeze out tears there.
     In Dust Town [Beth-le-aphrah]
          roll yourself in the dust.
11   You who live in Beauty Town [Shaphir]
          leave it shamefully naked.
     You who live in March Town [Zaanan]
          will not march out of it.
     The lamentation in Near Town [Beth-ezel]
          will remove from you anything to stand near.
12   You who live in Bitter Town [Maroth]
          will be tired of looking for better days.
     Disaster will come down from the LORD
          to the very gate of Jerusalem.

GENESIS 49:8-12, 22-26

8   Judah, your brothers will praise you—
          your hand will be on the necks of your enemies;
               your father's sons will bow down before you.

9   Judah is a young lion;
          you have come up from eating the prey, my son;
               he crouches and stretches out like a lion;
                    as a mature lion, who will rouse Him?

10   The scepter will not pass away from Judah
          or a ruler from between his feet
               until SHILOH [Man of Rest][20] comes,
                    whom the nations will obey.

11   He will tie His donkey to a vine,
          His donkey's colt to the choice vine.
     He will wash His clothes in wine,
          His garment in the blood of grapes.
12   His eyes are dark from wine,
          His teeth white from milk.

[20] From *shalah* "rest" or *shalom* "peace." Both mean basically the same. When one has *peace* he is at *rest*.

22 Joseph is a branch of a fruitful vine,
   a branch of a fruitful vine by a spring,
      whose branches climb over a wall.
23 And the archers bitterly opposed him
   and shot at him
   and kept attacking him,
24   but his bow stayed steady,
   and his arms moved nimbly
      with the help of[21] the Mighty One of Jacob—
      with the help of[22] the Shepherd, the Rock of Israel—yes,
25   with the help of the God of your father, who aids you,
      with the help of the Almighty, who blesses you
         with blessings from the heavens above,
         with blessings from the deep which lies below,
         with blessings of the breasts and womb.
26 The blessings your father received
   are greater than those received by my ancestors,
      ˌadvancingˌ, even to the borders of the everlasting hills.
May these blessings be placed on Joseph's head,
   on the brow of the one who is prince among his brothers.

[21] Literally: "from the hands of."
[22] Literally: "from there."

APPENDIX 16
NAMES/TITLES OF THE THREE PERSONS OF THE TRINITY

1. OF THE FATHER

A and Z
Rev 21:6

Alpha and Omega
Rev 21:6

Almighty
Rev 19:6

Almighty God
Rev 16:14; 19:15

Beginning and End
Rev 21:6

Being
Col 1:19
Heb 1:3

Blessed One
Mk 14:61

Caretaker
Jn 15:1

Creator
Rom 1:25

Father (selected)
Matt 5:16; 28:19
Mk 8:38
Lk 6:36
Jn 1:14
Acts 1:4
Rom 1:7
1 Cor 8:6
Gal 1:1
Eph 1:2
1 Pet 1:2
1 Jn 1:3
Rev 1:6

Father of lights
Jas 1:17

God (selected)
Gal 1:1
Rev 1:6

Head
1 Cor 11:3

Helper
Heb 13:6

Holy One
1 Pet 1:15
1 Jn 2:20
Rev 16:5

Judge
Jn 8:50
2 Tim 4:8
Heb 12:23
Jas 4:12

King
Rev 11:15,17; 19:6

King of the nations [ages]
Rev 15:3

Lawgiver
Jas 4:12

Light
1 Jn 1:5

Lord
Matt 11:25
Lk 2:22
Rev 11:15

Lord Almighty
2 Cor 6:18

Lord God Almighty
Rev 4:8; 11:17;
15:3; 16:7; 21:22

Lord of armies [hosts]
Jas 5:4

Lord of heaven
and earth
Lk 10:21

Lord of the harvest
Lk 10:2

Love
1 Jn 4:8,16

Majesty
Heb 1:3; 8:1

Master
Acts 4:24
Rom 8:20
Eph 6:9
2 Tim 2:21

Most High
Lk 1:35; 1:76; 6:35

Most High God
Mk 5:7
Lk 8:28
Acts 16:17
Heb 7:1

One-Who-Is,
One-Who-Was
Rev 11:17; 16:5

One-Who-Is,
One-Who-Was,
One-Who-Will-Be
Rev 1:4

Savior
Lk 1:47;
1 Tim 1:1

Who-Was, Who-Is,
Who-Will-Be
Rev 4:8

2. OF CHRIST

A and Z
Rev 22:13

Alpha and Omega
Rev 22:13

Amen
Rev 3:14

Angel
Acts 7:30,35,38
Rev 10:1,5,8,9,10;
20:1

Anointed (see Anointed
One, Messiah)
Acts 4:26

Anointed One
[Chosen One]
Matt 1:16n
Mk 1:1n
Lk 2:26n
Jn 1:41n
Acts 2:31n
2 Cor 1:21n

Apostle
Heb 3:1

Atonement Cover
Rom 3:25

Author
Acts 3:15
Heb 12:2n

Beginning
Col 1:18

Beginning and End
Rev 22:13

Beloved
Matt 3:17n

Branch (see Nazarene)
Matt 2:23n

Bread [Manna]
Jn 6:41,50,51,58

Bread [Manna] of Life
Jn 6:35,48

Bridegroom
Jn 3:29

Bright Morning Star
Rev 22:16

Caretaker
1 Pet 2:25

Christ (see Messiah)
Matt 1:16
Mk 8:29
Lk 24:26
Jn 1:41
Acts 3:20
1 Jn 2:22

Cornerstone
Matt 21:42
Mk 12:10
Lk 20:17
Acts 4:11
Eph 2:20
1 Pet 2:6,7

Covering
Rom 3:25n

Creator
Rev 22:16

Descendant
Acts 3:25
Rom 15:12
Gal 3:16,19
Rev 22:16

Door
Jn 10:7,9

Faithful
Rev 19:11

Father's Son
2 Jn 3

Finisher
Heb 12:2n

First (of the dead)
Rev 1:5

First and Last
Rev 1:17; 2:8;
22:13

Firstborn
Rom 8:29
Col 1:15

Firstfruit
1 Cor 15:23

Forerunner
Heb 6:20

Fruit
Lk 1:42n

Galilean
Matt 26:69
Lk 22:59

Glory
Lk 2:32

God (selected)
Jn 1:1; 20:28
Rom 9:5
1 Jn 5:20

Good Shepherd
Jn 10:11,14

Great Shepherd
Heb 13:20

Guarantee
Heb 7:22

Head
1 Cor 11:3
Eph 1:10,22; 4:15;
5:23

Head Shepherd
1 Pet 5:4

Heir
Heb 1:2

Helper
  Matt 1:16n
  Lk 1:31n

High Priest
  Heb 2:17; 3:1;
  4:14,15; 5:5,10; 6:20;
  7:26; 8:1; 9:11

Holy Being
  Lk 1:35

Holy One
  Acts 2:27; 13:35
  1 Jn 2:20

Holy One of God
  Mark 1:24
  Lk 4:34
  Jn 6:69

Holy and Righteous
  One
  Acts 3:14

Hope
  Col 1:27
  1 Tim 1:1

Horn of salvation
  Lk 1:69

Husband
  2 Cor 11:2

I AM
  Jn 8:58

Immanuel
  [God With Us]
  Matt 1:23

Jesus (selected)
  Matt 1:21; 21:11
  Mk 1:9; 10:47
  Lk 1:31; 2:21
  Jn 1:45
  Acts 18:5
  1 Jn 4:15
  Rev 22:16

Jew
  Jn 4:9

Judge
  2 Tim 4:8
  James 5:9

King
  Matt 5:35; 21:5;
  25:34,40
  Lk 1:33; 19:38; 23:2
  Jn 12:15; 19:14,15
  Acts 17:8
  1 Tim 1:17

King of Israel
  Matt 27:42
  Mk 15:32
  Jn 1:49; 12;13

King of kings and
  Lord of lords
  1 Tim 6:15
  Rev 19:16

King of the Jews
  Matt 2:2; 27:11,29,37
  Mk 15:2,9,12,18,26
  Lk 23:3,37,38
  Jn 18:33,39;
  19:3,19,21

Lamb
  1 Pet 1:19,20
  Rev 5:6,8,12,13;
  6:1,16; 7:9,10,14,17;
  12:11; 13:8, n;
  14:1,4,10; 15:3;
  17:14; 19:7,9;
  21:9,14,22,23,27;
  22:1,3

Lamb of God
  Jn 1:29,36

LAMP
  Rev 21:23

Leader
  Matt 2:6; 23:10
  Acts 5:31
  Heb 2:10

Life
  Jn 1:4; 11:25; 14:6
  Col 3:4
  1 Jn 1:1,2

Light
  Matt 4:16
  Lk 2:32
  Jn 1:4,5,7,8,9;
  3:19,20,21;
  12:35,36,46

Light of Life
  Jn 8:12

Light of the world
  Jn 8:12; 9:5

Living One
  Rev 1:18

Lion
  Rev 5:5

Lord (selected)
  Matt 21:3
  Mk 16:19
  Lk 2:11
  Jn 6:23; 20:28
  Acts 2:36
  1 Cor 12:3

Lord and Christ
  Acts 2:36

Lord and Savior
  2 Pet 1:11; 2:20;
  3:2,18

Lord of glory
  1 Cor 2:8
  James 2:1

Lord of lords and
  King of kings
  Rev 17:14

Lord of the Sabbath
  Matt 12:8
  Mk 2:28
  Lk 6:5

Man (selected)
  Jn 5:12
  1 Tim 2:5

Master
  Mk 10:51
  Lk 5:5; 8:24,45;
  9:33,49; 17:13
  Col 4:1
  Jude 4
  Rev 6:10

Mediator
  1 Tim 2:5
  Heb 8:6; 9:15; 12:24

Messenger (see Angel)

Messiah (see Anointed,
  Anointed One)
  Matt 2:4
  Mk 12:35
  Lk 2:26n; 3:15; 20:41;
  24:26,46
  Jn 1:20, 41; 4:25;
  7:26,31,41; 9:22;
  10:24
  Acts 2:31n; 4:26n;
  5:42; 9:22; 18:5,28
  2 Cor 1:21n
  1 Jn 2:22; 5:1

Miraculous Sign
  Lk 2:34n

Morning Star
  2 Pet 1:19
  Rev 2:28

NAME
  Acts 4:12; 5:41

Nazarene (see Branch)
  Matt 2:23

Owner
  Lk 13:25

Passover ₁Lamb₁
  1 Cor 5:7

Peace
  Eph 2:14

Priest
  Heb 5:6;
  7:11,15,17,21; 8:2;
  10:21

Prince
  Acts 3:15n

Prophet
  Matt 21:11
  Lk 24:19
  Jn 1:21,25; 6:14;
  7:40,52
  Acts 3:22,23; 7:37

Rabbi
  Matt 26:25,49
  Mk 9:5; 11:21; 14:45
  Jn 1:38,49; 3:2,26;
  4:31; 6:25; 9:2; 11:8

Rabboni
  Jn 20:16

Resurrection
  Jn 11:25

Rider
  Rev 19:11,19,21

Righteous One
  Acts 7:52; 22:14
  1 Pet 3:18

Rock
  Rom 9:33
  1 Cor 10:4
  1 Pet 2:8

Root (of David)
  Rev 5:5; 22:16n

Root (of Jesse)
  Rom 15:12n

Ruler
  1 Tim 6:15
  Heb 2:7
  Rev 1:5; 3:14n

Salvation
  Lk 2:30

Savior
  Matt 1:16n; 2:23n
  Lk 1:31n,47; 2:11
  Jn 4:42
  Acts 5:31; 13:23
  Rom 11:26
  Eph 5:23
  Phil 3:20
  1 Tim 2:3; 4:10
  2 Tim 1:10
  Titus 1:3,4; 2:10,13;
  3:4,6
  2 Pet 1:1,11;
  2:20; 3:2,18
  1 Jn 4:14

Second Adam
  1 Cor 15:45

Second Man
  1 Cor 15:47

Servant
  Matt 12:18
  Acts 3:13,26; 4:27,30
  Rom 15:8

Shepherd
  Matt 26:31
  Mk 14:27
  Jn 10:16
  1 Pet 2:25
  Rev 7:17

Sign
  Lk 2:34

Son (selected)
  Matt 3:17; 28:19
  Mk 1:11
  Lk 9:35
  Jn 3:16; 17:1
  Acts 13:33
  Rom 1:3; 8:3
  1 Cor 1:9
  Gal 4:4
  Heb 5:8
  2 Jn 3

Son of David (selected)
  Matt 9:27
  Mk 10:47
  Lk 18:38

Son of God (selected)
Matt 4:3
Mk 1:1
Lk 1:35
Jn 1:34; 10:36
Rom 1:4
2 Cor 1:19
Gal 2:20
Heb 4:14
1 Jn 3:8

Son of Man (selected)
Matt 8:20
Mk 2:10
Lk 5:24
Jn 1:51
Acts 7:56
Rev 1:13

Son of the Blessed One
Mk 14:61

Son of the living God
Matt 16:16

Son of the Most High
Lk 1:32

Son of the
Most High God
Mk 5:7
Lk 8:28

Source
Heb 5:9
Rev 3:14

Stone
Matt 21:42,44
Mk 12:10
Lk 20:17,18
Acts 4:11
Rom 9:33
1 Pet 2:4,7,8

Sun (KJV – "Dayspring"
or "Day Star")
Lk 1:78

Teacher
Matt 8:19; 9:11;
12:38; 17:24; 19:16;
22:16,24,36; 23:8;
26:18

Mk 4:38; 5:35;
9:17,38; 10:17,20,35;
12:14,19,32; 13:1;
14:14
Lk 3:12; 7:40; 8:49;
9:38; 10:25; 11:45;
12:13; 18:18; 19:39;
20:21,28,39; 21:7;
22:11
Jn 1:38; 3:2; 8:4;
11:28; 13:13; 20:16

Temple
Jn 2:19,21

True
Rev 19:11

Truth
Jn 5:33; 14:6

Vine
Jn 15:1,5

Way
Jn 14:6

Witness
Rev 1:5; 3:14

Word
Jn 1:1,14

Word of God
Rev 19:13

"Yes"
2 Cor 1:20

3. OF THE HOLY SPIRIT

Comforter
Jn 14:16,26; 15:26;
16:7

God
Acts 5:4

Oil of Joy
Heb 1:9

Holy Spirit (selected)
Matt 28:19
Mk 1:8
Lk 3:16
Jn 1:33

Seven Spirits
Rev 1:4; 3:1; 4:5; 5:6

Spirit (selected)
Matt 12:18
Jn 1:33
Rom 8:26
1 Cor 2:10,11
Rev 22:17

Spirit of Truth
Jn 14:17;
15:26; 16:13
1 Jn 5:6

GLOSSARY

Aaron The first high priest of Israel (Ex. 28:1-43; Lev. 8:1-9:24; Heb. 5:4). He was the older brother of Moses, who served as Moses' spokesman to the Israelites and to Pharaoh (Ex. 4:14-16); also the brother of Miriam (Num. 26:59).

Agrippa Two people are called by this name in the NT: (1) the grandson of Herod the Great, Herod Agrippa, who killed James the Apostle (Acts 12:1, 2; here simply called "Herod"); (2) Herod Agrippa's son, before whom Paul made his defense (Acts 25:13-26:32).

alabaster A vessel of any type material, without handles, in which perfume was sealed; the neck had to be broken to release its content.

aloes In the NT a bitter, succulent plant with a thick, fleshy leaf (Jn. 19:39). From the pressed leaves a bright violet liquid, called aloin, was obtained. This substance was then mixed with water and added to sweet-smelling spices for use in embalming; it was very expensive. The "aloes" of the OT refers to a plant different from that of the NT.

alpha and omega The first and last letters of the *Greek* alphabet, used by the Lord as a divine self-designation in Revelation 1:8; 21:6; 22:13.

altar A place/object upon which sacrifices were offered to God by His people; used from earliest times down to the time of Jesus. Since the sacrificial work of Jesus, altars with their sacrifices now belong to the past (Heb. 9-10; cf. Rom. 12:1). With the destruction of the Temple in A.D. 70, Daniel's prophecy in 9:27 was fulfilled and Jewish animal sacrifices have ceased to exist to this very day.

amen A Hebrew word meaning "it is true" or "so let it be"; it was used liturgically in worship to express agreement in response to a religious address (1 Chr. 16:36; Neh. 5:13; 8:6); Jesus frequently used the term to emphasize the importance of His teaching when He specifically mentioned the "truth" of what he was saying (e.g., Matt. 5:18, 26; 6:2,5,16); also a title for Jesus Himself (Rev. 3:14). "Amen, amen" (doubled), the famous "verily, verily" of the KJV or "truly, truly" of some modern translations is often used by Jesus in John's Gospel.

ancestors The honored, ancient *fathers* (patriarchs) of the Jews, such as Abraham (Heb. 7:4), Jacob and his twelve sons (Acts 7:8, 9), King David (Acts 2:29), etc. See Malachi 4:6; Romans 9:5; and Hebrews 1:1.

anoint (see **Christ Jesus**) "To put ₁olive₁ oil on" people or things; such anointing signified *separation* from the profane and a *choosing* for use in God's service. Thus, kings (1 Kgs. 1:34), priests (Ex. 28:41), and prophets (1 Kgs. 19:16) were *anointed* in ancient Israel. Such ceremony was meant to indicate that God had *chosen* persons to serve Him and His people. Eventually the term "Anointed One" ("Messiah") came to be used in describing the coming Savior-King who had been promised by the OT prophets (Ps. 2:2; Acts 10:38). In the NT the Greek term *Christos* ("Christ") means "Anointed One." When Christ was *anointed* at His baptism with the Holy Spirit, called the "Oil of Joy" in Psalm 45:7, this indicated—*via* that Spirit's anointing—that Jesus was the One whom the Father had *chosen* to be the Savior of the nations. In relation to the above, then, it can be said that *Christ Jesus* was God's "Anointed," as He was kept *separated from sin* by His special divine conception and human birth (Lk. 1:35; cf. 1 Pet. 1:19; 2:22) and was *chosen* to save the world from sin.

apostle This term means "one sent out" or "messenger"; *apostolos*, the Greek word for this term, has several meanings in the NT, such as "one sent" (Phil. 2:25), "a messenger of God" (Lk. 11:49), or "an honored believer with a commission" (Acts 14:14); most frequently, however, it describes the Twelve, chosen and authorized by Christ to be His witnesses and to serve as the leaders in His church.

Aretas A name held by a number of kings of Nabatea, an Arab country just southeast of the Jordan River. As early as 170 B.C., Aretas I gained control of the trade routes between the Mediterranean and the Orient, making Nabatea very wealthy; the king mentioned in 2 Corinthians 11:32 is Aretas IV Philopatris, who was apparently able to control commerce as far north as Damascus.

ark The vessel built by Noah, approximately 450' in length, 75' in width, and 45' in height, on which he and his wife, his three sons and their wives, and a great number of living creatures (at least one male and female of each kind) were saved from the Flood (see Gen. 6-8; Matt. 24:38).

ark of the covenant [testament] A rectangular, gold-covered box of acacia wood, about 4' in length and 2 1/2' in width and height, in which were kept the tablets of the Ten Commandments, a pot of manna, and Aaron's rod (Ex. 25:16; Heb. 9:4, 5). On top of this box was a golden lid or "atonement cover" (cf. Rom. 3:25), flanked on each side by golden cherubs who guarded it with outspread wings. The ark was at the very center of Israel's worship as the symbol of God's presence and was eventually placed in the Most Holy Place in Solomon's Temple. It was probably lost after the Babylonian destruction of Jerusalem in 588 B.C.

Armageddon A proper name found only in Revelation 16:16. The precise meaning of this name and its location are uncertain, although many scholars today think that "mountain (Hebrew: *har*) of Megiddo" is possible. Many important battles were fought near the city of Megiddo in ancient times (cf. Judg. 5:19).

Artemis A Greek goddess of fertility whose temple at Ephesus became one of the seven wonders of the ancient world. (Sometimes Artemis is erroneously translated "Diana," the parallel goddess of the Romans.) The riot described in Acts 19:23-41 arose because the Christian faith endangered businesses which depended on the popularity of the worship of Artemis and the sale of her images and *silver shrines*. (Most likely, the shrines represented Artemis sitting in a niche with her lions next to her.)

Asia The Roman province comprising approximately the western third of what is now Asia Minor. Its major cities were ancient centers of Greek culture and civilization, and by NT times Asia was among the most prosperous provinces of the Roman Empire. Ephesus was its most important city, a key center of Christian faith in the Early Church; other centers were Colossae, Hierapolis, Troas, as well as the six cities mentioned, along with Ephesus, in Revelation 2 and 3.

Atonement, Day of Known as *Yom Kippur* in Hebrew, this was one of the most sacred days in OT worship, in fact, the highest day of repentance and fasting. Once each year on the 10th of *Tishri* (September/October) the high priest would enter the Most Holy Place to make atonement for himself, the priesthood, and the whole congregation of people by sprinkling the blood of a bull and a goat on the "atonement cover" and before the ark (Lev. 16; Heb. 9). The ultimate Day of Atonement became Good Friday when Christ became our "Atonement Cover" by shedding His blood for sin (Rom. 3:25).

Augustus The term means "venerable" or "majestic"; an honorific name given to Caesar Octavianus, who ruled Rome at the time of Jesus' birth (Lk. 2:1). His rule brought a new era of peace and security to the Empire.

Babylon A leading city of Babylonia from the early second millennium, geographically located on both sides of the Euphrates River about 50 miles south of modern Baghdad. Its greatest glory was achieved under Nebuchadnezzer II in the sixth century B.C. Under his rule, many Jews were exiled to Babylon, where they remained until its overthrow by Cyrus the Persian. "Babylon" is a code name for "Rome" in Revelation 17:9 (note the mention of the "seven hills"). 1 Peter 5:13 seems to imply the same.

Balaam (see *Balak*) A soothsayer from Mesopotamia who was hired by Balak the king of Moab to *curse* Israel just before her invasion into Canaan (Num. 22-24). Because of God's hand upon him, Balaam could only *bless* Israel. In the NT Balaam is remembered as avaricious

(2 Pet. 2:15; Jude 11) and as a dangerous, spiritual enemy of God's people who cleverly advised Balak to destroy Israel by enticing her sexually to sin against her God (Rev. 2:14; Num. 31:16).

Balak (see **Balaam**) The king of Moab who hired Balaam to put a *curse* upon Israel (Num. 22–24; Rev. 2:14). Balak's frustrating experience with Balaam illustrates how powerless the occult is in opposing God's will and purpose for His people.

baptize *"To apply water"* by washing, dipping, sprinkling, immersing, etc. Utensils, even those very large in size, were *baptized* in or with water (cf. Mk 7:4; Matt. 28:19). The largeness of certain objects ("dining couches") would indicate that "baptism" was not only by immersion; heavy, bulky objects would be baptized [water being applied] by wiping them off with water.

barley A cereal grass, the grain of which was used to feed livestock, since it was less valued and cheaper than wheat. (Corn, as maize, and probably oats and alfalfa were unknown.) The poor often used *barley* grain to make inexpensive bread. Compare Judges 7:13 and John 6:9.

Beelzebul A title meaning "lord (*Beel*) of filth (*zebul*)"; refers to the prince of demons (Matt. 12:24); probably an alternate title for Satan himself (Mk. 3:22, 23). "*Zebul*" in Semitic expression may also have the alternate meaning "dwelling," indicating that Jesus in Matthew 10:25 would be engaging in a play on words.

believe *"To have faith, confidence, trust."* To *believe* in a Christian sense is to *trust* in Jesus as Savior and Lord, confident that His death and resurrection has won personal forgiveness, reconciliation with God, and eternal life for every individual.

Bernice The sister and companion of Agrippa II, who with her brother heard Paul's defense before Festus the Roman governor at Caesarea (Acts 25:13–26:32).

blasphemy An intentional and defiant act which dishonors the Name and work of God by word or action.

bless This term is defined in three ways: (1) God "blesses" people when He bestows on them qualities, both spiritual and material, which bring happiness and joy in order that they, in turn, may praise and glorify God; (2) people "bless" God when they give Him thanks and praise, acknowledging His great power and glory; and (3) people "bless" people when they express good wishes for one another and pray to God on behalf of others.

blessed Enjoying the state of being happy, blissful, joyful, especially as these qualities have their source in God.

Booths, Festival of *[Tabernacles, Festival of]* One of the three major Hebrew festivals (Deut. 16:16), celebrated from the 15th through the 22nd of *Tishri* (September/October). It was a time of rejoicing in which the Jews lived in small tents, tabernacles, or booths made of tree branches, recalling their own or their ancestors' years of wandering in the wilderness (Lev. 23:42,43; Jn. 7:2). Judgment Day, a day of rejoicing for believers, replaces this Festival in NT thought (Rev. 19:1,5-9).

bottomless pit, depths *[abyss]* The place of the dead (Rom. 10:7), of demons (Lk. 8:31), and of the "beast" of Revelation 11:7 and 17:8.

breastplate A protective covering for the chest and back, made of metal or linen or leather, fastened with metal studs or plates. In Ephesians 6:14, the "breastplate of righteousness" probably does not refer to the Christian's righteous conduct but to the righteousness that God gives to the Christian as a gift through faith in Christ; this is the Christian's best and truest spiritual defense.

caesar A cognomen of the aristocratic Julian family, whose most famous member was Julius Caesar (102-44 B.C.). It became a dynastic name of the Roman emperors from Augustus (ruler from 43 B.C.-14 A.D.) onward, being used as a title also by those not from the Julian family. In the NT "Caesar" is used primarily as an official title for "Emperor," and at times it is used symbolically to mean *the state* itself (see Matt. 22:17, 21).

census A population count; census taking was carried on in both OT and NT times. The Roman censuses mentioned in Luke 2:1, 2 and Acts 5:37 were done to form the list of names by which to assess the taxes that Palestine and other subject areas would have to pay the Roman government.

Christ, Messiah (see *anoint* and Matt. 1:16 and its accompanying footnote "d"). Meaning "Anointed One"; a title for the awaited Savior. Although Jesus accepted this title from His disciples in private (Matt. 16:13-17) and publicly accepted it at His trial (Mk. 14:61, 62), He carefully avoided it during His three-year ministry (Mk. 8:30), because almost everyone understood this term primarily in a *political* or *military* sense (cf. even the apostles in Acts 1:6). This kind of misunderstanding would have constantly undercut Jesus' teaching on the real nature of God's Kingdom that had its true center in suffering and dying on the cross (Mk. 8:31-33). The designation "Christian" is based on the name "Christ" (see THE EARLIEST CHRISTIAN CREEDS on page 557).

Christ Jesus (see *Christ, Messiah* and *Jesus, Savior*) In summary, this title means the "Anointed (or) Chosen Savior" ("Christ" = "Messiah" = "Anointed One" = "Chosen One") ("Jesus" = "Joshua" = "Helper" = "Savior"). Thus, *Christ Jesus* is the "Chosen Savior," *anointed* by God to *help* the world by dying for all sin, that is, *chosen* by God to *save* all people from sin.

circumcision Literally, the surgical removal of the foreskin of the male sexual organ. Also used in a figurative way when speaking about the circumcision of a person's heart (Deut. 10:16). Paul speaks of circumcision being spiritually replaced by baptism following the resurrection of Christ (Col. 2:11,12).

Claudius The Roman emperor from A.D. 41-54 (see Acts 11:28; 18:2).

Comforter Another name, special to John's Gospel, for the "Holy Spirit." The Greek word for "Comforter" is *Paraclete*, meaning "one called to one's side," used in a judicial sense, referring to an "advocate, defender, pleader, intercessor."

confess "To declare one's faith" in something or someone, or "to declare one's sins" for the purpose of receiving forgiveness. When a Christian *confesses*, either he is telling of his faith in Jesus or he is openly admitting his sins for the purpose of receiving forgiveness.

convert A person who has turned from one belief, conviction, or faith to another.

covenant See *DIATHEKE* on page 531.

cross [crucifix] An upright post, beam, or stick with another fastened across it near the top, on which convicted persons were executed in ancient times; a Christian symbol of Christ's death. The symbols of the *cross* and *crucifix* differ only in that a *crucifix* portrays the body of Christ on it while a *cross* does not. Because a cross is made of wood, it is also referred to as a "tree" or as "wood" (Gal. 3:13; cf. Rev. 22:2).

crucifix (see *cross*)

crucify (see *cross*) "To put to death by suspending from a cross," with hands and feet tied or nailed (the latter as in the case of Jesus and, most likely, the two men crucified with Him). Death by crucifixion occurred when victims *suffocated* because their lack of strength left them unable to pump themselves up by the legs to get oxygen into their lungs. When the legs of

crucified victims were broken, all their weight on their extended arms cut off the ability to breath, thus the practice of breaking the legs of the crucified victims at times so that they might die of suffocation sooner (Jn. 19:32). In the case of Jesus it had been predicted that none of His bones would be broken (Ex. 12:46), and therefore His death was not caused by suffocation since He could have pumped Himself up by His legs to get air; rather, Jesus at His own time of chosing died on the cross (cause not stated) after He had completed His task (Jn. 10:18; 19:30).

cummin   An aromatic, annual herb whose seeds are used as a spice in various foods.

Dalmatia   A Roman province covering the southern part of Illyricum, a mountainous region bordering the east coast of the Adriatic Sea just across from Italy (cf. 2 Tim. 4:10).

David's city   In the OT the southeast hill of Jerusalem, upon which the Jebusite citadel stood until its capture by David; in the NT the reference is to Bethlehem, the small village in which both David and Jesus were born. Compare Micah 5:2.

Dedication, Festival of   Also called the Festival of Lights (*Hanukka*), an extra-Biblical festival orginating during the Maccabean period in commemoration of the cleansing of the Temple in 164 B.C. It began on the 25th of *Kislev* (November/December) and lasted eight days.

demon (see *devil*)   Used in this present GWN translation as a reference to one of Satan's evil angels; the term can also be translated "devil."

depths (see *bottomless pit*)

descendant (see *ancestor*)   The offspring of an ancestor.

devil (see *Satan* and *demon*)   A reference to Satan; the term "Devil" is used as a proper noun only at Revelation 12:9 and 20:2; otherwise, it is a generic term, "devil, demon," meaning *deceiver, liar, slanderer* (Jn. 8:44).

dill   An annual herb of the parsley family whose leaves and aromatic seeds were used as a spice in foods and for medicinal purposes.

disciple   A follower or adherent of any teacher. John the Baptizer and Christ both had disciples.

dragon   In the OT a large sea creature or sea monster of some kind, at times symbolizing the enemies of God's people (Is. 51:9); in Revelation the "dragon" is Satan himself (12:9).

dropsy   A generalized accumulation of body fluids; edema. This affliction is only mentioned by Luke the physician (Lk. 14:2) and marks one of the several instances where he identifies a disease prevalent in NT times.

Drusilla   The youngest sister of Agrippa II and wife of Antonius Felix (governor of Judea, c. A.D. 52-59); see Acts 24:24-27.

elder   An OT term which often refers to the honored leaders of the tribes, towns, and villages of Israel. In Jesus' time they were leaders in the Sanhedrin and local synagogs and are often mentioned with the chief priests and scribes as Jesus' main opponents (Matt. 26:3, 4; Mk. 8:31; 14:43; 15:1). In the NT church "elders" were the leaders of local congregations, essentially equivalent to the "pastors" of today. "Elder" obviously denotes advancement in age, implying maturity *via* experience.

Elijah   One of the greatest prophets of the OT, who appeared in Israel at the time of a critical spiritual and political conflict involving the pagan Canaanite religion (1 Kgs. 17:1-2 Kgs. 2:11). Through a misunderstanding of Malachi 4:5, 6 the people of Jesus' day thought that

Elijah would return from his place in heaven (2 Kgs. 2:11) as the forerunner of the Messiah (Matt. 17:10), but Jesus explained that *Elijah* in this prophecy should be understood typologically as a reference to *John the Baptizer* (Matt. 11:14; 17:10-13; cf. Lk. 1:17).

Epicureans (see *Mars' Hill*)   Followers of the Greek philosopher Epicurus (341-270 B.C.), who believed that men should seek happiness as the highest good through an essentially conservative life-style. This life-style was to avoid excess in any area (even those considered "pleasurable") which could result in pain to body or soul. Essentially, Epicureans were materialists who denied the relevance of any divine powers in man's life. They also held that death involves no more than an untroubled non-existence. In his discourse before the Areopagus, the council that met on Mars' Hill, Paul's mention of God's judgment, along with the resurrection (Acts 17:18,31,32), would have offended Epicureans religiously as well as intellectually, since the fear of divine judgment was in their opinion one of the chief causes of man's troubled existence.

epileptic   One who is subject to seizures and fainting, popularly thought to be caused by the cycles of the moon. In the NT epilepsy is clearly distinguished from demon-possession (Matt. 4:24).

eunuch   An ambiguous term in both the Bible and ancient Near East; it may refer to (1) a castrated man or (2) a court official who may or may not have this condition.

fast   "*To abstain from food*" for a period of time for religious or personal reasons by an individual or a group. It may also refer to the period of time itself when this abstinence takes place. The first mention of *fasting* in the Bible is with Moses (Ex. 34:28), and, with the exception of the Day of Atonement, it appears to be only an occasional activity. Later in Israel's history its popularity grew into a regular religious practice. (Note the additional fast days listed in Zechariah 8:19; compare Esther 9:31.) By Jesus' time the pious were fasting regularly twice a week. In the best texts of the NT Jesus neither enjoins nor forbids fasting, but passages such as Mark 2:18-20 indicate that Christ's saving presence among His people (Matt. 28:20) now makes fasting (as a spiritual necessity) obsolete.

Felix   Roman governor of Judea (c. A.D. 52-59) before whom Paul made a defense (Acts 24); Tacitus, an ancient contemporary historian, writes that Felix "with savagery and lust... exercised the powers of a king with the disposition of a slave."

festival [feast]   A sacred season or holy day observed by God's decree.

Festus   Roman governor of Judea (c. A.D. 59-62); apparently an honorable man but under considerable pressure to accommodate the Jewish leadership of an increasingly rebellious Palestine (cf. Acts 25:9). Paul made a key legal defense before Festus and the visiting Jewish king, Agrippa II (Acts 25-26), before being sent to Rome, where he was probably acquitted (as anticipated by Acts 26:30-32).

forgive   "*To pardon or remit any claim or desire to give punishment*"; eternally speaking, "*to pardon human wrongdoing or sin completely and to receive no punishment.*"

frankincense (see *incense*)   A yellowish white resin obtained from a tree used as an aromatic ingredient in worship (cf. Ex. 30:34; Lev. 6:15). "Frankincense" is genuine or pure *incense*, the former serving as a base for the latter. Since frankincense was used as a symbol of *prayer* in OT worship (Ps. 141:2), the gift of the Wise Men may have been an indicator of Jesus' High Priestly office of intercession for His people (church).

fulfill   "*To carry out a promise or prediction.*" Many facts about Christ's life and NT events happened as the OT foretold them.

Gabbatha   An Aramaic name for a locality in Jerusalem whose meaning is uncertain. In John 19:13 Pilate pronounced the formal death sentence on Christ from this place.

Gabriel   An angel who served as God's messenger to Daniel in the OT (Dan. 8:16; 9:21) and in the NT to Zacharias (Lk. 1:11-20) and Mary (Lk. 1:26-38); with the exception of "Michael" (cf. Dan. 10:13,21; 12:1; Jude 9; Rev. 12:7), Gabriel is the only other angel mentioned by name in Scripture.

Galatia   Either (1) the ethnic kingdom in the north-central area of Asia Minor or (2) the larger Roman province containing the ethnic kingdom, plus other areas, in which a number of cities evangelized by Paul are found (Antioch, Iconium, Lystra and Derbe; see Acts 13-14). Scholars are evenly divided on which of these two "Galatias" is meant in Galatians 1:2.

gall, poison   Descriptive of a number of poisonous substances and bitter herbs often of uncertain identification; in Matthew 27:34 "gall" may have been a narcotic herb added to the wine which would work as a sedative. Jesus did not take it until His suffering was completed (cf. Jn. 19:28-30).

Gallio   Roman governor of Greece (A.D. 52-53) who presided over Paul's trial in Corinth (Acts 18:12-17); he was generally regarded by his contemporaries as a decent and just man. The date of his governorship is an important key for Pauline chronology.

Gamaliel   One of the most respected Jewish teachers in history; he represented a more tolerant and liberalizing trend within Pharisaism (cf. Acts 5:33-39); before becoming a Christian, Paul was one of Gamaliel's more zealous students.

generation, family history, genealogy   The varying translations of a Biblical term that correspond quite closely to parallel English usage. "Generation" is often used to refer to a given time period in the past, present, or future that covers the life span of the ancestors or descendants of a given individual or group of people (Matt. 11:16). It also refers to the extension and linking together of periods of time (Lk. 1:50). "Generation" can also refer to groupings of ancestors for purposes of communicating a certain idea (Matt. 1:17). Sometimes a period of *40 years* is referred to as the span of a *generation*, as based on Israel's wanderings (Josh. 5:6). Finally, "generation" is also used in a more general sense to describe a given type of people, such as an *evil* or *chosen* kind of people or generation (Matt. 12:39; 1 Pet. 2:9).

Gennesaret   An alternate name for the Sea of Galilee.

Gentiles, nations, people of the world   Terms used by Jews to describe people who are non-Jews.

glorify   With reference to the persons of the Godhead, *glorify* means "*to exalt, make glorious, honor*" God through the human life of the believer, that is, in line with the directives given in Scripture. Christ also *glorified* His Father through His own ministry, which was carried out in obedience to His Father's will (Jn. 17:4). In turn, He is *glorified* by His Father (Jn. 17:22, 24). Christ also *glorifies* His followers (Jn. 17:22) and is *glorified* by them (Lk. 17:18; 1 Cor. 6:20).

glory   Glory is a major Biblical concept with a variety of meanings. It may refer to the "honor" given to or proceeding from the Triune God, or it may be used to describe an object or person (Person) who reflects this glory (cf. Jn. 17:22, 24; Eph. 3:21; Josh. 7:19; 2 Cor. 3:7, 18). Jesus Christ is the perfect *Glory* of God who best reflects His Father's essence (Jn. 14:9,13). The *glorifying* of Jesus refers to His dying, rising, and ascension to heaven (Jn. 17:1-5). In John's Gospel Jesus is the "Glory" of God, having become flesh by living in the *tabernacle* of His own body (Jn. 1:14; cf. Is. 46:13). As such, Jesus is the ultimate *Shekinah* ("dwelling") of God. (*Shekinah* is the Jewish way of speaking of the *glory cloud* that led the people of Israel as a pillar of fire in the OT. It was Jesus Himself who had been in that cloud as we see from Exodus 14:19, and who in NT times showed Himself to the world, as is stated in Hebrews 1:1,2.)

Gomorrah (see *Lot*)   An ancient city which, together with Sodom, was destroyed by God because of its wickedness. These cities may have been located on a plain south of the Dead Sea, but with this sea expanding to the south over time, both locations would now be under water. Read Genesis 19:1-28 for more information, especially verses 24 and 25.

grave   See *HADES/GEHENNA* on page 540.

hades   See *HADES/GEHENNA* on page 540.

heaven   The place where God and His holy angels reside. All believers in Christ go to live in *heaven* for eternity after their existence on earth.

hell   See *HADES/GEHENNA* on page 540.

Hermes   A name twice used in Scripture: (1) in Romans 16:14 the name of a Christian; (2) in Acts 14:12 the name of a Greek god, known in mythology as the *messenger* of the gods.

Herod   Three people are called by this name in the NT: (1) Herod the Great, who tried to murder Jesus at His birth (Matt. 2:13); (2) Herod's son Antipas, who inherited his father's rule over Galilee (Herod's other sons, Archelaus and Philip, inherited other territories, cf. Matt. 2:22; Lk. 3:1) and was responsible for putting John the Baptizer to death (Matt. 14:1-12); and (3) Herod Agrippa I, the grandson of Herod the Great and persecutor of the Early Church (Acts 12:1-4).

Herodias   A granddaughter of Herod the Great; she married her uncle Philip (an ordinary citizen, not the Philip mentioned in Lk. 3:1), and after divorcing him, she married Philip's half-brother, Herod Antipas. John the Baptizer's denunciation of this marriage created intense hostility between John and Herodias, eventually leading to John's execution (cf. Mk. 6:17-28).

high priest   The priest who occupied the highest office in the Jewish priestly system and was president of the supreme council of the Jews (the Sanhedrin). Once a year (on the Day of Atonement) the high priest entered the Most Holy Place in the Tabernacle or Temple and offered up two sacrifices for sin: (1) for his own sins and those of his fellow priests and (2) for the sins of the people of Israel. Jesus is now our ultimate High Priest (see Heb. 3-10).

Holy Spirit (see *Comforter*)   The third person of the Godhead or Holy Trinity; also called the *Comforter* by Christ in His Farewell Address (Jn. 14-17).

homosexuals, those who sin sexually with others   Those who have sexual relations with persons of the same sex. Paul explicitly condemns this activity (Rom. 1:26, 27; 1 Cor. 6:9; 1 Tim. 1:10); Jesus (and also the rest of the NT) speaks against such sexual deviation under the general term "sexual sins" (Mk. 7:21), which by definition includes all sexual relations outside marriage.

hyssop   A small bushy plant, used in religious ceremonies to sprinkle liquids; its stems served as a brush (Ex. 12:22) and as a pole (Jn. 19:29).

I AM   An expression used in a series of statements by Christ, found in John's Gospel, which emphasizes His deity. Compare, for example, John 8:58 with Deuteronomy 32:39, Isaiah 43:13, etc. See also Exodus 3:14.

Illyricum   A Roman province north of Greece on the western part of the Balkan peninsula, approximately in the same area as modern Yugoslavia and Albania. Paul mentions Illyricum in Romans 15:19 as the westernmost extent of his missionary outreach.

incense (see *frankincense*)   A *mixture* of aromatic ingredients, of which *frankincense* was usually the base. "Incense" was burned to make a fragrant smoke in connection with OT worship (Lk. 1:9). The term can also be used of *sweet smoke* itself which was produced by such a mixture (Lev. 16:12). Christ and His work serve as a *fragrant smell* in the nostrils of the Father, thus blocking out the stench of sin (Eph. 5:2). In this way Jesus is our "Incense" before God.

Iscariot   There are several theories concerning the actual meaning of *Iscariot*: some have suggested "bag" (as in "Judas of the bag," since he carried the disciples' money), "strangling"

(since this is the way Judas died), "man from Kartan" (a town in Galilee), or more often, "dagger" (since Judas may have been a radical zealot or "dagger man"); all of these suggestions are based on Latin, Hebrew, or Aramaic words which sound something like *Iscariot*. The most prevalent (and probably correct) view held by scholars is that *Iscariot* is from the Hebrew "*ish Kerioth*," meaning "man of Kerioth"; "Kerioth," in turn, is probably a town in Judea a few miles south of Hebron (Josh. 15:25) or possibly in Moab (cf. Jer. 48:24).

Israel   The name given to Jacob in Genesis 32:28 when he wrestled with the Angel of the Lord (Jesus). "Israel" in a collective sense refers to Jacob's descendants (the Israelites); later it refers to the Northern Kingdom, its entire territory and people; and in the NT revealed sense it refers to all believers in Christ (the "New Israel," Rom. 9:6-8; 11:26).

Jerusalem   The city on Mount Zion. David made this city the capital of his kingdom, which included all twelve tribes of Israel. Spiritually, the term "Jerusalem" is used to describe *heaven* (Rev. 21:2).

Jesus Christ (see *Christ Jesus*)

Jesus, Savior   The predetermined name given to the Savior (Lk. 1:31; cf. Lk. 2:21); see Matthew 1:16 and its accompanying footnote "e."

Jew   See JEWS AND SAMARITANS on page 553.

judgment (see *Last Day*)   The evaluation of words or actions as to their conformity to God's laws of right and wrong and the consequent pronouncing of reward or punishment when these words and actions do or do not conform, respectively. Thus, "judgment" has both a negative and positive side. Since Scripture concludes that all people are sinners (Rom. 3:9-19, 23), Judgment Day would require punishment for all; but since Jesus kept the whole Law as mankind's Substitute and died for all as Substitute (Rom. 5:19; 2 Cor. 5:15), all believers in Jesus will be *judged* innocent and will therefore be rewarded with forgiveness and heaven, not on the basis of their own merits but because of Jesus' merits (Jn. 3:16; Rom. 3:28; 5:19; Jn. 5:28, 29, note that this last reference must be understood in the light of the other passages listed).

kingdom, Kingdom of heaven, Kingdom of God   Politically, the territory or realm of one's rule; the expression "Kingdom of heaven" or "Kingdom of God," as used in the Gospels, refers to the *rule* of Christ, whether presently in a person's heart (Lk. 17:21) or in the future at His Second Coming. In John's Gospel the receiving of "eternal life" (cf. Jn. 5:39) seems to mean much the same thing as does the phrase "enter the Kingdom of heaven" or "enter the Kingdom of God" in the Synoptic Gospels (Matt. 18:3); when John uses the term "Kingdom of God," it also seems to imply the concept of "eternal life" (cf. Jn. 3:5).

lamb   A young sheep. Lambs along with other animals were used in the Jewish sacrifices instituted by God. Christ is called the "Lamb of God" (Jn. 1:29).

Last Day   The Day of Judgment, when Christ will return to earth with His holy angels to judge the living and the dead.

law   See *NOMOS* on page 544.

leper   A person suffering from an infectious condition characterized by patches of skin discoloration. This skin abnormality was called *leprosy* but is not to be identified directly with modern leprosy (although it may be included here). Rather, Biblical leprosy involved a wide number of health problems affecting not only the skin (Lev. 13:1-46) but also clothing (Lev. 13:47-59) and even the walls of a house (Lev. 14:33-57). Jesus healed many lepers during His earthly minstry (Matt. 8:3; Lk. 17:12, 14). Such action was seen, in part, as proving that He was the Promised One from heaven (Matt. 11:5).

Levite   A man of the tribe of Levi chosen to assist the Jewish priests. "Levites" especially served in the area of *music* and as *guards* in connection with the Tabernacle/Temple (cf. Mk. 14:65).

linen wrappings   Pieces of linen cloth in which a dead body was wrapped. Jesus passed through such burial wrappings during His miraculous resurrection (Jn. 20:6-9).

LORD   Found in the OT portions of English Bibles as a translation of the Hebrew Name "*Yahweh*," the personal Name for God in the Hebrew OT. This is in keeping with the Greek NT which always translates "*Yahweh*" as "*Kyrios*," our English "Lord."

Lot   The nephew of Abraham. Lot seems to have valued material prosperity above the spiritual welfare of his family (cf. Gen. 13:10-13); this ultimately led to the loss of his wife (Gen. 19:26; Lk. 17:29,32) and to a fundamentally twisted relationship with his daughters (Gen. 19:31-36).

Macedonia   A Roman province covering approximately the northern half of modern Greece. Here Paul found some of his best and most responsive converts to the Christian message (cf. Acts 17:10-13; Phil. 1:3-5; 1 Thess. 1:2-10).

manna   Bread-like food that was miraculously provided for the Israelites in the wilderness (Ex. 16:14,31). Jesus calls himself the "Bread of Life" and says that unlike the manna of the OT, which gave people only a temporary relief from hunger, the "Bread" which He offers will give them eternal life (Jn. 6:48-58).

Mars' Hill   This translation of the Greek *Areopagus* is derived from "'the hill' (*pagos*) of 'Ares' (*Areios*)"; thus "Mars' Hill" since *Ares* and *Mars* were the Greek and Latin names, respectively, for the ancient god of war. This hill was located northwest of the Athenian Acropolis; there in ancient times a distinguished council met and, as a result, was itself also called the "Areopagus." By Paul's time the council usually assembled in the Athenian marketplace, which is probably where Paul's case was heard in Acts 17:16-34.

Messiah (see *Christ, Messiah*)

Michael   See MICHAEL THE ARCHANGEL on page 555.

mint   A garden herb used as a seasoning in foods.

Molech/Moloch   The national god of the Ammonites; his worship sometimes involved the sacrifice of children, a practice which at certain times infected Israel's history, even at the highest levels of her society (2 Chr. 28:3; 2 Kgs. 21:6; cf. 1 Kgs. 11:7; Acts 7:43).

Most Holy Place   The innermost room of the Tabernacle and Temple in which the ark of the covenant was kept. Only the high priest could enter this room and then only once a year on the Day of Atonement to offer sacrifices for himself, his fellow priests, and the people of Israel. See Diagram #1 on page 430.

Mount of Olives   A hilly ridge east of Jerusalem, running in a north-south direction, which witnessed the central events in Jesus' life during and after Passion week; compare 2 Samuel 15:30; Luke 22:39-44 (in both cases this mount witnessed the sorrow of God's two chosen ones, who were rejected by their people).

mustard   Probably the black mustard, whose tiny seeds produce a tree 10 feet or more in height.

myrrh   A sweet-smelling resin that was highly prized (cf. Matt. 2:11). It served as a medicine (Mk. 15:23) and was used by Jews in preparing bodies for burial. As one gift from the Wise Men (Magi), *myrrh* may have symbolized the coming burial of Christ (Matt. 2:11; Jn. 19:39).

name A word or group of words by which a person, thing, or class of things is known, called, or addressed. "Name" may also be used of some quality, characteristic, or description of a person or thing. In John 1:12 ("His Name") and Acts 5:41 ("NAME") this word stands for Christ Himself. See especially Isaiah 42:8; 48:11.

nard Any number of plants with heart-shaped leaves, small greenish-white flowers, and reddish berries; an ointment made from these roots. It was very expensive.

Nazarene A person from Nazareth (Hebrew meaning: "Branchtown," compare Matt. 2:23 with Is. 11:1 concerning Jesus); early Christians were also described by this term (Acts 24:5).

Nicolaitans A little known sect in the Early Church which apparently sought to accommodate the new Christian faith to the pagan practices and institutions prevalent in many cities in Asia Minor (cf. Rev. 2:1-6, 12-15); Christians were often under intense social pressure to make such accommodations (cf. 1 Pet. 1:6, 7; Rev. 2:13).

Nineveh A chief city of ancient Assyria; its ruins are next to modern Mosul in northern Iraq; Jesus mentions Nineveh as an example of repentance among pagans, which should have put His own generation in Israel to shame (Lk. 11:29-32; Jonah 3:10).

Nisan The first month of Israel's religious year, corresponding to March/April on our calendar (also called *Abib*). *Nisan* is the month in which Passover (14th) and the Festival of Unleavened Bread (15th-21st) were celebrated. As prophesied, Jesus was crucified and rose in the month of *Nisan* during the Passover season (Ex. 12:2-27; cf. Jn. 18:28, 39).

Noah (see *ark*) The last of the pre-Flood patriarchs; Jesus used the example of Noah's generation to warn all future Christians against the danger of being drawn into society's lack of concern for God's judgment (Matt. 24:36-44).

omega (see *alpha and omega*)

parable A method of teaching by which Jesus—through His use of illustrations from everyday life—describes the nature of God's Kingdom and His place within it. Often parables have a single, major point, the cumulative force of which is to call people to decide for or against the Savior, whose presence among men is at the very heart of the Kingdom's presence (cf. Mk. 3:22-27; 12:1-12; Lk. 11:14-23). It can be said that a *parable* uses earthly examples to convey spiritual meaning and truth; an earthly story with a Kingdom meaning.

Paradise A place to which the souls of God's people go immediately after death (Lk. 23:43; cf. 16:19-31). Paul believed that he had been taken there, but he did not know if this was an out-of-body experience or whether he also was there physically (2 Cor. 12:1-4). The Septuagint (LXX), the Greek translation of the Hebrew OT, translates the Hebrew word for "garden," as in *Garden* of Eden, with this same Greek word translated "paradise." Jesus was, therefore, saying to the criminal on the cross, "Today you will be with Me in the garden" (Lk. 23:43). Thus, paradise regained!

paralytic A person who is lame or unable to move parts of the body.

parchments The skins of animals, used as one type of writing material in ancient times; compare 2 Timothy 4:13 and its accompanying footnote.

Passover, Festival of One of the three major festivals of the Hebrews (cf. Ex. 23:14, 15; Deut. 16:16). God instituted it to commemorate their deliverance from Egyptian slavery (Ex. 12:13, 14); the angel of death killed the first-born in the Egyptian homes but *passed over* the Hebrew houses (Ex. 12:23-27). Jesus died on Passover Day (Jn. 19:14). The Jews still celebrate *Pesach*, as they call it.

Paul (see *Saul*) Famous NT apostle whose name was changed from the Hebrew *Saul* to the Greek *Paulos*; this name change fit his calling to be the "Apostle to the Gentiles" (Acts 9:15;

cf. Acts 9:29b; Gal. 1:16). (Note: The international language of the Gentiles in Paul's day was Greek, the language which Paul also spoke.)

Pentecost One of the three major festivals (cf. Deut. 16:16; Acts 2:1) celebrated by Israel from the time of Moses onward; it was held on the 50th day after Passover, originally as a day of joy and thanksgiving for God's bounty.

Pharaoh The rulers of Egypt, regarded as divine by their subjects.

Pharisees (see ***Sadducees***) The religious faction which came into existence some 100 years before Christ's time and with whom Jesus found Himself in greatest conflict. Much of Jesus' ministry was directed against the Pharisaic view that people are saved by human compliance to the Law of Moses. The Pharisees stood as champions for the ordinary people (against the aristocracy) and for pure religion (against the doctrinal errors and ecclesiastical manuverings of the Sadducees); however, the Pharisees put a severe overemphasis on *tradition* (Matt. 15:9). Such practice led to an emphasis on the outward, rather than on inward spirituality. Its end result was *pride.* This has led to the modern saying, "You little pharisee!" (cf. Lk. 12:1). But it should be said that Pharisees, in general, sought to live a pure, non-hypocritical life. Their basic problem lay in that they thought they could accomplish what only Christ really could do (Gal. 2:15,16).

Pilate The governor of Judea (A.D. 26-36) under whom Jesus was put to death. The NT makes it clear that Pilate did not believe that Jesus was a political rival to Roman power (Matt. 27:15-23; Mk. 15:6-15; Lk. 23:13-16; Jn. 19:1-6,12).

potter One who shapes vessels from clay, which are then hardened for use through the process of baking.

pray *"To speak to God,"* thereby praising Him, asking Him for something, or thanking Him.

prophet A person chosen by God to proclaim God's word to His people. In the OT a prophet was mainly a spokesman for God (*forthteller*), but on many occasions he also foretold (as a *foreteller*) events which would occur in the future; as such, he was a messenger who dealt with the past, present, and future as this related to God's covenantal relationship with His people. The NT prophets edified God's people by communicating Jesus' word to the various conditions and situations of the church (as do pastors, teachers, evangelists, etc., today). For this, they often need and receive special insight from God's Spirit (1 Cor. 14:30). However, their work must always be scrutinized by the church in the light of apostolic teaching (1 Cor. 14:29, 36-38; 15:1, 2), since the character of their work is often mixed, immature, or false (cf. 1 Cor. 1:4-7 with 3:1-3).

rabbi An authorized teacher of the Jewish religion who decides questions concerning the interpretation of OT Law and ritual.

reaper A person who cuts and harvests grain.

Red Sea This can refer to (1) the Bitter Lakes or perhaps Lake Timsah, where God divided the sea for Israel to cross over (Heb. 11:29), (2) the Gulf of Aqaba (1 Kgs. 9:26), or (3) the Gulf of Suez (Num. 33:10,11).

resurrection The state of having been revived and brought back from the dead.

righteousness "Uprightness" or "equity"; in Paul's thought, the primary emphasis is on *righteousness* as God's divine attribute of "sinless perfection" (a righteousness possessed only by God Himself) which He—by His grace or undeserved love—places upon sinful individuals through faith in Jesus Christ and thereby declares them to be fully righteous and holy in His sight (Rom. 1:16,17), despite the fact that in our own conduct and spirituality, we never attain

to this level of perfection (Phil. 3:9-12). It is simply the way God looks at us, as He views us through His Son Jesus and His substitutionary work of keeping the Law in our behalf and of dying and rising for our sins.

rue   An herb used as a spice in food and medicinally as an antiseptic.

Sabbath   The seventh day of the week, from sundown Friday to sundown Saturday; under the "Sabbath" commandment of the Sinai Covenant, God's people were expected to rest, not work, during this time period.

Sadducees   A small, wealthy, and aristocratic group of religious and political leaders, many of whom were priests, whose power was centered in the Temple and Sanhedrin at Jerusalem. In one sense they were "conservative," since they resisted the innovations (the "tradition of the elders," cf. Mk. 7:5-8), which added to and even altered Mosaic Law, but in Jesus' view they also misrepresented (perhaps under a Hellenistic/Epicurean influence) the most basic aspects of OT teaching (Mk. 12:24). This may be why Jesus supported the doctrinal leadership of the Pharisees (Matt. 23:1-3), despite His disagreements with them (Matt. 23:13-26), against the rival claims of the Sadducees and other groups at that time who, in another sense, were very "liberal" in their denials of doctrines, such as *resurrection* (Mk. 12:18; Acts 23:6-9).

salvation   A rescue from sin, death, and damnation through the atoning work of Christ. "Salvation" is derived from the word *save*.

Samaritan   A native of the territory of Samaria, the region between Galilee and Judea. Samaritans accepted only the Five Books of Moses and rejected the Temple of Jerusalem as the proper place of worship (cf. Jn. 4:19-21). Even though they traced their lineage to Jacob and had much in common with the Jews, there was a strong hostility between them and the Jewish community at the time of Christ (see JEWS AND SAMARITANS on page 553).

Sanhedrin   The chief religious and political ruling body of the Jews at the time of Jesus, composed of 71 members (possibly 72 when including its *nasi* or president) from the Sadducees and leading Pharisees. It was allowed considerable power by Rome over Jewish affairs, although Rome always reserved the right of final approval, especially in cases of capital punishment (cf. Jn. 18:31).

Satan   The proper name or title of the leader of the evil angels; compare its Hebrew meaning "accuser" in Zechariah 3:1 with Revelation 12:10.

Saul (see *Paul*)   Two very significant personages have this name on the pages of Scripture: (1) Israel's first king (1 Sam. 9-31); (2) Saul who became the Apostle Paul (Acts 7:58b; 9:1-30; 13:9).

scorpion   Related to the spider; it is 4 to 5 inches long with 4 pairs of legs and an upward curving tail at the end of which is a stinger capable of inflicting a painful and sometimes deadly wound.

Scripture(s)   A reference in the NT to the OT books that had been given by inspiration of the Holy Spirit (2 Tim. 3:15). In the church today the term encompasses all the books of the Bible, OT and NT.

serpent   A snake which may or may not be venomous. Under God's sovereignty it may bring either destruction (Num. 21:6) or salvation (Num. 21:8; cf. Jn. 3:14). Depending on a context of faith or unbelief, it can be *symbolic* either of a God-given intelligence (Matt. 10:16) or of a devilish and destructive cleverness (Matt. 23:33; cf. Gen. 3:1); ultimately, it becomes symbolic for Satan himself (Rev. 12:9), who with demonic brilliance is able to deceive the entire world because of its rejection of the call to repentance and faith in Jesus as Lord (Rev. 9:20,21).

GLOSSARY

sheepfold An enclosure for sheep.

shepherd A person who tends sheep; Jesus calls Himself the Good Shepherd (Jn. 10:11) of His people, who like sheep would certainly perish without His protection.

sickle A sharp, curved tool for harvesting grain.

sin In the synoptic Gospels and throughout the NT, especially 1 John, "sin" (as either a noun or verb) refers to a definite and often deliberate act of transgression against God's Law. This was its primary meaning in Jewish circles at Jesus' time and was often used by Him in this sense (Lk. 15:18, 21; 17:3; Jn. 5:14; 9:2, 3; cf. 1 Jn. 3:4). *Sin* is also seen in the NT as a defective condition in man (Rom. 3:20-23; Jn. 9:41; 1 Jn. 1:8) or (especially in Paul's epistles) as a negative "power" dwelling within him (Rom. 7:17,20) from which even the most dedicated Christian cannot free himself. In this sense the Christian cannot avoid sin, although he is no longer dominated by it (Rom. 6:14). However, the Christian does continually fall short of God's glory throughout life (Rom. 3:23). "Sin," in the first sense mentioned above, that is, as a clear and deliberate offense against a Biblical standard of conduct, is not to be a part of a Christian's manner of life. When this is the case, that is, when a person lives a life of murder, adultery, hatred, theft, etc., that person's life-style and claim to be a Christian is unacceptable (Matt. 7:16; 1 Cor. 6:9-11; cf. 1 Cor. 5:1-13; Gal. 5:19-21; 1 Jn. 3:4-10).

Sodom (see *Gomorrah*)

Solomon's porch The eastern side of the colonnade which ran along the outside edge of the Temple area within the walls; in these covered walkways the moneychangers had their booths, and scribes instructed their students.

Son of David A Messianic title (cf. Mk. 10:47, 48), since the Messiah was to be a descendant of King David (Jn. 7:42; Mk. 12:35-37).

Son of God A title understood by Jesus' contemporaries as a kingly designation (Jn. 1:49), but it was used by Christ to emphasize His special relationship to His heavenly Father and the divine status this implies (Jn. 5:17, 18; 10:36). Compare John 19:7-12, in which Jesus' accusers seem to make use of both meanings above: (1) the claim to deity, which was a basis for condemnation under Jewish Law (Jn. 10:33; 19:7); (2) the claim to kingship, which put one in conflict with Roman law (Jn. 19:12).

Son of Man The term "Son of Man" was used by Jesus concerning every phase of His ministry. Unlike the title "Messiah," the name "Son of Man" did not carry secular, political connotations with it in Jesus' day. Though this "Son of Man" designation had full Messianic implications in Daniel 7:13, 14, its meaning had been hidden from the minds of the people. Thus, it had remained a *neutral* term which Jesus was able to apply to virtually every phase of His ministry. For example, He associated it with His suffering and death (Mk. 9:30-32) and ultimately used it to identify Himself with the Person of Daniel 7 (Mk. 13:26; 14:62). For Jesus, "Son of Man" was a "revealing/concealing" term.

spices Aromatic oils or salves especially used in preparing a corpse for burial (Jn. 19:40).

Stoics (see *Mars' Hill*) Followers of a Greek philosophy begun by Zeno (335-263 B.C.). Stoics viewed the universe as determined by a kind of cosmic Reason, but not the result of chance events over which one might exercise some control; true happiness and peace of mind, therefore, could be attained only through a clear *knowledge* of this order and an acceptance of one's place in it, even if this entails personal difficulty and pain. Their reaction to Paul was one of amusement (Acts 17:18); they regarded him as offering only "scraps of learning," since he based his ethical views on the belief that God personally intervenes in human affairs (cf. 1 Cor. 1:18) and not on a rational, systematic philosophy.

sulfur A non-metallic element, often found in a yellow, crystalline form, which burns easily and is associated in the Bible with God's judgment (Lk. 17:29; Rev. 9:18).

synagog A building or place used by the Jews for worship and religious instruction, probably originating in the Babylonian Exile at the time of Ezekiel. By the first century A.D. synagogs are found in the Jewish dispersion throughout the Roman world and the Near East.

Tabernacle The tent-like portable sanctuary which served as the center of Israelite worship before Solomon built the Temple at Jerusalem (Ex. 26). See Diagram #1 on page 430. Jesus became the ultimate Tabernacle (see Jn. 1:14 and its accompanying footnote "e"; Rev. 21:2, 3).

tassels Objects placed on the four corners of the outer garment as commanded by God (Num. 15:37-39); they served as reminders of Israel's religious obligations. By Jesus' time they had become vehicles of religious pride (Matt. 23:5).

Temple Any of three buildings successively built on the eastern side of Jerusalem on Mount Moriah (2 Chr. 3:1): (1) Solomon's Temple (1 Kgs. 6), (2) the post-exilic second Temple (Ezra 3); and (3) the Herodian Temple (begun 19 B.C. and finished A.D. 64; cf. Matt. 24:1, 2). Jesus and the Lord God Almighty have become our ultimate Temple (Jn. 2:19-21; Rev. 21:22).

testament See *DIATHEKE* on page 531.

Theophilus The person to whom Luke dedicated his two books (Lk. 1:1; Acts 1:1). It is unlikely that the expression "most excellent Theophilus" is a symbolic title referring to all Christian readers (Theophilus means "friend of God"), since the first Christians regularly avoided honorific forms of address when speaking to each other (cf. Matt. 23:8-10).

Tiberias, Sea of Another name for the Sea of Galilee.

Tiberius Roman emperor from A.D. 14-37; he is the ruler referred to in Luke 3:1.

tomb A cave or cavity cut in rocks for the burial of the dead.

truth A primary attribute of God. Jesus identifies Himself with the truth (Jn. 14:6) and promises a knowledge of the truth, given by the Spirit (Jn. 16:13), to those who continue in His word (Jn. 8:32).

tunic A loose, gown-like inner garment worn under a cloak or coat by men and women in ancient Greece, Rome, and Palestine.

Unleavened Bread, Festival of One of the three major Hebrew festivals (Deut. 16:16), celebrated from the 15th through the 21st of *Abib* (March/April) in conjunction with Passover (14th of *Abib*). During this period, no yeast (leaven) was to be used.

vineyard Land devoted to the cultivation of grapevines.

vow A binding promise to God to do or not do something; such "vows" were carried out on the basis of religious dedication to God or in thankful response for His divine favor. Jesus strongly warned against false or insincere vows (Matt. 5:33-37); note that the "vow" taken by Paul in Acts 18:18 (cf. 21:23, 24) was no more than a temporary religious exercise, aimed perhaps at breaking down resistance to the Gospel among his countrymen (1 Cor. 9:20).

winnowing shovel A fork-like shovel, used to throw grain with its mixture of chaff into the wind; the heavier grain would fall back to the threshing floor, while the light chaff would be blown away.

witchcraft [divination, magic, fortune-telling] A human, Satan-guided, practice of seeking to look into the future or of obtaining information otherwise inaccessible, either through an inner spiritual awareness (e.g., a trance) or by consulting the stars, entrails of sacrificial animals, ghosts, etc. With few exceptions, this kind of activity is strongly condemned in Scripture (Deut. 18:9-14; Is. 47:12-15; Jer. 10:1, 2; Gal. 5:20; Rev. 21:8).

worship *"To show religious devotion or reverence to a deity."* Christian *worship* is centered in God's love for us as seen in the cross of His Son Jesus.

yoke A heavy wooden frame joining two draft animals together to enable them to pull together smoothly. In a symbolic sense, God's people in their life under the Sinai Covenant are described as being under a burdensome "yoke" of Law (Acts 15:10; Gal. 5:1; cf. "under the Law" in *NOMOS* on p. 544). Jesus, on the other hand, teaches that His leadership will not be a matter of authoritarian domination and subordination but one of gentleness and lowliness, which His people are to emulate (Matt. 11:29,30).

zeal Eager devotion and ardent enthusiasm for a cause.

Zeus The leading Greek god in mythology.

Zion The hill located in the southeast corner of Jerusalem; in poetic form it often stands for the entire city.

Zion, daughter(s) of This phrase occurs 24 times in the OT and twice in the Gospels. It is a poetic synonym in the singular for the city of Jerusalem (Lam. 1:6); in the plural (4 times) the phrase stands for the inhabitants of the city, maybe men and women in Isaiah 4:4, certainly its female residents in Isaiah 3:16,17, and Christians in general in Song of Solomon 3:11.

GWN ABRIDGED CONCORDANCE

This concordance is provided as a useful tool for studying the Scriptures. Most of the key word entries were chosen on the basis of the more common and frequently quoted verses. Also included for the benefit of many are a few of the well-known King James terms which are cross-referenced with updated GWN terminology. Proper *NAMES* and *PLACES* are found in separate listings at the end of the main concordance.

All key word entries are in alphabetical order. Each is followed by selected references and the corresponding context phrases containing the key word. The key word within the phrase is abbreviated to the first letter of the word which appears in boldface type, for example, "blessed" would appear as "**b**." If the key word entry is a phrase (e.g., **SON OF MAN**), only the first word appears abbreviated and the rest of the phrase is written out. For the sake of simplicity, the quoted context phrase of a reference contains no punctuation of any kind.

WORDS

"A" AND THE "Z"
Rev 21:6 I am the **A** and the **Z**
ABBA
Rom 8:15 by which we call out **A** Father
"ABC"
Heb 5:12 teach you the **ABC**'s of God's word
ABILITY
Acts 2:4 Spirit gave them the **a** to speak
1 Cor 3:5 the Lord gave him the **a**
ABLE
Lk 1:37 nothing that God will not be **a** to
ABOMINABLE
Tit 1:16 are **a** disobedient and not fit
1 Pet 4:3 the **a** worship of idols
ABOMINATION
Mk 13:14 see the devastating **a** standing
Rev 17:4 filled with **a** and unclean things
ABOVE
Col 3:1 be eager for the things that are **a**
ABSENCE
1 Cor 16:17 have made up for your **a**
ABSOLUTE
Jn 1:51 I tell you the **a** truth you will see
Jn 3:3 tell you the **a** truth Jesus answered
Jn 5:19 tell you the **a** truth Jesus answered
Jn 6:26 tell you the **a** truth Jesus answered
Jn 8:34 tell you the **a** truth Jesus answered
Jn 10:1 tell you the **a** truth the man who
Jn 12:24 tell you the **a** truth if a kernel
Jn 13:16 tell you the **a** truth a slave is no
Jn 14:12 tell you the **a** truth the person
Jn 16:20 tell you the **a** truth you will cry
Jn 21:18 tell you the **a** truth when you were
ABUSE
Heb 13:13 bear the **a** He suffered

1 Pet 2:23 When others **a** Him He did not **a**
2 Pet 2:11 angels . . . do not condemn and **a**
ACCEPT
Acts 2:41 who **a** what he said . . . baptized
Rom 11:15 when God **a** them what can it mean
Rom 14:18 who serves Christ . . . is **a** by God
1 Cor 2:14 person does not **a** things
1 Cor 15:1 Gospel . . . which you **a**
2 Cor 8:12 for God **a** a person's gift
Col 2:6 just as you **a** Christ Jesus as your
1 Thess 2:13 you **a** was not the word of men
1 Tim 4:9 you can . . . **a** absolutely
ACCORDING
Rom 2:6 every person **a** to what he has done
Rev 2:23 I will give each of you **a** to what
ACCOUNT
Matt 10:18 On My **a** you will be brought
Rom 14:12 have to give an **a** of himself
1 Pet 4:5 will have to give an **a** to Him
ACCUSATION
1 Tim 5:19 not accept **a** against a pastor
ACCUSE
Matt 12:10 something of which to **a** Him
Rom 2:15 either **a** them . . . or defend them
Rom 8:33 Who will **a** those God has chosen
1 Cor 1:8 no one can **a** you of anything
Rev 12:10 the one **a** them before our God
ACCUSER
Matt 5:25 so that your **a** may not hand you
ACQUITTED
Matt 12:37 By your words you will be **a**
ACT
Rom 14:23 Any **a** that is not based . . . is sin
1 Cor 3:3 flesh and **a** like other people
1 Cor 7:36 man thinks he is **a** improperly

Gal 4:12 **a** as I did because I am **a**
ACTION
1 Jn 3:18 let us put our love into **a**
ACTIVE
Gal 5:6 faith that is **a** in love
Jas 2:22 his faith was **a** with works
ADD
Matt 6:27 Can any of you **a a** single hour
Acts 2:41 day about 3000 persons were **a**
Gal 3:19 was **a** to point out trespasses
2 Pet 1:5 to your faith **a** excellence
Rev 22:18 if anyone **a** anything to this
ADDRESSED
Acts 2:14 Peter stood up . . . and **a** them
ADMINISTRATION
Eph 3:2 the **a** of His grace toward you
ADMIRED
2 Thess 1:10 **a** by all who . . . believe
ADOPTED
Rom 8:15 spirit of God's **a** children
Gal 4:5 we might be **a** as . . . sons
ADORNMENT
1 Tim 2:9 Their **a** is not a matter of
ADULTERER
Matt 5:32 marries a divorced woman . . . an **a**
ADULTERESS
Matt 5:32 her to be looked upon as an **a**
Rom 7:3 will be called an **a** if she lives
ADULTERY
Matt 5:28 **a** with her in his heart
Matt 15:19 out of heart come . . . **a**
Matt 19:9 divorces his wife except for **a**
Mk 7:21 people's hearts come . . . **a**
Mk 10:11 marries another he is living in **a**
Jn 8:4 woman who had been caught in **a**
ADVANCE
2 Cor 9:5 arrange in **a** this promised
ADVANTAGE
Rom 3:1 what is the **a** then of being a Jew
1 Cor 10:33 by not continuing to seek my **a**
ADVISER
Rom 11:34 who has become His **a**
AFFLICTION
Col 1:24 am enduring whatever **a** of Christ
AFRAID
Matt 8:26 Why are you **a** He asked them
Matt 10:28 Stop being **a** of those who kill
Matt 28:5 Don't be **a** any longer
Mk 11:18 They were **a** of Him
Mk 16:8 because they were **a**
Lk 2:10 Stop being **a** the angel said
Lk 12:32 Don't be **a** any longer . . . flock
Jn 14:27 Do not let your heart be . . . or **a**
Acts 18:9 Stop being **a**
Rom 13:3 do not . . . be **a** of those who rule
1 Cor 16:10 not have to be **a** while he is
Gal 4:11 I am **a** for you that the hard work
AGAINST
Matt 6:12 have forgiven those who sin **a** us
Matt 12:30 who is not with Me is **a** Me
Mk 9:40 Anyone who is not **a** us is for us

Mk 11:25 if you have anything **a** anyone
Lk 15:21 I have sinned **a** heaven and **a** you
Acts 4:26 join their forces **a** the Lord
Rom 8:31 If God is for us who can be **a** us
2 Cor 13:8 cannot do anything **a** the truth
1 Pet 3:12 Lord is **a** those who do wrong
AGREE
Mk 14:56 their statements did not **a**
Rom 7:16 I **a** that the Law is good
1 Cor 1:10 I urge you all to **a**
2 Cor 13:11 **A** with one another
AGROUND
Acts 27:41 They struck a bank . . . ship **a**
AHEAD
Matt 21:31 into Kingdom of God **a** of you
Mk 1:2 I am sending My messenger **a** of You
Mk 13:11 do not worry **a** of time about
AIMED
Mk 12:12 they knew His parable was **a**
AIR
1 Thess 4:17 to meet the Lord in the **a**
ALARMED
Matt 2:3 he became **a** and all Jerusalem
Matt 24:6 See that you do not become **a**
2 Cor 7:11 how **a** you were
2 Thess 2:2 become **a** either by a spirit
ALERT
Eph 6:18 be **a** and keep at it continually
ALIVE
Matt 4:4 will not be kept **a** by bread
Acts 1:3 convincing proofs that He was **a**
Rom 8:11 will make your dying bodies **a**
1 Cor 15:22 in Christ all will be made **a**
ALL
Mk 14:23 And they **a** drank of it
Rom 5:12 death spread to **a** people since **a**
2 Cor 5:15 died for **a** that those who live
ALLELUIA
Rev 19:1 **A** Salvation and glory and power
ALLEYS
Lk 14:21 streets and **a** of the city
ALLOW
Acts 28:16 Paul was **a** to live by himself
1 Cor 14:34 women . . . are not **a** to speak
1 Tim 2:12 I do not **a** a woman to teach
ALMIGHTY
Rev 1:8 the One-Who-Will-Be the **A**
ALONE
Matt 4:4 not be kept alive by bread **a**
Mk 2:7 Who but God **a** can forgive sins
Mk 7:33 from the crowd to be **a** with him
ALPHA
Rev 1:8 I am the **A** and the Omega
ALREADY
Mk 15:44 Has He died **a**
ALTAR
Matt 5:24 leave gift there before the **a**
Acts 17:23 found an **a** with the inscription
Heb 9:4 golden **a** of incense and the ark
Rev 6:9 under the **a** souls of those killed

ALWAYS

2 Tim 3:7 are **a** learning and never able
Heb 7:25 He **a** lives to pray for them

AM

Matt 26:64 Jesus answered him I **a**
Jn 8:58 before Abraham . . . I **A**

AMAZED

Matt 7:28 crowds were **a** at His teaching
Matt 8:27 men were **a** and asked
Matt 12:23 people were all **a**
Mk 11:18 He **a** all the people with His
Lk 2:48 parents saw Him they were **a**
Lk 5:9 were **a** to see fish they had caught
Lk 9:43 All were **a** to see God's wonderful
Acts 2:7 **A** and wondering they asked
Acts 3:10 They were very . . . **a** to see

AMBASSADORS

Lk 14:32 he sends **a** to ask for terms
2 Cor 5:20 we are **a** for Christ

AMBITION

Jas 3:14 selfish **a** in your hearts

AMBUSH

Acts 25:3 laying an **a** to kill him

AMEN

1 Cor 14:16 say **A** to your prayer of thanks
Rev 3:14 The **A** the Witness who is faithful

AMONG

Matt 18:20 together in My Name I am **a** them

ANCESTOR

Acts 2:29 our **a** David died and was buried
Rom 9:5 they have the **a** and from them
Gal 1:14 become for the traditions of my **a**
Heb 7:10 He was still in the body of his **a**

ANCHOR

Heb 6:19 we have this hope like an **a**

ANCIENT

Lk 9:19 one of the **a** prophets
2 Pet 2:5 He did not spare the **a** world

ANGEL

Matt 1:20 an **a** of the Lord appeared to him
Matt 4:6 He will order His **a** to help you
Matt 4:11 devil left Him and **a** came
Matt 18:10 their **a** in heaven always see
Matt 25:31 glory and all the **a** with Him
Matt 28:2 **a** of the Lord came . . . from heaven
Mk 1:13 and the **a** took care of Him
Lk 2:9 **a** of the Lord appeared to them
Lk 9:26 He shares with . . . holy **a**
Lk 16:22 **a** carried him to Abraham's side
Acts 7:30 **A** appeared to him in the flames
Acts 10:3 saw an **a** of God come to him
Acts 12:7 an **a** of the Lord stood near him
Acts 27:23 For an **a** stood by me last night
Rom 8:38 neither **a** nor rulers
1 Cor 6:3 we will judge **a**
1 Cor 10:10 the **a** of death destroyed them
1 Cor 11:10 under authority . . . for the **a**
1 Cor 13:1 languages of men and of **a**
2 Cor 11:14 Satan . . . masquerades as an **a**
Gal 1:8 but even if we or an **a** from heaven
Gal 3:19 was given through **a** by the hand

Col 2:18 false humility and worship of **a**
1 Tim 3:16 in spirit Was seen by **a**
Heb 1:4 He became . . . better than **a**
Heb 1:14 are not all **a** spirits who serve
Heb 2:7 You made Him lower than the **a**
Heb 13:2 this is how some entertained **a**
1 Pet 1:12 of which the **a** long to catch
1 Pet 3:22 where **a** rulers and powers
2 Pet 2:4 God did not spare **a** who sinned
2 Pet 2:11 even **a** although they are greater
Jude 6 **a** who did not keep their position
Rev 1:20 seven stars are the **a** of the
Rev 2:12 **a** of the church in Pergamum
Rev 7:1 after this I saw four **a** standing
Rev 10:1 I saw another mighty **A** come down
Rev 14:6 saw another **a** flying in mid-heaven

ANGER (see also WRATH)

Rom 1:18 **a** of God is being revealed
Eph 2:3 We deserved God's **a** just like
Eph 5:6 these sins bring God's **a**
Col 3:6 bring down the **a** of God
Col 3:8 rid of all such things as **a** fury
1 Tim 2:8 so I want the men . . . without **a**
Rev 15:7 golden bowls full of the **a** of God

ANGRY

Matt 5:22 anyone who is **a** with his brother
Eph 6:4 do not make your children **a**
Heb 3:10 I was **a** with those people
Heb 3:17 With whom was He **a** forty years
Jas 1:20 **a** person does not do what is right

ANIMALS

Mk 1:13 He was there with the wild **a**
Acts 10:12 all kinds of four-footed **a**
1 Cor 15:32 I have fought with wild **a**
1 Cor 15:39 **a** have another
2 Pet 2:12 like unthinking **a** they

ANNOUNCE

Lk 4:19 to **a** an acceptable year
1 Pet 1:12 **a** to you the things of which

ANNOYED

Lk 13:14 leader was **a** with Jesus

ANOINT

Matt 6:17 when you fast **a** your head
Lk 4:18 He **a** Me to preach the
Acts 4:26 against the Lord . . . against His **A**
Acts 10:38 God **a** Jesus from Nazareth
2 Cor 1:21 and also has **a** us
Heb 1:9 by **a** You with the Oil of Joy

ANOTHER

Jn 13:34 a new commandment Love one **a**
Rom 7:4 died to the Law to marry **A**—Him
Gal 1:6 turning to **a** kind of gospel

ANSWER

Matt 5:21 Whoever murders must **a** for it
2 Cor 5:12 you can **a** those who boast

ANTICHRIST

1 Jn 2:18 heard that an **a** is coming
1 Jn 4:3 spirit of the **A** which you have

ANXIOUSLY

Lk 2:48 See how **a** Your father and I

ANYTHING
Jn 14:14 If you ask Me for **a** in My Name
ANYONE
2 Cor 5:17 if **a** is in Christ
APART
Rom 3:21 from Him—a righteousness **a** from
Rom 3:28 justified by faith—a **a** from works
APOSTLE
Acts 1:2 Spirit to the **a** whom He had chosen
Acts 2:42 hold firmly to teaching of the **a**
1 Cor 1:1 Paul called as an **a** of Christ
1 Cor 12:28 God has appointed . . . **a** next
2 Cor 11:5 any way less than your super **a**
Gal 1:1 Paul an **a** not sent from men
Eph 2:20 foundation of the **a** and prophets
Eph 4:11 He gave some to be **a**
APOSTOLIC
Rom 1:5 holding the **a** office
APPEAL
Acts 25:12 You **a** to Caesar
Rom 12:1 I **a** to you fellow Christians
Phlm 10 My **a** to you concerns my child
1 Pet 5:1 I **a** to you pastors I who also
APPEAR
Acts 7:2 God of glory **a** to our father
Acts 7:35 help of the Angel who **a** to him
2 Cor 5:10 We must all **a** before judgment
Col 3:4 will **a** with Him in glory
1 Tim 3:16 He **a** in flesh
Heb 9:24 to **a** now before God for us
1 Pet 1:7 Jesus Christ **a** again
APPEARANCE
Mk 12:40 to put on a good **a**
APPOINT
Mk 3:14 He **a** twelve to be with Him
Jn 15:16 I chose you and **a** you to go
Acts 10:42 warn them that God has **a** Him
Rom 8:29 first He also **a** long ago
Eph 1:11 **a** us long ago in Christ and chose
1 Thess 5:9 God did not **a** us to be
1 Tim 1:12 Lord . . . **a** me to do His work
Tit 1:5 I left you behind . . . to **a** pastors
APPRECIATE
1 Thess 5:12 **a** the men who work with you
APPROVAL
Gal 1:10 say this now to win the **a** of men
Phlm 14 not . . . do anything without your **a**
Heb 11:2 men of long ago won God's **a**
APPROVE
Acts 8:1 Saul also **a** putting him to death
Rom 1:32 but **a** of others who do them
Rom 14:18 accepted by God and **a** by people
Rom 14:22 in regard to anything he **a**
1 Cor 16:3 have you **a** some men and I will
2 Tim 2:15 as one whom He **a**
ARAMAIC
Jn 5:2 in **A** is called Bethesda
Jn 19:13 Stone Pavement or Gabbatha in **A**
Jn 19:17 Skull . . . in **A** is called Golgotha
Jn 19:20 notice . . . was written in **A**
Jn 20:16 Rabboni she said to Him in **A**

Acts 6:1 against those who spoke **A**
Acts 21:40 spoke to them in **A**
ARCHANGEL
1 Thess 4:16 with the voice of the **a**
Jude 9 **a** Michael was debating with devil
ARGUE
Acts 6:9 rose up to **a** with Stephen
Rom 14:1 do not **a** about different opinions
1 Cor 11:16 anybody means to **a** about this
ARGUMENT
2 Cor 10:5 With them we tear down **a**
1 Tim 6:4 craving for debates and **a**
2 Tim 2:23 foolish and unintelligent **a**
Tit 3:9 keep away from foolish **a**
ARK
Heb 11:7 respected God and built an **a**
1 Pet 3:20 when God waited . . . while the **a**
Rev 11:19 the **A** of His COVENANT was seen
ARMS
Mk 9:36 put His **a** around him
ARMOR
Rom 13:12 put on the **a** of light
Eph 6:11 Put on God's whole **a**
ARMIES
Rom 9:29 If the Lord of **a** [hosts] had not
AROMA
2 Cor 2:16 to some an **a** of death
ARRESTED
Acts 12:1 King Herod **a** some members of
ARROWS
Eph 6:16 all the flaming **a** of the Evil One
ASHES
Matt 11:21 repented . . . in sackcloth and **a**
ASHAMED
Lk 9:26 whoever is **a** of Me and My words
Lk 14:9 Then you will feel **a**
Rom 1:16 For I am not **a** of the Gospel
1 Cor 6:5 I say this to make you feel **a**
2 Cor 9:4 you will make us . . . feel **a**
2 Thess 3:14 he will feel **a**
2 Tim 1:8 So do not be **a** to witness about
Tit 2:8 anyone who opposes us will be **a**
Heb 11:16 God is not **a** to be called
1 Pet 3:16 will feel **a** of their slander
1 Pet 4:16 do not feel **a** but praise God
ASK
Matt 5:42 If someone **a** for anything give
Matt 21:22 Whatever you **a** for in prayer
Mk 10:35 You to do for us whatever we **a**
Mk 11:24 anything you **a** for in prayer
Lk 11:13 give the Holy Spirit . . . **a** Him
Jn 14:13 will do anything you **a** in My Name
Jn 14:14 you **a** Me for anything in My Name
Jn 17:20 I am not **a** for them only but also
Jas 1:6 **a** in faith having no doubts
1 Jn 5:14 if we **a** for . . . according
ASLEEP
1 Cor 15:6 Some have fallen **a** in death
1 Thess 4:13 those who fall **a**
ASSIGNED
1 Cor 7:17 the life that the Lord **a** to him

ASSOCIATE
1 Cor 5:9 not to **a** with those who live
2 Thess 3:6 not to **a** with any Christian
ASSURING
Acts 18:5 solemnly **a** the Jews
ATHLETE
Col 1:29 struggling like an **a** by His power
ATONING
1 Jn 2:2 He is the **a** sacrifice
ATONEMENT COVER
Rom 3:25 Displayed Him as the **A** Cover
Heb 9:5 overshadowing the **a** cover
ATTACHED
Lk 15:15 went and **a** himself to . . . citizens
ATTACK
Acts 18:12 Jews united in an **a** on Paul
ATTENDANT
Lk 4:20 gave it back to the **a** and sat
ATTENTION
Matt 28:20 teaching them to pay close **a**
Jas 2:3 and you give special **a** to the one
ATTITUDE
Phil 2:5 have the same **a** that Christ Jesus
1 Pet 4:1 arm yourselves with the same **a**
AUTHOR
Acts 3:15 You killed the **A** of life
AUTHORITY
Matt 7:29 He taught them with **a**
Matt 9:6 Son of Man has **a** on earth
Matt 10:1 twelve disciples and gave them **a**
Matt 28:18 All **a** has been given to Me
Mk 1:22 one who had **a**
Mk 3:15 to have **a** to drive out demons
Mk 11:33 by what **a** I am doing these things
Acts 25:5 you who have the **a** come down
1 Cor 11:10 head to show she is under **a**
Eph 6:12 against the powers against the **a**
1 Tim 2:12 have **a** over a man
Tit 2:15 correct with full **a**
1 Pet 2:13 Be subordinate to every human **a**
Rev 13:7 was given **a** over every tribe
AVENGE
Acts 7:24 He **a** the man who was mistreated
Rom 12:19 I alone have the right to **a**
1 Thess 4:6 the Lord **a** all these things
AVENGER
Rom 13:4 it is God's servant an **a**
AWAIT
Gal 5:5 eagerly **a** by faith that hope
AWAKE
1 Thess 5:10 whether we are **a** or asleep
AWARE
Heb 4:1 We should be **a** of the situation
AWE
Acts 2:43 **A** came on everybody

BABBLE
Matt 6:7 pray do not **b** like the Gentiles
BABY
Lk 1:44 greeting the **b** leaped with delight
Lk 2:7 She wrapped Him in **b** clothes

1 Cor 3:1 people of world as **b** in Christ
Eph 4:14 we will not be **b** any longer
1 Pet 2:2 like newborn **b** thirst for
BABYLON
Rev 14:8 great **B** has fallen
Rev 18:2 great **B** has fallen
BACKS
2 Pet 2:21 turn their **b** . . . holy commandment
BAD
Matt 6:23 if your eye is **b** your whole body
BAG
Matt 10:10 nor a **b** for the way
BALANCE
2 Cor 8:13 we want to strike a **b**
BANDAGED
Lk 10:34 He went to him and **b** his wounds
BANKERS
Matt 25:27 should have invested . . . with **b**
BANQUET
Rev 19:17 together for great **b** of God
BAPTISM
Lk 3:3 preached the **b** of repentance
Acts 19:4 baptized with **b** of repentance
1 Cor 10:2 **b** in the cloud and in the sea
Eph 4:5 one Lord one faith one **b** one God
Col 2:12 you were buried with Him in **b**
1 Pet 3:21 same way also **b** now saves us
BAPTIZE
Matt 3:11 **b** you with water to bring about
Matt 3:13 at the Jordan . . . to be **b** by him
Matt 28:19 make disciples . . . **b** them in Name
Mk 1:4 should repent and be **b**
Lk 3:21 being **b** Jesus was **b** also
Jn 1:25 Why then do you **b** if you are not
Jn 1:28 Bethany . . . where John was **b**
Jn 1:31 I came and **b** with water to show
Jn 10:40 where John had been **b** earlier
Acts 1:5 will be **b** with the Holy Spirit
Acts 2:38 Repent and be **b** every one of you
Acts 2:41 who accepted what he said were **b**
Acts 8:36 to keep me from being **b**
Acts 9:18 He got up and was **b**
Acts 10:47 keep them from being **b**
Acts 16:15 she and her family were **b**
Acts 18:8 who heard . . . believed and were **b**
Acts 19:4 **b** with baptism of repentance
Acts 22:16 be **b** and have your sins washed
Rom 6:3 all of us who were **b** into Christ
1 Cor 1:14 I did not **b** any of you except
1 Cor 12:13 In one Spirit . . . were **b**
1 Cor 15:29 are **b** for the benefit of dead
Gal 3:27 all of you who were **b** into Christ
BARBARIAN
Col 3:11 there is no . . . **b** Scythian slave
BARLEY
Jn 6:9 boy here who has five **b** loaves
BARNS
Matt 6:26 reap or gather into **b**
BARRIER
1 Thess 2:18 Satan placed a **b** in our way

BATTLE
1 Cor 14:8 call who will get ready . . . **b**
BEAR
1 Cor 10:13 way out so that you can **b** it
1 Cor 13:7 It **b** everything believes
Col 3:13 **b** with one another and forgive
BEAST
Rev 13:1 And I saw a **b** coming up out of
BEAT
1 Cor 9:27 I **b** my body and make it
BEAUTIFUL
Acts 7:20 Moses was born and was a **b** child
Rom 10:15 How **b** are the feet of those
BEAUTY
1 Pet 3:3 your **b** be something outward
BECOME
Rom 6:16 who obey God and **b** righteous
1 Thess 1:6 and you **b** imitators of us
Phlm 10 Onesimus who **b** my son
Heb 2:17 He had the obligation to **b** like
Rev 2:8 who died and **b** alive
BEFORE
Mk 13:10 **B** the end comes Gospel must be
Jn 17:24 You gave Me . . . **b** the world was
Eph 1:4 **B** He made the world His love
Col 1:17 He was **b** everything and He holds
2 Tim 1:9 Jesus **b** the world began
BED
Jn 5:11 Pick up your **b** and walk
Acts 9:34 Get up and make your **b**
BEG
Matt 18:26 bowing low before him **b**
Mk 5:18 the demons **b** Jesus to let
Lk 15:28 father came out and **b** him
Acts 3:2 so that he could **b** for gifts
2 Cor 12:8 Three times I **b** the Lord
BEGGAR
Mk 10:46 a blind **b** was sitting by the road
Lk 16:20 **b** by the name of Lazarus was laid
2 Cor 6:10 as **b** but making many rich
BEGGARLY
Gal 4:9 so weak and **b** and be willing
BEGINNING
Mk 10:6 the **b** He made them male and female
Jn 1:1 In the **b** was the Word . . . with God
Jn 15:27 you have been with Me from the **b**
Col 1:18 He is the **B** first from the dead
2 Thess 2:13 in the **b** God chose you
Heb 1:10 Lord in the **b** You laid foundation
1 Jn 1:1 That which was from the **b**
BEGOTTEN
Acts 13:33 You are My Son today I have **b**
Heb 1:5 today I have **b** You
BEHALF
2 Cor 1:11 thank God on our **b** for the gift
Col 1:24 in **b** of His body the church
BEHAVE
Tit 2:3 **B** . . . fitting for holy women
BEHAVIOR
1 Tim 3:2 pastor . . . good judgment and fine **b**

BEHEAD
Mk 6:16 John whom I **b**
Lk 9:9 Herod said I **b** John
BEHIND
Lk 2:43 Jesus stayed **b** in Jerusalem
Phil 3:13 forget what is **b** reach for what
BEING
Col 1:19 His whole **B** live in Him
Heb 1:3 He . . . is the perfect copy of His **B**
BELIEVE
Matt 8:13 Go . . . Let it be as you **b**
Matt 9:28 Do you **b** that I can do this
Matt 18:6 one of these little ones who **b**
Matt 21:32 but you did not **b** him
Mk 5:36 to be afraid Only **b**
Mk 11:22 **B** in God Jesus answered them
Mk 16:11 been seen by her they did not **b**
Mk 16:16 He who **b** and is baptized . . . saved
Lk 1:20 you did not **b** what I said
Lk 8:13 They **b** for a while
Lk 22:67 you will not **b** Me
Lk 24:25 **b** everything the prophets said
Jn 2:11 His disciples **b** in Him
Jn 2:23 many **b** in His Name when
Jn 3:16 who **b** in Him would not perish
Jn 3:36 who **b** in the Son has everlasting
Jn 4:42 We no longer **b** because of
Jn 10:38 you do not **b** in Me **b** in My works
Jn 10:42 And many **b** in Him there
Jn 11:25 The person who **b** in Me will live
Jn 14:1 **B** in God and **b** in Me
Jn 14:10 **b** that I am in the Father
Jn 16:31 Jesus answered them Do you now **b**
Jn 17:20 through their word will **b** in Me
Jn 19:35 the truth so that you also will **b**
Jn 20:25 hand in His side I will never **b**
Jn 20:29 have not seen and still have **b**
Jn 20:31 things are written that you may **b**
Acts 6:7 priests came to **b** and obey
Acts 10:43 everyone who **b** in Him receives
Acts 13:39 Everyone who **b** in this Jesus
Acts 15:7 that they would hear it and **b**
Acts 16:31 **B** in the Lord Jesus . . . and you
Acts 17:31 everyone a good reason to **b**
Acts 17:34 Some men joined him and **b**
Acts 20:21 turn from sin to God and to **b**
Acts 24:14 **b** everything written in the Law
Rom 1:16 save everyone who **b** it
Rom 3:22 comes from God to all who **b**
Rom 4:3 Abraham **b** God and it was credited
Rom 4:11 was to be the father of all who **b**
Rom 9:30 righteousness . . . is received by **b**
Rom 10:4 righteousness to everyone who **b**
Rom 10:9 **b** that in your heart that God
Rom 10:11 Anyone who **b** in Him
Rom 14:23 live according to what he **b**
Rom 16:26 lead them to **b** and obey
1 Cor 13:7 **b** everything hopes for
1 Cor 15:11 this is what you **b**
2 Cor 4:13 I **b** and so I spoke
2 Cor 13:5 to see whether you really **b**

Gal 2:16 but only by **b** in Jesus Christ
Gal 3:26 you are all God's children by **b**
Eph 1:15 I heard how you **b** in Lord Jesus
Phil 1:29 not only to **b** in Christ but also
1 Thess 4:14 we **b** that Jesus died and rose
2 Thess 1:10 by all who have come to **b**
Phlm 5 I hear how you **b** in the Lord Jesus
Heb 3:19 come there since they did not **b**
Jas 2:19 demons also **b** that—and shudder
1 Pet 2:6 the person who **b** in Him
Jude 5 destroyed those who did not **b**

BELIEVERS
Acts 4:32 group of **b** was one in heart
Rom 8:27 He is pleading for the **b** [saints]
1 Cor 6:1 not before the **b**
1 Cor 6:2 that **b** will judge the world
Gal 6:10 especially to our family of **b**
Col 1:1 to the **b** and faithful brothers

BELONG
Mk 9:41 because you **b** to Christ
Rom 8:9 Spirit of Christ does not **b** to Him
1 Cor 1:12 I **b** to Paul or I **b** to Apollos
1 Cor 3:23 you **b** to Christ . . . Christ to God
1 Cor 6:19 You do not **b** to yourselves
2 Cor 10:7 that we **b** to Christ just as he

BELT
Acts 21:11 He came to us took Paul's **b**
Eph 6:14 having truth as a **b** fastened

BENEFICIAL
1 Cor 10:23 but not everything is **b**

BENEFIT
Rom 11:28 treated as enemies for your **b**
Phil 1:24 for your **b** it is more necessary

BESIDES
Mk 12:32 there is no other **b** Him

BEST
1 Cor 12:31 I will show you . . . the **b** way

BETRAY
Matt 10:21 A brother will **b** his brother
Matt 26:16 looking for a chance to **b** Him
Matt 26:23 the one who will **b** Me
Matt 26:24 woe . . . the Son of Man is **b**
Matt 26:25 Judas the one who was **b** Him
Matt 26:45 the Son of Man is being **b**
Matt 26:46 here comes the one who is **b** Me
Matt 27:4 have sinned by **b** innocent blood
Mk 13:12 brother will **b** his brother
Lk 21:16 friends will **b** you and kill
1 Cor 11:23 Lord Jesus . . . night He was **b**

BETTER
Matt 5:20 righteousness is much **b** than
Matt 5:29 It is **b** for you to lose a part
Rom 14:5 One person thinks one day is **b**
1 Cor 12:31 Eagerly desire the **b** gifts
Phil 2:3 think of others as being **b** than

BEWARE
Matt 7:15 Always **b** of false prophets
Mk 12:38 **B** of the scribes
Lk 20:46 **B** of the scribes

BEWILDERED
Mk 16:8 they were trembling and **b**

BEWITCHED
Gal 3:1 Who has **b** you—you who saw Jesus

BEYOND
1 Cor 4:6 not to go **b** what Scripture says

BIND
Matt 27:2 they **b** Him led Him away
Col 3:14 love which **b** it all together

BIRDS
Matt 6:26 Look at the **b** in the air
1 Cor 15:39 **b** have another
Rev 19:17 saying to all **b** flying

BIRTH
Acts 3:2 cripple from his **b**
Gal 4:19 I am suffering **b** pains for you
Jas 1:15 it gives **b** to sin and when sin

BITS
Jas 3:3 If we put **b** into the mouths

BITTER
Rev 10:9 it will be **b** in your stomach

BLAMELESS
Phil 3:6 keeping the Law I was **b**
1 Thess 2:10 holy righteous and **b**
1 Tim 3:2 pastor must be **b** the husband

BLANKET
Heb 1:12 You will roll them up like a **b**

BLASPHEME
Matt 26:65 the high priest . . . said He has **b**
1 Tim 1:20 teach them not to **b**
2 Tim 3:2 they will **b** they will disobey

BLASPHEMOUS
Rev 13:5 proud and **b** things and he was

BLASPHEMY
Jn 10:33 not for a good work but for **b**

BLAZING
Matt 20:12 who have endured . . . the **b** heat

BLESS
Mk 10:16 laid His hands on them and **b** them
Lk 1:30 God has chosen to **b** you
Lk 24:50 He raised His hands and **b** them
Heb 7:1 He **b** Abraham
Heb 11:21 Jacob **b** each of Joseph's sons

BLESSED
Matt 5:3 **B** are those who are poor in
Mk 14:61 Are You Christ Son of the **B** One
Lk 1:48 people will call me **b**
Lk 11:28 **b** are those who continue . . . God's
Lk 14:15 **B** is he who will eat bread
Jn 12:13 **B** is He who is coming in the Name
Jn 13:17 you are **b** if you do them
Jn 20:29 **B** are those who have not seen and
Acts 3:25 in Your Descendant all . . . be **b**
Rom 9:5 is God over everything **b** forever
Gal 3:8 Through you all nations will be **b**
1 Tim 1:11 Gospel of the **b** God
Rev 14:13 **B** are the dead who die in the
Rev 20:6 **B** and holy is he who shares
Rev 22:7 **B** is the one who keeps the words

BLESSING
1 Pet 3:9 speak a **b** instead

BLIND
Matt 9:27 two **b** men followed Him

Matt 11:5 **B** people see . . . lame are walking
Mk 8:22 There people brought a **b** man
Mk 10:46 a **b** beggar was sitting by road
Jn 9:1 He saw a man who had been **b**
Jn 10:21 demon cannot open . . . eyes of the **b**

BLOOD
Matt 9:20 woman who had . . . a flow of **b**
Matt 27:6 it is **b** money
Lk 13:1 Galileans whose **b** Pilate
Lk 22:20 cup is the new . . . testament in My **b**
Jn 1:13 born not of **b** nor of an urge of
Jn 6:53 Son of Man and drink His **b**
Jn 19:34 immediately **b** and water came out
Acts 15:20 eat anything strangled or any **b**
Acts 18:6 Your **b** be on your own heads
Acts 20:28 church . . . bought with His own **b**
Rom 3:25 Cover through faith in His **b**
Rom 5:9 Now that His **b** has justified us
1 Cor 10:16 communion with the **b** of Christ
1 Cor 11:25 cup is . . . testament in My **b**
1 Cor 11:27 against Lord's body and **b**
1 Cor 15:50 flesh and **b** cannot have share
Eph 1:7 paid our ransom price with his **b**
Col 1:20 peace made by the **b** of His cross
Heb 2:14 He also took on flesh and **b**
Heb 9:13 sprinkling the **b** of goats and
Heb 9:14 much more will the **b** of Christ
Heb 9:20 This is the **b** of the covenant
1 Jn 1:7 the **b** of Jesus His Son washes us
1 Jn 5:6 He who came by water and **b**
Rev 5:9 with Your **b** You bought us
Rev 7:14 made them white in the **b** of Lamb
Rev 16:3 turned to **b** like . . . of a dead man
Rev 17:6 drunk . . . the **b** of the witnesses

BLOT
Jude 12 They are a **b** on your love meals

BLOW
Matt 6:2 to poor don't **b** your own horn
Jn 3:8 wind **b** where it pleases

BLUSH
Rom 6:21 things that make you **b** now

BOAST
Rom 11:18 do not **b** of being more than
1 Cor 1:29 keep anyone from **b** before God
1 Cor 9:15 let anyone take away my **b**
2 Cor 11:16 fool and also **b** a little
Gal 6:13 that they can **b** of what was done
Eph 2:9 so no one may **b**
Phil 2:16 I can **b** on the Day of Christ

BOAT
Matt 4:21 were in the **b** with their father
Matt 8:23 Jesus stepped into a **b**
Lk 5:2 Jesus saw two **b** on the shore

BODILY
Lk 3:22 down on Him in **b** form

BODY
Matt 5:29 better . . . lose part of your **b**
Matt 10:28 those who kill the **b** but cannot
Lk 22:19 This is My **b** which is given
Acts 2:26 even My **b** will rest in hope
Rom 8:13 kill the activities of the **b**

Rom 12:1 your **b** as a living sacrifice
1 Cor 6:13 **b** is not for sexual sin
1 Cor 7:4 cannot do . . . likes with her **b**
1 Cor 9:27 beat my **b** and make it my slave
1 Cor 10:16 communion with the **b** of Christ
1 Cor 11:29 without recognizing Lord's **b**
1 Cor 12:12 the **b** is one and yet has many
1 Cor 15:35 what kind of **b** will they have
2 Cor 12:2 whether in his **b** or outside it
Gal 6:17 I bear on my **b** the scars of Jesus
Eph 1:23 which is His **b** completely filled
Eph 3:6 inheritance belong to the same **b**
Eph 4:4 There is one **b** and one Spirit
Eph 5:28 their wives . . . like their own **b**
Phil 3:21 who will change our humble **b**
Col 1:18 Head of church which is His **b**
Col 2:9 In Him that is in His **b** lives all
Heb 3:17 **b** dropped dead in wilderness
Heb 10:5 You prepared a **b** for Me
1 Pet 2:24 carried our sins in His **b**
1 Pet 4:1 Christ has suffered in His **b**
1 Pet 4:2 no longer live . . . in the **b**
Jude 8 with their dreams defile the **b**

BOLD
Rom 15:15 parts of which are rather **b**
2 Cor 10:1 but **b** toward you when I am away

BOLDLY
Acts 4:13 surprised to see how **b** they
Eph 3:12 we have confidence and can **b** come
Heb 4:16 let us come **b** to throne of grace
Heb 10:19 can now go **b** into the MOST HOLY

BOLDNESS
Acts 4:29 speak Your word with all **b**

BONES
Lk 24:39 A ghost does not have flesh and **b**
Jn 19:36 None of His **b** shall be broken

BOOK
Mk 12:26 read in the **b** of Moses
Jn 20:30 signs . . . not written in this **b**
Jn 21:25 would not have room for the **b**
Acts 1:1 first **b** Theophilus I wrote about
Acts 19:19 gathered their **b** and burned
Phil 4:3 whose names are in the **B** of Life
Rev 3:5 his name out of the **B** of Life
Rev 13:8 of the world in the **B** of Life
Rev 20:12 book was opened--the **B** of Life

BORN
Matt 1:18 This is how Jesus Christ was **b**
Lk 1:35 Holy Being to be **b** of you will be
Lk 2:11 Savior . . . Christ the Lord was **b**
Jn 1:13 **b** not of blood nor of an urge
Jn 3:3 if anyone is not **b** again he cannot
Jn 3:5 not **b** of water and the Spirit
Jn 3:8 it is with everyone **b** of the Spirit
1 Cor 15:8 who was like one **b** unexpectedly
Gal 2:15 we were **b** Jews and not Gentile

BORROW
Matt 5:42 wants to **b** anything from you

BOTHER
2 Cor 11:9 I did not **b** anyone to help me

BOTTOMLESS
Lk 8:31 order them to go into the **b** pit
BOUND
Acts 21:13 ready not only to be **b**
1 Cor 7:15 Christian man or woman is not **b**
1 Cor 7:39 A wife is **b** to her husband
BOUNDARY
Acts 17:26 **b** within which they live
BOW
Matt 9:18 official . . . **b** down before Him
Matt 14:33 men in boat **b** down before Him
Jn 19:30 He **b** His head and gave up His
Rev 4:10 the 24 elders **b** down before Him
BOWLS
Rev 15:7 seven golden **b** full of the anger
BOY
Matt 2:16 kill all the **b** in Bethlehem
Rev 12:5 birth to a Son a **B** who . . . rule
BRAG
2 Tim 3:2 they will **b** and be proud
BRANCHES
Jn 15:5 I am the Vine you are the **b**
Rom 11:17 if some of **b** have been broken
BRANDED
1 Tim 4:2 whose consciences have been **b**
Rev 13:16 to be **b** on their right hands
BRAVE
Rom 5:7 a person might be **b** enough to die
BREAD
Matt 4:4 not be kept alive by **b** alone
Matt 6:11 give us today our daily **b**
Matt 26:26 Jesus took **b** . . . This is My body
Lk 22:19 Jesus took **b** spoke a prayer
Jn 6:5 Where should we buy **b** for these
Jn 6:26 you have eaten of the loaves of **b**
Jn 6:31 He gave them **b** from heaven to eat
Jn 6:34 Lord always give us this **b**
Jn 6:35 I am the **B** of Life Jesus told them
Jn 6:41 I am the **B** that came . . . from heaven
Jn 6:58 This is the **B** that came down
BREAK
Lk 9:16 He . . . **b** them and kept giving
Jn 5:18 He was not only **b** the Sabbath
Jn 19:32 soldiers came and **b** the legs
Jn 19:36 None of His bones shall be **b**
Acts 2:42 **b** of the bread . . . to the prayers
Acts 21:13 crying and **b** my heart
Rom 2:23 by **b** the Law you are dishonoring
Rom 4:15 no Law there is no **b** of the Law
1 Cor 11:24 He gave thanks **b** it and said
Jas 2:10 person is guilty of **b** all of it
BREAKFAST
Jn 21:12 Jesus told them Come have **b**
BREASTPLATE
Eph 6:14 righteousness covering you as a **b**
1 Thess 5:8 faith and love as a **b**
BREATH
Jn 20:22 He **b** on them and said
Acts 17:25 gives everyone life and **b**
2 Thess 2:8 will destroy . . . with the **b**

BREED
2 Tim 2:23 you know they **b** quarrels
BRIDE
Rev 21:9 I will show you the **b** the wife
BRIDEGROOM
Matt 9:15 friends of the **b** cannot mourn
Jn 3:29 One who has the bride is the **B**
BRIGHT
Matt 28:3 He was as **b** as lightning
BRING
1 Cor 15:1 Gospel which I **b** to you
1 Thess 4:14 in the same way God will **b**
1 Tim 6:7 we did not **b** anything into the
1 Pet 3:18 Christ died . . . to **b** us to God
BROAD
Matt 7:13 way is **b** . . . leads to destruction
Eph 3:18 can grasp how **b** and long and high
BRONZE
Rev 1:15 His feet were like glowing **b**
Rev 2:18 whose feet are like glowing **b**
BROTHER
Matt 4:18 saw two **b** Simon called Peter
Matt 5:22 anyone who is angry with his **b**
Matt 5:23 your **b** has something against you
Matt 10:21 A **b** will betray his **b** to death
Matt 18:15 If your **b** sins against you go
Matt 18:21 how often shall I forgive my **b**
Matt 25:40 you did for one of My **b** here
Matt 28:10 Go tell My **b** to go to Galilee
Mk 3:35 My **b** and sister and mother
Mk 13:12 A **b** will betray his **b** to death
Lk 16:28 for I have five **b**
Jn 20:17 But go to My **b** and tell them
Acts 9:17 **B** Saul the Lord sent me
Heb 2:11 He is not ashamed to call them **b**
1 Jn 3:15 who hates his **b** is a murderer
1 Jn 4:20 does not love his **b** . . . cannot
BUILD
Matt 7:24 had sense enough to **b** his house
Lk 14:28 wants to **b** a tower
1 Cor 3:12 someone **b** on this foundation
2 Cor 13:10 the Lord gave me to **b** you up
Heb 3:4 every house is **b** by someone
Jude 20 while you **b** yourselves up
BUILDER
Heb 3:3 as the **b** of a house is honored
BUILDING
Mk 13:1 those magnificent stone **b**
1 Cor 3:9 You are God's field God's **b**
Eph 2:21 in Him the whole **b** is fitted
BULL
Rev 4:7 second like a young **b**
BURDEN
Matt 11:28 carrying a heavy **b**
2 Cor 11:9 I kept myself from being a **b**
Gal 6:2 Help one another bear these **b**
1 Tim 5:16 not allow them to become a **b**
Rev 2:24 I am putting no other **b** on you
BURDENSOME
1 Jn 5:3 His commands are not **b**

BURIAL
Matt 8:28 came out of **b** places and met Him
Jn 12:7 Let her do it for day of My **b**
BURN
1 Cor 7:9 better to marry than to to **b**
1 Cor 13:3 give up my body to be **b**
Rev 8:7 third of the earth was **b** up
Rev 16:8 allowed to **b** people with fire
BURNT OFFERINGS
Mk 12:33 more than all **b** offerings and
BURST
Matt 9:17 the skins **b** the wine runs out
BURY
Jn 19:40 Jewish custom of **b** the dead
Acts 2:29 ancestor David died and was **b**
1 Cor 15:4 He was **b** and He was raised on
Rom 6:4 into His death we were **b** with Him
BUSH
Mk 12:26 in the passage about the **b**
Acts 7:30 flames of a burning **b**
BUSINESS
Jn 2:16 My Father's House a place of **b**
Acts 19:25 a fine income from this **b**
1 Thess 4:11 mind your own **b** and to work
BUSY
1 Tim 5:10 if she . . . **b** doing every kind of
BUSYBODIES
2 Thess 3:11 not doing any work . . . being **b**
BUY
Acts 20:28 church of God . . . He **b** with
1 Cor 6:20 you were **b** with a price
Rev 5:9 with Your blood You **b** us
Rev 18:11 no one **b** their loads of goods

CALF
Acts 7:41 the time they made a **c**
CALL
Matt 9:12 I did not come to **c** righteous
Matt 10:1 Jesus **c** His twelve disciples
Acts 2:21 And everyone who **c** on the Name
Acts 2:39 all whom the Lord our God will **c**
Acts 22:16 **c** on His Name be baptized
Rom 1:6 who have been **c** to belong to Jesus
Rom 8:28 whom He **c** according to His plan
1 Cor 1:2 **c** to be holy with all
1 Cor 14:8 trumpet does not sound clear **c**
Gal 5:13 You were indeed **c** to be free
Eph 4:1 whom God has **c**
2 Thess 1:11 will make you worthy of His **c**
2 Thess 2:14 He **c** you by the Gospel
2 Tim 1:9 He saved us and **c** us to be holy
CALLOUS
Eph 4:19 Having become **c**
CANCEL
Matt 18:27 freed him and **c** his debt
Rom 3:31 Do we then by faith **c** the Law
Gal 3:17 null and void and so **c** its promise
CANCER
2 Tim 2:17 talk will spread like a **c**
CAPTAIN
Matt 8:5 a **c** came to Him and begged Him
Matt 27:54 the **c** and those watching Jesus

Acts 10:1 man by the name of Cornelius a **c**
CAPTIVATE
2 Tim 3:6 make their way into homes and **c**
CAPTURE
Eph 4:8 He took captive those who had **c** us
CARE
Matt 27:4 What do we **c** That's your problem
Mk 4:38 Teacher don't You **c**
Lk 10:35 Take **c** of him he said and anything
Acts 20:28 Take **c** of yourselves . . . flock
1 Pet 5:7 He **c** for you
CAREFUL
Matt 6:1 **c** not to do your good works before
Mk 1:44 Be **c** not to say anything to anyone
Mk 13:33 Be **c** and watch because you
1 Cor 8:9 be **c** or the weak may fall
1 Cor 10:12 be **c** that he does not fall
Eph 5:15 Be very **c** then as to how you live
Col 2:8 Be **c** or someone will capture you
CARELESS
Matt 12:36 give an account of every **c** word
CARNELIAN
Rev 4:3 and like a **c** stone
CARPENTER
Matt 13:55 Isn't He the **c** son
CARRY
Matt 4:6 they will **c** you in their hands
Matt 8:17 took . . . our sicknesses and **c** our
Mk 14:13 meet a man **c** a jar of water
CASE
1 Cor 6:1 when one of you has a **c** against
CASTRATE
Gal 5:12 who upset you would **c** themselves
CATCH
Matt 14:31 stretched out His hand and **c**
Lk 5:4 let down your nets for a **c**
Lk 5:5 worked hard all night and **c** nothing
Lk 5:10 you are going to **c** men
Gal 6:1 person is **c** in the trap of some sin
CAUSE
Matt 5:30 your right hand **c** you to stumble
CELEBRATE
Lk 15:23 and let's eat and begin to **c**
1 Cor 5:8 Let us then **c** our festival
Col 2:15 He **c** His victory in Christ
CENSER
Rev 8:3 another angel with a golden **c** came
CENSUS
Lk 2:1 ordered that a **c** be taken of whole
CENT
Matt 10:29 two sparrows sold for a **c**
CERTAIN
Rom 5:9 we are even more **c** that He will
CERTAINLY
Matt 17:25 **C** he answered
Matt 27:54 **C** this was the Son of God
Rom 6:2 **C** not We died to sin
1 Cor 14:25 God is **c** here among you
CHAIN
Mk 5:3 any longer not even with a **c**
Acts 9:2 back to Jerusalem in **c**

Acts 9:14 put in c . . . who call on Your Name
Acts 12:6 Peter bound . . . two c was sleeping
Phil 1:13 that I am in c for Christ
Col 4:18 I am in c Grace be with you
Rev 20:1 and a large c in His hand

CHANCE

Gal 6:10 we have a c let us do good

CHANGE

Matt 3:11 bring about a c of heart
Matt 21:29 Later he c his mind and went
Matt 21:32 not . . . c your mind and believe
Jn 4:46 Cana . . . where He . . . c water to wine
Rom 5:11 given us this c relationship
Rom 11:29 God never c His mind
1 Cor 15:51 we shall all be c
2 Cor 1:17 when I say yes or no it never c
Gal 1:7 c the Gospel [Good News] of Christ
Phil 3:21 who will c our humble bodies
2 Tim 2:25 Perhaps God will c their hearts
Heb 6:17 that He would not c His plan
Heb 7:21 Lord has sworn and will not c His

CHARGE

Mk 3:21 they went to take c of Him
Acts 6:3 put them in c of this work
2 Tim 4:1 I solemnly c you Preach the word
Phlm 18 or owes you anything c it to me
Heb 3:6 a Son in c of God's house

CHARIOT

Acts 8:29 Go over to that c and stay close

CHASM

Lk 16:26 wide c fixed between us and you

CHEEK

Matt 5:39 anyone slaps you on your right c

CHEER

Matt 9:2 C up son Your sins are forgiven
Mk 10:49 C up Get up He's calling for you
Phil 2:19 news about you that will c me up
1 Thess 5:14 c . . . those who are discouraged
2 Tim 1:16 Onesiphorus . . . often c me up

CHEERFUL

2 Cor 9:7 God loves a c giver

CHEERFULLY

Rom 12:8 people in need let him do it c

CHEST

Jn 13:25 leaning over . . . against His c

CHILD

Matt 1:18 she was found to be with C
Lk 2:5 fiancee who was going to have a c
Jn 16:21 When woman is giving birth to a c
1 Cor 13:11 when I was a c I used to talk

CHILDHOOD

2 Tim 3:15 since c you have known the

CHILDISH

1 Cor 14:20 not be c in use of your minds

CHILDREN

Matt 5:9 make peace . . . called the c of God
Matt 11:16 They are like little c sitting
Matt 11:25 revealing them to little c
Matt 17:25 collect toll . . . from their c
Matt 23:37 often I wanted to bring your c
Mk 7:27 First let the c eat all they want

Lk 3:8 God can raise c for Abraham
Lk 11:13 know enough to give your c good
Jn 1:12 gave the right to become c of God
Acts 2:39 promise is made to you and . . . c
Rom 4:19 could not have c anymore
Rom 9:7 are for that reason his real c
2 Cor 12:14 c are not obligated to save
Gal 3:26 you are all God's c by believing
Eph 6:1 C obey your parents in the Lord
1 Thess 5:5 you are all the c of light
1 Tim 2:15 women . . . be saved as they have c
1 Jn 2:12 I am writing to you little c
1 Jn 3:1 we are called God's c and
2 Jn 4 happy to find some of your c living

CHOICE

Lk 10:42 Mary has made the right c
2 Cor 8:17 coming to you by his own c

CHOOSE

Jn 15:16 You did not c Me but I c you
Eph 1:4 His love led Him to c us
Acts 22:14 God of our fathers c you to know
Rom 11:2 people whom He c long ago
1 Cor 1:27 God c the foolish things
1 Thess 1:4 He has c you because
2 Thess 2:13 God c you to be made holy

CHOSEN

Matt 22:14 many are invited but few are c
Matt 24:31 angels . . . will gather His c ones
Acts 9:15 this man is My c instrument
Acts 10:41 God has c to be witnesses
1 Pet 1:2 c according to the foreknowledge

CHRIST

Matt 26:63 are You the C the Son of God
Lk 2:11 Savior who is C the Lord was born
Jn 1:20 He confessed I am not the C
Jn 1:41 found the Messiah which means C
Jn 4:25 Messiah who is called C is coming
Jn 4:29 Could He be the C
Jn 7:26 not found out . . . He is the C
Jn 9:22 synagog anyone who confessed . . . C
Acts 2:31 concerning the resurrection of C
Rom 10:4 C is end of Law to give
1 Cor 10:16 communion with the body of C
2 Cor 5:14 For the love of C compels us
Col 1:27 This mystery is C in you
1 Jn 5:1 believes that Jesus is the C

CHRISTIAN

Acts 11:26 disciples were first called C
Rom 14:13 trap in way of a fellow C
1 Cor 7:12 a C man has a wife who does not

CHURCH

Matt 16:18 on this rock I will build My c
Matt 18:17 will not listen even to the c
Acts 8:3 Saul began to destroy the c
Acts 20:28 c of God . . . with His own blood
Rom 16:16 All the c of Christ greet you
1 Cor 14:19 in the c I would rather say
2 Cor 8:1 of God which He gave to the c
2 Cor 11:28 I am . . . concerned about all c
Eph 1:22 everything for the good of c
Col 4:16 have it read also in the c

1 Thess 1:1 Paul . . . to the c
Phlm 2 to the c that meets in your house
Rev 1:4 John to the seven c in the province
Rev 1:11 send it to the seven c—to Ephesus
Rev 2:1 to the angel of the c in Ephesus

CIRCUMCISE
Acts 15:1 If you are not c according to
Rom 3:30 He will justify the c by faith
1 Cor 7:18 Were you c when you were called
Gal 2:3 But no one forced him to be c
Gal 5:2 if you have yourselves c
Phil 3:3 we are really the c people
Col 2:11 in Him you were c not by human

CIRCUMCISION
Acts 7:8 He gave him the covenant of c
Rom 2:25 C benefits you only if you do

CITIZENS
Phil 1:27 live as c worthy of the Good News

CITY
Jn 19:20 Jesus was crucified was near the c
Acts 18:10 I have many people in this c
Heb 11:10 He was looking for the c
Heb 12:22 the C of the living God

CLAIM
Jn 10:33 because You c to be God
Acts 25:19 Paul c He is alive
1 Tim 6:21 some c to have it and have lost

CLEAN
Matt 8:2 want to . . . You can make me c
Mk 1:40 If You want to You can make me c
Acts 10:15 call unclean what God has made c
Heb 9:14 wash our consciences c from dead

CLEANSE
2 Cor 7:1 let us c ourselves . . . everything
2 Tim 2:21 if anyone will c himself from
Heb 9:22 almost everything is c by blood

CLEANSING
Acts 15:9 by c their hearts by faith He has
Heb 1:3 He made a c from sins

CLEAR
Rom 1:19 God has made it c to them
2 Tim 1:3 serve with a c conscience
2 Tim 4:5 keep a c head in everything

CLEVERNESS
1 Cor 1:17 using any c in my preaching for
2 Cor 1:12 without human c but with God's

CLIFF
Lk 4:29 led Him to a c of the hill

CLING
Rom 11:22 if you c to His kindness
1 Cor 15:2 saved if you c to the word
Col 2:19 a person does not c to the Head
1 Thess 5:21 C to what is good
Tit 1:9 to be one who c to the word
Heb 4:14 let us c to what we confess
Heb 10:23 Let us c to the confession
Rev 2:13 and you c to My Name and did
Rev 3:11 C to what you have so that no

CLOSE
Mk 6:52 Instead their minds were c
Lk 4:20 in the synagog was watching Him c

1 Cor 8:8 Food will not bring us c to God

CLOTH
Matt 9:16 no one sews piece of unshrunk c

CLOTHES
Jn 19:23 soldiers . . . took His c and divided
Acts 1:10 two men in white c were standing

CLOTHING
Matt 6:28 why worry about c

CLOUD
Matt 17:5 bright c suddenly overshadowed
Matt 24:30 see the Son of Man coming on c
Acts 1:9 lifted up and a c took Him away
1 Cor 10:1 fathers were all under the c
1 Thess 4:17 caught up . . . with them in the c

COALS
Jn 18:18 heap of burning c because it was
Rom 12:20 you will heap burning c . . . head

COAT
Matt 5:40 let him also have your c
2 Tim 4:13 bring the warm c I left

COIN
Matt 17:27 open its mouth . . . find a c
Mk 12:42 dropped in two small c

COLLECT
Matt 17:25 kings of world c toll or tax
Lk 3:13 Stop c more money than

COLLECTION
1 Cor 16:1 Concerning the c for believers

COLLECTORS
Matt 17:24 the c of the Temple tax came

COLT
Mk 11:5 What are you doing untying the c
Jn 12:15 Your King is coming riding . . . c

COME
Matt 3:11 One who is c after me is mightier
Matt 8:9 And another C and he comes
Matt 10:23 before . . . the Son of Man will c
Matt 11:3 Are You the One who is c
Matt 11:28 C to Me all you who are working
Matt 25:34 C you whom My Father has blessed
Mk 8:38 when He c with the holy angels
Mk 11:9 Blessed is He who is c in Name
Lk 17:20 When will the Kingdom of God c
Jn 1:27 the One who is c after me
Jn 1:51 angels of God going up and c down
Jn 6:37 Father gives Me will c to Me
Jn 7:36 Where I am you cannot c
Jn 11:20 when Martha heard Jesus is c
Jn 11:43 He called out . . . Lazarus c out
Jn 14:6 No one c to the Father except by Me
Acts 1:11 will c back in the same way
1 Cor 11:26 every time you eat . . . until He c
1 Thess 3:13 when our Lord Jesus c with all
2 Thess 2:1 Our Lord Jesus Christ is c
Heb 10:7 Then I said Look I have c
Jas 4:8 C close to God and He will c close
Rev 1:7 Look He is c in the clouds
Rev 18:4 c out of her My people
Rev 22:17 the Spirit and the bride say C
Rev 22:20 Yes I am c soon

COMFORT

Matt 5:4 mourn for they will be c
Acts 4:36 Barnabas which means Son of C
2 Cor 1:4 He c us in every trouble
2 Cor 2:7 forgive and c him
1 Thess 4:18 c one another with these words
2 Thess 2:16 grace gave us everlasting c

COMFORTER

Jn 14:26 C the Holy Spirit whom the Father
Jn 15:26 When the C [Helper] comes whom I
Jn 16:7 if I do not go away C will not come

COMMAND

Matt 28:20 teaching . . . everything I have c
1 Cor 7:10 I c . . . A wife should not leave
1 Cor 14:37 write to you is what Lord c

COMMANDMENT

Matt 5:19 sets aside one of least of . . . c
Mk 7:8 You abandon the c of God
Jn 13:34 I am giving you a new c Love one
Jn 14:15 If you love Me you will obey My c
Jn 14:21 person who has My c and obeys
Jn 15:10 If you obey My c you will remain
Rom 7:8 this c and worked . . . wrong desire
Rom 7:11 taking the c as a challenge
Rom 13:9 the c Do not commit adultery
Eph 6:2 is an important c with a promise
1 Jn 2:3 if we keep His c

COMMENDS

2 Cor 10:18 he whom the Lord c

COMMITTED

Rom 6:17 pattern of teaching to which . . . c

COMMON

2 Cor 6:15 a believer have in c with an

COMMUNION

1 Cor 10:16 not a c with blood of Christ

COMPELS

2 Cor 5:14 For the love of Christ c us

COMPETES

2 Tim 2:5 if he c according to the rules

COMPLAIN

1 Cor 10:10 Do not c as some of them did

COMPLAINT

Acts 6:1 a c was brought against those
Phil 2:14 everything without c or arguing

COMPLETE

1 Cor 13:10 when c thing comes
2 Cor 13:9 that God may make you c
Col 2:10 and in Him . . . you are c
Jas 1:4 so that you may be perfect and c
Rev 3:2 your works are not c in sight

COMPREHENDED

1 Cor 2:9 no mind has c what God

CONCEITED

1 Cor 13:4 It does not boast or become c
Gal 5:26 let us not become c challenge one

CONCEIVE

Matt 1:23 virgin will c and have a Son
Lk 1:31 You will c and give birth to

CONCERN

1 Cor 9:9 God is not c about oxen is He
1 Cor 12:25 parts might feel the same c for
2 Cor 11:28 am anxiously c about . . . churches

CONDEMN

Lk 6:37 Stop c and you will not be c
Mk 14:64 all c Him saying . . . He was guilty
Jn 3:17 Son into world to c the world
Jn 5:29 done evil will rise to c
Jn 7:51 Does our Law c anyone without first
Jn 8:10 Jesus asked her Did no one c you
Jn 12:48 has one that is c him the word
Acts 25:15 and asked me to c him
Rom 2:1 whoever you are if you c anyone
Rom 3:7 why am I still c as a sinner
Rom 8:34 Who will c It is Christ who died
2 Cor 3:9 if the ministry that c has glory
Tit 3:11 sinner who c himself

CONDEMNATION

Rom 5:18 one failure c came to all people
Rom 8:1 So now no c remains for those

CONFESS

Jn 1:20 John c and did not deny
Rom 10:9 you c with your mouth Jesus is
2 Cor 9:13 Good News of Christ which you c
Phil 2:11 everyone should c that JESUS
1 Tim 6:12 you c so beautifully before many
Jas 5:16 c your sins to one another
1 Jn 1:9 we c our sins He will keep His
1 Jn 4:2 spirit who c that Jesus . . . has come
Rev 3:5 I will c his name before My Father

CONFIDENCE

Eph 3:12 have c and can boldly come to God
1 Tim 3:13 deacons . . . great c in their faith

CONFIRM

Mk 16:20 c the word by the miraculous signs
Rom 4:11 a mark to c that righteousness
1 Cor 1:6 concerning Christ was c in you
Phil 1:7 defending and c the Gospel

CONFLICT

1 Thess 2:2 in the face of much c

CONGREGATION

Acts 7:38 Moses was in the c in the
Heb 2:12 in the c I will sing Your praise

CONQUER

Jn 16:33 I have c the world
Rom 12:21 c evil with good
Heb 11:33 by faith c kingdoms did righteous
1 Jn 5:5 one who c the world
Rev 6:2 rode off as a conqueror to c
Rev 17:14 Lamb will c them because He is

CONSCIENCE

Acts 24:16 a clear c before God and men
Rom 2:15 their c tells the same truth
Rom 9:1 my c assures me by the Holy Spirit
Rom 13:5 but also because your c tell you
1 Cor 8:7 their c being weak is stained
1 Cor 10:25 let your c trouble you
2 Cor 1:12 our c will testify
1 Tim 1:5 love . . . from a good c and . . . faith
1 Tim 3:9 with a clear c they must hold
2 Tim 1:3 whom I serve with a clear c
1 Pet 3:16 Keep a good c so that those
1 Pet 3:21 guaranteeing us a good c before
1 Jn 3:20 Whenever our c condemns us

CONSIDER
Acts 4:19 whether God c it right to listen
CONSTRUCTED
Lk 21:5 it is beautifully c
CONSUME
Jn 2:17 zeal for Your House will c Me
CONTAINER
Matt 5:15 lamp and put it under a c
CONTENT
Phil 4:11 I have learned to be c in any
CONTEST
2 Tim 2:5 if a person enters a c
CONTINUE
Gal 3:10 everyone who does not c to do
Heb 1:11 they will perish but You c
Heb 7:3 he c a priest forever
Heb 8:9 they did not c in My covenant
CONTRARY
1 Tim 1:10 found to be c to sound teaching
CONTRIBUTION
Mk 12:41 Jesus sat facing the c boxes
CONTROL
Heb 2:8 He left nothing outside His c
Jas 3:2 who can also c his whole body
CONVENIENT
2 Tim 4:2 be ready whether it is c or not c
CONVICT
Jude 15 to c all the ungodly of all
CONVICTION
1 Thess 1:5 with the Holy Spirit and with c
CONVINCE
Acts 28:24 Some . . . were c by what he said
Rom 4:21 was fully c that what God promised
Rom 8:38 I am c that neither death nor life
Rom 14:5 Let everyone be thoroughly c
Rom 14:14 I know and am c in Lord Jesus
1 Cor 14:24 all c him of sin
Col 2:2 be richly c in your understanding
Heb 11:1 being c of things we cannot see
CONVULSION
Mk 1:26 spirit threw the man into c
COPY
Heb 1:3 He . . . is the perfect c of His Being
CORBAN
Mk 7:11 I might help you is C
CORNERSTONE
Acts 4:11 become the C No one else . . . save
Eph 2:20 Christ Jesus Himself is the C
CORPSE
Mk 9:26 The boy became like a c
CORRECT
Lk 9:55 He turned and sternly c them
Acts 18:25 taught c about Jesus
Rom 15:14 able to c one another
1 Cor 2:14 have the Spirit to judge them c
1 Cor 11:32 Lord judges us we are being c
2 Cor 6:9 as c but not killed
1 Tim 5:20 go on sinning c before everyone
2 Tim 2:25 gentle in c those who oppose him
2 Tim 3:16 useful for . . . c for training
Tit 1:9 can encourage people and c those

CORRUPT
2 Tim 3:8 Their minds are c and they
Tit 1:15 their mind and conscience are c
CORRUPTION
2 Pet 1:4 you have escaped the c
COST
Lk 14:28 figure out what it c
1 Cor 9:18 I will not let it c anyone
COUNCIL
Mk 15:43 Joseph . . . member of Jewish c
COUNT
Matt 10:30 hairs on your head are all c
2 Cor 5:19 by not c their sins against them
COUNTRY
Mk 16:12 as they were walking into the c
COURAGE
Matt 14:27 Be c . . . It is I
Heb 3:6 continue unshaken in our c
COURT
Mk 11:16 item for sale across Temple c
Acts 17:22 Paul stood before the c of Mars
Acts 18:12 brought him into c
1 Cor 6:1 bring before a c of unrighteous
COVENANT
Acts 3:25 of the prophets and of the c that
Rom 9:4 they have the glory the c the law
Gal 4:24 the women are two c
Heb 8:7 if that first c . . . without fault
Heb 8:8 set up a new c
Rev 11:19 ARK of His C [Testament] was seen
COVERED
Mk 14:65 They c His face struck Him
Rom 4:7 Blessed . . . whose sins are c
1 Cor 11:4 every man who keeps his head c
COWARDLY
2 Tim 1:7 God did not give us a c spirit
CRASH
Matt 7:27 it went down with a loud c
CRAVING
1 Tim 6:4 he has a morbid c for debates
Jas 4:1 because of your c for pleasure
CRAZY
2 Cor 5:13 If we are c it was for God
CREATED
Mk 13:19 from beginning of God's c world
Eph 2:10 c us in Christ Jesus to do . . . works
Eph 3:9 in God who c all things
Col 1:16 in Him was c everything in heaven
1 Tim 4:4 everything God c is good
Heb 11:3 By faith we know God c the world
Rev 4:11 for You c everything
CREATION
Rom 1:20 since the c of the world they have
2 Cor 5:17 he is a new c
Gal 6:15 what matters is being a new c
Col 1:15 the Firstborn of all c
CREATOR
Rom 1:25 created instead of the C who is
CREATURE
Rev 4:6 throne there were four living c
Rev 5:13 And I heard every c in heaven

CREDITED
Rom 4:3 c to his account as righteousness
Gal 3:6 He believed God and it was c to him
CRIMES
Acts 25:18 accuse him of c I was suspecting
CRIMINAL
Jn 18:30 If He were not a c we would not
2 Tim 2:9 even chained like a c
CRIPPLE
Lk 13:11 woman whom a spirit had c
Acts 3:2 man who had been a c from birth
CRITICAL
Matt 20:15 are you c of me because I am
CRITICISM
2 Cor 8:20 we are trying to avoid any c of
CRITICIZE
Rom 14:10 why do you c fellow Christian
CROOKED
Lk 3:5 the c will be made straight
Acts 2:40 Be saved from this c kind
CROP
2 Tim 2:6 the first . . . share of the c
CROSS
Matt 10:38 take his c and follow Me
Matt 16:24 follow Me . . . take up your c
Matt 27:32 forced him to carry His c
Mk 8:34 take up his c and follow
Mk 15:21 forced him to carry the c of Jesus
Mk 15:30 come down from the c and save
Lk 14:27 whoever does not carry his c
Lk 16:26 might want to c from here over
Lk 23:26 they laid the c on him
Jn 19:17 Jesus carrying His own c He went
Jn 19:19 Pilate wrote notice . . . put it on c
Jn 19:31 did not want bodies to stay on c
Acts 13:29 they took Him down from the c
Rom 6:6 our old self was nailed . . . to the c
1 Cor 1:17 that the c of Christ might lose
2 Cor 13:4 He did indeed die on a c
Gal 6:12 persecuted for the c of Christ
Phil 2:8 point of death . . . on a c
Phil 3:18 enemies of the c of Christ
Col 2:14 out of way by nailing it to the c
Heb 12:2 He endured the c thinking nothing
1 Pet 2:24 sins in His body on the c so
CROSS-EXAMINED
Acts 4:9 if we are c today about helping
CROWED
Mk 14:72 Just then rooster c a second time
CROWD
Matt 8:18 When Jesus saw a c around Him
Acts 2:6 c gathered and was dumbfounded
Rev 7:9 and there was a large c
CROWN
Matt 27:29 twisted some thorns into a c
Jn 19:2 twisted some thorns into a c
Phil 4:1 my joy and c
2 Tim 4:8 waiting . . . the c of righteousness
Heb 2:7 then c Him with glory and honor
Jas 1:12 he will receive the c of life
1 Pet 5:4 win the unfading c of glory

Rev 2:10 give you the c of life
Rev 3:11 so that no one takes your c
Rev 4:4 there were golden c on heads
Rev 13:1 on his horns ten c
CRUCIFY
Matt 27:22 C Him they all said
Mk 15:13 C Him they shouted
Lk 23:21 But they kept yelling C c Him
Jn 19:15 Away with Him . . . C Him
Jn 19:16 handed Jesus over to them to be c
Jn 19:18 There they c Him with two others
Jn 19:20 place where Jesus was c was near
Acts 2:36 this Jesus whom you c
Acts 4:10 Jesus . . . whom you c but God raised
1 Cor 1:13 Was Paul c for you
Gal 2:19 I have been c with Christ
Gal 5:24 have c the flesh with its passions
Heb 6:6 they . . . c the Son of God again
CRUSH
Matt 12:20 He will not c a bruised reed
Mk 3:9 To keep the crowd from c Him
Rom 16:20 God of peace will soon c Satan
2 Cor 4:8 we are hard-pressed but not c
CRY (see also **WEEP**)
Matt 2:18 Rachel c over her children
Jn 20:15 Woman why are you c
Heb 5:7 Jesus while c loudly with tears
CULTIVATED
Rom 11:24 grafted into a c olive tree
CUP
Matt 26:27 He took the c and spoke a prayer
Matt 26:39 Father . . . let this c pass away
Lk 22:20 He did the same with the c
Lk 22:42 if You wish take this c away
Jn 18:11 the c My Father gave Me
1 Cor 10:16 Is the c of blessing . . . we bless
Rev 16:19 give great Babylon the c of wine
CURSE
Matt 25:41 Go away from Me you c ones
Mk 11:21 fig tree You c is dried up
1 Cor 12:3 No one . . . will say C be Jesus
1 Cor 16:22 not love the Lord a c on him
Gal 1:8 a c be on him
Gal 3:10 There is a c on all who depend
Gal 3:10 C is everyone who does not
Gal 3:13 C is everyone who hangs on a tree
Rev 16:11 c God of heaven for their pains
CURTAIN
Matt 27:51 inner c in the Temple was torn
Heb 6:19 strong and which goes behind the c
CUSHION
Mk 4:38 back of boat sleeping on the c
CUSTOM
Jn 18:39 have c that I set one person free
Jn 19:40 Jewish c of burying the dead
Acts 6:14 change the c that Moses gave
1 Cor 11:16 we do not have such a c
CUSTOMARY
Mk 14:12 it was c to kill Passover lamb
CUT
Acts 2:37 people heard this they were c
Heb 4:12 c better than any two-edged sword

CUT OFF
Acts 3:23 completely **c** off from the people
Rom 9:3 could wish myself **c** off from Christ
Gal 4:17 they want to **c** you off from me
Gal 5:4 have been **c** off from Christ
CYMBAL
1 Cor 13:1 I have become . . . a clashing **c**

DAMNED
Mk 16:16 he who does not believe will be **d**
Rom 9:3 **d** for my fellow Jews my own flesh
DANGER
1 Cor 15:30 Why are we in **d** every hour
2 Cor 11:26 **d** from my own people and
DARED
Mk 12:34 Nobody **d** to ask Him another
Mk 15:43 Joseph . . . **d** to go to Pilate
DARK
Matt 6:23 eye is bad your . . . body will be **d**
Mk 13:24 sun will turn **d** moon
Jn 1:5 The Light is shining in the **d**
Eph 6:12 rulers of this **d** world
DARKNESS
Matt 8:12 thrown out into outer **d**
Matt 27:45 At noon **d** came over the . . . land
Lk 1:79 shine on those who sit in **d**
Jn 8:12 you will never wander in **d**
Jn 12:35 Walk while you have Light so **d**
2 Cor 4:6 Let light shine out of the **d**
2 Cor 6:14 light have anything to do with **d**
Eph 5:8 you were **d** but now you are light
1 Pet 2:9 called you out of **d** into . . . light
DAUGHTER
Matt 9:18 My **d** just died he said
Jn 12:15 **d** of Zion Look your King
Acts 2:17 and your **d** speak God's word
Acts 7:21 Pharaoh's **d** took and raised him
2 Cor 6:18 you will be My sons and **d**
DAWNING
Matt 28:1 as Sunday was **d**
DAY
Matt 24:36 No one knows about that **D**
Mk 13:32 No one knows about that **D** or Hour
Lk 13:14 not on the **d** of rest
Jn 8:56 Abraham was delighted . . . see My **d**
Acts 3:24 Samuel . . . told about these **d**
Acts 17:31 He has set a **D** when He is going
Rom 2:5 on the **D** of His anger
Rom 14:5 One person thinks one **d** is better
1 Cor 3:13 that **D** will show what it is
2 Tim 1:3 I never fail to do **d** or night
DAY OF PREPARATION
Matt 27:62 after the **d** of preparation
DAY OF THE LORD
Acts 2:20 great splendid **d** of the Lord
1 Cor 5:5 save . . . on the **D** of the Lord
DAZZLING
Mk 9:3 His clothes became **d** white
DEACON
1 Tim 3:8 the **d** . . . must be serious

DEAD
Lk 15:24 son . . . was **d** and has come to life
Lk 24:5 Why do you look among the **d** for Him
Acts 3:15 God raised Him from the **d**
Acts 10:41 after He rose from the **d**
Acts 17:31 raising Him from **d** He has given
Acts 24:15 the **d** will rise both righteous
Eph 2:1 You also were once **d** in . . . sins
Col 2:13 Although you were **d** in sins
Jas 2:26 so faith without works is **d**
1 Pet 4:5 judge the living and the **d**
Rev 3:1 you are alive but you are **d**
Rev 20:12 I saw the **d** great and small
DEAF
Acts 7:51 pagan at heart and **d** to the truth
DEAR
1 Thess 2:8 our own lives—so **d** you had
1 Tim 6:2 are believers and are **d** to you
DEATH
Matt 2:15 stayed there until the **d** of Herod
Jn 8:51 My word he will never see **d**
Rom 5:10 were reconciled to God by **d** of Son
Rom 5:12 man and **d** through sin so **d** also
Rom 6:4 baptized into His **d** we were buried
Rom 7:5 to produce fruit for **d**
1 Cor 15:54 **D** is swallowed up in victory
2 Cor 3:6 because the letter brings **d**
2 Cor 4:12 so **d** is working in us
2 Cor 7:10 worldly sorrow produces **d**
2 Tim 1:10 took away the power of **d**
Heb 2:9 by God's grace . . . He might taste **d**
Heb 2:14 power of **d** that is the devil
Jas 1:15 it gives birth to **d**
DEATH TRAP
Rev 2:14 taught Balak how to put a **d** trap
DEBATE
Jude 9 When the archangel was **d** with devil
DEBATER
1 Cor 1:20 Where is the **d** of our time
DEBT
Rom 4:4 not considered a gift but a **d**
Col 2:14 wiping out **d** which was recorded
DECAY
Acts 2:27 allow Your Holy One experience **d**
1 Cor 15:42 when body is sown it **d**
DECEIT
Jn 1:47 Israelite in whom there is no **d**
Rom 1:29 murder quarreling **d** viciousness
DECEITFUL
1 Pet 3:10 saying anything **d**
DECEIVE
Mk 13:6 I am He and will **d** many
Rom 16:18 are **d** innocent people
1 Cor 3:18 Do not **d** yourself If any
2 Cor 11:3 snake by its trickery **d** Eve
1 Thess 2:3 we are not **d** you
1 Tim 2:14 Adam was not **d** but the woman
2 Tim 3:13 as they **d** and are **d**
Tit 1:10 who talk foolishly and **d**
1 Jn 1:8 we **d** ourselves and truth is not
Rev 20:8 will go out to **d** the Gentiles

DECEPTION
Heb 3:13 become stubborn through **d** of sin
DECISION
Mk 15:1 Jewish council came to a **d**
Rom 11:33 how impossible to find out His **d**
DECLARED
Rom 3:4 You may be **d** right when you speak
DECREE
Rom 1:32 they know God's righteous **d**
DEDICATION
Jn 10:22 then came the Festival of **D**
DEEDS
1 Pet 2:9 others about the wonderful **d** of
DEEP
Rom 11:33 how **d** are God's riches wisdom
DEFEAT
1 Cor 1:19 **d** the intelligence of the
DEFEND
Acts 22:1 as I now **d** myself before you
2 Cor 12:19 we were **d** ourselves before you
DEFILES
2 Cor 7:1 everything that **d** body and spirit
DEITY
Col 2:9 In Him . . . lives fullness of the **D**
DELAY
Acts 25:17 without any **d** I sat down on
DELIGHT
Matt 3:17 Son whom I love and in whom I **d**
Matt 17:5 Son whom I love and in whom I **d**
Lk 1:47 my spirit **d** in God my Savior
1 Cor 13:6 It does not **d** in wrongdoing
3 Jn 3 I was **d** when some fellow Christians
DELIVER
Matt 6:13 but **d** us from evil
DEMON
Matt 8:28 two men with **d** in them came out
Mk 16:9 out of whom He had driven seven **d**
Lk 11:14 driving out a **d** . . . When the **d** had
Jn 8:52 we know that there is a **d** in You
1 Cor 10:20 sacrifices . . . are made to **d**
Jas 2:19 **d** also believe that—and shudder
Rev 18:2 Babylon . . . has become home for **d**
DEMONSTRATE
Rom 9:17 I raised you to the throne to **d**
1 Tim 1:16 Christ might **d** in me
DENARII
Matt 18:28 slaves who owed him a hundred **d**
Mk 6:37 buy bread for two hundred **d**
DENOUNCE
Matt 11:20 He began to **d** the cities
1 Cor 10:30 I let myself be **d** for eating
DENY
Matt 16:24 want to follow Me **d** yourself
Matt 26:35 Peter told . . . I will never **d** You
Lk 9:23 **d** yourself take up your cross
Acts 3:13 you delivered and **d** before Pilate
1 Tim 5:8 does not take care . . . **d** the faith
Tit 1:16 they **d** Him by what they do
1 Jn 2:23 Everyone who **d** Son does not have
Rev 3:8 kept my word and have not **d** My Name

DEPART
Lk 2:29 You are letting Your servant **d**
DEPEND
Rom 9:16 does not **d** on anyone's desire
1 Cor 1:9 you can **d** on God who called you
Gal 3:10 a curse on all who **d** on doing
1 Thess 5:24 You can **d** on Him who calls you
2 Tim 2:11 You can **d** on this If we . . . died
Tit 3:8 You can **d** on this statement
DEPRIVE
1 Cor 7:5 Do not **d** one another
DESCENDED
2 Cor 11:22 Are they **d** from Abraham So am I
DESCENDANT
Matt 1:1 Christ a **d** of David
Lk 2:4 he was one of the **d** of David
Jn 8:33 We are Abraham's **d** and have never
Acts 2:30 place one of his **d** on his throne
Acts 3:25 And in your **D** all the people
Rom 1:3 was born a a **d** of David
Rom 4:13 Abraham of his **d** received promise
Rom 9:7 children will be called your **d**
Rom 15:12 Jesse will have **D** who will rise
Gal 3:7 believe are Abraham's real **d**
Gal 3:16 spoken to Abraham and . . . his **D**
Phil 3:5 a **d** of Israel of the tribe of
Rev 22:16 I am David's Creator and **D**
DESERTED
Gal 4:27 the **d** woman has more children
2 Tim 1:15 everyone in province . . . **d** me
DESERVE
Matt 10:11 person there who is **d** and stay
Lk 15:19 I do not **d** to be called your son
Rom 11:9 fall and receive what they **d**
2 Cor 5:10 each to receive what he **d**
2 Cor 11:15 get what they **d** for what they
Phil 4:8 excellent or that **d** praise
DESIRE
Rom 7:7 Do not wrongfully **d**
Rom 10:1 my heart's **d** and my prayer to God
Rom 13:9 Do not have wrongful **d**
Col 2:23 in curbing the constant **d** of the
1 Tim 6:9 foolish and harmful **d** which drown
2 Tim 4:3 following their own **d**
2 Tim 4:5 God **d** you to do as a pastor
Jas 1:14 person is tempted by his own **d**
2 Pet 3:12 **d** the coming of the Day
DESPAIRED
2 Cor 1:8 we even **d** of living
DESPISE
Matt 6:24 loyal to the one and **d** the other
Matt 18:10 careful not to **d** . . . little ones
Rom 14:10 do you **d** your fellow Christian
1 Thess 5:20 Do not **d** God's word when
DESTINED
1 Thess 3:3 we are **d** to suffer them
DESTROY
Acts 8:3 Saul began to **d** the church
1 Cor 3:17 God will **d** him because God's
Gal 5:15 you will be **d** by one another
Phil 1:28 they will be **d** and you . . . be saved
2 Pet 3:12 will **d** the heavens with fire

DESTRUCTION
Matt 7:13 gate is wide . . . leads to **d**
Rom 3:16 there is **d** and misery
Rom 9:22 prepared themselves for **d**
Gal 6:8 will from his flesh reap **d**
1 Thess 5:3 well and safe then **d** will come
DETERMINED
Lk 9:51 He was **d** to go to Jerusalem
1 Cor 2:2 I was **d** to know only Jesus Christ
DEVIL
Matt 4:1 wilderness to be tempted by the **d**
Matt 25:41 fire . . . for the **d** and his angels
Lk 4:2 the **d** continued to tempt Him
Jn 8:44 Your father is the **d**
Eph 6:11 tricky ways of the **d**
1 Tim 3:6 fall into the judgment of the **d**
Heb 2:14 power of death that is the **d**
1 Jn 3:8 Anyone who lives in sin is **d** child
DEVOTION
2 Cor 8:16 putting into the heart . . . **d**
2 Cor 11:3 sincere and pure **d** to Christ
DEVOUR
1 Pet 5:8 lion looking for someone to **d**
DICE
Matt 27:35 divided His clothes . . . throwing **d**
Jn 19:24 not tear it but let's throw **d**
DICTATE
Gal 2:5 we let them **d** to us
Col 2:20 do you let others **d** to you
DIE
Matt 26:52 all who take the sword will **d**
Matt 26:66 He . . . deserves to **d** they answered
Mk 15:37 Jesus cried out . . . and **d**
Lk 13:33 prophet to **d** outside Jerusalem
Jn 11:21 my brother would not have **d**
Jn 11:26 everyone who . . . believes . . . never **d**
Acts 9:37 that time she became sick and **d**
Acts 21:13 even to **d** . . . for Name . . . Jesus
Rom 5:6 Christ **d** for the ungodly
Rom 5:8 we . . . still sinners Christ **d** for us
Rom 6:2 We **d** to sin How can we then live in
Rom 8:11 will also make your **d** bodies alive
1 Cor 15:3 important . . . Christ **d** for sins
1 Cor 15:22 in Adam all **d** in Christ . . . alive
2 Cor 5:15 He **d** for all so those who live
Gal 2:19 by the Law I **d** to the Law
Phil 1:20 glorify Christ . . . living or by **d**
1 Pet 3:18 Christ **d** once for our sins
Rev 14:13 blessed are dead who **d** in Lord
DIFFERENCE
Rom 3:22 There is no **d** for all have sinned
Rom 10:12 is no **d** between Jew and Greek
DIFFERENT
Mk 16:12 He appeared in a **d** form to two
Acts 15:9 He has declared we are not **d**
1 Cor 12:4 gifts are given to **d** persons
Tit 3:10 chooses to be **d** in his teaching
DIFFICULT
Heb 5:11 it is **d** to explain because you
DILIGENT
Heb 4:11 Let us be **d** to come to that rest

DIPPED
Jn 13:26 So He **d** it and gave it to Judas
DIRECTED
Matt 27:10 as the Lord **d** me
DIRECTIONS
1 Cor 11:34 I will give **d** concerning
DIRT
1 Pet 3:21 not by washing **d** from the body
DISAPPOINTED
Rom 5:5 in this hope we will not be **d**
Rom 9:33 believes in Him will not be **d**
1 Pet 2:6 who believes . . . will never be **d**
DISCIPLE
Matt 9:14 Why is it that Your **d** do not fast
Matt 27:57 Joseph . . . had become a **d** of Jesus
Matt 28:19 Go and make **d** of all people
Lk 14:26 he cannot be My **d**
Jn 1:35 John . . . standing with two of his **d**
Jn 8:31 in My word you are really My **d**
Jn 19:27 Then He said to **d** . . . your mother
Acts 9:1 murder against the Lord's **d**
DISCIPLINE
Heb 12:5 not think lightly of the Lord's **d**
DISCOURAGED
2 Cor 4:1 Therefore we do not become **d**
DISCUSSION
Acts 15:7 After much **d** Peter stood up
DISGRACE
1 Cor 11:6 **d** for a woman . . . hair cut off
1 Cor 14:35 **d** for a woman to speak . . . church
DISGUISED
Matt 7:15 come to you **d** as sheep
DISGUSTED
2 Cor 7:11 how **d** with wrong also how
DISHONORS
1 Cor 11:5 nothing on her head **d** her head
DISOBEDIENCE
Rom 5:19 through the **d** of one man
Rom 11:32 God . . . all people in prison of **d**
Heb 2:2 every trespass and **d** received
DISOBEY
Rom 1:30 they **d** parents They are foolish
Eph 2:2 is now working in the people who **d**
2 Tim 3:2 They will **d** parents
1 Pet 2:8 Because they **d** word they stumble
1 Pet 3:20 who **d** long ago in the days
DISORDERLY
2 Cor 12:20 there may be . . . and **d** conduct
1 Thess 5:14 warn those who are **d** cheer up
DISOWN
2 Tim 2:12 If we **d** Him He will also **d** us
Jude 4 lust and **d** our only Master
DISPLAY
Phil 2:6 being equal . . . as a prize to be **d**
1 Jn 2:16 the vain **d** of property
DISQUALIFIED
1 Cor 9:27 I myself may not be **d**
DISTANCE
1 Pet 2:11 keep your **d** from the . . . flesh
DISTANT
Lk 15:13 left home for a **d** country

DISTINCTION
1 Cor 14:7 no **d** in the sounds how can you
DISTINGUISHING
2 Thess 3:17 is a **d** mark in every letter
DISTRESS
2 Cor 5:4 we sigh feeling **d** for this reason
DISTRIBUTED
Acts 4:35 then it was **d** to each one in
DISTURBED
Mk 6:20 John he was very much **d**
DIVIDED
Matt 27:35 they **d** His clothes among them
Lk 15:12 So he **d** his property between
Jn 19:23 His clothes and **d** them in four
1 Cor 1:10 all to agree and not to be **d**
1 Cor 1:13 Is Christ **d** Was Paul crucified
1 Cor 11:18 you gather . . . church you are **d**
DIVINE
2 Pet 1:4 promises share in the **d** nature
DIVISION
1 Cor 11:19 there must be **d** among you
DIVORCE
Matt 5:31 Whoever **d** his wife must give her
Matt 19:9 if anyone **d** his wife except for
Mk 10:12 And if a wife **d** her husband
1 Cor 7:11 husband should not **d** his wife
DO
Matt 5:18 from Law until everything is **d**
Matt 7:21 who continues to **d** the will of My
Mk 10:17 what should I **d** to inherit
Jn 6:6 He knew what He was going to **d**
Acts 2:37 Fellow Jews what should we **d**
2 Cor 5:18 But God has **d** it all
Gal 6:10 let us **d** good to everyone
Phil 4:13 I can **d** everything through Him
DOCTOR
Matt 9:12 healthy do not need a **d**
Lk 4:23 this proverb **D** heal yourself
DOCTRINES
Matt 15:9 what they teach for **d** are rules
DOCTRINAL
Eph 4:14 tossed and driven by every **d** wind
DOGS
Matt 7:6 give what is holy to **d** nor throw
Lk 16:21 **d** would even come and lick his
Phil 3:2 look out for those **d**
2 Pet 2:22 **d** goes back to what he vomited
DONKEY
Jn 12:14 Jesus found a **d** and sat on it
2 Pet 2:16 **d** . . . spoke with a human voice
DOOMED
2 Thess 2:3 man . . . who is **d** to destruction
DOOR
Matt 7:8 the **d** will be opened
Jn 10:7 I am the **D** for the sheep
Jn 20:19 Sunday evening the **d** were locked
Jn 20:26 The **d** were locked but Jesus came
1 Cor 16:9 a **d** has opened wide for me
DOT
Matt 5:18 **d** of an i will pass away . . . Law

DOUBLE
2 Cor 1:15 have the benefit of a **d** visit
DOUBT
Matt 14:31 Why did you **d**
Matt 28:17 they worshiped Him but some **d**
Rom 14:23 if a person **d** and still eats
DOUGH
Rom 11:16 if first handful of **d** is holy
DOVE
Matt 3:16 coming down on Him as a **d**
Matt 10:16 as snakes and innocent as **d**
Mk 1:10 Spirit coming down on Him as a **d**
DRAGON
Rev 12:3 large fire-red **d** with seven heads
DREAM
Matt 1:20 appeared to him in a **d**
Acts 2:17 your old men will **d d**
DRESS
Matt 6:29 Solomon in all glory . . . not **d**
1 Tim 2:9 women to **d** in decent clothes
DRIFT
Heb 2:1 so that we do not **d** away
DRINK
Matt 26:27 **D** of it all of you
Acts 10:41 who ate and **d** with Him after
Rom 14:17 Kingdom is not . . . eating and **d**
1 Cor 10:4 all drank the same spiritual **d**
1 Cor 11:28 eat bread and **d** from the cup
2 Tim 4:6 poured out as a **d** offering
DRIVE
Matt 10:1 to **d** out unclean spirits and heal
Mk 9:29 This kind can be **d** out only
Mk 11:15 began to **d** out those selling
Acts 18:16 And he **d** them out
DROPSY
Lk 14:2 man who had **d**
DROWN
Matt 8:25 Lord We're going to **d**
Matt 18:6 be **d** in the deepest part of sea
1 Tim 6:9 desires . . . **d** them in destruction
DRUNK
Acts 2:15 men are not **d** as you suppose
1 Cor 5:11 worships idols slanders gets **d**
Eph 5:18 do not get **d** on wine
DRUNKARD
1 Tim 3:3 no **d** not violent but gentle
DRUNKENNESS
Lk 21:34 carousing and **d**
Gal 5:21 envy **d** carousing and the like
DRY
Matt 12:43 he goes through **d** places
DULL
Acts 28:27 people have become **d** at heart
Rom 11:7 minds of the others were **d**
DUMBFOUNDED
Acts 2:6 crowd gathered and was **d**
Acts 3:11 They were **d**
DUNGEONS
2 Pet 2:4 put them into gloomy **d** of hell
DUST
Matt 10:14 shake the **d** off your feet

Mk 6:11 shake the **d** off soles of feet
Lk 9:5 shake the **d** off your feet
DWELL
2 Cor 12:9 Christ's power **d** in me
DWELLING PLACE
Eph 2:22 into God's spiritual **d** place

EAGER
Matt 6:33 to be **e** for God's rule
Rom 1:15 I am **e** to preach the Gospel also
1 Pet 3:11 be **e** for peace and pursue it
EAGERLY
Eph 6:7 serve **e** as you would serve the Lord
EAGLE
Rev 4:7 fourth was like a flying **e**
EAR
Lk 14:35 The one who has **e** to hear
Jn 18:10 cut off his right **e**
1 Cor 12:16 suppose an **e** says I am not
Rev 2:7 who has an **e** listen to what Spirit
EARLY
Mk 16:2 coming to the tomb very **e**
EARNESTLY
1 Thess 3:10 as we **e** pray day and night
EARTH
Matt 5:13 You are the salt of the **e**
Acts 7:49 throne and the **e** is My footstool
Acts 16:26 Suddenly the **e** quaked so
1 Cor 15:48 people of the **e** are like the
EARTHLY
Rom 15:27 serve them with their **e** goods
Col 3:2 keep your mind . . . not on **e** things
EARTHQUAKE
Matt 24:7 there will be famines and **e**
Matt 27:54 saw the **e** and the other things
Matt 28:2 There was a great **e**
Rev 6:12 and a great **e** took place
EAST
Matt 2:1 Then Wise Men came from the **e**
Matt 8:11 many will come from **e** . . . west
EASY
Matt 10:15 it will be **e** for the land of
Matt 11:22 it will be **e** for Tyre and Sidon
EAT
Matt 6:25 worrying about what you will **e**
Matt 8:11 will **e** with Abraham Isaac Jacob
Matt 26:26 Take and **e** this is My body
Mk 2:16 Why . . . does He **e** with tax collectors
Jn 6:5 buy bread for these people to **e**
Rom 14:2 One . . . believes he can **e** anything
Rom 14:15 ruin any person . . . by what you **e**
1 Cor 11:26 you **e** this bread
Gal 2:12 He had been **e** with the Gentiles
Col 2:16 say you are wrong . . . what you **e**
2 Thess 3:10 to work neither should he **e**
EDUCATED
Acts 7:22 Moses was **e** in all the wisdom
EDUCATION
Acts 4:13 Peter and John had no special **e**
EFFECTIVELY
Col 1:29 power which is **e** at work in me

EFFORT
Rom 9:16 anyone's desire or on anyone's **e**
EIGHTEEN
Lk 13:4 **e** on whom the tower at Siloam
Lk 13:11 spirit had crippled for **e** years
ELDER
Jas 5:14 anyone . . . sick Let him call for **e**
2 Jn 1:1 The **E** to the chosen lady
Rev 4:4 sat 24 **e** dressed in white clothes
ELEMENTARY
Gal 4:3 slaves under the **e** rules . . . world
ELEMENTS
2 Pet 3:10 **e** will be destroyed by heat
ELEVEN
Mk 16:14 He showed Himself to the **E**
ELIMINATED
Gal 5:11 cross would be **e** as a stumbling
ELSE
Matt 11:3 should we look for someone **e**
Mk 1:38 Let us go somewhere **e** He told
Acts 4:12 No one **e** can save us
1 Tim 6:3 anyone teaches anything **e**
EMPTY
Phil 2:7 but He **e** Himself made Himself
2 Tim 2:16 keep away from **e** worldly
ENABLES
Eph 2:18 He **e** . . . us to come to the Father
ENCOURAGE
Acts 14:22 **e** them to be loyal to the faith
Rom 12:8 If it is **e** others let him **e**
1 Thess 5:11 **e** one another and strengthen
1 Tim 5:1 but **e** him as a father
ENCOURAGEMENT
Acts 15:31 delighted with **e** it brought them
Rom 15:4 **e** which the Scriptures give us
END
Matt 12:42 came from the **e** of the earth
Matt 24:13 endures to the **e** will be saved
Matt 28:20 I am with you always until the **e**
Mk 13:27 from one **e** of world to the other
Lk 1:33 His Kingdom will never **e**
Rom 10:4 Christ is the **e** of the Law
1 Cor 10:11 us on whom the **e** of the ages
Heb 1:12 Your years will never **e**
1 Pet 4:17 how will it **e** for those who
ENDURANCE
Rom 5:3 suffering produces patient **e**
Rom 15:4 through the patient **e** and
2 Pet 1:6 to self-control patient **e**
ENDURE
Matt 24:13 who **e** to the end will be saved
Mk 13:13 who **e** to the end will be saved
Lk 21:19 Patiently **e** and you will gain
1 Cor 13:7 for everything **e** everything
2 Cor 1:6 patiently **e** the same sufferings
Col 1:11 you . . . **e** patiently whatever comes
2 Tim 2:10 why I can patiently **e** anything
2 Tim 2:12 If we patiently **e** we shall also
ENEMY
Matt 5:44 love your **e** always pray for those
Matt 22:44 until I put Your **e** under . . . feet

Lk 1:74 to rescue us from our **e**
Lk 13:17 all His **e** had to feel ashamed
Rom 5:10 when we were still His **e**
Rom 11:28 they are treated as **e** for your
1 Cor 15:25 puts all His **e** under His feet
Gal 4:16 I have become your **e** by telling
Phil 1:28 do not let your **e** frighten you
Phil 3:18 live as the **e** of cross of Christ
Col 1:21 mind you were His **e** doing wicked
1 Tim 5:14 give the **e** no chance to slander
2 Tim 3:3 never forgiving an **e** slanderous
Heb 1:13 until I make Your **e** a footstool
1 Pet 5:8 Your **e** the devil is prowling

ENGRAVED
2 Cor 3:7 Now if that ministry **e** in letters

ENJOY
Rom 11:31 while you **e** mercy
1 Pet 3:10 wants to love life and **e** happy
2 Pet 1:2 May you **e** more . . . of His grace

ENOUGH
2 Cor 2:6 that is **e** for such a person
2 Cor 12:9 My grace is **e** for you

ENTANGLED
2 Pet 2:20 **e** and conquered by them again

ENTER
Matt 5:20 you will never **e** the Kingdom
Acts 14:22 troubles . . . we must **e** Kingdom

ENTHUSIASM
2 Cor 9:2 and your **e** has stirred up most

ENTRUST
Lk 23:46 into Your hands I **e** My spirit
Acts 20:24 ministry that the Lord Jesus **e**
Rom 3:2 advantage is that God **e** His word
Gal 2:7 I had been **e** with bringing Gospel
1 Thess 2:4 to be **e** with the Gospel
2 Tim 1:12 what I have **e** to Him
2 Tim 2:2 **e** to faithful men who will be
Jude 3 faith once **e** to the believers

EPHPHATHA
Mk 7:34 Then He said to him **E**

EPILEPTICS
Matt 4:24 the demon-possessed the **e**

EQUAL
Phil 2:6 His being **e** with God as a prize

EQUIPPED
Rom 15:14 fully **e** with . . . knowledge

ERASE
Rev 3:5 I will never **e** his name out of Book

ERROR
2 Tim 3:16 useful for . . . pointing out **e**

ESCAPE
Mk 14:44 take Him away and do not let Him **e**
Lk 21:36 you may be able to **e**
Rom 2:3 do you think you will **e** being
2 Cor 11:33 I **e** from his hands
1 Thess 5:3 they will not **e**
2 Tim 2:26 they will **e** the snare of devil
Heb 11:34 **e** death by the sword
2 Pet 1:4 after you have **e** the corruption

ESPECIALLY
Gal 6:10 **e** to our family of believers
1 Tim 4:10 Savior of all people **e** of those

ESTABLISHED
Rom 13:1 exist have been **e** by God

ESTATE
Jude 6 left their **e** He put them

ETERNAL
2 Thess 1:9 punished with an **e** destruction

EUNUCH
Acts 8:27 a **e** who was a high official

EVALUATING
1 Cor 11:31 But if we were **e** ourselves

EVANGELISTS
Eph 4:11 He gave some men . . . some to be **e**

EVENING
Mk 11:19 Whenever **e** came they would leave
Jn 4:6 It was about six in the **e**

EVERLASTING
Mk 3:29 Yes he is guilty of an **e** sin
Jn 3:15 believes in Him might have **e** life
Jn 3:36 who believes in the Son has **e** life
Jn 4:14 spring . . . bubbling up to **e** life
Jn 12:25 will secure it for **e** life
Jn 17:3 This is **e** life—to know You
Rom 1:20 tell He has **e** power and is God
Rom 2:7 **e** life to those who . . . working good
Rom 6:23 the gift given freely . . . is **e** life
1 Jn 2:25 is what He promised us—**e** life

EVERYONE
Mk 13:37 What I tell you I tell **e** Watch

EVERYTHING
Matt 19:26 for God **e** is possible
Mk 10:28 Look We gave up **e** and followed
Mk 12:44 **e** she had to live on
Jn 1:3 **E** was made by Him
Rom 11:36 **E** is from Him by Him and for Him
1 Cor 3:22 future things—**e** is yours
1 Cor 15:27 for **e** is to be subordinated
Col 3:11 but Christ is **e** and in all of you
Heb 2:8 God put **e** under His feet
Heb 3:4 He who built **e** is God

EVERYWHERE
Mk 16:15 Go **e** in the world and preach
Mk 16:20 They went out and preached **e**
1 Tim 2:8 men to pray **e** lifting . . . hands

EVIL
Matt 5:39 do not oppose an **e** man
Matt 5:45 sun rise . . . whether they are **e**
Matt 6:13 but deliver us from **e**
Matt 12:35 **e** person . . . **e** from the **e** stored
Mk 9:39 turn right around and speak **e** of Me
Rom 7:21 **e** is there with me
1 Cor 12:10 tell true Spirit from **e** spirits
Eph 6:12 against the **e** spirits that are
2 Thess 3:3 protect you against the **E** One
1 Jn 2:13 you have conquered the **E** One

EXACT
Matt 2:7 **e** time the star appeared

EXALTED
Phil 2:9 very highly **e** Him and gave Him

EXAMINE
1 Cor 4:3 or any human court should **e** me
1 Cor 9:3 defend myself before . . . who **e** me

1 Cor 11:28 **e** himself then eat of the bread
2 Cor 13:5 **e** yourselves to see whether you
EXAMPLE
Gal 3:15 let me use an **e** from daily life
1 Tim 4:12 be an **e** to those who believe
Tit 2:7 In everything be an **e** of good works
1 Pet 2:21 Christ . . . left you an **e**
EXCLUDED
Rom 3:27 becomes of our pride It is **e**
Heb 4:1 may imagine that he is **e**
EXCUSE
Rom 1:20 Therefore they have no **e**
EXIST
Jn 1:15 above me because He **e** before
Rom 4:17 being that which does not **e**
1 Cor 11:11 woman . . . not **e** apart from man
Gal 4:8 slaves to gods who do not really **e**
Heb 2:10 for whom by whom everything **e**
Heb 11:6 he must believe that God **e**
EXISTENCE
1 Cor 11:12 man comes into **e** by woman
1 Cor 11:12 woman came into **e** from man
EXPECT
Matt 20:10 they **e** to receive more
Lk 8:40 because they were all **e** Him
EXPECTATION
1 Cor 9:10 with the **e** that he will receive
EXPENSIVE
Mk 14:3 real nard and very **e**
Jn 12:3 Mary took . . . perfume . . . very **e**
1 Tim 2:9 not . . . gold pearls or **e** clothes
EXPERIENCE
Acts 2:31 His body would not **e** decay
Gal 3:4 did you **e** so much for nothing
EXPLAIN
Mk 4:34 He fully **e** everything to them
Lk 24:27 with Moses . . . He **e** . . . Scriptures
Acts 18:26 and **e** God's way to him
1 Cor 2:13 **e** the things of the Spirit
1 Pet 3:15 asks you to **e** the hope you have
2 Pet 1:20 Scripture comes . . . human **e**
EXPOSED
Heb 4:13 Everything is uncovered and **e**
EXTRA
Mk 12:44 what they have **e** and dropped it in
EXTREME
Rom 7:13 that sin . . . would become **e** sinful
2 Cor 1:8 our suffering . . . was so **e**
EYE
Matt 5:29 If your . . . **e** causes you to stumble
Matt 5:38 An **e** for an **e** and a tooth
Matt 6:22 **e** is the lamp of the body
Lk 24:31 their **e** were opened . . . knew who He
Acts 9:8 When he opened his **e** he could not
Acts 9:40 She opened her **e** and seeing Peter
1 Cor 2:9 No **e** has seen no ear has heard
Gal 4:15 you would have torn out your **e**
1 Jn 2:16 lust of the **e** and vain display
Rev 4:6 covered with **e** in front

FACE
Matt 6:16 hypocrites put on the kind of **f**
Matt 18:10 angels in heaven . . . see **f** of My
Matt 26:39 with His **f** to the ground
Mk 15:39 When the captain who stood **f**
Acts 6:15 it was like the **f** of an angel
1 Cor 13:12 then we will see **f** to **f**
2 Cor 3:7 the **f** of Moses because it shone
2 Cor 11:23 beaten . . . more and often **f** death
Gal 2:11 I opposed him to his **f** . . . wrong
Rev 1:16 His **f** was like sun when it shines
FAIL
1 Cor 6:7 you already have completely **f**
2 Cor 13:5 unless you **f** in your test
FAILURES
Rom 4:25 to death because of our **f** and then
FAINT
Lk 21:26 People will **f** as they fearfully
FAITH
Matt 8:10 Israel have I found such **f**
Matt 9:22 your **f** has made you well
Mk 10:52 your **f** has made you well
Lk 7:50 Your **f** saved you
Acts 3:16 **f** that Jesus worked has given him
Acts 6:5 Stephen a man full of **f**
Acts 15:9 cleansing their hearts by **f** He
Acts 16:34 happy to have found **f**
Rom 1:5 listen and come to **f**
Rom 1:8 news of your **f** is spreading all
Rom 1:17 righteous will live by **f**
Rom 3:28 by **f**—apart from the works
Rom 4:5 **f** is credited . . . as righteousness
Rom 4:9 Abraham's **f** was credited to his
Rom 5:1 Now that we are justified by **f**
Rom 10:8 This is the word of **f** we preach
Rom 10:17 **f** comes from hearing the message
Rom 11:20 but you stand by **f**
1 Cor 2:5 your **f** might not depend
1 Cor 13:2 if I have **f** to move mountains
2 Cor 4:13 Having the same spirit of **f**
2 Cor 5:7 we live by **f** not by sight
Gal 1:23 persecute us is preaching the **f**
Gal 2:16 be justified by **f** in Christ
Gal 3:11 the just will live by **f**
Gal 5:5 await by **f** the righteousness
Eph 2:8 by grace you are saved through **f**
Eph 6:16 take **f** as the shield
Phil 2:17 in behalf of your **f** I am glad
Phil 3:9 which is through **f** in Christ
Col 2:5 firm you are in your **f** in Christ
Col 2:12 raised with Him through **f**
1 Tim 2:7 teacher of **f** and truth to
1 Tim 6:10 wandered away from the **f**
2 Tim 1:5 sincere your **f** was
Tit 1:13 they may be sound in their **f**
Heb 11:1 **f** is being sure of the things
Heb 11:3 By **f** we know God created the world
Heb 11:6 impossible to please God without **f**
Heb 11:39 By **f** all these won approval
Jas 2:20 **f** without works is dead
1 Pet 1:5 through **f** you are protected

1 Pet 1:7 **f** . . . more precious than gold
1 Pet 5:9 be strong in your **f** and resist
2 Pet 1:1 were given a **f** as precious as
1 Jn 5:4 our **f** is the victorious conqueror
Jude 20 build yourselves . . . most holy **f**
FAITHFUL
2 Tim 2:2 before . . . witnesses entrust to **f**
2 Tim 2:13 He remains **f** because He cannot
Heb 3:2 Moses was **f** in God's whole house
Heb 10:23 He who made the promise is **f**
Rev 2:10 continue to be **f** until death
Rev 19:11 its Rider is called **F** and True
FALL
Matt 7:25 it did not **f** because
Matt 24:10 Then many will **f** from faith
Mk 13:25 stars will be **f** from the sky
Lk 5:8 When Simon Peter saw . . . **f** down
Acts 7:60 said this he **f** asleep
Acts 9:4 He **f** . . . ground and heard a voice
Rom 11:11 by their **f** salvation has come
Rom 16:17 cause people to **f** from faith
1 Cor 10:12 be careful that he does not **f**
Gal 5:4 have **f** from grace
1 Tim 2:14 woman . . . deceived **f** into sin
Heb 4:11 so no one may **f** by following
Rev 2:5 Remember from where you have **f**
Rev 6:16 saying to mountains and rocks **F**
Rev 18:2 The great Babylon has **f**
FALSE
Matt 26:60 came forward with **f** testimony
2 Cor 11:13 such men are **f** apostles
1 Jn 4:1 many **f** prophets have gone out
FALSELY
1 Tim 6:20 what is **f** called knowledge
FALSIFYING
2 Cor 4:2 trickery nor are we **f** God's word
FAMILY
Matt 13:57 his hometown and in his **f**
Acts 16:31 you and your **f** will be saved
1 Cor 16:15 you know . . . **f** of Stephanas
Gal 6:10 especially to our **f** of believers
Eph 2:19 members of God's **f**
Eph 3:15 from whom the whole **f**
1 Tim 3:4 He must manage his own **f** well
1 Tim 3:15 people to behave within His **f**
FAMINE
Matt 24:7 there will be **f** and earthquakes
Lk 4:25 a severe **f** all over the land
Acts 11:28 severe **f** all over the world
FAR
Mk 12:34 not **f** away from the Kingdom
Acts 17:27 He is never **f** from any one of us
Eph 3:20 working in us can do **f f** more than
FARMS
Lk 9:12 Send the crowd to the . . . **f**
FARMER
2 Tim 2:6 hard-working **f** should . . . a share
FARTHEST
Acts 1:8 testify . . . to the **f** parts of world
Rom 10:18 their words to the **f** parts

FAST
Matt 6:16 when you **f** stop looking sad
Matt 9:14 Why is it . . . disciples do not **f**
FATHER
Matt 5:48 as your **F** in heaven is perfect
Matt 6:9 Our **F** in heaven may Your Name
Matt 6:14 your **F** in heaven . . . forgive you
Matt 6:18 **F** who sees what you do in private
Matt 10:20 Spirit of your **F** speaking
Matt 10:29 without your **F** permission
Matt 10:37 loves **f** or mother more than Me
Mk 7:10 who speaks evil of **f** or mother
Mk 11:25 so that your **F** in heaven
Lk 3:8 Abraham is our **f**
Lk 22:42 **F** if You wish take this cup away
Lk 23:34 **F** forgive them for they do not
Lk 23:46 **F** into Your hands I entrust
Jn 1:14 glory of the **F** one-and-only Son
Jn 5:23 does not honor Son does not honor **F**
Jn 8:19 knew Me you would know My **F** also
Jn 8:44 he is a liar and the **f** of lies
Jn 14:6 No one comes to the **F** except by Me
Jn 20:17 I am going up to My **F** and your **F**
Rom 4:11 He was . . . **f** of all who believe
1 Cor 4:15 in Christ Jesus I became your **f**
2 Cor 1:3 **F** of mercy and God of all
Eph 6:4 and **f** do not make your children
Col 3:21 **F** do not irritate your children
Heb 1:5 I will be His **F** He will be My Son
Heb 12:7 son whom his **f** does not discipline
1 Jn 2:13 I am writing to you **f**
FAULT
Rom 9:19 Why does He . . . find **f** with anyone
Col 1:22 stand before Him without sin or **f**
Rev 14:5 they are without **f**
FAVOR
Mk 12:14 do not **f** any individuals
Acts 25:3 begged him to do them a **f**
Rom 2:11 does not **f** one person over another
Eph 6:9 He does not **f** one person over
Jas 2:1 do not **f** one person over another
FAVORABLE
2 Cor 6:2 At a **f** time I have heard you
FEAR
Matt 28:8 hurried away . . . with **f** and great
Acts 10:2 was a religious man who **f** God
Rom 3:18 they have no **f** of God
2 Cor 5:11 Since we know the **f** of the Lord
Heb 5:7 He **f** God He was heard
1 Jn 4:18 His mature love throws out **f**
Rev 14:7 **F** God and give Him glory
FEED
Matt 6:26 Father . . . continues to **f** them
Jn 21:15 **F** My lambs Jesus told him
FEEL
Lk 24:39 it is I Myself **F** Me and see
Jn 14:1 Do not **f** troubled Believe in God
FEET
Lk 10:39 sat at the Lord's **f** and listened
Jn 12:3 poured it on Jesus' **f** dried His **f**
Acts 4:35 They laid it at the apostles' **f**

Rom 16:20 crush Satan under your **f**
Eph 1:22 put everything under His **f**
1 Tim 5:10 if she . . . washed **f** of believers
FELLOW
Matt 18:28 he found one of his **f** slaves
Eph 2:19 but **f** citizens with the believers
Phlm 1 Philemon our dear **f** worker
FELLOWSHIP
Acts 2:42 teaching of apostles and to the **f**
2 Cor 13:14 **f** of the Holy Spirit be with
Gal 2:9 gave . . . me the right hand of **f**
1 Jn 1:3 you too may have **f** with us
FENCES
Lk 14:23 roads and stone **f**
FERTILIZE
Lk 13:8 dig around it and **f** it
FESTIVAL
Jn 7:2 the Jewish **F** of Booths was near
Jn 7:10 gone up to the **F** He also went up
Jn 7:11 looking for Jesus . . . at the **F**
Jn 7:37 the great day of the **F** as Jesus
Jn 12:12 crowd . . . come to the **f** hearing that
Jn 13:29 Buy what we need for the **f**
Col 2:16 say you are wrong . . . do on a **f**
FEVER
Matt 8:14 lying in bed with a **f**
Lk 4:39 ordered the **f** to leave and it left
FEW
Matt 7:14 only a **f** are finding it
Mk 6:5 except lay His hands on a **f** sick
Lk 13:23 only a **f** people . . . saved
FIANCEE
Lk 2:5 to register with Mary his **f**
FIELD
Matt 27:8 has . . . been called the **F** of Blood
Lk 14:18 I bought a **f**
1 Cor 3:9 You are God's **f** God's building
FIERY
Heb 1:7 His servants **f** flames
Rev 20:14 death . . . were thrown into **f** lake
FIG
Lk 13:6 man had a **f** tree growing
Jn 1:50 I saw you under the **f** tree
FIGHT
Jn 18:36 My helpers would **f** to keep Me
2 Cor 10:3 we are not **f** in a fleshly way
1 Tim 1:18 **f** a good **f** while still holding
1 Tim 6:12 **f** the good **f** of faith
2 Tim 2:14 not to **f** about words
2 Tim 4:7 I have **f** the good **f** . . . completed
FIGURATIVE
Jn 16:25 I have used **f** language in speaking
Jn 16:29 talking . . . not using **f** language
FIGURATIVELY
Heb 11:19 **f** speaking he did get him back
FILL
Lk 5:7 they **f** both boats so . . . sink
Acts 2:4 were all **f** with the Holy Spirit
Acts 4:31 They were **f** with the Holy Spirit
Eph 1:23 Him who **f** everything in every way
Eph 4:10 above all heavens to **f** everything

FILTHY
Col 3:8 fury malice slander and **f** talk
FINGER
Mk 7:33 He put His **f** into the man's ears
Lk 16:24 dip the tip of his **f** in water and
Jn 20:25 put my **f** in the mark of the nails
FINISH
Matt 7:28 Jesus **f** speaking the crowds were
Phil 1:6 will go on to **f** it until the Day
Jn 19:30 Jesus said It is **f**
Heb 4:3 yet God **f** His work . . . He made world
FIRE
Matt 25:41 Go away . . . into the everlasting **f**
Mk 9:48 worm does not die and **f** is not put
Lk 16:24 I am suffering in this **f**
1 Cor 3:13 the **f** will reveal it and test it
1 Thess 5:19 Do not put out the **f** . . . Spirit
Heb 12:29 our God is a consuming **f**
Jas 3:6 tongue is also a **f**
2 Pet 3:7 heavens and the earth for **f** and
Rev 1:14 His eyes were like flames of **f**
FIRM
1 Cor 16:13 Watch stand **f** in your faith
2 Cor 1:21 both us and you **f** in Christ
FIRST
Matt 20:10 when **f** ones came they expected
Matt 20:16 last will be **f** and **f** last
Mk 9:35 If anyone wants to be **f**
Mk 10:31 **f** will be last and the last **f**
Mk 16:9 showed Himself **f** to Mary . . . Magdala
Lk 13:30 last will be **f** . . . who are **f** will be
Jn 2:11 the **f** of His miraculous signs
1 Cor 15:45 **f** man Adam became natural being
Col 1:18 Beginning the **f** from the dead
1 Thess 4:16 dead . . . in Christ will rise **f**
1 Tim 2:13 Adam was formed **f** then Eve
1 Jn 4:19 We love because He **f** loved us
FIRST AND THE LAST
Rev 1:17 I am the **F** and the **L**
FIRSTBORN
Rom 8:29 He would be the **F** among brothers
Col 1:15 the **F** of all creation
Heb 1:6 when He brings the **f** Son into world
FISH
Matt 12:40 Jonah . . . belly of the huge **f**
Matt 17:27 take the first **f** that comes up
Lk 5:6 caught a very large number of **f**
Jn 6:9 has five barley loaves and two **f**
Jn 21:3 Peter said to others I'm going **f**
1 Cor 15:39 **f** have still another
FISHERS
Matt 4:19 I will make you **f** of men
FISHERMEN
Matt 4:18 for they were **f**
Mk 1:16 for they were **f**
FISTS
Matt 26:67 struck Him with their **f**
FIT
Lk 9:62 not **f** for the Kingdom
Eph 4:16 He makes the whole body **f** together

FIVE

Matt 25:15 He gave one man f talents
Mk 8:19 When I broke the f loaves
Acts 4:4 men grew to about f thousand

FLAME

Acts 2:3 saw tongues like f that separated
Rev 1:14 His eyes were like f of fire
Rev 8:10 a huge star f like a torch fell

FLASH

Acts 9:3 light from heaven f around him

FLATTERED

1 Thess 2:5 we never f as you know

FLEE

Matt 10:23 they hunt you . . . f to another
1 Cor 6:18 f from sexual sin

FLESH

Matt 19:6 they are no longer two but one f
Mk 10:8 no longer two but one f
Lk 24:39 A ghost does not have f and bones
Jn 3:6 What is born of f is f
Jn 6:51 The Bread I will give . . . is My f
Rom 8:3 His Son to be like sinful f
1 Cor 3:3 influenced by your sinful f
1 Cor 15:39 Not all f is the same
1 Cor 15:50 f and blood cannot have a share
2 Cor 10:2 we are living according to the f
2 Cor 12:7 a thorn for my f
Gal 5:13 as a launching pad for the f
Gal 5:19 you know the works of the f
Eph 2:3 doing what our f and mind wanted to
Eph 5:31 the two will be one f
Eph 6:12 not fighting against f and blood
Heb 2:14 He also took on f and blood to be
1 Pet 2:11 the desires of your f because
1 Pet 3:18 death in f . . . alive in spirit
2 Pet 2:10 go lusting after sinful f
1 Jn 4:2 Jesus Christ has come in the f

FLESHLY

Rom 8:7 the f mind hates God
Col 2:18 puffed up by his f mind

FLOCK

Lk 2:8 shepherds . . . watching their f
Lk 12:32 afraid any longer little f
Acts 20:28 Take care of . . . the whole f

FLOOD

2 Pet 2:5 He brought a f on . . . ungodly

FLOWING

Lk 4:22 gracious words f from His

FLOWERS

Matt 6:28 Notice . . . the f grow in the field
1 Pet 1:24 glory like the f of the grass

FLUTE

Matt 11:17 We played a tune on f for you
1 Cor 14:7 Lifeless instruments such as a f

FOAMED

Mk 9:20 rolled around and f at the mouth

FOGS

2 Pet 2:17 they are . . . f driven by a storm

FOLLOW

Matt 4:20 they left their nets and f Him
Matt 7:24 My words and continues to f them

Matt 9:9 F Me He told him
Matt 10:38 take his cross and f Me
Matt 12:15 Many f Him and He healed them
Matt 27:55 women . . . had f Jesus from Galilee
Lk 21:8 Do not f them
Jn 10:27 I know them and they f Me
Acts 9:2 bring any of the f of Jesus
Rom 8:4 we who do not f the flesh
2 Tim 3:10 you have closely f my teaching

FOOD

Jn 4:32 I have f to eat you do not know
Acts 2:46 they shared their f
Acts 6:1 when the f was handed out
Rom 14:20 Do not ruin God's work just for f
1 Cor 10:3 all ate the same spiritual f
1 Tim 4:3 away from f which God created

FOOL

Matt 5:22 Anyone who calls him a f
Rom 1:22 claiming to be wise they became f
1 Cor 4:10 we are f for Christ's sake
2 Cor 11:16 should think that I am a f
2 Tim 3:9 to be the plain f they are

FOOLISH

Matt 7:26 man was so f . . . built his house
1 Cor 2:14 they are f and he cannot know
Gal 3:1 F Galatians Who has bewitched
Eph 5:17 so do not be f but understand

FOOLISHNESS

Mk 7:22 out of people's hearts come . . . f
1 Cor 1:18 story of the cross is f
1 Cor 1:25 God's f is wiser . . . man's wisdom
2 Cor 11:1 up with a little f from me

FOOT

1 Cor 12:15 Suppose a f says I am not a

FOOTSTOOL

Matt 5:35 earth for it is His f
Acts 2:35 until I make Your enemies a f

FOR

Rom 8:31 If God is f us who can be against

FORBADE

Mk 7:36 But the more He f them the more

FORCE

Matt 16:18 build My church and f of hell
Mk 15:21 they f him to carry cross of Jesus
Lk 4:29 got up f Him out of town
Acts 6:12 took him by f and brought
Gal 2:3 But no one f him to be circumcised

FOREHEAD

Rev 7:3 put the seal on the f of servants
Rev 13:16 right hands or on their f

FOREIGN

Acts 7:6 strangers in a f country
Acts 17:18 He . . . to be telling about f gods

FOREIGNERS

Eph 2:19 you are no longer f or strangers

FOREVER

Rom 5:21 in our living f through our Lord
2 Cor 4:18 what we do not see lasts f
2 Cor 9:9 his righteousness lasts f
1 Thess 2:16 anger has come upon them f
Heb 13:8 the same yesterday today and f

1 Jn 2:17 who does will of God remains **f**
Rev 11:15 He will rule as King **f**
FORGET
Phil 3:13 I **f** what is behind reach for what
1 Thess 1:3 never **f** before God and Father
Heb 6:10 For God is not so unjust as to **f**
FORGIVE
Matt 6:12 **f** us our sins as we have **f** those
Matt 6:14 if you **f** the sins of others
Matt 9:2 Your sins are **f**
Matt 9:6 authority on earth to **f** sins
Matt 12:31 slandering Spirit will not be **f**
Matt 18:21 how often shall I **f** my brother
Mk 2:7 Who but God alone can **f** sins
Mk 11:25 anything against anyone **f** him
Lk 6:37 **F** and you will be **f**
Lk 23:34 Father **f** them for they do not know
Jn 20:23 Whenever you **f** . . . sins they are **f**
Rom 4:7 Blessed . . . whose wrongs are **f**
2 Cor 2:7 So now instead **f** and comfort him
2 Cor 2:10 to whom you **f** anything so do I
Eph 4:32 **f** one another as God . . . has **f**
Col 2:13 alive . . . Christ when He **f** all sins
Col 3:13 **f** one another if you have any
Heb 8:12 I will **f** their wrongdoing
1 Jn 1:9 He will **f** our sins
FORGIVENESS
Matt 26:28 My blood . . . for the **f** of sins
Mk 1:4 be baptized for the **f** of sins
Lk 1:77 by the **f** of their sins
Lk 3:3 repentance for the **f** of sins
Lk 24:47 **f** of sins will be preached to all
Acts 13:38 through this Jesus **f** of sins
Col 1:14 redemption namely the **f** of sins
FORM
Mk 16:12 He appeared in a different **f**
Acts 17:29 **f** by the art and imagination of
Rom 9:20 thing which is **f** say . . . who **f** it
1 Tim 2:13 Adam was **f** first then Eve
FORSAKE
Matt 27:46 My God why did You **f** Me
Lk 13:35 now your house is **f**
2 Cor 4:9 persecuted but not **f**
1 Tim 5:5 widow alone and **f** puts her hope
FORTRESSES
2 Cor 10:4 to tear down **f**
FORTY
Matt 4:2 eat anything **f** days and **f** nights
Lk 4:2 to tempt Him for **f** days
Acts 7:23 When he was **f** years old
Heb 3:9 when they saw My works for **f** years
FOUND
Lk 15:32 He was lost and has been **f**
1 Cor 5:1 as is not **f** even among Gentiles
FOUNDATION
1 Cor 3:10 I laid a **f** as an expert master
Eph 2:20 you are built on **f** of the apostles
Col 1:23 stand firm on the **f** and not moved
2 Tim 2:19 there stands God's solid **f**
Rev 21:14 has twelve **f** stones on them

FOUR
Jn 19:23 divided them into **f** parts
FOURTEEN
2 Cor 12:2 I know a man in Christ **f** years
Gal 2:1 **f** years later I went . . . to Jerusalem
FOX
Matt 8:20 **F** have holes . . . Son of Man not
Lk 13:32 Go and tell that **f**
FRAGRANCE
2 Cor 2:14 spreads the **f** of knowing Him
Phil 4:18 it is a sweet **f** a sacrifice
FRANKLY
Mk 8:32 speaking this fact quite **f**
FREE
Matt 17:26 the children are certainly **f**
Matt 27:15 governor used to **f** one prisoner
Lk 13:16 to be **f** from her bond
Lk 24:21 One who was going to **f** Israel
Jn 8:32 know the truth . . . will set you **f**
Jn 8:36 Son sets you **f** you will . . . be **f**
Rom 5:15 the **f** gift is not at all like the
Rom 8:2 set you **f** from the law of sin
Rom 8:21 world also will be **f** from slavery
1 Cor 7:21 if you have a chance to become **f**
1 Cor 9:1 Am I not **f** Am I not an apostle
Gal 3:13 Christ paid the price to **f** us
Gal 4:5 to **f** [redeem] those under the Law
Gal 4:22 the other the son of the **f** woman
Gal 5:1 Christ has **f** us so we will be **f**
Tit 2:14 a payment for us to **f** us
Heb 2:15 thus might **f** those who were
Rev 1:5 by His blood has **f** us from our sins
FREELY
Rom 3:24 they are justified **f** by His grace
FREEDMEN
Acts 6:9 Synagog of the **F** as it was
FREEDOM
Rom 8:21 share the **f** of glory
2 Cor 3:17 where . . . Lord is there is **f**
Gal 2:4 they sneaked in to spy out the **f**
Gal 5:13 do not use your **f** as launching pad
FRIEND
Matt 20:13 **F** I am doing you no wrong
Jn 3:29 Bridegroom's **f** stands and listens
Jn 11:11 Our **f** Lazarus is asleep
3 Jn 14 **f** here send you their greetings
FROGS
Rev 16:13 saw three unclean spirits like **f**
FRONT
Mk 12:39 the **f** seats in the synagogs
FRUIT
Matt 12:33 tree good and then its **f** good
Jn 15:5 I in him he bears much **f**
Jn 15:8 glorify My Father . . . you bear much **f**
Rom 7:5 to produce **f** for death
Gal 5:22 the **f** of the spirit is love joy
Rev 22:2 tree of life . . . twelve kinds of **f**
FULFILL
Matt 2:15 through the prophet was **f**
Matt 3:15 that is how we should **f** all
Matt 5:17 not set them aside but to **f** them

Matt 26:54 then are the Scriptures to be **f**
Matt 26:56 what the prophets written . . . be **f**
Jn 12:38 Isaiah had said was **f**
Jn 13:18 the Scripture is **f** which says
Jn 15:25 the word is **f** which is written
Jn 17:12 so that the Scripture might be **f**
Jn 19:24 what Scripture said was **f**
Jn 19:36 Scripture said was **f** None of His
Col 1:25 in order to **f** the word of God
FULLNESS
Col 2:9 lives all the **f** of the Deity
FUNDAMENTAL
Heb 6:1 let us not repeat the **f** teachings
FUNERAL
Matt 11:17 We sang a **f** song but you did not
FURIOUS
Lk 4:28 all in the synagog became **f**
Acts 7:54 members of the council became **f**
FURY
Rom 2:8 **f** to those who are selfish
FUTURE
Rom 8:38 neither . . . in present nor in the **f**
1 Thess 5:1 God's plans for the **f**

GABBATHA
Jn 19:13 called . . . **G** in Aramaic
GAIN
Phil 1:21 to live is Christ to die is **g**
Phil 3:7 I counted as **g** I now consider
GALL
Matt 27:34 they offered . . . wine mixed with **g**
GARDEN
Jn 18:26 didn't I see you with Him in the **g**
GARDENER
Jn 19:41 there was a **g** at the place
Jn 20:15 thinking He was the **g**
GARMENT
Matt 9:21 If I only touch His **g** I'll
Acts 9:39 the inner and outer **g** Dorcas made
GATE
Matt 7:13 **g** is wide . . . leads to destruction
Rev 21:12 at the **g** twelve angels
GATHER
Matt 24:31 angels . . . will **g** His chosen ones
1 Cor 14:26 when you **g** each is ready
2 Thess 2:1 we will be **g** to meet Him
GENEALOGIES
1 Tim 1:4 myths and endless **g** that give
Tit 3:9 keep away from foolish arguments **g**
GENERATION
Matt 1:17 14 **g** from Abraham to David 14 **g**
Matt 11:16 picture people of this **g**
Matt 12:39 wicked and unfaithful **g** looks
Matt 12:45 will happen to this wicked **g**
Eph 3:21 in Christ Jesus through all **g**
GENEROUS
Matt 20:15 critical of me because I am **g**
Rom 12:8 is sharing let him be **g**
GENTILES
Matt 10:5 Do not go among the **G**
Lk 2:32 a Light to shine on the **G**

Acts 15:7 preach the Gospel to the **G**
Acts 22:21 I will send you away to the **G**
Rom 2:14 **G**—who do not have the Law—do
Rom 11:11 salvation has come to the **G**
Rom 15:9 have **G** praise God for His mercy
Eph 3:6 **G** have the same inheritance
Col 1:27 this mystery among the **G**
GENTLE
Matt 5:5 Blessed are those who are **g**
Matt 11:29 I am **g** and humble-minded
Phil 4:5 know how **g** you can be
1 Thess 2:7 we became **g** when we were with
2 Tim 2:25 and **g** in correcting those
GENTLENESS
Col 3:12 kindness humility **g** patience
GHOST
Matt 14:26 It's a **g** . . . and they cried out
Lk 24:39 A **g** does not have flesh and bones
GIFT
Matt 2:11 offered Him **g** gold frankincense
Matt 5:23 So if you are bringing your **g**
Mk 7:11 Corban that is a **g** to God
Lk 11:13 give your children good **g**
Lk 21:1 dropping their **g** into contribution
Jn 1:16 one **g** of grace after another
Acts 2:38 will receive the **g** of Holy
Rom 1:11 to share a spiritual **g** with you
Rom 4:16 it might come to us as a free **g**
Rom 5:15 free **g** is not at all like failure
Rom 12:6 We have **g** that are different
1 Cor 1:7 you do not lack any **g** as you
1 Cor 7:7 each one has the **g** God gave him
1 Cor 12:4 differing spiritual **g** are given
1 Cor 16:3 men . . . take your **g** to Jerusalem
2 Cor 9:15 thanks be to God for His . . . **g**
Eph 2:8 it is God's **g** It is not the result
Eph 4:8 and gave **g** to people
Phil 1:29 God's **g** to you not . . . to believe
2 Tim 1:6 fan into a flame the **g** of God
Heb 2:4 distributing **g** of the Holy Spirit
GIRL
Mk 5:41 Little **g** I tell you get up
GIVE
Matt 4:9 All this I will **g** You if You
Matt 5:15 **g** light to everyone in the house
Matt 5:42 someone ask for anything **g** it to
Matt 27:50 Jesus cried out . . . and **g** up His
Matt 28:18 All authority has been **g** to Me
Mk 10:45 **g** His life as a ransom for many
Jn 6:37 All the Father **g** Me will come to Me
Jn 19:30 bowed His head and **g** up His spirit
Acts 4:12 no other NAME **g** among mankind
Acts 6:2 not right for us to **g** up teaching
Rom 5:11 Jesus . . . who has now **g** us this
Rom 8:32 **g** Him up for all of us
1 Cor 15:57 God who continues to **g** us
2 Cor 8:5 they **g** themselves to Lord first
Gal 1:4 who **g** Himself for our sins
Gal 2:20 who loved me and **g** Himself for me
Eph 3:8 He **g** this grace to preach the Good
Eph 5:25 Christ loved church and **g** Himself

2 Tim 2:19 calls on . . . Lord **g** up wrongdoing
Heb 2:13 the children God has **g** Me
Heb 4:13 Him to whom we must **g** an account
Heb 13:17 For they must **g** an account
1 Jn 3:16 He **g** His life for us

GLAD
Lk 15:32 we had to celebrate and be **g**
Jn 8:56 My day he saw it and was **g**
Jn 16:22 your heart will be **g** and no one

GLASS
Rev 4:6 something like a sea of **g**

GLORIFY
Jn 11:4 order that Son of God may be **g** by
Jn 12:16 when Jesus was **g** they remembered
Jn 12:28 I have **g** My Name and will **g** it
Jn 13:32 yes He will **g** Him now
Jn 14:13 Father may be **g** in the Son
Jn 17:1 **G** Your Son so that Your Son will **g**
Jn 17:4 I have **g** You on earth by finishing
Acts 3:13 God . . . has **g** His Servant
Rom 8:30 whom He justified He also **g**
1 Cor 6:20 **g** God in your body
1 Cor 10:31 do everything to **g** God
Phil 1:20 always **g** Christ in my body
Phil 3:21 make them like His **g** body
2 Thess 1:10 to be **g** among His holy ones

GLORIOUS
Eph 5:27 to Himself as a **g** church

GLORY
Matt 4:8 kingdoms in the world and their **g**
Matt 24:30 in sky with power and great **g**
Matt 25:31 When the Son of Man comes . . . **g**
Mk 8:38 with holy angels in His Father's **g**
Lk 2:14 **G** to God in the highest heavens
Lk 9:26 He comes in the **g** which He shares
Jn 1:14 we saw His **g** the **g** of the
Jn 2:11 showed His **g** . . . disciples believed
Jn 11:4 but to show the **g** of God
Jn 17:24 may see My **g** which You gave Me
Acts 7:2 God of **g** appeared to our father
Acts 7:55 gazed up to heaven saw God's **g**
Rom 8:17 order that we may share in His **g**
Rom 8:18 the **g** to be revealed to us
Rom 9:23 show the riches of **g** that He has
Rom 11:36 to Him be **g** forever Amen
2 Cor 3:7 Moses because it shone with a **g**
2 Cor 3:18 same **g** which comes from Lord
2 Cor 4:6 knowledge of the **g** of God
Eph 3:21 to Him be **g** in the church
1 Thess 2:20 Yes you are our **g** and joy

GLOW
Lk 24:32 hearts **g** as He was talking
Rom 12:11 but let your spirit **g** and serve

GLUTTON
Matt 11:19 Look at the **g** and drunkard

GO
Matt 8:9 I tell one of them **G** and he **g**
Matt 8:32 **g** He told them They came out
Matt 15:18 what **g** out of the mouth comes
Matt 28:19 **G** and make disciples of all
Acts 1:10 As He was **g** up they were gazing

GOAL
1 Cor 9:26 run with a clear **g** ahead of me
Phil 3:12 reached the **g** or have
1 Tim 1:5 **g** of our instruction is love

GOAT
Matt 25:32 separates the sheep from the **g**
Lk 15:29 never gave me even a little **g**

GOD
Matt 1:23 Immanuel which means **G** with us
Matt 19:26 for **G** everything is possible
Matt 22:37 Love the Lord your **G** with all
Matt 27:46 My **G** My **G** why did You forsake
Lk 1:37 nothing that **G** will not be able to
Jn 1:1 and the Word was **G** . . . in beginning
Jn 1:18 The one-and-only Son who is **G**
Jn 1:29 Lamb of **G** who takes away the sin
Jn 10:35 called them **g** to whom **G** word
Jn 20:17 to My **G** and your **G**
Jn 20:28 Thomas answered . . . My Lord and my **G**
Acts 5:4 You did not lie to men but to **G**
Acts 10:4 to poor have gone up before **G**
Acts 12:22 people shouted A **g** is speaking
Rom 8:28 for good for those who love **G**
1 Cor 11:3 the Head of Christ is **G**
1 Cor 12:18 **G** arranged the parts fitting
2 Cor 4:4 whose . . . minds the **g** of this world
Phil 3:19 own feelings are their **g**
2 Thess 2:4 proclaims that he is **G**
Tit 3:4 when **G** our Savior showed how kind
1 Pet 1:23 cannot perish namely **G** . . . word
1 Jn 4:8 know **G** because **G** is Love

GODDESS
Acts 19:27 temple of the great **g** Artemis

GODLINESS
1 Tim 4:8 but **g** helps in every way
Tit 1:1 know the truth which promotes **g**
2 Pet 1:3 everything needed for life and **g**

GODLY
1 Tim 6:3 not agree . . . words . . . **g** teaching
2 Tim 3:12 all who want to live a **g** life

GOLD
Matt 2:11 offered Him gifts **g** frankincense
Acts 3:6 I do not have any silver or **g**
1 Cor 3:12 with **g** silver precious stones
2 Tim 2:20 there are not only things of **g**
1 Pet 1:7 more precious than **g**
Rev 21:18 city was of pure **g** like clear

GOLDEN
Rev 1:13 wore a **g** belt around His chest

GOLGOTHA
Jn 19:17 Skull . . . in Aramaic is called **G**

GOOD
Matt 5:13 It is no longer **g** for anything
Matt 5:16 see the **g** you do and praise your
Matt 12:35 A **g** person produces **g** things
Matt 28:9 Jesus met them and said **G** morning
Mk 10:17 **G** Teacher he asked Him
Jn 5:29 done **g** will rise to live
Jn 10:11 I am the **G** Shepherd
Acts 9:36 She was always doing **g** works
Acts 10:38 went around doing **g** and healing

Rom 3:8 evil that **g** may come of it
Rom 8:28 work together for **g** for those
2 Cor 10:12 they do not show **g** sense
Eph 2:10 do **g** works in which God
1 Tim 2:9 clothes but of **g** works
1 Tim 6:18 to be rich in **g** works to be glad
2 Tim 1:14 guard the **g** thing entrusted to
2 Tim 3:17 equipped for every **g** work
Tit 2:14 His own people eager to do **g** works
Tit 3:1 obey to be ready to do any **g** work
Jas 2:16 what **g** does it do

GOOD-BYE
Mk 6:46 After saying **g** to them He
Lk 9:61 let me say **g** to those at home
Acts 18:21 As he said **g** to them

GOOD NEWS (see also **GOSPEL**)
Matt 4:23 in synagogs preaching the **G** News
Matt 24:14 **G** News of the Kingdom . . . preached
Mk 1:1 The beginning of the **G** News of Jesus
Lk 2:10 I have **g** news for you A great joy
Lk 4:43 preach the **G** News of the Kingdom
Acts 8:35 He told him the **G** News of Jesus
Rom 10:15 messengers who bring **g** news
1 Cor 9:12 not hinder the **G** News of Christ
1 Thess 2:2 to tell you the **G** News of God
2 Thess 1:8 obey the **G** News of Lord Jesus

GOOD WILL
Lk 2:14 peace to people who have His **g** will
Acts 2:47 having the **g** will of all people

GOSPEL (see also **GOOD NEWS**)
Matt 11:5 poor people hear the **G**
Mk 10:30 Me and for the **G** will certainly
Mk 14:9 Wherever the **G** is preached
Mk 16:15 preach the **G** to whole creation
Lk 4:18 preach the **G** to the poor
Acts 15:7 one among you to preach the **G**
Rom 1:9 preaching the **G** of His Son
Rom 16:25 make you strong by the **G**
1 Cor 9:18 my right in preaching the **G**
Gal 1:6 turning to another kind of **g**
Col 1:5 in the word of truth the **G**
1 Pet 1:25 This word is the **G** . . . preached
1 Pet 4:6 dead also once heard the **G**
Rev 14:6 everlasting **G** to preach to those

GOSSIPING
1 Tim 5:13 not only idle but **g** and meddling

GOVERNMENT
Rom 13:1 let everyone be subordinate to **g**
Tit 3:1 people to be subordinate to **g**

GOVERNOR
Matt 27:2 handed Him over to Pilate the **g**
Lk 3:1 Pontius Pilate was **g** of Judea
1 Pet 2:14 or to **g** as men whom He sent

GRACE
Jn 1:14 Son . . . He is full of **g** and truth
Jn 1:17 **g** and truth came through Jesus
Acts 15:11 we are saved by the **g** of . . . Jesus
Acts 20:24 to the Gospel of the **g** of God
Rom 1:5 the **g** of holding apostolic office
Rom 5:15 God's **g** and the gracious gift
Rom 11:5 God has chosen by His **g**

Rom 16:20 **g** of our Lord Jesus be with you
1 Cor 1:4 because of His **g** which
1 Cor 15:10 God's **g** made me what I am
1 Cor 16:23 the **g** of Lord Jesus be with you
2 Cor 8:9 you know the **g** of our Lord Jesus
2 Cor 12:9 My **g** is enough for you
2 Cor 13:14 **g** of Lord Jesus . . . love of God
Gal 5:4 have fallen from **g**
Eph 2:5 You are saved by **g**
Eph 4:7 But **g** has been given
Phil 4:23 the **g** of our Lord Jesus be with
2 Tim 2:1 let God's **g** . . . make you strong
Tit 2:11 For the **g** of God has appeared
Tit 3:7 justified by His **g** . . . become heirs
Phlm 25 the **g** of Lord Jesus be with . . . you
Heb 4:16 throne of **g** to receive mercy . . . **g**
Rev 22:21 the **g** of Lord Jesus be with all

GRAFTED
Rom 11:17 you . . . have been **g** in among them

GRAIN
Matt 6:26 They do not sow or reap **g**
Matt 9:38 out workers to bring in His **g**
Jn 4:36 reaper . . . gathering **g** for

GRANDMOTHER
2 Tim 1:5 just as it lived in your **g** Lois

GRASS
1 Pet 1:24 All people are like **g**

GRAVE (see also **HADES**)
Jn 5:28 in their **g** will hear His voice
Acts 2:27 You will not leave Me in the **g**

GREAT
Matt 5:19 will be called **g** in Kingdom
Acts 2:20 before the coming of the **g** . . . day
Rev 16:19 the **g** city split into three parts

GREATER
Matt 11:11 least in the Kingdom . . . is **g** than
Matt 12:41 something **g** than Jonah is here
Jn 8:53 Are You **g** than our father Abraham
Jn 10:29 My Father . . . is **g** than all others
Jn 15:13 No one has **g** love than this
Jn 15:20 A slave is not **g** than his master
1 Jn 4:4 He who is in you is **g** than he

GREATEST
1 Cor 13:13 but the **g** of these is love

GREED
Mk 7:22 from people's hearts come . . . **g**
Col 3:5 kill . . . passion evil lust and **g**

GREEDY
1 Cor 5:10 from those who are **g** who rob
Eph 5:5 **g** such a person worships an idol
2 Pet 2:14 their hearts are trained to be **g**

GREEK
Jn 12:20 came up to worship . . . were some **G**
Jn 19:20 notice . . . written in Aramaic . . . **G**
Acts 6:1 by those who spoke **G**
Acts 21:37 Can you speak **G** he asked

GREET
Lk 20:46 around in long robes . . . to be **g**
Rom 16:3 **g** Prisca and Aquila my . . . workers
1 Cor 16:19 churches in . . . Asia **g** you
2 Jn 10 take him into your home or **g** him

GREETINGS
Lk 1:28 **G** you who are greatly blessed
GRIEVE
Eph 4:30 do not **g** God's Holy Spirit
1 Thess 4:13 you do not **g** like the others
GROAN
Rom 8:23 first taste of heaven **g** inwardly
Jas 5:4 the **g** of those who cut the grain
GROANING
Acts 7:34 I have heard their **g** and have
GROOM
Jn 2:9 the manager called the **g**
GROUP
Acts 6:5 The idea pleased the whole **g**
GROW
Rom 15:2 please his neighbor . . . help him **g**
1 Cor 3:6 Apollos watered but God made it **g**
1 Pet 2:2 cause you to **g** . . . saved
2 Pet 3:18 **g** in grace and knowing our Lord
Rev 2:3 I know . . . and have not **g** weary
GROWING
Phil 4:17 but the **g** profit in your account
GROWTH
1 Cor 10:23 not everything encourages **g**
GROUND
Mk 4:28 The **g** produces grain by itself
Acts 7:33 place . . . standing is holy **g**
GRUDGE
Mk 6:19 Herodias . . . hold a **g** against John
GRUMBLING
Matt 20:11 Although they took it . . . began **g**
Mk 14:5 And they were **g** at her
GUARANTEE
2 Cor 1:22 given . . . Spirit as a **g** in heart
Heb 2:3 those who heard Him **g** its truth
Heb 6:16 their oath **g** what they say
GUARD
Matt 10:17 Be on your **g** against men
Matt 28:4 The **g** were so afraid of him
Mk 13:9 Be on your **g** Men will hand
Jn 18:22 When He said this one of Temple **g**
Phil 4:7 will **g** your hearts and minds in
1 Tim 6:20 **g** what has been entrusted
2 Tim 1:14 **g** the good thing entrusted to
2 Pet 3:17 Be on your **g** so that you
GUARDIAN
Gal 3:24 thus the Law has been our **g** until
Gal 4:2 He is under **g** and managers until
GUEST
Rom 12:13 Eagerly welcome strangers as **g**
Phlm 22 have a **g** room ready for me
1 Pet 2:11 I urge you as **g** and stangers
GUIDE
Lk 1:79 **g** our feet into the way of peace
Acts 8:31 How can I unless someone **g** me
Rom 2:19 if . . . you are a **g** to blind
GUILT
1 Cor 8:7 conscience . . . is stained with **g**
GUILTY
Jn 18:38 not find this Man **g** of anything
Acts 25:11 Now if I am **g** and have done

HABITS
1 Cor 15:33 Bad company ruins good **h**
HADES (see also **GRAVE**)
Rev 1:18 keys of death and of **h**
Rev 6:8 and **H** cames close behind
HAIL
Matt 27:29 **H** King of the Jews
Jn 19:3 **H** King of the Jews and slapped His
Rev 16:21 huge **h** stones weighing . . . pounds
HAIR
Matt 10:31 As for you even **h** on your head
Acts 18:18 he had his **h** cut
1 Cor 11:14 for a man to have long **h**
Rev 1:14 His head and His **h** were white
HAIR-STYLING
1 Tim 2:9 matter of attractive **h** gold
HALF
Mk 6:23 I will give you anything . . . up to **h**
Lk 10:30 went away leaving him **h** dead
HAND
Matt 4:6 They will carry you in their **h**
Matt 5:30 if . . . **h** causes you to stumble
Matt 6:3 left **h** know what right **h** is doing
Matt 9:25 He went in and took her **h**
Matt 11:27 Father put everything in My **h**
Lk 24:39 Look at My **h** and My feet
Jn 10:29 tear them out of My Father's **h**
Jn 13:9 not only my feet but also my **h**
Jn 20:25 put my **h** in His side I will not
Acts 6:6 prayed and laid their **h** on
Acts 7:50 Did My **h** not make all . . . things
Acts 9:12 Ananias come . . . place his **h** on him
Rom 4:25 It was He who was **h** over to death
1 Cor 5:5 **h** such a person over to Satan
1 Cor 15:24 He **h** over the Kingdom to God
Col 3:1 sitting at the right **h** of God
1 Tim 2:8 men pray . . . lifting . . . holy **h**
1 Tim 4:14 when pastors laid their **h** on you
Heb 1:10 heavens are the works of Your **h**
HANDCUFFS
Mk 5:4 he had torn the **h** apart
HANDWRITING
2 Thess 3:17 this is my **h**
HANG
Matt 27:5 he . . . went away and **h** himself
Gal 3:13 Cursed is everyone who **h** on a tree
HAPPEN
Mk 10:32 going to **h** to Him
Lk 2:15 Lord has told us what has **h**
Lk 21:7 things are going to **h**
Lk 24:18 does not know what things **h** there
Rev 4:1 what must **h** after these
HAPPIER
2 Cor 7:7 and this made me even **h**
HAPPINESS
Rom 15:13 God of hope fill you with . . . **h**
HAPPY
Matt 2:10 They were extremely **h** to see star
Acts 16:34 everyone . . . **h** to have found faith
Rom 12:15 Be **h** with those who are **h**
1 Cor 7:40 she will be **h** if she stays

Phil 4:4 Be **h** in the Lord always
Heb 13:17 obey them so that they may be **h**
HARD
Matt 25:24 I knew that you are a **h** man
Mk 10:23 How **h** it will be for those . . . rich
Lk 5:5 we worked **h** all night
1 Pet 4:18 it is **h** for a righteous person
Rev 2:2 I know . . . how **h** you have worked
HARDSHIP
2 Cor 6:4 in troubles in need in **h**
2 Tim 2:3 share **h** with me like good soldier
HARMONY
Rom 12:16 Live in **h** with one another
1 Pet 3:8 all of you live in **h**
HARSH
Col 3:19 love your wives and do not be **h**
1 Tim 5:1 Do not be **h** with an older man
HARVEST
Matt 9:38 ask the Lord of the **h** to send
1 Cor 15:20 first in **h** of those who have
Rev 14:15 the **h** on the earth is very ripe
HATE
Matt 5:43 Love your neighbor **h** your enemy
Matt 10:22 Everybody will **h** you because of
Matt 24:9 and all nations will **h** you
Lk 14:26 comes to Me and does not **h**
Jn 15:23 person who **h** Me also **h** My Father
Rom 1:30 they slander and are **h** by God
Rom 7:15 instead . . . I do what I **h**
Rom 8:7 the fleshly mind **h** God
Rom 12:9 **h** evil cling to what is good
Jas 4:4 love the world is to **h** God
1 Jn 2:9 says I am . . . but **h** his brother
1 Jn 3:13 surprised . . . if world **h** you
HEAD
Matt 5:36 do not swear by your **h**
Jn 13:9 not only my feet but also . . . my **h**
1 Cor 11:3 the **H** of every man is Christ
Eph 1:10 organized under Christ as its **H**
Eph 1:22 established Him as **H** of everything
Eph 5:23 husband is **h** of his wife as Christ
Col 1:18 He is also **H** of church . . . His body
Rev 13:3 one of **h** seemed to have . . . wounded
HEAL
Matt 4:23 Kingdom and **h** every kind
Matt 10:1 **h** every kind of disease and
Lk 14:3 right to **h** on the Sabbath
Acts 4:10 this man stands before you **h**
Acts 4:30 stretch out Your hand to **h**
Acts 10:38 **h** all who were under the tyranny
1 Cor 12:9 same Spirit gives ability to **h**
HEALING
Lk 13:32 drive out demons and work **h**
Acts 28:27 they never turn to Me for **h**
HEALTH
Acts 3:16 given him this perfect **h** in front
HEALTHY
Matt 6:22 your eye is **h** you will have light
Matt 9:12 Those . . . **h** do not need a doctor
HEAR
Matt 5:21 You have **h** that long ago people

Mk 4:24 Be careful what you **h**
Lk 10:16 person who **h** you **h** Me
Jn 8:40 truth which I **h** from God
Jn 12:38 what they **h** from us
Acts 4:20 telling what we have seen and **h**
Acts 10:31 Cornelius . . . God has **h** prayer
Rom 10:14 if they have not **h** of Him
Rom 10:17 faith comes from **h** the message
1 Cor 2:9 No ear has **h** and no mind has
Heb 3:15 Today if you **h** Him speak
1 Pet 3:12 Lord watches the righteous and **h**
1 Pet 4:6 the dead also once **h** the Gospel
HEART
Matt 5:8 Blessed are those whose **h** are pure
Matt 6:21 where treasure is . . . **h** will be
Matt 12:40 Son of Man . . . in **h** of the earth
Matt 15:8 but their **h** are far from Me
Matt 15:18 out of the mouth comes from **h**
Matt 22:37 Love . . . God with all your **h**
Lk 2:19 Mary treasured all . . . in her **h**
Jn 1:18 is close to the Father's **h**
Jn 12:40 He blinded . . . and hardened their **h**
Acts 2:46 were one at **h** as they continued
Rom 1:21 their ignorant **h** were darkened
Rom 9:2 great sorrow . . . pain in my **h**
2 Cor 3:3 but on tablets of human **h**
2 Cor 7:3 I told you . . . you are in our **h**
Col 3:16 songs to God with thankful **h**
1 Thess 2:4 God who tests our **h**
Phlm 12 back to you—and my **h** goes with him
Heb 3:12 See . . . none of you has a wicked **h**
Heb 4:12 thoughts and intentions of the **h**
Heb 8:10 write them on their **h**
Heb 10:22 our **h** were sprinkled to take away
1 Pet 3:15 in your **h** have deep respect
1 Jn 3:17 shuts his **h** against him
HEARTILY
Matt 18:35 each of you will not **h** forgive
Col 3:23 whatever you do work **h** as for Lord
HEATHEN
Matt 18:17 treat like **h** and tax collector
HEAVEN
Matt 3:16 **h** opened and He saw the Spirit
Matt 5:12 you have a great reward in **h**
Matt 5:18 until **h** and earth pass away not
Matt 6:10 on earth as it is in **h**
Matt 10:7 The Kingdom of **h** is near
Matt 24:29 powers of **h** will be shaken
Matt 26:64 coming on the clouds of **h**
Matt 28:18 All authority . . . in **h** and earth
Lk 9:51 Jesus to be taken up to **h**
Jn 1:51 you will see **h** opened and angels
Jn 3:13 except the One who came down from **h**
Acts 1:11 you saw Him go to **h**
Acts 3:21 Jesus whom **h** must receive until
Acts 9:3 suddenly a light from **h** flashed
Rom 8:23 as our first taste of **h**
Eph 1:20 made Him sit at His . . . hand in **h**
Col 1:5 stored up for you in **h**
Col 1:16 created . . . in **h** and on earth
1 Thess 1:10 wait for Son to come from **h**

Heb 1:10 the **h** are the works of Your hand
Heb 11:16 longing for better land—I mean **h**
1 Pet 3:22 has gone to **h** and is at right
2 Pet 3:10 on that Day the **h** will pass away
Rev 4:1 door was standing open in **h**
Rev 19:1 loud sound . . . crowd in **h** saying

HEAVENLY
1 Cor 15:40 there are **h** bodies and earthly

HEIR
Matt 8:12 those who were born to be **h**
Rom 8:17 if children then **h** God's **h**
Gal 3:29 descendants and **h** . . . God promised
Tit 3:7 might become **h** in keeping . . . hope
Heb 1:2 Son whom He made **H** of everything

HELL
Matt 5:29 to have all of it thrown into **h**
Matt 10:28 both soul and body in **h**
Matt 11:23 you will go down to **h**
Mk 9:43 two hands and go to **h** where fire
Lk 16:23 being tormented in **h** [hades] he
2 Pet 2:4 put them . . . gloomy dungeons of **h**

HELLFIRE
Matt 5:22 calls him a fool must answer in **h**

HELMET
Eph 6:17 take salvation as your **h** and sword

HELP
Mk 9:24 I do believe **h** me with my
Lk 10:37 one who was kind enough to **h** him
Acts 7:35 free them with the **h** of the Angel
Acts 16:9 Come over to Macedonia and **h** us
Rom 8:37 He who loved us **h** us win . . . victory
Rom 12:8 it is **h** people in need let him
1 Cor 3:5 by whose **h** you came to believe
1 Cor 14:26 Do it all to **h** one another grow
2 Cor 1:11 you are also joining in **h** us
2 Cor 2:10 presence of Christ to **h** you
2 Tim 1:18 all he did to **h** me in Ephesus
Heb 1:14 sent to **h** those who . . . inherit
Heb 13:6 Lord is my **H** I will not be afraid

HELPLESS
Rom 5:6 while we were still **h** Christ died

HEN
Matt 23:37 bring children . . . as a **h** gathers

HERE
Matt 28:6 He is not **h** He has risen . . . said
Lk 17:21 will not say Look **h** it is

HEREAFTER
1 Tim 4:8 promise for life here and **h**

HIDDEN
Matt 5:14 town cannot be **h** . . . on hill
Lk 8:17 Everything **h** will be uncovered
Lk 9:45 it was **h** from them
1 Cor 2:7 we tell about God's **h** wisdom
Rev 1:20 The **h** meaning of the seven stars

HIDE
Matt 11:25 for **h** these things from wise
Heb 4:13 No creature can **h** from Him
Rev 6:15 slave and free man **h** themselves

HIGH
Eph 3:18 how broad long **h** deep His love is

HIGHER
Matt 8:24 waves were **h** than the boat
Heb 7:26 made **h** than the heavens

HIGHLY
1 Thess 5:13 Love them think very **h** of them

HIGHEST
Lk 2:14 Glory to God in the **h** heavens

HIGH PRIEST
Matt 26:63 Then **h** priest said to Him
Acts 23:2 **h** priest Ananias ordered the men
Heb 2:17 He might be . . . **H** Priest to pay for
Heb 3:1 consider Jesus Apostle and **H** Priest
Heb 4:14 we have a great **H** Priest who has
Heb 7:26 Here is the **H** Priest we needed
Heb 9:11 Christ came as **H** Priest of good

HILL
Lk 3:5 every mountain and **h** will be

HILLSIDE
Jn 6:3 Jesus went up **h** and sat down there

HIMSELF
Heb 7:27 and for all when He sacrificed **H**

HINDER
1 Cor 9:12 not to **h** the Good News of Christ

HIRED
Matt 20:7 Nobody has **h** us they answered him
Lk 15:17 How many of my father's **h** men

HIT
Matt 26:68 tell us Who **h** You

HOGS
Matt 8:30 Far away a herd of many **h** feeding
Mk 5:13 the herd about 2,000 **h** stampeded
Lk 15:15 sent him to his fields to feed **h**

HOLD
Jn 20:17 Jesus told her Stop **h** on to Me
Acts 2:42 continued to **h** firmly to teaching
Acts 5:2 he **h** back some of the money
Rom 6:9 Death no longer has any **h** on Him
Col 1:17 He **h** everything together
2 Thess 2:6 now you know what is **h** him back

HOLINESS
Lk 1:75 in **h** and righteousness before Him
1 Cor 1:30 wisdom righteousness **h** ransom
1 Tim 2:15 faith and love and **h** while using
Heb 12:10 to have us share His **h**

HOLY
Matt 7:6 Do not give what is **h** to dogs
Mk 6:20 he knew John was a just and **h** man
Jn 17:17 Make them **h** in truth Your word is
Rom 7:12 So the Law itself is **h**
1 Cor 1:2 called to be **h**
1 Cor 7:34 be **h** in body and in spirit
1 Thess 4:7 not call us to be unclean but **h**
1 Thess 5:23 God of peace make you **h** in
1 Tim 4:5 word of God and prayer make it **h**
Heb 10:10 we are made **h** by the sacrifice
2 Pet 3:11 continue living in a **h** and godly
Rev 4:8 **H H H** is the Lord God Almighty

HOLY CITY
Matt 4:5 devil took Him into the **H** City
Rev 21:2 I saw the **H** CITY NEW JERUSALEM
Rev 22:19 in the **H** City which are described

HOLY ONE
Mk 1:24 know who You are—the **H** One of God
Jn 6:69 know that You are the **H** One of God
HOLY PLACE
Heb 9:2 this is called the **H** Place
HOLY SCRIPTURE
Rom 1:2 through prophets in **H** Scriptures
HOLY SPIRIT
Matt 1:18 be with Child—by the **H** Spirit
Matt 12:32 a word against the **H** Spirit
Matt 28:19 baptizing in name . . . of **H** Spirit
Mk 1:8 He will baptize you with **H** Spirit
Mk 3:29 anyone who slanders the **H** Spirit
Lk 1:35 **H** Spirit will come over you
Jn 20:22 Receive **H** Spirit . . . you forgive
Acts 1:5 you will be baptized with **H** Spirit
Acts 2:4 They were all filled with **H** Spirit
Acts 4:31 filled with the **H** Spirit . . . word
Acts 5:3 tried to make the **H** Spirit a liar
Acts 7:51 you are always opposing **H** Spirit
Acts 10:44 the **H** Spirit came down . . . heard
Acts 19:2 have not heard there is **H** Spirit
Acts 20:28 **H** Spirit has made you overseers
Acts 28:25 **H** Spirit spoke truth to your
Rom 5:5 because **H** Spirit who has been given
Rom 14:17 joy in the **H** Spirit
1 Cor 6:19 body is a temple of the **H** Spirit
1 Cor 12:3 unless he is moved by **H** Spirit
Eph 1:13 were sealed in Him by **H** Spirit
Tit 3:5 **H** Spirit gives us new birth . . . life
HOME
Matt 2:23 He came and made his **h** in a town
Matt 4:13 made His **h** in Capernaum by sea
Matt 10:13 If the **h** is deserving
Matt 12:44 I will go back to the **h** I left
Lk 16:27 send him to my father's **h**
Jn 8:23 My **h** is not in this world
Acts 16:34 he took them up into his **h**
HOMETOWN
Matt 13:54 He went to His **h** taught people
Lk 4:24 no prophet is accepted in his **h**
HONOR
Matt 15:8 people **h** Me with their lips
Lk 14:7 trying to get the places of **h**
Lk 20:46 have the places of **h** at dinners
Jn 5:23 all might **h** Son as they **h** Father
Jn 12:26 If . . . serves Me the Father will **h**
Rom 13:7 if **h** then **h**
Rom 14:6 special day means to **h** the Lord
Eph 3:13 It is an **h** to you
Eph 6:2 **H** your father and mother
1 Tim 1:17 be **h** and glory forever and ever
1 Pet 1:7 praise and glory and **h** when Jesus
HONORABLE
1 Cor 12:23 we think less **h** we dress
1 Cor 12:26 If one is **h** all . . . are happy
2 Tim 2:20 Some are used in an **h** way
HOOK
Matt 17:27 go to the sea throw in a **h**
HOPE
Matt 12:21 His Name will be **h** of Gentiles

Acts 2:26 even My body will rest in **h**
Acts 28:20 it is for the **h** of Israel I wear
Rom 5:2 based on our **h** for God's glory
Rom 5:4 In this **h** we . . . not be disappointed
Rom 8:20 but it does so with **h**
Rom 8:24 if we **h** for something we see
Rom 8:24 who **h** for what he sees
Rom 15:13 God of **h** fill you with perfect
1 Cor 13:7 **h** for everything endures
Eph 1:12 first to **h** in Christ
Col 1:23 not moved from the **h** of the Gospel
Col 1:27 mystery is . . . in you **H** of glory
1 Thess 1:3 your **h** in our Lord Jesus Christ
1 Thess 5:8 the **h** of salvation as a helmet
1 Tim 4:10 our **h** is in the living God
Tit 2:13 we look for the blessed **h**
Heb 11:1 things we **h** for being convinced
HORSE
Rev 6:2 there was a white **h** and its rider
Rev 9:17 the way I saw the **h** in the vision
HOSANNA
Jn 12:13 **H** Blessed is He who is coming
HOST
Rom 16:23 Gaius my **h** and **h** of whole church
HOSTILITY
Eph 2:14 breaking down the wall of **h**
HOUR
Jn 5:25 the **h** is coming . . . dead will hear
HOUSE
Mk 12:40 they swallow up the **h** of widows
Lk 2:49 I must be in My Father's **H**
Lk 20:47 up the **h** of widows
Jn 2:16 stop making My Father's **H** a place
Jn 14:2 In My Father's **h** . . . are many rooms
Acts 2:2 filled the whole **h** where they were
Acts 7:49 What kind of **h** will you build Me
Acts 18:7 His **h** was right beside synagog
Acts 20:20 teaching you . . . **h** to **h**
Phlm 2 to the church that meets in your **h**
Heb 3:2 faithful in God's whole **h**
HUMAN
Mk 14:58 tear down this Temple made by **h**
Rom 6:19 I am speaking in a **h** way because
1 Cor 2:13 words not taught by **h** wisdom
2 Cor 5:1 not made by **h** hands but lasting
2 Cor 5:16 think of anyone only from a **h**
2 Cor 11:18 Since many boast in a **h** way
Gal 1:11 Gospel . . . is not a **h** message
Rev 4:7 face like that of a **h** being
HUMBLE
Lk 1:48 has looked kindly at His **h** servant
Lk 14:11 himself will be **h** . . . person who **h**
Acts 8:33 When He **h** Himself
2 Cor 10:1 I who am **h** when . . . face to face
Phil 2:8 became obedient and **h** Himself
Jas 4:6 God opposes proud . . . grace to the **h**
HUMBLY
Acts 20:19 how I served Lord very **h** with
HUMILITY
Col 2:18 delighting in false **h**
1 Pet 5:5 All of you wear **h** as a sign

HUNDRED
Mk 10:30 will certainly receive a **h** times
Rom 4:19 he was about a **h** years old
HUNGER
Matt 5:6 Blessed are those who **h** and thirst
HUNGRY
Matt 4:2 that time He was very **h**
Matt 25:35 I was **h** you gave Me something
Lk 1:53 **h** He has filled with good things
Rom 12:20 If your enemy is **h** feed him
1 Cor 11:21 so one stays **h** and another gets
1 Cor 13:3 all that I have to feed the **h**
HURLED
Rev 12:9 great dragon was **h** down
HURRICANE
Acts 27:14 a **h** called a northeaster
HURRY
Matt 28:8 They **h** away from the tomb
HURT
Acts 20:38 **h** them most of all
HUSBAND
Jn 4:16 Jesus told her Go call your **h**
1 Cor 7:2 each woman her own **h**
1 Cor 7:13 wife has a **h** . . . not believe
Gal 4:27 than the one who has the **h**
Eph 5:23 a **h** is the head of his wife
Col 3:19 **H** love your wives
1 Pet 3:5 They were subordinate to their **h**
1 Pet 3:7 you **h** live with wives
HUSH
Mk 4:39 **H** He said to the sea
HYMN
1 Cor 14:26 each is ready with a **h**
Eph 5:19 as you speak psalms **h** . . . songs
Col 3:16 singing psalms **h** spiritual songs
HYPOCRISY
1 Tim 4:2 led astray by **h** of liars
HYPOCRITE
Matt 6:2 don't blow your own horn as **h** do
Matt 7:5 You **h** first remove the log
Lk 13:15 You **h** Doesn't each of you
HYPOCRITICALLY
Gal 2:13 Jews acted just as **h** as he did

IDLE
2 Thess 3:7 we were not **i** when we were with
1 Tim 5:13 learn to be **i** and go around
IDOL
Acts 7:41 brought a sacrifice to the **i**
1 Cor 5:10 who rob or who worship **i**
1 Cor 8:4 there is no **i** that is truly alive
1 Cor 10:14 flee from the worship of **i**
Eph 5:5 such a person worships an **i**
Col 3:5 greed which is **i** worship
1 Jn 5:21 Little children keep away from **i**
Rev 2:20 eat food sacrificed to **i**
Rev 9:20 worshiping demons and **i** of gold
IGNORANCE
Eph 4:18 Their natural state of **i**
IGNORANT
2 Pet 3:16 who are **i** . . . twist their meaning

IGNORE
1 Cor 14:38 if anyone **i** this just **i** him
Tit 2:15 full authority—let no one **i** you
ILLEGITIMATE
Heb 12:8 you are not sons but are **i**
ILLUSTRATIONS
Mk 3:23 He called them said to them in **i**
Gal 4:24 use these historical events as **i**
IMAGE
Acts 7:43 star of god Rephan and **i** you made
Rom 1:23 likeness of an **i** of mortals
1 Cor 11:7 he is God's **i** and glory
1 Cor 13:12 we see a blurred **i** in a mirror
Col 1:15 He is the **i** of the invisible God
Rev 13:15 put breath into the **i** of beast
IMAGINE
2 Cor 4:17 greater than anything we can **i**
Eph 3:20 than anything we ask or **i**
IMITATE
1 Cor 11:1 I me as I **i** Christ
Eph 5:1 **i** God as His dear children
Phil 3:17 keep on **i** me and taking note
Heb 13:7 lives ended and **i** their faith
IMMEASURABLE
Eph 2:7 show . . . **i** riches of His grace
IMMEDIATELY
Mk 1:42 **I** the leprosy left him
Lk 13:13 **i** stood up straight
Acts 3:7 **I** his feet ankles were . . . strong
IMMORAL
Eph 5:5 no one who is **i** impure or greedy
2 Pet 2:2 many will follow their **i** ways
Rev 14:8 wine of her **i** passion
IMMORALITY
1 Pet 4:3 when you lived in unbridled **i**
IMMORALLY
Rom 1:24 handed them over to live **i** by
IMMORTAL
1 Cor 15:52 dead will be raised **i**
1 Tim 1:17 everlasting King **i** invisible
IMPORTANT
Mk 12:28 Which is the most **i** of all
Lk 14:8 someone more **i** than you
1 Cor 14:5 more **i** to prophesy than to speak
1 Cor 15:3 very **i** that Christ died for
IMPOSSIBLE
Rom 11:33 how **i** it is to figure out His
Heb 6:6 it is **i** when they fall away . . . back
IMPOSTER
Matt 27:63 we remember how that **i** said
IMPURITY
1 Thess 2:3 does not contain any error or **i**
INCENSE
Rev 5:8 golden bowls full of **i**
INDECENT
1 Cor 13:5 It is not **i** It is not selfish
INDECISIVE
Jas 1:8 He is **i**—wavering in everything
INDESCRIBABLE
2 Cor 9:15 God for His **i** gift

INFANT
Lk 2:12 you will find an **I** wrapped
INFERIOR
2 Cor 12:11 I was not . . . **i** to . . . apostles
INHERIT
Matt 25:34 whom My Father has blessed **i** the
Lk 10:25 what should I do to **i** . . . life
Heb 1:14 those who are going to **i** salvation
INHERITANCE
Acts 20:32 build you up and give you the **i**
Gal 3:18 For if we receive the **i** by the Law
Eph 1:14 guarantee of our **i**
Col 1:12 share believer's **i** in the light
Col 3:24 Lord will give you the **i** as reward
1 Pet 1:4 awaits **i** that cannot be destroyed
INNER
Rom 7:22 my **i** being I delight in God's Law
1 Cor 2:11 thinks except his own **i** spirit
INNKEEPER
Lk 10:35 two denarii and gave them to the **i**
INNOCENT
Matt 27:24 I am **i** of this Man's blood
Acts 18:6 I am **i** From now on
Acts 20:26 I am **i** of blood of any of you
Rom 16:19 **i** in respect to what is evil
2 Cor 7:11 that you are **i** in this matter
Heb 7:26 holy **i** spotless separated
INSANE
Acts 26:24 You are **i** Paul . . . great learning
1 Cor 14:23 they not say that you are **i**
INSIST
Gal 2:12 those who **i** on circumcision
Gal 6:12 **i** you have yourselves circumcised
Tit 3:8 I want you to **i** on these things
INSPIRED
2 Tim 3:16 All Scripture is **i** by God
INSTRUCTED
Rom 2:18 since you are **i** by the Law
INSTRUCTION
2 Thess 2:15 cling to **i** we handed . . . you
2 Thess 3:6 with the **i** you received from us
Eph 6:4 training and **i** of the Lord
INSTRUMENT
Acts 9:15 this man is My chosen **i**
INSULT
Matt 5:11 Blessed are you when people **i** you
Matt 27:44 the robbers . . . also were **i** Him
Acts 23:4 Do you **i** God's high priest
Rom 15:3 The **i** of those who are **i** You
Heb 10:29 and **i** the Spirit of grace
Jas 2:6 but you have **i** the poor man
INTENDED
Acts 2:23 God . . . planned and **i** to have
INTENSELY
1 Pet 1:22 love . . . **i** with a pure heart
INTERESTS
Phil 2:21 all look after their own **i**
INTERFERE
1 Pet 3:7 nothing will **i** with your prayers
INTERPRET
1 Cor 12:10 Another can **i** languages

INTIMIDATED
1 Pet 3:14 do not be **i**
INVISIBLE
Col 1:15 He is the image of the **i** God
1 Tim 1:17 everlasting King immortal **i**
INVITE
Matt 22:14 many are **i** but few are chosen
Lk 14:12 do not **i** your friends
Rev 19:9 blessed are those who are **i**
INWARDLY
Rom 2:29 a real Jew is one who is a Jew **i**
2 Cor 7:5 fighting and **i** afraid
2 Thess 2:17 comfort you **i** and strengthen
IRRITATE
Col 3:21 Fathers do not **i** your children
ISLAND
Rev 1:9 the **i** called Patmos for speaking
ISRAEL
Rom 11:26 in this way all **I** will be saved
ISRAELITES
Rom 10:1 prayer to God is to save the **I**

JAR
Mk 14:13 meet a man carrying a **j** of water
Jn 2:6 Six stone water **j** were standing
JAILER
Acts 16:27 The **j** woke up saw prison doors
JASPER
Rev 21:11 very precious stone like **j**
JEALOUS
Mk 7:22 from people's hearts come . . . **j** eye
Rom 10:19 I will make you **j** of those
1 Cor 3:3 when you are **j** quarreling and
2 Cor 11:2 I am **j** of you with a godly **j**
JERUSALEM
Jn 1:19 Jews in **J** sent priests and Levites
Jn 4:20 people must worship is in **J**
Jn 4:21 worshiping . . . this mountain or in **J**
Rev 21:10 showed me HOLY CITY **J** coming
JESUS
Matt 3:13 Then **J** came from Galilee to John
Matt 27:37 THIS IS **J** THE KING OF THE
Mk 1:9 **J** came from Nazareth in Galilee
Lk 1:31 Son and you will name Him **J**
Jn 1:45 prophets also wrote—**J** Joseph's son
Acts 4:30 Name of Your holy Servant **J**
Acts 7:59 Lord **J** receive my spirit
Acts 8:35 he told him the Good News of **J**
Acts 9:5 I am **J** . . . whom you are persecuting
Acts 19:4 the One coming after him . . . in **J**
Acts 22:8 I am **J** . . . Nazareth . . . persecuting
Acts 28:23 tried to convince them about **J**
Rom 3:22 by their believing in **J** Christ
Rom 5:17 rule even more through One Man **J**
Rom 7:25 does it through our Lord **J** Christ
1 Cor 6:11 justified . . . in . . . **J** Christ
1 Cor 11:23 Lord **J** on the night . . . betrayed
Eph 2:20 **J** Himself is the Cornerstone
Phil 2:10 at Name of **J** everyone in heaven
1 Thess 4:14 who have fallen asleep in **J**
1 Tim 2:5 the Man Christ **J** who gave Himself

Heb 7:24 because **J** lives forever His
Heb 12:24 here is **J** the Mediator
Heb 13:8 **J** Christ is same yesterday today
1 Jn 1:7 blood of **J** His Son washes us clean
Rev 1:5 from **J** . . . He is the faithful Witness
JEW
Matt 27:37 IS JESUS THE KING OF THE **J**
Jn 18:36 from being handed over to the **J**
Acts 2:5 **J** who feared God . . . were living
Acts 18:2 There he found a **J** by the
Acts 21:39 Paul answered I am a **J** from
Rom 1:16 save everyone . . . **J** first also Greek
Rom 3:1 advantage then of being a **J**
Rom 9:3 damned for my fellow **J** those who
2 Cor 11:22 Are they **J** So am I
Col 4:11 are the only **J** working with me
1 Thess 2:14 as they did from the **J**
JOB
2 Cor 8:11 finish the **j** so your eagerness
JOIN
Matt 19:6 what God has **j** together
2 Tim 1:8 **j** me in suffering for the Gospel
JOINT
Eph 4:16 the support of every **j**
Heb 4:12 divides soul spirit **j** marrow
JOY
Matt 28:8 ran with fear and great **j** to tell
Lk 2:10 A great **j** will come to all people
Lk 24:52 back to Jerusalem with great **j**
Acts 2:28 You will fill Me with **j** by being
Rom 14:17 peace and **j** in the Holy Spirit
2 Cor 8:2 overflowing **j** and their deep
Gal 5:22 fruit of spirit is love **j** peace
Phil 1:4 I always do it with **j**
1 Thess 2:19 who is our hope or **j** or crown
1 Pet 1:6 This brings you great **j**
1 Jn 1:4 so that our **j** may be complete
JUDGE
Matt 5:25 **j** may not hand you over . . . officer
Lk 6:37 Stop **j** and you will not be **j**
Jn 12:31 Now this world is being **j**
Jn 16:11 ruler of this world is **j**
Acts 4:19 **j** for yourselves for we cannot
Acts 7:27 Who made you ruler and **j** over us
Acts 10:42 God appointed Him to **j** living
Acts 17:31 He . . . **j** the world with justice
Rom 2:16 God through Christ . . . **j** the secrets
Rom 14:10 stand before God to be **j**
1 Cor 5:12 what business is it of mine to **j**
1 Cor 10:29 Why should my freedom be **j** by
Jas 4:12 who are you to **j** your neighbor
Jas 5:9 You know the **J** is standing at door
Rev 11:18 time You set to **j** the dead
Rev 14:7 has come for Him to **j**
Rev 18:8 the One who is **j** her is mighty
Rev 18:20 God has **j** her for the judgment
Rev 20:12 the dead were **j** on the basis of
JUDGMENT (see also **LAST DAY**)
Matt 12:36 on **J** Day people will . . . give
Matt 12:41 at time of **J** and will condemn
Jn 5:27 given Him authority to execute **j**

Jn 8:16 My **j** is valid
Jn 16:8 convict world of sin . . . and **j**
Acts 15:19 it is my **j** that we . . . not trouble
Rom 13:2 will bring **j** on themselves
1 Cor 1:10 united in understanding and **j**
1 Cor 5:3 I have already made a **j** in regard
1 Cor 11:29 body is there brings **j**
2 Cor 5:10 We must all appear before **j** seat
1 Tim 5:24 sins . . . go ahead of them to **j**
1 Pet 4:17 it is time for the **j** to start
2 Pet 2:4 hell to be kept for **j**
JUMP
Matt 4:6 the Son of God **j** down
Acts 3:8 He **j** up stood and started to walk
JUST
Gal 3:11 because the **j** will live by faith
JUSTIFY
Lk 10:29 But he wanted to **j** himself
Acts 13:39 believes in this Jesus is **j**
Rom 3:20 not one person will be **j**
Rom 3:24 they are **j** . . . freely by grace
Rom 3:26 the One who **j** [acquits] the person
Rom 3:28 **j** . . . by faith—apart from works
Rom 4:5 believes in Him who **j** . . . the ungodly
Rom 5:9 now that His blood has **j** . . . us
Rom 6:7 has been **j** [declared righteous]
Rom 8:30 those whom He called He also **j**
Rom 8:33 It is God who **j** [acquits] us
1 Cor 6:11 have been **j** [declared righteous]
Gal 2:16 know a person cannot be **j** by doing
Gal 2:17 we are seeking to be **j** in Christ
Gal 3:8 God would **j** [acquit] the nations by
Gal 5:4 You who try to be **j** by the Law
Tit 3:7 we who were **j** by His grace
Jas 2:21 Abraham considered **j** [declared
JUSTIFICATION
Rom 4:25 then was raised because of our **j**
Rom 5:18 **j** . . . came to all people
JUSTICE
Matt 12:18 He will announce **j** to Gentiles
Acts 28:4 **j** did not let him live
Rom 3:26 He wanted to show His **j**

KEEP
Lk 11:28 listen to God's word and **k** it
Rom 11:4 I have **k** for Myself seven thousand
Gal 3:21 righteousness . . . by **k** that law
1 Tim 6:14 you **k** this command without spot
2 Tim 1:12 sure that He can **k** for that Day
2 Tim 2:8 **K** in mind Jesus Christ who is
Tit 2:5 to **k** house . . . helpful . . . subordinate
Jas 2:10 whoever **k** the whole Law but fails
1 Jn 3:6 not **k** on sinning Anyone . . . **k** on
Jude 24 to Him who is able to **k** you
KERNEL
1 Cor 15:37 bare **k** maybe wheat
KEY
Rev 1:18 and I have **k** of death and of hades
Rev 3:7 One who has the **k** of David
Rev 20:1 Angel . . . holding **k** to bottomless

KIDNAPPER
1 Tim 1:10 homosexuals for **k** for . . . who lie
KILL
Mk 3:4 to save a life or to **k**
Jn 8:40 want to **k** Me a Man who told you
Acts 2:23 Him to a cross and you **k** Him
Acts 7:52 they **k** those who announced
Acts 16:27 was about to **k** himself
Rom 7:11 sin seduced me and . . . **k** me
Rom 8:13 by the Spirit you **k** the activities
Col 3:5 Therefore **k** what is earthly in you
1 Thess 2:15 these Jews **k** both the Lord
KIND
1 Cor 13:4 Love is **k** Love is not envious
1 Cor 15:35 what **k** of body will they have
Tit 3:4 God our Savior showed how **k** He is
KINDNESS
Rom 2:4 The **k** of God which leads you
Gal 5:22 fruit of spirit is . . . joy peace . . . **k**
Tit 3:2 to yield and show **k** to everyone
KING
Matt 2:1 in Judea when Herod was **k**
Matt 17:25 From whom do **k** . . . collect tax
Matt 18:23 like a **k** who wanted to settle
Matt 25:34 **K** will say to those at His right
Matt 27:37 THIS IS JESUS THE **K** OF
Mk 6:14 **K** Herod heard about Jesus
Lk 14:31 suppose a **k** is going into battle
Jn 6:15 people intended . . . to make Him **k**
Jn 12:13 in Name of Lord the **K** of Israel
Jn 12:15 Look Your **K** is coming riding
Jn 18:37 You are correct . . . I am a **k**
Jn 19:3 Hail **K** of the Jews and slapped His
Jn 19:19 JESUS FROM NAZARETH **K** OF
Acts 4:26 **k** of the earth stand ready and
Acts 9:15 My Name before Gentiles and **k**
1 Tim 2:2 for **k** and all who are over us
1 Tim 6:15 **K** of kings and Lord of lords
Rev 5:10 they rule as **k** on the earth
Rev 17:12 ten horns that you saw are ten **k**
Rev 18:3 **k** of earth have lived in sexual
Rev 19:16 He has a Name written **K** of **K**
KINGDOM
  (see also **KINGDOM OF GOD/HEAVEN**)
Matt 6:10 Your **K** come may Your will be done
Matt 12:25 Every **k** divided against itself
Mk 6:23 up to half of my **k**
Mk 11:10 Blessed is the coming **K**
Lk 1:33 His **K** will never end
Lk 12:32 your Father to give you the **k**
Lk 23:42 when You come into Your **K**
Jn 18:36 My **K** does not belong to this world
Acts 14:22 troubles we must enter into **K**
Rom 14:17 God's **K** is not a matter of eating
Heb 12:28 we have received a **K**
Rev 1:6 has made us a **k** priests to God
Rev 11:15 the **K** of . . . Lord and of His Christ
KINGDOM OF GOD
  (see also **KINGDOM,**
  KINGDOM OF HEAVEN)
Matt 21:31 prostitutes going into **K** of God

Mk 15:43 Joseph . . . waiting for the **K** of God
Lk 9:60 tell about the **K** of God
Lk 17:20 When will the **K** of God come
Jn 3:3 not born again he . . . see the **K** of God
Acts 1:3 spoke with them about the **K** of God
Acts 28:23 declared truth about **K** of God
1 Cor 4:20 **K** of God is not a matter of
1 Cor 6:9 will not be heirs of the **K** of God
1 Cor 15:50 cannot have share in **K** of God
KINGDOM OF HEAVEN
  (see also **KINGDOM,**
  KINGDOM OF GOD)
Matt 4:17 Repent for **K** of heaven is near
Matt 5:3 **K** of heaven belongs to them
Matt 5:19 be called least in **K** of heaven
Matt 11:12 **K** of heaven has been advancing
KISS
Matt 26:48 The one I **k** is the Man
Lk 15:20 put his arms around him and **k** him
Rom 16:16 greet one another with a holy **k**
KNEEL
Matt 2:11 They **k** and worshiped Him
Rom 14:11 everyone will **k** before Me
Eph 3:14 for this reason I **k** before Father
Phil 2:10 under the earth should **k**
KNOCKING
Matt 7:7 Keep **k** and door . . . be opened
KNOW
Mk 1:24 I **k** who You are—Holy One of God
Mk 13:32 No one **k** about that Day or Hour
Lk 8:46 for I **k** that power went
Lk 13:25 I do not **k** where you are from
Jn 1:10 made the world and world did not **k**
Jn 10:14 I **k** My own and My own **k** Me
Jn 14:7 **k** Me you will **k** My Father also
Jn 17:3 to **k** You the only true God Jesus
Rom 15:20 where Name of Christ was not **k**
1 Cor 2:12 we **k** the things which God has
2 Cor 8:9 You **k** the grace of our Lord
Eph 1:18 **k** the hope to which He called you
2 Tim 1:12 I **k** Him in whom I trust
2 Tim 2:19 Lord **k** those who are His own
Heb 8:11 say **K** the Lord For they will all
1 Jn 4:7 everyone who loves . . . **k** God
Rev 2:19 I **k** your works and your love
KNOWLEDGE
Rom 11:33 God's riches wisdom and **k**
1 Cor 1:5 in speech and **k** of every kind
1 Cor 8:1 **k** puffs up but love builds up
1 Cor 13:8 **k** it will be brought to an end
2 Cor 4:6 revealing the **k** of the glory
Phil 1:9 more in **k** and in every kind
Col 3:10 renewed in **k** to be like Him
1 Tim 6:20 what is falsely called **k**
2 Pet 1:5 to excellence **k** to **k** self-control

LACK
Mk 10:21 You **l** one thing Jesus told him
1 Thess 3:10 supply whatever is **l** in faith
LADY
2 Jn 1 The Elder to the chosen **l**

LAMB

Mk 14:12 customary to kill the Passover l
Jn 1:29 The L of God who takes away the sin
Jn 1:36 Look the L of God
Jn 21:15 Feed My l Jesus told him
Acts 8:32 as a l is dumb before man cuts
Rev 5:6 I saw a L standing
Rev 6:16 from the anger of the L
Rev 14:1 the L was standing on Mount
Rev 19:7 marriage of L has come

LAME

Matt 11:5 those who were l are walking

LAMP

Matt 5:15 you do not light a l
Matt 6:22 eye is the l of the body

LAMPSTAND

Heb 9:2 In the first part were the l
Rev 1:12 I saw seven golden l
Rev 2:5 I will . . . take your l from its place

LAND

Acts 7:3 come to the l that I will show you
Heb 11:15 If their hearts had been in the l

LANDOWNER

Matt 20:1 like the rich l who went out

LANGUAGE

Acts 2:4 began to speak in other l
Acts 19:6 started to talk in other l
1 Cor 12:10 can speak in various . . . l
1 Cor 12:30 not all can speak in other l
1 Cor 14:27 If anyone speaks in another l

LAST

Matt 20:16 In this way the l will be first
Mk 10:31 first will be l and the l first
Lk 13:30 Some who are l will be first
Acts 2:17 the l days God says I will pour
1 Cor 15:8 L of all I saw Him
2 Tim 3:1 the l days there will come times
Heb 1:2 l days spoken to us by His Son
1 Jn 2:18 children it is the l hour

LAST DAY (see also JUDGMENT)

Jn 6:39 I raise them on the L Day
Jn 12:48 will condemn Him on the L Day

LAST WILL AND TESTAMENT

Mk 14:24 My blood of l will and testament
Heb 13:20 everlasting l will and testament

LATIN

Jn 19:20 notice . . . written in Aramaic L and

LAUGHED

Matt 9:24 But they l at Him

LAW

Matt 5:17 not think I came to set aside L
Matt 7:12 That is the L and the Prophets
Jn 1:17 L was given through Moses but grace
Jn 7:23 circumcised on a Sabbath to keep L
Jn 7:51 Does our L condemn anyone
Jn 18:31 judge Him according to your l
Acts 18:13 ways that are against the L
Acts 25:8 sinned against the L of the Jews
Rom 2:12 All who sin without having the L
Rom 2:15 show what L requires them to do
Rom 3:19 we know that whatever the L says

Rom 4:13 It was not by the L that Abraham
Rom 7:1 speaking to people who know the L
Rom 7:7 Is the L the cause of sin
Rom 8:2 set you free from the l of sin
Rom 10:4 Christ is end of L to give
Rom 13:10 to love is to keep the whole L
1 Cor 15:56 the L gives sin its power
Gal 2:16 justified by the works of the L
Gal 3:2 Spirit by doing what the L says
Gal 3:10 depend on doing what the L says
Gal 4:21 not listen to what the L says
Eph 2:15 He put away the L
1 Tim 1:8 know the L is good if it is used
Heb 7:19 the L made nothing perfect
Heb 8:10 I will put My l into their minds
Jas 2:10 whoever keeps whole L but fails
1 Jn 3:4 sin is the breaking of the L

LAY

Mk 16:18 They will l their hands on sick
Jn 20:13 I don't know where they l Him
Acts 6:6 prayed and l their hands on
1 Cor 3:11 no one can l any . . . foundation
1 Tim 4:14 when pastors l their hands on

LAZY

2 Thess 3:11 you are living a l life

LEAD

2 Cor 11:3 may be l away from you
1 Thess 5:12 who work with you and l you

LEADING

Matt 2:6 least among the l towns of Judea

LEADER

Matt 2:6 from you will come a L who will
Gal 2:2 who were recognized as l
1 Tim 5:17 pastors who are good l . . . double
Heb 2:10 the L of their salvation perfect
Heb 13:7 Remember your l who have spoken

LEARN

Acts 18:24 He was a l man
Rom 7:7 did I l what sin is
Eph 4:20 is not what you l when you came

LEAST

Matt 5:19 aside . . . l of these commandments
Matt 11:11 Yet the l in Kingdom of heaven
Matt 25:40 here even the l important of
1 Cor 15:9 I am the l of the apostles

LEAVE

Matt 8:34 urged Him to l their territory
Lk 5:8 L me Lord . . . I am a sinful man
Lk 13:31 L here and go somewhere else
Acts 7:3 L your land and your relatives
Gal 1:6 you are so quickly l Him who called
Eph 5:31 man will l his father and mother
Phil 1:23 I want to l and be with Christ
Heb 13:5 I will never l you or desert you

LEAVING

Lk 9:31 talking about His l this world

LEFT

Matt 6:3 do not let your l hand know
Matt 25:33 right but the goats at His l
Lk 9:17 pieces that were l over
Acts 2:31 He would not be l in the grave

LEGS

Jn 19:32 soldiers . . . broke the l of first
Jn 19:33 they did not break His l

LEGAL

Acts 19:39 must be settled in a l meeting

LEGION

Mk 5:9 My name is **L** [Six Thousand]
Lk 8:30 **L** [Six Thousand] he answered

LEPER

Matt 8:2 l went to Him and bowed down
Matt 10:8 cleanse l drive out demons
Matt 11:5 l are made clean deaf . . . hear
Lk 4:27 There were many l in Israel
Lk 17:12 ten l came toward Him

LEPROSY

Matt 8:3 l left him and he was clean
Lk 5:12 a man who was covered with l

LESSON

1 Cor 10:6 these things happened as l
1 Cor 10:11 make them a l to others

LET

Mk 11:6 the men l them go
Lk 2:29 Lord now You are l Your servant
1 Cor 16:7 if the Lord will l me

LETTER

Acts 9:2 asked him for l to the synagogs
1 Cor 16:3 I will send them with l
2 Cor 3:2 you . . . our l written in our hearts
2 Cor 3:6 not of l but of spirit
2 Cor 10:9 to frighten you with my l
1 Thess 5:27 read this l to all Christians
1 Pet 5:12 I am writing you this short l

LEVITE

Lk 10:32 A **L** who came to the place did

LIAR

Rom 3:4 Let God be true and every man a l
1 Tim 4:2 led astray by the hypocrisy of l
Tit 1:12 Men of Crete are always l

LIBERTY

Jas 2:12 judged by the word that brings l

LIE

Matt 15:19 out of heart come . . . stealing l
Jn 8:44 Whenever he tells a l . . . his heart
Rom 3:7 if my l honors God by showing
1 Cor 15:15 we stand there as men who l
Eph 4:25 each of you has stripped off l
Tit 1:2 God who never l promised before
Heb 6:18 in which God cannot l

LIFE

Matt 7:14 way if difficult that leads to l
Matt 25:46 the righteous to everlasting l
Lk 14:26 hate . . . even his own l
Jn 1:4 In Him was l . . . **L** was Light of
Jn 3:16 would not perish but have . . . l
Jn 3:36 who rejects the Son will not see l
Jn 5:39 you think you have everlasting l
Jn 6:35 I am the Bread of **L** Jesus told them
Jn 6:47 one who believes in Me has . . . l
Jn 11:25 I am the Resurrection and the **L**
Jn 14:6 I am the Way the Truth and the **L**
Jn 20:31 by believing you . . . have l in His

Acts 3:15 You killed the Author of l
Rom 2:7 everlasting l to . . . working good
Rom 5:10 He will save us by His l
Rom 5:18 justification . . . brings l to
Rom 8:6 spirit has . . . gives l and peace
Rom 10:5 you will find l in them
1 Cor 15:19 if Christ is our hope in this l
2 Cor 3:6 but the spirit brings l
Gal 2:20 the l I now live in my body I live
Gal 3:15 let me use an example from daily l
Col 3:3 you have died and your l is hidden
2 Tim 1:1 promised l in Christ Jesus
Tit 1:2 is based on of everlasting l
Tit 3:7 heirs . . . the hope of everlasting l
1 Pet 3:10 person wants to love l and enjoy
1 Jn 5:11 this l is in His Son

LIFT

Lk 1:52 and l up lowly people
Jn 3:14 Moses l up snake in the wilderness
Acts 1:9 He was l up and a cloud took Him
Jas 4:10 Humble yourselves . . . He will l you

LIGAMENTS

Col 2:19 bound together by l and sinews

LIGHT

Matt 4:16 people . . . darkness have seen a l
Matt 5:14 You are the l of the world
Matt 11:30 My burden is l
Jn 1:4 the Life was the **L** of mankind
Jn 3:19 **L** came . . . world but people have
Jn 8:12 I am the **L** of the world
Jn 9:5 I am the **L** of the world
Jn 12:35 The **L** will be with you . . . a little
Acts 9:3 suddenly a l from heaven flashed
Acts 22:9 saw the l but did not understand
Eph 5:8 now you are l in the Lord
1 Tim 6:16 lives in a l to which no one can
Jas 1:17 from the Father of l with whom
1 Pet 2:9 out of darkness into His . . . l
2 Pet 1:19 a l shining in a gloomy place
1 Jn 1:5 God is **L** and in Him is no darkenss
Rev 21:23 the GLORY OF GOD gave it l

LIGHTNING

Matt 24:27 the Son of Man will be like l
Matt 28:3 was a bright as l and his
Rev 4:5 from the throne came flashes of l

LIKE

Mk 12:37 The large crowd l to hear Him
Acts 3:22 A Prophet . . . who is l me
Col 3:10 renewed . . . to be l Him who created
1 Jn 3:2 we will be l Him

LIMIT

Jn 3:34 gives Him His Spirit without l

LINEN

Matt 27:57 body wrapped . . . a clean l cloth
Mk 14:51 had nothing on but a l cloth
Jn 20:5 looked in He saw the l wrappings

LION

2 Tim 4:17 I was rescued from the l mouth
Heb 11:33 shut the mouths of l
1 Pet 5:8 prowling around like a roaring l
Rev 4:7 first living creature was like a l
Rev 5:5 you see the **L** from tribe of Judah

LIPS
Matt 15:8 people honor Me with their l
LIST
1 Tim 5:9 on your l of widows if she is not
LISTEN
Matt 11:15 The one who has ears . . . l
Matt 17:5 in whom I delight L to Him
Lk 4:21 Today while you are l
Lk 4:28 As they were l all in the
Lk 10:39 sat at the Lord's feet and l
Lk 11:28 who continue to l to God's word
Lk 16:29 They should l to them
Jn 5:25 those who l to it will live
Jn 8:47 person who belongs to God l
Acts 2:14 l closely to what I say
Acts 3:23 person will not l to . . . Prophet
Acts 28:28 out to Gentiles and they will l
Rom 1:5 they may l and come to faith
Gal 4:21 will you not l to . . . Law says
2 Tim 2:14 but only ruins those who are l
2 Tim 4:3 will not l to sound teaching
Heb 2:1 why we should l . . . more carefully
Rev 2:11 who has an ear l to what Spirit
Rev 3:20 if anyone l to My voice and opens
LITTLE
Matt 6:30 you who trust Him so l
Matt 8:26 You trust Me so l
Matt 18:6 causes one of these l ones
Matt 18:10 not to despise one these l ones
Mk 5:41 L girl I tell you get up
Mk 9:42 anyone causes one of these l ones
Mk 10:15 receive Kingdom . . . as a l child
Lk 9:48 Whoever welcomes this l child
Jn 14:19 Only a l while and world will not
Rev 12:12 knowing that he has l time
LIVE
Matt 9:18 lay Your hand on her she will l
Matt 19:9 marries . . . he is l in adultery
Lk 10:28 do this and you will l
Jn 1:14 Word became flesh and l among us
Jn 11:25 person who believes in Me will l
Jn 14:19 Because I l you also will l
Acts 20:18 You know how I l with you
Rom 1:17 The righteous will l by faith
Rom 4:16 not only to those who l by the Law
Rom 7:1 the Law only as long as you l
Rom 8:13 if you l according to the flesh
Rom 13:13 let us l decently as is proper
1 Cor 8:6 we l for Him
2 Cor 5:15 those who l would no longer l
Gal 2:20 is no longer I who l but . . . Christ
Eph 6:3 you may l long on the earth
Col 2:6 as your Lord so l in Him
1 Thess 4:11 make . . . ambition to l quietly
1 Tim 1:16 believe in Him and l forever
1 Tim 2:2 so that we may l quietly
1 Tim 5:6 one who l for pleasure is dead
2 Tim 2:11 If we have died with Him we . . . l
1 Jn 1:7 if we l in the light as He is
LIVING
Acts 10:42 to judge the l and the dead

Acts 18:3 they made tents for a l
1 Cor 9:14 receive their l from the Gospel
Eph 4:22 follows your former ways of l
Tit 1:6 accused of wild l or disobedience
LOAF
Matt 14:17 All we have here are five l
Matt 15:34 how many l do you have
Matt 15:36 took the seven l and the fish
Lk 9:13 All we have are five l
Jn 6:9 five barley l
1 Cor 10:17 There is one l . . . one body
LOG
Matt 7:3 not notice the l in your own eye
LONELY
Mk 1:45 He stayed out in l places
LONG
Matt 5:33 you have heard that l ago
Mk 9:21 How l has he been like this
Lk 20:47 a good appearance . . . make l prayers
1 Cor 10:6 that we might not l for . . . evil
1 Thess 2:8 we l for you so much
LOOK
Matt 5:28 anyone who l at a woman to lust
Mk 13:1 Teacher l at these magnificent
Jn 1:29 He said L The Lamb of God
Acts 3:4 L at us Peter said
Phil 3:20 l for Lord Jesus Christ to come
1 Tim 4:12 Do not let anyone l down on you
Tit 2:13 as we l for our blessed hope
Heb 12:2 l to Jesus who gives us our faith
LORD
Matt 7:21 Not everyone who says to Me L L
Matt 12:8 Son of Man is L of the Sabbath
Matt 22:44 The L said to my L Sit at My
Jn 20:28 Thomas answered My L and my God
Acts 25:26 reliable to write our l about
Rom 1:4 He is our L Jesus Christ
Rom 5:1 peace with God through our L Jesus
Rom 8:39 God has . . . in Christ Jesus our L
Rom 14:9 to be L of both dead and living
1 Cor 12:3 no one . . . to say Jesus is the L
2 Cor 3:17 where the Spirit of the L is
2 Cor 11:20 who l it over you or who slaps
Eph 4:5 one L one faith one baptism
Phil 2:11 JESUS CHRIST IS L to the glory
Col 1:16 thrones or l or powers
1 Pet 5:3 not l it over people entrusted
LORD'S DAY
Rev 1:10 under the Spirit's power on L day
LOSE
Lk 9:24 save his life will l it but . . . l his
Jn 12:25 The person who loves his life l it
1 Cor 8:8 we l nothing by not eating
LOSS
Acts 27:10 suffer hardship and a heavy l
Rom 11:12 their l made the Gentiles rich
Phil 3:7 consider as a l for Christ
LOST
Matt 10:6 But go to the l sheep of Israel
Lk 15:24 He was l and has been found
Lk 19:10 has come to seek and to save the l

Jn 10:28 They will never be l
Rom 11:11 They did not stumble . . . to be l
LOUD
Matt 27:50 Jesus cried out . . . with a l voice
Mk 15:37 Jesus cried out in a l voice
LOVE
Matt 5:44 l your enemies and always pray
Matt 10:37 Anyone l father . . . more than Me
Matt 22:37 L the Lord your God with all
Matt 22:39 L your neighbor as yourself
Mk 10:21 Jesus looked at him and l him
Jn 3:16 God l the world so much that He
Jn 13:34 a new commandment L one another
Jn 14:15 If you l Me you will obey My
Jn 15:13 No one has greater l than this
Jn 15:17 command you to do L one another
Jn 21:17 Simon . . . do you l Me
Rom 5:8 God shows His l for us by this
Rom 8:39 separate us from l God has for us
Rom 9:13 Jacob I l but Esau I hated
Rom 9:25 those who are not l I will call
Rom 12:9 L sincerely Hate evil
Rom 13:8 except to l one another
Rom 13:10 to l is to keep the whole Law
1 Cor 8:1 knowledge puffs up but l builds
1 Cor 13:2 but have no l I am nothing
1 Cor 16:24 My l be with you all in Christ
2 Cor 2:4 realize how very much I l you
2 Cor 6:6 a spirit of holiness by sincere l
2 Cor 9:7 because God l a cheerful giver
Gal 5:13 by l continue to serve one another
Eph 2:4 because of His deep l for us
Eph 3:18 broad long high deep His l is
Eph 5:2 live in l just as Christ also l
Eph 5:25 Husbands l your wives as Christ l
Col 3:14 top of all these virtues put on l
Col 3:19 husbands l your wives
1 Thess 1:3 your l is toiling and your hope
1 Tim 1:5 the goal of our instruction is l
1 Tim 6:10 l of money is root of all evils
2 Tim 3:4 will l pleasures rather than God
1 Pet 1:22 l one . . . with a pure heart
2 Pet 1:7 to brotherly kindness l
1 Jn 2:15 Do not l the world
1 Jn 3:11 L one another
1 Jn 3:23 l one another as He has commanded
1 Jn 4:8 because God is L
2 Jn 6 this is l that we live
Jude 2 mercy peace and l be yours
LOWER
Eph 4:9 gone down to the l earthly regions
Heb 2:7 You made Him l than the angels
LOWEST
Lk 14:9 have to take the l place
LOWLY
Rom 9:21 noble purpose another . . . l purpose
Jas 1:9 the l Christian be proud
LOYAL
Matt 6:24 be l to one and despise the other
Acts 14:22 to be l to the faith

LUKEWARM
Rev 3:16 you are l and not hot or cold
LUST
Matt 5:28 anyone who looks at a woman to l
Rom 1:24 followed the l of their hearts
Rom 7:5 the sinful l stirred up by the Law
Eph 2:3 lived . . . in our fleshly l
Eph 4:19 themselves over to a life of l to
1 Thess 4:5 in the way of passionate l
2 Tim 2:22 Flee from the l of young people
Tit 2:12 No to ungodliness and worldly l
1 Pet 4:2 in l of men but in the will of
1 Jn 2:16 the l of the flesh
Jude 4 into unrestrained l and who disown
LUSTFUL
2 Cor 12:21 sexual and l things they did
LUXURY
Lk 16:19 lived in l every day

MAD
2 Cor 11:23 I am m to talk like this
MAGIC
Acts 19:19 who had practiced m gathered
MAGNIFIES
Lk 1:46 My soul m the Lord and
MAINTAINS
Heb 1:3 copy of His Being m everything
MAJESTY
Jude 25 to Him be glory m power authority
MAKE
Matt 5:24 and m up with your brother
Matt 8:7 I will come m him well Jesus said
Matt 27:31 they had m fun of Him they took
Matt 28:19 Go and m disciples of all people
Mk 14:58 tear down this Temple m by human
Lk 14:29 watch him will m fun of him
Jn 1:3 Everything was m by Him
Acts 4:24 Master You m heaven and earth the
Acts 17:24 God who m the world and
2 Cor 5:21 God m Him who did not know sin
Heb 1:2 He m the Heir . . . and m the world
Heb 2:11 He who m people holy and those who
2 Pet 1:10 be all the more eager . . . m sure
MAN
Mk 2:27 The Sabbath was made for m not m
Jn 4:29 see a M who told me . . . I have done
Jn 8:40 kill Me a M who told you the truth
Jn 9:11 The m they call Jesus made some mud
Jn 11:47 This M is working many miraculous
Jn 11:50 better for you one M should die
Jn 18:14 one M should die for the people
Acts 2:22 a M whom God commended to you
Acts 5:29 We must obey God rather than m
Acts 10:26 Get up he said I am only a m
Acts 17:31 by a M whom He has appointed
Rom 5:12 sin came . . . through one m
Rom 5:15 gracious gift of the One M Jesus
Col 2:22 doing what m order and teach
2 Thess 2:3 the m of sin . . . to destruction
1 Tim 2:5 one Mediator between God and m
1 Tim 6:11 you m of God flee from these
Tit 2:2 Tell older m Be sober serious

MANAGE
Eph 1:10 to **m** everything in heaven . . . earth
1 Tim 3:4 He must **m** his own family well
MANAGER
Jn 2:8 take it to the **m** of the dinner
1 Cor 4:1 servants of Christ and **m** of God's
Tit 1:7 As a **m** appointed by God
MANGER
Lk 2:7 baby clothes and laid Him in a **m**
Lk 2:12 clothes and lying in a **m**
Lk 13:15 donkey from the **m** on the Sabbath
MANKIND
Jn 1:4 the Life was the Light of **m**
MANNA
Jn 6:31 Our fathers ate **m** in the wilderness
Heb 9:4 golden jar containing the **m**
MANURE
Lk 14:35 good . . . for the **m** pile
MANY
Mk 14:24 which is being poured out for **m**
Mk 15:41 There were also **m** other women
MARK
Jn 20:25 put my finger in the **m** of nails
Rom 4:11 circumcision as a **m** to confirm
Phil 3:14 with my eyes on the **m** I go after
MARKETPLACE
Matt 20:3 saw others standing in **m** doing
Mk 7:4 come from the **m** they do not eat
Acts 17:17 in the **m** every day with those
MARRIAGE
Mk 11:25 nor are given in **m** . . . like angels
Heb 13:4 everyone think highly of **m**
Rev 19:7 **m** of the Lamb has come
MARRY
Mk 12:25 they neither **m** nor are they given
Lk 14:20 I just got **m** and that's why
1 Cor 7:9 if they cannot control . . . get **m**
1 Cor 7:28 if a virgin gets **m** it is no sin
1 Tim 4:3 order people not to **m**
1 Tim 5:14 I want younger women to **m**
MASQUERADE
2 Cor 11:13 since they **m** as apostles
MASTER
Matt 6:24 No one can serve two **m**
1 Cor 3:10 as an expert **m** builder and
Eph 6:9 And **m** treat your slaves in the same
Col 4:1 **M** be just and fair to your slaves
1 Pet 2:18 servants be subordinate to **m**
MATTER
Gal 2:6 position in life does not **m** to God
MATURE
Heb 5:14 but solid food is for **m** people
MEANINGLESS
Eph 5:6 anyone fool you with **m** words
MEANT
1 Tim 1:8 as it was **m** to be used
MEASURE
Matt 7:2 the **m** with which you **m** will be
Mk 4:24 The **m** with which you **m**
Rom 12:3 God has given a **m** of faith
Eph 3:19 you . . . filled with God's full **m**

MEASURING STICK
Rev 11:1 I was given a **m** stick like a rod
MEAT
1 Cor 8:13 I will never eat **m**
MEDIATOR
Gal 3:19 through angels by the hand of a **m**
1 Tim 2:5 one **M** between God and men
Heb 8:6 of which He is the **M**
Heb 9:15 **M** of a new last will and testament
MEET
Acts 1:4 When He **m** with them He ordered
Acts 15:6 apostles and elders **m** to look
Phlm 2 to the church that **m** in your house
MEETING
1 Cor 5:4 Call a **m** My Spirit . . . will be with
MEMBER
Mk 15:43 Joseph . . . **m** of the Jewish council
Rom 6:13 presenting the **m** of your body to
Rom 7:5 sinful lusts . . . worked in the **m** of
1 Cor 6:15 your bodies are **m** of Christ
Eph 4:25 we are **m** of one another
MEMORIAL-OFFERING
Acts 10:4 before God as your **m**
MENTALLY
1 Pet 1:13 Now then get ready **m** for action
MENTION
Eph 5:3 even be **m** among you
1 Thess 1:2 **m** you in our prayers
MERCHANTS
Rev 18:3 has made **m** of the earth rich
MERCIFUL
Matt 5:7 Blessed are those who are **m**
Mk 5:19 how **m** He has been to you
Lk 1:50 who is **m** from generation
Lk 18:13 God be **m** to me the sinner
Rom 9:15 I will be **m** . . . to whom I wish to be
Rom 11:32 in order to be **m** to all
MERCIFULLY
Matt 18:33 treated . . . as **m** as I treated you
MERCY
Matt 9:12 I want **m** and not sacrifice
Lk 1:54 remembered His **m**
Rom 11:31 while you enjoy **m**
Rom 12:1 the **m** of God to offer your bodies
Rom 15:9 Gentiles praise God for His **m**
2 Cor 1:3 Father of **m** God of every comfort
1 Tim 1:13 I received **m** because I acted
Tit 3:5 but because of His **m**
Heb 4:16 receive **m** and find grace to help
Jas 2:13 **M** triumphs over judgment
MERE
1 Thess 1:5 come to you with **m** words but
MESSAGE
Rom 10:17 faith comes from hearing the **m**
2 Cor 5:19 He put into our hands the **m**
Gal 1:11 Gospel I preached is not a human **m**
Eph 1:13 When you heard the **m** of the truth
2 Thess 2:2 spirit **m** or . . . word or . . . letter
Tit 2:8 give a sound **m** that cannot be
Heb 4:2 the **m** they heard did not help them

MESSENGER
Matt 11:10 I am sending My **m** ahead of You
Matt 14:35 recognized Jesus and sent **m** all
Mk 1:2 I am sending My **m** ahead of you
Lk 9:52 He sent **m** ahead of Him
Rom 10:15 of the **m** who bring good news
MESSIAH
Jn 1:41 We found the **M** which means Christ
Jn 4:25 I know that the **M** who is called
METALWORKER
2 Tim 4:14 Alexander the **m** did me much harm
MIDDLE
Jn 19:18 one on each side and Jesus in **m**
MIGHTY
Lk 1:49 He who is **m** whose Name is holy
Lk 24:19 Prophet **m** in what He did and said
Acts 18:24 a learned man and **m**
MIND
Matt 22:37 Love the Lord . . . with all your **m**
Mk 3:21 He's out of His **m**
Mk 5:15 there dressed and in his right **m**
Mk 6:52 Instead their **m** were closed
Rom 7:25 I serve the Law of God with my **m**
Rom 8:5 their **m** set on the things of flesh
Rom 11:29 God never changes His **m** when He
Rom 12:2 renewing of your **m** so you can test
1 Cor 2:16 who has known the **m** of the Lord
1 Cor 14:14 my **m** is not productive
2 Cor 1:17 I easily changed my **m** do you
2 Cor 4:4 whose . . . **m** the god of this world
Eph 4:17 their **m** are set on worthless
Phil 4:7 will guard your hearts and **m** in
Tit 3:8 **m** set on being busy with good works
MILE
Matt 5:41 If anyone makes you go one **m**
MILK
1 Cor 3:2 I gave you **m** to drink not solid
Heb 5:12 you have come to need **m** instead
MILLSTONE
Matt 18:6 have a large **m** hung around neck
MINISTER
2 Cor 3:6 able **m** of a new last will
MIRACLE
Matt 11:20 He had worked most of His **m**
Mk 6:2 That He is able to do such great **m**
Mk 9:39 Anyone who works a **m** in My Name
Acts 2:22 by the **m** . . . signs which God worked
2 Cor 12:12 by miraculous signs . . . and **m**
2 Thess 2:9 Satan uses all . . . **m** and signs
Heb 2:4 different kinds of **m**
MIRACULOUS
Matt 12:38 we want You to show us a **m** sign
Mk 16:17 These are **m** signs . . . will accompany
Mk 16:20 the **m** signs that accompanied
Jn 2:23 when they saw the **m** signs
Jn 3:2 No one can work these **m** signs
Jn 4:54 the second **m** sign that Jesus worked
Jn 6:30 What **m** sign are You going to work
Jn 7:31 will He work even more **m** signs
Jn 10:41 John worked no **m** sign
Jn 12:37 they . . . Him work so many **m** signs

Acts 2:22 by the miracles . . . **m** signs which
Acts 2:43 apostles were working many . . . **m**
Acts 4:30 stretch out Your hand to . . . work **m**
Acts 6:8 wonderful proofs and great **m** signs
1 Cor 1:22 Jews ask for **m** signs and Greeks
2 Cor 12:12 by **m** signs . . . proofs miracles
MIRROR
Jas 1:23 person who in a **m** sees the face
MISERABLE
Rom 7:24 What a **m** person I am
Rev 3:17 do not know that you are **m**
MISERY
Lk 16:25 Lazarus had his **m** Now . . . comforted
MISLEAD
Col 2:4 no one will **m** you by . . . arguments
MISTAKE
Gal 6:7 Make no **m** about this
MISTAKEN
Mk 12:27 You are badly **m**
MISTREATED
Acts 7:34 I have . . . seen how My people are **m**
2 Cor 12:10 I am glad to be weak and **m**
1 Thess 2:2 We had suffered and been . . . **m**
MOCK
Acts 17:32 some started to **m**
MOCKERS
2 Pet 3:3 **m** . . . will come with their
MODEL
1 Thess 1:7 you became **m** for all believers
MODEST
1 Tim 2:9 decent clothes **m** and . . . judgment
MOMENT
1 Cor 15:52 in **m** in twinkling of an eye
MONEY
Matt 6:24 You cannot serve God and **m**
Matt 25:14 called his servants and put **m**
Matt 27:5 he threw the **m** into the Temple
Mk 6:8 no copper **m** in your pocket
Mk 12:41 watching how people put **m** into
Lk 9:3 Do not take . . . no **m**
Acts 4:34 brought the **m** from the things
Acts 5:3 holding back some of the **m** you
1 Thess 2:5 found excuses to make **m** as God
1 Tim 3:3 pastor . . . not one who loves **m**
1 Tim 6:10 love of **m** is root of all evils
2 Tim 3:2 People will love themselves and **m**
Tit 1:11 shameful purpose of making **m**
MONEYCHANGERS
Jn 2:14 He found . . . **m** sitting there
MOON
Matt 24:29 the **m** will not give its light
Acts 2:20 sun will turn dark . . . **m** to blood
Rev 6:12 the full **m** became like blood
MORE
Matt 5:37 Anything **m** . . . comes from Evil One
Mk 12:43 poor widow has contributed **m**
Lk 20:47 will receive a **m** severe punishment
Rom 5:3 **M** than that we also boast
Rom 5:20 God's grace overflowed even **m**
1 Cor 15:6 then **m** than 500 Christians
2 Cor 8:3 have given . . . **m** than they could
2 Cor 11:23 I have done much **m** hard work

MORNING
Acts 2:15 it is only nine in the **m**
MORNING STAR
2 Pet 1:19 day dawns and the **M** Star rises
Rev 2:28 I will give him the **M** Star
Rev 22:16 Creator Descendant Bright **M** Star
MOST
Eph 5:16 make the **m** of your opportunites
MOST HIGH
Lk 1:32 called the Son of the **M** High
Lk 1:35 power of the **M** High will overshadow
MOST HOLY PLACE
Heb 9:3 Tabernacle called the **M** Holy Place
Heb 10:19 go boldly into the **M** Holy Place
MOTHER
Mk 3:35 My brother and sister and **m**
Jn 19:27 to the disciple There is your **m**
2 Tim 1:5 lived in . . . your **m** Eunice before
Rev 17:5 Babylon THE **M** OF PROSTITUTES
MOTHER-IN-LAW
Matt 8:14 there He saw his **m** down in bed
MOTIVES
Phil 1:18 **m** that are honest or dishonest
MOUNTAIN
Matt 4:8 devil took Him to very high **m**
Jn 4:20 Our ancestors worshiped on this **m**
Jn 4:21 not be worshiping . . . on this **m**
1 Cor 13:2 if I have all faith to move **m**
Rev 6:15 among the rocks of the **m**
Rev 8:8 something like a hugh burning **m**
MOUNT OF OLIVES
Jn 8:1 Jesus went to the **M** of Olives
MOURN
Matt 5:4 Blessed are those who **m**
Matt 9:15 friends . . . cannot **m** while the
Matt 24:30 the . . . people on earth will **m**
Mk 16:10 were now **m** and crying
Rev 1:7 groups of people on earth will **m**
Rev 18:11 merchants of earth weep and **m**
MOUTH
Matt 15:18 goes out **m** comes from the heart
Acts 8:32 He does not open His **m**
Rom 3:19 that every **m** may become silent
Rom 10:8 word is near you in your **m**
Rev 2:16 fight . . . with the sword of My **m**
MOVE
Acts 7:4 God had him **m** from there to this
Acts 17:28 in Him we live and **m** and exist
Rom 8:14 all who are **m** by God's Spirit
MUD
2 Pet 2:22 goes back to roll around in **m**
MULTIPLY
Rom 5:20 The Law was added to **m** failure
2 Cor 9:10 will also provide and **m** seed
MURDER
Matt 5:21 people were told Do not **m**
Lk 13:34 Jerusalem you **m** the prophets
Jn 8:44 he has been **m** people
Rom 1:29 full of envy **m** quarreling
Rom 13:9 Do not **m** Do not steal

MURDERER
1 Tim 1:9 for those who are **m**
1 Jn 3:15 no **m** has everlasting life
MUSIC
Lk 15:25 he heard **m** and dancing
Eph 5:19 and making **m** to the Lord
Rev 14:2 like the **m** of harpists playing
MUZZLE
1 Cor 9:9 Do not **m** an ox when . . . treading
MYRRH
Mk 15:23 give Him wine mixed with **m** but He
Jn 19:39 brought a mixture of **m** and aloes
MYSTERY
Rom 11:25 I want you to know this **m**
1 Cor 4:1 managers of God's **m**
1 Cor 13:2 and understand all **m**
1 Cor 14:2 his spirit is speaking **m**
Eph 1:9 known to us the **m** of His will
Eph 3:3 made the **m** known
Col 1:26 This is the **m** hidden for ages
1 Tim 3:16 Deep is the **m** of our religion
MYTHS
1 Tim 1:4 to busy themselves with **m**
2 Tim 4:4 will turn to **m**
2 Pet 1:16 were not following any clever **m**

NAIL
Jn 20:25 finger in the mark of the **n**
Rom 6:6 old self was **n** with Him to cross
Col 2:14 by **n** it to the cross
NAKED
Matt 25:36 **n** and you gave Me . . . to wear
Mk 14:52 linen cloth and ran . . . **n**
2 Cor 5:3 we will not be found **n**
NAKEDNESS
Rev 3:18 keep your shameful **n** from showing
NAME
Matt 1:21 you will **n** Him JESUS because He
Matt 6:9 may Your **N** be kept holy
Matt 10:22 will hate you because of My **N**
Matt 12:21 His **N** will be hope of Gentiles
Matt 18:20 together in My **N** there I am
Matt 24:9 hate you on account of My **N**
Matt 28:19 baptizing . . . in **N** of the Father
Mk 5:9 My **n** is Legion [Six Thousand]
Mk 6:14 Jesus' **N** was now well known
Mk 16:17 In My **N** they will drive out demons
Lk 24:47 His **N** repentance and forgiveness
Jn 1:12 believe in His **N**
Jn 2:23 many believed in His **N**
Jn 3:18 not believe in **N** of God's one-and
Jn 5:43 come in My Father's **N**
Jn 10:25 works . . . in **N** of My Father testify
Jn 14:13 anything you ask in My **N**
Jn 16:23 He will give it to you in My **N**
Jn 16:24 asked for anything in My **N**
Jn 16:26 ask in My **N**
Jn 17:6 I made Your **N** known to the people
Jn 17:26 I made Your **N** known to them
Jn 20:31 believing . . . have life in His **N**
Acts 2:21 who calls on **N** of Lord will be

Acts 2:38 baptized . . . in the **N** of Jesus
Acts 3:6 In the **N** of Jesus Christ . . . walk
Acts 3:16 believed in Jesus' **N** that **N**
Acts 4:7 By what power or **N** did you do this
Acts 4:10 by the **N** of Jesus . . . you crucified
Acts 4:12 no other **N** given among mankind
Acts 4:30 proofs by the **N** of Your . . . Jesus
Acts 10:43 through His **N** everyone who
Acts 21:13 to die . . . for the **N** of the Lord
Rom 9:17 to spread My **N** over all the earth
Rom 15:20 only where **N** of Christ was not
Eph 1:21 any **n** that can be mentioned
Eph 5:20 thank God . . . in the **N** of our Lord
Phil 2:9 gave Him the **N** which is above
2 Thess 1:12 the **N** . . . Jesus may be glorified
Heb 1:4 He inherited a **N** . . . more excellent
Heb 2:12 proclaim Your **N** to My brothers
Heb 6:10 the love you showed for His **N**
Heb 12:23 whose **n** are written in heaven
Rev 14:1 had His **N** and His Father's **N** was
Rev 19:13 His **N** is called the Word of God
NARROW
Matt 7:13 Go through the **n** gate
NATION
Matt 24:7 **N** will fight against **n**
Matt 25:32 all **n** will be gathered . . . Him
Mk 11:17 a house of prayer for all **n**
Lk 24:47 will be preached to all **n**
Acts 2:5 Jews . . . from every **n**
Acts 4:25 the **n** rage and the peoples plan
Acts 17:26 He made every **n** of mankind
Rom 4:17 I have made you a father of many **n**
Gal 3:8 God would justify the **n** by faith
1 Tim 3:16 by angels Was preached among **n**
1 Pet 2:9 a holy **n** a people who are His own
Rev 18:3 all the **n** fell by the wine
NATIVE
Acts 2:8 hear his own **n** language
NATURAL
Rom 9:8 children who are born in a **n** way
Rom 11:21 God did not spare **n** branches
1 Cor 15:44 it is sown a **n** body
NATURALLY
Mk 7:35 he talked **n**
NATURE
Rom 2:14 do by **n** what the Law says
Rom 9:5 according to His human **n** came
Eph 2:3 By **n** we deserved God's anger
NEAR
Matt 4:17 the Kingdom of heaven is **n**
Phil 4:5 The Lord is **n**
1 Pet 4:7 end of everything is **n**
Rev 1:3 because the time is **n**
NEARER
Rom 13:11 salvation is now **n**
Eph 2:13 brought **n** through blood of Christ
NECESSARY
Phil 3:1 it is **n** for your safety
NEED
Matt 6:8 you what you **n** before you ask
Mk 12:44 she put in what she **n** for herself

Acts 4:34 none of the people was in **n**
Acts 17:25 as if He **n** anything
Heb 4:16 grace to help us when we **n** it
NEEDY
Acts 2:45 money to all the **n** in proportion
NEGLECT
Acts 6:1 their widows were being **n**
1 Tim 4:14 Do not **n** the gift you have
Heb 2:3 how . . . escape if we **n** a salvation
NEIGHBOR
Matt 5:43 Love your **n** and hate your enemy
Matt 22:39 Love your **n** as yourself
Lk 10:29 And who is my **n**
Rom 13:9 Love your **n** as yourself
NESTS
Matt 8:20 birds of air have **n** but the Son
NETS
Lk 5:2 fishermen . . . were washing their **n**
NEVER
Mk 2:12 **N** have we seen anything like this
Mk 3:29 slanders the Holy Spirit will **n** be
Jn 11:26 believes in Me will **n** die
Rom 3:4 **N** Let God be true and . . . man a liar
NEW
Mk 1:27 This is a **n** teaching
Mk 14:25 when I drink it in a **n** way
Acts 17:21 telling or hearing something **n**
Rom 6:4 we too will live a **n** life
2 Cor 5:17 is in Christ he is a **n** creation
Gal 2:6 did not teach me anything **n**
Eph 2:15 the two one **n** person in Himself
Col 3:10 have put on the **n** self
Tit 3:5 Spirit gives us **n** birth and **n** life
1 Pet 1:3 mercy given us a **n** birth
2 Pet 3:13 expect **n** heavens and a **n** earth
Rev 3:12 from My God and My **n** Name
Rev 21:1 I saw a **n** heaven and a **n** earth
Rev 21:5 Look I am making everything **n**
NEW "LAST WILL AND TESTAMENT"
Heb 8:13 calling it a **n** last will and
Heb 9:15 Mediator of a **n** last will and
NEWS
Matt 9:26 The **n** about this spread all over
Mk 1:45 spread the **n** so widely
Lk 4:14 The **n** about Him spread
Eph 3:8 preach Good **N** of the immeasurable
NIGHT
1 Thess 5:2 come just as a thief in the **n**
NINE
Mk 15:25 It was **n** in morning . . . crucified
NO
2 Cor 1:17 when I say yes or **n**
Phlm 16 **n** longer as a slave but more than a
NO ONE
Mk 11:2 on which **n** one has ever sat
Lk 4:27 But **n** one except Naaman from
Rom 3:10 **N** one is righteous no not one
1 Jn 4:12 **N** one has ever seen God
NOBLE
Rom 9:21 one thing for a **n** purpose
1 Cor 1:26 not many are born of **n** parents

Phil 4:8 all that is **n** all that is right
1 Tim 3:1 he desires to do a **n** work
NOBLY
1 Cor 7:35 to show . . . to live **n** for the Lord
NOISY
Matt 9:23 saw flute players and the **n** crowd
NOTE
2 Thess 3:14 take **n** of him and do not have
NOTICE
Jn 19:19 Pilate also wrote a **n** and put it
NOTHING
Lk 1:37 There is **n** that God will not be
Jn 15:5 for without Me you can do **n**
Rom 8:39 **n** above or below nor any other
Rom 14:14 **n** is unclean in itself
1 Cor 1:28 what it despises that which is **n**
1 Cor 13:2 but have no love I am **n**
1 Cor 15:2 unless your faith means **n**
1 Cor 15:14 our preaching means **n**
Gal 2:21 then Christ died for **n**
NOURISH
1 Tim 4:6 servant . . . **n** by words of the faith
NUMBER
Acts 2:47 added to . . . **n** those . . . being saved
Acts 6:1 as the **n** of the disciples
Rev 7:4 I heard the **n** of those who were
NUMBSKULL
Matt 5:22 anyone who calls his brother **n**

OATH
Lk 1:73 the **o** He swore to our father
Heb 7:20 established without an **o**
OBEY
Matt 8:27 Even winds and the sea **o** Him
Mk 1:27 unclean spirits and they **o** Him
Jn 15:10 If you **o** My commandments you will
Acts 5:29 We must **o** God rather than men
Acts 7:39 fathers were not willing to **o** him
Rom 6:17 you have heartily **o** the pattern
Rom 10:16 not all have **o** the Gospel
Rom 16:19 heard how you **o** and so I am happy
2 Cor 2:9 stand the test and **o** in every way
Eph 6:1 Children **o** your parents in the Lord
2 Thess 1:8 not **o** the Good News of our Lord
Heb 13:17 **O** your leaders and submit to them
Heb 13:17 **O** them so that they may be happy
OBEDIENCE
Rom 5:19 through the **o** of the One Man
2 Cor 10:5 thought a prisoner in **o** to
OBEDIENT
Rom 15:18 make the Gentiles **o**
OBLIGATION
1 Thess 5:27 put you under . . . **o** before Lord
OBSERVE
Lk 17:20 cannot **o** the coming
Gal 4:10 you **o** days months seasons years
OBTAIN
1 Thess 4:4 know how to **o** a husband or wife
OFFEND
(see **STUMBLE,STUMBLING BLOCK**)

OFFER
Heb 9:14 the everlasting Spirit **o** Himself
OFFERING
Rom 15:16 **o** made holy by the Holy Spirit
Eph 5:2 gave Himself for us as fragrant **o**
2 Tim 4:6 poured out as a drink **o**
Heb 11:4 when God approved of his **o**
OFFICIAL
Matt 9:18 an important **o** came to Him
OLD
Matt 9:16 piece of unshrunk cloth on an **o**
Rom 6:6 our **o** self was nailed
2 Cor 3:14 the reading of the **o** covenant
OLDER
Lk 15:25 his **o** son was out in the field
Rom 9:12 The **o** will serve the younger
OLIVE
Rom 11:24 be grafted back into own **o** tree
ONCE
1 Pet 2:10 **O** you were no people but now
ONE
Jn 3:34 **O** whom God has sent speaks God's
Jn 10:16 they will become **o** flock with **o**
Jn 10:30 I and the Father are **o**
Acts 3:14 denied the Holy and Righteous **O**
Acts 4:32 whole group of believers was **o**
Acts 17:26 From **o** man He made every nation
Rom 5:19 through the obedience of the **O** Man
1 Cor 10:17 there is **o** loaf . . . **o** body
1 Cor 14:27 **o** at a time someone interpret
Gal 3:28 you are all **o** in Christ Jesus
Phil 1:27 fighting side by side with **o** mind
Phil 2:2 happiness . . . be **o** in thought
1 Tim 2:5 is **o** God There is also **o** Mediator
2 Pet 3:8 **O** day is like a thousand years
ONENESS
Eph 4:3 Do your best to keep **o** of Spirit
ONLY
Matt 4:10 Lord your God and serve Him **o**
Jn 3:16 so much He gave His one-and-**o** Son
Rom 11:3 I am the **o** one left
Jude 25 to the **o** God who saves us through
OPEN
Matt 3:16 heavens were **o** and He saw Spirit
Mk 7:34 Ephphatha which means Be **o**
Lk 13:25 Lord **o** up for us
Jn 1:51 you will see heaven **o** and angels
Acts 16:14 Lord **o** her heart to accept
Col 4:3 God will **o** a door for the word
Rev 6:1 I saw when the Lamb **o** the first
OPINIONS
Rom 14:1 argue about different **o**
Jas 2:4 judges who give corrupt **o**
OPPORTUNITY
Rom 15:23 no more **o** for me to work
Col 4:5 make the most of your **o**
OPPOSE
Matt 5:39 do not **o** an evil man
Acts 7:51 You are always **o** the Holy Spirit
Acts 18:6 But they **o** him and slandered
Rom 10:21 although they disobeyed and **o** Me

Rom 13:2 government **o** what God established
Gal 2:11 I **o** him to his face because
2 Thess 2:4 He **o** and sets himself above
2 Tim 3:8 those people **o** the truth
Tit 2:8 anyone who **o** us will be ashamed
ORDAIN
1 Tim 5:22 Do not be in hurry to **o** anyone
ORDER
Matt 12:16 He **o** them not to tell people
Matt 27:58 Then Pilate **o** that it be given
Mk 3:12 He gave strict **o** not to reveal
Lk 4:39 **o** the fever to leave and
Lk 9:21 He gave them strict **o**
Acts 10:33 everything the Lord has **o** you
1 Tim 1:3 so that you may **o** certain men
ORDERLY
1 Cor 14:40 done in a proper and **o** way
Col 2:5 delight to see how **o** and firm you
ORPHANS
Jn 14:18 I will not leave you as **o**
Jas 1:27 if people look after **o** and widows
OTHER
Matt 6:15 forgive the sins of **o**
Matt 7:12 do for **o** everything you want them
OUTSIDE
Col 4:5 those who are **o**
Rev 22:15 **O** are dogs and people
OUTWARD
Rom 7:6 the old way of **o** obedience
1 Pet 3:3 beauty be something **o**
OUTWARDLY
Rom 2:28 Jew who is merely one **o**
2 Cor 7:5 we . . . afflicted in every way **o**
OVER
1 Cor 5:5 hand such a person **o** to Satan
OVERCOME
Rev 7:16 nor will the sun ever **o** them
OVERFLOW
2 Cor 1:5 sufferings of Christ **o** to us
2 Cor 9:8 His grace **o** every gift of
Col 2:7 **o** all the while with thanksgiving
1 Thess 3:12 grow in love and **o** with it
OVERPOWER
Matt 16:18 hell will not **o** it
OVERSEERS
Acts 20:28 Holy Spirit has made you **o**
OVERSHADOW
Lk 1:35 power of Most High will **o** you
OVERWHELM
2 Cor 2:7 too much grief may **o** someone
OWE
Rom 8:12 fellow Christians we do not **o** it
Rom 13:8 Do not **o** anyone anything
1 Cor 7:3 do for his wife what he **o** her
Phlm 19 you **o** me more . . . your own self
OWN
Jn 1:11 His **o** people did not welcome Him
Acts 2:6 the disciples speak his **o** language
OX
Lk 14:19 I bought five teams of **o**
1 Cor 9:9 muzzle an **o** when treading
1 Tim 5:18 When an **o** is treading out grain

PAGAN
Acts 7:51 stubborn you are and **p** at heart
PAID
Rom 3:24 through the ransom Christ Jesus **p**
Rom 11:35 for which he must be **p** back
Gal 3:13 Christ **p** the price to free us
Eph 1:7 His dear Son **p** our ransom price
PAIN
Acts 2:24 God set aside the **p** of death
1 Thess 5:3 them like labor **p** on a woman
1 Tim 6:10 pierced themselves with many **p**
PALACES
Matt 11:8 are in the **p** of kings
PALM
Jn 12:13 took branches from the **p** trees
Rev 7:9 robes and carrying **p** branches
PARADISE
Lk 23:43 today you will be with Me in **P**
2 Cor 12:4 was caught up to **P**
Rev 2:7 tree of life that stands in the **P**
PARALYTIC
Mk 2:4 bed on which the **p** was lying
PARCHMENTS
2 Tim 4:13 bring . . . scrolls especially the **p**
PARENTS
Mk 13:12 rebel against their **p**
Jn 9:3 man nor his **p** sinned
2 Cor 12:14 children save up for their **p**
Eph 6:1 Children obey your **p** in the Lord
PART
Lk 24:51 He **p** from them
Rom 12:4 we have many **p** in one body
1 Cor 12:12 body is one and yet has many **p**
Jas 3:5 tongue is small **p** but it can boast
PARTNER
Lk 5:7 waved to their **p** in the other boat
2 Cor 6:14 righteousness wickedness be **p**
2 Cor 8:23 As for Titus he is my **p**
Phlm 17 if . . . me as your **p** welcome him
PARTIES
1 Cor 3:3 quarreling forming different **p**
PASS
Lk 10:31 priest . . . **p** by on the other side
1 Cor 11:23 Lord what . . . I **p** on to you
PASS AWAY
Matt 24:35 Heaven and earth will **p** away but
Mk 13:31 My words will not **p** away
Lk 21:33 heaven and earth will **p** away
1 Cor 7:31 world . . . present form is **p** away
Jas 1:10 he will **p** away like a flower on a
2 Pet 3:10 heavens will **p** away with a roar
1 Jn 2:17 world with its lust is **p** away
Rev 21:4 the first things have **p** away
PASSION
1 Cor 7:36 if his **p** is very strong
Gal 5:24 crucified the flesh with its **p**
Col 3:5 kill . . . impurity **p** evil lust
Tit 3:3 many kinds of **p** and pleasures
Rev 18:3 wine of her immoral **p**
PASSOVER
Mk 14:16 so they prepared the **P**

Lk 2:41 to Jerusalem to celebrate the **P**
Jn 2:13 The Jewish **P** was near so Jesus went
Jn 6:4 Jewish Festival of the **P** was near
Jn 11:55 Jewish **P** was near and many came
Jn 12:1 Six days before the **P** Jesus came
Jn 13:1 Before the Festival of the **P** Jesus
Jn 18:28 they wanted to celebrate the **P**
Jn 18:39 set one person free for you at **P**
Jn 19:14 preparation of the **P**
1 Cor 5:7 our **P** has been sacrificed
Heb 11:28 By faith he celebrated the **P**
PAST
Rom 3:25 those sins . . . done in the **p**
PASTOR
Acts 20:17 asked the **p** of the church to
Eph 4:11 some to be **p** and teachers
Phil 1:1 together with the **p** and deacons
1 Tim 3:1 sets his heart on being a **p**
1 Tim 5:17 **p** who are good leaders
2 Tim 4:5 God desires you to do as a **p**
PASTURE
Jn 10:9 he will go . . . and find **p**
PATCH
Matt 9:16 the **p** will tear away some
PATIENCE
2 Cor 6:6 by knowledge by **p** and kindness
PATIENT
Matt 18:26 Be **p** with me I will repay you
Rom 15:1 Be **p** with weaknesses
1 Cor 13:4 Love is **p** Love is kind
1 Thess 5:14 be **p** with everyone else
2 Thess 3:5 love of God and the **p** endurance
Jas 5:7 Be **p** fellow Christians until the
PATIENTLY
Rom 8:25 we **p** wait for it with eager
Rom 9:22 He waited **p** before He punished
Heb 10:32 you **p** endured a . . . struggle
PATTERN
Heb 8:5 they serve as a **p** and a shadow
PAY
Matt 5:26 until you **p** the last cent
Matt 18:28 **P** what you owe
Matt 20:4 I shall **p** you whatever is right
Lk 3:14 be satisfied with your **p**
Lk 10:35 I will **p** back to you when I return
Lk 14:12 invite you and **p** you back
Rom 12:19 I will **p** back says the Lord
Col 3:25 wrong will be **p** back
2 Thess 1:6 God to **p** back suffering
2 Tim 4:14 Lord will **p** him back for what he
Phlm 19 I will **p** it back
PAYMENT
Tit 2:14 He gave Himself as a **p** for us
PARALYZED
Matt 8:6 my slave is lying at home **p**
PEACE
Matt 5:9 Blessed are those who make **p**
Mk 5:34 Go in **p** be healed from your
Mk 9:50 live in **p** with one another
Lk 2:14 on earth **p** to people
Lk 2:29 You are letting . . . depart in **p**

Lk 7:50 Your faith saved you Go in **p**
Jn 20:19 said to them **P**
Rom 5:1 we have **p** with God through . . . Jesus
Rom 8:6 what spirit has . . . gives life and **p**
Rom 12:18 live in **p** with everybody
Rom 14:17 righteousness **p** and joy in Holy
1 Cor 14:33 God is . . . of **p**
2 Cor 1:2 Christ give you grace and **p**
Eph 2:14 He is our **P** In His flesh
Phil 4:7 Then the **p** of God which goes
Col 1:2 Father give you grace and **p**
Col 3:15 let the **p** of Christ to which
1 Tim 2:2 live quietly and **p** and be godly
2 Tim 2:22 righteousness faith love **p**
Jas 3:18 righteousness in the field of **p**
Jude 2 May more and more mercy **p** and love
Rev 6:4 power to take away **p** from the earth
PEALS
Rev 8:5 there came **p** of thunder rumblings
PEARLS
Matt 7:6 nor throw your **p** to hogs
Rev 21:21 twelve gates were twelve **p**
PEDDLE
2 Cor 2:17 we do not **p** impure word of God
PENTECOST
Acts 2:1 day of **P** came and they were all
PEOPLE
Matt 5:16 let your light shine before **p**
Rom 9:25 I will call My **p**
Rom 15:10 Gentiles together with His own **p**
2 Cor 6:16 and they will be My **p**
Tit 3:14 **p** should learn to be busy
PERFECT
Matt 5:48 Be **p** as your Father in heaven
Col 1:28 to present everyone **p** in Christ
Heb 7:19 the Law made nothing **p**
PERFECTION
2 Cor 13:11 Strive for **p**
Heb 7:11 if priests . . . could have given us **p**
PERFUME
Jn 12:3 took a pound of **p** real nard
PERIODS
Acts 1:7 It is not for you to know what . . . **p**
PERISH
Jn 3:16 everyone would not **p**
1 Cor 1:18 foolishness to those who are **p**
1 Cor 15:18 fallen asleep in Christ have **p**
2 Cor 2:15 among those who **p**
PERMANENT
Heb 10:34 better and **p** possessions
PERSECUTE
Matt 5:10 Blessed . . . **p** for doing right
Lk 21:12 arrest you and **p** you
Jn 5:16 the Jews began to **p** Jesus
Acts 7:52 a prophet your fathers did not **p**
Acts 9:4 Why are you **p** Me
Rom 12:14 Bless those who **p** you
Gal 1:13 how violently I **p** God's church
Rev 12:13 he **p** woman who had given birth
PERSECUTION
Mk 10:30 fields along with **p**

Rom 8:35 hardship **p** hunger
2 Tim 3:11 those **p** which I endured
PERSECUTER
Phil 3:6 is concerned a **p** of the church
PERSIST
Heb 11:27 he **p** as one who was constantly
PERSON
Jn 8:47 **p** who belongs to God listens
2 Cor 4:6 in the **p** of Christ
PERSONALLY
Gal 1:22 were not acquainted with me **p**
PERSUADE
Matt 28:14 we will **p** him and see that you
1 Cor 2:4 clever words to **p** you
PERSUASION
Gal 5:8 This **p** does not come
PERVERSE
Phil 2:15 crooked and **p** people
PERVERSIONS
Acts 20:30 **p** of the truth in order to draw
PETITIONS
1 Tim 2:1 **p** prayers intercessions and
PHARISEE
Matt 5:20 righteousness . . . better than . . . **P**
Jn 7:32 ruling priests as well as the **P**
Phil 3:5 as far as the Law is concerned a **P**
PHILOSOPHERS
Acts 17:18 Stoic **p** also debated with him
PHILOSOPHY
Col 2:8 through an empty and foolish **p**
PHYSICAL
Phil 3:4 something **p** I could claim more
2 Pet 2:18 using **p** cravings they set traps
PHYSICIAN
Col 4:14 Luke the **p** whom we love and Demas
PICTURE
Gal 3:1 Christ so clearly **p** before your
Heb 9:9 this is a **p** which pointed to time
PIERCED
Rev 1:7 even the men who **p** Him
PILGRIMS
Heb 11:13 strangers and **p** on earth
PILLAR
Gal 2:9 Peter and John were considered **p**
1 Tim 3:15 church . . . **p** and support of truth
Rev 3:12 I will make a **p** in the TEMPLE
PIT
Mk 12:1 dug a **p** for the winepress
Rev 9:1 given the key to . . . bottomless **p**
Rev 20:1 key to bottomless **p**
PITY
Matt 9:27 Have **p** on us Son of David
Lk 16:24 have **p** on me
Rom 9:15 I will **p** anyone whom I wish to **p**
1 Cor 15:19 we should be **p** more than all
PLACE
Matt 8:20 **p** to lay His head
Matt 28:6 Come see the **p** where He was lying
Lk 4:17 He found the **p** where it says
Jn 14:2 I am going to prepare a **p** for you
Phlm 13 serve me in your **p** while I . . . chains
Rev 2:5 take your lampstand from its **p**

PLAGUE
Lk 21:11 famines and **p** in various places
2 Cor 12:7 messenger of Satan to **p** me
Rev 6:8 its rider's name was **P**
Rev 15:1 seven angels with seven **p**
PLAN
Acts 2:23 God definitely **p** and intended
Acts 20:27 the whole **p** of God
Rom 8:28 called according to His **p**
1 Cor 3:20 knows that the **p** of wise
Eph 1:11 carries out . . . His will **p** it
2 Tim 1:9 He **p** to give us His grace
PLANTED
1 Cor 3:6 I **p** Apollos watered but God
Jas 1:21 word is **p** in you which can save
PLATFORM
Acts 12:21 sat on the **p** and made a speech
PLAY
1 Cor 10:7 drink and got up to **p**
PLEAD
Rom 8:26 the Spirit Himself **p** for us
2 Cor 5:20 God were **p** through us
1 Jn 2:1 have One to **p** for us with Father
PLEASE
Rom 12:1 sacrifice holy and **p** to God
1 Cor 7:32 unmarried man . . . how he can **p** the
1 Cor 10:5 God was not **p** with most of them
2 Cor 5:9 we make it our goal to **p** Him
Col 1:10 aiming to **p** Him in every way
1 Tim 2:3 this is good and **p** God our Savior
2 Tim 2:4 wants to **p** the one who enlisted
Heb 11:5 that God was **p** with him
Heb 11:6 impossible to **p** God without faith
PLEASURE
1 Tim 5:6 one who lives for **p** is dead
Heb 11:25 enjoying the short-lived **p** of sin
Jas 4:3 to spend it on your **p**
PLEDGE
1 Tim 5:12 breaking **p** they originally made
PLOT
Matt 12:14 Pharisees left and **p** against Him
Acts 4:25 peoples **p** to no avail
PLUNGE
1 Pet 4:4 you do not **p** into the same
POCKET
Mk 6:8 no copper money in your **p**
PODS
Lk 15:16 glad to fill up on the **p** that the
POETS
Acts 17:28 as some of your **p** have said
POINT
Matt 18:15 and **p** out his sin to him
1 Tim 4:6 **P** these things out to our fellow
POISON
Mk 16:18 any deadly **p** . . . not hurt
Rom 3:13 the **p** of serpents
POLLUTED
Acts 15:20 things **p** by idols
POMP
Acts 25:23 came with great **p** and went

POOR

Matt 5:3 Blessed are those . . . **p** in spirit
Matt 11:5 **p** people hear the Gospel
Matt 26:11 the **p** you always have with you
Lk 14:13 invite the **p** the crippled
Acts 10:2 He gave much to **p** among people
2 Cor 8:9 was rich yet for you He became **p**
Gal 2:10 we keep remembering the **p**

POSITION

1 Cor 1:26 not many are in **p** of power

POSSESS

Matt 5:5 gentle for they will **p** the earth
Matt 8:16 many who were **p** by demons

POSSESSIONS

Acts 2:45 they sold their lands and . . . **p**

POSSIBLE

Matt 26:39 My Father if it is **p** let this
Mk 14:35 if it were **p** He might not have

POTS

Mk 7:4 washing cups huge wine jars **p**

POTTER

Matt 27:7 to buy the **p** field for the burial
Rom 9:21 not a **p** have right over his clay

POUR

Lk 22:20 cup . . . **p** out for you
Jn 12:3 **p** it on Jesus' feet dried His feet
Acts 2:17 God says I will **p** out
Rom 5:5 Spirit . . . **p** God's love into hearts
1 Tim 1:14 Our Lord **p** His grace on me
2 Tim 4:6 **p** out as a drink offering

POVERTY

2 Cor 8:2 and their deep **p** have overflowed
2 Cor 8:9 rich through His **p**

POWER

Matt 13:54 get this wisdom and the **p**
Matt 24:29 the **p** of heaven will be shaken
Lk 4:14 In the **p** of the Spirit
Lk 8:46 I know that **p** went out from Me
Acts 1:8 will receive **p** and will testify
Acts 3:12 as if by our own **p** or piety we
Acts 10:38 anointed . . . with . . . Spirit and **p**
Rom 1:16 Gospel . . . is God's **p** to save
Rom 9:22 and let them know His **p**
Rom 15:19 by the **p** of miraculous signs
1 Cor 1:18 cross . . . it is the **p** of God
1 Cor 12:6 Differing **p** are given to them
1 Cor 15:56 the Law gives sin its **p**
2 Cor 12:9 My **p** is at its best when
2 Cor 13:4 He lives by God's **p**
Eph 1:19 vast resources of His **p** working in
Eph 3:16 strengthen you with **p**
Eph 6:10 Lord and His mighty **p** make
Col 1:13 from the **p** of darkness
2 Tim 3:5 but refuse to let it be a **p**
Heb 6:5 the **p** of the coming age
2 Pet 1:3 His divine **p** has given to us
Jude 25 to Him be glory majesty **p**
Rev 5:12 worthy to receive **p** and wealth

PRACTICE

Col 3:7 you also **p** them
1 Thess 4:10 you are **p** it toward all

PRAETORIUM

Phil 1:13 the whole **P** and all the others

PRAISE

Matt 5:16 see the good you do and **p**
Matt 6:2 on streets to be **p** by people
Matt 11:25 I **p** You Father Lord of heaven
Lk 1:68 **P** the Lord the God of Israel
Lk 13:13 up straight and began **p** God
Lk 18:43 all the people . . . **p** God
Lk 24:53 they were . . . in the Temple **p** God
Acts 3:8 walking jumping and **p** God
Rom 3:23 are without the **p** that God gives
Rom 13:3 Do what is right and it will **p** you
Rom 15:6 you **p** the God and Father of our
1 Cor 4:5 receive his **p** from God
2 Cor 1:3 let us **p** the God and Father
Eph 1:3 let us **p** the God and Father of our
Eph 1:14 His glory might be **p**
Phil 4:8 anything . . . that deserves **p**
1 Thess 2:6 nor did we seek **p** from people
Rev 7:12 Amen **P** and glory and wisdom and

PRAY

Matt 6:6 when you **p** go into your own room
Matt 26:39 **p** My Father . . . let this cup pass
Matt 26:41 Stay awake and **p** that you may
Mk 1:35 lonely place and there He **p**
Mk 14:35 fell to ground and **p**
Jn 16:26 I will **p** to the Father for you
Acts 4:31 they had **p** the place . . . shaken
Acts 6:4 devote ourselves to **p**
Acts 9:11 For at this very moment he is **p**
Acts 9:40 He knelt and **p**
Acts 10:2 was continually **p** to God
Acts 12:5 earnestly **p** to God
Rom 1:10 whenever I **p** as I keep asking
Rom 8:34 right hand of God and He **p** for us
Eph 6:18 **p** in a spiritual way
Col 1:9 we have not stopped **p** for you
1 Thess 5:17 Always keep on **p**
1 Tim 2:8 to **p** everywhere lifting . . . hands
1 Tim 5:5 widow . . . asking and **p** day night
Heb 7:25 He always lives to **p** for them
Heb 13:18 **P** for us for we are sure
Jas 5:13 anyone . . . suffering Let him **p**

PRAYER

Matt 21:22 Whatever you ask for in **p**
Matt 26:27 took a cup spoke a **p** of thanks
Mk 9:29 can be driven out only by **p**
Mk 11:24 anything you ask for in **p** believe
Acts 2:42 breaking of the bread . . . the **p**
Rom 10:1 my **p** to God is to save Israelites
Rom 12:12 Be happy . . . and continue in **p**
2 Cor 1:11 in helping us through your **p**
Eph 1:16 as I remember you in my **p**
Col 4:2 Be persistent in **p**
1 Tim 2:1 **p** intercessions and thanksgivings
1 Tim 4:5 word of God and **p** make it holy
Jas 5:16 The earnest **p** of righteous man
1 Pet 3:7 interfere with your **p**
Rev 5:8 **p** of the believers
Rev 8:3 offer with the **p** of all believers

PREACH

Matt 10:7 As you go **p** The Kingdom of heaven
Matt 11:1 teach and **p** in their towns
Matt 12:41 they repented when Jonah **p**
Mk 1:38 so that I may **p** there also
Mk 6:12 and **p** that people should repent
Mk 13:10 Gospel must be **p** to all nations
Mk 16:15 Go everywhere . . . and **p** the Gospel
Lk 4:43 I have to **p** the Good News
Lk 9:2 He sent them to **p**
Lk 24:47 forgiveness of sins will be **p**
Acts 8:4 went . . . **p** the word
Acts 9:20 started to **p** in the synagogs
Acts 10:42 ordered us to **p** to the people
Acts 28:31 He **p** God's Kingdom
Rom 10:8 faith that we **p**
Rom 10:14 hear if no one **p**
1 Cor 1:17 to **p** the Gospel [Good News]
1 Cor 1:21 the foolishness of our **p**
1 Cor 15:14 our **p** means nothing
2 Cor 1:19 whom I . . . **p** to you was not yes
2 Cor 11:4 when someone comes along and **p**
Gal 1:23 to persecute us is now **p** the faith
Phil 1:18 Christ is being **p** and I am glad
Col 1:23 has been **p** to every creature
2 Tim 4:2 **P** the word be ready whether it is
1 Pet 3:19 He also went and **p** to spirits
Rev 14:6 Gospel [Good News] to **p** to those

PREACHER

1 Cor 12:28 God has appointed . . . **p**
1 Tim 2:7 appointed a **p** and an apostle
2 Tim 1:11 I was appointed a **p** apostle

PRECIOUS

1 Pet 2:4 God selected as **p**

PREDICT

Acts 3:18 He **p** by the mouth of all prophets
Acts 13:27 what the prophets had **p**
1 Pet 1:11 when He **p** the sufferings

PREFER

Heb 11:25 and **p** being mistreated with God's

PREFERENCE

1 Tim 5:21 without **p** for anyone in anything

PREGNANT

Rev 12:2 and she was **p** and she cried

PREJUDICE

1 Tim 5:21 keep . . . without **p** and

PREPARE

Matt 25:34 inherit the Kingdom **p** for you
Lk 1:76 go . . . to **p** His ways
Lk 2:31 You **p** for all people to see
Rom 9:23 whom He long ago **p**
1 Cor 2:9 God has **p** for those who love Him
2 Tim 2:21 useful to the Master and **p** to do
Heb 11:16 He has **p** a city for them

PRESENCE

2 Cor 2:10 I did so in the **p** of Christ

PRESENTING

Rom 6:13 not go on **p** members of your body

PRESERVED

Matt 9:17 then both are **p**

PRICE

1 Cor 6:20 you were bought for a **p**
Heb 9:12 paid a **p** that frees us forever

PRIDE

Rom 3:27 What then becomes of our **p**

PRIEST

Lk 10:31 a **p** came down that road
Acts 6:7 the **p** came to believe
Rom 15:16 Gospel of God as a **p**
Heb 5:6 You are a **P** forever
Heb 7:1 Melchizedek . . . **p** of the Most High
Rev 5:10 them a kingdom and **p** to our God
Rev 20:6 they will be **p** of God of Christ

PRIESTHOOD

Heb 7:24 His is an unchanging **p**
1 Pet 2:9 you are . . . a royal **p** a holy nation

PRINCIPLE

Rom 3:27 On what **p** On the **p** of works
Col 2:20 with Christ to basic **p** of world

PRISON

Matt 4:12 John had been put in **p**
Matt 11:2 When John who was in **p** heard
Matt 18:30 put him in **p** until he would pay
Matt 25:36 in **p** and you visited Me
Mk 6:17 put him in **p** because Herod had
Jn 3:24 John had not yet been put in **p**
Acts 8:3 he put them in **p**
Acts 12:4 put him in **p** and had . . . soldiers
Rom 11:32 all people in a **p**
Rom 16:7 who went to **p** with me
2 Cor 6:5 beaten or put in **p**
1 Pet 3:19 the spirits kept in **p**
Rev 20:7 freed from his **p**

PRISONER

Matt 27:15 free one **p** whom the crowd wanted
Rom 7:23 making me a **p** to the law of sin
Gal 3:22 everything is a **p** of sin
Eph 3:1 I Paul the **p** of Christ Jesus
Col 4:10 my fellow **p** sends greetings

PRIVATE

Matt 6:6 Father who is with you in **p**

PRIVATELY

Gal 2:2 I laid it **p** before those who were

PRIZE

1 Cor 9:24 only one wins the **p**
Phil 3:14 I go after heavenly **p** to which
2 Tim 2:5 he wins a **p** only if he competes

PROCLAIM

1 Cor 11:26 you are **p** the Lord's death
Heb 2:12 I will **p** Your Name to My bothers

PRODUCE

Matt 7:16 know them by what they **p**
Matt 12:35 good person **p** good things from
Rom 5:3 know suffering **p** patient endurance

PRODUCTS

2 Cor 9:10 increase **p** of your righteousness

PROFIT

Phil 4:17 but the growing **p** in your
1 Tim 6:5 religion is a way to make a **p**
2 Pet 2:3 twist meaning . . . to make a **p**

PROGRESS
1 Tim 4:15 everyone can see your **p**
PROMISE
Lk 1:55 as He **p** our fathers
Acts 1:4 the Father had **p**
Acts 2:39 this **p** is . . . to you and . . . children
Rom 1:2 He **p** this Good News in advance
Rom 4:16 **p** is by faith that it might come
Rom 9:4 Law the worship and the **p**
Rom 9:8 children of the **p** are counted as
2 Cor 11:2 I **p** you in marriage to one
Gal 3:14 receive the **p** Spirit
Gal 3:18 receive it by a **p**
Gal 4:23 free woman by the **p**
Eph 3:6 share the same **p**
1 Tim 4:8 godliness . . . has a **p** for life here
2 Tim 1:1 **p** life in Christ Jesus to Timothy
Tit 1:2 God who never lies **p** before time
Heb 7:6 him who had the **p**
2 Pet 1:4 His precious and very great **p**
2 Pet 3:9 to do what He **p**
PROMOTES
Tit 1:1 know the truth which **p** godliness
PROMPTLY
Mk 11:3 will **p** send it back here
PROOF
Acts 1:3 convincing **p** that He was alive
2 Cor 13:3 seeing that you want **p**
PROPER
1 Cor 14:40 done in a **p** and orderly way
Eph 5:4 These are not **p** Instead give thanks
PROPERTY
Lk 8:3 His disciples with their **p**
Lk 15:12 divided his **p** between them
PROPHECY
1 Cor 13:8 If . . . **p** they will be brought to
1 Cor 14:1 gifts of Spirit especially **p**
1 Tim 1:18 according to the **p** made earlier
2 Pet 1:21 for no **p** was ever spoken
Rev 1:3 the words of this **p** and
Rev 19:10 witness . . . is spirit of **p**
PROPHESY
Matt 26:68 **P** You Christ and tell us
1 Cor 12:10 another can **p**
Jude 14 from Adam **p** about them
PROPHET
Matt 5:12 they persecuted **p** who lived
Matt 8:17 this way what **p** Isaiah said
Matt 12:17 what **p** Isaiah said was fulfilled
Matt 12:39 sign . . . of **p** Jonah
Matt 13:57 only place a **p** is not honored
Matt 23:37 who murdered the **p** and stoned
Matt 27:9 what **p** Jeremiah said . . . fulfilled
Lk 1:76 will be called a **p** of the
Lk 4:24 no **p** is accepted in his hometown
Lk 13:33 **p** to die outside Jerusalem
Lk 16:29 They have Moses and the **p**
Lk 24:19 a **P** mighty in what He did
Jn 1:21 Are you the **P** No he answered
Jn 4:44 declared that a **p** is not
Jn 6:14 This . . . is the **P** who is coming

Jn 7:40 This is certainly the **P**
Acts 2:16 this is what the **p** Joel spoke
Acts 3:22 raise up a **P** for you from among
Acts 10:43 All the **p** testify about Him
Acts 13:27 messages of the **p** which were
Eph 2:20 foundation of apostles and **p**
Heb 1:1 God . . . spoke . . . by the **p**
1 Pet 1:10 **p** who wrote beforehand
2 Pet 3:2 words spoken . . . by the holy **p**
1 Jn 4:1 many false **p** have gone . . . world
PROSELYTES
Acts 2:10 Jews as well as **p**
PROSTITUTE
Matt 21:31 tax collectors and **p** are going
Lk 15:30 devoured your property with **p**
1 Cor 6:15 members of a **p**
Rev 17:1 great **p** who sits on many waters
PROTECTED
Mk 6:20 So he **p** him
PROTECTOR
Rom 16:2 she has become a **p** of many
PROUD
Lk 1:51 scattered those who think so **p**
Rom 1:30 they are haughty **p** boastful
1 Tim 6:4 is **p** and does not know anything
Jas 4:6 God opposes the **p** but gives grace
PROVED
Acts 18:28 vigorously he **p** that the Jews
PSALMS
Eph 5:19 as you speak **p** hymns
Col 3:16 by singing **p** hymns spiritual songs
PUBLICLY
Acts 20:20 teaching you **p** and from house to
3 Jn 6 have **p** told church about your love
PUNISH
Acts 7:7 **p** the people whom they will serve
Rom 9:22 He **p** those who deserved it
Rom 12:19 Do not take revenge . . . let God **p**
2 Thess 1:9 will be **p** with an . . . destruction
PUNISHMENT
Matt 25:46 these . . . go away to everlasting **p**
Mk 12:40 They will receive a more severe **p**
Lk 20:47 They will receive a more severe **p**
Rom 1:27 suffering in themselves the **p**
Gal 5:10 will have to take his **p**
Heb 2:2 received a just **p**
Heb 12:6 He gives **p** to everyone
PURE
2 Cor 6:6 by being **p** by knowledge
Phil 1:10 you may be **p** and without blame
Phil 4:8 all that is **p** all that is
1 Tim 1:5 flowing from a **p** heart
1 Tim 5:2 keeping yourself altogether **p**
Tit 1:15 Everything is **p** to those who are **p**
PURIFY
1 Jn 3:3 puts his hope in Him **p** himself
PURITY
1 Cor 5:8 the bread of **p** and truth
PURPLE
Mk 15:17 They put a **p** robe on Him
Lk 16:19 rich man who dressed in **p**

Jn 19:2 put a **p** robe on Him
Acts 16:14 a dealer in **p** goods
Rev 17:4 woman wore **p** and scarlet
PURPOSE
Rom 9:11 God might carry out His **p**
1 Cor 7:14 serves a holy **p**
Eph 1:9 it was His **p** in Christ to manage
Phil 2:2 keep one **p** in mind
1 Tim 2:7 for this **p** I was appointed a
PURSUE
Rom 9:30 Gentiles . . . **p** righteousness found
1 Tim 6:11 **p** righteousness godliness faith
PUT
Matt 25:23 I will **p** you in charge of many
2 Cor 11:19 being wise gladly **p** up
Col 2:11 by **p** away the sinful body
Col 3:9 you have **p** away your old self
1 Pet 3:18 He was **p** to death in flesh
1 Pet 3:22 angels . . . have been **p** under Him
3 Jn 10 tries to **p** them out of the church
PUZZLED
Acts 2:12 amazed and **p**

QUACKS
2 Tim 3:13 evil men and religious **q** will
QUARRELING
1 Cor 1:11 you are **q** my fellow Christians
2 Cor 12:20 there may be **q** jealousy
QUARRELSOME
1 Tim 3:3 pastor . . . not **q** not . . . loves money
QUEEN
Matt 12:42 **q** from the south will be raised
Rev 18:7 I am a **q** on a throne . . . not a widow
QUESTIONS
Lk 2:46 listening to them and asking them **q**
Acts 18:15 we have **q** here about words
1 Cor 10:27 do not ask any **q** or let
QUICK
Jas 1:19 everyone be **q** to listen
QUICKLY
Matt 28:7 go **q** tell disciples He has risen
QUIET
Matt 8:26 ordered winds and sea to be **q**
Mk 1:25 Be **q** and come out of him
QUIETNESS
1 Tim 2:11 Let a woman learn in **q**

RABBI
Jn 1:38 **R** (which means Teacher) where are
RABBONI
Jn 20:16 she turned **R** she said
RACE
1 Cor 9:24 those who run in a **r** all run but
RAIN
Matt 5:45 lets **r** fall on them whether they
Matt 7:25 **r** poured down the floods came
Lk 4:25 it did not **r** for three years
RAINBOW
Rev 10:1 there was a **r** over His head
RAISE
Jn 5:21 As the Father **r** the dead gives life

Acts 2:24 God set aside . . . death and **r** Him
Acts 3:15 But God **r** Him from the dead
Acts 3:22 The Lord . . . will **r** up a Prophet
Acts 10:40 God **r** Him on the third day
Acts 13:30 But God **r** Him from the dead
Acts 17:31 by **r** Him from the dead He has
Rom 4:24 Him who **r** our Lord . . . from the dead
Rom 4:25 was **r** because of our justification
Rom 6:4 as Christ was **r** from the dead
Rom 9:17 I **r** you to throne to demonstrate
1 Cor 6:14 God **r** the Lord . . . will also **r** us
1 Cor 15:4 buried and that He was **r** on
1 Cor 15:20 now Christ was **r** from the dead
Gal 1:1 God the Father who **r** Him from dead
Eph 1:20 **r** Him from the dead made Him sit
Eph 2:6 He **r** us with Him and had us sit
Col 3:1 now if you were **r** with Christ
Heb 11:19 God can even **r** him from the dead
RANSOM
Mk 10:45 give His life as a **r** for many
Lk 1:68 has prepared a **r** for them
Rom 3:24 through the **r** Christ Jesus paid
1 Cor 1:30 God made our wisdom . . . **r** from sin
Eph 1:7 Son paid our **r** price with His blood
1 Tim 2:6 who gave Himself as a **r** for all
RATIFIED
Gal 3:15 once last will and testament is **r**
RAVINE
Lk 3:5 Every **r** will be filled
REACHED
Phil 3:12 already **r** the goal or have
READ
Lk 4:16 He stood up to **r** and was
Acts 8:30 heard him **r** the prophet Isaiah
Col 4:16 also **r** the letter from Laodicea
READING
1 Tim 4:13 devote yourself to the public **r**
READY
Mk 4:29 As soon as the grain is **r**
Acts 10:33 we are . . . **r** to hear everything
2 Cor 9:2 Greece has been **r** since last year
2 Tim 3:17 God is **r** equipped for every
REAL
Rom 9:6 not all . . . are the **r** Israel
Col 2:23 it is of no **r** value to anyone
1 Tim 1:2 to Timothy my **r** son by faith
Tit 3:14 help in cases of **r** need
REALIZE
Lk 2:49 Didn't you **r** that I must be in My
Jn 6:15 when Jesus **r** the people intended to
Acts 4:13 Then they **r** that these men
REAP
1 Cor 9:11 too much if we **r** your earthly
REAPER
Jn 4:36 Already the **r** is getting paid
REASON
Acts 17:31 given everyone a . . . **r** to believe
REBEL
Mk 13:12 Children will **r** against parents
1 Tim 1:9 those who break Law those who **r**
Heb 3:8 as it happened when the people **r**
Jude 11 they have **r** like Korah and perished

REBELS
Mk 15:7 He was in prison with the r
REBELLIOUS
2 Thess 2:8 then the r one will be revealed
Tit 1:10 many who are r who talk foolishly
REBUKED
2 Cor 2:6 and more of you have r him
RECEIVE
Matt 7:8 Anyone who continues to ask r
Matt 10:8 Give these things as you r them
Matt 21:22 prayer believing you will r
Mk 10:15 whoever does not r Kingdom of God
Jn 20:22 R the Holy Spirit
Rom 11:7 Israel did not r what it wanted
2 Cor 5:10 judgment seat of Christ . . . to r
Heb 11:13 without having r what was
RECEIVING
Phil 4:15 balancing of giving and r
RECLINING
Mk 2:15 as Jesus was r at the table
RECOGNIZE
Matt 14:35 men of that place r Jesus
Rom 3:20 Law teaches us to r sin
RECOMMEND
2 Cor 3:1 Are we beginning to r ourselves
2 Cor 5:12 We are not r ourselves to you
RECONCILE
Rom 5:10 we were r to God by death of Son
Rom 11:15 the world is r to God
2 Cor 5:18 He r us to Himself through
Eph 2:16 r them both to God in one body
Col 1:20 by Him to r to Himself everything
Col 1:22 He r you by dying in human body
RECORD
Matt 1:1 A r of family history of Jesus
REDEMPTION
Lk 21:28 your r is drawing near
Col 1:14 In His Son we have r . . . forgiveness
REED
Matt 11:7 a r shaken by the wind
Matt 12:20 He will not crush a bruised r
REFRESH
Acts 3:20 the Lord r you
Phlm 20 R my heart in Christ
2 Pet 1:13 to r your memory
REFUSED
Matt 27:34 He r to drink it
REGARDED
Rom 1:28 they r it as worthless to hold on
REGION
2 Cor 10:16 by preaching Gospel to the r
Gal 1:21 to the r of Syria
REGISTER
Lk 2:3 went to r each to his own town
REGRET
2 Cor 7:10 leads to salvation free from r
REJECT
Lk 9:22 Son of Man . . . has to be r
Lk 10:16 person who r you r Me
Jn 3:36 one who r the Son will not see life
Jn 12:48 The person who r Me and does not

Rom 11:1 God did not r His people did He
1 Thess 4:7 he does not r a man but God
1 Tim 4:4 Nothing is to be r if it is
Heb 12:17 to inherit the blessing he was r
REJOICE
Matt 5:12 Continue to r and be glad
RELATIONSHIP
Rom 5:10 we have this changed r
RELEASED
Acts 4:23 When Peter and John were r they
RELIABLE
Acts 25:26 I have nothing r to write
RELIEF
Acts 11:29 to send r to the fellow
2 Thess 1:7 to give r to you who suffer
RELIGION
Acts 25:19 about their own r and about
Gal 1:13 I . . . lived according to Jewish r
1 Tim 6:5 r is a way to make a profit
RELIGIOUS
Acts 10:2 He was a r man
Acts 17:22 I see how very r you are
REMAIN
Jn 8:31 If you r with My word
Jn 9:41 We see . . . your sin r
1 Thess 4:17 we who r and are still living
1 Pet 1:25 word of the Lord r forever
2 Pet 3:4 everything has r as it was
1 Jn 4:16 whoever r in His love r in God
REMEMBER
Lk 1:54 He r His mercy
Lk 22:19 Do this to r Me
Lk 23:42 Jesus r me when You come . . . Kingdom
1 Cor 11:24 Do this to r Me
Gal 2:10 we keep r the poor the very thing
Heb 8:12 no longer r their sins
Rev 22:7 r I am coming soon
REMIND
Heb 10:3 these sacrifices r people of . . . sin
Jas 1:5 God does not keep on r a person
REMINDER
2 Pet 1:15 you have a constant r
REMNANT
Rom 11:5 then there is also right now a r
REMOVED
1 Cor 5:2 the man who did this might be r
RENEW
2 Cor 4:16 our inward person is being r
Col 3:10 continually r in knowledge . . . like
REPAY
1 Tim 5:4 family and r their parents
REPENT
Matt 3:8 produce works that show you have r
Matt 4:17 R for Kingdom of heaven is near
Matt 11:20 because they had not r
Mk 6:12 preached that people should r
Lk 16:30 from the dead they will r
Acts 2:38 R and be baptized every one of
Acts 3:19 R then and turn to have your sins
Rom 2:4 leads you to r of your sins
Rev 2:5 you have fallen and r and do as you
Rev 9:20 rest of mankind . . . did not r

REPENTANCE
Lk 3:3 baptism of **r** for the forgiveness
Lk 24:47 **r** and forgiveness of sins
2 Cor 7:10 godly sorrow produces **r**
2 Pet 3:9 wants all to come to **r**
REPRESENTATIVE
2 Thess 2:4 above everyone who is God's **r**
REQUIRES
Rom 2:15 what the Law **r** them to do
RESCUE
Lk 1:74 to **r** us from our enemies
Acts 7:34 have come down to **r** them
Acts 12:11 the Lord sent His angel and **r** me
Rom 7:24 Who will **r** me from this body
Rom 15:31 I may be **r** from those in Judea
2 Cor 1:10 He is One who **r** us from . . . death
1 Thess 1:10 Jesus who **r** us from coming
2 Tim 4:17 I was **r** from the lion's mouth
2 Pet 2:7 He **r** righteous Lot
RESERVED
2 Pet 3:7 same word has **r** the . . . earth
RESIST
Rom 9:19 Who can **r** His will
Eph 6:13 you may be able to **r** when things
Heb 12:4 you have not yet **r** to the point
1 Pet 5:9 strong in your faith and **r** him
RESOURCES
Eph 1:19 vast **r** of His power working in
RESPECT
Gal 2:6 the **r** leaders—what sort of people
Eph 5:33 let a wife **r** her husband
1 Tim 5:4 learn to **r** their own family
1 Tim 6:1 men who deserve every **r**
Heb 11:7 faith Noah . . . **r** God and built ark
RESPECTABILITY
1 Cor 12:23 unpresentable parts have . . . **r**
REST
Mk 6:31 where you can be alone and **r**
Acts 2:3 flames that separated and . . . **r**
Acts 2:26 even My body will **r** in hope
Rom 2:17 if you call yourself a Jew and **r**
Heb 3:11 never come to My place of **r**
Rev 14:13 let them **r** from their hard work
RESTORE
Acts 3:21 everything will be **r** as God said
1 Pet 5:10 will **r** you firm you up
RESULT
Rom 1:13 enjoy some of the **r** of working
Rom 6:21 What was the **r** then of doing
2 Cor 1:11 as a **r** of the prayers of many
RESURRECTION
Jn 11:25 I am the **R** and the Life
Acts 17:18 Gospel of Jesus and the **r**
Rom 1:4 declared by His **r**
1 Cor 15:21 Man also brought the **r** of dead
Phil 3:10 know Him both the power of His **r**
2 Tim 2:18 **r** has already taken place
1 Pet 3:21 good conscience . . . by **r** of Jesus
Rev 20:5 this is the first **r**
RETURN
1 Thess 3:9 how can we ever **r** thanks

REVEAL
Matt 11:25 **r** them to little children
Matt 11:27 the Son wants to **r** Him
Jn 12:38 the arm of the Lord been **r**
Rom 1:17 it **r** the righteousness which comes
Rom 8:18 the glory soon to be **r** to us
1 Cor 2:10 God has **r** it to us by His Spirit
1 Cor 14:30 If God **r** something to another
Gal 3:23 faith . . . about to come would be **r**
Eph 1:17 will **r** more and more to you as you
Eph 3:5 as it now has been **r** by the Spirit
Phil 3:15 God will also **r** this to you
2 Thess 2:3 man of sin . . . must be **r**
Tit 1:3 right times He **r** in His word
1 Pet 1:5 ready to be **r** at the end of time
1 Pet 1:20 He was **r** in the last period
1 Jn 1:2 which was **r** to us
Rev 15:4 judgments have been **r**
REVELATION
Rev 1:1 This is the **r** from JESUS CHRIST
REVENGE
Rom 12:19 not take **r** dear friends
REVERENTLY
1 Pet 1:17 live **r** as you spend your time
REVOLT
Mk 15:7 in their **r** had committed a murder
2 Thess 2:3 For the **r** must take place first
REVOLUTION
Lk 21:9 hear of wars and **r**
REWARD
Matt 5:12 you have a great **r** in heaven
Matt 6:1 Father in heaven will not **r** you
1 Cor 9:17 I receive a **r**
Eph 6:8 the Lord will **r** each one
Heb 10:35 There is a great **r** for it
Heb 11:6 God . . . **r** those who search for
Rev 11:18 **r** to Your servants the prophets
Rev 22:12 will have My **r** with Me to pay
RICH
Matt 27:57 came a **r** man from Arimathea
Mk 10:23 hard it will be for . . . who are **r**
Mk 12:41 Many **r** people put in much
Lk 1:53 **r** He has sent away empty-handed
Lk 16:19 There was a **r** man who dressed
Lk 21:1 He saw **r** people dropping
Rom 11:12 their loss made the Gentiles **r**
1 Cor 1:5 you have been made **r** in every way
2 Cor 8:7 As you are **r** in everything
2 Cor 8:9 was **r** yet for you He became poor
Eph 1:7 result of the **r** of His grace
Eph 2:4 God who is **r** in mercy because
Col 1:27 known the glorious **r** of mystery
Col 3:16 let Christ's word live **r** in you
1 Tim 6:9 people who want to get **r** fall
1 Tim 6:17 Tell those who are **r** in world
Heb 11:26 suffered for Christ greater **r**
Jas 1:11 the **r** person will fade away
Jas 5:1 come now you **r** people cry and howl
Rev 2:9 poor you are (but you are **r**)
RID
Lk 13:12 Woman you are **r** of your trouble

RIDE
Jn 12:15 King is coming r on a donkey's
RIDER
Rev 6:2 horse and its r had a bow
Rev 19:11 its **R** is called Faithful and True
RIDICULED
Matt 27:39 those who passed by r Him
RIGHT
Matt 20:15 Don't I have the r to do
Matt 22:44 Sit at My r hand until I put
Matt 25:33 have the sheep stand at His r
Matt 26:64 Son of Man sitting at r hand of
Matt 27:6 It is not r to put it into Temple
Mk 16:19 sat down at the r hand of God
Acts 2:25 Lord before Me He is at My r hand
Acts 4:19 God considers it r to listen
Acts 7:55 Jesus standing at God's r hand
1 Cor 7:4 her husband has a r to it
1 Cor 9:5 Do we not have a r to take along
Col 3:1 Christ is sitting at the r hand of
2 Thess 3:9 have a r to receive support
1 Tim 6:15 At His own r time God will show
Heb 1:3 He sat . . . at the r hand of Majesty
Jas 4:17 knows what is r but does not do it
1 Pet 3:17 suffer for doing r than . . . wrong
Rev 2:1 seven stars in His r hand
Rev 13:16 branded on their r hands or on
RIGHTEOUS
Matt 9:12 not come to call r people
Matt 25:37 Then the r will ask Him Lord
Matt 25:46 but the r to everlasting life
Lk 14:14 when the r rise from the dead
Jn 17:25 **R** Father the world did not know
Acts 3:14 You denied the Holy and **R** One
Acts 7:52 The **R** One will come
Acts 22:14 see the **R** One and hear Him speak
Rom 1:17 The r will live by faith
Rom 3:10 No one is r no not one
Rom 5:7 die for someone who is r
Rom 8:10 you are r And if the Spirit of Him
2 Cor 5:21 we might become r before God
1 Tim 1:9 Law is not meant for a r person
Heb 11:4 r when God approved his offerings
1 Pet 3:14 suffer because you are r
1 Pet 3:18 Christ died . . . **R** One for the
1 Jn 2:1 Jesus Christ who is r
Rev 15:4 Your r judgments . . . been revealed
RIGHTEOUSNESS
Matt 3:15 we should fulfill all r
Matt 5:20 unless your r is much better than
Matt 6:33 God's rule and His r
Matt 21:32 John came to you teaching . . . r
Lk 1:75 in holiness and r before Him
Jn 16:8 convict world of sin r and judgment
Rom 1:17 a r which comes from God by faith
Rom 3:21 God has shown a r that comes from
Rom 5:17 His gift of r will live and rule
Rom 9:30 Gentiles . . . not pursuing r found
Rom 10:3 not knowing the r which God gives
2 Cor 6:7 with weapons of r in right hand
Gal 3:21 certainly r would become ours

Gal 5:5 r for which we hope
Phil 3:9 not having my own r which comes
2 Tim 3:16 useful for . . . training in r
2 Tim 4:8 waiting for me the crown of r
Heb 11:7 of the r that comes by faith
2 Pet 1:1 people who by the r of our God
RING
Lk 15:22 put a r on his finger and sandals
RIOT
Matt 27:24 but that a r was breaking out
Acts 19:40 accused of a r today
RIPE
Rev 14:15 the harvest on earth is very r
RISE
Matt 28:6 He has r as He said
Lk 14:14 when the righteous r from the dead
Lk 16:31 will not be convinced . . . r from the
Lk 24:6 He is not here He has r
Jn 5:29 those who have done evil will r to
Jn 11:23 Your brother will r again
Acts 23:6 my hope that the dead will r
2 Cor 5:15 but for Him who died and r for
1 Thess 4:16 dead . . . in Christ will r first
2 Tim 2:8 Keep in mind Jesus Christ r
RISKED
Rom 16:4 who r their necks to save my life
Phil 2:30 he r his life and almost died
RIVER
Rev 9:14 who are held bound at the great r
ROAR
Lk 21:25 r and tossing of the sea
ROB
1 Cor 6:7 let yourself be r
1 Cor 6:10 greedy get drunk slander or r
2 Cor 11:8 I r other churches taking pay
ROBBER
Matt 27:38 they crucified two r with Him
Lk 10:30 fell into the hands of r
Jn 10:1 somewhere else is a thief and a r
ROBE
Matt 11:8 Those who wear soft r
Mk 12:38 parade around in long r
Mk 16:5 a young man dressed in white r
Lk 15:22 bring out a r—the best—and put
Lk 20:46 like to parade around in long r
Jn 19:2 put a purple r on Him
Rev 1:13 was clothed with a r that reached
ROCK
Matt 7:24 build his house on the r
Matt 16:18 on this r I will build My church
Rom 9:33 a r which will cause them to fall
1 Cor 10:4 drank from the spiritual **R**
ROD
Heb 9:4 manna Aaron's r that had budded
ROLLING
Matt 27:60 After r a large stone against
ROOF
Matt 8:8 worthy for You to come under my r
Mk 2:4 they opened up the r over the place
ROOM
Matt 6:6 when you pray go into your own r

Mk 2:2 was no **r** not even in front of door
Mk 14:15 show you a large **r** upstairs
Lk 2:7 because there was no **r** . . . in the inn
Lk 14:22 there still is **r**
Jn 14:2 Father's house there are many **r**
ROOSTER
Matt 26:34 before the **r** crows you will deny
Mk 14:68 Just then a **r** crowed a second time
Jn 18:27 just then a **r** crowed
ROOT
Rom 11:16 if the **r** is holy so are branches
Eph 3:17 you will be firmly **r** and built up
Col 2:7 be **r** and built up in Him
1 Tim 6:10 love of money is **r** of all evils
ROYAL
Jas 2:8 if you . . . do everything the **R** Law
1 Pet 2:9 a chosen people a **r** priesthood
RUBBISH
Phil 3:8 consider it **r** . . . to gain Christ
RUDDER
Jas 3:4 very small **r** steers them anywhere
RUIN
Rom 14:15 do not **r** any person . . . by what you
1 Cor 8:11 your knowledge is **r** the weak
RULE
Matt 6:33 eager for God's **r** . . . righteousness
Matt 15:9 teach for doctrines are **r** laid
Rom 5:14 Yet death **r** from Adam to Moses
Rom 6:12 not let sin go on **r** in your dying
Rom 7:21 I find this to be the **r**
1 Cor 15:25 He must **r** until God puts all
Heb 1:8 **r** Your Kingdom with . . . righteousness
Rev 5:10 they . . . **r** as kings on the earth
Rev 20:4 they lived and **r** with Christ
RULER
Acts 4:8 **R** of the people and elders
Eph 1:21 above all **r** authorities powers
Eph 2:2 **r** who governs the air the spirit
1 Tim 6:15 He the blessed and only **R** King
Heb 2:7 made Him **R** over what Your hands
RUMOR
Matt 24:6 hear of wars and **r** of wars
RUN
Lk 15:20 He **r** and put his arms around him
1 Cor 9:24 wins prize Like them **r** to win
Gal 2:2 to be **r** or to have **r** in vain
Heb 12:1 endurance **r** the race that is laid
RUST
Matt 6:19 treasures on earth where moth **r**

SABBATH
Matt 12:8 Lord of the **S**
Matt 12:10 Is it right to heal on a **S**
Mk 2:27 The **S** . . . not man for the **S**
Lk 4:16 On the **S** He went into
Lk 13:14 Jesus for healing on the **S**
Jn 5:18 not only breaking the **S**
Jn 7:23 circumcised on **S** to keep
Col 2:16 say you are wrong . . . on a **S**
Heb 4:9 still a **S** rest for people of God

SACKCLOTH
Matt 11:21 repented . . . in **s** and ashes
SACRED PLACE
Acts 6:13 against the **s** place and the Law
SACRIFICE
Matt 9:12 mercy and not **s**
Mk 1:44 offer the **s** for your cleansing
Mk 12:33 offerings and **s**
Lk 13:1 blood Pilate had mixed with their **s**
Rom 8:3 to be a **s** for sin and condemned sin
Rom 12:1 bodies as a living **s**
1 Cor 5:7 our Passover Lamb has been **s**
1 Cor 8:1 the meat **s** to idols
1 Cor 10:28 someone tells you This was **s**
Phil 2:17 part of the **s** and service
Heb 5:1 gifts and **s** on behalf of sins
Heb 7:27 He does not need to bring **s** every
Heb 11:4 faith Abel offered a richer **s** to
SAD
Matt 6:16 When you fast stop looking **s**
2 Cor 7:8 letter made you **s**
SAFELY
Lk 15:27 has him back **s** and sound
2 Tim 4:18 will take me **s** to . . . Kingdom
SAINTS
1 Cor 6:1 not before the believers [**s**]
1 Cor 16:1 collection for the believers [**s**]
2 Cor 1:1 to the church . . . all believers [**s**]
SAKE
Mk 13:20 for the **s** of the elect
SALT
Matt 5:13 You are the **s** of the earth
Mk 9:49 everyone will be **s** with fire
SALVATION
Lk 2:30 my eyes have seen Your **S**
Acts 28:28 the **s** . . . God has been sent
Rom 11:11 **s** has come to the Gentiles
2 Cor 6:2 now is the day of **s**
Eph 6:17 take **s** as your helmet and sword
Phil 2:12 work out your **s** with fear
1 Thess 5:9 to obtain **s** through . . . Christ
Heb 1:14 those who . . . inherit **s**
Heb 2:3 neglect a **s** as great as this
1 Pet 1:9 looking for . . . the **s** of your souls
2 Pet 3:15 patience . . . for our **s**
Rev 12:10 **s** and the power and the Kingdom
SALVE
Rev 3:18 and **s** to put on your eyes
SAMARITAN
Lk 10:33 a **S** as he was traveling came near
Jn 4:9 How is it You a Jew ask me a **S** woman
Jn 4:39 Many **S** in that town believed in Him
SAME
Rom 2:1 doing the **s** things
Eph 3:6 Gentiles have the **s** inheritance
Phil 3:1 no trouble to write the **s** things
Heb 1:12 but You are the **s**
Heb 13:8 Jesus . . . the **s** yesterday today
SANCTUARY
Rev 15:5 and the **S** of the TABERNACLE

SAND
Matt 7:26 built house on the s
Rom 9:27 many as the s by the sea
Heb 11:12 stars in the sky and s
SANDAL
Matt 3:11 worthy to carry His s
Mk 6:9 but wear s and do not put on two
Lk 15:22 put a ring . . . and s on
Jn 1:27 to untie His s strap
Acts 7:33 Take off your s
Eph 6:15 having eagerness tied . . . as s
SAP
Rom 11:17 the rich s from root of the olive
SATAN
Matt 4:10 Go away S For it is written
Mk 1:13 days while S continued to tempt Him
Mk 3:23 can S drive out S
Acts 5:3 did S fill your heart
1 Cor 5:5 hand such a person over to S
1 Cor 7:5 together . . . so S may not tempt
2 Cor 2:11 might keep S from getting
2 Cor 11:14 S . . . masquerades as an angel
2 Thess 2:9 is the work of S who uses all
Rev 2:13 where the throne of S is
Rev 12:9 snake called Devil and S who
Rev 20:2 serpent which is Devil and S
SATISFY
Matt 5:6 righteousness . . . they will be s
Mk 15:15 Pilate wanting to s the people
Rom 13:14 do not make plans to s . . . desires
1 Tim 6:6 to those . . . s with what . . . have
Heb 13:5 Be s with what you have
SAVAGE
Matt 8:28 They were so s nobody could go
SAVE
Matt 1:21 He will s His people from sins
Matt 8:25 Lord s us they said We're
Matt 10:22 who is faithful . . . will be s
Matt 14:30 Lord s me he cried
Matt 24:13 endures to the end will be s
Mk 3:4 to s a life or to kill
Mk 13:13 who endures to the end will be s
Lk 3:6 see that God has s them
Lk 9:24 wants to s his life
Lk 13:23 only a few people going to be s
Lk 19:10 to seek and to s
Jn 3:17 world would be s through Him
Acts 2:40 Be s from this crooked
Acts 2:47 those who were being s
Acts 4:12 No one else can s us because
Acts 15:1 not circumcised . . . cannot be s
Acts 16:30 what do I have to do to be s
Rom 1:16 God's power to s everyone who
Rom 5:10 He will s us by His life
Rom 10:9 you will be s
Rom 11:14 make . . . Jews jealous and s
Rom 11:26 all Israel will be s
1 Cor 5:5 s his spirit on Day of the Lord
1 Cor 7:16 wife . . . you may s your husband
1 Cor 10:33 so that they may be s
1 Cor 15:2 by which you are s if you cling

1 Cor 16:2 success provides and s it so
2 Cor 2:15 among those who are s
2 Cor 12:14 children . . . not obligated to s
Eph 1:13 you were s and when you believed
Eph 2:8 by grace you are s through faith
Phil 1:28 you will be s and this proof
1 Thess 2:16 Gentiles so they may be s
2 Thess 2:13 believe truth and so to be s
1 Tim 1:15 Jesus came into the world to s
1 Tim 4:16 you will s both yourself and
2 Tim 3:15 wise so that you may be s
Heb 7:25 He can . . . s those who come to God
Jas 5:20 back . . . will s his soul
Rev 7:10 We are s by our God who sits
SAVIOR
Lk 1:47 my spirit delights in God my S
Lk 2:11 the S who is Christ the Lord
1 Tim 4:10 God who is the S of all people
Tit 3:4 when God our S showed how kind He
SAWED
Heb 11:37 tempted s in half murdered
SAY
Jas 3:2 mistake in what he s
2 Pet 1:21 God gave them to s as they
SCALES
Acts 9:18 like s fell from his eyes
SCARS
Gal 6:17 I bear on my body the s of Jesus
SCATTER
Matt 12:30 does not join Me in gathering s
Mk 4:26 A man s seed on the ground
Lk 1:51 He has s those who think so proudly
Acts 8:4 people who were s went from place
2 Cor 9:9 He s his gifts to the poor
SCEPTER
Heb 1:8 with s of righteousness
SCOFFERS
Jude 18 there will be s following their
SCOLDED
Mk 16:14 He s them for their unbelief
SCORN
Gal 4:14 you did not despise or s me
SCOURGE (see **WHIP**)
SCRIBE
Matt 2:4 and s of the people
Mk 7:1 The Pharisees and some s
Mk 12:32 Right Teacher the s said
SCRIPTURE
Lk 24:27 said about Him in all the S
Jn 2:22 they believed S and this statement
Jn 5:39 You search the S since you think
Jn 7:49 crowd which does not know the S
Jn 10:34 Is it not written in your S
Jn 10:35 and the S cannot be set aside
Jn 12:34 We have heard from the S
Jn 13:18 the S is fulfilled which says
Jn 15:25 which is written in their S
Jn 17:12 the S might be fulfilled
Jn 19:24 what the S said was fulfilled
Jn 19:28 have the words of the S come true
Jn 19:36 way what the S said was fulfilled

Jn 20:9 did not know yet what **S** meant
Acts 8:35 that statement of the **S**
Rom 15:4 encouragement which the **S** give us
1 Cor 15:3 as the **S** said He would
2 Tim 3:15 you have known the Holy **S**
2 Pet 1:20 prophetic utterance of **S** comes
2 Pet 3:16 they do with the rest of the **S**

SCROLL
Lk 4:17 given the **s** of the prophet
2 Tim 4:13 bring . . . **s** especially parchments
Heb 10:7 writing in the **s** of the book
Rev 5:1 on the throne I saw a **s** with
Rev 10:9 give me the little **s**

SEA
Matt 8:26 ordered winds and **s** to be quiet
Matt 14:25 He came to them walking on the **s**
Acts 4:24 You made heaven and earth the **s**
2 Cor 11:26 in the wilderness and on the **s**
Rev 20:13 the **s** gave up the dead who were

SEASHORE
Mk 3:7 Jesus went . . . His disciples to the **s**

SEAL
1 Cor 9:2 you are the **s** which proves
Eph 1:13 you also were **s** in Him by the Holy
Eph 4:30 by whom you were **s** for the Day
Rev 5:1 scroll . . . **s** with seven **s**
Rev 6:1 Lamb opened the first of seven **s**
Rev 7:3 we have put the **s** on the foreheads

SEARCH
Matt 2:8 Go and **s** carefully for . . . Child
Matt 7:7 Keep **s** and you will find
Mk 1:36 those who were with him **s** for Him
Jn 5:39 You **s** Scriptures since you think
Rom 3:11 no one is **s** for God
Rom 8:27 He who **s** hearts knows what Spirit
2 Tim 1:17 coming to Rome he **s** hard for me
1 Pet 1:10 made a thorough **s** to learn all
Rev 2:23 One who **s** minds and hearts

SEASON
Mk 11:13 not the **s** for figs
Gal 4:10 days months **s** and years
Col 4:6 talk pleasantly **s** your speech

SEAT
Lk 9:15 got them all **s**
Acts 25:6 sat on the judge's **s**

SECOND
Mk 14:72 Just then rooster crowed a **s** time
Jn 4:54 was the **s** miraculous sign Jesus did
Rev 20:14 The fiery lake is the **s** death

SECRET
Matt 6:4 Father who sees what is done in **s**
Lk 8:17 and every **s** certainly will be known
1 Cor 14:25 **s** of his heart are shown
Phil 4:12 learned the **s** of being fully

SECRETLY
Matt 2:7 Herod **s** called Wise Men and found
Acts 6:11 Then they **s** got some men

SECT
Acts 28:22 talking against this **s**

SECURE
Matt 27:64 tomb to be made **s**

SEDUCED
Rom 7:11 sin **s** me and used the commandment

SEE
Matt 5:8 hearts are pure they will **s** God
Matt 6:5 in order to be **s** by people
Matt 28:7 Galilee There you will **s** Him
Lk 2:15 Let's go to Bethlehem and **s** it
Jn 1:18 No one has ever **s** God
Jn 14:19 a . . . while and world will not **s** Me
Jn 16:17 a . . . while and you will not **s** Me
Jn 20:29 Blessed are those who have not **s**
Acts 7:34 I have clearly **s** how My people
Acts 7:55 gazed up to heaven and **s** God's
Acts 9:17 so that you may **s** again and be
2 Cor 4:18 at the things that are not **s**
1 Tim 6:16 whom no one has ever **s** or can **s**
Heb 11:3 from what can be **s**

SEED
1 Cor 15:36 **s** you sow has to die

SEEK
Lk 19:10 Son of Man has come to **s** and save

SELECT
Acts 6:3 **s** seven men from among you

SELF
Col 3:9 put away your old **s** and its ways
Col 3:10 put on new **s** which is . . . renewed

SELF-CONTROL
2 Pet 1:6 to knowledge **s** to **s** patient

SELFISH
2 Cor 12:20 angry feelings **s** ambitions

SELFISHNESS
Gal 5:20 jealousy anger **s** quarreling

SEND
Matt 9:38 Lord of the harvest to **s** out
Mk 6:36 **S** them away to the farms
Mk 13:27 He will **s** the angels and gather
Lk 4:43 that is what I was **s** to do
Lk 10:16 rejects Me rejects the One who **s**
Jn 7:29 I come from Him and He **s** Me
Jn 9:7 pool of Siloam (name means **S**)
Acts 7:34 now come I will **s** you to Egypt
Acts 9:17 Brother Saul the Lord **s** me
Rom 10:15 preach if they are not **s**
2 Cor 8:23 who are **s** by the churches
Gal 4:4 time finally came God **s** out His Son
1 Jn 4:10 He loved us and **s** His Son to

SENSES
Lk 15:17 When he came to his **s**
2 Tim 2:26 they will come to their **s**

SENSIBLE
1 Cor 10:15 I am talking to **s** people

SENSIBLY
Mk 12:34 When Jesus saw how **s** he answered

SENTENCE
Rom 5:16 the **s** which followed the one sin
Rom 9:28 execute His **s** on the land
Rev 19:2 He has **s** the great prostitute

SEPARATE
Matt 19:6 let no one **s** what God has joined
Matt 25:32 He will **s** them from one another
Rom 8:39 creature can ever **s** us from
2 Cor 6:17 so come away . . . and **s** yourselves

SERIOUS
Tit 2:2 Tell older men be sober s sensible
SERPENT
Rev 12:9 the old s called Devil and Satan
SERVANT
Matt 12:18 Here is My S whom I have chosen
Matt 25:14 called his s and put his money
Mk 9:35 place and be a s to everyone else
Acts 3:13 God . . . has glorified His S Jesus
Acts 4:27 Your holy S Jesus . . . You anointed
Rom 13:4 it is God's s to help you
2 Cor 11:15 masquerade . . . s of righteousness
Phil 1:1 Paul and Timothy s of Christ Jesus
Jas 1:1 James a s of God
SERVE
Mk 10:45 Son of Man did not come to be s
Acts 6:2 in order to s at tables
Rom 7:25 I s the Law of God with my mind
Rom 12:7 person's gift is s then let him s
Rom 16:18 Such people are not s Christ
1 Cor 12:5 Differing ways of s are assigned
Gal 5:13 by love continue to s one another
Eph 6:7 S eagerly as you would s the Lord
1 Tim 6:2 s them all the better
1 Pet 4:11 if a person s let him do it with
SERVICE
Rev 2:19 and your love and faith and s
SET
Matt 5:17 not think I came to s aside Law
Jn 10:35 the Scripture cannot be s aside
Gal 3:15 nobody s it aside or adds to it
Gal 6:1 s him right again in a humble
Rev 20:3 he must be s free for a . . . while
SEVEN
Matt 12:45 he . . . takes home with him s
Matt 18:21 forgive my brother . . . s times
Mk 8:20 the s loaves for the four thousand
Acts 6:3 select s men from among you
Rev 1:4 John to the s churches in province
SEVENTH
Heb 4:4 On the s day God rested from all
SEVENTY
Matt 18:22 not seven times but s times
SEVERELY
Jas 3:1 who teach will be judged more s
SEWS
Matt 9:16 No one s piece of unshrunk cloth
SEXUAL
1 Cor 5:1 there is s sin among you
Gal 5:19 works of the flesh They are s sin
Eph 5:3 s sin impurity or greed
Col 3:5 kill . . . s sin impurity passion
1 Thess 4:3 keep away from s sin
Heb 12:16 that no one lives in s sin or is
Jude 7 committed s sins and gave themselves
Rev 17:2 kings of earth lived in s sin with
Rev 18:3 kings of earth have lived in s sin
SEXUALLY
Matt 5:32 she has been s unfaithful
1 Tim 1:10 for those who are s immoral

SHADOW
Matt 4:16 sitting in land of s of death
Lk 1:79 and in the s of death
Col 2:17 these are a s of things to come
SHAKE
Matt 27:51 The earth s and rocks were split
Mk 6:11 s the dust off soles of your feet
Acts 2:25 so that I will not be s
Acts 4:31 prayed . . . the place . . . was s
Acts 18:6 In protest he s the dust from his
SHAME
1 Cor 1:27 put those who are wise to s
1 Cor 1:27 to put those who are strong to s
Phil 3:19 they glory in their s and . . . mind
Jude 13 foaming out their own s
SHAMEFUL
Rom 1:26 God gave them up to s lusts
Eph 5:4 No s things foolish talk
SHARE
Lk 3:11 garments should s with him
Acts 2:44 All who believed . . . s everything
Acts 4:32 but they s everything
Rom 1:11 to s a spiritual gift with you
Rom 8:17 s in His suffering . . . s in His
Rom 12:8 gift is s let him be generous
1 Cor 9:10 expectation he will receive a s
2 Cor 1:7 s our sufferings you also s
2 Cor 8:4 that they might s in the help
Gal 5:21 no s in the Kingdom of God
Gal 6:6 s all good things with his teacher
Eph 5:5 has any s in the Kingdom of Christ
Phil 4:15 you were the only church to s
Heb 3:14 we s in Christ only if we keep
2 Jn 11 greets him s the wicked things
SHAVED
1 Cor 11:5 like the woman whose head is s
SHEEP
Matt 25:32 separates the s from the goats
Jn 10:2 one . . . the door is shepherd of the s
Jn 10:27 My s listen to My voice and I know
Jn 21:17 Jesus told him Feed My s
Acts 8:32 He was led away like a s
Rom 8:36 considered as s to be slaughtered
SHEEPFOLD
Jn 10:1 man . . . does not come into s through
SHELTERS
Lk 9:33 Let's put up three s
SHEPHERD
Matt 2:6 Leader who will s My people Israel
Matt 25:32 as s separates sheep from goats
Matt 26:31 I will strike down the S
Mk 6:34 like sheep without a s
Lk 2:15 the s said to one another
Jn 10:2 through the door is s of the sheep
Jn 10:11 I am the Good S . . . gives His life
Acts 20:28 You are to s the church of God
Heb 13:20 the Great S of the sheep
1 Pet 2:25 you have come back to the S
Rev 7:17 the throne will be their S
SHIELD
Eph 6:16 take faith as the s

SHINE
Lk 2:9 glory of the Lord s all around them
Lk 2:32 a Light to s on the Gentiles
Jn 1:5 The Light is s in the dark
1 Cor 15:41 s of sun is different . . . moon
2 Cor 3:7 Moses because it s with a glory
2 Cor 4:6 Let light s out of the darkness
Eph 5:14 Christ will s on you
Rev 22:5 Lord God will s on them
SHIP
Acts 27:10 loss . . . of the cargo and s
Jas 3:4 look at the s . . . even though they
SHIPWRECK
2 Cor 11:25 three times I was in a s
1 Tim 1:19 suffered s in their faith
SHIRT
Matt 5:40 someone . . . sue you for your s
SHORE
Matt 4:18 walking along the s of the sea
SHORTENED
1 Cor 7:29 the time has been s
SHOUTED
Acts 7:57 they s at the top of their voices
SHOW
Matt 5:45 you will s that you are
Mk 16:9 Jesus s Himself first to Mary
Acts 1:3 Jesus also s the apostles
Rom 3:25 to s that He is just even though
Rom 5:8 God s His love for us
Rom 9:22 What if God wanting to s people
1 Jn 3:2 has not yet been s what we are
Rev 4:1 Come up here and I will s you
SHREWD
Matt 10:16 So be s as snakes and innocent
SHRINK
Acts 20:20 how I did not s from telling you
Heb 10:38 if he s back I will not be
SHRIVELED
Matt 12:10 man with a s hand
SHUT
Acts 28:27 have s their eyes so . . . never see
1 Jn 3:17 s his heart against him
Rev 3:7 who s a door and no one opens it
SICK
Matt 9:12 but those who are s
Matt 14:35 people brought Him all the s
Mk 16:18 They will lay their hands on the s
Jn 11:6 when He heard that Lazarus was s
1 Cor 11:30 that is why many of you are s
Gal 4:13 first time because I was s
Phil 2:27 He was so s that he almost died
Jas 5:14 Is anyone among you s Let him call
SICKNESS
Matt 4:23 and s among the people
Matt 8:17 He took away our s and carried
SIDE
Lk 16:22 angels carried him to Abraham's s
Jn 20:25 put my hand in His s I will never
SIGHT
Matt 9:30 Then their s was restored
Jn 9:15 how he received his s
2 Cor 5:7 For we live by faith not by s

SIGN
Matt 24:30 miraculous s announcing the Son
Mk 8:11 asked Him for some miraculous s
Lk 21:25 will be miraculous s in the sun
Acts 2:19 miraculous s on the earth below
Rev 12:1 a great miraculous s was seen in
SILENCE
2 Cor 11:10 boast of mine will not be s
Tit 1:11 must be s because they are ruining
1 Pet 2:15 God wants you to s ignorant
Rev 8:1 there was s in heaven for about
SILENT
Matt 26:63 but Jesus was s
SILLY
1 Tim 1:6 have turned to s talk
SILVER
Acts 3:6 I do not have any s or gold
2 Tim 2:20 things of gold and s but also
SILVERSMITH
Acts 19:24 A s . . . provided a large income
SIN
Matt 1:21 He will save His people from . . . s
Matt 6:14 if you forgive the s of others
Matt 9:2 Your s are forgiven
Matt 18:15 If your brother s against you
Matt 27:4 I have s by betraying innocent
Mk 1:4 be baptized for the forgiveness of s
Mk 11:25 in heaven may forgive you your s
Lk 3:3 repentance for the forgiveness of s
Lk 15:18 Father I have s against heaven
Lk 15:21 I have s against heaven
Jn 1:29 Lamb of God who takes away the s of
Jn 8:34 everyone . . . keeps on s is slave to s
Jn 9:41 We see and your s remains
Jn 16:8 convict the world of s
Acts 2:38 so that your s will be forgiven
Acts 7:60 Lord do not hold this s against
Acts 10:43 believes . . . forgiveness for his s
Acts 25:8 I have in no way s against
Rom 3:9 that they are all under . . . s
Rom 3:23 all have s and are without praise
Rom 4:8 Blessed . . . the Lord never charges s
Rom 5:12 s came into the world through one
Rom 6:16 either of s which results in death
Rom 6:23 wages paid by s is death
Rom 7:20 rather it is s living in me
Rom 11:27 when I take away their s
Rom 13:13 not s sexually or living wildly
Rom 14:23 act . . . not based on . . . is s
1 Cor 6:18 person who s sexually s against
1 Cor 8:12 you s against Christ
1 Cor 10:8 let us not s sexually as some of
1 Cor 15:17 you are still in your s
1 Cor 15:56 S gives death its sting
2 Cor 5:21 did not know s to be s for us
Gal 6:1 is caught in the trap of some s
Eph 2:1 You also were once dead . . . s
1 Tim 5:20 those who keep on s correct
1 Tim 5:24 s of some people are obvious
Heb 1:3 after He had made cleaning from s
Heb 4:15 just as we are . . . without s

Heb 8:12 no longer remember their s
Heb 9:22 if no blood is poured out no s
Heb 10:3 sacrifices reminded people of . . . s
Heb 12:1 let us also rid . . . s into which we
Jas 1:15 when s becomes full-grown . . . death
Jas 4:17 knows what is right . . . he is s
1 Pet 2:22 He never s or was found to be
1 Pet 3:18 Christ died once for our s
1 Jn 1:7 washes us clean from every s
1 Jn 3:4 s is the breaking of the Law
1 Jn 5:16 If anyone sees his brother s
1 Jn 5:16 There is a s which leads to death
Rev 2:14 idols and to s sexually

SINCERE
2 Cor 2:17 speak a message . . . both s and
Eph 6:5 be s in your heart
Col 3:22 serve them with a s heart
2 Tim 1:5 I recall how s your faith was

SINFUL
Mk 8:38 in this unfaithful and s
Lk 5:8 Leave me Lord he said I am a s man
Rom 7:5 s lusts stirred up by the Law
Rom 7:13 so that sin . . . become extremely s
Rom 8:3 His Son to be like s flesh
Col 2:11 putting away the s body

SING
Eph 5:19 s with your hearts making music to
Jas 5:13 you happy Let him s song of praise

SINGLE
1 Cor 7:8 It is good for them to stay s

SINK
Matt 14:30 was frightened and started to s

SINNER
Matt 9:10 many tax collectors and s came
Mk 2:15 many tax collectors and s were
Lk 13:2 Galileans were worse s
Lk 18:13 God be merciful to me the s
Jn 9:25 I do not know if he is a s
Jn 9:31 We know that God does not hear s
Rom 5:8 While we were still s Christ died
Gal 2:15 we . . . born Jews and not Gentile s
Jude 15 ungodly s have said against Him

SITTING
Mk 14:62 you will see Son of Man s

SIX
Jn 19:14 Passover and about s

SKULL
Matt 27:33 Golgotha . . . means Place of the S
Jn 19:17 Place of the S which in Aramaic

SLAIN
Rev 5:6 Lamb seemed to have been s

SLANDER
Matt 12:31 s the Spirit . . . not be forgiven
Mk 3:29 anyone who s the Holy Spirit
Rom 3:8 Some s us and claim we say that
1 Cor 5:11 worships idols s gets drunk or
1 Tim 3:11 women . . . not s not drinking too
2 Pet 2:10 without trembling they s God's

SLANDEROUS
Acts 6:11 We heard him speak s things

SLAP
Matt 5:39 If anyone s you on . . . right cheek
Matt 26:67 some s Him saying Prophesy
Jn 19:3 Hail King of Jews and s His face
2 Cor 11:20 or who s your face

SLAVE
Matt 8:6 my s is at home lying paralyzed
Matt 18:23 settle accounts with his s
Mk 12:2 At the right time he sent a s
Jn 8:34 everyone . . . keeps on sinning is s to
Acts 2:18 even on My s . . . I will pour out
Rom 6:16 obey someone as s you are s
1 Cor 7:21 Were you a s when you . . . called
1 Cor 9:19 I have made myself a s to all
Gal 4:1 he is no better than a s
Gal 4:22 one was the son of the s woman
Eph 6:5 S obey your earthly masters
Phil 2:7 made Himself a s became like other
Col 3:11 here there is no . . . s or free
Col 3:22 S obey your earthly masters
Tit 2:9 Tell s Obey your masters in

SLAVERY
Rom 8:15 receive the spirit of s to make
1 Tim 6:1 under the yoke of s should think
Heb 2:15 free those who were subjected to s

SLAUGHTER
Jas 5:5 fattened yourselves in the day of s

SLEEP
Matt 8:24 But He was s
Matt 9:24 little girl is not dead she is s
Matt 28:13 stole Him while we were s
Mk 4:27 While he s by night
Rom 11:8 God . . . given them spirit of deep s

SLEEPER
Eph 5:14 Wake up s Rise from the dead

SLEEPLESS
2 Cor 11:27 toiled struggled . . . s hungry

SLOW
Lk 24:25 s you are in your heart to believe
Jas 1:19 quick to listen s to speak
2 Pet 3:9 is not s to do what He promised

SMOKE
Rev 9:2 s went up from the shaft
Rev 19:3 s goes up from her forever

SMOOTH
Lk 3:5 and the rough roads s

SNAKE
Mk 16:18 they will pick up s
Acts 28:3 heat made a poisonous s come out
1 Cor 10:9 the s killed them
2 Cor 11:3 the s by its trickery deceived

SNARE
Rom 11:9 let their table be a s and a trap
2 Tim 2:26 escape the s of the devil

SNATCH
Jude 23 s them from the fire

SNEAKED
Gal 2:4 They s in to spy out the freedom
Jude 4 who have s in among you

SNEERED
Acts 2:13 others s They are full of new

SNOW
Matt 28:3 clothes were as white as s
SOBER
1 Cor 15:34 come back to a s . . . life
1 Thess 5:6 but be awake and s
SOIL
1 Cor 15:47 made of the s of the earth
Rev 3:4 people . . . have not s their clothes
SOLD
Matt 18:25 all he had to be s in order to
Acts 2:45 they s their lands and other
SOLDIER
Lk 3:14 Some s also asked him
Acts 28:16 a s who was guarding Paul
1 Cor 9:7 Does a s ever pay his own
Phil 2:25 fellow worker and fellow s
2 Tim 2:3 like a good s of Christ Jesus
2 Tim 2:4 s will get mixed up with affairs
SOLID
1 Cor 3:2 not s food because you were not
Heb 5:12 need milk instead of s food
SOMEONE
Rev 4:2 and S was sitting on the throne
SOMETHING
1 Cor 1:28 do away with that which is s
SON
(see also **SON OF GOD,SON OF MAN**)
Matt 2:15 I called My S out of Egypt
Matt 3:17 This is My S whom I love and in
Matt 12:23 this Fellow is not S of David
Matt 17:5 This is My S whom I love
Matt 21:28 A man had two s
Matt 24:36 not even S but only the Father
Mk 2:5 S your sins are forgiven
Mk 13:32 nor the S but only the Father
Lk 2:7 she gave birth to her firstborn s
Lk 4:22 Isn't this the s of Joseph
Jn 1:14 glory of Father's one-and-only S
Jn 1:18 The one-and-only S who is God
Jn 3:16 that He gave His one-and-only S
Jn 3:35 Father loves S and . . . put everything
Jn 5:21 the S gives life to whom He wishes
Jn 5:23 all . . . honor S as they honor Father
Jn 8:36 If then the S sets you free you
Jn 19:26 Woman . . . there is your s
Acts 2:17 your s and your daughters will
Rom 9:9 Sarah will have a s
Rom 9:26 they . . . be called s of living God
2 Cor 1:19 For God's S Jesus Christ whom I
2 Cor 6:18 you will be My s and daughters
Gal 4:5 adopted as His full-fledged s
Gal 4:6 the Spirit of His S into our hearts
Eph 1:5 made His s by Jesus Christ
2 Tim 2:1 You my s let God's grace
Heb 1:2 days spoken to us by His S whom
Heb 12:6 everyone whom He accepts as His s
1 Jn 4:15 confess that Jesus is God's S
SON OF GOD
(see also **SON,SON OF MAN**)
Matt 8:29 have in common S of God
Matt 27:54 Certainly this was the S of God

Mk 1:1 Jesus Christ the S of God
Lk 1:35 of you will be called the S of God
Jn 1:34 testified This is the S of God
Jn 10:36 because I said I am the S of God
Jn 19:7 He has claimed to be the S of God
Jn 20:31 Jesus is the Christ the S of God
Acts 9:20 to preach . . . Jesus is the S of God
Rom 1:4 to be the powerful S of God
SON OF MAN
(see also **SON,SON OF GOD**)
Matt 8:20 S of Man . . . not have place to lay
Matt 9:6 know the S of Man has authority
Matt 10:23 the S of Man will come
Matt 11:19 The S of Man has come He eats
Matt 12:8 S of Man is Lord of the Sabbath
Matt 12:32 speaks . . . against the S of Man
Matt 12:40 S of Man will be in . . . earth
Matt 24:27 For the coming of the S of Man
Matt 24:30 the sign announcing the S of Man
Matt 26:64 S of Man sitting at right hand
Mk 8:38 the S of Man will also be ashamed
Mk 9:12 And what is written about S of Man
Mk 10:45 even the S of Man did not come to
Mk 13:26 people . . . see the S of Man coming
Mk 14:21 The S of Man is going away as it
Lk 19:10 S of Man has come to seek . . . save
Jn 3:13 One came down from heaven—S of Man
Jn 3:14 so the S of Man must be lifted up
Jn 5:27 authority . . . because He is S of Man
Jn 6:53 unless you eat flesh of S of Man
Jn 8:28 When you have lifted up S of Man
Jn 9:35 Do you believe in the S of Man
Jn 12:34 The S of Man must be lifted up
Acts 7:56 S of Man standing at right hand
Heb 2:6 or a s of man that You should care
Rev 14:14 One who was like the S of Man
SONG
Rev 5:9 and they sang a new s
SOON
Rev 22:20 Yes I am coming s
SORES
Lk 16:20 He was covered with s
Rev 16:2 painful s came on the people
SORROW
Jn 16:20 your s will turn to joy
Rom 8:35 will s hardship or persecution
Rom 9:2 I have great s and continuous pain
Phil 2:27 having one s after another
SORRY
Matt 18:27 master felt s for his slave
Matt 27:3 he felt s and brought 30 pieces
Mk 1:41 Jesus felt s for him
Mk 6:34 He saw a large crowd and felt s for
Lk 10:33 Samaritan . . . felt s for him
Lk 15:20 father saw him and felt s for him
2 Cor 7:8 I am not s if my letter made you
SOUL
Matt 10:28 cannot kill the s but fear Him
Matt 11:29 you will find rest for your s
Lk 1:46 My s magnifies the Lord and my
Acts 4:32 believers was one in heart and s

1 Pet 2:11 which constantly attack your **s**
2 Pet 2:8 tortured his righteous **s** day
3 Jn 2 your **s** is doing well
Rev 6:9 under the altar the **s** of those
Rev 20:4 the **s** of those who . . . been beheaded
SOUND
Acts 2:2 Suddenly a **s** like a violent blast
Tit 1:13 that they may be **s** in their faith
SOURCE
Rev 3:14 and true the **S** of God's creation
SOWER
Matt 13:37 **s** who sows the good seed
Mk 4:14 **s** sows the word
SOWN
1 Cor 15:42 when the body is **s** it decays
SPARE
Rom 8:32 He who did not **s** His own Son but
Rom 11:21 He will not **s** you
2 Cor 1:23 I stayed away . . . to **s** you
2 Cor 13:2 when I come . . . I will not **s** you
SPARINGLY
2 Cor 9:6 who plants **s** will harvest **s**
SPARK
Jas 3:5 set on fire by just a little **s**
SPARROWS
Matt 10:29 Are not two **s** sold for a cent
SPEAK
Matt 4:4 by every word that God **s**
Mk 13:11 you will not be ones who **s**
Acts 2:18 men and women . . . will **s** God's word
Acts 18:9 the Lord **s** to Paul in a vision
Rom 12:6 gift is **s** God's word let him **s**
Gal 4:20 could change my way of **s** to you
1 Cor 12:8 one . . . the ability to **s** wisely
2 Cor 4:13 I believed and so I **s**
2 Cor 13:3 Christ is **s** through me
Heb 1:1 God--who long ago **s** to our fathers
1 Pet 3:10 stop **s** evil or saying anything
1 Pet 4:11 if a person **s** let him say what
2 Pet 2:16 donkey **s** . . . **s** with a human voice
SPEAKER
2 Cor 10:10 he is a poor **s**
SPEAR
Jn 19:34 soldiers stuck a **s** into His side
SPECK
Matt 7:3 look at **s** in your brother's
SPECTACLE
1 Cor 4:9 we have become a **s** for world
SPECULATIONS
1 Tim 1:4 genealogies that give rise to **s**
SPEECH
Mk 7:32 brought . . . a man who had a **s** defect
Lk 21:15 give you such **s** and wisdom
SPEECHLESS
Mk 9:17 There is a **s** spirit in him
SPEND
2 Cor 12:15 I shall be very glad to **s**
SPICES
Mk 16:1 Salome bought **s** to go and anoint
SPIN
Matt 6:28 they do not work or **s**

SPIRIT
Matt 3:16 He saw the **S** of God coming down
Matt 8:16 He drove out the **s** by speaking
Matt 10:20 the **S** of your Father speaking
Matt 12:18 I will put My **S** upon Him
Matt 26:41 the **s** is willing but the flesh
Matt 27:50 Jesus cried . . . and gave up His **s**
Mk 2:8 Immediately Jesus knew in His **s**
Lk 1:47 my **s** delights in God my Savior
Lk 4:14 In the power of the **S**
Lk 4:18 The **S** of the Lord is upon Me
Lk 23:46 into Your hands I entrust My **s**
Jn 1:32 John testified I saw the **S** come
Jn 1:33 When you see the **S** come down
Jn 3:5 born of water and the **S** he cannot
Jn 3:6 what is born of **S** is **s**
Jn 6:63 The **S** is the One who gives life
Jn 7:39 By this He meant the **S**
Jn 15:26 the **S** of Truth who goes out
Jn 16:13 When the **S** of Truth comes He will
Jn 19:30 bowed His head and gave up His **s**
Acts 6:3 full of the **S** and wisdom
Acts 7:59 Lord Jesus receive my **s**
Acts 10:19 about the vision when the **S** said
Rom 8:6 **s** has in mind gives life and peace
Rom 8:9 if God's **S** lives in you
Rom 8:26 the **S** Himself pleads for us
1 Cor 2:11 only God's **S** knows what God
1 Cor 3:16 **S** of God lives in you
2 Cor 1:22 seal on us and given us the **S**
2 Cor 3:6 not of letter but of **s**
2 Cor 3:17 where the **S** of the Lord is
2 Cor 5:5 given us His **S** as a guarantee
Gal 4:6 the **S** of His Son into our hearts
Gal 6:18 grace . . . be with your **s** my fellow
Eph 2:2 **s** who is now working in the people
Eph 5:18 But let the **S** fill you
Phil 4:23 our Lord Jesus be with your **s**
1 Thess 5:19 Do not put out fire of the **S**
1 Tim 4:1 **S** says clearly . . . some will turn
2 Tim 1:7 God did not give us a cowardly **s**
Phlm 25 grace . . . be with the **s** of all of you
Heb 1:14 are not all angels **s** who serve
Jas 4:5 The **S** who dwells in us strongly
1 Pet 1:11 time the **S** of Christ in them
1 Jn 4:1 do not believe every **s** . . . test
1 Jn 4:3 This is the **s** of the Antichrist
Rev 1:4 from Seven **S** . . . before His throne
Rev 2:7 listen to what **S** says to churches
Rev 4:5 torches . . . these are Seven **S** of God
Rev 16:13 I saw three unclean **s** like frogs
SPIRITUAL
Rom 7:6 serve in new **s** way not in old way
Rom 7:14 we know that the Law is **s**
Rom 8:2 The law of the **s** life that we have
Rom 12:1 you will be worshiping in a **s** way
1 Cor 3:1 talk to you as **s** people
1 Cor 10:3 all ate same **s** food . . . all drank
1 Cor 15:44 it is raised a **s** body
Gal 4:29 persecuted the son born in a **s** way
Col 1:9 giving you every kind of **s** wisdom

SPIT
Matt 26:67 they **s** in His face and struck
Mk 7:33 He **s** and touched his tongue
Mk 8:23 Then He **s** on his eyes and laid
Rev 3:16 going to **s** you out of My mouth
SPLENDOR
1 Cor 15:40 the **s** of the heavenly bodies
Rev 18:14 your luxuries and **s** have perished
SPLIT
Matt 27:51 the rocks were **s** The tombs were
SPOT
Eph 5:27 church without **s** or wrinkle
SPREAD
Matt 9:31 they went out and **s** the news
Mk 1:45 to **s** the news so widely
Lk 4:14 The news about Him **s**
Acts 6:7 word of God kept on **s**
Phil 1:12 actually has helped **s** the Gospel
2 Thess 3:1 Lord's word may **s** rapidly and
SPRING
Jas 3:11 Does a **s** pour out both fresh
SPRINKLE
Heb 9:19 took the blood . . . and **s** the scroll
Heb 11:28 Passover and **s** the blood to keep
SPY
Gal 2:4 sneaked in to **s** out the freedom
SQUANDERED
Lk 15:13 younger son **s** all he had
STAFF
Mk 6:8 on the way except a **s** no bread
STAMPEDED
Matt 8:32 whole herd **s** down the cliff
STAND
Mk 3:24 that kingdom cannot **s**
Acts 1:11 why are you **s** here looking up
Acts 25:10 I am **s** before Caesar's judgment
Rom 5:2 into this grace in which we **s**
1 Cor 10:13 be tested more than you can **s**
1 Cor 15:58 **s** firm then my dear fellow
Eph 6:11 you may . . . **s** against . . . devil
2 Thess 2:15 **S** then fellow Christians cling
2 Tim 4:17 the Lord **s** by me and gave me
Heb 12:12 feel weak in your knees **s** firm
Rev 6:17 who is able to **s**
STANDARD
Matt 7:2 By the **s** with which you judge
STAR
Matt 2:2 We saw His **s** in the east
Matt 2:9 there was the **s** they had seen
Matt 24:29 the **s** will fall from sky
Phil 2:15 among whom you shine like **s**
Heb 11:12 **s** in sky and sand on the seashore
Rev 1:16 in His right hand He held seven **s**
Rev 8:10 a huge **s** flaming like a torch
Rev 9:1 saw a **s** had fallen out of the sky
STARING
Acts 3:12 why are you **s** at us as if by our
STARVING
Lk 15:17 here I am **s** to death
2 Cor 11:27 hungry and thirsty often **s** cold

STAY
Matt 2:13 **S** there until I tell you
Lk 24:29 **S** with us . . . It's getting late
STEAL
Matt 27:64 keep . . . from coming to **s** Him
Matt 28:13 His disciples came . . . and **s** Him
1 Cor 6:10 who **s** are greedy get drunk
Tit 2:10 Do not **s** but show that you can be
STEPS
1 Pet 2:21 example . . . follow in His **s**
STERNLY
Matt 9:30 He **s** ordered them
STICK
Matt 27:29 put a **s** in His right hand
STILL
Mk 4:39 Hush He said to the sea Be **s**
STING
1 Cor 15:55 Death where is your **s**
STIR
Acts 17:16 He was **s** inwardly when he saw
2 Pet 3:1 **s** up your pure minds by
STOMACH
1 Cor 6:13 food is for the **s** and the **s** for
1 Tim 5:23 use a little wine for your **s**
STONE
Matt 4:3 tell these **s** to become loaves
Matt 7:9 any of you give him a **s**
Matt 27:60 After rolling a large **s** against
Matt 28:2 angel . . . rolled the **s** away
Mk 13:1 look at those magnificent **s**
Jn 10:31 Jews picked up **s** to **s** Him
Acts 4:11 This One is the very **S** rejected
Acts 7:58 of the city and began to **s** him
Rom 9:33 I am putting in Zion a **S**
2 Cor 3:3 not on **s** tablets but on tablets
2 Cor 11:25 beaten with sticks once I was **s**
1 Pet 2:4 who is the living **S** whom men
Rev 2:17 I will give him a white **s**
Rev 21:19 foundations . . . kinds of precious **s**
STOP
Matt 2:9 came to a **s** over the place
Matt 14:32 When they stepped . . . the wind **s**
Acts 4:20 For we cannot **s** telling what
Acts 28:31 very boldly taught..no one **s** him
STORE
Matt 6:19 **s** up for yourselves treasures on
Col 1:5 the hope which is **s** up for you
STORM
Matt 8:24 a severe **s** churned the sea so
STORY
Matt 18:31 told their master the whole **s**
Matt 28:15 their **s** has been spread among
STRANGE
Acts 17:20 some things that sound **s** to our
STRANGER
Matt 25:38 we see You a **s** and take You into
Lk 24:18 Are you the only **s** living in
Jn 10:5 they do not know the voice of **s**
Acts 7:6 would be **s** in a foreign country
Acts 7:29 became a **s** living in . . . Midian
Col 1:21 once you were **s** to God

1 Tim 5:10 if she . . . welcomed **s** . . . washed
Heb 11:9 he lived as a **s** in Promised Land
Heb 11:13 they were **s** and pilgrims on earth
1 Pet 2:11 I urge you as guests and **s**
STRANGLED
Acts 15:20 not eat anything **s** or any blood
STRAW
1 Cor 3:12 precious stones wood hay or **s**
STREET
Matt 6:2 on **s** to be praised by people
Lk 14:21 into the **s** and alleys
Acts 9:11 go to the **s** called Straight
STRENGTH
Phil 4:13 through Him who gives me **s**
STRENGTHEN
Acts 3:16 that Name **s** the limbs
Acts 14:22 **s** the disciples and encouraging
Eph 3:16 Spirit will inwardly **s** you with
1 Thess 3:2 to **s** you and encourage you
STRESS
1 Cor 7:26 so full of **s** for us
STRETCHED
Rom 10:21 All day long I have **s** out My
STRIP
Eph 4:22 **s** off your old self which follows
STRONG
Lk 2:40 little Child grew and became **s**
Rom 15:1 But we who are **s** have a
Rom 16:25 can make you **s** by the Gospel
1 Cor 16:13 stand firm in your faith . . . be **s**
2 Tim 2:1 let God's grace . . . make you **s**
STRUCK
Matt 26:67 **s** Him with their fists
STRUGGLE
Lk 13:24 **S** to enter through the narrow door
Rom 15:30 join me in my **s** by praying for me
Col 2:1 how much I am **s** for you
STUBBORN
Acts 7:51 How **s** you are and pagan at heart
Rom 9:18 makes **s** whom He wishes to make **s**
Heb 3:8 do not make your hearts **s**
Heb 3:15 do not make your hearts **s**
STUMBLE
Matt 5:30 if . . . hand causes you to **s**
Matt 11:6 blessed is anyone who does not **s**
Matt 18:6 to **s** in his faith
Matt 18:7 people to **s** in their faith
Rom 11:11 did not **s** in order to be lost
Rom 14:20 it causes someone to **s**
1 Pet 2:8 Stone which makes them **s**
STUMBLING BLOCK
Matt 17:27 not become a **s** block to them
Rom 9:32 they stumbled over the **s** block
1 Cor 1:23 Jews this is a **s** block and
2 Cor 6:3 laying any kind of a **s** block
SUBMIT
Heb 13:17 Obey your leaders and **s** to them
SUBORDINATE
Rom 13:1 Let everyone be **s** to government
1 Cor 14:34 let them be **s** as the Law says
Eph 5:22 Wives be **s** to your husbands

Col 3:18 Wives be **s** to your husbands
Tit 2:5 be **s** to their husbands
Tit 3:1 people to be **s** to governments
Heb 12:9 not much more be **s** to Father
1 Pet 2:13 be **s** to every human authority
SUBORDINATION
2 Cor 9:13 glorifying God . . . show your **s**
SUCCEED
Matt 2:22 Archelaus had **s** his father Herod
Lk 13:24 try to enter and not **s**
SUDDENLY
Mk 13:36 Make sure he does not come **s**
Lk 2:13 **S** there was with the angel a large
1 Thess 5:3 come on them **s** like labor pains
SUE
Matt 5:25 If someone wants to **s** you
1 Cor 6:6 one Christian **s** another
SUFFER
Matt 4:24 brought to Him . . . all who were **s**
Matt 8:6 my slave . . . **s** terribly
Matt 24:9 those who will make you **s**
Mk 14:35 might not have to **s**
Lk 16:25 he is comforted . . . while you are **s**
Acts 3:18 His Christ would **s**
1 Cor 12:26 If one member **s** all others **s**
Col 1:24 I am now happy to **s** for you
1 Thess 2:14 since you **s** the same things
2 Tim 2:24 willing to **s** wrong
Heb 2:9 He **s** death so that by God's grace
1 Pet 3:17 is better . . . to **s** for doing right
SUFFERING
Rom 5:3 we also boast of our **s**
Rom 8:17 we share in His **s**
Rom 8:18 consider our present **s** to be
1 Pet 2:19 bears the pains of unjust **s**
SUGGESTION
Jas 1:17 no shifting nor **s** of change
SUN
Matt 5:45 He makes His **s** rise on people
Matt 24:29 the **s** will turn dark
Acts 2:20 **s** will turn dark and the moon
SUNDAY
Matt 28:1 as **S** was dawning
Jn 20:1 Early on **S** morning while it was
1 Cor 16:2 every **S** let each . . . you put aside
SUPER
2 Cor 11:5 way less than your **s** apostles
SUPPLY
2 Cor 8:14 your abundance will **s** what they
SUPPER
Jn 13:4 Jesus rose from **s** laid aside
SUPPORTED
Lk 8:3 They **s** Jesus and His disciples
Col 2:19 which is **s** and bound together
SUPPRESS
Rom 1:18 **s** truth by their unrighteousness
SURE
Rom 4:16 that the promise might be **s** to all
1 Pet 1:13 be perfectly **s** of what God's
SURPRISE
Matt 8:10 He was **s** and said to the people

Lk 2:18 everybody was s to hear the story
Lk 4:22 were s to hear the gracious words
Lk 21:34 Day will take you by s
1 Thess 5:4 let that Day take you by s
SURROUNDED
Lk 21:20 you see Jerusalem s
SURVIVORS
Rom 9:29 had not left us some s
SWALLOW
Mk 12:40 They s up the houses of widows
Lk 20:47 They s up the houses of widows
1 Cor 15:54 Death is s up in victory
SWEAR
Matt 5:33 Do not s falsely but give to Lord
Matt 26:63 high priest said S by the living
Lk 1:73 the oath He s to our father Abraham
Acts 2:30 knew that God had s to him
Heb 3:11 So because I was angry I s
Heb 6:13 He s by Himself
Heb 7:21 The Lord has s and will not change
Jas 5:12 do not s by heaven or by the earth
SWORD
Matt 26:52 Put your s back in its place
Rom 8:35 hunger or nakedness danger or s
Rom 13:4 government carries the s for a
Eph 6:17 the s of the Spirit which is word
Heb 4:12 cuts better than any two-edged s
Rev 1:16 out of His mouth came a sharp . . . s
SYMBOLS
Rev 1:1 revelation by way of s
SYMPATHIZE
Heb 4:15 unable to s with our weaknesses
SYNAGOG
Matt 13:54 taught the people in their s
Lk 4:15 continued to teach in their s
Lk 4:20 Everyone in the s was watching
Jn 6:59 He was teaching in a s in Capernaum
Jn 9:22 put out of s anyone who confessed
Acts 18:7 house was right beside the s
Rev 2:9 but rather are the s of Satan

TABERNACLE
Acts 7:44 fathers had T in which God spoke
Heb 9:2 a T was set up
Rev 15:5 the SANCTUARY of the T
TABLE
Matt 9:10 Jesus was reclining at the t
Acts 6:2 to serve at t
TABLETS
Heb 9:4 t on which the covenant was written
TAKE
Matt 26:52 all who t the sword will die
Mk 4:25 even what he has will be t away
Mk 16:19 Lord was t up to heaven and sat
Lk 24:51 parted from them and was t up
Jn 1:29 Lamb of God who t away sin of world
Acts 1:11 who was t away from you to heaven
Rom 11:27 when I t away their sins
1 Tim 3:16 in world Was t up in glory
1 Tim 5:8 If anyone does not t care of his
1 Tim 6:7 did not bring . . . cannot t anything

1 Tim 6:12 t hold of the everlasting life
1 Jn 3:5 in order to t away our sins
Rev 22:19 if anyone t away any words . . . book
TALENTS
Matt 18:24 one who owed him ten thousand t
TALK
Matt 9:32 a man unable to t because
Mk 7:35 set free to speak and he t
Lk 9:31 were t about His leaving
Rom 3:5 I am t like a man
Rom 9:20 who are you man to t back to God
Gal 1:16 I did not immediately t it over
Col 4:6 Always t pleasantly season your
TAME
Jas 3:8 not one person can t the tongue
TARNISH
Jas 5:3 their t will be evidence against
TASSEL
Matt 14:36 touch the t of His garment
TASTE
Matt 5:13 If salt loses its t how will it
Mk 9:1 who will never t death until they
Mk 9:50 how will you make it t salty
Lk 14:24 invited will t my dinner
Rom 8:23 as our first t of heaven
Heb 2:9 He might t death on behalf of
Heb 6:5 t the goodness of word of God
1 Pet 2:3 you have t that Lord is good
TAX
Matt 9:9 Matthew sitting in the t booth
Matt 17:24 the Temple t came to Peter
Rom 13:6 is why you also pay t
TAX COLLECTORS
Matt 9:10 t collectors and sinners . . . ate
Matt 21:31 I tell you the truth t collector
Mk 2:15 many t collectors and sinners
Lk 3:12 Some t collectors also came
TEACH
Matt 4:23 t in their synagogs
Matt 5:2 Then He began to t them
Matt 28:20 t them to pay close attention
Mk 9:31 He was t His disciples
Mk 10:1 Again He t them as was His custom
Lk 4:15 He continued to t in their
Acts 1:1 Jesus began to do and to t
Rom 12:7 If it is t let him t
1 Cor 2:13 words t . . . but t by the Spirit
Gal 6:6 person who is t the word
1 Tim 1:3 men not to t any
1 Tim 6:3 anyone t anything else
2 Tim 2:2 who will also be able to t others
2 Tim 3:16 Scripture . . . useful for t
Tit 2:3 T what is good
2 Jn 10 bring what Christ t do not
TEACHER
Matt 9:11 does your T eat with . . . sinners
Matt 17:24 T pay the Temple tax
Mk 4:38 T don't You care
Jn 1:38 Rabbi (which means T) where are You
Jn 8:4 T . . . this woman was caught
Jn 11:28 T is here and is calling for you

Jn 13:13 You call Me **T** and Lord and you are
1 Cor 12:28 God has appointed apostles . . . **t**
1 Tim 1:7 they want to be **t** of the Law
TEACHING
Matt 7:28 crowds were amazed at His **t**
Mk 1:27 This is a new **t** which has
Jn 7:17 know whether My **t** is from God
Acts 2:42 hold firmly to the **t** of apostle
Rom 16:17 going against the **t** you learned
1 Tim 4:6 the sound **t** you have followed
2 Tim 1:13 an example of sound **t**
Tit 1:9 by sound **t** he can encourage people
Tit 2:1 what is right according to sound **t**
2 Pet 2:1 bring in their own destructive **t**
TEAR
Matt 5:29 right eye . . . to stumble . . . **t** it out
Lk 5:6 their nets began to **t**
Jn 2:19 **T** down this Temple . . . I will raise
Jn 10:28 no one will **t** them out of My hand
2 Cor 13:10 authority . . . not to **t** you down
TEARS
Acts 20:19 I served the Lord . . . with **t**
2 Tim 1:4 I remember your **t** I long to see
TELL
Matt 11:4 **t** John what you hear and see
Matt 28:7 **t** His disciples He has risen
Mk 16:7 go and **t** His disciples and Peter
Lk 2:17 had seen Him they **t** others
Lk 9:60 go and **t** about the Kingdom
TEMPLE
Matt 4:5 stand on the ledge of the **T**
Matt 27:51 curtain in the **T** was torn in two
Mk 11:16 across the **T** court
Lk 2:46 they found Him in the **T**
Jn 2:15 out of the **T** together
Jn 2:19 Tear down this **T** . . . I will raise it
Jn 5:14 Jesus found him in the **T**
Jn 8:2 He came back into the **T**
Jn 8:20 while He was teaching in the **T**
Jn 10:23 Jesus was walking . . . in the **T**
Jn 18:20 always taught . . . in the **T**
Acts 2:46 go to the **T** every day
Acts 3:2 lay him every day at the **T** gate
1 Cor 3:16 know that you are the **t** of God
2 Cor 6:16 we are the **t** of the living God
Eph 2:21 a holy **t** in the Lord
2 Thess 2:4 in God's **t** and proclaims
Rev 3:12 pillar in the **T** of My God
Rev 11:19 seen in His **T**
TEMPT
Matt 4:1 into wilderness to be **t** by devil
Lk 4:2 the devil continued to **t** Him
1 Cor 7:5 Satan may not **t** you
Gal 6:1 you also are not **t**
Heb 4:15 He was **t** in every way just as we
Jas 1:13 when he is **t** God is **t** me
TEMPTATION
Matt 6:13 do not lead us into **t** but deliver
1 Cor 10:13 No **t** has taken hold of you
1 Tim 6:9 fall into **t** and a snare

TEMPTER
1 Thess 3:5 afraid the **T** had in some way
TENDERHEARTED
Eph 4:32 Be kind to one another and **t**
TENDERHEARTEDNESS
Col 3:12 dress yourselves with **t**
TENDERLY
Rom 12:10 one another **t** as fellow
TENT
Acts 18:3 they made **t** for a living
2 Cor 5:1 the earthly **t** we live in is torn
2 Pet 1:13 I am in the **t** of this body
TENTH
Heb 7:4 gave him a **t** from the best
TEN THOUSAND
Jude 14 come with **t** thousands of His
TERRIFIED
Jn 6:19 and they were **t**
TERRITORY
Lk 4:26 at Zarephath in the **t** of Sidon
TEST
Matt 4:7 Do not put . . . to a **t**
Jn 6:6 He asked this . . . to **t** him
Acts 15:10 why do you **t** God
1 Cor 3:13 fire will reveal it and **t** it
1 Cor 3:14 stands the **t**
1 Cor 10:9 not go . . . in **t** the Lord's
2 Cor 13:5 **T** yourselves Do you not know
Gal 6:4 **t** the genuineness of his own work
Eph 5:10 **t** things to see
1 Thess 2:4 God who **t** our hearts
1 Thess 5:21 But **t** everything
Heb 2:18 help others when they are **t**
Jas 1:2 when you are **t** in different ways
1 Pet 1:7 gold is **t** for its genuineness
1 Pet 4:12 you are being **t**
1 Jn 4:1 **t** the spirits to see
Rev 2:10 that you may be **t**
TESTAMENT
Matt 26:28 the last will and **t**
Mk 14:24 My blood of the . . . **t**
Lk 22:20 last will and **t** in My blood
Rom 11:27 this will be My last will and **t**
1 Cor 11:25 the new last will and **t**
TESTIFY
Matt 10:18 to **t** to them and to the Gentiles
Matt 26:62 these men **t** against You
Jn 1:7 He came to **t** that is to **t** about the
Jn 1:34 I have seen it and have **t**
Jn 3:32 He **t** to what He has seen
Jn 5:39 They **t** about Me
Jn 19:35 He who saw it has **t** about it
Acts 1:8 will **t** of Me in Jerusalem
Acts 4:33 apostles continued to **t**
Acts 10:43 all the prophets **t** about Him
Acts 13:31 who are **t** to the people
Rom 8:16 Spirit Himself **t** with our spirit
1 Tim 6:13 Christ . . . who **t** . . . before Pontius
Heb 3:5 as a servant who was to **t**
1 Jn 1:2 we have seen It and **t** to It
Rev 1:2 John **t** about what he saw

TESTIMONY
Matt 24:14 preached . . . as a t to all nations
Jn 1:19 this was John's t when the Jews
Jn 3:11 do not accept Our t
Jn 3:33 accepted His t has certified
Jn 19:35 his t is true
1 Jn 5:9 God's own t . . . about His Son
Rev 1:2 and t of Jesus Christ
Rev 12:17 who hold on to the t of Jesus
Rev 15:5 TABERNACLE of T was opened

THANK
Mk 6:41 looked up to heaven and gave t
Rom 1:8 I t my God through Jesus Christ
Rom 1:21 honor Him as God nor . . . they t Him
Rom 7:25 T be to God—He does it
Rom 14:6 for the Lord and he t God
1 Cor 15:57 But t be to God
2 Cor 4:15 to overflow with t so that God
Eph 5:20 always t God the Father for every
Phil 1:3 I think of you I t my God
Col 1:3 we are always t God the Father
1 Thess 3:9 how can we ever return t to God
Rev 7:12 wisdom and t and honor and power

THANKFUL
Col 3:15 and continue to be t

THANKSGIVING
2 Cor 9:12 through the many prayers of t
1 Tim 4:4 if it is received with t

THEATER
Acts 19:29 they all rushed into the t

THIEF
Matt 6:19 rust destroy t break in and steal
1 Thess 5:2 will come just as a t in night

THINGS
Lk 2:19 Mary treasured all these t

THINK
Matt 5:17 Do not t I came to set aside Law
Matt 12:25 He knew what they were t
Mk 2:6 they t to themselves
Lk 2:19 Mary treasured . . . kept t about them
Rom 6:11 t of yourselves as dead to sin
Rom 11:34 Who has found out how Lord t
Rom 14:14 person who t anything is unclean
1 Cor 2:11 God's Spirit knows what God t
2 Cor 12:6 keep anyone from t more of me
Gal 6:3 if anyone t he is something

THIRD
Jn 21:17 Peter . . . asked him a t time
Acts 10:40 God raised Him on the t day
2 Cor 12:2 was caught up to the t heaven

THIRST
1 Pet 2:2 t for the pure milk of the word

THIRSTY
Matt 25:35 I was t and you gave Me a drink
Jn 4:13 drinks this water will become t
Jn 19:28 Jesus said I am t
Rom 12:20 If he is t give him a drink
Rev 21:6 anyone who is t I will give water

THIRTY
Matt 26:15 offered him t pieces of silver
Lk 3:23 Jesus was about t years old

THIRTY-NINE
2 Cor 11:24 Five times Jews gave t lashes

THORN
Matt 27:29 They twisted some t into a crown
Jn 19:2 soldiers twisted some t into crown
2 Cor 12:7 a t for my flesh

THOROUGH
2 Tim 4:2 being very patient and t

THOUGHT
Matt 15:19 out of heart come evil t murders
Rom 12:3 Keep your t in bounds
2 Cor 10:5 make every t a prisoner
Heb 4:12 judge inner t and intentions of

THOUSAND
Lk 14:31 if with ten t men he can oppose
2 Pet 3:8 a t years are like one day
Rev 20:2 bound him for a t years

THREATS
Lk 3:14 Do not use t or blackmail
Acts 9:1 Saul still breathing t and murder

THREATENING
Eph 6:9 stop t them

THREE
Matt 27:46 About t o'clock Jesus called out
Jn 2:19 I will raise it in t days
Jn 13:38 until you have denied Me t times
Acts 9:9 for t days he could not see
Heb 11:23 his parents hid him t months

THROATS
Rom 3:13 their t are an open grave

THRONE
Matt 5:34 not by heaven for it is God's t
Matt 25:31 He will sit on His t of glory
Lk 1:32 give Him the t of His ancestor
Acts 7:49 Heaven is My t and earth is My
Heb 1:8 Your t . . . is forever and ever
Heb 12:2 sat down at right hand of God's t
Rev 2:13 where the t of Satan is
Rev 3:21 sitting with Me on My t just as I
Rev 20:4 I saw t and they sat on them
Rev 20:11 I saw a great white t and the One

THROW
Matt 22:13 Tie him hand . . . and t him out
Matt 27:5 Then he t the money into Temple
Lk 4:29 in order to t him over
1 Pet 5:7 T all you worry on Him
Rev 2:22 I am t her into a bed

THUNDER
Rev 8:5 came peals of t rumblings flashes

THUNDERBOLTS
Mk 3:17 Boanerges which means T

TIME
Matt 25:34 from t the world was created
Mk 6:31 there was not even t to eat
Lk 2:6 the t came for her to have her baby
Lk 4:27 lepers in Israel at the t of the
Jn 2:4 My t has not yet come
Jn 7:30 because His t had not yet come
Acts 1:7 It is not for you to know what t
Rom 5:6 at the set t . . . Christ died
Rom 13:11 you know the t in which we are

1 Cor 11:25 Every **t** you drink it do it to
2 Cor 6:2 At a favorable **t** I have heard you
Gal 4:4 when **t** finally came God sent . . . Son
Eph 1:10 when the right **t** would come
1 Thess 5:1 passing of **t** and God's plan
1 Pet 1:11 what **t** the Spirit of Christ in
Rev 1:3 because the **t** is near
TIRED
2 Thess 3:13 do not become **t** of doing good
TODAY
Matt 6:11 give us **t** our daily bread
Lk 23:43 **t** you wil be with Me in Paradise
Heb 3:13 encourage . . . as long as **t** lasts
TOILING
1 Thess 1:3 your love is **t** and your hope
TOLERATE
Rev 2:2 that you cannot **t** wicked people
TOMB
Matt 27:60 laid it in his own new **t**
Jn 11:17 Lazarus . . . been in the **t** four days
Jn 19:42 laid Jesus . . . the **t** was near
Jn 20:1 Mary from Magdala went to the **t**
TOMORROW
Matt 6:34 **t** will take care of itself
1 Cor 15:32 eat and drink for **t** we die
Jas 4:14 you do not know about **t**
TONGUE
Mk 7:33 He spit and touched his **t**
Lk 16:24 finger in water and cool off my **t**
Acts 2:3 They saw **t** like flames
Jas 1:26 if he does not control his **t**
Jas 3:5 **t** is a small part but it can boast
TOOLS
Rom 6:13 use the members of your body as **t**
TOOTH
Matt 5:38 eye for an eye and a **t** for a **t**
TORMENTED
Lk 16:23 being **t** in hell he looked up
TORTURE
Matt 8:29 Did You come to **t** us before
Lk 16:28 not come to this place of **t**
Heb 11:35 Some were **t** when they refused
Rev 14:10 will be **t** by fire and sulfur
Rev 20:10 they will be **t** day and night
TORTURER
Matt 18:34 handed him over to the **t**
TOUCH
Matt 8:15 He **t** her hand and fever left her
Matt 9:20 came to Him . . . and **t** the tassel
Matt 9:29 Then He **t** their eyes and said
Mk 3:10 rushed up to Him in order to **t** Him
1 Cor 7:1 man not to **t** a woman
2 Cor 6:17 do not **t** anything unclean
Col 2:20 do not taste do not **t**
1 Jn 1:1 our hands have **t**
TOWN
Matt 5:14 **t** cannot be hidden . . . on hill
Matt 8:34 whole **t** came out to meet Jesus
Lk 4:29 on which their **t** was built
Jn 7:42 from the little **t** of Bethlehem

TRADITION
Mk 7:3 to follow the **t** of their fathers
Gal 1:14 become for the **t** of my ancestors
Col 2:8 as he follows the **t** of men
TRAIN
1 Tim 4:7 **t** yourself for a godly life
TRAINING
1 Cor 9:25 goes into strict **t**
TRAMPLE
Matt 5:13 thrown out and **t** on by people
Heb 10:29 who **t** on God's Son treats as an
TRANCE
Acts 10:10 he fell into a **t**
TRANSFERRED
Col 1:13 power of darkness and **t** us into
TRAP
Rom 14:13 lay any stumbling . . . or death **t**
2 Cor 12:16 who **t** you with some trick
Jas 1:14 draws him away and tries to **t** him
2 Pet 2:14 They try to **t** weak souls
TRAVEL
Lk 2:44 with others who were **t** with
Jn 4:6 Jesus tired as He was from **t**
2 Cor 8:19 churches elected him to **t**
TREACHEROUS
2 Tim 3:4 they will be **t** reckless proud
TREASURE
Matt 2:11 opened their **t** chests and offered
Matt 6:19 store for yourselves **t** on earth
Lk 2:19 Mary **t** all . . . things in her heart
Acts 8:27 official in charge of all the **t**
2 Cor 4:7 Now we have this **t** in clay jars
Col 2:3 in whom are hidden all **t** of wisdom
1 Tim 6:19 storing up for themselves a **t**
TREASURY
Matt 27:6 not right . . . into the Temple **t**
TREAT
Matt 18:17 will not listen to church **t** him
Matt 18:33 Shouldn't you have **t** your fellow
Matt 20:12 you have **t** them exactly as . . . us
Eph 5:29 feeds his body and **t** it tenderly
Eph 6:9 masters **t** your slaves in same way
TREATMENT
Col 2:23 and harsh **t** of the body
TREE
Matt 12:33 Make a **t** good . . . fruit is good
Gal 3:13 Cursesd is . . . who hangs on a **t**
Rev 2:7 from the **t** of life that stands in
Rev 22:2 leaves of **t** are for the healing
Rev 22:2 the **t** of life visible
TREMBLING
Mk 16:8 they were **t** and bewildered
1 Cor 2:3 in fear and with much **t**
TRESPASS
Gal 3:19 It was added to point out **t**
Heb 2:2 every **t** and disobedience
TRIAL
Acts 23:6 I am on **t** for my hope
1 Pet 1:6 to suffer various **t**
1 Pet 4:12 not be surprised by this fiery **t**

TRIBE
Rom 11:1 descendant of Abraham and of the t
Heb 7:13 belongs to a different t
Jas 1:1 James . . . to the twelve t who are
Rev 7:4 were from every t of the people

TRIBUTE
Rom 13:7 if you owe anyone t pay t

TRICKED
Matt 2:16 Herod saw the Wise Men had t him

TRICKERY
1 Cor 3:19 with their own t and again
Eph 4:14 by the t of men and their clever

TRIED
Acts 25:9 up to Jerusalem to be t there
Rom 16:10 Greet Apollos a t and true

TRIFLES
1 Cor 6:2 are you not able to judge t

TROUBLE
Matt 6:34 Each day has enough t of its own
Mk 5:35 Why t the Teacher anymore
Jn 14:1 Do not feel t Believe in God and
Jn 14:27 not let your heart be t or afraid
Acts 14:22 through many t we must enter
Acts 15:19 we should not t these Gentiles
2 Cor 1:4 comforts us in every t
2 Cor 4:17 For the light t of this moment
Phil 1:17 intend to stir up t for me
Phil 2:26 is deeply t because you heard
Heb 5:2 he too is t with weakness

TRUE
Jn 17:3 the only t God and Jesus Christ
Acts 2:36 it is t that God made Him Lord
Acts 26:25 I am saying is . . . t and sensible
Rom 3:4 Let God be t and every man a liar
2 Cor 1:20 give glory . . . by saying It is t
1 Jn 5:20 know Him who is t and we are in

TRULY (see ABSOLUTE)

TRUMPET
Matt 24:31 He will send . . . with loud t call
1 Cor 14:8 if the t does not sound a clear
1 Cor 15:52 when the last t sounds
1 Thess 4:16 with the t sound of God
Rev 8:2 they were given seven t

TRUST
Matt 6:30 you who t Him so little
Matt 8:26 You t Me so little
Matt 14:31 How little you t Me
Matt 25:23 proved you could be t with a few
Mk 4:40 Have you still not learned to t
Lk 8:25 Where is your t He asked
2 Cor 1:9 learn not to t in ourselves
1 Tim 1:15 This is a statement we can t
2 Tim 1:12 I know Him in whom I t
1 Pet 4:19 you can t Him who created you

TRUSTWORTHY
1 Cor 4:2 any manager that he be found t

TRUTH
Mk 5:33 told Him the whole t
Mk 12:32 Teacher . . . You told the t
Jn 1:14 He is full of grace and t
Jn 1:17 grace and t came through Jesus

Jn 8:32 you will know the t and the t
Jn 8:44 there is no t in him
Jn 14:6 I am the Way the T and the Life
Jn 15:26 the Spirit of T who goes out
Jn 16:13 Spirit of T comes He will lead you
Jn 17:17 holy in the t Your word is t
Acts 7:51 pagan at heart and deaf to the t
Acts 28:23 declared the t about the Kingdom
Rom 1:18 people who suppress the t
Rom 9:1 I am telling the t in Christ
2 Cor 13:8 cannot do anything against the t
Gal 2:14 doing . . . right according to the t
Eph 4:21 as the t is in Jesus
Eph 6:14 stand then having t as a belt
2 Thess 2:10 refuse to love t . . . be saved
1 Tim 2:4 saved and to come to know the t
1 Jn 1:6 lying and not living the t
1 Jn 1:8 deceive ourselves and t is not in
1 Jn 4:6 is the spirit of t and . . . of error

TUNIC
Jn 19:23 the t was left over . . . without seam

TURN
Jn 6:37 comes to Me I will never t away
Acts 3:26 bless you by t every one of you
Acts 7:42 God t away from them . . . abandoned
Acts 28:27 they never t to Me for healing
Rom 16:17 T completely away
1 Cor 15:23 each one in his own t
1 Thess 1:9 t from idols to God in order
1 Tim 1:20 whom I t over to Satan to teach
1 Tim 6:20 t away from empty worldly talk
Heb 8:9 so I t away from them says the Lord

TWELVE
Matt 10:1 Jesus called His t disciples
Mk 3:14 He appointed t to be with Him
Lk 2:42 He was t years old they went up
Lk 9:1 Jesus called the T together
Jn 6:67 So Jesus asked the T Do you want
Jn 6:70 Didn't I choose the t of you
Jn 11:9 Are there not t hours in a day
Acts 6:2 The T called the whole group
Rev 7:5 t thousand from the tribe of Judah

TWENTY-FOUR
Rev 4:4 were t other thrones

TWICE
Mk 14:30 before the rooster crows t

TWINKLING
1 Cor 15:52 in t of an eye

TWIST
2 Pet 3:16 not well-grounded t . . . meaning

TWO
Matt 18:20 where t or three have come

TYPE
Rom 5:14 Adam was a t [picture] of Him who

UNBELIEF
Matt 13:58 miracles . . . because of their u
Mk 9:24 help me with my u
Rom 3:3 What if some were u Will their u
Rom 4:20 There was no u to make him doubt
Heb 3:18 to those who were u

UNBELIEVER
1 Cor 14:22 not for **u** but for believers
2 Cor 6:14 yoked together with **u**
UNCERTAIN
1 Tim 6:17 as **u** as riches but to trust
UNCIRCUMCISED
Rom 4:10 He was not circumcised but **u**
UNCLEAN
Matt 15:18 that makes a person **u**
Acts 10:14 I have never eaten anything . . . **u**
Rom 14:14 nothing is **u** in itself
1 Cor 7:14 otherwise . . . children would be **u**
2 Cor 12:21 not repented for the **u** sexual
Rev 21:27 nothing **u** . . . will ever come
UNCLEAN SPIRIT
Matt 12:43 When **u** spirit comes out of a
Mk 1:23 man in synagog with an **u** spirit
Mk 3:30 He has an **u** spirit
UNCOVERED
Lk 8:17 Everything hidden will be **u**
UNDER
Matt 8:9 soldiers **u** me I tell one
Rom 6:14 you are not **u** law but **u** grace
Heb 2:8 everything **u** His feet
Rev 6:9 **u** the altar the souls of those
UNDERHANDED
Mk 14:1 looking for some **u** way to arrest
UNDERSTAND
Lk 9:45 so that they did not **u** it
Acts 2:14 **u** this and listen closely to what
1 Cor 14:2 no one **u** him his spirit is
2 Tim 2:7 try to **u** what I say
UNDERSTANDING
Lk 2:47 His **u** and His answers surprised
UNFAIR
1 Pet 2:18 but also when they are **u**
UNFAITHFUL
Matt 5:32 she has been sexually **u**
UNFORGIVEN
Jn 20:23 not forgive them they are **u**
UNGODLINESS
Rom 1:18 anger of God . . . against all **u**
Rom 11:26 He will get rid of **u** in Jacob
UNGODLY
Rom 4:5 believes in Him who justifies the **u**
Rom 5:6 Christ died for the **u**
1 Tim 1:9 rebel against it for the **u**
Jude 15 convict all the **u** of all the
UNHAPPY
Mk 10:22 When he heard that he looked **u**
UNIMPRESSIVE
2 Cor 10:10 when he is with us he is **u**
UNITED
Rom 6:5 If we were **u** with Him in this
1 Cor 1:10 but to be perfectly **u**
UNJUST
Rom 9:14 Does this then mean that God is **u**
UNKNOWN
Acts 17:23 altar . . . inscription TO AN U GOD
2 Cor 6:9 as **u** we are well-known

UNNATURAL
Rom 1:26 natural relations for the **u**
UNNATURALLY
Rom 11:24 have been **u** grafted into
UNPRESENTABLE
1 Cor 12:23 our **u** parts have greater
UNPUNISHED
Rom 3:25 patience He had left **u** those sins
UNRIGHTEOUS
1 Cor 6:1 it before a court of **u** people
UNRIGHTEOUSNESS
Rom 1:18 against all ungodliness and **u**
Rom 3:5 but if our **u** shows how right God is
UNSPIRITUAL
Rom 7:14 spiritual but I am **u**
1 Cor 2:14 But an **u** person does not accept
UNSPOTTED
Jas 1:27 keep themselves **u** from the world
UNTIE
Mk 1:7 bend down and **u** His sandal straps
Lk 13:15 Doesn't each of you **u** his ox
Jn 1:27 I am not worthy to **u** His
UNVEILING
Rom 8:19 see the **u** of God's children
Rom 16:25 by **u** the mystery that was veiled
UNWORTHY
1 Cor 11:27 drinks Lord's cup in an **u** way
UPSTAIRS
Mk 14:15 large room **u** furnished and ready
URGE
Rom 16:17 I **u** you fellow Chrisians to take
Eph 4:1 I a prisoner in the Lord **u** you to
1 Tim 6:2 Teach and **u** them to do these
USE
Mk 15:6 Pilate **u** to free a prisoner
1 Cor 7:31 those who **u** the world as though
USEFUL
1 Cor 12:7 to each one to make him **u**
Phlm 11 he is quite **u** both to you and to me
USELESS
2 Pet 1:8 not made you **u** and unproductive

VAIN
Matt 15:9 They worship Me in **v**
Gal 2:2 be running or to have run in **v**
VALID
Heb 2:2 word spoken through angels was **v**
VALUE
Rom 12:3 not let your thoughts about your **v**
VANISHED
Lk 24:31 But Jesus **v** from them
VARIOUS
Heb 1:1 many times and in **v** ways God
VEGETABLES
Rom 14:2 one . . . faith is weak eats only **v**
VEIL
2 Cor 3:12 not like Moses who wore a **v**
VENGEANCE
Lk 21:22 will be a time of **v**
2 Thess 1:8 take **v** on those who do not know

VERDICT
Matt 26:66 what is your **v** He is guilty
VERIFY
Matt 18:16 have two or three witnesses to **v**
VERILY (see **ABSOLUTE**)
VEXED
2 Pet 2:7 wicked people **v** with . . . immoral
VICTORIOUS
Matt 12:20 He has made justice **v**
VICTORY
Rom 8:37 helps us win an overwhelming **v**
1 Cor 15:54 Death is swallowed up in **v**
Col 2:15 He celebrated His **v** in Christ
Rev 2:26 to the one who wins the **v**
Rev 21:7 one who wins the **v** will inherit
VIGOROUS
Acts 18:28 Publicly and **v** he proved
VILLAGE
Lk 9:6 went from **v** to **v** preaching
Lk 24:13 going to a **v** called Emmaus
VINE
Jn 15:1 I am the genuine **V** and My Father
VINEYARD
Matt 20:1 hire men to work in his **v**
Lk 13:7 man who worked the **v**
Jn 15:1 My Father is the Caretaker of the **v**
1 Cor 9:7 Does anyone plant a **v** and not eat
VIOLENT
Mk 4:37 Then a **v** storm came up
VIRGIN
Matt 1:23 **v** will conceive and have a Son
1 Cor 7:25 Now concerning **v**
VISION
Lk 24:23 seen a **v** of angels
Acts 2:17 your young men will see **v**
Acts 10:3 One day . . . he had a **v** in which he
Acts 16:9 One night Paul saw a **v**—a man
Col 2:18 goes on searching his **v**
VISIT
Lk 1:68 He has **v** His people
2 Cor 1:15 have the benefit of a double **v**
VISITORS
Acts 2:10 **v** from Rome Jews . . . proselytes
VOICE
Matt 3:17 a **v** from heaven said This is My
Matt 12:19 nor will anyone hear His **v**
Jn 1:23 I am a **v** calling out in wilderness
Jn 5:25 the dead will hear the **v** of the Son
Jn 5:28 who in their graves will hear His **v**
Jn 10:27 My sheep listen to My **v** and I know
Jn 12:28 A **v** came from heaven I have
Acts 4:24 raised their **v** together to God
Acts 9:4 heard a **v** saying to him Saul
Rom 10:18 their **v** has gone all over earth
2 Pet 1:18 We heard that **v** speak to Him
Rev 1:10 I heard a loud **v** behind me like a
VOW
Acts 18:18 he had been under a **v**
VULTURE
Matt 24:28 Where dead body is there the **v**

WAIT
Matt 8:15 She got up and began to **w** on
Mk 15:43 **w** for the Kingdom of God
Acts 22:16 what are you **w** for Get up
1 Thess 1:10 and to **w** for His Son to come
WALK
Matt 14:25 He came to them **w** on the sea
Matt 14:29 Peter got out of boat **w** on water
Mk 8:24 They look to me like tree **w**
Lk 4:30 But he **w** right through them
Jn 5:11 Pick up your bed and **w**
Jn 6:19 saw Jesus **w** on the sea and coming
Acts 3:6 in the Name of Jesus . . . **w**
WALL
Rev 21:12 a large high **w** with twelve gates
WANT
Matt 8:2 Lord if You **w** to . . . make me clean
Matt 11:26 I praise You for **w** it to be
Matt 21:31 Which . . . did what the father **w**
Matt 26:39 not be as I **w** it but as You **w**
Mk 1:40 If You **w** to You can make me clean
Jn 5:40 you do not **w** to come to Me
Jn 17:24 I **w** those You have given Me to be
Rom 7:16 if I do what I do not **w** to do
Rom 12:2 test and be sure of what God **w**
1 Tim 2:4 God . . . who **w** all people . . . saved
1 Tim 5:14 I **w** younger women to marry
1 Tim 6:9 people who **w** to get rich fall
2 Pet 3:9 does not **w** any to perish
1 Jn 2:5 accomplished in you what He **w**
WAR
Matt 24:6 to hear of **w** and rumors of **w**
Rev 12:7 then a **w** broke out in heaven
WARMING
Jn 18:18 and they were **w** themselves
WARN
Matt 2:12 God **w** them in dream not to go
Matt 2:22 being **w** in dream he went to
Lk 16:28 I have five brothers—to **w** them
Acts 2:40 He said much more to **w** them
Acts 10:42 He ordered us . . . to **w** them that
Acts 20:21 how I . . . **w** Jews and Greeks
1 Cor 4:14 I am **w** you as my dear children
Col 1:28 Him we preach **w** everyone
1 Thess 2:11 **w** every one of you to live
1 Thess 5:14 fellow Christians **w** those who
2 Thess 3:15 **w** him like a brother
2 Tim 2:14 Remind them of . . . and **w** them
Rev 22:18 I **w** everyone who hears the words
WARNING
Mk 1:43 Jesus sent him . . . with a stern **w**
Mk 6:11 soles of your feet as a **w** to them
Tit 3:10 Give a **w** to a person who chooses
2 Pet 2:6 made them a **w** to those . . . ungodly
Jude 7 lie before us as a **w** concerning
WASH
Matt 27:24 Pilate took water and **w** his
Mk 7:3 do not eat without **w** their hands
Lk 5:2 fishermen . . . were **w** their nets
Acts 9:37 she was **w** and laid in a room
Acts 22:16 baptized and . . . sins **w** away

1 Cor 6:11 you have been **w**
Tit 3:5 He saved us by the **w** in which the
Heb 9:14 **w** our consciences clean
1 Jn 1:7 blood of Jesus . . . **w** us clean
Rev 7:14 they have **w** their robes and made

WASTE
Rom 8:20 this created world must **w** away
1 Cor 15:58 your hard work is not **w**
2 Cor 6:1 do not let God's grace be **w** on
Gal 4:11 I did on you may have been **w**
Tit 3:14 not **w** their lives
Rev 18:17 all this wealth has been laid **w**

WATCH
Matt 27:36 sat . . . there and kept **w** over Him
Mk 13:33 Be careful and **w** because you
Lk 4:20 in the synagog was **w** Him closely
Acts 1:9 while they were **w** Him He was
Eph 6:6 serve only while you are being **w**
Col 3:22 only when they are **w** you
1 Tim 4:16 **W** yourself and your teaching
1 Pet 3:12 the Lord **w** the righteous
1 Pet 5:2 God's flock . . . **w** over it
1 Pet 5:8 Keep a clear head and **w**

WATER
Matt 3:16 He came out of the **w**
Mk 1:8 I have baptized you with **w**
Lk 13:15 take it out to **w**
Lk 16:24 finger in **w** and cool off my
Jn 3:5 not born of **w** and Spirit he cannot
Jn 19:34 immediately blood and **w** came out
1 Cor 3:6 Apollos **w** but God made it grow
1 Pet 3:20 eight persons were saved by **w**
2 Pet 3:5 the earth was formed out of **w**
1 Jn 5:6 He who came by **w** and blood
Rev 1:15 voice was like the sound of many **w**
Rev 7:17 to springs of the **w** of life
Rev 22:1 showed me a river of the **w** of life
Rev 22:17 take the **w** of life as a free gift

WAVES
Matt 8:24 **w** were higher than the boat

WAY
Jn 14:6 I am the **W** the Truth and the Life
Acts 1:11 will come back in the same **w**
Acts 3:26 turning every one of you from . . . **w**
Rom 5:2 who provided us with the **w** to come
1 Cor 10:13 He will also give you a **w** out
Heb 3:10 they have not known My **w**
Heb 9:8 the **w** into the MOST HOLY PLACE
Rev 15:3 righteous dependable are Your **w**

WEAK
Rom 6:19 you are naturally **w**
Rom 8:3 **w** by the flesh
Rom 14:1 the person who is **w** in faith
1 Cor 1:27 God chose **w** things in the world
1 Cor 8:7 conscience being **w** is stained
1 Cor 12:22 that we think are **w**
2 Cor 11:29 When anyone is **w** am I not **w** too
2 Cor 12:9 power is . . . best when you are **w**

WEAKER
1 Pet 3:7 woman she is **w** than you

WEAKNESS
Rom 8:26 Spirit helps us in our **w**
1 Cor 1:25 God's **w** is stronger than man's

WEAPON
2 Cor 6:7 by God's power with the **w** of
2 Cor 10:4 The **w** with which we fight

WEAR
Matt 6:25 what you will **w** on your bodies

WEDDING
Matt 22:11 man there without a **w** garment
Jn 2:2 disciples had also been invited to **w**

WEEP (see also **CRY**)
Matt 2:18 **W** and loud wailing Rachel crying
Rom 12:15 **w** with those who **w**
2 Cor 2:4 wrote to you with much **w**
2 Cor 12:21 I may have to **w** over many
Rev 18:15 merchants **w** and mourning

WEIGHT
2 Cor 4:17 producing for us everlasting **w**

WELCOME
Matt 10:14 If anyone does not **w** you
Mk 6:11 do not **w** you or listen to you
Mk 9:37 And whoever **w** Me **w** not Me but
Lk 8:40 the people **w** Him because
Lk 9:11 He **w** them talked to them
Lk 9:48 Whoever **w** this little child
Gal 4:14 scorn me but you **w** me as if I were

WELFARE
Phil 2:20 interest in your **w**

WELL
Matt 4:24 paralyzed and He made them **w**
Matt 8:13 slave was made **w** that same hour
Matt 9:22 that moment the woman was made **w**
Lk 4:22 All spoke **w** of Him and were
Lk 14:5 ox falls into a **w**
Jn 4:6 Jacob's **W** was there so Jesus tired
Jn 4:50 Go Jesus told him your son is **w**
Jn 5:15 Jesus who had made him **w**
Acts 9:34 Jesus Christ makes you **w**
1 Tim 3:13 they have served **w** as deacons

WELL-GROUNDED
2 Pet 1:12 **w** in the truth that you have

WENT
Mk 16:20 they **w** out and preached everywhere
Gal 1:18 Then three . . . I **w** up to Jerusalem
Eph 4:8 When He **w** up on high

WHEAT
Jn 12:24 if a kernel of **w** does not fall

WHILE
Jn 16:18 when He says A little **w**

WHIP
Matt 10:17 **w** you in their places of worship
Jn 19:1 Pilate took Jesus and had Him **w**

WHITE
Acts 1:10 two men in **w** clothes were
Rev 1:14 and His hair were **w** like **w** wool
Rev 3:4 they . . . walk with Me in **w** garments
Rev 6:11 each of them was given a **w** robe

WHITEWASHED
Acts 23:3 is going to strike you you **w** wall

WHOLE
Mk 1:33 The **w** town had gathered at His door
Mk 14:9 Gospel is preached in **w** world
Mk 16:15 preach Gospel to the **w** creation
WHY
Matt 27:46 My God **w** did You forsake Me
WICKED
Matt 12:39 A **w** and unfaithful generation
Lk 11:13 if you **w** as you are know enough
Acts 2:23 had **w** men nail Him to a cross
1 Cor 5:13 Remove the **w** man from among
Gal 1:4 from this present **w** world
2 Thess 3:2 rescued from **w** and evil people
Heb 3:12 none of you has a **w** heart which
WICKEDNESS
Mk 7:22 from people's hearts come . . . **w**
Rom 6:19 impurity and **w** to do wrong
1 Pet 2:1 get rid of . . . kind of **w** and deceit
WIDELY
Mk 7:36 the more **w** they spread the news
WIDOW
Mk 12:40 they swallow up the houses of **w**
Mk 12:42 a poor **w** also came dropped in two
Lk 4:25 were many **w** in Israel
Lk 21:2 a certain poor **w** drop in
Acts 6:1 their **w** were being neglected
Acts 9:39 There all the **w** stood around him
1 Cor 7:8 to those . . . are not married and **w**
1 Tim 5:3 Honor **w** who are all alone
WIFE
Matt 1:18 promised to Joseph to be his **w**
Acts 18:2 Aquila . . . and his **w** Priscilla
1 Cor 5:1 man has his father's **w**
1 Cor 7:2 let each man have his own **w**
1 Cor 7:12 man has a **w** who does not believe
Eph 5:22 **w** be subordinate to your
Col 3:18 **W** be subordinate to your husbands
1 Tim 3:12 deacons be the husbands of one **w**
1 Tim 4:7 to do with worldly old **w** tales
1 Pet 3:1 **w** be subordinate
WILD
Mk 1:13 He was there with the **w** animals
Lk 15:13 squandered all he had in **w** living
Tit 1:6 not accused of **w** living or
WILDERNESS
Jn 1:23 I am a voice calling out in the **w**
Jn 3:14 Moses lifted up snake in the **w**
Jn 6:31 our fathers ate manna in the **w**
Acts 7:38 Moses . . . the congregation in the **w**
WILL
Matt 6:10 Your **w** be done on earth
Matt 23:37 but you were not **w**
Jn 6:38 the **w** of Him who sent
Acts 21:14 May the Lord's **w** be done
Gal 3:15 once a last **w** and testament is
Eph 1:1 apostle of Christ Jesus by God's **w**
Phil 2:13 to be **w** and to be doing
Jas 4:15 If the Lord is **w** we will live
1 Jn 5:14 for anything according to His **w**
WIN
Matt 18:15 If he listens to you you have **w**

Lk 9:25 **w** the whole world and destroy
Acts 18:4 try to **w** Jews and Greeks
1 Cor 9:19 in order to **w** more of them
1 Cor 9:24 only one **w** the prize
1 Pet 3:1 listen to word you will **w** them
WIND
Jn 6:18 A strong **w** started to blow and stir
Acts 2:2 blast of **w** came from heaven
Heb 1:7 He makes His angels **w**
WINE
Matt 9:17 people pour new **w** into old
Lk 10:34 pouring on olive oil and **w**
Jn 2:10 Everybody serves his good **w** first
Acts 2:13 others sneered . . . full of new **w**
1 Tim 3:8 deacons . . . not drinking a lot of **w**
1 Tim 5:23 use a little **w** for your stomach
WINEPRESS
Rev 14:19 threw . . . into great **w** of . . . anger
Rev 19:15 will tread the **w** of fierce anger
WINESKINS
Matt 9:17 pour new wine into old **w**
WINGS
Matt 23:37 gathers her chicks under her **w**
Rev 4:8 creatures had six **w** which
WINTER
1 Cor 16:6 spend the **w** with you
2 Tim 4:21 Do your best to come before **w**
WIPE
Acts 3:19 turn to have your sins **w** away
Rev 7:17 **w** every tear from their eyes
WISDOM
Matt 11:19 And yet **w** is proved right
Matt 12:42 to hear Solomon's **w**
Lk 2:40 Child grew . . . filled with **w**
1 Cor 1:19 I will destroy the **w** of the wise
1 Cor 1:24 Christ God's power and God's **w**
1 Cor 2:6 we speak **w** to those . . . mature
Eph 1:8 giving us every kind of **w** and
Col 2:23 this looks like **w** with its
Col 3:16 as with all **w** you teach and warn
Jas 1:5 If anyone lacks **w** let him ask God
Jas 3:17 The **w** that comes from above is
WISE
Matt 2:1 **W** Men came from the east to
Matt 11:25 hiding these things from **w**
Rom 12:16 Do not think that you are **w**
Rom 16:19 I want you to be **w** concerning
Rom 16:27 to the only **w** God through Jesus
1 Cor 1:25 God's foolishness is **w** than
Eph 5:15 Do not be unwise but **w**
Col 4:5 Be **w** in the way you live with those
WISELY
1 Cor 12:8 one . . . the ability to speak **w**
2 Tim 3:15 you **w** so that you may be saved
WISH
Lk 22:42 Father if You **w** take this cup
WITCHCRAFT
Gal 5:20 worshiping of idols **w** hate
Rev 9:21 not repent of . . . their **w**
Rev 18:23 by your **w** . . . were deceived
Rev 21:8 and practice **w**
Rev 22:15 people who practice **w**

WITH

Matt 12:30 Anyone . . . not **w** Me is against
Lk 23:43 today you will be **w** Me in Paradise
Jn 17:24 want those . . . given Me to be **w** Me

WITHDRAWN

Jn 5:13 Jesus had **w** from the crowd

WITHERS

1 Cor 9:25 win wreath that **w** but . . . never **w**

WITHIN

Lk 17:21 Kingdom of God is **w** you

WITHOUT

Jn 15:5 for **w** Me you can do nothing

WITNESS

Matt 18:16 have two or three **w** to verify
Matt 26:65 Why do we need any more **w**
Acts 2:32 of that we are all **w**
Acts 3:15 we are **w** of that
2 Cor 1:23 I call on God . . . as my **w**
2 Cor 13:1 what two or three **w** say
1 Tim 5:19 supported by two or three **w**
Heb 12:1 with all these **w** around us
Rev 1:5 Christ—He is the faithful **W**
Rev 2:13 My faithful **w** who was killed
Rev 3:14 The Amen the **W** who is faithful
Rev 11:3 to My two **w** who are dressed
Rev 17:6 blood of the **w** of Jesus

WOE

Matt 11:21 **W** to you Chorazin **W** to you
Matt 18:7 **W** to the world when it causes
1 Cor 9:16 **W** to me if I do not preach
Rev 8:13 **W w w** to those living
Rev 18:19 **W w** to the great city

WOLVES

Matt 7:15 in their hearts they are greedy **w**
Matt 10:16 sending you like sheep among **w**
Acts 20:29 fierce **w** will come in among you

WOMAN

Matt 9:20 a **w** who had been suffering
Matt 27:55 Many **w** were there watching
Mk 15:41 There were also many other **w**
Lk 13:11 **w** whom a spirit had crippled
Jn 2:4 What do we have in common **w**
Jn 16:21 When a **w** is giving birth
Acts 16:14 there was a **w** by name of Lydia
Rom 7:2 a married **w** to her husband
1 Cor 11:3 the head of a **w** is the man
1 Cor 14:34 **w** keep silent in your churches
Gal 4:4 sent out His Son to be born of a **w**
Gal 4:24 the **w** are two covenants
1 Tim 2:9 I want **w** to dress in . . . clothes
1 Tim 2:12 I do not allow a **w** to teach
1 Tim 3:11 the **w** must be serious not
1 Tim 5:2 encourage . . . younger **w** as sisters
2 Tim 3:6 way into homes captivate weak **w**
Tit 2:3 tell older **w** Behave in a way
Rev 2:20 you tolerate that **w** Jezebel
Rev 12:1 a **w** with the sun for her garment

WOMB

Lk 1:42 Child who will come from your **w**
Lk 1:44 baby leaped with delight in my **w**
Jn 3:4 his mother's **w** and be born a second
Gal 1:15 separated me from my mother's **w**

WONDER

Acts 2:11 hear them tell . . . the **w** which God

WONDERFUL

Acts 2:19 will give you **w** proofs in the sky
Heb 2:4 by . . . signs and **w** proofs

WOOD

1 Cor 3:12 silver precious stones **w** hay

WORD (see also **WORD OF GOD**)

Matt 4:4 by every **w** that God
Matt 7:24 everyone who hears these **w** of
Matt 8:8 say a **w** and my slave made well
Matt 24:35 but My **w** will never pass away
Mk 2:2 He was speaking the **w** to them
Lk 11:28 listen to God's **w** and keep it
Jn 1:1 In beginning was the **W** . . . with God
Jn 1:14 **W** became flesh and lived among us
Jn 3:34 God has sent speaks God's **w**
Jn 8:31 you remain in My **w** . . . My disciples
Jn 8:55 I do know Him and I obey His **w**
Jn 10:35 gods to whom God's **w** came
Jn 12:48 the **w** I spoke will condemn him
Jn 17:17 in the truth Your **w** is truth
Jn 17:20 who through their **w** will believe
Acts 2:18 men and women . . . speak God's **w**
Acts 8:4 from . . . to place preaching the **w**
Acts 10:44 came down on all who heard the **w**
Acts 20:32 entrust you to God and to the **w**
Rom 3:2 God entrusted His **w** to the Jews
Rom 10:8 The **w** is near you in your mouth
Rom 10:17 comes through the **w** of Christ
1 Cor 2:13 human **w** but taught by the Spirit
Col 3:16 Let Christ's **w** live richly in you
1 Thess 1:8 not only has Lord's **w** spread
1 Thess 4:18 comfort one . . . with these **w**
1 Thess 5:20 Do not despise God's **w** when
2 Tim 2:14 not to fight about **w**
2 Tim 2:15 teaches **w** of truth in correct
Tit 1:3 revealed in His **w** through preaching
Heb 1:3 everything by His mighty **w**
Heb 5:12 teach you the ABC's of God's **w**
Jas 1:18 gave birth to us by **w** of truth
Jas 1:21 welcome the **w** that is planted
1 Pet 1:23 not perish . . . God's ever-living **w**
1 Pet 2:2 pure milk of the **w** . . . you grow
2 Pet 1:19 we have . . . the prophetic **w**
1 Jn 1:1 namely the **W** who is the Life
1 Jn 1:10 His **w** is not in us
1 Jn 2:14 God's **w** remains in you
Rev 1:9 for speaking God's **w** and testifying
Rev 6:9 slain because of God's **w**
Rev 22:6 these **w** are faithful and genuine

WORD OF GOD (see also **WORD**)

Acts 4:31 speak the **w** of God with boldness
2 Cor 2:17 peddle an impure **w** of God like
Eph 6:17 sword of Spirit which is **w** of God
1 Thess 2:13 it was in truth the **w** of God
2 Tim 2:9 But the **w** of God is not chained
Heb 4:12 the **w** of God is living and active
Heb 13:7 leaders who have spoken **w** of God
2 Pet 3:5 **w** of God the heavens existed
Rev 19:13 His Name is called the **W** of God
Rev 20:4 because of the **w** of God

WORK

Matt 3:8 produce **w** that show . . . repented
Matt 6:1 careful not to do your good **w**
Matt 11:2 John . . . heard about **w** of Christ
Matt 11:28 Come to Me all you who are **w**
Matt 13:58 He did not **w** many miracles
Matt 21:28 Son go and **w** in the vineyard
Jn 6:29 This is the **w** of God—that you
Jn 14:10 the Father . . . is doing His **w**
Acts 20:34 these hands **w** for my own needs
Rom 4:4 Now when a person **w** his pay
Rom 8:28 We know that all things **w** together
Rom 9:32 . . . not pursue it by faith but by **w**
1 Cor 9:1 Are you not my **w** in the Lord
1 Cor 9:13 men who **w** at the Temple receive
1 Cor 15:58 always do more **w** for the Lord
2 Cor 2:12 do the **w** of the Lord
2 Cor 6:1 who are **w** with God we plead
2 Cor 11:23 I have done much more hard **w**
Gal 2:16 justified by faith . . . and not by **w**
Phil 2:12 to **w** out your salvation with fear
Col 3:23 Whatever you do **w** heartily
Col 4:17 you do all the **w** you undertook
2 Thess 2:7 rebellious thing is already **w**
2 Thess 3:10 If anyone does not want to **w**
Jas 2:14 have faith but do not have any **w**
Jas 2:24 You see a person is justified by **w**
Rev 15:3 Great and wonderful are Your **w**

WORKERS

Matt 9:38 send out **w** to bring in His grain
Matt 20:2 agreed with the **w** to pay them
Eph 4:12 prepare believers for service as **w**

WORLD

Jn 1:10 He was in the **w** and He made the **w**
Jn 14:19 little while longer and **w** will not
Jn 16:11 ruler of this **w** is judged
Jn 17:24 You loved Me before the **w** was made
Jn 18:36 Kingdom does not belong to this **w**
Acts 1:8 testify . . . farthest parts of the **w**
Acts 17:31 judge the **w** with justice
Rom 3:19 whole **w** may stand guilty before
Rom 8:19 the created **w** is waiting on tiptoe
1 Cor 7:31 whose who use the **w**
Gal 6:14 whom the **w** is crucified to me
Col 2:8 principles of this **w** rather than
Heb 11:3 By faith we know God created the **w**
Jas 4:4 do you now know that to love the **w**
1 Jn 2:2 sins of the whole **w**
1 Jn 2:15 Do not love the **w**
1 Jn 4:5 the **w** listens to them

WORM

Mk 9:48 where their **w** does not die
Acts 12:23 he was eaten by **w** and he died

WORMWOOD

Rev 8:11 third of the waters turned to **w**

WORRY

Matt 6:25 stop **w** about what you will eat
Matt 6:31 Do not **w** then and say
Matt 6:34 So do not **w** about tomorrow
Matt 10:19 do not **w** how you will speak
Lk 10:41 you **w** and fuss about a lot
1 Pet 5:7 throw all your **w** on Him . . . He

WORSE

Matt 12:45 seven . . . spirits **w** than himself
Lk 13:2 Galileans were **w** sinners
2 Pet 2:20 **w** off in end than they . . . before

WORSHIP

Matt 2:2 and have come to **w** Him
Matt 4:9 if You will bow down and **w** me
Matt 4:10 **W** the Lord your God and serve Him
Matt 28:9 took hold of His feet and **w** Him
Jn 4:20 Our ancestors **w** on this mountain
Jn 9:38 he bowed down to **w** Him
Acts 7:7 **w** Me in this place
Rom 1:25 **w** and served what was created
1 Cor 10:7 Do not **w** idols as some of them
Heb 1:6 let all angels of God **w** Him
Heb 9:14 may **w** the living God
Rev 14:7 **w** Him who made heaven
Rev 19:10 I bowed down at his feet to **w** him

WORST

1 Tim 1:15 sinners—of whom I am the **w**

WORTHLESS

Rom 3:12 together have become **w**
Jas 1:26 his religion is **w**

WORTHY

Matt 8:8 Lord I am not **w** for You
Matt 10:37 more than Me is not **w** of Me
Col 1:10 so that you live **w** of the Lord
1 Thess 2:12 to live **w** of God who is
2 Thess 1:5 are counted **w** of His Kingdom
Rev 4:11 You are **w** to receive glory honor

WOUNDS

1 Pet 2:24 His **w** have healed you

WRANGLING

1 Tim 6:5 continued **w** of people . . . corrupt

WRAPPED

Lk 2:7 She **w** Him in baby clothes

WRAPPINGS

Jn 19:40 **w** . . . in linen **w** according to Jewish

WRATH (see also ANGER)

Jn 3:36 rejects the Son . . . **w** of God rests
Rom 5:9 He will save us from the **w** of God

WRENCHED

Mk 9:26 It screamed and **w** him violently

WRESTLING

Col 4:12 He is always **w** in prayer for you

WRIST

Mk 7:3 washing their hands up to the **w**

WRITE

Mk 9:12 And what is **w** about the Son of Man
Mk 14:21 Son of Man is going away as is **w**
Jn 8:8 He bent down again and **w** on ground
Jn 10:34 Is it not **w** in your Scriptures
Jn 21:25 **w** . . . room for books that would be **w**
Acts 24:14 believe everything **w** in the Law
Rom 2:15 is **w** in their hearts
Rom 4:23 were **w** not only for him but . . . us
Rom 15:4 All that was **w** long ago was **w** to
1 Cor 14:37 what I **w** to you is what the
1 Cor 16:21 I Paul **w** with my own hand
2 Cor 3:2 you are our letter **w** in . . . hearts
Gal 3:10 everything **w** in book of the Law

Gal 6:11 when I **w** to you with my own hand
Phil 3:1 it is no trouble to **w** same things
Col 4:18 I Paul am **w** this greeting with my
Heb 10:7 The **w** in the scroll of the book
Rev 2:8 to the angel of church in Smyrna **w**
Rev 21:27 who are **w** in Lamb's Book of Life

WRONG
Matt 20:13 Friend I am doing you no **w**
Acts 9:13 heard ... tell how much **w** this man
Acts 28:18 because I had done no **w**
Gal 2:11 because he was completely **w**
Eph 5:11 continue to expose them as **w**
Col 2:16 say that you are **w** in what you eat
Col 3:25 man who does **w** will be paid back
2 Tim 2:19 must give up **w**
Tit 3:11 person is set in his **w** way

YARDSTICK
2 Cor 10:12 measure themselves by ... own **y**
YEARS
Matt 2:16 up to two **y** old according to
YEAST
1 Cor 5:6 a little **y** spreads ... whole batch
1 Cor 5:8 with bread that has no **y**
Gal 5:9 A little **y** spreads through
YES
2 Cor 1:17 so that when I say **y** or no

YOKE
Matt 11:29 Take My **y** upon you and learn
Acts 15:10 why ... test God by putting a **y** on
2 Cor 6:14 do not be **y** ... with unbelievers
Gal 5:1 do not get caught again under a **y**
YOUNG
Mk 14:51 a ... **y** man who also was following
Mk 16:5 they saw a **y** man dressed
1 Tim 5:11 but do not put **y** widows on list
2 Tim 2:22 Flee from lusts of **y** people
Tit 2:4 in order to train **y** women to love
1 Jn 2:13 I am writing to you **y** men
YOUNGER
Lk 15:12 **y** of them said to his father
1 Tim 4:12 down on you because you are **y**
YOURS
Jn 17:10 All that is Mine is **Y** what is **Y**
YOURSELF
Matt 22:39 Love your neighbor as **y**
Rom 2:1 condemn anyone else you condemn **y**
Rom 2:21 do you fail to teach **y**

ZEAL
Jn 2:17 **z** for Your House will consume Me
ZEALOUS
Rom 10:2 I can testify they are **z** for God
ZION
Jn 12:15 not ... be afraid daughter of **Z**

NAMES

AARON
Lk 1:5; Acts 7:40; Heb 9:4
ABEL
Matt 23:35; Heb 11:4
ABRAHAM
Matt 1:1; Lk 13:28;16:23;
Jn 8:57,58; Rom 4:2,13;11:1;
Gal 3:6,16;4:22;
Heb 2:16;6:13;11:8
ADAM
1 Cor 15:22,45; 1 Tim 2:13,14
AGAR
Gal 4:24,25
ANDREW
Mk 1:29;13:3; Jn 1:40,44
ANNA
Lk 2:36
ANNAS
Lk 3:2; Jn 18:13,24
ANTICHRIST
1 Jn 2:18,22;4:3; 2 Jn 7
APOLLOS
Acts 18:24; 1 Cor 1:12;3:4-6
AQUILA
Acts 18:2; 1 Cor 16:19
ARTEMIS (DIANA)
Acts 19:24,28,35
AUGUSTUS
Lk 2:1; Acts 25:21

BALAAM
2 Pet 2:15; Rev 2:14
BARABBAS
Jn 18:40
BARAK
Heb 11:32
BARNABAS
Acts 4:36;13:2;14:12;15:2,37;
Gal 2:1,13
BARTHOLOMEW
Matt 10:3; Acts 1:13
BARTIMAEUS
Mk 10:46
BEELZEBUB
Matt 10:25;12:24; Lk 11:15,18
BELIAL
2 Cor 6:15
BENJAMIN
Acts 13:21

CAIAPHAS
Matt 26:3,57; Jn 11:49;18:14,28
CAIN
Heb 11:4; 1 Jn 3:12; Jude 11
CEPHAS
Jn 1:42; 1 Cor 1:12;15:5;
Gal 2:9
CAESAR
Matt 22:17; Lk 2:1; Jn 19:12;
Acts 25:11, Phil 4:22

CORNELIUS
Acts 10:1,7,25,31

DANIEL
Matt 24:15
DAVID
Matt 9:27;12:3;21:9;
Mk 10:47; Lk 6:3;18:38;
Jn 7:42;
Acts 2:29; Heb 4:7;11:32;
Rev 3:7;5:5;22:16
DEMAS
Col 4:14; 2 Tim 4:10
DEMETRIUS
Acts 19:24,38
DORCAS
Acts 9:36

ELIJAH
Matt 11:14;16:14;17:3;
Lk 1:17;9:54; Jn 1:21; Jas 5:17
ELIZABETH
Lk 1:5,24,40,57
ELISHA
Lk 4:27
ENOCH
Heb 11:5; Jude 14
ESAU
Rom 9:13; Heb 11:20;12:16

EVE
2 Cor 11:3; 1 Tim 2:13
EUNICE
2 Tim 1:5

FELIX
Acts 23:24;24:24
FESTUS
Acts 24:27;25:9;26:25

GABRIEL
Lk 1:19,26
GAMALIEL
Acts 5:34,22:3
GIDEON
Heb 11:32

HEROD
Matt 2:12,16;14:3;
Mk 6:20;8:15;
Lk 9:7;13:31;23:7;
Acts 4:27;12:1,21

ISAAC
Matt 8:11; Gal 4:28;
Heb 11:9,17,20
ISAIAH
Matt 3:3; Lk 4:17; Jn 12:39;
Acts 8:28;28:25;
Rom 9:27;10:16;15:12

JACOB
Matt 8:11; Lk 13:28; Jn 4:6;
Rom 9:13;11:26; Heb 11:9,20
JAMES
Matt 4:21; Mk 1:19;5:37;13:3;
Acts 12:2; 1 Cor 15:7;
Gal 1:19
JEREMIAH
Matt 2:17;16:14
JESSE
Matt 1:5
JESUS (see entry above)
JOB
Jas 5:11
JOEL
Acts 2:16
JOHN (Baptizer)
Matt 3:4;4:12;9:14; Mk 6:20;
Lk 9:7; Jn 1:6;5:33;
Acts 1:5;13:24
JOHN (Apostle)
Matt 4:21; Lk 22:8; Acts 3:1;
Rev 1:1
JONAH
Matt 12:39; Lk 11:29
JOSEPH
Jn 4:5; Acts 7:9; Heb 11:21
JOSEPH (husband of Mary)
Matt 1:18; Lk 2:4;4:22

JUDAH
Matt 1:2; Heb 7:14
JUDAS
Matt 13:55; Mk 14:43;
Jn 18:3;27:3; Acts 1:16

KORAH
Jude 11

LAZARUS
Lk. 16:20; Jn 11:2,43;12:9
LEVI
Mk 2:14; Lk 5:27; Heb 7:9
LOIS
2 Tim 1:5
LUKE
Col 4:14; 2 Tim 4:11
LYDIA
Acts 16:14,40

MARK
Acts 12:12;15:39; 2 Tim 4:11
MARTHA
Lk 10:38; Jn 11:1;12:2
MARY
Matt 1:16;2:11;13:55;27:56;
Lk 2:5;10:39;
Jn 11:1;12:3;19:25;20:11;
Acts 1:14; Rom 16:6
MARY MAGDALENE
Matt 27:56; Lk 8:2;24:10;
Jn 20:18
MATTHEW
Matt 9:9;10:3
MELCHIZEDEK
Heb 7:1,11
MESSIAH (see entry above)
MICHAEL
Jude 9; Rev 12:7
MOSES
Matt 17:3;19:7;23:2;
Mk 10:3;12:19; Lk 16:29;20:37;
Jn 1:17;3:14;5:45;9:28;
Acts 3:22;7:20; Rom 5:14;
1 Cor 10:2;
2 Cor 3:7; 2 Tim 3:8;
Heb 3:2;7:14;10:28;11:24;
Jude 9;
Rev 15:3

NATHANAEL
Jn 1:45;21:2
NICODEMUS
Jn 3:1;7:50;19:39
NOAH
Matt 24:37; Heb 11:7;
1 Pet 3:20; 2 Pet 2:5

ONESIMUS
Col 4:9; Phlm 10

PAUL (SAUL)
Acts 7:58;9:4;13:1;15:38;
16:25;26:24; 1 Cor 1:12;
2 Pet 3:15
PETER
Matt 16:18;26:37; Lk 22:61;
Jn 1:44; Acts
1:15;4:8;9:40;10:13;12:3
PHARAOH
Acts 7:13; Rom 9:17; Heb 11:24
PHILIP
Matt 10:3
PILATE
Matt 27:2; Lk 3:1;23:12;
Jn 18:29;19:8; Acts 3:13;13:28;
1 Tim 6:13

RAHAB
Matt 1:5; Heb 11:31; Jas 2:25
REBEKAH
Rom 9:10
RUTH
Matt 1:5

SAMSON
Heb 11:32
SAMUEL
Acts 3:24;13:20; Heb 11:32
SAPPHIRA
Acts 5:1
SARAH
Rom 4:19; Heb 11:11; 1 Pet 3:6
SILAS
Acts 15:22;16:25;17:4
SIMEON
Lk 2:25,34
SOLOMON
Matt 1:6;6:29;12:42; Jn 10:23;
Acts 3:11
STEPHEN
Acts 6:5;7:59;22:20

TABITHA
Acts 9:40
THEOPHILUS
Lk 1:3; Acts 1:1
THOMAS
Matt 10:3; Jn 11:16;20:24
TIMOTHY
Acts 16:1; 1 Cor 16:10;
Phil 2:19; 1 Thess 3:2; 1 Tim 1:2
TITUS
2 Cor 2:13; Gal 2:3

ZACHARIAS
Lk 1:13,59
ZEBEDEE
Matt 4:21;10:2;20:20

PLACES

ANTIOCH
Acts 11:19,26,15:22; Gal 2:11;
2 Tim 3:11
ARABIA
Gal 1:17,4:25
ARIMATHEA
Matt 27:57
ARMAGEDDON
Rev 16:16
ASIA
Acts 6:9;16:6;19:10,27;
2 Tim 1:15
ATHENS
Acts 17:15,22;18:1; 1 Thess 3:1

BABYLON
Matt 1:17; Acts 7:43;
Rev 16:19;17:5;18:10
BEREA
Acts 17:10;20:4
BETHANY
Matt 21:17; Mk 11:12;
Lk 24:50; Jn 11:1
BETHESDA
Jn 5:2
BETHLEHEM
Matt 2:1,16; Lk 2:4,15; Jn 7:42
BETHPHAGE
Matt 21:1
BETHSAIDA
Matt 11:21; Mk 6:45;8:22;
Lk 9:10; Jn 1:44;12:21
BITHYNIA
Acts 16:7

CALVARY
Lk 23:33
CANA
Jn 2:1;4:46;21:2
CANAAN
Matt 15:22; Acts 7:11;13:19
CAPERNAUM
Matt 4:13;11:23; Mk 1:21;
Lk 4:23; Jn 2:12;4:46;6:17
CAPPADOCIA
Acts 2:9; 1 Pet 1:1
CAESAREA
Matt 16:13; Mk 8:27;
Acts 8:40;11:11;23:23;25:1
CORINTH
Acts 18:1;19:1; 2 Cor 1:23
CRETE
Acts 27:7; Tit 1:5
CYPRUS
Acts 4:36;11:19;15:39;27:4

DAMASCUS
Acts 9:2;22:6; 2 Cor 11:32;
Gal 1:17
DECAPOLIS
Matt 4:25; Mk 5:20;7:31

EGYPT
Acts 7:10; Heb 11:27; Rev 11:8

EPHESUS
Acts 19:26
EPHRAIM
Jn 11:54
ETHIOPIA
Acts 8:27
EUPHRATES
Rev 9:14;16:12

GABBATHA
Jn 19:13
GALATIA
Acts 16:6; 1 Cor 16:1;
2 Tim 4:10
GALILEE
Matt 2:2; Mk 1:16,39; Lk 4:14;
Jn 7:41;12:21; Acts 1:11;5:37
GAZA
Acts 8:26
GENNESARET
Matt 14:34; Lk 5:1
GADARENES
Matt 8:28
GETHSEMANE
Matt 26:36; Mk 14:32
GOG
Rev 20:8
GOLGOTHA
Matt 27:33
GOMORRAH
Matt 10:15
GREECE
Acts 18:12;20:2; Rom 15:26;
2 Cor 9:2; 1 Thess 1:7

ICONIUM
Acts 13:51;14:1,19; 2 Tim 3:11
IDUMEA
Mk 3:8
ISRAEL
Lk 1:54; Jn 3:10, 12:13;
Acts 1:6; Rom 9:4,6;11:7;
1 Cor 10:18; Gal 6:16;
Rev 21:12
ITALY
Acts 18:2;27:1; Heb 13:24

JERICHO
Lk 10:30; Heb 11:30
JERUSALEM
Matt 4:25;23:37; Mk 10:33;
Lk 10:30;23:7;24:47; Jn 4:21;
Acts 1:19;6:7;15:2; Gal 1:17
JOPPA
Acts 9:36;10:5;11:5
JORDAN
Matt 3:6
JUDEA
Matt 24:16; Jn 4:3;
Acts 1:8;9:31; Rom 15:31;
1 Thess 2:14

KIDRON
Jn 18:1

LAODICEA
Col 2:1;4:13
LYSTRA
Acts 14:6;16:1; 2 Tim 3:11

MACEDONIA
Acts 16:9;18:5;19:21;
Rom 15:26;
2 Cor 7:5;8:1;9:2;11:9;
1 Thess 1:7
MAGOG
Rev 20:8
MESOPOTAMIA
Acts 2:9;7:2

NAIN
Lk 7:11

PAMPHYLIA
Acts 13:13;15:38;27:5
PATMOS
Rev 1:9
PHILADELPHIA
Rev 1:11;3:7
PHILIPPI
Acts 16:12; 1 Thess 2:2

ROME
Acts 2:10;18:2;23:11;
Rom 1:15; 2 Tim 1:17

SAMARIA
Lk 17:11; Jn 4:4; Acts 8:1;9:31
SARDIS
Rev 1:11;3:4
SMYRNA
Rev 1:11;2:8
SODOM
Matt 10:15; Lk 17:29;
Rom 9:29; 2 Pet 2:6;
Jude 7; Rev 11:8
SPAIN
Rom 15:24
SYRIA
Matt 4:24; Lk 2:2;
Acts 15:23;18:18

TARSUS
Acts 9:11;11:25;21:39
THESSALONICA
Acts 17:1;27:2; Phil 4:16;
2 Tim 4:10
THYATIRA
Acts 16:14; Rev 1:11;2:24
TIBERIAS
Jn 6:1,23
TYRE
Matt 11:21; Acts 12:20

ZION (see entry above)